45TH
ANNUAL EDITION

2014 ALMANAC OF
BUSINESS AND
INDUSTRIAL
FINANCIAL RATIOS

Leo Troy, Ph.D.

Wolters Kluwer
CCH

EDITORIAL STAFF

Production .... Christopher Zwirek
Design.. Kathie Luzod, Craig Arritola

ISBN: 978-0-8080-3495-7

Certified Chain of Custody
Product Line Contains At Least
20% Certified Forest Content
www.sfiprogram.org
SFI-00756

DEDICATED

To Alexander, Suzannah, Dale, Ariel Sarah Troy, Abigayle Hannah Troy, and Rachel Ilana Troy

PREFACE

Now in its 45th Edition, the *Almanac of Business and Industrial Financial Ratios* provides a precise benchmark for evaluating an individual company's financial performance. The performance data is derived from the latest available IRS figures on U.S. and international companies, and tracks 50 operating and financial factors in nearly 200 industries. The *Almanac* provides competitive norms in actual dollar amounts for revenue and capital factors, as well as important average operating costs in percent of net sales. It also provides other critical financial factors in percentage, including debt ratio, return on assets, return on equity, profit margin, and more. Beyond its reliable insights into corporate behavior, the *Almanac* can be used by other countries looking to model their economies on American performance.

Also included with the text, in a special pocket provided in the inside cover of the book, is a CD-ROM that contains all the materials found in the book including the explanatory discussion, the data tables, and the supporting index. Also included on the CD, but not in the book itself, is a special template that allows the reader to add individual company data of interest to compare and contrast with data from the book.

2014 Edition Highlights

The 2014 Edition of the *Almanac of Business and Industrial Financial Ratios* has been updated to include the following:

- **Broad scope:** *2014 Almanac* features the North American Industry Classification System (NAICS), so you can benchmark or analyze results consistently with corporations in the United States, Canada, and Mexico.

- **Most industry types:** *2014 Almanac* highlights most industry types, including industries with advanced technologies and newly emerging industries such as paging and wireless communications.

- **A truer picture** of corporate financial performance, since the data isn't based on a mixed bag of averages that might include partnerships or sole proprietors. *2014 Almanac* features a homogeneous universe of American corporate financial performance.

- **Many classifications:** *2014 Almanac* analyzes 195 industries with 50 financial performance items.

- **Benchmarks:** *2014 Almanac* provides 13 benchmarks, including such critical measures as Receipts to Cash Flow, Debt to Total Assets, and Return on Equity both before and after taxes.

■ **Analytical tables:** *Table I, Corporations with and without Net Income (All Corporations), and Table II, Corporations with Net Income.*

■ **Easier apples-to-apples comparisons:** Each table is divided into 13 asset sizes.

■ **More comprehensive:** Total receipts of all corporations covered by *2014 Almanac* is $26.2 trillion, making the *Almanac* the Anatomy of American Corporate Capitalism.

Leo Troy, Ph. D.

June 2013

ABOUT THE AUTHOR

Dr. Leo Troy is Professor Emeritus of Economics at Rutgers University. He was a faculty member of Rutgers for 50 years. In addition to authoring the widely praised *Almanac*, he has written many other books and articles published in leading journals. Professor Troy has been the recipient of numerous awards including two from the National Science Foundation, and two Fulbright grants. In addition, he has received numerous awards from private foundations. Dr. Troy received his Ph.D. from Columbia University and is a member of Phi Beta Kappa. He is a veteran of World War II with three battle stars and the combat infantry badge. He is the father of two children and is also a grandfather of three girls, including twins.

ACKNOWLEDGMENTS

I wish to acknowledge the contributions of five people in particular for the development of the 45th Edition of the *Almanac:* Phil Wilson, Alan Kovar of Brighton Best, Lawrence R. Chodor, CPA, CVA, Wiss & Company, Marvin Sunshine, and Karen Kane.

Philip is responsible for the programming, which dealt with a very large amount of data, covering both the current and trend information. Alan, drawing upon his knowledge and experience as a CPA and Partner of Wiss and Company of Livingston, N.J., contributed significantly to the new content of the book. To Marvin Sunshine, Esq, my appreciation for actions and support that helped make the *Almanac* a continuing publication. Karen Kane is acknowledged for her contributions to the graphics of this issue.

Special acknowledgement is due my late friends and colleagues, Stan Katz, CPA, and Professor Emeritus of Accounting, Rutgers University, John Gilmour. I thank, too, Professor of Accounting, Rutgers University, David Zaumeyer, Ph.D., CPA, for recommending several ratios that continue to be included in the *Almanac*. I thank Mr. Ka-Neng Au, Business Librarian, Rutgers University, for significant contributions to the *Almanac*.

I wish to recognize, too, the cooperation of members of the Statistics of Income Division of the Internal Revenue Service—in particular, Ken Szeflinksi, Martha A. Harris, and Phyllis J. Whiles of the Corporation Returns Analysis Section. Without their data and its reliability, the Almanac would not be possible. Responsibility for the use of their facts and figures is, of course, solely my own. In this regard, I recall the valuable assistance I received from Barry Rosenstein, MBA, CPA, in checking procedures, in earlier editions, and which have continued into the current one. Finally, I wish to recognize the help of Suzannah B. Troy in bringing about the 45th annual edition of the *Almanac*. I anticipate continuation of her valuable assistance in subsequent editions.

INTRODUCTION

QUESTIONS, ANSWERS AND COMMENTS ON THE *ALMANAC*

Some users have requested further information on the use of the *Almanac's* ratios and statistics. This Q & A addition to the *Almanac* is in response to that demand.

1. What are the general purposes of the Almanac?

The goal of the *Almanac* is to provide users with a reliable and comprehensive source of standard financial ratios and financial statistics on all corporations, public and private, including those filing 1120S returns in the United States. Excluded are all individual proprietorships and partnerships. The *Almanac* makes available key business and financial statistics, which are consistent and neutral (unbiased by any commercial publisher or trade association).

2. What is the source and reliability of the Almanac's results?

The *Almanac's* results are computed from the Department of the Treasury, Internal Revenue Service's statistical sampling of the tax returns of all corporations. Dividends received from foreign corporations are included in total receipts of those corporations affected. The statistics apply to the company rather than the establishment.

3. Are international comparisons available?

Yes. Because of the adoption of a common system of industrial classification by the U.S., Canada and Mexico, known as the North American Industrial Classification System of industries (NAICS), under the North American Free Trade Agreement, users in Canada and Mexico can compare and contrast their results with those corporations in the United States.

4. What about comparisons within the U.S?

These are the most important applications of the *Almanac*. Results are available for each and every corporation within the U.S., whether public or private, and include small business corporations, those which file the 1120S tax return. Therefore, users can compare their corporate performance with that of their industry and asset size group of corporate enterprise in the United States.

5. How many corporations are covered in the Almanac?

The *Almanac's* results are derived from more than 5.8 million corporation tax returns. Furthermore, the user can easily determine the number of enterprises for the total of each industry and by each of the 12 asset size groups. This makes for a total of 13 asset size comparisons.

6. What about differences in the size of corporations?

In addition to the results for each industry, the *Almanac* displays 12 columns of performance by the size of assets. Again, this makes for a total of 13 asset size comparisons.

7. Does the Almanac distinguish between the profitability of corporations?

In a word, yes. Each industry is divided between two tables: Table I reports the results of all corporations in an industry, that is, those with and without net income. It is followed by a second table for the same industry, Table II, which reports only those corporations with net income.

8. How many items of information are there for each industry?

There are 50 indicators of corporate performance in each table and each industry and for all asset size groups, except where the IRS' data sample is too small, or it does not supply the necessary information.

9. Who are the users of the Almanac?

Accountants, corporate managers, business consultants, investors evaluating a corporate takeover, entrepreneurs considering new businesses, lawyers, and students of accounting, business, and management.

10. What accounting time period is covered?

The Internal Revenue Service provides the most recent statistics publicly available for the *Almanac*. For the 2014 *Almanac*, these statistics apply to the accounting period from July 2010 through June 2011.

WHAT'S NEW IN THIS EDITION

Beginning with the year 2002, the *Almanac of Business and Industrial Financial Ratios* began using the North American Industry Classification System (NAICS). NAICS replaces the Internal Revenue Service's own system, which it had used for many years, an adaptation of Standard Industrial Classification (SIC); all previous *Almanacs* had used that adaptation.

The new industrial classification system is the product of the North American Free Trade Agreement (NAFTA), and it replaces the existing classification systems not only of the United States but also of Canada and Mexico. Hence, the new system applies uniformly to the three countries, and users of the *Almanac 2014*, utilizing the new international industrial classification system, can now compare their results with corporations in all three nations.

In the United States, the new manual was created by the Office of Management and Budget (OMB). The NAICS system gives special attention to industries producing and furnishing advanced technologies, new and emerging industries, as well as service industries in general. NAICS divides the economy into 21 sectors, five in the predominantly goods-producing area, and 16 in the service producing area.

INDUSTRY SECTORS

In 2007, NAICS was revised and reorganized; several of those changes apply to the *Almanac 2014*. The Real Estate Investment Trust category (525930) was deleted. In its place, Mortgage REIT's were reclassified to Other Financial Vehicles (525995) while Equity REIT's were reclassified either to Lessors of Buildings (531115) or Lessors of Miniwarehouses, Self-Storage Units and other Real Estate (531135), depending on the content of the REIT portfolio.

The other major changes were in the information sector. The Internet Publishing and Broadcasting category (516100) was deleted and reclassified with Other Information Services (519100). Internet Service Providers (518115) were reclassified to Telecommunications (517000). Web Search Portals (also part of 518115) were reclassified to the expanded category, Other Information Services

(519100). The remainder of the 518115 category was reorganized as Data processing, Hosting and Related Services (518210).

The source of the IRS's data are the tax returns of all *active* public and private corporations. Because the *Almanac's* data are derived only from corporate tax returns, there is a mixture of corporate with the financial performance of partnerships and individual proprietorships; the *Almanac's* information constitutes a **homogeneous universe**. The tax returns are classified by the IRS on the basis of the business activity which accounts for a corporation's largest percentage of total receipts. Large corporations with dissimilar business activities are included in only one industry, despite operations that are unrelated to the industry in which they are grouped.

The data developed by the IRS are derived from a stratified probability sample of corporation income tax returns. Where the sample data from the sample are small and should those numbers be used in a denominator, the result is reported as a dot (·) in the *Almanac*. Returns of the largest corporations are generally in the sample from year to year, but comparability can be affected by consolidations and mergers, changes in the law and the tax forms, and changes in the industrial classification system used over the years.

REPRESENTATIVE INDUSTRIES

The *Almanac* reports on nearly 200 industries. Minor industries are denoted by a six-digit code; major industries are designated by a three-digit industry code; industrial sectors by a two-digit code; and industrial divisions by a two-digit code. When the data are the same for minor, major, sector, and industrial division, the IRS reports only the industrial division, and similarly for other identities applicable to the major and sectoral industries; the *Almanac* follows this procedure.

Almanac 2014 continues the previous coverage of reporting information: for all industries, **Table I, Corporations with and without Net Income** (that is, the entire universe of active reporting corporations), and **Table II, Corporations with Net Income**, a subset of the universe. In the *Almanac 2014*, Table I covers over 5.8 million enterprises (corporations), and Table II covers 3.3 million corporations with net income. This implies that 2.5 million corporations reported deficits. The IRS defines net income (or deficit) as the companies' net profit or loss from taxable sources of income reduced by allowable deductions. Total receipts of the 5.8 million corporations reported in *Almanac 2014* was $26.2 trillion, up by $1.4 trillion.

The *Almanac* continues to report performance results not only by the total for each industry, but by 12 other asset size groups (a total of 13 asset size groups), providing 50 items of data and/or ratios on corporate performance:

TOTAL

Zero

$1 to $500,000

$500,001 to $1,000,000

$1,000,001 to $5,000,000

$5,000,001 to $10,000,000

$10,000,001 to $25,000,000

$25,000,001 to $50,000,000

$50,000,001 to $100,000,000

$100,000,001 to $250,000,000

$250,000,001 to $500,000,000

$500,000,001 to $2,500,000,000

$2,500,000,001 or more

All data in Tables I and II cover an accounting period identified on all tables and are the most recent information available from the IRS. For the *Almanac 2014*, the accounting period is July 2010 through June 2011. The dating of the data is counterbalanced by the most extensive industrial coverage available in any report on financial performance, the number of items of corporate performance, and their availability in thirteen asset size groups. Moreover, the timing of the data are also counterbalanced by the stability of the *Almanac's* values as past trends have indicated. Therefore, the *Almanac's* financial results are reliable in assessing current corporate performance.

Beyond its reliable insights into corporate behavior on a micro basis, its comprehensive and detailed coverage make the *Almanac* the **Anatomy of American Corporate Capitalism**. In this macro sense, it constitutes **the** example to those countries desirous of modeling their economies on the American performance.

HOW TO USE THE ALMANAC

On the micro level, the *Almanac* multiplies manyfold the power of financial analysis to evaluate an individual company's financial performance: In contrast to many standard reports, the *Almanac* gives management, and analysts independent of any company, more of the fundamental analytical tools needed to compare their company with companies in the same industry and of the same asset size. The *Almanac* can enhance the value of any company's annual report because it affords the analyst and the stockholder detailed background of financial information for comparison.

All items and ratios are listed in Both Table I and Table II. No figures are reported in the *Almanac* when the IRS has either suppressed the underlying data, or the sample size, or other reasons affecting a calculated result, and where the ratio/item was not applicable to an industry. The 50 tax-based items that provide that financial analysis are as follows:

1. Number of Enterprises

These are the count of corporate tax returns filed by active corporations on one of the Form 1120-series returns.

> **SPECIAL NOTE:** Net Sales is used to compute the percentage of items 3 to 7 to Net Sales for all industries, except Finance, Insurance, and Real Estate (FIRE). For the FIRE industries, Total Receipts are used to compute the percentage of items 3 to 7.

REVENUES ($ IN THOUSANDS), ITEMS 2 TO 9

2. Operating Income (Net Sales)

This is the IRS item Business Receipts, the gross operating receipts reduced by the cost of returned goods and allowances.

3. Interest

Taxable interest includes interest on U.S. Government obligations, loans, notes, mortgages, arbitrage bonds, nonexempt private activity bonds, corporate bonds, bank deposits, and tax refunds; interest received from tax-exempt state or local municipal bonds and ESOP loans are not included in this item.

4. Rents

These are the gross amounts received from the use or occupancy of property by corporations whose principal activities did not involve operating rental properties.

5. Royalties

These are gross payments received for the use of property rights before taking deductions.

6. Other Portfolio Income

These consist of cash, notes, and accounts receivable, less allowance for bad debts and inventories.

7. Other Receipts

These receipts include such items as income from minor operations, cash discounts, claims, license rights, judgments, and joint ventures.

8. Total Receipts

Total receipts are the sum of ten items: 1. Business receipts; 2. Interest; 3. Interest on government obligations: state and local; 4. Rents; 5. Royalties; 6. Net capital gains (excluding long-term gains from regulated investment companies); 7. Net gain, noncapital assets; 8. Dividends received from domestic corporations; 9. Dividends received from foreign corporations; 10. Other receipts.

9. Average Total Receipts

Total receipts divided by the number of enterprises.

OPERATING COSTS/OPERATING INCOME, ITEMS 10 TO 22

10. Cost of Operations

This is the IRS's Costs of Goods Sold; it consists of the costs incurred in producing the goods or furnishing the services that generated the corporations' business receipts.

11. Salaries and Wages

These include the amount of salaries and wages paid as well as bonuses and director's fees, but no contributions to pension plans (see item 16) nor compensation of officers (see item 20).

12. Taxes Paid

Excludes Federal Income Taxes; they are the amounts paid for ordinary state and local taxes, social security, payroll taxes, unemployment insurance taxes, excise taxes, import and tariff duties, and business license and privilege taxes.

13. Interest Paid

These amounts consist of interest paid on all business indebtedness.

14. Depreciation

The charges allowed are governed principally by the IRS rules in effect in 1997, basically enacted in 1986, but also include other modifications. Hence, depreciation could represent amounts computed by different sets of rules.

15. Amortization and Depletion

Most amortization is calculated on a straight-line basis. Depletion is allowed for the exhaustion of natural deposits and timber.

16. Pensions, Profit-Sharing, Stock Bonus, and Annuity Plans

These are amounts deducted during the current year for qualified pension, profit-sharing, or other funded deferred compensation plans.

17. Employee Benefits

These are employer contributions to death benefit, insurance, health, accident, and sickness, and other welfare plans.

18. Advertising

Amounts include promotion and publicity expenses.

19. Other Expenses

These include expenses for repairs, bad debts, rent paid on business property, domestic production activities, contributions and gifts, and expenses not allocable to specific deductible items.

20. Officers' Compensation

Salaries, wages, stock bonuses, bonds, and other forms of compensation are included in this item.

21. Operating Margin

This is the net income after all operating costs have been deducted.

22. Operating Margin Before Officers' Compensation

This measure takes into account the effect of Officers' Compensation on the operating margin.

SELECTED AVERAGE BALANCE SHEET ITEMS ($ IN THOUSANDS) ITEMS 23 TO 29

23. Average Net Receivables

The total of Notes and Accounts Receivable, less Allowance for Bad Debts, divided by the number of enterprises. Notes and Accounts Receivable are the gross amounts arising from business sales or services to customers on credit in the course of ordinary trade or business. This includes commercial paper, charge accounts, current intercompany receivables, property investment loans, and trade acceptances.

24. Average Inventories

Total inventories are divided by the number of enterprises. Inventories include finished goods, partially finished goods, new materials and supplies acquired for sale, merchandise on hand or in transit, and growing crops reported as assets by agricultural enterprises.

25. Average Net Property, Plant and Equipment

This includes depreciable assets less accumulated depreciation, depletable assets less accumulated depletion, and land; the sum is divided by the number of enterprises. Depreciable assets consist of end-of-year balance sheet tangible property, such as buildings and equipment used in trade or business, or held for the production of income, and that has a useful life of one year or more. The amount of accumulated depreciation represents the portion written off in the current year, as well as in prior years. Depletable assets represent the end-of-year value of mineral property, oil and gas wells, and other natural resources; standing timber; intangible development and drilling costs capitalized; and leases and leaseholds, subject to depletion. Accumulated depletion represents the cumulative adjustment of these assets.

26. Average Total Assets

Total Assets (and Total Liabilities) are amounts reported in the end-of-year balance sheet. Total Assets are net amounts after reduction from accumulated depreciation, accumulated amortization, accumulated depletion, and the reserve for bad debts. Total Liabilities include the claims of creditors and stockholders' equity, and were net after reduction by the cost of treasury stock. The average of total assets was obtained by dividing it by the number of enterprises.

27. Average of Notes and Loans Payable, and Mortgages

These liabilities were separated on the balance sheet according to the time to maturity of the obligations. Time to maturity was based on the date of the balance sheet, rather than the date of issue of the obligations. The total was divided by the number of enterprises.

28. Average of All Other Liabilities

These included accounts payable, and other liabilities including other current liabilities. The total was divided by the number of enterprises.

29. Average Net Worth

Net Worth represents the stockholders' equity in the corporation (total assets minus the claims of creditors). It consists of Capital Stock, Paid-In Capital Surplus, Retained Earnings Appropriated, Retained Earnings Unappropriated, less cost of treasury stock.

SELECTED FINANCIAL RATIOS, NUMBER OF TIMES TO ONE, RATIOS 30 TO 44

30. CURRENT RATIO

The items that used Current Assets for this ratio are Cash; Notes and Accounts Receivable, Less: Allowance for Bad Debts; Inventories; Government Obligations; Tax-Exempt Securities; and Other Current Assets. For Current Liabilities, the following items were included: Accounts Payable; Mortgages and Notes Maturing in Less than 1 Year; and Other Current Liabilities.

This ratio, rated highest by CPAs as a measure of liquidity, gauges the ability of a company to meet its short-term financial obligations should it be compelled to liquidate its assets. However, it is not an absolute measure of the company's ability to meet its obligations. It is obtained by dividing current assets by current liabilities. The standard guideline has been a ratio of 2 to 1; however, some companies have found that in their experience, a ratio less than 2 to 1 is adequate, while others consider a larger one to be necessary. The ratio is affected by the method of valuation of inventory (LIFO or FIFO) and by inflation. The *Almanac* provides measures that can be treated as standards by size of asset.

31. Quick Ratio

This ratio is also known as the "Acid Test Ratio" because it is often used to estimate a company's general liquidity. There is some disagreement about the inclusion of inventory in the numerator because it may be slow moving, obsolete, or pledged to specific creditors, and, therefore, not be readily convertible into cash. The *Almanac* adopts a conservative approach and does not include the item in calculating the ratio. Excluding inventories and other current assets, the numerator is the same as that used in determining current assets. The denominator, current liabilities, is unchanged. The ratio of 1 to 1 has been considered a reasonable standard, but it is jeopardized because accounts and notes receivable may not be convertible into cash at face value and at short notice. The *Almanac* provides measures that can be treated as standards by size of asset.

32. Net Sales to Working Capital

This is an efficiency, or turnover, ratio that measures the rate at which current assets less current liabilities (Working Capital) is used in making sales. (In industries in Finance, Insurance, and Real Estate, total receipts rather than net sales is used.) A low ratio indicates a less efficient (profitable) use of working capital in making sales. The *Almanac* provides measures that can be treated as standards by size of asset. Working Capital is the difference between current assets and current liabilities.

33. Coverage Ratio

This ratio measures the number of times all interest paid by the company is covered by earnings before interest charges and taxes (EBIT). For that reason, the ratio is also known as the "times interest earned ratio." The ratio indicates the company's ability to service its debt based on its income.

34. Total Asset Turnover

The ratio is an efficiency ratio because it indicates the effectiveness of the company's use of its total assets in generating sales. It is measured by dividing net sales by total assets.

35. Inventory Turnover

Inventory turnover measures the liquidity of the inventory. It is computed by dividing the cost of goods sold by the average inventory. The result shows the number of times that the average inventory can be converted into receivables or cash. The ratio reflects both on the quality of the inventory and the efficiency of management. Typically, the higher the turnover rate, the more likely profits will be higher.

> **SPECIAL NOTE:** Inventory turnover is not computed for industries in Finance, Insurance, and Real Estate.

36. Receivables Turnover

This ratio measures the liquidity of accounts receivable. It indicates the average collection period throughout the year. It is obtained by dividing sales average by net receivables. It is not computed in the Finance, Insurance, and Real Estate industries (although it is calculated for all other industries even though conventional analysis typically omits it) for many of the industries in the *Almanac*.

37. Total Liabilities to Net Worth

This ratio indicates the extent to which the company's funds are supplied by short- and long-term creditors compared to its owners. It is an indicator of the company's long-term debt paying ability. The ratio is one of the most important bearing on the company's capital structure. Net worth is defined in ratio 29.

38. Current Assets to Working Capital

The dependence of Working Capital in part on current assets is important to understanding this part of the source of Working Capital. Current Assets are defined in ratio 30 and Working Capital is defined in ratio 32.

39. Current Liabilities to Working Capital

The dependence of Working Capital in part on current liabilities is important to understanding this part of the source of Working Capital. Current Liabilities are defined in ratio 30 and Working Capital is defined in ratio 32.

40. Working Capital to Net Sales or Total Receipts

The purpose of this ratio is to determine the working capital needed in relation to projected sales or receipts. Working Capital is defined in ratio 32.

41. Inventory to Working Capital

This ratio, by showing the proportion of Working Capital invested in Inventory, indicates the part of Current Assets that are least liquid. Inventories which exceed working capital indicate that current liabilities exceed liquid current assets. Working Capital is defined in ratio 32.

42. Total Receipts to Cash Flow

Cash Flow is the difference between cash receipts and cash disbursements. The ratio of total receipts to cash flow could suggest steps which management might take to improve the company's cash position.

43. Cost of Goods to Cash Flow

This ratio can be the basis for projections of cash requirements needed to fund projected costs of production. Cash flow is defined in ratio 42.

44. Cash Flow to Total Debt

This ratio indicates the extent to which a company could service its total debt from cash flow. It is analogous to the coverage ratio; refer to ratio 33. Cash flow is defined in ratio 42.

SELECTED FINANCIAL FACTORS (IN PERCENTAGES), ITEMS 45 TO 50

45. Debt Ratio (Total Liabilities to Total Assets)

This ratio indicates the company's ability to pay all its debts. It measures the creditors' and owners' of the company's ability to withstand losses. It is an indicator of the long-run solvency of the firm.

46. Return on Total Assets

The ratio combines the turnover and profit ratios (Sales/Total Assets x [times] Profit/Sales) and yields the return on investment (Total Assets). The result is the end product of the DuPont System of financial analysis. The system takes into account both operating income and operating assets. In Table I of each industry, the Return on Investment (ROI) is net income less deficit before income taxes divided by total assets. In Table II of each industry, the ROI is net income before income taxes divided by Total Assets. Total Assets are used because management has discretion in the investment of the resources provided by both the creditors and owners.

47. Return on Equity Before Income Taxes

This ratio measures the profitability of the company's operations to owners, before income taxes. For Table I this is net income, less deficit before income taxes and before credits. For Table II this is net income minus income tax before credits.

48. Return on Equity After Income Taxes

This ratio measures the profitability of the company's operations to owners, after income taxes. For Table I this is net income, less deficit and minus income tax before credits. For Table II this is net income minus income tax and before credits.

49. Profit Margin (Before Income Tax)

This is net income before income tax divided by net sales (or total receipts) and indicates the contribution of sales to the profitability of the company. Competition, capital structure, and operating characteristics cause the margin to vary within and among industries. For Table I, net income less deficit and before income taxes is the numerator; for Table II it is net income before tax.

50. Profit Margin (After Income Tax)

This ratio is the same as ratio 49 except that income taxes are taken into account.

TABLE OF CONTENTS

Page references to tables for industries with net income are in italic

PRINCIPAL BUSINESS ACTIVITY (BASED ON NAICS)

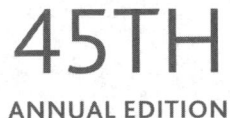

45TH
ANNUAL EDITION

2014 ALMANAC OF
BUSINESS AND INDUSTRIAL FINANCIAL RATIOS

Table I

Corporations with and without Net Income

AGRICULTURAL PRODUCTION

MONEY AMOUNTS AND SIZE OF ASSETS IN THOUSANDS OF DOLLARS

Item Description for Accounting Period 7/10 Through 6/11	Total	Zero Assets	Under 500	500 to 1,000	1,000 to 5,000	5,000 to 10,000	10,000 to 25,000	25,000 to 50,000	50,000 to 100,000	100,000 to 250,000	250,000 to 500,000	500,000 to 2,500,000	2,500,000 and over
Number of Enterprises **1**	101952	10155	57130	16577	15929	1201	618	161	96	53	21	11	0
Revenues ($ in Thousands)													
Net Sales **2**	108983081	1653484	12717370	13630716	22872172	6723000	8499977	3631321	7761813	8824291	9552034	13316901	0
Interest **3**	215390	1856	19393	50766	56297	27044	11106	9704	6012	13719	6399	13093	0
Rents **4**	983962	37198	259198	147684	287762	60738	22071	24254	14174	68827	45871	16184	0
Royalties **5**	110284	891	3464	14305	19441	5545	1686	10629	2094	30610	9313	12307	0
Other Portfolio Income **6**	1343475	90951	200449	220231	404135	120566	43966	89216	48368	54009	53879	17708	0
Other Receipts **7**	16449137	267699	3516617	2747756	6604792	1468029	913227	315351	216089	212358	8184	179033	0
Total Receipts **8**	128085329	2052079	16716491	16811458	30244599	8404922	9492033	4080475	8048550	9203814	9675680	13355226	0
Average Total Receipts **9**	1256	202	293	1014	1899	6998	15359	25345	83839	173657	460747	1214111	•
Operating Costs/Operating Income (%)													
Cost of Operations **10**	51.5	67.0	15.5	38.4	38.1	40.7	65.3	58.6	67.8	68.7	73.9	78.9	•
Salaries and Wages **11**	7.8	3.7	9.0	11.6	10.6	11.9	6.2	9.1	5.6	5.7	2.7	3.7	•
Taxes Paid **12**	2.4	2.0	3.3	3.6	3.2	2.2	1.6	1.9	1.2	1.5	1.2	1.5	•
Interest Paid **13**	2.3	2.1	2.7	2.0	3.6	2.8	1.9	2.3	1.4	1.5	1.0	2.1	•
Depreciation **14**	6.4	3.0	10.0	8.1	9.3	6.6	5.2	5.4	3.6	3.8	2.8	3.9	•
Amortization and Depletion **15**	0.3	0.1	0.2	0.2	0.1	0.1	0.1	0.5	0.6	0.4	0.8	0.7	•
Pensions and Other Deferred Comp. **16**	0.2	0.0	0.1	0.1	0.1	0.1	0.3	0.2	0.2	0.2	0.4	0.3	•
Employee Benefits **17**	1.0	0.3	1.4	1.0	0.9	1.0	0.9	0.7	0.6	0.9	0.4	1.5	•
Advertising **18**	0.3	0.1	0.4	0.2	0.2	0.2	0.3	0.2	0.2	0.2	0.3	0.9	•
Other Expenses **19**	40.9	36.9	82.0	52.1	62.3	54.7	26.7	29.3	18.5	16.8	14.2	6.6	•
Officers' Compensation **20**	1.9	0.9	4.4	3.1	2.6	1.6	1.4	1.3	0.9	0.7	0.3	0.4	•
Operating Margin **21**	•	•	•	•	•	•	•	•	•	•	1.9	•	•
Operating Margin Before Officers' Comp. **22**	•	•	•	•	•	•	•	•	0.3	•	0.2	2.2	•

Selected Average Balance Sheet ($ in Thousands)

	1	2	3	4	5	6	7	8	9	10	11	12	13
Net Receivables 23	98	0	3	27	88	522	1769	5546	10564	24117	38840	205860	•
Inventories 24	119	0	10	38	167	649	2129	4219	10084	28252	59671	168488	•
Net Property, Plant and Equipment 25	500	0	86	366	1094	3759	6143	12761	27949	60544	128570	326388	•
Total Assets 26	1108	0	182	711	1999	6749	15198	33995	69352	159779	335707	1256557	•
Notes and Loans Payable 27	606	0	201	392	1202	4254	7320	13094	26571	57145	114892	449280	•
All Other Liabilities 28	162	0	16	53	195	791	2627	5055	9751	27671	53483	429891	•
Net Worth 29	340	0	-35	266	602	1704	5252	15846	33030	74964	167332	377386	•

Selected Financial Ratios (Times to 1)

	1	2	3	4	5	6	7	8	9	10	11	12
Current Ratio 30	1.6	•	1.6	1.5	1.4	1.2	1.4	1.8	1.7	1.7	2.3	1.5
Quick Ratio 31	0.8	•	1.0	1.0	0.8	0.7	0.7	1.1	0.8	0.8	0.8	0.7
Net Sales to Working Capital 32	8.0	•	11.4	12.2	9.8	18.4	7.6	3.5	7.2	5.6	5.1	6.6
Coverage Ratio 33	2.1	4.8	1.9	2.4	1.4	2.1	1.9	2.2	3.4	3.4	4.1	1.8
Total Asset Turnover 34	1.0	•	1.2	1.2	0.7	0.8	0.9	0.7	1.2	1.0	1.4	0.9
Inventory Turnover 35	4.6	•	3.4	8.3	3.3	3.5	4.2	3.1	5.4	4.0	5.6	5.6
Receivables Turnover 36	11.1	•	79.1	34.4	18.3	•	8.4	4.0	8.6	6.9	12.4	•
Total Liabilities to Net Worth 37	2.3	•	•	1.7	2.3	3.0	1.9	1.1	1.1	1.1	1.0	2.3
Current Assets to Working Capital 38	2.8	•	2.8	3.0	3.4	6.0	3.3	2.2	2.5	2.5	1.8	2.9
Current Liabilities to Working Capital 39	1.8	•	1.8	2.0	2.4	5.0	2.3	1.2	1.5	1.5	0.8	1.9
Working Capital to Net Sales 40	0.1	•	0.1	0.1	0.1	0.1	0.1	0.3	0.1	0.2	0.2	0.2
Inventory to Working Capital 41	1.0	•	0.6	0.6	1.2	2.1	1.3	0.6	1.0	1.0	0.8	0.9
Total Receipts to Cash Flow 42	3.1	2.9	1.7	2.6	2.1	2.1	4.4	3.9	5.3	5.5	6.5	16.2
Cost of Goods to Cash Flow 43	1.6	1.9	0.3	1.0	0.8	0.9	2.9	2.3	3.6	3.8	4.8	12.8
Cash Flow to Total Debt 44	0.5	•	0.6	0.7	0.5	0.5	0.3	0.3	0.4	0.4	0.4	0.1

Selected Financial Factors (in Percentages)

	1	2	3	4	5	6	7	8	9	10	11	12
Debt Ratio 45	69.3	•	119.2	62.5	69.9	74.7	65.4	53.4	52.4	53.1	50.2	70.0
Return on Total Assets 46	4.6	•	6.5	5.7	3.5	4.9	3.4	3.3	5.3	5.4	5.7	3.6
Return on Equity Before Income Taxes 47	7.9	•	•	9.0	3.2	10.3	4.8	3.8	7.9	8.2	8.7	5.3
Return on Equity After Income Taxes 48	6.2	•	•	7.5	2.1	8.5	4.2	2.4	6.9	6.0	6.7	3.8
Profit Margin (Before Income Tax) 49	2.5	8.2	2.5	2.9	1.3	3.1	1.8	2.7	3.2	3.7	3.2	1.7
Profit Margin (After Income Tax) 50	2.0	7.2	2.1	2.4	0.9	2.6	1.6	1.7	2.8	2.7	2.5	1.2

Table II

Corporations with Net Income

AGRICULTURAL PRODUCTION

MONEY AMOUNTS AND SIZE OF ASSETS IN THOUSANDS OF DOLLARS

Item Description for Accounting Period 7/10 Through 6/11	Total	Zero Assets	Under 500	500 to 1000	1,000 to 5,000	5,000 to 10,000	10,000 to 25,000	25,000 to 50,000	50,000 to 100,000	100,000 to 250,000	250,000 to 500,000	500,000 to 2,500,000	2,500,000 and over
Number of Enterprises **1**	54845	4884	27328	11680	9796	618	329	95	59	•	13	•	0
Revenues ($ in Thousands)													
Net Sales **2**	76000599	1294550	9082248	6289844	15581710	5029294	4725485	2201377	5604692	•	7576439	•	0
Interest **3**	173626	1676	14515	39629	43581	22249	8264	7922	4487	•	5530	•	0
Rents **4**	774080	18712	200699	120277	226598	43819	13557	19963	9329	•	39016	•	0
Royalties **5**	87593	891	1650	14305	14143	5545	1686	3309	0	•	3147	•	0
Other Portfolio Income **6**	958989	78845	112770	199029	248932	97897	22899	59709	22154	•	49248	•	0
Other Receipts **7**	12947363	297078	1908327	2257047	6038276	943009	769921	202788	172180	•	38481	•	0
Total Receipts **8**	90942250	1691752	11320209	8920131	22153240	6141813	5541812	2495068	5812842	•	7711861	•	0
Average Total Receipts **9**	1658	346	414	764	2261	9938	16844	26264	98523	•	593220	•	•
Operating Costs/Operating Income (%)													
Cost of Operations **10**	53.4	71.9	14.8	24.4	39.2	45.4	61.0	44.9	71.3	•	84.3	•	•
Salaries and Wages **11**	6.7	2.3	7.1	7.8	10.6	9.0	6.6	11.4	5.1	•	2.1	•	•
Taxes Paid **12**	2.1	2.0	2.6	3.5	3.0	1.9	2.0	2.0	1.1	•	1.1	•	•
Interest Paid **13**	1.8	1.5	1.8	2.7	2.4	1.7	2.1	2.1	1.1	•	1.0	•	•
Depreciation **14**	5.8	2.5	7.7	12.8	8.1	5.6	5.3	5.8	3.3	•	2.3	•	•
Amortization and Depletion **15**	0.3	0.1	0.2	0.3	0.0	0.1	0.1	0.4	0.6	•	0.0	•	•
Pensions and Other Deferred Comp. **16**	0.2	0.0	0.1	0.1	0.1	0.1	0.3	0.2	0.1	•	0.5	•	•
Employee Benefits **17**	1.0	0.3	1.1	1.6	0.9	1.1	1.1	0.6	0.5	•	0.4	•	•
Advertising **18**	0.3	0.1	0.3	0.3	0.2	0.2	0.1	0.2	0.1	•	0.4	•	•
Other Expenses **19**	36.7	25.1	68.9	69.4	63.7	45.6	26.6	32.1	12.6	•	4.1	•	•
Officers' Compensation **20**	1.9	0.6	4.0	4.8	2.8	1.8	1.8	1.1	0.7	•	0.2	•	•
Operating Margin **21**	•	•	•	•	•	•	•	•	3.5	•	3.4	•	•
Operating Margin Before Officers' Comp. **22**	•	•	•	•	•	•	0.4	0.4	4.2	•	3.7	•	•

Selected Average Balance Sheet ($ in Thousands)

Line Item										
Net Receivables 23	130	0	5	31	80	653	1763	6707	12812	50602
Inventories 24	133	0	9	31	165	834	1891	3299	10254	80213
Net Property, Plant and Equipment 25	528	0	80	353	1007	2733	5647	12343	24711	137799
Total Assets 26	1303	0	194	706	1951	6688	15667	34572	69036	338478
Notes and Loans Payable 27	529	0	117	283	871	3546	5420	11951	24959	109922
All Other Liabilities 28	217	0	25	52	178	841	2604	5813	11521	72453
Net Worth 29	557	0	52	371	903	2301	7643	16808	32556	156103

Selected Financial Ratios (Times to 1)

Line Item										
Current Ratio 30	1.6	2.2	•	1.8	1.3	1.3	2.0	1.7	2.0	1.7
Quick Ratio 31	0.9	1.6	•	1.2	0.8	0.6	1.3	0.8	0.9	0.7
Net Sales to Working Capital 32	7.9	8.8	•	6.2	12.4	16.1	3.2	5.7	7.0	7.5
Coverage Ratio 33	6.1	9.9	17.2	6.3	5.6	6.7	7.1	6.0	7.6	6.2
Total Asset Turnover 34	1.1	1.7	•	0.8	0.8	1.2	0.7	0.9	1.4	1.7
Inventory Turnover 35	5.6	5.8	•	4.3	3.8	4.4	3.2	4.6	6.6	6.1
Receivables Turnover 36	13.1	88.0	•	23.7	20.5	16.8	•	8.0	8.7	•
Total Liabilities to Net Worth 37	1.3	2.8	•	0.9	1.2	1.9	1.1	1.0	1.1	1.2
Current Assets to Working Capital 38	2.7	1.9	•	2.3	4.1	4.8	2.0	2.3	2.4	2.0
Current Liabilities to Working Capital 39	1.7	0.9	•	1.3	3.1	3.8	1.0	1.3	1.4	1.0
Working Capital to Net Sales 40	0.1	0.1	•	0.2	0.1	0.1	0.3	0.2	0.1	0.1
Inventory to Working Capital 41	0.9	0.3	•	0.4	1.2	2.0	0.5	0.9	0.9	1.0
Total Receipts to Cash Flow 42	2.8	1.6	2.4	1.7	1.7	2.2	2.7	3.3	5.9	13.5
Cost of Goods to Cash Flow 43	1.5	0.2	1.7	0.4	0.7	1.0	1.2	2.0	4.2	11.4
Cash Flow to Total Debt 44	0.7	1.5	•	0.9	0.9	0.9	0.5	0.5	0.4	0.2

Selected Financial Factors (in Percentages)

Line Item										
Debt Ratio 45	57.2	73.4	•	47.4	53.7	65.6	51.4	51.2	52.8	53.9
Return on Total Assets 46	12.0	30.6	•	12.9	11.0	14.0	9.8	11.3	11.4	10.8
Return on Equity Before Income Taxes 47	23.6	103.3	•	20.6	19.5	34.6	17.2	19.3	21.0	19.5
Return on Equity After Income Taxes 48	21.7	99.5	•	19.2	18.4	32.1	15.0	18.6	19.5	16.2
Profit Margin (Before Income Tax) 49	9.5	16.0	24.3	14.2	11.1	9.8	12.5	10.3	7.2	5.2
Profit Margin (After Income Tax) 50	8.7	15.4	23.0	13.2	10.4	9.1	10.9	9.9	6.7	4.3

Table I
Corporations with and without Net Income

FORESTRY AND LOGGING

MONEY AMOUNTS AND SIZE OF ASSETS IN THOUSANDS OF DOLLARS

Item Description for Accounting Period 7/10 Through 6/11	Total	Zero Assets	Under 500	500 to 1,000	1,000 to 5,000	5,000 to 10,000	10,000 to 25,000	25,000 to 50,000	50,000 to 100,000	100,000 to 250,000	250,000 to 500,000	500,000 to 2,500,000	2,500,000 and over
Number of Enterprises 1	8779	998	6088	711	758	103	77	27	13	0	5	0	0
Revenues ($ in Thousands)													
Net Sales 2	10813687	161185	3298134	1472822	1418191	1141679	1041701	583229	568064	0	1128683	0	0
Interest 3	50311	2	1681	77	2313	195	1112	74	5686	0	39171	0	0
Rents 4	33803	0	14716	24	3414	1526	3771	991	441	0	8921	0	0
Royalties 5	21099	0	1529	0	0	15119	296	0	0	0	4154	0	0
Other Portfolio Income 6	253246	21270	101418	29927	17471	4250	51400	878	275	0	26357	0	0
Other Receipts 7	90061	73	13295	2778	14275	-3742	40644	9022	-3204	0	16920	0	0
Total Receipts 8	11262207	182530	3430773	1505628	1455664	1159027	1138924	594194	571262	0	1224206	0	0
Average Total Receipts 9	1283	183	564	2118	1920	11253	14791	22007	43943	•	244841	•	•
Operating Costs/Operating Income (%)													
Cost of Operations 10	56.3	88.5	19.3	68.0	34.4	87.3	85.2	93.0	86.5	•	80.3	•	•
Salaries and Wages 11	8.9	2.8	11.0	6.5	21.5	3.5	4.9	1.1	2.6	•	7.0	•	•
Taxes Paid 12	2.4	0.7	2.2	1.5	5.5	1.8	1.7	2.0	1.2	•	2.3	•	•
Interest Paid 13	1.8	2.2	1.8	1.9	1.8	0.4	1.3	1.4	4.7	•	1.8	•	•
Depreciation 14	5.3	4.8	9.3	6.8	5.9	2.2	2.3	0.9	1.5	•	1.5	•	•
Amortization and Depletion 15	0.8	0.0	0.0	•	0.1	0.2	0.3	1.5	2.5	•	4.7	•	•
Pensions and Other Deferred Comp. 16	0.1	•	•	0.0	0.3	0.0	0.2	0.1	0.1	•	0.2	•	•
Employee Benefits 17	1.1	0.0	1.4	0.3	2.5	0.2	0.8	0.5	0.6	•	1.8	•	•
Advertising 18	0.1	0.0	0.0	0.1	0.1	0.1	0.0	0.0	0.0	•	0.2	•	•
Other Expenses 19	24.1	10.7	52.8	13.2	23.7	3.7	10.5	6.5	7.3	•	7.5	•	•
Officers' Compensation 20	2.2	0.3	2.8	3.2	3.9	0.9	2.0	0.5	0.8	•	0.3	•	•
Operating Margin 21	•	•	•	•	0.4	•	•	•	•	•	•	•	•
Operating Margin Before Officers' Comp. 22	•	•	2.3	1.6	4.3	0.7	•	•	•	•	•	•	•

Selected Average Balance Sheet ($ in Thousands)

Item										
Net Receivables 23	67	0	1	50	76	123	850	1564	3252	64320
Inventories 24	58	0	2	52	110	330	3126	2496	2057	3063
Net Property, Plant and Equipment 25	463	0	68	361	966	2759	6655	22318	30593	173712
Total Assets 26	1131	0	109	673	1974	7604	15856	37947	78488	648710
Notes and Loans Payable 27	540	0	100	604	1324	887	3805	9535	28188	338055
All Other Liabilities 28	75	0	11	23	115	1563	1154	2112	9345	12166
Net Worth 29	515	0	-3	46	534	5155	10898	26300	40955	298489

Selected Financial Ratios (Times to 1)

Item										
Current Ratio 30	1.8	•	1.2	1.5	1.2	1.0	3.9	3.9	1.6	2.1
Quick Ratio 31	0.9	•	0.9	0.6	0.6	0.6	1.1	2.8	0.6	1.3
Net Sales to Working Capital 32	9.3	•	99.7	23.2	30.7	217.7	3.3	3.3	6.4	2.6
Coverage Ratio 33	1.6	2.5	2.9	1.4	2.7	3.9	1.0	•	•	1.4
Total Asset Turnover 34	1.1	•	5.0	3.1	0.9	1.5	0.9	0.6	0.6	0.3
Inventory Turnover 35	12.0	•	58.9	27.0	5.9	29.3	3.7	8.0	18.4	59.2
Receivables Turnover 36	17.9	•	276.4	36.4	17.5	•	18.8	16.8	14.7	4.8
Total Liabilities to Net Worth 37	1.2	•	•	13.7	2.7	0.5	0.5	0.4	0.9	1.2
Current Assets to Working Capital 38	2.3	•	5.6	2.9	7.4	42.0	1.3	1.3	2.7	1.9
Current Liabilities to Working Capital 39	1.3	•	4.6	1.9	6.4	41.0	0.3	0.3	1.7	0.9
Working Capital to Net Sales 40	0.1	•	0.0	0.0	0.0	0.0	0.3	0.3	0.2	0.4
Inventory to Working Capital 41	0.4	•	0.3	0.2	1.2	6.5	0.9	0.3	0.1	0.0
Total Receipts to Cash Flow 42	4.8	21.6	2.0	9.4	5.1	23.3	21.0	2790.6	•	20.2
Cost of Goods to Cash Flow 43	2.7	19.2	0.4	6.4	1.8	20.4	17.9	2594.9	•	16.2
Cash Flow to Total Debt 44	0.4	•	2.4	0.4	0.3	0.2	0.1	0.0	•	0.0

Selected Financial Factors (in Percentages)

Item										
Debt Ratio 45	54.4	•	102.7	93.2	72.9	32.2	31.3	30.7	47.8	54.0
Return on Total Assets 46	3.2	•	26.4	8.1	4.6	2.6	1.2	•	•	0.9
Return on Equity Before Income Taxes 47	2.7	•	•	30.9	10.6	2.8	0.1	•	•	0.5
Return on Equity After Income Taxes 48	1.4	•	•	29.8	10.1	1.9	•	•	•	•
Profit Margin (Before Income Tax) 49	1.1	3.2	3.5	0.7	3.0	1.3	0.1	•	•	0.7
Profit Margin (After Income Tax) 50	0.6	3.1	3.2	0.7	2.9	0.9	0.1	•	•	•

Table II
Corporations with Net Income

FORESTRY AND LOGGING

MONEY AMOUNTS AND SIZE OF ASSETS IN THOUSANDS OF DOLLARS

Item Description for Accounting Period 7/10 Through 6/11	Total	Zero Assets	Under 500	500 to 1,000	1,000 to 5,000	5,000 to 10,000	10,000 to 25,000	25,000 to 50,000	50,000 to 100,000	100,000 to 250,000	250,000 to 500,000	500,000 to 2,500,000	2,500,000 and over
Number of Enterprises 1	4784	32	3834	508	324	52	21	•	•	•	0	0	0

Revenues ($ in Thousands)

Item Description for Accounting Period 7/10 Through 6/11	Total	Zero Assets	Under 500	500 to 1,000	1,000 to 5,000	5,000 to 10,000	10,000 to 25,000	25,000 to 50,000	50,000 to 100,000	100,000 to 250,000	250,000 to 500,000	500,000 to 2,500,000	2,500,000 and over
Net Sales 2	7420062	35666	2952862	952473	699409	780030	384609	•	•	•	0	0	0
Interest 3	46285	0	1616	74	1135	195	447	•	•	•	0	0	0
Rents 4	28368	0	14716	0	319	1526	2900	•	•	•	0	0	0
Royalties 5	21099	0	1529	0	0	15119	296	•	•	•	0	0	0
Other Portfolio Income 6	194367	20780	75836	22671	8344	2855	43760	•	•	•	0	0	0
Other Receipts 7	90608	-3	12226	2646	8271	3273	32502	•	•	•	0	0	0
Total Receipts 8	7800789	56443	3058785	977864	717478	802998	464514	•	•	•	0	0	0
Average Total Receipts 9	1631	1764	798	1925	2214	15442	22120	•	•	•	•	•	•

Operating Costs/Operating Income (%)

Item Description for Accounting Period 7/10 Through 6/11	Total	Zero Assets	Under 500	500 to 1,000	1,000 to 5,000	5,000 to 10,000	10,000 to 25,000	25,000 to 50,000	50,000 to 100,000	100,000 to 250,000	250,000 to 500,000	500,000 to 2,500,000	2,500,000 and over
Cost of Operations 10	50.8	92.4	16.5	54.8	57.9	80.6	87.9	•	•	•	•	•	•
Salaries and Wages 11	7.0	9.3	9.6	9.0	1.3	5.1	5.0	•	•	•	•	•	•
Taxes Paid 12	2.2	0.9	1.8	1.8	4.8	2.6	2.0	•	•	•	•	•	•
Interest Paid 13	1.5	7.8	1.5	2.4	1.3	0.7	0.2	•	•	•	•	•	•
Depreciation 14	5.3	16.5	7.8	7.9	5.5	3.2	0.9	•	•	•	•	•	•
Amortization and Depletion 15	0.1	0.1	0.0	•	•	0.3	0.1	•	•	•	•	•	•
Pensions and Other Deferred Comp. 16	0.0	•	•	0.0	0.1	0.0	0.3	•	•	•	•	•	•
Employee Benefits 17	1.3	•	1.2	0.4	3.6	0.2	1.2	•	•	•	•	•	•
Advertising 18	0.1	0.0	0.0	0.1	0.2	0.1	0.0	•	•	•	•	•	•
Other Expenses 19	27.5	6.6	55.7	18.0	12.9	1.7	11.3	•	•	•	•	•	•
Officers' Compensation 20	2.4	•	2.4	4.1	6.2	1.3	2.7	•	•	•	•	•	•
Operating Margin 21	1.7	•	3.4	1.5	6.2	4.3	•	•	•	•	•	•	•
Operating Margin Before Officers' Comp. 22	4.1	•	5.8	5.6	12.4	5.5	•	•	•	•	•	•	•

Selected Average Balance Sheet ($ in Thousands)

Net Receivables 23	45	0	1	49	71	124	1415
Inventories 24	36	0		72	28	416	855
Net Property, Plant and Equipment 25	358	0	74	394	798	4499	9699
Total Assets 26	1028	0	130	667	2078	6569	17379
Notes and Loans Payable 27	584	0	103	651	943	1757	749
All Other Liabilities 28	69	0	12	9	153	255	1072
Net Worth 29	375	0	16	8	982	4557	15557

Selected Financial Ratios (Times to 1)

Current Ratio 30	2.2	•	1.2	1.4	2.4	1.2	2.8
Quick Ratio 31	1.2	•	0.9	0.5	1.1	0.7	2.2
Net Sales to Working Capital 32	10.1	•	110.9	24.7	5.4	54.2	8.3
Coverage Ratio 33	5.5	4.2	5.6	2.7	7.7	12.0	42.0
Total Asset Turnover 34	1.5	•	5.9	2.8	1.0	2.3	1.1
Inventory Turnover 35	22.0	•	110.8	14.2	44.8	29.0	18.8
Receivables Turnover 36	31.1	•	1059.3	28.6	49.4	95.5	13.4
Total Liabilities to Net Worth 37	1.7	•	7.3	84.4	1.1	0.4	0.1
Current Assets to Working Capital 38	1.8	•	5.8	3.5	1.7	5.7	1.5
Current Liabilities to Working Capital 39	0.8	•	4.8	2.5	0.7	4.7	0.5
Working Capital to Net Sales 40	0.1	•	0.0	0.0	0.2	0.0	0.1
Inventory to Working Capital 41	0.2	•	0.2	0.4	0.1	2.4	0.3
Total Receipts to Cash Flow 42	3.4	•	1.8	5.5	7.0	12.4	11.9
Cost of Goods to Cash Flow 43	1.7	•	0.3	3.0	4.1	10.0	10.5
Cash Flow to Total Debt 44	0.7	•	3.8	0.5	0.3	0.6	0.8

Selected Financial Factors (in Percentages)

Debt Ratio 45	63.5	•	88.0	98.8	52.7	30.6	10.5
Return on Total Assets 46	12.6	•	50.3	18.5	10.5	18.0	9.9
Return on Equity Before Income Taxes 47	28.1	•	343.5	1003.9	19.3	23.7	10.8
Return on Equity After Income Taxes 48	24.9		326.8	995.4	18.7	21.7	8.5
Profit Margin (Before Income Tax) 49	6.8	24.8	7.0	4.2	8.8	7.2	9.2
Profit Margin (After Income Tax) 50	6.0	24.2	6.6	4.1	8.5	6.6	7.2

Table I
Corporations with and without Net Income

SUPPORT ACTIVITIES AND FISHING, HUNTING AND TRAPPING

MONEY AMOUNTS AND SIZE OF ASSETS IN THOUSANDS OF DOLLARS

Item Description for Accounting Period 7/10 Through 6/11	Total	Zero Assets	Under 500	500 to 1,000	1,000 to 5,000	5,000 to 10,000	10,000 to 25,000	25,000 to 50,000	50,000 to 100,000	100,000 to 250,000	250,000 to 500,000	500,000 to 2,500,000	2,500,000 and over
Number of Enterprises **1**	26237	4706	17490	1533	1942	376	114	55	14	6	0	0	0
Revenues ($ in Thousands)													
Net Sales **2**	27227741	325312	6120598	2025258	7769983	2994574	2881384	2246234	861203	2003196	0	0	0
Interest **3**	16608	154	990	631	6712	1199	4247	1759	342	572	0	0	0
Rents **4**	39609	409	27566	2050	3861	2909	1006	1808	0	0	0	0	0
Royalties **5**	2435	0	0	0	0	818	0	798	0	819	0	0	0
Other Portfolio Income **6**	140127	20984	18348	15517	52162	5374	5404	18698	993	2648	0	0	0
Other Receipts **7**	1190776	48370	380010	121175	265520	133185	67468	82027	39886	53135	0	0	0
Total Receipts **8**	28617296	395229	6547512	2164631	8098238	3138059	2959509	2351324	902424	2060370	0	0	0
Average Total Receipts **9**	1091	84	374	1412	4170	8346	25961	42751	64459	343395	•	•	•
Operating Costs/Operating Income (%)													
Cost of Operations **10**	59.9	46.3	38.0	48.1	60.5	72.2	74.8	77.2	69.0	74.9	•	•	•
Salaries and Wages **11**	9.1	6.0	10.9	8.8	11.9	6.8	6.4	3.3	10.3	6.7	•	•	•
Taxes Paid **12**	1.9	2.7	2.5	1.7	2.0	1.3	1.6	0.9	2.1	2.2	•	•	•
Interest Paid **13**	0.9	1.5	0.8	0.6	1.0	1.1	1.0	0.8	1.4	1.0	•	•	•
Depreciation **14**	3.4	3.9	3.2	5.1	3.2	4.1	2.5	2.5	3.8	4.2	•	•	•
Amortization and Depletion **15**	0.1	•	0.1	0.0	0.1	0.2	0.0	0.0	0.3	0.2	•	•	•
Pensions and Other Deferred Comp. **16**	0.1	0.1	0.2	0.2	0.1	0.0	0.2	0.2	0.2	0.1	•	•	•
Employee Benefits **17**	0.7	0.2	0.9	0.8	0.4	0.6	0.6	0.6	1.3	1.7	•	•	•
Advertising **18**	0.3	0.4	0.6	0.1	0.2	0.2	0.2	0.0	0.6	0.2	•	•	•
Other Expenses **19**	20.0	37.9	32.2	32.3	20.1	13.5	9.3	12.3	7.3	5.7	•	•	•
Officers' Compensation **20**	2.8	5.7	6.9	1.2	1.7	1.6	2.3	0.6	1.9	0.6	•	•	•
Operating Margin **21**	0.8	•	3.6	1.0	•	•	1.0	1.4	1.8	2.5	•	•	•
Operating Margin Before Officers' Comp. **22**	3.6	1.1	10.5	2.2	0.5	•	3.4	2.1	3.7	3.1	•	•	•

Selected Average Balance Sheet ($ in Thousands)

Net Receivables 23	98	0	7	85	314	1332	3903	6317	13485	34862
Inventories 24	69	0	5	47	196	362	3135	3415	8730	78271
Net Property, Plant and Equipment 25	185	0	44	247	642	2105	4049	10168	13909	74749
Total Assets 26	589	0	106	683	1942	6478	15320	33542	68752	300164
Notes and Loans Payable 27	233	0	58	231	1045	2020	4962	13019	16346	74308
All Other Liabilities 28	131	0	16	47	452	1541	5134	7547	19392	61599
Net Worth 29	225	0	32	405	445	2918	5224	12977	33014	164257

Selected Financial Ratios (Times to 1)

Current Ratio 30	1.8	•	2.1	3.3	1.9	1.7	1.5	1.7	1.4	2.7
Quick Ratio 31	1.1	•	1.5	2.2	1.1	1.3	0.9	1.1	0.8	0.9
Net Sales to Working Capital 32	7.6	•	14.6	5.6	9.3	5.7	7.4	6.6	7.0	3.3
Coverage Ratio 33	7.3	12.1	14.5	15.0	4.2	3.7	4.8	8.3	5.8	6.1
Total Asset Turnover 34	1.8	•	3.3	1.9	2.1	1.2	1.6	1.2	0.9	1.1
Inventory Turnover 35	9.0	•	25.8	13.5	12.4	15.9	6.0	9.2	4.9	3.2
Receivables Turnover 36	11.4	•	46.5	24.2	14.5	6.3	7.0	5.8	5.9	9.7
Total Liabilities to Net Worth 37	1.6	•	2.3	0.7	3.4	1.2	1.9	1.6	1.1	0.8
Current Assets to Working Capital 38	2.2	•	1.9	1.4	2.2	2.4	3.0	2.5	3.8	1.6
Current Liabilities to Working Capital 39	1.2	•	0.9	0.4	1.2	1.4	2.0	1.5	2.8	0.6
Working Capital to Net Sales 40	0.1	•	0.1	0.2	0.1	0.2	0.1	0.2	0.1	0.3
Inventory to Working Capital 41	0.5	•	0.2	0.1	0.5	0.3	0.9	0.6	1.1	0.8
Total Receipts to Cash Flow 42	4.7	2.4	3.0	3.2	4.9	7.0	10.0	6.4	9.1	10.0
Cost of Goods to Cash Flow 43	2.8	1.1	1.1	1.5	2.9	5.1	7.5	5.0	6.3	7.5
Cash Flow to Total Debt 44	0.6	•	1.6	1.5	0.5	0.3	0.3	0.3	0.2	0.2

Selected Financial Factors (in Percentages)

Debt Ratio 45	61.9	•	70.0	40.7	77.1	55.0	65.9	61.3	52.0	45.3
Return on Total Assets 46	12.0	•	37.6	16.3	8.2	5.1	7.8	8.4	7.1	7.0
Return on Equity Before Income Taxes 47	27.1	•	116.7	25.7	27.3	8.3	18.1	19.2	12.2	10.7
Return on Equity After Income Taxes 48	26.0	•	116.0	25.4	26.6	7.5	14.9	17.3	11.3	10.2
Profit Margin (Before Income Tax) 49	5.9	17.0	10.6	7.9	3.0	3.0	3.7	6.1	6.5	5.3
Profit Margin (After Income Tax) 50	5.6	15.7	10.5	7.8	3.0	2.7	3.1	5.5	6.1	5.0

SUPPORT ACTIVITIES AND FISHING, HUNTING AND TRAPPING

Table II
Corporations with Net Income

MONEY AMOUNTS AND SIZE OF ASSETS IN THOUSANDS OF DOLLARS

Item Description for Accounting Period 7/10 Through 6/11	Total	Zero Assets	Under 500	500 to 1,000	1,000 to 5,000	5,000 to 10,000	10,000 to 25,000	25,000 to 50,000	50,000 to 100,000	100,000 to 250,000	250,000 to 500,000	500,000 to 2,500,000	2,500,000 and over
Number of Enterprises **1**	16396	2706	10445	1383	1461	258	81	•	•	•	0	0	0
Revenues ($ in Thousands)													
Net Sales **2**	22163255	273870	4562341	1810039	6551341	1598599	2459710	•	•	•	0	0	0
Interest **3**	13782	149	522	619	5735	1199	3548	•	•	•	0	0	0
Rents **4**	17993	238	9249	1967	2165	2840	552	•	•	•	0	0	0
Royalties **5**	2435	0	0	0	0	818	0	•	•	•	0	0	0
Other Portfolio Income **6**	129608	20984	16511	13621	45859	5352	4991	•	•	•	0	0	0
Other Receipts **7**	914063	48369	328070	72656	128620	131919	39215	•	•	•	0	0	0
Total Receipts **8**	2324136	343610	4916693	1899902	6733720	1740727	2508016	•	•	•	0	0	0
Average Total Receipts **9**	1417	127	471	1373	4609	6747	30963	•	•	•	•	•	•
Operating Costs/Operating Income (%)													
Cost of Operations **10**	58.4	53.6	36.7	52.8	55.8	65.2	73.0	•	•	•	•	•	•
Salaries and Wages **11**	9.3	7.1	9.9	8.8	13.1	9.3	6.6	•	•	•	•	•	•
Taxes Paid **12**	1.9	2.2	2.2	1.8	2.1	1.7	1.7	•	•	•	•	•	•
Interest Paid **13**	0.7	0.6	0.6	0.3	0.5	1.3	0.8	•	•	•	•	•	•
Depreciation **14**	3.0	3.3	2.6	4.0	3.0	3.1	2.4	•	•	•	•	•	•
Amortization and Depletion **15**	0.1	•	0.1	0.0	0.1	0.2	0.0	•	•	•	•	•	•
Pensions and Other Deferred Comp. **16**	0.2	0.1	0.2	0.2	0.1	0.1	0.2	•	•	•	•	•	•
Employee Benefits **17**	0.7	0.2	0.5	0.9	0.4	0.8	0.6	•	•	•	•	•	•
Advertising **18**	0.2	0.5	0.3	0.1	0.1	0.1	0.2	•	•	•	•	•	•
Other Expenses **19**	18.5	26.9	29.8	25.8	20.6	14.5	8.6	•	•	•	•	•	•
Officers' Compensation **20**	2.8	5.2	7.2	1.0	1.9	2.6	2.1	•	•	•	•	•	•
Operating Margin **21**	4.2	0.3	9.9	4.2	2.2	1.2	4.0	•	•	•	•	•	•
Operating Margin Before Officers' Comp. **22**	7.0	5.5	17.1	5.3	4.1	3.9	6.1	•	•	•	•	•	•

Selected Average Balance Sheet ($ in Thousands)

Net Receivables 23	136	0	8	94	340	1933	4191
Inventories 24	79	0	3	51	195	312	3837
Net Property, Plant and Equipment 25	180	0	32	214	448	1330	3959
Total Assets 26	733	0	116	681	1945	6726	16135
Notes and Loans Payable 27	201	0	47	181	525	1803	4505
All Other Liabilities 28	164	0	14	50	449	1485	6009
Net Worth 29	368	0	55	450	971	3438	5621

Selected Financial Ratios (Times to 1)

Current Ratio 30	2.0	•	2.8	3.2	1.9	2.3	1.4
Quick Ratio 31	1.3	•	2.4	2.2	1.1	1.9	0.9
Net Sales to Working Capital 32	6.8	•	11.5	5.2	9.3	2.6	8.8
Coverage Ratio 33	13.9	45.5	29.1	37.2	10.9	8.7	8.7
Total Asset Turnover 34	1.8	•	3.8	1.9	2.3	0.9	1.9
Inventory Turnover 35	10.0	•	53.8	13.5	12.9	12.9	5.8
Receivables Turnover 36	11.1	•	46.8	23.9	15.6	3.5	7.3
Total Liabilities to Net Worth 37	1.0	•	1.1	0.5	1.0	1.0	1.9
Current Assets to Working Capital 38	2.0	•	1.6	1.4	2.1	1.8	3.3
Current Liabilities to Working Capital 39	1.0	•	0.6	0.4	1.1	0.8	2.3
Working Capital to Net Sales 40	0.1	•	0.1	0.2	0.1	0.4	0.1
Inventory to Working Capital 41	0.5	•	0.1	0.1	0.5	0.1	1.0
Total Receipts to Cash Flow 42	4.3	2.5	2.5	3.7	4.4	4.7	8.8
Cost of Goods to Cash Flow 43	2.5	1.3	0.9	1.9	2.4	3.1	6.4
Cash Flow to Total Debt 44	0.9	•	2.9	1.5	1.1	0.4	0.3

Selected Financial Factors (in Percentages)

Debt Ratio 45	49.8	•	52.8	33.9	50.1	48.9	65.2
Return on Total Assets 46	18.0	•	68.9	18.1	12.7	10.5	12.6
Return on Equity Before Income Taxes 47	33.3	•	140.8	26.6	23.0	18.3	32.1
Return on Equity After Income Taxes 48	32.2	•	140.1	26.3	22.6	17.3	27.9
Profit Margin (Before Income Tax) 49	9.1	25.8	17.7	9.1	5.0	10.1	5.9
Profit Margin (After Income Tax) 50	8.8	24.3	17.6	9.1	4.9	9.6	5.2

Table I

Corporations with and without Net Income

OIL AND GAS EXTRACTION

MONEY AMOUNTS AND SIZE OF ASSETS IN THOUSANDS OF DOLLARS

Item Description for Accounting Period 7/10 Through 6/11		Total	Zero Assets	Under 500	500 to 1,000	1,000 to 5,000	5,000 to 10,000	10,000 to 25,000	25,000 to 50,000	50,000 to 100,000	100,000 to 250,000	250,000 to 500,000	500,000 to 2,500,000	2,500,000 and over
Number of Enterprises	1	21741	3823	12550	1711	2039	672	408	191	109	97	46	55	40
Revenues ($ in Thousands)														
Net Sales	2	187749477	3109708	3570841	728058	2934676	1887529	2512431	2744242	2055774	5198299	3706401	17039906	142261613
Interest	3	1834911	4536	1858	3570	8519	5488	7897	4057	16928	29687	37789	36342	1678239
Rents	4	422528	408	0	47	28867	12339	16303	79213	19918	6597	1249	3891	253695
Royalties	5	709574	55169	45015	1525	40965	37596	92596	52210	33572	23217	4487	23708	299513
Other Portfolio Income	6	16241850	184162	96935	16822	51705	261308	173809	131087	473772	248504	712011	1189699	12702037
Other Receipts	7	12469780	284181	93191	6105	348020	222699	306750	206280	341278	608972	271600	1797518	7983185
Total Receipts	8	219428120	3638164	3807840	756127	3412752	2426959	3109786	3217089	2941242	6115276	4733537	20091064	165178282
Average Total Receipts	9	10093	952	303	442	1674	3612	7622	16843	26984	63044	102903	365292	4129457
Operating Costs/Operating Income (%)														
Cost of Operations	10	54.2	7.2	31.6	11.4	26.4	14.8	36.2	33.8	20.4	47.6	23.4	44.8	60.5
Salaries and Wages	11	4.9	2.9	4.7	11.8	16.2	12.4	9.1	9.9	19.4	9.3	5.4	4.6	4.1
Taxes Paid	12	2.9	2.7	3.0	5.7	4.7	5.3	4.3	3.7	6.4	2.7	3.7	3.1	2.6
Interest Paid	13	4.9	12.0	0.7	2.6	2.3	2.4	2.3	3.6	4.5	4.8	6.9	5.9	4.9
Depreciation	14	8.6	7.9	3.4	5.5	6.3	8.3	11.6	11.5	14.9	10.1	13.4	10.0	8.2
Amortization and Depletion	15	7.1	19.9	0.9	4.1	3.0	2.7	6.9	7.2	14.2	8.9	20.2	15.2	5.6
Pensions and Other Deferred Comp.	16	0.6	0.1	0.6	•	0.1	0.8	0.4	0.4	0.3	0.5	0.4	0.3	0.6
Employee Benefits	17	0.7	0.1	0.6	0.6	1.5	1.0	1.0	0.9	1.2	0.8	0.9	0.5	0.6
Advertising	18	0.0	0.1	0.1	0.1	0.3	0.1	0.2	0.1	0.1	0.0	0.0	0.0	0.0
Other Expenses	19	28.1	30.9	32.3	39.2	36.3	47.0	31.5	38.8	44.6	34.9	36.5	30.4	26.3
Officers' Compensation	20	1.1	3.1	8.8	8.1	7.4	6.1	3.2	2.8	3.1	1.7	2.8	0.9	0.5
Operating Margin	21	•	13.0	13.3	10.9	•	•	•	•	•	•	•	•	•
Operating Margin Before Officers' Comp.	22	•	16.1	22.0	19.0	3.0	5.1	•	•	•	•	•	•	•

Selected Average Balance Sheet ($ in Thousands)

Net Receivables 23	1874	0	23	43	390	1031	1571	3578	4805	15060	36034	56224	770696
Inventories 24	262	0	2	30	22	82	189	293	614	2180	3447	7909	112565
Net Property, Plant and Equipment 25	13286	0	39	150	537	1732	5390	14121	28844	81377	200319	641728	5635440
Total Assets 26	23738	0	121	698	2423	7067	16151	34496	69583	168843	350434	1118167	9723309
Notes and Loans Payable 27	6179	0	76	277	631	1150	3643	8566	17566	42872	79491	289980	2551156
All Other Liabilities 28	6543	0	19	212	1068	2139	3498	9426	12071	51756	66009	261210	2776369
Net Worth 29	11017	0	25	208	724	3778	9010	16504	39946	74215	204934	566977	4395784

Selected Financial Ratios (Times to 1)

Current Ratio 30	1.0	•	3.3	1.7	1.1	1.7	1.6	1.3	1.7	1.2	2.5	1.1	0.9
Quick Ratio 31	0.8	•	3.1	1.2	0.9	1.3	1.3	1.0	1.3	0.9	1.8	0.8	0.7
Net Sales to Working Capital 32	134.8	•	5.9	2.6	15.9	1.9	2.8	6.1	2.2	5.7	1.6	23.3	•
Coverage Ratio 33	2.1	3.5	28.9	6.7	6.2	12.4	8.4	2.2	4.2	0.2	3.2	1.4	1.9
Total Asset Turnover 34	0.4	•	2.3	0.6	0.6	0.4	0.4	0.4	0.3	0.3	0.2	0.3	0.4
Inventory Turnover 35	17.9	•	40.9	1.6	16.9	5.1	11.8	16.6	6.3	11.7	5.5	17.5	19.1
Receivables Turnover 36	4.3	•	14.0	8.0	4.5	2.3	3.6	4.2	3.9	3.6	2.2	4.9	4.3
Total Liabilities to Net Worth 37	1.2	•	3.8	2.3	2.3	0.9	0.8	1.1	0.7	1.3	0.7	1.0	1.2
Current Assets to Working Capital 38	60.0	•	1.4	2.4	13.6	2.5	2.6	5.0	2.4	5.1	1.7	14.0	•
Current Liabilities to Working Capital 39	59.0	•	0.4	1.4	12.6	1.6	1.5	4.0	1.4	4.1	0.7	13.0	•
Working Capital to Net Sales 40	0.0	•	0.2	0.4	0.1	0.5	0.4	0.2	0.5	0.2	0.6	0.0	•
Inventory to Working Capital 41	3.9	•	0.0	0.1	0.3	0.0	0.1	0.1	0.1	0.2	0.1	0.7	•
Total Receipts to Cash Flow 42	3.8	1.9	2.1	2.5	2.4	1.7	2.5	2.7	2.0	3.9	2.8	4.1	4.2
Cost of Goods to Cash Flow 43	2.0	0.1	0.7	0.3	0.6	0.2	0.9	0.9	0.4	1.8	0.6	1.9	2.5
Cash Flow to Total Debt 44	0.2	•	1.4	0.3	0.4	0.5	0.4	0.3	0.3	0.1	0.2	0.1	0.2

Selected Financial Factors (in Percentages)

Debt Ratio 45	53.6	•	79.1	70.1	70.1	46.5	44.2	52.2	42.6	56.0	41.5	49.3	54.8
Return on Total Assets 46	3.8	•	48.4	10.5	8.3	11.9	7.3	3.3	5.1	0.3	5.1	2.3	3.4
Return on Equity Before Income Taxes 47	4.3	•	223.5	30.1	23.4	20.5	11.5	3.9	6.7	•	6.0	1.2	3.5
Return on Equity After Income Taxes 48	2.1	•	219.0	28.2	21.7	19.7	10.6	2.6	5.7	•	3.8	•	1.2
Profit Margin (Before Income Tax) 49	5.5	30.0	19.9	14.7	11.8	27.5	16.8	4.4	14.2	•	15.2	2.3	4.3
Profit Margin (After Income Tax) 50	2.6	21.2	19.5	13.8	10.9	26.5	15.4	3.0	12.1	•	9.7	•	1.5

Table II

Corporations with Net Income

OIL AND GAS EXTRACTION

MONEY AMOUNTS AND SIZE OF ASSETS IN THOUSANDS OF DOLLARS

Item Description for Accounting Period 7/10 Through 6/11	Total	Zero Assets	Under 500	500 to 1,000	1,000 to 5,000	5,000 to 10,000	10,000 to 25,000	25,000 to 50,000	50,000 to 100,000	100,000 to 250,000	250,000 to 500,000	500,000 to 2,500,000	2,500,000 and over
Number of Enterprises 1	14792	1696	9842	1090	1215	401	262	109	62	47	24	26	18
Revenues ($ in Thousands)													
Net Sales 2	128866591	2260679	3190469	554339	2208339	1352302	1921998	2198028	1510124	3912340	2685685	12336604	94735684
Interest 3	1332505	3571	996	3513	7016	2348	4280	1678	15173	21725	25044	24478	1222684
Rents 4	174751	408	0	0	27443	704	14296	77882	19277	4066	157	2545	27973
Royalties 5	631815	49665	44975	1456	33448	17595	88908	43021	26936	19323	2160	15157	289172
Other Portfolio Income 6	12357108	173050	61135	15162	23700	252951	147499	114315	397121	161275	696813	1067615	9246471
Other Receipts 7	8063012	276898	76998	29599	308941	211834	286216	177354	264664	470409	206225	1180810	4573066
Total Receipts 8	151425782	2764271	3374573	604069	2608887	1837734	2463197	2612278	2233295	4589138	3616084	14627209	110095050
Average Total Receipts 9	10237	1630	343	554	2147	4583	9402	23966	36021	97641	150670	562585	6116392
Operating Costs/Operating Income (%)													
Cost of Operations 10	58.1	1.2	28.8	12.3	27.4	7.7	32.1	38.6	16.8	53.5	25.1	52.8	65.7
Salaries and Wages 11	4.0	1.9	2.8	5.3	9.6	9.4	8.8	8.0	17.2	8.4	3.7	3.5	3.3
Taxes Paid 12	2.9	3.0	2.6	5.7	4.2	5.8	4.5	3.6	6.3	2.4	3.7	2.1	2.8
Interest Paid 13	3.5	12.6	0.5	0.2	1.1	1.4	1.0	1.7	1.6	2.2	5.1	3.1	3.6
Depreciation 14	7.1	5.4	2.6	4.7	4.8	7.0	11.5	8.0	11.8	7.5	8.8	6.5	7.2
Amortization and Depletion 15	4.3	19.6	0.5	4.6	2.4	3.5	5.9	3.1	6.9	2.5	13.2	6.2	3.6
Pensions and Other Deferred Comp. 16	0.7	0.0	0.7	•	0.0	0.7	0.4	0.4	0.3	0.5	0.1	0.2	0.8
Employee Benefits 17	0.7	0.2	0.6	0.6	1.2	0.9	0.9	0.8	1.2	0.6	0.8	0.4	0.7
Advertising 18	0.0	0.0	0.1	0.1	0.3	0.1	0.2	0.1	0.0	0.0	0.0	0.0	0.0
Other Expenses 19	18.6	24.4	29.0	30.2	27.0	39.2	20.0	23.2	34.0	20.8	25.0	18.8	16.9
Officers' Compensation 20	1.1	4.0	9.5	6.7	6.2	4.7	3.2	2.0	2.9	1.2	2.4	0.6	0.5
Operating Margin 21	•	27.7	22.2	29.6	15.9	19.6	11.6	10.4	0.9	0.4	12.2	5.9	•
Operating Margin Before Officers' Comp. 22	0.2	31.7	31.7	36.3	22.1	24.3	14.8	12.4	3.8	1.7	14.5	6.5	•

Selected Average Balance Sheet ($ in Thousands)

Net Receivables 23	1941	0	28	49	512	817	1526	3712	4837	17640	55418	88379	1215041
Inventories 24	225	0	3	13	20	55	140	423	596	3655	4780	10235	142317
Net Property, Plant and Equipment 25	8676	0	41	55	517	1844	3636	12180	25459	56499	171496	588776	5586547
Total Assets 26	17543	0	127	682	2513	7198	15977	34017	69886	168737	343732	1144463	10744150
Notes and Loans Payable 27	3715	0	75	72	395	402	1965	5254	8661	32307	70617	262925	2322978
All Other Liabilities 28	4855	0	6	188	853	2221	2978	7394	10833	40465	62607	244637	3200228
Net Worth 29	8973	0	46	422	1264	4576	11035	21369	50392	95965	210509	636900	5220944

Selected Financial Ratios (Times to 1)

Current Ratio 30	1.4	•	4.3	2.7	1.6	1.6	2.0	2.0	2.9	2.4	3.3	1.8	1.2
Quick Ratio 31	1.1	•	4.0	1.8	1.5	1.4	1.6	1.6	2.3	1.8	2.4	1.2	1.0
Net Sales to Working Capital 32	7.7	•	5.9	1.5	3.5	2.4	2.2	3.5	1.5	2.3	1.4	3.9	17.5
Coverage Ratio 33	6.5	5.0	52.2	174.4	31.3	40.9	41.8	18.1	31.3	9.0	10.3	9.0	5.0
Total Asset Turnover 34	0.5	•	2.6	0.7	0.7	0.5	0.5	0.6	0.3	0.5	0.3	0.4	0.5
Inventory Turnover 35	22.6	•	33.2	4.9	24.7	4.7	16.8	18.4	6.9	12.2	5.9	24.5	24.3
Receivables Turnover 36	4.6	•	13.3	11.9	4.8	3.0	4.7	6.9	6.9	4.5	2.1	6.2	4.3
Total Liabilities to Net Worth 37	1.0	•	1.8	0.6	1.0	0.6	0.4	0.6	0.4	0.8	0.6	0.8	1.1
Current Assets to Working Capital 38	3.4	•	1.3	1.6	2.7	2.6	2.0	2.0	1.5	1.7	1.4	2.3	6.4
Current Liabilities to Working Capital 39	2.4	•	0.3	0.6	1.7	1.6	1.0	1.0	0.5	0.7	0.4	1.3	5.4
Working Capital to Net Sales 40	0.1	•	0.2	0.7	0.3	0.4	0.5	0.3	0.7	0.4	0.7	0.3	0.1
Inventory to Working Capital 41	0.2	•	0.0	0.1	0.1	0.0	0.0	0.1	0.0	0.1	0.1	0.1	0.5
Total Receipts to Cash Flow 42	3.3	1.5	1.9	1.5	1.8	1.3	1.9	2.2	1.3	3.0	1.9	2.7	4.3
Cost of Goods to Cash Flow 43	1.9	0.0	0.5	0.2	0.5	0.1	0.6	0.8	0.2	1.6	0.5	1.4	2.8
Cash Flow to Total Debt 44	0.3	•	2.1	1.3	0.8	1.0	0.8	0.7	0.9	0.4	0.5	0.3	0.2

Selected Financial Factors (in Percentages)

Debt Ratio 45	48.9	•	63.9	38.1	49.7	36.4	30.9	37.2	27.9	43.1	38.8	44.3	51.4
Return on Total Assets 46	11.1	•	72.8	28.9	25.4	26.6	18.5	18.3	17.5	9.8	17.0	11.4	8.8
Return on Equity Before Income Taxes 47	18.4	•	197.9	46.5	48.8	40.8	26.2	27.5	23.5	15.3	25.0	18.2	14.5
Return on Equity After Income Taxes 48	14.5	•	194.7	45.0	47.1	39.8	25.0	25.7	22.1	13.2	21.0	14.6	10.4
Profit Margin (Before Income Tax) 49	19.0	50.0	28.0	38.6	33.9	55.4	39.3	29.1	48.6	17.6	47.0	24.4	14.4
Profit Margin (After Income Tax) 50	14.9	38.0	27.5	37.4	32.8	54.0	37.6	27.3	45.8	15.2	39.5	19.6	10.3

Table I

Corporations with and without Net Income

COAL MINING

MONEY AMOUNTS AND SIZE OF ASSETS IN THOUSANDS OF DOLLARS

Item Description for Accounting Period 7/10 Through 6/11		Total	Zero Assets	Under 500	500 to 1,000	1,000 to 5,000	5,000 to 10,000	10,000 to 25,000	25,000 to 50,000	50,000 to 100,000	100,000 to 250,000	250,000 to 500,000	500,000 to 2,500,000	2,500,000 and over
Number of Enterprises	1	1166	272	507	31	125	113	63	14	13	12	0	11	6
Revenues ($ in Thousands)														
Net Sales	2	33537150	557071	0	256553	1082641	743212	1357455	453121	933137	2056987	0	8330625	17766348
Interest	3	275828	427	358	39	607	307	2407	223	403	921	0	119803	150332
Rents	4	22509	657	0	0	0	42	4297	0	0	76	0	1520	15916
Royalties	5	303601	2068	0	0	0	1171	1094	0	7791	13586	0	30420	247471
Other Portfolio Income	6	784922	10289	0	0	0	19674	14359	355	1827	5246	0	7339	725831
Other Receipts	7	1888464	82711	2095	0	197	14935	35286	18967	7209	15278	0	443196	1268595
Total Receipts	8	36812474	653223	2453	256592	1083445	779341	1414898	472666	950367	2092094	0	8932903	20174493
Average Total Receipts	9	31572	2402	5	8277	8668	6897	22459	33762	73105	174341	•	812082	3362416
Operating Costs/Operating Income (%)														
Cost of Operations	10	59.4	67.8	•	85.7	59.5	67.0	69.2	74.2	69.5	73.9	•	65.7	52.1
Salaries and Wages	11	5.2	5.7	•	•	5.5	2.0	3.2	2.5	3.1	1.1	•	1.9	7.7
Taxes Paid	12	6.0	6.6	•	0.2	5.0	7.6	2.8	3.0	4.7	3.9	•	3.4	7.8
Interest Paid	13	4.2	2.7	•	•	0.5	0.5	1.5	2.7	1.8	1.6	•	5.5	4.7
Depreciation	14	7.8	14.8	•	0.2	1.6	5.2	6.2	6.2	7.8	8.2	•	6.9	8.7
Amortization and Depletion	15	5.5	6.9	•	•	0.1	0.2	2.2	2.8	5.2	3.6	•	5.8	6.5
Pensions and Other Deferred Comp.	16	0.9	0.0	•	•	•	0.2	0.1	0.3	0.3	0.2	•	0.5	1.4
Employee Benefits	17	4.1	16.3	•	•	0.8	1.5	1.3	1.4	1.6	2.3	•	3.8	4.9
Advertising	18	0.1	0.1	•	•	•	0.0	0.0	0.1	0.1	0.0	•	0.0	0.1
Other Expenses	19	11.1	10.8	•	4.9	21.9	22.5	17.7	17.1	5.7	8.7	•	5.3	12.6
Officers' Compensation	20	0.4	•	•	•	0.4	1.2	2.0	0.9	0.6	0.5	•	0.7	0.2
Operating Margin	21	•	•	•	9.0	4.6	•	•	•	•	•	•	0.5	•
Operating Margin Before Officers' Comp.	22	•	•	•	9.0	5.0	•	•	•	•	0.2	•	1.2	•

Selected Average Balance Sheet ($ in Thousands)

Net Receivables 23	29635	0	0	565	514	464	3574	11660	4924	28003	•	64152	5487765
Inventories 24	1585	0	0	0	0	213	859	1881	2478	8084	•	48492	180069
Net Property, Plant and Equipment 25	26714	0	0	36	409	1315	4785	9492	21584	96786	•	536165	3862333
Total Assets 26	78707	0	78	739	1539	7663	15992	38983	65315	192469	•	1215561	12094754
Notes and Loans Payable 27	14619	0	102	4	974	973	5927	6582	18685	55287	•	337584	1946196
All Other Liabilities 28	45135	0	88	568	1102	679	5016	13663	14277	57977	•	475721	7621575
Net Worth 29	18953	0	-111	167	-537	6011	5049	18738	32352	79205	•	402256	2526982

Selected Financial Ratios (Times to 1)

Current Ratio 30	1.1	•	0.9	1.2	1.3	2.7	1.8	4.1	1.7	0.7	•	1.3	1.0
Quick Ratio 31	1.0	•	0.1	1.1	1.2	2.6	1.5	3.5	1.4	0.5	•	0.9	1.0
Net Sales to Working Capital 32	12.6	•	•	64.3	39.1	4.5	7.7	1.8	10.4	•	•	11.4	12.1
Coverage Ratio 33	2.4	•	•	•	10.6	•	•	•	1.8	•	•	2.4	2.7
Total Asset Turnover 34	0.4	•	•	11.2	5.6	0.9	1.3	0.8	1.1	0.9	•	0.6	0.2
Inventory Turnover 35	10.8	•	•	•	•	20.7	17.4	12.8	20.1	15.7	•	10.3	8.6
Receivables Turnover 36	1.1	•	•	8.1	26.7	13.7	7.3	2.5	15.9	7.1	•	11.8	0.6
Total Liabilities to Net Worth 37	3.2	•	•	3.4	•	0.3	2.2	1.1	1.0	1.4	•	2.0	3.8
Current Assets to Working Capital 38	15.9	•	•	5.4	4.4	1.6	2.2	1.3	2.4	•	•	4.0	25.7
Current Liabilities to Working Capital 39	14.9	•	•	4.4	3.4	0.6	1.2	0.3	1.4	•	•	3.0	24.7
Working Capital to Net Sales 40	0.1	•	•	0.0	0.0	0.2	0.1	0.6	0.1	•	•	0.1	0.1
Inventory to Working Capital 41	0.7	•	•	•	•	0.1	0.3	0.1	0.4	•	•	0.8	0.8
Total Receipts to Cash Flow 42	7.5	•	•	7.6	4.1	7.0	9.4	14.6	24.3	26.7	•	9.0	6.1
Cost of Goods to Cash Flow 43	4.4	•	•	6.5	2.5	4.7	6.5	10.8	16.9	19.7	•	5.9	3.2
Cash Flow to Total Debt 44	0.1	•	•	1.9	1.0	0.6	0.2	0.1	0.1	0.1	•	0.1	0.1

Selected Financial Factors (in Percentages)

Debt Ratio 45	75.9	•	241.8	77.4	134.9	21.6	68.4	51.9	50.5	58.8	•	66.9	79.1
Return on Total Assets 46	3.6	•	•	100.6	29.1	•	•	•	3.6	•	•	8.3	3.1
Return on Equity Before Income Taxes 47	8.8	•	45.4	445.4	•	•	•	•	3.2	•	•	14.6	9.5
Return on Equity After Income Taxes 48	6.7	•	45.4	436.6	•	•	•	•	2.7	•	•	13.3	6.8
Profit Margin (Before Income Tax) 49	5.8	•	•	9.0	4.7	•	•	•	1.4	•	•	7.8	8.1
Profit Margin (After Income Tax) 50	4.4	•	•	8.8	4.7	•	•	•	1.2	•	•	7.1	5.8

Table II
Corporations with Net Income

COAL MINING

MONEY AMOUNTS AND SIZE OF ASSETS IN THOUSANDS OF DOLLARS

Item Description for Accounting Period 7/10 Through 6/11	Total	Zero Assets	Under 500	500 to 1,000	1,000 to 5,000	5,000 to 10,000	10,000 to 25,000	25,000 to 50,000	50,000 to 100,000	100,000 to 250,000	250,000 to 500,000	500,000 to 2,500,000	2,500,000 and over
1 Number of Enterprises	207	•	0	31	74	•	32	7	8	3	0	5	•
Revenues ($ in Thousands)													
2 Net Sales	19646316	•	0	256553	413218	•	614239	400064	829321	519756	0	3830057	•
3 Interest	132176	•	0	39	0	•	1525	20	114	65	0	2484	•
4 Rents	20071	•	0	0	0	•	4297	0	0	0	0	49	•
5 Royalties	67036	•	0	0	0	•	1034	0	7791	0	0	13647	•
6 Other Portfolio Income	702386	•	0	0	0	•	9371	68	352	538	0	1964	•
7 Other Receipts	1435993	•	0	0	4894	•	24961	5518	4621	8557	0	295971	•
8 Total Receipts	22003978	•	0	256592	418112	•	655427	405670	842199	528916	0	4144172	•
9 Average Total Receipts	106299	•	•	8277	5650	•	20482	57953	105275	176305	•	828834	•
Operating Costs/Operating Income (%)													
10 Cost of Operations	48.0	•	•	85.7	14.5	•	45.7	77.0	67.6	62.1	•	54.8	•
11 Salaries and Wages	8.1	•	•	•	13.4	•	4.7	1.0	2.8	0.8	•	3.1	•
12 Taxes Paid	6.0	•	•	0.2	1.5	•	1.7	2.7	5.2	4.5	•	2.3	•
13 Interest Paid	3.9	•	•	•	0.0	•	2.1	0.7	1.0	0.9	•	4.1	•
14 Depreciation	7.3	•	•	0.2	1.0	•	10.2	4.6	7.7	7.6	•	5.8	•
15 Amortization and Depletion	5.6	•	•	•	•	•	3.1	2.3	5.5	6.2	•	5.7	•
16 Pensions and Other Deferred Comp.	1.2	•	•	•	•	•	0.1	0.1	0.3	0.4	•	0.5	•
17 Employee Benefits	4.2	•	•	•	2.1	•	0.8	1.2	1.8	2.0	•	3.0	•
18 Advertising	0.1	•	•	•	•	•	0.1	0.0	0.1	0.0	•	0.0	•
19 Other Expenses	12.9	•	•	4.9	43.5	•	26.9	6.8	4.1	5.0	•	5.1	•
20 Officers' Compensation	0.4	•	•	•	1.0	•	2.3	1.0	0.5	0.5	•	1.0	•
21 Operating Margin	2.5	•	•	9.0	23.0	•	2.3	2.7	3.4	10.1	•	14.7	•
22 Operating Margin Before Officers' Comp.	2.8	•	•	9.0	24.0	•	4.6	3.7	3.9	10.6	•	15.6	•

Selected Average Balance Sheet ($ in Thousands)

Net Receivables 23	7882	565	2448	7310	6961	24033	92770
Inventories 24	5510	0	1024	2683	3058	3097	59879
Net Property, Plant and Equipment 25	91234	36	4127	8694	27166	85725	286983
Total Assets 26	171906	739	14956	35538	67575	138622	1162494
Notes and Loans Payable 27	42602	4	4066	9313	19399	15310	220267
All Other Liabilities 28	61367	568	4090	10031	17692	28980	453088
Net Worth 29	67937	167	6800	16195	30484	94332	489139

Selected Financial Ratios (Times to 1)

Current Ratio 30	1.5	1.2	1.8	1.9	1.4	2.5	3.2
Quick Ratio 31	1.0	1.1	1.4	1.4	1.0	2.3	2.1
Net Sales to Working Capital 32	8.8	64.3	6.4	6.1	22.8	6.3	3.3
Coverage Ratio 33	5.0	1204.3	5.3	6.8	5.8	13.7	6.6
Total Asset Turnover 34	0.6	11.2	1.3	1.6	1.5	1.2	0.7
Inventory Turnover 35	8.3	•	8.6	16.4	22.9	34.7	7.0
Receivables Turnover 36	1.6	8.1	7.2	3.8	15.4	•	•
Total Liabilities to Net Worth 37	1.5	3.4	1.2	1.2	1.2	0.5	1.4
Current Assets to Working Capital 38	2.9	5.4	2.3	2.1	3.8	1.7	1.5
Current Liabilities to Working Capital 39	1.9	4.4	1.3	1.1	2.8	0.7	0.5
Working Capital to Net Sales 40	0.1	0.0	0.2	0.2	0.0	0.2	0.3
Inventory to Working Capital 41	0.4	•	0.4	0.2	0.7	0.1	0.3
Total Receipts to Cash Flow 42	4.0	7.6	3.5	12.7	13.9	7.2	3.8
Cost of Goods to Cash Flow 43	1.9	6.5	1.6	9.8	9.4	4.5	2.1
Cash Flow to Total Debt 44	0.2	1.9	0.7	0.2	0.2	0.5	0.3

Selected Financial Factors (in Percentages)

Debt Ratio 45	60.5	77.4	54.5	54.4	54.9	32.0	57.9
Return on Total Assets 46	10.7	100.6	14.0	7.8	9.2	15.9	17.7
Return on Equity Before Income Taxes 47	21.7	445.4	25.0	14.5	17.0	21.7	35.8
Return on Equity After Income Taxes 48	18.5	436.6	24.3	13.2	16.1	21.6	33.4
Profit Margin (Before Income Tax) 49	15.5	9.0	8.9	4.1	5.0	11.8	22.9
Profit Margin (After Income Tax) 50	13.2	8.8	8.6	3.8	4.7	11.7	21.3

Table I

Corporations with and without Net Income

METAL ORE MINING

MONEY AMOUNTS AND SIZE OF ASSETS IN THOUSANDS OF DOLLARS

Item Description for Accounting Period 7/10 Through 6/11	Total	Zero Assets	Under 500	500 to 1,000	1,000 to 5,000	5,000 to 10,000	10,000 to 25,000	25,000 to 50,000	50,000 to 100,000	100,000 to 250,000	250,000 to 500,000	500,000 to 2,500,000	2,500,000 and over
Number of Enterprises **1**	1501	3	1029	90	190	51	44	35	18	14	6	12	10
Revenues ($ in Thousands)													
Net Sales **2**	53570826	0	7677	258	1245	1352	346223	302105	435169	266276	906594	4390753	46913173
Interest **3**	599437	2	187	15	239	1774	150	1592	15380	1627	2128	39280	537064
Rents **4**	44266	0	6711	0	1034	0	0	160	0	26	595	30	35711
Royalties **5**	423767	0	0	0	1126	133	0	30934	5186	0	0	215550	170839
Other Portfolio Income **6**	4396277	901	19283	538	66808	0	0	24457	6340	101	26361	60597	4190892
Other Receipts **7**	1546411	162	22097	0	10122	1063	5213	-46158	21315	17329	7243	370453	1137569
Total Receipts **8**	60580984	1065	55955	811	80574	4322	351586	313090	483390	285359	942921	5076663	52985248
Average Total Receipts **9**	40360	355	54	9	424	85	7991	8945	26855	20383	157154	423055	5298525
Operating Costs/Operating Income (%)													
Cost of Operations **10**	49.0	•	1.7	•	29.5	35.4	96.7	62.4	53.8	70.5	51.8	64.3	46.9
Salaries and Wages **11**	1.6	•	•	•	888.8	1452.4	4.0	8.2	10.0	9.1	0.4	1.5	1.3
Taxes Paid **12**	1.5	•	28.6	26.7	58.2	107.8	0.1	3.2	2.2	1.9	1.0	1.7	1.5
Interest Paid **13**	2.8	•	33.9	•	661.8	288.8	0.0	2.8	1.7	3.2	0.5	1.1	3.1
Depreciation **14**	5.2	•	9.6	4.7	458.2	252.9	0.7	12.8	7.9	10.7	14.7	6.2	4.9
Amortization and Depletion **15**	12.1	•	27.4	•	720.2	1130.4	2.5	19.0	8.5	29.9	9.1	13.4	11.9
Pensions and Other Deferred Comp. **16**	0.6	•	•	•	•	•	•	0.7	0.7	•	•	0.1	0.6
Employee Benefits **17**	0.7	•	26.3	•	•	3.8	0.0	1.2	1.1	0.8	2.8	0.1	0.7
Advertising **18**	0.1	•	•	•	36.8	13.8	0.1	0.1	0.0	0.1	0.0	0.0	0.1
Other Expenses **19**	8.9	•	889.8	517.8	15521.4	4228.3	19.7	31.1	22.3	24.7	15.3	6.9	7.8
Officers' Compensation **20**	0.5	•	77.7	•	703.5	367.0	1.5	1.3	1.8	1.9	0.4	0.7	0.4
Operating Margin **21**	17.0	•	•	•	•	•	•	•	•	•	4.1	4.0	20.7
Operating Margin Before Officers' Comp. **22**	17.4	•	•	•	•	•	•	•	•	•	4.6	4.7	21.1

Selected Average Balance Sheet ($ in Thousands)

Net Receivables 23	16353	0	0	0	5	10	1653	780	9925	9915	11747	45136	2351436
Inventories 24	5068	0	0	0	80	70	0	1030	3466	8076	29890	89627	612248
Net Property, Plant and Equipment 25	24888	0	5	357	666	2119	4921	13746	25810	33914	173842	508294	2830530
Total Assets 26	101184	0	91	795	2040	7514	15088	33777	75929	161269	377106	1275332	12790426
Notes and Loans Payable 27	15710	0	4	71	1601	5664	3803	21574	41390	57932	94916	140677	1817812
All Other Liabilities 28	29476	0	8	74	755	2690	4596	12541	19238	42292	118604	203752	3915014
Net Worth 29	55999	0	-53	783	-317	-840	6690	-337	15301	61046	163586	930904	7057601

Selected Financial Ratios (Times to 1)

Current Ratio 30	1.8	•	4.9	20.4	1.1	0.3	2.3	2.1	2.3	1.3	2.5	2.2	1.7
Quick Ratio 31	1.3	•	3.9	20.4	0.5	0.1	2.1	1.3	1.6	0.7	1.9	1.4	1.3
Net Sales to Working Capital 32	2.5	•	0.2	0.0	0.1	•	3.2	1.5	1.5	1.9	1.7	1.9	2.7
Coverage Ratio 33	12.2	•	•	•	•	•	•	•	1.6	•	17.6	21.3	12.7
Total Asset Turnover 34	0.4	•	0.1	0.0	0.0	0.0	0.5	0.3	0.3	0.1	0.4	0.3	0.4
Inventory Turnover 35	3.4	•	•	•	0.0	0.1	•	5.2	3.7	1.7	2.6	2.6	3.6
Receivables Turnover 36	1.9	•	•	•	2.5	0.6	6.2	17.3	4.4	2.9	16.8	6.3	1.7
Total Liabilities to Net Worth 37	0.8	•	•	0.0	•	•	1.3	•	4.0	1.6	1.3	0.4	0.8
Current Assets to Working Capital 38	2.3	•	1.3	1.1	9.2	•	1.9	•	1.8	4.4	1.7	1.9	2.3
Current Liabilities to Working Capital 39	1.3	•	0.3	0.1	8.2	•	0.9	•	0.8	3.4	0.7	0.9	1.3
Working Capital to Net Sales 40	0.4	•	4.3	82.3	11.1	•	0.7	0.3	0.7	0.5	0.6	0.5	0.4
Inventory to Working Capital 41	0.4	•	•	•	2.2	•	•	0.3	0.2	0.8	0.3	0.5	0.4
Total Receipts to Cash Flow 42	2.8	•	0.6	•	0.1	•	•	•	5.8	•	5.3	4.0	2.6
Cost of Goods to Cash Flow 43	1.4	•	0.0	•	0.0	•	•	•	3.1	•	2.7	2.5	1.2
Cash Flow to Total Debt 44	0.3	•	0.1	•	0.0	•	•	•	0.1	•	0.1	0.3	0.3

Selected Financial Factors (in Percentages)

Debt Ratio 45	44.7	•	158.0	1.5	115.5	111.2	55.7	101.0	79.8	62.1	56.6	27.0	44.8
Return on Total Assets 46	12.3	•	•	•	•	•	•	•	0.9	•	3.5	6.5	14.2
Return on Equity Before Income Taxes 47	20.4	•	52.5	•	260.5	238.7	•	1004.6	1.7	•	7.5	8.4	23.7
Return on Equity After Income Taxes 48	13.8	•	52.5	•	260.5	238.7	•	1066.9	1.2	•	4.4	6.2	16.3
Profit Margin (Before Income Tax) 49	31.9	•	•	•	•	•	•	•	1.1	•	8.1	21.4	35.7
Profit Margin (After Income Tax) 50	21.7	•	•	•	•	•	•	•	0.8	•	4.8	15.8	24.6

11

Table II

Corporations with Net Income

METAL ORE MINING

MONEY AMOUNTS AND SIZE OF ASSETS IN THOUSANDS OF DOLLARS

Item Description for Accounting Period 7/10 Through 6/11	Total	Zero Assets	Under 500	500 to 1,000	1,000 to 5,000	5,000 to 10,000	10,000 to 25,000	25,000 to 50,000	50,000 to 100,000	100,000 to 250,000	250,000 to 500,000	500,000 to 2,500,000	2,500,000 and over
Number of Enterprises **1**	554	0	498	0	10	0	8	8	8	0	•	•	9
Revenues ($ in Thousands)													
Net Sales **2**	45466337	0	7071	0	0	0	344721	298343	383207	0	•	2839358	•
Interest **3**	532834	0	11	0	24	0	89	585	14123	0	•	25055	•
Rents **4**	43754	0	6711	0	1034	0	0	14	0	0	•	30	•
Royalties **5**	372028	0	0	0	0	0	0	30850	5186	0	•	215312	•
Other Portfolio Income **6**	4369455	0	19283	0	66755	0	0	8009	374	0	•	60597	•
Other Receipts **7**	1246231	0	22097	0	2025	0	3438	1120	20720	0	•	366838	•
Total Receipts **8**	52030639	0	55173	0	69838	0	348248	338921	423610	0	•	3507190	•
Average Total Receipts **9**	93918	•	111	•	6984	•	43531	42365	52951	•	•	389688	•
Operating Costs/Operating Income (%)													
Cost of Operations **10**	41.1	•	•	•	•	•	97.1	62.7	50.3	•	•	48.6	•
Salaries and Wages **11**	1.5	•	•	•	•	•	•	1.4	9.0	•	•	2.0	•
Taxes Paid **12**	1.6	•	29.0	•	•	•	0.1	2.7	2.4	•	•	2.3	•
Interest Paid **13**	3.1	•	20.9	•	•	•	•	0.5	1.3	•	•	1.5	•
Depreciation **14**	5.5	•	9.6	•	•	•	•	3.1	7.6	•	•	7.4	•
Amortization and Depletion **15**	13.6	•	•	•	•	•	•	13.4	7.4	•	•	19.9	•
Pensions and Other Deferred Comp. **16**	0.6	•	•	•	•	•	•	0.7	0.7	•	•	0.2	•
Employee Benefits **17**	0.7	•	16.5	•	•	•	•	0.4	1.0	•	•	0.1	•
Advertising **18**	0.1	•	•	•	•	•	•	0.0	0.0	•	•	0.0	•
Other Expenses **19**	8.8	•	206.3	•	•	•	1.7	8.5	16.2	•	•	9.3	•
Officers' Compensation **20**	0.4	•	84.4	•	•	•	•	0.8	0.5	•	•	0.8	•
Operating Margin **21**	23.0	•	•	•	•	•	1.1	5.8	3.6	•	•	7.8	•
Operating Margin Before Officers' Comp. **22**	23.4	•	•	•	•	•	1.1	6.6	4.1	•	•	8.6	•

Selected Average Balance Sheet ($ in Thousands)

Net Receivables 23	33157	0	0	5905	3347	22170	23886
Inventories 24	11627	0	0	143	7185	5737	110441
Net Property, Plant and Equipment 25	55426	11	191	2139	9613	29036	414949
Total Assets 26	228945	88	1902	12570	35258	78846	1136358
Notes and Loans Payable 27	34394	3	288	237	22769	57504	163850
All Other Liabilities 28	64540	45	1195	2837	12463	25932	207250
Net Worth 29	130011	39	418	9495	26	-4590	765258

Selected Financial Ratios (Times to 1)

Current Ratio 30	1.9	8.6	1.2	2.8	3.2	3.9	2.3
Quick Ratio 31	1.4	8.6	1.1	2.8	1.2	2.9	1.4
Net Sales to Working Capital 32	2.5	0.3	8.6	•	2.1	1.6	1.4
Coverage Ratio 33	13.8	20.5	9.4	•	41.8	11.9	23.9
Total Asset Turnover 34	0.4	0.2	3.4	•	1.1	0.6	0.3
Inventory Turnover 35	2.9	•	292.7	•	3.3	4.2	1.4
Receivables Turnover 36	2.1	•	7.4	•	22.3	4.3	•
Total Liabilities to Net Worth 37	0.8	1.2	0.3	3.5	1342.2	0.5	0.5
Current Assets to Working Capital 38	2.1	1.1	1.6	6.9	1.4	1.3	1.8
Current Liabilities to Working Capital 39	1.1	0.1	0.6	5.9	0.4	0.3	0.8
Working Capital to Net Sales 40	0.4	3.1	0.1	•	0.5	0.6	0.7
Inventory to Working Capital 41	0.4	•	•	•	0.4	0.2	0.5
Total Receipts to Cash Flow 42	2.3	0.3	26.0	•	4.1	4.1	2.6
Cost of Goods to Cash Flow 43	1.0	•	25.2	•	2.6	2.1	1.3
Cash Flow to Total Debt 44	0.4	0.9	0.5	3.8	0.3	0.1	0.3

Selected Financial Factors (in Percentages)

Debt Ratio 45	43.2	55.0	78.0	24.5	99.9	105.8	32.7
Return on Total Assets 46	15.3	69.1	104.9	7.4	21.0	9.4	9.7
Return on Equity Before Income Taxes 47	25.0	146.3	425.8	9.8	27596.7	•	13.8
Return on Equity After Income Taxes 48	17.5	146.3	425.8	7.7	24098.6	•	10.2
Profit Margin (Before Income Tax) 49	39.6	406.5	•	2.2	19.4	14.2	33.4
Profit Margin (After Income Tax) 50	27.7	406.5	•	1.7	17.0	13.8	24.7

Table I
Corporations with and without Net Income

NONMETALLIC MINERAL MINING AND QUARRYING

MONEY AMOUNTS AND SIZE OF ASSETS IN THOUSANDS OF DOLLARS

Item Description for Accounting Period 7/10 Through 6/11	Total	Zero Assets	Under 500	500 to 1,000	1,000 to 5,000	5,000 to 10,000	10,000 to 25,000	25,000 to 50,000	50,000 to 100,000	100,000 to 250,000	250,000 to 500,000	500,000 to 2,500,000	2,500,000 and over
Number of Enterprises 1	4036	376	2102	323	826	176	109	51	33	19	10	9	0
Revenues ($ in Thousands)													
Net Sales 2	22344573	54801	136220	468498	2186436	1170751	1330654	1481069	1550211	2110383	2963489	8892061	0
Interest 3	37437	1115	54	49	3374	2433	717	1009	1657	1696	1273	24061	0
Rents 4	41002	0	0	1423	1111	676	545	1227	1207	1603	1431	31779	0
Royalties 5	27772	0	401	0	0	0	0	258	214	117	326	26457	0
Other Portfolio Income 6	204147	12256	0	32128	16634	13157	8009	16077	15751	5090	7997	77046	0
Other Receipts 7	332710	12666	238	-6685	16227	26204	54671	-2450	16229	3511	26178	185921	0
Total Receipts 8	22987641	80838	136913	495413	2223782	1213221	1394596	1497190	1585269	2122400	3000694	9237325	0
Average Total Receipts 9	5696	215	65	1534	2692	6893	12794	29357	48038	111705	300069	1026369	•
Operating Costs/Operating Income (%)													
Cost of Operations 10	65.3	56.0	62.8	69.4	56.2	64.9	65.7	71.2	65.1	69.5	66.6	64.9	•
Salaries and Wages 11	5.0	3.6	1.6	0.5	3.3	4.6	5.6	3.4	6.4	3.4	10.7	4.3	•
Taxes Paid 12	2.4	13.7	3.3	3.8	4.5	3.1	3.3	2.0	1.6	1.7	1.2	2.3	•
Interest Paid 13	3.2	8.7	2.2	2.1	0.8	3.0	1.8	1.7	1.5	1.9	2.6	5.0	•
Depreciation 14	7.5	14.2	12.7	7.2	4.5	10.1	8.4	7.2	8.2	6.3	6.3	8.2	•
Amortization and Depletion 15	3.2	4.4	0.0	0.5	1.1	0.7	3.1	2.3	1.6	2.3	4.7	4.4	•
Pensions and Other Deferred Comp. 16	0.9	0.2	•	•	0.8	0.4	0.4	0.6	0.7	0.5	1.5	1.2	•
Employee Benefits 17	2.3	2.2	•	1.5	2.5	2.0	2.5	1.6	2.5	2.3	1.7	2.7	•
Advertising 18	0.2	0.1	1.1	0.1	0.5	0.2	0.3	0.2	0.2	0.2	0.1	0.3	•
Other Expenses 19	10.0	73.5	21.4	6.8	18.7	11.1	7.4	6.4	14.2	8.4	8.4	8.4	•
Officers' Compensation 20	1.4	2.8	0.7	2.1	3.6	2.4	3.2	1.4	1.3	1.4	0.7	0.6	•
Operating Margin 21	•	•	•	6.0	3.5	•	•	2.0	•	2.2	•	•	•
Operating Margin Before Officers' Comp. 22	•	•	•	8.1	7.0	•	1.5	3.4	•	3.6	•	•	•

Selected Average Balance Sheet ($ in Thousands)

Net Receivables 23	744	0	0	23	280	1053	1920	4197	5889	18524	35540	139505
Inventories 24	716	0	2	21	198	679	2255	3795	6402	17620	22866	153500
Net Property, Plant and Equipment 25	3583	0	19	355	1036	3770	7338	13551	28980	62440	178177	818767
Total Assets 26	8821	0	33	658	2371	6995	16127	32850	65070	150034	361328	2231513
Notes and Loans Payable 27	2861	0	20	641	789	3564	3618	10330	15686	34999	160609	701110
All Other Liabilities 28	1886	0	24	43	228	1125	2679	4468	10524	29381	80483	548215
Net Worth 29	4073	0	-10	-27	1355	2306	9830	18053	38860	85654	120236	982188

Selected Financial Ratios (Times to 1)

Current Ratio 30	2.0	•	1.1	4.5	3.4	1.8	2.1	2.4	2.4	2.5	1.9	1.6
Quick Ratio 31	1.1	•	0.7	3.8	2.6	1.1	1.3	1.4	1.6	1.4	1.2	0.7
Net Sales to Working Capital 32	4.9	65.4	7.4	6.5	3.5	6.3	3.8	4.1	3.5	3.2	5.7	6.5
Coverage Ratio 33	1.5	•	6.5	7.7	1.4	1.0	2.7	2.8	0.5	2.4	•	1.4
Total Asset Turnover 34	0.6	1.9	2.2	1.1	1.0	0.8	0.8	0.9	0.7	0.7	0.8	0.4
Inventory Turnover 35	5.0	24.9	47.7	7.5	6.4	6.4	3.6	5.4	4.8	4.4	8.6	4.2
Receivables Turnover 36	7.4	18.9	109.9	6.4	7.0	5.6	7.3	8.2	5.4	9.9	•	7.6
Total Liabilities to Net Worth 37	1.2	•	•	0.7	2.0	0.6	0.8	0.7	0.8	2.0	2.0	1.3
Current Assets to Working Capital 38	2.0	9.1	1.3	1.4	0.4	0.7	1.9	1.2	1.7	1.7	2.1	2.7
Current Liabilities to Working Capital 39	1.0	8.1	0.3	0.4	0.3	0.9	0.9	0.3	0.7	0.7	1.1	1.7
Working Capital to Net Sales 40	0.2	0.0	0.1	0.3	0.3	0.3	0.2	0.3	0.3	0.5	0.2	0.2
Inventory to Working Capital 41	0.6	•	0.1	0.3	0.3	0.6	0.5	0.5	0.5	0.5	0.5	1.0
Total Receipts to Cash Flow 42	13.8	3.0	8.7	8.5	6.8	12.3	11.8	15.6	10.8	11.8	39.0	17.5
Cost of Goods to Cash Flow 43	9.0	1.7	5.4	5.9	3.8	8.0	7.7	11.1	7.0	8.2	26.0	11.4
Cash Flow to Total Debt 44	0.1	0.2	0.2	0.4	0.1	0.2	0.1	0.2	0.3	0.5	0.1	0.0

Selected Financial Factors (in Percentages)

Debt Ratio 45	53.8	130.8	104.0	42.9	67.0	39.0	45.0	40.3	42.9	66.7	56.0	
Return on Total Assets 46	3.0	•	30.7	6.6	4.0	3.6	4.3	0.5	3.5	•	3.0	
Return on Equity Before Income Taxes 47	2.1	32.9	•	10.1	3.5	3.8	5.0	•	3.6	1.8		
Return on Equity After Income Taxes 48	1.0	33.1	•	9.6	2.4	3.4	4.6	•	2.2	0.6		
Profit Margin (Before Income Tax) 49	1.6	11.8	11.8	5.2	1.2	3.0	3.1	•	2.7	1.8		
Profit Margin (After Income Tax) 50	0.7	11.6	4.9	0.8	2.8	2.9	•	1.7	0.6			

13

Table II
Corporations with Net Income

NONMETALLIC MINERAL MINING AND QUARRYING

MONEY AMOUNTS AND SIZE OF ASSETS IN THOUSANDS OF DOLLARS

Item Description for Accounting Period 7/10 Through 6/11	Total	Zero Assets	Under 500	500 to 1,000	1,000 to 5,000	5,000 to 10,000	10,000 to 25,000	25,000 to 50,000	50,000 to 100,000	100,000 to 250,000	250,000 to 500,000	500,000 to 2,500,000	2,500,000 and over
Number of Enterprises 1	1936	•	906	323	462	•	59	28	18	15	•	6	0
Revenues ($ in Thousands)													
Net Sales 2	13965838	•	22673	468498	1632026	•	824060	975072	1068646	1902252	•	4628742	0
Interest 3	26456	•	54	49	2345	•	191	515	1076	1620	•	16010	0
Rents 4	26658	•	0	1423	440	•	144	91	1027	1319	•	20850	0
Royalties 5	26287	•	401	0	0	•	0	54	214	0	•	25572	0
Other Portfolio Income 6	134466	•	0	32128	16379	•	2265	14063	9559	4368	•	25135	0
Other Receipts 7	295570	•	93	-6685	10488	•	32133	2914	13384	11997	•	165275	0
Total Receipts 8	14475275	•	23221	495413	1661678	•	858793	992709	1093906	1921556	•	4881584	0
Average Total Receipts 9	7477	•	26	1534	3597	•	14556	35454	60773	128104	•	813597	•
Operating Costs/Operating Income (%)													
Cost of Operations 10	65.4	•	24.3	69.4	50.3	•	62.6	66.3	67.7	69.7	•	66.5	•
Salaries and Wages 11	3.8	•	0.1	0.5	3.4	•	5.0	4.6	4.3	3.1	•	3.7	•
Taxes Paid 12	2.1	•	8.8	3.8	4.4	•	2.3	2.0	1.6	1.6	•	1.7	•
Interest Paid 13	1.8	•	4.3	2.1	0.8	•	1.6	0.7	0.9	1.7	•	2.9	•
Depreciation 14	6.9	•	18.2	7.2	3.1	•	8.4	7.1	6.4	6.1	•	8.2	•
Amortization and Depletion 15	3.1	•	0.2	0.5	1.1	•	3.4	2.2	1.9	2.2	•	5.3	•
Pensions and Other Deferred Comp. 16	1.0	•	•	•	1.1	•	0.3	0.6	0.7	0.5	•	1.3	•
Employee Benefits 17	1.8	•	•	1.5	2.7	•	1.7	1.9	1.8	2.2	•	1.5	•
Advertising 18	0.2	•	2.3	0.1	0.5	•	0.2	0.2	0.1	0.1	•	0.2	•
Other Expenses 19	8.8	•	13.4	6.8	21.9	•	5.4	7.8	10.1	8.1	•	6.3	•
Officers' Compensation 20	1.6	•	0.0	2.1	3.0	•	3.2	1.5	1.3	1.2	•	1.1	•
Operating Margin 21	3.6	•	28.2	6.0	7.6	•	5.8	4.9	3.3	3.4	•	1.3	•
Operating Margin Before Officers' Comp. 22	5.2	•	28.3	8.1	10.6	•	9.0	6.4	4.6	4.5	•	2.4	•

Selected Average Balance Sheet ($ in Thousands)

Net Receivables 23	988	0	23	357	2045	4405	7270	21352	112144
Inventories 24	907	0	24	288	2112	5262	7059	18727	121388
Net Property, Plant and Equipment 25	3848	7	355	1096	8595	14138	30312	66909	541236
Total Assets 26	9605	35	658	2706	18208	33738	66040	161551	1480464
Notes and Loans Payable 27	2134	9	641	661	3067	5895	10766	32829	341394
All Other Liabilities 28	2323	0	43	285	3312	5448	13902	34423	449698
Net Worth 29	5148	27	-27	1761	11828	22395	41372	94298	689372

Selected Financial Ratios (Times to 1)

Current Ratio 30	2.2	16.6	4.5	3.0	2.5	2.9	2.1	2.5	1.7
Quick Ratio 31	1.2	11.1	3.8	2.1	1.8	1.8	1.3	1.4	0.8
Net Sales to Working Capital 32	4.2	1.7	7.4	4.4	3.2	3.6	4.5	3.3	5.0
Coverage Ratio 33	5.1	8.1	6.5	12.9	7.2	10.0	7.6	3.6	3.5
Total Asset Turnover 34	0.8	0.7	2.2	1.3	0.8	1.0	0.9	0.8	0.5
Inventory Turnover 35	5.2		41.8	6.2	4.1	4.4	5.7	4.7	4.2
Receivables Turnover 36	7.1			5.9	5.7	8.2	8.4	5.5	7.3
Total Liabilities to Net Worth 37	0.9	0.3		0.5	0.5	0.5	0.6	0.7	1.1
Current Assets to Working Capital 38	1.9	1.1	1.3	1.5	1.6	1.5	1.9	1.7	2.4
Current Liabilities to Working Capital 39	0.9	0.1	0.3	0.5	0.6	0.5	0.9	0.7	1.4
Working Capital to Net Sales 40	0.2	0.6	0.1	0.2	0.3	0.3	0.2	0.3	0.2
Inventory to Working Capital 41	0.5		0.1	0.4	0.4	0.5	0.6	0.4	0.7
Total Receipts to Cash Flow 42	8.3	2.5	8.5	5.0	7.2	9.2	7.4	10.2	10.4
Cost of Goods to Cash Flow 43	5.4	0.6	5.9	2.5	4.5	6.1	5.0	7.1	6.9
Cash Flow to Total Debt 44	0.2	1.1	0.2	0.8	0.3	0.3	0.3	0.2	0.1

Selected Financial Factors (in Percentages)

Debt Ratio 45	46.4	24.8	104.0	34.9	35.0	33.6	37.4	41.6	53.4
Return on Total Assets 46	6.9	24.7	30.7	13.3	8.8	7.7	6.2	4.8	5.2
Return on Equity Before Income Taxes 47	10.4	28.8		18.9	11.7	10.5	8.6	5.9	8.1
Return on Equity After Income Taxes 48	8.6	28.6		18.2	11.1	9.9	8.0	4.4	5.6
Profit Margin (Before Income Tax) 49	7.4	30.7	11.8	9.4	9.9	6.7	6.0	4.4	7.2
Profit Margin (After Income Tax) 50	6.1	30.4	11.6	9.1	9.4	6.4	5.6	3.3	5.0

14

Table I
Corporations with and without Net Income

SUPPORT ACTIVITIES FOR MINING

MONEY AMOUNTS AND SIZE OF ASSETS IN THOUSANDS OF DOLLARS

Item Description for Accounting Period 7/10 Through 6/11	Total	Zero Assets	Under 500	500 to 1,000	1,000 to 5,000	5,000 to 10,000	10,000 to 25,000	25,000 to 50,000	50,000 to 100,000	100,000 to 250,000	250,000 to 500,000	500,000 to 2,500,000	2,500,000 and over
Number of Enterprises **1**	11381	2371	6071	1231	1162	234	124	66	45	24	11	24	19
Revenues ($ in Thousands)													
Net Sales **2**	78003953	1544947	2886805	1695236	3782759	2431894	3173227	2492257	3182054	2329751	1843639	11616366	41025019
Interest **3**	717137	12298	428	2061	2064	1708	2556	1841	2651	6012	1736	41376	642404
Rents **4**	1529554	71772	0	0	12405	2265	3573	333	314	29449	3452	228301	1177689
Royalties **5**	340874	18	0	327	459	46227	15843	71	0	902	140	20540	256347
Other Portfolio Income **6**	2399887	4290	6902	1948	51097	25554	28981	6167	15066	24280	69801	338584	1826315
Other Receipts **7**	2267587	98356	8013	1933	-20847	15743	29575	22329	53128	84179	54949	356737	1563497
Total Receipts **8**	85258092	1731681	2902148	1701505	3827937	2523391	3253755	2522998	3253213	2474573	1973717	12601904	46491271
Average Total Receipts **9**	7491	730	478	1382	3294	10784	26240	38227	72294	103107	179429	525079	2446909
Operating Costs/Operating Income (%)													
Cost of Operations **10**	49.0	60.9	5.3	22.3	39.0	50.1	61.1	52.0	56.1	46.3	58.2	50.1	51.4
Salaries and Wages **11**	10.4	13.5	30.3	16.9	13.2	11.7	10.4	11.8	10.7	18.5	6.6	10.7	7.9
Taxes Paid **12**	2.3	1.6	4.7	2.5	3.2	4.0	2.0	2.9	2.6	2.8	2.9	2.4	1.8
Interest Paid **13**	4.4	6.4	1.2	0.8	1.0	0.4	1.0	1.6	3.0	3.5	3.8	5.4	5.7
Depreciation **14**	12.6	8.0	4.2	7.0	7.7	5.9	5.9	8.0	10.1	13.2	20.9	18.8	13.3
Amortization and Depletion **15**	0.8	0.6	0.1	0.1	0.2	0.2	0.4	0.4	0.5	1.7	1.4	1.9	0.8
Pensions and Other Deferred Comp. **16**	0.4	0.1	0.4	0.2	0.2	0.1	0.1	0.5	0.1	0.2	0.8	0.2	0.6
Employee Benefits **17**	2.3	5.6	1.1	0.6	2.0	0.8	1.0	2.3	1.1	2.3	1.8	1.8	2.8
Advertising **18**	0.1	0.1	0.4	0.4	0.2	0.2	0.2	0.3	0.2	0.2	0.1	0.1	0.1
Other Expenses **19**	18.9	27.9	35.1	31.0	25.4	19.0	14.1	15.4	16.6	24.9	17.2	17.2	17.4
Officers' Compensation **20**	1.4	5.8	6.3	2.7	5.7	2.3	1.3	1.3	0.8	1.8	1.3	0.9	0.5
Operating Margin **21**	•	•	10.9	15.5	2.2	5.2	2.6	3.5	•	•	•	•	•
Operating Margin Before Officers' Comp. **22**	•	•	17.3	18.2	8.0	7.5	3.9	4.8	•	•	•	•	•

Selected Average Balance Sheet ($ in Thousands)

Item													
Net Receivables 23	2127	0	19	105	254	1353	5152	7960	13570	35582	35072	138395	895279
Inventories 24	479	0	1	10	53	210	366	1035	1506	4985	58765	23536	200593
Net Property, Plant and Equipment 25	4762	0	43	227	507	1296	5710	9525	24878	65483	124764	454523	1918728
Total Assets 26	13180	0	120	707	1897	6254	16175	34215	67595	173904	369942	1068849	5448754
Notes and Loans Payable 27	4038	0	89	193	619	694	5084	10864	24101	43066	58801	248649	1800864
All Other Liabilities 28	2984	0	10	484	291	1177	4643	10592	22301	67620	79113	284289	1110355
Net Worth 29	6157	0	21	31	987	4383	6447	12759	21193	63218	232029	535911	2537535

Selected Financial Ratios (Times to 1)

Item													
Current Ratio 30	2.0	•	2.0	0.8	2.8	5.1	1.6	2.0	1.3	1.4	•	3.1	2.1
Quick Ratio 31	1.5	•	1.9	0.7	2.2	4.0	1.4	1.5	1.2	1.1	•	1.4	1.5
Net Sales to Working Capital 32	3.4	•	14.2	•	5.2	3.1	8.5	5.4	10.8	5.2	1.8	3.6	2.6
Coverage Ratio 33	2.6	•	10.7	21.7	4.5	21.6	6.0	3.9	1.1	•	•	1.0	3.1
Total Asset Turnover 34	0.5	•	4.0	1.9	1.7	1.7	1.6	1.1	1.0	0.6	0.5	0.5	0.4
Inventory Turnover 35	7.0	•	17.2	32.0	24.1	24.8	42.8	19.0	26.3	9.0	1.7	10.3	5.5
Receivables Turnover 36	3.6	•	29.5	16.8	13.1	11.2	7.2	5.2	6.5	3.4	2.6	3.9	2.7
Total Liabilities to Net Worth 37	1.1	•	4.8	22.1	0.9	0.4	1.5	1.7	2.2	1.8	0.6	1.0	1.1
Current Assets to Working Capital 38	2.0	•	2.0	•	1.5	1.2	2.7	2.0	4.0	3.5	1.5	1.9	1.9
Current Liabilities to Working Capital 39	1.0	•	1.0	•	0.5	0.2	1.7	1.0	3.0	2.5	0.5	0.9	0.9
Working Capital to Net Sales 40	0.3	•	0.1	•	0.2	0.3	0.1	0.2	0.1	0.2	0.6	0.3	0.4
Inventory to Working Capital 41	0.2	•	0.0	•	0.1	0.1	0.2	0.1	0.2	0.3	0.6	0.2	0.2
Total Receipts to Cash Flow 42	5.7	16.0	2.4	2.4	4.2	4.1	6.9	7.0	7.9	30.8	23.3	9.9	5.3
Cost of Goods to Cash Flow 43	2.8	9.8	0.1	0.5	1.7	2.1	4.2	3.6	4.4	14.2	13.6	5.0	2.7
Cash Flow to Total Debt 44	0.2	•	2.0	0.9	0.8	1.3	0.4	0.3	0.2	0.0	0.1	0.1	0.1

Selected Financial Factors (in Percentages)

Item													
Debt Ratio 45	53.3	•	82.9	95.7	48.0	29.9	62.7	60.1	68.6	63.6	37.3	49.9	53.4
Return on Total Assets 46	6.0	•	50.0	32.3	7.5	15.6	7.0	9.7	3.6	•	•	2.4	7.1
Return on Equity Before Income Taxes 47	8.0	•	264.6	712.9	11.2	21.2	20.3	14.0	1.4	•	•	•	10.4
Return on Equity After Income Taxes 48	4.6	•	263.8	711.8	10.0	18.2	17.6	11.1	0.9	•	•	•	6.1
Profit Margin (Before Income Tax) 49	7.1	•	11.5	15.8	3.4	8.9	4.7	5.1	0.4	•	•	•	12.2
Profit Margin (After Income Tax) 50	4.1	•	11.4	15.8	3.0	7.7	3.7	4.4	0.3	•	•	•	7.2

Table II
Corporations with Net Income

SUPPORT ACTIVITIES FOR MINING

MONEY AMOUNTS AND SIZE OF ASSETS IN THOUSANDS OF DOLLARS

Item Description for Accounting Period 7/10 Through 6/11	Total	Zero Assets	Under 500	500 to 1,000	1,000 to 5,000	5,000 to 10,000	10,000 to 25,000	25,000 to 50,000	50,000 to 100,000	100,000 to 250,000	250,000 to 500,000	500,000 to 2,500,000	2,500,000 and over
Number of Enterprises **1**	8095	1107	4797	1084	721	202	83	44	19	9	4	11	13
Revenues ($ in Thousands)													
Net Sales **2**	56966313	850377	2574239	1458201	2452591	2351958	2730840	1942359	2036311	1278830	953335	7744345	30592927
Interest **3**	549059	118	287	448	1089	243	1289	1118	299	4071	1052	10554	528490
Rents **4**	1096167	1164	0	0	4413	1349	1904	333	0	193	490	182782	903539
Royalties **5**	321153	18	0	0	459	46227	7133	0	0	2577	0	18036	249279
Other Portfolio Income **6**	2139170	2299	6901	753	43178	23749	27886	5346	9457	2577	47030	270444	1699551
Other Receipts **7**	1819237	98907	3945	1612	7336	16495	28005	21433	39012	4349	11377	210146	1376620
Total Receipts **8**	62891099	952883	2585372	1461014	2509066	2440021	2797057	1970589	2085079	1290020	1013284	8436307	35350406
Average Total Receipts **9**	7769	861	539	1348	3480	12079	33699	44786	109741	143336	253321	766937	2719262
Operating Costs/Operating Income (%)													
Cost of Operations **10**	48.5	67.7	4.3	24.5	34.0	48.5	66.6	54.9	60.5	54.0	56.4	46.9	51.1
Salaries and Wages **11**	10.0	6.6	29.6	10.9	11.8	11.4	7.8	9.7	7.4	7.4	9.1	11.4	8.3
Taxes Paid **12**	2.3	1.2	4.8	2.8	2.2	3.8	1.8	2.7	2.7	1.8	2.7	2.5	1.9
Interest Paid **13**	2.6	0.6	1.3	0.8	0.5	0.3	0.5	1.2	0.8	3.3	2.3	2.4	3.6
Depreciation **14**	9.5	2.9	4.0	7.1	6.6	5.7	4.3	6.1	5.4	7.3	11.1	16.4	10.0
Amortization and Depletion **15**	0.6	0.2	0.0	•	0.2	0.2	0.2	0.2	0.1	1.0	0.5	1.5	0.6
Pensions and Other Deferred Comp. **16**	0.5	0.3	0.4	0.1	0.1	0.1	0.1	0.5	0.1	0.4	1.0	0.2	0.8
Employee Benefits **17**	2.1	0.9	1.2	0.7	1.1	0.8	0.6	2.2	0.7	0.6	1.1	1.4	3.0
Advertising **18**	0.1	0.1	0.4	0.4	0.2	0.2	0.2	0.2	0.2	0.2	0.1	0.1	0.1
Other Expenses **19**	18.1	16.7	32.5	28.4	27.8	18.7	10.6	13.6	11.5	14.7	9.6	18.1	17.4
Officers' Compensation **20**	1.4	1.9	6.7	2.9	6.0	2.3	1.1	0.9	0.7	2.3	1.5	0.9	0.5
Operating Margin **21**	4.4	0.9	14.7	21.3	9.5	7.9	6.1	7.7	9.8	7.0	4.6	•	2.8
Operating Margin Before Officers' Comp. **22**	5.7	2.8	21.4	24.2	15.5	10.2	7.2	8.7	10.5	9.3	6.1	•	3.3

Selected Average Balance Sheet ($ in Thousands)

Net Receivables	23	2243	0	20	108	249	1414	6307	8995	18334	41207	46801	212314	1024156
Inventories	24	373	0	1	6	45	230	438	866	1659	3262	25583	30712	181166
Net Property, Plant and Equipment	25	3789	0	41	255	347	1350	4087	8654	16557	47519	113291	494121	1717213
Total Assets	26	12035	0	117	700	1847	6276	15905	35688	68252	168814	314879	1151220	5682879
Notes and Loans Payable	27	2547	0	79	216	343	538	2298	8643	10666	41852	29983	228870	1220362
All Other Liabilities	28	2633	0	9	62	204	971	5429	12875	17916	37013	123454	344313	1145478
Net Worth	29	6855	0	30	422	1299	4766	8178	14170	39671	89950	161442	578038	3317038

Selected Financial Ratios (Times to 1)

Current Ratio	30	2.3	•	2.0	4.2	4.3	5.5	1.8	2.1	1.9	2.2	2.7	1.9	2.3
Quick Ratio	31	1.7	•	2.0	3.5	3.5	4.1	1.6	1.7	1.7	1.8	1.8	1.3	1.7
Net Sales to Working Capital	32	3.0	•	15.2	5.1	4.4	3.2	7.3	5.2	7.0	4.0	2.6	4.3	2.2
Coverage Ratio	33	7.0	21.8	12.8	26.7	22.9	36.6	16.8	8.3	16.7	3.4	5.7	4.4	6.5
Total Asset Turnover	34	0.6	•	4.6	1.9	1.8	1.9	2.1	1.2	1.6	0.8	0.8	0.6	0.4
Inventory Turnover	35	9.1	•	33.6	56.9	25.9	24.5	50.1	28.0	39.1	23.5	5.3	10.8	6.6
Receivables Turnover	36	3.7	•	35.7	22.1	12.6	14.0	8.2	5.7	6.9	4.1	2.0	5.3	2.6
Total Liabilities to Net Worth	37	0.8	•	2.9	0.7	0.4	0.3	0.9	1.5	0.7	0.9	1.0	1.0	0.7
Current Assets to Working Capital	38	1.8	•	2.0	1.3	1.3	1.2	2.2	1.9	2.2	1.8	1.6	2.2	1.7
Current Liabilities to Working Capital	39	0.8	•	1.0	0.3	0.3	0.2	1.2	0.9	1.2	0.8	0.6	1.2	0.7
Working Capital to Net Sales	40	0.3	•	0.1	0.2	0.2	0.3	0.1	0.2	0.1	0.2	0.4	0.2	0.4
Inventory to Working Capital	41	0.2	•	0.0	0.1	0.1	0.1	0.1	0.1	0.1	0.1	0.3	0.2	0.2
Total Receipts to Cash Flow	42	4.1	3.7	2.4	2.2	2.8	3.7	6.4	5.8	4.8	9.0	6.7	5.2	4.1
Cost of Goods to Cash Flow	43	2.0	2.5	0.1	0.5	1.0	1.8	4.3	3.2	2.9	4.8	3.8	2.5	2.1
Cash Flow to Total Debt	44	0.3	•	2.6	2.2	2.2	2.1	0.7	0.4	0.8	0.2	0.2	0.2	0.2

Selected Financial Factors (in Percentages)

Debt Ratio	45	43.0	•	74.5	39.7	29.6	24.1	48.6	60.3	41.9	46.7	48.7	49.8	41.6
Return on Total Assets	46	10.6	•	75.5	42.9	22.8	22.1	18.8	12.9	20.4	9.4	10.0	6.4	9.6
Return on Equity Before Income Taxes	47	16.0	•	273.3	68.5	31.0	28.3	34.3	28.5	33.1	12.4	16.1	9.9	13.9
Return on Equity After Income Taxes	48	11.8	•	272.6	68.4	29.5	25.2	31.1	24.5	32.4	9.3	14.1	7.4	9.2
Profit Margin (Before Income Tax)	49	15.6	12.9	15.1	21.5	11.8	11.6	8.5	9.1	12.2	7.8	10.9	8.1	19.7
Profit Margin (After Income Tax)	50	11.5	11.0	15.1	21.4	11.3	10.3	7.7	7.9	12.0	5.9	9.6	6.0	13.0

Table I

Corporations with and without Net Income

ELECTRIC POWER GENERATION, TRANSMISSION AND DISTRIBUTION

MONEY AMOUNTS AND SIZE OF ASSETS IN THOUSANDS OF DOLLARS

Item Description for Accounting Period 7/10 Through 6/11	Total	Zero Assets	Under 500	500 to 1,000	1,000 to 5,000	5,000 to 10,000	10,000 to 25,000	25,000 to 50,000	50,000 to 100,000	100,000 to 250,000	250,000 to 500,000	500,000 to 2,500,000	2,500,000 and over
Number of Enterprises **1**	1249	102	504	265	93	39	59	26	31	29	22	32	46
Revenues ($ in Thousands)													
Net Sales **2**	308262448	851752	2880	73545	1993	139420	275463	2002632	1532455	2558349	2040743	12676639	286106577
Interest **3**	3480095	804	268906	0	1815	89	1838	5752	40958	31194	27005	176955	2924780
Rents **4**	1307933	219	0	0	1060	1263	86	0	1017	504	14604	8208	1280971
Royalties **5**	25638	0	0	0	0	0	0	503	89	0	0	331	24715
Other Portfolio Income **6**	7998159	263275	0	0	393	22015	4275	2812	605	3784	263259	213000	7224741
Other Receipts **7**	9712143	34736	6421	2533	34	1959	2721	22673	249818	254842	213807	323344	8599252
Total Receipts **8**	33078416	1150786	278207	76078	5295	164746	284383	2034372	1824942	2844673	2559418	13398477	306161036
Average Total Receipts **9**	264841	11282	552	287	57	4224	4820	78245	58869	98230	116337	418702	6655675
Operating Costs/Operating Income (%)													
Cost of Operations **10**	55.4	62.1	211.9	12.2	•	61.7	54.1	89.1	62.6	79.5	55.4	61.4	54.6
Salaries and Wages **11**	3.4	11.1	90.0	6.8	311.6	14.1	17.4	2.5	2.9	2.9	2.3	5.1	3.3
Taxes Paid **12**	4.3	2.2	3.4	12.8	50.3	5.6	3.4	0.4	1.3	1.1	2.3	2.4	4.5
Interest Paid **13**	6.9	7.7	8457.5	3.4	81.5	5.1	2.8	0.5	3.4	3.3	12.3	6.7	6.9
Depreciation **14**	13.0	13.3	7.4	2.1	36.3	14.8	13.0	1.4	4.6	7.7	15.2	11.5	13.3
Amortization and Depletion **15**	1.5	1.1	11.4	0.3	23.5	0.2	0.4	0.5	1.1	0.4	1.5	1.5	1.5
Pensions and Other Deferred Comp. **16**	1.7	0.1	0.1	•	0.6	0.6	1.3	0.2	0.2	0.7	0.6	1.0	1.8
Employee Benefits **17**	1.2	1.1	15.7	0.4	5.6	1.2	2.5	1.1	0.5	0.4	0.8	0.9	1.2
Advertising **18**	0.1	0.5	0.0	0.4	48.9	•	0.2	0.0	0.3	0.0	0.1	0.1	0.1
Other Expenses **19**	19.5	24.3	1203.7	55.0	1273.2	31.8	37.0	6.8	50.6	11.1	26.0	19.7	19.3
Officers' Compensation **20**	0.3	1.1	•	33.1	180.0	1.2	3.7	0.5	1.2	0.5	0.8	0.6	0.3
Operating Margin **21**	•	•	•	•	•	•	•	•	•	•	•	•	•
Operating Margin Before Officers' Comp. **22**	•	•	•	6.5	•	•	•	•	•	•	•	•	•

Selected Average Balance Sheet ($ in Thousands)

Item													
Net Receivables 23	43760	0	0	21	7	659	1116	9909	18832	9901	12070	79195	1100645
Inventories 24	12605	0	0	2	48	239	634	138	1189	1320	7902	31802	313528
Net Property, Plant and Equipment 25	423391	0	1	193	269	3380	5520	10907	23438	72495	177797	648062	10880847
Total Assets 26	718269	0	15	766	1917	6796	15633	35406	71598	153665	371971	1150164	18325157
Notes and Loans Payable 27	291299	0	38	4	376	3601	3550	15446	30767	71953	189102	574443	7335712
All Other Liabilities 28	246145	0	1	332	-603	1268	5075	32362	29034	32127	86082	256357	6397459
Net Worth 29	180826	0	-24	430	2144	1927	7007	-12402	11797	49585	96787	319364	4591986

Selected Financial Ratios (Times to 1)

Item													
Current Ratio 30	1.0	•	10.4	1.6	12.9	1.8	1.3	0.5	1.2	1.3	1.3	1.6	1.0
Quick Ratio 31	0.6	•	9.2	1.6	1.1	1.2	1.0	0.4	1.0	0.9	1.0	1.0	0.6
Net Sales to Working Capital 32	55.0	•	1.0	1.3	0.0	3.5	4.1	•	8.1	15.7	8.8	4.1	140.0
Coverage Ratio 33	1.0	2.3	1.0	•	•	•	•	•	•	2.2	1.6	0.2	1.1
Total Asset Turnover 34	0.3	•	0.4	0.4	0.0	0.5	0.3	2.2	0.7	0.6	0.2	0.3	0.3
Inventory Turnover 35	10.8	•	28.3	18.8	•	9.2	4.0	496.8	26.0	53.1	6.5	7.6	10.8
Receivables Turnover 36	5.3	•	•	26.0	•	6.0	5.9	11.1	2.7	9.4	6.8	5.2	5.3
Total Liabilities to Net Worth 37	3.0	•	•	0.8	•	2.5	1.2	5.1	2.1	2.8	2.6	•	3.0
Current Assets to Working Capital 38	24.5	•	1.1	2.6	1.1	2.3	4.7	•	5.3	4.6	4.4	2.8	61.2
Current Liabilities to Working Capital 39	23.5	•	0.1	1.6	0.1	1.3	3.7	•	4.3	3.6	3.4	1.8	60.2
Working Capital to Net Sales 40	0.0	•	1.0	0.8	49.7	0.3	0.2	0.1	0.1	0.1	0.1	0.2	0.0
Inventory to Working Capital 41	2.6	•	•	0.0	•	0.2	0.1	0.3	0.3	0.2	0.4	0.4	6.4
Total Receipts to Cash Flow 42	7.2	147.7	1.1	6.3	•	10.7	•	26.8	2.8	7.9	5.0	12.2	7.1
Cost of Goods to Cash Flow 43	4.0	91.7	2.3	0.8	•	6.6	•	23.9	1.7	6.3	2.7	7.5	3.9
Cash Flow to Total Debt 44	0.1	•	0.1	0.1	0.6	0.1	•	0.1	0.3	0.1	0.1	0.0	0.1

Selected Financial Factors (in Percentages)

Item													
Debt Ratio 45	74.8	•	253.0	43.9	•	71.6	55.2	135.0	83.5	67.7	74.0	72.2	74.9
Return on Total Assets 46	2.4	•	3003.8	•	•	•	•	•	•	4.1	5.0	0.5	2.5
Return on Equity Before Income Taxes 47	0.3	•	82.5	•	•	•	•	9.5	•	6.9	7.5	•	0.6
Return on Equity After Income Taxes 48	•	•	84.6	•	•	•	•	11.9	•	2.7	6.4	•	•
Profit Margin (Before Income Tax) 49	0.2	10.3	•	•	•	•	•	•	•	2.7	7.8	3.9	0.5
Profit Margin (After Income Tax) 50	•	9.7	•	•	•	•	•	•	•	1.5	6.7	•	•

Table II

Corporations with Net Income

ELECTRIC POWER GENERATION, TRANSMISSION AND DISTRIBUTION

MONEY AMOUNTS AND SIZE OF ASSETS IN THOUSANDS OF DOLLARS

Item Description for Accounting Period 7/10 Through 6/11	Total	Zero Assets	Under 500	500 to 1,000	1,000 to 5,000	5,000 to 10,000	10,000 to 25,000	25,000 to 50,000	50,000 to 100,000	100,000 to 250,000	250,000 to 500,000	500,000 to 2,500,000	2,500,000 and over
Number of Enterprises 1	379	25	34	197	28	19	4	3	10	18	11	9	21
Revenues ($ in Thousands)													
Net Sales 2	165116534	673589	0	60740	0	71822	252452	65613	919395	2331728	1028204	4532517	155180474
Interest 3	1406672	268891	0	0	0	3	1256	195	1520	24452	11321	7805	1091106
Rents 4	926321	0	0	0	1060	1263	86	0	170	484	0	82	923174
Royalties 5	15087	0	0	0	0	0	0	503	89	0	0	331	14164
Other Portfolio Income 6	7156236	262499	0	0	0	21831	1033	989	157	3740	262064	6197	6597725
Other Receipts 7	7472645	-275	274	2530	34	1699	296	10277	41603	243710	127815	175800	6868886
Total Receipts 8	182093495	935934	269165	63270	1094	96618	255123	77577	962934	2604114	1429404	4722732	170675529
Average Total Receipts 9	480458	37437	7917	321	274	3451	13428	25859	96293	144673	129946	524748	8127406
Operating Costs/Operating Income (%)													
Cost of Operations 10	56.7	70.2	•	•	•	49.5	55.9	16.1	83.3	83.2	54.6	56.5	56.1
Salaries and Wages 11	4.2	10.8	•	1.0	•	4.6	4.9	2.7	2.7	2.6	1.4	4.9	4.2
Taxes Paid 12	4.4	0.8	•	12.8	•	7.4	3.0	5.3	1.2	1.0	2.7	3.7	4.5
Interest Paid 13	6.0	0.7	•	•	•	7.9	0.4	4.8	1.8	2.6	12.1	6.7	5.9
Depreciation 14	11.5	1.0	•	1.4	•	15.3	6.5	3.1	1.5	2.5	11.8	11.1	11.8
Amortization and Depletion 15	1.8	0.2	•	•	•	•	0.0	13.0	0.2	0.4	1.2	1.3	1.9
Pensions and Other Deferred Comp. 16	1.7	0.1	•	•	•	1.1	1.3	0.1	0.2	0.2	0.1	1.2	1.8
Employee Benefits 17	1.4	1.0	•	•	•	2.2	1.2	0.3	0.3	0.3	0.8	0.9	1.4
Advertising 18	0.1	0.6	•	•	•	•	0.2	0.0	0.5	0.0	0.0	0.0	0.1
Other Expenses 19	16.9	18.1	•	44.4	•	9.9	18.8	26.8	6.3	8.3	21.3	11.8	17.2
Officers' Compensation 20	0.3	0.8	•	35.6	•	•	1.3	4.1	1.3	0.5	0.7	0.5	0.3
Operating Margin 21	•	•	•	4.7	•	2.1	6.5	23.6	0.8	•	•	1.3	•
Operating Margin Before Officers' Comp. 22	•	•	•	40.4	•	2.1	7.8	27.7	2.1	•	•	1.9	•

Selected Average Balance Sheet ($ in Thousands)

Net Receivables 23	66299	0	0	0	485	2568	1225	14406	13857	12309	71903	1137401
Inventories 24	24454	0	0	0	180	988	148	1260	1570	4072	73003	415365
Net Property, Plant and Equipment 25	724004	0	167	2138	3724	8455	19482	20001	55131	196030	861863	12520347
Total Assets 26	1197121	10	737	2154	6665	15970	44271	68076	149088	382748	1341883	20632403
Notes and Loans Payable 27	473685	0	0	295	3573	2819	10727	22422	71715	163669	647672	8104527
All Other Liabilities 28	381990	0	179	0	1171	6622	14872	23151	43060	110736	277282	6657884
Net Worth 29	341446	10	558	1870	1920	6529	18672	22503	34313	108343	416929	5869991

Selected Financial Ratios (Times to 1)

Current Ratio 30	1.1	•	•	3.2	2.1	1.6	1.7	1.6	1.5	1.4	1.3	3.5	1.0
Quick Ratio 31	0.6	•	•	3.2	1.7	1.4	1.1	1.4	1.3	0.9	0.9	2.1	0.6
Net Sales to Working Capital 32	30.8	•	•	0.8	4.2	5.9	4.5	9.8	13.3	8.1	2.4	53.4	
Coverage Ratio 33	1.9	•	50.2	1.1	3.6	1.8	9.6	4.1	4.8	3.6	1.8	1.9	
Total Asset Turnover 34	0.4	•	•	0.4	0.4	0.8	0.5	1.4	0.9	0.2	0.4	0.4	
Inventory Turnover 35	10.1	•	•	7.1	7.5	23.8	60.8	68.6	12.5	3.9	10.0		
Receivables Turnover 36	6.8	•	•	5.7	8.6	•	5.7	10.4	10.4	2.2	6.9		
Total Liabilities to Net Worth 37	2.5	•	0.3	1.5	2.5	1.4	2.3	2.0	3.3	2.5	2.2	2.5	
Current Assets to Working Capital 38	12.7	•	1.0	1.9	2.6	2.8	3.0	3.7	4.1	1.4	21.9		
Current Liabilities to Working Capital 39	11.7	•	0.5	0.9	1.6	1.8	2.0	2.7	3.1	0.4	20.9		
Working Capital to Net Sales 40	0.0	•	1.3	0.2	0.2	0.2	0.1	0.1	0.1	0.4	0.0		
Inventory to Working Capital 41	1.9	•	•	0.3	0.2	0.3	0.2	0.2	0.5	0.3	3.3		
Total Receipts to Cash Flow 42	6.1	7.9	2.5	2.2	4.3	1.7	9.7	6.2	3.1	7.5	6.1		
Cost of Goods to Cash Flow 43	3.4	5.5	•	1.1	2.4	0.3	8.1	5.1	1.7	4.2	3.4		
Cash Flow to Total Debt 44	0.1	•	0.7	0.3	0.3	0.5	0.2	0.1	0.1	0.1	0.1		

Selected Financial Factors (in Percentages)

Debt Ratio 45	71.5	•	24.3	13.2	71.2	59.1	57.8	66.9	77.0	71.7	68.9	71.5
Return on Total Assets 46	4.2	82566.0	3.7	2.9	5.4	6.6	23.0	9.8	10.9	10.7	4.6	3.9
Return on Equity Before Income Taxes 47	7.1	7992.9	4.9	2.4	8.3	15.3	49.0	22.5	37.6	27.4	6.7	6.5
Return on Equity After Income Taxes 48	5.3	79917.2	4.9	2.4	8.3	13.1	35.1	17.4	27.8	25.5	5.7	4.8
Profit Margin (Before Income Tax) 49	5.5	34.7	8.9	•	6.2	7.5	6.2	41.8	31.8	10.0	5.5	5.1
Profit Margin (After Income Tax) 50	4.2	34.0	8.9	•	6.2	6.4	6.4	29.9	29.5	7.4	4.7	3.8

Table I

Corporations with and without Net Income

NATURAL GAS DISTRIBUTION

MONEY AMOUNTS AND SIZE OF ASSETS IN THOUSANDS OF DOLLARS

Item Description for Accounting Period 7/10 Through 6/11	Total	Zero Assets	Under 500	500 to 1,000	1,000 to 5,000	5,000 to 10,000	10,000 to 25,000	25,000 to 50,000	50,000 to 100,000	100,000 to 250,000	250,000 to 500,000	500,000 to 2,500,000	2,500,000 and over
Number of Enterprises 1	936	•	355	0	112	24	•	18	7	•	4	12	16
Revenues ($ in Thousands)													
Net Sales 2	78411371	•	27918	0	450565	466558	•	816844	500736	•	3260884	23586470	46164454
Interest 3	302512	•	0	0	601	287	•	524	411	•	13751	16781	269694
Rents 4	53680	•	0	0	0	150	•	0	6	•	2370	2051	47004
Royalties 5	2603	•	0	0	0	0	•	0	18	•	248	0	279
Other Portfolio Income 6	479906	•	0	0	34	862	•	26	114	•	105115	66138	303562
Other Receipts 7	2987365	•	0	0	5775	3911	•	-2030	2805	•	53562	131646	2779104
Total Receipts 8	82237437	•	27918	0	456975	471768	•	815364	504090	•	3435930	23803086	49564097
Average Total Receipts 9	87861	•	79	•	4080	19657	•	45298	72013	•	858982	1983590	3097756
Operating Costs/Operating Income (%)													
Cost of Operations 10	78.2	•	84.2	•	73.0	85.5	•	80.5	71.2	•	95.7	93.0	68.7
Salaries and Wages 11	3.0	•	•	•	4.3	0.7	•	6.0	5.2	•	1.0	0.8	4.3
Taxes Paid 12	2.0	•	0.2	•	1.0	1.0	•	1.1	1.6	•	0.8	0.6	2.9
Interest Paid 13	3.6	•	•	•	0.9	0.4	•	0.5	1.6	•	3.2	0.7	5.4
Depreciation 14	5.8	•	•	•	2.3	2.4	•	1.3	3.7	•	0.8	1.8	8.6
Amortization and Depletion 15	0.6	•	•	•	0.0	0.5	•	0.1	0.7	•	0.0	0.2	0.9
Pensions and Other Deferred Comp. 16	0.7	•	•	•	1.1	0.1	•	0.1	0.8	•	0.1	0.2	1.0
Employee Benefits 17	0.8	•	•	•	0.2	1.0	•	0.6	1.0	•	0.4	0.3	1.2
Advertising 18	0.1	•	•	•	0.1	0.1	•	0.2	0.8	•	0.0	0.0	0.1
Other Expenses 19	10.9	•	17.4	•	9.5	5.0	•	5.9	8.4	•	7.0	3.2	15.7
Officers' Compensation 20	0.4	•	•	•	2.7	1.1	•	1.4	1.5	•	0.2	0.2	0.5
Operating Margin 21	•	•	•	•	5.0	2.3	•	2.2	3.6	•	•	•	•
Operating Margin Before Officers' Comp. 22	•	•	•	•	7.7	3.4	•	3.6	5.0	•	•	•	•

Selected Average Balance Sheet ($ in Thousands)

Net Receivables 23	13022	125	•	373	522	•	12975	9714	•	32458	188437	567774
Inventories 24	4300	0	•	18	506	•	907	4184	•	62710	95793	156162
Net Property, Plant and Equipment 25	82266	17	•	396	3947	•	9502	22239	•	50232	377888	4432836
Total Assets 26	181873	146	•	1735	9081	•	31074	72431	•	304461	1077947	9545834
Notes and Loans Payable 27	87391	12	•	600	1743	•	5052	16623	•	225124	365812	4736723
All Other Liabilities 28	54681	107	•	516	1934	•	14177	16676	•	254388	385332	2774028
Net Worth 29	39801	27	•	619	5403	•	11846	39132	•	-175051	326803	2035084

Selected Financial Ratios (Times to 1)

Current Ratio 30	1.0	1.2	•	1.7	4.2	•	1.3	2.0	•	1.0	1.1	1.0
Quick Ratio 31	0.4	1.2	•	1.6	2.6	•	1.2	1.0	•	0.3	0.6	0.4
Net Sales to Working Capital 32	121.2	3.6	•	10.4	6.5	•	10.0	4.5	•	•	45.4	•
Coverage Ratio 33	0.7	•	•	8.1	8.9	•	4.8	3.7	•	•	1.0	0.7
Total Asset Turnover 34	0.5	0.5	•	2.3	2.1	•	1.5	1.0	•	2.7	1.8	0.3
Inventory Turnover 35	15.2	•	•	160.1	32.9	•	40.2	12.2	•	12.4	19.1	12.7
Receivables Turnover 36	6.2	0.8	•	16.1	68.4	•	•	•	•	9.3	13.4	4.6
Total Liabilities to Net Worth 37	3.6	4.3	•	1.8	0.7	•	1.6	0.9	•	•	2.3	3.7
Current Assets to Working Capital 38	60.3	5.9	•	2.5	1.3	•	4.2	2.0	•	•	9.4	•
Current Liabilities to Working Capital 39	59.3	4.9	•	1.5	0.3	•	3.2	1.0	•	•	8.4	•
Working Capital to Net Sales 40	0.0	0.3	•	0.1	0.2	•	0.1	0.2	•	•	0.0	•
Inventory to Working Capital 41	6.0	•	•	0.1	0.2	•	0.2	0.3	•	•	2.2	•
Total Receipts to Cash Flow 42	13.7	13.3	•	6.7	12.5	•	14.4	8.5	•	•	35.2	9.6
Cost of Goods to Cash Flow 43	10.7	11.2	•	4.9	10.7	•	11.6	6.0	•	•	32.8	6.6
Cash Flow to Total Debt 44	0.0	0.0	•	0.5	0.4	•	0.2	0.3	•	•	0.1	0.0

Selected Financial Factors (in Percentages)

Debt Ratio 45	78.1	81.3	•	64.3	40.5	•	61.9	46.0	•	157.5	69.7	78.7
Return on Total Assets 46	1.1	•	•	17.0	7.9	•	3.7	5.8	•	•	1.2	1.1
Return on Equity Before Income Taxes 47	•	•	•	41.8	11.8	•	7.6	7.8	•	16.9	•	•
Return on Equity After Income Taxes 48	•	•	•	29.2	10.2	•	5.3	6.4	•	17.0	•	•
Profit Margin (Before Income Tax) 49	•	•	•	6.4	3.3	•	2.0	4.3	•	•	•	•
Profit Margin (After Income Tax) 50	•	•	•	4.5	2.8	•	1.4	3.5	•	•	•	•

Table II
Corporations with Net Income

NATURAL GAS DISTRIBUTION

MONEY AMOUNTS AND SIZE OF ASSETS IN THOUSANDS OF DOLLARS

Item Description for Accounting Period 7/10 Through 6/11	Total	Zero Assets	Under 500	500 to 1,000	1,000 to 5,000	5,000 to 10,000	10,000 to 25,000	25,000 to 50,000	50,000 to 100,000	100,000 to 250,000	250,000 to 500,000	500,000 to 2,500,000	2,500,000 and over
Number of Enterprises **1**	258	0	107	0	84	24	6	9	•	9	0	•	8
Revenues ($ in Thousands)													
Net Sales **2**	42753512	0	3530	0	450565	466558	20919	736265	•	4602303	0	•	27851409
Interest **3**	200239	0	0	0	601	287	21	42	•	275	0	•	187366
Rents **4**	23209	0	0	0	0	150	0	0	•	262	0	•	20980
Royalties **5**	2354	0	0	0	0	0	0	0	•	2058	0	•	278
Other Portfolio Income **6**	269475	0	0	0	34	862	1673	26	•	411	0	•	265502
Other Receipts **7**	2391296	0	0	0	5775	3911	598	23	•	7058	0	•	2360350
Total Receipts **8**	45640085	0	3530	0	456975	471768	23211	736356	•	4612367	0	•	30685885
Average Total Receipts **9**	176900	•	33	•	5440	19657	3868	81817	•	512485	•	•	3835736
Operating Costs/Operating Income (%)													
Cost of Operations **10**	77.4	•	•	•	73.0	85.5	23.9	86.5	•	94.9	•	•	72.5
Salaries and Wages **11**	3.0	•	•	•	4.3	0.7	4.4	3.4	•	0.8	•	•	3.9
Taxes Paid **12**	2.1	•	1.6	•	1.0	1.0	5.0	0.9	•	0.3	•	•	2.7
Interest Paid **13**	4.1	•	•	•	0.9	0.4	•	0.1	•	0.3	•	•	5.8
Depreciation **14**	5.6	•	•	•	2.3	2.4	12.6	0.6	•	0.9	•	•	7.3
Amortization and Depletion **15**	0.4	•	•	•	0.0	0.5	•	0.1	•	0.0	•	•	0.6
Pensions and Other Deferred Comp. **16**	0.8	•	•	•	1.1	0.1	2.5	0.1	•	0.1	•	•	1.0
Employee Benefits **17**	1.0	•	•	•	0.2	1.0	1.8	0.3	•	0.1	•	•	1.3
Advertising **18**	0.1	•	•	•	0.1	0.1	0.3	0.0	•	0.0	•	•	0.1
Other Expenses **19**	9.0	•	88.5	•	4.6	5.0	11.2	2.5	•	1.6	•	•	11.3
Officers' Compensation **20**	0.3	•	•	•	2.7	1.1	•	0.9	•	0.1	•	•	0.3
Operating Margin **21**	•	•	9.8	•	9.9	2.3	38.4	4.6	•	0.8	•	•	•
Operating Margin Before Officers' Comp. **22**	•	•	9.8	•	12.6	3.4	38.4	5.5	•	0.9	•	•	•

Selected Average Balance Sheet ($ in Thousands)

	C1	C2	C3	C4	C5	C6	C7	C8
Net Receivables 23	34305	414	497	522	90	11609	35334	880248
Inventories 24	10135	0	30	506	1376	1811	12603	187277
Net Property, Plant and Equipment 25	182630	57	528	3947	6582	6975	53672	5402951
Total Assets 26	447718	483	1922	9081	12684	27773	162328	13131036
Notes and Loans Payable 27	221867	39	800	1743	129	1857	27981	6782052
All Other Liabilities 28	143426	354	567	1934	823	11960	78384	4129549
Net Worth 29	82426	90	555	5403	11732	13957	55963	2219434

Selected Financial Ratios (Times to 1)

	C1	C2	C3	C4	C5	C6	C7	C8
Current Ratio 30	1.0	1.2	1.9	4.2	7.3	1.8	1.2	1.0
Quick Ratio 31	0.4	1.2	1.9	2.6	2.3	1.6	0.7	0.4
Net Sales to Working Capital 32	113.3	0.5	8.7	6.5	0.7	9.8	37.7	•
Coverage Ratio 33	1.8	•	13.5	8.9	•	50.5	4.3	1.6
Total Asset Turnover 34	0.4	0.1	2.8	2.1	0.3	2.9	3.2	0.3
Inventory Turnover 35	12.6	•	129.3	32.9	0.6	39.1	38.5	13.5
Receivables Turnover 36	4.1	0.2	17.2	74.5	1.8	•	•	3.3
Total Liabilities to Net Worth 37	4.4	4.3	2.5	0.7	0.1	1.0	1.9	4.9
Current Assets to Working Capital 38	62.7	5.9	2.1	1.3	1.2	2.3	6.5	•
Current Liabilities to Working Capital 39	61.7	4.9	1.1	0.3	0.2	1.3	5.5	•
Working Capital to Net Sales 40	0.0	2.2	0.1	0.2	1.5	0.1	0.0	•
Inventory to Working Capital 41	5.9	•	0.0	0.2	0.0	0.2	0.9	•
Total Receipts to Cash Flow 42	9.7	2.9	6.7	12.5	1.7	15.5	43.0	8.0
Cost of Goods to Cash Flow 43	7.5	•	4.9	10.7	0.4	13.4	40.8	5.8
Cash Flow to Total Debt 44	0.0	0.0	0.6	0.4	2.2	0.4	0.1	0.0

Selected Financial Factors (in Percentages)

	C1	C2	C3	C4	C5	C6	C7	C8
Debt Ratio 45	81.6	81.3	71.1	40.5	7.5	49.7	65.5	83.1
Return on Total Assets 46	2.7	0.7	34.1	7.9	13.6	14.0	4.2	2.5
Return on Equity Before Income Taxes 47	6.2	3.6	109.3	11.8	14.7	27.2	9.3	5.5
Return on Equity After Income Taxes 48	4.2	3.6	90.6	10.2	9.8	23.3	8.1	3.4
Profit Margin (Before Income Tax) 49	3.1	9.8	11.3	3.3	49.4	4.6	1.0	3.5
Profit Margin (After Income Tax) 50	2.1	9.8	9.4	2.8	32.9	4.0	0.9	2.2

Table I

Corporations with and without Net Income

WATER, SEWAGE AND OTHER SYSTEMS

MONEY AMOUNTS AND SIZE OF ASSETS IN THOUSANDS OF DOLLARS

Item Description for Accounting Period 7/10 Through 6/11	Total	Zero Assets	Under 500	500 to 1,000	1,000 to 5,000	5,000 to 10,000	10,000 to 25,000	25,000 to 50,000	50,000 to 100,000	100,000 to 250,000	250,000 to 500,000	500,000 to 2,500,000	2,500,000 and over
Number of Enterprises **1**	4427	754	2612	359	476	98	64	27	12	9	6	7	3
Revenues ($ in Thousands)													
Net Sales **2**	9184210	201471	729115	253137	507778	369094	402689	197483	81720	213571	448605	1570343	4209205
Interest **3**	32115	432	365	215	1091	45	446	2343	1132	871	1890	7309	15976
Rents **4**	19243	0	1290	0	2284	0	414	1793	141	735	1198	7920	3467
Royalties **5**	103	0	0	0	0	42	0	61	0	0	0	0	0
Other Portfolio Income **6**	75184	15790	2868	0	11	267	15367	3662	71	2973	159	31383	2633
Other Receipts **7**	106590	297	7785	1292	32546	7819	9859	1388	-98	-24427	2515	15865	51748
Total Receipts **8**	9417445	217990	741423	254644	543710	377267	428775	206730	82966	193723	454367	1632820	4283029
Average Total Receipts **9**	2127	289	284	709	1142	3850	6700	7657	6914	21525	75728	233260	1427676
Operating Costs/Operating Income (%)													
Cost of Operations **10**	31.4	14.1	22.8	16.2	20.7	38.0	55.2	29.3	42.0	32.5	41.3	26.6	29.7
Salaries and Wages **11**	8.1	1.4	12.7	15.5	7.9	6.3	9.7	6.7	19.8	8.9	10.7	5.3	7.9
Taxes Paid **12**	7.2	2.6	2.9	5.6	3.4	7.6	4.8	12.6	7.8	7.5	7.2	5.8	9.2
Interest Paid **13**	8.3	0.1	1.1	0.9	5.3	2.3	4.0	5.7	4.4	13.2	8.4	10.4	10.8
Depreciation **14**	18.0	0.9	4.2	8.4	15.6	7.9	15.4	11.7	14.8	35.1	17.3	19.4	22.3
Amortization and Depletion **15**	1.1	•	0.0	0.2	0.2	0.1	0.4	1.5	16.1	6.2	0.9	0.4	1.5
Pensions and Other Deferred Comp. **16**	2.5	0.0	0.6	2.1	0.4	0.3	1.2	0.8	0.3	2.4	1.8	3.3	3.4
Employee Benefits **17**	3.0	0.4	1.9	2.1	1.3	1.6	6.5	4.4	2.7	3.0	2.5	2.8	3.3
Advertising **18**	0.2	0.2	0.0	0.4	0.0	0.0	0.2	0.1	0.1	0.2	0.1	0.0	0.3
Other Expenses **19**	21.9	49.5	35.2	41.7	43.3	23.0	14.7	27.1	47.2	22.1	20.1	11.7	18.4
Officers' Compensation **20**	2.6	33.3	8.9	5.5	3.8	3.4	3.0	5.2	2.8	1.6	3.8	1.0	0.2
Operating Margin **21**	•	•	9.7	1.5	•	9.6	•	•	•	2.9	•	•	•
Operating Margin Before Officers' Comp. **22**	•	30.8	18.6	7.0	1.9	13.0	0.1	•	0.1	4.5	•	•	•

Selected Average Balance Sheet ($ in Thousands)

	23–29												
Net Receivables 23	242	0	7	82	40	486	1755	756	1101	3592	11245	34080	157582
Inventories 24	49	0	1	35	8	36	32	244	52	2816	1152	14207	17297
Net Property, Plant and Equipment 25	6288	0	109	583	1331	3964	10140	18638	35099	123928	308329	724284	5570073
Total Assets 26	8719	0	171	765	2809	5931	17129	33178	70435	183153	382696	1040943	7296657
Notes and Loans Payable 27	3323	0	68	181	1562	1579	5879	8852	13031	95735	122006	375810	2858028
All Other Liabilities 28	2705	0	39	49	213	1019	7531	9315	15985	49910	158374	360996	2267209
Net Worth 29	2691	0	65	535	1033	3333	3719	15011	41419	37507	102316	304137	2171420

Selected Financial Ratios (Times to 1)

Current Ratio 30	0.8	•	1.3	8.3	2.1	1.1	1.3	1.2	1.5	1.5	0.5	0.6	0.6
Quick Ratio 31	0.5	•	1.3	6.3	2.0	0.8	1.1	0.8	0.6	0.9	0.3	0.3	0.3
Net Sales to Working Capital 32	•	•	19.4	4.5	2.6	25.4	7.9	11.4	1.9	4.1	•	•	•
Coverage Ratio 33	0.8	45.6	11.2	3.3	2.0	6.2	•	0.9	•	•	1.5	1.2	0.5
Total Asset Turnover 34	0.2	•	1.6	0.9	0.4	0.6	0.4	0.2	0.1	0.1	0.2	0.2	0.2
Inventory Turnover 35	13.4	•	56.9	3.3	29.2	39.7	109.6	8.8	54.8	2.7	17.3	6.5	24.1
Receivables Turnover 36	9.0	•	42.8	7.2	33.0	6.5	5.3	10.7	4.1	7.8	6.8	8.5	8.3
Total Liabilities to Net Worth 37	2.2	•	1.6	0.4	1.7	0.8	3.6	1.2	0.7	3.9	2.7	2.4	2.4
Current Assets to Working Capital 38	•	•	4.2	1.1	1.9	8.9	4.7	5.4	2.8	2.9	•	•	•
Current Liabilities to Working Capital 39	•	•	3.2	0.1	0.9	7.9	3.7	4.4	1.8	1.9	•	•	•
Working Capital to Net Sales 40	•	•	0.1	0.2	0.4	0.0	0.1	0.1	0.5	0.2	•	•	•
Inventory to Working Capital 41	•	•	•	0.0	0.0	•	0.0	0.6	0.0	0.9	•	•	•
Total Receipts to Cash Flow 42	7.8	1.9	2.4	2.7	2.3	4.5	568.8	4.9	4.9	1.9	4.9	12.2	24.2
Cost of Goods to Cash Flow 43	2.5	0.3	0.6	0.4	0.5	1.7	314.1	1.4	•	•	1.3	5.0	7.2
Cash Flow to Total Debt 44	0.0	•	1.1	1.1	0.3	0.3	0.0	0.1	•	•	0.1	0.0	0.0

Selected Financial Factors (in Percentages)

Debt Ratio 45	69.1	•	62.1	30.1	63.2	43.8	78.3	54.8	41.2	79.5	73.3	70.8	70.2
Return on Total Assets 46	1.5	•	20.5	2.8	4.0	8.9	•	1.1	•	•	2.4	2.8	1.1
Return on Equity Before Income Taxes 47	•	•	49.2	2.8	5.4	13.3	•	•	•	•	3.0	1.9	•
Return on Equity After Income Taxes 48	•	•	49.2	2.7	5.1	13.3	•	•	•	•	1.3	0.4	•
Profit Margin (Before Income Tax) 49	•	5.8	11.4	2.1	5.2	11.8	•	•	•	•	4.1	2.5	•
Profit Margin (After Income Tax) 50	•	5.3	11.4	2.1	4.9	11.7	•	•	•	•	1.7	0.5	•

Table II

Corporations with Net Income

WATER, SEWAGE AND OTHER SYSTEMS

MONEY AMOUNTS AND SIZE OF ASSETS IN THOUSANDS OF DOLLARS

Item Description for Accounting Period 7/10 Through 6/11	Total	Zero Assets	Under 500	500 to 1,000	1,000 to 5,000	5,000 to 10,000	10,000 to 25,000	25,000 to 50,000	50,000 to 100,000	100,000 to 250,000	250,000 to 500,000	500,000 to 2,500,000	2,500,000 and over
Number of Enterprises **1**	3412	•	1997	226	298	69	31	19	4	5	•	•	0
Revenues ($ in Thousands)													
Net Sales **2**	4585102	•	615496	74157	390612	338253	81620	164676	60154	185745	•	•	0
Interest **3**	15846	•	0	45	956	32	294	96	20	795	•	•	0
Rents **4**	11381	•	0	0	0	0	314	1689	0	735	•	•	0
Royalties **5**	0	•	0	0	0	0	0	0	0	0	•	•	0
Other Portfolio Income **6**	48854	•	0	0	8	267	382	973	0	670	•	•	0
Other Receipts **7**	60023	•	7606	1291	10386	7395	3424	1764	367	8216	•	•	0
Total Receipts **8**	4721206	•	623102	75493	401962	345947	86034	169198	60541	196161	•	•	0
Average Total Receipts **9**	1384	•	312	334	1349	5014	2775	8905	15135	39232	•	•	•
Operating Costs/Operating Income (%)													
Cost of Operations **10**	35.1	•	27.0	12.1	23.5	40.8	14.8	26.4	51.2	28.2	•	•	•
Salaries and Wages **11**	7.0	•	12.2	14.8	8.6	4.4	8.4	3.3	15.0	7.3	•	•	•
Taxes Paid **12**	6.5	•	2.2	6.7	3.2	7.5	8.2	14.4	5.7	8.2	•	•	•
Interest Paid **13**	6.0	•	1.0	2.7	5.0	2.1	7.9	4.3	1.2	6.8	•	•	•
Depreciation **14**	12.5	•	3.3	11.0	8.3	7.9	17.8	12.6	3.6	21.1	•	•	•
Amortization and Depletion **15**	0.8	•	0.0	•	0.2	0.1	1.5	0.1	3.9	0.1	•	•	•
Pensions and Other Deferred Comp. **16**	1.8	•	•	0.1	0.4	0.3	1.2	0.9	0.5	2.7	•	•	•
Employee Benefits **17**	2.3	•	0.2	0.2	1.3	1.7	2.5	4.3	2.7	3.0	•	•	•
Advertising **18**	0.1	•	0.0	0.0	0.0	0.0	0.0	0.0	0.1	•	•	•	•
Other Expenses **19**	18.2	•	32.7	39.2	33.6	19.0	29.5	22.6	12.7	16.1	•	•	•
Officers' Compensation **20**	3.8	•	5.4	7.2	4.3	3.7	3.4	4.1	1.9	3.9	•	•	•
Operating Margin **21**	5.9	•	16.0	6.0	11.6	12.5	4.8	6.9	1.6	2.5	•	•	•
Operating Margin Before Officers' Comp. **22**	9.8	•	21.5	13.2	15.9	16.2	8.2	11.0	3.5	6.5	•	•	•

Selected Average Balance Sheet ($ in Thousands)

Net Receivables 23	164	2	16	25	674	770	741	2670	3525
Inventories 24	21	0	1	8	46	10	121	60	778
Net Property, Plant and Equipment 25	3055	104	719	1199	3785	11926	24018	31199	158516
Total Assets 26	4378	164	796	2901	5645	17642	33154	66896	197605
Notes and Loans Payable 27	1598	66	232	2071	1793	3882	5919	13716	59527
All Other Liabilities 28	1402	38	11	281	922	7486	10863	25272	63037
Net Worth 29	1378	61	553	550	2930	6274	16372	27908	75042

Selected Financial Ratios (Times to 1)

Current Ratio 30	0.8	1.5	5.8	2.2	1.1	2.0	1.1	0.6	1.2
Quick Ratio 31	0.6	1.5	4.9	2.0	0.7	1.9	0.7	0.5	0.9
Net Sales to Working Capital 32	•	15.6	5.1	2.4	24.2	2.5	34.9	•	15.6
Coverage Ratio 33	2.5	17.9	3.9	3.9	7.9	2.3	3.2	2.8	2.2
Total Asset Turnover 34	0.3	1.9	0.4	0.5	0.9	0.1	0.3	0.2	0.2
Inventory Turnover 35	22.4	•	28.7	37.8	43.0	37.8	18.9	128.2	13.5
Receivables Turnover 36	10.0	141.9	6.1	58.6	6.5	5.3	11.3	•	•
Total Liabilities to Net Worth 37	2.2	1.7	0.4	4.3	0.9	1.8	1.0	1.4	1.6
Current Assets to Working Capital 38	•	2.9	1.2	1.9	8.2	2.0	11.0	•	6.7
Current Liabilities to Working Capital 39	•	1.9	0.2	0.9	7.2	1.0	10.0	•	5.7
Working Capital to Net Sales 40	•	0.1	0.2	0.4	0.0	0.4	0.0	•	0.1
Inventory to Working Capital 41	•	•	0.0	0.0	•	0.0	0.5	•	0.3
Total Receipts to Cash Flow 42	4.5	2.2	2.3	2.3	4.7	3.0	3.4	9.6	4.8
Cost of Goods to Cash Flow 43	1.6	0.6	0.3	0.5	1.9	0.4	0.9	4.9	1.3
Cash Flow to Total Debt 44	0.1	1.4	0.6	0.2	0.4	0.1	0.2	0.0	0.1

Selected Financial Factors (in Percentages)

Debt Ratio 45	68.5	62.9	30.5	81.0	48.1	64.4	50.6	58.3	62.0
Return on Total Assets 46	4.6	34.4	4.3	8.8	14.6	2.7	3.6	0.8	2.8
Return on Equity Before Income Taxes 47	8.6	87.4	4.6	34.6	24.6	4.3	5.0	1.2	4.0
Return on Equity After Income Taxes 48	7.5	87.4	4.5	33.6	24.6	3.7	3.9	1.0	2.7
Profit Margin (Before Income Tax) 49	8.9	17.3	7.8	14.5	14.7	10.2	9.5	2.2	8.1
Profit Margin (After Income Tax) 50	7.7	17.3	7.5	14.1	14.7	8.9	7.3	1.9	5.5

Table I

Corporations with and without Net Income

COMBINATION GAS AND ELECTRIC

MONEY AMOUNTS AND SIZE OF ASSETS IN THOUSANDS OF DOLLARS

Item Description for Accounting Period 7/10 Through 6/11		Total	Zero Assets	Under 500	500 to 1,000	1,000 to 5,000	5,000 to 10,000	10,000 to 25,000	25,000 to 50,000	50,000 to 100,000	100,000 to 250,000	250,000 to 500,000	500,000 to 2,500,000	2,500,000 and over
Number of Enterprises	1	42	•	0	0	0	0	•	0	0	•	0	4	27
Revenues ($ in Thousands)														
Net Sales	2	188736305	•	0	0	0	0	•	0	0	•	0	1961393	183014229
Interest	3	1047817	•	0	0	0	0	•	0	0	•	0	7758	972772
Rents	4	852650	•	0	0	0	0	•	0	0	•	0	7317	841880
Royalties	5	6380	•	0	0	0	0	•	0	0	•	0	0	6380
Other Portfolio Income	6	2315408	•	0	0	0	0	•	0	0	•	0	5577	2261168
Other Receipts	7	4391364	•	0	0	0	0	•	0	0	•	0	21864	4303376
Total Receipts	8	197734924	•	0	0	0	0	•	0	0	•	0	2003909	191399805
Average Total Receipts	9	4698808	•	•	•	•	•	•	•	•	•	•	500977	7088882
Operating Costs/Operating Income (%)														
Cost of Operations	10	51.9	•	•	•	•	•	•	•	•	•	•	61.7	51.5
Salaries and Wages	11	6.5	•	•	•	•	•	•	•	•	•	•	2.4	6.6
Taxes Paid	12	3.9	•	•	•	•	•	•	•	•	•	•	2.5	3.9
Interest Paid	13	5.0	•	•	•	•	•	•	•	•	•	•	4.7	4.9
Depreciation	14	12.9	•	•	•	•	•	•	•	•	•	•	7.6	13.0
Amortization and Depletion	15	0.8	•	•	•	•	•	•	•	•	•	•	0.2	0.8
Pensions and Other Deferred Comp.	16	2.7	•	•	•	•	•	•	•	•	•	•	2.3	2.7
Employee Benefits	17	1.7	•	•	•	•	•	•	•	•	•	•	0.7	1.7
Advertising	18	0.1	•	•	•	•	•	•	•	•	•	•	0.3	0.1
Other Expenses	19	18.1	•	•	•	•	•	•	•	•	•	•	18.0	18.4
Officers' Compensation	20	0.2	•	•	•	•	•	•	•	•	•	•	0.6	0.2
Operating Margin	21	•	•	•	•	•	•	•	•	•	•	•	•	•
Operating Margin Before Officers' Comp.	22	•	•	•	•	•	•	•	•	•	•	•	•	•

Selected Average Balance Sheet ($ in Thousands)

Net Receivables 23	607672	47274	924703
Inventories 24	259546	22991	399771
Net Property, Plant and Equipment 25	6220987	599900	9581173
Total Assets 26	10579582	984764	16263715
Notes and Loans Payable 27	3667477	405157	5627908
All Other Liabilities 28	4130661	263219	6370872
Net Worth 29	2781444	316388	4264935

Selected Financial Ratios (Times to 1)

Current Ratio 30	0.9	1.1	0.9
Quick Ratio 31	0.5	0.5	0.5
Net Sales to Working Capital 32	•	53.6	•
Coverage Ratio 33	1.2	1.2	1.1
Total Asset Turnover 34	0.4	0.5	0.4
Inventory Turnover 35	9.0	13.2	8.7
Receivables Turnover 36	7.5	6.5	7.4
Total Liabilities to Net Worth 37	2.8	2.1	2.8
Current Assets to Working Capital 38	•	14.5	•
Current Liabilities to Working Capital 39	•	13.5	•
Working Capital to Net Sales 40	•	0.0	•
Inventory to Working Capital 41	•	1.6	•
Total Receipts to Cash Flow 42	7.2	6.9	7.1
Cost of Goods to Cash Flow 43	3.7	4.3	3.7
Cash Flow to Total Debt 44	0.1	0.1	0.1

Selected Financial Factors (in Percentages)

Debt Ratio 45	73.7	67.9	73.8
Return on Total Assets 46	2.4	2.9	2.3
Return on Equity Before Income Taxes 47	1.2	1.7	1.1
Return on Equity After Income Taxes 48	0.1	0.7	0.1
Profit Margin (Before Income Tax) 49	0.7	1.1	0.7
Profit Margin (After Income Tax) 50	0.1	0.4	•

Table II

Corporations with Net Income

COMBINATION GAS AND ELECTRIC

MONEY AMOUNTS AND SIZE OF ASSETS IN THOUSANDS OF DOLLARS

Item Description for Accounting Period 7/10 Through 6/11	Total	Zero Assets	Under 500	500 to 1,000	1,000 to 5,000	5,000 to 10,000	10,000 to 25,000	25,000 to 50,000	50,000 to 100,000	100,000 to 250,000	250,000 to 500,000	500,000 to 2,500,000	2,500,000 and over
Number of Enterprises **1**	19	•	0	0	0	0	0	0	•	0	•	0	14
Revenues ($ in Thousands)													
Net Sales **2**	122437317	•	0	0	0	0	0	0	•	0	•	0	118668445
Interest **3**	888108	•	0	0	0	0	0	0	•	0	•	0	817920
Rents **4**	645338	•	0	0	0	0	0	0	•	0	•	0	641884
Royalties **5**	1089	•	0	0	0	0	0	0	•	0	•	0	1089
Other Portfolio Income **6**	1414019	•	0	0	0	0	0	0	•	0	•	0	1361612
Other Receipts **7**	3426249	•	0	0	0	0	0	0	•	0	•	0	3365389
Total Receipts **8**	128812120	•	0	0	0	0	0	0	•	0	•	0	124856339
Average Total Receipts **9**	6779585	•	•	•	•	•	•	•	•	•	•	•	8918310
Operating Costs/Operating Income (%)													
Cost of Operations **10**	55.8	•	•	•	•	•	•	•	•	•	•	•	55.6
Salaries and Wages **11**	5.4	•	•	•	•	•	•	•	•	•	•	•	5.5
Taxes Paid **12**	3.7	•	•	•	•	•	•	•	•	•	•	•	3.7
Interest Paid **13**	4.3	•	•	•	•	•	•	•	•	•	•	•	4.2
Depreciation **14**	10.4	•	•	•	•	•	•	•	•	•	•	•	10.3
Amortization and Depletion **15**	0.7	•	•	•	•	•	•	•	•	•	•	•	0.7
Pensions and Other Deferred Comp. **16**	3.3	•	•	•	•	•	•	•	•	•	•	•	3.4
Employee Benefits **17**	1.4	•	•	•	•	•	•	•	•	•	•	•	1.4
Advertising **18**	0.2	•	•	•	•	•	•	•	•	•	•	•	0.2
Other Expenses **19**	16.4	•	•	•	•	•	•	•	•	•	•	•	16.6
Officers' Compensation **20**	0.2	•	•	•	•	•	•	•	•	•	•	•	0.2
Operating Margin **21**	•	•	•	•	•	•	•	•	•	•	•	•	•
Operating Margin Before Officers' Comp. **22**	•	•	•	•	•	•	•	•	•	•	•	•	•

Selected Average Balance Sheet ($ in Thousands)

Net Receivables 23	793209	1066120
Inventories 24	280086	377563
Net Property, Plant and Equipment 25	7585689	10186474
Total Assets 26	13732213	18440673
Notes and Loans Payable 27	4550594	6103930
All Other Liabilities 28	5543936	7479128
Net Worth 29	3637683	4857616

Selected Financial Ratios (Times to 1)

Current Ratio 30	0.9	0.9
Quick Ratio 31	0.5	0.5
Net Sales to Working Capital 32	•	•
Coverage Ratio 33	1.8	1.8
Total Asset Turnover 34	0.5	0.5
Inventory Turnover 35	12.8	12.5
Receivables Turnover 36	9.5	9.4
Total Liabilities to Net Worth 37	2.8	2.8
Current Assets to Working Capital 38	•	•
Current Liabilities to Working Capital 39	•	•
Working Capital to Net Sales 40	•	•
Inventory to Working Capital 41	•	•
Total Receipts to Cash Flow 42	6.7	6.7
Cost of Goods to Cash Flow 43	3.7	3.7
Cash Flow to Total Debt 44	0.1	0.1

Selected Financial Factors (in Percentages)

Debt Ratio 45	73.5	73.7
Return on Total Assets 46	3.6	3.5
Return on Equity Before Income Taxes 47	6.1	5.8
Return on Equity After Income Taxes 48	4.2	4.0
Profit Margin (Before Income Tax) 49	3.4	3.3
Profit Margin (After Income Tax) 50	2.4	2.3

Table I

Corporations with and without Net Income

CONSTRUCTION OF BUILDINGS

MONEY AMOUNTS AND SIZE OF ASSETS IN THOUSANDS OF DOLLARS

Item Description for Accounting Period 7/10 Through 6/11	Total	Zero Assets	Under 500	500 to 1,000	1,000 to 5,000	5,000 to 10,000	10,000 to 25,000	25,000 to 50,000	50,000 to 100,000	100,000 to 250,000	250,000 to 500,000	500,000 to 2,500,000	2,500,000 and over
Number of Enterprises 1	210334	42495	128005	16647	17898	2920	1614	374	198	110	25	•	•
Revenues ($ in Thousands)													
Net Sales 2	401344580	7593191	54756394	23004078	72079379	42385011	43104295	21864174	25514609	26594642	10328555		
Interest 3	785595	19484	9189	9807	47653	17700	17262	9545	5962	24599	20553		
Rents 4	435119	3185	23986	30434	60027	38575	45110	26257	24050	40668	56737		
Royalties 5	25122	0	0	0	0	2	1056	542	0	10363	417		
Other Portfolio Income 6	941922	37578	219784	67363	140264	44916	50355	23417	50324	54921	47178		
Other Receipts 7	4615285	346394	215563	353309	575138	386137	209313	55330	194324	372925	143805		
Total Receipts 8	408147623	7999832	55224916	23464991	72902461	42872341	43427391	21979265	25789269	27098118	10597245		
Average Total Receipts 9	1940	188	431	1410	4073	14682	26907	58768	130249	246347	423890		
Operating Costs/Operating Income (%)													
Cost of Operations 10	85.8	68.9	70.5	79.6	86.1	90.7	89.0	89.7	90.7	89.7	90.0		
Salaries and Wages 11	3.9	3.2	6.5	5.3	3.8	2.1	2.8	2.5	2.6	3.0	3.6		
Taxes Paid 12	1.1	1.4	2.2	1.6	1.3	0.7	0.8	0.7	0.7	0.7	0.9		
Interest Paid 13	0.8	0.9	0.5	0.8	0.5	0.4	0.5	0.4	0.4	0.5	1.5		
Depreciation 14	0.7	1.1	1.1	0.9	0.6	0.5	0.5	0.5	0.4	0.7	0.7		
Amortization and Depletion 15	0.1	0.0	0.0	0.0	0.0	0.0	0.0	0.0	0.0	0.3	0.2		
Pensions and Other Deferred Comp. 16	0.2	0.0	0.1	0.3	0.2	0.1	0.2	0.2	0.2	0.2	0.1		
Employee Benefits 17	0.7	0.5	0.9	1.0	0.7	0.4	0.7	0.4	0.6	0.5	0.6		
Advertising 18	0.3	0.3	0.5	0.3	0.3	0.2	0.2	0.1	0.2	0.2	0.2		
Other Expenses 19	6.3	25.4	13.4	8.4	5.2	3.1	3.4	2.9	2.2	3.9	3.1		
Officers' Compensation 20	2.1	3.2	5.0	3.8	2.4	1.4	1.6	1.8	1.0	0.8	1.0		
Operating Margin 21	•	•	•	•	•	0.6	0.3	0.8	1.0	•	•		
Operating Margin Before Officers' Comp. 22	0.2	•	4.4	1.9	1.3	2.0	2.0	2.6	2.0	0.4	•		

Selected Average Balance Sheet ($ in Thousands)

	•	•	•	•	•	•	•	•	•	•	•
Net Receivables **23**	263	0	10	118	471	1854	4809	9754	22713	42702	67515
Inventories **24**	226	0	13	145	465	1397	2848	5848	7813	19043	49141
Net Property, Plant and Equipment **25**	141	0	24	182	309	915	1947	3010	7206	21607	37419
Total Assets **26**	1246	0	101	732	2137	6978	15222	34296	69265	153226	331726
Notes and Loans Payable **27**	446	0	72	475	788	2353	4796	8213	15825	42034	127226
All Other Liabilities **28**	466	0	28	153	817	2577	6430	15131	33764	64768	114280
Net Worth **29**	335	0	1	103	533	2048	3996	10952	19676	46424	90221

Selected Financial Ratios (Times to 1)

	•	•	•	•	•	•	•	•	•	•	•
Current Ratio **30**	1.6	•	1.5	1.8	1.6	1.5	1.6	1.5	1.5	1.4	1.5
Quick Ratio **31**	0.9	•	0.8	0.8	0.9	1.0	1.0	1.0	1.0	1.0	0.8
Net Sales to Working Capital **32**	6.1	•	20.9	6.7	7.7	6.7	6.2	8.2	8.2	7.7	6.6
Coverage Ratio **33**	0.7	1.5	1.5	0.9	5.7	3.3	4.5	6.7	6.7	3.8	1.4
Total Asset Turnover **34**	1.5	•	4.2	1.9	2.1	1.8	1.7	1.9	1.9	1.6	1.2
Inventory Turnover **35**	7.2	•	23.6	7.6	9.4	8.3	9.0	11.4	15.0	11.4	7.6
Receivables Turnover **36**	6.8	•	40.8	11.2	7.6	5.4	6.0	8.6	•	5.7	4.3
Total Liabilities to Net Worth **37**	2.7	•	132.6	6.1	2.4	2.8	2.1	2.5	2.5	2.3	2.7
Current Assets to Working Capital **38**	2.7	•	3.0	2.3	2.7	2.9	2.8	3.4	3.4	3.4	3.0
Current Liabilities to Working Capital **39**	1.7	•	2.0	1.3	1.7	1.9	1.8	2.4	2.4	2.4	2.0
Working Capital to Net Sales **40**	0.2	•	0.0	0.2	0.1	0.1	0.2	0.1	0.1	0.1	0.2
Inventory to Working Capital **41**	0.7	•	0.7	0.7	0.6	0.6	0.5	0.5	0.5	0.5	0.7
Total Receipts to Cash Flow **42**	21.1	4.2	9.0	15.0	25.0	29.4	31.2	29.1	29.1	22.2	39.2
Cost of Goods to Cash Flow **43**	18.1	2.9	6.3	12.0	22.7	26.1	28.0	26.4	26.4	19.9	35.3
Cash Flow to Total Debt **44**	0.1	•	0.5	0.1	0.1	0.1	0.1	0.1	0.1	0.1	0.0

Selected Financial Factors (in Percentages)

	•	•	•	•	•	•	•	•	•	•	•
Debt Ratio **45**	73.1	•	99.3	85.9	75.1	70.6	73.8	68.1	71.6	69.7	72.8
Return on Total Assets **46**	0.9	•	3.3	1.4	1.1	4.4	2.7	2.8	4.5	3.2	2.7
Return on Equity Before Income Taxes **47**	•	•	145.2	•	0.2	12.2	7.1	6.7	13.4	7.8	3.0
Return on Equity After Income Taxes **48**	•	•	136.5	•	•	11.5	6.6	6.2	12.9	6.7	1.5
Profit Margin (Before Income Tax) **49**	0.4	0.3	•	0.0	1.7	1.1	1.3	2.0	2.0	1.5	0.7
Profit Margin (After Income Tax) **50**	0.3	0.2	•	•	1.6	1.0	1.2	2.0	2.0	1.3	0.3

25

CONSTRUCTION OF BUILDINGS

Table II

Corporations with Net Income

MONEY AMOUNTS AND SIZE OF ASSETS IN THOUSANDS OF DOLLARS

Item Description for Accounting Period 7/10 Through 6/11	Total	Zero Assets	Under 500	500 to 1,000	1,000 to 5,000	5,000 to 10,000	10,000 to 25,000	25,000 to 50,000	50,000 to 100,000	100,000 to 250,000	250,000 to 500,000	500,000 to 2,500,000	2,500,000 and over
Number of Enterprises **1**	107299	21892	65037	8153	8993	1820	914	252	134	64	•	•	•
Revenues ($ in Thousands)													
Net Sales **2**	272884063	4768600	35169861	13617707	47984009	25060681	33341697	18070069	21401584	22570710	•	•	•
Interest **3**	210121	956	5448	4479	30443	11947	12753	3727	2534	20933	•	•	•
Rents **4**	178312	168	3188	8467	16896	22499	19260	14956	10057	4766	•	•	•
Royalties **5**	18694	0	0	0	0	2	1056	514	0	9964			•
Other Portfolio Income **6**	607236	35250	170620	29531	64445	36864	34897	16707	44737	47461	•	•	•
Other Receipts **7**	2782382	294450	117883	97403	281597	242534	161680	116368	100387	340025	•	•	•
Total Receipts **8**	276680808	5099424	35467000	13757587	48377390	25374527	33571343	18222341	21559299	22993859	•	•	•
Average Total Receipts **9**	2579	233	545	1687	5379	13942	36730	72311	160890	359279	•	•	•
Operating Costs/Operating Income (%)													
Cost of Operations **10**	83.5	65.5	65.0	76.8	84.1	86.3	87.7	89.8	90.1	89.6	•	•	•
Salaries and Wages **11**	3.5	2.7	6.7	3.3	3.5	2.4	2.5	2.0	2.2	2.5	•	•	•
Taxes Paid **12**	1.0	1.2	2.2	1.2	1.1	0.7	0.7	0.6	0.7	0.5	•	•	•
Interest Paid **13**	0.3	0.6	0.4	0.6	0.3	0.3	0.2	0.1	0.2	0.2	•	•	•
Depreciation **14**	0.6	1.2	0.8	0.9	0.5	0.6	0.4	0.4	0.3	0.6	•	•	•
Amortization and Depletion **15**	0.0	0.0	0.0	0.0	0.0	0.0	0.0	0.0	0.0	0.1	•	•	•
Pensions and Other Deferred Comp. **16**	0.2	0.0	0.1	0.2	0.2	0.1	0.2	0.2	0.2	0.2	•	•	•
Employee Benefits **17**	0.6	0.5	0.6	0.7	0.5	0.4	0.7	0.4	0.6	0.4	•	•	•
Advertising **18**	0.2	0.2	0.5	0.3	0.3	0.2	0.2	0.1	0.1	0.1	•	•	•
Other Expenses **19**	4.8	19.6	11.9	7.7	4.3	3.6	2.9	2.1	1.6	2.9	•	•	•
Officers' Compensation **20**	2.1	2.7	5.0	3.5	2.4	1.7	1.6	1.7	1.0	0.8	•	•	•
Operating Margin **21**	3.2	5.7	6.7	4.7	2.8	3.6	2.8	2.6	3.0	2.2	•	•	•
Operating Margin Before Officers' Comp. **22**	5.2	8.5	11.7	8.3	5.2	5.3	4.4	4.3	4.1	2.9	•	•	•

Selected Average Balance Sheet ($ in Thousands)

Net Receivables 23	342	0	11	121	547	2028	6304	11671	27716	61083
Inventories 24	109	0	8	89	456	1079	1697	3939	3827	4004
Net Property, Plant and Equipment 25	123	0	25	176	228	841	1156	1578	5370	14982
Total Assets 26	1145	0	94	705	2163	6968	15499	33814	69870	155407
Notes and Loans Payable 27	219	0	48	372	593	1798	2426	3169	8755	18444
All Other Liabilities 28	526	0	25	158	844	2940	8079	17263	39880	89627
Net Worth 29	400	0	21	175	726	2230	4994	13382	21235	47336

Selected Financial Ratios (Times to 1)

Current Ratio 30	1.5	•	1.6	1.8	1.8	1.5	1.5	1.6	1.4	1.3
Quick Ratio 31	1.0	•	1.2	1.0	0.9	0.9	1.1	1.2	1.2	1.1
Net Sales to Working Capital 32	9.6	•	26.0	8.5	7.2	7.3	9.0	6.7	9.5	13.4
Coverage Ratio 33	14.6	20.9	18.1	10.3	11.7	17.3	18.1	25.2	24.2	17.2
Total Asset Turnover 34	2.2	•	5.8	2.4	2.5	2.0	2.4	2.1	2.3	2.3
Inventory Turnover 35	19.5	•	44.0	14.4	9.8	11.0	18.9	16.4	37.6	78.9
Receivables Turnover 36	7.4	•	47.9	13.5	9.7	6.6	5.6	6.0	5.5	5.8
Total Liabilities to Net Worth 37	1.9	•	3.5	3.0	2.0	2.1	2.1	1.5	2.3	2.3
Current Assets to Working Capital 38	3.1	•	2.6	2.3	2.3	2.9	3.2	2.7	3.4	4.5
Current Liabilities to Working Capital 39	2.1	•	1.6	1.3	1.3	1.9	2.2	1.7	2.4	3.5
Working Capital to Net Sales 40	0.1	•	0.0	0.1	0.1	0.1	0.1	0.2	0.1	0.1
Inventory to Working Capital 41	0.4	•	0.5	0.4	0.6	0.6	0.3	0.3	0.2	0.1
Total Receipts to Cash Flow 42	12.3	3.2	5.7	8.4	15.1	13.4	18.3	21.1	22.0	16.0
Cost of Goods to Cash Flow 43	10.2	2.1	3.7	6.4	12.7	11.6	16.1	19.0	19.8	14.4
Cash Flow to Total Debt 44	0.3	•	1.3	0.4	0.2	0.2	0.2	0.2	0.1	0.2

Selected Financial Factors (in Percentages)

Debt Ratio 45	65.0	•	77.7	75.1	66.4	68.0	67.8	60.4	69.6	69.5
Return on Total Assets 46	10.8	•	46.3	15.1	9.6	10.2	8.6	7.6	8.9	9.7
Return on Equity Before Income Taxes 47	28.9	•	196.3	54.9	26.3	29.9	25.2	18.5	28.1	29.8
Return on Equity After Income Taxes 48	27.6	•	195.7	54.4	25.3	29.0	24.5	17.8	27.4	28.1
Profit Margin (Before Income Tax) 49	4.5	12.7	7.6	5.8	3.6	4.8	3.4	3.4	3.7	4.0
Profit Margin (After Income Tax) 50	4.3	12.5	7.6	5.7	3.5	4.7	3.4	3.3	3.6	3.8

Table I
Corporations with and without Net Income

HEAVY AND CIVIL ENGINEERING CONSTRUCTION

MONEY AMOUNTS AND SIZE OF ASSETS IN THOUSANDS OF DOLLARS

Item Description for Accounting Period 7/10 Through 6/11	Total	Zero Assets	Under 500	500 to 1,000	1,000 to 5,000	5,000 to 10,000	10,000 to 25,000	25,000 to 50,000	50,000 to 100,000	100,000 to 250,000	250,000 to 500,000	500,000 to 2,500,000	2,500,000 and over
Number of Enterprises **1**	23270	2285	11938	2012	4210	1572	721	282	140	64	23	18	4
Revenues ($ in Thousands)													
Net Sales **2**	180887277	728942	7322509	3621956	21509601	22502315	21476442	18132702	13993333	13407356	10832163	17712689	30247270
Interest **3**	167655	861	4971	5257	24464	9269	13940	4952	12221	9617	12549	29361	40192
Rents **4**	107377	321	2670	6105	11098	13501	17706	14366	16331	7206	1515	10231	6327
Royalties **5**	87128	0	0	0	0	1932	685	290	19335	84	1132	22204	41466
Other Portfolio Income **6**	1211549	132286	94146	45597	134820	270159	79766	124461	54438	40697	40635	79588	114958
Other Receipts **7**	3232135	255426	32926	10003	125877	69885	133761	142129	201092	554052	260406	206735	1239842
Total Receipts **8**	185693121	1117836	7457222	3688918	21805860	22887061	21722300	18818900	14296750	14019012	11148400	17460808	31690055
Average Total Receipts **9**	7980	489	625	1833	5180	14546	30128	65315	102120	219047	484713	970045	7922514
Operating Costs/Operating Income (%)													
Cost of Operations **10**	77.7	61.5	48.7	54.8	71.2	77.7	81.2	81.5	80.0	78.0	85.0	78.1	83.6
Salaries and Wages **11**	3.9	7.0	10.3	7.5	5.8	3.9	2.9	3.2	3.2	3.6	2.4	3.8	3.0
Taxes Paid **12**	1.7	2.5	3.2	2.7	2.5	1.9	1.5	1.5	1.5	1.4	0.9	2.3	1.0
Interest Paid **13**	0.6	2.3	0.8	1.0	0.6	0.5	0.4	0.6	0.5	0.7	0.5	0.9	0.5
Depreciation **14**	3.2	7.6	2.8	4.4	4.1	3.3	3.0	3.3	3.6	3.4	3.6	4.1	1.8
Amortization and Depletion **15**	0.2	0.7	0.1	0.0	0.0	0.0	0.0	0.1	0.2	0.3	0.3	0.8	0.5
Pensions and Other Deferred Comp. **16**	0.3	1.6	0.1	0.1	0.2	0.7	0.3	0.2	0.5	0.5	0.3	0.2	0.2
Employee Benefits **17**	1.2	1.2	1.1	0.8	1.1	1.6	1.4	1.1	1.7	1.4	0.9	1.3	0.6
Advertising **18**	0.1	0.2	0.6	0.2	0.2	0.1	0.1	0.1	0.1	0.1	0.1	0.4	0.0
Other Expenses **19**	7.6	40.6	25.6	21.1	11.3	6.0	5.1	5.8	6.5	6.7	4.0	7.4	4.4
Officers' Compensation **20**	2.1	3.3	8.2	3.5	3.0	2.7	1.8	1.5	1.3	1.2	1.3	0.7	1.5
Operating Margin **21**	1.3	•	•	3.9	•	1.6	2.2	1.1	0.9	2.8	0.9	0.0	3.0
Operating Margin Before Officers' Comp. **22**	3.4	•	6.8	7.4	2.9	4.3	4.0	2.7	2.3	4.0	2.1	0.7	4.5

Selected Average Balance Sheet ($ in Thousands)

Net Receivables 23	1115	0	26	86	617	2238	4816	10489	15775	32534	68257	139142	1137840
Inventories 24	142	0	2	33	50	236	376	1076	2074	7183	12269	42359	65990
Net Property, Plant and Equipment 25	1293	0	60	337	780	1693	3642	8524	18804	34332	103520	297118	1293262
Total Assets 26	5015	0	167	663	2325	7033	15225	34570	70027	157771	364157	898730	6838312
Notes and Loans Payable 27	895	0	111	376	648	1307	2552	6235	12310	24192	62773	227001	389928
All Other Liabilities 28	1725	0	57	137	521	2765	4699	11310	21098	49422	118205	364005	2671091
Net Worth 29	2395	0	-2	150	1156	2961	7974	17025	36618	84157	183179	307724	3777293

Selected Financial Ratios (Times to 1)

Current Ratio 30	1.5	•	1.1	1.1	1.9	1.6	1.9	1.8	1.9	1.8	1.8	1.5	0.9
Quick Ratio 31	1.1	•	0.8	0.9	1.5	1.2	1.5	1.4	1.4	1.3	1.3	0.8	0.7
Net Sales to Working Capital 32	9.0	•	105.2	81.8	8.4	8.1	6.5	6.8	5.2	5.3	5.6	7.0	•
Coverage Ratio 33	7.8	11.7	1.6	6.7	3.2	6.9	9.7	5.4	7.3	11.9	8.4	3.2	17.4
Total Asset Turnover 34	1.6	•	3.7	2.7	2.2	2.0	2.0	1.9	1.4	1.3	1.3	1.1	1.1
Inventory Turnover 35	42.5	•	152.0	29.9	72.2	47.0	64.3	48.7	38.5	22.7	32.6	17.5	95.7
Receivables Turnover 36	6.9	•	18.3	15.1	8.3	7.3	5.8	6.1	6.5	6.5	6.8	6.7	6.2
Total Liabilities to Net Worth 37	1.1	•	•	3.4	1.0	1.4	0.9	1.0	0.9	0.9	1.0	1.9	0.8
Current Assets to Working Capital 38	2.9	•	14.6	11.7	2.2	2.7	2.2	2.3	2.1	2.3	2.2	2.9	•
Current Liabilities to Working Capital 39	1.9	•	13.6	10.7	1.2	1.7	1.2	1.3	1.1	1.3	1.2	1.9	•
Working Capital to Net Sales 40	0.1	•	0.0	0.0	0.1	0.1	0.2	0.1	0.2	0.2	0.2	0.1	•
Inventory to Working Capital 41	0.2	0.3	1.3	1.3	0.2	0.2	0.1	0.1	0.1	0.2	0.2	0.3	•
Total Receipts to Cash Flow 42	11.6	1.7	4.8	4.8	12.2	17.3	18.5	17.7	15.2	9.0	15.3	15.1	9.0
Cost of Goods to Cash Flow 43	9.0	1.1	2.4	2.6	8.7	13.5	15.0	14.4	12.1	7.0	13.0	11.8	7.6
Cash Flow to Total Debt 44	0.3	•	0.8	0.7	0.4	0.2	0.2	0.2	0.2	0.2	0.2	0.1	0.3

Selected Financial Factors (in Percentages)

Debt Ratio 45	52.3	•	101.1	77.4	50.3	57.9	47.6	50.8	47.7	46.7	49.7	65.8	44.8
Return on Total Assets 46	7.1	•	4.6	18.3	4.3	6.4	7.2	6.1	5.0	10.6	5.5	3.2	9.8
Return on Equity Before Income Taxes 47	13.0	•	•	69.2	6.0	13.0	12.4	10.1	8.3	18.1	9.7	6.5	16.8
Return on Equity After Income Taxes 48	11.4	•	•	65.1	5.0	12.0	11.7	9.2	7.5	16.9	8.4	4.5	14.3
Profit Margin (Before Income Tax) 49	4.0	24.8	0.5	5.7	1.4	2.7	3.3	2.7	3.0	7.3	3.8	2.1	8.4
Profit Margin (After Income Tax) 50	3.5	21.3	0.5	5.4	1.1	2.5	3.1	2.4	2.8	6.8	3.3	1.4	7.1

Table II
Corporations with Net Income

HEAVY AND CIVIL ENGINEERING CONSTRUCTION

MONEY AMOUNTS AND SIZE OF ASSETS IN THOUSANDS OF DOLLARS

Item Description for Accounting Period 7/10 Through 6/11		Total	Zero Assets	Under 500	500 to 1,000	1,000 to 5,000	5,000 to 10,000	10,000 to 25,000	25,000 to 50,000	50,000 to 100,000	100,000 to 250,000	250,000 to 500,000	500,000 to 2,500,000	2,500,000 and over
Number of Enterprises	1	11478	1236	4593	1123	2450	1146	537	199	109	50	19	11	4
Revenues ($ in Thousands)														
Net Sales	2	144956571	557453	3443608	2871018	14574992	17375550	16148075	13969371	11754908	11331049	10355645	12327632	30247270
Interest	3	122325	836	2909	723	15191	5999	8988	3811	7357	7871	11071	17377	40192
Rents	4	57002	321	0	0	2396	10064	10232	1830	12822	4033	1515	7462	6327
Royalties	5	86276	0	0	0	0	1932	15	287	19335	0	1132	22108	41466
Other Portfolio Income	6	920042	117086	61641	40794	62160	230422	50937	70306	49177	34888	39344	48330	114958
Other Receipts	7	3037299	267600	24106	2064	96075	57004	118154	130328	184622	548163	248396	120945	1239842
Total Receipts	8	149179515	943296	3532264	2914599	14750814	17680971	16336401	14175933	12028221	11926004	10657103	12543854	31690055
Average Total Receipts	9	12997	763	769	2595	6021	15428	30422	71236	110351	238520	560900	1140350	7922514
Operating Costs/Operating Income (%)														
Cost of Operations	10	77.0	61.7	41.8	50.5	66.8	75.6	78.7	79.4	79.8	78.8	85.3	76.0	83.6
Salaries and Wages	11	3.5	7.0	7.3	7.9	6.5	2.9	3.0	3.0	2.8	3.5	2.1	3.5	3.0
Taxes Paid	12	1.6	2.6	3.2	2.1	2.4	1.7	1.6	1.5	1.6	1.5	0.8	2.8	1.0
Interest Paid	13	0.5	1.2	0.6	0.9	0.5	0.4	0.3	0.4	0.4	0.5	0.5	0.9	0.5
Depreciation	14	2.9	6.8	1.7	4.1	3.9	3.1	2.7	2.9	3.4	2.8	3.3	3.9	1.8
Amortization and Depletion	15	0.2	0.8	0.1	0.0	0.0	0.0	0.0	0.1	0.1	0.2	0.3	0.9	0.5
Pensions and Other Deferred Comp.	16	0.4	0.6	0.1	0.1	0.2	0.9	0.3	0.2	0.5	0.5	0.2	0.1	0.2
Employee Benefits	17	1.2	1.2	0.9	0.7	1.0	1.7	1.4	1.1	1.7	1.5	0.9	1.5	0.6
Advertising	18	0.1	0.3	0.6	0.1	0.3	0.1	0.1	0.1	0.1	0.0	0.0	0.5	0.0
Other Expenses	19	6.8	37.6	28.8	23.3	10.9	6.5	5.4	5.4	5.3	5.2	3.2	6.8	4.4
Officers' Compensation	20	1.9	3.0	7.2	2.0	3.0	2.7	1.9	1.5	1.4	1.3	1.1	0.7	1.5
Operating Margin	21	3.8	•	7.8	8.1	4.6	4.4	4.6	4.3	3.0	4.3	2.3	2.3	3.0
Operating Margin Before Officers' Comp.	22	5.6	•	15.0	10.2	7.6	7.1	6.5	5.8	4.4	5.6	3.4	2.3	4.5

Selected Average Balance Sheet ($ in Thousands)

Net Receivables **23**	1771	0	22	48	674	2299	5043	10640	16699	33903	74339	143722	1137840
Inventories **24**	236	0	2	44	72	275	343	1112	2006	7312	13536	31331	65970
Net Property, Plant and Equipment **25**	1823	0	42	341	801	1505	3227	7913	18694	31160	105118	234867	1293262
Total Assets **26**	7847	163	637	2371	7022	15130	35425	70152	156972	377024	868871		6833312
Notes and Loans Payable **27**	1070	0	91	488	569	1150	1977	5360	10641	18862	57642	156420	389928
All Other Liabilities **28**	2722	0	111	112	471	2852	4861	11255	19968	49357	125067	330377	2671091
Net Worth **29**	4054	-38	37	1331	3019	8292	18810	39543	88754	194316	382074		3777293

Selected Financial Ratios (Times to 1)

Current Ratio **30**	1.6	•	0.9	1.0	2.1	1.6	2.0	1.9	2.0	1.8	2.0	1.4	0.9
Quick Ratio **31**	1.2	•	0.8	0.7	1.8	1.2	1.6	1.5	1.5	1.4	1.4	0.9	0.7
Net Sales to Working Capital **32**	9.2	•	•	492.7	8.0	7.9	6.0	6.4	5.0	5.2	5.2	9.8	•
Coverage Ratio **33**	14.9	38.9	18.5	11.5	12.7	16.2	20.6	17.0	15.5	21.3	12.2	5.4	17.4
Total Asset Turnover **34**	1.6	•	4.6	4.0	2.5	2.2	2.0	2.0	1.5	1.4	1.4	1.3	1.1
Inventory Turnover **35**	41.2	173.8	•	29.6	55.3	41.7	69.0	50.1	42.9	24.4	34.4	27.2	95.8
Receivables Turnover **36**	7.0	•	23.9	29.6	9.5	7.8	5.9	6.2	6.5	•	7.6	•	•
Total Liabilities to Net Worth **37**	0.9	•	•	16.3	0.8	1.3	0.8	0.9	0.8	0.8	0.9	1.3	0.8
Current Assets to Working Capital **38**	2.8	•	•	44.1	1.9	2.6	2.0	2.1	2.0	2.2	2.0	3.3	•
Current Liabilities to Working Capital **39**	1.8	•	•	43.1	0.9	1.6	1.0	1.1	1.0	1.2	1.0	2.3	•
Working Capital to Net Sales **40**	0.1	•	•	0.0	0.1	0.1	0.2	0.2	0.2	0.2	0.2	0.1	•
Inventory to Working Capital **41**	0.2	•	•	7.6	0.1	0.2	0.1	0.1	0.1	0.2	0.2	0.3	•
Total Receipts to Cash Flow **42**	9.4	1.3	3.0	3.7	8.1	11.1	12.4	11.9	12.5	8.5	13.7	13.5	9.0
Cost of Goods to Cash Flow **43**	7.2	0.8	1.2	1.9	5.4	8.4	9.8	9.5	10.0	6.7	11.7	10.3	7.6
Cash Flow to Total Debt **44**	0.4	•	1.3	1.1	0.7	0.3	0.4	0.4	0.3	0.4	0.2	0.2	0.3

Selected Financial Factors (in Percentages)

Debt Ratio **45**	48.3	•	123.4	94.2	43.9	57.0	45.2	46.9	43.6	43.5	48.5	56.0	44.8
Return on Total Assets **46**	11.5	•	50.4	42.4	15.8	12.7	12.0	12.1	8.7	14.4	8.1	6.4	9.8
Return on Equity Before Income Taxes **47**	20.8	•	•	669.9	25.9	27.6	20.9	21.5	14.5	24.2	14.4	11.9	16.8
Return on Equity After Income Taxes **48**	19.0	•	•	640.5	24.3	26.3	20.1	20.4	13.5	22.7	13.0	9.3	14.3
Profit Margin (Before Income Tax) **49**	6.7	46.2	10.4	9.7	5.8	5.5	5.8	5.8	5.3	9.5	5.1	4.1	8.4
Profit Margin (After Income Tax) **50**	6.1	41.6	10.3	9.2	5.4	5.2	5.5	5.5	5.0	8.9	4.6	3.2	7.1

Table I

Corporations with and without Net Income

LAND SUBDIVISION

MONEY AMOUNTS AND SIZE OF ASSETS IN THOUSANDS OF DOLLARS

Item Description for Accounting Period 7/10 Through 6/11		Total	Zero Assets	Under 500	500 to 1,000	1,000 to 5,000	5,000 to 10,000	10,000 to 25,000	25,000 to 50,000	50,000 to 100,000	100,000 to 250,000	250,000 to 500,000	500,000 to 2,500,000	2,500,000 and over
Number of Enterprises	1	36120	5071	17113	2852	8935	1208	619	183	70	41	16	12	0
Revenues ($ in Thousands)														
Net Sales	2	16813282	909043	1997178	1022783	5598424	743173	1374415	1538600	1141685	952814	967000	568167	0
Interest	3	154448	1034	2583	980	12682	1878	6195	6802	10312	26747	37344	47891	0
Rents	4	299290	0	4	747	11685	35111	53741	15319	29912	48933	5624	98214	0
Royalties	5	16042	0	0	0	1368	0	286	482	0	182	0	13724	0
Other Portfolio Income	6	164457	1377	3448	887	36629	10149	19522	9915	14781	18547	785	48418	0
Other Receipts	7	657086	73345	232677	42275	114289	76510	30291	4558	9625	69543	55700	-51729	0
Total Receipts	8	18104605	984799	2235890	1067672	5775077	866821	1484450	1575676	1206315	1116766	1066453	724685	0
Average Total Receipts	9	501	194	131	374	646	718	2398	8610	17233	27238	66653	60390	•
Operating Costs/Operating Income (%)														
Cost of Operations	10	80.6	152.8	58.1	91.0	82.1	88.5	82.4	82.7	73.4	63.7	47.2	90.8	•
Salaries and Wages	11	9.1	0.5	24.9	2.2	5.1	4.3	10.1	5.9	6.2	13.7	20.4	10.6	•
Taxes Paid	12	3.4	0.8	5.3	1.2	2.3	5.2	3.1	2.6	2.5	5.1	8.7	6.0	•
Interest Paid	13	5.8	1.7	2.0	1.7	3.0	13.1	9.4	5.2	7.6	9.3	16.4	17.1	•
Depreciation	14	2.6	0.2	1.9	2.9	1.3	3.5	2.4	4.3	3.1	5.1	5.2	6.9	•
Amortization and Depletion	15	0.2	0.0	0.0	0.0	0.0	0.2	0.2	0.1	0.2	0.6	0.9	0.3	•
Pensions and Other Deferred Comp.	16	0.3	0.3	0.0	0.0	0.2	0.1	0.2	0.1	0.1	1.0	1.1	0.9	•
Employee Benefits	17	1.0	0.2	3.6	0.5	0.5	0.2	0.5	0.4	0.6	2.0	1.1	1.6	•
Advertising	18	0.6	0.2	0.1	0.0	0.4	0.8	1.1	0.5	0.6	1.3	1.3	1.4	•
Other Expenses	19	17.9	16.0	19.8	16.1	11.1	16.8	21.8	14.8	27.3	23.0	28.5	39.9	•
Officers' Compensation	20	3.1	4.9	6.6	0.3	3.0	1.5	2.6	1.5	2.9	3.7	1.0	4.6	•
Operating Margin	21	•	•	•	•	•	•	•	•	•	•	•	•	•
Operating Margin Before Officers' Comp.	22	•	•	•	•	•	•	•	•	•	•	•	•	•

Selected Average Balance Sheet ($ in Thousands)

	•	•	•	•	•	•	•	•	•	•	•	•
Net Receivables 23	132	0	3	15	151	95	1022	3498	4922	9826	54872	25311
Inventories 24	574	0	29	337	565	2858	5311	9628	22218	32625	80639	130956
Net Property, Plant and Equipment 25	641	0	50	81	567	2188	4128	11446	14471	50259	87348	436589
Total Assets 26	2060	0	143	659	1990	6781	15650	35780	68691	151053	354885	931979
Notes and Loans Payable 27	1248	0	142	438	1290	4885	11004	20065	46056	94323	196529	270738
All Other Liabilities 28	314	0	23	127	243	534	2190	6639	10202	22009	89522	180027
Net Worth 29	498	0	-22	94	457	1361	2456	9076	12433	34720	68834	481214

Selected Financial Ratios (Times to 1)

	•	•	•	•	•	•	•	•	•	•	•	•
Current Ratio 30	2.4	•	2.6	3.4	2.6	3.3	2.3	2.5	3.5	2.0	2.9	1.3
Quick Ratio 31	0.6	•	0.8	0.7	0.6	0.3	0.4	0.8	0.9	0.6	1.1	0.3
Net Sales to Working Capital 32	0.8	•	2.8	1.2	1.0	0.3	0.5	0.8	0.7	0.7	0.5	0.8
Coverage Ratio 33	•	•	•	•	•	•	•	•	•	•	•	•
Total Asset Turnover 34	0.2	•	0.8	0.5	0.3	0.1	0.1	0.2	0.2	0.2	0.2	0.1
Inventory Turnover 35	0.7	•	2.4	1.0	0.9	0.2	0.3	0.7	0.5	0.5	0.4	0.3
Receivables Turnover 36	3.5	•	22.7	13.0	4.4	5.5	2.0	2.5	3.3	1.9	1.2	1.6
Total Liabilities to Net Worth 37	3.1	•	•	6.0	3.4	4.0	5.4	2.9	4.5	3.4	4.2	0.9
Current Assets to Working Capital 38	1.7	•	1.6	1.4	1.6	1.4	1.8	1.7	1.4	2.0	1.5	4.0
Current Liabilities to Working Capital 39	0.7	•	0.6	0.4	0.6	0.4	0.8	0.7	0.4	1.0	0.5	3.0
Working Capital to Net Sales 40	1.2	•	0.4	0.8	1.0	3.8	2.2	1.2	1.5	1.4	2.0	1.2
Inventory to Working Capital 41	0.9	•	0.7	0.9	0.9	0.9	1.0	0.9	0.8	1.0	0.6	1.9
Total Receipts to Cash Flow 42	•	•	22.8	27.4	53.8	•	•	•	•	14.5	30.5	•
Cost of Goods to Cash Flow 43	•	•	13.2	25.0	44.2	•	•	•	•	9.2	14.4	•
Cash Flow to Total Debt 44	•	•	0.0	0.0	0.0	•	•	•	•	0.0	0.0	•

Selected Financial Factors (in Percentages)

	•	•	•	•	•	•	•	•	•	•	•	•
Debt Ratio 45	75.8	•	115.4	85.7	77.0	79.9	84.3	74.6	81.9	77.0	80.6	48.4
Return on Total Assets 46	•	•	•	•	•	•	•	•	•	•	•	•
Return on Equity Before Income Taxes 47	•	•	54.3	•	•	•	•	•	•	•	•	•
Return on Equity After Income Taxes 48	•	•	54.4	•	•	•	•	•	•	•	•	•
Profit Margin (Before Income Tax) 49	•	•	•	•	•	•	•	•	•	•	•	•
Profit Margin (After Income Tax) 50	•	•	•	•	•	•	•	•	•	•	•	•

Table II
Corporations with Net Income

LAND SUBDIVISION

MONEY AMOUNTS AND SIZE OF ASSETS IN THOUSANDS OF DOLLARS

Item Description for Accounting Period 7/10 Through 6/11	Total	Zero Assets	Under 500	500 to 1,000	1,000 to 5,000	5,000 to 10,000	10,000 to 25,000	25,000 to 50,000	50,000 to 100,000	100,000 to 250,000	250,000 to 500,000	500,000 to 2,500,000	2,500,000 and over
Number of Enterprises **1**	7545	777	2863	733	2532	466	106	34	16	12	0	5	0
Revenues ($ in Thousands)													
Net Sales **2**	7132177	100674	709747	747178	2450779	360133	403642	921399	704296	679726	0	54603	0
Interest **3**	91333	551	2131	409	8858	1113	1965	820	2191	29665	0	43630	0
Rents **4**	143358	0	0	465	1129	23239	50760	7064	4772	7788	0	48142	0
Royalties **5**	15185	0	0	0	1279	0	0	0	0	182	0	13724	0
Other Portfolio Income **6**	95838	1374	1789	247	23780	60	14471	537	1230	5203	0	47146	0
Other Receipts **7**	723664	27369	204673	10248	197417	66063	9422	11865	30174	57601	0	108832	0
Total Receipts **8**	8201555	129968	918340	758547	2683242	450608	480260	941685	742663	780165	0	316077	0
Average Total Receipts **9**	1087	167	321	1035	1060	967	4531	27697	46416	65014	•	63215	•
Operating Costs/Operating Income (%)													
Cost of Operations **10**	73.7	38.8	84.3	92.5	73.3	75.1	57.5	82.5	67.6	52.9	•	60.9	•
Salaries and Wages **11**	5.4	0.0	4.0	0.7	4.2	4.7	13.0	2.0	5.1	15.0	•	39.2	•
Taxes Paid **12**	2.8	2.1	4.7	0.1	2.6	4.2	3.5	2.0	1.5	3.6	•	28.6	•
Interest Paid **13**	2.9	0.1	0.9	0.2	2.1	7.0	5.7	0.8	1.1	3.9	•	99.7	•
Depreciation **14**	1.5	0.2	0.4	0.0	0.6	2.7	2.9	2.8	0.6	3.6	•	24.9	•
Amortization and Depletion **15**	0.1	•	•	0.0	0.0	0.2	0.8	0.0	0.0	0.2	•	5.6	•
Pensions and Other Deferred Comp. **16**	0.4	2.4	•	0.0	0.0	0.0	0.4	0.1	0.1	2.8	•	9.0	•
Employee Benefits **17**	0.5	1.3	•	•	0.3	0.3	1.1	0.2	0.4	2.0	•	4.4	•
Advertising **18**	0.5	0.2	0.0	0.0	0.5	0.4	0.4	0.2	0.2	1.0	•	10.2	•
Other Expenses **19**	10.1	3.8	9.4	6.4	6.9	7.6	11.6	5.6	13.6	18.4	•	154.3	•
Officers' Compensation **20**	2.3	43.1	0.5	•	0.9	1.3	4.7	0.9	3.0	4.0	•	28.4	•
Operating Margin **21**	•	7.9	•	0.1	8.6	•	•	2.9	6.7	•	•	•	•
Operating Margin Before Officers' Comp. **22**	2.2	51.0	•	0.1	9.5	•	3.1	3.8	9.7	•	•	•	•

Selected Average Balance Sheet ($ in Thousands)

Net Receivables 23	184	0	3	30	49	146	56	960	9243	7405	30250	10195
Inventories 24	541	0	30	130	515	2574	3636	8754	15327	14063	5960	
Net Property, Plant and Equipment 25	973	0	67	158	651	2350	4244	8558	14038	50056	544702	
Total Assets 26	2711	0	188	589	2178	6795	16955	36272	71172	169410	920506	
Notes and Loans Payable 27	1187	0	45	226	1080	4022	10177	16803	27836	76645	207972	
All Other Liabilities 28	335	0	14	144	155	564	1795	9678	12537	36629	113409	
Net Worth 29	1189	0	130	219	942	2210	4984	9791	30799	56136	599125	

Selected Financial Ratios (Times to 1)

Current Ratio 30	3.1	•	6.1	1.7	4.6	4.0	2.7	1.9	3.3	2.5	0.8
Quick Ratio 31	1.0	•	3.1	1.7	1.2	0.2	1.7	0.5	1.9	1.2	0.6
Net Sales to Working Capital 32	1.3	•	2.7	9.4	1.1	0.3	2.2	1.2	2.1	1.2	•
Coverage Ratio 33	6.2	349.5	28.1	9.2	9.5	4.1	7.4	4.1	12.3	2.8	2.1
Total Asset Turnover 34	0.3	•	1.3	1.7	0.4	0.1	0.7	0.2	0.6	0.3	0.0
Inventory Turnover 35	1.3	•	7.0	7.2	1.4	0.2	2.6	0.6	1.9	2.1	1.1
Receivables Turnover 36	5.0	•	16.4	24.1	7.2	7.5	3.8	3.0	6.2	2.3	1.1
Total Liabilities to Net Worth 37	1.3	•	0.4	1.7	1.3	2.1	2.7	2.4	1.3	2.0	0.5
Current Assets to Working Capital 38	1.5	•	1.2	2.4	1.3	1.3	1.6	2.1	1.4	1.7	•
Current Liabilities to Working Capital 39	0.5	•	0.2	1.4	0.3	0.3	0.6	1.1	0.4	0.7	•
Working Capital to Net Sales 40	0.8	•	0.4	0.1	0.9	3.4	0.5	0.8	0.5	0.8	•
Inventory to Working Capital 41	0.7	•	0.2	•	0.5	1.0	0.5	1.1	0.4	0.6	•
Total Receipts to Cash Flow 42	4.6	2.5	3.1	12.7	4.4	3.6	12.0	4.3	4.1	4.9	0.6
Cost of Goods to Cash Flow 43	3.4	1.0	2.6	11.7	3.2	2.7	9.9	2.5	2.8	2.6	0.3
Cash Flow to Total Debt 44	0.1	•	1.4	0.2	0.2	0.0	0.1	0.1	0.3	0.1	0.1

Selected Financial Factors (in Percentages)

Debt Ratio 45	56.1	•	30.9	62.8	56.7	67.5	70.6	73.0	56.7	66.9	34.9
Return on Total Assets 46	6.2	•	34.5	3.2	9.0	3.3	5.2	4.4	8.1	3.7	2.5
Return on Equity Before Income Taxes 47	11.8	•	48.1	7.6	18.6	7.6	13.3	14.1	17.2	7.3	2.1
Return on Equity After Income Taxes 48	11.2	•	48.0	7.2	17.9	7.3	11.8	12.4	16.6	6.4	1.6
Profit Margin (Before Income Tax) 49	14.9	37.0	25.2	1.6	18.1	21.6	17.4	5.1	12.0	7.2	113.7
Profit Margin (After Income Tax) 50	14.1	35.7	25.2	1.6	17.4	20.9	15.5	4.5	11.6	6.3	85.9

Table I
Corporations with and without Net Income

ELECTRICAL CONTRACTORS

MONEY AMOUNTS AND SIZE OF ASSETS IN THOUSANDS OF DOLLARS

Item Description for Accounting Period 7/10 Through 6/11	Total	Zero Assets	Under 500	500 to 1,000	1,000 to 5,000	5,000 to 10,000	10,000 to 25,000	25,000 to 50,000	50,000 to 100,000	100,000 to 250,000	250,000 to 500,000	500,000 to 2,500,000	2,500,000 and over
Number of Enterprises **1**	59096	9243	40965	4615	3175	721	257	61	39	12	•	•	•
Revenues ($ in Thousands)													
Net Sales **2**	78923039	588561	16840741	9350830	16210995	10998659	8440816	3960774	5848732	3193703	•	•	•
Interest **3**	34841	0	2749	2443	7888	3536	6694	2149	2839	2511	•	•	•
Rents **4**	8485	0	4298	3	867	878	593	1205	583	57	•	•	•
Royalties **5**	0	0	0	0	0	0	0	0	0	0			
Other Portfolio Income **6**	174614	15460	23747	11278	14154	11203	10399	9037	4255	51487	•	•	•
Other Receipts **7**	1028191	-68555	68501	113094	44529	50451	25586	11763	20538	23974	•	•	•
Total Receipts **8**	80169170	535466	16940036	9477648	16278433	11064727	8484088	3984928	5876947	3271732	•	•	•
Average Total Receipts **9**	1357	58	414	2054	5127	15346	33012	65327	150691	272644	•	•	•
Operating Costs/Operating Income (%)													
Cost of Operations **10**	68.2	31.0	51.2	62.3	73.7	74.7	75.1	77.7	79.1	71.4	•	•	•
Salaries and Wages **11**	7.3	11.4	10.4	7.5	6.4	6.5	5.4	4.9	5.9	6.5	•	•	•
Taxes Paid **12**	2.7	4.1	3.5	3.0	2.7	2.7	2.0	1.8	1.8	2.6	•	•	•
Interest Paid **13**	0.4	0.8	0.5	0.5	0.4	0.3	0.4	0.3	0.3	0.4	•	•	•
Depreciation **14**	1.5	4.5	1.6	1.5	1.2	1.2	0.9	1.2	0.8	1.4	•	•	•
Amortization and Depletion **15**	0.1	0.0	0.0	0.1	0.1	0.0	0.0	0.1	0.1	0.4	•	•	•
Pensions and Other Deferred Comp. **16**	0.5	0.0	0.3	0.4	0.4	0.4	0.5	0.9	0.5	0.7	•	•	•
Employee Benefits **17**	2.6	2.9	1.1	2.4	3.5	3.0	3.5	2.7	1.7	1.7	•	•	•
Advertising **18**	0.3	0.8	0.7	0.3	0.2	0.2	0.2	0.1	0.1	0.1	•	•	•
Other Expenses **19**	9.7	33.0	18.0	11.6	6.7	6.7	5.1	3.8	4.3	12.2	•	•	•
Officers' Compensation **20**	5.1	10.4	9.5	8.8	3.5	2.6	3.1	3.7	2.0	1.9	•	•	•
Operating Margin **21**	1.5	1.2	3.0	1.7	1.3	1.6	3.9	2.7	3.4	0.8	•	•	•
Operating Margin Before Officers' Comp. **22**	6.6	11.6	12.5	10.5	4.8	4.2	6.9	6.4	5.5	2.7	•	•	•

Selected Average Balance Sheet ($ in Thousands)

Net Receivables 23	209	0	16	214	894	3087	6841	16118	30778	50320
Inventories 24	24	0	10	53	74	180	769	459	1055	6039
Net Property, Plant and Equipment 25	86	0	21	170	215	733	1483	3893	5451	14642
Total Assets 26	593	0	85	741	1947	6826	15219	35161	66435	151774
Notes and Loans Payable 27	106	0	47	200	280	1007	2337	3872	7276	18616
All Other Liabilities 28	214	0	24	176	775	2793	6247	16551	29460	71966
Net Worth 29	272	0	14	365	892	3026	6635	14738	29698	61192

Selected Financial Ratios (Times to 1)

Current Ratio 30	1.8	•	1.6	2.2	2.0	1.8	1.8	1.6	1.8	1.6
Quick Ratio 31	1.5	•	1.2	1.7	1.6	1.4	1.5	1.4	1.4	1.2
Net Sales to Working Capital 32	7.0	•	19.9	7.4	6.8	6.5	5.6	6.0	6.4	6.6
Coverage Ratio 33	8.1	•	7.8	6.9	5.5	7.5	13.5	12.1	16.2	9.5
Total Asset Turnover 34	2.3	•	4.8	2.7	2.6	2.2	2.2	1.8	2.3	1.8
Inventory Turnover 35	37.4	•	20.3	23.8	50.7	63.3	32.1	110.0	112.5	31.4
Receivables Turnover 36	6.5	•	20.6	10.4	6.4	5.0	4.7	3.9	•	4.5
Total Liabilities to Net Worth 37	1.2	•	4.9	1.0	1.2	1.3	1.3	1.4	1.2	1.5
Current Assets to Working Capital 38	2.2	•	2.5	1.8	2.0	2.3	2.2	2.6	2.3	2.6
Current Liabilities to Working Capital 39	1.2	•	1.5	0.8	1.0	1.3	1.2	1.6	1.3	1.6
Working Capital to Net Sales 40	0.1	•	0.1	0.1	0.1	0.2	0.2	0.2	0.2	0.2
Inventory to Working Capital 41	0.1	•	0.5	0.2	0.1	0.1	0.2	0.0	0.0	0.2
Total Receipts to Cash Flow 42	9.6	4.7	5.4	8.3	15.0	14.8	13.3	19.2	15.5	8.3
Cost of Goods to Cash Flow 43	6.5	1.5	2.8	5.2	11.1	11.0	10.0	14.9	12.2	5.9
Cash Flow to Total Debt 44	0.4	•	1.1	0.6	0.3	0.3	0.3	0.2	0.3	0.4

Selected Financial Factors (in Percentages)

Debt Ratio 45	54.1	•	83.2	50.7	54.2	55.7	56.4	58.1	55.3	59.7
Return on Total Assets 46	7.9	•	20.1	9.8	5.5	5.6	10.2	6.7	9.4	6.3
Return on Equity Before Income Taxes 47	15.1	•	104.3	17.0	9.8	11.0	21.6	14.6	19.8	14.1
Return on Equity After Income Taxes 48	13.7	•	102.2	16.1	8.3	9.4	20.2	13.5	18.8	10.6
Profit Margin (Before Income Tax) 49	3.1	•	3.6	3.1	1.7	2.2	4.4	3.3	3.9	3.2
Profit Margin (After Income Tax) 50	2.8	•	3.5	2.9	1.5	1.9	4.1	3.1	3.7	2.4

Table II
Corporations with Net Income

ELECTRICAL CONTRACTORS

MONEY AMOUNTS AND SIZE OF ASSETS IN THOUSANDS OF DOLLARS

Item Description for Accounting Period 7/10 Through 6/11	Total	Zero Assets	Under 500	500 to 1,000	1,000 to 5,000	5,000 to 10,000	10,000 to 25,000	25,000 to 50,000	50,000 to 100,000	100,000 to 250,000	250,000 to 500,000	500,000 to 2,500,000	2,500,000 and over
Number of Enterprises 1	33583	4310	24010	2720	1782	443	219	53	32	•	•	0	•
Revenues ($ in Thousands)													
Net Sales 2	55650558	263056	11310373	5986799	10105045	7054879	7481904	3367881	4998792	•	•	0	•
Interest 3	19795	0	1763	1166	3445	2345	2632	2137	1093	•	•	0	•
Rents 4	7073	0	3597	3	157	878	592	1205	583	•	•	0	•
Royalties 5	0	0	0	0	0	0	0	0	0	•	•	0	•
Other Portfolio Income 6	150321	8823	23017	10076	5637	9724	6688	8690	3540	•	•	0	•
Other Receipts 7	1017820	1217	62536	80280	18520	42819	19318	13259	19741	•	•	0	•
Total Receipts 8	56845567	273096	11401286	6078324	10132804	7110645	7511134	3393172	5023749	•	•	0	•
Average Total Receipts 9	1693	63	475	2235	5686	16051	34297	64022	156992	•	•	•	•
Operating Costs/Operating Income (%)													
Cost of Operations 10	66.1	15.6	46.5	58.6	70.9	70.4	74.3	77.7	78.9	•	•	•	•
Salaries and Wages 11	7.3	6.7	11.5	7.3	6.0	6.4	5.0	4.8	5.7	•	•	•	•
Taxes Paid 12	2.6	3.0	3.1	3.1	2.6	2.8	2.1	1.6	1.7	•	•	•	•
Interest Paid 13	0.3	0.4	0.4	0.4	0.4	0.2	0.2	0.1	0.2	•	•	•	•
Depreciation 14	1.5	1.4	1.6	1.6	1.1	1.3	0.7	1.0	0.8	•	•	•	•
Amortization and Depletion 15	0.2	•	0.0	0.1	0.1	0.1	0.0	0.0	0.1	•	•	•	•
Pensions and Other Deferred Comp. 16	0.5	•	0.2	0.3	0.4	0.3	0.3	1.1	0.5	•	•	•	•
Employee Benefits 17	2.7	0.2	0.9	2.8	3.5	3.7	3.7	2.7	1.5	•	•	•	•
Advertising 18	0.2	0.5	0.4	0.3	0.1	0.2	0.2	0.1	0.1	•	•	•	•
Other Expenses 19	8.8	34.2	17.4	9.1	6.1	7.1	4.9	2.6	4.3	•	•	•	•
Officers' Compensation 20	5.1	15.1	8.6	9.8	3.9	3.0	3.3	4.1	2.0	•	•	•	•
Operating Margin 21	4.8	22.9	9.4	6.7	5.1	4.5	5.3	4.3	4.4	•	•	•	•
Operating Margin Before Officers' Comp. 22	9.9	38.0	17.9	16.5	8.9	7.5	8.6	8.4	6.4	•	•	•	•

Selected Average Balance Sheet ($ in Thousands)

Net Receivables 23	260	0	14	199	964	3130	7029	15659	31794
Inventories 24	29	0	12	62	80	211	615	489	987
Net Property, Plant and Equipment 25	99	0	24	134	213	707	1207	3407	5279
Total Assets 26	748	0	94	747	2123	6931	15295	34349	68275
Notes and Loans Payable 27	86	0	37	172	300	709	1654	1004	3635
All Other Liabilities 28	274	0	20	154	785	3265	6253	17140	31546
Net Worth 29	388	0	37	421	1038	2957	7388	16205	33094

Selected Financial Ratios (Times to 1)

Current Ratio 30	1.9	•	2.1	2.7	2.1	1.5	1.9	1.8	1.7
Quick Ratio 31	1.5	•	1.6	2.2	1.8	1.2	1.6	1.6	1.4
Net Sales to Working Capital 32	6.4	•	16.3	6.7	6.0	8.3	5.3	5.2	6.5
Coverage Ratio 33	23.4	72.7	24.5	20.2	15.5	23.7	27.2	36.1	30.7
Total Asset Turnover 34	2.2	•	5.0	2.9	2.7	2.3	2.2	1.8	2.3
Inventory Turnover 35	37.4	•	19.0	20.9	50.3	53.1	41.3	101.0	124.9
Receivables Turnover 36	6.1	•	20.5	11.5	6.1	4.4	4.8	3.6	•
Total Liabilities to Net Worth 37	0.9	•	1.5	0.8	1.0	1.3	1.1	1.1	1.1
Current Assets to Working Capital 38	2.1	•	1.9	1.6	1.9	2.9	2.1	2.2	2.3
Current Liabilities to Working Capital 39	1.1	•	0.9	0.6	0.9	1.9	1.1	1.2	1.3
Working Capital to Net Sales 40	0.2	•	0.1	0.1	0.2	0.1	0.2	0.2	0.2
Inventory to Working Capital 41	0.1	•	0.4	0.2	0.1	0.1	0.1	0.0	0.0
Total Receipts to Cash Flow 42	7.4	1.7	4.0	6.7	10.0	10.0	11.6	16.5	13.7
Cost of Goods to Cash Flow 43	4.9	0.3	1.9	3.9	7.1	7.0	8.6	12.8	10.8
Cash Flow to Total Debt 44	0.6	•	2.0	1.0	0.5	0.4	0.4	0.2	0.3

Selected Financial Factors (in Percentages)

Debt Ratio 45	48.1	•	60.7	43.6	51.1	57.3	51.7	52.8	51.5
Return on Total Assets 46	16.1	•	52.8	25.5	15.2	12.5	13.1	9.6	11.5
Return on Equity Before Income Taxes 47	29.7	•	128.8	42.9	29.1	28.0	26.1	19.7	23.0
Return on Equity After Income Taxes 48	27.9	•	127.4	41.7	26.9	25.4	24.6	18.5	21.9
Profit Margin (Before Income Tax) 49	7.0	26.7	10.2	8.2	5.3	5.2	5.6	5.0	4.9
Profit Margin (After Income Tax) 50	6.5	26.4	10.0	8.0	4.7	4.7	5.3	4.7	4.6

Table I

Corporations with and without Net Income

PLUMBING, HEATING, AND AIR-CONDITIONING CONTRACTORS

MONEY AMOUNTS AND SIZE OF ASSETS IN THOUSANDS OF DOLLARS

Item Description for Accounting Period 7/10 Through 6/11	Total	Zero Assets	Under 500	500 to 1,000	1,000 to 5,000	5,000 to 10,000	10,000 to 25,000	25,000 to 50,000	50,000 to 100,000	100,000 to 250,000	250,000 to 500,000	500,000 to 2,500,000	2,500,000 and over
Number of Enterprises **1**	77856	8503	60818	3664	3806	637	327	66	25	6	•	•	•
Revenues ($ in Thousands)													
Net Sales **2**	102897851	1131612	32185410	8388588	21902704	11938828	10629327	5369549	3664213	1650043	•	•	•
Interest **3**	29715	1079	4599	4237	7797	4901	2872	951	816	815	•	•	•
Rents **4**	15560	0	1779	246	515	2094	8445	18	369	0	•	•	•
Royalties **5**	0	0	0	0	0	0	0	0	0	0			•
Other Portfolio Income **6**	200595	23926	31745	27051	95478	7893	4522	2118	1502	476	•	•	•
Other Receipts **7**	342422	38552	15326	75341	62344	87485	30301	8491	6199	5559	•	•	•
Total Receipts **8**	103486143	1195169	32238859	8495463	22068838	12041201	10675467	5381127	3673099	1655893	•	•	•
Average Total Receipts **9**	1329	141	530	2319	5798	18903	32647	81532	146924	276149			•
Operating Costs/Operating Income (%)													
Cost of Operations **10**	66.0	55.4	50.0	59.4	71.1	75.1	77.9	80.4	79.8	80.4	•	•	•
Salaries and Wages **11**	8.4	5.3	12.2	11.0	7.0	6.5	5.5	4.7	4.9	5.8	•	•	•
Taxes Paid **12**	2.8	2.6	3.2	3.5	2.7	2.5	2.2	2.7	1.9	1.6	•	•	•
Interest Paid **13**	0.5	0.4	0.6	0.4	0.4	0.3	0.5	0.2	0.1	0.8	•	•	•
Depreciation **14**	1.1	1.8	1.5	1.5	0.9	0.6	0.6	0.5	0.7	0.6	•	•	•
Amortization and Depletion **15**	0.1	0.3	0.1	0.0	0.1	0.1	0.1	0.1	0.1	0.5	•	•	•
Pensions and Other Deferred Comp. **16**	0.4	0.0	0.2	0.8	0.5	0.4	0.5	0.7	0.4	0.5	•	•	•
Employee Benefits **17**	2.0	1.3	1.7	2.3	1.8	2.4	2.6	1.7	3.6	0.7	•	•	•
Advertising **18**	0.8	1.5	1.2	1.1	1.1	0.3	0.1	0.1	0.1	0.1	•	•	•
Other Expenses **19**	10.3	33.2	16.8	11.4	8.9	6.8	4.8	3.2	3.2	2.8	•	•	•
Officers' Compensation **20**	5.1	3.0	8.5	6.7	4.6	2.8	2.6	1.9	1.7	1.8	•	•	•
Operating Margin **21**	2.6	•	4.1	1.8	0.8	2.2	2.4	3.8	3.5	4.3	•	•	•
Operating Margin Before Officers' Comp. **22**	7.7	•	12.6	8.5	5.4	5.0	5.1	5.7	5.2	6.1	•	•	•

Selected Average Balance Sheet ($ in Thousands)

	1	2	3	4	5	6	7	8	9	10
Net Receivables 23	178	0	22	223	857	3745	6766	18985	31722	53005
Inventories 24	23	0	7	54	173	233	475	1184	2058	1027
Net Property, Plant and Equipment 25	56	0	24	137	219	795	1202	3070	7134	8616
Total Assets 26	443	0	95	673	2131	7407	14085	35546	68705	145118
Notes and Loans Payable 27	100	0	55	161	452	953	2153	2765	4961	14303
All Other Liabilities 28	182	0	23	221	825	3237	6559	18197	34800	94104
Net Worth 29	161	0	16	291	854	3217	5372	14584	28944	36711

Selected Financial Ratios (Times to 1)

	1	2	3	4	5	6	7	8	9	10
Current Ratio 30	1.7	•	1.9	1.8	1.8	1.7	1.7	1.6	1.5	1.1
Quick Ratio 31	1.4	•	1.7	1.5	1.5	1.4	1.4	1.4	1.3	1.0
Net Sales to Working Capital 32	9.5	•	17.9	10.9	7.5	7.3	7.0	8.0	8.3	21.9
Coverage Ratio 33	7.9	2.9	8.5	7.9	4.7	12.0	6.2	21.4	29.3	6.6
Total Asset Turnover 34	3.0	•	5.6	3.4	2.7	2.5	2.3	2.3	2.1	1.9
Inventory Turnover 35	38.4	•	36.9	25.3	23.6	60.4	53.3	55.3	56.8	215.5
Receivables Turnover 36	7.6	•	25.8	10.7	6.6	5.8	4.4	4.6	•	5.1
Total Liabilities to Net Worth 37	1.8	•	4.7	1.3	1.5	1.3	1.6	1.4	1.4	3.0
Current Assets to Working Capital 38	2.4	•	2.1	2.3	2.2	2.4	2.5	2.8	3.1	8.8
Current Liabilities to Working Capital 39	1.4	•	1.1	1.3	1.2	1.4	1.5	1.8	2.1	7.8
Working Capital to Net Sales 40	0.1	•	0.1	0.1	0.1	0.1	0.1	0.1	0.1	0.0
Inventory to Working Capital 41	0.2	•	0.2	0.2	0.2	0.1	0.1	0.1	0.1	0.1
Total Receipts to Cash Flow 42	9.0	3.4	5.5	8.3	12.3	13.4	15.8	16.3	17.4	16.3
Cost of Goods to Cash Flow 43	5.9	1.9	2.7	4.9	8.7	10.1	12.3	13.1	13.9	13.1
Cash Flow to Total Debt 44	0.5	•	1.2	0.7	0.4	0.3	0.2	0.2	0.2	0.2

Selected Financial Factors (in Percentages)

	1	2	3	4	5	6	7	8	9	10
Debt Ratio 45	63.7	•	82.6	56.7	59.9	56.6	61.9	59.0	57.9	74.7
Return on Total Assets 46	10.8	•	27.2	12.0	5.3	8.2	7.9	9.7	8.2	10.5
Return on Equity Before Income Taxes 47	26.0	•	137.7	24.3	10.5	17.4	17.3	22.5	18.8	35.3
Return on Equity After Income Taxes 48	24.5	•	135.0	22.6	9.5	16.5	16.2	21.7	18.3	35.3
Profit Margin (Before Income Tax) 49	3.2	0.8	4.3	3.1	1.6	3.0	2.9	4.0	3.7	4.7
Profit Margin (After Income Tax) 50	3.0	0.7	4.2	2.9	1.4	2.8	2.7	3.9	3.6	4.7

Table II
Corporations with Net Income

PLUMBING, HEATING, AND AIR-CONDITIONING CONTRACTORS

MONEY AMOUNTS AND SIZE OF ASSETS IN THOUSANDS OF DOLLARS

Item Description for Accounting Period 7/10 Through 6/11	Total	Zero Assets	Under 500	500 to 1,000	1,000 to 5,000	5,000 to 10,000	10,000 to 25,000	25,000 to 50,000	50,000 to 100,000	100,000 to 250,000	250,000 to 500,000	500,000 to 2,500,000	2,500,000 and over
Number of Enterprises **1**	49821	4307	39927	2335	2410	510	247	54	22	•	•	•	•
Revenues ($ in Thousands)													
Net Sales **2**	80868539	477370	25639911	5916025	15779165	9754604	8226034	4806597	3251580	•	•	•	•
Interest **3**	16025	1075	1830	1324	5343	2078	1613	475	813	•	•	•	•
Rents **4**	12812	0	1768	246	163	127	8445	18	369	•	•	•	•
Royalties **5**	0	0	0	0	0	0	0	0	0				
Other Portfolio Income **6**	158709	23844	21551	2968	90518	6750	3706	1774	1502	•	•	•	•
Other Receipts **7**	302944	4953	58859	63462	45749	78216	25156	8240	5726	•	•	•	•
Total Receipts **8**	81359029	507242	25723919	5984025	15920938	9841775	8264954	4817104	3259990	•	•	•	•
Average Total Receipts **9**	1633	118	644	2563	6606	19298	33461	89206	148181	•	•	•	•
Operating Costs/Operating Income (%)													
Cost of Operations **10**	66.1	48.2	50.6	58.8	70.0	75.0	76.3	80.1	79.5	•	•	•	•
Salaries and Wages **11**	7.8	9.8	10.9	10.3	7.4	5.7	5.2	4.6	4.4	•	•	•	•
Taxes Paid **12**	2.6	2.9	2.9	2.8	2.5	2.5	2.1	2.8	2.1	•	•	•	•
Interest Paid **13**	0.3	0.2	0.4	0.3	0.2	0.3	0.3	0.1	0.1	•	•	•	•
Depreciation **14**	0.8	1.9	1.2	1.0	0.7	0.5	0.5	0.5	0.7	•	•	•	•
Amortization and Depletion **15**	0.1	0.0	0.1	0.0	0.0	0.0	0.1	0.0	0.0	•	•	•	•
Pensions and Other Deferred Comp. **16**	0.4	•	0.2	0.9	0.5	0.5	0.6	0.7	0.4	•	•	•	•
Employee Benefits **17**	1.8	2.0	1.7	1.6	1.5	2.4	2.5	1.8	3.2	•	•	•	•
Advertising **18**	0.7	1.1	1.1	1.0	0.9	0.2	0.2	0.1	0.1	•	•	•	•
Other Expenses **19**	9.4	25.1	15.7	10.6	8.4	6.5	4.8	2.7	2.9	•	•	•	•
Officers' Compensation **20**	5.1	1.2	8.4	7.1	4.3	2.9	3.0	2.0	1.9	•	•	•	•
Operating Margin **21**	5.0	7.6	6.9	5.6	3.5	3.5	4.4	4.7	4.7	•	•	•	•
Operating Margin Before Officers' Comp. **22**	10.0	8.8	15.2	12.6	7.8	6.4	7.4	6.7	6.6	•	•	•	•

Selected Average Balance Sheet ($ in Thousands)

Net Receivables 23	218	0	23	257	914	3911	6864	20674	31924
Inventories 24	25	0	6	54	202	242	542	1318	1800
Net Property, Plant and Equipment 25	55	0	23	93	194	691	1292	3088	7252
Total Assets 26	518	0	98	678	2194	7412	14137	36958	69121
Notes and Loans Payable 27	80	0	41	116	312	964	1904	1832	4470
All Other Liabilities 28	217	0	24	189	825	3356	6495	19572	34618
Net Worth 29	221	0	33	373	1056	3093	5738	15554	30033

Selected Financial Ratios (Times to 1)

Current Ratio 30	1.8	•	2.1	2.4	2.1	1.7	1.7	1.6	1.5
Quick Ratio 31	1.5	•	1.8	2.2	1.7	1.4	1.4	1.4	1.3
Net Sales to Working Capital 32	9.1	•	19.3	8.1	6.9	7.7	6.7	8.3	8.1
Coverage Ratio 33	19.2	60.9	18.4	20.6	19.3	17.6	20.3	48.9	43.5
Total Asset Turnover 34	3.1	•	6.6	3.7	3.0	2.6	2.4	2.4	2.1
Inventory Turnover 35	42.6	•	57.6	27.4	22.7	59.3	46.8	54.1	65.3
Receivables Turnover 36	7.2	•	32.6	10.5	6.4	5.4	4.0	4.5	•
Total Liabilities to Net Worth 37	1.3	•	1.9	0.8	1.1	1.4	1.5	1.4	1.3
Current Assets to Working Capital 38	2.3	•	1.9	1.7	2.0	2.5	2.4	2.8	3.0
Current Liabilities to Working Capital 39	1.3	•	0.9	0.7	1.0	1.5	1.4	1.8	2.0
Working Capital to Net Sales 40	0.1	•	0.1	0.1	0.1	0.1	0.1	0.1	0.1
Inventory to Working Capital 41	0.1	•	0.2	0.1	0.2	0.1	0.1	0.1	0.1
Total Receipts to Cash Flow 42	7.8	3.2	5.0	6.6	9.4	11.6	12.1	15.1	14.8
Cost of Goods to Cash Flow 43	5.2	1.5	2.5	3.9	6.6	8.7	9.2	12.1	11.8
Cash Flow to Total Debt 44	0.7	•	2.0	1.3	0.6	0.4	0.3	0.3	0.3

Selected Financial Factors (in Percentages)

Debt Ratio 45	57.3	•	66.1	45.0	51.9	58.3	59.4	57.9	56.6
Return on Total Assets 46	18.3	•	50.1	26.4	13.9	11.8	12.0	12.1	10.9
Return on Equity Before Income Taxes 47	40.7	•	139.5	45.6	27.4	26.8	28.0	28.2	24.4
Return on Equity After Income Taxes 48	39.0	•	137.4	43.6	26.1	25.5	26.7	27.3	23.9
Profit Margin (Before Income Tax) 49	5.5	13.9	7.2	6.7	4.4	4.3	4.8	4.9	5.0
Profit Margin (After Income Tax) 50	5.3	13.9	7.1	6.4	4.2	4.1	4.6	4.8	4.9

Table I

Corporations with and without Net Income

OTHER SPECIALTY TRADE CONTRACTORS

MONEY AMOUNTS AND SIZE OF ASSETS IN THOUSANDS OF DOLLARS

Item Description for Accounting Period 7/10 Through 6/11	Total	Zero Assets	Under 500	500 to 1,000	1,000 to 5,000	5,000 to 10,000	10,000 to 25,000	25,000 to 50,000	50,000 to 100,000	100,000 to 250,000	250,000 to 500,000	500,000 to 2,500,000	2,500,000 and over
Number of Enterprises **1**	311701	54930	228340	12197	12866	2081	957	204	72	36	•	•	0
Revenues ($ in Thousands)													
Net Sales **2**	285511751	5636658	99272698	24952353	60983111	30747067	26462176	12259029	7781299	6833191	•	•	0
Interest **3**	103301	2829	11390	10530	27348	13781	9878	6024	4445	8610	•	•	0
Rents **4**	332479	2692	14349	4174	17925	7748	6818	10473	4081	132747	•	•	0
Royalties **5**	8225	3743	0	0	0	131	0	3093	9	2	•	•	0
Other Portfolio Income **6**	941870	218055	223157	61668	214539	51402	42294	57186	18550	38553	•	•	0
Other Receipts **7**	1508246	-98468	494306	70599	419964	109929	200397	100426	61228	48746	•	•	0
Total Receipts **8**	288405872	5765509	100015900	25099324	61662887	30930058	26721563	12436231	7869612	7061849	•	•	0
Average Total Receipts **9**	925	105	438	2058	4793	14863	27922	60962	109300	196162	•	•	•
Operating Costs/Operating Income (%)													
Cost of Operations **10**	64.3	46.3	51.3	60.3	68.9	77.3	76.6	79.9	75.4	74.4	•	•	•
Salaries and Wages **11**	7.7	7.5	10.6	8.6	6.6	4.8	4.7	4.6	5.6	7.2	•	•	•
Taxes Paid **12**	2.4	1.9	3.0	2.9	2.4	1.8	2.0	2.0	1.4	1.8	•	•	•
Interest Paid **13**	0.6	1.3	0.6	0.6	0.6	0.4	0.4	0.6	0.4	0.6	•	•	•
Depreciation **14**	2.1	2.5	2.1	2.0	1.8	1.7	2.0	2.6	2.3	3.6	•	•	•
Amortization and Depletion **15**	0.1	0.0	0.0	0.0	0.0	0.0	0.1	0.2	0.1	0.4	•	•	•
Pensions and Other Deferred Comp. **16**	0.4	0.1	0.3	0.2	0.4	0.4	0.9	0.3	0.4	0.5	•	•	•
Employee Benefits **17**	1.7	1.0	1.6	2.3	1.8	1.5	2.1	2.5	1.5	1.3	•	•	•
Advertising **18**	0.5	1.5	0.8	0.5	0.2	0.2	0.1	0.2	0.1	0.1	•	•	•
Other Expenses **19**	14.0	31.3	20.3	16.6	11.8	7.4	6.5	5.5	8.5	8.1	•	•	•
Officers' Compensation **20**	4.4	8.0	6.7	4.7	3.8	2.7	2.2	1.4	1.9	1.4	•	•	•
Operating Margin **21**	1.8	•	2.7	1.2	1.6	1.7	2.4	0.2	2.2	0.6	•	•	•
Operating Margin Before Officers' Comp. **22**	6.2	6.4	9.4	5.9	5.5	4.4	4.6	1.6	4.1	1.9	•	•	•

Selected Average Balance Sheet ($ in Thousands)

Net Receivables 23	114	0	13	186	765	2985	5990	11994	23424	42211
Inventories 24	16	0	5	49	104	258	402	1101	1930	3644
Net Property, Plant and Equipment 25	75	0	26	163	425	1056	2617	6535	11061	35922
Total Assets 26	351	0	79	697	2028	6827	14928	33492	70573	148596
Notes and Loans Payable 27	107	0	47	235	538	1391	2837	7412	12255	32829
All Other Liabilities 28	118	0	26	157	597	2605	5470	14073	26080	50350
Net Worth 29	126	0	7	305	892	2831	6621	12007	32239	65418

Selected Financial Ratios (Times to 1)

Current Ratio 30	1.6	•	1.3	2.0	1.9	1.7	1.8	1.5	1.5	1.6
Quick Ratio 31	1.3	•	1.0	1.6	1.5	1.3	1.5	1.2	1.3	1.3
Net Sales to Working Capital 32	10.5	•	47.0	8.9	7.0	7.3	6.0	8.2	6.6	6.3
Coverage Ratio 33	5.5	1.6	6.9	3.9	5.4	6.3	9.0	3.7	8.4	7.0
Total Asset Turnover 34	2.6	•	5.5	2.9	2.3	2.2	1.9	1.8	1.5	1.3
Inventory Turnover 35	37.8	•	44.5	25.1	31.5	44.3	52.7	43.6	42.2	38.8
Receivables Turnover 36	8.0	•	34.8	10.9	5.9	5.4	4.4	4.9	4.3	4.6
Total Liabilities to Net Worth 37	1.8	•	10.8	1.3	1.3	1.4	1.3	1.8	1.2	1.3
Current Assets to Working Capital 38	2.6	•	4.4	2.0	2.1	2.5	2.3	3.1	2.9	2.6
Current Liabilities to Working Capital 39	1.6	•	3.4	1.0	1.1	1.5	1.3	2.1	1.9	1.6
Working Capital to Net Sales 40	0.1	•	0.0	0.1	0.1	0.1	0.2	0.1	0.2	0.2
Inventory to Working Capital 41	0.2	•	0.5	0.2	0.1	0.1	0.1	0.2	0.1	0.1
Total Receipts to Cash Flow 42	7.5	4.0	5.0	7.0	8.8	15.7	14.3	20.7	11.1	11.8
Cost of Goods to Cash Flow 43	4.8	1.9	2.6	4.2	6.0	12.2	11.0	16.6	8.4	8.7
Cash Flow to Total Debt 44	0.5	•	1.2	0.7	0.5	0.2	0.2	0.1	0.3	0.2

Selected Financial Factors (in Percentages)

Debt Ratio 45	64.2	•	91.5	56.2	56.0	58.5	55.6	64.1	54.3	56.0
Return on Total Assets 46	9.1	•	21.9	7.0	7.8	5.8	7.1	4.1	5.7	5.8
Return on Equity Before Income Taxes 47	20.7	•	221.1	11.9	14.5	11.8	14.2	8.4	10.9	11.3
Return on Equity After Income Taxes 48	19.7	•	218.3	11.4	13.7	10.9	13.5	6.6	9.8	10.9
Profit Margin (Before Income Tax) 49	2.8	0.7	3.4	1.8	2.7	2.3	3.4	1.7	3.3	3.9
Profit Margin (After Income Tax) 50	2.7	0.7	3.4	1.7	2.6	2.1	3.2	1.3	2.9	3.8

Table II
Corporations with Net Income

OTHER SPECIALTY TRADE CONTRACTORS

MONEY AMOUNTS AND SIZE OF ASSETS IN THOUSANDS OF DOLLARS

Item Description for Accounting Period 7/10 Through 6/11	Total	Zero Assets	Under 500	500 to 1,000	1,000 to 5,000	5,000 to 10,000	10,000 to 25,000	25,000 to 50,000	50,000 to 100,000	100,000 to 250,000	250,000 to 500,000	500,000 to 2,500,000	2,500,000 and over
Number of Enterprises **1**	189171	30602	140548	7645	8070	1390	704	125	52	24	7	4	0
Revenues ($ in Thousands)													
Net Sales **2**	200119016	3357506	65487746	18705010	43430822	22024243	20428186	8119807	6294398	5204427	3073344	3993526	0
Interest **3**	55319	138	3314	8099	9688	9433	6584	3820	3852	7597	739	2054	0
Rents **4**	197848	0	3133	2140	13920	5413	2282	3493	3814	132192	0	31462	0
Royalties **5**	4482	0	0	0	0	131	0	3093	9	2	1247	0	0
Other Portfolio Income **6**	655882	137925	177493	17642	173062	42881	29994	35045	13272	21609	5015	1942	0
Other Receipts **7**	1223497	5230	324161	54065	363800	78550	154916	54007	51055	40461	70769	26486	0
Total Receipts **8**	202256044	3500799	65995847	18786956	43391292	22160651	20621962	8219265	6366400	5406288	3151114	4055470	0
Average Total Receipts **9**	1069	114	470	2457	5451	15943	29293	65754	122431	225262	450159	1013868	•
Operating Costs/Operating Income (%)													
Cost of Operations **10**	62.8	38.0	48.1	60.8	68.1	74.9	74.7	75.8	75.1	74.2	77.4	76.2	•
Salaries and Wages **11**	7.0	3.5	10.0	7.3	6.3	4.6	4.4	4.5	5.2	7.0	4.4	4.0	•
Taxes Paid **12**	2.3	1.8	2.9	2.4	2.2	1.8	2.0	1.9	1.3	1.9	1.2	1.7	•
Interest Paid **13**	0.5	0.5	0.5	0.5	0.4	0.3	0.3	0.3	0.4	0.5	1.1	1.0	•
Depreciation **14**	1.7	1.8	1.6	1.5	1.4	1.5	1.8	2.4	1.9	2.6	2.3	2.3	•
Amortization and Depletion **15**	0.1	0.0	0.0	0.0	0.0	0.0	0.0	0.1	0.1	0.3	0.7	1.2	•
Pensions and Other Deferred Comp. **16**	0.4	0.1	0.2	0.2	0.4	0.6	1.1	0.3	0.5	0.6	0.2	0.2	•
Employee Benefits **17**	1.7	0.8	1.6	2.4	1.5	1.2	2.5	2.9	1.0	1.3	1.2	1.4	•
Advertising **18**	0.4	2.2	0.7	0.4	0.2	0.2	0.1	0.1	0.1	0.1	0.2	0.1	•
Other Expenses **19**	13.0	28.2	20.0	15.9	10.6	6.6	5.4	4.7	8.7	7.1	5.7	7.0	•
Officers' Compensation **20**	4.1	8.6	6.0	4.1	3.9	2.9	2.3	1.6	1.8	1.5	1.4	1.0	•
Operating Margin **21**	6.1	14.6	8.2	4.4	4.9	5.2	5.4	5.3	4.0	3.1	4.4	4.0	•
Operating Margin Before Officers' Comp. **22**	10.2	23.1	14.2	8.5	8.8	8.1	7.7	6.9	5.8	4.5	5.8	4.9	•

Selected Average Balance Sheet ($ in Thousands)

	•	•	•	•	•	•	•	•	•	•	•	•
Net Receivables 23	129	0	12	198	814	2927	6178	13327	25205	48089	81758	377789
Inventories 24	17	0	5	49	96	312	438	1165	1679	3247	1398	81301
Net Property, Plant and Equipment 25	72	0	23	170	415	1116	2279	6183	9215	25087	35192	113312
Total Assets 26	378	0	79	708	2089	6976	14884	34571	72213	151275	345033	971915
Notes and Loans Payable 27	86	0	34	218	450	1134	2227	5626	8301	27626	72999	204560
All Other Liabilities 28	124	0	20	170	568	2470	5661	13623	29566	55684	100117	540089
Net Worth 29	168	0	26	320	1071	3373	6996	15322	34345	67965	171917	227266

Selected Financial Ratios (Times to 1)

	•	•	•	•	•	•	•	•	•	•	•	•
Current Ratio 30	1.8	•	1.8	2.0	2.3	1.9	1.8	1.7	1.8	1.7	1.4	1.2
Quick Ratio 31	1.5	•	1.5	1.6	1.9	1.5	1.4	1.6	1.4	1.0	1.0	1.0
Net Sales to Working Capital 32	9.1	•	25.3	10.8	6.4	6.5	5.9	6.9	5.2	5.8	7.8	8.9
Coverage Ratio 33	16.5	39.1	18.2	10.5	15.0	18.3	23.4	21.6	14.6	15.2	7.5	6.6
Total Asset Turnover 34	2.8	•	5.9	3.5	2.6	2.3	1.9	1.9	1.7	1.4	1.3	1.0
Inventory Turnover 35	39.8	47.1	30.3	38.4	38.0	49.4	42.3	54.1	49.6	242.9	9.4	
Receivables Turnover 36	8.1	38.4	12.7	6.3	6.0	4.3	4.5	4.5	4.7	•	3.3	
Total Liabilities to Net Worth 37	1.3	•	2.0	1.2	1.0	1.1	1.3	1.1	1.2	1.0	3.3	
Current Assets to Working Capital 38	2.2	•	2.3	2.0	1.8	2.2	2.5	2.3	2.4	3.6	5.7	
Current Liabilities to Working Capital 39	1.2	•	1.3	1.0	0.8	1.2	1.5	1.3	1.4	2.6	4.7	
Working Capital to Net Sales 40	0.1	•	0.0	0.1	0.2	0.2	0.1	0.2	0.2	0.1	0.1	
Inventory to Working Capital 41	0.1	•	0.2	0.2	0.1	0.1	0.1	0.1	0.1	0.0	0.7	
Total Receipts to Cash Flow 42	5.9	2.3	3.9	5.8	7.2	10.7	11.2	10.9	8.9	8.9	10.8	9.9
Cost of Goods to Cash Flow 43	3.7	0.9	1.9	3.5	4.9	8.0	8.5	8.1	6.7	6.6	8.4	7.6
Cash Flow to Total Debt 44	0.9	•	2.2	1.1	0.7	0.4	0.3	0.3	0.4	0.3	0.2	0.1

Selected Financial Factors (in Percentages)

	•	•	•	•	•	•	•	•	•	•	•	•
Debt Ratio 45	55.6	•	67.2	54.8	48.7	51.7	53.0	55.7	52.4	55.1	50.2	76.6
Return on Total Assets 46	21.2	•	55.7	18.5	17.0	14.0	12.9	12.8	9.2	10.6	10.1	6.7
Return on Equity Before Income Taxes 47	44.9	•	160.4	37.0	30.9	27.3	26.2	27.5	18.0	22.1	17.6	24.3
Return on Equity After Income Taxes 48	43.6	•	159.3	36.3	29.8	26.2	25.2	25.3	16.6	21.6	16.1	18.2
Profit Margin (Before Income Tax) 49	7.1	18.8	8.9	4.8	6.2	5.8	6.3	6.5	5.1	6.9	6.9	5.5
Profit Margin (After Income Tax) 50	6.9	18.7	8.9	4.7	5.9	5.6	6.1	6.0	4.7	6.8	6.3	4.1

Table I

Corporations with and without Net Income

ANIMAL FOOD AND GRAIN AND OILSEED MILLING

MONEY AMOUNTS AND SIZE OF ASSETS IN THOUSANDS OF DOLLARS

Item Description for Accounting Period 7/10 Through 6/11		Total	Zero Assets	Under 500	500 to 1,000	1,000 to 5,000	5,000 to 10,000	10,000 to 25,000	25,000 to 50,000	50,000 to 100,000	100,000 to 250,000	250,000 to 500,000	500,000 to 2,500,000	2,500,000 and over
Number of Enterprises	1	1840	445	858	0	236	80	99	45	26	30	9	6	5
Revenues ($ in Thousands)														
Net Sales	2	121429375	478442	150524	0	1702914	1741593	3658724	4047953	3825698	9101671	3181450	4459708	89080697
Interest	3	221368	0	331	0	1161	308	1531	1105	262	3679	14730	6467	191794
Rents	4	200642	0	0	0	529	457	82	505	22	659	1135	284	196969
Royalties	5	426776	0	0	0	0	0	0	0	0	224	2675	3034	420844
Other Portfolio Income	6	565610	116	0	0	1604	40	2142	92	659	43392	31456	988	485121
Other Receipts	7	2501811	587	1	0	3040	6567	48794	35812	36684	58269	17715	21798	2272543
Total Receipts	8	125345582	479145	150856	0	1709248	1748965	3711273	4085467	3863325	9207894	3249161	4492279	92647968
Average Total Receipts	9	68123	1077	176	•	7243	21862	37488	90788	148589	306930	361018	748713	18529594
Operating Costs/Operating Income (%)														
Cost of Operations	10	80.8	78.3	68.5	•	71.4	88.6	82.9	78.7	79.8	82.5	75.1	73.4	81.3
Salaries and Wages	11	2.7	5.6	5.4	•	6.6	2.1	3.7	4.1	4.3	2.7	4.2	4.7	2.3
Taxes Paid	12	0.6	1.0	9.9	•	0.9	0.6	0.6	0.8	0.9	0.7	0.9	0.8	0.6
Interest Paid	13	1.5	1.3	0.3	•	0.6	0.5	0.3	0.6	0.4	0.8	2.0	1.7	1.7
Depreciation	14	2.3	2.1	0.8	•	0.9	1.2	2.0	2.6	2.2	2.5	3.8	4.3	2.2
Amortization and Depletion	15	0.2	0.0	•	•	•	0.1	0.0	0.2	0.2	0.2	0.8	1.9	0.1
Pensions and Other Deferred Comp.	16	0.7	0.5	•	•	0.1	0.1	0.2	0.4	0.3	0.3	0.5	0.7	0.8
Employee Benefits	17	0.8	0.5	0.8	•	1.1	0.4	0.5	0.8	0.8	0.8	0.8	0.6	0.8
Advertising	18	5.4	1.1	0.2	•	3.9	0.6	0.2	0.7	1.0	0.4	0.6	1.5	7.1
Other Expenses	19	4.7	8.2	17.2	•	7.3	3.2	5.1	6.6	5.8	5.4	7.8	8.2	4.1
Officers' Compensation	20	0.4	0.4	10.9	•	1.7	0.8	1.1	0.9	0.7	0.6	1.7	0.5	0.2
Operating Margin	21	•	1.0	•	•	5.5	2.0	3.5	3.6	3.8	3.1	1.6	1.6	•
Operating Margin Before Officers' Comp.	22	0.2	1.4	•	•	7.2	2.8	4.6	4.5	4.4	3.7	3.4	2.2	•

Selected Average Balance Sheet ($ in Thousands)

Net Receivables 23	4239	0	5	•	996	2106	3819	5982	14444	29411	62206	63685	909075
Inventories 24	6281	0	13	•	1430	1109	2972	8973	15386	31521	34016	75982	1662722
Net Property, Plant and Equipment 25	9662	0	11	•	432	1055	4089	12896	20078	48883	89787	270369	2435748
Total Assets 26	48409	0	39	•	3009	6286	15189	35622	66783	164495	345911	824022	13998059
Notes and Loans Payable 27	22043	0	93	•	2077	607	2961	9207	15583	45242	149414	151042	7043803
All Other Liabilities 28	13376	0	32	•	1166	3260	4139	8928	16226	36861	70330	165635	4016535
Net Worth 29	12990	0	-86	•	-234	2419	8089	17487	34974	82393	126166	507345	2937721

Selected Financial Ratios (Times to 1)

Current Ratio 30	1.3	•	0.8	•	1.1	1.3	1.7	1.8	2.3	1.8	1.5	2.0	1.1
Quick Ratio 31	0.5	•	0.2	•	0.5	1.0	1.0	1.0	1.1	0.9	0.9	0.8	0.3
Net Sales to Working Capital 32	19.2	•	•	•	28.0	18.6	9.7	10.6	6.8	8.3	8.4	7.0	32.6
Coverage Ratio 33	3.3	1.9	•	•	10.4	6.3	16.8	8.6	11.8	6.7	3.1	2.4	2.9
Total Asset Turnover 34	1.4	•	4.5	•	2.4	3.5	2.4	2.5	2.2	1.8	1.0	0.9	1.3
Inventory Turnover 35	8.5	•	9.4	•	3.6	17.4	10.3	7.9	7.6	7.9	7.8	7.2	8.7
Receivables Turnover 36	16.6	•	38.3	•	7.1	7.6	10.4	12.7	10.0	11.3	7.8	12.8	21.0
Total Liabilities to Net Worth 37	2.7	•	•	•	1.6	0.9	0.9	1.0	0.9	1.0	1.7	0.6	3.8
Current Assets to Working Capital 38	4.9	•	•	•	9.6	4.0	2.4	2.2	1.8	2.2	3.2	2.0	8.2
Current Liabilities to Working Capital 39	3.9	•	•	•	8.6	3.0	1.4	1.2	0.8	1.2	2.2	1.0	7.2
Working Capital to Net Sales 40	0.1	•	•	•	0.0	0.1	0.1	0.1	0.1	0.1	0.1	0.1	0.0
Inventory to Working Capital 41	2.1	•	•	•	4.7	0.9	0.9	0.9	0.8	1.0	1.1	0.9	3.6
Total Receipts to Cash Flow 42	16.8	18.5	•	•	9.1	20.2	10.9	10.3	11.2	12.2	10.2	10.7	20.3
Cost of Goods to Cash Flow 43	13.6	14.5	•	•	6.5	17.9	9.1	8.1	8.9	10.1	7.7	7.8	16.5
Cash Flow to Total Debt 44	0.1	•	0.0	•	0.2	0.3	0.5	0.5	0.4	0.3	0.2	0.2	0.1

Selected Financial Factors (in Percentages)

Debt Ratio 45	73.2	•	317.9	•	107.8	61.5	46.7	50.9	47.6	49.9	63.5	38.4	79.0
Return on Total Assets 46	6.8	•	•	•	15.7	9.8	12.8	12.8	11.4	9.4	6.4	3.7	6.4
Return on Equity Before Income Taxes 47	17.9	•	28.0	•	21.5	22.7	23.1	19.9	16.0	12.0	•	3.4	20.2
Return on Equity After Income Taxes 48	12.3	•	28.0	•	19.1	22.2	21.4	17.8	13.7	7.0	•	2.5	12.5
Profit Margin (Before Income Tax) 49	3.5	1.1	•	•	5.9	2.4	5.0	4.5	4.7	4.3	4.3	2.3	3.3
Profit Margin (After Income Tax) 50	2.4	•	•	•	5.9	2.1	4.9	4.2	4.2	3.7	2.5	1.7	2.1

Table II

Corporations with Net Income

ANIMAL FOOD AND GRAIN AND OILSEED MILLING

MONEY AMOUNTS AND SIZE OF ASSETS IN THOUSANDS OF DOLLARS

Item Description for Accounting Period 7/10 Through 6/11	Total	Zero Assets	Under 500	500 to 1,000	1,000 to 5,000	5,000 to 10,000	10,000 to 25,000	25,000 to 50,000	50,000 to 100,000	100,000 to 250,000	250,000 to 500,000	500,000 to 2,500,000	2,500,000 and over
Number of Enterprises **1**	788	•	288	0	•	72	88	•	18	25	6	•	•
Revenues ($ in Thousands)													
Net Sales **2**	113354307	•	1997	0	•	1384399	3475984	•	3252711	7568367	2236835	•	•
Interest **3**	211378	•	0	0	•	308	1531	•	211	2056	9699	•	•
Rents **4**	200594	•	0	0	•	457	82	•	22	648	1134	•	•
Royalties **5**	423173	•	0	0	•	0	0	•	0	117	2518	•	•
Other Portfolio Income **6**	547670	•	0	0	•	40	2142	•	652	42918	21707	•	•
Other Receipts **7**	2461042	•	0	0	•	5006	47984	•	28196	50318	13877	•	•
Total Receipts **8**	117798164	•	1997	0	•	1390210	3527723	•	3281792	7664424	2285770	•	•
Average Total Receipts **9**	148729	•	7	•	•	19308	40088	•	182322	306577	380962	•	•
Operating Costs/Operating Income (%)													
Cost of Operations **10**	80.9	•	42.5	•	•	87.9	83.0	•	80.1	81.7	72.2	•	•
Salaries and Wages **11**	2.7	•	9.4	•	•	2.1	3.4	•	3.9	2.7	4.1	•	•
Taxes Paid **12**	0.6	•	10.6	•	•	0.6	0.6	•	0.9	0.6	1.1	•	•
Interest Paid **13**	1.4	•	0.8	•	•	0.2	0.3	•	0.4	0.7	0.9	•	•
Depreciation **14**	2.2	•	3.9	•	•	0.6	2.0	•	1.7	2.2	3.4	•	•
Amortization and Depletion **15**	0.2	•	•	•	•	0.1	0.0	•	0.1	0.2	0.6	•	•
Pensions and Other Deferred Comp. **16**	0.7	•	•	•	•	0.2	0.2	•	0.3	0.3	0.5	•	•
Employee Benefits **17**	0.8	•	0.4	•	•	0.4	0.5	•	0.8	0.9	0.8	•	•
Advertising **18**	5.8	•	0.9	•	•	0.7	0.1	•	1.0	0.5	0.8	•	•
Other Expenses **19**	4.1	•	26.6	•	•	3.1	4.4	•	4.9	5.0	8.1	•	•
Officers' Compensation **20**	0.4	•	•	•	•	1.1	1.1	•	0.7	0.7	2.1	•	•
Operating Margin **21**	0.3	•	5.0	•	•	2.9	4.3	•	5.3	4.5	5.5	•	•
Operating Margin Before Officers' Comp. **22**	0.7	•	5.0	•	•	4.0	5.4	•	6.0	5.1	7.6	•	•

Selected Average Balance Sheet ($ in Thousands)

Net Receivables 23	9101	0	2323	4100	17372	32320	70803
Inventories 24	13528	17	1039	2990	18193	31577	48632
Net Property, Plant and Equipment 25	19607	1	665	4293	16989	45602	87644
Total Assets 26	103166	2	6201	15325	68113	163244	316580
Notes and Loans Payable 27	45345	1	675	2982	14064	41916	93161
All Other Liabilities 28	28899	59	2330	3844	18635	36909	63345
Net Worth 29	28922	-58	3196	8500	35414	84418	159474

Selected Financial Ratios (Times to 1)

Current Ratio 30	1.2	0.0	1.9	1.8	2.2	1.8	1.5
Quick Ratio 31	0.4	0.0	1.5	1.0	1.1	0.9	0.9
Net Sales to Working Capital 32	20.2	•	7.8	9.2	7.3	7.9	7.6
Coverage Ratio 33	4.1	7.7	14.6	21.4	17.5	9.5	10.3
Total Asset Turnover 34	1.4	3.7	3.1	2.6	2.7	1.9	1.2
Inventory Turnover 35	8.6	0.2	16.3	11.0	8.0	7.8	5.5
Receivables Turnover 36	17.0	1.0	8.2	11.0	•	10.5	•
Total Liabilities to Net Worth 37	2.6	•	0.9	0.8	0.9	0.9	1.0
Current Assets to Working Capital 38	5.1	•	2.1	2.3	1.8	2.2	2.9
Current Liabilities to Working Capital 39	4.1	•	1.1	1.3	0.8	1.2	1.9
Working Capital to Net Sales 40	0.0	•	0.1	0.1	0.1	0.1	0.1
Inventory to Working Capital 41	2.2	•	0.4	0.9	0.7	0.9	1.0
Total Receipts to Cash Flow 42	15.8	3.8	17.2	10.7	10.4	10.8	7.0
Cost of Goods to Cash Flow 43	12.8	1.6	15.2	8.9	8.4	8.9	5.1
Cash Flow to Total Debt 44	0.1	0.0	0.4	0.5	0.5	0.4	0.3

Selected Financial Factors (in Percentages)

Debt Ratio 45	72.0	3223.8	48.5	44.5	48.0	48.3	49.6
Return on Total Assets 46	7.8	21.7	11.1	15.7	17.5	12.0	10.6
Return on Equity Before Income Taxes 47	20.9	•	20.0	26.9	31.8	20.8	19.0
Return on Equity After Income Taxes 48	15.1	•	18.1	26.5	28.7	18.1	13.0
Profit Margin (Before Income Tax) 49	4.2	5.1	3.3	5.8	6.2	5.8	8.1
Profit Margin (After Income Tax) 50	3.0	5.0	3.0	5.7	5.6	5.1	5.6

Table I

Corporations with and without Net Income

SUGAR AND CONFECTIONERY PRODUCT

MONEY AMOUNTS AND SIZE OF ASSETS IN THOUSANDS OF DOLLARS

Item Description for Accounting Period 7/10 Through 6/11	Total	Zero Assets	Under 500	500 to 1,000	1,000 to 5,000	5,000 to 10,000	10,000 to 25,000	25,000 to 50,000	50,000 to 100,000	100,000 to 250,000	250,000 to 500,000	500,000 to 2,500,000	2,500,000 and over
Number of Enterprises **1**	1185	9	792	194	67	43	31	18	12	7	4	6	3
Revenues ($ in Thousands)													
Net Sales **2**	60228481	1039015	856803	283377	127637	564511	1213050	1353867	1681120	1190511	2544105	5742072	43632414
Interest **3**	115280	19016	0	0	21	534	334	168	285	250	144	7921	86607
Rents **4**	47761	0	0	0	0	421	15	4929	0	1931	5	22645	17815
Royalties **5**	406028	110687	0	0	0	0	12065	1285	23	426	2643	4788	274112
Other Portfolio Income **6**	1365325	0	0	0	0	117	107	2721	121	124	325	213780	1148032
Other Receipts **7**	249864	0	0	990	665	226	3734	4401	5334	4736	-399	11496	218675
Total Receipts **8**	62412739	1168718	856803	284367	128323	565809	1229305	1367371	1686883	1197978	2546823	6002702	45377655
Average Total Receipts **9**	52669	129858	1082	1466	1915	13158	39655	75965	140574	171140	636706	1000450	15125885
Operating Costs/Operating Income (%)													
Cost of Operations **10**	53.4	42.5	60.3	59.0	64.3	63.8	75.1	78.9	66.8	67.8	72.1	75.9	47.0
Salaries and Wages **11**	5.7	12.6	7.7	16.4	1.4	7.1	5.3	2.7	7.6	5.5	4.9	2.1	6.0
Taxes Paid **12**	1.2	1.0	6.4	1.6	3.5	2.0	1.5	1.0	1.2	1.2	1.3	0.7	1.1
Interest Paid **13**	3.8	6.5	0.5	1.2	0.3	1.1	0.6	0.7	0.9	2.6	1.4	0.9	4.6
Depreciation **14**	3.0	2.6	0.0	2.3	0.7	3.9	1.3	3.0	1.8	4.7	3.2	4.0	2.9
Amortization and Depletion **15**	1.6	14.5	•	•	0.0	0.6	0.0	0.1	0.3	1.8	0.3	0.9	1.6
Pensions and Other Deferred Comp. **16**	0.7	5.5	•	3.8	0.6	0.6	0.6	0.2	0.6	0.4	0.3	0.6	0.7
Employee Benefits **17**	1.2	2.5	•	•	0.4	0.5	0.9	0.3	2.3	1.0	1.0	1.8	1.2
Advertising **18**	6.3	16.1	1.5	0.4	0.1	1.4	0.7	0.3	3.7	2.1	3.2	0.8	7.8
Other Expenses **19**	19.2	8.4	15.0	12.0	9.9	15.4	9.2	7.6	11.4	10.5	10.2	9.2	22.7
Officers' Compensation **20**	0.8	1.8	1.1	3.0	17.6	3.6	1.8	2.0	1.1	1.2	0.9	0.6	0.6
Operating Margin **21**	3.1	•	7.5	0.1	•	0.1	3.1	3.2	2.2	1.2	1.2	2.4	3.8
Operating Margin Before Officers' Comp. **22**	3.9	•	8.6	3.1	17.4	3.7	4.9	5.2	3.4	2.4	2.1	3.0	4.4

Selected Average Balance Sheet ($ in Thousands)

Net Receivables 23	8332	0	16	187	263	1527	2838	6652	13828	17287	74994	66975	2848111
Inventories 24	4204	0	58	311	398	1092	4999	6587	27582	25975	116336	129315	955084
Net Property, Plant and Equipment 25	9865	0	3	219	201	3028	3961	13971	17596	39997	131575	308056	2753848
Total Assets 26	82025	0	112	764	1088	7554	15675	35564	69328	130237	405424	1001506	28668045
Notes and Loans Payable 27	35983	0	0	467	328	2525	4576	9532	21285	78106	183991	180858	13160521
All Other Liabilities 28	26831	0	50	152	88	1754	4539	8648	19601	28967	127779	287067	9558957
Net Worth 29	19211	0	63	145	672	3275	6560	17384	28441	23165	93654	533580	5968567

Selected Financial Ratios (Times to 1)

Current Ratio 30	1.0	•	2.2	2.5	3.3	2.2	2.1	1.9	2.1	0.8	2.1	1.5	0.9
Quick Ratio 31	0.5	•	1.1	0.9	2.0	1.4	0.9	0.9	1.0	0.4	1.0	0.5	0.5
Net Sales to Working Capital 32	•	•	18.7	4.6	3.1	7.3	7.1	8.2	6.3	•	5.0	8.2	•
Coverage Ratio 33	4.2	0.8	17.5	1.4	2.2	1.3	8.8	7.1	3.7	3.1	1.9	9.0	4.2
Total Asset Turnover 34	0.6	•	9.6	1.9	1.8	1.7	2.5	2.1	2.0	1.3	1.6	1.0	0.5
Inventory Turnover 35	6.5	•	11.3	2.8	3.1	7.7	5.9	9.0	3.4	4.4	3.9	5.6	7.2
Receivables Turnover 36	7.5	•	41.8	8.2	4.2	8.8	14.6	12.9	7.7	19.7	10.2	10.7	6.5
Total Liabilities to Net Worth 37	3.3	•	0.8	4.3	0.6	1.3	1.4	1.0	1.4	4.6	3.3	0.9	3.8
Current Assets to Working Capital 38	•	•	1.9	1.7	1.4	1.8	1.9	2.1	1.9	•	1.9	2.9	•
Current Liabilities to Working Capital 39	•	•	0.9	0.7	0.4	0.8	0.9	1.1	0.9	•	0.9	1.9	•
Working Capital to Net Sales 40	•	•	0.1	0.2	0.3	0.1	0.1	0.1	0.2	•	0.2	0.1	•
Inventory to Working Capital 41	•	•	0.9	1.1	0.6	0.6	1.1	0.8	0.9	•	0.9	1.1	•
Total Receipts to Cash Flow 42	4.2	19.2	5.9	11.6	19.8	8.1	8.7	10.1	7.8	10.0	10.0	9.2	3.5
Cost of Goods to Cash Flow 43	2.2	8.2	3.6	6.9	12.7	5.2	6.5	7.9	5.2	6.8	7.2	7.0	1.6
Cash Flow to Total Debt 44	0.2	•	3.7	0.2	0.2	0.4	0.5	0.4	0.4	0.2	0.2	0.2	0.2

Selected Financial Factors (in Percentages)

Debt Ratio 45	76.6	•	44.2	81.1	38.2	56.6	58.2	51.1	59.0	82.2	76.9	46.7	79.2
Return on Total Assets 46	9.7	•	76.5	3.2	1.0	2.5	12.4	10.5	7.1	10.4	4.3	8.0	9.9
Return on Equity Before Income Taxes 47	31.7	•	129.2	4.5	0.9	1.3	26.3	18.5	12.8	39.5	9.0	13.4	36.2
Return on Equity After Income Taxes 48	21.0	•	129.2	4.5	0.6		24.0	16.9	11.4	33.5	8.5	9.1	23.6
Profit Margin (Before Income Tax) 49	12.0	•	7.5	0.4	0.4	0.3	4.4	4.3	2.6	5.4	1.3	7.5	14.8
Profit Margin (After Income Tax) 50	8.0	•	7.5	0.4	0.2	•	4.0	3.9	2.3	4.6	1.3	5.1	9.7

Table II
Corporations with Net Income

SUGAR AND CONFECTIONERY PRODUCT

MONEY AMOUNTS AND SIZE OF ASSETS IN THOUSANDS OF DOLLARS

Item Description for Accounting Period 7/10 Through 6/11	Total	Zero Assets	Under 500	500 to 1,000	1,000 to 5,000	5,000 to 10,000	10,000 to 25,000	25,000 to 50,000	50,000 to 100,000	100,000 to 250,000	250,000 to 500,000	500,000 to 2,500,000	2,500,000 and over
Number of Enterprises 1	1051	0	792	129	33	33	21	•	•	•	•	•	3
Revenues ($ in Thousands)													
Net Sales 2	55742650	0	856803	160223	82457	478467	866658	•	•	•	•	•	43632414
Interest 3	95071	0	0	0	0	534	155	•	•	•	•	•	86607
Rents 4	47756	0	0	0	0	421	15	•	•	•	•	•	17815
Royalties 5	292928	0	0	0	0	0	12065	•	•	•	•	•	274112
Other Portfolio Income 6	1364779	0	0	0	0	117	15	•	•	•	•	•	1148032
Other Receipts 7	245122	0	0	0	0	226	1597	•	•	•	•	•	218675
Total Receipts 8	57788306	0	856803	160223	82457	479765	880505	•	•	•	•	•	45377655
Average Total Receipts 9	54984	•	1082	1242	2499	14538	41929	•	•	•	•	•	15125885
Operating Costs/Operating Income (%)													
Cost of Operations 10	52.0	•	60.3	51.8	79.9	65.9	76.3	•	•	•	•	•	47.0
Salaries and Wages 11	5.7	•	7.7	18.8	2.2	6.5	4.6	•	•	•	•	•	6.0
Taxes Paid 12	1.2	•	6.4	2.5	3.2	2.1	1.1	•	•	•	•	•	1.1
Interest Paid 13	3.9	•	0.5	1.1	0.4	1.1	0.4	•	•	•	•	•	4.6
Depreciation 14	3.0	•	0.0	1.1	0.2	4.3	1.1	•	•	•	•	•	2.9
Amortization and Depletion 15	1.3	•	•	•	•	0.0	0.0	•	•	•	•	•	1.6
Pensions and Other Deferred Comp. 16	0.6	•	•	6.8	•	0.7	0.4	•	•	•	•	•	0.7
Employee Benefits 17	1.2	•	•	•	0.5	0.6	0.8	•	•	•	•	•	1.2
Advertising 18	6.4	•	1.5	0.8	•	1.6	0.9	•	•	•	•	•	7.8
Other Expenses 19	20.1	•	15.0	13.3	9.4	9.7	8.0	•	•	•	•	•	22.7
Officers' Compensation 20	0.7	•	1.1	1.8	2.9	4.2	1.7	•	•	•	•	•	0.6
Operating Margin 21	3.9	•	7.5	2.0	1.2	3.4	4.7	•	•	•	•	•	3.8
Operating Margin Before Officers' Comp. 22	4.6	•	8.6	3.8	4.1	7.5	6.4	•	•	•	•	•	4.4

Selected Average Balance Sheet ($ in Thousands)

Net Receivables 23	9104	•	16	220	453	1656	2288	•	•	•	•	2844111
Inventories 24	4114	•	26	389	695	1406	4492	•	•	•	•	975876
Net Property, Plant and Equipment 25	10636	•	3	145	174	2650	4124	•	•	•	•	2753848
Total Assets 26	90378	•	112	772	1106	8112	14868	•	•	•	•	28688045
Notes and Loans Payable 27	39887	•	0	613	665	3178	2583	•	•	•	•	13160521
All Other Liabilities 28	29535	•	50	73	94	1354	3713	•	•	•	•	9558957
Net Worth 29	20957	•	63	86	347	3580	8572	•	•	•	•	5968567

Selected Financial Ratios (Times to 1)

Current Ratio 30	1.0	•	2.2	4.2	2.0	4.3	2.9	•	•	•	•	0.9
Quick Ratio 31	0.5	•	1.1	1.5	1.0	2.5	1.3	•	•	•	•	0.5
Net Sales to Working Capital 32	•	•	18.7	2.7	5.3	4.9	6.5	•	•	•	•	•
Coverage Ratio 33	4.4	•	17.5	2.7	3.8	4.4	15.3	•	•	•	•	4.2
Total Asset Turnover 34	0.6	•	9.6	1.6	2.3	1.8	2.8	•	•	•	•	0.5
Inventory Turnover 35	6.7	•	25.3	1.7	2.9	6.8	7.0	•	•	•	•	7.0
Receivables Turnover 36	7.2	•	125.6	•	2.9	9.5	15.1	•	•	•	•	•
Total Liabilities to Net Worth 37	3.3	•	0.8	8.0	2.2	1.3	0.7	•	•	•	•	3.8
Current Assets to Working Capital 38	•	•	1.9	1.3	2.0	1.3	1.5	•	•	•	•	•
Current Liabilities to Working Capital 39	•	•	0.9	0.3	1.0	0.3	0.5	•	•	•	•	•
Working Capital to Net Sales 40	•	•	0.1	0.4	0.2	0.2	0.2	•	•	•	•	•
Inventory to Working Capital 41	•	•	0.9	0.8	1.0	0.5	0.8	•	•	•	•	•
Total Receipts to Cash Flow 42	3.9	•	5.9	10.5	35.0	9.8	7.5	•	•	•	•	3.5
Cost of Goods to Cash Flow 43	2.0	•	3.6	5.5	28.0	6.5	5.7	•	•	•	•	1.6
Cash Flow to Total Debt 44	0.2	•	3.7	0.2	0.1	0.3	0.9	•	•	•	•	0.2

Selected Financial Factors (in Percentages)

Debt Ratio 45	76.8	•	44.2	88.9	68.6	55.9	42.3	•	•	•	•	79.2
Return on Total Assets 46	10.0	•	76.5	5.0	3.7	8.4	18.7	•	•	•	•	9.9
Return on Equity Before Income Taxes 47	33.3	•	129.2	28.5	8.8	14.8	30.3	•	•	•	•	36.2
Return on Equity After Income Taxes 48	22.3	•	129.2	28.5	7.7	9.9	27.7	•	•	•	•	23.6
Profit Margin (Before Income Tax) 49	13.1	•	7.5	2.0	1.2	3.6	6.3	•	•	•	•	14.8
Profit Margin (After Income Tax) 50	8.8	•	7.5	2.0	1.1	2.4	5.7	•	•	•	•	9.7

Table I

Corporations with and without Net Income

FRUIT AND VEGETABLE PRESERVING AND SPECIALTY FOOD

MONEY AMOUNTS AND SIZE OF ASSETS IN THOUSANDS OF DOLLARS

Item Description for Accounting Period 7/10 Through 6/11	Total	Zero Assets	Under 500	500 to 1,000	1,000 to 5,000	5,000 to 10,000	10,000 to 25,000	25,000 to 50,000	50,000 to 100,000	100,000 to 250,000	250,000 to 500,000	500,000 to 2,500,000	2,500,000 and over
Number of Enterprises **1**	588	•	•	0	•	100	109	43	26	25	7	4	8
Revenues ($ in Thousands)													
Net Sales **2**	50856204	•	•	0	•	1802175	3218835	2173180	2934293	5740850	4229153	6827924	21714490
Interest **3**	109194	•	•	0	•	0	884	822	1734	1737	14378	6709	82902
Rents **4**	18804	•	•	0	•	0	48	478	3277	2131	1239	2985	6643
Royalties **5**	262893	•	•	0	•	0	0	0	0	0	0	6	262875
Other Portfolio Income **6**	363505	•	•	0	•	24176	347	1651	2399	898	344	2771	330874
Other Receipts **7**	1362476	•	•	0	•	50257	12572	16309	20707	29014	8852	61010	1162811
Total Receipts **8**	52973076	•	•	0	•	1876608	3232686	2192440	2962410	5774630	4253966	6901405	23560595
Average Total Receipts **9**	90090	•	•	•	•	18766	29658	50987	113939	230985	607709	1725351	2945074
Operating Costs/Operating Income (%)													
Cost of Operations **10**	67.5	•	•	•	•	71.5	70.6	76.4	79.3	77.6	77.3	54.9	62.4
Salaries and Wages **11**	4.9	•	•	•	•	3.2	6.5	4.2	2.7	3.8	2.2	9.2	4.9
Taxes Paid **12**	1.1	•	•	•	•	1.2	1.3	1.1	1.1	1.2	1.3	1.4	0.8
Interest Paid **13**	2.1	•	•	•	•	0.2	1.0	1.0	1.2	0.7	1.7	1.2	3.4
Depreciation **14**	3.5	•	•	•	•	3.6	3.3	3.2	2.9	3.1	4.0	2.8	4.1
Amortization and Depletion **15**	1.0	•	•	•	•	0.4	0.1	0.1	0.3	0.1	0.2	1.0	1.7
Pensions and Other Deferred Comp. **16**	0.6	•	•	•	•	0.0	0.3	0.1	0.3	0.4	0.1	0.2	1.2
Employee Benefits **17**	1.3	•	•	•	•	2.1	1.0	0.8	0.9	1.2	0.8	2.7	1.1
Advertising **18**	2.7	•	•	•	•	0.2	2.9	1.7	0.9	0.8	1.6	8.9	2.4
Other Expenses **19**	12.9	•	•	•	•	12.8	8.1	8.5	8.3	7.4	9.1	15.0	17.0
Officers' Compensation **20**	0.9	•	•	•	•	0.4	1.3	1.2	0.7	0.8	0.2	0.4	1.0
Operating Margin **21**	1.5	•	•	•	•	4.4	3.7	1.7	1.4	2.8	1.6	2.4	0.1
Operating Margin Before Officers' Comp. **22**	2.4	•	•	•	•	4.8	5.0	2.9	2.1	3.6	1.8	2.7	1.0

Selected Average Balance Sheet ($ in Thousands)

Net Receivables **23**	13180	884	3527	5377	10436	22600	42147	88347	672617
Inventories **24**	14111	749	5204	11061	22319	50211	109794	298804	405577
Net Property, Plant and Equipment **25**	17702	1210	5135	10349	22084	37870	118241	343301	664679
Total Assets **26**	136212	8134	16445	33843	69279	152921	358745	1030224	7878096
Notes and Loans Payable **27**	33674	475	5341	12834	23737	34908	90952	299514	1881759
All Other Liabilities **28**	29199	1325	5211	5405	14319	45282	118981	285010	1570705
Net Worth **29**	73339	6334	5893	15604	31223	72731	148812	445700	4425633

Selected Financial Ratios (Times to 1)

Current Ratio **30**	1.6	2.9	1.7	2.1	1.7	2.0	1.3	1.9	1.5
Quick Ratio **31**	0.8	1.1	0.7	0.8	0.7	0.6	0.4	0.9	0.8
Net Sales to Working Capital **32**	6.6	7.0	6.9	5.0	7.7	4.9	11.2	7.8	6.0
Coverage Ratio **33**	3.8	34.8	5.0	3.5	3.0	5.8	2.3	4.0	3.7
Total Asset Turnover **34**	0.6	2.2	1.8	1.5	1.6	1.5	1.7	1.7	0.3
Inventory Turnover **35**	4.1	17.2	4.0	3.5	4.0	3.6	4.3	3.1	4.2
Receivables Turnover **36**	7.4	32.9	9.5	8.8	10.4	12.6	15.0	12.2	4.9
Total Liabilities to Net Worth **37**	0.9	0.3	1.8	1.2	1.2	1.1	1.4	1.3	0.8
Current Assets to Working Capital **38**	2.6	1.5	2.4	1.9	2.4	2.0	4.0	2.1	3.0
Current Liabilities to Working Capital **39**	1.6	0.5	1.4	0.9	1.4	1.0	3.0	1.1	2.0
Working Capital to Net Sales **40**	0.2	0.1	0.1	0.2	0.1	0.2	0.1	0.1	0.2
Inventory to Working Capital **41**	1.1	0.5	1.3	1.1	1.3	1.3	2.1	1.0	1.0
Total Receipts to Cash Flow **42**	6.2	5.1	10.5	11.1	11.1	11.9	10.5	6.4	4.4
Cost of Goods to Cash Flow **43**	4.2	3.7	7.4	8.5	8.8	9.2	8.1	3.5	2.7
Cash Flow to Total Debt **44**	0.2	2.0	0.3	0.3	0.3	0.2	0.3	0.5	0.2

Selected Financial Factors (in Percentages)

Debt Ratio **45**	46.2	22.1	64.2	53.9	54.9	52.4	58.5	56.7	43.8
Return on Total Assets **46**	5.0	16.4	9.2	5.3	5.9	6.3	6.6	7.6	4.3
Return on Equity Before Income Taxes **47**	6.8	20.5	20.6	8.3	8.6	10.9	8.9	13.2	5.5
Return on Equity After Income Taxes **48**	4.8	20.5	20.1	7.1	6.5	9.8	5.9	9.8	3.5
Profit Margin (Before Income Tax) **49**	5.8	7.2	4.1	2.5	2.4	3.4	2.2	3.4	9.0
Profit Margin (After Income Tax) **50**	4.1	7.2	4.0	2.2	1.8	3.1	1.4	2.6	5.7

41

Table II
Corporations with Net Income

FRUIT AND VEGETABLE PRESERVING AND SPECIALTY FOOD

MONEY AMOUNTS AND SIZE OF ASSETS IN THOUSANDS OF DOLLARS

Item Description for Accounting Period 7/10 Through 6/11	Total	Zero Assets	Under 500	500 to 1,000	1,000 to 5,000	5,000 to 10,000	10,000 to 25,000	25,000 to 50,000	50,000 to 100,000	100,000 to 250,000	250,000 to 500,000	500,000 to 2,500,000	2,500,000 and over
Number of Enterprises 1	481	•	0	•	•	96	90	28	14	20	•	4	5
Revenues ($ in Thousands)													
Net Sales 2	40294442	•	0	0	•	1758783	2930686	1587747	1907097	4588604	•	6827924	15770449
Interest 3	101527	•	0	0	•	0	568	747	947	1269	•	6709	77204
Rents 4	15221	•	0	0	•	0	48	330	2925	1983	•	2985	5698
Royalties 5	258442	•	0	0	•	0	0	0	0	0	•	6	258436
Other Portfolio Income 6	362402	•	0	0	•	24176	200	1621	2225	227	•	2771	330874
Other Receipts 7	1317198	•	0	0	•	50258	5022	15845	10220	15543	•	61010	1156083
Total Receipts 8	42349232	•	0	0	•	1833217	2936524	1606290	1923414	4607626	•	6901405	17598744
Average Total Receipts 9	88044	•	•	•	•	19096	32628	57368	137387	230381	•	1725351	3519749
Operating Costs/Operating Income (%)													
Cost of Operations 10	65.4	•	•	•	•	70.4	69.9	75.6	76.7	76.7	•	54.9	59.5
Salaries and Wages 11	4.9	•	•	•	•	3.1	6.7	3.9	1.9	3.9	•	9.2	4.5
Taxes Paid 12	1.2	•	•	•	•	1.3	1.2	1.2	1.0	1.1	•	1.4	1.0
Interest Paid 13	1.6	•	•	•	•	0.2	0.9	1.1	0.6	0.8	•	1.2	2.5
Depreciation 14	3.6	•	•	•	•	3.7	3.0	2.9	2.5	2.9	•	2.8	4.6
Amortization and Depletion 15	0.7	•	•	•	•	0.4	0.2	0.0	0.1	0.1	•	1.0	1.1
Pensions and Other Deferred Comp. 16	0.7	•	•	•	•	0.0	0.3	0.2	0.3	0.3	•	0.2	1.4
Employee Benefits 17	1.5	•	•	•	•	2.2	0.9	0.9	0.8	1.2	•	2.7	1.4
Advertising 18	3.1	•	•	•	•	0.2	3.2	1.6	0.9	0.6	•	8.9	2.5
Other Expenses 19	13.8	•	•	•	•	13.0	7.4	7.0	8.8	7.3	•	15.0	19.9
Officers' Compensation 20	0.7	•	•	•	•	0.3	1.2	1.4	0.7	0.8	•	0.4	0.8
Operating Margin 21	2.9	•	•	•	•	5.3	5.1	4.1	5.7	4.4	•	2.4	0.9
Operating Margin Before Officers' Comp. 22	3.7	•	•	•	•	5.6	6.4	5.5	6.4	5.1	•	2.7	1.7

Selected Average Balance Sheet ($ in Thousands)

Item									
Net Receivables	23	13567	843	3286	6785	12332	21112	88347	924563
Inventories	24	13216	696	4947	12624	30835	61284	298804	374026
Net Property, Plant and Equipment	25	15648	1252	5070	8246	19931	35112	343301	711087
Total Assets	26	125894	8244	17152	34650	71557	146997	1030224	9349209
Notes and Loans Payable	27	21898	342	4993	13355	18953	35984	299514	1389555
All Other Liabilities	28	25971	1284	4876	5270	14026	46395	285010	1749220
Net Worth	29	78025	6619	7282	16025	38579	64618	445700	6210434

Selected Financial Ratios (Times to 1)

Item									
Current Ratio	30	1.5	3.0	1.9	2.1	2.1	2.1	1.9	1.3
Quick Ratio	31	0.8	1.1	0.7	0.8	1.0	0.6	0.9	0.8
Net Sales to Working Capital	32	7.6	7.2	6.1	4.5	6.2	4.8	7.8	9.4
Coverage Ratio	33	6.3	49.0	7.1	5.8	12.2	7.2	4.0	6.3
Total Asset Turnover	34	0.7	2.2	1.9	1.6	1.9	1.6	1.7	0.3
Inventory Turnover	35	4.1	18.5	4.6	3.4	3.4	2.9	3.1	5.0
Receivables Turnover	36	6.7	35.6	12.8	8.0	9.0	•	12.2	•
Total Liabilities to Net Worth	37	0.6	0.2	1.4	1.2	0.9	1.3	1.3	0.5
Current Assets to Working Capital	38	2.8	1.5	2.1	1.9	1.9	1.9	2.1	4.5
Current Liabilities to Working Capital	39	1.8	0.5	1.1	0.9	0.9	0.9	1.1	3.5
Working Capital to Net Sales	40	0.1	0.1	0.2	0.2	0.2	0.2	0.1	0.1
Inventory to Working Capital	41	1.1	0.4	1.2	1.0	0.9	1.3	1.0	1.1
Total Receipts to Cash Flow	42	5.2	4.8	9.7	9.7	7.3	10.3	6.4	3.4
Cost of Goods to Cash Flow	43	3.4	3.4	6.8	7.3	5.6	7.9	3.5	2.0
Cash Flow to Total Debt	44	0.3	2.3	0.3	0.3	0.6	0.3	0.5	0.3

Selected Financial Factors (in Percentages)

Item									
Debt Ratio	45	38.0	19.7	57.5	53.8	46.1	56.0	56.7	33.6
Return on Total Assets	46	6.5	18.5	11.8	10.4	13.6	8.7	7.6	5.2
Return on Equity Before Income Taxes	47	8.8	22.5	23.9	18.7	23.2	17.2	13.2	6.6
Return on Equity After Income Taxes	48	6.5	22.5	23.4	17.0	20.1	15.7	9.8	4.3
Profit Margin (Before Income Tax)	49	8.2	8.1	5.3	5.3	6.6	4.8	3.4	13.1
Profit Margin (After Income Tax)	50	6.1	8.1	5.2	4.8	5.7	4.4	2.6	8.5

Table I
Corporations with and without Net Income

DAIRY PRODUCT

MONEY AMOUNTS AND SIZE OF ASSETS IN THOUSANDS OF DOLLARS

Item Description for Accounting Period 7/10 Through 6/11	Total	Zero Assets	Under 500	500 to 1,000	1,000 to 5,000	5,000 to 10,000	10,000 to 25,000	25,000 to 50,000	50,000 to 100,000	100,000 to 250,000	250,000 to 500,000	500,000 to 2,500,000	2,500,000 and over
Number of Enterprises 1	1189	•	•	•	•	81	53	37	17	20	5	10	0

Revenues ($ in Thousands)

Item Description for Accounting Period 7/10 Through 6/11	Total	Zero Assets	Under 500	500 to 1,000	1,000 to 5,000	5,000 to 10,000	10,000 to 25,000	25,000 to 50,000	50,000 to 100,000	100,000 to 250,000	250,000 to 500,000	500,000 to 2,500,000	2,500,000 and over
Net Sales 2	49120428	•	•	•	•	1293926	2552205	3635682	2688644	5172975	4062028	27735787	0
Interest 3	27257	•	•	•	•	177	1236	2088	1643	3088	9	18304	0
Rents 4	7560	•	•	•	•	128	982	124	3378	1180	72	1696	0
Royalties 5	97189	•	•	•	•	0	0	900	3030	0	0	93258	0
Other Portfolio Income 6	131730	•	•	•	•	9465	454	2491	1026	4566	287	107807	0
Other Receipts 7	345628	•	•	•	•	23672	1474	12107	26227	16944	15338	223740	0
Total Receipts 8	49729792	•	•	•	•	1327368	2556351	3653392	2723948	5198753	4077734	28180592	0
Average Total Receipts 9	41825	•	•	•	•	16387	48233	98740	160232	259938	815547	2818059	•

Operating Costs/Operating Income (%)

Item Description for Accounting Period 7/10 Through 6/11	Total	Zero Assets	Under 500	500 to 1,000	1,000 to 5,000	5,000 to 10,000	10,000 to 25,000	25,000 to 50,000	50,000 to 100,000	100,000 to 250,000	250,000 to 500,000	500,000 to 2,500,000	2,500,000 and over
Cost of Operations 10	76.4	•	•	•	•	85.3	80.1	77.0	74.4	77.6	75.7	75.4	•
Salaries and Wages 11	4.6	•	•	•	•	2.5	4.6	4.9	4.9	4.0	4.0	4.8	•
Taxes Paid 12	1.0	•	•	•	•	1.3	1.1	1.2	1.0	0.9	0.9	1.0	•
Interest Paid 13	1.2	•	•	•	•	0.4	0.5	0.6	0.6	1.0	0.8	1.6	•
Depreciation 14	3.2	•	•	•	•	1.3	1.8	2.2	3.2	3.6	3.5	3.5	•
Amortization and Depletion 15	0.5	•	•	•	•	0.0	0.0	0.1	0.1	0.3	0.4	0.7	•
Pensions and Other Deferred Comp. 16	0.5	•	•	•	•	0.2	0.3	0.5	0.4	0.3	0.6	0.6	•
Employee Benefits 17	0.8	•	•	•	•	0.6	0.5	1.0	0.9	0.8	1.4	0.7	•
Advertising 18	1.6	•	•	•	•	0.7	0.4	0.3	1.0	2.2	1.8	2.0	•
Other Expenses 19	8.2	•	•	•	•	5.5	6.7	8.4	11.0	5.4	6.4	8.8	•
Officers' Compensation 20	0.8	•	•	•	•	2.2	2.1	1.0	0.8	0.5	0.5	0.6	•
Operating Margin 21	1.2	•	•	•	•	0.0	1.7	2.8	1.6	3.5	3.9	0.3	•
Operating Margin Before Officers' Comp. 22	1.9	•	•	•	•	2.2	3.8	3.8	2.4	3.9	4.4	0.9	•

Selected Average Balance Sheet ($ in Thousands)

Net Receivables 23	3151	1605	5071	8192	16018	16340	52937	200508
Inventories 24	2500	1836	2931	4313	14061	18560	71932	143713
Net Property, Plant and Equipment 25	7720	2148	5363	11882	23788	55830	156071	576883
Total Assets 26	22963	6688	14901	34762	72897	153682	367340	1782085
Notes and Loans Payable 27	9349	1875	4341	8387	17715	55636	103811	817547
All Other Liabilities 28	7070	2101	3944	10284	24864	26838	99963	598927
Net Worth 29	6544	2713	6617	16091	30318	71208	163565	365610

Selected Financial Ratios (Times to 1)

Current Ratio 30	1.5	1.3	1.7	1.6	1.6	2.1	1.9	1.4
Quick Ratio 31	0.7	0.7	1.1	1.0	0.8	1.1	0.9	0.6
Net Sales to Working Capital 32	14.4	18.6	12.6	14.0	11.3	9.2	10.5	17.8
Coverage Ratio 33	3.1	5.7	4.6	6.8	6.0	4.9	6.7	2.4
Total Asset Turnover 34	1.8	2.4	3.2	2.8	2.2	1.7	2.2	1.6
Inventory Turnover 35	12.6	7.4	13.2	17.6	8.4	10.8	8.6	14.6
Receivables Turnover 36	14.3	•	10.0	14.1	10.7	18.6	15.7	14.5
Total Liabilities to Net Worth 37	2.5	1.5	1.3	1.2	1.4	1.2	1.2	3.9
Current Assets to Working Capital 38	2.9	4.4	2.4	2.6	2.8	1.9	2.1	3.5
Current Liabilities to Working Capital 39	1.9	3.4	1.4	1.6	1.8	0.9	1.1	2.5
Working Capital to Net Sales 40	0.1	0.1	0.1	0.1	0.1	0.1	0.1	0.1
Inventory to Working Capital 41	1.0	2.1	0.8	0.6	1.1	0.7	1.0	1.0
Total Receipts to Cash Flow 42	11.2	15.0	14.1	10.2	8.0	11.7	10.5	11.3
Cost of Goods to Cash Flow 43	8.6	12.8	11.3	7.8	5.9	9.1	7.9	8.5
Cash Flow to Total Debt 44	0.2	0.3	0.4	0.5	0.5	0.3	0.4	0.2

Selected Financial Factors (in Percentages)

Debt Ratio 45	71.5	59.4	55.6	53.7	58.4	53.7	55.5	79.5
Return on Total Assets 46	7.0	5.5	7.6	10.7	7.5	8.4	11.3	6.1
Return on Equity Before Income Taxes 47	16.6	11.1	13.5	19.7	15.1	14.4	21.5	17.5
Return on Equity After Income Taxes 48	13.5	11.0	11.5	17.5	12.8	12.9	19.7	12.9
Profit Margin (Before Income Tax) 49	2.6	1.9	1.8	3.2	2.9	4.0	4.3	2.3
Profit Margin (After Income Tax) 50	2.1	1.9	1.6	2.9	2.5	3.5	4.0	1.7

Table II
Corporations with Net Income

DAIRY PRODUCT

MONEY AMOUNTS AND SIZE OF ASSETS IN THOUSANDS OF DOLLARS

Item Description for Accounting Period 7/10 Through 6/11	Total	Zero Assets	Under 500	500 to 1,000	1,000 to 5,000	5,000 to 10,000	10,000 to 25,000	25,000 to 50,000	50,000 to 100,000	100,000 to 250,000	250,000 to 500,000	500,000 to 2,500,000	2,500,000 and over
Number of Enterprises 1	287	0	0	0	115	70	33	28	•	17	•	7	0
Revenues ($ in Thousands)													
Net Sales 2	40724502	0	0	0	1174076	1103946	1541750	2560775	•	4954172	•	23945875	0
Interest 3	14716	0	0	0	284	156	969	1940	•	3088	•	7552	0
Rents 4	3835	0	0	0	0	0	610	0	•	1125	•	1696	0
Royalties 5	96788	0	0	0	0	0	0	900	•	0	•	93063	0
Other Portfolio Income 6	129924	0	0	0	5632	9362	454	2411	•	4566	•	106495	0
Other Receipts 7	252616	0	0	0	23848	23625	991	8779	•	16761	•	139869	0
Total Receipts 8	41222381	0	0	0	1203840	1137089	1544774	2574805	•	4979712	•	24294550	0
Average Total Receipts 9	143632	•	•	•	10468	16244	46811	91957	•	292924	•	3470650	•
Operating Costs/Operating Income (%)													
Cost of Operations 10	75.8	•	•	•	81.1	84.7	74.4	78.1	•	78.4	•	74.6	•
Salaries and Wages 11	4.4	•	•	•	3.7	2.0	5.3	3.7	•	4.1	•	4.6	•
Taxes Paid 12	1.0	•	•	•	1.9	1.2	1.3	1.0	•	0.9	•	1.0	•
Interest Paid 13	1.3	•	•	•	0.5	0.5	0.3	0.6	•	0.9	•	1.7	•
Depreciation 14	3.2	•	•	•	1.4	1.2	2.0	2.1	•	3.5	•	3.5	•
Amortization and Depletion 15	0.5	•	•	•	0.0	0.0	0.0	0.1	•	0.2	•	0.8	•
Pensions and Other Deferred Comp. 16	0.5	•	•	•	0.1	0.2	0.3	0.4	•	0.3	•	0.6	•
Employee Benefits 17	0.8	•	•	•	0.7	0.7	0.3	0.6	•	0.8	•	0.7	•
Advertising 18	1.7	•	•	•	0.3	0.7	0.4	0.3	•	1.5	•	2.1	•
Other Expenses 19	7.7	•	•	•	6.1	5.3	8.2	7.1	•	5.0	•	8.6	•
Officers' Compensation 20	0.8	•	•	•	2.5	2.5	3.2	1.3	•	0.5	•	0.6	•
Operating Margin 21	2.3	•	•	•	1.8	1.0	4.1	4.8	•	4.0	•	1.1	•
Operating Margin Before Officers' Comp. 22	3.1	•	•	•	4.3	3.5	7.3	6.1	•	4.5	•	1.7	•

Selected Average Balance Sheet ($ in Thousands)

Net Receivables 23	10882	1185	1672	5609	8483	18722	246084
Inventories 24	8289	899	1269	2705	4713	23660	153747
Net Property, Plant and Equipment 25	26757	654	1970	4356	9755	59200	734073
Total Assets 26	81295	3297	6651	14505	33182	156818	2289557
Notes and Loans Payable 27	32718	639	2129	3027	8065	45616	1062171
All Other Liabilities 28	25198	1260	2137	4540	8798	29386	753733
Net Worth 29	23379	1399	2385	6938	16319	81816	473653

Selected Financial Ratios (Times to 1)

Current Ratio 30	1.6	1.8	1.2	1.8	1.9	2.3	1.4
Quick Ratio 31	0.7	1.1	0.6	1.2	1.1	1.2	0.6
Net Sales to Working Capital 32	13.0	9.5	23.0	10.7	10.2	8.5	16.7
Coverage Ratio 33	3.9	9.2	8.1	13.8	10.3	6.2	2.7
Total Asset Turnover 34	1.7	3.1	2.4	3.2	2.8	1.9	1.5
Inventory Turnover 35	13.0	9.2	10.5	12.9	15.2	9.7	16.6
Receivables Turnover 36	14.6	10.3	14.3	8.2	12.4		15.6
Total Liabilities to Net Worth 37	2.5	1.4	1.8	1.1	1.0	0.9	3.8
Current Assets to Working Capital 38	2.7	2.2	5.5	2.3	2.2	1.8	3.4
Current Liabilities to Working Capital 39	1.7	1.2	4.5	1.3	1.2	0.8	2.4
Working Capital to Net Sales 40	0.1	0.1	0.0	0.1	0.1	0.1	0.1
Inventory to Working Capital 41	0.9	0.9	2.6	0.7	0.5	0.7	1.0
Total Receipts to Cash Flow 42	10.5	13.1	12.8	9.5	9.6	11.4	10.7
Cost of Goods to Cash Flow 43	8.0	10.6	10.8	7.0	7.5	8.9	8.0
Cash Flow to Total Debt 44	0.2	0.4	0.3	0.7	0.6	0.3	0.2

Selected Financial Factors (in Percentages)

Debt Ratio 45	71.2	57.6	64.1	52.2	50.8	47.8	79.3
Return on Total Assets 46	8.8	14.9	8.6	14.9	16.2	10.1	7.1
Return on Equity Before Income Taxes 47	22.7	31.3	21.1	28.9	29.8	16.2	21.9
Return on Equity After Income Taxes 48	19.1	28.6	20.9	25.9	27.0	14.6	16.8
Profit Margin (Before Income Tax) 49	3.7	4.3	3.2	4.3	5.3	4.5	3.0
Profit Margin (After Income Tax) 50	3.1	3.9	3.2	3.9	4.8	4.1	2.3

Table I

Corporations with and without Net Income

MEAT AND SEAFOOD PROCESSING

MONEY AMOUNTS AND SIZE OF ASSETS IN THOUSANDS OF DOLLARS

Item Description for Accounting Period 7/10 Through 6/11	Total	Zero Assets	Under 500	500 to 1,000	1,000 to 5,000	5,000 to 10,000	10,000 to 25,000	25,000 to 50,000	50,000 to 100,000	100,000 to 250,000	250,000 to 500,000	500,000 to 2,500,000	2,500,000 and over
Number of Enterprises **1**	3470	19	2444	130	513	83	127	65	39	25	12	9	4
Revenues ($ in Thousands)													
Net Sales **2**	123335687	685831	1702234	253400	4734237	2471972	7791808	7970623	7403690	10153310	8378444	12846910	58943227
Interest **3**	97528	4	1	296	584	14	2461	1138	544	3721	7905	15237	65623
Rents **4**	23591	0	404	288	220	0	854	741	449	1615	7091	997	10931
Royalties **5**	14842	0	0	0	0	0	0	24	100	0	0	161	14557
Other Portfolio Income **6**	448612	63140	0	1133	88	0	1300	4125	35600	1781	13981	52179	275285
Other Receipts **7**	791401	9183	377	477	162568	3889	24083	15883	30448	33899	12219	94921	403455
Total Receipts **8**	124711661	758158	1703016	255594	4897697	2475875	7820506	7992534	7470831	10194326	8419640	13010405	59713078
Average Total Receipts **9**	35940	39903	697	1966	9547	29830	61579	122962	191560	407773	701637	1445601	14928270
Operating Costs/Operating Income (%)													
Cost of Operations **10**	84.7	75.0	77.0	73.3	75.8	79.0	86.3	85.1	81.2	86.3	81.9	84.7	86.3
Salaries and Wages **11**	2.6	5.1	4.1	4.1	3.8	5.8	3.5	3.9	4.0	2.2	1.5	2.0	2.1
Taxes Paid **12**	0.8	0.6	1.8	2.6	1.4	0.8	0.7	0.9	0.9	0.7	0.7	0.8	0.7
Interest Paid **13**	0.9	0.6	0.3	0.1	0.5	0.4	0.3	0.6	0.8	0.6	0.8	0.9	1.2
Depreciation **14**	1.8	2.2	0.5	1.2	1.6	2.2	1.0	1.5	2.7	2.0	2.3	3.2	1.5
Amortization and Depletion **15**	0.3	0.3	0.5	•	0.0	0.3	0.0	0.1	0.2	0.1	0.3	0.9	0.2
Pensions and Other Deferred Comp. **16**	0.4	0.0	0.0	0.1	0.5	0.1	0.1	0.1	0.2	0.1	0.2	0.2	0.2
Employee Benefits **17**	0.7	2.2	0.0	1.0	1.3	0.6	0.6	0.5	1.4	0.6	0.9	0.9	0.5
Advertising **18**	0.5	0.7	1.2	1.5	0.3	0.1	0.1	0.7	2.0	0.5	0.9	0.4	0.3
Other Expenses **19**	4.7	9.9	12.6	12.4	8.7	10.5	4.6	5.1	4.7	4.4	6.7	4.6	3.6
Officers' Compensation **20**	0.6	2.2	3.2	3.7	3.4	0.4	0.9	0.5	0.7	0.2	1.0	0.6	0.2
Operating Margin **21**	2.2	1.2	•	0.1	2.6	•	1.9	0.9	1.2	2.2	2.8	0.6	2.9
Operating Margin Before Officers' Comp. **22**	2.7	3.4	1.9	3.8	6.0	0.0	2.8	1.4	1.9	2.4	3.8	1.2	3.1

Selected Average Balance Sheet ($ in Thousands)

Net Receivables 23	2164	0	14	100	730	1857	3555	7945	12829	32150	66523	98142	744508
Inventories 24	3004	0	2	50	405	1170	1921	9595	14163	37454	85353	191356	1251419
Net Property, Plant and Equipment 25	4506	0	18	95	1096	3524	4424	10832	27331	54755	100646	326820	1718760
Total Assets 26	15925	0	82	732	3264	7105	13468	33797	68545	164468	374831	1129016	6837372
Notes and Loans Payable 27	4491	0	92	53	1658	4288	3327	14609	17434	54091	123660	391926	1432751
All Other Liabilities 28	4008	0	14	48	799	1735	2941	8272	16154	52699	100686	193192	1877122
Net Worth 29	7425	0	-25	631	808	1082	7200	10916	34957	57678	150485	543898	3527499

Selected Financial Ratios (Times to 1)

Current Ratio 30	1.7	•	0.8	2.3	1.8	0.6	2.1	1.5	1.6	1.5	1.7	1.6	1.8
Quick Ratio 31	0.7	•	0.7	1.4	1.1	0.4	1.2	0.7	0.8	0.7	0.7	0.3	0.8
Net Sales to Working Capital 32	12.2	•	•	15.9	11.1	•	15.2	18.8	15.5	13.8	9.2	6.6	12.2
Coverage Ratio 33	4.8	20.9	•	14.4	12.9	0.4	8.7	2.9	3.8	5.7	5.0	3.3	4.7
Total Asset Turnover 34	2.2	•	8.5	2.7	2.8	4.2	4.6	3.6	2.8	2.5	1.9	1.3	2.2
Inventory Turnover 35	10.0	•	233.8	28.4	17.3	20.1	27.6	10.9	10.9	9.4	6.7	6.3	10.2
Receivables Turnover 36	17.4	•	52.8	18.9	13.1	11.9	20.8	14.9	16.5	13.5	11.8	17.9	20.2
Total Liabilities to Net Worth 37	1.1	•	•	0.2	3.0	5.6	0.9	2.1	1.0	1.9	1.5	1.1	0.9
Current Assets to Working Capital 38	2.5	•	•	1.8	2.2	•	1.9	3.2	2.7	2.9	2.5	2.6	2.3
Current Liabilities to Working Capital 39	1.5	•	•	0.8	1.2	•	0.9	2.2	1.7	1.9	1.5	1.6	1.3
Working Capital to Net Sales 40	0.1	•	•	0.1	0.1	•	0.1	0.1	0.1	0.1	0.1	0.2	0.1
Inventory to Working Capital 41	1.1	•	•	0.6	0.5	•	0.6	1.5	1.2	1.3	1.2	1.1	1.1
Total Receipts to Cash Flow 42	14.7	5.2	14.8	11.3	7.9	17.4	17.0	19.4	16.9	16.3	11.0	19.6	14.6
Cost of Goods to Cash Flow 43	12.4	3.9	11.4	8.2	6.0	13.8	14.7	16.5	13.7	14.0	9.0	16.6	12.6
Cash Flow to Total Debt 44	0.3	•	0.4	1.7	0.5	0.3	0.6	0.3	0.3	0.2	0.3	0.1	0.3

Selected Financial Factors (in Percentages)

Debt Ratio 45	53.4	•	130.3	13.8	75.2	84.8	46.5	67.7	49.0	64.9	59.9	51.8	48.4
Return on Total Assets 46	9.4	•	•	2.1	18.6	0.7	11.6	6.4	8.0	7.9	7.7	3.9	11.7
Return on Equity Before Income Taxes 47	15.9	•	34.1	2.3	69.4	•	19.2	12.8	11.6	18.5	15.5	5.6	17.8
Return on Equity After Income Taxes 48	11.8	•	34.2	2.0	68.4	•	18.3	11.6	10.6	14.8	14.0	2.5	12.2
Profit Margin (Before Income Tax) 49	3.3	11.5	•	0.7	6.1	•	2.3	1.1	2.1	2.6	3.3	2.1	4.3
Profit Margin (After Income Tax) 50	2.5	11.4	•	0.6	6.0	•	2.2	1.0	1.9	2.1	3.0	1.0	2.9

Table II

Corporations with Net Income

MEAT AND SEAFOOD PROCESSING

MONEY AMOUNTS AND SIZE OF ASSETS IN THOUSANDS OF DOLLARS

Item Description for Accounting Period 7/10 Through 6/11	Total	Zero Assets	Under 500	500 to 1,000	1,000 to 5,000	5,000 to 10,000	10,000 to 25,000	25,000 to 50,000	50,000 to 100,000	100,000 to 250,000	250,000 to 500,000	500,000 to 2,500,000	2,500,000 and over
Number of Enterprises 1	2208	4	1329	130	468	60	104	42	30	•	•	•	6
Revenues ($ in Thousands)													
Net Sales 2	103741593	586246	1161946	253400	4280297	2201731	6342211	4952587	5578350	•	•	5664880	•
Interest 3	91258	4	0	296	569	0	704	987	506	•	•	11195	•
Rents 4	21822	0	0	288	220	0	260	741	449	•	•	997	•
Royalties 5	14682	0	0	0	0	0	0	24	100	•	•	0	•
Other Portfolio Income 6	421385	63129	0	1133	88	0	749	4037	24692	•	•	36559	•
Other Receipts 7	805883	906	100	477	162445	3411	23732	9417	23180	•	•	71181	•
Total Receipts 8	105096623	650285	1162046	255594	4443619	2205142	6367656	4967793	5627277	•	•	5784812	•
Average Total Receipts 9	47598	162571	874	1966	9495	36752	61227	118281	187576	•	•	964135	•
Operating Costs/Operating Income (%)													
Cost of Operations 10	84.0	72.1	80.6	73.3	75.9	78.5	85.8	84.9	80.1	•	•	78.5	•
Salaries and Wages 11	2.6	5.5	4.5	4.1	3.6	5.9	3.5	4.1	4.5	•	•	2.0	•
Taxes Paid 12	0.8	0.5	0.8	2.6	1.4	0.8	0.8	1.0	0.8	•	•	1.2	•
Interest Paid 13	0.9	0.7	0.1	0.1	0.5	0.2	0.3	0.5	0.7	•	•	0.7	•
Depreciation 14	1.8	2.3	0.1	1.2	1.6	2.3	0.8	1.6	2.4	•	•	3.9	•
Amortization and Depletion 15	0.2	0.2	0.8	•	0.0	0.2	0.0	0.0	0.1	•	•	0.5	•
Pensions and Other Deferred Comp. 16	0.4	•	0.0	0.1	0.5	0.1	0.1	0.1	0.2	•	•	0.4	•
Employee Benefits 17	0.7	2.4	0.0	1.0	1.4	0.5	0.7	0.3	1.5	•	•	1.5	•
Advertising 18	0.5	0.7	1.7	1.5	0.3	0.0	0.2	0.5	1.8	•	•	0.1	•
Other Expenses 19	4.6	7.9	6.1	12.4	7.8	11.2	4.2	3.8	4.5	•	•	5.9	•
Officers' Compensation 20	0.5	2.2	2.6	3.7	3.7	0.0	1.0	0.6	0.7	•	•	0.2	•
Operating Margin 21	3.1	5.5	2.7	0.1	3.3	0.3	2.7	2.6	2.6	•	•	5.2	•
Operating Margin Before Officers' Comp. 22	3.6	7.7	5.3	3.8	7.0	0.3	3.7	3.2	3.3	•	•	5.5	•

Selected Average Balance Sheet ($ in Thousands)

Item												
Net Receivables	**23**	2865	0	23	100	724	2249	3500	7674	12884	•	74998
Inventories	**24**	3720	0	2	48	374	625	1785	11561	12856	•	174618
Net Property, Plant and Equipment	**25**	6112	0	1	95	1104	4068	4038	11042	26460	•	355003
Total Assets	**26**	21741	0	107	732	3327	7452	13063	33467	67041	•	1064713
Notes and Loans Payable	**27**	5549	0	6	53	1655	4846	2567	13774	14859	•	346428
All Other Liabilities	**28**	5503	0	2	48	799	1970	2688	7927	15619	•	139256
Net Worth	**29**	10690	0	99	631	873	636	7808	11766	36564	•	579030

Selected Financial Ratios (Times to 1)

Item												
Current Ratio	**30**	1.7	•	11.5	2.3	1.9	0.6	2.4	1.5	1.7	•	1.7
Quick Ratio	**31**	0.7	•	10.5	1.4	1.2	0.4	1.4	0.7	0.9	•	0.3
Net Sales to Working Capital	**32**	11.4	•	30.1	15.9	10.5	•	13.5	15.9	14.6	•	4.6
Coverage Ratio	**33**	5.9	25.7	41.9	14.4	16.1	3.3	13.3	6.5	6.0	•	12.7
Total Asset Turnover	**34**	2.2	•	8.2	2.7	2.7	4.9	4.7	3.5	2.8	•	0.9
Inventory Turnover	**35**	10.6	•	455.8	29.9	18.5	46.1	29.3	8.7	11.6	•	4.2
Receivables Turnover	**36**	17.6	•	75.8	18.9	13.4	21.8	22.3	12.0	15.7	•	11.3
Total Liabilities to Net Worth	**37**	1.0	•	0.1	0.2	2.8	10.7	0.7	1.8	0.8	•	0.8
Current Assets to Working Capital	**38**	2.4	•	1.1	1.8	2.1	•	1.7	2.8	2.5	•	2.5
Current Liabilities to Working Capital	**39**	1.4	•	0.1	0.8	1.1	•	0.7	1.8	1.5	•	1.5
Working Capital to Net Sales	**40**	0.1	•	0.0	0.1	0.1	•	0.1	0.1	0.1	•	0.2
Inventory to Working Capital	**41**	1.0	•	0.1	0.6	0.5	•	0.5	1.3	1.0	•	0.6
Total Receipts to Cash Flow	**42**	12.9	4.6	12.6	11.3	7.8	14.7	15.8	17.3	14.1	•	8.7
Cost of Goods to Cash Flow	**43**	10.8	3.3	10.1	8.2	5.9	11.5	13.6	14.7	11.3	•	6.9
Cash Flow to Total Debt	**44**	0.3	•	8.4	1.7	0.5	0.4	0.7	0.3	0.4	•	0.2

Selected Financial Factors (in Percentages)

Item												
Debt Ratio	**45**	50.8	•	7.7	13.8	73.8	91.5	40.2	64.8	45.5	•	45.6
Return on Total Assets	**46**	11.4	•	22.9	2.1	21.0	3.4	15.6	12.2	11.7	•	7.6
Return on Equity Before Income Taxes	**47**	19.3	•	24.3	2.3	75.0	27.7	24.1	29.4	17.8	•	12.9
Return on Equity After Income Taxes	**48**	14.9	•	24.3	2.0	74.1	27.7	23.2	27.6	16.5	•	8.6
Profit Margin (Before Income Tax)	**49**	4.4	16.2	2.7	0.7	7.2	0.5	3.1	2.9	3.5	•	7.9
Profit Margin (After Income Tax)	**50**	3.4	16.1	2.7	0.6	7.1	0.5	3.0	2.8	3.2	•	5.3

Table I

Corporations with and without Net Income

BAKERIES AND TORTILLA

MONEY AMOUNTS AND SIZE OF ASSETS IN THOUSANDS OF DOLLARS

Item Description for Accounting Period 7/10 Through 6/11	Total	Zero Assets	Under 500	500 to 1,000	1,000 to 5,000	5,000 to 10,000	10,000 to 25,000	25,000 to 50,000	50,000 to 100,000	100,000 to 250,000	250,000 to 500,000	500,000 to 2,500,000	2,500,000 and over
Number of Enterprises 1	4061	817	2539	59	303	145	100	42	23	13	4	13	3
Revenues ($ in Thousands)													
Net Sales 2	45951653	1357457	985485	36432	1238025	2669912	2874376	2271984	2768891	2758114	2781909	11114183	15094885
Interest 3	67899	25	5	3	301	30	1805	303	555	1485	2567	30869	29950
Rents 4	10421	246	15	0	19	300	0	668	54	583	26	6783	1729
Royalties 5	51476	0	0	0	0	0	0	86	4575	25860	5035	9043	6876
Other Portfolio Income 6	136340	398	2843	40	125	983	1830	398	2111	11776	0	27472	88364
Other Receipts 7	219634	-5346	8172	1700	4061	6960	6837	3665	20167	25687	993	105561	41176
Total Receipts 8	46437423	1352780	996520	38175	1242531	2678185	2884848	2277104	2796353	2823505	2790530	11293911	15262980
Average Total Receipts 9	11435	1656	392	647	4101	18470	28848	54217	121581	217193	697632	868762	5087660
Operating Costs/Operating Income (%)													
Cost of Operations 10	61.6	50.5	52.5	52.1	63.7	68.0	69.2	68.0	61.1	66.4	66.2	59.0	59.8
Salaries and Wages 11	9.1	15.5	18.1	1.3	6.5	7.1	5.6	5.2	10.9	8.2	8.6	10.9	8.3
Taxes Paid 12	2.0	1.8	4.7	2.6	2.3	2.1	1.9	1.5	2.1	1.9	1.3	2.2	1.8
Interest Paid 13	1.4	0.8	1.9	0.0	0.3	0.4	0.8	1.6	0.9	1.3	0.6	1.4	2.1
Depreciation 14	3.3	3.8	2.4	18.9	1.7	2.4	4.5	3.8	4.2	4.0	2.0	3.1	3.2
Amortization and Depletion 15	0.6	0.7	0.3	1.4	0.4	0.1	0.0	0.6	0.6	0.7	0.7	0.7	0.8
Pensions and Other Deferred Comp. 16	1.2	0.2	0.0	0.0	0.4	0.1	0.1	0.2	1.6	1.6	0.4	1.8	1.4
Employee Benefits 17	3.2	4.1	0.1	0.2	1.1	1.6	1.8	1.1	4.0	2.8	1.5	3.9	4.0
Advertising 18	2.0	4.1	0.3	4.6	1.1	0.4	0.6	0.7	1.2	1.1	2.7	1.7	3.2
Other Expenses 19	12.8	15.9	20.2	42.0	12.5	10.1	8.4	10.3	9.8	11.7	10.3	14.1	14.1
Officers' Compensation 20	1.1	1.9	3.2	0.8	6.2	1.8	2.5	3.2	1.5	0.9	0.5	0.6	0.2
Operating Margin 21	1.8	0.5	•	•	3.6	6.0	4.5	3.9	2.2	•	5.1	0.4	1.3
Operating Margin Before Officers' Comp. 22	2.9	2.4	•	•	9.9	7.7	7.0	7.0	3.7	0.4	5.6	1.1	1.5

Selected Average Balance Sheet ($ in Thousands)

Item													
Net Receivables 23	1124	0	8	4	256	1452	1990	3908	8787	24954	66965	160318	338443
Inventories 24	574	0	12	8	241	758	1667	2999	5096	11076	64008	39568	264050
Net Property, Plant and Equipment 25	2465	0	38	331	523	3057	6391	12989	29225	58435	97359	225860	1116573
Total Assets 26	9851	0	97	538	1832	7196	15751	33466	67163	150412	407597	1016477	5601128
Notes and Loans Payable 27	3225	0	145	618	501	2041	4995	15053	21639	45572	39333	271767	2109923
All Other Liabilities 28	2654	0	17	18	305	2721	2980	5914	14938	38685	99882	306442	1490504
Net Worth 29	3972	0	-65	-98	1025	2434	7775	12499	30586	66155	268382	438268	2000700

Selected Financial Ratios (Times to 1)

Item													
Current Ratio 30	1.0	•	2.7	3.0	1.5	2.0	1.2	1.4	1.3	1.7	0.9	0.8	
Quick Ratio 31	0.7	•	1.4	1.4	1.0	1.4	0.9	0.9	0.9	1.1	0.6	0.4	
Net Sales to Working Capital 32	135.9	13.1	•	5.8	14.1	7.8	25.2	19.6	16.7	11.1	•	4.6	
Coverage Ratio 33	4.1	1.2	•	12.5	16.0	3.5	16.0	4.7	2.4	9.8	2.4	4.6	
Total Asset Turnover 34	1.1	•	4.0	2.2	1.6	1.8	2.6	1.8	1.4	1.7	0.8	0.9	
Inventory Turnover 35	12.1	17.0	42.5	10.8	12.3	11.9	16.5	14.4	12.7	7.2	12.8	11.4	
Receivables Turnover 36	10.1	29.1	282.4	11.9	15.5	15.1	16.2	13.3	9.3	9.2	5.9	12.5	
Total Liabilities to Net Worth 37	1.5	•	•	0.8	1.7	1.0	2.0	1.2	1.3	0.5	1.3	1.8	
Current Assets to Working Capital 38	30.6	1.6	•	1.5	3.0	2.0	5.0	3.5	4.4	2.5	•	•	
Current Liabilities to Working Capital 39	29.6	0.6	•	0.5	2.0	1.0	4.0	2.5	3.4	1.5	•	•	
Working Capital to Net Sales 40	0.0	0.1	•	0.2	0.1	0.1	0.0	0.1	0.1	0.1	•	•	
Inventory to Working Capital 41	7.1	0.5	•	0.3	0.9	0.4	1.2	0.9	0.7	0.7	•	•	
Total Receipts to Cash Flow 42	8.1	13.3	12.4	7.9	8.4	8.8	7.4	10.0	10.1	7.4	7.7	7.8	
Cost of Goods to Cash Flow 43	5.0	7.0	6.5	5.1	5.7	6.1	5.0	6.1	6.7	4.9	4.6	4.6	
Cash Flow to Total Debt 44	0.2	0.2	0.1	0.6	0.3	0.4	0.5	0.3	0.2	0.7	0.2	0.2	

Selected Financial Factors (in Percentages)

Item													
Debt Ratio 45	59.7	•	166.9	118.2	44.0	62.7	50.6	66.2	54.5	56.0	34.2	56.9	64.3
Return on Total Assets 46	6.8	•	•	9.7	17.1	10.3	9.3	7.4	4.4	10.3	2.9	8.5	
Return on Equity Before Income Taxes 47	12.8	•	14.5	121.5	16.0	47.4	18.0	17.7	12.7	5.8	14.1	4.0	18.7
Return on Equity After Income Taxes 48	9.6	•	15.2	121.7	13.5	47.4	15.8	17.0	10.9	5.2	11.3	2.0	13.5
Profit Margin (Before Income Tax) 49	4.5	0.2	•	4.0	6.3	4.9	6.3	4.1	3.2	1.8	5.4	2.0	7.4
Profit Margin (After Income Tax) 50	3.4	•	•	3.4	6.3	4.3	3.9	2.8	4.4	1.6	5.4	1.0	5.4

Table II
Corporations with Net Income

BAKERIES AND TORTILLA

MONEY AMOUNTS AND SIZE OF ASSETS IN THOUSANDS OF DOLLARS

Item Description for Accounting Period 7/10 Through 6/11	Total	Zero Assets	Under 500	500 to 1,000	1,000 to 5,000	5,000 to 10,000	10,000 to 25,000	25,000 to 50,000	50,000 to 100,000	100,000 to 250,000	250,000 to 500,000	500,000 to 2,500,000	2,500,000 and over
Number of Enterprises **1**	1109	3	741	3	116	114	61	32	16	9	4	7	3
Revenues ($ in Thousands)													
Net Sales **2**	37994913	1266977	579386	3574	909625	1972736	2176505	1675754	2302767	1734627	2781909	7496170	15094885
Interest **3**	51425	25	5	3	135	0	970	237	176	272	2567	17085	29950
Rents **4**	9028	1	0	0	0	300	0	232	54	104	26	6583	1729
Royalties **5**	18364	0	0	0	0	0	0	0	0	0	5035	6452	6876
Other Portfolio Income **6**	106433	398	2843	40	9	734	314	248	1079	11776	0	628	88364
Other Receipts **7**	167448	-5815	1147	0	2682	6341	2819	2886	13088	23919	993	78211	41176
Total Receipts **8**	38347611	1261586	583381	3617	912451	1980111	2180608	1679357	2317164	1770698	2790530	7605129	15262980
Average Total Receipts **9**	34579	420529	787	1206	7866	17369	35748	52480	144823	196744	697632	1086447	5087660
Operating Costs/Operating Income (%)													
Cost of Operations **10**	61.5	49.1	63.0	55.0	64.3	65.3	68.7	68.6	61.0	60.3	66.2	60.7	59.8
Salaries and Wages **11**	7.8	14.9	7.9	13.7	6.0	6.9	4.4	4.0	10.6	10.6	8.6	5.9	8.3
Taxes Paid **12**	1.8	1.7	1.9	3.1	2.1	1.9	1.7	1.3	2.1	1.9	1.3	1.8	1.8
Interest Paid **13**	1.2	0.6	0.5	0.1	0.3	0.2	0.5	0.8	0.5	1.0	0.6	1.0	2.1
Depreciation **14**	3.3	3.7	1.7	0.5	1.0	2.3	3.1	4.4	3.9	3.8	2.0	3.8	3.2
Amortization and Depletion **15**	0.6	0.5	•	•	0.1	0.1	0.0	0.1	0.2	0.2	0.7	0.8	0.8
Pensions and Other Deferred Comp. **16**	1.0	0.2	•	0.2	0.5	0.1	0.2	0.2	1.5	2.1	0.4	1.1	1.4
Employee Benefits **17**	2.8	4.3	0.0	1.7	0.7	1.2	1.8	0.7	3.8	2.9	1.5	2.0	4.0
Advertising **18**	2.1	4.4	0.3	1.0	1.2	0.5	0.2	0.5	1.2	1.3	2.7	1.6	3.2
Other Expenses **19**	12.9	15.3	18.4	14.7	10.6	10.7	7.5	8.4	8.8	10.7	10.3	16.1	14.1
Officers' Compensation **20**	1.0	1.9	3.1	8.1	6.0	0.8	3.1	3.9	1.6	0.7	0.5	0.4	0.2
Operating Margin **21**	4.0	3.3	3.1	1.9	7.2	9.9	8.8	7.0	4.9	4.5	5.1	4.9	1.3
Operating Margin Before Officers' Comp. **22**	5.0	5.2	6.2	10.0	13.2	10.7	11.9	10.9	6.4	5.2	5.6	5.3	1.5

Selected Average Balance Sheet ($ in Thousands)

Net Receivables 23	2500	0	22	17	485	1511	2201	3438	10364	24015	66965	88268	338443
Inventories 24	1783	0	22	69	448	748	2236	2787	6229	7871	64008	49666	264050
Net Property, Plant and Equipment 25	6965	0	45	89	683	2866	6445	14966	32156	46477	97359	248707	1116573
Total Assets 26	26814	0	187	635	2515	7030	16023	31534	69391	133250	407597	824749	5601128
Notes and Loans Payable 27	8152	0	81	26	493	1766	3886	11088	13239	43718	39333	148226	2109923
All Other Liabilities 28	7146	0	51	5	660	2726	3494	5140	16708	24046	99882	252383	1490504
Net Worth 29	11516	0	54	604	1362	2537	8644	15306	39444	65486	268382	424139	2000700

Selected Financial Ratios (Times to 1)

Current Ratio 30	1.2	•	2.0	78.6	2.3	1.3	1.6	2.1	1.5	2.3	1.7	1.4	0.8
Quick Ratio 31	0.7	•	1.2	25.1	1.4	1.0	1.1	1.4	1.0	1.7	1.1	0.9	0.4
Net Sales to Working Capital 32	32.0	•	15.1	3.3	8.4	20.5	12.7	8.5	17.5	6.0	11.1	15.4	•
Coverage Ratio 33	6.6	6.2	8.8	28.2	26.2	42.2	10.0	17.7	12.5	7.4	9.8	7.7	4.6
Total Asset Turnover 34	1.3	•	4.2	1.9	3.1	2.5	1.7	2.2	2.1	1.4	1.7	1.3	0.9
Inventory Turnover 35	11.8	•	22.2	9.5	11.3	15.1	12.9	11.0	14.1	14.8	7.2	13.1	11.4
Receivables Turnover 36	12.7	•	140.2	12.7	14.2	16.6	14.8	12.8	•	•	•	9.2	12.5
Total Liabilities to Net Worth 37	1.3	•	2.4	0.1	1.0	0.8	1.1	0.9	0.8	1.0	0.5	0.9	1.8
Current Assets to Working Capital 38	5.9	•	2.0	1.0	1.8	4.4	2.7	1.9	3.1	1.8	2.5	3.3	•
Current Liabilities to Working Capital 39	4.9	•	1.0	0.0	0.8	3.4	1.7	0.9	2.1	0.8	1.5	2.3	•
Working Capital to Net Sales 40	0.0	•	0.1	0.3	0.1	0.0	0.1	0.1	0.1	0.2	0.1	0.1	•
Inventory to Working Capital 41	1.7	•	0.4	0.2	0.5	0.7	0.7	0.5	0.8	0.2	0.7	0.8	•
Total Receipts to Cash Flow 42	6.8	6.3	8.0	7.1	6.5	5.4	7.2	6.7	8.6	6.8	7.4	5.2	7.8
Cost of Goods to Cash Flow 43	4.2	3.1	5.0	3.9	4.2	3.6	5.0	4.6	5.3	4.1	4.9	3.1	4.6
Cash Flow to Total Debt 44	0.3	•	0.7	5.4	1.1	0.7	0.4	0.7	0.6	0.4	0.7	0.5	0.2

Selected Financial Factors (in Percentages)

Debt Ratio 45	57.1	•	70.9	45.8	63.9	46.1	51.5	43.2	50.9	34.2	48.6	64.3
Return on Total Assets 46	10.5	•	18.0	24.5	25.9	21.2	13.4	12.3	10.9	10.3	9.5	8.5
Return on Equity Before Income Taxes 47	20.7	•	55.0	43.5	70.1	37.1	24.8	20.0	19.2	14.1	16.1	18.7
Return on Equity After Income Taxes 48	16.7	•	52.2	38.7	70.1	33.8	24.0	18.0	18.4	11.3	12.3	13.5
Profit Margin (Before Income Tax) 49	6.9	2.9	3.8	7.5	10.3	9.0	7.2	5.5	6.5	5.4	6.4	7.4
Profit Margin (After Income Tax) 50	5.6	2.3	3.6	6.7	10.3	8.2	7.0	4.9	6.3	4.4	4.9	5.4

48

Table I

Corporations with and without Net Income

OTHER FOOD

MONEY AMOUNTS AND SIZE OF ASSETS IN THOUSANDS OF DOLLARS

Item Description for Accounting Period 7/10 Through 6/11	Total	Zero Assets	Under 500	500 to 1,000	1,000 to 5,000	5,000 to 10,000	10,000 to 25,000	25,000 to 50,000	50,000 to 100,000	100,000 to 250,000	250,000 to 500,000	500,000 to 2,500,000	2,500,000 and over
Number of Enterprises **1**	3355	994	1039	81	682	201	189	65	40	33	15	12	3
Revenues ($ in Thousands)													
Net Sales **2**	121197136	140264	206065	235718	2901570	3550116	6620244	5903341	4999766	8309650	5630972	14481334	68218095
Interest **3**	2845269	46	1	6	848	400	929	428	1496	4929	3076	38251	2794857
Rents **4**	237274	0	0	0	11	98	510	199	3425	1532	15120	1715	214664
Royalties **5**	1023606	406	0	0	0	0	8	0	1145	12954	1512	687	1006893
Other Portfolio Income **6**	3717911	38004	0	0	313	962	1978	3978	87118	13659	81760	24222	3465916
Other Receipts **7**	4426851	496	6	6758	6435	68533	49176	3193	20775	36566	66983	379073	3788861
Total Receipts **8**	133448047	179216	206072	242482	2909177	3620109	6672845	5911139	5113725	8379290	5799423	14925282	79489286
Average Total Receipts **9**	39776	180	198	2994	4266	18010	35306	90941	127843	253918	386628	1243774	26496429
Operating Costs/Operating Income (%)													
Cost of Operations **10**	70.8	59.5	21.8	41.2	62.1	69.4	72.7	79.4	70.6	68.3	70.2	72.7	70.5
Salaries and Wages **11**	5.7	8.9	18.3	8.9	11.8	7.3	6.4	4.5	6.2	6.9	5.7	5.7	5.1
Taxes Paid **12**	1.4	3.8	3.4	2.2	2.3	1.8	1.3	0.8	1.2	1.4	1.0	1.1	1.4
Interest Paid **13**	5.1	2.4	2.1	0.5	0.7	0.5	0.4	0.5	1.2	0.9	1.3	2.9	8.0
Depreciation **14**	2.4	1.6	4.6	3.3	1.6	1.1	2.6	1.5	2.9	3.0	3.1	3.4	2.2
Amortization and Depletion **15**	0.4	1.6	0.9	0.1	0.1	0.0	0.0	0.1	0.8	0.4	0.6	0.9	0.4
Pensions and Other Deferred Comp. **16**	0.8	•	•	0.2	0.2	0.2	0.6	0.3	0.4	0.4	0.6	0.8	1.0
Employee Benefits **17**	1.6	1.7	•	0.0	1.1	0.4	1.5	1.0	1.1	1.8	0.9	1.2	1.8
Advertising **18**	2.8	0.5	6.5	0.3	1.6	0.3	0.6	1.0	2.2	2.0	4.4	1.1	3.7
Other Expenses **19**	11.8	23.5	36.1	39.3	13.0	11.1	7.8	5.8	8.8	10.8	7.6	9.5	13.6
Officers' Compensation **20**	0.7	2.2	2.0	0.6	4.4	2.8	1.4	1.1	1.3	1.1	0.8	0.9	0.1
Operating Margin **21**	•	4.3	•	3.5	1.1	5.0	4.7	4.0	3.3	2.9	3.8	•	•
Operating Margin Before Officers' Comp. **22**	•	6.3	•	4.1	5.5	7.8	6.1	5.1	4.6	4.0	4.6	0.8	•

Selected Average Balance Sheet ($ in Thousands)

Net Receivables 23	101636	0	0	29	320	1610	3078	7935	12333	20477	39741	139957	111966919
Inventories 24	2795	0	6	72	364	1607	3735	9975	14976	28736	41709	130069	1261856
Net Property, Plant and Equipment 25	6066	0	66	195	525	1655	4879	9018	19264	41175	78229	274500	3824418
Total Assets 26	166134	0	96	653	1918	6730	15894	34911	74792	146319	309724	1257253	173913125
Notes and Loans Payable 27	22409	0	106	958	635	2372	4304	8436	27172	33204	90163	575580	20759538
All Other Liabilities 28	113631	0	19	111	384	2510	3868	10131	19962	53688	70833	304733	123918949
Net Worth 29	30095	0	-29	-416	899	1848	7721	16344	27658	59427	148728	376941	29234638

Selected Financial Ratios (Times to 1)

Current Ratio 30	1.0	•	0.5	1.5	2.6	1.7	1.9	1.6	1.7	1.7	1.7	1.5	1.0
Quick Ratio 31	0.9	•	0.1	0.8	1.4	0.9	1.0	0.8	0.9	0.7	0.7	0.7	0.9
Net Sales to Working Capital 32	•	•	•	48.7	5.6	9.9	7.7	12.3	8.5	8.5	7.9	8.8	•
Coverage Ratio 33	2.4	10.3	3.1	13.9	3.0	13.9	13.7	8.7	5.5	5.1	6.2	2.1	2.2
Total Asset Turnover 34	0.2	•	2.1	4.5	2.2	2.6	2.2	2.6	1.7	1.7	1.2	1.0	0.1
Inventory Turnover 35	9.1	6.7	6.7	16.6	7.3	7.6	6.8	7.2	5.9	6.0	6.3	6.7	12.7
Receivables Turnover 36	0.4	•	203.6	15.4	•	11.7	12.3	12.3	10.9	12.6	9.6	9.9	0.2
Total Liabilities to Net Worth 37	4.5	•	•	1.1	2.6	1.1	1.1	1.7	1.7	1.5	1.1	2.3	4.9
Current Assets to Working Capital 38	•	•	•	2.9	1.6	2.5	2.1	2.7	2.5	2.5	2.3	2.9	•
Current Liabilities to Working Capital 39	•	•	1.9	•	0.6	1.5	1.1	1.7	1.5	1.5	1.3	1.9	•
Working Capital to Net Sales 40	•	•	0.0	0.2	0.1	0.1	0.1	0.1	0.1	0.1	0.1	0.1	•
Inventory to Working Capital 41	•	•	1.4	0.5	0.9	1.2	0.9	1.0	1.1	1.0	0.9	1.1	•
Total Receipts to Cash Flow 42	7.2	2.4	2.3	9.3	6.1	8.9	11.2	8.0	8.0	9.0	9.5	6.4	
Cost of Goods to Cash Flow 43	5.1	0.9	1.0	5.8	4.2	6.5	8.9	5.6	5.5	6.3	6.9	4.5	
Cash Flow to Total Debt 44	0.0	0.4	1.2	0.6	0.4	0.5	0.4	0.3	0.4	0.3	0.1	0.0	

Selected Financial Factors (in Percentages)

Debt Ratio 45	81.9	•	130.4	163.6	53.1	72.5	51.4	53.2	63.0	59.4	52.0	70.0	83.2
Return on Total Assets 46	2.7	•	13.4	30.5	4.6	19.7	13.1	12.2	11.4	8.1	9.8	5.7	2.3
Return on Equity Before Income Taxes 47	8.6	•	•	6.4	6.4	66.6	24.9	23.1	25.2	16.0	17.1	9.7	7.2
Return on Equity After Income Taxes 48	6.0	•	•	4.9	4.9	61.0	24.0	22.2	23.2	12.5	15.4	5.6	4.7
Profit Margin (Before Income Tax) 49	7.1	22.0	4.3	6.4	1.4	7.0	5.5	4.2	5.6	3.8	6.8	3.0	9.2
Profit Margin (After Income Tax) 50	5.0	11.9	4.3	6.3	1.0	6.4	5.3	4.0	5.1	3.0	6.1	1.8	6.0

Table II
Corporations with Net Income

OTHER FOOD

MONEY AMOUNTS AND SIZE OF ASSETS IN THOUSANDS OF DOLLARS

Item Description for Accounting Period 7/10 Through 6/11	Total	Zero Assets	Under 500	500 to 1,000	1,000 to 5,000	5,000 to 10,000	10,000 to 25,000	25,000 to 50,000	50,000 to 100,000	100,000 to 250,000	250,000 to 500,000	500,000 to 2,500,000	2,500,000 and over
Number of Enterprises 1	2056	19	1039	48	515	145	150	58	29	29	12	9	3
Revenues ($ in Thousands)													
Net Sales 2	113626539	108113	206065	176349	2234197	3079977	5786065	5468238	4129616	7363050	4855763	12001012	68218095
Interest 3	2838945	19	1	0	457	291	616	106	420	4877	2433	34870	2794857
Rents 4	236718	0	0	0	5	98	430	199	2959	1532	15114	1715	214664
Royalties 5	1022281	0	0	0	0	0	8	0	245	12934	1512	687	1006893
Other Portfolio Income 6	3711889	37976	0	0	313	962	637	3840	86372	13654	78175	24044	3465916
Other Receipts 7	4265186	406	6	33	1800	62598	39056	2457	11424	19701	65872	272975	3788861
Total Receipts 8	125701558	146514	206072	176382	2236772	3143926	5826812	5474840	4231036	7415748	5018869	12335303	79489286
Average Total Receipts 9	61139	7711	198	3675	4343	21682	38845	94394	145898	255715	418239	1370589	26496429
Operating Costs/Operating Income (%)													
Cost of Operations 10	70.6	49.0	21.8	49.1	58.9	68.8	71.5	79.7	70.4	67.9	71.3	71.6	70.5
Salaries and Wages 11	5.4	10.6	18.3	0.1	12.9	6.9	5.9	4.5	5.9	6.4	3.9	5.3	5.1
Taxes Paid 12	1.4	4.4	3.4	1.7	2.3	1.9	1.3	0.8	1.1	1.3	0.9	1.1	1.4
Interest Paid 13	5.3	0.2	2.1	0.7	0.5	0.4	0.4	0.5	1.1	0.8	1.2	2.7	8.0
Depreciation 14	2.3	1.8	4.6	2.4	1.4	0.8	2.3	1.3	2.3	2.9	2.8	3.1	2.2
Amortization and Depletion 15	0.4	1.6	0.9	•	0.0	0.0	0.0	0.1	0.6	0.4	0.5	0.8	0.4
Pensions and Other Deferred Comp. 16	0.8	•	•	•	0.1	0.2	0.4	0.3	0.4	0.5	0.4	0.9	1.0
Employee Benefits 17	1.6	2.1	•	0.0	0.8	0.2	1.6	1.0	0.9	1.9	0.6	1.4	1.8
Advertising 18	2.8	0.3	6.5	0.0	1.4	0.3	0.6	0.9	2.0	1.6	5.1	1.1	3.7
Other Expenses 19	11.7	22.5	36.1	28.8	11.4	10.8	7.7	5.2	7.8	10.7	6.8	9.4	13.6
Officers' Compensation 20	0.6	2.6	2.0	0.8	4.1	2.6	1.4	1.1	1.3	1.2	0.9	1.0	0.1
Operating Margin 21	•	4.9	4.3	16.4	6.1	6.9	6.9	4.8	6.1	4.5	5.5	1.8	•
Operating Margin Before Officers' Comp. 22	•	7.5	6.3	17.2	10.3	9.6	8.3	5.8	7.5	5.7	6.4	2.8	•

Selected Average Balance Sheet ($ in Thousands)

Net Receivables 23	165518	0	0	48	335	1705	3275	8410	13647	22606	41766	161068	111966919
Inventories 24	4016	0	7	61	358	1128	3650	9555	16424	29921	38925	147829	1261856
Net Property, Plant and Equipment 25	8849	0	66	126	502	1876	4734	8598	19264	38258	77007	257053	3824418
Total Assets 26	267406	0	96	626	1837	6701	15820	35293	77354	146551	308146	1265472	173913125
Notes and Loans Payable 27	34618	0	106	135	591	1292	3706	8431	25282	33207	89502	497002	20759538
All Other Liabilities 28	184298	0	19	177	347	2688	3854	9763	20640	46955	57590	307639	123918949
Net Worth 29	48489	-29	314	900	2721	8260	17099	31432	66389	161054	460831		29234638

Selected Financial Ratios (Times to 1)

Current Ratio 30	1.0	•	0.5	0.4	2.9	1.4	2.0	1.6	1.8	1.7	1.8	2.2	1.0
Quick Ratio 31	0.9	•	0.1	0.3	1.6	0.9	1.1	0.8	0.9	0.7	0.8	1.1	0.9
Net Sales to Working Capital 32	•	•	•	•	5.6	16.6	7.8	12.5	8.0	8.1	8.0	5.8	•
Coverage Ratio 33	2.5	194.5	3.1	25.9	12.5	21.1	22.3	10.8	8.9	7.8	8.3	2.7	2.2
Total Asset Turnover 34	0.2	•	2.1	5.9	2.4	3.2	2.4	2.7	1.8	1.7	1.3	1.1	0.1
Inventory Turnover 35	9.7	•	6.0	29.5	7.1	12.9	7.6	7.9	6.1	5.8	7.4	6.5	12.7
Receivables Turnover 36	0.4	•	29.6	152.3	13.7	17.4	12.5	12.7	•	12.1	9.7	•	0.2
Total Liabilities to Net Worth 37	4.5	•	•	1.0	1.0	1.5	0.9	1.1	1.5	1.2	0.9	1.7	4.9
Current Assets to Working Capital 38	•	•	•	•	1.5	3.3	2.0	2.7	2.2	2.4	2.3	1.9	•
Current Liabilities to Working Capital 39	•	•	•	•	0.5	2.3	1.0	1.7	1.2	1.4	1.3	0.9	•
Working Capital to Net Sales 40	•	•	•	0.2	0.2	0.1	0.1	0.1	0.1	0.1	0.1	0.2	•
Inventory to Working Capital 41	•	•	•	0.4	0.4	1.2	0.8	1.2	0.9	1.1	0.8	0.6	•
Total Receipts to Cash Flow 42	6.8	1.7	4.3	2.3	7.0	5.5	7.4	11.0	6.9	7.1	8.0	8.4	6.4
Cost of Goods to Cash Flow 43	4.8	0.8	0.9	1.1	4.2	3.8	5.3	8.8	4.8	4.8	5.7	6.0	4.5
Cash Flow to Total Debt 44	0.0	•	0.4	5.1	0.7	1.0	0.7	0.5	0.5	0.4	0.3	0.2	0.0

Selected Financial Factors (in Percentages)

Debt Ratio 45	81.9	•	130.4	49.9	51.0	59.4	47.8	51.6	59.4	54.7	47.7	63.6	83.2
Return on Total Assets 46	2.8	•	13.4	100.1	16.1	30.0	19.4	14.5	17.8	10.5	13.2	7.7	2.3
Return on Equity Before Income Taxes 47	9.3	•	•	191.9	30.2	70.4	35.5	27.1	38.9	20.2	22.3	13.4	7.2
Return on Equity After Income Taxes 48	6.7	•	•	191.5	28.2	65.2	34.3	26.1	36.5	16.7	20.4	9.0	4.7
Profit Margin (Before Income Tax) 49	8.1	40.4	4.3	16.4	6.3	9.0	7.6	4.9	8.6	5.3	8.9	4.6	9.2
Profit Margin (After Income Tax) 50	5.9	27.3	4.3	16.3	5.8	8.3	7.3	4.7	8.1	4.4	8.1	3.1	6.0

Table I
Corporations with and without Net Income

SOFT DRINK AND ICE

MONEY AMOUNTS AND SIZE OF ASSETS IN THOUSANDS OF DOLLARS

Item Description for Accounting Period 7/10 Through 6/11	Total	Zero Assets	Under 500	500 to 1,000	1,000 to 5,000	5,000 to 10,000	10,000 to 25,000	25,000 to 50,000	50,000 to 100,000	100,000 to 250,000	250,000 to 500,000	500,000 to 2,500,000	2,500,000 and over
Number of Enterprises **1**	351	•	•	•	56	9	19	29	15	12	8	4	4
Revenues ($ in Thousands)													
Net Sales **2**	47162827	•	•	•	203236	133359	694174	2113062	2007058	3164436	2291852	4144844	20794392
Interest **3**	78397	•	•	•	583	7	35	709	1892	540	2154	2000	66951
Rents **4**	33303	•	•	•	429	0	225	0	25	214	1505	4	28098
Royalties **5**	1388333	•	•	•	0	0	161	0	0	0	10785	0	1377387
Other Portfolio Income **6**	1917317	•	•	•	105	3705	300	13198	702	2216	5309	10161	1857166
Other Receipts **7**	2423591	•	•	•	482	29068	16682	7789	31613	32097	45462	125945	2059683
Total Receipts **8**	53003768	•	•	•	204835	166139	711577	2134758	2041290	3199503	3057067	4282954	26183677
Average Total Receipts **9**	151008	•	•	•	3658	18460	37451	73612	136086	266625	382133	1070738	6545919
Operating Costs/Operating Income (%)													
Cost of Operations **10**	52.4	•	•	•	59.5	70.0	75.1	71.7	60.3	70.0	60.1	56.2	40.8
Salaries and Wages **11**	13.7	•	•	•	5.8	15.1	7.3	6.4	12.9	7.5	12.4	16.1	13.9
Taxes Paid **12**	1.9	•	•	•	3.6	2.2	1.4	1.5	1.6	1.1	2.5	2.1	1.8
Interest Paid **13**	4.6	•	•	•	1.0	0.0	0.7	0.8	1.1	0.6	4.9	3.7	7.0
Depreciation **14**	4.6	•	•	•	4.9	3.5	1.7	3.7	3.6	3.4	4.5	5.3	5.5
Amortization and Depletion **15**	1.2	•	•	•	0.0	•	1.0	0.1	0.5	0.7	1.8	1.0	1.5
Pensions and Other Deferred Comp. **16**	0.6	•	•	•	0.1	1.2	0.2	0.4	0.2	0.4	0.5	0.6	0.9
Employee Benefits **17**	2.5	•	•	•	0.5	3.0	1.2	1.9	1.9	1.8	1.7	2.9	2.4
Advertising **18**	4.4	•	•	•	6.0	0.7	3.1	6.6	3.4	2.4	2.2	0.7	7.5
Other Expenses **19**	17.1	•	•	•	23.0	23.9	8.7	5.5	8.2	8.3	10.6	12.6	27.3
Officers' Compensation **20**	0.5	•	•	•	6.1	0.3	0.9	1.8	1.4	0.5	0.6	0.5	0.3
Operating Margin **21**	•	•	•	•	•	•	•	•	4.7	3.3	•	•	•
Operating Margin Before Officers' Comp. **22**	•	•	•	•	•	•	•	1.4	6.2	3.8	•	•	•

Selected Average Balance Sheet ($ in Thousands)

Item												
Net Receivables 23	13183	•	•	276	1376	2424	5953	13805	35299	26447	134571	736046
Inventories 24	7500	•	•	304	1061	1859	4954	6417	14700	23268	53721	430154
Net Property, Plant and Equipment 25	38808	•	•	1619	1257	3449	13130	29687	49418	97138	315457	2497950
Total Assets 26	220854	•	•	3444	5851	14958	36712	70510	157636	330921	909584	16640464
Notes and Loans Payable 27	89977	•	•	1662	0	5678	16072	23478	29704	141465	602472	6648927
All Other Liabilities 28	50410	•	•	921	961	2622	18588	20849	38286	89390	322536	3553085
Net Worth 29	80468	•	•	861	4891	6658	2051	26183	89645	100065	-15424	6438452

Selected Financial Ratios (Times to 1)

Item												
Current Ratio 30	0.7	•	•	0.6	3.2	2.1	1.0	2.1	2.2	2.0	1.4	0.6
Quick Ratio 31	0.4	•	•	0.4	2.0	1.2	0.6	1.4	1.5	1.2	0.9	0.3
Net Sales to Working Capital 32	•	•	•	6.9	12.0	•	9.2	7.9	8.9	13.1	•	•
Coverage Ratio 33	3.7	•	•	•	6169.0	2.7	1.7	7.1	7.9	1.1	1.4	4.5
Total Asset Turnover 34	0.6	•	•	1.1	2.5	2.4	2.0	1.9	1.7	1.1	1.1	0.3
Inventory Turnover 35	9.4	•	•	7.1	9.8	14.8	10.5	12.6	12.6	9.7	10.8	4.9
Receivables Turnover 36	8.0	•	•	•	•	15.6	13.0	8.2	9.5	13.5	8.0	4.9
Total Liabilities to Net Worth 37	1.7	•	•	3.0	0.2	1.2	16.9	1.7	0.8	2.3	•	1.6
Current Assets to Working Capital 38	•	•	•	•	1.4	1.9	•	1.9	1.8	2.0	3.5	•
Current Liabilities to Working Capital 39	•	•	•	•	0.4	0.9	•	0.9	0.8	1.0	2.5	•
Working Capital to Net Sales 40	•	•	•	•	0.1	0.1	•	0.1	0.1	0.1	0.1	•
Inventory to Working Capital 41	•	•	•	•	0.5	0.7	•	0.5	0.5	0.5	0.9	•
Total Receipts to Cash Flow 42	4.4	•	•	10.2	6.9	13.2	23.3	8.2	8.8	14.0	9.4	2.5
Cost of Goods to Cash Flow 43	2.3	•	•	6.0	4.8	9.9	16.7	4.9	6.2	8.4	5.3	1.0
Cash Flow to Total Debt 44	0.2	•	•	0.1	2.2	0.3	0.1	0.4	0.4	0.1	0.1	0.2

Selected Financial Factors (in Percentages)

Item												
Debt Ratio 45	63.6	•	•	75.0	16.4	55.5	94.4	62.9	43.1	69.8	101.7	61.3
Return on Total Assets 46	10.2	•	•	•	11.7	5.0	2.8	14.2	8.4	5.9	6.1	9.9
Return on Equity Before Income Taxes 47	20.4	•	•	•	14.0	7.2	20.1	32.9	13.0	1.2	•	20.0
Return on Equity After Income Taxes 48	13.5	•	•	•	11.2	7.1	14.7	32.0	10.3	•	•	13.0
Profit Margin (Before Income Tax) 49	12.2	•	•	•	4.6	1.3	0.6	6.4	4.4	0.3	1.6	24.7
Profit Margin (After Income Tax) 50	8.1	•	•	•	3.7	1.3	0.4	6.3	3.5	•	0.9	16.1

Table II

Corporations with Net Income

SOFT DRINK AND ICE

MONEY AMOUNTS AND SIZE OF ASSETS IN THOUSANDS OF DOLLARS

Item Description for Accounting Period 7/10 Through 6/11	Total	Zero Assets	Under 500	500 to 1000	1,000 to 5,000	5,000 to 10,000	10,000 to 25,000	25,000 to 50,000	50,000 to 100,000	100,000 to 250,000	250,000 to 500,000	500,000 to 2,500,000	2,500,000 and over
Number of Enterprises **1**	150	•	0	65	18	9	10	•	11	9	5	•	4
Revenues ($ in Thousands)													
Net Sales **2**	42981787	•	0	218319	124189	133359	165750	•	1761732	2762310	1996229	•	20794392
Interest **3**	76868	•	0	12	556	7	0	•	1394	505	1620	•	66951
Rents **4**	30949	•	0	0	0	0	0	•	10	180	338	•	28098
Royalties **5**	1388171	•	0	0	0	0	0	•	0	0	10785	•	1377387
Other Portfolio Income **6**	1909055	•	0	0	29	3705	285	•	642	615	3628	•	1857166
Other Receipts **7**	2385624	•	0	1	444	29068	16483	•	29916	19765	30047	•	2059683
Total Receipts **8**	48772454	•	0	218332	125218	166139	182518	•	1793694	2783375	2042647	•	26183677
Average Total Receipts **9**	325150	•	•	3359	6957	18460	18252	•	163063	309264	408529	•	6545919
Operating Costs/Operating Income (%)													
Cost of Operations **10**	51.2	•	•	65.8	50.7	70.0	51.9	•	58.3	70.4	63.4	•	40.8
Salaries and Wages **11**	13.8	•	•	0.4	1.1	15.1	14.8	•	14.4	6.9	10.9	•	13.9
Taxes Paid **12**	1.9	•	•	2.7	2.1	2.2	2.1	•	1.5	1.0	2.6	•	1.8
Interest Paid **13**	4.5	•	•	0.3	•	0.0	1.0	•	0.8	0.4	0.9	•	7.0
Depreciation **14**	4.5	•	•	1.1	2.1	3.5	1.2	•	2.6	2.7	4.1	•	5.5
Amortization and Depletion **15**	1.2	•	•	0.3	•	•	2.5	•	0.5	0.5	1.3	•	1.5
Pensions and Other Deferred Comp. **16**	0.7	•	•	1.5	0.1	1.2	0.4	•	0.2	0.3	0.7	•	0.9
Employee Benefits **17**	2.5	•	•	0.2	•	3.0	1.6	•	1.8	1.7	1.5	•	2.4
Advertising **18**	4.7	•	•	2.0	2.7	0.7	8.7	•	3.9	2.6	3.0	•	7.5
Other Expenses **19**	17.6	•	•	19.6	16.7	23.9	7.7	•	8.4	6.9	8.2	•	27.3
Officers' Compensation **20**	0.5	•	•	2.8	1.1	0.3	1.9	•	1.4	0.3	0.5	•	0.3
Operating Margin **21**	•	•	•	3.4	23.4	•	6.1	•	6.1	6.1	3.0	•	•
Operating Margin Before Officers' Comp. **22**	•	•	•	6.1	24.5	•	8.0	•	7.6	6.5	3.5	•	•

Selected Average Balance Sheet ($ in Thousands)

Net Receivables 23	27731	181	521	1376	1640	16356	33274	28947	736046
Inventories 24	14700	357	54	1061	1504	6758	14939	24460	408373
Net Property, Plant and Equipment 25	80733	22	1272	1257	2070	22571	42958	75777	2497950
Total Assets 26	493651	687	4187	5851	14644	67713	145414	296828	16640464
Notes and Loans Payable 27	193580	190	4	0	3726	15629	21923	52346	6648927
All Other Liabilities 28	111823	146	461	961	1498	23212	38285	119930	3553085
Net Worth 29	188248	351	3722	4891	9420	28873	85206	124553	6438452

Selected Financial Ratios (Times to 1)

Current Ratio 30	0.7	4.4	2.6	3.2	2.8	2.2	2.0	2.2	0.6
Quick Ratio 31	0.4	1.7	2.2	2.0	2.1	1.5	1.3	1.3	0.3
Net Sales to Working Capital 32	•	6.7	9.3	6.9	8.3	9.2	11.2	7.4	•
Coverage Ratio 33	4.1	11.7	•	6169.0	16.8	10.5	17.2	6.6	4.5
Total Asset Turnover 34	0.6	4.9	1.6	2.5	1.1	2.4	2.1	1.3	0.3
Inventory Turnover 35	10.0	6.2	64.4	9.8	5.7	13.8	14.5	10.4	5.2
Receivables Turnover 36	8.6	17.5	19.9	•	7.2	•	11.3	•	•
Total Liabilities to Net Worth 37	1.6	1.0	0.1	0.2	0.6	1.3	0.7	1.4	1.6
Current Assets to Working Capital 38	•	1.3	1.6	1.4	1.6	1.9	2.0	1.9	•
Current Liabilities to Working Capital 39	•	0.3	0.6	0.4	0.6	0.9	1.0	0.9	•
Working Capital to Net Sales 40	•	0.1	0.1	0.1	0.1	0.1	0.1	0.1	•
Inventory to Working Capital 41	•	0.8	0.1	0.5	0.3	0.4	0.6	0.5	•
Total Receipts to Cash Flow 42	4.0	5.7	2.7	6.9	4.7	7.2	8.1	8.7	2.5
Cost of Goods to Cash Flow 43	2.0	3.7	1.4	4.8	2.4	4.2	5.7	5.5	1.0
Cash Flow to Total Debt 44	0.2	1.8	5.5	2.2	0.7	0.6	0.6	0.3	0.2

Selected Financial Factors (in Percentages)

Debt Ratio 45	61.9	49.0	11.1	16.4	35.7	57.4	41.4	58.0	61.3
Return on Total Assets 46	10.8	17.9	39.8	11.7	19.4	20.8	15.4	8.3	9.9
Return on Equity Before Income Taxes 47	21.4	32.2	44.8	14.0	28.4	44.0	24.8	16.7	20.0
Return on Equity After Income Taxes 48	14.5	24.4	35.5	11.2	28.4	42.9	21.1	12.9	13.0
Profit Margin (Before Income Tax) 49	14.1	3.4	24.2	4.6	16.1	7.9	6.9	5.2	24.7
Profit Margin (After Income Tax) 50	9.5	2.5	19.1	3.7	16.1	7.7	5.9	4.0	16.1

Table I

Corporations with and without Net Income

BREWERIES

MONEY AMOUNTS AND SIZE OF ASSETS IN THOUSANDS OF DOLLARS

Item Description for Accounting Period 7/10 Through 6/11	Total	Zero Assets	Under 500	500 to 1,000	1,000 to 5,000	5,000 to 10,000	10,000 to 25,000	25,000 to 50,000	50,000 to 100,000	100,000 to 250,000	250,000 to 500,000	500,000 to 2,500,000	2,500,000 and over
Number of Enterprises **1**	759	437	107	0	164	10	16	15	0	6	0	0	3
Revenues ($ in Thousands)													
Net Sales **2**	20043638	55603	129210	0	492354	64428	456569	840171	0	1524494	0	0	16480808
Interest **3**	234219	3	0	0	0	2	29	169	0	249	0	0	233767
Rents **4**	9479	0	0	0	0	0	0	0	0	0	0	0	9479
Royalties **5**	333756	0	0	0	0	0	0	0	0	0	0	0	333756
Other Portfolio Income **6**	674677	2499	0	0	0	218	443	58	0	2571	0	0	668888
Other Receipts **7**	934735	809	10	0	2122	3	1125	7325	0	6578	0	0	916765
Total Receipts **8**	22230504	58914	129220	0	494476	64651	458166	847723	0	1533892	0	0	18643463
Average Total Receipts **9**	29289	135	1208	•	3015	6465	28635	56515	•	255649	•	•	6214488
Operating Costs/Operating Income (%)													
Cost of Operations **10**	39.8	64.7	61.8	•	34.9	48.0	55.9	57.6	•	55.2	•	•	36.8
Salaries and Wages **11**	7.4	8.7	1.6	•	6.4	3.8	9.3	6.6	•	6.1	•	•	7.6
Taxes Paid **12**	12.9	8.3	4.0	•	2.9	1.6	3.4	4.3	•	5.9	•	•	14.7
Interest Paid **13**	14.2	2.9	0.0	•	2.7	1.3	1.0	1.4	•	0.6	•	•	17.0
Depreciation **14**	3.4	4.0	0.2	•	12.7	15.6	7.4	6.6	•	3.9	•	•	2.8
Amortization and Depletion **15**	1.2	0.4	•	•	0.0	0.1	0.1	0.2	•	0.5	•	•	1.4
Pensions and Other Deferred Comp. **16**	0.7	•	0.4	•	0.2	2.6	0.5	0.3	•	0.3	•	•	0.8
Employee Benefits **17**	1.6	1.6	0.3	•	0.5	2.9	0.9	1.1	•	1.1	•	•	1.7
Advertising **18**	4.2	11.2	0.0	•	1.8	0.3	2.1	1.8	•	5.0	•	•	4.4
Other Expenses **19**	12.1	6.7	2.0	•	11.9	13.1	11.7	8.5	•	10.9	•	•	12.4
Officers' Compensation **20**	0.5	1.0	1.3	•	2.8	3.0	2.0	1.6	•	0.8	•	•	0.3
Operating Margin **21**	2.1	•	28.3	•	23.1	7.8	5.6	9.9	•	9.9	•	•	0.0
Operating Margin Before Officers' Comp. **22**	2.5	•	29.6	•	25.9	10.8	7.6	11.5	•	10.6	•	•	0.3

Selected Average Balance Sheet ($ in Thousands)

Item									
Net Receivables 23	6515	0	141	58	501	2234	4570	26188	1551420
Inventories 24	1083	0	19	412	1152	2001	3056	10216	200147
Net Property, Plant and Equipment 25	10227	0	5	1503	2398	9464	23030	71894	2187580
Total Assets 26	120661	0	185	2640	5213	16893	40658	193172	29679310
Notes and Loans Payable 27	60278	0	0	1266	1990	4950	12359	35264	1015768
All Other Liabilities 28	29192	0	21	359	888	3800	6102	46138	7219172
Net Worth 29	31192	0	164	1015	2334	8142	22197	111770	7444370

Selected Financial Ratios (Times to 1)

Item									
Current Ratio 30	2.1		2.3	2.5	2.4	1.5	2.1	2.2	2.1
Quick Ratio 31	1.7		2.0	1.3	1.1	0.9	1.4	1.7	1.8
Net Sales to Working Capital 32	3.7		12.0	4.9	4.2	12.8	7.9	5.6	3.3
Coverage Ratio 33	2.0		1355.0	9.6	7.3	6.8	8.6	17.4	1.8
Total Asset Turnover 34	0.2		6.5	1.1	1.2	1.7	1.4	1.3	0.2
Inventory Turnover 35	9.7		39.4	2.5	2.7	8.0	10.6	13.7	10.1
Receivables Turnover 36	4.0		17.2	42.1	25.7	14.4	16.7	13.6	3.4
Total Liabilities to Net Worth 37	2.9		0.1	1.6	1.2	1.1	0.8	0.7	3.0
Current Assets to Working Capital 38	1.9		1.8	1.7	1.7	2.8	1.9	1.8	1.9
Current Liabilities to Working Capital 39	0.9		0.8	0.7	0.7	1.8	0.9	0.8	0.9
Working Capital to Net Sales 40	0.3		0.1	0.2	0.2	0.1	0.1	0.2	0.3
Inventory to Working Capital 41	0.1		0.2	0.8	0.8	1.0	0.5	0.2	0.1
Total Receipts to Cash Flow 42	4.5	37.2	3.4	3.5	5.5	7.2	5.6	4.9	4.4
Cost of Goods to Cash Flow 43	1.8	24.1	2.1	1.2	2.6	4.0	3.2	2.7	1.6
Cash Flow to Total Debt 44	0.1		17.2	0.5	0.4	0.5	0.5	0.6	0.1

Selected Financial Factors (in Percentages)

Item									
Debt Ratio 45	74.1		11.1	61.6	55.2	51.8	45.4	42.1	74.9
Return on Total Assets 46	6.1		184.8	29.9	11.6	11.8	16.9	14.4	5.8
Return on Equity Before Income Taxes 47	11.7		207.7	69.7	22.4	20.8	27.3	23.5	10.5
Return on Equity After Income Taxes 48	8.3		194.2	69.7	16.4	20.1	26.1	20.2	7.0
Profit Margin (Before Income Tax) 49	13.9		28.3	23.6	8.1	5.9	10.8	10.3	14.2
Profit Margin (After Income Tax) 50	9.8		26.5	23.6	5.9	5.7	10.3	8.9	9.5

Table II
Corporations with Net Income

BREWERIES

MONEY AMOUNTS AND SIZE OF ASSETS IN THOUSANDS OF DOLLARS

Item Description for Accounting Period 7/10 Through 6/11	Total	Zero Assets	Under 500	500 to 1,000	1,000 to 5,000	5,000 to 10,000	10,000 to 25,000	25,000 to 50,000	50,000 to 100,000	100,000 to 250,000	250,000 to 500,000	500,000 to 2,500,000	2,500,000 and over
Number of Enterprises **1**	302	•	107	0	146	10	•	•	0	6	0	0	3
Revenues ($ in Thousands)													
Net Sales **2**	19945348	•	129210	0	491867	64428	•	•	0	1524494	0	0	16480808
Interest **3**	234218	•	0	0	0	2	•	•	0	249	0	0	233767
Rents **4**	9479	•	0	0	0	0	•	•	0	0	0	0	9479
Royalties **5**	333756	•	0	0	0	0	•	•	0	0	0	0	333756
Other Portfolio Income **6**	674646	•	0	0	0	218	•	•	0	2571	0	0	668888
Other Receipts **7**	934735	•	10	0	2122	3	•	•	0	6578	0	0	916765
Total Receipts **8**	22132182	•	129220	0	493989	64651	•	•	0	1533892	0	0	18643463
Average Total Receipts **9**	73285	•	1208	•	3383	6465	•	•	•	255649	•	•	6214488
Operating Costs/Operating Income (%)													
Cost of Operations **10**	39.6	•	61.8	•	34.8	48.0	•	•	•	55.2	•	•	36.8
Salaries and Wages **11**	7.4	•	1.6	•	6.3	3.8	•	•	•	6.1	•	•	7.6
Taxes Paid **12**	13.0	•	4.0	•	2.9	1.6	•	•	•	5.9	•	•	14.7
Interest Paid **13**	14.2	•	0.0	•	2.8	1.3	•	•	•	0.6	•	•	17.0
Depreciation **14**	3.4	•	0.2	•	12.7	15.6	•	•	•	3.9	•	•	2.8
Amortization and Depletion **15**	1.2	•	•	•	0.0	0.1	•	•	•	0.5	•	•	1.4
Pensions and Other Deferred Comp. **16**	0.7	•	0.4	•	0.2	2.6	•	•	•	0.3	•	•	0.8
Employee Benefits **17**	1.6	•	0.3	•	0.5	2.9	•	•	•	1.1	•	•	1.7
Advertising **18**	4.2	•	0.0	•	1.8	0.3	•	•	•	5.0	•	•	4.4
Other Expenses **19**	12.1	•	2.0	•	11.7	13.1	•	•	•	10.9	•	•	12.4
Officers' Compensation **20**	0.5	•	1.3	•	2.8	3.0	•	•	•	0.8	•	•	0.3
Operating Margin **21**	2.1	•	28.3	•	23.5	7.8	•	•	•	9.9	•	•	0.0
Operating Margin Before Officers' Comp. **22**	2.6	•	29.6	•	26.3	10.8	•	•	•	10.6	•	•	0.3

Selected Average Balance Sheet ($ in Thousands)

Net Receivables 23	16338	141	62	501	26188	1551420
Inventories 24	2603	19	296	1152	10216	200147
Net Property, Plant and Equipment 25	25589	5	1689	2398	71894	2187580
Total Assets 26	302782	185	2661	5213	193172	29679310
Notes and Loans Payable 27	151333	0	1422	1990	35264	15015768
All Other Liabilities 28	73249	21	246	888	46138	7219172
Net Worth 29	78200	164	993	2334	111770	7444370

Selected Financial Ratios (Times to 1)

Current Ratio 30	2.1	2.3	3.3	2.4	2.2	2.1
Quick Ratio 31	1.7	2.0	1.9	1.1	1.7	1.8
Net Sales to Working Capital 32	3.7	12.0	5.0	4.2	5.6	3.3
Coverage Ratio 33	2.0	1355.0	9.7	7.3	17.4	1.8
Total Asset Turnover 34	0.2	6.5	1.3	1.2	1.3	0.2
Inventory Turnover 35	10.0	39.4	4.0	2.7	13.7	10.1
Receivables Turnover 36	4.0	17.2	54.2	25.7	13.6	3.4
Total Liabilities to Net Worth 37	2.9	0.1	1.7	1.2	0.7	3.0
Current Assets to Working Capital 38	1.9	1.8	1.4	1.7	1.8	1.9
Current Liabilities to Working Capital 39	0.9	0.8	0.4	0.7	0.8	0.9
Working Capital to Net Sales 40	0.3	0.1	0.2	0.2	0.2	0.3
Inventory to Working Capital 41	0.1	0.2	0.5	0.8	0.2	0.1
Total Receipts to Cash Flow 42	4.5	3.4	3.5	5.5	4.9	4.4
Cost of Goods to Cash Flow 43	1.8	2.1	1.2	2.6	2.7	1.6
Cash Flow to Total Debt 44	0.1	17.2	0.6	0.4	0.6	0.1

Selected Financial Factors (in Percentages)

Debt Ratio 45	74.2	11.1	62.7	55.2	42.1	74.9
Return on Total Assets 46	6.2	184.8	33.7	11.6	14.4	5.8
Return on Equity Before Income Taxes 47	11.8	207.7	81.0	22.4	23.5	10.5
Return on Equity After Income Taxes 48	8.4	194.2	81.0	16.4	20.2	7.0
Profit Margin (Before Income Tax) 49	14.0	28.3	23.9	8.1	10.3	14.2
Profit Margin (After Income Tax) 50	9.9	26.5	23.9	5.9	8.9	9.5

Table I
Corporations with and without Net Income

WINERIES AND DISTILLERIES

MONEY AMOUNTS AND SIZE OF ASSETS IN THOUSANDS OF DOLLARS

Item Description for Accounting Period 7/10 Through 6/11	Total	Zero Assets	Under 500	500 to 1,000	1,000 to 5,000	5,000 to 10,000	10,000 to 25,000	25,000 to 50,000	50,000 to 100,000	100,000 to 250,000	250,000 to 500,000	500,000 to 2,500,000	2,500,000 and over
Number of Enterprises 1	1782	•	•	•	249	94	62	45	21	10	3	5	4
Revenues ($ in Thousands)													
Net Sales 2	23843302	•	•	•	364969	360395	660551	773107	1038544	949305	713559	3029510	15729089
Interest 3	89548	•	•	•	269	336	248	513	3234	68	50	11880	72951
Rents 4	11968	•	•	•	496	26	0	147	775	0	448	345	9731
Royalties 5	638619	•	•	•	0	0	7361	3150	0	0	0	150	627958
Other Portfolio Income 6	109896	•	•	•	216	2640	13653	1927	9074	590	5	927	77490
Other Receipts 7	639146	•	•	•	24442	21446	6176	23598	13333	22525	-7352	41731	491431
Total Receipts 8	25332479	•	•	•	390392	384843	687989	802442	1064960	972488	706710	3084543	17008650
Average Total Receipts 9	14216	•	•	•	1568	4094	11097	17832	50712	97249	235570	616909	4252162
Operating Costs/Operating Income (%)													
Cost of Operations 10	55.5	•	•	•	45.5	42.2	52.0	41.6	62.7	55.3	88.9	51.6	55.3
Salaries and Wages 11	6.6	•	•	•	10.9	25.2	13.5	12.1	6.6	8.2	1.3	5.0	6.1
Taxes Paid 12	10.3	•	•	•	3.3	6.0	4.3	3.0	8.1	6.0	0.6	13.0	11.6
Interest Paid 13	5.1	•	•	•	1.4	6.4	2.7	3.3	2.1	1.7	2.6	3.0	6.3
Depreciation 14	3.3	•	•	•	3.9	5.1	4.1	8.2	5.9	4.4	2.2	4.8	2.4
Amortization and Depletion 15	1.9	•	•	•	0.1	0.8	0.3	0.2	0.4	3.9	0.0	0.6	2.4
Pensions and Other Deferred Comp. 16	0.9	•	•	•	1.3	0.1	0.2	0.3	0.4	0.2	0.7	0.5	1.1
Employee Benefits 17	1.3	•	•	•	2.3	1.7	0.8	1.8	0.7	1.1	0.2	0.9	1.4
Advertising 18	5.3	•	•	•	0.8	2.0	1.4	2.9	1.1	1.8	1.1	4.0	6.7
Other Expenses 19	11.1	•	•	•	26.9	18.5	14.1	17.9	8.6	6.4	3.1	9.4	11.2
Officers' Compensation 20	1.2	•	•	•	8.2	1.4	2.0	2.2	1.8	1.4	0.3	0.7	0.8
Operating Margin 21	•	•	•	•	•	•	4.5	6.5	1.6	9.5	•	6.5	•
Operating Margin Before Officers' Comp. 22	3.6	•	•	•	•	•	6.5	8.7	3.5	10.9	•	7.2	•

Selected Average Balance Sheet ($ in Thousands)

Net Receivables 23	1793	99	333	1235	2526	5653	12558	27771	72485	563834
Inventories 24	4632	903	2672	6171	9078	18614	69022	106271	291620	1035701
Net Property, Plant and Equipment 25	3557	421	3473	4020	16221	28522	40529	113017	213529	602355
Total Assets 26	19711	2067	7533	15264	36273	70973	134986	313878	841582	5778435
Notes and Loans Payable 27	8945	796	4794	6311	10258	24972	37336	135055	155245	3042908
All Other Liabilities 28	3441	140	515	3665	5588	10811	23475	87591	174228	959410
Net Worth 29	7325	1131	2223	5288	20427	35190	74175	91233	512109	1776117

Selected Financial Ratios (Times to 1)

Current Ratio 30	3.4	3.5	5.1	2.0	2.2	2.0	2.7	1.8	2.6	4.9
Quick Ratio 31	0.9	0.9	1.1	0.3	0.7	0.5	0.6	0.4	0.5	1.6
Net Sales to Working Capital 32	2.5	1.3	1.4	2.4	2.1	3.1	2.0	3.8	2.3	2.7
Coverage Ratio 33	1.9	2.7	0.6	4.2	4.1	3.0	7.9	0.2	3.8	1.6
Total Asset Turnover 34	0.7	0.7	0.5	0.7	0.5	0.7	0.7	0.8	0.7	0.7
Inventory Turnover 35	1.6	0.7	0.6	0.9	0.8	1.7	0.8	2.0	1.1	2.1
Receivables Turnover 36	6.6	•	•	9.9	7.1	9.1	6.7	17.1	8.6	5.8
Total Liabilities to Net Worth 37	1.7	0.8	2.4	1.9	0.8	1.0	0.8	2.4	0.6	2.3
Current Assets to Working Capital 38	1.4	1.4	1.2	2.0	1.8	2.0	1.6	2.2	1.6	1.3
Current Liabilities to Working Capital 39	0.4	0.4	0.2	1.0	0.8	1.0	0.6	1.2	0.6	0.3
Working Capital to Net Sales 40	0.4	0.7	0.7	0.4	0.5	0.3	0.5	0.3	0.4	0.4
Inventory to Working Capital 41	0.9	0.8	1.0	1.6	1.1	1.2	1.2	1.7	1.1	0.7
Total Receipts to Cash Flow 42	9.6	4.7	8.6	5.3	4.2	9.9	6.1	133.0	7.0	11.2
Cost of Goods to Cash Flow 43	5.3	2.1	3.6	2.8	1.7	6.2	3.4	118.2	3.6	6.2
Cash Flow to Total Debt 44	0.1	0.3	0.1	0.2	0.3	0.1	0.3	0.0	0.3	0.1

Selected Financial Factors (in Percentages)

Debt Ratio 45	62.8	45.3	70.5	65.4	43.7	50.4	45.1	70.9	39.1	69.3
Return on Total Assets 46	6.5	2.7	1.9	7.9	6.4	4.3	9.6	0.4	8.2	6.9
Return on Equity Before Income Taxes 47	8.2	3.1	•	17.4	8.6	5.9	15.3	•	9.9	8.6
Return on Equity After Income Taxes 48	5.5	2.8	•	16.8	8.2	5.4	15.1	•	8.4	4.4
Profit Margin (Before Income Tax) 49	4.5	2.4	•	8.7	10.2	4.2	11.9	•	8.4	3.9
Profit Margin (After Income Tax) 50	3.0	2.1	•	8.3	3.8	7.1	11.8	•	7.1	2.0

Table II
Corporations with Net Income

WINERIES AND DISTILLERIES

MONEY AMOUNTS AND SIZE OF ASSETS IN THOUSANDS OF DOLLARS

Item Description for Accounting Period 7/10 Through 6/11	Total	Zero Assets	Under 500	500 to 1,000	1,000 to 5,000	5,000 to 10,000	10,000 to 25,000	25,000 to 50,000	50,000 to 100,000	100,000 to 250,000	250,000 to 500,000	500,000 to 2,500,000	2,500,000 and over
Number of Enterprises **1**	880	•	0	268	199	59	45	33	11	10	0	•	•
Revenues ($ in Thousands)													
Net Sales **2**	19933459	•	0	176144	225514	281953	562833	711267	802103	1568681	0	•	•
Interest **3**	67925	•	0	0	203	91	164	511	697	18	0	•	•
Rents **4**	10726	•	0	0	0	24	0	147	39	439	0	•	•
Royalties **5**	636227	•	0	0	0	0	7361	3150	0	0	0	•	•
Other Portfolio Income **6**	80451	•	0	0	216	74	13610	1917	2751	590	0	•	•
Other Receipts **7**	398433	•	0	0	24055	19394	4365	16165	8395	15518	0	•	•
Total Receipts **8**	21127221	•	0	176144	249988	301536	588333	733157	813985	1585246	0	•	•
Average Total Receipts **9**	24008	•	•	657	1256	5111	13074	22217	73999	158525	•	•	•
Operating Costs/Operating Income (%)													
Cost of Operations **10**	54.0	•	•	44.4	34.2	34.7	51.3	42.3	61.5	70.8	•	•	•
Salaries and Wages **11**	6.4	•	•	•	9.4	25.1	12.7	10.4	5.7	5.0	•	•	•
Taxes Paid **12**	12.0	•	•	7.0	3.5	5.4	4.3	3.1	9.8	3.6	•	•	•
Interest Paid **13**	4.0	•	•	6.7	0.4	5.9	2.8	1.8	0.8	0.9	•	•	•
Depreciation **14**	2.7	•	•	1.6	3.3	4.4	3.0	6.9	3.6	2.8	•	•	•
Amortization and Depletion **15**	1.8	•	•	0.4	•	0.1	0.2	0.2	0.2	2.4	•	•	•
Pensions and Other Deferred Comp. **16**	1.0	•	•	•	2.1	0.1	0.2	0.3	0.3	0.4	•	•	•
Employee Benefits **17**	1.0	•	•	1.2	2.2	1.3	0.6	1.9	0.6	0.7	•	•	•
Advertising **18**	5.5	•	•	3.7	0.9	1.9	1.4	2.7	0.9	1.3	•	•	•
Other Expenses **19**	8.7	•	•	6.0	26.9	21.2	14.9	15.4	8.1	4.4	•	•	•
Officers' Compensation **20**	1.2	•	•	24.4	10.3	1.5	2.0	2.4	1.8	1.0	•	•	•
Operating Margin **21**	1.7	•	•	4.7	6.9	•	6.7	12.7	6.6	6.7	•	•	•
Operating Margin Before Officers' Comp. **22**	2.9	•	•	29.1	17.2	•	8.7	15.1	8.4	7.7	•	•	•

Selected Average Balance Sheet ($ in Thousands)

Net Receivables 23	2911	10	41	342	1564	3205	8682	18403
Inventories 24	7472	312	619	2521	6918	9103	24121	71236
Net Property, Plant and Equipment 25	4252	349	276	3557	3328	14416	18592	40266
Total Assets 26	25544	766	1676	6924	15809	35831	63793	159586
Notes and Loans Payable 27	12804	697	579	4551	6139	8443	13719	44213
All Other Liabilities 28	4870	5	82	636	4599	6420	9401	40534
Net Worth 29	7870	64	1015	1737	5070	20968	40673	74838

Selected Financial Ratios (Times to 1)

Current Ratio 30	3.4	3.8	2.8	3.5	2.0	2.4	2.3	2.4
Quick Ratio 31	1.0	0.4	0.6	0.6	0.4	0.8	0.9	0.6
Net Sales to Working Capital 32	2.7	2.4	1.4	2.1	2.4	2.2	3.5	2.8
Coverage Ratio 33	3.0	1.7	48.8	1.9	5.0	9.9	11.6	9.2
Total Asset Turnover 34	0.9	0.9	0.7	0.7	0.8	0.6	1.1	1.0
Inventory Turnover 35	1.6	0.9	0.6	0.7	0.9	1.0	1.9	1.6
Receivables Turnover 36	6.2	92.8	27.1	•	9.3	7.4	8.4	9.6
Total Liabilities to Net Worth 37	2.2	11.0	0.7	3.0	2.1	0.7	0.6	1.1
Current Assets to Working Capital 38	1.4	1.4	1.6	1.4	2.0	1.7	1.8	1.7
Current Liabilities to Working Capital 39	0.4	0.4	0.6	0.4	1.0	0.7	0.8	0.7
Working Capital to Net Sales 40	0.4	0.4	0.7	0.5	0.4	0.5	0.3	0.4
Inventory to Working Capital 41	0.8	1.2	0.8	1.1	1.6	1.0	1.0	1.3
Total Receipts to Cash Flow 42	7.1	12.1	2.7	4.4	4.6	3.7	7.2	9.0
Cost of Goods to Cash Flow 43	3.8	5.4	0.9	1.5	2.3	1.6	4.4	6.4
Cash Flow to Total Debt 44	0.2	0.1	0.6	0.2	0.3	0.4	0.4	0.2

Selected Financial Factors (in Percentages)

Debt Ratio 45	69.2	91.7	39.4	74.9	67.9	41.5	36.2	53.1
Return on Total Assets 46	10.5	9.7	12.2	7.8	11.1	10.5	10.1	8.6
Return on Equity Before Income Taxes 47	22.5	47.9	19.8	15.0	27.7	16.2	14.5	16.3
Return on Equity After Income Taxes 48	17.4	47.8	19.3	15.0	26.9	15.6	13.6	15.9
Profit Margin (Before Income Tax) 49	7.8	4.7	17.7	5.5	11.2	15.7	8.1	7.8
Profit Margin (After Income Tax) 50	6.0	4.6	17.3	5.4	10.9	15.2	7.6	7.6

Table I

Corporations with and without Net Income

TOBACCO MANUFACTURING

MONEY AMOUNTS AND SIZE OF ASSETS IN THOUSANDS OF DOLLARS

Item Description for Accounting Period 7/10 Through 6/11	Total	Zero Assets	Under 500	500 to 1,000	1,000 to 5,000	5,000 to 10,000	10,000 to 25,000	25,000 to 50,000	50,000 to 100,000	100,000 to 250,000	250,000 to 500,000	500,000 to 2,500,000	2,500,000 and over
Number of Enterprises **1**	33	0	0	0	0	0	22	0	4	0	0	4	3
Revenues ($ in Thousands)													
Net Sales **2**	49014297	0	0	0	0	0	1389368	0	552035	0	0	3919142	43153753
Interest **3**	84235	0	0	0	0	0	768	0	13	0	0	16521	66933
Rents **4**	899959	0	0	0	0	0	0	0	8	0	0	364	899586
Royalties **5**	5912	0	0	0	0	0	0	0	267	0	0	1	5643
Other Portfolio Income **6**	854535	0	0	0	0	0	340	0	0	0	0	23963	830231
Other Receipts **7**	143776	0	0	0	0	0	18413	0	2374	0	0	26457	96533
Total Receipts **8**	51002714	0	0	0	0	0	1408889	0	554697	0	0	3986448	45052679
Average Total Receipts **9**	1545537	•	•	•	•	•	64040	•	138674	•	•	996612	15017560
Operating Costs/Operating Income (%)													
Cost of Operations **10**	38.0	•	•	•	•	•	39.5	•	35.0	•	•	36.1	38.2
Salaries and Wages **11**	3.6	•	•	•	•	•	3.1	•	2.6	•	•	3.4	3.7
Taxes Paid **12**	29.7	•	•	•	•	•	44.1	•	45.4	•	•	32.3	28.8
Interest Paid **13**	2.5	•	•	•	•	•	0.1	•	0.5	•	•	3.3	2.5
Depreciation **14**	1.3	•	•	•	•	•	0.7	•	0.9	•	•	1.4	1.3
Amortization and Depletion **15**	0.8	•	•	•	•	•	0.0	•	0.2	•	•	4.0	0.6
Pensions and Other Deferred Comp. **16**	2.0	•	•	•	•	•	0.2	•	0.2	•	•	0.6	2.2
Employee Benefits **17**	0.9	•	•	•	•	•	0.2	•	0.5	•	•	0.5	0.9
Advertising **18**	0.8	•	•	•	•	•	0.6	•	0.6	•	•	0.7	0.9
Other Expenses **19**	7.4	•	•	•	•	•	6.5	•	6.1	•	•	7.8	7.4
Officers' Compensation **20**	0.5	•	•	•	•	•	2.6	•	1.1	•	•	1.4	0.4
Operating Margin **21**	12.5	•	•	•	•	•	2.2	•	6.9	•	•	8.6	13.2
Operating Margin Before Officers' Comp. **22**	13.0	•	•	•	•	•	4.8	•	8.0	•	•	10.0	13.6

Selected Average Balance Sheet ($ in Thousands)

Net Receivables 23	13435	3327	7522	14646	93833
Inventories 24	118403	3273	28800	131237	1057281
Net Property, Plant and Equipment 25	124209	3978	3718	88846	1213712
Total Assets 26	1901116	17166	84119	1427899	18770365
Notes and Loans Payable 27	610394	3427	114970	477781	5898873
All Other Liabilities 28	884416	8809	57068	297924	9190651
Net Worth 29	406306	4930	-87919	652195	3680840

Selected Financial Ratios (Times to 1)

Current Ratio 30	1.1	1.4	0.8	2.8	1.0
Quick Ratio 31	0.6	0.6	0.3	1.7	0.6
Net Sales to Working Capital 32	31.8	17.7		3.4	110.3
Coverage Ratio 33	7.7	29.8	16.3	4.1	8.1
Total Asset Turnover 34	0.8	3.7	1.6	0.7	0.8
Inventory Turnover 35	4.8	7.6	1.7	2.7	5.2
Receivables Turnover 36	104.4	19.6	18.0	65.3	142.3
Total Liabilities to Net Worth 37	3.7	2.5		1.2	4.1
Current Assets to Working Capital 38	9.3	3.5		1.6	30.9
Current Liabilities to Working Capital 39	8.3	2.5		0.6	29.9
Working Capital to Net Sales 40	0.0	0.1		0.3	0.0
Inventory to Working Capital 41	2.5	1.2		0.5	7.8
Total Receipts to Cash Flow 42	4.5	11.3	7.9	6.1	4.3
Cost of Goods to Cash Flow 43	1.7	4.5	2.8	2.2	1.6
Cash Flow to Total Debt 44	0.2	0.5	0.1	0.2	0.2

Selected Financial Factors (in Percentages)

Debt Ratio 45	78.6	71.3	204.5	54.3	80.4
Return on Total Assets 46	15.1	13.6	12.8	9.3	15.8
Return on Equity Before Income Taxes 47	61.7	45.6		15.3	70.4
Return on Equity After Income Taxes 48	40.7	43.3		11.8	45.8
Profit Margin (Before Income Tax) 49	16.9	3.6	7.3	10.2	18.0
Profit Margin (After Income Tax) 50	11.1	3.4	7.3	7.8	11.7

Table II

Corporations with Net Income

TOBACCO MANUFACTURING

MONEY AMOUNTS AND SIZE OF ASSETS IN THOUSANDS OF DOLLARS

Item Description for Accounting Period 7/10 Through 6/11		Total	Zero Assets	Under 500	500 to 1,000	1,000 to 5,000	5,000 to 10,000	10,000 to 25,000	25,000 to 50,000	50,000 to 100,000	100,000 to 250,000	250,000 to 500,000	500,000 to 2,500,000	2,500,000 and over
Number of Enterprises	1	27	0	0	0	0	0	0	0	0	0	0	4	•
Revenues ($ in Thousands)														
Net Sales	2	48563366	0	0	0	0	0	0	0	0	0	0	3919142	•
Interest	3	84160	0	0	0	0	0	0	0	0	0	0	16521	•
Rents	4	899950	0	0	0	0	0	0	0	0	0	0	364	•
Royalties	5	5645	0	0	0	0	0	0	0	0	0	0	1	•
Other Portfolio Income	6	854257	0	0	0	0	0	0	0	0	0	0	23963	•
Other Receipts	7	141873	0	0	0	0	0	0	0	0	0	0	26457	•
Total Receipts	8	50549251	0	0	0	0	0	0	0	0	0	0	3986448	•
Average Total Receipts	9	1872194	•	•	•	•	•	•	•	•	•	•	996612	•
Operating Costs/Operating Income (%)														
Cost of Operations	10	37.9	•	•	•	•	•	•	•	•	•	•	36.1	•
Salaries and Wages	11	3.6	•	•	•	•	•	•	•	•	•	•	3.4	•
Taxes Paid	12	29.6	•	•	•	•	•	•	•	•	•	•	32.3	•
Interest Paid	13	2.5	•	•	•	•	•	•	•	•	•	•	3.3	•
Depreciation	14	1.3	•	•	•	•	•	•	•	•	•	•	1.4	•
Amortization and Depletion	15	0.8	•	•	•	•	•	•	•	•	•	•	4.0	•
Pensions and Other Deferred Comp.	16	2.0	•	•	•	•	•	•	•	•	•	•	0.6	•
Employee Benefits	17	0.9	•	•	•	•	•	•	•	•	•	•	0.5	•
Advertising	18	0.8	•	•	•	•	•	•	•	•	•	•	0.7	•
Other Expenses	19	7.4	•	•	•	•	•	•	•	•	•	•	7.8	•
Officers' Compensation	20	0.5	•	•	•	•	•	•	•	•	•	•	1.4	•
Operating Margin	21	12.6	•	•	•	•	•	•	•	•	•	•	8.6	•
Operating Margin Before Officers' Comp.	22	13.2	•	•	•	•	•	•	•	•	•	•	10.0	•

Selected Average Balance Sheet ($ in Thousands)

Net Receivables 23	15711	14646
Inventories 24	143092	131237
Net Property, Plant and Equipment 25	151474	88846
Total Assets 26	2312447	1427899
Notes and Loans Payable 27	728000	477781
All Other Liabilities 28	1069437	297924
Net Worth 29	515010	652195

Selected Financial Ratios (Times to 1)

Current Ratio 30	1.1	2.8
Quick Ratio 31	0.6	1.7
Net Sales to Working Capital 32	28.9	3.4
Coverage Ratio 33	7.7	4.1
Total Asset Turnover 34	0.8	0.7
Inventory Turnover 35	4.8	2.7
Receivables Turnover 36	106.3	65.3
Total Liabilities to Net Worth 37	3.5	1.2
Current Assets to Working Capital 38	8.4	1.6
Current Liabilities to Working Capital 39	7.4	0.6
Working Capital to Net Sales 40	0.0	0.3
Inventory to Working Capital 41	2.2	0.5
Total Receipts to Cash Flow 42	4.5	6.1
Cost of Goods to Cash Flow 43	1.7	2.2
Cash Flow to Total Debt 44	0.2	0.2

Selected Financial Factors (in Percentages)

Debt Ratio 45	77.7	54.3
Return on Total Assets 46	15.2	9.3
Return on Equity Before Income Taxes 47	59.6	15.3
Return on Equity After Income Taxes 48	39.4	11.8
Profit Margin (Before Income Tax) 49	17.1	10.2
Profit Margin (After Income Tax) 50	11.3	7.8

58

Table I
Corporations with and without Net Income

TEXTILE MILLS

Money Amounts and Size of Assets in Thousands of Dollars

Item Description for Accounting Period 7/10 Through 6/11	Total	Zero Assets	Under 500	500 to 1,000	1,000 to 5,000	5,000 to 10,000	10,000 to 25,000	25,000 to 50,000	50,000 to 100,000	100,000 to 250,000	250,000 to 500,000	500,000 to 2,500,000	2,500,000 and over
Number of Enterprises 1	1659	362	884	56	172	66	65	16	20	9	4	5	0
Revenues ($ in Thousands)													
Net Sales 2	12255094	283275	370489	232128	354569	1292920	1449236	688416	1938922	1861464	1848556	1939119	0
Interest 3	42642	1228	0	1	2432	528	1795	64	1986	1362	3071	30175	0
Rents 4	7365	0	0	0	0	65	5879	26	146	0	898	351	0
Royalties 5	22855	2201	0	0	0	0	0	10	172	6307	0	14166	0
Other Portfolio Income 6	45301	0	0	0	3229	1973	36	804	3050	1857	2219	32132	0
Other Receipts 7	122411	375	0	91	336	1727	7003	3815	11260	12361	36072	49372	0
Total Receipts 8	12499668	287079	370489	232220	360566	1297213	1463949	693135	1955536	1883351	1890816	2065315	0
Average Total Receipts 9	7534	793	419	4147	2096	19655	22522	43321	97777	209261	472704	413063	•
Operating Costs/Operating Income (%)													
Cost of Operations 10	74.8	48.6	65.9	74.0	72.2	78.4	83.0	74.1	75.7	75.8	79.6	66.5	•
Salaries and Wages 11	5.6	18.8	4.4	2.4	5.1	4.7	4.2	6.8	6.2	4.2	4.0	8.0	•
Taxes Paid 12	1.6	2.6	1.6	3.9	2.8	1.4	1.1	1.9	1.5	1.1	1.8	1.7	•
Interest Paid 13	2.2	1.2	2.6	0.1	0.3	0.8	1.4	1.7	1.1	2.1	2.6	5.6	•
Depreciation 14	2.4	0.5	0.5	0.4	1.6	1.1	2.4	4.8	2.6	3.3	2.1	2.7	•
Amortization and Depletion 15	0.8	0.6	•	•	•	0.1	0.0	0.4	0.2	0.5	0.2	4.1	•
Pensions and Other Deferred Comp. 16	0.4	0.4	0.1	0.0	0.1	0.2	0.1	0.0	0.6	0.2	0.9	0.7	•
Employee Benefits 17	1.5	0.6	2.3	2.3	3.6	0.7	0.6	1.2	0.9	1.2	1.9	3.1	•
Advertising 18	0.3	0.1	0.0	0.1	0.2	0.1	0.2	0.3	0.5	0.1	0.5	0.3	•
Other Expenses 19	9.0	16.9	22.2	10.0	14.4	8.2	6.1	4.4	6.9	7.5	5.4	15.2	•
Officers' Compensation 20	1.6	4.5	2.5	6.8	5.1	0.9	1.4	0.6	1.6	0.8	1.8	1.1	•
Operating Margin 21	•	5.3	•	0.0	•	3.4	•	3.8	2.2	3.1	•	•	•
Operating Margin Before Officers' Comp. 22	1.3	9.9	0.3	6.8	4.2	•	0.9	4.4	3.8	3.9	1.1	•	•

Selected Average Balance Sheet ($ in Thousands)

Net Receivables 23	1125	0	76	326	351	1738	3968	7054	11025	27795	89982	80896	•
Inventories 24	954	0	1	114	402	2451	3807	5771	13802	21080	72124	50177	•
Net Property, Plant and Equipment 25	1365	0	10	142	371	1177	4246	11724	21051	56390	76032	81952	•
Total Assets 26	6597	0	124	630	2105	7234	16633	32634	70299	152742	420384	779143	•
Notes and Loans Payable 27	2310	0	77	123	187	2998	7227	13332	15174	63607	131583	288438	•
All Other Liabilities 28	1482	0	105	310	473	2552	1849	5101	16388	31927	90307	184357	•
Net Worth 29	2805	0	-58	197	1445	1683	7557	14201	38737	57208	198494	306348	•

Selected Financial Ratios (Times to 1)

Current Ratio 30	2.1	•	0.7	1.1	6.5	1.7	3.2	2.3	2.2	2.2	2.6	1.5	•
Quick Ratio 31	1.1	•	0.7	0.8	4.2	0.6	1.7	1.0	1.0	1.4	1.4	0.7	•
Net Sales to Working Capital 32	5.0	•	•	122.8	1.7	9.0	3.2	4.5	5.2	5.2	4.2	6.1	•
Coverage Ratio 33	1.8	6.4	0.2	1.5	•	5.6	1.3	3.6	3.9	3.0	1.6	0.7	•
Total Asset Turnover 34	1.1	•	3.4	6.6	1.0	2.7	1.3	1.3	1.4	1.4	1.1	0.5	•
Inventory Turnover 35	5.8	•	327.8	26.9	3.7	6.3	4.9	5.5	5.3	7.4	5.1	5.1	•
Receivables Turnover 36	7.6	•	•	12.8	6.3	13.0	5.7	7.5	10.3	8.9	6.1	•	•
Total Liabilities to Net Worth 37	1.4	•	•	2.2	0.5	3.3	1.2	1.3	0.8	1.7	1.1	1.5	•
Current Assets to Working Capital 38	1.9	•	•	13.3	1.2	2.5	1.5	1.8	1.8	1.8	1.6	3.0	•
Current Liabilities to Working Capital 39	0.9	•	•	12.3	0.2	1.5	0.5	0.8	0.8	0.8	0.6	2.0	•
Working Capital to Net Sales 40	0.2	•	•	0.0	0.6	0.1	0.3	0.2	0.2	0.2	0.2	0.2	•
Inventory to Working Capital 41	0.7	•	•	3.4	0.3	1.3	0.6	0.7	0.8	0.6	0.7	0.8	•
Total Receipts to Cash Flow 42	12.0	6.1	9.4	17.4	13.5	10.2	19.9	16.6	12.8	9.9	17.1	9.4	•
Cost of Goods to Cash Flow 43	9.0	3.0	6.2	12.8	9.8	8.0	16.5	12.3	9.7	7.5	13.6	6.2	•
Cash Flow to Total Debt 44	0.2	•	0.2	0.6	0.2	0.3	0.1	0.1	0.2	0.2	0.1	0.1	•

Selected Financial Factors (in Percentages)

Debt Ratio 45	57.5	•	147.2	68.7	31.4	76.7	54.6	56.5	44.9	62.5	52.8	60.7	•
Return on Total Assets 46	4.5	•	1.7	1.5	•	12.2	2.5	8.2	5.8	8.8	4.5	2.0	•
Return on Equity Before Income Taxes 47	4.8	•	15.5	1.7	•	43.0	1.3	13.6	7.9	15.7	3.6	•	•
Return on Equity After Income Taxes 48	3.4	•	15.5	1.3	•	39.1	0.8	11.5	5.7	14.6	2.5	•	•
Profit Margin (Before Income Tax) 49	1.8	6.7	•	0.1	•	3.7	0.5	4.5	3.1	4.3	1.5	•	•
Profit Margin (After Income Tax) 50	1.3	6.7	•	0.1	•	3.4	0.3	3.8	2.3	4.0	1.1	•	•

Table II

Corporations with Net Income

TEXTILE MILLS

MONEY AMOUNTS AND SIZE OF ASSETS IN THOUSANDS OF DOLLARS

Item Description for Accounting Period 7/10 Through 6/11	Total	Zero Assets	Under 500	500 to 1,000	1,000 to 5,000	5,000 to 10,000	10,000 to 25,000	25,000 to 50,000	50,000 to 100,000	100,000 to 250,000	250,000 to 500,000	500,000 to 2,500,000	2,500,000 and over
Number of Enterprises **1**	994	•	397	•	67	44	38	12	•	0	0	•	0
Revenues ($ in Thousands)													
Net Sales **2**	8267633	•	115346	•	188527	1036605	1044992	558637	•	0	0	0	0
Interest **3**	7407	•	0	•	939	0	329	11	•	0	0	0	0
Rents **4**	4525	•	0	•	0	0	3460	0	•	0	0	•	0
Royalties **5**	6492	•	0	•	0	0	0	10	•	0	0	•	0
Other Portfolio Income **6**	22164	•	0	•	0	1705	36	786	•	0	0	•	0
Other Receipts **7**	58942	•	0	•	22	1665	2091	3813	•	0	0	•	0
Total Receipts **8**	8367163	•	115346	•	189488	1039975	1050908	563257	•	0	0	•	0
Average Total Receipts **9**	8418	•	291	•	2828	23636	27655	46938	•	•	•	•	•
Operating Costs/Operating Income (%)													
Cost of Operations **10**	72.0	•	20.2	•	74.3	77.0	83.5	72.3	•	•	•	•	•
Salaries and Wages **11**	5.8	•	14.2	•	0.6	5.5	3.7	7.4	•	•	•	•	•
Taxes Paid **12**	1.4	•	1.2	•	2.5	1.0	0.8	1.8	•	•	•	•	•
Interest Paid **13**	1.5	•	3.0	•	0.0	0.9	1.5	1.9	•	•	•	•	•
Depreciation **14**	2.0	•	1.6	•	1.3	0.8	1.2	3.0	•	•	•	•	•
Amortization and Depletion **15**	0.3	•	•	•	•	0.1	0.0	0.1	•	•	•	•	•
Pensions and Other Deferred Comp. **16**	0.4	•	•	•	0.1	0.2	0.1	0.0	•	•	•	•	•
Employee Benefits **17**	1.6	•	7.4	•	4.5	0.6	0.2	1.3	•	•	•	•	•
Advertising **18**	0.3	•	•	•	0.0	0.1	0.2	0.3	•	•	•	•	•
Other Expenses **19**	8.8	•	43.8	•	15.1	7.8	5.3	4.2	•	•	•	•	•
Officers' Compensation **20**	1.4	•	1.7	•	0.6	0.5	1.2	0.6	•	•	•	•	•
Operating Margin **21**	4.6	•	6.8	•	0.9	5.5	2.2	6.9	•	•	•	•	•
Operating Margin Before Officers' Comp. **22**	5.9	•	8.5	•	1.5	6.0	3.4	7.5	•	•	•	•	•

Selected Average Balance Sheet ($ in Thousands)

Net Receivables 23	1218		0	492	1755	4000	8310
Inventories 24	886		0	569	2445	4477	6199
Net Property, Plant and Equipment 25	1237		19	60	957	3031	9952
Total Assets 26	6211		49	1782	7232	16133	32135
Notes and Loans Payable 27	2065		90	6	3510	6806	12666
All Other Liabilities 28	1016		36	148	1891	1950	5006
Net Worth 29	3130		-77	1628	1831	7377	14463

Selected Financial Ratios (Times to 1)

Current Ratio 30	2.1	0.8	11.7	1.8	2.5	2.4
Quick Ratio 31	1.1	0.8	8.0	0.7	1.1	1.1
Net Sales to Working Capital 32	5.2	3.3	1.8	9.0	4.3	3.9
Coverage Ratio 33	4.9	3.3	34.1	7.2	2.8	5.1
Total Asset Turnover 34	1.3	5.9	1.6	3.3	1.7	1.4
Inventory Turnover 35	6.8		3.7	7.4	5.1	5.4
Receivables Turnover 36	9.2	32.1	5.2	16.1	7.9	7.5
Total Liabilities to Net Worth 37	1.0		0.1	2.9	1.2	1.2
Current Assets to Working Capital 38	1.9		1.1	2.2	1.7	1.7
Current Liabilities to Working Capital 39	0.9		0.1	1.2	0.7	0.7
Working Capital to Net Sales 40	0.2		0.6	0.1	0.2	0.3
Inventory to Working Capital 41	0.7		0.3	1.1	0.8	0.7
Total Receipts to Cash Flow 42	8.4	4.1	7.7	8.7	14.3	11.6
Cost of Goods to Cash Flow 43	6.0	0.8	5.7	6.7	11.9	8.4
Cash Flow to Total Debt 44	0.3	0.6	2.4	0.5	0.2	0.2

Selected Financial Factors (in Percentages)

Debt Ratio 45	49.6	257.2	8.6	74.7	54.3	55.0
Return on Total Assets 46	9.9	58.1	2.3	22.1	7.4	14.0
Return on Equity Before Income Taxes 47	15.6		2.4	75.1	10.5	25.0
Return on Equity After Income Taxes 48	13.6		2.0	69.8	9.6	22.3
Profit Margin (Before Income Tax) 49	5.9	6.8	1.4	5.8	2.8	7.8
Profit Margin (After Income Tax) 50	5.1	6.8	1.1	5.4	2.6	6.9

Table I

Corporations with and without Net Income

TEXTILE PRODUCT MILLS

MONEY AMOUNTS AND SIZE OF ASSETS IN THOUSANDS OF DOLLARS

Item Description for Accounting Period 7/10 Through 6/11	Total	Zero Assets	Under 500	500 to 1,000	1,000 to 5,000	5,000 to 10,000	10,000 to 25,000	25,000 to 50,000	50,000 to 100,000	100,000 to 250,000	250,000 to 500,000	500,000 to 2,500,000	2,500,000 and over
1 Number of Enterprises	2541	329	1148	234	670	41	59	29	11	8	9	3	0
Revenues ($ in Thousands)													
2 Net Sales	21624949	97244	716215	319056	3041083	571699	2197488	1794485	1323568	1613138	4173416	5777558	0
3 Interest	12327	1	49	0	415	8	478	253	434	1160	4911	4618	0
4 Rents	7686	0	0	0	1199	987	0	2002	0	2225	172	1100	0
5 Royalties	41471	0	0	0	0	0	0	388	20	0	13134	27929	0
6 Other Portfolio Income	70517	0	0	0	158	112	2442	2136	1579	5897	16340	41854	0
7 Other Receipts	203842	4920	737	6	11848	1165	18161	7050	8724	6716	9948	134565	0
8 Total Receipts	21960792	102165	717001	319062	3054703	573971	2218569	1806314	1334325	1629136	4217921	5987624	0
9 Average Total Receipts	8643	311	625	1364	4559	13999	37603	62287	121302	203642	468658	1995875	•
Operating Costs/Operating Income (%)													
10 Cost of Operations	68.4	101.7	45.6	63.1	56.0	73.0	79.5	79.2	76.4	78.3	78.6	57.5	•
11 Salaries and Wages	10.2	5.0	13.1	3.4	13.0	4.3	6.2	4.8	5.9	4.9	6.3	17.9	•
12 Taxes Paid	1.7	1.4	1.8	3.9	1.9	2.7	0.9	1.1	1.6	1.3	1.4	2.1	•
13 Interest Paid	1.8	0.7	1.7	0.7	0.7	1.7	0.9	1.6	0.9	0.9	2.8	2.8	•
14 Depreciation	2.5	0.2	0.2	0.2	3.8	1.5	1.6	1.3	2.3	2.5	1.8	3.6	•
15 Amortization and Depletion	0.4	•	0.6	•	0.1	0.7	0.4	0.6	0.3	0.1	0.7	0.4	•
16 Pensions and Other Deferred Comp.	0.5	•	•	•	0.2	0.3	0.2	0.3	0.3	0.3	0.5	0.9	•
17 Employee Benefits	1.3	0.0	0.7	1.5	0.9	0.4	1.1	1.3	1.4	1.0	1.1	2.0	•
18 Advertising	0.7	0.4	3.0	0.1	1.1	0.1	0.4	0.3	0.5	0.2	1.2	0.5	•
19 Other Expenses	10.8	20.1	18.6	19.8	16.6	8.6	6.9	6.0	7.3	7.1	5.7	14.9	•
20 Officers' Compensation	1.9	0.5	11.7	7.6	3.5	6.6	1.8	1.0	0.5	1.3	0.9	0.5	•
21 Operating Margin	•	•	3.2	•	2.3	0.1	0.1	2.6	2.7	2.1	•	•	•
22 Operating Margin Before Officers' Comp.	1.7	•	14.9	7.3	5.8	6.7	1.9	3.6	3.2	3.4	•	•	•

Selected Average Balance Sheet ($ in Thousands)

Net Receivables 23	937	0	17	154	492	1836	3138	8204	17903	30483	68091	148328
Inventories 24	1284	0	24	458	538	2694	6622	8822	20774	35701	67771	312565
Net Property, Plant and Equipment 25	1148	0	28	12	484	1855	2366	6515	12844	31055	52295	430975
Total Assets 26	6819	0	115	815	2074	6869	16606	37150	69557	151543	367380	2664243
Notes and Loans Payable 27	2135	0	50	550	641	2873	3819	12660	30407	42677	150419	690324
All Other Liabilities 28	1895	0	34	126	574	1163	6321	6959	17377	32430	123251	726076
Net Worth 29	2789	0	31	139	858	2834	6467	17531	21772	76436	93710	1247843

Selected Financial Ratios (Times to 1)

Current Ratio 30	1.6	•	1.5	2.2	1.8	2.3	1.9	2.0	2.5	1.6	1.7	1.3
Quick Ratio 31	0.8	•	0.8	0.5	0.9	1.0	0.7	0.9	1.2	0.7	0.8	0.7
Net Sales to Working Capital 32	7.2	•	34.7	3.5	7.1	5.4	6.4	5.8	4.5	6.7	6.3	11.3
Coverage Ratio 33	1.8	•	2.9	0.6	5.1	1.3	2.2	3.0	4.7	4.6	1.1	1.3
Total Asset Turnover 34	1.2	•	5.4	1.7	2.2	2.0	2.2	1.7	1.7	1.3	1.3	0.7
Inventory Turnover 35	4.5	•	12.0	1.9	4.7	3.8	4.5	5.6	4.4	4.4	5.4	3.5
Receivables Turnover 36	9.9	•	•	7.1	11.4	9.7	10.9	7.5	7.5	6.9	7.1	•
Total Liabilities to Net Worth 37	1.4	•	2.7	4.9	1.4	1.4	1.6	1.1	2.2	1.0	2.9	1.1
Current Assets to Working Capital 38	2.6	•	2.9	1.9	2.3	1.8	2.1	2.0	1.7	2.6	2.5	4.8
Current Liabilities to Working Capital 39	1.6	•	1.9	0.9	1.3	0.8	1.1	1.0	0.7	1.6	1.5	3.8
Working Capital to Net Sales 40	0.1	•	0.0	0.3	0.1	0.2	0.2	0.2	0.2	0.1	0.2	0.1
Inventory to Working Capital 41	1.2	•	1.3	1.4	1.1	0.9	1.1	1.0	0.8	1.3	0.9	1.8
Total Receipts to Cash Flow 42	10.6	•	5.8	8.2	6.8	13.3	16.0	13.2	11.3	11.8	25.7	8.2
Cost of Goods to Cash Flow 43	7.3	•	2.6	5.1	3.8	9.7	12.8	10.4	8.7	9.2	20.2	4.7
Cash Flow to Total Debt 44	0.2	•	1.3	0.2	0.6	0.3	0.2	0.2	0.2	0.2	0.1	0.2

Selected Financial Factors (in Percentages)

Debt Ratio 45	59.1	•	73.0	82.9	58.6	58.7	61.1	52.8	68.7	49.6	74.5	53.2
Return on Total Assets 46	4.2	•	27.0	0.6	7.5	4.5	4.4	7.9	7.7	5.2	4.0	2.6
Return on Equity Before Income Taxes 47	4.5	•	65.5	•	14.6	2.4	6.1	11.3	19.3	8.1	2.0	1.1
Return on Equity After Income Taxes 48	3.3	•	65.0	•	12.5	1.0	3.3	10.8	19.2	6.4	•	0.7
Profit Margin (Before Income Tax) 49	1.5	•	3.3	•	2.8	0.5	1.1	3.2	3.5	3.1	0.4	0.7
Profit Margin (After Income Tax) 50	1.1	•	3.2	•	2.4	0.2	0.6	3.0	3.5	2.4	•	0.4

Table II

Corporations with Net Income

TEXTILE PRODUCT MILLS

MONEY AMOUNTS AND SIZE OF ASSETS IN THOUSANDS OF DOLLARS

Item Description for Accounting Period 7/10 Through 6/11	Total	Zero Assets	Under 500	500 to 1,000	1,000 to 5,000	5,000 to 10,000	10,000 to 25,000	25,000 to 50,000	50,000 to 100,000	100,000 to 250,000	250,000 to 500,000	500,000 to 2,500,000	2,500,000 and over
Number of Enterprises **1**	1747	0	824	173	632	31	42	25	•	•	6	0	0
Revenues ($ in Thousands)													
Net Sales **2**	13243534	0	621344	174595	2970377	435156	1357138	1529601	•	•	3990512	0	0
Interest **3**	4441	0	0	0	415	7	462	240	•	•	1996	0	0
Rents **4**	4546	0	0	0	0	987	0	1727	•	•	993	0	0
Royalties **5**	29504	0	0	0	0	0	0	0	•	•	29484	0	0
Other Portfolio Income **6**	48844	0	0	0	0	74	2442	2136	•	•	41839	0	0
Other Receipts **7**	113366	0	736	0	11802	231	6889	6310	•	•	74692	0	0
Total Receipts **8**	13444235	0	622080	174595	2982594	436455	1366931	1540014	•	•	4139516	0	0
Average Total Receipts **9**	7696	•	755	1009	4719	14079	32546	61601	•	•	689919	•	•
Operating Costs/Operating Income (%)													
Cost of Operations **10**	68.2	•	46.6	50.7	55.0	72.1	80.5	77.7	•	•	69.5	•	•
Salaries and Wages **11**	7.3	•	11.3	0.5	13.0	3.1	3.0	5.1	•	•	6.6	•	•
Taxes Paid **12**	1.5	•	1.5	6.1	1.8	3.3	0.9	1.1	•	•	1.2	•	•
Interest Paid **13**	1.0	•	2.0	0.5	0.6	2.3	0.4	0.9	•	•	1.3	•	•
Depreciation **14**	2.5	•	0.2	0.2	3.9	1.7	1.9	1.3	•	•	2.8	•	•
Amortization and Depletion **15**	0.3	•	0.7	•	0.1	•	0.1	0.1	•	•	0.6	•	•
Pensions and Other Deferred Comp. **16**	0.5	•	•	•	0.2	0.4	0.1	0.3	•	•	1.2	•	•
Employee Benefits **17**	1.4	•	0.8	2.1	1.0	0.3	1.3	1.5	•	•	2.1	•	•
Advertising **18**	0.7	•	2.6	0.1	1.1	0.1	0.3	0.3	•	•	0.6	•	•
Other Expenses **19**	11.0	•	17.7	28.0	16.5	7.3	5.2	6.3	•	•	11.8	•	•
Officers' Compensation **20**	2.4	•	11.7	9.4	3.5	8.5	1.6	1.0	•	•	0.7	•	•
Operating Margin **21**	3.3	•	5.1	2.4	3.5	1.0	4.9	4.3	•	•	1.5	•	•
Operating Margin Before Officers' Comp. **22**	5.6	•	16.7	11.8	7.0	9.5	6.4	5.4	•	•	2.2	•	•

Selected Average Balance Sheet ($ in Thousands)

Net Receivables 23	1027	14	119	508	1486	3655	7931			119458
Inventories 24	1034	19	381	470	2567	6478	8631			82179
Net Property, Plant and Equipment 25	865	37	2	487	1392	2700	6028			92186
Total Assets 26	5137	116	894	2111	6719	16019	36392			697444
Notes and Loans Payable 27	1584	70	594	634	3799	3258	9471			218334
All Other Liabilities 28	1349	3	105	603	1370	5114	6489			200268
Net Worth 29	2205	43	195	873	1550	7647	20431			278842

Selected Financial Ratios (Times to 1)

Current Ratio 30	2.0	9.4	2.2	1.8	1.9	2.3	2.1			2.0
Quick Ratio 31	1.1	7.6	0.3	0.9	0.7	1.0	1.0			1.4
Net Sales to Working Capital 32	4.9	29.1	2.3	7.1	6.7	4.8	5.3			3.6
Coverage Ratio 33	5.8	3.6	5.4	7.0	1.6	13.5	6.3			5.1
Total Asset Turnover 34	1.5	6.5	1.1	2.2	2.1	2.0	1.7			1.0
Inventory Turnover 35	5.0	19.0	1.3	5.5	3.9	4.0	5.5			5.6
Receivables Turnover 36	8.3	31.0	10.7	13.5	11.3	8.6	8.1			
Total Liabilities to Net Worth 37	1.3	1.7	3.6	1.4	3.3	1.1	0.8			1.5
Current Assets to Working Capital 38	2.0	1.1	1.8	2.3	2.2	1.8	1.9			2.0
Current Liabilities to Working Capital 39	1.0	0.1	0.8	1.3	1.2	0.8	0.9			1.0
Working Capital to Net Sales 40	0.2	0.0	0.4	0.1	0.1	0.2	0.2			0.3
Inventory to Working Capital 41	0.8	0.2	1.5	1.1	1.3	0.9	0.9			0.4
Total Receipts to Cash Flow 42	7.6	5.5	5.2	6.3	14.1	10.5	10.5			6.5
Cost of Goods to Cash Flow 43	5.2	2.6	2.7	3.5	10.2	8.5	8.2			4.5
Cash Flow to Total Debt 44	0.3	1.9	0.3	0.6	0.2	0.4	0.4			0.2

Selected Financial Factors (in Percentages)

Debt Ratio 45	57.1	62.7	78.2	58.6	76.9	52.3	43.9			60.0
Return on Total Assets 46	8.7	46.6	3.3	10.1	7.5	12.1	10.0			6.5
Return on Equity Before Income Taxes 47	16.7	90.3	12.3	20.8	11.8	23.5	15.0			13.2
Return on Equity After Income Taxes 48	14.4	89.8	12.3	18.7	8.3	20.2	14.5			10.3
Profit Margin (Before Income Tax) 49	4.9	5.2	2.4	3.9	1.3	5.6	5.0			5.5
Profit Margin (After Income Tax) 50	4.2	5.1	2.4	3.5	0.9	4.8	4.8			4.3

Table I
Corporations with and without Net Income

APPAREL KNITTING MILLS

MONEY AMOUNTS AND SIZE OF ASSETS IN THOUSANDS OF DOLLARS

Item Description for Accounting Period 7/10 Through 6/11	Total	Zero Assets	Under 500	500 to 1,000	1,000 to 5,000	5,000 to 10,000	10,000 to 25,000	25,000 to 50,000	50,000 to 100,000	100,000 to 250,000	250,000 to 500,000	500,000 to 2,500,000	2,500,000 and over
Number of Enterprises 1	205	0	144	0	19	10	19	4	5	0	4	0	0
Revenues ($ in Thousands)													
Net Sales 2	7212153	0	151197	0	19017	166589	501005	229113	613285	0	5531947	0	0
Interest 3	5795	0	0	0	1866	0	1311	231	2057	0	330	0	0
Rents 4	47	0	0	0	0	0	12	0	34	0	0	0	0
Royalties 5	51846	0	0	0	0	0	562	0	10753	0	40532	0	0
Other Portfolio Income 6	18526	0	0	0	0	113	457	119	1456	0	16380	0	0
Other Receipts 7	12108	0	328	0	0	135	6003	1226	3259	0	1159	0	0
Total Receipts 8	7300475	0	151525	0	20883	166837	509350	230689	630844	0	5590348	0	0
Average Total Receipts 9	35612	•	1052	•	1099	16684	26808	57672	126169	•	1397587	•	•
Operating Costs/Operating Income (%)													
Cost of Operations 10	75.9	•	66.6	•	56.2	65.7	78.6	78.5	72.9	•	76.5	•	•
Salaries and Wages 11	6.6	•	13.2	•	23.3	3.6	5.9	4.6	5.6	•	6.7	•	•
Taxes Paid 12	1.2	•	4.2	•	5.7	2.1	1.5	1.8	1.8	•	1.0	•	•
Interest Paid 13	2.5	•	0.6	•	0.2	0.7	1.2	0.1	0.7	•	3.0	•	•
Depreciation 14	0.9	•	6.2	•	0.2	0.7	0.9	1.5	2.6	•	0.6	•	•
Amortization and Depletion 15	0.3	•	•	•	•	•	0.6	0.0	0.2	•	0.3	•	•
Pensions and Other Deferred Comp. 16	0.2	•	•	•	0.1	•	0.1	0.4	0.9	•	0.1	•	•
Employee Benefits 17	1.5	•	•	•	2.8	1.5	0.5	0.6	1.0	•	1.8	•	•
Advertising 18	3.2	•	0.9	•	0.5	0.2	0.1	1.7	3.8	•	3.6	•	•
Other Expenses 19	7.8	•	9.6	•	18.5	9.2	6.9	7.1	12.5	•	7.2	•	•
Officers' Compensation 20	0.7	•	8.4	•	7.8	1.4	1.1	1.9	0.9	•	0.3	•	•
Operating Margin 21	•	•	•	•	•	14.8	2.7	1.9	•	•	•	•	•
Operating Margin Before Officers' Comp. 22	•	•	•	•	•	16.2	3.8	3.8	•	•	•	•	•

Selected Average Balance Sheet ($ in Thousands)

	1	2	3	4	5	6	7	8
Net Receivables 23	3984	115	113	2366	3926	8728	13865	148897
Inventories 24	6836	98	141	3483	2052	8245	18531	324961
Net Property, Plant and Equipment 25	1967	2	50	503	1624	2279	21580	62310
Total Assets 26	34589	261	2408	6567	16629	28916	102765	1499054
Notes and Loans Payable 27	13141	74	7	1198	6133	1782	25247	605279
All Other Liabilities 28	20140	66	222	1059	1791	7618	25060	978652
Net Worth 29	1308	121	2179	4310	8705	19516	52457	-84877

Selected Financial Ratios (Times to 1)

	1	2	3	4	5	6	7	8
Current Ratio 30	2.1	3.5	1.7	3.0	2.2	2.7	2.0	2.1
Quick Ratio 31	0.7	2.0	0.9	1.3	1.6	1.5	0.6	0.6
Net Sales to Working Capital 32	4.6	6.3	6.8	4.4	4.6	4.4	4.3	4.7
Coverage Ratio 33	1.3	•	•	21.1	4.6	29.5	1.0	1.1
Total Asset Turnover 34	1.0	4.0	0.4	2.5	1.6	2.0	1.2	0.9
Inventory Turnover 35	3.9	7.1	4.0	3.1	10.1	5.5	4.8	3.3
Receivables Turnover 36	9.2	18.3	8.1	5.3	6.2	•	12.4	18.6
Total Liabilities to Net Worth 37	25.4	1.2	0.1	0.5	0.9	0.5	1.0	•
Current Assets to Working Capital 38	1.9	1.4	2.5	1.5	1.8	1.6	2.0	1.9
Current Liabilities to Working Capital 39	0.9	0.4	1.5	0.5	0.8	0.6	1.0	0.9
Working Capital to Net Sales 40	0.2	0.2	0.1	0.2	0.2	0.2	0.2	0.2
Inventory to Working Capital 41	1.0	0.6	1.0	0.8	0.4	0.6	0.9	1.1
Total Receipts to Cash Flow 42	15.4	•	154.6	4.9	10.4	12.0	8.9	18.4
Cost of Goods to Cash Flow 43	11.7	•	86.9	3.2	8.2	9.4	6.5	14.1
Cash Flow to Total Debt 44	0.1	•	0.0	1.5	0.3	0.5	0.3	0.0

Selected Financial Factors (in Percentages)

	1	2	3	4	5	6	7	8
Debt Ratio 45	96.2	53.6	9.5	34.4	47.7	32.5	49.0	105.7
Return on Total Assets 46	3.3	•	•	39.8	8.6	5.3	0.9	3.0
Return on Equity Before Income Taxes 47	19.8	•	•	57.7	12.9	7.5	•	•
Return on Equity After Income Taxes 48	12.8	•	•	48.2	12.9	6.5	•	•
Profit Margin (Before Income Tax) 49	0.7	•	•	14.9	4.2	2.6	0.3	0.3
Profit Margin (After Income Tax) 50	0.5	•	•	12.5	4.2	2.2	0.1	0.1

63

Table II

Corporations with Net Income

APPAREL KNITTING MILLS

MONEY AMOUNTS AND SIZE OF ASSETS IN THOUSANDS OF DOLLARS

Item Description for Accounting Period 7/10 Through 6/11	Total	Zero Assets	Under 500	500 to 1,000	1,000 to 5,000	5,000 to 10,000	10,000 to 25,000	25,000 to 50,000	50,000 to 100,000	100,000 to 250,000	250,000 to 500,000	500,000 to 2,500,000	2,500,000 and over
Number of Enterprises **1**	117	0	•	0	0	0	10	•	•	•	•	0	0

Revenues ($ in Thousands)

Net Sales **2**	6276904	0	•	0	0	166589	280237	•	•	•	•	0	0
Interest **3**	794	0	•	0	0	0	0	•	•	•	•	0	0
Rents **4**	0	0	•	0	0	0	0	•	•	•	•	0	0
Royalties **5**	42364	0	•	0	0	0	0	•	•	•	•	0	0
Other Portfolio Income **6**	16139	0	•	0	0	113	0	•	•	•	•	0	0
Other Receipts **7**	8647	0	•	0	0	135	5909	•	•	•	•	0	0
Total Receipts **8**	6344848	0	•	0	0	166837	286146	•	•	•	•	0	0
Average Total Receipts **9**	54229	•	•	•	•	16684	28615	•	•	•	•	•	•

Operating Costs/Operating Income (%)

Cost of Operations **10**	74.5	•	•	•	•	65.7	71.6	•	•	•	•	•	•
Salaries and Wages **11**	6.8	•	•	•	•	3.6	7.4	•	•	•	•	•	•
Taxes Paid **12**	1.1	•	•	•	•	2.1	0.9	•	•	•	•	•	•
Interest Paid **13**	2.6	•	•	•	•	0.7	1.0	•	•	•	•	•	•
Depreciation **14**	1.0	•	•	•	•	0.7	0.2	•	•	•	•	•	•
Amortization and Depletion **15**	0.3	•	•	•	•	•	0.0	•	•	•	•	•	•
Pensions and Other Deferred Comp. **16**	0.1	•	•	•	•	•	0.0	•	•	•	•	•	•
Employee Benefits **17**	1.6	•	•	•	•	1.5	0.4	•	•	•	•	•	•
Advertising **18**	3.6	•	•	•	•	0.2	0.1	•	•	•	•	•	•
Other Expenses **19**	7.5	•	•	•	•	9.2	8.5	•	•	•	•	•	•
Officers' Compensation **20**	0.6	•	•	•	•	1.4	1.7	•	•	•	•	•	•
Operating Margin **21**	0.3	•	•	•	•	14.8	8.3	•	•	•	•	•	•
Operating Margin Before Officers' Comp. **22**	0.9	•	•	•	•	16.2	10.0	•	•	•	•	•	•

Selected Average Balance Sheet ($ in Thousands)

Net Receivables	23	5856	2366	4682
Inventories	24	7520	3029	1889
Net Property, Plant and Equipment	25	2887	503	623
Total Assets	26	53852	6567	14540
Notes and Loans Payable	27	20633	1198	4362
All Other Liabilities	28	33766	1059	1847
Net Worth	29	-547	4310	8331

Selected Financial Ratios (Times to 1)

Current Ratio	30	2.2	3.0	1.7
Quick Ratio	31	0.7	1.3	1.2
Net Sales to Working Capital	32	4.7	4.4	8.9
Coverage Ratio	33	1.6	21.1	11.9
Total Asset Turnover	34	1.0	2.5	1.9
Inventory Turnover	35	5.3	3.6	10.6
Receivables Turnover	36	12.6	•	4.8
Total Liabilities to Net Worth	37	•	0.5	0.7
Current Assets to Working Capital	38	1.8	1.5	2.4
Current Liabilities to Working Capital	39	0.8	0.5	1.4
Working Capital to Net Sales	40	0.2	0.2	0.1
Inventory to Working Capital	41	1.0	0.8	0.5
Total Receipts to Cash Flow	42	14.2	4.9	5.9
Cost of Goods to Cash Flow	43	10.6	3.2	4.2
Cash Flow to Total Debt	44	0.1	1.5	0.8

Selected Financial Factors (in Percentages)

Debt Ratio	45	101.0	34.4	42.7
Return on Total Assets	46	4.3	39.8	21.9
Return on Equity Before Income Taxes	47	•	57.7	35.0
Return on Equity After Income Taxes	48	•	48.2	35.0
Profit Margin (Before Income Tax)	49	1.7	14.9	10.4
Profit Margin (After Income Tax)	50	1.4	12.5	10.4

Table I

Corporations with and without Net Income

CUT AND SEW APPAREL CONTRACTORS AND MFRS.

MONEY AMOUNTS AND SIZE OF ASSETS IN THOUSANDS OF DOLLARS

Item Description for Accounting Period 7/10 Through 6/11	Total	Zero Assets	Under 500	500 to 1,000	1,000 to 5,000	5,000 to 10,000	10,000 to 25,000	25,000 to 50,000	50,000 to 100,000	100,000 to 250,000	250,000 to 500,000	500,000 to 2,500,000	2,500,000 and over
Number of Enterprises **1**	6749	2125	3109	600	572	181	87	29	•	•	4	•	0
Revenues ($ in Thousands)													
Net Sales **2**	33659374	355827	866848	1072144	3368440	2091907	2765046	2457160	•	•	1550520	•	0
Interest **3**	21943	0	3	710	2776	230	691	2317	•	•	40	•	0
Rents **4**	10906	0	0	0	99	0	0	199	•	•	0	•	0
Royalties **5**	615195	0	0	145	25471	0	0	3439	•	•	0	•	0
Other Portfolio Income **6**	205457	3557	0	0	26	817	191	259	•	•	1355	•	0
Other Receipts **7**	264460	4745	9832	3	27915	44452	39461	9417	•	•	20921	•	0
Total Receipts **8**	34777335	364129	876683	1073002	3424727	2137406	2805389	2472791	•	•	1572836	•	0
Average Total Receipts **9**	5153	171	282	1788	5987	11809	32246	85269	•	•	393209	•	•
Operating Costs/Operating Income (%)													
Cost of Operations **10**	59.6	41.3	30.8	66.4	68.9	68.3	73.8	72.0	•	•	52.1	•	•
Salaries and Wages **11**	10.4	13.9	31.6	12.1	8.8	11.4	5.0	8.2	•	•	12.9	•	•
Taxes Paid **12**	2.0	1.9	4.6	2.3	2.9	2.1	1.8	1.1	•	•	3.9	•	•
Interest Paid **13**	1.4	0.6	0.1	1.1	1.0	0.9	1.1	0.6	•	•	3.3	•	•
Depreciation **14**	1.4	2.1	0.9	1.3	0.4	0.4	0.5	0.7	•	•	2.4	•	•
Amortization and Depletion **15**	0.6	•	0.2	0.8	0.0	0.1	0.0	0.2	•	•	0.6	•	•
Pensions and Other Deferred Comp. **16**	1.1	0.3	•	0.1	0.3	0.2	0.1	0.6	•	•	0.9	•	•
Employee Benefits **17**	0.9	4.0	0.4	0.8	0.7	0.5	0.4	0.6	•	•	0.7	•	•
Advertising **18**	2.5	4.1	0.3	3.2	0.2	2.4	1.2	1.0	•	•	4.5	•	•
Other Expenses **19**	16.8	18.3	28.7	19.2	8.3	10.9	11.9	9.4	•	•	16.9	•	•
Officers' Compensation **20**	2.2	6.9	5.9	3.5	4.7	3.0	2.9	1.2	•	•	1.6	•	•
Operating Margin **21**	1.1	6.6	•	•	3.8	•	1.3	4.4	•	•	0.1	•	•
Operating Margin Before Officers' Comp. **22**	3.3	13.5	2.4	•	8.4	2.7	4.2	5.6	•	•	1.7	•	•

Selected Average Balance Sheet ($ in Thousands)

	•	•	•	•	•	•	•	•	•
Net Receivables 23	583	0	12	182	294	1264	3894	6391	47581
Inventories 24	746	0	10	128	1230	1994	6925	11418	127055
Net Property, Plant and Equipment 25	403	0	12	107	248	2348	999	3783	53469
Total Assets 26	3442	0	63	681	2320	7153	16284	32447	353742
Notes and Loans Payable 27	1005	0	38	243	611	2056	5021	3545	101877
All Other Liabilities 28	1148	0	49	382	985	1950	4592	12705	83801
Net Worth 29	1288	0	-24	56	724	3146	6671	16197	168064

Selected Financial Ratios (Times to 1)

	•	•	•	•	•	•	•	•	•
Current Ratio 30	1.8	•	1.8	1.2	1.8	1.5	1.8	2.2	2.4
Quick Ratio 31	0.9	•	1.5	0.7	0.6	0.6	0.7	0.8	1.1
Net Sales to Working Capital 32	6.2	•	14.0	26.3	6.6	9.0	4.9	6.0	3.3
Coverage Ratio 33	4.5	16.2	•	•	6.6	3.0	3.6	9.5	1.5
Total Asset Turnover 34	1.4	•	4.4	2.6	2.5	1.6	2.0	2.6	1.1
Inventory Turnover 35	4.0	•	8.3	9.3	3.3	4.0	3.4	5.3	1.6
Receivables Turnover 36	8.6	•	15.9	13.2	15.8	9.4	7.3	•	6.3
Total Liabilities to Net Worth 37	1.7	•	•	11.2	2.2	1.3	1.4	1.0	1.1
Current Assets to Working Capital 38	2.2	•	2.3	6.0	2.2	3.1	2.2	1.8	1.7
Current Liabilities to Working Capital 39	1.2	•	1.3	5.0	1.2	2.1	1.2	0.8	0.7
Working Capital to Net Sales 40	0.2	•	0.1	0.0	0.2	0.1	0.2	0.2	0.3
Inventory to Working Capital 41	0.9	•	0.2	1.7	1.3	1.6	0.9	0.8	0.9
Total Receipts to Cash Flow 42	5.7	4.4	4.7	18.8	9.2	9.1	8.0	8.2	8.2
Cost of Goods to Cash Flow 43	3.4	1.8	1.4	12.5	6.3	6.2	5.9	5.9	4.3
Cash Flow to Total Debt 44	0.4	0.7	0.7	0.2	0.4	0.3	0.4	0.6	0.3

Selected Financial Factors (in Percentages)

	•	•	•	•	•	•	•	•	•
Debt Ratio 45	62.6	•	138.6	91.8	68.8	56.0	59.0	50.1	52.5
Return on Total Assets 46	9.3	•	•	•	16.2	4.5	7.4	14.7	5.3
Return on Equity Before Income Taxes 47	19.2	•	27.4	•	44.1	6.9	13.0	26.4	3.6
Return on Equity After Income Taxes 48	14.4	•	27.5	•	43.6	6.7	11.4	25.2	3.1
Profit Margin (Before Income Tax) 49	5.0	8.9	•	•	5.4	1.9	2.7	5.0	1.6
Profit Margin (After Income Tax) 50	3.7	8.9	•	•	5.4	1.8	2.4	4.8	1.3

Table II

Corporations with Net Income

CUT AND SEW APPAREL CONTRACTORS AND MFRS.

MONEY AMOUNTS AND SIZE OF ASSETS IN THOUSANDS OF DOLLARS

Item Description for Accounting Period 7/10 Through 6/11	Total	Zero Assets	Under 500	500 to 1,000	1,000 to 5,000	5,000 to 10,000	10,000 to 25,000	25,000 to 50,000	50,000 to 100,000	100,000 to 250,000	250,000 to 500,000	500,000 to 2,500,000	2,500,000 and over
Number of Enterprises **1**	2149	407	849	91	561	123	62	21	15	•	•	7	0
Revenues ($ in Thousands)													
Net Sales **2**	28173783	323619	311946	122878	3237620	986110	1898871	2058304	1728454	•	•	14151364	0
Interest **3**	20434	0	0	5	2707	207	80	2300	868	•	•	13587	0
Rents **4**	10747	0	0	0	99	0	0	199	2032	•	•	7649	0
Royalties **5**	596033	0	0	0	25471	0	0	2800	570	•	•	567102	0
Other Portfolio Income **6**	201622	3557	0	0	6	817	49	259	982	•	•	193481	0
Other Receipts **7**	200884	4737	1712	1	27808	18995	24740	2947	21521	•	•	68620	0
Total Receipts **8**	29203503	331913	313658	122884	3293711	1006129	1923740	2066809	1754427	•	•	15001803	0
Average Total Receipts **9**	13589	816	369	1350	5871	8180	31028	98419	116962	•	•	2143115	•
Operating Costs/Operating Income (%)													
Cost of Operations **10**	58.9	42.1	38.3	58.8	67.7	67.0	72.8	72.7	62.2	•	•	52.1	•
Salaries and Wages **11**	9.3	15.2	0.8	7.3	8.9	8.3	4.5	7.1	10.5	•	•	10.4	•
Taxes Paid **12**	1.8	2.1	1.0	3.2	3.0	1.6	1.5	1.1	3.0	•	•	1.6	•
Interest Paid **13**	1.4	0.6	0.1	0.7	0.9	0.5	0.7	0.5	0.7	•	•	1.8	•
Depreciation **14**	1.5	1.5	1.1	0.8	0.4	0.8	0.5	0.7	1.2	•	•	2.1	•
Amortization and Depletion **15**	0.6	•	0.1	•	0.0	0.2	0.0	0.0	0.2	•	•	1.0	•
Pensions and Other Deferred Comp. **16**	1.2	0.3	•	•	0.4	0.4	0.1	0.7	0.6	•	•	2.0	•
Employee Benefits **17**	0.9	4.4	0.0	0.0	0.7	0.9	0.4	0.4	1.3	•	•	0.9	•
Advertising **18**	2.5	3.9	0.1	1.5	0.2	1.8	0.7	0.7	1.7	•	•	3.5	•
Other Expenses **19**	16.7	10.4	47.6	17.5	8.3	7.5	10.4	8.4	8.9	•	•	23.1	•
Officers' Compensation **20**	2.1	6.5	1.7	6.9	4.8	4.9	2.9	1.1	2.1	•	•	1.3	•
Operating Margin **21**	3.1	12.9	9.2	3.3	4.6	6.0	5.4	6.6	7.7	•	•	0.3	•
Operating Margin Before Officers' Comp. **22**	5.2	19.3	11.0	10.2	9.5	10.9	8.3	7.7	9.8	•	•	1.5	•

Selected Average Balance Sheet ($ in Thousands)

Net Receivables 23	1645	0	39	193	289	1079	4867	6689	13740	•	301476
Inventories 24	1828	0	4	484	1038	1133	5356	12210	17143	•	232895
Net Property, Plant and Equipment 25	1119	0	13	43	244	3333	1115	4489	7497	•	177270
Total Assets 26	9635	0	107	844	2300	7197	16304	32529	70592	•	1852384
Notes and Loans Payable 27	2765	0	76	145	613	1549	5147	3606	19130	•	553750
All Other Liabilities 28	3137	0	107	83	938	1909	4297	10993	15152	•	668113
Net Worth 29	3733	0	-76	616	749	3739	6860	17929	36310	•	630520

Selected Financial Ratios (Times to 1)

Current Ratio 30	1.9	•	3.7	1.9	1.1	1.9	2.5	3.1	•	•	1.7
Quick Ratio 31	1.0	•	3.4	0.6	0.6	0.8	0.9	1.5	•	•	0.9
Net Sales to Working Capital 32	5.8	•	6.5	6.3	25.1	4.4	6.0	3.3	•	•	7.2
Coverage Ratio 33	6.2	25.0	142.8	7.8	17.2	10.0	16.1	13.4	•	•	5.1
Total Asset Turnover 34	1.4	•	3.4	2.5	1.1	1.9	3.0	1.6	•	•	1.6
Inventory Turnover 35	4.2	•	33.1	3.8	4.7	4.2	5.8	4.2	•	•	4.5
Receivables Turnover 36	8.3	•	•	17.0	10.2	6.1	11.9	10.1	•	•	7.2
Total Liabilities to Net Worth 37	1.6	•	•	2.1	0.9	1.4	0.8	0.9	•	•	1.9
Current Assets to Working Capital 38	2.1	•	1.4	2.2	8.7	2.1	1.6	1.5	•	•	2.5
Current Liabilities to Working Capital 39	1.1	•	0.4	1.2	7.7	1.1	0.6	0.5	•	•	1.5
Working Capital to Net Sales 40	0.2	•	0.2	0.2	0.0	0.2	0.2	0.3	•	•	0.1
Inventory to Working Capital 41	0.8	•	0.1	0.6	1.3	4.0	0.7	0.8	0.6	•	0.9
Total Receipts to Cash Flow 42	5.0	4.5	1.8	8.5	7.3	6.5	7.6	6.7	•	•	4.0
Cost of Goods to Cash Flow 43	2.9	1.9	0.7	5.7	4.9	4.8	5.5	4.1	•	•	2.1
Cash Flow to Total Debt 44	0.4	•	1.1	0.4	0.3	0.5	0.9	0.5	•	•	0.4

Selected Financial Factors (in Percentages)

Debt Ratio 45	61.3	•	171.5	27.0	67.4	48.0	57.9	44.9	48.6	•	66.0
Return on Total Assets 46	12.0	33.9	6.4	18.3	9.5	14.1	22.6	16.1	•	•	10.3
Return on Equity Before Income Taxes 47	26.0	•	7.2	49.1	17.2	30.1	38.4	29.0	•	•	24.4
Return on Equity After Income Taxes 48	20.7	•	6.8	48.6	16.9	27.9	36.9	26.0	•	•	16.0
Profit Margin (Before Income Tax) 49	7.4	15.4	9.8	3.3	6.4	8.0	6.7	7.0	9.1	•	7.6
Profit Margin (After Income Tax) 50	5.9	15.4	9.7	3.1	6.3	7.9	6.7	6.3	6.8	•	5.0

Table I
Corporations with and without Net Income

APPAREL ACCESSORIES AND OTHER APPAREL

MONEY AMOUNTS AND SIZE OF ASSETS IN THOUSANDS OF DOLLARS

Item Description for Accounting Period 7/10 Through 6/11	Total	Zero Assets	Under 500	500 to 1,000	1,000 to 5,000	5,000 to 10,000	10,000 to 25,000	25,000 to 50,000	50,000 to 100,000	100,000 to 250,000	250,000 to 500,000	500,000 to 2,500,000	2,500,000 and over
Number of Enterprises **1**	4027	778	2773	117	239	57	33	21	•	•	0	•	0
Revenues ($ in Thousands)													
Net Sales **2**	7759171	250398	1338176	124312	702847	833312	1030045	1250392	•	•	0	•	0
Interest **3**	2712	241	0	0	34	0	1933	103	•	•	0	•	0
Rents **4**	334	0	0	0	0	4	0	150	•	•	0	•	0
Royalties **5**	2844	0	0	0	0	0	1975	50	•	•	0	•	0
Other Portfolio Income **6**	1797	0	1262	0	0	0	386	3	•	•	0	•	0
Other Receipts **7**	54042	175	3328	1	4817	4322	6778	10988	•	•	0	•	•
Total Receipts **8**	7820900	250814	1342766	124313	707698	837673	1041117	1261686	•	•	0	•	•
Average Total Receipts **9**	1942	322	484	1063	2961	14696	31549	60080	•	•	•	•	•
Operating Costs/Operating Income (%)													
Cost of Operations **10**	60.8	48.2	52.9	73.0	54.9	72.8	72.7	67.4	•	•	•	•	•
Salaries and Wages **11**	9.7	13.8	6.5	11.2	7.5	10.7	7.4	9.9	•	•	•	•	•
Taxes Paid **12**	3.0	1.3	1.5	4.4	2.4	1.7	2.1	1.4	•	•	•	•	•
Interest Paid **13**	1.5	2.3	0.1	4.4	0.1	1.1	2.4	0.9	•	•	•	•	•
Depreciation **14**	1.1	0.3	0.2	1.8	0.5	0.5	1.0	1.7	•	•	•	•	•
Amortization and Depletion **15**	0.7	0.2	0.2	3.7	0.0	0.3	0.3	0.1	•	•	•	•	•
Pensions and Other Deferred Comp. **16**	0.4	0.0	•	•	3.0	0.0	0.8	0.1	•	•	•	•	•
Employee Benefits **17**	0.9	0.1	1.5	1.5	1.8	0.6	1.1	0.7	•	•	•	•	•
Advertising **18**	1.2	0.8	0.3	0.9	0.4	0.2	0.9	1.9	•	•	•	•	•
Other Expenses **19**	16.0	33.1	29.1	21.5	11.5	7.1	7.2	9.6	•	•	•	•	•
Officers' Compensation **20**	2.7	7.9	3.2	2.0	10.3	2.1	1.5	1.4	•	•	•	•	•
Operating Margin **21**	2.0	•	5.9	•	7.6	2.9	2.7	4.8	•	•	•	•	•
Operating Margin Before Officers' Comp. **22**	4.7	•	9.0	•	17.9	5.0	4.2	6.2	•	•	•	•	•

Selected Average Balance Sheet ($ in Thousands)

Net Receivables 23	211	0	14	106	490	2644	4154	7022
Inventories 24	365	0	50	267	524	2334	7671	15570
Net Property, Plant and Equipment 25	96	0	2	56	132	218	1813	4579
Total Assets 26	1007	0	106	700	2013	6160	16342	31113
Notes and Loans Payable 27	444	0	69	1290	106	1522	5909	12183
All Other Liabilities 28	401	0	36	134	396	3524	4859	8448
Net Worth 29	162	0	2	-724	1510	1114	5574	10482

Selected Financial Ratios (Times to 1)

Current Ratio 30	1.5	•	2.6	3.1	4.2	1.3	1.4	1.7
Quick Ratio 31	0.7	•	1.4	1.2	3.3	0.7	0.6	0.5
Net Sales to Working Capital 32	8.4	•	8.0	3.2	2.4	13.4	7.9	6.1
Coverage Ratio 33	2.9	•	46.0	•	83.1	4.0	2.6	7.2
Total Asset Turnover 34	1.9	•	4.5	1.5	1.5	2.4	1.9	1.9
Inventory Turnover 35	3.2	•	5.1	2.9	3.1	4.6	3.0	2.6
Receivables Turnover 36	8.5	•	26.0	12.6	4.7	6.0	6.5	•
Total Liabilities to Net Worth 37	5.2	•	53.5	•	0.3	4.5	1.9	2.0
Current Assets to Working Capital 38	3.0	•	1.6	1.5	1.3	4.8	3.3	2.5
Current Liabilities to Working Capital 39	2.0	•	0.6	0.5	0.3	3.8	2.3	1.5
Working Capital to Net Sales 40	0.1	•	0.1	0.3	0.4	0.1	0.1	0.2
Inventory to Working Capital 41	1.5	•	0.8	0.9	0.3	2.2	1.5	1.6
Total Receipts to Cash Flow 42	6.6	4.6	3.2	•	5.8	12.0	10.3	7.3
Cost of Goods to Cash Flow 43	4.0	2.2	1.7	•	3.2	8.7	7.5	4.9
Cash Flow to Total Debt 44	0.3	•	1.4	•	1.0	0.2	0.3	0.4

Selected Financial Factors (in Percentages)

Debt Ratio 45	83.9	•	98.2	203.4	25.0	81.9	65.9	66.3
Return on Total Assets 46	8.2	•	28.8	•	12.3	10.8	11.8	12.6
Return on Equity Before Income Taxes 47	33.4	•	1536.2	35.7	16.1	44.8	21.3	32.2
Return on Equity After Income Taxes 48	31.5	•	1526.4	35.7	15.7	42.6	20.2	30.0
Profit Margin (Before Income Tax) 49	2.8	•	6.2	•	8.3	3.4	3.8	5.7
Profit Margin (After Income Tax) 50	2.6	•	6.2	•	8.1	3.2	3.6	5.3

Table II
Corporations with Net Income

APPAREL ACCESSORIES AND OTHER APPAREL

MONEY AMOUNTS AND SIZE OF ASSETS IN THOUSANDS OF DOLLARS

Item Description for Accounting Period 7/10 Through 6/11	Total	Zero Assets	Under 500	500 to 1,000	1,000 to 5,000	5,000 to 10,000	10,000 to 25,000	25,000 to 50,000	50,000 to 100,000	100,000 to 250,000	250,000 to 500,000	500,000 to 2,500,000	2,500,000 and over
Number of Enterprises **1**	3333	254	•	0	198	53	29	•	•	0	0	0	0

Revenues ($ in Thousands)

Item Description for Accounting Period 7/10 Through 6/11	Total	Zero Assets	Under 500	500 to 1,000	1,000 to 5,000	5,000 to 10,000	10,000 to 25,000	25,000 to 50,000	50,000 to 100,000	100,000 to 250,000	250,000 to 500,000	500,000 to 2,500,000	2,500,000 and over
Net Sales **2**	6055661	69403	•	0	659735	794516	967260	•	•	0	0	0	0
Interest **3**	2378	0	•	0	20	0	1854	•	•	0	0	0	0
Rents **4**	329	0	•	0	0	0	0	•	•	0	0	0	0
Royalties **5**	2844	0	•	0	0	0	1975	•	•	0	0	0	0
Other Portfolio Income **6**	1702	0	•	0	0	33	386	•	•	0	0	0	0
Other Receipts **7**	26952	0	•	0	4235	225	6775	•	•	0	0	0	0
Total Receipts **8**	6088866	69403	•	0	663990	794774	978250	•	•	0	0	0	0
Average Total Receipts **9**	1827	273	•	•	3353	14996	33733	•	•	•	•	•	•

Operating Costs/Operating Income (%)

Item Description for Accounting Period 7/10 Through 6/11	Total	Zero Assets	Under 500	500 to 1,000	1,000 to 5,000	5,000 to 10,000	10,000 to 25,000	25,000 to 50,000	50,000 to 100,000	100,000 to 250,000	250,000 to 500,000	500,000 to 2,500,000	2,500,000 and over
Cost of Operations **10**	62.9	13.7	•	•	53.5	72.8	72.6	•	•	•	•	•	•
Salaries and Wages **11**	8.0	•	•	•	6.7	10.4	7.1	•	•	•	•	•	•
Taxes Paid **12**	2.4	0.6	•	•	2.3	1.7	2.0	•	•	•	•	•	•
Interest Paid **13**	0.7	•	•	•	0.0	1.1	1.4	•	•	•	•	•	•
Depreciation **14**	0.8	•	•	•	0.5	0.4	0.9	•	•	•	•	•	•
Amortization and Depletion **15**	0.1	•	•	•	0.0	0.3	0.2	•	•	•	•	•	•
Pensions and Other Deferred Comp. **16**	0.5	•	•	•	3.2	•	0.8	•	•	•	•	•	•
Employee Benefits **17**	0.8	•	•	•	1.8	0.4	1.1	•	•	•	•	•	•
Advertising **18**	1.2	0.4	•	•	0.2	0.2	0.8	•	•	•	•	•	•
Other Expenses **19**	14.3	83.6	•	•	9.9	7.0	7.2	•	•	•	•	•	•
Officers' Compensation **20**	2.9	•	•	•	10.8	2.1	1.4	•	•	•	•	•	•
Operating Margin **21**	5.4	1.8	•	•	11.1	3.7	4.5	•	•	•	•	•	•
Operating Margin Before Officers' Comp. **22**	8.3	1.8	•	•	21.9	5.8	5.9	•	•	•	•	•	•

Selected Average Balance Sheet ($ in Thousands)

Net Receivables 23	203	0	•	322	•	2756	4427
Inventories 24	296	0	•	537	•	2343	7458
Net Property, Plant and Equipment 25	72	0	•	151	210	1722	
Total Assets 26	809	0	•	2010	6050	16514	
Notes and Loans Payable 27	225	0	•	88	1378	4381	
All Other Liabilities 28	258	0	•	442	3653	5066	
Net Worth 29	326	0	•	1480	1019	7067	

Selected Financial Ratios (Times to 1)

Current Ratio 30	1.9	•	3.8	1.3	1.5	
Quick Ratio 31	0.9		2.9	0.7	0.6	
Net Sales to Working Capital 32	5.9		2.7	12.6	8.1	
Coverage Ratio 33	10.1		447.4	4.4	4.9	
Total Asset Turnover 34	2.2		1.7	2.5	2.0	
Inventory Turnover 35	3.9		3.3	4.7	3.2	
Receivables Turnover 36	8.6		7.7	•	6.6	
Total Liabilities to Net Worth 37	1.5		0.4	4.9	1.3	
Current Assets to Working Capital 38	2.1		1.4	4.5	3.1	
Current Liabilities to Working Capital 39	1.1		0.4	3.5	2.1	
Working Capital to Net Sales 40	0.2		0.4	0.1	0.1	
Inventory to Working Capital 41	1.0	•	0.3	2.0	1.4	
Total Receipts to Cash Flow 42	1.3	5.6	5.2	11.6	8.7	
Cost of Goods to Cash Flow 43	0.2	3.5	2.8	8.4	6.3	
Cash Flow to Total Debt 44	0.7		1.2	0.3	0.4	

Selected Financial Factors (in Percentages)

Debt Ratio 45	59.8	•	26.4	83.2	57.2	
Return on Total Assets 46	14.8	•	19.6	11.9	14.2	
Return on Equity Before Income Taxes 47	33.1	•	26.5	54.8	26.5	
Return on Equity After Income Taxes 48	32.0	•	26.0	52.3	25.5	
Profit Margin (Before Income Tax) 49	5.9	1.8	11.8	3.7	5.6	
Profit Margin (After Income Tax) 50	5.7	1.8	11.5	3.6	5.4	

Table I

Corporations with and without Net Income

LEATHER AND ALLIED PRODUCT MANUFACTURING

MONEY AMOUNTS AND SIZE OF ASSETS IN THOUSANDS OF DOLLARS

Item Description for Accounting Period 7/10 Through 6/11	Total	Zero Assets	Under 500	500 to 1,000	1,000 to 5,000	5,000 to 10,000	10,000 to 25,000	25,000 to 50,000	50,000 to 100,000	100,000 to 250,000	250,000 to 500,000	500,000 to 2,500,000	2,500,000 and over
1 Number of Enterprises	1665	604	866	0	132	3	31	13	7	5	0	4	0
Revenues ($ in Thousands)													
2 Net Sales	7229426	43250	303700	0	418987	48474	795800	766771	741923	1491989	0	2618533	0
3 Interest	4537	0	1	0	300	19	352	261	505	2347	0	753	0
4 Rents	481	0	0	0	0	6	4	0	0	385	0	86	0
5 Royalties	146857	0	0	0	0	0	0	0	719	1198	0	144939	0
6 Other Portfolio Income	28740	0	18	0	1130	14	8	14	3	2735	0	24816	0
7 Other Receipts	98534	142	-1	0	-1	1	1488	21362	3559	11370	0	60614	0
8 Total Receipts	7508575	43392	303718	0	420416	48514	797652	788408	746709	1510024	0	2849741	0
9 Average Total Receipts	4510	72	351	•	3185	16171	25731	60647	106673	302005	•	712435	•
Operating Costs/Operating Income (%)													
10 Cost of Operations	62.4	63.6	19.4	•	70.7	70.6	61.0	66.4	62.4	64.9	•	63.8	•
11 Salaries and Wages	11.8	13.0	21.5	•	7.9	8.5	8.9	8.2	10.1	9.4	•	15.0	•
12 Taxes Paid	1.8	2.5	4.7	•	2.9	1.1	1.6	1.6	1.9	1.4	•	1.7	•
13 Interest Paid	0.6	•	0.8	•	•	0.6	0.4	0.2	1.2	0.5	•	0.7	•
14 Depreciation	1.5	0.2	0.8	•	0.6	0.6	1.2	1.4	1.4	2.1	•	1.6	•
15 Amortization and Depletion	0.4	0.0	0.2	•	•	0.1	0.1	0.0	0.6	0.6	•	0.6	•
16 Pensions and Other Deferred Comp.	0.6	•	0.0	•	•	0.1	0.3	0.1	0.2	1.4	•	0.6	•
17 Employee Benefits	1.2	•	3.6	•	0.2	1.0	1.0	0.6	0.7	1.0	•	1.6	•
18 Advertising	3.6	0.1	4.0	•	0.7	0.2	3.6	0.9	3.0	2.2	•	5.9	•
19 Other Expenses	10.6	41.6	25.1	•	13.5	8.7	9.5	11.4	10.8	11.3	•	7.6	•
20 Officers' Compensation	1.9	6.7	1.4	•	2.7	3.0	3.0	1.7	1.8	1.9	•	1.5	•
21 Operating Margin	3.5	•	18.6	•	0.8	5.6	9.1	7.2	5.9	3.2	•	•	•
22 Operating Margin Before Officers' Comp.	5.4	•	20.0	•	3.5	8.6	12.1	8.9	7.7	5.1	•	0.9	•

Selected Average Balance Sheet ($ in Thousands)

Net Receivables 23	1904	0	0	285	1280	2735	8358	14240	47714	649346
Inventories 24	722	0	34	510	3791	4580	8202	28278	41773	109825
Net Property, Plant and Equipment 25	317	0	2	150	810	1467	2661	8023	28310	56524
Total Assets 26	4506	0	90	1665	7035	15574	34180	79146	223417	1146269
Notes and Loans Payable 27	462	0	65	0	1166	1682	5981	20948	56623	37568
All Other Liabilities 28	2284	0	0	860	1628	2785	8140	14080	69044	762203
Net Worth 29	1760	0	25	806	4241	11107	20059	44117	97750	346498

Selected Financial Ratios (Times to 1)

Current Ratio 30	1.5	6.8	•	1.7	2.3	3.6	2.1	4.4	1.5	1.3
Quick Ratio 31	1.0	1.2	•	0.6	1.2	1.9	1.1	2.0	0.9	1.0
Net Sales to Working Capital 32	3.9	10.2	•	5.6	4.7	2.8	4.6	2.5	7.3	3.3
Coverage Ratio 33	14.1	23.4	•	•	11.0	24.6	42.9	6.4	9.6	14.5
Total Asset Turnover 34	1.0	3.9	•	1.9	2.3	1.6	1.7	1.3	1.3	0.6
Inventory Turnover 35	3.8	2.0	•	4.4	3.0	3.4	4.8	2.3	4.6	3.8
Receivables Turnover 36	2.9	6135.4	•	11.5	6.9	8.5	9.9	6.2	7.0	1.3
Total Liabilities to Net Worth 37	1.6	2.6	•	1.1	0.7	0.4	0.7	0.8	1.3	2.3
Current Assets to Working Capital 38	3.1	1.2	•	2.5	1.8	1.4	1.9	1.3	3.0	4.7
Current Liabilities to Working Capital 39	2.1	0.2	•	1.5	0.8	0.4	0.9	0.3	2.0	3.7
Working Capital to Net Sales 40	0.3	0.1	•	0.2	0.2	0.4	0.2	0.4	0.1	0.3
Inventory to Working Capital 41	0.7	1.0	•	0.9	0.7	0.5	0.8	0.6	1.1	0.6
Total Receipts to Cash Flow 42	6.5	2.4	7.1	9.4	7.6	5.9	4.8	6.9	8.4	7.5
Cost of Goods to Cash Flow 43	4.1	0.5	4.5	6.6	5.3	3.6	3.2	4.3	5.4	4.8
Cash Flow to Total Debt 44	0.2	2.2	•	0.4	0.8	1.0	0.9	0.4	0.3	0.1

Selected Financial Factors (in Percentages)

Debt Ratio 45	61.0	71.9	•	51.6	39.7	28.7	41.3	44.3	56.2	69.8
Return on Total Assets 46	8.0	75.3	•	1.8	14.5	16.0	17.7	10.4	6.7	5.6
Return on Equity Before Income Taxes 47	19.0	256.8	•	3.7	21.8	21.6	29.5	15.8	13.8	17.2
Return on Equity After Income Taxes 48	16.5	256.8	•	3.3	21.0	20.4	29.5	14.7	12.8	12.8
Profit Margin (Before Income Tax) 49	7.7	18.6	•	0.9	5.7	9.3	10.0	6.6	4.5	9.1
Profit Margin (After Income Tax) 50	6.7	18.6	•	0.8	5.5	8.8	10.0	6.1	4.2	6.8

Table II
Corporations with Net Income

LEATHER AND ALLIED PRODUCT MANUFACTURING

MONEY AMOUNTS AND SIZE OF ASSETS IN THOUSANDS OF DOLLARS

Item Description for Accounting Period 7/10 Through 6/11	Total	Zero Assets	Under 500	500 to 1,000	1,000 to 5,000	5,000 to 10,000	10,000 to 25,000	25,000 to 50,000	50,000 to 100,000	100,000 to 250,000	250,000 to 500,000	500,000 to 2,500,000	2,500,000 and over
Number of Enterprises **1**	827	0	642	0	132	3	27	•	•	•	0	4	0
Revenues ($ in Thousands)													
Net Sales **2**	6316536	0	286349	0	418987	48474	695014	•	•	•	0	2618533	0
Interest **3**	2032	0	0	0	300	19	352	•	•	•	0	753	0
Rents **4**	95	0	0	0	0	6	4	•	•	•	0	86	0
Royalties **5**	146400	0	0	0	0	0	0	•	•	•	0	144939	0
Other Portfolio Income **6**	27104	0	0	0	1130	14	8	•	•	•	0	24816	0
Other Receipts **7**	96441	0	0	0	-1	1	1482	•	•	•	0	60614	0
Total Receipts **8**	6588608	0	286349	0	420416	48514	696860	•	•	•	0	2849741	0
Average Total Receipts **9**	7967	•	446	•	3185	16171	25810	•	•	•	•	712435	•
Operating Costs/Operating Income (%)													
Cost of Operations **10**	60.5	•	18.8	•	70.7	70.6	59.0	•	•	•	•	63.8	•
Salaries and Wages **11**	12.7	•	22.8	•	7.9	8.5	8.8	•	•	•	•	15.0	•
Taxes Paid **12**	1.9	•	2.5	•	2.9	1.1	2.1	•	•	•	•	1.7	•
Interest Paid **13**	0.5	•	0.9	•	•	0.6	0.4	•	•	•	•	0.7	•
Depreciation **14**	1.5	•	0.8	•	0.6	0.6	1.1	•	•	•	•	1.6	•
Amortization and Depletion **15**	0.3	•	0.2	•	•	0.1	0.1	•	•	•	•	0.6	•
Pensions and Other Deferred Comp. **16**	0.6	•	•	•	•	•	0.3	•	•	•	•	0.6	•
Employee Benefits **17**	1.3	•	3.8	•	0.2	1.0	1.1	•	•	•	•	1.6	•
Advertising **18**	4.0	•	4.2	•	0.7	0.2	3.7	•	•	•	•	5.9	•
Other Expenses **19**	10.4	•	24.0	•	13.5	8.7	9.8	•	•	•	•	7.6	•
Officers' Compensation **20**	1.7	•	1.5	•	2.7	3.0	2.9	•	•	•	•	1.5	•
Operating Margin **21**	4.6	•	20.6	•	0.8	5.6	10.7	•	•	•	•	10.7	•
Operating Margin Before Officers' Comp. **22**	6.3	•	22.1	•	3.5	8.6	13.6	•	•	•	•	0.9	•

Selected Average Balance Sheet ($ in Thousands)

Net Receivables 23	3659	0	285	1280	2585	649346
Inventories 24	1260	26	322	3184	3617	122580
Net Property, Plant and Equipment 25	536	2	150	810	1452	56524
Total Assets 26	8069	103	1665	7035	15697	1146269
Notes and Loans Payable 27	565	29	0	1166	1496	37568
All Other Liabilities 28	4430	0	860	1628	2597	762203
Net Worth 29	3074	75	806	4241	11604	346498

Selected Financial Ratios (Times to 1)

Current Ratio 30	1.4	7.9	1.7	2.3	4.0	1.3
Quick Ratio 31	1.0	1.8	0.6	1.2	2.2	1.0
Net Sales to Working Capital 32	3.9	14.0	5.6	4.7	2.7	3.3
Coverage Ratio 33	20.8	24.7	•	11.0	30.5	14.5
Total Asset Turnover 34	0.9	4.3	1.9	2.3	1.6	0.6
Inventory Turnover 35	3.7	3.2	7.0	3.6	4.2	3.4
Receivables Turnover 36	2.6	13015.9	12.0	7.8	13.1	•
Total Liabilities to Net Worth 37	1.6	0.4	1.1	0.7	0.4	2.3
Current Assets to Working Capital 38	3.2	1.1	2.5	1.8	1.3	4.7
Current Liabilities to Working Capital 39	2.2	0.1	1.5	0.8	0.3	3.7
Working Capital to Net Sales 40	0.3	0.1	0.2	0.2	0.4	0.3
Inventory to Working Capital 41	0.7	0.9	0.9	0.7	0.5	0.6
Total Receipts to Cash Flow 42	5.9	2.4	9.4	7.6	5.3	7.5
Cost of Goods to Cash Flow 43	3.6	0.4	6.6	5.3	3.2	4.8
Cash Flow to Total Debt 44	0.3	6.6	0.4	0.8	1.2	0.1

Selected Financial Factors (in Percentages)

Debt Ratio 45	61.9	27.7	51.6	39.7	26.1	69.8
Return on Total Assets 46	9.2	92.4	1.8	14.5	18.5	5.6
Return on Equity Before Income Taxes 47	23.1	122.7	3.7	21.8	24.2	17.2
Return on Equity After Income Taxes 48	20.2	122.6	3.3	21.0	22.9	12.8
Profit Margin (Before Income Tax) 49	9.3	20.6	0.9	5.7	10.9	9.1
Profit Margin (After Income Tax) 50	8.1	20.6	0.8	5.5	10.3	6.8

Table I

Corporations with and without Net Income

WOOD PRODUCT MANUFACTURING

MONEY AMOUNTS AND SIZE OF ASSETS IN THOUSANDS OF DOLLARS

Item Description for Accounting Period 7/10 Through 6/11	Total	Zero Assets	Under 500	500 to 1,000	1,000 to 5,000	5,000 to 10,000	10,000 to 25,000	25,000 to 50,000	50,000 to 100,000	100,000 to 250,000	250,000 to 500,000	500,000 to 2,500,000	2,500,000 and over
Number of Enterprises 1	11142	491	6863	1069	1785	527	224	71	53	34	9	15	0
Revenues ($ in Thousands)													
Net Sales 2	64778200	212627	4470614	1724982	7963603	7278230	5781794	3767606	4149697	5553514	4112670	19762864	0
Interest 3	177266	219	42	237	5408	2545	4542	2473	6597	20740	17039	117425	0
Rents 4	33541	0	0	290	6549	705	3124	1541	2863	2664	2558	13247	0
Royalties 5	30361	0	0	0	0	119	306	413	41	2191	780	26510	0
Other Portfolio Income 6	381111	417	1484	5012	10217	8801	3993	6051	26485	4118	68653	245879	0
Other Receipts 7	546159	3831	13543	5942	14670	22682	54592	18208	40729	102893	39160	229911	0
Total Receipts 8	65946638	217094	4485683	1736463	8000447	7313082	5848351	3796292	4226412	5686120	4240860	20395836	0
Average Total Receipts 9	5919	442	654	1624	4482	13877	26109	53469	79744	167239	471207	1359722	•
Operating Costs/Operating Income (%)													
Cost of Operations 10	75.0	75.5	56.1	57.6	70.9	80.2	76.1	79.5	82.0	78.3	81.6	75.5	•
Salaries and Wages 11	6.6	2.7	14.7	15.0	6.8	5.5	5.0	4.4	4.5	5.4	5.1	6.5	•
Taxes Paid 12	1.8	1.7	3.1	3.6	2.6	1.6	2.1	2.1	1.6	1.4	1.5	1.3	•
Interest Paid 13	2.0	4.2	0.9	1.7	0.7	0.8	1.2	0.7	1.7	2.3	1.4	3.8	•
Depreciation 14	3.5	9.0	1.9	2.8	1.9	2.7	3.9	4.7	3.5	5.3	2.8	4.0	•
Amortization and Depletion 15	0.4	3.4	0.2	0.1	0.0	0.1	0.1	0.1	0.6	0.5	0.2	0.8	•
Pensions and Other Deferred Comp. 16	0.4	0.1	0.7	0.1	0.2	0.1	0.2	0.4	0.1	0.3	0.3	0.6	•
Employee Benefits 17	1.4	0.8	1.0	0.7	1.5	1.5	1.3	1.1	1.3	1.4	0.7	1.8	•
Advertising 18	0.6	0.3	0.7	0.4	0.3	0.4	0.2	0.2	0.4	1.0	1.0	0.8	•
Other Expenses 19	8.4	22.0	14.8	14.1	9.7	5.6	8.9	6.4	6.1	8.4	9.2	7.5	•
Officers' Compensation 20	1.6	1.6	5.0	4.9	3.9	1.6	1.3	1.2	0.9	1.1	0.4	0.4	•
Operating Margin 21	•	•	1.0	•	1.5	•	•	•	•	•	•	•	•
Operating Margin Before Officers' Comp. 22	•	•	6.0	4.0	5.4	1.4	1.0	0.4	•	•	•	•	•

Selected Average Balance Sheet ($ in Thousands)

	•	•	•	•	•	•	•	•	•	•	•	•
Net Receivables 23	618	0	20	119	505	1248	2230	7022	9358	15965	30818	183750
Inventories 24	643	0	14	245	458	2052	3682	7802	12766	17313	56709	117074
Net Property, Plant and Equipment 25	1651	0	50	233	613	2228	6062	12613	25798	64629	122255	574635
Total Assets 26	4654	0	144	760	2059	6829	15444	36338	70880	147021	362015	1648085
Notes and Loans Payable 27	1799	0	136	464	679	2613	4501	9898	23112	59028	120410	667006
All Other Liabilities 28	1149	0	44	192	380	1144	3175	5721	13811	28425	96460	488903
Net Worth 29	1705	0	-35	105	1001	3072	7768	20719	33957	59567	145146	492176

Selected Financial Ratios (Times to 1)

	•	•	•	•	•	•	•	•	•	•	•	•
Current Ratio 30	1.8	•	0.9	1.8	2.2	2.0	2.3	2.4	2.1	1.6	1.3	1.6
Quick Ratio 31	0.9	•	0.6	0.7	1.4	0.8	1.0	1.4	1.0	0.9	0.4	0.8
Net Sales to Working Capital 32	7.4	•	•	8.8	6.5	6.9	5.6	4.4	5.0	9.2	12.7	7.5
Coverage Ratio 33	1.0	•	2.5	0.8	4.0	1.4	1.7	1.0	0.6	•	0.1	1.1
Total Asset Turnover 34	1.2	•	4.5	2.1	2.2	2.0	1.7	1.5	1.1	1.1	1.3	0.8
Inventory Turnover 35	6.8	•	25.6	3.8	6.9	5.4	5.3	5.4	5.0	7.4	6.6	8.5
Receivables Turnover 36	9.4	•	34.9	12.8	8.8	12.0	11.5	7.9	9.4	11.1	10.4	7.0
Total Liabilities to Net Worth 37	1.7	•	•	6.3	1.1	1.2	1.0	0.8	1.1	1.5	1.5	2.3
Current Assets to Working Capital 38	2.3	•	•	2.3	1.8	2.0	1.8	1.7	1.9	2.7	3.9	2.6
Current Liabilities to Working Capital 39	1.3	•	•	1.3	0.8	1.0	0.8	0.7	0.9	1.7	2.9	1.6
Working Capital to Net Sales 40	0.1	•	•	0.1	0.2	0.1	0.2	0.2	0.2	0.1	0.1	0.1
Inventory to Working Capital 41	0.8	•	•	0.1	0.6	1.1	0.9	0.7	0.8	1.0	1.6	0.7
Total Receipts to Cash Flow 42	17.7	•	8.8	12.8	11.5	23.1	14.8	22.7	25.5	25.6	21.3	22.2
Cost of Goods to Cash Flow 43	13.3	•	4.9	7.4	8.2	18.5	11.3	18.1	20.9	20.0	17.4	16.8
Cash Flow to Total Debt 44	0.1	•	0.4	0.2	0.4	0.2	0.2	0.1	0.1	0.1	0.1	0.1

Selected Financial Factors (in Percentages)

	•	•	•	•	•	•	•	•	•	•	•	•
Debt Ratio 45	63.4	•	124.3	86.2	51.4	55.0	49.7	43.0	52.1	59.5	59.9	70.1
Return on Total Assets 46	2.6	•	10.3	2.9	5.7	2.3	3.4	1.0	1.2		0.1	3.2
Return on Equity Before Income Taxes 47	0.3	•	•	•	8.8	1.3	2.9	•	•	•	•	0.6
Return on Equity After Income Taxes 48	•	•	•	•	8.2	1.0	2.1	•	•	•	•	•
Profit Margin (Before Income Tax) 49	0.1	•	1.4	•	2.0	0.3	0.9	•	•	•	•	0.2
Profit Margin (After Income Tax) 50	•	•	1.4	•	1.8	0.2	0.6	•	•	•	•	•

71

Table II

Corporations with Net Income

WOOD PRODUCT MANUFACTURING

MONEY AMOUNTS AND SIZE OF ASSETS IN THOUSANDS OF DOLLARS

Item Description for Accounting Period 7/10 Through 6/11	Total	Zero Assets	Under 500	500 to 1,000	1,000 to 5,000	5,000 to 10,000	10,000 to 25,000	25,000 to 50,000	50,000 to 100,000	100,000 to 250,000	250,000 to 500,000	500,000 to 2,500,000	2,500,000 and over
Number of Enterprises **1**	5546	101	3470	394	1023	297	157	52	26	12	4	9	0
Revenues ($ in Thousands)													
Net Sales **2**	44258060	132709	3368838	579574	5142968	5613835	4346491	2834976	2449433	2384033	1791678	15613524	0
Interest **3**	125769	14	3	1	3431	1530	1924	1747	1096	2194	575	113254	0
Rents **4**	22208	0	0	0	3027	532	1086	1287	701	309	2081	13186	0
Royalties **5**	19020	0	0	0	0	119	0	413	0	100	46	18342	0
Other Portfolio Income **6**	352152	412	1484	4188	7576	3730	2855	3403	14084	958	67719	245741	0
Other Receipts **7**	267692	42	2667	4362	6913	10749	28820	7970	27518	70441	1751	106462	0
Total Receipts **8**	45044901	133177	3372992	588125	5163915	5630495	4381176	2849796	2492832	2458035	1863850	16110509	0
Average Total Receipts **9**	8122	1319	972	1493	5048	18958	27906	54804	95878	204836	465962	1790057	•
Operating Costs/Operating Income (%)													
Cost of Operations **10**	73.3	65.2	52.6	61.9	67.8	80.3	74.2	77.9	79.6	73.4	74.2	75.5	•
Salaries and Wages **11**	6.4	2.2	15.9	8.8	5.6	5.0	4.2	4.1	3.9	5.4	4.9	6.8	•
Taxes Paid **12**	1.7	1.5	2.8	2.4	2.5	1.3	2.1	1.5	1.4	1.3	2.6	1.1	•
Interest Paid **13**	2.0	1.5	0.4	1.5	0.4	0.3	0.7	0.6	1.3	1.1	1.6	4.4	•
Depreciation **14**	2.8	11.4	1.3	2.1	1.8	2.0	3.3	3.1	2.9	4.1	2.3	3.4	•
Amortization and Depletion **15**	0.3	0.3	0.2	0.3	0.0	0.0	0.0	0.1	0.4	0.3	0.4	0.7	•
Pensions and Other Deferred Comp. **16**	0.4	0.2	0.9	•	0.3	0.1	0.1	0.2	0.2	0.3	•	0.5	•
Employee Benefits **17**	1.3	0.1	1.2	0.3	1.3	0.9	1.2	1.2	1.3	1.2	0.5	1.7	•
Advertising **18**	0.5	0.1	0.8	0.1	0.3	0.2	0.2	0.2	0.2	1.2	1.7	0.6	•
Other Expenses **19**	7.4	10.8	11.3	9.9	8.9	5.0	7.4	6.5	5.1	9.0	11.3	6.7	•
Officers' Compensation **20**	1.6	1.7	5.1	7.9	4.2	1.5	1.2	1.2	0.8	1.4	0.5	0.4	•
Operating Margin **21**	2.2	4.8	7.5	4.9	6.9	3.2	5.4	3.5	2.8	1.3	0.1	•	•
Operating Margin Before Officers' Comp. **22**	3.9	6.6	12.6	12.8	11.1	4.8	6.6	4.7	3.6	2.7	0.6	•	•

Selected Average Balance Sheet ($ in Thousands)

Net Receivables 23	765	0	27	146	465	1231	2382	8092	7197	23339	33384	206128
Inventories 24	703	0	12	215	480	2518	3239	6841	13311	18724	59944	108912
Net Property, Plant and Equipment 25	1905	0	43	276	503	2160	5404	10950	23555	65845	95891	660537
Total Assets 26	5836	0	176	720	2095	7144	15518	35266	69954	154630	317314	1999306
Notes and Loans Payable 27	2261	0	74	183	530	1814	4335	8681	20172	35422	121300	951287
All Other Liabilities 28	1342	0	33	250	378	1134	2293	5213	10820	29272	64485	553987
Net Worth 29	2233	0	69	287	1186	4196	8889	21372	38963	89936	131529	494031

Selected Financial Ratios (Times to 1)

Current Ratio 30	2.3	•	2.1	1.3	3.0	2.5	2.6	2.6	2.4	2.2	2.9	2.0
Quick Ratio 31	1.2	•	1.5	0.9	1.9	1.2	1.4	0.9	0.9	1.5	1.0	1.0
Net Sales to Working Capital 32	6.1	•	19.1	18.5	5.6	6.8	5.2	4.2	5.1	5.8	4.8	6.1
Coverage Ratio 33	3.0	4.4	19.9	5.2	18.8	11.6	9.7	8.2	4.4	5.3	3.6	1.3
Total Asset Turnover 34	1.4	•	5.5	2.0	2.4	2.6	1.8	1.5	1.3	1.3	1.4	0.9
Inventory Turnover 35	8.3	•	42.2	4.2	7.1	6.0	6.3	6.2	5.6	7.8	5.5	12.0
Receivables Turnover 36	12.9	•	38.0	7.7	10.0	14.7	11.9	7.9	15.7	10.5	26.8	13.1
Total Liabilities to Net Worth 37	1.6	•	1.5	1.5	0.8	0.7	0.7	0.7	0.8	0.7	1.4	3.0
Current Assets to Working Capital 38	1.8	•	1.9	4.4	1.5	1.7	1.7	1.6	1.7	1.8	1.5	2.0
Current Liabilities to Working Capital 39	0.8	•	0.9	3.4	0.5	0.7	0.7	0.6	0.7	0.8	0.5	1.0
Working Capital to Net Sales 40	0.2	•	0.1	0.1	0.2	0.1	0.2	0.2	0.2	0.2	0.2	0.2
Inventory to Working Capital 41	0.6	•	0.3	0.9	0.5	1.0	0.8	0.7	0.8	0.5	0.6	0.5
Total Receipts to Cash Flow 42	11.3	7.1	6.6	8.6	7.3	13.9	8.3	12.1	12.7	8.4	10.9	18.8
Cost of Goods to Cash Flow 43	8.3	4.7	3.5	5.3	5.0	11.2	6.2	9.4	10.1	6.2	8.1	14.2
Cash Flow to Total Debt 44	0.2	•	1.4	0.4	0.8	0.5	0.5	0.3	0.2	0.4	0.2	0.1

Selected Financial Factors (in Percentages)

Debt Ratio 45	61.7	•	60.7	60.1	43.4	41.3	42.7	39.4	44.3	41.8	58.5	75.3
Return on Total Assets 46	8.2	•	44.3	16.0	18.5	10.2	12.3	7.1	7.9	7.4	8.1	5.0
Return on Equity Before Income Taxes 47	14.3	•	106.9	32.4	30.9	15.9	19.2	10.2	11.0	10.3	14.1	5.0
Return on Equity After Income Taxes 48	13.5	•	106.9	31.8	30.0	15.4	18.2	9.5	10.5	9.5	12.8	4.0
Profit Margin (Before Income Tax) 49	4.0	5.2	7.6	6.3	7.3	3.5	6.2	4.0	4.6	4.7	4.1	1.4
Profit Margin (After Income Tax) 50	3.8	3.5	7.6	6.2	7.1	3.4	5.8	3.7	4.3	4.3	3.8	1.1

Table I

Corporations with and without Net Income

PULP, PAPER, AND PAPERBOARD MILLS

MONEY AMOUNTS AND SIZE OF ASSETS IN THOUSANDS OF DOLLARS

Item Description for Accounting Period 7/10 Through 6/11	Total	Zero Assets	Under 500	500 to 1,000	1,000 to 5,000	5,000 to 10,000	10,000 to 25,000	25,000 to 50,000	50,000 to 100,000	100,000 to 250,000	250,000 to 500,000	500,000 to 2,500,000	2,500,000 and over
Number of Enterprises 1	315	4	4	58	124	30	16	22	11	14	9	16	7
Revenues ($ in Thousands)													
Net Sales 2	79377792	6077613	0	163143	765745	351797	584278	1417619	1698981	2012470	4004179	16346263	45955705
Interest 3	541401	8733	49	35	24	0	172	3	1610	10542	6164	16027	498042
Rents 4	22806	1535	0	0	0	0	67	19	289	105	4144	6250	10396
Royalties 5	80207	1033	0	0	0	0	0	0	0	0	11	4763	74401
Other Portfolio Income 6	963884	96175	0	0	0	0	3969	276	1268	596	4405	502893	354302
Other Receipts 7	533040	-36468	0	0	7607	6885	623	-144	2803	5760	9746	203864	332364
Total Receipts 8	81519130	6148621	49	163178	773376	358682	589109	1417773	1704951	2029473	4028649	17080060	47225210
Average Total Receipts 9	258791	1537155	12	2813	6237	11956	36819	64444	154996	144962	447628	1067504	6746459
Operating Costs/Operating Income (%)													
Cost of Operations 10	76.1	79.9	•	36.3	85.1	75.4	93.2	78.9	84.5	80.4	76.6	77.4	74.3
Salaries and Wages 11	4.4	4.2	•	7.6	5.1	4.7	2.8	5.3	2.7	3.0	7.2	3.6	4.6
Taxes Paid 12	1.1	0.3	•	1.9	0.5	1.8	1.0	1.4	0.8	1.0	1.1	1.1	1.1
Interest Paid 13	4.0	2.0	•	0.0	0.9	2.1	0.6	0.8	0.6	3.0	2.9	2.6	5.2
Depreciation 14	4.5	3.6	•	0.4	0.6	3.4	0.9	2.7	2.5	4.1	4.9	5.7	4.4
Amortization and Depletion 15	0.6	1.5	•	•	0.9	0.1	0.3	0.1	0.2	0.6	0.3	0.3	0.7
Pensions and Other Deferred Comp. 16	0.9	•	•	13.8	•	0.0	1.7	0.7	0.4	0.5	1.0	1.0	1.0
Employee Benefits 17	1.9	1.6	•	5.1	0.3	1.4	1.7	1.3	1.1	1.7	2.0	2.2	1.9
Advertising 18	0.2	0.6	•	0.2	0.1	0.1	0.2	0.0	0.3	0.4	0.3	0.3	0.2
Other Expenses 19	8.3	8.2	•	10.1	7.0	18.9	4.5	7.0	6.4	4.5	5.0	5.1	10.0
Officers' Compensation 20	0.4	0.3	•	23.2	1.1	0.6	1.0	1.0	0.6	0.9	0.5	0.6	0.2
Operating Margin 21	•	•	•	1.4	•	•	•	0.6	•	•	•	0.2	•
Operating Margin Before Officers' Comp. 22	•	•	•	24.6	•	•	1.7	•	0.6	0.9	•	•	0.8

Selected Average Balance Sheet ($ in Thousands)

Net Receivables 23	38723	0	0	261	140	1050	2106	6119	18931	11433	51694	141854	1266020
Inventories 24	22628	0	423	225	203	1452	3081	4535	17721	16855	40168	124447	588331
Net Property, Plant and Equipment 25	107576	0	0	5	230	3663	4037	12038	30360	50337	146299	478340	3344224
Total Assets 26	382233	0	155	679	1388	6827	15766	33187	74583	157668	364638	1061465	13673015
Notes and Loans Payable 27	170188	0	0	0	1133	7771	4641	9791	21639	65511	104569	322673	6526700
All Other Liabilities 28	90943	0	0	603	227	2232	11674	20621	11363	40819	117387	299725	3046853
Net Worth 29	121102	0	155	76	28	-3176	-549	2776	41581	51338	142681	439067	4099462

Selected Financial Ratios (Times to 1)

Current Ratio 30	0.9	•	0.9	1.9	1.1	2.1	1.0	2.1	1.6	1.5	2.4	0.7
Quick Ratio 31	0.5	•	0.5	1.2	0.4	1.3	0.4	1.1	0.6	0.8	1.5	0.4
Net Sales to Working Capital 32	•	0.5	•	29.4	63.5	6.9	•	7.3	7.7	10.7	4.8	•
Coverage Ratio 33	1.2	•	63.2	0.2	•	•	1.9	1.6	1.3	0.6	2.8	1.0
Total Asset Turnover 34	0.7	•	4.1	4.4	1.7	2.3	1.9	2.1	0.9	1.2	1.0	0.5
Inventory Turnover 35	8.5	•	4.5	25.8	6.1	11.0	11.2	7.4	6.9	8.5	6.4	8.3
Receivables Turnover 36	5.5	•	21.6	19.9	14.0	11.4	11.4	9.7	13.4	8.9	5.6	4.4
Total Liabilities to Net Worth 37	2.2	•	7.9	47.8	•	•	11.0	0.8	2.1	1.6	1.4	2.3
Current Assets to Working Capital 38	•	1.0	•	2.1	16.8	1.9	•	1.9	2.8	2.9	1.7	•
Current Liabilities to Working Capital 39	•	•	•	1.1	15.8	0.9	•	0.9	1.8	1.9	0.7	•
Working Capital to Net Sales 40	•	•	•	0.0	0.0	0.1	•	0.1	0.1	0.1	0.2	•
Inventory to Working Capital 41	•	•	•	0.8	9.1	0.5	•	0.9	1.0	1.0	0.5	•
Total Receipts to Cash Flow 42	17.0	25.7	16.7	62.0	10.8	16.0	17.4	24.0	62.0	12.2	16.9	
Cost of Goods to Cash Flow 43	13.0	20.6	6.1	52.8	8.1	12.6	14.7	19.3	47.5	9.5	12.5	
Cash Flow to Total Debt 44	0.1	•	0.3	0.1	0.1	0.1	0.3	0.1	0.0	0.1	0.0	

Selected Financial Factors (in Percentages)

Debt Ratio 45	68.3	•	88.7	97.9	146.5	103.5	91.6	44.2	67.4	60.9	58.6	70.0
Return on Total Assets 46	3.1	•	5.9	0.9	•	2.8	1.9	3.5	2.1	7.0	2.5	
Return on Equity Before Income Taxes 47	1.5	•	51.9	•	24.2	476.9	15.2	1.2	2.3	•	10.8	•
Return on Equity After Income Taxes 48	0.6	•	44.1	•	24.2	476.9	5.4	0.4	•	•	7.0	•
Profit Margin (Before Income Tax) 49	0.7	•	1.4	•	•	0.7	0.3	0.8	•	4.7	•	
Profit Margin (After Income Tax) 50	0.3	•	1.2	•	•	0.2	0.1	0.1	0.0	3.0	•	

73

Table II

Corporations with Net Income

PULP, PAPER, AND PAPERBOARD MILLS

MONEY AMOUNTS AND SIZE OF ASSETS IN THOUSANDS OF DOLLARS

Item Description for Accounting Period 7/10 Through 6/11	Total	Zero Assets	Under 500	500 to 1,000	1,000 to 5,000	5,000 to 10,000	10,000 to 25,000	25,000 to 50,000	50,000 to 100,000	100,000 to 250,000	250,000 to 500,000	500,000 to 2,500,000	2,500,000 and over
Number of Enterprises **1**	227	•	0	58	120	0	5	•	7	7	3	11	•
Revenues ($ in Thousands)													
Net Sales **2**	55764037	•	0	163143	741185	0	113675	•	877177	1328357	1655523	9894065	•
Interest **3**	486464	•	0	35	24	0	0	•	1032	1028	860	13246	•
Rents **4**	13817	•	0	0	0	0	0	•	266	0	404	1973	•
Royalties **5**	79227	•	0	0	0	0	0	•	0	0	0	4763	•
Other Portfolio Income **6**	750301	•	0	0	0	0	0	•	480	160	76	475718	•
Other Receipts **7**	446166	•	0	0	2141	0	0	•	1742	3146	462	104153	•
Total Receipts **8**	57540012	•	0	163178	743350	0	113675	•	880697	1332691	1657325	10493918	•
Average Total Receipts **9**	253480	•	•	2813	6195	•	22735	•	125814	190384	552442	953993	•
Operating Costs/Operating Income (%)													
Cost of Operations **10**	73.2	•	•	36.3	83.6	•	83.9	•	83.0	76.9	76.8	75.1	•
Salaries and Wages **11**	4.8	•	•	7.6	4.5	•	0.8	•	2.5	3.0	7.3	3.7	•
Taxes Paid **12**	1.1	•	•	1.9	0.5	•	0.8	•	0.7	1.2	1.0	1.3	•
Interest Paid **13**	3.9	•	•	0.0	0.9	•	•	•	1.0	2.5	2.2	1.5	•
Depreciation **14**	4.4	•	•	0.4	0.4	•	0.1	•	2.9	3.1	3.2	3.6	•
Amortization and Depletion **15**	0.8	•	•	•	0.9	•	•	•	0.3	0.8	0.1	0.3	•
Pensions and Other Deferred Comp. **16**	0.8	•	•	13.8	•	•	0.0	•	0.4	0.5	0.1	1.3	•
Employee Benefits **17**	1.9	•	•	5.1	0.1	•	0.3	•	2.0	1.8	0.6	1.8	•
Advertising **18**	0.3	•	•	0.2	0.1	•	•	•	0.1	0.4	0.1	0.4	•
Other Expenses **19**	9.0	•	•	10.1	6.6	•	3.4	•	3.5	4.6	4.7	5.5	•
Officers' Compensation **20**	0.4	•	•	23.2	1.1	•	•	•	0.7	1.0	0.5	0.7	•
Operating Margin **21**	•	•	•	1.4	1.3	•	10.7	•	2.9	4.3	3.7	4.9	•
Operating Margin Before Officers' Comp. **22**	•	•	•	24.6	2.4	•	10.7	•	3.6	5.3	4.1	5.6	•

Selected Average Balance Sheet ($ in Thousands)

Net Receivables 23	43895	261	132	3126	19262	16799	56336	154714
Inventories 24	19922	225	141	4836	14687	29416	51517	210514
Net Property, Plant and Equipment 25	98031	5	49	2991	30643	46079	72830	394647
Total Assets 26	440399	679	1320	12050	77696	165658	353484	981957
Notes and Loans Payable 27	193939	0	932	793	26699	64700	121361	196108
All Other Liabilities 28	95543	603	145	1290	10895	49384	96717	295719
Net Worth 29	150917	76	243	9968	40102	51574	135406	490131

Selected Financial Ratios (Times to 1)

Current Ratio 30	0.7	0.9	2.0	4.7	1.8	1.6	2.4	2.7
Quick Ratio 31	0.5	0.5	1.7	3.9	1.1	0.6	1.3	1.8
Net Sales to Working Capital 32	•	•	40.1	3.2	7.7	9.7	6.7	4.0
Coverage Ratio 33	1.9	63.2	2.8	•	4.3	2.8	2.7	8.2
Total Asset Turnover 34	0.6	4.1	4.7	1.9	1.6	1.1	1.6	0.9
Inventory Turnover 35	9.0	4.5	36.5	3.9	7.1	5.0	8.2	3.2
Receivables Turnover 36	6.0	21.6	23.3	3.4	7.4	•	19.6	2.0
Total Liabilities to Net Worth 37	1.9	7.9	4.4	0.2	0.9	2.2	1.6	1.0
Current Assets to Working Capital 38	•	•	2.0	1.3	2.3	2.7	1.7	1.6
Current Liabilities to Working Capital 39	•	•	1.0	0.3	1.3	1.7	0.7	0.6
Working Capital to Net Sales 40	•	•	0.0	0.3	0.1	0.1	0.1	0.3
Inventory to Working Capital 41	•	•	0.3	0.2	0.8	1.5	0.6	0.4
Total Receipts to Cash Flow 42	11.3	16.7	28.5	7.6	16.5	13.1	14.8	6.7
Cost of Goods to Cash Flow 43	8.3	6.1	23.8	6.4	13.7	10.1	11.4	5.0
Cash Flow to Total Debt 44	0.1	0.3	0.2	1.4	0.2	0.1	0.2	0.3

Selected Financial Factors (in Percentages)

Debt Ratio 45	65.7	88.7	81.6	17.3	48.4	68.9	61.7	50.1
Return on Total Assets 46	4.1	5.9	11.4	20.2	6.9	8.1	9.3	11.5
Return on Equity Before Income Taxes 47	5.7	51.9	39.6	24.4	10.3	17.0	15.3	20.2
Return on Equity After Income Taxes 48	4.6	44.1	39.6	24.4	8.9	11.4	12.1	15.2
Profit Margin (Before Income Tax) 49	3.5	1.4	1.6	10.7	3.3	4.6	3.8	11.0
Profit Margin (After Income Tax) 50	2.8	1.2	1.6	10.7	2.8	3.1	3.0	8.3

Table I

Corporations with and without Net Income

CONVERTED PAPER PRODUCT

MONEY AMOUNTS AND SIZE OF ASSETS IN THOUSANDS OF DOLLARS

Item Description for Accounting Period 7/10 Through 6/11		Total	Zero Assets	Under 500	500 to 1,000	1,000 to 5,000	5,000 to 10,000	10,000 to 25,000	25,000 to 50,000	50,000 to 100,000	100,000 to 250,000	250,000 to 500,000	500,000 to 2,500,000	2,500,000 and over
Number of Enterprises	1	2373	18	860	253	735	158	185	78	32	23	11	12	8
Revenues ($ in Thousands)														
Net Sales	2	94662378	473640	610107	722178	4766256	2796733	6421159	5329547	3587929	5187767	5460590	11951821	47354651
Interest	3	564012	20	1011	0	71	356	1317	3704	1606	6530	14589	99406	435401
Rents	4	36962	0	0	0	26	695	570	1052	1516	108	17448	8957	6589
Royalties	5	2046474	172	0	0	0	0	309	532	0	2497	2833	6412	2033719
Other Portfolio Income	6	1234652	6923	0	0	18772	14870	16980	41873	1705	5401	47200	59730	1021197
Other Receipts	7	1034469	17660	871	294	5323	33108	33126	31722	13226	15522	11880	89062	782679
Total Receipts	8	99578947	498415	611989	722472	4790448	2845762	6473461	5408430	3605982	5217825	5554540	12215388	51634236
Average Total Receipts	9	41963	27690	712	2856	6518	18011	34992	69339	112687	226862	504958	1017949	6454280
Operating Costs/Operating Income (%)														
Cost of Operations	10	68.8	71.3	70.2	57.5	65.3	82.3	74.0	76.6	78.2	73.9	79.6	73.3	63.2
Salaries and Wages	11	8.4	6.3	3.8	8.2	12.1	3.8	5.6	6.2	4.9	6.5	4.1	5.7	10.6
Taxes Paid	12	1.3	4.6	2.3	1.7	2.5	1.8	1.6	1.5	1.1	1.0	1.1	1.6	1.1
Interest Paid	13	2.5	1.1	0.5	0.0	0.9	0.9	1.0	1.0	1.1	1.2	1.4	3.8	3.2
Depreciation	14	4.2	2.7	1.0	1.3	1.8	2.2	3.1	3.3	3.4	3.9	2.3	3.8	5.2
Amortization and Depletion	15	0.7	0.6	0.4	•	0.2	0.0	0.1	0.1	0.3	0.4	0.7	0.6	1.0
Pensions and Other Deferred Comp.	16	1.5	0.7	0.2	•	0.4	0.2	0.2	0.3	0.4	0.8	0.7	0.6	2.6
Employee Benefits	17	1.8	1.0	0.1	0.6	2.3	0.7	1.3	1.6	1.2	0.9	1.8	1.5	2.2
Advertising	18	0.8	0.0	0.2	0.0	0.2	0.1	0.1	0.1	0.2	0.3	0.6	0.1	1.3
Other Expenses	19	7.9	6.4	18.0	11.3	9.2	7.2	7.6	6.6	4.7	7.5	7.5	7.0	8.4
Officers' Compensation	20	0.8	1.1	2.2	5.9	2.3	1.7	2.4	1.1	0.9	0.8	0.6	0.4	0.4
Operating Margin	21	1.4	4.2	1.2	13.6	2.9	•	3.1	1.6	3.7	2.7	•	1.7	0.7
Operating Margin Before Officers' Comp.	22	2.2	5.2	3.3	19.4	5.2	0.8	5.5	2.7	4.6	3.5	0.3	2.1	1.1

Selected Average Balance Sheet ($ in Thousands)

Item													
Net Receivables 23	5394	0	80	319	754	1873	3757	7744	13106	34398	63727	144001	857621
Inventories 24	3422	0	19	48	424	1139	3077	6096	15905	23966	51076	81582	494324
Net Property, Plant and Equipment 25	10301	0	26	63	576	2218	5193	14003	19632	47672	100316	363467	1798672
Total Assets 26	51305	0	224	821	2155	6576	15784	36531	68797	158923	338217	1140157	11211940
Notes and Loans Payable 27	17276	0	64	46	917	2619	5546	12444	24012	43463	77064	506628	3643769
All Other Liabilities 28	11865	0	90	110	524	2551	3995	7772	16926	48939	123325	248199	2489464
Net Worth 29	22163	0	70	665	714	1406	6243	16315	27859	66521	137828	385330	5078708

Selected Financial Ratios (Times to 1)

Item													
Current Ratio 30	1.3	•	1.7	6.4	2.0	1.2	1.7	1.6	1.7	1.7	1.6	1.4	1.1
Quick Ratio 31	0.7	•	1.2	6.0	1.4	0.7	0.9	0.9	0.9	0.9	0.8	0.8	0.6
Net Sales to Working Capital 32	15.6	9.2	9.1	4.5	8.6	24.8	8.9	10.1	7.7	8.1	8.7	10.9	43.1
Coverage Ratio 33	4.2	9.2	4.1	507.7	4.9	1.9	5.0	4.0	3.6	1.4	2.2	2.1	4.9
Total Asset Turnover 34	0.8	•	3.2	3.5	3.0	2.7	2.2	1.9	1.6	1.4	1.5	0.9	0.5
Inventory Turnover 35	8.0	•	26.0	34.5	10.0	12.8	8.3	8.6	5.5	7.0	7.7	8.9	7.6
Receivables Turnover 36	7.0	•	10.7	10.8	8.0	10.2	10.7	9.3	7.6	6.8	9.4	7.6	5.9
Total Liabilities to Net Worth 37	1.3	•	2.2	0.2	2.0	3.7	1.5	1.2	1.5	1.4	1.5	2.0	1.2
Current Assets to Working Capital 38	4.6	•	2.5	1.2	2.0	5.3	2.3	2.8	2.3	2.5	2.8	3.3	13.5
Current Liabilities to Working Capital 39	3.6	•	1.5	0.2	1.0	4.3	1.3	1.8	1.3	1.5	1.8	2.3	12.5
Working Capital to Net Sales 40	0.1	•	0.1	0.2	0.1	0.0	0.1	0.1	0.1	0.1	0.1	0.1	0.0
Inventory to Working Capital 41	1.5	•	0.3	0.1	0.6	1.8	0.9	1.0	1.0	0.9	1.0	1.1	3.9
Total Receipts to Cash Flow 42	8.4	7.5	11.4	5.3	12.5	21.9	11.2	15.5	13.6	10.8	13.8	12.4	6.3
Cost of Goods to Cash Flow 43	5.7	5.4	8.0	3.1	8.2	18.0	8.3	11.9	10.7	8.0	11.0	9.1	4.0
Cash Flow to Total Debt 44	0.2	•	0.4	3.4	0.4	0.2	0.3	0.2	0.2	0.2	0.2	0.1	0.2

Selected Financial Factors (in Percentages)

Item													
Debt Ratio 45	56.8	•	68.9	19.0	66.9	78.6	60.4	55.3	59.5	58.1	59.2	66.2	54.7
Return on Total Assets 46	8.2	•	6.2	47.4	12.8	4.5	10.7	7.7	8.6	6.4	4.4	6.8	8.4
Return on Equity Before Income Taxes 47	14.5	•	15.1	58.4	30.8	10.1	21.8	12.9	17.1	11.1	5.8	10.3	14.7
Return on Equity After Income Taxes 48	10.0	•	14.8	57.3	30.8	8.3	20.1	11.2	16.0	8.9	3.6	6.7	9.6
Profit Margin (Before Income Tax) 49	8.0	9.4	1.5	13.6	3.4	0.8	3.9	3.1	4.2	3.3	1.6	4.0	12.6
Profit Margin (After Income Tax) 50	5.5	7.7	1.5	13.3	3.4	0.7	3.6	2.7	4.0	2.6	1.0	2.6	8.3

Table II

Corporations with Net Income

CONVERTED PAPER PRODUCT

MONEY AMOUNTS AND SIZE OF ASSETS IN THOUSANDS OF DOLLARS

Item Description for Accounting Period 7/10 Through 6/11	Total	Zero Assets	Under 500	500 to 1,000	1,000 to 5,000	5,000 to 10,000	10,000 to 25,000	25,000 to 50,000	50,000 to 100,000	100,000 to 250,000	250,000 to 500,000	500,000 to 2,500,000	2,500,000 and over
Number of Enterprises **1**	1736	14	482	•	642	68	152	•	26	17	7	8	8
Revenues ($ in Thousands)													
Net Sales **2**	82089893	450271	610107	•	4141710	1080649	5338632	•	3074521	3936580	3184402	8017104	47354651
Interest **3**	538384	20	1011	•	65	331	1308	•	827	2485	6138	89946	435401
Rents **4**	34978	0	0	•	26	695	537	•	14	108	17234	8861	6589
Royalties **5**	2046352	172	0	•	0	0	309	•	0	2376	2833	6412	2033719
Other Portfolio Income **6**	1161197	6923	0	•	18720	11078	8002	•	564	5318	39606	48583	1021197
Other Receipts **7**	982793	17660	871	•	4344	6707	29041	•	11117	14975	11137	84220	782679
Total Receipts **8**	86853597	475046	611989	•	4164865	1099460	5377829	•	3087043	3961842	3261350	8255126	51634236
Average Total Receipts **9**	50031	33932	1270	•	6487	16169	35380	•	118732	233050	465907	1031891	6454280
Operating Costs/Operating Income (%)													
Cost of Operations **10**	67.3	70.0	70.2	•	65.7	73.3	72.3	•	76.7	73.3	78.2	73.2	63.2
Salaries and Wages **11**	8.7	6.3	3.8	•	11.3	6.1	5.7	•	5.2	6.1	4.3	5.0	10.6
Taxes Paid **12**	1.3	4.8	2.1	•	2.3	1.5	1.7	•	1.1	1.0	1.3	1.6	1.1
Interest Paid **13**	2.4	1.2	0.5	•	0.8	0.5	0.9	•	1.2	1.2	1.1	2.5	3.2
Depreciation **14**	4.3	2.6	1.0	•	1.2	2.6	3.0	•	3.4	3.7	2.8	4.0	5.2
Amortization and Depletion **15**	0.7	0.7	0.4	•	0.2	0.0	0.1	•	0.3	0.4	0.7	0.5	1.0
Pensions and Other Deferred Comp. **16**	1.7	0.7	0.2	•	0.5	0.4	0.2	•	0.4	0.8	0.6	0.4	2.6
Employee Benefits **17**	1.9	1.0	0.1	•	2.2	1.3	1.3	•	1.3	1.1	1.5	1.2	2.2
Advertising **18**	0.9	0.0	0.2	•	0.2	0.1	0.1	•	0.1	0.1	0.8	0.2	1.3
Other Expenses **19**	7.8	6.3	16.3	•	8.4	7.5	7.5	•	4.5	6.5	7.2	7.1	8.4
Officers' Compensation **20**	0.8	1.1	2.2	•	2.6	3.1	2.5	•	0.8	0.8	0.5	0.5	0.4
Operating Margin **21**	2.3	5.4	3.0	•	4.7	3.6	4.7	•	4.9	5.0	1.0	3.8	0.7
Operating Margin Before Officers' Comp. **22**	3.1	6.5	5.2	•	7.3	6.7	7.3	•	5.7	5.8	1.5	4.3	1.1

Selected Average Balance Sheet ($ in Thousands)

Line Item													
Net Receivables 23	6326	0	143	•	796	1829	3760	•	12982	33280	58979	122278	857621
Inventories 24	3947	0	36	•	380	1403	2950	•	13477	24364	43356	78914	537997
Net Property, Plant and Equipment 25	12532	0	46	•	484	2330	5239	•	20422	48527	80393	410440	1798672
Total Assets 26	65302	0	388	•	2115	6663	15882	•	70390	154807	337617	1257203	11211940
Notes and Loans Payable 27	20956	0	115	•	592	1985	5513	•	26260	42554	76864	404123	3643769
All Other Liabilities 28	14578	0	160	•	460	1739	3678	•	16194	40869	110504	242814	2489464
Net Worth 29	29767	0	113	•	1063	2938	6691	•	27937	71384	150250	610266	5078708

Selected Financial Ratios (Times to 1)

Line Item													
Current Ratio 30	1.3	•	1.6	•	2.5	2.1	1.7	•	1.8	1.7	1.7	1.5	1.1
Quick Ratio 31	0.7	•	1.1	•	1.8	1.3	0.9	•	0.9	1.0	0.9	0.8	0.6
Net Sales to Working Capital 32	15.8	•	9.6	•	7.0	8.1	9.1	•	7.9	8.8	6.7	10.7	43.1
Coverage Ratio 33	5.0	10.3	•	•	8.0	11.9	6.8	•	5.5	5.6	4.5	3.7	4.9
Total Asset Turnover 34	0.7	•	3.3	•	3.1	2.4	2.2	•	1.7	1.5	1.3	0.8	0.5
Inventory Turnover 35	8.1	•	24.4	•	11.1	8.3	8.6	•	6.7	7.0	8.2	9.3	7.0
Receivables Turnover 36	7.0	•	•	•	9.3	7.0	11.0	•	9.5	•	11.1	8.3	•
Total Liabilities to Net Worth 37	1.2	•	2.4	•	1.0	1.3	1.4	•	1.5	1.2	1.2	1.1	1.2
Current Assets to Working Capital 38	4.7	•	2.6	•	1.7	2.0	2.3	•	2.2	2.5	2.4	3.1	13.5
Current Liabilities to Working Capital 39	3.7	•	1.6	•	0.7	1.0	1.3	•	1.2	1.5	1.4	2.1	12.5
Working Capital to Net Sales 40	0.1	•	0.1	•	0.1	0.1	0.1	•	0.1	0.1	0.1	0.1	0.0
Inventory to Working Capital 41	1.5	•	0.3	•	0.4	0.5	0.9	•	1.0	0.9	0.9	1.0	3.9
Total Receipts to Cash Flow 42	7.5	6.8	•	•	10.7	10.7	9.7	•	12.2	9.3	11.8	9.2	6.3
Cost of Goods to Cash Flow 43	5.0	4.7	•	•	7.0	7.8	7.0	•	9.4	6.8	9.2	6.8	4.0
Cash Flow to Total Debt 44	0.2	•	0.4	•	0.6	0.4	0.4	•	0.2	0.3	0.2	0.2	0.2

Selected Financial Factors (in Percentages)

Line Item													
Debt Ratio 45	54.4	70.9	•	•	49.7	55.9	57.9	•	60.3	53.9	55.5	51.5	54.7
Return on Total Assets 46	8.8	12.5	•	•	18.2	14.0	14.2	•	10.8	10.3	6.5	7.6	8.4
Return on Equity Before Income Taxes 47	15.4	37.4	•	•	31.7	29.0	28.7	•	22.3	18.3	11.3	11.4	14.7
Return on Equity After Income Taxes 48	10.9	37.1	•	•	31.7	26.9	26.8	•	21.0	15.5	8.2	8.0	9.6
Profit Margin (Before Income Tax) 49	9.7	10.9	3.3	•	5.2	5.4	5.5	•	5.3	5.7	3.7	6.9	12.6
Profit Margin (After Income Tax) 50	6.8	9.1	3.3	•	5.2	5.0	5.1	•	5.0	4.8	2.7	4.9	8.3

Table I
Corporations with and without Net Income

PRINTING AND RELATED SUPPORT ACTIVITIES

MONEY AMOUNTS AND SIZE OF ASSETS IN THOUSANDS OF DOLLARS

Item Description for Accounting Period 7/10 Through 6/11	Total	Zero Assets	Under 500	500 to 1,000	1,000 to 5,000	5,000 to 10,000	10,000 to 25,000	25,000 to 50,000	50,000 to 100,000	100,000 to 250,000	250,000 to 500,000	500,000 to 2,500,000	2,500,000 and over
Number of Enterprises **1**	26863	3266	18620	1781	2340	398	292	95	34	14	13	8	3
Revenues ($ in Thousands)													
Net Sales **2**	73907636	1972924	9636184	4537791	11221174	5155703	8407758	4153033	2913900	2873963	512432	6165651	11757122
Interest **3**	90659	143	115	248	7438	1004	2415	1377	1706	2138	3454	43362	27259
Rents **4**	22243	33	86	6216	2666	579	2631	538	142	2541	1556	3434	1820
Royalties **5**	66819	0	1342	0	1840	1061	5334	215	0	5683	3374	46624	1345
Other Portfolio Income **6**	204580	39411	19733	12018	17283	6909	41925	8882	2818	493	14692	10776	29638
Other Receipts **7**	885981	23377	37711	47005	84237	26669	73004	110578	285396	18280	29047	84417	66264
Total Receipts **8**	75177918	2035888	9695171	4603278	11334638	5191925	8533067	4274623	3203962	2903098	5164555	6354264	11883448
Average Total Receipts **9**	2799	623	521	2585	4844	13045	29223	44996	94234	207364	397273	794283	3961149
Operating Costs/Operating Income (%)													
Cost of Operations **10**	60.4	63.4	47.0	54.0	63.4	64.5	68.3	68.7	69.4	62.4	61.5	38.4	68.7
Salaries and Wages **11**	10.8	7.2	9.3	14.3	11.0	9.3	9.3	9.8	10.9	14.4	12.3	17.1	8.3
Taxes Paid **12**	2.4	1.4	2.4	3.0	2.7	2.3	2.3	1.9	2.1	2.1	1.8	3.0	2.2
Interest Paid **13**	2.1	1.5	0.7	0.7	1.2	0.7	0.9	2.2	1.6	4.8	3.5	4.4	3.6
Depreciation **14**	3.6	3.4	2.1	1.3	2.7	3.7	4.2	5.3	4.7	3.7	4.8	4.6	4.0
Amortization and Depletion **15**	0.8	0.9	0.1	0.0	0.2	0.2	0.3	0.6	0.6	1.5	1.8	2.8	1.1
Pensions and Other Deferred Comp. **16**	0.5	2.4	0.4	0.1	0.3	0.4	0.2	0.2	0.4	0.2	1.7	0.5	0.6
Employee Benefits **17**	1.6	1.8	1.2	0.8	1.5	1.6	1.8	1.7	2.5	1.9	3.1	3.0	0.7
Advertising **18**	0.8	0.5	0.5	0.9	0.3	0.4	0.4	0.5	3.3	0.7	0.2	4.0	0.3
Other Expenses **19**	12.4	18.6	23.1	13.2	10.7	11.9	9.0	9.5	8.9	7.9	8.9	21.3	6.6
Officers' Compensation **20**	2.9	1.0	7.3	5.4	5.1	2.5	2.3	1.9	1.9	1.1	0.5	1.1	0.2
Operating Margin **21**	1.7	5.9	5.9	6.2	0.9	2.4	0.9	•	•	•	•	•	3.8
Operating Margin Before Officers' Comp. **22**	4.6	•	13.2	11.6	5.9	4.9	3.2	•	•	0.5	0.4	0.9	3.9

Selected Average Balance Sheet ($ in Thousands)

Net Receivables 23	386	0	22	198	541	1888	4368	7439	13403	29550	56405	225180	732958
Inventories 24	148	0	7	63	201	1333	1924	3419	7503	15526	30664	78293	239553
Net Property, Plant and Equipment 25	490	0	39	194	550	2201	5157	9545	19831	41823	83147	145028	1337901
Total Assets 26	2099	0	111	714	2073	7297	16469	33796	70554	167893	400412	1230336	5818655
Notes and Loans Payable 27	860	0	74	221	851	2765	5327	11506	19925	88078	185405	499602	2423276
All Other Liabilities 28	617	0	49	174	558	2064	4814	7588	20624	43508	110186	316402	1939590
Net Worth 29	622	0	-11	319	664	2468	6328	14703	30006	36307	104822	414332	1455789

Selected Financial Ratios (Times to 1)

Current Ratio 30	1.5	•	1.5	1.9	1.5	1.6	1.6	2.0	1.6	1.9	1.6	1.7	1.2
Quick Ratio 31	1.1	•	1.2	1.5	1.1	1.0	1.1	1.4	1.1	1.2	1.0	1.3	0.9
Net Sales to Working Capital 32	10.5	•	26.8	12.1	12.3	8.4	8.9	5.4	7.2	6.5	9.7	5.2	24.7
Coverage Ratio 33	2.7	2.0	10.6	11.7	2.7	5.3	3.6	1.3	3.4	1.2	1.3	1.8	2.3
Total Asset Turnover 34	1.3	•	4.6	3.6	2.3	1.8	1.7	1.3	1.2	1.2	1.0	0.6	0.7
Inventory Turnover 35	11.2	•	35.7	21.8	15.1	6.3	10.2	8.8	7.9	8.2	7.9	3.8	11.2
Receivables Turnover 36	7.2	•	21.1	13.2	8.4	6.3	6.8	6.1	6.9	7.6	6.6	2.3	10.7
Total Liabilities to Net Worth 37	2.4	•	•	1.2	2.1	2.0	1.6	1.3	1.4	3.6	2.8	2.0	3.0
Current Assets to Working Capital 38	2.9	•	3.2	2.1	2.9	2.8	2.7	2.0	2.7	2.2	2.8	2.5	7.7
Current Liabilities to Working Capital 39	1.9	•	2.2	1.1	1.9	1.8	1.7	1.0	1.7	1.2	1.8	1.5	6.7
Working Capital to Net Sales 40	0.1	•	0.0	0.1	0.1	0.1	0.1	0.2	0.1	0.2	0.1	0.2	0.0
Inventory to Working Capital 41	0.6	•	0.4	0.5	0.5	0.9	0.6	0.5	0.7	0.5	0.8	0.2	1.5
Total Receipts to Cash Flow 42	8.5	6.7	4.3	6.8	12.0	9.2	12.4	13.3	10.2	17.6	16.2	5.1	11.1
Cost of Goods to Cash Flow 43	5.1	4.3	2.0	3.7	7.6	5.9	8.5	9.1	7.1	11.0	9.9	2.0	7.6
Cash Flow to Total Debt 44	0.2	•	1.0	0.3	0.3	0.2	0.2	0.2	0.2	0.1	0.1	0.2	0.1

Selected Financial Factors (in Percentages)

Debt Ratio 45	70.4	•	110.2	55.3	68.0	66.2	61.6	56.5	57.5	78.4	73.8	66.3	75.0
Return on Total Assets 46	7.3	•	33.3	29.9	7.1	6.8	6.0	3.5	6.5	6.8	4.3	5.1	5.7
Return on Equity Before Income Taxes 47	15.5	•	•	61.1	13.7	16.4	11.3	1.7	10.7	4.7	3.5	6.8	13.1
Return on Equity After Income Taxes 48	12.7	•	•	60.7	13.0	16.3	9.9	0.5	8.8	1.5	0.0	3.0	8.6
Profit Margin (Before Income Tax) 49	3.5	1.4	6.5	7.6	1.9	3.1	2.5	0.6	3.8	0.8	0.9	3.7	4.9
Profit Margin (After Income Tax) 50	2.9	0.9	6.5	7.6	1.8	3.1	2.2	0.2	3.1	0.3	0.0	1.6	3.2

Table II
Corporations with Net Income

PRINTING AND RELATED SUPPORT ACTIVITIES

MONEY AMOUNTS AND SIZE OF ASSETS IN THOUSANDS OF DOLLARS

Item Description for Accounting Period 7/10 Through 6/11	Total	Zero Assets	Under 500	500 to 1,000	1,000 to 5,000	5,000 to 10,000	10,000 to 25,000	25,000 to 50,000	50,000 to 100,000	100,000 to 250,000	250,000 to 500,000	500,000 to 2,500,000	2,500,000 and over
Number of Enterprises **1**	16197	1864	11296	1433	1049	257	192	57	25	11	7	4	3
Revenues ($ in Thousands)													
Net Sales **2**	54258025	1848448	6527408	4230372	7168029	3460413	5815597	2639447	2289301	1888487	2571067	4062333	11757122
Interest **3**	80914	143	21	62	6777	462	1938	909	1191	2035	2469	37646	27259
Rents **4**	16955	33	86	5869	522	0	1534	538	110	2533	480	3430	1820
Royalties **5**	63637	0	0	0	0	1061	5334	215	0	5683	3374	46624	1345
Other Portfolio Income **6**	167295	28614	17649	12018	7390	6256	40425	2636	1630	493	14388	6160	29638
Other Receipts **7**	724400	22121	9754	44959	68072	19038	53842	98739	278146	10422	15079	37967	66264
Total Receipts **8**	55311226	1899359	6554918	4293280	7250790	3487230	5918670	2742484	2570378	1909653	2606857	4194160	11883448
Average Total Receipts **9**	3415	1019	580	2996	6912	13569	30826	48114	102815	173605	372408	1048540	3961149
Operating Costs/Operating Income (%)													
Cost of Operations **10**	59.6	63.9	39.8	54.3	63.6	63.7	66.7	70.6	67.9	70.6	59.7	30.9	68.7
Salaries and Wages **11**	10.5	7.4	8.4	14.2	10.6	11.0	9.6	8.6	12.0	6.8	10.9	20.0	8.3
Taxes Paid **12**	2.2	1.4	2.2	3.0	2.3	2.0	2.1	1.7	2.1	1.6	2.2	2.8	2.2
Interest Paid **13**	1.8	0.2	0.7	0.6	0.7	0.8	0.9	1.3	1.4	2.2	2.9	3.5	3.6
Depreciation **14**	3.0	2.6	1.4	1.1	2.1	2.9	3.0	4.5	4.7	4.5	4.1	3.6	4.0
Amortization and Depletion **15**	0.6	0.8	0.1	0.1	0.2	0.1	0.2	0.3	0.4	0.8	1.7	1.9	1.1
Pensions and Other Deferred Comp. **16**	0.5	2.5	0.5	0.0	0.3	0.2	0.3	0.2	0.4	0.3	0.9	0.6	0.6
Employee Benefits **17**	1.6	1.8	1.3	0.6	1.6	1.8	1.8	1.4	2.6	1.6	3.2	3.7	0.7
Advertising **18**	0.8	0.2	0.6	0.8	0.3	0.6	0.4	0.3	4.1	0.8	0.4	3.1	0.3
Other Expenses **19**	12.0	18.1	26.0	12.7	9.1	9.0	8.7	7.8	9.1	6.5	8.0	23.7	6.6
Officers' Compensation **20**	2.8	0.7	8.1	5.2	4.7	2.2	2.4	2.0	2.0	1.4	0.9	1.0	0.2
Operating Margin **21**	4.6	0.5	10.8	7.3	4.5	5.7	3.9	1.1	•	2.8	5.3	5.2	3.8
Operating Margin Before Officers' Comp. **22**	7.4	1.2	18.9	12.5	9.2	7.9	6.3	3.1	•	4.2	6.1	6.2	3.9

Selected Average Balance Sheet ($ in Thousands)

Net Receivables	23	475	0	20	221	744	2001	4627	7050	14527	22612	46362	356492	732958
Inventories	24	174	0	7	45	331	1647	1970	3409	6894	15995	27333	106330	239553
Net Property, Plant and Equipment	25	573	0	29	212	527	2138	4620	8876	18720	44336	79104	159553	1337901
Total Assets	26	2542	0	117	711	2398	6989	16785	33768	67826	158668	393638	1431221	5818655
Notes and Loans Payable	27	908	0	57	200	759	1947	4524	6879	18658	41225	147127	500289	2423276
All Other Liabilities	28	778	0	45	193	666	2198	4719	7008	19886	36344	80160	494502	1939590
Net Worth	29	856	0	15	317	972	2844	7542	19881	29282	81100	166351	436430	1455789

Selected Financial Ratios (Times to 1)

Current Ratio	30	1.6	•	2.4	2.0	2.0	1.4	1.8	2.4	1.7	2.0	1.7	1.5	1.2
Quick Ratio	31	1.1	•	2.1	1.7	1.5	0.7	1.2	1.7	1.2	1.2	1.1	1.2	0.9
Net Sales to Working Capital	32	9.8	•	12.8	12.9	8.8	11.7	7.0	4.8	6.6	5.2	8.5	5.7	24.7
Coverage Ratio	33	4.8	20.0	17.0	14.7	9.4	8.9	7.4	4.8	5.0	2.8	3.3	3.8	2.3
Total Asset Turnover	34	1.3	•	4.9	4.2	2.8	1.9	1.8	1.4	1.4	1.1	0.9	0.7	0.7
Inventory Turnover	35	11.5	•	31.6	35.3	13.1	5.2	10.3	9.6	9.0	7.6	8.0	3.0	11.2
Receivables Turnover	36	7.6	•	40.9	14.0	8.6	6.5	7.6	7.4	7.4	7.7	8.4	1.9	10.7
Total Liabilities to Net Worth	37	2.0	•	6.6	1.2	1.5	1.2	1.2	0.7	1.3	1.0	1.4	2.3	3.0
Current Assets to Working Capital	38	2.7	•	1.7	2.0	2.0	3.8	2.2	1.7	2.4	2.0	2.5	2.9	7.7
Current Liabilities to Working Capital	39	1.7	•	0.7	1.0	1.0	2.8	1.2	0.7	1.4	1.0	1.5	1.9	6.7
Working Capital to Net Sales	40	0.1	•	0.1	0.1	0.1	0.1	0.1	0.2	0.2	0.2	0.1	0.2	0.0
Inventory to Working Capital	41	0.5	•	0.2	0.3	0.4	1.5	0.5	0.4	0.6	0.5	0.7	0.2	1.5
Total Receipts to Cash Flow	42	6.7	5.8	3.3	6.4	9.2	8.2	8.6	9.1	8.3	12.3	8.3	3.4	11.1
Cost of Goods to Cash Flow	43	4.0	3.7	1.3	3.5	5.8	5.2	5.8	6.4	5.6	8.7	4.9	1.1	7.6
Cash Flow to Total Debt	44	0.3	•	1.7	1.2	0.5	0.4	0.4	0.4	0.3	0.2	0.2	0.3	0.1

Selected Financial Factors (in Percentages)

Debt Ratio	45	66.3	•	86.8	55.4	59.5	59.3	55.1	41.1	56.8	48.9	57.7	69.5	75.0
Return on Total Assets	46	11.1	•	58.6	39.3	18.1	14.1	12.0	8.7	9.6	6.6	9.0	9.4	5.7
Return on Equity Before Income Taxes	47	26.1	•	417.8	82.0	39.9	30.8	23.2	11.8	17.8	8.3	14.8	22.5	13.1
Return on Equity After Income Taxes	48	22.7	•	417.1	81.4	38.8	30.7	21.5	10.3	15.1	6.4	10.8	15.4	8.6
Profit Margin (Before Income Tax)	49	6.7	3.6	11.2	8.8	5.7	6.5	5.8	5.1	5.7	3.9	6.7	9.7	4.9
Profit Margin (After Income Tax)	50	5.8	3.1	11.2	8.7	5.5	6.5	5.3	4.4	4.8	3.0	4.9	6.6	3.2

Table I

Corporations with and without Net Income

PETROLEUM REFINERIES (INCLUDING INTEGRATED)

MONEY AMOUNTS AND SIZE OF ASSETS IN THOUSANDS OF DOLLARS

Item Description for Accounting Period 7/10 Through 6/11	Total	Zero Assets	Under 500	500 to 1,000	1,000 to 5,000	5,000 to 10,000	10,000 to 25,000	25,000 to 50,000	50,000 to 100,000	100,000 to 250,000	250,000 to 500,000	500,000 to 2,500,000	2,500,000 and over
Number of Enterprises 1	246	•	0	0	•	•	22	5	8	14	0	9	20
Revenues ($ in Thousands)													
Net Sales 2	1783351216	•	0	0	•	•	242998	186098	1107037	5029538	0	34566221	1736538698
Interest 3	10773913	•	0	0	•	•	281	259	519	2697	0	48105	10719805
Rents 4	1276838	•	0	0	•	•	1093	0	0	693	0	30504	1244522
Royalties 5	1128523	•	0	0	•	•	0	0	0	8	0	11469	1117045
Other Portfolio Income 6	52029507	•	0	0	•	•	1415	0	498	12236	0	263921	51729588
Other Receipts 7	35753303	•	0	0	•	•	6979	516	6989	88246	0	307919	35173613
Total Receipts 8	1884313300	•	0	0	•	•	252766	186873	1115043	5133418	0	35228139	1836523271
Average Total Receipts 9	7659810	•	•	•	•	•	11489	37375	139380	366673	•	3914238	91826164
Operating Costs/Operating Income (%)													
Cost of Operations 10	90.5	•	•	•	•	•	67.3	85.3	93.3	93.7	•	92.1	90.4
Salaries and Wages 11	1.3	•	•	•	•	•	8.2	4.6	0.8	1.1	•	1.8	1.3
Taxes Paid 12	1.3	•	•	•	•	•	2.9	0.9	0.5	0.4	•	1.0	1.4
Interest Paid 13	1.1	•	•	•	•	•	4.9	0.1	1.3	0.5	•	1.2	1.0
Depreciation 14	1.1	•	•	•	•	•	5.3	3.7	4.3	1.9	•	1.8	1.1
Amortization and Depletion 15	0.4	•	•	•	•	•	0.3	•	0.2	0.2	•	0.6	0.4
Pensions and Other Deferred Comp. 16	0.3	•	•	•	•	•	0.3	•	0.2	0.1	•	0.1	0.3
Employee Benefits 17	0.3	•	•	•	•	•	1.9	0.0	0.5	0.2	•	0.2	0.3
Advertising 18	0.1	•	•	•	•	•	0.0	•	0.0	0.0	•	0.1	0.1
Other Expenses 19	3.8	•	•	•	•	•	34.9	5.4	2.7	2.8	•	2.7	3.8
Officers' Compensation 20	0.0	•	•	•	•	•	3.3	0.3	0.5	0.2	•	0.2	0.0
Operating Margin 21	•	•	•	•	•	•	•	•	•	•	•	0.1	•
Operating Margin Before Officers' Comp. 22	•	•	•	•	•	•	0.0	0.0	•	•	•	0.2	•

Selected Average Balance Sheet ($ in Thousands)

Net Receivables	23	3470889	1609	2634	12158	33968	155824	42590669
Inventories	24	138786	1503	1775	6767	23193	229157	1617311
Net Property, Plant and Equipment	25	1275548	4333	14429	34274	61437	696450	15308562
Total Assets	26	9401752	14153	27755	85844	183946	1357147	114825598
Notes and Loans Payable	27	2069266	6916	4734	22341	41942	447363	25202508
All Other Liabilities	28	3517501	2002	3604	26583	49771	460204	43008188
Net Worth	29	3814985	5235	19417	36920	92233	449580	46614902

Selected Financial Ratios (Times to 1)

Current Ratio	30	1.3	0.7	3.6	1.1	1.9	1.9	1.3
Quick Ratio	31	1.2	0.5	3.0	0.7	1.2	1.0	1.2
Net Sales to Working Capital	32	9.3	•	4.2	53.3	8.9	13.7	9.2
Coverage Ratio	33	8.0	•	3.2	•	3.1	1.1	8.2
Total Asset Turnover	34	0.8	0.8	1.3	1.6	2.0	2.8	0.8
Inventory Turnover	35	47.3	4.9	17.9	19.1	14.5	15.4	48.6
Receivables Turnover	36	2.5	5.2	28.3	10.6	•	22.0	•
Total Liabilities to Net Worth	37	1.5	1.7	0.4	1.3	1.0	2.0	1.5
Current Assets to Working Capital	38	4.9	•	1.4	10.1	2.1	2.1	5.0
Current Liabilities to Working Capital	39	3.9	•	0.4	9.1	1.1	1.1	4.0
Working Capital to Net Sales	40	0.1	•	0.2	0.0	0.1	0.1	0.1
Inventory to Working Capital	41	0.2	•	0.2	2.6	0.6	0.8	0.2
Total Receipts to Cash Flow	42	12.0	19.7	18.7	•	29.6	76.3	11.7
Cost of Goods to Cash Flow	43	10.9	13.2	15.9	•	27.8	70.3	10.6
Cash Flow to Total Debt	44	0.1	0.1	0.2	•	0.1	0.1	0.1

Selected Financial Factors (in Percentages)

Debt Ratio	45	59.4	63.0	30.0	57.0	49.9	66.9	59.4
Return on Total Assets	46	6.5	•	0.3	•	3.0	4.0	6.5
Return on Equity Before Income Taxes	47	13.9	•	0.3	•	4.0	1.4	14.0
Return on Equity After Income Taxes	48	9.0	•	0.2	•	2.6	•	9.0
Profit Margin (Before Income Tax)	49	7.3	•	0.2	•	1.0	0.2	7.5
Profit Margin (After Income Tax)	50	4.7	•	0.1	•	0.7	•	4.9

Table II

Corporations with Net Income

PETROLEUM REFINERIES (INCLUDING INTEGRATED)

MONEY AMOUNTS AND SIZE OF ASSETS IN THOUSANDS OF DOLLARS

Item Description for Accounting Period 7/10 Through 6/11		Total	Zero Assets	Under 500	500 to 1,000	1,000 to 5,000	5,000 to 10,000	10,000 to 25,000	25,000 to 50,000	50,000 to 100,000	100,000 to 250,000	250,000 to 500,000	500,000 to 2,500,000	2,500,000 and over
Number of Enterprises	1	169	•	0	0	120	4	15	0	•	•	0	•	•
Revenues ($ in Thousands)														
Net Sales	2	1375229923	•	0	0	0	0	426920	0	•	•	0	•	•
Interest	3	9741483	•	0	0	0	9	503	0	•	•	0	•	•
Rents	4	1143349	•	0	0	0	0	1093	0	•	•	0	•	•
Royalties	5	1074282	•	0	0	0	0	0	0	•	•	0	•	•
Other Portfolio Income	6	51487662	•	0	0	0	0	1415	0	•	•	0	•	•
Other Receipts	7	32499085	•	0	0	48361	20486	3884	0	•	•	0	•	•
Total Receipts	8	1471175784	•	0	0	48361	20495	433815	0	•	•	0	•	•
Average Total Receipts	9	8705182	•	•	•	403	5124	28921	•	•	•	•	•	•
Operating Costs/Operating Income (%)														
Cost of Operations	10	88.4	•	•	•	•	•	74.9	•	•	•	•	•	•
Salaries and Wages	11	1.6	•	•	•	•	•	5.7	•	•	•	•	•	•
Taxes Paid	12	1.7	•	•	•	•	•	1.4	•	•	•	•	•	•
Interest Paid	13	1.2	•	•	•	•	•	0.5	•	•	•	•	•	•
Depreciation	14	1.1	•	•	•	•	•	2.2	•	•	•	•	•	•
Amortization and Depletion	15	0.5	•	•	•	•	•	•	•	•	•	•	•	•
Pensions and Other Deferred Comp.	16	0.4	•	•	•	•	•	0.1	•	•	•	•	•	•
Employee Benefits	17	0.3	•	•	•	•	•	0.9	•	•	•	•	•	•
Advertising	18	0.1	•	•	•	•	•	0.0	•	•	•	•	•	•
Other Expenses	19	4.5	•	•	•	•	•	12.4	•	•	•	•	•	•
Officers' Compensation	20	0.0	•	•	•	•	•	2.0	•	•	•	•	•	•
Operating Margin	21	0.3	•	•	•	•	•	•	•	•	•	•	•	•
Operating Margin Before Officers' Comp.	22	0.3	•	•	•	•	•	1.7	•	•	•	•	•	•

Selected Average Balance Sheet ($ in Thousands)

Net Receivables 23	4990008	0	128	3221
Inventories 24	143709	0	0	2134
Net Property, Plant and Equipment 25	1581910	0	463	1191
Total Assets 26	13040864	2209	6688	14968
Notes and Loans Payable 27	2782243	0	1948	4582
All Other Liabilities 28	4910915	0	2	3145
Net Worth 29	5347707	2209	4738	7242

Selected Financial Ratios (Times to 1)

Current Ratio 30	1.3			2.0
Quick Ratio 31	1.2			1.5
Net Sales to Working Capital 32	7.3			5.7
Coverage Ratio 33	9.0		1026.9	4.1
Total Asset Turnover 34	0.6			1.9
Inventory Turnover 35	50.1			10.0
Receivables Turnover 36	1.9			10.5
Total Liabilities to Net Worth 37	1.4		0.4	1.1
Current Assets to Working Capital 38	4.9	1.0	1.0	2.0
Current Liabilities to Working Capital 39	3.9			1.0
Working Capital to Net Sales 40	0.1			0.2
Inventory to Working Capital 41	0.1			0.4
Total Receipts to Cash Flow 42	9.3			7.9
Cost of Goods to Cash Flow 43	8.2			5.9
Cash Flow to Total Debt 44	0.1		2.5	0.5

Selected Financial Factors (in Percentages)

Debt Ratio 45	59.0		29.1	51.6
Return on Total Assets 46	6.8	18.2	72.9	3.5
Return on Equity Before Income Taxes 47	14.8	18.2	102.8	5.4
Return on Equity After Income Taxes 48	9.6	18.2	67.9	3.7
Profit Margin (Before Income Tax) 49	9.7			1.4
Profit Margin (After Income Tax) 50	6.3			0.9

ASPHALT PAVING, ROOFING, OTHER PETROLEUM AND COAL PRODUCTS

Table I

Corporations with and without Net Income

MONEY AMOUNTS AND SIZE OF ASSETS IN THOUSANDS OF DOLLARS

Item Description for Accounting Period 7/10 Through 6/11	Total	Zero Assets	Under 500	500 to 1,000	1,000 to 5,000	5,000 to 10,000	10,000 to 25,000	25,000 to 50,000	50,000 to 100,000	100,000 to 250,000	250,000 to 500,000	500,000 to 2,500,000	2,500,000 and over
Number of Enterprises 1	562	•	6	135	•	•	49	11	12	13	3	4	0
Revenues ($ in Thousands)													
Net Sales 2	15682868	•	22112	458449	•	•	1448444	480369	1797110	3632652	1395882	3077354	0
Interest 3	11959	•	0	117	•	•	71	340	184	5080	335	5760	0
Rents 4	3294	•	0	454	•	•	378	0	0	613	91	0	0
Royalties 5	12103	•	0	0	•	•	0	0	290	293	0	11520	0
Other Portfolio Income 6	51266	•	0	338	•	•	2616	35	463	10903	959	32613	0
Other Receipts 7	218286	•	3945	1074	•	•	9264	1228	7614	79770	5988	10398	0
Total Receipts 8	15979776	•	26057	460432	•	•	1460773	481972	1805661	3729311	1403255	3137645	0
Average Total Receipts 9	28434	•	4343	3411	•	•	29812	43816	150472	286870	467752	784411	•
Operating Costs/Operating Income (%)													
Cost of Operations 10	70.5	•	129.3	76.3	•	•	72.9	60.3	81.0	82.0	63.2	48.4	•
Salaries and Wages 11	4.5	•	6.9	3.9	•	•	4.7	7.4	2.9	3.1	8.9	4.8	•
Taxes Paid 12	1.3	•	0.5	2.4	•	•	1.3	1.2	0.9	0.7	1.4	1.9	•
Interest Paid 13	2.5	•	6.4	0.2	•	•	0.7	0.1	1.1	0.6	0.1	9.9	•
Depreciation 14	2.8	•	0.3	2.8	•	•	4.3	3.0	2.9	1.4	5.1	3.6	•
Amortization and Depletion 15	0.2	•	8.1	0.0	•	•	0.0	0.1	0.2	0.2	0.2	0.2	•
Pensions and Other Deferred Comp. 16	0.2	•	•	0.0	•	•	0.1	0.3	0.2	0.2	0.6	0.1	•
Employee Benefits 17	0.9	•	0.1	1.9	•	•	1.8	1.1	0.5	0.3	1.4	1.5	•
Advertising 18	1.0	•	•	1.1	•	•	2.6	1.6	0.2	0.9	0.5	0.6	•
Other Expenses 19	9.0	•	60.6	6.9	•	•	7.5	11.3	4.1	5.7	6.7	16.5	•
Officers' Compensation 20	1.2	•	2.8	4.9	•	•	1.2	3.0	1.1	0.6	1.3	0.1	•
Operating Margin 21	6.0	•	•	•	•	•	2.9	10.6	4.8	4.3	10.5	12.5	•
Operating Margin Before Officers' Comp. 22	7.2	•	•	4.5	•	•	4.1	13.6	5.9	5.0	11.8	12.6	•

Selected Average Balance Sheet ($ in Thousands)

Net Receivables 23	2932	74	113	3502	6085	12779	26977	46803	73933
Inventories 24	1860	58	66	2916	6302	11912	19272	39801	56716
Net Property, Plant and Equipment 25	4819	8	479	6771	5372	19075	24555	97755	248586
Total Assets 26	22348	180	848	16301	36112	66373	157664	338298	1520548
Notes and Loans Payable 27	5818	6247	211	4471	4925	14630	46092	3944	228858
All Other Liabilities 28	10210	6405	197	2486	3415	15745	30285	90557	966832
Net Worth 29	6320	-12472	440	9344	27772	35998	81287	243797	324858

Selected Financial Ratios (Times to 1)

Current Ratio 30	1.5	0.0	1.5	2.0	6.9	2.5	2.9	2.6	1.1
Quick Ratio 31	0.9	0.0	1.2	1.2	4.2	1.3	1.6	0.8	0.8
Net Sales to Working Capital 32	8.7	•	29.9	7.4	2.4	7.0	5.3	4.4	14.6
Coverage Ratio 33	4.2	•	1.3	6.6	150.5	5.7	12.2	156.5	2.5
Total Asset Turnover 34	1.2	20.5	4.0	1.8	1.2	2.3	1.8	1.4	0.5
Inventory Turnover 35	10.6	82.4	39.5	7.4	4.2	10.2	11.9	7.4	6.6
Receivables Turnover 36	9.8	98.9	22.0	9.3	•	11.0	•	9.6	10.3
Total Liabilities to Net Worth 37	2.5	•	0.9	0.7	0.3	0.8	0.9	0.4	3.7
Current Assets to Working Capital 38	2.9	•	3.1	2.0	1.2	1.7	1.5	1.6	8.4
Current Liabilities to Working Capital 39	1.9	•	2.1	1.0	0.2	0.7	0.5	0.6	7.4
Working Capital to Net Sales 40	0.1	•	0.0	0.1	0.4	0.1	0.2	0.2	0.1
Inventory to Working Capital 41	0.6	•	0.5	0.7	0.3	0.6	0.4	0.4	1.3
Total Receipts to Cash Flow 42	6.9	•	17.8	10.4	4.8	12.3	8.6	6.2	4.0
Cost of Goods to Cash Flow 43	4.9	•	13.6	7.6	2.9	10.0	7.1	3.9	2.0
Cash Flow to Total Debt 44	0.3	•	0.5	0.4	1.1	0.4	0.4	0.8	0.2

Selected Financial Factors (in Percentages)

Debt Ratio 45	71.7	•	48.1	42.7	23.1	45.8	48.4	27.9	78.6
Return on Total Assets 46	13.0	7041.7	1.2	8.0	13.3	14.5	13.7	15.3	12.4
Return on Equity Before Income Taxes 47	35.1	28.7	0.5	11.8	17.1	22.0	24.4	21.0	34.5
Return on Equity After Income Taxes 48	27.6	28.7	•	10.9	14.7	18.3	17.7	20.1	22.6
Profit Margin (Before Income Tax) 49	8.0	•	0.1	3.7	10.9	5.3	7.1	11.0	14.6
Profit Margin (After Income Tax) 50	6.3	•	•	3.4	9.3	4.4	5.2	10.5	9.5

Table II

Corporations with Net Income

ASPHALT PAVING, ROOFING, OTHER PETROLEUM AND COAL PRODUCTS

MONEY AMOUNTS AND SIZE OF ASSETS IN THOUSANDS OF DOLLARS

Item Description for Accounting Period 7/10 Through 6/11	Total	Zero Assets	Under 500	500 to 1,000	1,000 to 5,000	5,000 to 10,000	10,000 to 25,000	25,000 to 50,000	50,000 to 100,000	100,000 to 250,000	250,000 to 500,000	500,000 to 2,500,000	2,500,000 and over
Number of Enterprises **1**	343	•	0	68	82	113	41	•	•	•	•	•	•
Revenues ($ in Thousands)													
Net Sales **2**	14823683	0	0	241310	836433	2309199	1372098	•	•	•	•	•	•
Interest **3**	7776	0	0	13	1	2	71	•	•	•	•	•	•
Rents **4**	2463	0	0	0	0	1757	0	•	•	•	•	•	•
Royalties **5**	495	0	0	0	0	0	0	•	•	•	•	•	•
Other Portfolio Income **6**	31252	0	0	338	2512	58	2616	•	•	•	•	•	•
Other Receipts **7**	145732	0	0	1	29103	7867	1805	•	•	•	•	•	•
Total Receipts **8**	15011401	0	0	241662	868049	2318883	1376590	•	•	•	•	•	•
Average Total Receipts **9**	43765	•	•	3554	10586	20521	33575	•	•	•	•	•	•
Operating Costs/Operating Income (%)													
Cost of Operations **10**	70.3	•	•	70.7	62.9	79.3	72.0	•	•	•	•	•	•
Salaries and Wages **11**	4.3	•	•	6.5	3.3	3.8	5.0	•	•	•	•	•	•
Taxes Paid **12**	1.2	•	•	1.6	2.1	1.1	1.3	•	•	•	•	•	•
Interest Paid **13**	2.3	•	•	0.2	0.2	1.0	0.5	•	•	•	•	•	•
Depreciation **14**	2.8	•	•	4.5	2.0	2.0	3.2	•	•	•	•	•	•
Amortization and Depletion **15**	0.1	•	•	•	•	0.1	0.0	•	•	•	•	•	•
Pensions and Other Deferred Comp. **16**	0.2	•	•	•	0.0	0.2	0.1	•	•	•	•	•	•
Employee Benefits **17**	0.9	•	•	0.9	1.2	0.5	1.9	•	•	•	•	•	•
Advertising **18**	1.0	•	•	0.1	0.5	1.7	2.7	•	•	•	•	•	•
Other Expenses **19**	8.3	•	•	8.8	13.7	5.5	7.6	•	•	•	•	•	•
Officers' Compensation **20**	1.0	•	•	5.9	2.4	1.3	1.2	•	•	•	•	•	•
Operating Margin **21**	7.6	•	•	0.9	11.6	3.5	4.6	•	•	•	•	•	•
Operating Margin Before Officers' Comp. **22**	8.7	•	•	6.8	14.0	4.8	5.8	•	•	•	•	•	•

Selected Average Balance Sheet ($ in Thousands)

Net Receivables 23	3944	193	1019	2314	3139
Inventories 24	2788	0	20	636	3403
Net Property, Plant and Equipment 25	6906	434	432	2489	6385
Total Assets 26	29969	895	3333	6978	16614
Notes and Loans Payable 27	5597	212	715	3666	3538
All Other Liabilities 28	14037	366	1109	1893	2410
Net Worth 29	10335	316	1509	1419	10666

Selected Financial Ratios (Times to 1)

Current Ratio 30	1.9	1.3	2.3	1.6	2.5
Quick Ratio 31	1.1	1.3	1.4	1.2	1.4
Net Sales to Working Capital 32	6.8	35.8	6.3	13.0	6.5
Coverage Ratio 33	5.0	5.4	70.2	5.2	10.9
Total Asset Turnover 34	1.4	4.0	3.1	2.9	2.0
Inventory Turnover 35	10.9	•	326.3	25.5	7.1
Receivables Turnover 36	11.6	14.4	•	14.2	10.8
Total Liabilities to Net Worth 37	1.9	1.8	1.2	3.9	0.6
Current Assets to Working Capital 38	2.2	4.6	1.8	2.7	1.6
Current Liabilities to Working Capital 39	1.2	3.6	0.8	1.7	0.6
Working Capital to Net Sales 40	0.1	0.0	0.2	0.1	0.2
Inventory to Working Capital 41	0.5	•	0.0	0.5	0.6
Total Receipts to Cash Flow 42	6.8	11.5	4.1	12.7	9.2
Cost of Goods to Cash Flow 43	4.8	8.1	2.6	10.1	6.6
Cash Flow to Total Debt 44	0.3	0.5	1.4	0.3	0.6

Selected Financial Factors (in Percentages)

Debt Ratio 45	65.5	64.6	54.7	79.7	35.8
Return on Total Assets 46	16.1	5.0	47.7	14.4	10.9
Return on Equity Before Income Taxes 47	37.3	11.6	103.9	57.0	15.4
Return on Equity After Income Taxes 48	29.7	9.8	103.7	53.0	14.4
Profit Margin (Before Income Tax) 49	8.9	1.0	15.4	4.0	4.9
Profit Margin (After Income Tax) 50	7.1	0.9	15.3	3.7	4.6

Table I
Corporations with and without Net Income

BASIC CHEMICAL

MONEY AMOUNTS AND SIZE OF ASSETS IN THOUSANDS OF DOLLARS

Item Description for Accounting Period 7/10 Through 6/11	Total	Zero Assets	Under 500	500 to 1,000	1,000 to 5,000	5,000 to 10,000	10,000 to 25,000	25,000 to 50,000	50,000 to 100,000	100,000 to 250,000	250,000 to 500,000	500,000 to 2,500,000	2,500,000 and over
Number of Enterprises **1**	1311	412	124	316	80	49	112	77	32	24	21	37	27
Revenues ($ in Thousands)													
Net Sales **2**	197960710	658154	85270	734017	851828	563993	3097737	3263485	3254641	6158953	7643066	28490241	143159325
Interest **3**	2154228	876	12	6	136	341	795	4364	1897	3103	7137	137762	1997799
Rents **4**	204910	0	0	0	0	0	1044	785	1150	6965	8955	14200	171811
Royalties **5**	3366530	217	1082	0	0	0	16	432	1474	14375	32000	137559	3179376
Other Portfolio Income **6**	3692858	19893	0	0	2555	306	12951	77250	14703	20577	64562	207668	3272390
Other Receipts **7**	452865	-277	12407	8911	24915	2254	33744	-1999	224551	134349	143584	428729	357699
Total Receipts **8**	211908101	678863	98771	742934	879434	566894	3146287	3344317	3498416	6338322	7899304	29416159	155298400
Average Total Receipts **9**	161639	1648	797	2351	10993	11569	28092	43433	109326	264097	376157	795031	5751793
Operating Costs/Operating Income (%)													
Cost of Operations **10**	75.4	70.9	67.9	74.2	51.8	67.3	63.2	66.5	74.7	84.1	73.6	72.4	76.4
Salaries and Wages **11**	6.0	10.6	4.7	2.4	16.1	4.1	7.6	7.1	5.0	4.8	6.5	5.7	5.9
Taxes Paid **12**	0.9	1.2	2.0	0.7	1.6	1.5	1.9	1.1	1.2	0.6	0.8	0.8	0.9
Interest Paid **13**	3.9	0.5	1.1	0.2	1.7	0.4	0.6	0.9	1.2	1.2	2.0	3.1	4.5
Depreciation **14**	3.6	4.4	0.6	3.2	1.8	2.4	2.4	4.0	3.8	2.5	3.7	5.5	3.2
Amortization and Depletion **15**	0.8	0.4	0.8	0.0	0.0	0.0	0.2	0.2	0.7	0.4	0.7	1.0	0.9
Pensions and Other Deferred Comp. **16**	1.3	0.0	•	•	0.0	0.8	0.4	0.5	0.4	0.5	1.1	1.1	1.4
Employee Benefits **17**	1.3	0.4	2.4	0.7	1.5	0.9	1.4	1.8	1.1	0.6	1.0	1.7	1.3
Advertising **18**	0.4	0.1	0.0	0.5	1.1	0.6	0.2	0.3	0.1	0.1	0.2	0.1	0.4
Other Expenses **19**	8.3	5.2	62.1	9.3	16.8	8.4	11.1	9.9	17.3	6.7	9.4	8.3	7.9
Officers' Compensation **20**	0.5	2.0	4.3	3.8	2.9	5.4	2.5	2.1	1.7	1.1	0.7	0.5	0.3
Operating Margin **21**	•	4.3	•	5.0	3.8	8.3	8.6	5.5	•	•	0.4	•	•
Operating Margin Before Officers' Comp. **22**	•	6.3	•	8.7	6.7	13.7	11.1	7.7	•	•	1.1	0.2	•

Selected Average Balance Sheet ($ in Thousands)

Net Receivables 23	58104	0	87	294	1029	1088	3668	6354	14970	26414	83182	125852	2500675
Inventories 24	14459	0	106	66	962	728	3326	5292	10445	20134	38957	91916	481193
Net Property, Plant and Equipment 25	42199	0	10	284	283	758	3735	9260	21508	40261	113164	270582	1481420
Total Assets 26	283756	0	354	848	3333	6515	15209	32956	70785	154311	371431	1105268	11563051
Notes and Loans Payable 27	114952	0	2	96	2568	721	3314	14270	19159	48494	139147	405795	4786956
All Other Liabilities 28	84428	0	28	118	2024	962	3138	11864	16840	50475	99895	304205	3483950
Net Worth 29	84376	0	324	633	-1260	4832	8757	6822	34786	55341	132388	395268	3292144

Selected Financial Ratios (Times to 1)

Current Ratio 30	1.1	•	11.5	3.0	1.4	4.9	2.5	1.8	1.8	1.8	2.0	1.4	1.1
Quick Ratio 31	0.8	•	7.5	1.9	0.7	2.5	1.5	1.1	1.1	1.1	1.3	0.8	0.7
Net Sales to Working Capital 32	13.5	•	2.3	6.3	11.9	3.2	4.5	5.1	6.4	7.6	4.7	8.5	21.6
Coverage Ratio 33	2.6	15.7	•	28.7	5.1	24.2	18.9	9.9	1.3	1.3	3.0	2.2	2.6
Total Asset Turnover 34	0.5	•	1.9	2.7	3.2	1.8	1.8	1.3	1.4	1.7	1.0	0.7	0.5
Inventory Turnover 35	7.9	•	4.4	25.9	5.7	10.6	5.3	5.3	7.3	10.7	6.9	6.1	8.4
Receivables Turnover 36	2.6	•	6.4	8.7	10.0	9.3	8.4	7.1	7.6	9.1	4.9	6.0	2.1
Total Liabilities to Net Worth 37	2.4	•	0.1	0.3	•	0.3	0.7	3.8	1.0	1.8	1.8	1.8	2.5
Current Assets to Working Capital 38	9.2	•	1.1	1.5	3.3	1.3	1.7	2.2	2.3	2.3	2.0	3.7	17.0
Current Liabilities to Working Capital 39	8.2	•	0.1	0.5	2.3	0.3	0.7	1.2	1.3	1.3	1.0	2.7	16.0
Working Capital to Net Sales 40	0.1	•	0.4	0.2	0.1	0.3	0.2	0.2	0.2	0.1	0.2	0.1	0.0
Inventory to Working Capital 41	1.5	•	0.4	0.2	1.7	0.2	0.6	0.7	0.7	0.6	0.6	1.1	2.3
Total Receipts to Cash Flow 42	9.4	9.9	•	7.6	4.7	7.1	5.2	6.2	13.2	20.6	9.2	11.8	9.1
Cost of Goods to Cash Flow 43	7.1	7.0	•	5.6	2.5	4.8	3.3	4.1	9.9	17.3	6.8	8.5	6.9
Cash Flow to Total Debt 44	0.1	•	•	1.4	0.5	1.0	0.8	0.3	0.2	0.2	0.1	0.1	0.1

Selected Financial Factors (in Percentages)

Debt Ratio 45	70.3	•	8.3	25.3	137.8	25.8	42.4	79.3	50.9	64.1	64.4	64.2	71.5
Return on Total Assets 46	5.3	•	•	17.5	27.9	16.1	19.5	11.5	2.1	2.5	5.8	4.7	5.3
Return on Equity Before Income Taxes 47	11.0	•	•	22.6	•	20.8	32.1	49.9	0.9	1.4	10.8	7.0	11.4
Return on Equity After Income Taxes 48	7.6	•	•	22.5	•	20.4	29.1	43.9	•	6.5	6.5	3.9	7.9
Profit Margin (Before Income Tax) 49	6.2	7.4	•	6.2	7.0	8.7	10.2	8.0	0.3	•	3.9	3.6	7.1
Profit Margin (After Income Tax) 50	4.3	5.1	•	6.1	6.6	8.6	9.2	7.1	•	•	2.3	2.0	4.9

Table II
Corporations with Net Income

BASIC CHEMICAL

MONEY AMOUNTS AND SIZE OF ASSETS IN THOUSANDS OF DOLLARS

Item Description for Accounting Period 7/10 Through 6/11	Total	Zero Assets	Under 500	500 to 1,000	1,000 to 5,000	5,000 to 10,000	10,000 to 25,000	25,000 to 50,000	50,000 to 100,000	100,000 to 250,000	250,000 to 500,000	500,000 to 2,500,000	2,500,000 and over
Number of Enterprises 1	741	8	108	281	62	27	98	57	23	13	15	27	23
Revenues ($ in Thousands)													
Net Sales 2	180027530	610576	85222	733640	819317	244153	2792963	2952042	2408060	4354754	6895355	22491128	135640320
Interest 3	1963106	876	0	6	18	307	789	3092	1339	1287	7017	100405	1847971
Rents 4	195353	0	0	0	0	0	1044	311	686	22	8955	13867	170470
Royalties 5	3261116	217	0	0	0	0	16	0	1474	13965	31941	129832	3083672
Other Portfolio Income 6	3615103	19797	0	0	2396	280	12951	77211	14190	9937	64546	182999	3230793
Other Receipts 7	3984248	-4056	0	8911	16958	1762	35096	-6335	25029	71042	143320	370966	3321552
Total Receipts 8	193046456	627410	85222	742557	838689	246502	2842859	3026321	2450778	4451007	7151134	23289197	147294778
Average Total Receipts 9	260522	78426	789	2643	13527	9130	29009	53093	106556	342385	476742	862563	6404121
Operating Costs/Operating Income (%)													
Cost of Operations 10	75.3	69.8	67.8	73.8	53.2	39.0	62.3	66.9	71.4	85.4	74.1	74.0	76.1
Salaries and Wages 11	5.9	10.8	4.7	2.3	14.5	5.9	7.7	5.6	5.0	2.6	6.6	4.7	6.1
Taxes Paid 12	0.9	1.2	1.9	0.7	1.3	2.6	1.8	1.1	1.4	0.6	0.7	0.8	0.9
Interest Paid 13	3.8	0.3	•	0.2	0.5	0.9	0.5	0.8	0.8	0.7	1.7	2.4	4.5
Depreciation 14	3.3	4.5	0.5	2.6	1.5	3.1	2.0	3.3	3.3	2.0	3.4	4.1	3.2
Amortization and Depletion 15	0.8	0.2	•	•	•	0.0	0.1	0.2	0.6	0.1	0.4	0.6	0.9
Pensions and Other Deferred Comp. 16	1.3	0.1	•	•	0.8	1.8	0.5	0.5	0.3	0.3	1.1	1.1	1.4
Employee Benefits 17	1.3	0.3	2.4	0.7	1.3	0.9	1.4	1.6	1.2	0.3	1.1	1.6	1.3
Advertising 18	0.4	0.1	0.0	0.0	1.1	1.4	0.2	0.3	0.1	0.1	0.2	0.1	0.5
Other Expenses 19	7.8	5.0	10.9	8.0	12.9	14.8	10.9	7.9	7.8	4.3	8.4	7.4	7.9
Officers' Compensation 20	0.5	2.2	4.3	3.6	2.6	9.2	2.6	2.2	2.0	1.3	0.6	0.5	0.3
Operating Margin 21	•	5.4	7.4	8.2	10.2	20.5	10.1	9.5	5.9	2.2	1.8	2.6	•
Operating Margin Before Officers' Comp. 22	•	7.6	11.8	11.7	12.8	29.6	12.7	11.7	7.9	3.5	2.4	3.1	•

Selected Average Balance Sheet ($ in Thousands)

Net Receivables 23	97583	0	100	331	1300	1278	3710	6884	16873	34835	95693	138644	2839745
Inventories 24	20749	0	124	80	1222	648	3410	6013	10974	20521	41376	80112	490211
Net Property, Plant and Equipment 25	62986	0	11	293	86	775	3737	9220	20440	34655	115432	229023	1601531
Total Assets 26	455145	0	382	884	3596	6765	14747	34240	69528	159427	385046	1073682	12814506
Notes and Loans Payable 27	181717	0	2	108	644	1022	2666	6734	18166	36715	118299	336966	5310503
All Other Liabilities 28	135369	0	32	131	1608	729	3171	8015	15711	50915	116777	284238	3866595
Net Worth 29	138059	0	348	645	1343	5014	8909	19491	35651	71797	149970	452479	3637408

Selected Financial Ratios (Times to 1)

Current Ratio 30	1.1	•	10.9	2.9	2.1	5.9	2.7	2.8	1.8	1.6	2.0	1.8	1.0
Quick Ratio 31	0.8	•	7.0	1.8	0.9	2.8	1.6	1.6	1.1	1.0	1.3	1.1	0.7
Net Sales to Working Capital 32	15.2	•	2.5	6.8	7.1	2.0	4.5	4.3	6.2	10.1	5.5	5.5	33.9
Coverage Ratio 33	3.0	28.3	•	43.2	28.0	25.8	26.7	15.3	10.3	7.8	4.3	3.9	2.7
Total Asset Turnover 34	0.5	•	2.1	3.0	3.7	1.3	1.9	1.5	1.5	2.1	1.2	0.8	0.5
Inventory Turnover 35	8.8	•	4.3	24.2	5.8	5.4	5.2	5.8	6.8	13.9	8.2	7.7	9.2
Receivables Turnover 36	2.5	•	•	•	9.8	5.2	8.4	7.9	7.2	10.8	5.3	7.0	2.1
Total Liabilities to Net Worth 37	2.3	•	0.1	0.4	1.7	0.3	0.7	0.8	1.0	1.2	1.6	1.4	2.5
Current Assets to Working Capital 38	10.4	•	1.1	1.5	1.9	1.2	1.6	1.6	2.3	2.6	2.0	2.3	26.8
Current Liabilities to Working Capital 39	9.4	•	0.1	0.5	0.9	0.2	0.6	0.6	1.3	1.6	1.0	1.3	25.8
Working Capital to Net Sales 40	0.1	•	0.4	0.1	0.1	0.5	0.2	0.2	0.2	0.1	0.2	0.2	0.0
Inventory to Working Capital 41	1.5	•	0.4	0.2	1.0	0.1	0.6	0.6	0.7	0.7	0.5	0.7	3.3
Total Receipts to Cash Flow 42	8.6	9.3	7.0	6.5	4.3	3.2	4.8	5.5	7.5	13.3	8.8	9.0	8.8
Cost of Goods to Cash Flow 43	6.5	6.5	4.8	4.8	2.3	1.3	3.0	3.7	5.4	11.4	6.5	6.6	6.7
Cash Flow to Total Debt 44	0.1	•	3.3	1.7	1.4	1.6	1.0	0.6	0.4	0.3	0.2	0.1	0.1

Selected Financial Factors (in Percentages)

Debt Ratio 45	69.7	•	8.9	27.0	62.6	25.9	39.6	43.1	48.7	55.0	61.1	57.9	71.6
Return on Total Assets 46	6.1	•	15.4	28.3	48.0	29.7	23.9	19.5	12.8	10.6	8.7	7.3	5.5
Return on Equity Before Income Taxes 47	13.3	•	16.9	37.9	123.9	38.5	38.1	32.0	22.5	20.6	17.2	12.9	12.3
Return on Equity After Income Taxes 48	9.6	•	15.5	37.8	120.2	37.8	34.7	29.2	18.6	15.7	11.9	9.1	8.6
Profit Margin (Before Income Tax) 49	7.6	8.2	7.4	9.4	12.6	21.4	11.9	12.0	7.7	4.4	5.6	7.0	7.6
Profit Margin (After Income Tax) 50	5.4	5.7	6.8	9.3	12.2	20.9	10.9	11.0	6.3	3.4	3.9	5.0	5.3

Table I

Corporations with and without Net Income

RESIN, SYNTHETIC RUBBER AND FIBERS AND FILAMENTS

MONEY AMOUNTS AND SIZE OF ASSETS IN THOUSANDS OF DOLLARS

Item Description for Accounting Period 7/10 Through 6/11	Total	Zero Assets	Under 500	500 to 1,000	1,000 to 5,000	5,000 to 10,000	10,000 to 25,000	25,000 to 50,000	50,000 to 100,000	100,000 to 250,000	250,000 to 500,000	500,000 to 2,500,000	2,500,000 and over
Number of Enterprises 1	587	22	330	0	111	11	49	14	11	15	9	8	6
Revenues ($ in Thousands)													
Net Sales 2	54915912	258123	92082	0	426349	192139	1134609	796823	1194865	4109648	5307257	9822430	31581585
Interest 3	646104	353	0	0	96	0	152	1146	205	6141	7541	24855	605614
Rents 4	26315	0	0	0	0	0	0	0	0	190	276	2157	23692
Royalties 5	638121	0	0	0	0	0	0	382	0	4700	4180	12028	616831
Other Portfolio Income 6	460072	0	0	0	0	0	2890	0	2012	9010	131286	79879	234995
Other Receipts 7	1726663	175	0	0	27772	0	4148	277	5674	12799	79485	146337	1449998
Total Receipts 8	58413187	258651	92082	0	454217	192139	1141799	798628	1202756	4142488	5530025	10087686	34512715
Average Total Receipts 9	99511	11757	279	•	4092	17467	23302	57045	109341	276166	614447	1260961	5752119
Operating Costs/Operating Income (%)													
Cost of Operations 10	71.5	81.0	70.4	•	53.0	55.6	71.1	80.3	78.9	80.9	88.6	81.2	64.2
Salaries and Wages 11	3.0	4.9	•	•	6.0	10.1	4.9	2.6	4.9	3.2	2.9	3.4	2.6
Taxes Paid 12	0.6	1.3	1.1	•	2.0	1.2	1.6	1.2	1.5	0.9	0.4	0.5	0.5
Interest Paid 13	3.8	0.6	0.2	•	7.5	0.1	0.8	0.7	0.6	1.1	0.9	2.0	5.5
Depreciation 14	5.8	2.7	3.3	•	2.6	1.2	3.6	2.8	3.0	2.3	4.1	2.8	7.7
Amortization and Depletion 15	0.8	1.3	0.2	•	0.1	•	0.3	0.3	0.1	0.4	0.1	0.5	1.1
Pensions and Other Deferred Comp. 16	0.8	0.3	•	•	3.5	•	0.3	0.2	0.7	0.3	0.3	1.0	0.9
Employee Benefits 17	1.6	1.7	3.6	•	1.7	2.2	1.4	0.7	0.8	0.7	0.9	0.9	2.2
Advertising 18	0.2	0.0	0.1	•	0.2	0.3	0.5	0.2	0.1	0.1	0.1	0.1	0.3
Other Expenses 19	14.0	17.0	17.0	•	41.1	20.1	7.5	7.0	4.4	5.6	3.6	4.8	20.1
Officers' Compensation 20	0.4	•	1.5	•	6.2	•	2.9	0.6	0.8	0.8	0.3	0.5	0.1
Operating Margin 21	•	•	2.7	•	•	9.3	5.1	3.5	4.3	3.7	•	2.3	•
Operating Margin Before Officers' Comp. 22	•	•	4.2	•	•	9.3	8.0	4.1	5.0	4.5	•	2.8	•

Selected Average Balance Sheet ($ in Thousands)

Item													
Net Receivables 23	16033	0	33	•	659	3430	3854	7460	17597	31970	69604	165854	1061658
Inventories 24	10678	0	10	•	681	953	2105	6384	15599	26595	46963	107208	689207
Net Property, Plant and Equipment 25	37448	0	34	•	711	245	5539	11493	16587	57228	104723	212377	2962398
Total Assets 26	159137	0	99	•	3217	6891	16119	37030	73413	169235	351650	1231049	12546685
Notes and Loans Payable 27	92843	0	32	•	1089	125	2994	5851	12321	41081	105232	536087	8024973
All Other Liabilities 28	34666	0	13	•	456	1382	6245	15065	20852	52125	103464	347470	2506568
Net Worth 29	31628	0	53	•	1671	5384	6879	16113	40240	76030	142955	347491	2015144

Selected Financial Ratios (Times to 1)

Item														
Current Ratio 30	1.7	•	4.3	•	3.2	•	4.6	1.5	1.7	2.5	2.0	1.6	1.5	1.8
Quick Ratio 31	1.1	•	3.2	•	2.0	•	3.2	0.9	1.0	1.4	1.0	0.9	0.9	1.1
Net Sales to Working Capital 32	5.5	•	6.3	•	3.6	•	3.8	7.7	7.4	3.6	6.1	10.6	7.3	4.7
Coverage Ratio 33	2.4	•	18.7	•	•	•	63.4	7.8	6.7	9.4	5.1	3.8	3.5	2.1
Total Asset Turnover 34	0.6	•	2.8	•	1.2	•	2.5	1.4	1.5	1.5	1.6	1.7	1.0	0.4
Inventory Turnover 35	6.3	•	19.7	•	3.0	•	10.2	7.8	7.2	5.5	8.3	11.1	9.3	4.9
Receivables Turnover 36	6.4	•	6.8	•	4.8	•	3.3	7.9	8.0	6.2	8.5	7.6	9.2	5.5
Total Liabilities to Net Worth 37	4.0	•	0.9	•	0.9	•	0.3	1.3	1.3	0.8	1.2	1.5	2.5	5.2
Current Assets to Working Capital 38	2.3	•	1.3	•	1.5	•	1.3	2.9	2.4	1.7	2.0	2.7	2.8	2.3
Current Liabilities to Working Capital 39	1.3	•	0.3	•	0.5	•	0.3	1.9	1.4	0.7	1.0	1.7	1.8	1.3
Working Capital to Net Sales 40	0.2	•	0.2	•	0.3	•	0.3	0.1	0.1	0.3	0.2	0.1	0.1	0.2
Inventory to Working Capital 41	0.7	•	0.2	•	0.5	•	0.8	0.8	0.8	0.5	0.6	1.0	0.8	0.7
Total Receipts to Cash Flow 42	6.5	19.5	7.0	•	4.3	•	3.8	10.3	9.0	12.3	11.0	20.2	12.9	4.8
Cost of Goods to Cash Flow 43	4.7	15.8	4.9	•	2.3	•	2.1	8.3	6.4	9.7	8.9	17.9	10.5	3.1
Cash Flow to Total Debt 44	0.1	•	0.9	•	0.6	•	3.1	0.3	0.3	0.3	0.6	0.1	0.1	0.1

Selected Financial Factors (in Percentages)

Item														
Debt Ratio 45	80.1	•	46.4	•	48.0	•	21.9	57.3	56.5	45.2	55.1	59.3	71.8	83.9
Return on Total Assets 46	5.3	•	8.0	•	•	•	23.9	9.5	6.8	8.1	9.1	6.1	7.1	4.9
Return on Equity Before Income Taxes 47	15.4	•	14.2	•	•	•	30.1	19.4	13.2	13.3	16.3	11.0	18.1	16.1
Return on Equity After Income Taxes 48	9.2	•	14.2	•	•	•	19.9	18.1	6.6	8.9	13.4	6.6	12.5	9.0
Profit Margin (Before Income Tax) 49	5.2	•	2.7	•	•	•	9.3	5.8	3.7	4.9	4.5	2.7	5.1	6.2
Profit Margin (After Income Tax) 50	3.1	•	2.7	•	•	•	6.1	5.4	1.9	3.3	3.7	1.6	2.7	3.5

Table II
Corporations with Net Income

RESIN, SYNTHETIC RUBBER AND FIBERS AND FILAMENTS

MONEY AMOUNTS AND SIZE OF ASSETS IN THOUSANDS OF DOLLARS

Item Description for Accounting Period 7/10 Through 6/11		Total	Zero Assets	Under 500	500 to 1,000	1,000 to 5,000	5,000 to 10,000	10,000 to 25,000	25,000 to 50,000	50,000 to 100,000	100,000 to 250,000	250,000 to 500,000	500,000 to 2,500,000	2,500,000 and over
Number of Enterprises	1	282	•	86	0	94	11	42	11	•	12	6	•	3
Revenues ($ in Thousands)														
Net Sales	2	44044062	•	92082	0	423674	192139	1023486	663307	•	3167515	3924988	•	24357299
Interest	3	503181		0	0	0	0	76	1124	•	539	7497	•	470977
Rents	4	16791		0	0	0	0	0	0	•	190	276	•	15565
Royalties	5	601537		0	0	0	0	0	0	•	4700	3421	•	581388
Other Portfolio Income	6	396842	•	0	0	0	0	2869	0	•	8107	117738	•	234766
Other Receipts	7	1670222	•	0	0	616	0	3823	224	•	6189	80386	•	1441601
Total Receipts	8	47232635	•	92082	0	424290	192139	1030254	664655	•	3187240	4134306	•	27101596
Average Total Receipts	9	167492	•	1071	•	4514	17467	24530	60423	•	265603	689051	•	9033865
Operating Costs/Operating Income (%)														
Cost of Operations	10	72.7	•	70.0	•	52.2	55.6	71.4	81.1	•	79.2	89.3	•	65.4
Salaries and Wages	11	2.0	•	•	•	5.3	10.1	4.9	1.2	•	3.3	3.4	•	1.0
Taxes Paid	12	0.5	•	1.1	•	1.9	1.2	1.5	1.1	•	1.0	0.4	•	0.4
Interest Paid	13	2.8	•	•	•	5.4	0.1	0.9	0.4	•	0.8	0.6	•	4.0
Depreciation	14	4.2	•	3.0	•	2.2	1.2	3.3	2.3	•	2.3	2.0	•	5.7
Amortization and Depletion	15	0.4	•	0.2	•	•	•	0.3	0.2	•	0.2	0.2	•	0.5
Pensions and Other Deferred Comp.	16	0.8	•	•	•	3.5	•	0.3	0.1	•	0.3	0.3	•	0.9
Employee Benefits	17	1.8	•	3.6	•	1.5	2.2	1.4	0.7	•	0.8	1.0	•	2.7
Advertising	18	0.3	•	0.0	•	0.1	0.3	0.5	0.2	•	0.1	0.1	•	0.4
Other Expenses	19	14.7	•	14.7	•	10.8	20.1	6.8	5.4	•	5.3	2.8	•	23.0
Officers' Compensation	20	0.4	•	1.5	•	5.5	•	2.8	0.6	•	0.9	0.4	•	0.1
Operating Margin	21	•	•	5.9	•	11.6	9.3	5.9	6.7	•	6.0	•	•	•
Operating Margin Before Officers' Comp.	22	•	•	7.4	•	17.0	9.3	8.7	7.4	•	6.9	0.1	•	•

Selected Average Balance Sheet ($ in Thousands)

Net Receivables 23	28653	128	413	3430	3696	7971	30233	70436	1844099
Inventories 24	13171	40	789	953	1908	5457	25129	36175	1225958
Net Property, Plant and Equipment 25	57750	131	799	245	5224	12143	55079	90616	4412624
Total Assets 26	279440	380	3136	6891	14986	35434	164168	349174	21709608
Notes and Loans Payable 27	154386	125	508	125	3334	5827	30425	59829	13189386
All Other Liabilities 28	64747	52	144	1382	4736	14124	52785	98580	4677201
Net Worth 29	60307	204	2484	5384	6915	15483	80958	190764	3843021

Selected Financial Ratios (Times to 1)

Current Ratio 30	1.8	4.3	5.8	4.6	1.7	1.8	2.2	1.9	1.6
Quick Ratio 31	1.1	3.2	2.9	3.2	1.1	1.0	1.0	1.2	1.1
Net Sales to Working Capital 32	5.0	6.3	4.4	3.8	7.2	7.0	5.2	8.9	4.8
Coverage Ratio 33	4.0	•	3.2	63.4	8.1	18.4	9.5	11.6	3.5
Total Asset Turnover 34	0.6	2.8	1.4	2.5	1.6	1.7	1.6	1.9	0.4
Inventory Turnover 35	8.6	18.5	3.0	10.2	9.1	9.0	8.3	16.2	4.3
Receivables Turnover 36	8.7	16.8	5.8	3.3	8.8	8.3	8.6	12.0	8.8
Total Liabilities to Net Worth 37	3.6	0.9	0.3	0.3	1.2	1.3	1.0	0.8	4.6
Current Assets to Working Capital 38	2.3	1.3	1.2	1.3	2.5	2.2	1.8	2.1	2.5
Current Liabilities to Working Capital 39	1.3	0.3	0.2	0.3	1.5	1.2	0.8	1.1	1.5
Working Capital to Net Sales 40	0.2	0.2	0.2	0.3	0.1	0.1	0.2	0.1	0.2
Inventory to Working Capital 41	0.6	0.2	0.5	0.3	0.7	0.8	0.6	0.7	0.7
Total Receipts to Cash Flow 42	5.4	6.5	4.6	3.8	8.9	8.8	9.2	13.9	3.8
Cost of Goods to Cash Flow 43	3.9	4.5	2.4	2.1	6.3	7.2	7.2	12.4	2.5
Cash Flow to Total Debt 44	0.1	0.9	1.5	3.1	0.3	0.3	0.3	0.3	0.1

Selected Financial Factors (in Percentages)

Debt Ratio 45	78.4	46.4	20.8	21.9	53.9	56.3	50.7	45.4	82.3
Return on Total Assets 46	6.2	16.5	24.5	23.9	12.2	12.5	11.9	12.1	5.2
Return on Equity Before Income Taxes 47	21.5	30.9	21.2	30.1	23.2	27.0	21.6	20.2	21.2
Return on Equity After Income Taxes 48	14.7	30.9	21.2	19.9	21.7	18.3	18.1	15.2	13.8
Profit Margin (Before Income Tax) 49	8.3	5.9	11.7	9.3	6.6	6.9	6.6	5.9	10.0
Profit Margin (After Income Tax) 50	5.7	5.9	11.7	6.1	6.2	4.7	5.6	4.4	6.5

Table I
Corporations with and without Net Income

PHARMACEUTICAL AND MEDICINE

MONEY AMOUNTS AND SIZE OF ASSETS IN THOUSANDS OF DOLLARS

Item Description for Accounting Period 7/10 Through 6/11		Total	Zero Assets	Under 500	500 to 1,000	1,000 to 5,000	5,000 to 10,000	10,000 to 25,000	25,000 to 50,000	50,000 to 100,000	100,000 to 250,000	250,000 to 500,000	500,000 to 2,500,000	2,500,000 and over
Number of Enterprises	1	1377	19	603	74	150	162	131	68	47	54	15	26	27
Revenues ($ in Thousands)														
Net Sales	2	323784477	1120440	48760	41232	700989	1590478	2472906	2282810	2399713	6638480	2736238	23779118	279955313
Interest	3	3790567	12162	42	0	106	2879	2421	4475	7421	25778	9638	42765	3682879
Rents	4	176958	263	0	0	0	0	559	1436	1748	2581	1381	3966	165024
Royalties	5	27341229	296124	0	0	0	0	27184	14951	115966	125200	70237	637740	26053827
Other Portfolio Income	6	12021961	107	158	56451	0	11192	5878	566	139281	114535	40633	22265	11630894
Other Receipts	7	29085669	1178564	29928	36	10537	3896	27801	90094	203328	138599	27324	1582863	25792700
Total Receipts	8	396200861	2607660	78888	97719	711632	1608445	2536749	2394332	2867457	7045173	2885451	26086717	347280637
Average Total Receipts	9	287728	137245	131	1321	4744	9929	19364	35211	61010	130466	192363	1003335	12862246
Operating Costs/Operating Income (%)														
Cost of Operations	10	51.4	43.0	81.1	51.2	63.8	61.7	58.9	63.4	46.5	47.6	46.6	49.7	51.5
Salaries and Wages	11	14.0	31.5	9.0	13.2	9.1	11.1	9.8	9.3	19.8	12.9	14.1	12.8	14.1
Taxes Paid	12	1.6	7.4	7.2	4.0	1.1	3.1	2.4	2.8	2.7	1.8	2.2	1.7	1.5
Interest Paid	13	4.7	17.2	23.4	4.2	0.4	1.0	1.7	2.6	1.4	1.5	2.9	1.1	5.2
Depreciation	14	3.0	2.2	3.6	0.1	1.8	2.8	4.9	3.5	4.3	4.0	5.5	3.6	2.9
Amortization and Depletion	15	1.8	4.3	1.4	•	2.3	1.2	0.9	4.1	1.6	1.8	3.8	2.0	1.7
Pensions and Other Deferred Comp.	16	1.4	0.4	•	•	0.1	0.6	0.4	1.3	1.0	0.6	0.6	0.7	1.5
Employee Benefits	17	2.5	0.9	•	0.0	2.1	2.1	1.7	2.1	2.1	1.9	1.9	2.0	2.6
Advertising	18	4.0	4.5	13.4	1.1	0.2	0.2	1.3	1.1	1.7	2.9	1.3	1.4	4.3
Other Expenses	19	25.8	99.9	115.6	68.7	17.1	18.4	18.3	21.9	35.9	21.2	21.3	22.1	26.0
Officers' Compensation	20	0.5	2.0	41.8	5.1	7.6	5.0	4.2	3.0	3.6	1.8	3.0	1.1	0.2
Operating Margin	21	•	•	•	•	•	•	•	•	•	2.0	•	1.8	•
Operating Margin Before Officers' Comp.	22	•	•	•	3.0	3.0	•	•	•	3.8	3.8	•	2.9	•

Selected Average Balance Sheet ($ in Thousands)

Net Receivables 23	59305	0	50	8	462	1249	2835	4876	9728	20473	36346	137490	2776852
Inventories 24	31307	0	10	1	276	2004	2318	6174	8290	17115	27243	163106	1335210
Net Property, Plant and Equipment 25	51578	0	1	0	120	2714	4411	7136	12928	31141	54660	208380	2252777
Total Assets 26	790678	0	152	735	1540	7947	16258	35336	71215	158835	340919	1118817	38386664
Notes and Loans Payable 27	263457	0	351	7	314	1769	7921	10872	21352	36850	77019	188730	13014883
All Other Liabilities 28	175573	0	87	95	932	1324	5184	10681	21373	43641	73592	325327	8408209
Net Worth 29	351648	0	-287	633	295	4854	3154	13782	28489	78344	190309	604760	16963573

Selected Financial Ratios (Times to 1)

Current Ratio 30	1.1	•	1.3	7.9	1.5	3.3	1.2	1.3	2.3	2.2	3.1	1.7	1.1
Quick Ratio 31	0.5	•	1.2	7.7	0.9	1.9	0.8	0.8	1.5	1.2	2.0	0.8	0.5
Net Sales to Working Capital 32	12.6	•	1.5	0.9	11.0	3.1	9.8	6.6	2.1	3.0	1.6	4.4	20.1
Coverage Ratio 33	4.1	2.1	•	22.5	•	•	•	•	0.2	6.8	1.9	11.9	4.1
Total Asset Turnover 34	0.3	•	0.5	0.8	3.0	1.2	1.2	1.0	0.7	0.8	0.5	0.8	0.3
Inventory Turnover 35	3.9	•	6.7	257.4	10.8	3.0	4.8	3.4	2.9	3.4	3.1	2.8	4.0
Receivables Turnover 36	4.1	•	1.4	134.5	18.2	6.5	7.4	5.9	5.4	6.6	5.1	7.0	3.9
Total Liabilities to Net Worth 37	1.2	•	•	0.2	4.2	0.6	4.2	1.6	1.5	1.0	0.8	0.9	1.3
Current Assets to Working Capital 38	9.5	•	4.4	1.1	3.0	1.4	5.1	4.2	1.7	1.8	1.5	2.5	15.6
Current Liabilities to Working Capital 39	8.5	•	3.4	0.1	2.0	0.4	4.1	3.2	0.7	0.8	0.5	1.5	14.6
Working Capital to Net Sales 40	0.1	•	0.6	1.2	0.1	0.3	0.1	0.2	0.5	0.3	0.6	0.2	0.0
Inventory to Working Capital 41	1.7	•	0.1	0.0	1.1	0.5	1.3	1.1	0.3	0.5	0.2	0.8	2.7
Total Receipts to Cash Flow 42	3.0	0.9	•	•	8.8	12.6	7.6	13.5	4.0	3.8	4.8	3.2	3.0
Cost of Goods to Cash Flow 43	1.6	0.4	•	•	5.6	7.8	4.5	8.6	1.9	1.8	2.3	1.6	1.5
Cash Flow to Total Debt 44	0.2	•	•	•	0.4	0.3	0.2	0.1	0.3	0.4	0.3	0.6	0.2

Selected Financial Factors (in Percentages)

Debt Ratio 45	55.5	•	288.8	13.8	80.9	38.9	80.6	61.0	60.0	50.7	44.2	45.9	55.8
Return on Total Assets 46	5.8	•	•	71.0	•	•	•	•	0.2	7.9	3.0	10.4	5.7
Return on Equity Before Income Taxes 47	9.9	•	38.1	78.8	•	•	•	•	•	13.6	2.6	17.6	9.8
Return on Equity After Income Taxes 48	6.4	•	41.4	78.8	•	•	•	•	•	8.9	•	11.5	6.4
Profit Margin (Before Income Tax) 49	14.8	19.4	•	89.5	•	•	•	•	•	8.7	2.7	11.7	16.0
Profit Margin (After Income Tax) 50	9.6	•	•	89.5	•	•	•	•	•	•	5.7	7.6	10.5

Table II
Corporations with Net Income

PHARMACEUTICAL AND MEDICINE

MONEY AMOUNTS AND SIZE OF ASSETS IN THOUSANDS OF DOLLARS

Item Description for Accounting Period 7/10 Through 6/11	Total	Zero Assets	Under 500	500 to 1,000	1,000 to 5,000	5,000 to 10,000	10,000 to 25,000	25,000 to 50,000	50,000 to 100,000	100,000 to 250,000	250,000 to 500,000	500,000 to 2,500,000	2,500,000 and over
Number of Enterprises 1	684	11	153	71	127	103	76	34	24	31	8	22	23
Revenues ($ in Thousands)													
Net Sales 2	308435924	81136	48590	35633	680832	1213084	1779949	1631789	1781597	4711556	1993277	23330633	271147850
Interest 3	3731970	7888	42	0	0	2446	871	1959	4583	11422	3173	33271	3666314
Rents 4	171249	263	0	0	0	0	559	505	1748	1240	1183	3759	161993
Royalties 5	26528830	233812	0	0	0	0	292	8798	112667	75999	24478	283292	25787490
Other Portfolio Income 6	11948872	104	158	56451	0	414	428	499	135195	104612	15146	22078	11613786
Other Receipts 7	27148821	1175273	19979	0	8031	-495	11370	65941	85433	109914	13168	457105	25203104
Total Receipts 8	377963666	1498476	68769	92084	688863	1215449	1793469	1709491	2121223	5014743	2050425	24130138	337580537
Average Total Receipts 9	552578	136225	449	1297	5424	11800	23598	50279	88384	161766	256303	1096824	14677415
Operating Costs/Operating Income (%)													
Cost of Operations 10	51.9	13.5	81.4	39.8	64.0	58.0	56.1	64.8	43.8	44.6	45.1	49.8	52.1
Salaries and Wages 11	13.6	28.2	5.8	14.6	5.0	8.1	7.0	6.2	14.4	10.1	11.6	10.5	14.0
Taxes Paid 12	1.6	62.8	3.0	4.6	0.8	3.0	2.0	2.5	2.3	1.7	1.5	1.5	1.5
Interest Paid 13	4.6	1.1	0.1	4.8	0.3	0.9	0.6	1.2	1.2	0.9	1.8	1.0	5.1
Depreciation 14	2.9	1.6	0.0	0.1	1.6	1.8	4.3	3.6	3.0	3.4	3.8	3.1	2.9
Amortization and Depletion 15	1.6	1.5	•	•	0.0	0.1	0.3	0.3	0.7	1.3	3.3	1.6	1.6
Pensions and Other Deferred Comp. 16	1.4	1.6	•	•	0.0	0.7	0.4	0.7	0.4	0.5	0.6	0.7	1.6
Employee Benefits 17	2.5	•	•	0.0	0.5	2.2	1.1	1.9	1.3	1.4	1.7	1.8	2.6
Advertising 18	3.9	1.1	0.3	1.3	0.1	0.2	1.1	1.2	1.7	2.8	1.4	1.4	4.2
Other Expenses 19	24.9	768.9	13.9	42.3	7.4	12.3	11.5	13.2	22.9	19.2	17.7	16.7	25.8
Officers' Compensation 20	0.4	2.3	•	5.9	5.9	4.6	3.5	1.8	3.2	1.7	1.4	0.9	0.2
Operating Margin 21	•	•	•	•	14.5	8.3	11.9	2.7	5.3	12.4	10.2	11.0	•
Operating Margin Before Officers' Comp. 22	•	•	•	•	20.4	12.9	15.5	4.6	8.4	14.1	11.6	11.9	•

Selected Average Balance Sheet ($ in Thousands)

Net Receivables 23	115316	0	196	8	533	1520	3639	5403	12169	20822	53528	154634	3191015
Inventories 24	59317	0	0	1	320	2481	2599	6739	9616	22891	31270	180562	1585399
Net Property, Plant and Equipment 25	93862	0	0	0	60	3229	4524	10067	11576	29284	58520	189817	2493283
Total Assets 26	1530177	0	343	746	1278	8284	16313	34606	71374	156483	336852	1166382	43834104
Notes and Loans Payable 27	520725	0	13	0	35	1731	4198	8036	13921	34032	74766	214757	15516296
All Other Liabilities 28	337634	0	63	94	779	973	5472	8358	22396	40727	85559	340636	9567284
Net Worth 29	671818	0	267	651	464	5580	6643	18212	35057	81724	176527	610989	19106523

Selected Financial Ratios (Times to 1)

Current Ratio 30	1.1	•	11.6	7.9	1.6	4.7	2.1	1.8	2.4	2.1	2.6	1.6	1.1
Quick Ratio 31	0.5	•	10.2	7.7	0.9	2.8	1.3	0.9	1.5	1.1	1.4	0.8	0.5
Net Sales to Working Capital 32	13.2	•	0.5	0.8	12.3	3.2	4.4	5.3	2.7	3.7	2.4	5.0	18.6
Coverage Ratio 33	4.6	861.7	313.3	31.4	55.1	10.5	22.0	7.1	22.0	21.9	8.5	15.1	4.3
Total Asset Turnover 34	0.3	•	0.9	0.7	4.2	1.4	1.4	1.4	1.0	1.0	0.7	0.9	0.3
Inventory Turnover 35	3.9	•	•	172.8	10.7	2.8	5.1	4.6	3.4	3.0	3.6	2.9	3.9
Receivables Turnover 36	4.1	•	•	116.3	18.4	5.9	7.7	8.2	5.7	7.2	5.1	7.3	•
Total Liabilities to Net Worth 37	1.3	•	0.3	0.1	1.8	0.5	1.5	0.9	1.0	0.9	0.9	0.9	1.3
Current Assets to Working Capital 38	10.0	•	1.1	1.1	2.8	1.3	1.9	2.3	1.7	1.9	1.6	2.5	14.7
Current Liabilities to Working Capital 39	9.0	•	0.1	0.1	1.8	0.3	0.9	1.3	0.7	0.9	0.6	1.5	13.7
Working Capital to Net Sales 40	0.1	•	2.1	1.3	0.1	0.3	0.2	0.2	0.4	0.3	0.4	0.2	0.1
Inventory to Working Capital 41	1.8	•	•	0.0	1.2	0.5	0.6	0.9	0.3	0.6	0.3	0.8	2.5
Total Receipts to Cash Flow 42	3.0	0.1	2.1	3.8	4.6	5.6	4.5	6.0	2.8	2.9	3.6	3.5	3.0
Cost of Goods to Cash Flow 43	1.5	0.0	1.7	1.5	3.0	3.2	2.5	3.9	1.2	1.3	1.6	1.7	1.5
Cash Flow to Total Debt 44	0.2	•	2.0	1.4	1.4	0.8	0.5	0.5	0.7	0.7	0.4	0.6	0.2

Selected Financial Factors (in Percentages)

Debt Ratio 45	56.1	•	22.3	12.7	63.7	32.6	59.3	47.4	50.9	47.8	47.6	47.6	56.4
Return on Total Assets 46	6.3	•	34.0	100.9	67.0	13.4	19.2	12.1	26.5	19.8	11.5	14.3	5.8
Return on Equity Before Income Taxes 47	11.2	•	43.6	111.9	181.2	18.0	45.0	19.7	51.5	36.2	19.3	25.6	10.2
Return on Equity After Income Taxes 48	7.5	•	29.4	111.9	181.2	16.6	39.0	17.3	44.2	28.4	12.8	18.4	6.8
Profit Margin (Before Income Tax) 49	16.7	964.3	36.6	145.1	15.7	8.5	12.8	7.5	24.3	19.5	13.7	14.7	16.6
Profit Margin (After Income Tax) 50	11.2	626.8	24.7	145.1	15.7	7.9	11.1	6.6	20.9	15.2	9.1	10.6	11.0

Table I

Corporations with and without Net Income

PAINT, COATING, AND ADHESIVE

MONEY AMOUNTS AND SIZE OF ASSETS IN THOUSANDS OF DOLLARS

Item Description for Accounting Period 7/10 Through 6/11	Total	Zero Assets	Under 500	500 to 1,000	1,000 to 5,000	5,000 to 10,000	10,000 to 25,000	25,000 to 50,000	50,000 to 100,000	100,000 to 250,000	250,000 to 500,000	500,000 to 2,500,000	2,500,000 and over
Number of Enterprises **1**	1573	10	229	505	649	32	71	32	14	13	6	5	7
Revenues ($ in Thousands)													
Net Sales **2**	47587232	235104	191123	1154148	3862293	512718	1836427	1402181	1260976	2182821	2133810	3345818	29469812
Interest **3**	273133	1	0	186	93	20	636	223	691	1512	14583	36906	218284
Rents **4**	26949	0	0	304	0	1707	1644	823	101	311	1632	4353	16073
Royalties **5**	377172	0	0	0	0	0	0	1645	1976	1425	3297	45759	323069
Other Portfolio Income **6**	627212	14139	0	0	1487	690	1560	5636	323	373	8146	27878	566981
Other Receipts **7**	398604	0	0	49	6008	4763	11861	3662	17399	5468	66885	18533	263977
Total Receipts **8**	49290302	249244	191123	1154687	3869881	519898	1852128	1414170	1281466	2191910	2228353	3479247	30858196
Average Total Receipts **9**	31335	24924	835	2287	5963	16247	26086	44193	91533	168608	371392	695849	4408314
Operating Costs/Operating Income (%)													
Cost of Operations **10**	63.6	72.4	37.2	58.9	63.3	64.4	65.4	69.9	64.4	64.4	64.3	65.9	63.0
Salaries and Wages **11**	9.9	10.2	22.1	7.3	5.9	12.1	10.7	7.9	8.5	10.3	11.7	11.2	10.1
Taxes Paid **12**	1.8	1.4	4.2	3.3	2.5	2.8	1.6	1.5	2.1	1.7	1.9	1.5	1.6
Interest Paid **13**	2.8	0.7	•	0.9	0.4	0.3	0.8	0.5	1.1	1.6	2.9	2.4	3.7
Depreciation **14**	2.2	0.5	•	0.7	1.1	2.6	1.5	1.9	2.7	3.0	2.9	2.1	2.4
Amortization and Depletion **15**	1.1	0.8	•	0.0	0.2	0.1	0.3	0.2	0.8	1.5	2.0	1.3	1.3
Pensions and Other Deferred Comp. **16**	1.5	0.3	•	0.9	0.4	0.4	0.8	0.4	1.2	0.6	0.8	2.0	1.8
Employee Benefits **17**	2.0	1.3	•	1.9	0.8	1.3	0.5	1.5	1.8	1.7	1.7	2.8	2.3
Advertising **18**	1.7	1.0	4.3	0.2	1.4	0.4	0.3	0.3	0.7	0.4	0.8	0.5	2.2
Other Expenses **19**	12.0	12.6	35.7	10.3	11.2	7.5	10.3	9.0	12.1	11.9	13.3	10.3	12.4
Officers' Compensation **20**	1.6	3.8	•	7.2	7.8	2.4	3.6	2.5	1.8	1.2	0.8	0.9	0.5
Operating Margin **21**	•	•	•	8.5	4.9	5.7	4.4	4.6	2.7	1.6	•	•	•
Operating Margin Before Officers' Comp. **22**	1.6	•	•	15.6	12.7	8.1	8.0	7.1	4.5	2.8	•	•	0.1

Selected Average Balance Sheet ($ in Thousands)

Net Receivables 23	4385	74	330	594	2723	3689	6244	13144	25446	48074	70346	660696
Inventories 24	2850	0	188	414	3252	3577	5253	11262	16116	39577	74178	374254
Net Property, Plant and Equipment 25	4437	0	81	252	779	2301	4717	18201	36967	50782	113928	689369
Total Assets 26	31995	151	760	2119	8270	14314	32409	72981	151692	366742	909863	5210397
Notes and Loans Payable 27	12807	753	281	514	1514	4060	5929	12318	46282	129618	166371	2369665
All Other Liabilities 28	13483	29	240	415	3078	4027	5854	22777	37975	98258	244102	2516731
Net Worth 29	5705	-630	239	1191	3679	6228	20627	37886	67435	138867	499391	324001

Selected Financial Ratios (Times to 1)

Current Ratio 30	1.0	•	2.0	2.9	1.7	2.1	2.7	1.4	1.7	1.9	1.9	0.8
Quick Ratio 31	0.6	•	1.3	2.0	0.9	1.1	1.7	0.7	0.9	1.0	1.2	0.4
Net Sales to Working Capital 32	151.1	23.4	7.6	6.2	5.2	5.4	3.7	9.7	6.4	5.5	5.1	•
Coverage Ratio 33	2.5	2.5	11.0	12.7	23.4	7.7	13.0	5.0	2.5	1.4	2.4	2.1
Total Asset Turnover 34	0.9	•	3.0	2.8	1.9	1.8	1.4	1.2	1.1	1.0	0.7	0.8
Inventory Turnover 35	6.7	•	7.1	9.1	3.2	4.7	5.8	5.1	6.7	5.8	5.9	7.1
Receivables Turnover 36	7.1	•	•	11.4	4.4	7.0	8.3	6.3	8.0	7.3	6.8	6.7
Total Liabilities to Net Worth 37	4.6	•	2.2	0.8	1.2	1.3	0.6	0.9	1.2	1.6	0.8	15.1
Current Assets to Working Capital 38	54.2	4.2	2.0	1.5	2.3	1.9	1.6	3.5	2.4	2.1	2.1	•
Current Liabilities to Working Capital 39	53.2	3.2	1.0	0.5	1.3	0.9	0.6	2.5	1.4	1.1	1.1	•
Working Capital to Net Sales 40	0.0	0.0	0.1	0.2	0.2	0.2	0.3	0.1	0.2	0.2	0.2	•
Inventory to Working Capital 41	14.4	•	0.6	0.4	1.0	0.8	0.5	1.2	0.9	0.7	0.3	•
Total Receipts to Cash Flow 42	7.8	12.8	6.4	7.9	7.7	7.1	8.0	6.8	8.7	9.3	8.6	7.7
Cost of Goods to Cash Flow 43	5.0	9.3	3.8	5.0	5.0	4.7	5.6	4.3	5.6	6.0	5.6	4.9
Cash Flow to Total Debt 44	0.1	0.3	0.7	0.8	0.5	0.4	0.5	0.4	0.2	0.2	0.2	0.1

Selected Financial Factors (in Percentages)

Debt Ratio 45	82.2	•	68.5	43.8	55.5	56.5	36.4	48.1	55.5	62.1	45.1	93.8
Return on Total Assets 46	6.6	515.6	28.2	15.3	14.3	10.9	8.0	7.0	4.4	3.9	4.2	6.4
Return on Equity Before Income Taxes 47	22.0	•	81.4	25.1	30.7	21.7	11.6	10.7	6.0	2.9	4.4	54.5
Return on Equity After Income Taxes 48	15.5	4.7	81.2	24.3	30.6	20.9	10.2	8.0	5.0	•	2.5	33.9
Profit Margin (Before Income Tax) 49	4.2	1.1	8.5	5.0	7.1	5.2	5.5	4.5	2.4	1.1	3.3	4.2
Profit Margin (After Income Tax) 50	2.9	1.0	8.5	4.9	7.0	5.0	4.8	3.4	2.0	•	1.9	2.6

Table II

Corporations with Net Income

PAINT, COATING, AND ADHESIVE

MONEY AMOUNTS AND SIZE OF ASSETS IN THOUSANDS OF DOLLARS

Item Description for Accounting Period 7/10 Through 6/11		Total	Zero Assets	Under 500	500 to 1,000	1,000 to 5,000	5,000 to 10,000	10,000 to 25,000	25,000 to 50,000	50,000 to 100,000	100,000 to 250,000	250,000 to 500,000	500,000 to 2,500,000	2,500,000 and over
Number of Enterprises	1	1192	•	0	401	642	14	71	24	•	8	•	•	•
Revenues ($ in Thousands)														
Net Sales	2	34050981	•	0	996059	3829280	275429	1836427	1197096	•	1061691	•	•	•
Interest	3	111548	•	0	146	93	5	636	223	•	732	•	•	•
Rents	4	11115	•	0	304	0	0	1644	823	•	223	•	•	•
Royalties	5	363104	•	0	0	0	0	0	186	•	979	•	•	•
Other Portfolio Income	6	589876	•	0	0	1487	690	1560	5636	•	22	•	•	•
Other Receipts	7	262254	•	0	0	5572	366	11861	2785	•	3209	•	•	•
Total Receipts	8	35388878	•	0	996509	3836432	276490	1852128	1206749	•	1066856	•	•	•
Average Total Receipts	9	29689	•	•	2485	5976	19749	26086	50281	•	133357	•	•	•
Operating Costs/Operating Income (%)														
Cost of Operations	10	63.5	•	•	56.8	63.0	54.8	65.4	67.8	•	63.2	•	•	•
Salaries and Wages	11	9.8	•	•	8.3	5.9	13.6	10.7	8.1	•	9.5	•	•	•
Taxes Paid	12	1.7	•	•	3.2	2.5	3.5	1.6	1.7	•	2.1	•	•	•
Interest Paid	13	2.5	•	•	1.0	0.4	0.4	0.8	0.4	•	0.9	•	•	•
Depreciation	14	2.2	•	•	0.7	0.9	2.9	1.5	1.9	•	2.3	•	•	•
Amortization and Depletion	15	0.7	•	•	0.0	0.2	0.0	0.3	0.2	•	1.7	•	•	•
Pensions and Other Deferred Comp.	16	1.5	•	•	1.0	0.4	0.7	0.8	0.4	•	0.6	•	•	•
Employee Benefits	17	1.7	•	•	2.0	0.8	1.8	0.5	1.6	•	1.5	•	•	•
Advertising	18	1.2	•	•	0.1	1.4	0.3	0.3	0.3	•	0.4	•	•	•
Other Expenses	19	10.8	•	•	9.5	11.2	6.7	10.3	8.7	•	10.5	•	•	•
Officers' Compensation	20	2.0	•	•	7.4	7.9	2.6	3.6	2.8	•	2.0	•	•	•
Operating Margin	21	2.4	•	•	10.1	5.3	12.8	4.4	6.0	•	5.4	•	•	•
Operating Margin Before Officers' Comp.	22	4.4	•	•	17.4	13.2	15.4	8.0	8.8	•	7.4	•	•	•

Selected Average Balance Sheet ($ in Thousands)

Net Receivables 23	4093	•	359	590	3141	3689	6397	•	28050
Inventories 24	2638	•	201	373	4334	3258	6091	•	20026
Net Property, Plant and Equipment 25	3821	•	92	241	1000	2301	5069	•	24951
Total Assets 26	30588	•	785	2110	9205	14314	30591	•	137714
Notes and Loans Payable 27	12569	•	345	480	2431	4060	6174	•	32242
All Other Liabilities 28	12785	•	279	408	3483	4027	6006	•	32406
Net Worth 29	5234	•	161	1223	3290	6228	18410	•	73067

Selected Financial Ratios (Times to 1)

Current Ratio 30	1.0	•	1.7	3.0	1.4	2.1	2.7	•	1.8
Quick Ratio 31	0.6	•	1.2	2.0	0.8	1.1	1.5	•	0.9
Net Sales to Working Capital 32	197.6	•	9.4	6.2	7.9	5.4	4.3	•	4.8
Coverage Ratio 33	3.9	•	11.5	14.0	31.0	7.7	18.3	•	8.2
Total Asset Turnover 34	0.9	•	3.2	2.8	2.1	1.8	1.6	•	1.0
Inventory Turnover 35	6.9	•	7.0	10.1	2.5	5.2	5.6	•	4.2
Receivables Turnover 36	7.1	•	•	12.5	3.4	7.6	8.8	•	•
Total Liabilities to Net Worth 37	4.8	•	3.9	0.7	1.8	1.3	0.7	•	0.9
Current Assets to Working Capital 38	72.4	•	2.4	1.5	3.3	1.9	2.3	•	2.3
Current Liabilities to Working Capital 39	71.4	•	1.4	0.5	2.3	0.9	0.6	•	1.3
Working Capital to Net Sales 40	0.0	•	0.1	0.2	0.1	0.2	0.2	•	0.2
Inventory to Working Capital 41	18.5	•	0.8	0.4	1.3	0.8	0.6	•	0.7
Total Receipts to Cash Flow 42	7.0	•	6.2	7.6	5.5	7.1	7.5	•	6.9
Cost of Goods to Cash Flow 43	4.5	•	3.5	4.8	3.0	4.7	5.1	•	4.4
Cash Flow to Total Debt 44	0.2	•	0.6	0.9	0.6	0.4	0.5	•	0.3

Selected Financial Factors (in Percentages)

Debt Ratio 45	82.9	•	79.4	42.1	64.3	56.5	39.8	•	46.9
Return on Total Assets 46	9.0	•	35.1	16.7	29.1	10.9	11.8	•	7.3
Return on Equity Before Income Taxes 47	38.9	•	156.0	26.8	78.8	21.7	18.5	•	12.0
Return on Equity After Income Taxes 48	29.6	•	155.5	25.9	78.4	20.9	16.4	•	10.5
Profit Margin (Before Income Tax) 49	7.1	•	10.1	5.5	13.2	5.2	6.8	•	6.6
Profit Margin (After Income Tax) 50	5.4	•	10.1	5.3	13.1	5.0	6.1	•	5.8

Table I
Corporations with and without Net Income

SOAP, CLEANING COMPOUND, AND TOILET PREPARATION

MONEY AMOUNTS AND SIZE OF ASSETS IN THOUSANDS OF DOLLARS

Item Description for Accounting Period 7/10 Through 6/11	Total	Zero Assets	Under 500	500 to 1,000	1,000 to 5,000	5,000 to 10,000	10,000 to 25,000	25,000 to 50,000	50,000 to 100,000	100,000 to 250,000	250,000 to 500,000	500,000 to 2,500,000	2,500,000 and over
Number of Enterprises 1	1509	6	707	203	350	99	68	27	16	8	8	7	11
Revenues ($ in Thousands)													
Net Sales 2	8960299	0	403887	404877	2381767	1431061	2419086	1356272	1519207	1690336	3566269	8383977	66047561
Interest 3	372162	0	51	49	63	782	799	2306	6249	563	1869	25710	333719
Rents 4	25069	0	0	0	2186	0	210	108	0	827	0	3467	18270
Royalties 5	3809245	0	0	0	9327	34	1035	1676	447	6	8965	92780	3694974
Other Portfolio Income 6	3713284	0	0	0	2517	307	19244	382	1513	434	20715	119361	3548812
Other Receipts 7	2305100	62801	316	12	36882	8969	44170	10374	77476	41772	12485	77236	1932610
Total Receipts 8	99829159	62801	404254	404938	2432742	1441153	2484544	1371118	1604892	1733938	3610303	8702531	75575946
Average Total Receipts 9	66156	10467	572	1995	6951	14557	36537	50782	100306	216742	451288	1243219	6870541
Operating Costs/Operating Income (%)													
Cost of Operations 10	43.6	•	68.5	66.0	63.1	48.5	62.9	62.9	65.5	71.1	51.2	51.5	38.7
Salaries and Wages 11	9.6	•	5.0	9.8	14.4	23.5	11.3	11.0	8.0	5.9	10.4	9.8	9.1
Taxes Paid 12	2.1	•	3.2	2.8	2.2	0.9	1.8	1.8	1.6	1.0	1.7	2.0	2.1
Interest Paid 13	3.2	•	•	0.6	0.5	0.3	0.6	1.0	2.0	3.1	1.1	3.1	3.7
Depreciation 14	2.7	•	0.3	1.0	0.6	2.2	1.8	2.2	2.4	2.3	2.4	2.0	3.0
Amortization and Depletion 15	1.6	•	0.0	0.0	0.0	0.3	0.2	0.6	1.8	2.3	1.0	0.6	1.9
Pensions and Other Deferred Comp. 16	1.5	•	•	0.6	0.5	0.8	0.2	0.3	0.0	0.2	0.6	1.1	1.8
Employee Benefits 17	1.6	•	•	1.6	0.7	0.2	1.5	1.3	1.2	0.2	0.7	1.3	1.8
Advertising 18	7.4	•	10.4	0.3	0.7	1.0	1.8	2.8	0.6	1.0	11.3	3.9	8.7
Other Expenses 19	20.1	•	14.7	7.6	14.7	14.1	12.9	11.2	12.2	10.9	16.1	18.2	21.8
Officers' Compensation 20	1.1	•	11.6	8.2	3.5	2.9	2.4	2.6	2.2	1.0	1.1	1.3	0.7
Operating Margin 21	5.6	•	•	1.7	•	5.4	2.5	2.3	2.3	1.0	2.6	5.2	6.7
Operating Margin Before Officers' Comp. 22	6.7	•	•	9.8	2.6	8.3	5.0	4.8	4.5	2.0	3.7	6.5	7.4

Selected Average Balance Sheet ($ in Thousands)

Line Item													
Net Receivables 23	22594	0	45	224	617	1456	3738	9062	18400	29372	49366	89393	2873426
Inventories 24	6032	0	48	162	645	1490	4178	6217	9180	30330	40916	152856	583930
Net Property, Plant and Equipment 25	11473	0	20	113	337	2460	3402	6138	10763	29545	62081	143602	1327914
Total Assets 26	162743	0	259	790	2948	7339	17557	36713	73870	167736	340559	1300274	20631085
Notes and Loans Payable 27	44391	0	206	314	893	291	5461	10815	40328	78035	84019	587408	5428901
All Other Liabilities 28	42613	0	13	88	645	2510	4972	11492	22449	44600	112549	377738	5353827
Net Worth 29	75740	0	40	387	1410	4539	7124	14406	11092	45102	143991	335128	9848357

Selected Financial Ratios (Times to 1)

Line Item													
Current Ratio 30	0.9	•	17.4	3.6	1.9	1.9	1.8	2.0	1.9	1.3	1.4	1.7	0.9
Quick Ratio 31	0.7	•	11.0	2.2	0.8	1.1	1.0	1.1	1.1	0.7	0.6	0.9	0.7
Net Sales to Working Capital 32	•	•	2.6	4.3	8.3	7.6	6.9	5.2	5.3	13.1	10.1	6.5	•
Coverage Ratio 33	7.6	•	•	3.8	3.4	23.5	10.3	4.3	5.0	2.1	4.7	4.1	8.2
Total Asset Turnover 34	0.4	•	2.2	2.5	2.3	2.0	2.0	1.4	1.3	1.3	1.3	0.9	0.3
Inventory Turnover 35	4.3	•	8.2	8.1	6.7	4.7	5.4	5.1	6.8	5.0	5.6	4.0	4.0
Receivables Turnover 36	2.6	•	9.9	10.7	11.3	10.8	8.5	6.5	6.2	5.7	9.8	10.6	2.1
Total Liabilities to Net Worth 37	1.1	•	5.4	1.0	1.1	0.6	1.5	1.5	5.7	2.7	1.4	2.9	1.1
Current Assets to Working Capital 38	•	•	1.1	1.4	2.2	2.1	2.3	2.0	2.1	4.3	3.3	2.5	•
Current Liabilities to Working Capital 39	•	•	0.1	0.4	1.2	1.1	1.3	1.0	1.1	3.3	2.3	1.5	•
Working Capital to Net Sales 40	•	•	0.4	0.2	0.1	0.1	0.1	0.2	0.2	0.1	0.1	0.2	•
Inventory to Working Capital 41	•	•	0.3	0.4	0.7	0.9	0.9	0.7	0.6	1.8	1.2	0.7	•
Total Receipts to Cash Flow 42	2.9	•	13.4	8.2	5.8	6.4	8.1	5.5	7.9	5.5	4.3	2.5	
Cost of Goods to Cash Flow 43	1.3	0.6	8.8	5.1	2.8	4.0	5.1	3.6	5.6	2.8	2.2	1.0	
Cash Flow to Total Debt 44	0.2	•	0.4	0.5	0.9	0.5	0.3	0.3	0.2	0.4	0.3	0.2	

Selected Financial Factors (in Percentages)

Line Item													
Debt Ratio 45	53.5	84.5	•	51.0	52.2	38.2	59.4	60.8	85.0	73.1	57.7	74.2	52.3
Return on Total Assets 46	8.9	•	•	5.8	4.0	12.5	11.7	6.0	12.8	8.4	6.5	11.7	8.8
Return on Equity Before Income Taxes 47	16.6	•	•	8.8	6.0	19.3	26.0	11.7	68.3	16.7	12.1	34.2	16.3
Return on Equity After Income Taxes 48	10.9	•	•	7.3	4.5	18.1	23.4	10.7	50.5	13.8	8.0	22.7	10.5
Profit Margin (Before Income Tax) 49	21.2	•	•	1.7	1.2	6.1	5.2	3.4	8.0	3.6	3.9	9.6	26.7
Profit Margin (After Income Tax) 50	13.9	•	•	1.4	0.9	5.7	4.7	3.1	5.9	2.9	2.6	6.4	17.3

Table II

Corporations with Net Income

SOAP, CLEANING COMPOUND, AND TOILET PREPARATION

MONEY AMOUNTS AND SIZE OF ASSETS IN THOUSANDS OF DOLLARS

Item Description for Accounting Period 7/10 Through 6/11	Total	Zero Assets	Under 500	500 to 1,000	1,000 to 5,000	5,000 to 10,000	10,000 to 25,000	25,000 to 50,000	50,000 to 100,000	100,000 to 250,000	250,000 to 500,000	500,000 to 2,500,000	2,500,000 and over
Number of Enterprises 1	987	6	300	203	283	74	63	20	11	•	•	•	8
Revenues ($ in Thousands)													
Net Sales 2	82732843	0	286266	404877	2019677	1272372	2246965	1027125	1254790	•	•	•	62125981
Interest 3	332868	0	0	49	26	704	799	2057	6144	•	•	•	295174
Rents 4	21645	0	0	0	227	0	210	0	0	•	•	•	17381
Royalties 5	3588389	0	0	0	9327	0	905	1554	0	•	•	•	3483686
Other Portfolio Income 6	3672058	0	0	0	2517	158	19244	379	434	•	•	•	3510961
Other Receipts 7	2251333	62801	315	12	36194	8739	44167	8480	77429	•	•	•	1903679
Total Receipts 8	92599136	62801	286581	404938	2067968	1281973	2312290	1039595	1338797	•	•	•	71336862
Average Total Receipts 9	93819	10467	955	1995	7307	17324	36703	51980	121709	•	•	•	8917108
Operating Costs/Operating Income (%)													
Cost of Operations 10	42.3	•	64.5	66.0	62.2	46.1	63.7	64.4	68.3	•	•	•	37.7
Salaries and Wages 11	9.7	•	4.4	9.8	14.7	25.5	11.6	10.1	6.1	•	•	•	9.2
Taxes Paid 12	2.0	•	3.5	2.8	2.1	0.8	1.8	1.6	1.4	•	•	•	2.1
Interest Paid 13	3.0	•	•	0.6	0.4	0.1	0.6	0.8	1.8	•	•	•	3.4
Depreciation 14	2.7	•	0.1	1.0	0.6	2.3	1.9	1.7	2.4	•	•	•	3.0
Amortization and Depletion 15	1.4	•	•	0.0	0.0	0.1	0.1	0.4	0.8	•	•	•	1.7
Pensions and Other Deferred Comp. 16	1.6	•	•	0.6	0.5	0.9	0.2	0.3	0.0	•	•	•	1.9
Employee Benefits 17	1.6	•	•	1.6	0.7	0.1	1.5	1.1	1.1	•	•	•	1.8
Advertising 18	7.5	•	0.1	0.3	0.6	0.5	1.6	3.5	0.7	•	•	•	8.7
Other Expenses 19	20.2	•	10.8	7.6	13.6	13.0	11.8	10.1	11.3	•	•	•	22.0
Officers' Compensation 20	1.0	•	14.5	8.2	3.2	2.4	1.4	2.3	2.2	•	•	•	0.7
Operating Margin 21	7.0	•	2.0	1.7	1.4	8.1	3.9	3.7	3.9	•	•	•	7.9
Operating Margin Before Officers' Comp. 22	8.0	•	16.6	9.8	4.6	10.5	5.2	6.0	6.1	•	•	•	8.6

Selected Average Balance Sheet ($ in Thousands)

Net Receivables 23	33285	87	224	643	1549	3695	10264	22684	•	3840802
Inventories 24	8139	32	126	570	1650	4029	6074	9757	•	549418
Net Property, Plant and Equipment 25	16460	33	113	335	3251	3468	5084	13889	•	1737421
Total Assets 26	235413	320	790	3133	7409	17520	37698	77653	•	26992786
Notes and Loans Payable 27	60707	0	314	529	218	3200	9628	20901	•	6762895
All Other Liabilities 28	62169	26	88	624	2228	4575	13689	26816	•	7072814
Net Worth 29	112537	293	387	1980	4963	9745	14381	29936	•	13157077

Selected Financial Ratios (Times to 1)

Current Ratio 30	0.9	10.9	3.6	2.2	1.9	1.8	1.9	1.9	•	0.9
Quick Ratio 31	0.7	7.6	2.2	0.9	1.0	1.0	1.0	1.3	•	0.7
Net Sales to Working Capital 32	•	3.7	4.3	7.0	9.8	7.1	5.5	5.3	•	•
Coverage Ratio 33	8.9	•	3.8	9.9	76.6	12.5	7.5	6.9	•	9.5
Total Asset Turnover 34	0.4	3.0	2.5	2.3	2.3	2.0	1.4	1.5	•	0.3
Inventory Turnover 35	4.4	19.0	10.5	7.8	4.8	5.6	5.4	8.0	•	5.3
Receivables Turnover 36	2.6	15.8	12.7	13.4	11.7	9.8	6.1	6.6	•	•
Total Liabilities to Net Worth 37	1.1	0.1	1.0	0.6	0.5	0.8	1.6	1.6	•	1.1
Current Assets to Working Capital 38	•	1.1	1.4	1.8	2.1	2.2	2.1	2.1	•	•
Current Liabilities to Working Capital 39	•	0.1	0.4	0.8	1.1	1.2	1.1	1.1	•	•
Working Capital to Net Sales 40	0.3	0.2	0.1	0.1	0.1	0.2	0.2	0.2	•	•
Inventory to Working Capital 41	•	0.2	0.4	0.6	0.9	0.9	0.8	0.6	•	•
Total Receipts to Cash Flow 42	2.8	7.7	13.4	7.2	5.3	6.1	7.6	5.0	•	2.4
Cost of Goods to Cash Flow 43	1.2	5.0	8.8	4.5	2.5	3.9	4.9	3.4	0.6	0.9
Cash Flow to Total Debt 44	0.2	4.7	0.4	0.9	1.3	0.8	0.3	0.5	•	0.2

Selected Financial Factors (in Percentages)

Debt Ratio 45	52.2	8.3	51.0	36.8	33.0	44.4	61.9	61.4	•	51.3
Return on Total Assets 46	9.4	6.4	5.8	9.6	20.9	15.0	7.8	18.2	•	9.2
Return on Equity Before Income Taxes 47	17.4	7.0	8.8	13.7	30.8	24.9	17.8	40.5	•	16.9
Return on Equity After Income Taxes 48	11.5	7.0	7.3	12.4	29.2	22.8	16.3	30.9	•	11.0
Profit Margin (Before Income Tax) 49	23.4	2.2	1.7	3.8	8.9	6.8	5.0	10.6	•	28.6
Profit Margin (After Income Tax) 50	15.4	2.2	1.4	3.4	8.4	6.2	4.6	8.1	•	18.6

Table I

Corporations with and without Net Income

CHEMICAL PRODUCT AND PREPARATION

MONEY AMOUNTS AND SIZE OF ASSETS IN THOUSANDS OF DOLLARS

Item Description for Accounting Period 7/10 Through 6/11	Total	Zero Assets	Under 500	500 to 1,000	1,000 to 5,000	5,000 to 10,000	10,000 to 25,000	25,000 to 50,000	50,000 to 100,000	100,000 to 250,000	250,000 to 500,000	500,000 to 2,500,000	2,500,000 and over
Number of Enterprises 1	1989	111	805	399	301	88	113	74	44	25	11	10	9
Revenues ($ in Thousands)													
Net Sales 2	68830616	999023	739917	586698	1504058	1115372	3230770	3630430	4736707	4634088	2580538	9367120	35705896
Interest 3	330583	3550	295	134	417	290	4122	1899	3186	8937	6389	12541	288824
Rents 4	30080	0	0	2153	0	3050	444	230	86	367	836	12533	10381
Royalties 5	499079	0	0	0	0	1	2657	133	5654	28105	22342	17850	422335
Other Portfolio Income 6	693711	64960	3176	5820	7553	79	1028	23257	4861	5986	63186	34165	479640
Other Receipts 7	900166	-9224	20652	337	4883	14638	16739	78120	24400	53485	50746	254923	390467
Total Receipts 8	71284235	1058309	764040	595142	1516911	1133430	3255760	3734069	4774894	4730968	2724037	9699132	37297543
Average Total Receipts 9	35839	9534	949	1492	5040	12880	28812	50460	108520	189239	247640	969913	4144171
Operating Costs/Operating Income (%)													
Cost of Operations 10	68.1	62.1	50.0	47.0	61.1	67.4	65.7	72.9	73.2	69.7	66.9	67.7	68.3
Salaries and Wages 11	6.5	13.2	7.2	4.2	6.9	8.1	10.1	5.7	5.8	7.6	6.6	7.2	5.8
Taxes Paid 12	1.2	0.9	3.8	2.1	2.7	1.7	1.9	1.4	1.2	1.3	1.4	1.4	0.9
Interest Paid 13	3.0	2.2	0.3	0.3	0.8	0.5	0.6	1.1	0.9	1.9	2.7	1.5	4.6
Depreciation 14	4.3	1.6	0.1	1.6	0.8	3.0	2.5	2.8	2.2	3.5	3.4	3.0	5.8
Amortization and Depletion 15	0.9	0.0	0.4	•	0.1	0.2	0.2	0.3	0.4	0.8	1.7	0.9	1.2
Pensions and Other Deferred Comp. 16	0.9	1.6	0.0	6.5	1.1	0.4	0.9	0.3	0.5	0.8	0.8	2.0	0.7
Employee Benefits 17	1.1	2.1	2.6	1.7	1.7	1.6	0.8	0.6	0.9	1.1	2.0	2.3	0.8
Advertising 18	0.5	0.1	0.3	0.2	0.2	0.7	0.9	0.9	0.4	0.6	0.5	2.0	0.1
Other Expenses 19	10.3	7.5	15.9	8.6	14.4	12.5	11.7	10.0	8.1	7.9	11.0	10.1	10.6
Officers' Compensation 20	1.2	0.9	15.1	13.7	4.7	2.8	2.7	2.7	1.6	1.1	1.4	1.0	0.2
Operating Margin 21	1.9	7.8	4.5	15.4	5.4	1.1	2.1	1.3	4.7	3.5	1.7	0.9	1.1
Operating Margin Before Officers' Comp. 22	3.1	8.7	19.5	29.1	10.0	3.9	4.8	4.0	6.3	4.7	3.1	1.9	1.3

Selected Average Balance Sheet ($ in Thousands)

Net Receivables 23	4837	0	25	77	703	1458	3862	6141	14991	32509	53558	188455	488099
Inventories 24	4929	0	62	134	354	2083	3587	7439	13755	30919	53922	134082	571127
Net Property, Plant and Equipment 25	7379	0	61	91	259	1857	4018	7745	12939	42425	39336	192161	1037612
Total Assets 26	42607	0	226	731	2622	6892	16774	35330	72325	172984	378379	1101976	6186358
Notes and Loans Payable 27	11448	0	31	74	339	3810	4113	9164	18279	45678	135849	283306	1651222
All Other Liabilities 28	12003	0	7	58	593	1905	3868	10180	16724	51559	84247	342490	1770153
Net Worth 29	19157	0	188	599	1690	1177	8794	15986	37322	75747	158283	476179	2764983

Selected Financial Ratios (Times to 1)

Current Ratio 30	1.4	•	2.9	5.3	2.7	1.8	2.4	2.0	2.3	1.7	1.3	1.4	1.2
Quick Ratio 31	0.7	•	1.3	3.6	2.1	0.9	1.4	1.0	1.3	0.9	0.7	0.8	0.5
Net Sales to Working Capital 32	8.1	•	12.8	3.8	4.6	6.1	4.5	4.7	4.2	4.8	9.2	7.7	13.4
Coverage Ratio 33	3.0	7.1	27.9	50.7	8.4	6.1	5.9	4.9	7.1	4.0	4.1	4.5	2.4
Total Asset Turnover 34	0.8	•	4.1	2.0	1.9	1.8	1.7	1.4	1.5	1.1	0.6	0.9	0.6
Inventory Turnover 35	4.8	•	7.5	5.2	8.6	4.1	5.2	4.8	5.7	4.2	2.9	4.7	4.7
Receivables Turnover 36	5.7	•	•	•	9.6	6.5	7.5	7.1	7.4	6.5	3.1	5.2	5.3
Total Liabilities to Net Worth 37	1.2	•	0.2	0.2	0.6	4.9	0.9	1.2	0.9	1.3	1.4	1.3	1.2
Current Assets to Working Capital 38	3.5	•	1.5	1.2	1.6	2.2	1.7	2.0	1.7	2.5	5.0	3.5	5.8
Current Liabilities to Working Capital 39	2.5	•	0.5	0.2	0.6	1.2	0.7	1.0	0.7	1.5	4.0	2.5	4.8
Working Capital to Net Sales 40	0.1	•	0.1	0.3	0.2	0.2	0.2	0.2	0.2	0.2	0.1	0.1	0.1
Inventory to Working Capital 41	1.1	•	0.9	0.3	0.3	0.7	0.6	0.7	0.5	0.8	1.8	1.0	1.8
Total Receipts to Cash Flow 42	7.4	5.3	4.8	4.5	5.7	7.7	8.4	7.9	8.3	8.5	6.4	8.4	7.2
Cost of Goods to Cash Flow 43	5.0	3.3	2.4	2.1	3.5	5.2	5.5	5.7	6.1	5.9	4.3	5.7	5.0
Cash Flow to Total Debt 44	0.2	•	5.0	2.5	0.9	0.3	0.4	0.3	0.4	0.2	0.2	0.2	0.2

Selected Financial Factors (in Percentages)

Debt Ratio 45	55.0	•	17.0	18.1	35.5	82.9	47.6	54.8	48.4	56.2	58.2	56.8	55.3
Return on Total Assets 46	7.4	•	32.6	34.6	13.5	5.9	5.9	7.3	9.9	8.2	6.7	5.6	7.0
Return on Equity Before Income Taxes 47	10.9	•	37.8	41.4	18.4	29.0	9.3	12.9	16.5	13.9	12.1	10.2	9.1
Return on Equity After Income Taxes 48	7.5	•	37.8	41.0	15.5	21.5	6.9	9.4	11.9	9.5	8.6	6.5	5.8
Profit Margin (Before Income Tax) 49	6.0	13.7	7.7	16.8	6.2	2.7	2.9	4.2	5.7	5.7	8.2	5.2	6.3
Profit Margin (After Income Tax) 50	4.2	13.7	7.7	16.7	5.3	2.0	2.1	3.1	4.1	3.9	5.8	3.3	4.1

Table II

Corporations with Net Income

CHEMICAL PRODUCT AND PREPARATION

MONEY AMOUNTS AND SIZE OF ASSETS IN THOUSANDS OF DOLLARS

Item Description for Accounting Period 7/10 Through 6/11	Total	Zero Assets	Under 500	500 to 1,000	1,000 to 5,000	5,000 to 10,000	10,000 to 25,000	25,000 to 50,000	50,000 to 100,000	100,000 to 250,000	250,000 to 500,000	500,000 to 2,500,000	2,500,000 and over
Number of Enterprises **1**	1526	6	711	331	202	67	86	40	35	•	•	•	•
Revenues ($ in Thousands)													
Net Sales **2**	60796650	726492	738519	447923	1166040	981103	2833796	2533171	3801139	•	•	•	•
Interest **3**	301250	1	0	131	332	149	3379	1672	2959	•	•	•	•
Rents **4**	28304	0	0	2153	0	3050	0	127	86	•	•	•	•
Royalties **5**	484698	0	0	0	0	1	947	133	5638		•	•	•
Other Portfolio Income **6**	671580	64955	3176	5820	1130	17	1010	23257	4807	•	•	•	•
Other Receipts **7**	799348	1122	20628	338	1250	193	15529	58465	23034	•	•	•	•
Total Receipts **8**	63081830	792570	762323	456365	1168752	984513	2854661	2616825	3837663	•	•	•	•
Average Total Receipts **9**	41338	132095	1072	1379	5786	14694	33194	65421	109648				
Operating Costs/Operating Income (%)													
Cost of Operations **10**	67.8	61.7	50.1	35.8	55.7	67.7	63.7	71.6	70.1	•	•	•	•
Salaries and Wages **11**	6.1	7.9	7.1	4.3	6.7	6.0	9.7	4.8	6.1	•	•	•	•
Taxes Paid **12**	1.2	1.0	3.8	2.1	2.8	1.5	1.8	1.2	1.3	•	•	•	•
Interest Paid **13**	2.5	0.2	0.3	0.4	0.3	0.4	0.5	0.5	0.9	•	•	•	•
Depreciation **14**	4.3	1.2	0.1	1.8	0.7	1.5	2.0	2.7	1.9	•	•	•	•
Amortization and Depletion **15**	0.9	0.0	0.4	•	0.1	0.1	0.1	0.3	0.3	•	•	•	•
Pensions and Other Deferred Comp. **16**	0.7	0.4	•	8.6	1.4	0.4	1.0	0.2	0.6	•	•	•	•
Employee Benefits **17**	1.1	2.6	2.6	0.5	1.6	1.5	0.7	0.5	0.9	•	•	•	•
Advertising **18**	0.5	0.1	0.3	0.3	0.3	0.8	1.0	0.9	0.5	•	•	•	•
Other Expenses **19**	9.5	7.0	14.3	9.5	13.6	11.0	9.7	9.1	8.2	•	•	•	•
Officers' Compensation **20**	1.1	1.1	15.1	14.7	5.3	2.7	2.6	2.8	1.8	•	•	•	•
Operating Margin **21**	4.3	16.6	6.1	22.2	11.5	6.4	7.1	5.7	7.4	•	•	•	•
Operating Margin Before Officers' Comp. **22**	5.4	17.8	21.2	36.9	16.8	9.1	9.7	8.5	9.2	•	•	•	•

Selected Average Balance Sheet ($ in Thousands)

Net Receivables 23	5563	0	28	80	904	1226	4128	6480	15170
Inventories 24	5411	0	70	110	410	1926	3758	8480	15179
Net Property, Plant and Equipment 25	8263	0	69	88	239	1765	3683	9610	11426
Total Assets 26	47727	0	254	770	2342	6637	16414	35932	71892
Notes and Loans Payable 27	11759	0	35	86	148	1321	3055	7602	16095
All Other Liabilities 28	13351	0	8	52	450	1725	3885	9038	18004
Net Worth 29	22617	0	211	633	1744	3591	9474	19291	37793

Selected Financial Ratios (Times to 1)

Current Ratio 30	1.4	•	2.9	5.4	4.5	1.8	2.5	2.1	2.5
Quick Ratio 31	0.7	•	1.3	4.2	3.6	0.9	1.4	1.1	1.4
Net Sales to Working Capital 32	8.1	•	12.9	3.4	3.6	7.7	5.0	5.5	3.9
Coverage Ratio 33	4.5	104.3	33.5	57.7	41.2	17.4	15.4	20.1	11.0
Total Asset Turnover 34	0.8	•	4.1	1.8	2.5	2.2	2.0	1.8	1.5
Inventory Turnover 35	5.0	•	7.5	4.4	7.9	5.2	5.6	5.3	5.0
Receivables Turnover 36	5.8	•	•	13.4	8.5	9.0	7.9	8.4	•
Total Liabilities to Net Worth 37	1.1	•	0.2	0.2	0.3	0.8	0.7	0.9	0.9
Current Assets to Working Capital 38	3.4	•	1.5	1.2	1.3	2.2	1.7	1.9	1.7
Current Liabilities to Working Capital 39	2.4	•	0.5	0.2	0.3	1.2	0.7	0.9	0.7
Working Capital to Net Sales 40	0.1	•	0.1	0.3	0.3	0.1	0.2	0.2	0.3
Inventory to Working Capital 41	1.1	•	0.9	0.2	0.2	0.9	0.6	0.8	0.5
Total Receipts to Cash Flow 42	6.5	3.2	4.8	3.4	4.4	6.4	6.5	6.1	6.7
Cost of Goods to Cash Flow 43	4.4	2.0	2.4	1.2	2.4	4.4	4.1	4.4	4.7
Cash Flow to Total Debt 44	0.2	•	5.1	2.9	2.2	0.7	0.7	0.6	0.5

Selected Financial Factors (in Percentages)

Debt Ratio 45	52.6	•	17.0	17.8	25.6	45.9	42.3	46.3	47.4
Return on Total Assets 46	9.3	•	39.4	43.0	29.6	15.9	16.8	16.6	14.4
Return on Equity Before Income Taxes 47	15.3	•	46.1	51.4	38.7	27.7	27.2	29.4	24.9
Return on Equity After Income Taxes 48	11.5	•	46.1	51.0	34.6	24.4	24.3	24.1	19.1
Profit Margin (Before Income Tax) 49	8.7	25.7	9.3	24.1	11.7	6.8	7.8	9.0	8.7
Profit Margin (After Income Tax) 50	6.5	25.7	9.3	23.9	10.4	6.0	7.0	7.3	6.7

Table I

Corporations with and without Net Income

PLASTICS PRODUCT

MONEY AMOUNTS AND SIZE OF ASSETS IN THOUSANDS OF DOLLARS

Item Description for Accounting Period 7/10 Through 6/11		Total	Zero Assets	Under 500	500 to 1,000	1,000 to 5,000	5,000 to 10,000	10,000 to 25,000	25,000 to 50,000	50,000 to 100,000	100,000 to 250,000	250,000 to 500,000	500,000 to 2,500,000	2,500,000 and over
Number of Enterprises	1	8950	925	3004	1183	2296	684	407	184	112	99	22	30	4
Revenues ($ in Thousands)														
Net Sales	2	117047371	2670943	1314237	2128876	12383013	9040001	11297653	9988966	11411581	19170277	8111862	19451317	10078646
Interest	3	175083	1649	427	810	3094	1805	1723	9181	10035	33102	14742	69914	28601
Rents	4	29741	0	0	114	1074	2143	3436	2629	1721	3655	9101	5868	0
Royalties	5	174245	95	0	0	0	1027	54	3552	6531	18185	52732	62022	30047
Other Portfolio Income	6	597934	92072	1807	543	46279	6852	9616	60907	20317	97307	49671	189452	23112
Other Receipts	7	921866	-78918	12299	6961	44392	27775	60216	263310	50028	270479	72179	171388	21755
Total Receipts	8	118946240	2685841	1328770	2137304	12477852	9079603	11372698	10328545	11500213	19593005	8310287	19949961	10182161
Average Total Receipts	9	13290	2904	442	1807	5435	13274	27943	56133	102680	197909	377740	664999	2545540
Operating Costs/Operating Income (%)														
Cost of Operations	10	72.8	86.3	57.6	63.0	67.9	71.8	71.0	70.6	73.8	73.8	74.9	76.5	72.8
Salaries and Wages	11	5.3	2.1	8.0	5.0	5.8	6.0	6.4	6.7	6.1	5.2	5.2	4.4	3.6
Taxes Paid	12	1.5	0.6	3.0	3.1	2.3	2.0	1.7	1.8	1.4	1.3	1.4	1.1	1.0
Interest Paid	13	2.4	1.4	0.3	1.2	1.0	0.7	1.0	1.2	1.2	1.9	2.6	5.1	5.7
Depreciation	14	3.6	1.7	1.0	3.0	2.2	2.9	3.1	3.9	3.8	3.9	3.6	4.4	5.2
Amortization and Depletion	15	0.6	0.5	0.0	0.1	0.2	0.1	0.3	0.4	0.6	0.7	0.8	0.9	1.0
Pensions and Other Deferred Comp.	16	0.4	0.1	0.0	0.0	0.3	0.4	0.4	0.4	0.4	0.5	0.6	0.3	0.4
Employee Benefits	17	1.6	0.9	0.3	1.4	1.4	1.2	1.5	1.7	1.5	1.4	2.1	1.3	3.0
Advertising	18	0.3	0.2	0.7	0.3	0.3	0.4	0.4	0.5	0.5	0.3	0.3	0.3	0.1
Other Expenses	19	8.5	5.0	17.0	11.6	9.3	9.1	8.5	10.0	7.3	8.7	7.9	7.0	8.6
Officers' Compensation	20	1.8	1.7	6.6	6.4	5.1	2.9	1.9	1.6	0.9	0.8	0.9	1.0	0.2
Operating Margin	21	1.2	•	5.5	4.9	4.3	2.5	3.7	1.2	2.5	1.5	•	•	•
Operating Margin Before Officers' Comp.	22	2.9	1.2	12.0	11.3	9.3	5.4	5.7	2.8	3.4	2.2	0.7	•	•

Selected Average Balance Sheet ($ in Thousands)

Net Receivables 23	1881	0	40	167	590	1740	3856	6874	14627	24556	57306	135289	437512
Inventories 24	1353	0	21	127	475	1174	3222	6297	12089	21300	39606	75341	234819
Net Property, Plant and Equipment 25	2555	0	19	176	504	1915	4777	11580	19249	46158	78560	173404	601660
Total Assets 26	11540	0	174	729	2137	7247	15847	35317	70523	155043	359298	876623	5407050
Notes and Loans Payable 27	4600	0	55	246	923	1991	5001	10590	21798	52187	125428	392860	2773594
All Other Liabilities 28	2767	0	78	208	506	2095	5356	9908	18117	35898	118814	222883	702276
Net Worth 29	4172	0	41	275	709	3161	5491	14819	30607	66958	115056	260881	1931181

Selected Financial Ratios (Times to 1)

Current Ratio 30	1.6	•	1.2	1.3	2.2	1.5	1.5	1.6	1.8	1.8	1.6	1.4	2.0
Quick Ratio 31	0.9	•	0.9	0.9	1.3	0.9	0.8	0.9	1.0	1.0	0.8	0.9	1.0
Net Sales to Working Capital 32	7.4	•	20.1	14.3	7.1	10.0	8.2	8.3	6.5	6.6	7.1	9.4	4.2
Coverage Ratio 33	2.2	1.0	20.4	5.5	6.1	5.1	5.3	4.9	3.0	3.9	2.0	1.1	0.9
Total Asset Turnover 34	1.1	•	2.5	2.5	2.5	1.8	1.8	1.5	1.2	1.4	1.0	0.7	0.5
Inventory Turnover 35	7.0	•	12.2	8.9	7.7	8.1	6.1	6.1	6.7	6.2	7.0	6.6	7.8
Receivables Turnover 36	7.7	•	9.0	11.7	9.7	8.5	8.2	8.1	8.8	7.5	7.6	5.2	6.9
Total Liabilities to Net Worth 37	1.8	•	3.2	1.7	2.0	1.3	1.9	1.4	1.3	1.3	2.1	2.4	1.8
Current Assets to Working Capital 38	2.6	•	5.1	4.0	1.8	3.1	2.8	2.8	2.2	2.3	2.8	3.8	2.0
Current Liabilities to Working Capital 39	1.6	•	4.1	3.0	0.8	2.1	1.8	1.8	1.2	1.3	1.8	2.8	1.0
Working Capital to Net Sales 40	0.1	•	0.0	0.1	0.1	0.1	0.1	0.1	0.2	0.2	0.1	0.1	0.2
Inventory to Working Capital 41	0.8	•	0.9	1.1	0.7	1.0	1.1	1.0	0.8	0.9	0.8	1.2	0.5
Total Receipts to Cash Flow 42	11.2	27.1	5.4	10.0	9.1	10.7	9.4	8.5	9.7	11.3	11.8	18.0	17.2
Cost of Goods to Cash Flow 43	8.1	23.4	3.1	6.3	6.2	7.7	6.7	6.0	7.1	8.3	8.9	13.8	12.5
Cash Flow to Total Debt 44	0.2	•	0.6	0.4	0.4	0.3	0.3	0.3	0.2	0.2	0.1	0.1	0.0

Selected Financial Factors (in Percentages)

Debt Ratio 45	63.8	•	76.3	62.3	66.8	56.4	65.4	58.0	56.8	56.6	68.0	70.2	64.3
Return on Total Assets 46	6.0	•	17.4	16.0	15.1	6.7	9.5	8.9	7.0	6.6	5.2	4.1	2.4
Return on Equity Before Income Taxes 47	9.1	•	69.6	34.7	38.2	12.3	22.2	16.9	10.7	11.3	8.0	1.2	•
Return on Equity After Income Taxes 48	7.4	•	69.4	34.1	37.3	11.5	20.4	15.0	8.6	9.2	5.1	•	•
Profit Margin (Before Income Tax) 49	2.9	0.0	6.6	5.3	5.0	2.9	4.4	4.6	3.7	3.4	2.5	0.5	•
Profit Margin (After Income Tax) 50	2.4	•	6.6	5.2	4.9	2.8	4.0	4.1	3.0	2.8	1.6	•	•

Table II
Corporations with Net Income

PLASTICS PRODUCT

MONEY AMOUNTS AND SIZE OF ASSETS IN THOUSANDS OF DOLLARS

Item Description for Accounting Period 7/10 Through 6/11	Total	Zero Assets	Under 500	500 to 1,000	1,000 to 5,000	5,000 to 10,000	10,000 to 25,000	25,000 to 50,000	50,000 to 100,000	100,000 to 250,000	250,000 to 500,000	500,000 to 2,500,000	2,500,000 and over
Number of Enterprises 1	5386	346	•	884	1972	402	300	134	82	74	•	19	0
Revenues ($ in Thousands)													
Net Sales 2	83208339	736271	•	1875088	11297997	6287518	8914202	7667360	8424450	14998395	•	17200607	0
Interest 3	75441	998	•	809	1520	1544	1255	4858	3974	17689	•	38232	0
Rents 4	17457	0	•	114	1074	1662	624	2054	789	3575	•	826	0
Royalties 5	124106	95	•	0	0	890	0	3552	5618	13044	•	60847	0
Other Portfolio Income 6	468146	92072	•	0	45700	2796	7724	52874	13763	82548	•	128812	0
Other Receipts 7	599961	-24840	•	6612	55784	13874	52190	72518	37644	196252	•	131975	0
Total Receipts 8	84493450	804596	•	1882623	11402075	6308284	8975995	7803216	8486238	15311503	•	17561299	0
Average Total Receipts 9	15688	2325	•	2130	5782	15692	29920	58233	103491	206912	•	924279	•
Operating Costs/Operating Income (%)													
Cost of Operations 10	71.2	69.6	•	68.0	66.6	70.8	69.2	70.0	71.7	72.6	•	74.2	•
Salaries and Wages 11	5.3	2.9	•	3.0	5.9	5.2	6.5	5.9	6.4	5.1	•	4.1	•
Taxes Paid 12	1.6	1.6	•	3.0	2.2	1.8	1.7	1.9	1.4	1.3	•	1.0	•
Interest Paid 13	1.6	1.6	•	1.0	0.9	0.7	0.8	0.9	0.9	1.4	•	3.6	•
Depreciation 14	3.3	4.1	•	2.6	2.1	2.7	2.8	3.4	3.4	3.9	•	4.2	•
Amortization and Depletion 15	0.4	1.1	•	0.1	0.1	0.0	0.1	0.4	0.3	0.6	•	0.8	•
Pensions and Other Deferred Comp. 16	0.4	0.2	•	•	0.3	0.6	0.4	0.4	0.4	0.5	•	0.4	•
Employee Benefits 17	1.6	1.6	•	0.9	1.5	1.2	1.6	1.7	1.5	1.4	•	1.8	•
Advertising 18	0.3	0.2	•	0.3	0.3	0.4	0.3	0.4	0.3	0.3	•	0.2	•
Other Expenses 19	7.7	10.7	•	9.6	9.0	7.4	8.0	7.8	6.5	7.7	•	7.1	•
Officers' Compensation 20	1.9	3.0	•	5.5	5.2	2.5	2.1	1.7	1.0	0.8	•	0.5	•
Operating Margin 21	4.8	3.3	•	6.0	6.1	6.8	6.4	5.7	6.1	4.2	•	2.2	•
Operating Margin Before Officers' Comp. 22	6.7	6.3	•	11.4	11.3	9.3	8.5	7.4	7.1	5.0	•	2.7	•

Selected Average Balance Sheet ($ in Thousands)

Net Receivables 23	2153	0	197	635	1883	4079	7259	13917	24948	172379
Inventories 24	1503	0	101	457	1168	3162	6393	12271	19304	93380
Net Property, Plant and Equipment 25	2802	0	157	495	2196	4680	11507	19701	46500	220763
Total Assets 26	11956	0	737	2170	7182	16238	35987	69895	158214	1289002
Notes and Loans Payable 27	4376	0	246	794	1877	5015	9474	18267	47040	619451
All Other Liabilities 28	2970	0	257	461	2139	4072	8384	15262	38010	316506
Net Worth 29	4609	0	233	915	3166	7152	18128	36367	73164	353044

Selected Financial Ratios (Times to 1)

Current Ratio 30	1.8	•	1.2	2.5	1.7	1.9	1.9	2.1	1.9	1.6
Quick Ratio 31	1.0	•	0.8	1.5	1.0	1.1	1.1	1.1	1.0	0.9
Net Sales to Working Capital 32	6.4	•	25.8	6.6	8.5	6.3	6.3	5.5	6.4	5.9
Coverage Ratio 33	5.0	9.1	7.1	9.0	10.9	10.3	9.3	8.8	5.5	2.3
Total Asset Turnover 34	1.3	•	2.9	2.6	2.2	1.8	1.6	1.5	1.3	0.7
Inventory Turnover 35	7.3	•	14.3	8.3	9.5	6.5	6.3	6.0	7.6	7.2
Receivables Turnover 36	8.1	•	14.6	10.4	10.2	8.7	8.6	7.7	9.7	•
Total Liabilities to Net Worth 37	1.6	•	2.2	1.4	1.3	1.3	1.0	0.9	1.2	2.7
Current Assets to Working Capital 38	2.2	•	6.4	1.7	2.4	2.2	2.1	1.9	2.1	2.6
Current Liabilities to Working Capital 39	1.2	•	5.4	0.7	1.4	1.2	1.1	0.9	1.1	1.6
Working Capital to Net Sales 40	0.2	•	0.0	0.2	0.1	0.2	0.2	0.2	0.2	0.2
Inventory to Working Capital 41	0.7	•	1.7	0.6	0.7	0.8	0.8	0.7	0.7	0.6
Total Receipts to Cash Flow 42	8.5	5.0	11.5	7.9	8.2	7.6	8.0	8.5	8.4	10.4
Cost of Goods to Cash Flow 43	6.1	3.5	7.8	5.2	5.8	5.3	5.6	6.1	6.1	7.7
Cash Flow to Total Debt 44	0.2	•	0.4	0.6	0.5	0.4	0.4	0.4	0.3	0.1

Selected Financial Factors (in Percentages)

Debt Ratio 45	61.4	•	68.3	57.8	55.9	56.0	49.6	48.0	53.8	72.6
Return on Total Assets 46	10.4	•	21.3	20.7	17.0	14.5	13.3	11.6	9.9	5.7
Return on Equity Before Income Taxes 47	21.5	•	57.8	43.6	35.0	29.6	23.6	19.7	17.6	11.7
Return on Equity After Income Taxes 48	19.1	•	56.8	42.8	33.7	27.8	21.5	17.4	15.0	9.1
Profit Margin (Before Income Tax) 49	6.4	12.6	6.4	7.0	7.1	7.1	7.5	7.0	6.3	4.6
Profit Margin (After Income Tax) 50	5.7	10.9	6.2	6.8	6.8	6.7	6.8	6.1	5.4	3.5

Table I

Corporations with and without Net Income

RUBBER PRODUCT

MONEY AMOUNTS AND SIZE OF ASSETS IN THOUSANDS OF DOLLARS

Item Description for Accounting Period 7/10 Through 6/11	Total	Zero Assets	Under 500	500 to 1,000	1,000 to 5,000	5,000 to 10,000	10,000 to 25,000	25,000 to 50,000	50,000 to 100,000	100,000 to 250,000	250,000 to 500,000	500,000 to 2,500,000	2,500,000 and over
Number of Enterprises **1**	864	30	408	0	244	58	63	7	24	9	8	10	3
Revenues ($ in Thousands)													
Net Sales **2**	52547947	466038	81486	0	1136108	1184891	1982074	386680	2206342	1058306	2439686	12959972	28646365
Interest **3**	246161	8	0	0	814	1112	224	198	625	876	6942	87958	147403
Rents **4**	15025	0	2	0	0	0	0	731	2252	483	674	3470	7412
Royalties **5**	523427	918	0	0	0	0	0	1234	2	0	18794	58202	444276
Other Portfolio Income **6**	226438	4	0	0	95	197	741	22341	4646	467	29805	80366	87778
Other Receipts **7**	284164	1405	5023	0	874	1114	18401	1105	11	3784	12249	70987	169210
Total Receipts **8**	53843162	468373	86511	0	1137891	1187314	2001440	412289	2213878	1063916	2508150	13260955	29502444
Average Total Receipts **9**	62318	15612	212	•	4663	20471	31769	58898	92245	118213	313519	1326096	9834148
Operating Costs/Operating Income (%)													
Cost of Operations **10**	70.1	68.0	40.0	•	69.2	66.6	65.9	66.4	71.9	67.1	72.5	77.1	67.3
Salaries and Wages **11**	6.5	6.4	13.3	•	6.2	9.8	7.7	6.8	6.2	5.9	4.9	4.3	7.4
Taxes Paid **12**	1.5	1.4	3.4	•	1.9	1.8	1.9	2.2	1.7	1.6	1.2	0.7	1.8
Interest Paid **13**	1.9	1.3	2.1	•	1.7	0.4	0.3	0.9	1.5	2.3	2.1	2.3	1.9
Depreciation **14**	3.4	19.5	1.6	•	2.4	0.4	2.2	2.8	2.7	3.2	2.6	3.5	3.4
Amortization and Depletion **15**	0.8	1.2	•	•	0.0	0.0	0.2	1.0	0.8	1.3	1.0	0.8	0.9
Pensions and Other Deferred Comp. **16**	2.0	0.3	0.0	•	0.4	0.6	0.3	0.2	0.5	0.6	0.8	1.2	2.9
Employee Benefits **17**	2.9	1.8	1.4	•	0.9	2.1	1.5	2.7	2.3	1.5	1.9	3.2	3.2
Advertising **18**	1.3	0.5	2.0	•	0.3	0.0	2.5	0.4	0.5	0.1	0.7	0.9	1.8
Other Expenses **19**	9.8	15.7	20.4	•	11.3	7.4	7.4	11.1	7.6	9.2	10.4	5.5	12.0
Officers' Compensation **20**	0.6	0.3	6.1	•	4.3	4.6	1.5	1.4	1.0	1.6	0.7	0.5	0.1
Operating Margin **21**	•	•	9.7	•	1.5	6.4	8.6	4.1	3.4	5.7	1.2	•	•
Operating Margin Before Officers' Comp. **22**	•	•	15.8	•	5.8	11.0	10.1	5.5	4.4	7.3	1.9	•	0.4

Selected Average Balance Sheet ($ in Thousands)

Net Receivables 23	9716	0	9	•	698	2689	4021	7437	11440	18904	110884	228794	1379861
Inventories 24	7457	0	7	•	630	1712	2970	12275	10834	16693	33802	145525	1255426
Net Property, Plant and Equipment 25	11299	0	5	•	397	891	4140	8440	18302	18110	51739	277136	1834663
Total Assets 26	52560	0	254	•	2132	7094	15904	42885	68041	138152	335166	1435559	7720213
Notes and Loans Payable 27	16517	0	107	•	665	1313	2095	5657	24932	45710	98586	510141	2305795
All Other Liabilities 28	25326	0	42	•	860	2098	3462	8504	18167	32087	180200	594794	4380356
Net Worth 29	10716	0	105	•	607	3683	10347	28724	24943	60354	56381	330624	1034063

Selected Financial Ratios (Times to 1)

Current Ratio 30	1.5	•	3.6	•	1.7	2.5	2.6	2.2	1.7	1.7	1.1	1.4	1.5
Quick Ratio 31	0.8	•	3.3	•	0.8	1.6	1.7	0.7	0.9	0.8	0.8	0.8	0.8
Net Sales to Working Capital 32	8.9	•	4.8	•	6.4	6.5	4.9	3.9	7.5	5.4	16.8	9.4	9.5
Coverage Ratio 33	2.1	•	8.7	•	2.0	18.2	37.1	12.6	3.5	3.8	3.1	2.1	1.3
Total Asset Turnover 34	1.2	•	0.8	•	2.2	2.9	2.0	1.3	1.4	0.9	0.9	0.9	1.2
Inventory Turnover 35	5.7	•	10.9	•	5.1	7.9	7.0	3.0	6.1	4.7	6.5	6.9	5.1
Receivables Turnover 36	7.3	•	11.1	•	7.7	8.2	8.0	4.8	8.5	6.5	4.5	6.9	7.7
Total Liabilities to Net Worth 37	3.9	•	1.4	•	2.5	0.9	0.5	0.5	1.7	1.3	4.9	3.3	6.5
Current Assets to Working Capital 38	3.2	•	1.4	•	2.4	1.7	1.6	1.8	2.4	2.4	9.6	3.8	3.1
Current Liabilities to Working Capital 39	2.2	•	0.4	•	1.4	0.7	0.6	0.8	1.4	1.4	8.6	2.8	2.1
Working Capital to Net Sales 40	0.1	•	0.2	•	0.2	0.2	0.2	0.3	0.1	0.2	0.1	0.1	0.1
Inventory to Working Capital 41	1.2	•	0.1	•	1.1	0.6	0.5	0.6	0.9	0.9	2.4	1.1	1.4
Total Receipts to Cash Flow 42	11.4	•	3.1	•	9.8	8.0	6.7	5.6	10.1	7.5	8.0	16.6	11.3
Cost of Goods to Cash Flow 43	8.0	•	1.3	•	6.8	5.3	4.4	3.7	7.2	5.0	5.8	12.8	7.6
Cash Flow to Total Debt 44	0.1	•	0.4	•	0.3	0.8	0.8	0.7	0.2	0.2	0.1	0.1	0.1

Selected Financial Factors (in Percentages)

Debt Ratio 45	79.6	•	58.5	•	71.5	48.1	34.9	33.0	63.3	56.3	83.2	77.0	86.6
Return on Total Assets 46	4.5	•	14.1	•	7.3	20.2	19.6	15.2	7.1	7.4	5.9	4.4	3.1
Return on Equity Before Income Taxes 47	11.3	•	30.1	•	12.7	36.8	29.3	20.9	13.8	12.5	23.7	10.0	6.0
Return on Equity After Income Taxes 48	8.3	•	30.0	•	10.6	32.9	28.8	13.8	11.9	7.9	20.6	6.3	3.7
Profit Margin (Before Income Tax) 49	2.0	•	15.9	•	1.7	6.6	9.6	10.9	3.7	6.4	4.4	2.5	0.7
Profit Margin (After Income Tax) 50	1.5	•	15.8	•	1.4	5.9	9.5	7.2	3.2	4.0	3.8	1.6	0.4

Table II

Corporations with Net Income

RUBBER PRODUCT

MONEY AMOUNTS AND SIZE OF ASSETS IN THOUSANDS OF DOLLARS

Item Description for Accounting Period 7/10 Through 6/11	Total	Zero Assets	Under 500	500 to 1,000	1,000 to 5,000	5,000 to 10,000	10,000 to 25,000	25,000 to 50,000	50,000 to 100,000	100,000 to 250,000	250,000 to 500,000	500,000 to 2,500,000	2,500,000 and over
Number of Enterprises **1**	444	3	•	0	186	58	55	7	20	6	•	10	0

Revenues ($ in Thousands)

Item	Total	Zero Assets	Under 500	500 to 1,000	1,000 to 5,000	5,000 to 10,000	10,000 to 25,000	25,000 to 50,000	50,000 to 100,000	100,000 to 250,000	250,000 to 500,000	500,000 to 2,500,000	2,500,000 and over
Net Sales **2**	40253132	55084	•	0	944691	1184891	1623604	386680	2051992	832339	•	30885712	0
Interest **3**	191576	8	•	0	640	1112	171	198	599	155	•	181976	0
Rents **4**	13992	0	•	0	0	0	0	731	1702	1	•	10882	0
Royalties **5**	100724	0	•	0	0	0	0	1234	2	0	•	82667	0
Other Portfolio Income **6**	141969	4	•	0	95	197	534	22341	4579	5	•	84673	0
Other Receipts **7**	245531	0	•	0	818	1114	15281	1105	-643	2105	•	208787	0
Total Receipts **8**	40946924	55096	•	0	946244	1187314	1639590	412289	2058231	834605	•	31145470	0
Average Total Receipts **9**	92223	18365	•	•	5087	20471	29811	58898	102912	139101	•	3145470	•

Operating Costs/Operating Income (%)

Item	Total	Zero Assets	Under 500	500 to 1,000	1,000 to 5,000	5,000 to 10,000	10,000 to 25,000	25,000 to 50,000	50,000 to 100,000	100,000 to 250,000	250,000 to 500,000	500,000 to 2,500,000	2,500,000 and over
Cost of Operations **10**	70.4	39.6	•	•	69.6	66.6	64.2	66.4	71.5	64.4	•	71.0	•
Salaries and Wages **11**	5.7	7.5	•	•	5.9	9.8	7.9	6.8	6.3	5.5	•	5.4	•
Taxes Paid **12**	1.4	2.1	•	•	1.6	1.8	2.1	2.2	1.7	1.6	•	1.3	•
Interest Paid **13**	1.5	0.1	•	•	1.7	0.4	0.3	0.9	1.2	2.7	•	1.5	•
Depreciation **14**	2.8	2.7	•	•	2.3	0.4	2.2	2.8	2.8	3.5	•	3.0	•
Amortization and Depletion **15**	0.3	0.3	•	•	0.0	0.0	0.1	1.0	0.6	1.5	•	0.3	•
Pensions and Other Deferred Comp. **16**	1.9	•	•	•	0.4	0.6	0.3	0.2	0.5	0.5	•	2.3	•
Employee Benefits **17**	3.0	1.2	•	•	1.1	2.1	1.4	2.7	2.4	1.5	•	3.3	•
Advertising **18**	1.4	0.2	•	•	0.2	0.0	0.4	0.4	0.4	0.1	•	1.7	•
Other Expenses **19**	9.2	18.6	•	•	10.4	7.4	7.7	11.1	7.7	8.7	•	9.3	•
Officers' Compensation **20**	0.7	0.1	•	•	4.5	4.6	1.3	1.4	0.9	1.9	•	0.3	•
Operating Margin **21**	1.8	27.6	•	•	2.4	6.4	12.1	4.1	3.9	8.2	•	0.6	•
Operating Margin Before Officers' Comp. **22**	2.5	27.7	•	•	6.9	11.0	13.4	5.5	4.9	10.1	•	0.9	•

Selected Average Balance Sheet ($ in Thousands)

Item	No.											
Net Receivables	23	15228	0	•	•	788	2689	4348	7437	12235	16029	522807
Inventories	24	10501	0	•	•	649	1690	3044	10912	10154	13239	399701
Net Property, Plant and Equipment	25	15035	0	•	•	395	891	3856	8440	17336	23312	554583
Total Assets	26	75092	0	•	•	2326	7094	16476	42885	68989	142488	2704554
Notes and Loans Payable	27	19538	0	•	•	684	1313	2085	5657	19722	52264	705365
All Other Liabilities	28	36410	0	•	•	981	2098	3098	8504	18229	31148	1380377
Net Worth	29	19144	0	•	•	661	3683	11293	28724	31038	59077	618812

Selected Financial Ratios (Times to 1)

Item	No.											
Current Ratio	30	1.4	•	•	•	1.7	2.5	3.0	2.2	1.6	1.5	1.4
Quick Ratio	31	0.8	•	•	•	0.9	1.6	2.0	0.7	0.9	0.8	0.8
Net Sales to Working Capital	32	10.3	•	•	•	6.2	6.5	3.9	3.9	8.0	9.5	11.0
Coverage Ratio	33	3.5	215.2	•	•	2.5	18.2	45.2	12.6	4.6	4.2	2.7
Total Asset Turnover	34	1.2	•	•	•	2.2	2.9	1.8	1.3	1.5	1.0	1.1
Inventory Turnover	35	6.1	•	•	•	5.4	8.0	6.2	3.4	7.2	6.7	5.5
Receivables Turnover	36	6.7	•	•	•	9.5	8.3	7.3	5.6	10.6	9.1	•
Total Liabilities to Net Worth	37	2.9	•	•	•	2.5	0.9	0.5	0.5	1.2	1.4	3.4
Current Assets to Working Capital	38	3.6	•	•	•	2.3	1.7	1.5	1.8	2.6	2.9	3.8
Current Liabilities to Working Capital	39	2.6	•	•	•	1.3	0.7	0.5	0.8	1.6	1.9	2.8
Working Capital to Net Sales	40	0.1	•	•	•	0.2	0.2	0.3	0.3	0.1	0.1	0.1
Inventory to Working Capital	41	1.3	•	•	•	1.0	0.6	0.4	0.6	1.0	1.1	1.4
Total Receipts to Cash Flow	42	9.6	2.2	•	•	9.5	8.0	5.3	5.6	9.5	6.7	10.8
Cost of Goods to Cash Flow	43	6.8	0.9	•	•	6.6	5.3	3.4	3.7	6.8	4.3	7.6
Cash Flow to Total Debt	44	0.2	•	•	•	0.3	0.8	1.1	0.7	0.3	0.2	0.1

Selected Financial Factors (in Percentages)

Item	No.											
Debt Ratio	45	74.5	•	•	•	71.6	48.1	31.5	33.0	55.0	58.5	77.1
Return on Total Assets	46	6.2	•	•	•	9.3	20.2	23.9	15.2	8.1	11.1	4.7
Return on Equity Before Income Taxes	47	17.2	•	•	•	19.9	36.8	34.2	20.9	14.1	20.3	12.8
Return on Equity After Income Taxes	48	14.0	•	•	•	17.3	32.9	33.7	13.8	12.3	13.3	9.7
Profit Margin (Before Income Tax)	49	3.6	27.6	•	•	2.6	6.6	13.1	10.9	4.3	8.7	2.6
Profit Margin (After Income Tax)	50	3.0	26.9	•	•	2.2	5.9	12.9	7.2	3.7	5.7	2.0

Table I
Corporations with and without Net Income

CLAY, REFRACTORY AND OTHER NONMETALLIC MINERAL PRODUCT

MONEY AMOUNTS AND SIZE OF ASSETS IN THOUSANDS OF DOLLARS

Item Description for Accounting Period 7/10 Through 6/11	Total	Zero Assets	Under 500	500 to 1,000	1,000 to 5,000	5,000 to 10,000	10,000 to 25,000	25,000 to 50,000	50,000 to 100,000	100,000 to 250,000	250,000 to 500,000	500,000 to 2,500,000	2,500,000 and over
Number of Enterprises **1**	2597	11	2043	233	174	9	53	31	13	16	6	8	0
Revenues ($ in Thousands)													
Net Sales **2**	17753927	398561	1393164	607753	851610	215588	1137080	1003616	812408	2245327	2075636	6793183	0
Interest **3**	45712	3472	395	33	5	0	1204	96	221	2952	1876	35458	0
Rents **4**	3668	0	0	0	0	0	36	262	0	299	178	2893	0
Royalties **5**	76046	0	0	0	0	0	1894	103	0	1967	891	71191	0
Other Portfolio Income **6**	29391	400	2983	0	5	499	143	576	592	6888	1991	15315	0
Other Receipts **7**	363161	-8590	3927	7846	177	689	2564	4933	12019	11441	19166	308990	0
Total Receipts **8**	18051905	393843	1400469	615632	851797	216776	1142921	1009586	825240	2266874	2099738	7227030	0
Average Total Receipts **9**	6951	35804	685	2642	4895	24086	21565	32567	63480	141805	349956	903379	•
Operating Costs/Operating Income (%)													
Cost of Operations **10**	67.5	76.8	62.1	54.5	73.8	51.7	69.2	64.2	68.4	63.3	70.8	69.5	•
Salaries and Wages **11**	6.8	4.7	3.8	7.4	6.3	11.7	4.1	7.6	8.5	7.4	6.4	7.5	•
Taxes Paid **12**	1.8	0.7	2.1	4.4	1.9	2.3	1.9	2.3	2.0	1.5	1.1	1.7	•
Interest Paid **13**	1.9	1.8	0.3	0.2	0.5	0.1	0.9	1.3	1.5	2.3	1.9	2.9	•
Depreciation **14**	4.6	15.8	1.7	0.5	2.5	4.4	3.0	5.6	5.4	4.7	3.8	5.5	•
Amortization and Depletion **15**	0.6	0.2	•	0.4	0.0	0.3	0.3	0.6	0.4	0.6	0.9	1.0	•
Pensions and Other Deferred Comp. **16**	1.6	0.1	3.2	•	0.2	0.4	0.4	0.6	0.2	0.7	0.8	2.8	•
Employee Benefits **17**	1.7	0.6	0.4	•	1.3	1.5	1.9	1.7	1.0	2.7	1.9	2.0	•
Advertising **18**	0.9	0.6	0.1	1.1	0.0	0.3	0.8	0.5	0.7	0.6	1.0	1.2	•
Other Expenses **19**	12.4	8.4	20.5	17.0	11.4	10.3	9.8	11.0	15.3	9.8	9.3	12.8	•
Officers' Compensation **20**	2.0	2.0	6.1	11.4	2.0	0.9	3.5	2.6	0.8	1.5	0.4	0.8	•
Operating Margin **21**	•	•	•	3.3	2.0	16.0	4.2	2.1	•	4.9	1.8	•	•
Operating Margin Before Officers' Comp. **22**	0.0	•	5.7	14.7	2.0	17.0	7.7	4.7	•	6.4	2.2	•	•

Selected Average Balance Sheet ($ in Thousands)

•	•	•	•	•	•	•	•	•	•	•	•
Net Receivables 23	1085	0	12	297	337	2384	2792	6992	12126	22398	45333	186372
Inventories 24	955	0	27	109	400	1944	3950	5348	16343	24826	64190	117930
Net Property, Plant and Equipment 25	2215	0	25	248	738	3006	4366	13619	29504	48979	93423	388390
Total Assets 26	9215	0	125	849	2537	7229	14840	35008	73496	164177	337776	1936165
Notes and Loans Payable 27	2879	0	48	70	1353	527	4610	12744	26071	29961	82364	646326
All Other Liabilities 28	2069	0	25	150	859	1996	3597	7786	17619	47308	100411	387470
Net Worth 29	4266	0	52	630	325	4705	6633	14479	29806	86908	155001	902370

Selected Financial Ratios (Times to 1)

Current Ratio 30	•	1.9	3.9	2.7	1.6	2.1	2.0	2.3	1.9	2.5	1.7	1.8
Quick Ratio 31	•	0.9	2.4	2.3	1.1	1.3	0.9	1.3	1.0	1.3	0.9	0.7
Net Sales to Working Capital 32	•	4.2	9.5	8.5	8.5	10.9	5.3	3.5	4.2	3.1	4.5	3.5
Coverage Ratio 33	•	1.6	1.4	26.6	1.1	140.2	6.0	3.0	•	3.5	3.0	0.5
Total Asset Turnover 34	•	0.7	5.4	3.1	1.9	3.3	1.4	0.9	0.9	0.9	1.0	0.4
Inventory Turnover 35	•	4.8	15.8	13.0	9.0	6.4	3.8	3.9	2.6	3.6	3.8	5.0
Receivables Turnover 36	•	7.5	86.4	9.4	11.1	7.3	8.4	5.8	4.5	7.8	6.8	6.4
Total Liabilities to Net Worth 37	•	1.2	1.4	0.3	6.8	0.5	1.2	1.4	1.5	0.9	1.2	1.1
Current Assets to Working Capital 38	•	2.1	1.3	1.6	2.6	1.9	2.0	1.8	2.1	1.6	2.4	2.3
Current Liabilities to Working Capital 39	•	1.1	0.3	0.6	1.6	0.9	1.0	0.8	1.1	0.6	1.4	1.3
Working Capital to Net Sales 40	•	0.2	0.1	0.1	0.1	0.1	0.2	0.3	0.2	0.3	0.2	0.3
Inventory to Working Capital 41	•	0.6	0.5	0.2	0.6	0.7	1.0	0.7	0.9	0.6	0.9	0.5
Total Receipts to Cash Flow 42	•	9.7	7.1	5.6	10.4	4.7	8.0	8.4	10.2	7.8	9.4	12.3
Cost of Goods to Cash Flow 43	•	6.6	4.4	3.0	7.7	2.4	5.6	5.4	7.0	4.9	6.7	8.6
Cash Flow to Total Debt 44	•	0.1	1.3	2.1	0.2	2.0	0.3	0.2	0.1	0.2	0.2	0.1

Selected Financial Factors (in Percentages)

Debt Ratio 45	•	53.7	58.3	25.9	87.2	34.9	55.3	58.6	59.4	47.1	54.1	53.4
Return on Total Assets 46	•	2.3	2.4	14.6	1.1	55.4	8.2	3.7	•	7.1	6.0	0.7
Return on Equity Before Income Taxes 47	•	1.8	1.7	18.9	0.7	84.5	15.3	6.0	•	9.6	8.7	•
Return on Equity After Income Taxes 48	•	0.7	1.7	18.8	•	84.5	14.4	3.8	•	7.5	5.9	•
Profit Margin (Before Income Tax) 49	•	1.1	0.1	4.6	0.0	16.6	4.7	2.7	•	5.9	3.9	•
Profit Margin (After Income Tax) 50	•	0.5	0.1	4.5	•	16.6	4.4	1.7	•	4.7	2.6	•

Table II
Corporations with Net Income

CLAY, REFRACTORY AND OTHER NONMETALLIC MINERAL PRODUCT

MONEY AMOUNTS AND SIZE OF ASSETS IN THOUSANDS OF DOLLARS

Item Description for Accounting Period 7/10 Through 6/11	Total	Zero Assets	Under 500	500 to 1,000	1,000 to 5,000	5,000 to 10,000	10,000 to 25,000	25,000 to 50,000	50,000 to 100,000	100,000 to 250,000	250,000 to 500,000	500,000 to 2,500,000	2,500,000 and over
Number of Enterprises **1**	1535	•	1084	233	114	•	41	18	6	13	•	•	0
Revenues ($ in Thousands)													
Net Sales **2**	12252925	•	844554	607753	565339	•	1025969	716828	353430	1978211	•	•	0
Interest **3**	22847	•	395	33	5	•	1201	91	217	2829	•	•	0
Rents **4**	3016	•	0	0	0	•	36	26	0	299	•	•	0
Royalties **5**	16553	•	0	0	0	•	60	103	0	1967	•	•	0
Other Portfolio Income **6**	22546	•	428	0	0	•	131	174	9	6483	•	•	0
Other Receipts **7**	311580	•	128	7846	173	•	4103	986	10633	9601	•	•	0
Total Receipts **8**	12629467	•	845505	615632	565517	•	1031500	718208	364289	1999390	•	•	0
Average Total Receipts **9**	8228	•	780	2642	4961	•	25159	39900	60715	153799	•	•	•
Operating Costs/Operating Income (%)													
Cost of Operations **10**	65.4	•	62.0	54.5	70.8	•	68.3	66.5	71.6	61.7	•	•	•
Salaries and Wages **11**	6.5	•	2.9	7.4	6.2	•	3.5	5.5	5.3	7.5	•	•	•
Taxes Paid **12**	1.7	•	1.8	4.4	2.5	•	1.9	1.8	1.3	1.5	•	•	•
Interest Paid **13**	1.8	•	0.4	0.2	0.1	•	0.9	0.7	0.9	2.7	•	•	•
Depreciation **14**	4.2	•	2.1	0.5	0.5	•	2.6	4.2	3.1	4.3	•	•	•
Amortization and Depletion **15**	0.5	•	•	0.4	0.0	•	0.3	0.4	0.7	0.6	•	•	•
Pensions and Other Deferred Comp. **16**	1.4	•	•	•	0.3	•	0.4	0.8	0.2	0.7	•	•	•
Employee Benefits **17**	1.5	•	0.1	•	1.1	•	2.0	1.4	0.7	2.6	•	•	•
Advertising **18**	0.9	•	0.1	1.1	0.1	•	0.8	0.5	0.1	0.6	•	•	•
Other Expenses **19**	11.9	•	22.3	17.0	14.8	•	9.6	8.8	7.1	10.5	•	•	•
Officers' Compensation **20**	2.0	•	3.0	11.4	2.1	•	3.5	3.0	0.5	1.5	•	•	•
Operating Margin **21**	2.1	•	5.3	3.3	1.2	•	6.2	6.5	8.4	5.9	•	•	•
Operating Margin Before Officers' Comp. **22**	4.1	•	8.3	14.7	3.4	•	9.7	9.5	9.0	7.4	•	•	•

Selected Average Balance Sheet ($ in Thousands)

Net Receivables 23	1470	0	297	299	3205	9630	14267	25158
Inventories 24	968	17	109	504	3998	5185	11192	20599
Net Property, Plant and Equipment 25	2509	37	248	142	4147	10797	20241	47614
Total Assets 26	8311	81	849	2028	14266	33644	69362	166483
Notes and Loans Payable 27	2078	52	70	582	3334	6550	6016	35680
All Other Liabilities 28	1811	5	150	1189	3068	8603	19931	51421
Net Worth 29	4422	24	630	257	7864	18491	43416	79382

Selected Financial Ratios (Times to 1)

Current Ratio 30	2.5	9.3	2.7	1.5	2.6	2.8	2.9	2.3
Quick Ratio 31	1.6	4.1	2.3	1.0	1.1	1.8	2.0	1.2
Net Sales to Working Capital 32	4.0	19.9	8.5	8.4	4.5	3.1	3.0	3.3
Coverage Ratio 33	3.9	13.8	26.6	9.5	8.3	10.7	13.3	3.6
Total Asset Turnover 34	1.0	9.7	3.1	2.4	1.8	1.2	0.8	0.9
Inventory Turnover 35	5.4	28.8	13.0	7.0	4.3	5.1	3.8	4.6
Receivables Turnover 36	7.5	15496.4	9.4	8.9	9.7	5.8	3.1	8.9
Total Liabilities to Net Worth 37	0.9	2.4	0.3	6.9	0.8	0.8	0.6	1.1
Current Assets to Working Capital 38	1.6	1.1	1.6	3.1	1.6	1.6	1.5	1.8
Current Liabilities to Working Capital 39	0.6	0.1	0.6	2.1	0.6	0.6	0.5	0.8
Working Capital to Net Sales 40	0.3	0.1	0.1	0.1	0.2	0.3	0.3	0.3
Inventory to Working Capital 41	0.5	0.6	0.2	0.5	0.8	0.5	0.4	0.6
Total Receipts to Cash Flow 42	7.3	5.0	5.6	7.3	7.0	7.2	5.9	7.0
Cost of Goods to Cash Flow 43	4.8	3.1	3.0	5.2	4.8	4.8	4.2	4.3
Cash Flow to Total Debt 44	0.3	2.8	2.1	0.4	0.6	0.4	0.4	0.2

Selected Financial Factors (in Percentages)

Debt Ratio 45	46.8	70.3	25.9	87.3	44.9	45.0	37.4	52.3
Return on Total Assets 46	6.8	56.8	14.6	3.4	13.5	8.7	10.6	8.8
Return on Equity Before Income Taxes 47	9.5	177.5	18.9	24.3	21.5	14.3	15.6	13.4
Return on Equity After Income Taxes 48	7.8	177.5	18.8	22.7	20.5	11.4	11.5	10.6
Profit Margin (Before Income Tax) 49	5.2	5.5	4.6	1.3	6.7	6.6	11.5	7.0
Profit Margin (After Income Tax) 50	4.3	5.5	4.5	1.2	6.4	5.3	8.4	5.5

Table I
Corporations with and without Net Income

GLASS AND GLASS PRODUCT

MONEY AMOUNTS AND SIZE OF ASSETS IN THOUSANDS OF DOLLARS

Item Description for Accounting Period 7/10 Through 6/11	Total	Zero Assets	Under 500	500 to 1,000	1,000 to 5,000	5,000 to 10,000	10,000 to 25,000	25,000 to 50,000	50,000 to 100,000	100,000 to 250,000	250,000 to 500,000	500,000 to 2,500,000	2,500,000 and over
Number of Enterprises **1**	1875	347	1011	67	331	68	20	10	4	5	3	7	3
Revenues ($ in Thousands)													
Net Sales **2**	23657842	2918	487907	87543	1417798	1154025	689184	354071	215762	637927	1527480	6953412	10129817
Interest **3**	41973	28	0	94	807	64	623	240	429	43	2855	12143	24647
Rents **4**	6509	0	563	0	435	408	735	70	960	0	0	216	3122
Royalties **5**	1145545	0	0	0	0	0	0	0	0	8	0	11510	1134027
Other Portfolio Income **6**	746844	0	1633	0	2280	174	185	4	1577	12754	14747	116672	596816
Other Receipts **7**	394709	-4138	2755	36	-408	11922	2758	7758	1802	3005	18930	99376	250913
Total Receipts **8**	25993422	-1192	492858	87673	1420912	1166593	693485	362143	220530	653737	1564012	7193329	12139342
Average Total Receipts **9**	13863	-3	487	1309	4293	17156	34674	36214	55132	130747	521337	1027618	4046447
Operating Costs/Operating Income (%)													
Cost of Operations **10**	67.6	•	41.7	51.1	55.6	69.0	81.3	70.8	73.6	69.4	74.0	70.1	66.6
Salaries and Wages **11**	6.1	•	15.3	27.2	9.7	4.8	3.1	9.1	6.6	5.3	4.2	7.1	4.8
Taxes Paid **12**	1.9	•	2.7	3.7	3.1	1.8	1.8	2.3	2.9	2.7	0.9	2.0	1.7
Interest Paid **13**	2.1	•	0.0	2.4	1.9	0.6	0.8	3.1	0.9	4.2	3.9	1.3	2.7
Depreciation **14**	4.4	•	0.4	4.7	7.6	3.2	1.8	2.6	4.1	5.8	6.6	6.0	3.0
Amortization and Depletion **15**	0.9	•	•	0.0	0.0	0.0	0.1	1.6	0.8	0.7	0.4	0.4	1.6
Pensions and Other Deferred Comp. **16**	1.1	•	•	0.0	0.0	0.1	0.1	0.2	1.1	0.6	1.5	1.3	1.2
Employee Benefits **17**	2.7	•	2.2	3.6	1.7	0.8	1.6	0.8	4.1	2.2	2.6	3.3	2.7
Advertising **18**	0.3	•	2.1	0.6	0.2	0.2	0.1	0.3	0.2	0.2	0.1	0.1	0.4
Other Expenses **19**	17.5	643.5	19.1	18.8	18.7	10.3	4.7	9.9	8.5	6.4	5.2	9.8	27.0
Officers' Compensation **20**	1.5	•	10.7	8.3	3.3	1.1	1.3	2.5	0.6	1.1	0.4	1.2	1.1
Operating Margin **21**	•	•	5.7	•	•	8.2	3.4	•	•	1.5	0.3	•	•
Operating Margin Before Officers' Comp. **22**	•	•	16.4	•	1.3	9.3	4.6	•	•	2.6	0.7	•	•

Selected Average Balance Sheet ($ in Thousands)

Net Receivables 23	2295	0	24	121	532	1400	3444	6563	8267	10671	80597	202253	706630
Inventories 24	1577	0	105	81	419	2491	1914	5174	13379	38804	60353	109940	446714
Net Property, Plant and Equipment 25	5188	0	16	136	1361	2578	6812	6414	22134	42258	148662	386119	1809474
Total Assets 26	30615	0	202	586	2859	7370	17022	36614	73467	150574	429439	1190540	14778646
Notes and Loans Payable 27	6881	0	376	383	1619	4132	4003	11938	30832	59131	289325	186091	2963516
All Other Liabilities 28	7647	0	36	150	636	1955	4400	9401	17504	33450	154171	474390	3248362
Net Worth 29	16087	0	-210	53	604	1282	8619	15275	25130	57993	-14056	530059	8566769

Selected Financial Ratios (Times to 1)

Current Ratio 30	1.4	•	4.9	1.0	1.4	1.6	1.8	1.4	0.8	4.7	1.1	1.2	1.4
Quick Ratio 31	0.9	•	2.2	0.5	0.6	1.0	1.3	1.0	0.4	3.0	0.6	0.8	1.0
Net Sales to Working Capital 32	6.2	•	3.3	314.9	13.7	8.9	9.0	6.5	•	1.9	41.0	12.4	4.3
Coverage Ratio 33	4.6	•	308.3	•	16.1	0.1	5.9	0.7	•	2.0	1.7	4.7	5.8
Total Asset Turnover 34	0.4	•	2.4	2.2	2.3	1.5	2.0	1.0	0.7	0.8	1.2	0.8	0.2
Inventory Turnover 35	5.4	•	1.9	8.2	4.7	5.7	14.6	4.8	3.0	2.3	6.2	6.3	5.0
Receivables Turnover 36	5.1	•	19.5	13.6	10.2	7.0	10.2	5.3	3.9	3.8	12.6	7.4	3.5
Total Liabilities to Net Worth 37	0.9	•	•	10.1	4.7	3.7	1.0	1.4	1.9	1.6	•	1.2	0.7
Current Assets to Working Capital 38	3.5	•	1.3	107.2	3.7	2.7	2.3	3.5	•	1.3	13.5	5.1	3.4
Current Liabilities to Working Capital 39	2.5	•	0.3	106.2	2.7	1.7	1.3	2.5	•	0.3	12.5	4.1	2.4
Working Capital to Net Sales 40	0.2	•	0.3	0.0	0.1	0.1	0.1	0.2	•	0.5	0.0	0.1	0.2
Inventory to Working Capital 41	0.8	•	0.7	30.8	1.7	0.9	0.6	0.9	•	0.4	4.9	1.7	0.6
Total Receipts to Cash Flow 42	5.6	•	5.4	•	6.5	9.4	13.9	14.4	19.3	12.2	14.8	12.7	3.4
Cost of Goods to Cash Flow 43	3.8	•	2.3	•	4.5	5.2	11.3	10.2	14.2	8.4	10.9	8.9	2.2
Cash Flow to Total Debt 44	0.2	•	0.2	•	0.4	0.2	0.3	0.1	0.1	0.1	0.1	0.1	0.2

Selected Financial Factors (in Percentages)

Debt Ratio 45	47.5	•	203.6	91.0	82.6	78.9	49.4	58.3	65.8	61.5	103.3	55.5	42.0
Return on Total Assets 46	4.1	•	16.1	•	22.8	0.3	9.6	2.0	•	6.9	7.9	4.9	3.6
Return on Equity Before Income Taxes 47	6.1	•	•	•	122.9	•	15.8	•	•	8.8	•	8.7	5.2
Return on Equity After Income Taxes 48	5.1	•	•	•	121.0	•	11.4	•	•	7.4	•	5.8	4.7
Profit Margin (Before Income Tax) 49	7.7	•	6.7	9.3	9.3	•	4.0	•	•	4.0	2.8	4.6	13.2
Profit Margin (After Income Tax) 50	6.5	•	6.7	9.1	9.1	•	2.8	•	•	3.3	2.1	3.1	11.8

Table II

Corporations with Net Income

GLASS AND GLASS PRODUCT

MONEY AMOUNTS AND SIZE OF ASSETS IN THOUSANDS OF DOLLARS

Item Description for Accounting Period 7/10 Through 6/11		Total	Zero Assets	Under 500	500 to 1000	1,000 to 5,000	5,000 to 10,000	10,000 to 25,000	25,000 to 50,000	50,000 to 100,000	100,000 to 250,000	250,000 to 500,000	500,000 to 2,500,000	2,500,000 and over
Number of Enterprises	1	977	•	281	51	201	•	11	6	•	5	0	•	0
Revenues ($ in Thousands)														
Net Sales	2	17849658	•	287704	64126	693406	•	624936	279669	•	1245862	0	•	0
Interest	3	29673	•	0	94	802	•	46	176	•	2858	0	•	0
Rents	4	2800	•	0	0	0	•	624	70	•	0	0	•	0
Royalties	5	1050632	•	0	0	0	•	0	0	•	1	0	•	0
Other Portfolio Income	6	715939	•	1633	0	112	•	162	3	•	14900	0	•	0
Other Receipts	7	323151	•	114	36	639	•	1885	6638	•	19861	0	•	0
Total Receipts	8	19971853	•	289451	64256	694959	•	627653	286556	•	1283482	0	•	0
Average Total Receipts	9	20442	•	1030	1260	3458	•	57059	47759	•	256696	•	•	•
Operating Costs/Operating Income (%)														
Cost of Operations	10	66.7	•	29.3	31.6	53.2	•	82.2	74.4	•	71.6	•	•	•
Salaries and Wages	11	5.9	•	17.9	30.2	5.2	•	2.8	5.7	•	5.3	•	•	•
Taxes Paid	12	1.8	•	3.1	3.9	3.9	•	1.5	1.9	•	1.5	•	•	•
Interest Paid	13	1.2	•	•	2.0	1.2	•	0.3	0.8	•	1.9	•	•	•
Depreciation	14	4.1	•	0.3	5.4	7.0	•	1.3	2.3	•	4.8	•	•	•
Amortization and Depletion	15	1.1	•	•	0.0	0.0	•	0.1	0.0	•	0.6	•	•	•
Pensions and Other Deferred Comp.	16	1.3	•	•	•	0.0	•	0.1	0.3	•	1.4	•	•	•
Employee Benefits	17	2.3	•	3.0	4.4	2.3	•	1.8	0.4	•	1.6	•	•	•
Advertising	18	0.3	•	1.8	•	0.2	•	0.1	0.2	•	0.2	•	•	•
Other Expenses	19	18.2	•	23.5	15.9	22.3	•	3.6	6.5	•	6.2	•	•	•
Officers' Compensation	20	1.4	•	8.3	6.0	3.5	•	1.2	2.9	•	0.6	•	•	•
Operating Margin	21	•	•	12.8	0.6	1.2	•	5.1	4.5	•	4.2	•	•	•
Operating Margin Before Officers' Comp.	22	•	•	21.1	6.6	4.7	•	6.3	7.4	•	4.8	•	•	•

Selected Average Balance Sheet ($ in Thousands)

Net Receivables 23	3059	31	108	418	5607	9604	51935
Inventories 24	2219	8	42	481	3901	5013	31941
Net Property, Plant and Equipment 25	7838	8	176	934	5301	9098	51269
Total Assets 26	50348	226	582	2526	16143	39436	248457
Notes and Loans Payable 27	8387	78	202	1221	3292	6576	78234
All Other Liabilities 28	11136	29	160	335	7413	13874	96714
Net Worth 29	30824	119	220	969	5437	18986	73508

Selected Financial Ratios (Times to 1)

Current Ratio 30	1.5	7.4	1.2	2.5	1.1	1.2	1.4
Quick Ratio 31	1.0	7.1	0.7	1.3	0.8	0.8	0.9
Net Sales to Working Capital 32	5.2	5.5	19.1	4.4	54.1	11.8	6.4
Coverage Ratio 33	11.9	•	1.4	2.3	22.8	9.3	4.8
Total Asset Turnover 34	0.4	4.5	2.2	1.4	3.5	1.2	1.0
Inventory Turnover 35	5.5	38.1	9.6	3.8	12.0	6.9	5.6
Receivables Turnover 36	4.9	37.3	23.3	7.0	8.8	9.7	5.2
Total Liabilities to Net Worth 37	0.6	0.9	1.6	1.6	2.0	1.1	2.4
Current Assets to Working Capital 38	3.0	1.2	6.1	1.7	9.1	5.9	3.3
Current Liabilities to Working Capital 39	2.0	0.2	5.1	0.7	8.1	4.9	2.3
Working Capital to Net Sales 40	0.2	0.2	0.1	0.2	0.0	0.1	0.2
Inventory to Working Capital 41	0.7	0.0	0.6	0.7	2.2	1.3	0.9
Total Receipts to Cash Flow 42	4.5	3.6	8.5	6.4	12.7	7.9	8.3
Cost of Goods to Cash Flow 43	3.0	1.1	2.7	3.4	10.5	5.9	5.9
Cash Flow to Total Debt 44	0.2	2.7	0.4	0.3	0.4	0.3	0.2

Selected Financial Factors (in Percentages)

Debt Ratio 45	38.8	47.1	62.2	61.6	66.3	51.9	70.4
Return on Total Assets 46	5.0	60.9	6.1	3.6	20.3	9.3	9.2
Return on Equity Before Income Taxes 47	7.5	115.1	4.7	5.2	57.5	17.1	24.6
Return on Equity After Income Taxes 48	6.6	115.1	4.0	4.4	44.8	12.1	20.9
Profit Margin (Before Income Tax) 49	12.7	13.4	0.8	1.5	5.5	7.0	7.3
Profit Margin (After Income Tax) 50	11.1	13.4	0.7	1.2	4.3	4.9	6.2

Table I

Corporations with and without Net Income

CEMENT, CONCRETE, LIME AND GYPSUM PRODUCT

MONEY AMOUNTS AND SIZE OF ASSETS IN THOUSANDS OF DOLLARS

Item Description for Accounting Period 7/10 Through 6/11	Total	Zero Assets	Under 500	500 to 1,000	1,000 to 5,000	5,000 to 10,000	10,000 to 25,000	25,000 to 50,000	50,000 to 100,000	100,000 to 250,000	250,000 to 500,000	500,000 to 2,500,000	2,500,000 and over
Number of Enterprises 1	4734	677	1697	678	1185	254	126	36	25	21	9	19	8
Revenues ($ in Thousands)													
Net Sales 2	51980810	537432	1102979	1037185	4857781	2693639	2543249	1385658	1368495	2775770	2159596	9259277	22259750
Interest 3	344401	965	602	606	5626	2118	3180	1082	1037	3590	10437	110347	204811
Rents 4	64644	616	0	0	3343	1433	1212	1464	1232	193	8881	9760	36511
Royalties 5	54719	322	0	0	0	0	1	24	1252	221	34	45568	7296
Other Portfolio Income 6	1185819	8027	501	529	14956	30584	33142	7813	25195	10932	7964	188057	858119
Other Receipts 7	565505	3770	1298	10416	110048	58219	12544	11157	14947	-664	24940	158996	159835
Total Receipts 8	54195898	551132	1105380	1048736	4991754	2785993	2593328	1407198	1412158	2790042	2211852	9772005	23526322
Average Total Receipts 9	11448	814	651	1547	4212	10968	20582	39089	56486	132859	245761	514316	2940790
Operating Costs/Operating Income (%)													
Cost of Operations 10	71.7	93.0	47.3	56.8	65.6	69.9	72.1	69.9	75.4	71.4	77.6	71.5	73.9
Salaries and Wages 11	6.2	1.3	14.1	8.4	6.0	5.8	7.1	6.4	5.1	5.7	3.9	4.9	6.8
Taxes Paid 12	2.3	3.1	5.1	2.7	2.8	2.8	2.7	1.8	2.3	2.5	1.7	1.8	2.1
Interest Paid 13	5.1	4.5	0.9	0.8	1.2	1.6	1.1	1.1	1.7	1.8	1.3	5.9	8.1
Depreciation 14	7.7	1.3	3.8	3.3	3.6	4.9	5.2	5.7	8.8	6.3	6.4	13.0	7.9
Amortization and Depletion 15	1.5	3.6	0.1	0.0	0.0	0.3	0.2	0.5	0.6	0.6	1.4	2.9	1.9
Pensions and Other Deferred Comp. 16	0.9	0.1	0.2	0.7	0.4	1.0	0.5	0.4	0.7	0.7	0.6	1.2	1.0
Employee Benefits 17	2.0	4.3	0.4	2.6	1.6	1.3	2.0	1.1	2.3	2.8	1.5	2.6	1.9
Advertising 18	0.4	0.1	0.5	0.8	1.2	0.2	0.6	0.7	0.6	0.4	0.2	0.2	0.3
Other Expenses 19	11.2	12.1	20.8	17.4	14.3	14.0	10.6	8.7	7.4	8.5	7.1	10.6	10.8
Officers' Compensation 20	1.4	0.5	8.1	3.8	4.6	3.9	1.6	2.4	1.3	1.0	0.8	0.6	0.3
Operating Margin 21	•	•	2.6	•	•	•	•	1.1	•	•	•	•	•
Operating Margin Before Officers' Comp. 22	•	6.8	6.4	3.2	•	•	•	3.6	•	•	•	•	•

Selected Average Balance Sheet ($ in Thousands)

Item													
Net Receivables 23	1756	0	132	486	1796	3200	5605	11337	20165	36960	74263	510154	
Inventories 24	1242	0	63	257	881	2095	5029	7502	13604	19847	66293	364784	
Net Property, Plant and Equipment 25	9339	0	83	285	736	3649	5945	13928	35312	56487	118277	576074	3343698
Total Assets 26	22482	197	678	2417	7728	15576	33595	71572	141580	315871	1143970	8536693	
Notes and Loans Payable 27	8284	0	132	163	1123	3830	8687	25205	38898	26883	356455	3424875	
All Other Liabilities 28	4831	0	59	261	470	2336	3252	5489	11094	36327	26384	270454	1802407
Net Worth 29	9367	0	7	255	824	1864	8494	19419	35273	66355	262603	517061	3309411

Selected Financial Ratios (Times to 1)

Item													
Current Ratio 30	1.6	•	1.0	1.5	2.3	1.3	2.0	2.5	1.5	2.2	3.5	1.6	1.5
Quick Ratio 31	1.0	•	0.6	1.1	1.7	0.8	1.3	1.5	1.0	1.4	2.4	0.9	0.9
Net Sales to Working Capital 32	5.8	•	•	15.7	5.3	14.8	4.9	4.0	6.3	4.5	2.8	5.9	5.8
Coverage Ratio 33	•	•	•	5.5	2.1	•	3.4	0.9	0.4	•	0.9	•	
Total Asset Turnover 34	0.5	3.3	2.3	1.7	1.4	1.3	1.1	0.8	0.9	0.8	0.4	0.3	
Inventory Turnover 35	6.3	15.7	13.9	10.4	8.4	6.9	5.4	5.5	6.9	9.4	5.3	5.6	
Receivables Turnover 36	6.0	22.6	11.3	9.6	5.2	7.1	5.8	4.6	6.8	6.8	5.5	5.4	
Total Liabilities to Net Worth 37	1.4	28.8	1.7	1.9	3.1	0.8	0.7	1.0	1.1	0.2	1.2	1.6	
Current Assets to Working Capital 38	2.6	•	3.2	1.8	4.4	2.0	1.7	2.9	1.8	1.4	2.8	3.2	
Current Liabilities to Working Capital 39	1.6	•	2.2	0.8	3.4	1.0	0.7	1.9	0.8	0.4	1.8	2.2	
Working Capital to Net Sales 40	0.2	•	0.1	0.2	0.1	0.2	0.3	0.2	0.2	0.4	0.2	0.2	
Inventory to Working Capital 41	0.6	•	0.7	0.4	1.2	0.5	0.5	0.7	0.5	0.2	0.8	0.7	
Total Receipts to Cash Flow 42	73.6	7.2	6.3	8.6	11.6	17.9	11.0	49.5	20.2	21.4	•	0.7	
Cost of Goods to Cash Flow 43	52.8	3.4	3.6	5.6	8.1	12.9	7.7	37.3	14.4	16.6	•	•	
Cash Flow to Total Debt 44	0.0	0.5	0.6	0.3	0.2	0.2	0.2	0.0	0.1	0.2	•	•	

Selected Financial Factors (in Percentages)

Item												
Debt Ratio 45	58.3	96.6	62.5	65.9	75.9	45.5	42.2	50.7	53.1	16.9	54.8	61.2
Return on Total Assets 46	•	•	10.2	4.4	•	•	4.3	•	0.9	•	•	
Return on Equity Before Income Taxes 47	•	•	22.2	6.8	•	•	5.3	•	•	•	•	
Return on Equity After Income Taxes 48	•	•	22.0	5.5	•	•	4.2	•	•	•	•	
Profit Margin (Before Income Tax) 49	•	•	3.7	1.4	•	•	2.7	•	•	•	•	
Profit Margin (After Income Tax) 50	•	•	3.7	1.1	•	•	2.1	•	•	•	•	

Table II
Corporations with Net Income

CEMENT, CONCRETE, LIME AND GYPSUM PRODUCT

MONEY AMOUNTS AND SIZE OF ASSETS IN THOUSANDS OF DOLLARS

Item Description for Accounting Period 7/10 Through 6/11	Total	Zero Assets	Under 500	500 to 1,000	1,000 to 5,000	5,000 to 10,000	10,000 to 25,000	25,000 to 50,000	50,000 to 100,000	100,000 to 250,000	250,000 to 500,000	500,000 to 2,500,000	2,500,000 and over
Number of Enterprises **1**	2288	424	507	524	631	92	57	25	•	9	•	7	0
Revenues ($ in Thousands)													
Net Sales **2**	15212261	35777	380103	749778	2614066	1027681	1311571	1048160	•	1203996	•	5047292	0
Interest **3**	64439	0	556	145	1028	445	2132	213	•	3361	•	52070	0
Rents **4**	14157	52	0	0	189	958	557	1254	•	180	•	2099	0
Royalties **5**	8838	0	0	0	0	0	0	24	•	221	•	7307	0
Other Portfolio Income **6**	669538	753	0	529	12577	24462	21125	7127	•	4580	•	588297	0
Other Receipts **7**	122399	57	219	10069	89780	5193	6544	7143	•	-6659	•	-6307	0
Total Receipts **8**	16091632	36639	380878	760521	2717640	1058739	1341929	1063921	•	1205679	•	5690758	0
Average Total Receipts **9**	7033	86	751	1451	4307	11508	23543	42557	•	133964	•	812965	•
Operating Costs/Operating Income (%)													
Cost of Operations **10**	64.0	60.8	51.8	53.6	60.6	67.0	68.7	68.6	•	62.0	•	63.0	•
Salaries and Wages **11**	6.1	3.7	10.8	8.7	5.3	5.6	7.1	6.2	•	4.7	•	6.9	•
Taxes Paid **12**	2.4	1.3	5.3	3.2	2.7	2.4	2.2	1.9	•	2.3	•	2.4	•
Interest Paid **13**	2.8	3.6	1.1	0.9	1.0	0.4	0.8	0.9	•	1.7	•	6.8	•
Depreciation **14**	7.0	8.6	5.8	3.9	3.4	6.9	3.8	5.3	•	6.8	•	10.4	•
Amortization and Depletion **15**	1.2	•	•	0.0	0.1	0.1	0.2	0.2	•	0.9	•	2.7	•
Pensions and Other Deferred Comp. **16**	0.8	•	0.2	0.6	0.5	0.4	0.5	0.4	•	0.8	•	1.3	•
Employee Benefits **17**	1.7	0.8	0.7	3.2	1.2	1.0	1.5	1.1	•	3.1	•	2.2	•
Advertising **18**	0.5	0.8	1.2	0.9	0.6	0.2	0.7	0.8	•	0.7	•	0.2	•
Other Expenses **19**	10.0	18.4	13.8	16.4	13.0	9.6	9.8	7.7	•	10.4	•	9.3	•
Officers' Compensation **20**	2.0	•	5.3	3.7	4.1	1.6	1.8	2.4	•	0.9	•	1.1	•
Operating Margin **21**	1.4	2.0	4.0	4.8	7.6	4.7	2.8	4.3	•	5.6	•	•	•
Operating Margin Before Officers' Comp. **22**	3.4	2.0	9.3	8.5	11.7	6.3	4.6	6.8	•	6.5	•	•	•

Selected Average Balance Sheet ($ in Thousands)

	•	•	•	•	•	•	•	•	•	•	•
Net Receivables 23	912	0	43	123	449	1283	3869	6257	17890	115201	•
Inventories 24	620	0	21	59	240	1346	2105	4710	17828	75004	•
Net Property, Plant and Equipment 25	4326	0	146	243	680	4465	5193	13719	58115	963453	•
Total Assets 26	9336	0	323	658	2440	7984	15874	34278	135397	1891529	•
Notes and Loans Payable 27	3562	0	100	172	709	1569	2895	7703	40811	933657	•
All Other Liabilities 28	1714	0	32	187	377	3846	2709	4513	28139	339898	•
Net Worth 29	4060	0	192	298	1354	2569	10270	22063	66447	617975	•

Selected Financial Ratios (Times to 1)

Current Ratio 30	2.3	•	2.0	1.6	2.9	1.4	2.5	2.8	2.1	1.8	•
Quick Ratio 31	1.5	•	1.5	1.2	2.2	0.8	1.8	1.9	1.3	1.1	•
Net Sales to Working Capital 32	4.6	•	12.0	11.7	4.1	14.5	4.1	3.5	4.5	6.0	•
Coverage Ratio 33	3.6	2.2	4.9	8.1	13.1	20.2	7.3	7.2	4.3	2.1	•
Total Asset Turnover 34	0.7	•	2.3	2.2	1.7	1.4	1.4	1.2	1.0	0.4	•
Inventory Turnover 35	6.9	•	18.4	13.1	10.5	5.6	7.5	6.1	4.7	6.1	•
Receivables Turnover 36	7.5	•	33.7	10.7	10.4	4.3	7.0	6.7	5.8	8.2	•
Total Liabilities to Net Worth 37	1.3	•	0.7	1.2	0.8	2.1	0.5	0.6	1.0	2.1	•
Current Assets to Working Capital 38	1.8	•	2.0	2.5	1.5	3.6	1.7	1.5	1.9	2.3	•
Current Liabilities to Working Capital 39	0.8	•	1.0	1.5	0.5	2.6	0.7	0.5	0.9	1.3	•
Working Capital to Net Sales 40	0.2	•	0.1	0.1	0.2	0.1	0.2	0.3	0.2	0.2	•
Inventory to Working Capital 41	0.4	•	0.4	0.5	0.3	1.0	0.4	0.4	0.6	0.6	•
Total Receipts to Cash Flow 42	7.2	7.5	5.9	6.0	5.0	7.5	8.6	8.4	6.9	8.4	•
Cost of Goods to Cash Flow 43	4.6	4.6	3.1	3.2	3.0	5.0	5.9	5.8	4.3	5.3	•
Cash Flow to Total Debt 44	0.2	•	1.0	0.7	0.8	0.3	0.5	0.4	0.3	0.1	•

Selected Financial Factors (in Percentages)

Debt Ratio 45	56.5	•	40.6	54.6	44.5	67.8	35.3	35.6	50.9	67.3	•
Return on Total Assets 46	7.3	•	12.2	15.4	21.3	11.3	8.6	8.3	7.4	5.4	•
Return on Equity Before Income Taxes 47	12.2	•	16.3	29.7	35.4	33.5	11.5	11.1	11.6	8.6	•
Return on Equity After Income Taxes 48	10.6	•	14.4	29.5	34.0	31.5	10.7	9.7	10.4	6.6	•
Profit Margin (Before Income Tax) 49	7.4	4.4	4.2	6.2	11.6	7.7	5.1	5.8	5.8	7.4	•
Profit Margin (After Income Tax) 50	6.5	4.2	3.7	6.1	11.1	7.2	4.8	5.1	5.2	5.7	•

Table I
Corporations with and without Net Income

IRON, STEEL MILLS AND STEEL PRODUCT

MONEY AMOUNTS AND SIZE OF ASSETS IN THOUSANDS OF DOLLARS

Item Description for Accounting Period 7/10 Through 6/11		Total	Zero Assets	Under 500	500 to 1,000	1,000 to 5,000	5,000 to 10,000	10,000 to 25,000	25,000 to 50,000	50,000 to 100,000	100,000 to 250,000	250,000 to 500,000	500,000 to 2,500,000	2,500,000 and over
Number of Enterprises	1	3156	372	1580	279	432	176	135	68	39	31	19	12	12
Revenues ($ in Thousands)														
Net Sales	2	12683269	271699	1556083	287563	1826583	2966056	3501958	3847926	4578299	7690299	7658411	19426912	73211480
Interest	3	576849	630	2	250	254	1550	2020	6459	1932	29165	20046	50295	464246
Rents	4	61599	2376	0	0	0	0	1527	199	571	1044	10546	12280	33055
Royalties	5	61123	0	0	0	0	0	0	0	135	363	2065	4018	54542
Other Portfolio Income	6	197991	18113	53964	719	7805	1444	8525	8735	9327	7359	11659	6906	63436
Other Receipts	7	1412769	35612	53673	568	18785	37085	18300	14823	26120	46831	53665	507138	600170
Total Receipts	8	129133600	328430	1663722	289100	1853427	3006135	3532330	3878142	4616384	7775061	7756392	20007549	74426929
Average Total Receipts	9	40917	883	1053	1036	4290	17080	26165	57032	118369	250808	408231	1667296	6202244
Operating Costs/Operating Income (%)														
Cost of Operations	10	84.4	90.7	59.1	68.2	73.7	84.0	73.2	78.3	82.0	83.5	85.3	84.4	86.4
Salaries and Wages	11	2.5	1.5	23.3	0.7	6.1	3.6	5.5	3.8	3.3	3.2	2.3	2.9	1.6
Taxes Paid	12	0.8	1.3	3.6	2.2	1.9	0.9	1.7	1.3	1.0	0.9	0.8	0.7	0.6
Interest Paid	13	2.1	1.6	1.4	0.4	0.8	0.8	0.4	1.2	0.6	1.4	1.5	2.0	2.7
Depreciation	14	3.5	1.3	2.1	3.5	2.4	1.6	2.8	2.5	2.4	2.1	3.8	2.7	4.1
Amortization and Depletion	15	0.7	•	0.1	•	0.2	0.0	0.2	0.2	0.2	0.2	0.4	1.2	0.8
Pensions and Other Deferred Comp.	16	0.5	0.2	0.3	0.1	0.0	0.1	0.7	0.5	0.6	0.3	0.3	0.4	0.5
Employee Benefits	17	1.4	2.5	1.2	4.8	1.0	1.4	1.8	1.3	1.1	1.2	0.9	1.2	1.5
Advertising	18	0.1	0.0	0.1	0.4	0.1	0.2	0.1	0.3	0.1	0.1	0.1	0.1	0.0
Other Expenses	19	5.9	4.4	19.7	19.5	5.2	3.4	6.4	5.8	3.2	4.8	3.0	4.6	6.6
Officers' Compensation	20	0.6	1.0	5.9	3.0	7.8	2.5	2.0	1.4	1.0	0.6	0.4	0.4	0.2
Operating Margin	21	•	•	•	•	0.7	1.4	5.3	3.3	4.5	1.7	1.4	•	•
Operating Margin Before Officers' Comp.	22	•	•	•	0.2	8.5	3.9	7.3	4.7	5.5	2.3	1.7	•	•

Selected Average Balance Sheet ($ in Thousands)

Net Receivables 23	4536	0	67	126	438	2104	3845	7874	14572	34624	39185	141882	705870
Inventories 24	5140	0	33	90	783	1936	3689	8197	17859	41197	62034	160637	777540
Net Property, Plant and Equipment 25	11078	0	76	94	469	2150	4169	8747	14489	40668	103292	353078	2087610
Total Assets 26	35170	0	192	855	2052	7644	16155	35702	67983	152165	345030	1235611	6238442
Notes and Loans Payable 27	11884	0	319	227	771	2532	3356	15594	16639	40471	111398	342862	2209459
All Other Liabilities 28	12405	0	65	116	577	2423	3578	13545	22210	56867	102471	376266	2320373
Net Worth 29	10880	0	-192	513	704	2688	9221	6564	29134	54827	131162	516482	1708610

Selected Financial Ratios (Times to 1)

Current Ratio 30	1.6	•	1.5	1.8	2.1	1.4	2.3	1.5	1.7	2.0	2.2	1.5	1.5
Quick Ratio 31	0.7	•	1.2	1.3	1.2	0.8	1.3	0.7	0.8	0.9	0.9	0.7	0.7
Net Sales to Working Capital 32	8.0	•	27.4	10.3	5.4	13.2	4.6	8.1	6.5	5.0	4.5	9.4	9.1
Coverage Ratio 33	0.7	11.0	•	•	3.7	4.3	17.2	4.4	9.4	3.0	2.8	2.2	•
Total Asset Turnover 34	1.1	•	5.1	1.2	2.1	2.2	1.6	1.6	1.7	1.6	1.2	1.3	1.0
Inventory Turnover 35	6.6	•	17.7	7.8	4.0	7.3	5.1	5.4	5.4	5.0	5.5	8.5	6.8
Receivables Turnover 36	9.3	•	13.6	9.5	8.1	9.7	6.7	8.0	9.0	8.1	10.9	13.4	8.8
Total Liabilities to Net Worth 37	2.2	•	•	0.7	1.9	1.8	0.8	4.4	1.3	1.8	1.6	1.4	2.7
Current Assets to Working Capital 38	2.7	•	3.1	2.3	1.9	3.8	1.8	3.0	2.4	2.0	1.8	2.9	3.2
Current Liabilities to Working Capital 39	1.7	•	2.1	1.3	0.9	2.8	0.8	2.0	1.4	1.0	0.8	1.9	2.2
Working Capital to Net Sales 40	0.1	•	0.0	0.1	0.2	0.1	0.2	0.1	0.2	0.2	0.2	0.1	0.1
Inventory to Working Capital 41	1.1	•	0.5	0.6	0.7	1.5	0.6	1.3	1.1	0.9	0.8	1.1	1.3
Total Receipts to Cash Flow 42	37.3	7.2	16.0	9.9	19.1	20.6	10.0	12.4	13.4	15.7	21.0	16.7	•
Cost of Goods to Cash Flow 43	31.5	6.6	9.4	6.7	14.1	17.3	7.3	9.7	11.0	13.1	17.9	14.1	•
Cash Flow to Total Debt 44	0.0	•	0.2	0.3	0.2	0.2	0.4	0.2	0.2	0.2	0.1	0.1	•

Selected Financial Factors (in Percentages)

Debt Ratio 45	69.1	•	199.8	40.0	65.7	64.8	42.9	81.6	57.1	64.0	62.0	58.2	72.6
Return on Total Assets 46	1.7	•	•	•	6.2	7.9	10.5	8.5	10.4	7.0	4.9	5.8	•
Return on Equity Before Income Taxes 47	•	•	51.1	•	13.3	17.2	17.4	35.5	21.6	12.9	8.2	7.7	•
Return on Equity After Income Taxes 48	•	•	51.1	•	11.5	16.3	16.2	30.7	17.6	10.2	4.8	4.7	•
Profit Margin (Before Income Tax) 49	•	16.4	•	•	2.2	2.7	6.2	4.1	5.4	2.9	2.7	2.5	•
Profit Margin (After Income Tax) 50	•	16.4	•	•	1.9	2.6	5.8	3.6	4.4	2.2	2.7	1.6	1.5

Table II

Corporations with Net Income

IRON, STEEL MILLS AND STEEL PRODUCT

MONEY AMOUNTS AND SIZE OF ASSETS IN THOUSANDS OF DOLLARS

Item Description for Accounting Period 7/10 Through 6/11	Total	Zero Assets	Under 500	500 to 1,000	1,000 to 5,000	5,000 to 10,000	10,000 to 25,000	25,000 to 50,000	50,000 to 100,000	100,000 to 250,000	250,000 to 500,000	500,000 to 2,500,000	2,500,000 and over
Number of Enterprises **1**	1162	12	639	52	86	136	105	47	35	23	12	9	5
Revenues ($ in Thousands)													
Net Sales **2**	68801017	172174	364275	116329	665285	2469403	3033091	3167761	4336478	5974202	4336710	16979399	27185911
Interest **3**	178493	628	2	242	232	1498	1793	2007	1901	28040	14792	21654	105704
Rents **4**	38255	2312	0	0	0	0	1527	199	571	901	11470	11470	11207
Royalties **5**	42213	0	0	0	0	0	0	0	64	363	62	3903	37821
Other Portfolio Income **6**	133660	18065	51951	0	7705	883	5753	2120	9231	4840	11524	4796	16796
Other Receipts **7**	787685	35296	15459	140	1499	36545	14633	8782	24876	48645	40198	368235	193371
Total Receipts **8**	69981323	228475	431687	116711	674721	2508329	3056797	3180869	4373121	6056991	4413354	17389457	27550810
Average Total Receipts **9**	60225	19040	676	2244	7846	18444	29112	67678	124946	263347	367780	1932162	5510162
Operating Costs/Operating Income (%)													
Cost of Operations **10**	81.5	92.0	57.2	62.3	52.6	83.3	71.0	77.6	81.4	82.8	81.1	84.0	82.2
Salaries and Wages **11**	2.9	1.6	22.0	•	6.5	3.5	5.8	3.6	3.4	3.2	2.2	3.0	1.9
Taxes Paid **12**	0.9	1.4	0.4	3.4	2.1	1.0	1.6	1.2	1.0	1.0	0.9	0.6	0.8
Interest Paid **13**	1.4	2.0	3.0	0.5	0.2	0.3	0.3	0.7	0.4	1.6	0.7	0.8	2.3
Depreciation **14**	3.0	0.5	2.1	5.1	1.2	1.7	2.0	2.3	2.3	1.7	4.0	2.7	3.8
Amortization and Depletion **15**	0.5	•	0.5	0.5	0.4	0.0	0.2	0.1	0.2	0.1	0.1	1.3	0.5
Pensions and Other Deferred Comp. **16**	0.4	0.0	0.2	•	0.0	0.1	0.7	0.6	0.6	0.4	0.4	0.4	0.3
Employee Benefits **17**	0.9	0.0	1.9	8.7	0.4	1.0	1.7	1.3	1.1	1.2	0.8	0.9	0.8
Advertising **18**	0.1	0.0	0.1	0.3	0.1	0.2	0.1	0.4	0.1	0.1	0.1	0.1	0.0
Other Expenses **19**	5.4	5.7	14.9	15.8	7.6	3.2	6.1	4.9	3.1	4.7	3.4	4.7	6.5
Officers' Compensation **20**	0.7	0.2	0.2	2.4	14.4	2.4	2.1	1.4	1.0	0.6	0.5	0.4	0.2
Operating Margin **21**	2.3	•	•	1.5	14.3	3.4	8.4	5.9	5.4	2.8	5.8	1.2	0.5
Operating Margin Before Officers' Comp. **22**	3.0	•	•	3.9	28.8	5.8	10.5	7.3	6.4	3.4	6.3	1.6	0.7

Selected Average Balance Sheet ($ in Thousands)

Net Receivables 23	6688	0	54	259	643	2134	4058	9103	15435	35552	34314	164406	654862
Inventories 24	5333	0	9	185	175	2008	3629	7351	13822	33912	49423	194977	706054
Net Property, Plant and Equipment 25	11991	0	13	359	200	2063	3447	9285	14954	39003	85620	353482	1436263
Total Assets 26	51461	0	108	902	2502	7854	15999	35479	69328	151150	331310	1256117	6773577
Notes and Loans Payable 27	14533	0	0	444	1436	1968	14105	12088	38066	61050	224160	2345690	
All Other Liabilities 28	11727	0	11	80	350	2181	3595	10081	22067	57740	88518	388086	1156412
Net Worth 29	25201	0	96	684	1709	4236	10436	11293	35174	55344	181741	643871	3271474

Selected Financial Ratios (Times to 1)

Current Ratio 30	2.1	•	8.2	5.8	5.0	1.9	2.4	1.7	1.8	1.9	2.5	1.5	2.8
Quick Ratio 31	1.0	•	7.4	4.9	3.4	1.1	1.4	0.8	0.9	0.9	1.1	0.8	1.3
Net Sales to Working Capital 32	5.3	•	6.9	5.8	4.8	7.4	4.6	6.7	6.0	5.2	3.8	10.3	4.1
Coverage Ratio 33	3.9	15.3	6.2	4.6	66.7	20.5	36.5	9.5	15.5	3.6	11.1	5.8	1.8
Total Asset Turnover 34	1.2	•	5.3	2.5	3.1	2.3	1.8	1.9	1.8	1.7	1.1	1.5	0.8
Inventory Turnover 35	9.0	•	36.8	7.5	23.2	7.5	5.7	7.1	7.3	6.3	5.9	8.1	6.3
Receivables Turnover 36	12.2	•	18.5	7.4	•	10.4	7.2	10.1	10.8	9.6	10.8	•	16.6
Total Liabilities to Net Worth 37	1.0	•	0.1	0.3	0.5	0.9	0.5	2.1	1.0	1.7	0.8	1.0	1.1
Current Assets to Working Capital 38	1.9	•	1.1	1.2	1.3	2.1	1.7	2.4	2.3	2.1	1.7	3.0	1.5
Current Liabilities to Working Capital 39	0.9	•	0.1	0.2	0.3	1.1	0.7	1.4	1.3	1.1	0.7	2.0	0.5
Working Capital to Net Sales 40	0.2	•	0.1	0.2	0.2	0.1	0.2	0.1	0.2	0.2	0.3	0.1	0.2
Inventory to Working Capital 41	0.7	•	0.1	0.1	0.1	0.9	0.6	1.0	1.0	1.0	0.6	1.1	0.5
Total Receipts to Cash Flow 42	12.4	4.1	4.0	7.9	4.9	14.2	7.9	10.2	12.2	13.2	10.2	13.6	14.2
Cost of Goods to Cash Flow 43	10.1	3.8	2.3	4.9	2.6	11.8	5.6	7.9	10.0	10.9	8.3	11.4	11.6
Cash Flow to Total Debt 44	0.2	•	12.7	1.3	2.0	0.4	0.7	0.3	0.3	0.2	0.2	0.2	0.1

Selected Financial Factors (in Percentages)

Debt Ratio 45	51.0	•	10.5	24.2	31.7	46.1	34.8	68.2	49.3	63.4	45.1	48.7	51.7
Return on Total Assets 46	6.3	•	100.2	5.7	49.5	12.1	17.1	13.4	11.9	9.9	9.0	6.7	3.4
Return on Equity Before Income Taxes 47	9.5	•	93.9	5.9	71.4	21.3	25.5	37.7	21.9	19.6	15.0	10.9	3.1
Return on Equity After Income Taxes 48	7.6	•	93.9	5.0	67.7	20.5	24.2	33.7	18.3	15.9	11.1	7.6	2.0
Profit Margin (Before Income Tax) 49	4.1	29.2	15.9	1.8	15.8	5.0	9.2	6.3	6.2	4.2	7.5	3.7	1.8
Profit Margin (After Income Tax) 50	3.2	29.1	15.9	1.5	15.0	4.8	8.8	5.6	5.2	3.4	5.6	2.6	1.2

Table I
Corporations with and without Net Income

NONFERROUS METAL PRODUCTION AND PROCESSING

MONEY AMOUNTS AND SIZE OF ASSETS IN THOUSANDS OF DOLLARS

Item Description for Accounting Period 7/10 Through 6/11	Total	Zero Assets	Under 500	500 to 1,000	1,000 to 5,000	5,000 to 10,000	10,000 to 25,000	25,000 to 50,000	50,000 to 100,000	100,000 to 250,000	250,000 to 500,000	500,000 to 2,500,000	2,500,000 and over
Number of Enterprises 1	824	17	8	0	411	104	128	66	31	16	20	24	•
Revenues ($ in Thousands)													
Net Sales 2	88888696	1513862	110	0	2213092	3524693	6547982	6949792	3967924	3366398	11481874	49322968	•
Interest 3	1356149	3381	0	0	112	15	399	729	4098	4774	13912	1328730	•
Rents 4	41274	1	0	0	3223	363	1593	572	691	0	16822	18009	•
Royalties 5	46522	20	0	0	0	30	2227	133	2955	878	0	40279	•
Other Portfolio Income 6	1045888	43834	4587	0	46	48	1265	7321	6606	3371	14378	964432	•
Other Receipts 7	1430857	7003	8158	0	5493	-27280	19575	14695	18477	38642	147181	1198913	•
Total Receipts 8	92809386	1568101	12855	0	2221966	3497869	6573041	6973242	4000751	3414063	11674167	52873331	•
Average Total Receipts 9	112633	92241	1607	•	5406	33633	51352	105655	129056	213379	583708	2203055	•
Operating Costs/Operating Income (%)													
Cost of Operations 10	87.4	89.9	15.5	•	80.3	89.2	88.1	90.6	84.7	83.7	86.5	87.6	•
Salaries and Wages 11	2.7	4.0	133.6	•	1.4	1.2	2.3	1.5	2.7	2.9	2.3	3.1	•
Taxes Paid 12	0.6	0.4	77.3	•	0.7	0.7	0.7	0.5	0.8	1.0	0.5	0.5	•
Interest Paid 13	3.1	18.8	1250.0	•	0.8	0.8	0.3	0.4	0.7	1.9	1.9	4.3	•
Depreciation 14	2.0	1.0	132.7	•	1.6	0.5	1.1	1.4	1.6	3.0	2.2	2.2	•
Amortization and Depletion 15	0.3	0.3	0.9	•	0.0	0.0	0.0	0.1	0.1	0.8	0.4	0.3	•
Pensions and Other Deferred Comp. 16	0.4	0.2	•	•	0.3	0.7	0.3	0.1	0.4	0.2	0.7	0.5	•
Employee Benefits 17	0.9	0.2	20.0	•	0.4	1.3	0.6	0.5	0.5	1.4	1.4	0.8	•
Advertising 18	0.1	0.0	•	•	0.2	0.0	0.1	0.1	0.0	0.1	0.1	0.1	•
Other Expenses 19	4.9	10.1	15729.1	•	7.5	1.6	3.6	2.7	4.4	5.3	5.4	5.2	•
Officers' Compensation 20	0.4	0.3	•	•	2.1	1.2	0.9	0.9	0.8	0.3	0.3	0.2	•
Operating Margin 21	•	•	•	•	4.6	2.9	1.9	1.2	3.1	•	•	•	•
Operating Margin Before Officers' Comp. 22	•	•	•	•	6.7	4.1	2.8	2.1	3.9	•	•	•	•

Selected Average Balance Sheet ($ in Thousands)

Net Receivables **23**	59620	0	0	•	313	1773	4035	9247	15232	25098	83847	1880685	•
Inventories **24**	10278	0	0	•	340	2835	3717	8769	14816	43743	67847	153103	•
Net Property, Plant and Equipment **25**	17150	0	52	•	319	826	3268	8134	12717	34906	92525	423168	•
Total Assets **26**	176375	0	153	•	1688	7972	15192	34465	65827	149749	370659	5322484	•
Notes and Loans Payable **27**	61141	0	2039	•	1858	4184	6077	10188	19682	44309	135595	1820175	•
All Other Liabilities **28**	52260	0	4446	•	1101	3695	3853	11181	16899	57828	122475	1544150	•
Net Worth **29**	62974	0	-6332	•	-1271	93	5262	13096	29247	47612	112589	1958160	•

Selected Financial Ratios (Times to 1)

Current Ratio **30**	1.2		0.0	•	1.0	1.5	2.2	1.5	2.2	1.5	1.8	1.2	•
Quick Ratio **31**	0.9		0.0	•	0.5	0.5	1.2	0.8	1.1	0.6	1.0	1.0	•
Net Sales to Working Capital **32**	6.9		•	•	104.8	14.1	9.2	13.0	5.5	8.6	6.5	5.8	•
Coverage Ratio **33**	1.7		•	•	7.3	3.6	9.0	5.1	6.8	1.5	1.2	1.8	•
Total Asset Turnover **34**	0.6		0.1	•	3.2	4.3	3.4	3.1	1.9	1.4	1.5	0.4	•
Inventory Turnover **35**	9.2		•	•	12.7	10.7	12.1	10.9	7.3	4.0	7.3	11.8	•
Receivables Turnover **36**	1.8		•	•	•	29.8	12.4	12.9	10.0	7.2	8.3	2.0	•
Total Liabilities to Net Worth **37**	1.8		•	•	•	84.8	1.9	1.6	1.3	2.1	2.3	1.7	•
Current Assets to Working Capital **38**	5.3		•	•	25.0	2.9	1.8	2.9	1.9	3.2	2.2	6.8	•
Current Liabilities to Working Capital **39**	4.3		•	•	24.0	1.9	0.8	1.9	0.9	2.2	1.2	5.8	•
Working Capital to Net Sales **40**	0.1		•	•	0.0	0.1	0.1	0.1	0.2	0.1	0.2	0.2	•
Inventory to Working Capital **41**	0.7		•	•	6.6	1.9	0.7	1.2	0.8	1.5	0.8	0.6	•
Total Receipts to Cash Flow **42**	19.3		0.0	•	9.4	30.2	20.2	29.1	13.6	21.1	23.3	16.7	•
Cost of Goods to Cash Flow **43**	16.8		0.0	•	7.6	26.9	17.8	26.4	11.6	17.7	20.1	14.7	•
Cash Flow to Total Debt **44**	0.0		0.1	•	0.2	0.1	0.3	0.2	0.3	0.1	0.1	0.0	•

Selected Financial Factors (in Percentages)

Debt Ratio **45**	64.3		•	•	175.3	98.8	65.4	62.0	55.6	68.2	69.6	63.2	•
Return on Total Assets **46**	3.4		4238.2	•	18.3	12.4	8.8	6.3	9.0	3.8	3.7	3.0	•
Return on Equity Before Income Taxes **47**	4.0	•	12.3	•	•	765.7	22.6	13.3	17.3	3.8	2.2	3.7	•
Return on Equity After Income Taxes **48**	2.9	12.3	•	•	•	745.0	20.3	10.2	15.7	•	•	2.7	•
Profit Margin (Before Income Tax) **49**	2.3		•	•	5.0	2.1	2.3	1.7	4.0	0.9	0.4	3.5	•
Profit Margin (After Income Tax) **50**	1.7		•	•	4.9	2.0	2.1	1.3	3.6	•	•	2.6	•

Table II
Corporations with Net Income

NONFERROUS METAL PRODUCTION AND PROCESSING

MONEY AMOUNTS AND SIZE OF ASSETS IN THOUSANDS OF DOLLARS

Item Description for Accounting Period 7/10 Through 6/11		Total	Zero Assets	Under 500	500 to 1,000	1,000 to 5,000	5,000 to 10,000	10,000 to 25,000	25,000 to 50,000	50,000 to 100,000	100,000 to 250,000	250,000 to 500,000	500,000 to 2,500,000	2,500,000 and over
Number of Enterprises	1	595	•	•	0	315	59	100	48	27	8	•	18	•
Revenues ($ in Thousands)														
Net Sales	2	68845271	•	•	0	1986575	2677813	5834588	5489206	3472877	2049208	•	40725569	•
Interest	3	1282795	•	•	0	22	15	272	577	4072	1033	•	1266886	•
Rents	4	24662	•	•	0	3223	0	1558	572	691	0	•	17780	•
Royalties	5	43712	•	•	0	0	30	0	0	2955	449	•	40279	•
Other Portfolio Income	6	984038	•	•	0	46	1	522	5438	6376	432	•	953091	•
Other Receipts	7	1167143	•	•	0	854	-32734	17489	8952	16866	7840	•	111437	•
Total Receipts	8	72347621	•	•	0	1990720	2645125	5854429	5504745	3503837	2058962	•	44115042	•
Average Total Receipts	9	121593	•	•	•	6320	44833	58544	114682	129772	257370	•	2450836	•
Operating Costs/Operating Income (%)														
Cost of Operations	10	86.9	•	•	•	80.3	90.7	88.0	89.4	83.5	79.4	•	87.4	•
Salaries and Wages	11	2.7	•	•	•	1.4	0.8	2.2	1.4	2.9	3.1	•	3.2	•
Taxes Paid	12	0.5	•	•	•	0.5	0.3	0.7	0.6	0.8	0.6	•	0.5	•
Interest Paid	13	3.1	•	•	•	0.5	0.1	0.3	0.3	0.7	1.6	•	4.7	•
Depreciation	14	1.8	•	•	•	0.6	0.2	0.8	1.5	1.5	1.5	•	2.1	•
Amortization and Depletion	15	0.2	•	•	•	0.0	0.0	0.0	0.0	0.1	0.4	•	0.3	•
Pensions and Other Deferred Comp.	16	0.4	•	•	•	0.3	0.2	0.2	0.1	0.5	0.2	•	0.5	•
Employee Benefits	17	0.7	•	•	•	0.3	0.2	0.5	0.5	0.6	1.6	•	0.8	•
Advertising	18	0.1	•	•	•	0.2	0.0	0.1	0.1	0.0	0.1	•	0.1	•
Other Expenses	19	4.7	•	•	•	5.5	1.0	3.2	2.6	4.4	5.6	•	5.3	•
Officers' Compensation	20	0.5	•	•	•	2.1	1.2	0.8	1.0	0.9	0.3	•	0.2	•
Operating Margin	21	•	•	•	•	8.4	5.3	3.2	2.5	4.1	5.5	•	•	•
Operating Margin Before Officers' Comp.	22	•	•	•	•	10.4	6.6	4.0	3.5	5.0	5.8	•	•	•

Selected Average Balance Sheet ($ in Thousands)

Net Receivables 23	78534	402	1919	4441	8822	15313	27023	2433711
Inventories 24	9231	401	3492	3087	8360	13398	31246	160910
Net Property, Plant and Equipment 25	18493	193	628	2856	9102	12840	22429	490722
Total Assets 26	220442	1524	9111	15482	35457	65722	144717	6675988
Notes and Loans Payable 27	75656	819	1558	4021	10318	17640	34929	2323727
All Other Liabilities 28	64913	245	4702	3455	11186	16535	53097	1955407
Net Worth 29	79873	461	2851	8006	13952	31547	56691	2396854

Selected Financial Ratios (Times to 1)

Current Ratio 30	1.2	3.1	1.4	2.3	1.8	2.3	1.5	1.1
Quick Ratio 31	1.0	1.9	0.4	1.3	0.9	1.3	0.7	1.0
Net Sales to Working Capital 32	6.4	7.1	20.0	9.3	11.1	5.3	10.1	5.7
Coverage Ratio 33	2.4	18.2	48.5	14.3	9.6	8.4	4.6	2.0
Total Asset Turnover 34	0.5	4.1	5.0	3.8	3.2	2.0	1.8	0.3
Inventory Turnover 35	10.9	12.6	11.8	16.6	12.2	8.0	6.5	12.3
Receivables Turnover 36	2.6	•	39.1	15.3	17.1	10.9	•	1.7
Total Liabilities to Net Worth 37	1.8	2.3	2.2	0.9	1.5	1.1	1.6	1.8
Current Assets to Working Capital 38	5.7	1.5	3.7	1.8	2.3	1.7	3.2	7.7
Current Liabilities to Working Capital 39	4.7	0.5	2.7	0.8	1.3	0.7	2.2	6.7
Working Capital to Net Sales 40	0.2	0.1	0.1	0.1	0.1	0.2	0.1	0.2
Inventory to Working Capital 41	0.6	0.5	2.4	0.7	1.0	0.7	1.2	0.5
Total Receipts to Cash Flow 42	14.8	8.1	21.1	17.3	22.6	12.1	10.0	14.9
Cost of Goods to Cash Flow 43	12.9	6.5	19.1	15.3	20.2	10.1	8.0	13.0
Cash Flow to Total Debt 44	0.1	0.7	0.3	0.4	0.2	0.3	0.3	0.0

Selected Financial Factors (in Percentages)

Debt Ratio 45	63.8	69.8	68.7	48.3	60.6	52.0	60.8	64.1
Return on Total Assets 46	3.9	37.5	20.8	14.2	10.5	11.0	13.5	3.1
Return on Equity Before Income Taxes 47	6.3	117.2	65.1	25.6	23.9	20.2	27.0	4.3
Return on Equity After Income Taxes 48	5.0	116.9	63.9	23.7	20.0	18.4	17.8	3.2
Profit Margin (Before Income Tax) 49	4.4	8.6	4.1	3.5	2.9	4.9	6.0	4.5
Profit Margin (After Income Tax) 50	3.5	8.5	4.0	3.3	2.4	4.5	3.9	3.4

Table I
Corporations with and without Net Income

FOUNDRIES

MONEY AMOUNTS AND SIZE OF ASSETS IN THOUSANDS OF DOLLARS

Item Description for Accounting Period 7/10 Through 6/11	Total	Zero Assets	Under 500	500 to 1,000	1,000 to 5,000	5,000 to 10,000	10,000 to 25,000	25,000 to 50,000	50,000 to 100,000	100,000 to 250,000	250,000 to 500,000	500,000 to 2,500,000	2,500,000 and over
Number of Enterprises 1	1311	11	889	0	205	112	55	13	10	4	4	8	0
Revenues ($ in Thousands)													
Net Sales 2	21281444	99361	505354	0	1515243	1269243	1304465	615922	966671	660065	2018809	12326312	0
Interest 3	9110	127	0	0	1083	853	460	42	83	10	2145	4307	0
Rents 4	3541	0	0	0	607	27	982	282	37	0	757	849	0
Royalties 5	17358	0	0	0	0	0	0	7	56	1798	0	15497	0
Other Portfolio Income 6	85488	1213	0	0	27152	222	239	24	664	2567	1919	51489	0
Other Receipts 7	188608	2319	0	0	13100	5635	3677	7133	6404	2892	23381	124065	0
Total Receipts 8	21585549	103020	505354	0	1557185	1275980	1309823	623410	973915	667332	2047011	12522519	0
Average Total Receipts 9	16465	9365	568	•	7596	11393	23815	47955	97392	166833	511753	1565315	•
Operating Costs/Operating Income (%)													
Cost of Operations 10	73.6	74.6	60.0	•	69.2	65.2	74.6	80.8	72.4	71.4	80.2	74.1	•
Salaries and Wages 11	4.9	5.1	8.7	•	6.2	5.7	4.6	1.8	4.9	5.1	6.3	4.4	•
Taxes Paid 12	1.6	2.4	3.0	•	2.8	1.9	1.8	1.9	2.2	0.7	1.4	1.3	•
Interest Paid 13	1.1	0.7	0.1	•	0.5	1.3	1.0	3.7	0.5	0.8	1.1	1.2	•
Depreciation 14	2.9	4.8	1.1	•	1.2	2.2	4.7	3.4	4.3	3.0	3.3	2.8	•
Amortization and Depletion 15	0.7	0.1	0.5	•	0.0	0.0	0.1	0.5	0.1	0.3	0.3	1.1	•
Pensions and Other Deferred Comp. 16	0.5	0.8	0.4	•	1.2	0.6	0.3	0.5	0.5	0.7	0.8	0.4	•
Employee Benefits 17	1.8	2.1	•	•	2.0	2.9	2.6	2.1	1.0	2.9	0.7	1.9	•
Advertising 18	0.1	0.0	0.1	•	0.1	0.1	0.1	0.1	0.3	0.0	0.3	0.1	•
Other Expenses 19	5.5	13.2	10.6	•	9.8	12.4	5.3	6.7	5.2	6.8	1.0	4.7	•
Officers' Compensation 20	1.7	3.1	8.4	•	5.6	2.2	3.4	0.8	1.3	0.8	0.5	1.0	•
Operating Margin 21	5.6	•	7.1	•	1.4	5.4	1.4	•	7.3	7.5	4.1	7.0	•
Operating Margin Before Officers' Comp. 22	7.3	•	15.6	•	7.0	7.6	4.8	•	8.6	8.3	4.6	8.0	•

Selected Average Balance Sheet ($ in Thousands)

Net Receivables 23	2339	0	45	•	1124	1992	3465	9147	12834	22604	69955	220512
Inventories 24	2256	0	10	•	682	1420	2716	6705	10050	24230	80540	236909
Net Property, Plant and Equipment 25	3381	0	8	•	576	1650	5422	13514	26970	27191	124918	346340
Total Assets 26	14782	0	104	•	3323	6738	14827	39632	73219	142304	436574	1684036
Notes and Loans Payable 27	2229	0	128	•	610	2145	4036	17582	13968	50380	49980	181478
All Other Liabilities 28	4303	0	47	•	911	1257	3220	14072	11222	41741	111817	523203
Net Worth 29	8250	0	-70	•	1802	3336	7570	7978	48029	50183	274778	979354

Selected Financial Ratios (Times to 1)

Current Ratio 30	2.3	•	1.7	•	2.3	4.1	2.0	1.3	3.4	1.9	2.9	2.2
Quick Ratio 31	1.4	•	1.4	•	1.6	2.8	1.1	0.7	2.2	0.9	2.0	1.3
Net Sales to Working Capital 32	4.3	•	17.6	•	5.2	3.1	5.9	10.4	3.8	4.4	3.6	4.1
Coverage Ratio 33	7.5	•	56.4	•	9.4	5.4	2.8	0.7	16.2	11.9	6.0	8.7
Total Asset Turnover 34	1.1	•	5.5	•	2.2	1.7	1.6	1.2	1.3	1.2	1.2	0.9
Inventory Turnover 35	5.3	•	32.7	•	7.5	5.2	6.5	5.7	7.0	4.9	5.0	4.8
Receivables Turnover 36	7.5	•	•	•	•	6.3	8.4	5.5	8.4	5.6	5.0	8.5
Total Liabilities to Net Worth 37	0.8	•	•	•	0.8	1.0	1.0	4.0	0.5	1.8	0.6	0.7
Current Assets to Working Capital 38	1.8	•	2.5	•	1.7	1.3	2.0	4.0	1.4	2.1	1.5	1.8
Current Liabilities to Working Capital 39	0.8	•	1.5	•	0.7	0.3	1.0	3.0	0.4	1.1	0.5	0.8
Working Capital to Net Sales 40	0.2	•	0.1	•	0.2	0.3	0.2	0.1	0.3	0.2	0.3	0.2
Inventory to Working Capital 41	0.6	•	0.3	•	0.5	0.4	0.8	1.5	0.4	0.5	0.4	0.7
Total Receipts to Cash Flow 42	9.5	•	7.1	•	9.9	7.8	17.7	33.3	8.1	6.9	23.3	8.5
Cost of Goods to Cash Flow 43	7.0	•	4.2	•	6.9	5.1	13.2	26.9	5.9	4.9	18.7	6.3
Cash Flow to Total Debt 44	0.3	•	0.5	•	0.5	0.4	0.2	0.0	0.5	0.3	0.1	0.3

Selected Financial Factors (in Percentages)

Debt Ratio 45	44.2	•	167.5	•	45.8	50.5	48.9	79.9	34.4	64.7	37.1	41.8
Return on Total Assets 46	9.1	•	39.6	•	10.1	12.2	4.4	3.1	11.3	10.4	7.6	9.2
Return on Equity Before Income Taxes 47	14.1	•	•	•	16.7	20.0	5.5	•	16.1	27.1	10.1	14.1
Return on Equity After Income Taxes 48	10.1	•	•	•	15.6	19.6	3.9	•	14.3	24.4	8.6	9.1
Profit Margin (Before Income Tax) 49	7.2	•	7.1	•	4.1	5.9	1.8	•	8.0	8.2	5.5	8.9
Profit Margin (After Income Tax) 50	5.1	•	7.1	•	3.8	5.8	1.3	•	7.1	7.4	4.7	5.8

Table II
Corporations with Net Income

FOUNDRIES

MONEY AMOUNTS AND SIZE OF ASSETS IN THOUSANDS OF DOLLARS

Item Description for Accounting Period 7/10 Through 6/11		Total	Zero Assets	Under 500	500 to 1,000	1,000 to 5,000	5,000 to 10,000	10,000 to 25,000	25,000 to 50,000	50,000 to 100,000	100,000 to 250,000	250,000 to 500,000	500,000 to 2,500,000	2,500,000 and over
Number of Enterprises	1	531	•	•	0	187	102	44	8	7	4	•	5	0
Revenues ($ in Thousands)														
Net Sales	2	18069898	•	•	0	1454670	1051822	1135598	484133	737110	660065	•	10571781	0
Interest	3	6509	•	•	0	964	25	450	42	9	10	•	4068	0
Rents	4	3432	•	•	0	607	27	982	282	0	0	•	814	0
Royalties	5	17351	•	•	0	0	0	0	0	56	1798	•	15497	0
Other Portfolio Income	6	82875	•	•	0	27073	179	120	24	529	2567	•	51124	0
Other Receipts	7	177067	•	•	0	12956	1716	3410	6389	5217	2892	•	120292	0
Total Receipts	8	18357132	•	•	0	1496270	1053769	1140560	490870	742921	667332	•	10763576	0
Average Total Receipts	9	34571	•	•	•	8001	10331	25922	61359	106132	166833	•	2152715	•
Operating Costs/Operating Income (%)														
Cost of Operations	10	73.1	•	•	•	69.8	67.3	74.2	83.3	70.3	71.4	•	73.0	•
Salaries and Wages	11	4.4	•	•	•	5.6	3.4	4.6	1.1	4.7	5.1	•	4.8	•
Taxes Paid	12	1.5	•	•	•	2.7	1.7	1.8	1.8	2.0	0.7	•	1.3	•
Interest Paid	13	0.9	•	•	•	0.3	1.2	0.9	1.4	0.3	0.8	•	0.9	•
Depreciation	14	2.6	•	•	•	1.1	2.0	4.2	2.6	4.0	3.0	•	2.5	•
Amortization and Depletion	15	0.8	•	•	•	0.0	0.0	0.0	0.2	0.0	0.3	•	1.3	•
Pensions and Other Deferred Comp.	16	0.5	•	•	•	1.2	0.6	0.3	0.3	0.5	0.7	•	0.3	•
Employee Benefits	17	1.8	•	•	•	2.1	3.3	2.7	1.6	1.1	2.9	•	1.7	•
Advertising	18	0.1	•	•	•	0.1	0.1	0.1	0.0	0.4	0.0	•	0.1	•
Other Expenses	19	4.9	•	•	•	9.7	4.9	4.9	5.5	4.5	6.8	•	4.3	•
Officers' Compensation	20	1.8	•	•	•	5.7	2.3	3.6	0.3	1.4	0.8	•	1.1	•
Operating Margin	21	7.8	•	•	•	1.6	13.1	2.5	1.8	10.6	7.5	•	8.9	•
Operating Margin Before Officers' Comp.	22	9.6	•	•	•	7.3	15.4	6.2	2.1	12.0	8.3	•	10.0	•

Selected Average Balance Sheet ($ in Thousands)

Net Receivables 23	4944	1190	2066	3870	9169	14216	22604	303351
Inventories 24	4631	574	1415	2286	5192	9781	20610	333100
Net Property, Plant and Equipment 25	6688	575	1436	5390	13832	24708	27191	455552
Total Assets 26	30613	3213	6704	15439	36522	75221	142304	2315405
Notes and Loans Payable 27	4192	432	2026	3848	14872	12745	50380	230655
All Other Liabilities 28	7798	975	1310	3501	13630	12116	41741	593375
Net Worth 29	18623	1806	3368	8090	8020	50359	50183	1491375

Selected Financial Ratios (Times to 1)

Current Ratio 30	2.5	2.1	4.1	2.0	1.2	3.6	1.9	2.6
Quick Ratio 31	1.5	1.6	2.9	1.2	0.7	2.4	0.9	1.6
Net Sales to Working Capital 32	4.0	6.5	2.7	5.7	21.7	3.6	4.4	3.5
Coverage Ratio 33	11.8	15.1	11.7	4.2	3.3	33.7	11.9	13.2
Total Asset Turnover 34	1.1	2.4	1.5	1.7	1.7	1.4	1.2	0.9
Inventory Turnover 35	5.4	9.5	4.9	8.4	9.7	7.6	5.7	4.6
Receivables Turnover 36	7.7	6.2	5.5	10.5	7.3	9.1	•	
Total Liabilities to Net Worth 37	0.6	0.8	1.0	0.9	3.6	0.5	1.8	0.6
Current Assets to Working Capital 38	1.7	1.9	1.3	2.0	6.3	1.4	2.1	1.6
Current Liabilities to Working Capital 39	0.7	0.9	0.3	1.0	5.3	0.4	1.1	0.6
Working Capital to Net Sales 40	0.3	0.2	0.4	0.2	0.0	0.3	0.2	0.3
Inventory to Working Capital 41	0.5	0.4	0.4	0.7	2.2	0.4	0.5	0.6
Total Receipts to Cash Flow 42	8.0	9.7	6.1	15.7	17.3	6.6	6.9	7.5
Cost of Goods to Cash Flow 43	5.8	6.8	4.1	11.7	14.4	4.6	4.9	5.4
Cash Flow to Total Debt 44	0.4	0.6	0.5	0.2	0.1	0.6	0.3	0.3

Selected Financial Factors (in Percentages)

Debt Ratio 45	39.2	43.8	49.8	47.6	78.0	33.1	64.7	35.6
Return on Total Assets 46	11.7	11.2	22.3	6.5	7.6	16.5	10.4	10.9
Return on Equity Before Income Taxes 47	17.5	18.6	40.6	9.5	24.1	23.9	27.1	15.7
Return on Equity After Income Taxes 48	13.1	17.4	40.1	7.6	20.5	21.4	24.4	10.4
Profit Margin (Before Income Tax) 49	9.6	4.3	13.2	3.0	3.2	11.4	8.2	11.1
Profit Margin (After Income Tax) 50	7.2	4.0	13.1	2.4	2.7	10.2	7.4	7.4

Table I

Corporations with and without Net Income

FORGING AND STAMPING

MONEY AMOUNTS AND SIZE OF ASSETS IN THOUSANDS OF DOLLARS

Item Description for Accounting Period 7/10 Through 6/11	Total	Zero Assets	Under 500	500 to 1,000	1,000 to 5,000	5,000 to 10,000	10,000 to 25,000	25,000 to 50,000	50,000 to 100,000	100,000 to 250,000	250,000 to 500,000	500,000 to 2,500,000	2,500,000 and over
Number of Enterprises **1**	1615	3	560	343	426	71	133	30	31	13	6	0	0
Revenues ($ in Thousands)													
Net Sales **2**	16182722	75219	174760	368872	2090878	1124116	3600079	1834020	2726008	2172258	2016512	0	0
Interest **3**	33349	0	11	22	531	325	695	57	860	969	29881	0	0
Rents **4**	2799	0	0	0	0	96	45	0	106	2289	263	0	0
Royalties **5**	8	0	0	0	7	0	0	1	0	0	0	0	0
Other Portfolio Income **6**	28049	10234	506	0	23	380	1140	2399	10773	2559	34	0	0
Other Receipts **7**	149893	8	718	922	12944	15458	22957	6799	26226	31524	32339	0	0
Total Receipts **8**	16396820	85461	175995	369816	2104383	1140375	3624916	1843276	2763973	2209599	2079029	0	0
Average Total Receipts **9**	10153	28487	314	1078	4940	16062	27255	61443	89160	169969	346505	•	•
Operating Costs/Operating Income (%)													
Cost of Operations **10**	72.0	72.1	52.5	61.8	66.7	68.8	73.0	75.5	76.7	73.1	70.5	•	•
Salaries and Wages **11**	4.5	1.9	0.9	1.1	6.5	3.5	4.7	4.0	5.1	4.1	4.0	•	•
Taxes Paid **12**	1.9	1.4	3.2	2.5	2.5	2.5	1.9	1.5	1.6	1.5	1.5	•	•
Interest Paid **13**	1.2	•	0.1	0.5	0.8	0.7	0.5	0.9	1.1	1.4	3.9	•	•
Depreciation **14**	3.4	1.3	0.2	0.7	2.5	3.1	2.9	2.7	4.3	5.0	3.9	•	•
Amortization and Depletion **15**	0.3	•	0.0	0.1	0.0	0.3	0.0	0.5	0.5	0.2	0.6	•	•
Pensions and Other Deferred Comp. **16**	0.7	•	3.0	0.0	1.5	0.4	0.6	0.3	0.4	0.4	1.1	•	•
Employee Benefits **17**	2.4	1.3	0.2	4.2	3.7	1.9	2.6	2.3	1.9	2.9	1.0	•	•
Advertising **18**	0.1	•	•	0.4	0.2	0.2	0.3	0.1	0.0	0.1	0.1	•	•
Other Expenses **19**	5.6	•	18.2	15.7	5.7	8.4	5.0	5.2	4.7	4.4	5.6	•	•
Officers' Compensation **20**	2.5	•	12.9	7.5	5.9	3.5	2.7	1.2	1.5	1.2	0.6	•	•
Operating Margin **21**	5.3	24.4	8.9	5.5	4.1	6.6	5.8	6.0	2.1	5.8	7.2	•	•
Operating Margin Before Officers' Comp. **22**	7.9	24.4	21.8	13.0	10.0	10.1	8.6	7.1	3.6	6.9	7.8	•	•

Selected Average Balance Sheet ($ in Thousands)

Net Receivables 23	1555	0	31	187	692	2097	3663	9210	14984	30421	60536
Inventories 24	1214	0	30	179	566	1738	2530	6442	9671	24563	61550
Net Property, Plant and Equipment 25	2034	0	3	21	577	1653	4062	12083	20807	44225	131858
Total Assets 26	8126	0	144	638	2116	8153	13532	35421	70944	160286	699731
Notes and Loans Payable 27	2101	0	19	89	555	1548	2666	10097	20577	31277	217167
All Other Liabilities 28	1984	0	44	109	524	1477	3388	8976	18419	37148	173344
Net Worth 29	4041	0	80	440	1036	5127	7478	16349	31948	91861	309220

Selected Financial Ratios (Times to 1)

Current Ratio 30	2.1	•	2.3	4.0	2.5	3.0	2.2	1.5	2.0	2.1	1.9
Quick Ratio 31	1.3	•	1.6	3.1	1.8	2.0	1.4	1.0	1.2	1.4	0.8
Net Sales to Working Capital 32	5.0	•	5.4	2.5	5.5	4.2	5.8	9.7	4.9	4.0	4.1
Coverage Ratio 33	6.5	•	117.8	12.7	7.0	12.3	15.3	8.5	4.4	6.3	3.6
Total Asset Turnover 34	1.2	•	2.2	1.7	2.3	1.9	2.0	1.7	1.2	1.0	0.5
Inventory Turnover 35	5.9	•	5.5	3.7	5.8	6.3	7.8	7.2	7.0	5.0	3.8
Receivables Turnover 36	7.0	•	7.7	5.5	7.1	7.4	8.8	6.3	7.3	5.4	6.8
Total Liabilities to Net Worth 37	1.0	•	0.8	0.5	1.0	0.6	0.8	1.2	1.2	0.7	1.3
Current Assets to Working Capital 38	1.9	•	1.8	1.3	1.7	1.5	1.8	3.0	2.0	1.9	2.1
Current Liabilities to Working Capital 39	0.9	•	0.8	0.3	0.7	0.5	0.8	2.0	1.0	0.9	1.1
Working Capital to Net Sales 40	0.2	•	0.2	0.4	0.2	0.2	0.2	0.1	0.2	0.3	0.2
Inventory to Working Capital 41	0.6	•	0.5	0.3	0.4	0.4	0.6	0.9	0.7	0.5	0.9
Total Receipts to Cash Flow 42	10.0	2.8	5.6	6.3	14.9	8.6	10.5	10.2	15.2	9.4	6.7
Cost of Goods to Cash Flow 43	7.2	2.0	2.9	3.9	9.9	5.9	7.7	7.7	11.7	6.9	4.7
Cash Flow to Total Debt 44	0.2	•	0.9	0.9	0.3	0.6	0.4	0.3	0.1	0.3	0.1

Selected Financial Factors (in Percentages)

Debt Ratio 45	50.3	•	44.1	31.1	51.0	37.1	44.7	53.8	55.0	42.7	55.8
Return on Total Assets 46	9.7	•	21.1	10.5	12.9	17.0	14.0	12.7	5.7	9.2	6.8
Return on Equity Before Income Taxes 47	16.5	•	37.4	14.0	22.5	24.9	23.7	24.2	9.7	13.5	11.2
Return on Equity After Income Taxes 48	15.1	•	35.9	13.8	21.6	22.3	22.5	22.7	8.2	12.4	9.6
Profit Margin (Before Income Tax) 49	6.7	38.0	9.6	5.7	4.7	8.1	6.5	6.5	3.5	7.4	10.3
Profit Margin (After Income Tax) 50	6.1	38.0	9.2	5.7	4.6	7.2	6.2	6.1	3.0	6.8	8.8

Table II
Corporations with Net Income

FORGING AND STAMPING

MONEY AMOUNTS AND SIZE OF ASSETS IN THOUSANDS OF DOLLARS

Item Description for Accounting Period 7/10 Through 6/11	Total	Zero Assets	Under 500	500 to 1,000	1,000 to 5,000	5,000 to 10,000	10,000 to 25,000	25,000 to 50,000	50,000 to 100,000	100,000 to 250,000	250,000 to 500,000	500,000 to 2,500,000	2,500,000 and over
Number of Enterprises **1**	1522	3	•	343	378	52	124	25	23	•	6	0	0
Revenues ($ in Thousands)													
Net Sales **2**	14809139	75219	•	368872	1945645	979532	3432071	1704660	2179385	•	2016512	0	0
Interest **3**	32984	0	•	22	516	323	375	53	833	•	29881	0	0
Rents **4**	2714	0	•	0	0	96	45	0	21	•	263	0	0
Royalties **5**	1	0	•	0	0	0	0	1	0	•	0	0	0
Other Portfolio Income **6**	25470	10234	•	0	15	362	1082	2399	8369	•	34	0	0
Other Receipts **7**	129351	8	•	922	11964	14462	21170	6799	14683	•	32339	0	0
Total Receipts **8**	14999659	85461	•	369816	1958140	994775	3454743	1713912	2203291	•	2079029	0	0
Average Total Receipts **9**	9855	28487	•	1078	5180	19130	27861	68556	95795	•	346505		
Operating Costs/Operating Income (%)													
Cost of Operations **10**	71.5	72.1	•	61.8	66.7	69.0	72.5	75.4	74.9	•	70.5	•	•
Salaries and Wages **11**	4.4	1.9	•	1.1	6.5	2.8	4.7	4.1	4.3	•	4.0	•	•
Taxes Paid **12**	1.8	1.4	•	2.5	2.4	2.4	1.9	1.6	1.4	•	1.5	•	•
Interest Paid **13**	1.1	•	•	0.5	0.8	0.8	0.4	0.6	0.8	•	3.9	•	•
Depreciation **14**	3.1	1.3	•	0.7	2.3	2.6	2.5	2.4	3.9	•	3.9	•	•
Amortization and Depletion **15**	0.2	•	•	0.1	0.0	0.3	0.0	0.3	0.5	•	0.6	•	•
Pensions and Other Deferred Comp. **16**	0.7	•	•	0.0	1.5	0.4	0.6	0.3	0.5	•	1.1	•	•
Employee Benefits **17**	2.3	1.3	•	4.2	3.5	1.1	2.6	2.3	2.0	•	1.0	•	•
Advertising **18**	0.1	•	•	0.4	0.2	0.1	0.3	0.1	0.1	•	0.1	•	•
Other Expenses **19**	5.6	•	•	15.7	5.4	7.8	5.0	5.2	5.3	•	5.6	•	•
Officers' Compensation **20**	2.5	•	•	7.5	5.9	3.3	2.8	1.0	1.4	•	0.6	•	•
Operating Margin **21**	6.6	24.4	•	5.5	4.7	9.5	6.8	6.7	4.8	•	7.2	•	•
Operating Margin Before Officers' Comp. **22**	9.1	24.4	•	13.0	10.6	12.8	9.5	7.7	6.1	•	7.8	•	•

Selected Average Balance Sheet ($ in Thousands)

	Col 1	Col 2	Col 3	Col 4	Col 5	Col 6	Col 7	Col 8	Col 9
Net Receivables 23	1502	0	187	736	2553	3781	10285	15590	60536
Inventories 24	971	0	108	303	1598	2256	5713	9577	74832
Net Property, Plant and Equipment 25	1848	0	21	561	1669	3883	12131	19360	131858
Total Assets 26	7628	0	638	2149	8684	13563	36831	69701	699731
Notes and Loans Payable 27	1745	0	89	607	1859	2501	8524	11226	217167
All Other Liabilities 28	1874	0	109	542	1502	3292	9996	18637	173344
Net Worth 29	4008	0	440	999	5322	7770	18312	39838	309220

Selected Financial Ratios (Times to 1)

	Col 1	Col 2	Col 3	Col 4	Col 5	Col 6	Col 7	Col 8	Col 9
Current Ratio 30	2.2		4.0	2.5	3.2	2.4	1.6	2.1	1.9
Quick Ratio 31	1.4		3.1	1.8	2.1	1.5	1.1	1.3	0.8
Net Sales to Working Capital 32	4.8		2.5	5.6	4.4	5.5	8.8	4.6	4.1
Coverage Ratio 33	8.4		12.7	7.4	15.8	19.5	13.3	8.2	3.6
Total Asset Turnover 34	1.3		1.7	2.4	2.2	2.0	1.9	1.4	0.5
Inventory Turnover 35	7.2		6.2	11.3	8.1	8.9	9.0	7.4	3.2
Receivables Turnover 36	8.4		8.4	9.2	9.2	9.9	7.7	8.0	
Total Liabilities to Net Worth 37	0.9		0.5	1.2	0.6	0.7	1.0	0.7	1.3
Current Assets to Working Capital 38	1.8		1.3	1.7	1.5	1.7	2.7	1.9	2.1
Current Liabilities to Working Capital 39	0.8		0.3	0.7	0.5	0.7	1.7	0.9	1.1
Working Capital to Net Sales 40	0.2		0.4	0.2	0.2	0.2	0.1	0.2	0.2
Inventory to Working Capital 41	0.6		0.3	0.4	0.4	0.6	0.8	0.6	0.9
Total Receipts to Cash Flow 42	8.9	2.8	6.3	14.5	7.0	9.6	9.5	10.3	6.7
Cost of Goods to Cash Flow 43	6.3	2.0	3.9	9.7	4.9	7.0	7.2	7.7	4.7
Cash Flow to Total Debt 44	0.3		0.9	0.3	0.8	0.5	0.4	0.3	0.1

Selected Financial Factors (in Percentages)

	Col 1	Col 2	Col 3	Col 4	Col 5	Col 6	Col 7	Col 8	Col 9
Debt Ratio 45	47.5		31.1	53.5	38.7	42.7	50.3	42.8	55.8
Return on Total Assets 46	11.4		10.5	14.8	25.7	16.0	14.5	9.1	6.8
Return on Equity Before Income Taxes 47	19.1		14.0	27.5	39.2	26.5	27.0	14.0	11.2
Return on Equity After Income Taxes 48	17.6		13.8	26.5	35.8	25.3	25.4	12.4	9.6
Profit Margin (Before Income Tax) 49	7.9	38.0	5.7	5.3	11.1	7.4	7.3	5.9	10.3
Profit Margin (After Income Tax) 50	7.3	38.0	5.7	5.2	10.1	7.1	6.8	5.2	8.8

Table I

Corporations with and without Net Income

CUTLERY, HARDWARE, SPRING AND WIRE MACHINE SHOPS, NUT, BOLT

MONEY AMOUNTS AND SIZE OF ASSETS IN THOUSANDS OF DOLLARS

Item Description for Accounting Period 7/10 Through 6/11	Total	Zero Assets	Under 500	500 to 1,000	1,000 to 5,000	5,000 to 10,000	10,000 to 25,000	25,000 to 50,000	50,000 to 100,000	100,000 to 250,000	250,000 to 500,000	500,000 to 2,500,000	2,500,000 and over
Number of Enterprises **1**	20810	3441	12535	1374	2493	455	362	73	33	20	13	8	3
Revenues ($ in Thousands)													
Net Sales **2**	65600741	501797	5037638	2892470	9057258	5479887	8501550	4043555	2879348	2997215	4594532	5736401	13879090
Interest **3**	320206	647	389	988	6669	4647	3959	13880	3979	2618	8133	7353	266944
Rents **4**	19565	45	18	0	1848	1935	3546	484	820	6388	320	2848	1312
Royalties **5**	362315	0	0	0	29	0	1555	29	2792	2807	3193	11979	339930
Other Portfolio Income **6**	303151	9232	8456	7114	26310	4751	9216	16432	10158	17466	128810	43891	21314
Other Receipts **7**	821951	199	10156	7816	60324	14014	42984	28643	18652	14996	213591	119094	291485
Total Receipts **8**	67427929	511920	5056657	2908388	9152438	5505234	8562810	4103023	2915749	3041490	4948579	5921566	14800075
Average Total Receipts **9**	3240	149	403	2117	3671	12099	23654	56206	88356	152074	380660	740196	4933358
Operating Costs/Operating Income (%)													
Cost of Operations **10**	63.8	41.7	52.6	57.2	60.3	65.6	67.8	75.2	72.6	70.8	76.0	62.3	58.8
Salaries and Wages **11**	7.8	10.4	7.9	8.1	8.7	5.0	6.7	5.0	5.7	6.5	7.4	7.9	10.5
Taxes Paid **12**	2.2	4.7	2.9	3.8	3.3	2.7	2.1	1.7	1.5	1.9	1.4	1.3	1.6
Interest Paid **13**	2.4	4.7	0.9	0.9	1.4	0.5	1.3	0.9	1.0	1.4	3.7	2.1	6.1
Depreciation **14**	2.8	5.6	2.0	4.2	3.1	2.5	3.7	2.8	3.4	3.1	2.8	2.7	1.7
Amortization and Depletion **15**	1.0	0.2	0.2	0.0	0.1	0.1	0.3	0.4	0.5	0.9	1.1	1.9	2.7
Pensions and Other Deferred Comp. **16**	1.1	0.2	0.8	0.8	0.4	0.6	0.4	0.4	0.8	0.4	0.7	0.8	2.9
Employee Benefits **17**	1.7	0.6	1.2	1.1	2.4	1.6	2.0	1.4	1.6	1.5	1.5	1.7	1.6
Advertising **18**	0.8	0.1	0.7	0.1	0.3	0.4	0.8	0.3	0.6	0.7	0.7	1.9	1.3
Other Expenses **19**	11.6	26.9	17.9	12.1	9.8	8.1	8.0	6.4	7.1	8.4	7.2	12.6	17.4
Officers' Compensation **20**	3.2	8.8	7.1	8.9	6.7	5.0	2.8	1.4	1.3	1.1	0.8	0.8	0.8
Operating Margin **21**	1.8	•	5.8	2.9	3.6	7.9	4.1	4.2	3.9	3.3	•	4.0	•
Operating Margin Before Officers' Comp. **22**	5.0	5.0	12.9	11.8	10.3	12.9	6.8	5.6	5.2	4.4	•	4.8	•

Selected Average Balance Sheet ($ in Thousands)

Net Receivables 23	449	0	23	267	503	1593	3069	8110	12516	28747	72667	83614	806616
Inventories 24	370	0	20	85	392	1980	3733	9273	14964	22191	51876	112056	308764
Net Property, Plant and Equipment 25	426	0	31	180	578	1361	4437	8846	16379	28059	47073	131670	385372
Total Assets 26	7075	0	135	741	2224	7014	15490	35781	68658	147973	369560	940051	36673536
Notes and Loans Payable 27	2184	0	85	277	845	1152	5129	6801	18546	38054	165460	274930	11097739
All Other Liabilities 28	3124	0	26	201	465	1138	3099	9022	17250	44396	89731	203682	18895810
Net Worth 29	1768	0	24	263	914	4723	7261	19958	32862	65522	114370	461439	6679987

Selected Financial Ratios (Times to 1)

Current Ratio 30	1.5	•	2.2	1.7	2.1	3.4	2.0	2.5	2.1	1.8	2.1	2.8	0.7
Quick Ratio 31	0.9	•	1.5	1.3	1.3	2.1	1.0	1.2	1.1	1.0	1.2	1.6	0.4
Net Sales to Working Capital 32	7.6	•	8.7	10.5	5.4	3.6	5.2	4.1	4.8	4.7	4.7	2.7	•
Coverage Ratio 33	3.2	0.6	8.0	5.0	4.3	18.7	4.7	7.7	6.1	4.5	2.3	4.4	1.8
Total Asset Turnover 34	0.4	•	3.0	2.8	1.6	1.7	1.5	1.5	1.3	1.0	1.0	0.8	0.1
Inventory Turnover 35	5.4	•	10.6	14.1	5.6	4.0	4.3	4.5	4.2	4.8	5.2	4.0	8.8
Receivables Turnover 36	7.5	•	18.9	7.3	7.6	7.5	8.3	7.7	7.1	6.5	4.7	9.4	6.4
Total Liabilities to Net Worth 37	3.0	•	4.6	1.8	1.4	0.5	1.1	0.8	1.1	1.3	2.2	1.0	4.5
Current Assets to Working Capital 38	3.0	•	1.8	2.5	1.9	1.4	2.0	1.7	1.9	2.3	1.9	1.6	•
Current Liabilities to Working Capital 39	2.0	•	0.8	1.5	0.9	0.4	1.0	0.7	0.9	1.3	0.9	0.6	•
Working Capital to Net Sales 40	0.1	•	0.1	0.1	0.2	0.3	0.2	0.2	0.2	0.2	0.2	0.4	•
Inventory to Working Capital 41	0.9	•	0.5	0.4	0.6	0.5	0.9	0.7	0.8	0.8	0.7	0.5	•
Total Receipts to Cash Flow 42	7.5	5.4	5.2	9.6	9.4	7.6	9.4	9.9	9.3	8.9	11.5	5.8	5.9
Cost of Goods to Cash Flow 43	4.8	2.2	2.8	5.5	5.7	5.0	6.4	7.4	6.8	6.3	8.8	3.6	3.5
Cash Flow to Total Debt 44	0.1	•	0.7	0.5	0.3	0.7	0.3	0.4	0.3	0.2	0.1	0.3	0.0

Selected Financial Factors (in Percentages)

Debt Ratio 45	75.0	•	82.2	64.5	58.9	32.7	53.1	44.2	52.1	55.7	69.1	50.9	81.8
Return on Total Assets 46	3.5	•	21.0	12.2	9.7	15.1	9.2	10.1	7.8	6.5	8.2	7.0	1.4
Return on Equity Before Income Taxes 47	9.6	•	103.6	27.6	18.1	21.3	15.5	15.8	13.6	11.4	15.1	11.0	3.5
Return on Equity After Income Taxes 48	7.8	•	102.1	23.8	16.4	19.8	13.8	13.0	11.7	8.6	11.3	7.6	2.2
Profit Margin (Before Income Tax) 49	5.4	•	6.2	3.4	4.6	8.4	4.8	5.7	5.1	5.0	4.9	7.1	5.0
Profit Margin (After Income Tax) 50	4.3	•	6.1	3.0	4.1	7.8	4.3	4.7	4.4	3.8	3.7	4.9	3.1

113

Table II

Corporations with Net Income

CUTLERY, HARDWARE, SPRING AND WIRE MACHINE SHOPS, NUT, BOLT

MONEY AMOUNTS AND SIZE OF ASSETS IN THOUSANDS OF DOLLARS

Item Description for Accounting Period 7/10 Through 6/11	Total	Zero Assets	Under 500	500 to 1,000	1,000 to 5,000	5,000 to 10,000	10,000 to 25,000	25,000 to 50,000	50,000 to 100,000	100,000 to 250,000	250,000 to 500,000	500,000 to 2,500,000	2,500,000 and over
Number of Enterprises **1**	13227	•	7407	1082	1945	435	263	55	•	16	10	•	0
Revenues ($ in Thousands)													
Net Sales **2**	51682885	•	3528741	2266055	7869976	5315465	6911908	3009245	•	2557141	3616771	0	0
Interest **3**	299379	•	343	881	6110	2061	3636	12660	•	2486	7522	0	0
Rents **4**	18575	•	0	0	1759	1935	3093	121	•	6375	265	0	0
Royalties **5**	42007	•	0	0	29	0	1555	29	•	2642	3193	0	0
Other Portfolio Income **6**	265995	•	7092	6981	13279	4479	5693	4016	•	17341	128170	0	0
Other Receipts **7**	746595	•	2081	6604	52961	13539	28269	25509	•	13344	210237	0	0
Total Receipts **8**	53055436	•	3538257	2280521	7944114	5337479	6954154	3051580	•	2599329	3966158	0	0
Average Total Receipts **9**	4011	•	478	2108	4084	12270	26442	55483	•	162458	396616	•	•
Operating Costs/Operating Income (%)													
Cost of Operations **10**	62.7	•	49.8	55.7	58.8	65.8	65.8	72.0	•	70.7	76.0	•	•
Salaries and Wages **11**	7.3	•	6.4	8.7	8.8	4.9	6.6	5.6	•	6.4	8.0	•	•
Taxes Paid **12**	2.1	•	2.5	3.4	3.1	2.6	2.0	1.7	•	1.9	1.3	•	•
Interest Paid **13**	2.3	•	0.8	0.5	1.1	0.4	1.0	0.6	•	1.2	3.9	•	•
Depreciation **14**	2.5	•	1.7	2.8	3.0	2.3	3.0	2.7	•	2.9	3.0	•	•
Amortization and Depletion **15**	0.9	•	0.3	0.0	0.1	0.1	0.1	0.2	•	0.5	1.0	•	•
Pensions and Other Deferred Comp. **16**	0.9	•	1.1	0.6	0.4	0.6	0.4	0.4	•	0.5	0.6	•	•
Employee Benefits **17**	1.7	•	0.9	0.9	2.2	1.6	2.1	1.6	•	1.5	1.6	•	•
Advertising **18**	0.8	•	0.8	0.1	0.3	0.4	1.0	0.4	•	0.8	0.7	•	•
Other Expenses **19**	10.7	•	17.0	11.4	9.4	7.9	8.0	6.1	•	7.9	6.9	•	•
Officers' Compensation **20**	3.4	•	6.9	9.3	6.5	5.1	2.9	1.4	•	1.1	0.8	•	•
Operating Margin **21**	4.6	•	11.8	6.7	6.3	8.4	7.2	7.2	•	4.7	•	•	•
Operating Margin Before Officers' Comp. **22**	7.9	•	18.7	16.0	12.8	13.5	10.1	8.7	•	5.8	•	•	•

Selected Average Balance Sheet ($ in Thousands)

Net Receivables 23	570	•	21	312	562	1611	3333	8638	• 32196	70962
Inventories 24	425	•	12	81	349	1864	3730	9712	• 25717	37280
Net Property, Plant and Equipment 25	485	•	33	94	549	1261	4242	7896	• 28652	41247
Total Assets 26	8759	•	114	749	2131	7045	15830	36201	• 151168	361218
Notes and Loans Payable 27	2553	•	72	223	795	1048	4065	5257	• 33579	158302
All Other Liabilities 28	4520	•	19	218	380	1141	2928	8547	• 47754	82272
Net Worth 29	1685	•	24	309	956	4856	8837	22397	• 69835	120645

Selected Financial Ratios (Times to 1)

Current Ratio 30	1.8	•	1.8	2.0	2.4	3.5	2.5	2.7	• 1.8	2.1
Quick Ratio 31	1.0	•	1.3	1.6	1.6	2.1	1.3	1.3	• 0.9	1.2
Net Sales to Working Capital 32	5.8	•	15.1	7.5	5.3	3.5	4.5	3.5	• 4.8	4.8
Coverage Ratio 33	4.5	•	15.4	15.4	7.5	23.3	9.0	15.6	• 6.3	2.7
Total Asset Turnover 34	0.4	•	4.2	2.8	1.9	1.7	1.7	1.5	• 1.1	1.0
Inventory Turnover 35	5.8	•	19.0	14.4	6.8	4.3	4.6	4.1	• 4.4	7.4
Receivables Turnover 36	7.5	•	25.1	7.9	8.4	8.0	8.7	7.4	•	5.7
Total Liabilities to Net Worth 37	4.2	•	3.8	1.4	1.2	0.5	0.8	0.6	• 1.2	2.0
Current Assets to Working Capital 38	2.3	•	2.2	2.0	1.7	1.4	1.7	1.6	• 2.3	1.9
Current Liabilities to Working Capital 39	1.3	•	1.2	1.0	0.7	0.4	0.7	0.6	• 1.3	0.9
Working Capital to Net Sales 40	0.2	•	0.1	0.1	0.2	0.3	0.2	0.3	• 0.2	0.2
Inventory to Working Capital 41	0.7	•	0.4	0.3	0.5	0.5	0.7	0.7	• 0.8	0.7
Total Receipts to Cash Flow 42	6.6	•	4.1	7.2	7.7	7.5	7.3	7.5	• 8.0	10.8
Cost of Goods to Cash Flow 43	4.1	•	2.0	4.0	4.6	4.9	4.8	5.4	• 5.7	8.2
Cash Flow to Total Debt 44	0.1	•	1.3	0.7	0.4	0.7	0.5	0.5	• 0.2	0.1

Selected Financial Factors (in Percentages)

Debt Ratio 45	80.8	•	79.2	58.8	55.1	31.1	44.2	38.1	• 53.8	66.6
Return on Total Assets 46	4.7	•	54.1	21.8	15.9	16.0	14.5	14.0	• 8.3	10.5
Return on Equity Before Income Taxes 47	18.9	•	242.9	49.6	30.6	22.2	23.1	21.2	• 15.0	19.6
Return on Equity After Income Taxes 48	15.9	•	240.5	45.5	28.5	20.7	21.2	18.0	• 11.8	14.9
Profit Margin (Before Income Tax) 49	8.2	•	12.1	7.3	7.2	8.8	7.8	8.7	• 6.6	6.5
Profit Margin (After Income Tax) 50	6.8	•	12.0	6.7	6.7	8.2	7.1	7.3	• 5.1	5.0

114

Table I

Corporations with and without Net Income

ARCHITECTURAL AND STRUCTURAL METALS

MONEY AMOUNTS AND SIZE OF ASSETS IN THOUSANDS OF DOLLARS

Item Description for Accounting Period 7/10 Through 6/11	Total	Zero Assets	Under 500	500 to 1,000	1,000 to 5,000	5,000 to 10,000	10,000 to 25,000	25,000 to 50,000	50,000 to 100,000	100,000 to 250,000	250,000 to 500,000	500,000 to 2,500,000	2,500,000 and over
Number of Enterprises **1**	7270	267	3940	853	1616	250	221	68	23	13	10	9	0
Revenues ($ in Thousands)													
Net Sales **2**	42698372	248441	1977988	1603379	7192913	3484883	5589245	3325467	2109460	2993043	3418835	10754719	0
Interest **3**	91862	16	696	370	2596	1218	2416	2534	2670	4939	30795	43613	0
Rents **4**	10206	0	0	0	335	7	1404	332	231	556	52	7290	0
Royalties **5**	45007	0	0	0	1343	81	0	109	0	235	138	43101	0
Other Portfolio Income **6**	160240	15368	36278	812	13090	1482	3727	3006	5441	457	6916	73662	0
Other Receipts **7**	422645	1852	2424	9252	81957	36348	28163	21019	10209	19933	44854	166633	0
Total Receipts **8**	43428332	265677	2017386	1613813	7292234	3524019	5624955	3352467	2128011	3019163	3501590	11089018	0
Average Total Receipts **9**	5974	995	512	1892	4513	14096	25452	49301	92522	232243	350159	1232113	•
Operating Costs/Operating Income (%)													
Cost of Operations **10**	73.4	61.0	66.5	71.7	71.2	78.9	70.6	75.8	70.4	70.4	79.4	75.3	•
Salaries and Wages **11**	6.9	8.4	5.7	8.3	6.7	4.8	7.6	6.2	8.0	8.0	5.8	7.3	•
Taxes Paid **12**	2.0	2.8	3.5	1.9	2.8	2.6	1.9	1.6	1.7	1.8	1.2	1.5	•
Interest Paid **13**	1.9	1.7	0.7	0.7	0.6	0.5	0.7	1.4	0.9	1.3	3.7	4.1	•
Depreciation **14**	2.7	1.6	2.2	1.1	2.2	2.1	2.2	2.5	2.3	2.4	3.3	3.7	•
Amortization and Depletion **15**	0.4	1.2	0.0	0.0	0.0	0.0	0.4	0.3	0.3	0.5	1.3	0.4	•
Pensions and Other Defered Comp. **16**	0.7	0.2	0.7	0.1	0.4	0.9	0.4	0.3	0.4	0.4	3.0	0.9	•
Employee Benefits **17**	2.1	5.7	1.1	2.8	3.0	0.7	2.0	1.3	1.5	2.5	0.8	2.7	•
Advertising **18**	0.5	0.3	0.4	0.6	0.4	0.3	0.3	0.4	0.5	0.6	0.2	0.8	•
Other Expenses **19**	9.6	11.2	17.0	11.7	11.4	8.3	9.1	7.8	8.5	8.4	8.5	8.8	•
Officers' Compensation **20**	2.0	2.3	7.3	4.1	3.1	3.7	1.9	1.5	2.2	0.6	0.9	0.5	•
Operating Margin **21**	•	3.3	•	•	•	•	3.0	1.0	3.3	3.0	•	•	•
Operating Margin Before Officers' Comp. **22**	•	5.6	2.3	1.0	1.3	0.8	4.8	2.5	5.5	3.5	•	•	•

Selected Average Balance Sheet ($ in Thousands)

Net Receivables 23	940	0	54	217	770	2566	3591	7340	14006	33833	47208	225330
Inventories 24	617	0	16	116	413	1432	2967	6529	12712	25237	26170	146071
Net Property, Plant and Equipment 25	1067	0	38	205	471	1866	3979	7267	12844	41292	75932	359660
Total Assets 26	4587	0	163	796	2235	7851	15583	33693	72671	165183	337079	1503077
Notes and Loans Payable 27	1659	0	80	307	722	2217	4206	7331	17386	56144	88688	702283
All Other Liabilities 28	1191	0	48	229	632	1801	3481	9804	17057	43949	87084	392687
Net Worth 29	1737	0	35	259	882	3833	7896	16558	38228	65090	161306	408107

Selected Financial Ratios (Times to 1)

Current Ratio 30	1.7	•	1.2	2.2	2.1	1.9	2.0	1.8	2.3	1.6	2.2	1.4
Quick Ratio 31	1.1	•	0.9	1.7	1.5	1.2	1.2	1.0	1.4	1.0	1.3	0.7
Net Sales to Working Capital 32	6.1	•	31.6	6.3	5.3	5.3	5.5	5.2	4.3	7.6	3.9	8.9
Coverage Ratio 33	0.9	7.1	•	•	0.4	•	6.5	2.3	5.7	3.9	•	0.5
Total Asset Turnover 34	1.3	•	3.1	2.4	2.0	1.8	1.6	1.5	1.3	1.4	1.0	0.8
Inventory Turnover 35	7.0	•	20.6	11.6	7.7	7.7	6.0	5.7	5.1	6.4	10.4	6.2
Receivables Turnover 36	6.5	•	9.2	10.2	5.4	6.9	6.6	6.2	6.2	6.8	8.5	5.9
Total Liabilities to Net Worth 37	1.6	•	3.6	2.1	1.5	1.0	1.0	1.0	0.9	1.5	1.1	2.7
Current Assets to Working Capital 38	2.4	•	7.2	1.9	1.9	2.2	2.0	2.2	1.8	2.7	1.9	3.7
Current Liabilities to Working Capital 39	1.4	•	6.2	0.9	0.9	1.2	1.0	1.2	0.8	1.7	0.9	2.7
Working Capital to Net Sales 40	0.2	•	0.0	0.2	0.2	0.2	0.2	0.2	0.2	0.1	0.3	0.1
Inventory to Working Capital 41	0.7	•	0.9	0.4	0.4	0.6	0.7	0.7	0.5	0.8	0.4	1.4
Total Receipts to Cash Flow 42	16.2	5.5	16.2	19.4	14.6	24.4	9.5	14.8	9.0	10.0	240.9	27.2
Cost of Goods to Cash Flow 43	11.9	3.4	10.8	13.9	10.4	19.3	6.7	11.3	6.3	7.1	191.2	20.5
Cash Flow to Total Debt 44	0.1	•	0.2	0.2	0.2	0.1	0.3	0.2	0.3	0.2	0.0	0.0

Selected Financial Factors (in Percentages)

Debt Ratio 45	62.1	•	78.4	67.4	60.6	51.2	49.3	50.9	47.4	60.6	52.1	72.8
Return on Total Assets 46	2.1	•	•	•	0.6	•	6.9	4.6	6.4	7.2	•	1.8
Return on Equity Before Income Taxes 47	•	•	•	•	•	•	11.5	5.3	10.1	13.6	•	•
Return on Equity After Income Taxes 48	•	•	•	•	•	•	10.6	4.1	8.6	12.1	•	•
Profit Margin (Before Income Tax) 49	•	10.3	•	•	•	•	3.6	1.8	4.2	3.8	•	•
Profit Margin (After Income Tax) 50	•	9.3	•	•	•	•	3.3	1.4	3.6	3.4	•	•

Table II
Corporations with Net Income

ARCHITECTURAL AND STRUCTURAL METALS

MONEY AMOUNTS AND SIZE OF ASSETS IN THOUSANDS OF DOLLARS

Item Description for Accounting Period 7/10 Through 6/11	Total	Zero Assets	Under 500	500 to 1,000	1,000 to 5,000	5,000 to 10,000	10,000 to 25,000	25,000 to 50,000	50,000 to 100,000	100,000 to 250,000	250,000 to 500,000	500,000 to 2,500,000	2,500,000 and over
Number of Enterprises 1	3330	261	•	363	753	97	165	44	15	•	4	4	0
Revenues ($ in Thousands)													
Net Sales 2	23520977	194849	•	862810	3664997	1171680	4457379	2188578	1818964	•	1592952	4320492	0
Interest 3	42320	16	•	126	1417	459	1700	1787	211	•	16060	17679	0
Rents 4	3897	0	•	0	335	7	790	0	214	•	5	1990	0
Royalties 5	25178	0	•	0	1343	0	0	0	0	•	0	23599	0
Other Portfolio Income 6	64346	12987	•	0	10304	93	2710	1672	5320	•	0	4818	0
Other Receipts 7	201754	1118	•	6663	15131	1902	26102	14829	11360	•	10243	97617	0
Total Receipts 8	23858472	208970	•	869599	3693527	1174141	4488681	2206866	1836069	•	1619260	4466195	0
Average Total Receipts 9	7165	801	•	2396	4905	12105	27204	50156	122405	•	404815	1116549	•
Operating Costs/Operating Income (%)													
Cost of Operations 10	70.9	64.5	•	74.1	65.8	67.2	69.1	75.1	70.5	•	82.1	73.1	•
Salaries and Wages 11	6.0	6.9	•	5.8	4.8	4.3	7.8	5.3	7.2	•	2.0	6.4	•
Taxes Paid 12	1.9	2.2	•	1.7	2.5	2.5	1.9	1.7	1.7	•	1.0	1.6	•
Interest Paid 13	1.0	1.2	•	0.3	0.4	0.4	0.5	0.9	0.4	•	0.7	2.3	•
Depreciation 14	2.6	1.4	•	0.8	2.4	3.0	2.1	2.1	2.4	•	3.7	3.8	•
Amortization and Depletion 15	0.2	1.5	•	•	0.0	0.0	0.2	0.2	0.2	•	0.9	0.2	•
Pensions and Other Deferred Comp. 16	0.6	0.2	•	0.0	0.3	0.5	0.4	0.2	0.4	•	0.1	1.5	•
Employee Benefits 17	1.8	2.2	•	2.5	2.3	0.7	1.9	0.9	1.0	•	0.8	2.3	•
Advertising 18	0.5	0.1	•	0.6	0.6	0.4	0.3	0.4	0.4	•	0.0	0.7	•
Other Expenses 19	8.9	9.6	•	9.6	11.6	9.6	8.8	5.8	7.3	•	4.1	10.3	•
Officers' Compensation 20	2.0	1.0	•	3.2	3.2	3.6	1.9	1.6	2.2	•	0.8	0.5	•
Operating Margin 21	3.8	9.1	•	1.4	6.0	7.8	5.1	5.7	6.3	•	3.7	•	•
Operating Margin Before Officers' Comp. 22	5.8	10.1	•	4.6	9.2	11.4	7.1	7.3	8.5	•	4.5	•	•

Selected Average Balance Sheet ($ in Thousands)

Net Receivables **23**	1040	0	•	253	660	2096	3593	6410	15666	55431	220247
Inventories **24**	702	0	•	121	393	1526	3156	6541	14349	18426	152935
Net Property, Plant and Equipment **25**	1033	0	•	98	388	1564	3811	7502	16683	92778	223647
Total Assets **26**	5376	0	•	738	2069	7220	15460	34449	69514	322909	1731121
Notes and Loans Payable **27**	1533	0	•	157	410	1475	3162	6524	9966	53783	677184
All Other Liabilities **28**	1311	0	•	310	468	1754	3330	9408	16667	86508	406112
Net Worth **29**	2533	0	•	271	1191	3991	8968	18516	42880	182617	647825

Selected Financial Ratios (Times to 1)

Current Ratio **30**	1.7	•	•	2.5	3.1	2.9	2.3	2.1	2.4	3.0	0.9
Quick Ratio **31**	1.1	•	•	1.8	2.1	1.9	1.4	1.0	1.4	2.2	0.5
Net Sales to Working Capital **32**	6.2	•	•	6.2	4.4	3.3	4.9	4.8	4.6	3.0	•
Coverage Ratio **33**	6.8	14.9	•	9.8	17.9	20.6	12.8	8.5	20.4	8.3	2.1
Total Asset Turnover **34**	1.3	•	•	3.2	2.4	1.7	1.7	1.4	1.7	1.2	0.6
Inventory Turnover **35**	7.1	•	•	14.5	8.2	5.3	5.9	5.7	6.0	17.7	5.2
Receivables Turnover **36**	6.8	•	•	13.5	6.6	6.7	6.5	6.3	7.2	•	•
Total Liabilities to Net Worth **37**	1.1	•	•	1.7	0.7	0.8	0.7	0.9	0.6	0.8	1.7
Current Assets to Working Capital **38**	2.4	•	•	1.7	1.5	1.5	1.8	1.9	1.7	1.5	•
Current Liabilities to Working Capital **39**	1.4	•	•	0.7	0.5	0.5	0.8	0.9	0.7	0.5	•
Working Capital to Net Sales **40**	0.2	•	•	0.2	0.2	0.3	0.2	0.2	0.2	0.3	•
Inventory to Working Capital **41**	0.7	•	•	0.4	0.4	0.5	0.6	0.7	0.5	0.1	•
Total Receipts to Cash Flow **42**	8.5	4.5	•	11.8	6.8	6.9	7.9	10.1	7.6	12.0	10.8
Cost of Goods to Cash Flow **43**	6.1	2.9	•	8.7	4.5	4.6	5.5	7.6	5.4	9.8	7.9
Cash Flow to Total Debt **44**	0.3	•	•	0.4	0.8	0.5	0.5	0.3	0.6	0.2	0.1

Selected Financial Factors (in Percentages)

Debt Ratio **45**	52.9	•	•	63.2	42.4	44.7	42.0	46.3	38.3	43.4	62.6
Return on Total Assets **46**	8.6	•	•	8.0	16.9	14.1	11.0	10.7	13.3	7.5	3.0
Return on Equity Before Income Taxes **47**	15.5	•	•	19.6	27.7	24.3	17.5	17.5	20.5	11.7	4.2
Return on Equity After Income Taxes **48**	13.8	•	•	17.4	26.4	22.3	16.5	16.0	18.5	7.9	2.8
Profit Margin (Before Income Tax) **49**	5.6	16.3	•	2.2	6.8	8.0	5.8	6.5	7.2	5.4	2.5
Profit Margin (After Income Tax) **50**	5.0	15.1	•	2.0	6.5	7.4	5.5	5.9	6.6	3.6	1.7

Table I

Corporations with and without Net Income

BOILER, TANK, AND SHIPPING CONTAINER

MONEY AMOUNTS AND SIZE OF ASSETS IN THOUSANDS OF DOLLARS

Item Description for Accounting Period 7/10 Through 6/11	Total	Zero Assets	Under 500	500 to 1,000	1,000 to 5,000	5,000 to 10,000	10,000 to 25,000	25,000 to 50,000	50,000 to 100,000	100,000 to 250,000	250,000 to 500,000	500,000 to 2,500,000	2,500,000 and over
Number of Enterprises **1**	542	•	0	•	235	28	44	•	16	7	6	4	3
Revenues ($ in Thousands)													
Net Sales **2**	22393831	•	0	•	719700	185589	1213934	•	1355660	906852	1698235	3577281	11561378
Interest **3**	34793	•	0	•	313	96	428	•	336	1679	3044	3010	25795
Rents **4**	11571	•	0	•	2183	525	0	•	3	0	1629	2789	4100
Royalties **5**	117955	•	0	•	0	0	0	•	538	17	149	14952	102299
Other Portfolio Income **6**	245102	•	0	•	25995	39	225	•	1239	81	30394	29366	157555
Other Receipts **7**	304851	•	0	•	6	943	6711	•	14738	10074	16175	31187	218478
Total Receipts **8**	23108103	•	0	•	748197	187192	1221298	•	1372514	918703	1749626	3658585	12069605
Average Total Receipts **9**	42635	•	•	•	3184	6685	27757	•	85782	131243	291604	914646	4023202
Operating Costs/Operating Income (%)													
Cost of Operations **10**	78.1	•	•	•	67.8	70.0	77.0	•	71.1	70.2	74.1	78.7	81.5
Salaries and Wages **11**	3.3	•	•	•	6.2	6.7	6.0	•	5.7	4.4	4.9	2.7	2.2
Taxes Paid **12**	1.1	•	•	•	3.2	1.7	1.9	•	1.6	1.4	1.8	1.2	0.6
Interest Paid **13**	2.8	•	•	•	0.3	0.9	0.3	•	2.0	4.2	4.9	2.6	3.2
Depreciation **14**	3.3	•	•	•	0.9	1.8	2.6	•	2.7	9.3	3.8	3.7	3.0
Amortization and Depletion **15**	0.9	•	•	•	•	0.2	0.1	•	0.7	0.8	0.7	0.4	1.4
Pensions and Other Deferred Comp. **16**	0.6	•	•	•	0.5	0.2	0.3	•	0.7	0.5	0.1	0.6	0.7
Employee Benefits **17**	1.6	•	•	•	3.4	0.9	1.9	•	2.6	1.4	0.9	1.3	1.6
Advertising **18**	0.1	•	•	•	0.6	0.2	0.1	•	0.4	0.2	0.3	0.1	0.0
Other Expenses **19**	5.6	•	•	•	9.9	10.5	5.3	•	6.3	7.9	4.3	4.1	5.5
Officers' Compensation **20**	1.1	•	•	•	4.6	2.0	2.4	•	1.9	0.6	2.1	0.1	0.7
Operating Margin **21**	1.5	•	•	•	2.6	4.8	2.1	•	4.3	•	2.2	4.5	•
Operating Margin Before Officers' Comp. **22**	2.6	•	•	•	7.2	6.9	4.5	•	6.2	•	4.3	4.7	0.3

Selected Average Balance Sheet ($ in Thousands)

Net Receivables 23	4119	381	1229	3660	13990	15659	44526	87303	291305
Inventories 24	5260	514	391	4074	9046	11176	71406	126764	404928
Net Property, Plant and Equipment 25	7575	179	1888	2842	13834	34347	48930	230708	682156
Total Assets 26	43992	1470	6931	16818	65853	157956	357127	1179412	4292058
Notes and Loans Payable 27	20579	139	3376	2870	17879	67027	145898	480439	2390556
All Other Liabilities 28	12778	322	1220	4238	18770	30967	153243	245292	1355724
Net Worth 29	10634	1008	2335	9711	29204	59962	57987	453680	545778

Selected Financial Ratios (Times to 1)

Current Ratio 30	1.4	3.5	3.2	3.6	1.3	2.2	1.3	1.9	1.0
Quick Ratio 31	0.7	2.0	2.3	2.4	0.8	1.1	0.5	1.0	0.4
Net Sales to Working Capital 32	10.7	3.4	2.3	3.4	9.5	4.2	7.6	6.1	•
Coverage Ratio 33	2.7	25.2	7.5	9.5	3.8	1.1	2.1	3.7	2.3
Total Asset Turnover 34	0.9	2.1	1.0	1.6	1.3	0.8	0.8	0.8	0.9
Inventory Turnover 35	6.1	4.0	11.9	5.2	6.7	8.1	2.9	5.6	7.8
Receivables Turnover 36	10.6	7.3	8.5	6.4	7.6	6.6	5.9	10.9	16.1
Total Liabilities to Net Worth 37	3.1	0.5	2.0	0.7	1.3	1.6	5.2	1.6	6.9
Current Assets to Working Capital 38	3.3	1.4	1.5	1.4	4.0	1.9	4.1	2.1	•
Current Liabilities to Working Capital 39	2.3	0.4	0.5	0.4	3.0	0.9	3.1	1.1	•
Working Capital to Net Sales 40	0.1	0.3	0.4	0.3	0.1	0.2	0.1	0.2	•
Inventory to Working Capital 41	1.4	0.5	0.2	0.4	1.2	0.4	1.9	0.9	•
Total Receipts to Cash Flow 42	11.8	11.3	8.0	15.3	9.7	13.4	13.8	12.3	11.9
Cost of Goods to Cash Flow 43	9.2	7.6	5.6	11.8	6.9	9.4	10.2	9.7	9.7
Cash Flow to Total Debt 44	0.1	0.6	0.2	0.3	0.2	0.1	0.1	0.1	0.1

Selected Financial Factors (in Percentages)

Debt Ratio 45	75.8	31.4	66.3	42.3	55.7	62.0	83.8	61.5	87.3
Return on Total Assets 46	7.2	14.2	6.3	5.0	9.6	3.8	8.2	7.3	6.8
Return on Equity Before Income Taxes 47	19.0	19.8	16.2	7.8	16.0	0.9	26.6	13.8	30.4
Return on Equity After Income Taxes 48	15.0	16.3	15.7	6.3	13.6	0.7	19.6	9.1	24.9
Profit Margin (Before Income Tax) 49	4.9	6.5	5.7	2.7	5.5	0.4	5.4	7.0	4.3
Profit Margin (After Income Tax) 50	3.9	5.4	5.5	2.2	4.7	0.3	4.0	4.6	3.5

Table II
Corporations with Net Income

BOILER, TANK, AND SHIPPING CONTAINER

MONEY AMOUNTS AND SIZE OF ASSETS IN THOUSANDS OF DOLLARS

Item Description for Accounting Period 7/10 Through 6/11		Total	Zero Assets	Under 500	500 to 1,000	1,000 to 5,000	5,000 to 10,000	10,000 to 25,000	25,000 to 50,000	50,000 to 100,000	100,000 to 250,000	250,000 to 500,000	500,000 to 2,500,000	2,500,000 and over
Number of Enterprises	1	507	•	0	180	235	9	36	19	13	4	•	•	4
Revenues ($ in Thousands)														
Net Sales	2	21116873	•	0	162489	719700	100945	1007938	907802	1144618	551299	•	•	3577281
Interest	3	33162	•	0	0	313	67	428	0	204	262	•	•	3010
Rents	4	11348	•	0	0	2183	525	0	0	3	0	•	•	2789
Royalties	5	117475	•	0	0	0	0	0	0	58	17	•	•	14952
Other Portfolio Income	6	245008	•	0	0	25995	0	225	209	1239	42	•	•	29366
Other Receipts	7	296359	•	0	4285	6	256	6471	1595	11101	7597	•	•	31187
Total Receipts	8	21820225	•	0	166774	748197	101793	1015062	909606	1157223	559217	•	•	3658585
Average Total Receipts	9	43038	•	•	927	3184	11310	28196	47874	89017	139804	•	•	914646
Operating Costs/Operating Income (%)														
Cost of Operations	10	78.2	•	•	47.1	67.8	61.8	76.6	73.9	71.8	68.0	•	•	78.7
Salaries and Wages	11	3.2	•	•	13.9	6.2	5.9	6.1	4.4	5.2	5.3	•	•	2.7
Taxes Paid	12	1.1	•	•	3.7	3.2	2.7	2.0	1.7	1.8	1.4	•	•	1.2
Interest Paid	13	2.7	•	•	0.9	0.3	0.2	0.4	0.7	1.0	3.9	•	•	2.6
Depreciation	14	3.0	•	•	0.9	0.9	0.8	2.0	2.1	2.3	2.3	•	•	3.7
Amortization and Depletion	15	0.9	•	•	0.9	•	•	0.1	0.1	0.4	0.5	•	•	0.4
Pensions and Other Deferred Comp.	16	0.6	•	•	1.0	0.5	•	0.3	0.7	0.8	0.2	•	•	0.6
Employee Benefits	17	1.6	•	•	2.6	3.4	1.7	1.9	1.8	2.3	1.1	•	•	1.3
Advertising	18	0.1	•	•	1.0	0.6	0.0	0.1	0.3	0.4	0.2	•	•	0.1
Other Expenses	19	5.5	•	•	9.7	9.9	11.6	4.5	6.7	5.8	9.3	•	•	4.1
Officers' Compensation	20	1.1	•	•	8.1	4.6	2.5	1.9	2.0	1.4	0.6	•	•	0.1
Operating Margin	21	2.0	•	•	11.2	2.6	12.8	4.2	5.7	6.8	7.2	•	•	4.5
Operating Margin Before Officers' Comp.	22	3.1	•	•	19.3	7.2	15.3	6.1	7.7	8.2	7.8	•	•	4.7

Selected Average Balance Sheet ($ in Thousands)

Item												
Net Receivables 23	4094	•	•	75	381	1318	3874	5817	13970	21950	•	87303
Inventories 24	4948	•	•	115	425	453	3716	6172	11174	9722	•	138952
Net Property, Plant and Equipment 25	7412	•	•	284	179	633	2869	5793	12712	16069	•	230708
Total Assets 26	43966	•	•	734	1470	7104	16735	28198	65728	167332	•	1179412
Notes and Loans Payable 27	20245	•	•	107	139	229	3179	8275	12494	48610	•	480439
All Other Liabilities 28	12989	•	•	43	322	354	4109	7196	17446	39472	•	245292
Net Worth 29	10732	•	•	584	1008	6521	9446	12727	35788	79250	•	453680

Selected Financial Ratios (Times to 1)

Item											
Current Ratio 30	1.4	•	6.4	3.5	16.8	3.8	2.3	1.9	2.6	•	1.9
Quick Ratio 31	0.7	•	4.2	2.0	14.2	2.4	1.3	1.2	1.5	•	1.0
Net Sales to Working Capital 32	10.8	•	2.4	3.4	1.9	3.3	4.4	5.1	3.0	•	6.1
Coverage Ratio 33	3.1	•	17.0	25.2	88.8	15.1	9.2	8.9	3.2	•	3.7
Total Asset Turnover 34	0.9	•	1.2	2.1	1.6	1.7	1.7	1.3	0.8	•	0.8
Inventory Turnover 35	6.6	•	3.7	4.9	15.3	5.8	5.7	5.7	9.6	•	5.1
Receivables Turnover 36	12.1	•	9.6	9.0	17.0	6.1	7.8	•	•	•	1.6
Total Liabilities to Net Worth 37	3.1	•	0.3	0.5	0.1	0.8	1.2	0.8	1.1	•	1.6
Current Assets to Working Capital 38	3.3	•	1.2	1.4	1.1	1.4	1.8	2.1	1.6	•	2.1
Current Liabilities to Working Capital 39	2.3	•	0.2	0.4	0.1	0.4	0.8	1.1	0.6	•	1.1
Working Capital to Net Sales 40	0.1	•	0.4	0.3	0.5	0.3	0.2	0.2	0.3	•	0.2
Inventory to Working Capital 41	1.4	•	0.3	0.5	0.1	0.4	0.6	0.6	0.2	•	0.9
Total Receipts to Cash Flow 42	11.0	•	7.3	11.3	5.0	12.5	8.9	8.2	5.9	•	12.3
Cost of Goods to Cash Flow 43	8.6	•	3.5	7.6	3.1	9.6	6.5	5.9	4.0	•	9.7
Cash Flow to Total Debt 44	0.1	•	0.8	0.6	3.9	0.3	0.3	0.4	0.3	•	0.1

Selected Financial Factors (in Percentages)

Item											
Debt Ratio 45	75.6	•	20.4	31.4	8.2	43.6	54.9	45.6	52.6	•	61.5
Return on Total Assets 46	7.8	•	18.0	14.2	21.8	8.8	11.2	11.9	10.3	•	7.3
Return on Equity Before Income Taxes 47	21.6	•	21.3	19.8	23.5	14.6	22.2	19.3	15.0	•	13.8
Return on Equity After Income Taxes 48	17.4	•	21.3	16.3	22.9	12.7	22.2	16.9	14.8	•	9.1
Profit Margin (Before Income Tax) 49	5.6	•	13.8	6.5	13.6	4.9	5.9	7.9	8.6	•	7.0
Profit Margin (After Income Tax) 50	4.5	•	13.8	5.4	13.3	4.3	5.9	6.9	8.5	•	4.6

Table I

Corporations with and without Net Income

COATING, ENGRAVING, HEAT TREATING, AND ALLIED ACTIVITIES

MONEY AMOUNTS AND SIZE OF ASSETS IN THOUSANDS OF DOLLARS

Item Description for Accounting Period 7/10 Through 6/11	Total	Zero Assets	Under 500	500 to 1,000	1,000 to 5,000	5,000 to 10,000	10,000 to 25,000	25,000 to 50,000	50,000 to 100,000	100,000 to 250,000	250,000 to 500,000	500,000 to 2,500,000	2,500,000 and over
Number of Enterprises **1**	3851	•	1413	•	690	89	75	•	7	7	0	6	0

Revenues ($ in Thousands)

Item Description for Accounting Period 7/10 Through 6/11	Total	Zero Assets	Under 500	500 to 1,000	1,000 to 5,000	5,000 to 10,000	10,000 to 25,000	25,000 to 50,000	50,000 to 100,000	100,000 to 250,000	250,000 to 500,000	500,000 to 2,500,000	2,500,000 and over
Net Sales **2**	12211942	•	944479	•	2968306	1084164	1417788	•	730586	723230	0	2974663	0
Interest **3**	20340	•	313	•	547	1064	503	•	750	4924	0	12112	0
Rents **4**	11995	•	0	•	3124	571	1808	•	0	2150	0	2403	0
Royalties **5**	24492	•	0	•	0	594	0	•	465	14180	0	9252	0
Other Portfolio Income **6**	33779	•	127	•	6836	658	641	•	461	4904	0	20147	0
Other Receipts **7**	107485	•	5120	•	25984	5781	-1028	•	2180	3301	0	44715	0
Total Receipts **8**	12310033	•	950039	•	3004797	1092832	1419712	•	734442	752689	0	3063292	0
Average Total Receipts **9**	3197	•	672	•	4355	12279	18929	•	104920	107527	•	510549	•

Operating Costs/Operating Income (%)

Item Description for Accounting Period 7/10 Through 6/11	Total	Zero Assets	Under 500	500 to 1,000	1,000 to 5,000	5,000 to 10,000	10,000 to 25,000	25,000 to 50,000	50,000 to 100,000	100,000 to 250,000	250,000 to 500,000	500,000 to 2,500,000	2,500,000 and over
Cost of Operations **10**	60.7	•	40.0	•	55.1	62.5	65.0	•	68.9	69.5	•	68.0	•
Salaries and Wages **11**	7.4	•	10.4	•	9.9	5.1	7.0	•	7.6	7.8	•	6.1	•
Taxes Paid **12**	2.8	•	3.4	•	4.1	2.5	2.7	•	2.4	1.4	•	2.1	•
Interest Paid **13**	3.1	•	0.2	•	0.5	1.1	1.4	•	1.6	4.6	•	8.0	•
Depreciation **14**	4.0	•	1.6	•	4.0	4.9	4.2	•	3.2	6.9	•	4.2	•
Amortization and Depletion **15**	0.5	•	•	•	0.0	0.2	0.2	•	1.7	1.0	•	1.1	•
Pensions and Other Deferred Comp. **16**	0.5	•	0.2	•	0.7	0.2	1.0	•	0.3	0.5	•	0.6	•
Employee Benefits **17**	2.3	•	2.8	•	3.3	0.6	2.2	•	1.9	2.4	•	2.2	•
Advertising **18**	0.2	•	0.0	•	0.2	0.1	0.2	•	0.1	0.4	•	0.3	•
Other Expenses **19**	10.6	•	14.6	•	10.3	10.7	7.1	•	5.4	7.2	•	9.6	•
Officers' Compensation **20**	4.3	•	15.0	•	7.5	2.2	3.3	•	1.8	0.4	•	1.0	•
Operating Margin **21**	3.5	•	11.7	•	4.3	9.9	5.7	•	5.1	•	•	•	•
Operating Margin Before Officers' Comp. **22**	7.7	•	26.7	•	11.8	12.1	9.0	•	6.9	•	•	•	•

Selected Average Balance Sheet ($ in Thousands)

Net Receivables 23	480	47	544	1386	2922	12080	17977	120318
Inventories 24	226	9	128	619	995	10416	13091	64924
Net Property, Plant and Equipment 25	715	100	667	2429	5297	26813	48721	134509
Total Assets 26	3252	235	1995	8156	14861	68318	154547	1126492
Notes and Loans Payable 27	1188	79	643	2468	5320	24261	43502	466912
All Other Liabilities 28	790	35	429	1573	2032	16112	39117	313420
Net Worth 29	1273	121	923	4115	7509	27945	71928	346160

Selected Financial Ratios (Times to 1)

Current Ratio 30	2.0	2.5	2.3	1.3	2.4	2.3	1.9	1.9
Quick Ratio 31	1.4	2.4	1.8	1.0	1.8	1.3	1.2	1.2
Net Sales to Working Capital 32	5.7	9.5	7.7	17.5	4.8	5.4	4.9	3.8
Coverage Ratio 33	2.6	52.5	12.1	11.1	5.2	4.6	1.5	1.0
Total Asset Turnover 34	1.0	2.8	2.2	1.5	1.3	1.5	0.7	0.4
Inventory Turnover 35	8.5	28.9	18.5	12.3	12.3	6.9	5.5	5.2
Receivables Turnover 36	6.9	12.3	8.4	5.8	7.5	8.2	5.7	5.1
Total Liabilities to Net Worth 37	1.6	0.9	1.2	1.0	1.0	1.4	1.1	2.3
Current Assets to Working Capital 38	2.0	1.7	1.8	3.9	1.7	1.8	2.1	2.1
Current Liabilities to Working Capital 39	1.0	0.7	0.8	2.9	0.7	0.8	1.1	1.1
Working Capital to Net Sales 40	0.2	0.1	0.1	0.1	0.2	0.2	0.2	0.3
Inventory to Working Capital 41	0.4	0.1	0.2	0.8	0.3	0.5	0.6	0.6
Total Receipts to Cash Flow 42	7.8	4.2	8.0	5.8	9.2	11.6	13.9	13.3
Cost of Goods to Cash Flow 43	4.7	1.7	4.4	3.6	6.0	8.0	9.7	9.1
Cash Flow to Total Debt 44	0.2	1.4	0.5	0.5	0.3	0.2	0.1	0.0

Selected Financial Factors (in Percentages)

Debt Ratio 45	60.8	48.5	53.7	49.5	49.5	59.1	53.5	69.3
Return on Total Assets 46	8.0	35.5	13.1	17.6	9.1	11.3	4.8	3.5
Return on Equity Before Income Taxes 47	12.7	67.6	25.9	31.7	14.6	21.5	3.6	0.0
Return on Equity After Income Taxes 48	11.3	67.6	25.0	30.9	13.8	16.2	1.2	•
Profit Margin (Before Income Tax) 49	5.2	12.2	5.6	10.7	5.8	5.8	2.5	0.0
Profit Margin (After Income Tax) 50	4.6	12.2	5.4	10.4	5.5	4.3	0.8	•

Table II
Corporations with Net Income

COATING, ENGRAVING, HEAT TREATING, AND ALLIED ACTIVITIES

MONEY AMOUNTS AND SIZE OF ASSETS IN THOUSANDS OF DOLLARS

Item Description for Accounting Period 7/10 Through 6/11	Total	Zero Assets	Under 500	500 to 1,000	1,000 to 5,000	5,000 to 10,000	10,000 to 25,000	25,000 to 50,000	50,000 to 100,000	100,000 to 250,000	250,000 to 500,000	500,000 to 2,500,000	2,500,000 and over
Number of Enterprises **1**	2661	917	748	379	476	66	53	8	•	3	0	•	0
Revenues ($ in Thousands)													
Net Sales **2**	8379584	73774	704444	551665	2118321	922668	1185058	401178	•	229958	0	•	0
Interest **3**	11767	0	0	31	458	295	94	81	•	374	0	•	0
Rents **4**	5315	0	0	211	1912	0	1808	0	•	0	0	•	0
Royalties **5**	14180	0	0	0	0	0	0	0	•	14180	0	•	0
Other Portfolio Income **6**	13682	0	0	0	780	608	455	4	•	4377	0	•	0
Other Receipts **7**	50888	60	108	159	6461	4582	3049	1114	•	2376	0	•	0
Total Receipts **8**	8475416	73834	704552	552066	2127932	928153	1190464	402377	•	251265	0	•	0
Average Total Receipts **9**	3185	81	942	1457	4470	14063	22462	50297	•	83755	•	•	•
Operating Costs/Operating Income (%)													
Cost of Operations **10**	55.7	3.2	31.4	42.9	50.9	63.6	64.5	73.0	•	50.3	•	•	•
Salaries and Wages **11**	7.9	4.6	12.2	5.3	11.7	4.3	6.6	3.6	•	8.8	•	•	•
Taxes Paid **12**	2.8	2.8	3.3	1.8	4.0	2.5	2.7	2.4	•	1.6	•	•	•
Interest Paid **13**	1.6	0.2	0.3	0.5	0.3	1.0	0.9	1.6	•	1.2	•	•	•
Depreciation **14**	3.0	0.6	1.4	1.7	2.7	3.0	2.7	4.1	•	3.2	•	•	•
Amortization and Depletion **15**	0.3	•	0.0	0.0	0.0	0.0	0.1	0.1	•	0.7	•	•	•
Pensions and Other Deferred Comp. **16**	0.6	•	•	0.7	0.7	0.2	1.0	0.6	•	1.2	•	•	•
Employee Benefits **17**	2.2	0.4	2.7	0.6	2.6	0.4	2.2	1.8	•	2.7	•	•	•
Advertising **18**	0.2	0.2	0.1	0.0	0.2	0.0	0.2	0.1	•	0.8	•	•	•
Other Expenses **19**	10.7	50.7	11.7	28.0	10.8	9.6	6.6	3.7	•	12.5	•	•	•
Officers' Compensation **20**	4.9	20.2	19.2	3.3	7.3	1.9	2.8	1.0	•	1.1	•	•	•
Operating Margin **21**	10.0	17.1	17.8	15.1	8.9	13.4	9.9	8.1	•	15.8	•	•	•
Operating Margin Before Officers' Comp. **22**	15.0	37.3	37.0	18.4	16.2	15.3	12.7	9.0	•	17.0	•	•	•

Selected Average Balance Sheet ($ in Thousands)

Net Receivables 23	495	0	54	130	496	1674	3483	6606	•	16255
Inventories 24	171	0	12	66	97	498	941	4282	•	24843
Net Property, Plant and Equipment 25	582	0	173	99	578	1675	4045	13679	•	17553
Total Assets 26	3108	0	323	671	1935	8286	14465	33921	•	174590
Notes and Loans Payable 27	684	0	129	97	207	2772	2852	6742	•	17109
All Other Liabilities 28	851	0	16	91	329	1513	2050	8944	•	51996
Net Worth 29	1574	0	178	483	1398	4001	9562	18236	•	105485

Selected Financial Ratios (Times to 1)

Current Ratio 30	2.4	•	5.4	3.8	2.8	1.2	3.0	1.8	•	2.8
Quick Ratio 31	1.7	•	5.1	2.9	2.2	0.9	2.4	1.5	•	1.9
Net Sales to Working Capital 32	4.8	•	7.9	4.2	7.1	30.3	4.7	7.8	•	2.2
Coverage Ratio 33	8.1	79.6	68.4	30.2	34.3	14.7	13.1	6.2	•	23.6
Total Asset Turnover 34	1.0	•	2.9	2.2	2.3	1.7	1.5	1.5	•	0.4
Inventory Turnover 35	10.2	•	24.3	9.4	23.3	17.9	15.3	8.5	•	1.6
Receivables Turnover 36	7.8	•	16.5	17.3	11.8	5.5	7.5	5.4	•	2.4
Total Liabilities to Net Worth 37	1.0	•	0.8	0.4	0.4	1.1	0.5	0.9	•	0.7
Current Assets to Working Capital 38	1.7	•	1.2	1.4	1.6	6.3	1.5	2.2	•	1.5
Current Liabilities to Working Capital 39	0.7	•	0.2	0.4	0.6	5.3	0.5	1.2	•	0.5
Working Capital to Net Sales 40	0.2	•	0.1	0.2	0.1	0.0	0.2	0.1	•	0.5
Inventory to Working Capital 41	0.3	•	0.1	0.3	0.2	1.2	0.3	0.3	•	0.4
Total Receipts to Cash Flow 42	5.3	2.0	3.6	2.6	6.1	5.1	6.7	9.2	•	2.8
Cost of Goods to Cash Flow 43	2.9	0.1	1.1	1.1	3.1	3.2	4.3	6.7	•	1.4
Cash Flow to Total Debt 44	0.4	•	1.8	2.9	1.4	0.6	0.7	0.3	•	0.4

Selected Financial Factors (in Percentages)

Debt Ratio 45	49.4	•	44.8	28.0	27.7	51.7	33.9	46.2	•	39.6
Return on Total Assets 46	13.0	•	52.8	34.1	22.1	25.3	17.2	14.8	•	12.1
Return on Equity Before Income Taxes 47	22.5	•	94.4	45.8	29.6	48.9	24.1	23.0	•	19.3
Return on Equity After Income Taxes 48	20.7	•	94.4	45.7	28.8	47.8	23.2	20.2	•	15.4
Profit Margin (Before Income Tax) 49	11.2	17.1	17.8	15.2	9.3	14.0	10.3	8.4	•	26.5
Profit Margin (After Income Tax) 50	10.4	17.1	17.8	15.2	9.0	13.7	9.9	7.3	•	21.2

Table I
Corporations with and without Net Income

OTHER FABRICATED METAL PRODUCT

MONEY AMOUNTS AND SIZE OF ASSETS IN THOUSANDS OF DOLLARS

Item Description for Accounting Period 7/10 Through 6/11		Total	Zero Assets	Under 500	500 to 1,000	1,000 to 5,000	5,000 to 10,000	10,000 to 25,000	25,000 to 50,000	50,000 to 100,000	100,000 to 250,000	250,000 to 500,000	500,000 to 2,500,000	2,500,000 and over
Number of Enterprises	1	15979	1952	8628	1092	2863	785	321	159	84	45	19	21	8

Revenues ($ in Thousands)

Net Sales	2	117364106	571382	3848980	2015690	12115106	8846790	7849924	8351071	8402605	7334858	5302823	17986225	34738651
Interest	3	1046688	1405	657	1256	3912	2275	2796	2642	5334	20543	7752	75551	922564
Rents	4	31202	166	0	305	148	480	2120	2237	4941	682	385	7891	11847
Royalties	5	1231606	0	0	0	0	0	4234	1259	11734	9927	5345	26675	1172432
Other Portfolio Income	6	1112963	29429	5319	13298	48975	58265	24752	7015	19790	25666	13517	67673	799266
Other Receipts	7	1266330	42054	38760	1561	83372	50338	67187	41571	26354	54060	89994	257140	513939
Total Receipts	8	122052895	644436	3893716	2032110	12251513	8958148	7951013	8405795	8470758	7445736	5419816	18421155	38158699
Average Total Receipts	9	7638	330	451	1861	4279	11412	24770	52867	100842	165461	285253	877198	4769837

Operating Costs/Operating Income (%)

Cost of Operations	10	67.5	69.7	58.4	60.2	64.8	66.5	68.9	66.4	71.2	66.6	63.8	71.6	67.9
Salaries and Wages	11	7.4	14.6	6.9	11.4	6.7	7.7	7.0	8.0	6.6	8.3	9.0	5.4	8.0
Taxes Paid	12	1.9	4.3	3.1	2.5	2.9	2.1	1.9	2.0	1.8	1.5	2.0	1.6	1.6
Interest Paid	13	2.8	1.4	1.1	1.1	0.8	0.7	0.7	1.1	1.2	1.3	0.9	4.2	5.6
Depreciation	14	2.4	2.5	1.7	2.3	2.1	2.1	3.1	2.9	2.8	3.0	3.2	2.7	1.8
Amortization and Depletion	15	1.2	1.6	0.1	0.3	0.0	0.0	0.2	0.4	0.4	0.8	0.6	1.1	2.8
Pensions and Other Deferred Comp.	16	1.2	1.4	0.1	0.6	0.6	0.4	0.6	0.6	0.8	0.7	1.3	1.5	2.2
Employee Benefits	17	2.1	1.7	1.8	1.1	1.7	1.7	1.9	1.7	2.0	1.9	2.1	1.8	2.7
Advertising	18	0.8	0.4	0.3	0.3	0.6	0.2	0.3	0.7	0.5	0.6	1.1	0.5	1.3
Other Expenses	19	9.0	20.0	12.6	14.4	10.6	9.4	7.5	9.4	6.5	8.6	8.3	8.0	9.1
Officers' Compensation	20	2.1	6.0	8.1	5.8	6.1	4.0	2.7	2.0	1.5	1.5	1.6	0.6	0.5
Operating Margin	21	1.5	•	5.9	•	3.1	5.2	5.3	4.8	4.9	5.2	6.3	1.2	•
Operating Margin Before Officers' Comp.	22	3.7	•	14.0	5.8	9.1	9.2	7.9	6.8	6.3	6.6	7.8	1.7	•

Selected Average Balance Sheet ($ in Thousands)

Item													
Net Receivables 23	1498	0	33	223	547	1655	3532	7014	13650	25835	50915	128455	1540671
Inventories 24	975	0	26	131	504	1725	4065	10013	15352	27603	54428	128408	406993
Net Property, Plant and Equipment 25	1097	0	45	137	529	1374	3953	8380	17068	30163	58499	145590	605630
Total Assets 26	17169	0	142	741	2134	6625	15731	35350	72394	155868	326792	1183843	25770780
Notes and Loans Payable 27	6845	0	116	311	653	1637	3337	10675	16866	28074	54929	498964	10989168
All Other Liabilities 28	2463	0	43	157	568	1437	3208	7801	19022	49963	81090	343083	2649712
Net Worth 29	7861	0	-17	273	912	3550	9186	16873	36505	77831	190773	341796	12131900

Selected Financial Ratios (Times to 1)

Item													
Current Ratio 30	1.8	•	1.1	1.8	2.1	2.8	2.2	1.9	2.2	2.8	2.1		1.3
Quick Ratio 31	1.0	•	0.8	1.2	1.3	1.7	1.6	1.1	1.0	1.3	1.5	1.0	0.9
Net Sales to Working Capital 32	4.7	•	42.6	9.5	5.6	3.8	3.6	4.2	5.4	3.7	2.6	3.8	6.1
Coverage Ratio 33	3.1	•	7.5	1.7	6.4	10.4	10.7	5.8	5.9	6.2	10.1	1.9	2.4
Total Asset Turnover 34	0.4	•	3.1	2.5	2.0	1.7	1.6	1.5	1.4	1.0	0.9	0.7	0.2
Inventory Turnover 35	5.1	•	9.9	8.5	5.4	4.3	4.1	3.5	4.6	3.9	3.3	4.8	7.2
Receivables Turnover 36	6.3	•	14.8	8.2	8.2	7.5	7.0	7.4	7.8	7.2	5.7	7.4	4.5
Total Liabilities to Net Worth 37	1.2	•	•	1.7	1.3	0.9	0.7	1.1	1.0	1.0	0.7	2.5	1.1
Current Assets to Working Capital 38	2.3	•	7.7	2.3	1.9	1.5	1.6	1.8	2.2	1.6	1.9		3.9
Current Liabilities to Working Capital 39	1.3	•	6.7	1.3	0.9	0.5	0.6	0.8	1.2	0.8	0.6	0.9	2.9
Working Capital to Net Sales 40	0.2	•	0.0	0.1	0.2	0.3	0.3	0.2	0.2	0.3	0.4	0.3	0.2
Inventory to Working Capital 41	0.7	•	2.0	0.6	0.7	0.6	0.6	0.8	0.9	0.6	0.5	0.7	0.6
Total Receipts to Cash Flow 42	8.2	19.4	6.8	12.2	9.0	7.7	8.4	7.7	9.4	7.4	6.9	10.1	7.6
Cost of Goods to Cash Flow 43	5.5	13.6	3.9	7.3	5.8	5.1	5.8	5.1	6.7	4.9	4.4	7.2	5.2
Cash Flow to Total Debt 44	0.1	0.4	0.3	0.3	0.4	0.5	0.4	0.4	0.3	0.3	0.3	0.1	0.0

Selected Financial Factors (in Percentages)

Item													
Debt Ratio 45	54.2	•	112.3	63.1	57.2	46.4	41.6	52.3	49.6	50.1	41.6	71.1	52.9
Return on Total Assets 46	3.8	•	25.6	4.8	9.8	12.2	11.3	9.8	9.7	8.4	8.0	5.7	2.2
Return on Equity Before Income Taxes 47	5.6	•	•	5.4	19.3	20.5	17.5	16.9	16.0	14.2	12.3	9.2	2.8
Return on Equity After Income Taxes 48	4.3	•	•	2.1	18.5	19.5	15.9	15.1	13.5	12.1	8.8	6.0	1.8
Profit Margin (Before Income Tax) 49	6.0	•	7.1	0.8	4.2	6.5	6.6	5.4	5.8	6.8	8.4	3.7	7.8
Profit Margin (After Income Tax) 50	4.6	•	6.8	0.3	4.0	6.1	6.0	4.9	5.8	6.0		2.4	5.0

Table II

Corporations with Net Income

OTHER FABRICATED METAL PRODUCT

MONEY AMOUNTS AND SIZE OF ASSETS IN THOUSANDS OF DOLLARS

Item Description for Accounting Period 7/10 Through 6/11	Total	Zero Assets	Under 500	500 to 1,000	1,000 to 5,000	5,000 to 10,000	10,000 to 25,000	25,000 to 50,000	50,000 to 100,000	100,000 to 250,000	250,000 to 500,000	500,000 to 2,500,000	2,500,000 and over
Number of Enterprises 1	10751	866	6307	451	1965	650	247	125	66	36	•	•	17
Revenues ($ in Thousands)													
Net Sales 2	90525988	252622	3179568	1132597	8252761	7657686	6556952	6971742	6740741	6041304	•	14941757	•
Interest 3	567036	1361	319	402	3468	1973	2588	1719	4555	13755	•	62323	•
Rents 4	27848	166	0	186	131	480	1906	2017	4672	464	•	7776	•
Royalties 5	1163885	0	0	0	0	0	205	1090	11734	7576	•	21291	•
Other Portfolio Income 6	1055678	27395	4611	13298	37001	57724	20117	6805	17946	25145	•	59721	•
Other Receipts 7	1062499	25356	32846	496	27097	45889	56780	36216	22190	49571	•	250188	•
Total Receipts 8	94402934	306900	3217344	1146979	8320458	7763752	6638548	7019589	6801838	6137815	•	15343056	•
Average Total Receipts 9	8781	354	510	2543	4234	11944	26877	56157	103058	170495	•	902533	•
Operating Costs/Operating Income (%)													
Cost of Operations 10	67.4	64.9	56.1	54.4	63.3	63.7	67.6	64.5	69.1	65.4	•	72.4	•
Salaries and Wages 11	7.2	5.5	7.5	13.9	6.5	7.8	7.1	7.5	6.6	8.3	•	5.6	•
Taxes Paid 12	1.9	1.4	3.1	2.3	2.8	2.2	1.8	2.0	1.7	1.5	•	1.2	•
Interest Paid 13	2.2	2.1	1.0	0.7	0.6	0.6	0.6	0.8	0.8	1.0	•	4.0	•
Depreciation 14	2.3	4.3	1.4	1.9	2.1	2.0	2.8	2.5	2.9	3.0	•	2.5	•
Amortization and Depletion 15	1.2	0.3	0.1	0.0	0.0	0.0	0.1	0.1	0.3	0.3	•	1.0	•
Pensions and Other Deferred Comp. 16	1.3	0.4	0.1	1.1	0.7	0.4	0.5	0.7	0.8	0.8	•	1.3	•
Employee Benefits 17	1.9	0.7	1.2	0.4	1.7	1.8	1.7	1.7	2.1	1.8	•	1.6	•
Advertising 18	0.6	0.3	0.2	0.2	0.4	0.2	0.3	0.8	0.5	0.7	•	0.5	•
Other Expenses 19	8.1	14.9	11.5	16.2	9.5	9.1	7.1	9.7	6.7	8.2	•	6.8	•
Officers' Compensation 20	2.0	0.9	8.2	6.8	4.9	4.1	2.5	2.1	1.6	1.5	•	0.5	•
Operating Margin 21	4.0	4.3	9.5	2.1	7.6	8.0	7.7	7.6	7.0	7.4	•	2.6	•
Operating Margin Before Officers' Comp. 22	6.0	5.2	17.7	8.9	12.5	12.1	10.2	9.7	8.6	9.0	•	3.1	•

Selected Average Balance Sheet ($ in Thousands)

	•	•	•	•	•	•	•	•	•	•	•	•
Net Receivables 23	1416	0	53	301	550	1729	3772	7292	14258	24505	•	135374
Inventories 24	1066	0	10	142	442	1816	4209	10271	16152	27974	•	113685
Net Property, Plant and Equipment 25	1218	0	41	88	562	1372	3749	7707	16180	29226	•	138096
Total Assets 26	20305	0	134	777	2207	6550	15801	35784	71712	154025	•	1145938
Notes and Loans Payable 27	7918	0	98	264	510	1327	3295	9459	12096	30661	•	504760
All Other Liabilities 28	2476	0	41	183	552	1304	3211	7481	17664	35671	•	282461
Net Worth 29	9911	0	-4	330	1144	3918	9294	18844	41952	87694	•	358717

Selected Financial Ratios (Times to 1)

	•	•	•	•	•	•	•	•	•	•	•	•
Current Ratio 30	2.0	•	1.3	1.8	2.7	3.3	2.8	2.8	2.5	2.2	•	1.9
Quick Ratio 31	1.2	•	1.0	1.3	1.7	2.0	1.6	1.4	1.3	1.3	•	1.0
Net Sales to Working Capital 32	4.6	•	29.3	9.6	4.5	3.5	3.6	3.6	4.1	3.8	•	4.4
Coverage Ratio 33	5.1	13.4	11.4	5.8	15.1	16.3	15.5	10.7	10.7	9.8	•	2.4
Total Asset Turnover 34	0.4	•	3.7	3.2	1.9	1.8	1.7	1.6	1.4	1.1	•	0.8
Inventory Turnover 35	5.3	•	27.5	9.6	6.0	4.1	4.3	3.5	4.4	3.9	•	5.6
Receivables Turnover 36	7.2	•	23.0	7.7	8.6	7.3	7.3	7.7	•	7.7	•	7.9
Total Liabilities to Net Worth 37	1.0	•	•	1.4	0.9	0.7	0.7	0.9	0.7	0.8	•	2.2
Current Assets to Working Capital 38	2.0	•	4.5	2.2	1.6	1.4	1.5	1.6	1.7	1.8	•	2.1
Current Liabilities to Working Capital 39	1.0	•	3.5	1.2	0.6	0.4	0.5	0.6	0.7	0.8	•	1.1
Working Capital to Net Sales 40	0.2	•	0.0	0.1	0.2	0.3	0.3	0.3	0.2	0.3	•	0.2
Inventory to Working Capital 41	0.6	•	0.9	0.5	0.5	0.5	0.6	0.7	0.6	0.6	•	0.7
Total Receipts to Cash Flow 42	7.1	2.6	5.6	9.4	6.9	6.2	7.1	6.2	7.7	6.5	•	9.4
Cost of Goods to Cash Flow 43	4.8	1.7	3.1	5.1	4.4	4.0	4.8	4.0	5.3	4.2	•	6.8
Cash Flow to Total Debt 44	0.1	•	0.7	0.6	0.6	0.7	0.6	0.5	0.4	0.4	•	0.1

Selected Financial Factors (in Percentages)

	•	•	•	•	•	•	•	•	•	•	•	•
Debt Ratio 45	51.2	•	103.0	57.5	48.2	40.2	41.2	47.3	41.5	43.1	•	68.7
Return on Total Assets 46	4.6	•	44.0	13.0	17.2	18.0	16.0	14.1	12.7	11.1	•	7.2
Return on Equity Before Income Taxes 47	7.6	•	•	25.3	31.0	28.2	25.5	24.3	19.7	17.5	•	13.2
Return on Equity After Income Taxes 48	6.1	•	•	18.6	30.0	27.1	23.5	22.3	16.9	15.2	•	9.5
Profit Margin (Before Income Tax) 49	9.0	26.4	10.7	3.3	8.4	9.4	8.9	8.2	8.1	9.2	•	5.4
Profit Margin (After Income Tax) 50	7.2	23.8	10.4	2.4	8.2	9.0	8.2	7.5	7.0	8.0	•	3.9

Table I

Corporations with and without Net Income

AGRICULTURE, CONSTRUCTION, AND MINING MACHINERY

MONEY AMOUNTS AND SIZE OF ASSETS IN THOUSANDS OF DOLLARS

Item Description for Accounting Period 7/10 Through 6/11	Total	Zero Assets	Under 500	500 to 1,000	1,000 to 5,000	5,000 to 10,000	10,000 to 25,000	25,000 to 50,000	50,000 to 100,000	100,000 to 250,000	250,000 to 500,000	500,000 to 2,500,000	2,500,000 and over
Number of Enterprises 1	2878	201	1109	276	884	156	108	45	37	23	13	13	13
Revenues ($ in Thousands)													
Net Sales 2	127694653	37085	492514	602177	4473892	1738792	2117059	2316587	2789218	4200557	4163291	11838367	92925115
Interest 3	2839500	4	105	901	445	1226	8016	2526	2588	10863	12976	35013	2764835
Rents 4	1348807	0	0	185	8561	571	9498	53	497	2813	2051	74305	1250073
Royalties 5	895326	0	0	0	0	0	0	2015	293	1328	2623	48521	840546
Other Portfolio Income 6	1976107	20	82	0	67873	14693	14839	29496	3813	44402	10630	254890	1535371
Other Receipts 7	2497758	369	350	5573	49788	12202	38768	19143	25968	46059	68070	44574	2186892
Total Receipts 8	137251951	37478	493051	608836	4600559	1767484	2188180	2369820	2822377	4306022	4259641	12295670	101502832
Average Total Receipts 9	47690	186	445	2206	5204	11330	20261	52663	76280	187218	327665	945821	7807910
Operating Costs/Operating Income (%)													
Cost of Operations 10	70.1	65.4	60.1	48.5	71.9	63.9	68.9	72.2	69.2	71.4	70.0	73.4	69.8
Salaries and Wages 11	7.8	12.4	8.0	15.7	6.8	9.5	10.1	6.5	8.1	5.9	7.6	6.4	8.0
Taxes Paid 12	1.0	1.8	2.1	3.0	1.6	2.2	2.0	1.9	1.5	1.3	1.7	1.2	0.8
Interest Paid 13	3.0	0.9	1.4	2.4	0.9	1.2	1.2	0.7	1.7	1.1	2.4	1.9	3.6
Depreciation 14	3.8	1.7	1.7	5.6	4.5	3.6	2.7	1.8	2.3	3.3	2.8	3.4	4.0
Amortization and Depletion 15	0.4	0.2	0.0	•	0.1	0.1	0.2	0.1	0.5	0.5	1.2	0.4	0.4
Pensions and Other Deferred Comp. 16	1.0	0.4	•	0.3	0.3	0.2	0.4	0.6	0.7	0.7	0.5	1.1	1.1
Employee Benefits 17	1.9	1.5	1.0	0.5	0.9	1.2	2.0	1.6	1.6	1.1	1.3	0.9	2.2
Advertising 18	0.3	0.1	0.4	0.7	0.6	1.9	0.8	0.7	0.5	0.5	0.7	0.6	0.2
Other Expenses 19	11.4	24.9	18.2	16.7	6.6	12.1	7.3	7.2	8.3	8.3	10.2	8.2	12.4
Officers' Compensation 20	0.7	0.7	10.3	3.2	3.8	3.6	2.8	1.6	1.4	1.1	0.7	0.4	0.3
Operating Margin 21	•	•	•	3.4	2.1	0.6	1.6	5.1	4.1	4.6	0.8	2.0	•
Operating Margin Before Officers' Comp. 22	•	6.9	6.9	6.6	5.9	4.2	4.4	6.7	5.6	5.8	1.5	2.4	•

Selected Average Balance Sheet ($ in Thousands)

Net Receivables 23	23502	0	17	134	378	1555	4101	8656	12318	30796	66743	149244	4784764
Inventories 24	6795	0	101	160	671	2500	4530	12442	17844	43194	65334	169211	973620
Net Property, Plant and Equipment 25	8198	0	22	338	418	1267	2302	5125	11606	27638	47693	172710	1423098
Total Assets 26	81832	0	154	898	1948	6383	14494	36394	70461	158402	327982	1123830	15696107
Notes and Loans Payable 27	29867	0	108	643	812	1349	3231	5720	19495	27475	97363	353047	5916590
All Other Liabilities 28	28493	0	54	76	529	2132	4550	11116	22045	40835	94339	295832	5638693
Net Worth 29	23472	0	-9	179	607	2901	6713	19558	28921	90092	136280	474951	4140823

Selected Financial Ratios (Times to 1)

Current Ratio 30	1.5	•	2.0	8.1	2.5	1.6	2.1	2.2	1.7	2.1	1.8	1.8	1.5
Quick Ratio 31	1.0	•	0.3	5.3	1.1	0.7	1.1	1.1	0.8	1.0	0.9	0.9	1.1
Net Sales to Working Capital 32	3.5	•	6.7	5.3	6.0	6.4	3.6	3.6	4.3	3.8	4.1	4.8	3.2
Coverage Ratio 33	3.7	•	•	2.9	6.6	2.9	4.9	11.2	4.2	7.5	2.3	4.6	3.6
Total Asset Turnover 34	0.5	•	2.9	2.4	2.6	1.7	1.4	1.4	1.1	1.2	1.0	0.8	0.5
Inventory Turnover 35	4.6	•	2.6	6.6	5.4	2.8	3.0	3.0	2.9	3.0	3.4	3.9	5.1
Receivables Turnover 36	2.2	•	•	•	15.7	7.4	5.4	6.1	6.9	5.8	4.9	6.2	1.8
Total Liabilities to Net Worth 37	2.5	•	•	4.0	2.2	1.2	1.2	0.9	1.4	0.8	1.4	1.4	2.8
Current Assets to Working Capital 38	3.0	•	2.0	1.1	1.7	2.6	1.9	1.8	2.4	1.9	2.2	2.2	3.2
Current Liabilities to Working Capital 39	2.0	•	1.0	0.1	0.7	1.6	0.9	0.8	1.4	0.9	1.2	1.2	2.2
Working Capital to Net Sales 40	0.3	•	0.1	0.2	0.2	0.2	0.3	0.3	0.2	0.3	0.2	0.2	0.3
Inventory to Working Capital 41	0.6	•	1.5	0.4	0.9	1.3	0.8	0.8	1.0	0.8	0.9	0.8	0.5
Total Receipts to Cash Flow 42	6.5	6.7	9.0	5.4	10.4	8.8	10.2	8.3	8.1	7.5	9.2	8.0	6.0
Cost of Goods to Cash Flow 43	4.5	4.4	5.4	2.6	7.4	5.6	7.1	6.0	5.6	5.3	6.5	5.8	4.2
Cash Flow to Total Debt 44	0.1	•	0.3	0.6	0.4	0.4	0.2	0.4	0.2	0.4	0.2	0.2	0.1

Selected Financial Factors (in Percentages)

Debt Ratio 45	71.3	•	105.7	80.0	68.8	54.5	53.7	46.3	59.0	43.1	58.4	57.7	73.6
Return on Total Assets 46	6.2	•	•	16.9	15.0	6.0	8.3	11.4	7.5	9.5	5.5	7.2	5.9
Return on Equity Before Income Taxes 47	15.7	•	165.3	54.8	40.7	8.7	14.4	19.3	14.0	14.5	7.6	13.4	16.1
Return on Equity After Income Taxes 48	10.5	•	168.6	47.3	38.4	5.2	10.7	16.5	11.3	11.3	5.0	8.4	10.5
Profit Margin (Before Income Tax) 49	8.3	•	•	4.5	4.9	2.3	4.9	7.3	5.4	7.2	3.2	7.0	9.3
Profit Margin (After Income Tax) 50	5.5	•	•	3.9	4.6	1.4	3.7	6.3	4.3	5.6	2.1	4.4	6.1

Table II

Corporations with Net Income

AGRICULTURE, CONSTRUCTION, AND MINING MACHINERY

MONEY AMOUNTS AND SIZE OF ASSETS IN THOUSANDS OF DOLLARS

Item Description for Accounting Period 7/10 Through 6/11	Total	Zero Assets	Under 500	500 to 1,000	1,000 to 5,000	5,000 to 10,000	10,000 to 25,000	25,000 to 50,000	50,000 to 100,000	100,000 to 250,000	250,000 to 500,000	500,000 to 2,500,000	2,500,000 and over
Number of Enterprises **1**	1750	•	485	276	691	108	79	36	•	19	•	10	10
Revenues ($ in Thousands)													
Net Sales **2**	117636297	•	178970	602177	4124314	1382613	1557358	1898288	•	3801879	•	10821027	87353006
Interest **3**	2744336	•	105	901	419	1209	7822	2252	•	6412	•	30843	2683250
Rents **4**	1347777	•	0	185	8561	571	9498	0	•	2438	•	74305	1250070
Royalties **5**	768842	•	0	0	0	0	0	0	•	486	•	20962	744478
Other Portfolio Income **6**	1940310	•	82	0	67873	14693	14695	29432	•	31433	•	232836	1535371
Other Receipts **7**	2187131	•	350	5573	41243	11547	33009	17051	•	44263	•	39426	1902570
Total Receipts **8**	126627693	•	179507	608836	4242410	1410633	1622382	1947023	•	3886911	•	11219399	95468745
Average Total Receipts **9**	72359	•	370	2206	6140	13061	20536	54084	•	204574	•	1121940	9546874
Operating Costs/Operating Income (%)													
Cost of Operations **10**	69.6	•	57.8	48.5	71.7	67.4	64.7	71.2	•	71.3	•	74.3	69.2
Salaries and Wages **11**	7.7	•	5.9	15.7	5.5	8.3	9.6	6.2	•	5.4	•	6.2	8.1
Taxes Paid **12**	0.9	•	1.3	3.0	1.3	2.1	1.8	1.8	•	1.3	•	1.2	0.7
Interest Paid **13**	2.8	•	0.4	2.4	0.6	0.6	1.3	0.7	•	1.0	•	1.1	3.5
Depreciation **14**	3.8	•	3.4	5.6	4.4	3.1	2.2	1.7	•	3.3	•	2.7	4.1
Amortization and Depletion **15**	0.4	•	0.0	•	0.1	0.1	0.2	0.1	•	0.5	•	0.4	0.4
Pensions and Other Deferred Comp. **16**	1.1	•	0.0	0.3	0.4	0.2	0.5	0.4	•	0.7	•	1.2	1.2
Employee Benefits **17**	1.9	•	1.5	0.5	0.6	1.4	1.7	1.1	•	1.0	•	0.9	2.2
Advertising **18**	0.3	•	0.4	0.7	0.6	1.8	1.0	0.6	•	0.5	•	0.7	0.1
Other Expenses **19**	11.3	•	13.6	16.7	6.1	9.1	8.2	7.0	•	7.3	•	7.5	12.5
Officers' Compensation **20**	0.6	•	8.7	3.2	4.0	3.2	3.2	1.7	•	0.9	•	0.4	0.3
Operating Margin **21**	•	•	6.9	3.4	4.8	2.7	5.7	7.5	•	6.8	•	3.4	•
Operating Margin Before Officers' Comp. **22**	0.1	•	15.7	6.6	8.7	5.9	8.9	9.2	•	7.7	•	3.8	•

Selected Average Balance Sheet ($ in Thousands)

Net Receivables 23	37365	•	10	134	435	1807	4036	8538	•	29432	•	178310 6075861
Inventories 24	8741	•	68	149	527	2026	4296	10834	•	37476	•	197296 995153
Net Property, Plant and Equipment 25	12366	•	15	338	485	1153	2312	4444	•	28033	•	150959 1784200
Total Assets 26	123579	•	86	898	1943	6958	14469	35850	•	159403	•	1156873 19154861
Notes and Loans Payable 27	45801	•	10	643	559	1373	2970	5453	•	29348	•	348375 7363830
All Other Liabilities 28	43038	•	25	76	431	2372	4043	10118	•	40256	•	289490 6876363
Net Worth 29	34740	•	52	179	953	3213	7457	20280	•	89799	•	519008 4914668

Selected Financial Ratios (Times to 1)

Current Ratio 30	1.5	•	2.6	8.1	3.4	1.7	2.4	2.3	•	2.0	•	1.8 1.5
Quick Ratio 31	1.1	•	0.4	5.3	1.8	0.8	1.4	1.2	•	1.0	•	0.9 1.1
Net Sales to Working Capital 32	3.4	•	7.1	5.3	6.1	6.2	3.1	3.6	•	4.4	•	4.8 3.1
Coverage Ratio 33	4.4	•	17.3	2.9	13.6	9.0	8.8	15.5	•	10.5	•	8.3 3.9
Total Asset Turnover 34	0.5	•	4.3	2.4	3.1	1.8	1.4	1.5	•	1.3	•	0.9 0.5
Inventory Turnover 35	5.4	•	3.2	7.1	8.1	4.3	3.0	3.5	•	3.8	•	4.1 6.1
Receivables Turnover 36	2.3	•	•	20.8	16.8	10.8	5.2	6.2	•	8.0	•	• 1.9
Total Liabilities to Net Worth 37	2.6	•	0.7	4.0	1.0	1.2	0.9	0.8	•	0.8	•	1.2 2.9
Current Assets to Working Capital 38	3.0	•	1.6	1.1	1.4	2.5	1.7	1.8	•	2.0	•	2.2 3.2
Current Liabilities to Working Capital 39	2.0	•	0.6	0.1	0.4	1.5	0.7	0.8	•	1.0	•	1.2 2.2
Working Capital to Net Sales 40	0.3	•	0.1	0.2	0.2	0.2	0.3	0.3	•	0.2	•	0.2 0.3
Inventory to Working Capital 41	0.5	•	1.3	0.4	0.6	1.3	0.6	0.7	•	0.9	•	0.9 0.5
Total Receipts to Cash Flow 42	6.1	•	5.4	5.4	8.2	8.5	6.4	7.0	•	7.0	•	7.6 5.7
Cost of Goods to Cash Flow 43	4.2	•	3.1	2.6	5.9	5.7	4.1	5.0	•	5.0	•	5.6 4.0
Cash Flow to Total Debt 44	0.1	•	2.0	0.6	0.7	0.4	0.4	0.5	•	0.4	•	0.2 0.1

Selected Financial Factors (in Percentages)

Debt Ratio 45	71.9	•	40.4	80.0	51.0	53.8	48.5	43.4	•	43.7	•	55.1 74.3
Return on Total Assets 46	6.7	•	32.7	16.9	25.3	9.8	15.2	15.8	•	12.5	•	8.8 6.1
Return on Equity Before Income Taxes 47	18.4	•	51.7	54.8	47.7	18.8	26.1	26.1	•	20.2	•	17.3 17.8
Return on Equity After Income Taxes 48	12.5	•	50.4	47.3	45.9	14.3	21.6	22.7	•	16.3	•	11.4 11.7
Profit Margin (Before Income Tax) 49	9.5	•	7.2	4.5	7.6	4.7	9.9	10.0	•	9.0	•	8.3 10.0
Profit Margin (After Income Tax) 50	6.5	•	7.0	3.9	7.3	3.6	8.2	8.7	•	7.3	•	5.4 6.6

Table I

Corporations with and without Net Income

INDUSTRIAL MACHINERY

Money Amounts and Size of Assets in Thousands of Dollars

Item Description for Accounting Period 7/10 Through 6/11	Total	Zero Assets	Under 500	500 to 1,000	1,000 to 5,000	5,000 to 10,000	10,000 to 25,000	25,000 to 50,000	50,000 to 100,000	100,000 to 250,000	250,000 to 500,000	500,000 to 2,500,000	2,500,000 and over
Number of Enterprises **1**	3059	26	1228	416	820	301	123	48	37	33	10	16	0
Revenues ($ in Thousands)													
Net Sales **2**	46328952	247471	495781	503667	4178413	2657115	2566226	1942443	2801675	4107475	3603334	23325352	0
Interest **3**	109713	155	65	4	2923	861	1671	2320	7118	16516	7741	70339	0
Rents **4**	88894	0	0	446	1009	73	72	5531	956	17750	8	63049	0
Royalties **5**	446367	0	0	0	0	947	90	1039	220	31416	34468	378187	0
Other Portfolio Income **6**	469700	534	49	12431	1362	22398	6785	4348	12141	51643	8618	349390	0
Other Receipts **7**	510450	3396	1007	1440	15461	12772	23726	21816	24043	41475	44493	320821	0
Total Receipts **8**	47954076	251556	496902	517988	4199168	2694166	2598570	1977497	2846153	4266275	3698662	24407138	0
Average Total Receipts **9**	15676	9675	405	1245	5121	8951	21127	41198	76923	129281	369866	1525446	•
Operating Costs/Operating Income (%)													
Cost of Operations **10**	64.1	76.3	59.6	58.9	64.3	65.2	70.5	67.4	68.9	66.9	64.1	61.9	•
Salaries and Wages **11**	10.4	4.0	9.4	2.7	10.0	11.6	9.7	9.5	9.5	11.0	8.9	10.9	•
Taxes Paid **12**	1.6	1.7	3.3	2.5	2.4	2.2	1.7	2.1	1.9	1.4	1.3	1.3	•
Interest Paid **13**	1.5	5.5	0.3	1.4	1.3	1.0	0.7	1.4	1.6	1.7	1.7	1.7	•
Depreciation **14**	2.3	3.0	0.9	0.1	2.0	2.3	1.7	3.8	2.2	2.2	2.0	2.5	•
Amortization and Depletion **15**	0.9	1.7	0.0	0.0	0.3	0.2	0.3	0.3	1.1	1.3	2.0	1.0	•
Pensions and Other Deferred Comp. **16**	0.8	0.3	•	0.0	0.2	0.9	0.5	0.5	1.0	0.7	0.9	1.0	•
Employee Benefits **17**	2.2	1.2	1.6	2.2	2.5	2.5	2.3	1.8	2.0	2.2	2.9	2.0	•
Advertising **18**	0.5	0.2	1.3	1.7	0.3	0.7	0.6	0.8	0.4	0.4	0.5	0.4	•
Other Expenses **19**	9.6	14.1	19.0	12.5	6.4	8.7	7.0	10.1	6.9	10.3	9.1	10.4	•
Officers' Compensation **20**	1.5	1.9	7.5	8.2	4.5	2.9	2.9	2.0	1.3	1.3	0.7	0.6	•
Operating Margin **21**	4.7	•	•	9.6	5.8	1.9	2.0	0.4	3.2	0.7	6.1	6.3	•
Operating Margin Before Officers' Comp. **22**	6.2	•	4.5	17.8	10.3	4.8	4.9	2.4	4.5	2.0	6.8	6.9	•

Selected Average Balance Sheet ($ in Thousands)

Net Receivables 23	4186	0	28	150	877	1231	3505	7223	15117	24114	75040	546033
Inventories 24	2187	0	60	217	628	2017	4304	8934	11281	19673	62833	119667
Net Property, Plant and Equipment 25	1907	0	43	13	571	1645	2081	8143	11976	16854	36446	175080
Total Assets 26	18446	0	132	816	2941	7330	16328	34303	73361	149771	346458	2283168
Notes and Loans Payable 27	3645	0	26	412	1078	2721	3478	6841	18982	34277	80754	365437
All Other Liabilities 28	5792	0	60	226	901	2021	5029	10812	22335	46460	127542	714431
Net Worth 29	9009	0	46	178	963	2588	7821	16650	32044	69034	138162	1203301

Selected Financial Ratios (Times to 1)

Current Ratio 30	1.7	•	1.4	2.0	2.0	2.2	2.0	2.0	1.8	2.1	1.8	1.6
Quick Ratio 31	1.1	•	0.6	0.8	1.2	1.3	1.2	1.1	1.1	1.2	1.0	1.2
Net Sales to Working Capital 32	3.7	•	18.0	3.2	5.2	3.1	3.8	3.5	4.1	3.0	4.3	3.6
Coverage Ratio 33	6.7	•	•	9.7	5.9	4.2	5.5	2.6	4.0	3.8	6.4	8.5
Total Asset Turnover 34	0.8	•	3.1	1.5	1.7	1.2	1.3	1.2	1.0	0.8	1.0	0.6
Inventory Turnover 35	4.4	•	4.0	3.3	5.2	2.9	3.4	3.1	4.6	4.2	3.7	7.5
Receivables Turnover 36	3.4	•	16.8	7.4	6.6	7.4	6.2	4.6	5.3	5.1	4.0	4.5
Total Liabilities to Net Worth 37	1.0	•	1.9	3.6	2.1	1.8	1.1	1.1	1.3	1.2	1.5	0.9
Current Assets to Working Capital 38	2.3	•	3.7	2.0	2.0	1.8	2.0	2.0	2.2	1.9	2.2	2.6
Current Liabilities to Working Capital 39	1.3	•	2.7	1.0	1.0	0.8	1.0	1.0	1.2	0.9	1.2	1.6
Working Capital to Net Sales 40	0.3	•	0.1	0.3	0.2	0.3	0.3	0.3	0.2	0.3	0.2	0.3
Inventory to Working Capital 41	0.5	•	1.9	0.8	0.7	0.7	0.7	0.7	0.7	0.5	0.7	0.4
Total Receipts to Cash Flow 42	6.6	21.7	10.3	4.6	9.8	10.7	11.7	9.7	10.0	8.4	6.3	5.3
Cost of Goods to Cash Flow 43	4.3	16.6	6.2	2.7	6.3	7.0	8.3	6.5	6.9	5.6	4.0	3.3
Cash Flow to Total Debt 44	0.2	•	0.5	0.4	0.3	0.2	0.2	0.2	0.2	0.2	0.3	0.3

Selected Financial Factors (in Percentages)

Debt Ratio 45	51.2	•	65.0	78.2	67.3	64.7	52.1	51.5	56.3	53.9	60.1	47.3
Return on Total Assets 46	8.5	•	•	20.6	13.2	5.2	5.1	4.2	6.6	5.3	11.3	9.1
Return on Equity Before Income Taxes 47	14.8	•	•	84.7	33.4	11.2	8.7	5.3	11.3	8.6	23.8	15.2
Return on Equity After Income Taxes 48	10.6	•	•	84.7	31.4	10.0	7.7	3.4	9.1	6.4	16.1	10.4
Profit Margin (Before Income Tax) 49	8.8	•	•	12.4	6.3	3.3	3.3	2.2	4.8	4.8	9.1	12.6
Profit Margin (After Income Tax) 50	6.3	•	•	12.4	5.9	2.9	2.9	1.4	3.9	3.6	6.2	8.6

Table II
Corporations with Net Income

INDUSTRIAL MACHINERY

MONEY AMOUNTS AND SIZE OF ASSETS IN THOUSANDS OF DOLLARS

Item Description for Accounting Period 7/10 Through 6/11	Total	Zero Assets	Under 500	500 to 1,000	1,000 to 5,000	5,000 to 10,000	10,000 to 25,000	25,000 to 50,000	50,000 to 100,000	100,000 to 250,000	250,000 to 500,000	500,000 to 2,500,000	2,500,000 and over
Number of Enterprises **1**	2624	11	•	416	588	205	81	32	30	23	•	16	0
Revenues ($ in Thousands)													
Net Sales **2**	41742065	81792	•	503667	3175712	2162475	1838516	1450681	2385134	3163275	•	23225352	0
Interest **3**	95644	24	•	4	2470	213	1374	799	3857	8893	•	70339	0
Rents **4**	84879	0	•	446	324	73	72	4868	710	15328	•	63049	0
Royalties **5**	441290	0	•	0	0	0	90	1039	220	27818	•	378187	0
Other Portfolio Income **6**	466435	34	•	12431	264	22398	6372	3593	11928	51362	•	349390	0
Other Receipts **7**	470498	3355	•	1440	12701	10707	13343	18249	20619	24507	•	320821	0
Total Receipts **8**	43300811	85205	•	517988	3191471	2195866	1859767	1479229	2422468	3291183	•	24407138	0
Average Total Receipts **9**	16502	7746	•	1245	5428	10712	22960	46226	80749	143095	•	1525446	•
Operating Costs/Operating Income (%)													
Cost of Operations **10**	62.9	81.3	•	58.9	60.7	62.7	67.4	65.3	68.1	66.4	•	61.9	•
Salaries and Wages **11**	10.4	1.2	•	2.7	9.9	11.9	9.9	9.6	9.8	10.7	•	10.9	•
Taxes Paid **12**	1.6	1.7	•	2.5	2.7	2.1	1.7	1.9	1.9	1.2	•	1.3	•
Interest Paid **13**	1.4	0.0	•	1.4	0.8	0.8	0.6	1.2	1.4	1.2	•	1.7	•
Depreciation **14**	2.3	0.8	•	0.1	1.7	2.0	1.7	3.5	2.2	2.2	•	2.5	•
Amortization and Depletion **15**	0.9	0.3	•	0.0	0.1	0.1	0.2	0.1	1.0	1.3	•	1.0	•
Pensions and Other Deferred Comp. **16**	0.9	0.3	•	0.0	0.1	1.1	0.5	0.6	0.9	0.8	•	1.0	•
Employee Benefits **17**	2.1	0.4	•	2.2	2.7	2.5	2.3	1.6	2.1	1.9	•	2.0	•
Advertising **18**	0.4	0.1	•	1.7	0.2	0.5	0.5	1.0	0.4	0.3	•	0.4	•
Other Expenses **19**	9.3	4.6	•	12.5	6.0	6.7	6.5	9.8	6.6	8.4	•	10.4	•
Officers' Compensation **20**	1.4	1.5	•	8.2	5.2	2.9	2.4	2.1	1.3	1.4	•	0.6	•
Operating Margin **21**	6.3	7.8	•	9.6	9.9	6.7	6.3	3.3	4.4	4.2	•	6.3	•
Operating Margin Before Officers' Comp. **22**	7.7	9.3	•	17.8	15.1	9.7	8.7	5.4	5.7	5.5	•	6.9	•

Selected Average Balance Sheet ($ in Thousands)

Net Receivables 23	4542	0	•	150	943	1323	3555	7659	16334	23348	•	546033
Inventories 24	1713	0	•	214	653	1213	3502	6904	10799	17681	•	174045
Net Property, Plant and Equipment 25	1916	0	•	13	506	1713	2405	7499	10709	18427	•	175080
Total Assets 26	19550	0	•	816	2707	7618	15930	34205	73009	147573	•	2283168
Notes and Loans Payable 27	3476	0	•	412	718	1730	2654	6620	15579	27961	•	365437
All Other Liabilities 28	6024	0	•	226	739	1970	5053	10335	20786	36335	•	714431
Net Worth 29	10050	0	•	178	1250	3918	8222	17250	36644	83277	•	1203301

Selected Financial Ratios (Times to 1)

Current Ratio 30	1.8	•	•	2.0	2.7	2.7	1.9	2.0	1.9	2.3	•	1.6
Quick Ratio 31	1.2	•	•	0.8	1.7	1.7	1.1	1.2	1.1	1.4	•	1.2
Net Sales to Working Capital 32	3.7	•	•	3.2	4.3	3.2	4.5	4.0	4.0	2.9	•	3.6
Coverage Ratio 33	8.5	259.7	•	9.7	13.6	11.8	13.7	5.4	5.4	7.8	•	8.5
Total Asset Turnover 34	0.8	•	•	1.5	2.0	1.4	1.4	1.3	1.1	0.9	•	0.6
Inventory Turnover 35	5.8	•	•	3.3	5.0	5.5	4.4	4.3	5.0	5.2	•	5.2
Receivables Turnover 36	4.5	•	•	7.5	5.9	9.9	8.5	6.2	6.3	7.0	•	•
Total Liabilities to Net Worth 37	0.9	•	•	3.6	1.2	0.9	0.9	1.0	1.0	0.8	•	0.9
Current Assets to Working Capital 38	2.3	•	•	2.0	1.6	1.6	2.1	2.0	2.1	1.8	•	2.6
Current Liabilities to Working Capital 39	1.3	•	•	1.0	0.6	0.6	1.1	1.0	1.1	0.8	•	1.6
Working Capital to Net Sales 40	0.3	•	•	0.3	0.2	0.3	0.2	0.3	0.2	0.3	•	0.3
Inventory to Working Capital 41	0.5	•	•	0.8	0.5	0.5	0.8	0.7	0.7	0.5	•	0.4
Total Receipts to Cash Flow 42	6.0	6.3	•	4.6	7.4	8.0	8.2	7.8	9.2	7.3	•	5.3
Cost of Goods to Cash Flow 43	3.8	5.1	•	2.7	4.5	5.0	5.5	5.1	6.3	4.9	•	3.3
Cash Flow to Total Debt 44	0.3	•	•	0.4	0.5	0.4	0.4	0.3	0.2	0.3	•	0.3

Selected Financial Factors (in Percentages)

Debt Ratio 45	48.6	•	•	78.2	53.8	48.6	48.4	49.6	49.8	43.6	•	47.3
Return on Total Assets 46	9.9	•	•	20.6	22.4	12.5	11.4	8.6	8.1	8.8	•	9.1
Return on Equity Before Income Taxes 47	17.0	•	•	84.7	44.9	22.3	20.4	13.9	13.2	13.6	•	15.2
Return on Equity After Income Taxes 48	12.6	•	•	84.7	42.8	21.1	18.8	11.1	10.8	11.0	•	10.4
Profit Margin (Before Income Tax) 49	10.7	12.0	•	12.4	10.4	8.3	7.4	5.3	6.1	8.2	•	12.6
Profit Margin (After Income Tax) 50	7.9	7.9	•	12.4	9.9	7.9	6.8	4.2	5.0	6.7	•	8.6

Table I
Corporations with and without Net Income

COMMERCIAL AND SERVICE INDUSTRY MACHINERY

MONEY AMOUNTS AND SIZE OF ASSETS IN THOUSANDS OF DOLLARS

Item Description for Accounting Period 7/10 Through 6/11	Total	Zero Assets	Under 500	500 to 1,000	1,000 to 5,000	5,000 to 10,000	10,000 to 25,000	25,000 to 50,000	50,000 to 100,000	100,000 to 250,000	250,000 to 500,000	500,000 to 2,500,000	2,500,000 and over
Number of Enterprises **1**	1924	18	1203	177	275	109	68	30	16	12	6	5	4
Revenues ($ in Thousands)													
Net Sales **2**	40795671	220019	448434	156281	1206697	1345551	1573844	951018	1401413	2422543	2099618	3301675	25568577
Interest **3**	535255	45	65	1	797	1312	1927	3655	3118	3896	3340	5158	511943
Rents **4**	126416	45	923	0	0	244	255	3023	166	4106	226	29977	87450
Royalties **5**	1332566	449	0	0	0	1840	72	2452	470	454	20712	35713	1270403
Other Portfolio Income **6**	681212	11192	0	0	1230	463	138	2792	1887	65616	833	14578	582484
Other Receipts **7**	1507220	13689	4994	0	14342	15783	17151	11388	17314	38946	1061	35881	1336671
Total Receipts **8**	44978340	245439	454416	156282	1223066	1365193	1593387	974328	1424368	2535561	2125790	3422982	29457528
Average Total Receipts **9**	23378	13636	378	883	4448	12525	23432	32478	89023	211297	354298	684596	7364382
Operating Costs/Operating Income (%)													
Cost of Operations **10**	51.3	45.9	66.5	77.3	62.8	68.0	71.7	67.3	60.2	66.3	64.4	44.1	45.7
Salaries and Wages **11**	18.6	10.3	4.8	9.6	8.3	10.3	7.8	8.4	11.0	12.5	8.8	20.7	22.4
Taxes Paid **12**	2.7	24.3	1.5	0.1	1.9	1.8	1.9	1.9	1.8	2.3	1.5	2.3	2.9
Interest Paid **13**	3.2	2.0	0.4	0.5	1.1	0.9	0.8	1.9	1.9	0.8	3.7	2.6	4.0
Depreciation **14**	5.3	1.4	3.5	0.1	1.0	1.3	1.6	1.8	2.3	1.5	1.9	3.9	7.1
Amortization and Depletion **15**	1.9	0.1	•	•	0.2	0.4	0.4	0.7	0.9	1.2	2.8	1.6	2.3
Pensions and Other Deferred Comp. **16**	2.1	0.1	0.9	0.0	0.6	0.3	0.2	0.4	0.5	1.0	0.5	0.7	3.0
Employee Benefits **17**	2.1	2.3	5.6	0.3	2.1	3.3	1.7	1.8	2.9	2.4	1.8	2.4	1.9
Advertising **18**	1.2	0.9	1.3	0.0	0.7	2.0	0.6	1.5	1.1	1.0	0.6	0.5	1.4
Other Expenses **19**	18.1	11.2	11.4	19.7	9.5	12.1	6.8	12.4	10.8	11.0	12.3	18.6	21.4
Officers' Compensation **20**	0.9	0.3	13.1	0.2	3.2	1.9	1.9	2.9	1.7	1.1	0.8	0.6	0.4
Operating Margin **21**	•	1.2	•	•	8.6	•	4.7	•	4.8	•	1.0	2.0	•
Operating Margin Before Officers' Comp. **22**	•	1.5	4.2	•	11.7	•	6.6	1.9	6.5	1.7	1.7	2.6	•

Selected Average Balance Sheet ($ in Thousands)

Net Receivables 23	9339	0	49	212	355	1719	3496	8506	12648	51846	68891	104052	3833794
Inventories 24	1890	0	25	130	1147	1576	4521	6795	13177	30878	51536	95853	304042
Net Property, Plant and Equipment 25	2475	0	22	1	251	917	2592	3961	8215	22241	38634	111628	770795
Total Assets 26	39736	0	136	876	2289	6584	15085	36516	74127	167094	448732	928497	15534945
Notes and Loans Payable 27	12995	0	99	166	1085	1341	4207	6260	13364	21623	254930	281807	5130666
All Other Liabilities 28	17847	0	8	685	300	3019	4186	17236	32523	71594	91477	260634	7440301
Net Worth 29	8895	0	29	25	904	2224	6692	13021	28240	73878	102325	386056	2963978

Selected Financial Ratios (Times to 1)

Current Ratio 30	1.2	•	4.0	0.4	2.6	1.3	1.7	1.3	1.4	1.4	1.8	1.4	1.2
Quick Ratio 31	0.8	•	3.3	0.3	1.3	0.7	0.9	0.7	0.7	0.8	1.0	0.7	0.8
Net Sales to Working Capital 32	7.4	•	4.9	•	4.2	13.0	5.3	5.3	6.7	7.6	5.4	7.7	7.8
Coverage Ratio 33	2.2	7.4	•	•	9.6	0.1	8.0	2.2	4.7	5.7	1.6	3.4	1.9
Total Asset Turnover 34	0.5	•	2.7	1.0	1.9	1.9	1.5	0.9	1.2	1.2	0.8	0.7	0.4
Inventory Turnover 35	5.8	•	10.1	5.2	2.4	5.3	3.7	3.1	4.0	4.3	4.4	3.0	9.6
Receivables Turnover 36	3.0	•	12.2	3.2	6.2	8.9	7.7	4.2	7.9	4.2	5.3	5.0	2.3
Total Liabilities to Net Worth 37	3.5	•	3.8	33.6	1.5	2.0	1.3	1.8	1.6	1.3	3.4	1.4	4.2
Current Assets to Working Capital 38	5.5	•	1.3	•	1.6	4.2	2.3	4.2	3.3	3.8	2.3	3.4	7.2
Current Liabilities to Working Capital 39	4.5	•	0.3	•	0.6	3.2	1.3	3.2	2.3	2.8	1.3	2.4	6.2
Working Capital to Net Sales 40	0.1	•	0.2	0.2	0.2	0.1	0.2	0.2	0.1	0.1	0.2	0.1	0.1
Inventory to Working Capital 41	0.7	•	0.2	•	0.7	1.7	0.9	1.4	1.2	1.2	0.9	1.1	0.5
Total Receipts to Cash Flow 42	5.8	7.2	30.9	8.9	6.3	10.6	8.8	10.0	6.4	7.7	7.6	4.7	5.3
Cost of Goods to Cash Flow 43	3.0	3.3	20.5	6.9	3.9	7.2	6.3	6.7	3.9	5.1	4.9	2.1	2.4
Cash Flow to Total Debt 44	0.1	•	0.1	0.1	0.5	0.3	0.3	0.1	0.3	0.3	0.1	0.3	0.1

Selected Financial Factors (in Percentages)

Debt Ratio 45	77.6	•	79.0	97.1	60.5	66.2	55.6	64.3	61.9	55.8	77.2	58.4	80.9
Return on Total Assets 46	3.8	•	•	•	21.2	0.1	10.4	3.7	10.6	5.8	4.6	6.5	3.2
Return on Equity Before Income Taxes 47	9.5	•	•	•	48.1	•	20.4	5.7	21.9	10.8	7.5	11.0	8.1
Return on Equity After Income Taxes 48	5.5	•	•	•	47.5	•	16.9	4.9	18.5	7.6	3.7	7.5	3.9
Profit Margin (Before Income Tax) 49	4.0	12.8	•	•	9.9	•	5.9	2.3	7.1	3.9	2.2	6.4	3.8
Profit Margin (After Income Tax) 50	2.3	8.5	•	•	9.8	•	4.9	2.0	6.0	2.8	1.1	4.4	1.8

Table II
Corporations with Net Income

COMMERCIAL AND SERVICE INDUSTRY MACHINERY

MONEY AMOUNTS AND SIZE OF ASSETS IN THOUSANDS OF DOLLARS

Item Description for Accounting Period 7/10 Through 6/11	Total	Zero Assets	Under 500	500 to 1,000	1,000 to 5,000	5,000 to 10,000	10,000 to 25,000	25,000 to 50,000	50,000 to 100,000	100,000 to 250,000	250,000 to 500,000	500,000 to 2,500,000	2,500,000 and over
Number of Enterprises 1	820	10	409	0	214	85	50	18	•	8	•	•	0
Revenues ($ in Thousands)													
Net Sales 2	27834677	220019	240804	0	943360	1127784	1176191	671706	•	1216912	•	•	0
Interest 3	510285	44	1	0	168	370	1682	1040	•	2177	•	•	0
Rents 4	11988	45	0	0	0	244	255	2896	•	2027	•	•	0
Royalties 5	472123	0	0	0	0	1828	0	0	•	285	•	•	0
Other Portfolio Income 6	639101	11192	0	0	1230	450	138	2792	•	65615	•	•	0
Other Receipts 7	1311419	13690	0	0	12763	6739	13907	10705	•	13054	•	•	0
Total Receipts 8	30779593	244990	240805	0	957521	1137415	1192173	689139	•	1300070	•	•	•
Average Total Receipts 9	37536	24499	589	•	4474	13381	23843	38286	•	162509	•	•	•
Operating Costs/Operating Income (%)													
Cost of Operations 10	43.2	45.9	73.8	•	57.2	70.0	67.1	70.7	•	63.5	•	•	•
Salaries and Wages 11	19.3	10.3	1.1	•	9.5	9.5	7.3	7.3	•	11.8	•	•	•
Taxes Paid 12	2.8	24.3	0.6	•	2.0	1.7	1.9	1.6	•	2.1	•	•	•
Interest Paid 13	3.5	2.0	0.0	•	1.0	0.5	0.9	1.2	•	1.3	•	•	•
Depreciation 14	5.8	1.4	0.3	•	0.5	1.1	1.6	1.8	•	1.7	•	•	•
Amortization and Depletion 15	2.5	0.1	•	•	0.2	0.1	0.5	0.3	•	1.1	•	•	•
Pensions and Other Deferred Comp. 16	2.3	0.1	0.0	•	0.7	0.3	0.3	0.3	•	1.6	•	•	•
Employee Benefits 17	1.6	2.3	0.0	•	2.3	2.1	1.8	1.7	•	2.7	•	•	•
Advertising 18	0.9	0.9	0.5	•	0.7	2.2	0.6	1.1	•	0.7	•	•	•
Other Expenses 19	20.6	10.8	4.4	•	9.9	7.2	8.2	7.3	•	9.6	•	•	•
Officers' Compensation 20	0.9	0.3	6.9	•	3.3	1.8	1.8	2.6	•	1.6	•	•	•
Operating Margin 21	•	1.5	12.4	•	12.7	3.5	8.0	4.2	•	2.3	•	•	•
Operating Margin Before Officers' Comp. 22	•	1.8	19.3	•	16.0	5.3	9.8	6.8	•	4.0	•	•	•

Selected Average Balance Sheet ($ in Thousands)

Net Receivables 23	20044	0	1	•	377	1674	3962	8525	•	55905
Inventories 24	2569	0	5	•	900	1461	4239	5986	•	28050
Net Property, Plant and Equipment 25	4046	0	3	•	118	907	2203	3836	•	22046
Total Assets 26	73472	0	105	•	2222	6654	14994	35068	•	156797
Notes and Loans Payable 27	20639	0	0	•	716	962	3741	1807	•	17682
All Other Liabilities 28	34295	0	1	•	263	2170	3693	20131	•	83134
Net Worth 29	18537	0	103	•	1243	3522	7560	13130	•	55981

Selected Financial Ratios (Times to 1)

Current Ratio 30	1.3	•	72.2	•	4.7	1.4	2.2	1.4	•	1.3
Quick Ratio 31	1.0	•	71.9	•	2.9	0.7	1.2	0.7	•	0.9
Net Sales to Working Capital 32	4.6	•	5.9	•	3.3	10.9	4.3	4.3	•	7.5
Coverage Ratio 33	3.5	7.5	5956.6	•	15.0	9.3	11.2	7.8	•	8.8
Total Asset Turnover 34	0.5	•	5.6	•	2.0	2.0	1.6	1.1	•	1.0
Inventory Turnover 35	5.7	•	93.0	•	2.8	6.4	3.7	4.4	•	3.4
Receivables Turnover 36	2.2	•	2046.4	•	6.8	10.3	7.2	7.2	•	•
Total Liabilities to Net Worth 37	3.0	•	C.0	•	0.8	0.9	1.0	1.7	•	1.8
Current Assets to Working Capital 38	3.9	•	1.0	•	1.3	3.3	1.9	3.3	•	5.0
Current Liabilities to Working Capital 39	2.9	•	0.0	•	0.3	2.3	0.9	2.3	•	4.0
Working Capital to Net Sales 40	0.2	•	0.2	•	0.3	0.1	0.2	0.2	•	0.1
Inventory to Working Capital 41	0.4	•	0.0	•	0.5	1.3	0.7	1.3	•	1.4
Total Receipts to Cash Flow 42	4.3	7.4	6.0	•	4.9	10.4	6.3	7.8	•	5.9
Cost of Goods to Cash Flow 43	1.8	3.4	4.1	•	2.8	7.3	4.2	5.5	•	3.7
Cash Flow to Total Debt 44	0.1	•	65.4	•	0.9	0.4	0.5	0.2	•	0.3

Selected Financial Factors (in Percentages)

Debt Ratio 45	74.8	•	1.6	•	44.1	47.1	49.6	62.6	•	64.3
Return on Total Assets 46	5.6	•	69.4	•	30.3	9.8	16.0	9.7	•	11.0
Return on Equity Before Income Taxes 47	15.8	•	70.4	•	50.5	16.4	29.0	22.6	•	27.2
Return on Equity After Income Taxes 48	11.3	•	70.3	•	50.0	13.7	24.8	21.3	•	21.0
Profit Margin (Before Income Tax) 49	8.6	12.9	12.4	•	14.2	4.4	9.3	8.0	•	10.0
Profit Margin (After Income Tax) 50	6.2	8.7	12.4	•	14.1	3.6	8.0	7.5	•	7.7

VENTILATION, HEATING, A.C. & COMMERCIAL REFRIGERATION EQUIP.

Table I

Corporations with and without Net Income

MONEY AMOUNTS AND SIZE OF ASSETS IN THOUSANDS OF DOLLARS

Item Description for Accounting Period 7/10 Through 6/11		Total	Zero Assets	Under 500	500 to 1,000	1,000 to 5,000	5,000 to 10,000	10,000 to 25,000	25,000 to 50,000	50,000 to 100,000	100,000 to 250,000	250,000 to 500,000	500,000 to 2,500,000	2,500,000 and over
Number of Enterprises	1	948	•	369	•	•	115	47	47	23	19	5	8	3
Revenues ($ in Thousands)														
Net Sales	2	33177586	•	54294	•	•	2067467	1068082	3020739	2293749	3541723	1246733	8982006	9822635
Interest	3	86468	•	0	•	•	226	841	2075	2240	3617	5957	34448	36459
Rents	4	11586	•	0	•	•	401	229	444	390	2067	203	7551	300
Royalties	5	301272	•	0	•	•	0	0	5887	4227	2992	12404	243649	32112
Other Portfolio Income	6	170941	•	1	•	•	388	1082	2320	6073	27983	18282	101325	13163
Other Receipts	7	326252	•	30	•	•	15140	6924	13092	9876	23335	8932	185579	61917
Total Receipts	8	34074105	•	54325	•	•	2083622	1077158	3044557	2316555	3601717	1292511	9554558	9966586
Average Total Receipts	9	35943	•	147	•	•	18118	22918	64778	100720	189564	258502	1194320	3322195
Operating Costs/Operating Income (%)														
Cost of Operations	10	70.7	•	53.0	•	•	80.7	67.5	70.1	68.7	67.9	70.8	67.0	74.4
Salaries and Wages	11	8.4	•	15.8	•	•	4.4	9.9	8.0	7.9	7.8	6.7	11.1	7.1
Taxes Paid	12	1.2	•	6.1	•	•	0.9	1.6	1.4	1.6	1.8	0.9	1.7	0.3
Interest Paid	13	3.4	•	2.8	•	•	0.3	0.6	0.9	0.8	1.8	4.8	2.6	7.2
Depreciation	14	1.8	•	1.3	•	•	0.9	1.7	1.9	2.2	2.4	1.7	2.4	1.3
Amortization and Depletion	15	1.1	•	0.1	•	•	0.0	0.6	0.2	0.5	0.4	2.1	0.9	2.1
Pensions and Other Deferred Comp.	16	0.9	•	•	•	•	0.3	0.6	0.5	0.5	0.9	0.1	1.0	1.4
Employee Benefits	17	2.1	•	4.8	•	•	0.6	1.3	2.2	1.8	2.5	2.1	1.8	2.7
Advertising	18	0.8	•	3.8	•	•	1.0	1.0	0.7	0.7	0.7	0.4	1.2	0.6
Other Expenses	19	9.8	•	28.3	•	•	6.0	8.2	9.7	8.7	8.2	12.6	12.1	8.6
Officers' Compensation	20	1.2	•	12.3	•	•	1.4	3.2	1.0	2.8	0.6	0.8	1.0	0.4
Operating Margin	21	•	•	•	•	•	3.5	3.8	3.4	3.9	5.1	•	•	•
Operating Margin Before Officers' Comp.	22	•	•	•	•	•	4.9	7.0	4.4	6.7	5.7	•	•	•

Selected Average Balance Sheet ($ in Thousands)

Net Receivables 23	5254	24	•	1870	3563	8602	14804	33303	90166	172168	409048
Inventories 24	3765	7	•	1699	4458	5436	11485	24190	39704	128525	286456
Net Property, Plant and Equipment 25	4398	5	•	1203	2677	7325	13583	25814	31578	203551	307837
Total Assets 26	41364	41	•	6993	15548	36546	70166	140357	417699	1500091	5697653
Notes and Loans Payable 27	12359	109	•	1988	3051	7383	19847	32848	174755	450418	1757035
All Other Liabilities 28	14589	24	•	1706	3454	13271	17196	70578	132238	458555	2186848
Net Worth 29	14417	-91	•	3299	9042	15891	33123	36932	110706	591118	1753770

Selected Financial Ratios (Times to 1)

Current Ratio 30	1.7	0.4	•	4.7	2.2	1.8	2.1	1.3	1.9	2.0	1.3
Quick Ratio 31	1.0	0.3	•	2.9	1.3	1.2	1.2	0.7	1.4	1.2	0.6
Net Sales to Working Capital 32	6.4	•	•	4.2	4.1	6.9	4.9	10.1	3.5	4.5	16.5
Coverage Ratio 33	1.6	•	•	17.1	8.6	5.7	7.2	4.8	1.2	3.1	0.4
Total Asset Turnover 34	0.8	3.6	•	2.6	1.5	1.8	1.4	1.3	0.6	0.7	0.6
Inventory Turnover 35	6.6	11.4	•	8.5	3.4	8.3	6.0	5.2	4.4	5.9	8.5
Receivables Turnover 36	6.3	2.1	•	10.0	4.8	8.1	6.6	7.0	2.9	6.9	5.7
Total Liabilities to Net Worth 37	1.9	•	•	1.1	0.7	1.3	1.1	2.8	2.8	1.5	2.2
Current Assets to Working Capital 38	2.4	•	•	1.3	1.8	2.2	1.9	4.5	2.1	2.0	4.4
Current Liabilities to Working Capital 39	1.4	•	•	0.3	0.8	1.2	0.9	3.5	1.1	1.0	3.4
Working Capital to Net Sales 40	0.2	•	•	0.2	0.2	0.1	0.2	0.1	0.3	0.2	0.1
Inventory to Working Capital 41	0.7	•	•	0.4	0.7	0.6	0.6	1.6	0.5	0.5	1.5
Total Receipts to Cash Flow 42	10.5	•	•	10.8	8.9	7.8	8.8	7.6	8.4	7.2	30.6
Cost of Goods to Cash Flow 43	7.4	•	•	8.7	6.0	5.5	6.0	5.2	5.9	4.8	22.8
Cash Flow to Total Debt 44	0.1	•	•	0.5	0.4	0.4	0.3	0.2	0.1	0.2	0.0

Selected Financial Factors (in Percentages)

Debt Ratio 45	65.1	320.2	•	52.8	41.8	56.5	52.8	73.7	73.5	60.6	69.2
Return on Total Assets 46	4.5	•	•	11.8	7.5	8.9	8.0	11.5	3.4	6.0	1.7
Return on Equity Before Income Taxes 47	4.6	45.6	•	23.5	11.4	16.9	14.6	34.6	1.8	10.2	•
Return on Equity After Income Taxes 48	2.8	45.6	•	19.7	9.2	13.8	11.7	27.0	1.7	7.8	•
Profit Margin (Before Income Tax) 49	1.9	•	•	4.3	4.5	4.2	4.9	6.9	0.8	5.4	•
Profit Margin (After Income Tax) 50	1.2	•	•	3.6	3.7	3.4	3.9	5.4	0.8	4.1	•

Table II
Corporations with Net Income

VENTILATION, HEATING, A.C. & COMMERCIAL REFRIGERATION EQUIP.

MONEY AMOUNTS AND SIZE OF ASSETS IN THOUSANDS OF DOLLARS

Item Description for Accounting Period 7/10 Through 6/11	Total	Zero Assets	Under 500	500 to 1,000	1,000 to 5,000	5,000 to 10,000	10,000 to 25,000	25,000 to 50,000	50,000 to 100,000	100,000 to 250,000	250,000 to 500,000	500,000 to 2,500,000	2,500,000 and over
Number of Enterprises 1	373	•	•	63	85	101	35	38	19	•	•	•	0
Revenues ($ in Thousands)													
Net Sales 2	20043309	•	•	127794	555049	1868322	890845	2382073	2032190	•	•	•	0
Interest 3	46715	•	•	2	371	188	475	1185	1173	•	•	•	0
Rents 4	10764	•	•	0	0	391	229	425	32	•	•	•	0
Royalties 5	263449	•	•	0	0	0	0	5887	4227	•	•	•	0
Other Portfolio Income 6	147601	•	•	0	99	388	1078	1858	5928	•	•	•	0
Other Receipts 7	237334	•	•	83	40	1925	4478	12266	7629	•	•	•	0
Total Receipts 8	20749172	•	•	127879	555559	1871214	897105	2403694	2051179	•	•	•	0
Average Total Receipts 9	55628	•	•	2030	6536	18527	25632	63255	107957	•	•	•	•
Operating Costs/Operating Income (%)													
Cost of Operations 10	68.1	•	•	70.9	64.5	79.3	67.7	65.8	67.9	•	•	•	•
Salaries and Wages 11	9.0	•	•	3.6	12.2	3.9	9.7	8.7	7.4	•	•	•	•
Taxes Paid 12	1.5	•	•	2.6	2.5	0.9	1.6	1.4	1.5	•	•	•	•
Interest Paid 13	1.7	•	•	0.1	0.2	0.2	0.3	0.8	0.8	•	•	•	•
Depreciation 14	2.0	•	•	0.2	1.5	0.7	1.3	1.8	2.0	•	•	•	•
Amortization and Depletion 15	0.6	•	•	•	0.1	0.0	0.5	0.2	0.5	•	•	•	•
Pensions and Other Deferred Comp. 16	0.8	•	•	0.0	0.4	0.3	0.6	0.5	0.5	•	•	•	•
Employee Benefits 17	1.9	•	•	1.7	0.7	0.5	1.5	2.5	1.8	•	•	•	•
Advertising 18	1.0	•	•	0.0	0.7	0.8	0.7	0.9	0.7	•	•	•	•
Other Expenses 19	9.7	•	•	8.1	9.7	5.0	5.3	10.3	8.2	•	•	•	•
Officers' Compensation 20	1.5	•	•	9.7	6.3	1.5	2.7	1.2	3.1	•	•	•	•
Operating Margin 21	2.1	•	•	3.0	1.3	6.8	8.1	5.9	5.7	•	•	•	•
Operating Margin Before Officers' Comp. 22	3.7	•	•	12.7	7.6	8.3	10.8	7.1	8.7	•	•	•	•

Selected Average Balance Sheet ($ in Thousands)

	1	2	3	4	5	6	7
Net Receivables 23	7827	118	810	2036	3940	7921	15464
Inventories 24	5782	233	604	1727	4006	4608	10521
Net Property, Plant and Equipment 25	7406	32	333	1230	2173	7504	13508
Total Assets 26	51242	595	2526	6725	15111	35951	69216
Notes and Loans Payable 27	14283	22	410	1089	2665	6840	19414
All Other Liabilities 28	16398	41	573	1573	3234	11745	17510
Net Worth 29	20560	532	1544	4063	9211	17366	32293

Selected Financial Ratios (Times to 1)

	1	2	3	4	5	6	7
Current Ratio 30	1.9		3.5	5.0	2.3	2.0	2.0
Quick Ratio 31	1.1		2.2	3.1	1.5	1.3	1.2
Net Sales to Working Capital 32	5.1		4.2	4.4	4.2	6.5	5.2
Coverage Ratio 33	4.7		6.8	30.0	25.8	9.6	9.0
Total Asset Turnover 34	1.0		2.6	2.8	1.7	1.7	1.5
Inventory Turnover 35	6.3		7.0	8.5	4.3	9.0	6.9
Receivables Turnover 36	8.0	•	8.6	9.3	5.7	8.6	7.6
Total Liabilities to Net Worth 37	1.5		0.6	0.7	0.6	1.1	1.1
Current Assets to Working Capital 38	2.1		1.4	1.2	1.8	2.0	2.0
Current Liabilities to Working Capital 39	1.1		0.4	0.2	0.8	1.0	1.0
Working Capital to Net Sales 40	0.2		0.2	0.2	0.2	0.2	0.2
Inventory to Working Capital 41	0.6		0.5	0.4	0.6	0.6	0.6
Total Receipts to Cash Flow 42	7.3		13.5	9.1	7.9	6.3	7.9
Cost of Goods to Cash Flow 43	5.0		8.7	7.2	5.4	4.1	5.4
Cash Flow to Total Debt 44	0.2		0.5	0.8	0.5	0.5	0.4

Selected Financial Factors (in Percentages)

	1	2	3	4	5	6	7
Debt Ratio 45	59.9	10.5	38.9	39.6	39.0	51.7	53.3
Return on Total Assets 46	8.5	10.9	4.1	19.9	15.2	13.2	11.5
Return on Equity Before Income Taxes 47	16.7	11.8	5.7	31.8	23.9	24.5	21.9
Return on Equity After Income Taxes 48	13.6	9.8	4.4	28.4	21.1	20.9	18.3
Profit Margin (Before Income Tax) 49	6.4	3.1	1.3	7.0	8.7	6.8	6.6
Profit Margin (After Income Tax) 50	5.2	2.6	1.0	6.2	7.6	5.8	5.5

Table I

Corporations with and without Net Income

METALWORKING MACHINERY

MONEY AMOUNTS AND SIZE OF ASSETS IN THOUSANDS OF DOLLARS

Item Description for Accounting Period 7/10 Through 6/11		Total	Zero Assets	Under 500	500 to 1,000	1,000 to 5,000	5,000 to 10,000	10,000 to 25,000	25,000 to 50,000	50,000 to 100,000	100,000 to 250,000	250,000 to 500,000	500,000 to 2,500,000	2,500,000 and over
Number of Enterprises	1	7359	751	4369	961	936	140	119	41	23	12	3	4	0
Revenues ($ in Thousands)														
Net Sales	2	21818194	552131	1849112	1315825	3136927	1384938	2098392	1841197	1420473	1676320	941203	5601676	0
Interest	3	54317	1035	738	2060	3944	269	406	366	2667	2809	1345	38677	0
Rents	4	14309	0	4382	0	1304	3221	164	548	0	4465	0	224	0
Royalties	5	4910	8	0	0	0	102	0	0	229	1789	0	2782	0
Other Portfolio Income	6	226045	31695	5766	1580	41501	6460	5958	13445	15188	17378	317	86757	0
Other Receipts	7	172277	127	5064	3992	30784	7406	18184	8623	10587	24991	1002	61521	0
Total Receipts	8	22290052	584996	1865062	1323457	3214460	1402396	2123104	1864179	1449144	1727752	943867	5791637	0
Average Total Receipts	9	3029	779	427	1377	3434	10017	17841	45468	63006	143979	314622	1447909	•
Operating Costs/Operating Income (%)														
Cost of Operations	10	63.5	49.2	36.3	56.3	68.1	67.2	66.7	69.3	68.7	64.7	69.2	66.2	•
Salaries and Wages	11	8.2	10.9	11.5	10.0	7.0	5.0	5.6	6.4	7.3	11.5	9.2	8.4	•
Taxes Paid	12	2.3	2.3	3.9	3.8	3.3	2.8	2.7	2.0	2.1	2.0	1.9	0.9	•
Interest Paid	13	2.1	3.9	1.6	1.9	0.6	0.7	0.8	1.2	1.4	2.2	2.0	4.2	•
Depreciation	14	3.9	2.9	3.0	4.3	3.3	4.6	4.3	4.1	3.6	2.8	3.6	4.5	•
Amortization and Depletion	15	0.6	0.7	0.0	0.1	0.0	0.1	0.1	0.2	0.4	0.7	0.5	1.6	•
Pensions and Other Deferred Comp.	16	0.6	0.4	0.1	0.0	0.3	0.7	0.4	0.9	0.5	0.6	0.3	1.0	•
Employee Benefits	17	3.3	0.8	2.7	3.4	1.5	1.7	3.1	2.3	2.2	3.4	1.4	6.3	•
Advertising	18	0.4	0.4	0.2	0.2	0.3	0.3	0.4	0.3	0.5	0.5	0.2	0.6	•
Other Expenses	19	11.2	19.0	31.8	9.9	11.1	6.3	7.7	7.8	8.6	10.2	10.4	8.7	•
Officers' Compensation	20	3.0	2.0	7.9	6.4	4.4	7.8	2.5	1.5	1.3	1.2	0.2	0.6	•
Operating Margin	21	1.1	7.4	0.9	3.8	0.2	2.9	5.7	4.0	3.3	0.1	1.4	•	•
Operating Margin Before Officers' Comp.	22	4.1	9.4	8.9	10.1	4.6	10.7	8.2	5.5	4.6	1.4	1.6	•	•

Selected Average Balance Sheet ($ in Thousands)

	•	•	•	•	•	•	•	•	•	•	•	•
Net Receivables 23	452	0	39	197	508	1313	3353	7916	11780	21313	48218	228880
Inventories 24	423	0	6	94	530	1189	2924	10369	12893	29272	97182	191602
Net Property, Plant and Equipment 25	498	0	30	251	496	1944	4008	7501	13971	23388	52989	253051
Total Assets 26	2913	0	110	715	2451	6346	15075	35589	65544	161138	334780	2346147
Notes and Loans Payable 27	960	0	169	503	494	1358	3594	8287	14218	59736	89957	777998
All Other Liabilities 28	808	0	40	190	534	1419	3829	10338	17464	28821	108919	733964
Net Worth 29	1144	0	-100	23	1423	3569	7652	16963	33862	72581	135904	834186

Selected Financial Ratios (Times to 1)

	•	•	•	•	•	•	•	•	•	•	•	•
Current Ratio 30	1.3	•	1.3	1.2	2.4	2.1	1.8	2.0	1.9	1.6	1.7	0.7
Quick Ratio 31	0.7	•	1.2	0.7	1.3	1.4	1.0	1.0	0.9	1.0	0.8	0.4
Net Sales to Working Capital 32	9.3	•	23.8	24.7	3.5	5.2	4.1	4.2	3.3	5.3	3.8	•
Coverage Ratio 33	2.8	4.4	2.1	3.3	5.5	6.9	9.3	5.5	4.7	2.7	2.2	1.5
Total Asset Turnover 34	1.0	•	3.8	1.9	1.4	1.6	1.2	1.3	0.9	0.9	0.9	0.6
Inventory Turnover 35	4.5	•	26.9	8.2	4.3	5.6	4.0	3.0	3.3	3.1	2.2	4.8
Receivables Turnover 36	6.9	•	12.1	7.6	6.6	7.0	5.8	5.5	6.7	4.9	13.0	6.6
Total Liabilities to Net Worth 37	1.5	•	•	30.7	0.7	0.8	1.0	1.1	0.9	1.2	1.5	1.8
Current Assets to Working Capital 38	3.9	•	4.1	7.4	1.7	1.9	2.2	2.0	2.1	2.6	2.4	•
Current Liabilities to Working Capital 39	2.9	•	3.1	6.4	0.7	0.9	1.2	1.0	1.1	1.6	1.4	•
Working Capital to Net Sales 40	0.1	•	0.0	0.0	0.3	0.2	0.2	0.2	0.3	0.2	0.3	•
Inventory to Working Capital 41	1.4	•	0.2	2.2	0.5	0.5	0.8	0.8	0.9	0.8	1.2	•
Total Receipts to Cash Flow 42	8.5	3.6	3.9	9.7	9.5	11.8	8.4	9.1	8.9	8.3	9.8	13.0
Cost of Goods to Cash Flow 43	5.4	1.7	1.4	5.4	6.5	8.0	5.6	6.3	6.1	5.4	6.8	8.6
Cash Flow to Total Debt 44	0.2	•	0.5	0.2	0.3	0.3	0.3	0.3	0.2	0.2	0.2	0.1

Selected Financial Factors (in Percentages)

	•	•	•	•	•	•	•	•	•	•	•	•
Debt Ratio 45	60.7	•	190.6	96.8	42.0	43.8	49.2	52.3	48.3	55.0	59.4	64.4
Return on Total Assets 46	5.9	•	13.2	12.0	4.4	7.5	9.0	8.0	6.4	5.0	4.1	3.7
Return on Equity Before Income Taxes 47	9.7	•	•	264.4	6.3	11.5	15.8	13.8	9.8	6.9	5.4	3.4
Return on Equity After Income Taxes 48	7.7	•	•	254.5	5.5	10.0	14.6	11.7	7.0	3.9	4.5	1.3
Profit Margin (Before Income Tax) 49	3.7	13.4	1.8	4.4	2.7	4.1	6.9	5.2	5.4	3.6	2.4	2.0
Profit Margin (After Income Tax) 50	3.0	13.4	1.8	4.2	2.3	3.6	6.3	4.4	3.8	2.0	1.9	0.8

Table II
Corporations with Net Income

METALWORKING MACHINERY

MONEY AMOUNTS AND SIZE OF ASSETS IN THOUSANDS OF DOLLARS

Item Description for Accounting Period 7/10 Through 6/11	Total	Zero Assets	Under 500	500 to 1,000	1,000 to 5,000	5,000 to 10,000	10,000 to 25,000	25,000 to 50,000	50,000 to 100,000	100,000 to 250,000	250,000 to 500,000	500,000 to 2,500,000	2,500,000 and over
Number of Enterprises 1	4665	498	2325	787	794	101	99	31	18	•	0	•	0
Revenues ($ in Thousands)													
Net Sales 2	16314727	514223	1268309	1007565	2824642	990151	1810143	1504373	1171257	•	0	•	0
Interest 3	44073	1035	84	405	2570	269	333	326	2589	•	0	•	0
Rents 4	9788	0	1335	0	1304	3180	0	0	0	•	0	•	0
Royalties 5	4808	8	0	0	0	0	0	0	229	•	0	•	0
Other Portfolio Income 6	215905	31695	0	1580	40542	6460	2958	13385	14881	•	0	•	0
Other Receipts 7	124873	128	3171	3993	30019	6766	16728	6638	10109	•	0	•	0
Total Receipts 8	16714174	547089	1272899	1013543	2899077	1006826	1830162	1524722	1199065	•	0	•	0
Average Total Receipts 9	3583	1099	547	1288	3651	9969	18486	49185	66615	•	•	•	•
Operating Costs/Operating Income (%)													
Cost of Operations 10	62.8	49.2	34.0	48.8	68.3	64.8	66.7	66.8	67.7	•	•	•	•
Salaries and Wages 11	8.2	10.2	13.1	12.2	7.3	4.5	5.5	7.0	7.7	•	•	•	•
Taxes Paid 12	2.6	2.5	4.2	4.3	3.2	2.8	2.5	2.0	2.1	•	•	•	•
Interest Paid 13	1.7	4.2	1.9	1.7	0.4	0.8	0.8	0.8	0.8	•	•	•	•
Depreciation 14	3.8	3.2	3.5	4.3	2.6	3.9	3.6	4.5	3.9	•	•	•	•
Amortization and Depletion 15	0.3	0.7	0.0	0.0	0.0	0.2	0.1	0.1	0.2	•	•	•	•
Pensions and Other Deferred Comp. 16	0.5	0.4	0.0	0.0	0.3	1.0	0.4	1.0	0.6	•	•	•	•
Employee Benefits 17	2.6	0.6	3.3	4.1	1.4	2.1	3.0	2.3	2.0	•	•	•	•
Advertising 18	0.4	0.4	0.1	0.2	0.3	0.4	0.4	0.3	0.4	•	•	•	•
Other Expenses 19	9.8	18.0	24.3	11.1	8.9	4.6	7.0	7.9	7.2	•	•	•	•
Officers' Compensation 20	3.4	2.1	10.1	6.9	4.6	8.7	2.5	1.6	1.3	•	•	•	•
Operating Margin 21	3.9	8.4	5.5	6.3	2.6	6.3	7.6	5.8	6.1	•	•	•	•
Operating Margin Before Officers' Comp. 22	7.3	10.5	15.6	13.2	7.2	15.0	10.1	7.4	7.4	•	•	•	•

Selected Average Balance Sheet ($ in Thousands)

Net Receivables 23	516	0	46	203	553	1170	3496	8393	11384
Inventories 24	445	0	1	60	530	995	2400	8203	11517
Net Property, Plant and Equipment 25	616	0	49	250	470	1864	4144	8235	15705
Total Assets 26	2911	0	137	697	2531	6692	14819	36440	65605
Notes and Loans Payable 27	1018	0	278	356	434	1530	2675	6409	10588
All Other Liabilities 28	729	0	43	101	594	1539	3329	10785	17576
Net Worth 29	1165	0	-183	240	1503	3623	8815	19246	37442

Selected Financial Ratios (Times to 1)

Current Ratio 30	1.4	•	1.1	1.7	2.4	2.0	2.4	2.2	2.1
Quick Ratio 31	0.8	•	1.1	1.1	1.3	1.4	1.5	1.2	1.0
Net Sales to Working Capital 32	7.9	•	55.7	7.5	3.5	5.2	3.4	3.9	3.1
Coverage Ratio 33	5.1	4.5	4.2	5.0	15.7	11.4	12.3	10.4	12.1
Total Asset Turnover 34	1.2	•	4.0	1.8	1.4	1.5	1.2	1.3	1.0
Inventory Turnover 35	4.9	•	346.1	10.4	4.6	6.4	5.1	4.0	3.8
Receivables Turnover 36	7.6	•	•	9.1	6.5	8.6	6.6	6.5	7.5
Total Liabilities to Net Worth 37	1.5	•	•	1.9	0.7	0.8	0.7	0.9	0.8
Current Assets to Working Capital 38	3.4	•	8.2	2.4	1.7	2.0	1.7	1.9	1.9
Current Liabilities to Working Capital 39	2.4	•	7.2	1.4	0.7	1.0	0.7	0.9	0.9
Working Capital to Net Sales 40	0.1	•	0.0	0.1	0.7	0.2	0.3	0.3	0.3
Inventory to Working Capital 41	1.2	•	0.1	0.7	0.6	0.5	0.6	0.8	0.7
Total Receipts to Cash Flow 42	7.5	3.5	4.4	7.5	9.0	8.9	7.7	7.9	8.0
Cost of Goods to Cash Flow 43	4.7	1.7	1.5	3.6	6.1	5.7	5.1	5.3	5.4
Cash Flow to Total Debt 44	0.3	•	0.4	0.4	0.4	0.4	0.4	0.4	0.3

Selected Financial Factors (in Percentages)

Debt Ratio 45	60.0	•	233.2	65.6	40.6	45.9	40.5	47.2	42.9
Return on Total Assets 46	10.3	•	30.8	15.8	7.8	12.8	11.7	10.5	9.1
Return on Equity Before Income Taxes 47	20.7	•	•	36.6	12.3	21.6	18.0	18.0	14.7
Return on Equity After Income Taxes 48	17.7	•	•	35.4	11.5	19.6	16.7	15.6	11.5
Profit Margin (Before Income Tax) 49	6.9	14.8	5.9	6.8	5.2	8.0	8.7	7.1	8.4
Profit Margin (After Income Tax) 50	5.9	14.7	5.8	6.6	4.9	7.3	8.1	6.2	6.6

Table I

Corporations with and without Net Income

ENGINE, TURBINE AND POWER TRANSMISSION EQUIPMENT

MONEY AMOUNTS AND SIZE OF ASSETS IN THOUSANDS OF DOLLARS

Item Description for Accounting Period 7/10 Through 6/11		Total	Zero Assets	Under 500	500 to 1,000	1,000 to 5,000	5,000 to 10,000	10,000 to 25,000	25,000 to 50,000	50,000 to 100,000	100,000 to 250,000	250,000 to 500,000	500,000 to 2,500,000	2,500,000 and over
Number of Enterprises	1	154	•	0	•	•	36	38	12	10	10	7	6	4
Revenues ($ in Thousands)														
Net Sales	2	28245973	•	0	•	•	503125	475313	369040	648763	1568635	2051014	8916168	13586948
Interest	3	151745	•	0	•	•	74	76	290	296	7273	6308	23888	113532
Rents	4	4806	•	0	•	•	0	0	0	0	107	8	1316	3374
Royalties	5	255275	•	0	•	•	0	0	0	0	218	2060	36070	216927
Other Portfolio Income	6	296378	•	0	•	•	133	78255	0	394	2820	4510	106039	104225
Other Receipts	7	378044	•	0	•	•	1520	2131	9832	7698	11552	33491	55428	246808
Total Receipts	8	29332221	•	0	•	•	504852	555775	379162	657151	1590605	2097391	9138909	14271814
Average Total Receipts	9	190469	•	•	•	•	14024	14626	31597	65715	159060	299627	1523152	3567954
Operating Costs/Operating Income (%)														
Cost of Operations	10	69.0	•	•	•	•	70.3	69.8	83.4	67.7	76.0	65.7	71.4	66.7
Salaries and Wages	11	8.0	•	•	•	•	4.3	10.8	9.3	9.6	5.8	11.2	8.0	7.7
Taxes Paid	12	1.4	•	•	•	•	2.8	3.0	2.5	1.9	1.1	2.0	1.4	1.3
Interest Paid	13	2.6	•	•	•	•	0.4	2.9	0.6	2.6	1.2	2.3	2.9	2.9
Depreciation	14	2.8	•	•	•	•	2.3	4.5	5.5	2.6	3.8	2.5	2.8	2.6
Amortization and Depletion	15	0.8	•	•	•	•	0.0	0.6	0.2	0.8	0.9	0.6	1.5	0.4
Pensions and Other Deferred Comp.	16	1.7	•	•	•	•	0.2	0.3	1.1	0.2	1.5	0.7	1.9	1.9
Employee Benefits	17	3.1	•	•	•	•	0.9	3.8	1.7	2.2	1.8	2.0	2.9	3.6
Advertising	18	0.4	•	•	•	•	0.3	0.3	0.2	0.2	0.4	0.3	0.7	0.1
Other Expenses	19	12.3	•	•	•	•	5.0	19.3	10.7	18.4	7.8	8.1	6.5	16.6
Officers' Compensation	20	0.7	•	•	•	•	2.0	3.7	0.3	1.8	0.8	1.0	0.5	0.5
Operating Margin	21	•	•	•	•	•	11.4	•	•	•	•	3.7	•	•
Operating Margin Before Officers' Comp.	22	•	•	•	•	•	13.4	•	•	•	•	4.7	•	•

Selected Average Balance Sheet ($ in Thousands)

Net Receivables 23	450470	368030	72935	27772	12484	4353	2281	1492	• · 33304
Inventories 24	416721	244307	37695	30130	12295	7600	3315	2103	• · 26900
Net Property, Plant and Equipment 25	643909	231823	36517	36608	13618	7641	4346	2045	• · 32984
Total Assets 26	3720024	1737006	369994	174371	65172	31212	15794	7710	• · 205337
Notes and Loans Payable 27	918819	359920	142917	37582	13622	3488	6635	2282	• · 50648
All Other Liabilities 28	1392204	767728	203648	75559	21338	14745	3297	1124	• · 84023
Net Worth 29	1409002	609358	23428	61230	30211	12980	5862	4304	• · 70666

Selected Financial Ratios (Times to 1)

Current Ratio 30	1.0	1.6	1.2	1.7	1.7	1.4	1.5	2.6	• · 1.3
Quick Ratio 31	0.5	1.0	0.5	0.9	1.1	0.7	0.7	1.4	• · 0.7
Net Sales to Working Capital 32	85.9	4.9	7.5	4.3	4.1	4.8	5.2	4.2	• · 9.2
Coverage Ratio 33	1.6	2.0	3.6	1.5	•	•	0.3	29.2	• · 1.7
Total Asset Turnover 34	0.9	0.9	0.8	0.9	1.0	1.0	0.8	1.8	• · 0.9
Inventory Turnover 35	5.4	4.3	5.1	4.0	3.6	3.4	2.6	4.7	• · 4.7
Receivables Turnover 36	8.1	3.9	3.8	6.1	5.0	8.6	5.6	10.9	• · 5.6
Total Liabilities to Net Worth 37	1.6	1.9	14.8	1.8	1.2	1.4	1.7	0.8	• · 1.9
Current Assets to Working Capital 38	32.2	2.7	6.0	2.5	2.5	3.2	2.9	1.6	• · 4.4
Current Liabilities to Working Capital 39	31.2	1.7	5.0	1.5	1.5	2.2	1.9	0.6	• · 3.4
Working Capital to Net Sales 40	0.0	0.2	0.1	0.2	0.2	0.2	0.2	0.2	• · 0.1
Inventory to Working Capital 41	11.7	0.8	1.0	0.9	0.7	1.4	1.3	0.7	• · 1.4
Total Receipts to Cash Flow 42	6.5	14.0	8.3	14.5	10.9	•	262.2	6.5	• · 8.8
Cost of Goods to Cash Flow 43	4.4	10.0	5.4	11.0	7.4	•	183.0	4.6	• · 6.1
Cash Flow to Total Debt 44	0.2	0.1	0.1	0.1	0.2	•	0.0	0.6	• · 0.2

Selected Financial Factors (in Percentages)

Debt Ratio 45	62.1	64.9	93.7	64.9	53.6	58.4	62.9	44.2	• · 65.6
Return on Total Assets 46	4.2	4.9	6.5	1.6	•	•	0.6	22.0	• · 4.1
Return on Equity Before Income Taxes 47	4.2	6.9	74.4	1.6	•	•	•	38.1	• · 4.9
Return on Equity After Income Taxes 48	2.3	4.8	50.9	•	•	•	•	26.9	• · 2.3
Profit Margin (Before Income Tax) 49	1.7	2.8	5.9	0.6	•	•	•	11.7	• · 1.9
Profit Margin (After Income Tax) 50	0.9	2.0	4.1	•	•	•	•	8.3	• · 0.9

Table II
Corporations with Net Income

ENGINE, TURBINE AND POWER TRANSMISSION EQUIPMENT

MONEY AMOUNTS AND SIZE OF ASSETS IN THOUSANDS OF DOLLARS

Item Description for Accounting Period 7/10 Through 6/11	Total	Zero Assets	Under 500	500 to 1,000	1,000 to 5,000	5,000 to 10,000	10,000 to 25,000	25,000 to 50,000	50,000 to 100,000	100,000 to 250,000	250,000 to 500,000	500,000 to 2,500,000	2,500,000 and over
Number of Enterprises **1**	99	•	0	0	23	32	14	5	5	6	4	•	•
Revenues ($ in Thousands)													
Net Sales **2**	22456257	•	•	0	117942	503125	289647	260871	461573	1320856	1696098	•	•
Interest **3**	40948	•	0	0	1	74	50	0	196	1849	2413	•	•
Rents **4**	3521	•	0	0	1	0	0	0	0	13	8	•	•
Royalties **5**	235515	•	0	0	0	0	0	0	0	218	2060	•	•
Other Portfolio Income **6**	196840	•	0	0	0	133	42545	0	27	2012	3726	•	•
Other Receipts **7**	354414	•	0	0	9585	1520	1899	98	6335	6994	33428	•	•
Total Receipts **8**	23287495	•	0	0	127529	504852	334141	260969	468131	1331942	1737733	•	•
Average Total Receipts **9**	235227	•	•	•	5545	15777	23867	52194	93626	221990	434433	•	•
Operating Costs/Operating Income (%)													
Cost of Operations **10**	68.6	•	•	•	51.4	70.3	62.5	75.2	66.1	76.1	66.5	•	•
Salaries and Wages **11**	7.7	•	•	•	11.9	3.2	10.7	6.7	5.7	5.3	10.4	•	•
Taxes Paid **12**	1.4	•	•	•	1.9	2.8	2.7	2.6	1.8	0.7	2.3	•	•
Interest Paid **13**	1.4	•	•	•	1.8	0.4	1.1	0.5	1.6	0.3	1.3	•	•
Depreciation **14**	2.7	•	•	•	1.1	2.2	1.8	1.8	1.8	3.0	2.4	•	•
Amortization and Depletion **15**	0.6	•	•	•	0.0	0.0	0.2	0.0	0.2	0.2	0.6	•	•
Pensions and Other Deferred Comp. **16**	1.8	•	•	•	0.6	0.2	0.4	1.5	0.2	1.4	0.6	•	•
Employee Benefits **17**	2.5	•	•	•	0.0	0.8	4.7	1.6	1.6	1.8	2.4	•	•
Advertising **18**	0.2	•	•	•	1.6	0.3	0.3	0.1	0.1	0.4	0.3	•	•
Other Expenses **19**	12.4	•	•	•	18.7	4.2	12.8	5.9	10.5	6.0	7.4	•	•
Officers' Compensation **20**	0.7	•	•	•	1.9	1.7	4.7	0.4	1.3	0.6	1.0	•	•
Operating Margin **21**	•	•	•	•	9.2	13.9	•	3.8	9.2	4.3	4.9	•	•
Operating Margin Before Officers' Comp. **22**	0.6	•	•	•	11.1	15.6	2.8	4.2	10.5	4.9	5.9	•	•

Selected Average Balance Sheet ($ in Thousands)

Net Receivables 23	41795	511	1679	4502	7698	16917	38175	48379
Inventories 24	30487	844	2132	5979	15263	13465	34754	51978
Net Property, Plant and Equipment 25	38229	966	2252	3798	6135	6823	40236	50564
Total Assets 26	236265	2825	8039	17898	33913	61618	187951	337927
Notes and Loans Payable 27	34765	1659	1717	4968	5437	10347	37601	64821
All Other Liabilities 28	91953	255	1047	2476	16784	19470	80916	103301
Net Worth 29	109547	911	5275	10454	11692	31801	69434	169805

Selected Financial Ratios (Times to 1)

Current Ratio 30	1.3	6.0	3.5	2.1	1.4	1.8	1.7	2.3
Quick Ratio 31	0.7	2.1	1.9	1.0	0.5	1.1	1.0	1.1
Net Sales to Working Capital 32	10.2	3.3	4.1	3.3	6.1	4.7	4.6	3.6
Coverage Ratio 33	4.2	10.8	38.1	13.0	8.8	7.7	16.4	6.7
Total Asset Turnover 34	1.0	1.8	2.0	1.2	1.5	1.5	1.2	1.3
Inventory Turnover 35	5.1	3.1	5.2	2.2	2.6	4.5	4.8	5.4
Receivables Turnover 36	6.0	18.8	12.0	4.3	7.2	6.9	7.0	•
Total Liabilities to Net Worth 37	1.2	2.1	0.5	0.7	1.9	0.9	1.7	1.0
Current Assets to Working Capital 38	4.7	1.2	1.4	1.9	3.2	2.3	2.4	1.8
Current Liabilities to Working Capital 39	3.7	0.2	0.4	0.9	2.2	1.3	1.4	0.8
Working Capital to Net Sales 40	0.1	0.3	0.2	0.3	0.2	0.2	0.2	0.3
Inventory to Working Capital 41	1.6	0.7	0.6	0.7	1.8	0.8	0.9	0.4
Total Receipts to Cash Flow 42	7.1	3.2	5.8	12.3	11.2	5.2	9.7	8.0
Cost of Goods to Cash Flow 43	4.9	1.6	4.1	7.7	8.4	3.5	7.4	5.3
Cash Flow to Total Debt 44	0.3	0.8	1.0	0.2	0.2	0.6	0.2	0.3

Selected Financial Factors (in Percentages)

Debt Ratio 45	53.6	67.7	34.4	41.6	65.5	48.4	63.1	49.8
Return on Total Assets 46	5.6	34.7	28.7	16.8	6.6	18.2	6.7	10.8
Return on Equity Before Income Taxes 47	9.3	97.6	42.6	26.5	17.0	30.7	17.0	18.4
Return on Equity After Income Taxes 48	6.7	97.6	32.3	22.7	14.2	21.2	12.8	12.7
Profit Margin (Before Income Tax) 49	4.5	17.3	14.3	13.4	3.8	10.6	5.3	7.4
Profit Margin (After Income Tax) 50	3.2	17.3	10.8	11.5	3.2	7.3	4.0	5.1

Table I

Corporations with and without Net Income

OTHER GENERAL PURPOSE MACHINERY

MONEY AMOUNTS AND SIZE OF ASSETS IN THOUSANDS OF DOLLARS

Item Description for Accounting Period 7/10 Through 6/11	Total	Zero Assets	Under 500	500 to 1,000	1,000 to 5,000	5,000 to 10,000	10,000 to 25,000	25,000 to 50,000	50,000 to 100,000	100,000 to 250,000	250,000 to 500,000	500,000 to 2,500,000	2,500,000 and over
Number of Enterprises 1	5784	549	3020	830	699	324	211	56	36	22	14	16	7
Revenues ($ in Thousands)													
Net Sales 2	60224739	311030	1006577	2122448	2873057	3287011	4539025	2663744	3010438	3680443	4899778	14028730	17802458
Interest 3	422465	1049	325	1854	1143	654	2382	1835	1806	10609	15512	194311	190986
Rents 4	14224	3620	0	458	123	2258	2589	510	54	934	624	2497	556
Royalties 5	249837	0	0	0	0	179	1787	2017	1527	9551	3911	135715	95150
Other Portfolio Income 6	979648	14	7	757	1122	12675	15002	545	22307	49823	33743	159558	684093
Other Receipts 7	642092	1381	0	3149	10680	32111	68901	17961	32335	21594	31298	94850	327834
Total Receipts 8	62553005	317094	1006909	2128666	2886125	3334888	4629686	2686612	3068467	3772954	4984866	14615661	19101077
Average Total Receipts 9	10811	578	333	2565	4129	10293	21942	47975	85235	171498	356062	913479	2728725
Operating Costs/Operating Income (%)													
Cost of Operations 10	66.8	66.1	36.0	55.9	56.2	63.9	69.3	72.3	68.7	66.0	66.5	66.2	70.9
Salaries and Wages 11	9.6	13.2	16.5	9.1	8.1	9.8	9.1	7.8	10.1	11.3	7.4	9.6	10.0
Taxes Paid 12	1.7	2.3	3.1	2.8	2.3	2.4	2.1	1.4	1.8	1.5	1.7	2.0	0.9
Interest Paid 13	2.2	2.0	2.0	0.3	0.6	1.3	0.7	1.1	1.4	1.6	2.4	2.9	3.2
Depreciation 14	3.5	2.6	2.9	0.5	2.4	1.9	2.2	1.7	2.6	1.7	2.5	3.1	6.3
Amortization and Depletion 15	0.8	1.4	0.1	0.0	0.2	0.0	0.2	0.3	0.8	0.7	0.8	0.9	1.3
Pensions and Other Deferred Comp. 16	1.3	•	0.2	1.6	0.5	0.6	0.3	0.4	0.9	0.6	2.0	1.1	2.1
Employee Benefits 17	2.3	0.2	1.9	0.9	2.6	2.2	2.0	1.2	1.7	2.0	2.0	3.1	2.4
Advertising 18	0.6	0.1	0.3	1.1	0.4	0.8	0.5	0.2	0.7	0.5	0.5	0.5	0.7
Other Expenses 19	9.2	14.8	23.1	12.1	14.4	11.0	8.3	6.6	8.1	10.7	7.9	9.9	7.1
Officers' Compensation 20	1.8	0.4	7.7	9.4	5.2	2.7	2.9	2.2	1.2	1.0	1.1	0.9	0.6
Operating Margin 21	0.3	•	6.1	6.5	7.3	3.2	2.4	4.8	2.0	2.5	5.4	•	•
Operating Margin Before Officers' Comp. 22	2.0	•	13.8	15.9	12.4	5.9	5.3	7.0	3.2	3.5	6.5	0.8	•

Selected Average Balance Sheet ($ in Thousands)

	1	2	3	4	5	6	7	8	9	10	11	12	13
Net Receivables 23	2388	0	16	119	495	1415	3303	10725	14478	32268	57558	162670	989201
Inventories 24	1450	0	18	120	596	1904	3280	8493	13838	24847	41919	109632	377847
Net Property, Plant and Equipment 25	1906	0	42	52	413	1176	2745	4653	11930	18410	46216	113862	862861
Total Assets 26	16187	0	102	602	2211	6960	15109	34708	68569	156177	315776	852943	8559054
Notes and Loans Payable 27	4243	0	97	309	531	1899	2633	7105	17834	42494	66288	261260	2194828
All Other Liabilities 28	4950	0	18	134	645	2187	4106	11914	21186	48582	54668	347706	2515890
Net Worth 29	6995	0	-13	159	1034	2874	8370	15689	29548	65101	194819	243978	3848337

Selected Financial Ratios (Times to 1)

	1	2	3	4	5	6	7	8	9	10	11	12	13
Current Ratio 30	1.2	•	1.8	2.1	2.0	2.2	2.1	2.0	1.8	1.4	1.8	1.6	0.9
Quick Ratio 31	0.7	•	1.3	1.1	1.2	1.1	1.2	1.2	0.9	0.8	1.0	0.9	0.5
Net Sales to Working Capital 32	10.4	•	17.3	11.8	5.4	3.8	4.0	3.9	4.4	6.6	4.8	6.0	•
Coverage Ratio 33	3.2	0.4	4.1	28.2	14.3	4.6	7.5	6.3	3.9	4.4	4.1	2.7	2.0
Total Asset Turnover 34	0.6	•	3.3	4.3	1.9	1.5	1.4	1.4	1.2	1.1	1.1	1.0	0.3
Inventory Turnover 35	4.8	•	6.8	11.9	3.9	3.4	4.5	4.1	4.2	4.4	5.5	5.3	4.8
Receivables Turnover 36	5.3	•	17.1	31.1	8.4	8.0	7.4	5.2	6.7	4.9	6.9	6.3	3.4
Total Liabilities to Net Worth 37	1.3	•	•	2.8	1.1	1.4	0.8	1.2	1.3	1.4	0.6	2.5	1.2
Current Assets to Working Capital 38	5.8	•	2.2	1.9	2.0	1.9	1.9	2.0	2.2	3.4	2.2	2.6	•
Current Liabilities to Working Capital 39	4.8	•	1.2	0.9	1.0	0.9	0.9	1.0	1.2	2.4	1.2	1.6	•
Working Capital to Net Sales 40	0.1	•	0.1	0.1	0.2	0.3	0.3	0.3	0.2	0.2	0.2	0.2	•
Inventory to Working Capital 41	1.6	•	0.7	0.9	0.7	0.8	0.6	0.8	0.9	0.9	0.7	0.8	•
Total Receipts to Cash Flow 42	8.9	9.2	4.9	5.8	5.1	8.3	9.2	9.3	9.7	7.1	7.6	8.5	13.6
Cost of Goods to Cash Flow 43	5.9	6.1	1.8	3.2	2.9	5.3	6.4	6.7	6.7	4.7	5.1	5.6	9.6
Cash Flow to Total Debt 44	0.1	0.6	0.6	1.0	0.7	0.3	0.3	0.3	0.2	0.3	0.4	0.2	0.0

Selected Financial Factors (in Percentages)

	1	2	3	4	5	6	7	8	9	10	11	12	13
Debt Ratio 45	56.8	•	112.5	73.6	53.2	58.7	44.6	54.8	56.9	58.3	38.3	71.4	55.0
Return on Total Assets 46	4.6	•	26.6	30.0	15.5	8.7	7.2	9.4	6.8	7.7	10.9	8.1	2.0
Return on Equity Before Income Taxes 47	7.2	•	•	109.6	30.8	16.5	11.3	17.4	11.8	14.3	13.3	17.9	2.3
Return on Equity After Income Taxes 48	4.8	•	•	109.3	27.6	13.2	10.0	14.2	7.6	10.0	8.5	11.0	0.9
Profit Margin (Before Income Tax) 49	4.9	•	6.2	6.8	7.7	4.7	4.4	5.7	4.2	5.6	7.4	5.0	3.4
Profit Margin (After Income Tax) 50	3.3	•	6.1	6.8	6.9	3.7	3.9	4.7	2.7	3.9	4.7	3.1	1.4

Table II
Corporations with Net Income

OTHER GENERAL PURPOSE MACHINERY

MONEY AMOUNTS AND SIZE OF ASSETS IN THOUSANDS OF DOLLARS

Item Description for Accounting Period 7/10 Through 6/11	Total	Zero Assets	Under 500	500 to 1,000	1,000 to 5,000	5,000 to 10,000	10,000 to 25,000	25,000 to 50,000	50,000 to 100,000	100,000 to 250,000	250,000 to 500,000	500,000 to 2,500,000	2,500,000 and over
Number of Enterprises **1**	3491	3	1795	746	459	216	154	43	29	17	•	12	•
Revenues ($ in Thousands)													
Net Sales **2**	44276762	199726	641890	2107789	2452964	2399398	3555151	2182957	2312917	2700589	•	11932405	•
Interest **3**	115540	1044	325	79	995	409	1713	1765	1394	10575	•	21593	•
Rents **4**	6070	209	0	0	79	0	2528	349	54	876	•	1255	•
Royalties **5**	227926	0	0	0	0	0	1787	2017	1294	903	•	134762	•
Other Portfolio Income **6**	666261	14	7	0	693	12571	13807	220	22234	47961	•	149714	•
Other Receipts **7**	326706	244	-1	3146	5125	23850	51340	12316	28395	19133	•	75307	•
Total Receipts **8**	45619265	201237	642221	2111014	2459856	2436228	3626326	2199624	2366288	2780037	•	12315036	•
Average Total Receipts **9**	13068	67079	358	2830	5359	11279	23548	51154	81596	163532	•	1026253	•
Operating Costs/Operating Income (%)													
Cost of Operations **10**	64.1	54.6	20.8	56.0	53.9	60.0	67.6	71.8	64.5	63.6	•	65.4	•
Salaries and Wages **11**	9.8	15.3	20.3	8.9	8.1	9.0	8.3	7.6	9.8	12.0	•	10.0	•
Taxes Paid **12**	1.7	2.4	3.9	2.7	2.1	2.3	2.1	1.3	1.9	1.7	•	2.0	•
Interest Paid **13**	1.4	2.4	1.5	0.2	0.4	0.7	0.6	0.8	1.2	1.3	•	1.0	•
Depreciation **14**	2.2	3.5	2.4	0.5	2.2	1.8	1.9	1.6	2.6	2.0	•	3.2	•
Amortization and Depletion **15**	0.7	1.0	0.0	0.0	0.2	0.0	0.1	0.3	0.7	0.5	•	0.7	•
Pensions and Other Deferred Comp. **16**	1.1	•	0.4	1.6	0.5	0.5	0.4	0.4	1.0	0.5	•	1.0	•
Employee Benefits **17**	2.0	0.1	2.1	0.9	2.5	2.1	1.9	1.2	1.9	1.6	•	3.1	•
Advertising **18**	0.7	0.0	0.4	1.1	0.5	0.8	0.5	0.2	0.4	0.4	•	0.5	•
Other Expenses **19**	9.2	16.3	25.0	12.0	13.8	12.5	6.9	5.6	8.5	10.4	•	9.6	•
Officers' Compensation **20**	1.9	0.6	9.6	9.3	4.4	2.8	3.0	2.4	1.3	0.9	•	1.0	•
Operating Margin **21**	5.2	3.9	13.6	6.9	11.5	7.4	6.6	6.9	6.2	4.9	•	2.6	•
Operating Margin Before Officers' Comp. **22**	7.1	4.5	23.2	16.1	15.8	10.3	9.7	9.3	7.5	5.9	•	3.6	•

Selected Average Balance Sheet ($ in Thousands)

Net Receivables 23	2301	0	22	131	602	1575	3173	11302	13469	31651	186639
Inventories 24	1630	0	28	111	588	1945	2940	6332	11754	23453	142080
Net Property, Plant and Equipment 25	1441	0	50	50	435	1019	2829	4115	12168	16470	116830
Total Assets 26	16937	0	127	587	2455	7245	15003	33804	67347	159624	858072
Notes and Loans Payable 27	4258	0	64	331	487	1207	2111	5374	14652	36295	212487
All Other Liabilities 28	3957	0	22	147	633	2060	3963	11621	19127	39695	362907
Net Worth 29	8722	0	41	109	1336	3979	8929	16808	33568	83634	282678

Selected Financial Ratios (Times to 1)

Current Ratio 30	1.5	•	1.9	2.0	2.3	2.7	2.1	2.3	2.1	1.7	1.6
Quick Ratio 31	0.8	•	1.2	1.1	1.4	1.5	1.2	1.5	1.0	0.9	0.9
Net Sales to Working Capital 32	5.7	•	13.0	13.2	5.2	3.0	4.3	3.7	4.0	4.4	6.4
Coverage Ratio 33	7.7	3.0	9.8	30.4	32.3	14.0	15.1	10.3	8.5	7.5	8.1
Total Asset Turnover 34	0.7	•	2.8	4.8	2.2	1.5	1.5	1.5	1.2	1.0	1.2
Inventory Turnover 35	5.0	•	2.7	14.3	4.9	3.4	5.3	5.8	4.4	4.3	4.6
Receivables Turnover 36	6.6	•	12.2	32.6	10.0	7.6	8.6	5.9	7.5	5.6	•
Total Liabilities to Net Worth 37	0.9	•	2.1	4.4	0.8	0.8	0.7	1.0	1.0	0.9	2.0
Current Assets to Working Capital 38	3.0	•	2.1	2.0	1.8	1.6	1.9	1.8	1.9	2.5	2.8
Current Liabilities to Working Capital 39	2.0	•	1.1	1.0	0.8	0.6	0.9	0.8	0.9	1.5	1.8
Working Capital to Net Sales 40	0.2	•	0.1	0.1	0.2	0.3	0.2	0.3	0.3	0.2	0.2
Inventory to Working Capital 41	0.9	•	0.8	0.8	0.7	0.6	0.7	0.6	0.8	0.7	0.9
Total Receipts to Cash Flow 42	6.5	5.3	3.3	5.8	4.3	5.7	7.3	8.5	6.5	6.0	7.7
Cost of Goods to Cash Flow 43	4.2	2.9	0.7	3.2	2.3	3.4	4.9	6.1	4.2	3.8	5.0
Cash Flow to Total Debt 44	0.2	•	1.3	1.0	1.1	0.6	0.5	0.4	0.4	0.3	0.2

Selected Financial Factors (in Percentages)

Debt Ratio 45	48.5	•	67.3	81.5	45.6	45.1	40.5	50.3	50.2	47.6	67.1
Return on Total Assets 46	7.9	•	42.8	34.9	26.4	14.8	14.2	12.8	11.8	9.8	9.0
Return on Equity Before Income Taxes 47	13.4	•	117.5	182.0	47.1	25.0	22.3	23.2	20.8	16.2	24.0
Return on Equity After Income Taxes 48	10.2	•	117.3	181.5	43.3	21.5	20.6	19.3	16.4	11.9	16.1
Profit Margin (Before Income Tax) 49	9.2	4.7	13.6	7.0	11.8	9.0	8.6	7.7	8.8	8.6	6.8
Profit Margin (After Income Tax) 50	7.0	3.8	13.6	7.0	10.8	7.7	8.0	6.4	6.9	6.3	4.6

Table I
Corporations with and without Net Income

COMPUTER AND PERIPHERAL EQUIPMENT

MONEY AMOUNTS AND SIZE OF ASSETS IN THOUSANDS OF DOLLARS

Item Description for Accounting Period 7/10 Through 6/11	Total	Zero Assets	Under 500	500 to 1,000	1,000 to 5,000	5,000 to 10,000	10,000 to 25,000	25,000 to 50,000	50,000 to 100,000	100,000 to 250,000	250,000 to 500,000	500,000 to 2,500,000	2,500,000 and over
Number of Enterprises 1	1873	434	708	63	370	66	100	48	29	14	15	11	13
Revenues ($ in Thousands)													
Net Sales 2	200099107	181155	494290	133566	1101132	445396	2804185	2043394	2477535	2776959	4482585	6772678	176386234
Interest 3	1558414	30	101	7	2520	542	2205	1793	3081	4922	11752	24561	1506900
Rents 4	1518682	0	0	0	0	0	203	66	169	86	1819	2838	1513502
Royalties 5	32501951	0	0	0	945	0	0	3800	33690	9295	77470	261205	32115546
Other Portfolio Income 6	6617330	33	0	0	1401	10	1990	2353	88798	1845	97877	5654	6417369
Other Receipts 7	1735966	-1	1232	1	17660	1382	1823	-629	45971	53040	115358	401838	1098287
Total Receipts 8	244031450	181217	495623	133574	1123658	447330	2810406	2050777	2649244	2846147	4788861	7468774	219037838
Average Total Receipts 9	130289	418	700	2120	3037	6778	28104	42725	91353	203296	319124	678979	16849064
Operating Costs/Operating Income (%)													
Cost of Operations 10	63.3	44.5	66.4	59.5	55.9	50.5	62.6	60.3	63.6	70.7	61.9	66.6	63.3
Salaries and Wages 11	16.0	27.2	16.0	17.0	20.1	23.7	14.2	15.7	16.3	12.7	15.0	17.0	16.0
Taxes Paid 12	1.9	2.8	1.8	5.0	2.8	2.3	1.6	1.8	1.8	1.0	1.8	1.7	1.9
Interest Paid 13	1.2	0.6	2.3	2.4	1.1	4.3	0.6	0.7	1.5	0.4	1.0	0.6	1.2
Depreciation 14	3.1	1.2	0.5	3.9	2.2	2.7	1.3	2.3	1.7	1.6	2.9	1.6	3.3
Amortization and Depletion 15	0.5	1.6	0.0	0.3	0.7	0.4	0.7	1.1	1.2	0.4	0.8	1.3	0.4
Pensions and Other Deferred Comp. 16	0.5	0.1	0.1	0.4	0.5	0.0	0.1	0.2	0.2	0.2	0.2	0.1	0.5
Employee Benefits 17	1.5	5.8	1.3	2.1	1.8	2.8	1.1	1.7	1.2	1.5	1.0	1.5	1.5
Advertising 18	1.5	0.1	0.0	0.3	0.8	1.8	1.4	1.3	1.1	0.5	1.1	0.9	1.5
Other Expenses 19	20.0	19.2	11.2	21.3	18.8	22.3	10.4	16.3	15.8	11.3	16.5	13.7	20.7
Officers' Compensation 20	0.9	7.8	3.1	10.6	5.6	4.4	2.4	2.3	2.3	1.5	2.4	1.0	0.7
Operating Margin 21	•	•	•	•	•	•	3.5	•	•	•	•	•	•
Operating Margin Before Officers' Comp. 22	•	•	0.3	•	•	•	6.0	•	•	•	•	•	•

Selected Average Balance Sheet ($ in Thousands)

Net Receivables 23	27589	0	12	333	437	1481	5257	8732	15232	40840	58482	132410	3622542
Inventories 24	4465	0	75	78	376	1089	3171	5730	7977	18088	27782	51737	463939
Net Property, Plant and Equipment 25	13108	0	17	39	184	1554	1216	2701	3906	11789	20619	35327	1779909
Total Assets 26	203719	0	210	636	2189	7367	16597	34437	71141	161228	368704	875812	27483356
Notes and Loans Payable 27	40140	0	120	752	922	1531	2966	6371	28874	20138	25692	188171	5417793
All Other Liabilities 28	68201	0	258	130	513	1771	5621	12510	30394	73246	138662	183255	9236714
Net Worth 29	95378	0	-167	-246	754	4065	8009	15557	11873	67844	204350	504386	12828850

Selected Financial Ratios (Times to 1)

Current Ratio 30	1.2	•	0.9	1.2	2.4	2.4	2.0	2.0	1.6	1.4	2.2	1.8	1.2
Quick Ratio 31	0.7	•	0.5	0.8	1.5	1.7	1.4	1.2	1.0	1.0	1.4	1.3	0.6
Net Sales to Working Capital 32	9.1	•	•	18.6	3.1	3.0	4.3	3.4	5.0	7.9	2.6	3.9	11.1
Coverage Ratio 33	14.3	•	•	•	•	•	7.0	•	1.2	3.1	3.5	8.6	15.6
Total Asset Turnover 34	0.5	•	3.3	3.3	1.4	0.9	1.7	1.2	1.2	1.2	0.8	0.7	0.5
Inventory Turnover 35	15.2	•	6.2	16.2	4.4	3.1	5.5	4.5	6.8	7.8	6.7	7.9	18.5
Receivables Turnover 36	4.1	•	12.6	3.7	7.2	4.3	6.1	5.4	6.2	5.3	5.7	3.8	4.0
Total Liabilities to Net Worth 37	1.1	•	1.9	0.8	2.0	1.1	1.2	5.0	1.4	0.8	2.2	0.7	1.1
Current Assets to Working Capital 38	5.6	•	•	5.2	1.7	2.0	2.0	2.8	3.4	1.8	2.2	6.9	•
Current Liabilities to Working Capital 39	4.6	•	•	4.2	0.7	1.0	1.0	1.8	2.4	0.8	1.2	5.9	•
Working Capital to Net Sales 40	0.1	•	•	0.1	0.3	0.2	0.3	0.2	0.1	0.4	0.3	0.1	•
Inventory to Working Capital 41	0.4	•	•	1.4	0.5	0.5	0.6	0.5	0.8	0.3	0.2	0.4	•
Total Receipts to Cash Flow 42	3.4	18.0	29.1	•	35.1	8.0	8.9	9.4	6.4	9.0	6.3	3.1	•
Cost of Goods to Cash Flow 43	2.1	8.0	19.3	8.5	17.7	5.0	5.4	6.0	6.4	6.0	4.2	2.0	•
Cash Flow to Total Debt 44	0.3	•	0.1	0.1	0.1	0.4	0.3	0.2	0.3	0.3	0.3	0.3	•

Selected Financial Factors (in Percentages)

Debt Ratio 45	53.2	179.8	138.7	44.8	65.5	51.7	54.8	83.3	57.9	44.6	42.4	53.3	•
Return on Total Assets 46	8.7	•	•	•	•	7.4	•	2.2	1.5	2.9	3.7	9.2	•
Return on Equity Before Income Taxes 47	17.3	10.8	194.0	•	•	13.2	•	2.4	2.4	3.8	5.7	18.4	•
Return on Equity After Income Taxes 48	12.0	10.8	195.3	•	•	10.7	•	•	1.5	2.3	3.9	12.9	•
Profit Margin (Before Income Tax) 49	15.5	•	•	•	•	3.8	•	0.3	0.8	2.6	4.7	17.4	•
Profit Margin (After Income Tax) 50	10.7	•	•	•	•	3.1	•	•	0.5	1.6	3.2	12.2	•

137

Table II

Corporations with Net Income

COMPUTER AND PERIPHERAL EQUIPMENT

MONEY AMOUNTS AND SIZE OF ASSETS IN THOUSANDS OF DOLLARS

Item Description for Accounting Period 7/10 Through 6/11	Total	Zero Assets	Under 500	500 to 1,000	1,000 to 5,000	5,000 to 10,000	10,000 to 25,000	25,000 to 50,000	50,000 to 100,000	100,000 to 250,000	250,000 to 500,000	500,000 to 2,500,000	2,500,000 and over
Number of Enterprises 1	952	13	583	•	125	•	66	27	12	10	10	•	•
Revenues ($ in Thousands)													
Net Sales 2	193042214	156808	394312	•	691140	•	2105320	1274138	1443239	2279954	3295976	•	•
Interest 3	1538010	29	0	•	873	•	1205	599	1786	3156	5248	•	•
Rents 4	1518268	0	0	•	0	•	203	0	169	86	1471	•	•
Royalties 5	32462023	0	0	•	0	•	0	3383	8670	7942	75099	•	•
Other Portfolio Income 6	6515870	33	0	•	71	•	46	1341	86137	1845	8529	•	•
Other Receipts 7	1654974	1	1233	•	11988	•	711	-4024	27109	5545	112620	•	•
Total Receipts 8	236731359	156871	395545	•	704072	•	2107485	1275437	1567110	2298528	3449943	•	•
Average Total Receipts 9	248667	12067	678	•	5633	•	31932	47238	130592	229853	349894	•	•
Operating Costs/Operating Income (%)													
Cost of Operations 10	63.8	40.5	71.5	•	58.7	•	64.9	57.7	65.0	73.2	63.0	•	•
Salaries and Wages 11	15.6	17.4	12.6	•	10.9	•	10.4	14.1	11.4	11.0	13.8	•	•
Taxes Paid 12	1.9	2.0	0.9	•	1.6	•	1.5	1.4	1.4	0.9	1.8	•	•
Interest Paid 13	1.1	0.1	1.8	•	0.2	•	0.4	0.7	0.5	0.3	1.1	•	•
Depreciation 14	3.1	1.2	0.5	•	0.5	•	1.0	1.8	1.6	1.3	3.1	•	•
Amortization and Depletion 15	0.4	1.8	•	•	0.0	•	0.2	0.3	0.3	0.3	0.7	•	•
Pensions and Other Deferred Comp. 16	0.5	0.0	•	•	0.8	•	0.1	0.3	0.2	0.2	0.2	•	•
Employee Benefits 17	1.5	0.0	•	•	0.7	•	0.7	1.3	0.8	1.4	0.9	•	•
Advertising 18	1.5	0.1	•	•	0.5	•	1.5	0.8	0.3	0.6	1.3	•	•
Other Expenses 19	19.8	10.5	8.5	•	9.0	•	7.5	10.6	11.6	6.5	13.8	•	•
Officers' Compensation 20	0.8	6.0	1.2	•	3.5	•	2.0	2.4	1.4	1.5	1.5	•	•
Operating Margin 21	•	14.6	3.0	•	13.7	•	9.8	8.6	5.5	2.8	•	•	•
Operating Margin Before Officers' Comp. 22	•	20.6	4.2	•	17.2	•	11.8	11.0	6.9	4.3	0.4	•	•

Selected Average Balance Sheet ($ in Thousands)

Net Receivables **23**	52785	0	14	448	5210	9469	17520	42732	65423
Inventories **24**	7631	0	21	507	3353	5453	12748	16525	31305
Net Property, Plant and Equipment **25**	24820	0	19	142	1065	3012	6097	12586	25535
Total Assets **26**	389301	0	209	2127	15754	33690	69216	162472	366690
Notes and Loans Payable **27**	75036	0	0	111	2248	5216	7092	12178	32266
All Other Liabilities **28**	130669	0	269	559	4029	11510	30149	83484	138172
Net Worth **29**	183595	0	-60	1457	9477	16964	31975	66810	196252

Selected Financial Ratios (Times to 1)

Current Ratio **30**	1.2	•	1.5	3.1	3.0	2.0	1.9	1.4	2.2
Quick Ratio **31**	0.7	•	0.6	2.2	1.9	1.2	1.2	0.9	1.5
Net Sales to Working Capital **32**	9.4	•	29.0	4.8	3.6	3.7	4.6	9.7	2.9
Coverage Ratio **33**	16.1	270.5	2.9	89.5	25.1	13.7	31.2	12.1	5.7
Total Asset Turnover **34**	0.5	•	3.2	2.6	2.0	1.4	1.7	1.4	0.9
Inventory Turnover **35**	16.9	•	23.1	6.4	6.2	5.0	6.1	10.1	6.6
Receivables Turnover **36**	4.2	•	19.1	8.9	8.1	6.3	6.7	6.5	5.6
Total Liabilities to Net Worth **37**	1.1	•	•	0.5	0.7	1.0	1.2	1.4	0.9
Current Assets to Working Capital **38**	5.7	•	3.0	1.5	1.5	2.0	2.1	3.7	1.8
Current Liabilities to Working Capital **39**	4.7	•	2.0	0.5	0.5	1.0	1.1	2.7	0.8
Working Capital to Net Sales **40**	0.1	•	0.0	0.2	0.3	0.3	0.2	0.1	0.3
Inventory to Working Capital **41**	0.4	•	1.6	0.4	0.5	0.6	0.5	0.9	0.3
Total Receipts to Cash Flow **42**	3.3	4.4	12.9	4.6	6.3	5.5	5.5	10.8	6.0
Cost of Goods to Cash Flow **43**	2.1	1.8	9.2	2.7	4.1	3.2	3.6	7.9	3.8
Cash Flow to Total Debt **44**	0.3	•	0.2	1.8	0.8	0.5	0.6	0.2	0.3

Selected Financial Factors (in Percentages)

Debt Ratio **45**	52.8	•	128.5	31.5	39.8	49.6	53.8	58.9	46.5
Return on Total Assets **46**	9.2	•	16.3	40.9	20.9	13.2	25.7	5.6	5.6
Return on Equity Before Income Taxes **47**	18.4	•	•	59.0	33.3	24.2	53.8	12.5	8.7
Return on Equity After Income Taxes **48**	13.0	•	•	52.8	30.1	19.7	44.8	11.2	6.4
Profit Margin (Before Income Tax) **49**	16.6	14.6	3.3	15.6	9.9	8.7	14.3	3.7	5.2
Profit Margin (After Income Tax) **50**	11.7	11.0	3.3	13.9	8.9	7.1	11.9	3.3	3.8

Table I
Corporations with and without Net Income

COMMUNICATIONS EQUIPMENT

MONEY AMOUNTS AND SIZE OF ASSETS IN THOUSANDS OF DOLLARS

Item Description for Accounting Period 7/10 Through 6/11	Total	Zero Assets	Under 500	500 to 1,000	1,000 to 5,000	5,000 to 10,000	10,000 to 25,000	25,000 to 50,000	50,000 to 100,000	100,000 to 250,000	250,000 to 500,000	500,000 to 2,500,000	2,500,000 and over
Number of Enterprises **1**	1328	38	723	63	300	29	65	47	18	16	5	17	7

Revenues ($ in Thousands)

Item Description for Accounting Period 7/10 Through 6/11	Total	Zero Assets	Under 500	500 to 1,000	1,000 to 5,000	5,000 to 10,000	10,000 to 25,000	25,000 to 50,000	50,000 to 100,000	100,000 to 250,000	250,000 to 500,000	500,000 to 2,500,000	2,500,000 and over
Net Sales **2**	78485075	893214	67247	74327	1528342	484333	1704633	2098883	1573742	2697551	1459075	11663429	54240300
Interest **3**	370734	4660	2	229	383	38	379	3101	1708	7089	17254	65432	270459
Rents **4**	67793	4	0	0	1237	0	295	2	0	7	6163	37246	22840
Royalties **5**	1326917	2567	0	0	0	0	0	15846	1	16555	435	35954	1255558
Other Portfolio Income **6**	682104	16440	0	0	10927	4092	2103	10175	169	3581	5186	61918	567513
Other Receipts **7**	652992	2466	5	-4743	605	4	52470	29096	4125	81272	72443	141258	273989
Total Receipts **8**	81585615	919351	67254	69813	1541494	488467	1759880	2157103	1579745	2806055	1560556	12005237	56630659
Average Total Receipts **9**	61435	24193	93	1108	5138	16844	27075	45896	87764	175378	312111	706190	8090094

Operating Costs/Operating Income (%)

Item Description for Accounting Period 7/10 Through 6/11	Total	Zero Assets	Under 500	500 to 1,000	1,000 to 5,000	5,000 to 10,000	10,000 to 25,000	25,000 to 50,000	50,000 to 100,000	100,000 to 250,000	250,000 to 500,000	500,000 to 2,500,000	2,500,000 and over
Cost of Operations **10**	62.2	69.8	41.8	20.9	47.7	55.6	67.5	54.5	59.3	63.6	67.2	66.5	61.7
Salaries and Wages **11**	11.2	23.8	2.7	59.7	22.2	10.7	12.6	13.6	13.3	13.8	14.9	10.4	10.3
Taxes Paid **12**	2.0	2.0	3.6	6.0	4.5	1.6	2.7	1.5	1.8	1.4	1.5	1.5	2.1
Interest Paid **13**	2.4	2.3	1.8	0.7	0.2	1.0	1.1	1.9	0.4	0.4	2.1	2.6	2.6
Depreciation **14**	2.3	2.3	4.0	2.1	0.8	1.0	1.4	2.4	1.9	2.4	3.6	3.1	2.1
Amortization and Depletion **15**	3.2	5.0	•	0.1	0.4	0.1	0.6	2.9	0.8	1.6	0.9	2.4	3.8
Pensions and Other Deferred Comp. **16**	1.6	0.4	•	0.2	0.1	0.1	0.4	0.2	0.3	0.6	0.4	0.6	2.1
Employee Benefits **17**	2.0	1.3	•	6.1	1.3	0.8	1.9	2.2	1.7	1.8	2.5	2.3	1.9
Advertising **18**	0.9	0.2	0.3	3.1	1.2	1.8	0.5	0.4	0.7	0.4	0.5	0.4	1.0
Other Expenses **19**	10.7	13.8	20.1	30.4	16.5	12.2	8.6	14.4	10.4	14.5	12.5	13.4	9.5
Officers' Compensation **20**	0.7	5.3	5.5	25.3	6.6	3.3	2.8	1.9	1.4	1.0	0.7	0.8	0.2
Operating Margin **21**	1.0	•	20.1	•	•	11.9	•	4.1	8.0	•	•	•	2.6
Operating Margin Before Officers' Comp. **22**	1.7	•	25.6	•	5.1	15.2	2.5	5.9	9.5	•	•	•	2.9

Selected Average Balance Sheet ($ in Thousands)

Net Receivables 23	14434	0	8	214	720	2545	3687	6824	15340	42897	57579	139085	2097821
Inventories 24	5064	0	25	133	665	2240	2261	4646	10459	21794	32642	74717	585468
Net Property, Plant and Equipment 25	5282	0	5	30	382	475	1250	3684	5940	9965	40117	103413	628763
Total Assets 26	75192	0	90	877	2589	6593	16299	35383	70267	170644	359501	1095881	10231565
Notes and Loans Payable 27	21039	0	17	693	972	1741	4695	11305	9573	18758	120032	285832	2967672
All Other Liabilities 28	35072	0	35	147	1241	2850	5395	10561	25322	46038	98518	604473	4754133
Net Worth 29	19080	0	38	38	376	2002	6210	13517	35372	105848	140951	205576	2509760

Selected Financial Ratios (Times to 1)

Current Ratio 30	1.6	•	1.6	2.4	1.7	2.1	1.7	1.6	2.0	2.8	1.3	1.0	1.8
Quick Ratio 31	1.0	•	0.9	2.0	1.1	1.3	1.2	1.1	1.3	2.0	0.8	0.7	1.2
Net Sales to Working Capital 32	4.9	•	3.8	2.7	6.1	5.4	6.0	5.7	4.0	2.5	9.1	•	4.0
Coverage Ratio 33	3.4	•	12.4	•	•	13.8	3.8	4.6	21.7	7.4	1.4	0.7	4.0
Total Asset Turnover 34	0.8	•	1.0	1.3	2.0	2.5	1.6	1.3	1.2	1.0	0.8	0.6	0.8
Inventory Turnover 35	7.3	•	1.6	1.9	3.7	4.1	7.8	5.2	5.0	4.9	6.0	6.1	8.2
Receivables Turnover 36	3.5	•	21.7	7.0	8.1	6.6	6.7	6.3	6.2	4.1	3.0	5.1	3.1
Total Liabilities to Net Worth 37	2.9	•	1.4	22.3	5.9	2.3	1.6	1.6	1.0	0.6	1.6	4.3	3.1
Current Assets to Working Capital 38	2.8	•	2.7	1.7	2.5	1.9	2.4	2.5	2.0	1.6	4.2	•	2.2
Current Liabilities to Working Capital 39	1.8	•	1.7	0.7	1.5	0.9	1.4	1.5	1.0	0.6	3.2	•	1.2
Working Capital to Net Sales 40	0.2	•	0.3	0.4	0.2	0.2	0.2	0.2	0.3	0.4	0.1	•	0.3
Inventory to Working Capital 41	0.4	•	1.2	0.3	0.7	0.7	0.5	0.7	0.5	0.3	0.9	•	0.3
Total Receipts to Cash Flow 42	7.4	•	2.9	•	9.2	4.4	10.1	5.3	6.0	7.6	10.8	10.5	6.7
Cost of Goods to Cash Flow 43	4.6	•	1.2	•	4.4	2.5	6.8	2.9	3.6	4.9	7.3	7.0	4.1
Cash Flow to Total Debt 44	0.1	•	0.6	•	0.2	0.8	0.3	0.4	0.4	0.3	0.1	0.1	0.1

Selected Financial Factors (in Percentages)

Debt Ratio 45	74.6	•	57.6	95.7	85.5	69.6	61.9	61.8	49.7	38.0	60.8	81.2	75.5
Return on Total Assets 46	6.3	•	22.6	•	•	34.7	6.5	11.1	11.5	3.3	2.3	1.2	7.9
Return on Equity Before Income Taxes 47	17.5	•	49.0	•	•	106.1	12.6	22.9	21.7	4.5	1.5	•	24.2
Return on Equity After Income Taxes 48	10.5	•	49.0	•	•	100.4	8.4	15.8	15.5	2.7	•	•	15.6
Profit Margin (Before Income Tax) 49	5.6	•	20.1	•	•	12.7	3.0	6.9	8.8	2.9	0.7	•	7.9
Profit Margin (After Income Tax) 50	3.4	•	20.1	•	•	12.0	2.0	4.8	6.3	1.7	•	•	5.1

Table II

Corporations with Net Income

COMMUNICATIONS EQUIPMENT

MONEY AMOUNTS AND SIZE OF ASSETS IN THOUSANDS OF DOLLARS

Item Description for Accounting Period 7/10 Through 6/11		Total	Zero Assets	Under 500	500 to 1,000	1,000 to 5,000	5,000 to 10,000	10,000 to 25,000	25,000 to 50,000	50,000 to 100,000	100,000 to 250,000	250,000 to 500,000	500,000 to 2,500,000	2,500,000 and over
Number of Enterprises	1	1025	3	631	0	254	•	45	25	13	11	•	7	•
Revenues ($ in Thousands)														
Net Sales	2	58611247	35947	49641	0	1442924	•	1455853	1342015	1223368	1989067	•	6163180	•
Interest	3	169008	4	0	0	301	•	320	2355	1610	5308	•	19765	•
Rents	4	22324	0	0	0	1237	•	71	2	0	7	•	0	•
Royalties	5	1184817	0	0	0	0	•	0	15846	0	15306	•	9209	•
Other Portfolio Income	6	610632	0	0	0	10927	•	1961	7273	147	3453	•	40424	•
Other Receipts	7	395593	1484	0	0	594	•	6374	28200	1773	80086	•	36083	•
Total Receipts	8	60993621	37435	49641	0	1455983	•	1464579	1395691	1226898	2093227	•	6268661	•
Average Total Receipts	9	59506	12478	79	•	5732	•	32546	55828	94377	190293	•	895523	•
Operating Costs/Operating Income (%)														
Cost of Operations	10	64.8	51.7	40.5	•	46.6	•	64.8	54.6	56.0	61.9	•	73.3	•
Salaries and Wages	11	8.7	19.0	•	•	21.9	•	9.7	10.9	12.7	13.2	•	5.5	•
Taxes Paid	12	2.0	1.8	3.2	•	4.8	•	2.7	1.2	1.8	1.5	•	1.2	•
Interest Paid	13	1.3	0.8	2.4	•	0.2	•	0.5	1.9	0.4	0.3	•	0.7	•
Depreciation	14	2.1	4.3	5.1	•	0.8	•	1.2	1.3	2.1	2.4	•	1.7	•
Amortization and Depletion	15	2.3	•	•	•	0.1	•	0.3	0.6	0.6	0.8	•	0.5	•
Pensions and Other Deferred Comp.	16	1.9	1.2	•	•	0.1	•	0.4	0.2	0.2	0.7	•	0.7	•
Employee Benefits	17	1.3	•	•	•	1.3	•	1.4	1.9	1.8	1.3	•	1.3	•
Advertising	18	0.9	•	•	•	1.1	•	0.5	0.3	0.8	0.3	•	0.3	•
Other Expenses	19	8.4	3.4	17.7	•	15.3	•	5.9	10.2	10.6	14.0	•	7.7	•
Officers' Compensation	20	0.6	4.6	•	•	5.7	•	2.5	1.6	1.2	0.9	•	0.7	•
Operating Margin	21	5.6	13.3	31.1	•	2.2	•	10.2	15.3	11.9	2.7	•	6.3	•
Operating Margin Before Officers' Comp.	22	6.3	17.8	31.1	•	7.9	•	12.7	16.9	13.1	3.6	•	7.0	•

Selected Average Balance Sheet ($ in Thousands)

	All								
Net Receivables 23	8936	0	0	775	4684	6258	17112	35832	140870
Inventories 24	4881	0	0	711	2366	4496	6841	25462	108878
Net Property, Plant and Equipment 25	4427	0	6	444	1093	4396	7222	11905	65056
Total Assets 26	57290	0	46	2640	15415	33352	70871	172544	916256
Notes and Loans Payable 27	11372	0	20	1059	4459	16694	10277	17992	101242
All Other Liabilities 28	24478	0	15	1294	5463	7013	27520	33121	315882
Net Worth 29	21440	0	11	288	5493	9645	33074	121431	499132

Selected Financial Ratios (Times to 1)

	All								
Current Ratio 30	1.8	•	0.8	1.6	2.2	1.7	2.0	3.0	2.0
Quick Ratio 31	1.1	•	0.8	1.0	1.6	1.2	1.3	2.1	1.4
Net Sales to Working Capital 32	5.2	•	•	7.4	5.1	6.7	4.7	2.5	3.5
Coverage Ratio 33	8.6	24.1	14.1	15.8	20.8	11.4	33.2	29.3	13.2
Total Asset Turnover 34	1.0	•	1.7	2.2	2.1	1.6	1.3	1.0	1.0
Inventory Turnover 35	7.6	•	3.7	3.7	8.9	6.5	7.7	4.4	5.9
Receivables Turnover 36	4.9	•	•	8.8	7.4	8.8	8.6	4.6	5.2
Total Liabilities to Net Worth 37	1.7	•	3.1	8.2	1.8	2.5	1.1	0.4	0.8
Current Assets to Working Capital 38	2.3	•	•	2.7	1.8	2.3	2.0	1.5	2.0
Current Liabilities to Working Capital 39	1.3	•	•	1.7	0.8	1.3	1.0	0.5	1.0
Working Capital to Net Sales 40	0.2	•	•	0.1	0.2	0.1	0.2	0.4	0.3
Inventory to Working Capital 41	0.4	•	•	0.9	0.4	0.6	0.4	0.3	0.3
Total Receipts to Cash Flow 42	6.1	5.5	2.2	7.5	6.5	3.7	4.8	5.3	7.2
Cost of Goods to Cash Flow 43	4.0	2.8	0.9	3.5	4.2	2.0	2.7	3.3	5.3
Cash Flow to Total Debt 44	0.3	•	•	1.0	0.5	0.6	0.5	0.7	0.3

Selected Financial Factors (in Percentages)

	All								
Debt Ratio 45	62.6	•	75.5	89.1	64.4	71.1	53.3	29.6	45.5
Return on Total Assets 46	11.4	•	57.4	7.2	23.8	34.3	17.3	8.8	8.7
Return on Equity Before Income Taxes 47	27.0	•	218.0	61.5	63.7	108.3	35.9	12.1	14.7
Return on Equity After Income Taxes 48	18.9	•	218.0	57.8	56.7	89.5	26.7	9.8	11.8
Profit Margin (Before Income Tax) 49	10.1	•	31.1	3.1	10.8	19.5	12.6	8.2	8.3
Profit Margin (After Income Tax) 50	7.1	•	31.1	2.9	9.6	16.1	9.4	6.6	6.7

Table I

Corporations with and without Net Income

AUDIO AND VIDEO EQUIP., REPRODUCING MAGNETIC & OPTICAL MEDIA

MONEY AMOUNTS AND SIZE OF ASSETS IN THOUSANDS OF DOLLARS

Item Description for Accounting Period 7/10 Through 6/11	Total	Zero Assets	Under 500	500 to 1,000	1,000 to 5,000	5,000 to 10,000	10,000 to 25,000	25,000 to 50,000	50,000 to 100,000	100,000 to 250,000	250,000 to 500,000	500,000 to 2,500,000	2,500,000 and over
Number of Enterprises 1	837	12	468	0	250	19	46	10	14	5	5	7	0
Revenues ($ in Thousands)													
Net Sales 2	23760004	256800	185842	0	929262	232141	1289027	438963	1184675	1448568	1262422	16532304	0
Interest 3	31218	166	27	0	180	417	591	141	419	3740	1253	24285	0
Rents 4	7627	0	0	0	0	0	1125	0	0	0	2195	4307	0
Royalties 5	153030	0	0	0	0	0	0	0	0	0	3227	149803	0
Other Portfolio Income 6	44599	217	0	0	0	14	2075	133	2386	7523	13487	18764	0
Other Receipts 7	321500	6812	0	0	9775	48420	4053	-3	4940	1653	8992	236856	0
Total Receipts 8	24317978	263995	185869	0	939217	280992	1296871	439234	1192420	1461484	1291576	16966319	0
Average Total Receipts 9	29054	22000	397	•	3757	14789	28193	43923	85173	292297	258315	2423760	•
Operating Costs/Operating Income (%)													
Cost of Operations 10	58.6	48.6	29.1	•	49.4	48.9	59.5	63.7	54.9	81.8	57.5	57.9	•
Salaries and Wages 11	12.0	21.6	23.3	•	13.5	27.0	13.6	9.6	14.7	7.3	14.2	11.4	•
Taxes Paid 12	1.1	2.4	2.7	•	2.8	3.7	1.8	1.7	2.5	1.2	1.8	0.7	•
Interest Paid 13	3.2	1.9	0.1	•	0.4	0.2	2.9	1.6	3.8	4.5	1.7	3.4	•
Depreciation 14	2.2	3.1	0.1	•	1.3	1.8	1.7	2.9	2.5	2.4	3.0	2.2	•
Amortization and Depletion 15	1.1	0.1	0.0	•	0.1	0.2	0.5	0.6	1.7	0.2	0.8	1.3	•
Pensions and Other Deferred Comp. 16	2.1	0.0	0.7	•	1.0	0.2	0.2	0.1	0.4	0.1	1.0	2.8	•
Employee Benefits 17	2.0	3.0	1.3	•	1.7	0.6	1.3	3.4	2.5	0.3	1.6	2.2	•
Advertising 18	2.3	2.6	0.7	•	2.4	0.2	0.7	0.4	2.5	0.5	2.2	2.6	•
Other Expenses 19	15.4	24.4	21.7	•	18.6	31.1	14.4	14.7	18.1	10.7	18.1	15.0	•
Officers' Compensation 20	1.0	6.8	13.1	•	6.4	7.4	2.0	2.2	1.8	0.2	1.1	0.3	•
Operating Margin 21	•	•	7.2	•	2.4	•	1.5	•	•	•	•	0.2	•
Operating Margin Before Officers' Comp. 22	0.1	•	20.2	•	8.8	•	3.5	1.5	•	•	•	0.6	•

Selected Average Balance Sheet ($ in Thousands)

	1	2	3	4	5	6	7	8	9	10	11	12
Net Receivables 23	4434	0	17	•	296	2330	4505	6940	16631	33866	37055	388666
Inventories 24	4190	0	24	•	550	1526	3204	13254	13854	31519	50892	232127
Net Property, Plant and Equipment 25	2795	0	2	•	85	523	1553	4420	9281	27448	34302	250359
Total Assets 26	51972	0	168	•	2223	7434	17605	36281	66510	175502	323514	5446553
Notes and Loans Payable 27	21646	0	8	•	354	419	47009	8178	47706	865	109615	2079050
All Other Liabilities 28	11708	0	58	•	291	5091	13576	8394	26032	56451	98018	1108177
Net Worth 29	18618	0	102	•	1578	1924	-42980	19709	-7229	118187	115881	2259326

Selected Financial Ratios (Times to 1)

	1	2	3	4	5	6	7	8	9	10	11	12
Current Ratio 30	1.4	•	2.4	•	4.8	1.3	1.0	2.0	1.6	2.3	1.4	1.3
Quick Ratio 31	0.7	•	2.0	•	2.8	1.0	0.5	1.0	0.8	1.1	0.7	0.6
Net Sales to Working Capital 32	7.4	•	4.4	•	2.8	9.1	•	4.0	5.5	4.2	6.5	8.3
Coverage Ratio 33	1.5	•	94.5	•	10.2	•	1.8	0.6	•	•	1.3	1.9
Total Asset Turnover 34	0.5	•	2.4	•	1.7	1.6	1.6	1.2	1.3	1.7	0.8	0.4
Inventory Turnover 35	4.0	•	4.8	•	3.3	3.9	5.2	2.1	3.4	7.5	2.9	5.9
Receivables Turnover 36	5.9	•	22.6	•	12.7	6.1	6.6	3.9	4.9	9.8	4.8	8.8
Total Liabilities to Net Worth 37	1.8	•	0.7	•	0.4	2.9	•	0.8	•	0.5	1.8	1.4
Current Assets to Working Capital 38	3.6	•	1.7	•	1.3	4.9	•	2.0	2.7	1.8	3.6	4.2
Current Liabilities to Working Capital 39	2.6	•	0.7	•	0.3	3.9	•	1.0	1.7	0.8	2.6	3.2
Working Capital to Net Sales 40	0.1	•	0.2	•	0.4	0.1	•	0.2	0.2	0.2	0.2	0.1
Inventory to Working Capital 41	1.2	•	0.3	•	0.5	0.6	•	0.9	0.9	0.6	0.9	1.3
Total Receipts to Cash Flow 42	6.7	•	3.9	9.4	5.7	3.6	7.1	8.1	8.8	54.6	7.0	6.2
Cost of Goods to Cash Flow 43	3.9	•	1.1	4.6	2.8	1.8	4.2	5.1	4.8	44.7	4.0	3.6
Cash Flow to Total Debt 44	0.1	•	1.6	1.6	1.0	0.6	0.1	0.3	0.1	0.1	0.2	0.1

Selected Financial Factors (in Percentages)

	1	2	3	4	5	6	7	8	9	10	11	12
Debt Ratio 45	64.2	•	39.5	•	29.0	74.1	344.1	45.7	110.9	32.7	64.2	58.5
Return on Total Assets 46	2.6	•	17.2	•	6.3	•	8.4	1.1	•	•	1.7	2.8
Return on Equity Before Income Taxes 47	2.4	•	28.1	•	8.1	•	•	•	54.1	•	1.1	3.1
Return on Equity After Income Taxes 48	1.1	•	27.8	•	4.6	•	•	•	61.7	•	•	2.4
Profit Margin (Before Income Tax) 49	1.6	•	7.2	•	3.4	•	2.4	•	•	•	0.5	3.0
Profit Margin (After Income Tax) 50	0.7	•	7.1	•	1.9	•	1.9	•	•	•	•	2.2

Table II
Corporations with Net Income

AUDIO AND VIDEO EQUIP., REPRODUCING MAGNETIC & OPTICAL MEDIA

MONEY AMOUNTS AND SIZE OF ASSETS IN THOUSANDS OF DOLLARS

Item Description for Accounting Period 7/10 Through 6/11	Total	Zero Assets	Under 500	500 to 1,000	1,000 to 5,000	5,000 to 10,000	10,000 to 25,000	25,000 to 50,000	50,000 to 100,000	100,000 to 250,000	250,000 to 500,000	500,000 to 2,500,000	2,500,000 and over
Number of Enterprises **1**	748	•	441	0	239	15	27	6	8	•	0	•	0
Revenues ($ in Thousands)													
Net Sales **2**	18811633	•	183354	0	919446	218891	796464	239203	864113	•	•	•	0
Interest **3**	25836	•	0	0	124	403	512	59	2	•	0	•	0
Rents **4**	5581	•	0	0	0	0	1125	0	0	•	0	•	0
Royalties **5**	152940	•	0	0	0	0	0	0	0	•	•	•	0
Other Portfolio Income **6**	23170	•	0	0	0	14	152	133	158	•	0	•	0
Other Receipts **7**	302069	•	0	0	9806	48421	2056	-4	1446	•	0	•	0
Total Receipts **8**	19321229	•	183354	0	929376	267729	800309	239391	865719	•	•	•	0
Average Total Receipts **9**	25831	•	416	•	3889	17849	29641	39898	108215	•	•	•	•
Operating Costs/Operating Income (%)													
Cost of Operations **10**	54.7	•	28.5	•	49.7	47.2	54.3	64.1	55.5	•	•	•	•
Salaries and Wages **11**	12.0	•	17.9	•	11.8	22.0	11.8	5.4	11.6	•	•	•	•
Taxes Paid **12**	1.0	•	2.1	•	2.6	3.5	1.9	1.0	2.2	•	•	•	•
Interest Paid **13**	3.2	•	0.0	•	0.3	0.0	0.5	0.2	3.5	•	•	•	•
Depreciation **14**	2.2	•	•	•	1.1	0.8	1.7	1.9	1.9	•	•	•	•
Amortization and Depletion **15**	1.2	•	•	•	0.0	0.0	0.3	0.1	0.5	•	•	•	•
Pensions and Other Deferred Comp. **16**	2.6	•	0.7	•	1.0	0.1	0.3	0.2	0.5	•	•	•	•
Employee Benefits **17**	2.2	•	1.2	•	1.6	0.3	1.1	4.8	2.7	•	•	•	•
Advertising **18**	2.6	•	0.5	•	2.5	0.2	0.3	0.8	2.7	•	•	•	•
Other Expenses **19**	14.9	•	9.2	•	14.5	28.8	12.5	13.6	9.1	•	•	•	•
Officers' Compensation **20**	1.0	•	10.8	•	6.2	6.5	2.1	3.0	1.5	•	•	•	•
Operating Margin **21**	2.3	•	29.2	•	8.8	•	13.1	5.0	8.3	•	•	•	•
Operating Margin Before Officers' Comp. **22**	3.3	•	40.0	•	15.0	•	15.2	7.9	9.8	•	•	•	•

Selected Average Balance Sheet ($ in Thousands)

Net Receivables 23	3647	16	276	2731	3611	5763	17391
Inventories 24	2916	22	570	1506	2301	15384	16533
Net Property, Plant and Equipment 25	2662	0	79	325	2109	3061	10337
Total Assets 26	52546	165	2177	7317	17803	34962	66723
Notes and Loans Payable 27	20024	0	276	227	2580	699	31379
All Other Liabilities 28	10212	26	264	5639	2732	6593	17434
Net Worth 29	22310	139	1636	1450	12491	27670	17910

Selected Financial Ratios (Times to 1)

Current Ratio 30	1.5	6.0	5.4	1.2	2.6	3.4	2.3
Quick Ratio 31	0.7	5.1	3.0	1.0	1.6	1.2	1.3
Net Sales to Working Capital 32	6.6	3.2	2.9	13.8	4.6	2.5	4.4
Coverage Ratio 33	2.6	2437.2	35.7	499.5	30.5	29.1	3.5
Total Asset Turnover 34	0.5	2.5	1.8	2.0	1.7	1.1	1.6
Inventory Turnover 35	4.7	5.4	3.4	4.6	7.0	1.7	3.6
Receivables Turnover 36	8.0	•	14.3	7.3	8.9	3.9	6.2
Total Liabilities to Net Worth 37	1.4	0.2	0.3	4.0	0.4	0.3	2.7
Current Assets to Working Capital 38	3.2	1.2	1.2	6.5	1.6	1.4	1.8
Current Liabilities to Working Capital 39	2.2	0.2	0.2	5.5	0.6	0.4	0.8
Working Capital to Net Sales 40	0.2	0.3	0.3	0.1	0.2	0.4	0.2
Inventory to Working Capital 41	1.0	0.2	0.5	0.7	0.5	0.8	0.7
Total Receipts to Cash Flow 42	5.6	2.8	5.0	2.6	4.1	5.7	6.1
Cost of Goods to Cash Flow 43	3.1	0.8	2.5	1.2	2.2	3.7	3.4
Cash Flow to Total Debt 44	0.1	5.8	1.4	1.0	1.4	1.0	0.4

Selected Financial Factors (in Percentages)

Debt Ratio 45	57.5	15.8	24.8	80.2	29.8	20.9	73.2
Return on Total Assets 46	4.0	73.6	18.1	25.9	23.3	6.0	19.4
Return on Equity Before Income Taxes 47	5.8	87.3	23.3	130.6	32.1	7.3	51.4
Return on Equity After Income Taxes 48	4.6	87.1	19.8	88.0	30.2	4.9	46.1
Profit Margin (Before Income Tax) 49	5.1	29.2	9.9	13.0	13.6	5.1	8.5
Profit Margin (After Income Tax) 50	4.1	29.1	8.4	8.7	12.8	3.4	7.6

Table I

Corporations with and without Net Income

SEMICONDUCTOR AND OTHER ELECTRONIC COMPONENT

MONEY AMOUNTS AND SIZE OF ASSETS IN THOUSANDS OF DOLLARS

Item Description for Accounting Period 7/10 Through 6/11	Total	Zero Assets	Under 500	500 to 1,000	1,000 to 5,000	5,000 to 10,000	10,000 to 25,000	25,000 to 50,000	50,000 to 100,000	100,000 to 250,000	250,000 to 500,000	500,000 to 2,500,000	2,500,000 and over
Number of Enterprises **1**	4668	578	1778	357	1124	319	210	77	48	60	37	60	20
Revenues ($ in Thousands)													
Net Sales **2**	204864055	826203	906399	518912	6400949	3483166	4966900	2969971	3792988	10352587	11112957	42775857	116757166
Interest **3**	874180	3414	1376	2183	983	1538	3425	4728	6661	24714	23183	220790	581184
Rents **4**	56874	0	0	0	201	953	2453	49	3261	2538	7802	9739	29878
Royalties **5**	10287326	17656	0	0	1109	57	0	4216	339	84092	109128	1286574	8784155
Other Portfolio Income **6**	1990933	477	3406	1035	34636	4441	11581	25745	11686	44113	98116	376124	1379573
Other Receipts **7**	2469354	38162	94	1146	18801	22198	22289	42926	99874	355145	340440	1217895	310384
Total Receipts **8**	220542722	885912	911275	523276	6456679	3512353	5006648	3047635	3914809	10863189	11691626	45886979	127842340
Average Total Receipts **9**	47246	1533	513	1466	5744	11011	23841	39580	81559	181053	315990	764783	6392117
Operating Costs/Operating Income (%)													
Cost of Operations **10**	61.6	57.4	46.2	45.2	58.8	62.3	71.2	63.6	69.1	76.0	64.8	67.7	57.5
Salaries and Wages **11**	11.2	15.7	2.2	15.8	11.3	8.5	9.3	10.2	8.9	10.9	12.8	14.0	10.4
Taxes Paid **12**	1.3	2.6	1.1	3.3	2.6	2.3	1.8	2.2	1.5	1.2	1.5	1.4	1.2
Interest Paid **13**	2.0	1.2	1.5	1.0	0.9	0.6	1.3	1.1	1.0	0.7	2.2	2.0	2.4
Depreciation **14**	4.2	3.5	0.4	5.0	2.6	2.0	2.2	3.6	3.0	3.1	4.3	4.2	4.7
Amortization and Depletion **15**	1.3	1.0	0.0	0.1	0.4	0.7	0.6	0.3	1.0	1.1	2.7	1.2	1.3
Pensions and Other Deferred Comp. **16**	0.5	0.2	0.0	0.0	0.7	0.7	0.4	0.8	0.6	0.2	0.4	0.5	0.5
Employee Benefits **17**	1.8	1.5	2.7	0.6	1.5	1.7	1.3	2.5	1.3	1.3	1.8	1.9	1.8
Advertising **18**	1.2	1.4	0.6	0.3	1.1	0.9	0.2	0.7	0.3	0.3	0.6	0.3	1.8
Other Expenses **19**	9.0	23.2	31.5	25.3	11.1	9.5	7.9	13.0	10.2	15.6	9.3	10.0	7.5
Officers' Compensation **20**	0.9	3.6	9.0	6.8	6.1	4.4	2.4	2.2	1.8	1.2	1.3	1.1	0.2
Operating Margin **21**	4.9	•	4.9	•	2.9	6.5	1.5	•	1.3	•	•	•	10.9
Operating Margin Before Officers' Comp. **22**	5.8	•	13.9	3.5	9.0	10.9	3.9	2.1	3.1	•	•	•	11.1

Selected Average Balance Sheet ($ in Thousands)

Net Receivables 23	13766	0	26	219	613	1455	3431	6139	15055	34334	63842	154860	2367584
Inventories 24	3323	0	11	150	600	1616	3193	6076	10898	20481	31462	56193	341165
Net Property, Plant and Equipment 25	8467	0	9	82	681	1104	2121	6038	11540	22839	42070	140209	1277890
Total Assets 26	67491	0	145	679	2672	6716	15572	34293	70469	161276	353664	1096017	10579181
Notes and Loans Payable 27	9608	0	38	183	903	1622	4344	6734	12871	31412	68084	207403	1214546
All Other Liabilities 28	21726	0	61	158	635	1303	4450	9428	21878	49172	75952	265922	3784648
Net Worth 29	36157	0	46	338	1133	3791	6778	18131	35721	80693	209627	622693	5579987

Selected Financial Ratios (Times to 1)

Current Ratio 30	1.8	•	1.3	3.2	2.1	2.8	2.0	2.1	1.9	2.0	2.4	2.5	1.6
Quick Ratio 31	1.3	•	1.1	2.0	1.2	1.7	1.2	1.2	1.3	1.2	1.5	1.8	1.2
Net Sales to Working Capital 32	3.2	•	21.5	4.0	6.5	3.6	4.5	3.5	4.3	3.7	2.7	2.2	3.6
Coverage Ratio 33	7.8	•	4.7	•	5.1	12.8	2.8	3.2	5.8	•	2.9	3.4	10.4
Total Asset Turnover 34	0.7	•	3.5	2.1	2.1	1.6	1.5	1.1	1.1	1.1	0.8	0.7	0.6
Inventory Turnover 35	8.1	•	21.7	4.4	5.6	4.2	5.3	4.0	5.0	6.4	6.2	8.6	9.8
Receivables Turnover 36	3.3	•	27.4	6.5	10.3	7.1	7.8	6.9	4.9	5.6	4.9	4.7	2.5
Total Liabilities to Net Worth 37	0.9	•	2.1	1.0	1.4	0.8	1.3	0.9	1.0	1.0	0.7	0.8	0.9
Current Assets to Working Capital 38	2.3	•	4.0	1.4	1.9	1.6	2.0	1.9	2.1	2.0	1.7	1.6	2.8
Current Liabilities to Working Capital 39	1.3	•	3.0	0.4	0.9	0.6	1.0	0.9	1.1	1.0	0.7	0.6	1.8
Working Capital to Net Sales 40	0.3	•	0.0	0.2	0.2	0.3	0.2	0.3	0.2	0.3	0.4	0.4	0.3
Inventory to Working Capital 41	0.3	•	0.5	0.5	0.7	0.5	0.7	0.6	0.5	0.5	0.3	0.2	0.2
Total Receipts to Cash Flow 42	5.4	6.5	3.6	7.1	9.0	7.5	12.8	8.3	7.8	54.5	9.5	10.8	3.9
Cost of Goods to Cash Flow 43	3.3	3.7	1.7	3.2	5.3	4.6	9.1	5.3	5.4	41.4	6.1	7.3	2.3
Cash Flow to Total Debt 44	0.3	•	1.4	0.6	0.4	0.5	0.2	0.3	0.3	0.0	0.2	0.1	0.3

Selected Financial Factors (in Percentages)

Debt Ratio 45	46.4	•	68.1	50.3	57.6	43.6	56.5	47.1	49.3	50.0	40.7	43.2	47.3
Return on Total Assets 46	10.4	•	24.1	•	10.1	12.9	5.3	4.2	6.4	•	5.2	4.5	13.5
Return on Equity Before Income Taxes 47	16.9	•	59.6	•	19.2	21.0	7.9	5.4	10.4	•	5.8	5.5	23.2
Return on Equity After Income Taxes 48	11.0	•	54.2	•	18.5	19.7	5.6	3.8	7.9	•	3.6	3.1	15.3
Profit Margin (Before Income Tax) 49	14.0	•	5.4	•	3.8	7.3	2.3	2.6	4.7	•	4.0	4.8	22.2
Profit Margin (After Income Tax) 50	9.1	•	4.9	•	3.7	6.9	1.6	1.8	3.6	•	2.5	2.7	14.7

Table II
Corporations with Net Income

SEMICONDUCTOR AND OTHER ELECTRONIC COMPONENT

MONEY AMOUNTS AND SIZE OF ASSETS IN THOUSANDS OF DOLLARS

Item Description for Accounting Period 7/10 Through 6/11	Total	Zero Assets	Under 500	500 to 1,000	1,000 to 5,000	5,000 to 10,000	10,000 to 25,000	25,000 to 50,000	50,000 to 100,000	100,000 to 250,000	250,000 to 500,000	500,000 to 2,500,000	2,500,000 and over
Number of Enterprises **1**	3024	4	1172	•	882	254	161	54	29	•	25	41	16
Revenues ($ in Thousands)													
Net Sales **2**	164286275	360059	585276	•	5614160	3140526	4443587	2441614	2681894	•	7966441	28290411	102597027
Interest **3**	685018	2144	1310	•	688	1261	1656	2781	3930	•	12750	148285	499598
Rents **4**	46207	0	0	•	193	112	2453	49	3261	•	7744	9483	22099
Royalties **5**	9907471	715	0	•	127	0	0	2668	339	•	100964	1218680	8578948
Other Portfolio Income **6**	1870155	477	0	•	34636	1612	10857	23185	6583	•	73083	359359	1323857
Other Receipts **7**	2064305	1104	-1	•	18862	10082	21029	28932	58905	•	266761	951957	602626
Total Receipts **8**	178859431	364499	586585	•	5668466	3153593	4479582	2499229	2754912	•	8427743	30978175	113624155
Average Total Receipts **9**	59147	91125	500	•	6427	12416	27823	46282	94997	•	337110	755565	7101510
Operating Costs/Operating Income (%)													
Cost of Operations **10**	58.4	39.1	31.1	•	58.5	59.7	71.9	62.3	66.0	•	62.6	58.7	56.5
Salaries and Wages **11**	10.2	20.2	1.4	•	10.1	6.9	7.4	8.2	8.3	•	12.2	16.2	8.8
Taxes Paid **12**	1.4	3.7	1.3	•	2.5	2.2	1.6	2.2	1.4	•	1.4	1.7	1.1
Interest Paid **13**	1.3	0.8	1.5	•	0.7	0.4	0.9	0.9	0.7	•	0.8	1.7	1.4
Depreciation **14**	4.3	5.1	0.3	•	1.9	1.5	1.8	3.1	2.5	•	2.8	4.7	4.8
Amortization and Depletion **15**	0.9	0.8	0.0	•	0.2	0.4	0.2	0.1	0.8	•	1.4	1.5	0.9
Pensions and Other Deferred Comp. **16**	0.6	0.0	•	•	0.7	0.7	0.4	0.9	0.4	•	0.5	0.6	0.6
Employee Benefits **17**	1.9	1.3	2.1	•	1.3	1.5	1.2	2.5	1.2	•	1.7	2.3	1.9
Advertising **18**	1.2	0.8	0.7	•	1.2	0.9	0.2	0.7	0.3	•	0.7	0.3	1.7
Other Expenses **19**	8.4	17.8	23.4	•	10.0	8.0	6.1	10.4	8.7	•	8.8	9.9	7.8
Officers' Compensation **20**	0.9	1.8	12.7	•	5.9	3.9	2.4	1.9	1.5	•	1.3	1.4	0.2
Operating Margin **21**	10.4	8.6	25.5	•	7.0	13.8	6.0	6.9	8.2	•	5.9	1.0	14.1
Operating Margin Before Officers' Comp. **22**	11.3	10.3	38.2	•	12.9	17.8	8.4	8.8	9.7	•	7.1	2.4	14.3

Selected Average Balance Sheet ($ in Thousands)

Net Receivables 23	17534	0	26	•	679	1644	3981	6815	14587	•	47408	158971	2611398
Inventories 24	3634	0	6	•	634	1685	3265	6698	9083	•	31486	44074	345349
Net Property, Plant and Equipment 25	10719	0	5	•	560	907	2235	5795	11066	•	40706	137181	1466372
Total Assets 26	86288	0	167	•	2556	6490	15717	34296	71075	•	344542	1153028	11839860
Notes and Loans Payable 27	8033	0	13	•	722	1423	4164	4625	11344	•	39498	175245	821628
All Other Liabilities 28	28168	0	84	•	518	1397	4529	10181	17134	•	62486	281535	4253542
Net Worth 29	50087	0	70	•	1316	3671	7025	19490	42597	•	242558	696249	6764689

Selected Financial Ratios (Times to 1)

Current Ratio 30	1.8	•	1.3	•	2.5	3.1	2.1	2.4	2.3	•	2.4	3.0	1.6
Quick Ratio 31	1.4	•	1.1	•	1.5	1.9	1.2	1.3	1.5	•	1.4	2.2	1.2
Net Sales to Working Capital 32	3.1	•	19.4	•	6.0	3.7	4.7	3.6	4.3	•	3.0	1.8	3.6
Coverage Ratio 33	16.6	12.6	18.4	•	12.0	36.2	8.3	11.4	16.6	•	16.7	8.8	19.5
Total Asset Turnover 34	0.6	•	3.0	•	2.5	1.9	1.8	1.3	1.3	•	0.9	0.6	0.5
Inventory Turnover 35	8.7	•	26.9	•	5.9	4.4	6.1	4.2	6.7	•	6.3	9.2	10.5
Receivables Turnover 36	4.4	•	24.5	•	12.2	7.4	9.2	7.5	8.1	•	7.3	5.6	3.6
Total Liabilities to Net Worth 37	0.7	•	1.4	•	0.9	0.8	1.2	0.8	0.7	•	0.4	0.7	0.8
Current Assets to Working Capital 38	2.2	•	4.3	•	1.6	1.5	1.9	1.7	1.8	•	1.7	1.5	2.8
Current Liabilities to Working Capital 39	1.2	•	3.3	•	0.6	0.5	0.9	0.7	0.8	•	0.7	0.5	1.8
Working Capital to Net Sales 40	0.3	•	0.1	•	0.2	0.3	0.2	0.3	0.2	•	0.3	0.6	0.3
Inventory to Working Capital 41	0.2	•	0.4	•	0.7	0.4	0.8	0.6	0.5	•	0.3	0.1	0.2
Total Receipts to Cash Flow 42	4.0	4.3	2.4	•	7.1	5.2	9.2	6.2	5.6	•	5.6	5.7	3.3
Cost of Goods to Cash Flow 43	2.3	1.7	0.8	•	4.2	3.1	6.6	3.8	3.7	•	3.5	3.3	1.9
Cash Flow to Total Debt 44	0.4	•	2.1	•	0.7	0.8	0.3	0.5	0.6	•	0.6	0.3	0.4

Selected Financial Factors (in Percentages)

Debt Ratio 45	42.0	•	58.2	•	48.5	43.4	55.3	43.2	40.1	•	29.6	39.6	42.9
Return on Total Assets 46	14.1	•	81.2	•	21.7	27.8	13.6	13.3	15.3	•	12.0	9.0	15.3
Return on Equity Before Income Taxes 47	22.8	•	183.6	•	38.6	47.8	26.8	21.4	24.0	•	16.0	13.2	25.5
Return on Equity After Income Taxes 48	16.2	•	178.1	•	37.9	46.2	23.9	19.3	20.5	•	13.3	9.9	17.4
Profit Margin (Before Income Tax) 49	21.0	9.8	25.7	•	8.0	14.2	6.8	9.2	11.0	•	12.2	13.3	26.9
Profit Margin (After Income Tax) 50	14.9	9.3	24.9	•	7.8	13.7	6.1	8.3	9.4	•	10.1	10.0	18.3

Table I

Corporations with and without Net Income

NAVIGATIONAL, MEASURING, ELECTROMEDICAL, AND CONTROL

MONEY AMOUNTS AND SIZE OF ASSETS IN THOUSANDS OF DOLLARS

Item Description for Accounting Period 7/10 Through 6/11	Total	Zero Assets	Under 500	500 to 1,000	1,000 to 5,000	5,000 to 10,000	10,000 to 25,000	25,000 to 50,000	50,000 to 100,000	100,000 to 250,000	250,000 to 500,000	500,000 to 2,500,000	2,500,000 and over
Number of Enterprises 1	2869	54	1231	400	429	393	159	70	35	35	20	26	17
Revenues ($ in Thousands)													
Net Sales 2	103492646	1104021	719970	724373	1640139	4563465	3598902	2866780	2801631	5998314	5223937	15440542	58810571
Interest 3	1648952	829	8	654	150	1251	2788	1406	4875	24536	39646	39530	1533280
Rents 4	79203	684	0	1280	0	1445	160	2439	6713	2456	1414	37002	25609
Royalties 5	838570	12525	0	0	35	0	149	803	4768	14370	10265	223783	571873
Other Portfolio Income 6	1447099	2077	50	0	24537	9059	35898	5909	16978	69491	39512	181790	1061798
Other Receipts 7	1735573	-9973	22735	5124	7192	26303	6592	39693	14005	54412	80836	176833	1311822
Total Receipts 8	109242043	1142871	710055	731431	1672053	4601523	3644489	2917030	2848970	6163579	5395610	16099480	63314953
Average Total Receipts 9	38077	21164	577	1829	3898	11709	22921	41672	81399	176102	269780	619211	3724409
Operating Costs/Operating Income (%)													
Cost of Operations 10	57.4	39.8	34.6	41.7	54.3	56.4	58.3	55.7	58.1	60.9	50.3	57.2	58.7
Salaries and Wages 11	14.2	35.4	16.1	25.8	18.1	12.7	15.6	14.7	12.9	11.6	17.9	15.0	13.3
Taxes Paid 12	1.9	1.1	2.6	3.9	2.9	2.5	2.2	2.3	1.6	1.6	1.9	1.6	2.0
Interest Paid 13	3.4	5.4	0.5	0.4	1.1	0.6	0.8	1.8	0.5	1.1	2.8	2.4	4.7
Depreciation 14	2.2	3.1	0.4	0.7	1.3	1.8	1.6	1.9	1.6	2.4	2.5	2.6	2.2
Amortization and Depletion 15	1.4	4.6	0.0	0.0	0.4	0.4	0.5	0.5	0.8	0.8	2.1	1.8	1.5
Pensions and Other Deferred Comp. 16	1.2	1.8	•	0.6	0.1	0.5	0.6	0.7	0.6	0.5	0.4	1.2	1.6
Employee Benefits 17	2.2	4.0	2.1	2.2	1.6	2.6	2.0	2.3	2.2	2.8	2.7	1.7	2.3
Advertising 18	0.7	0.7	1.4	0.9	1.8	1.1	0.7	0.8	1.8	0.5	1.9	0.6	0.4
Other Expenses 19	12.7	20.5	20.7	16.4	17.0	14.0	10.7	11.5	11.9	14.2	16.0	11.4	12.2
Officers' Compensation 20	1.4	7.8	10.5	6.3	5.7	3.4	3.9	2.6	2.0	1.6	1.2	1.0	0.6
Operating Margin 21	1.3	•	11.0	1.0	•	4.0	3.0	5.0	6.0	2.0	0.3	3.3	0.6
Operating Margin Before Officers' Comp. 22	2.7	•	21.5	7.3	1.5	7.4	6.9	7.6	7.9	3.6	1.5	4.4	1.2

Selected Average Balance Sheet ($ in Thousands)

Net Receivables **23**	6648	0	33	207	708	2133	3426	6823	14095	33779	66051	129831	612597
Inventories **24**	3744	0	69	85	595	1027	3476	6131	11995	21447	29991	84477	295004
Net Property, Plant and Equipment **25**	4059	0	3	72	194	965	2064	4840	6305	18927	29345	79646	408417
Total Assets **26**	71122	0	188	660	2038	7097	15388	33876	69629	154719	354195	1167866	8810139
Notes and Loans Payable **27**	17585	0	101	158	759	1436	2329	7860	8673	22117	96020	274539	2253995
All Other Liabilities **28**	18556	0	15	223	944	1945	4028	10289	17960	39660	83862	309395	2285906
Net Worth **29**	34981	0	71	280	335	3716	9031	15727	42996	92941	174312	583932	4270239

Selected Financial Ratios (Times to 1)

Current Ratio **30**	1.2	•	9.8	2.2	1.4	1.9	2.3	2.0	1.9	2.3	1.7	1.3	1.0
Quick Ratio **31**	0.7	•	5.8	1.7	0.9	1.3	1.4	1.1	1.2	1.4	1.1	0.8	0.5
Net Sales to Working Capital **32**	11.4	•	4.4	5.9	8.6	4.8	3.9	4.2	4.2	3.5	4.4	6.5	777.6
Coverage Ratio **33**	3.4	•	19.9	5.7	•	8.8	6.7	4.8	18.3	5.7	2.6	5.1	3.0
Total Asset Turnover **34**	0.5	•	3.1	2.7	1.9	1.6	1.5	1.2	1.1	1.1	0.7	0.5	0.4
Inventory Turnover **35**	5.5	•	2.9	8.9	3.5	6.4	3.8	3.7	3.9	4.9	4.4	4.0	6.9
Receivables Turnover **36**	5.0	•	11.7	15.0	3.9	7.6	6.7	6.1	5.4	5.6	4.4	4.1	4.9
Total Liabilities to Net Worth **37**	1.0	•	1.6	1.4	5.1	0.9	0.7	1.2	0.6	0.7	1.0	1.0	1.1
Current Assets to Working Capital **38**	5.6	•	1.1	1.9	3.7	2.1	1.8	2.0	2.1	1.8	2.5	4.4	355.9
Current Liabilities to Working Capital **39**	4.6	•	0.1	0.9	2.7	1.1	0.8	1.0	1.1	0.8	1.5	3.4	354.9
Working Capital to Net Sales **40**	0.1	•	0.2	0.2	0.1	0.2	0.3	0.2	0.2	0.3	0.2	0.2	0.0
Inventory to Working Capital **41**	1.2	•	0.4	0.3	1.2	0.5	0.6	0.6	0.6	0.5	0.5	1.0	68.7
Total Receipts to Cash Flow **42**	5.8	•	3.7	6.8	12.5	6.2	8.1	6.1	5.9	5.9	5.7	5.9	5.5
Cost of Goods to Cash Flow **43**	3.3	•	1.3	2.8	6.8	3.5	4.7	3.4	3.4	3.6	2.9	3.4	3.2
Cash Flow to Total Debt **44**	0.2	•	1.3	0.7	0.2	0.6	0.4	0.4	0.5	0.5	0.3	0.2	0.1

Selected Financial Factors (in Percentages)

Debt Ratio **45**	50.8	•	62.1	57.6	83.6	47.6	41.3	53.6	38.2	39.9	50.8	50.0	51.5
Return on Total Assets **46**	5.8	•	31.7	6.7	•	9.0	7.5	10.7	9.6	7.1	5.4	6.3	5.6
Return on Equity Before Income Taxes **47**	8.3	•	79.4	13.0	•	15.2	10.8	18.2	14.7	9.7	6.7	10.1	7.8
Return on Equity After Income Taxes **48**	5.7	•	78.3	11.8	•	14.0	8.9	15.2	12.5	6.4	3.9	7.0	5.3
Profit Margin (Before Income Tax) **49**	8.1	•	9.7	2.0	•	4.9	4.3	7.0	7.9	5.3	4.5	10.0	9.6
Profit Margin (After Income Tax) **50**	5.5	•	9.5	1.8	•	4.5	3.5	5.8	6.7	5.3	2.6	6.8	6.5

NAVIGATIONAL, MEASURING, ELECTROMEDICAL, AND CONTROL

Table II

Corporations with Net Income

MONEY AMOUNTS AND SIZE OF ASSETS IN THOUSANDS OF DOLLARS

Item Description for Accounting Period 7/10 Through 6/11	Total	Zero Assets	Under 500	500 to 1,000	1,000 to 5,000	5,000 to 10,000	10,000 to 25,000	25,000 to 50,000	50,000 to 100,000	100,000 to 250,000	250,000 to 500,000	500,000 to 2,500,000	2,500,000 and over
Number of Enterprises **1**	1900	•	673	305	277	347	135	55	29	27	•	21	•
Revenues ($ in Thousands)													
Net Sales **2**	92278307	•	592110	539744	1288889	4204560	3226699	2555369	2438920	4735545	•	12797371	•
Interest **3**	1624665	•	2	72	48	426	1650	1221	3564	22804	•	34102	•
Rents **4**	76783	•	0	1280	0	1195	160	2439	6713	2428	•	37002	•
Royalties **5**	714470	•	0	0	0	0	0	49	4618	7307	•	198118	•
Other Portfolio Income **6**	1392132	•	0	0	24293	793	34274	5585	16931	65528	•	181600	•
Other Receipts **7**	1661432	•	1	1564	879	23492	4323	39427	13705	42382	•	154460	•
Total Receipts **8**	97747789	•	592113	542660	1314109	4230466	3267106	2604090	2484451	4875994	•	13402653	•
Average Total Receipts **9**	51446	•	880	1779	4744	12192	24201	47347	85671	180592	•	638222	•
Operating Costs/Operating Income (%)													
Cost of Operations **10**	57.3	•	32.4	47.5	50.3	55.8	58.2	55.8	58.0	58.8	•	54.7	•
Salaries and Wages **11**	13.3	•	18.3	19.3	16.7	11.4	13.2	14.0	11.5	10.9	•	15.6	•
Taxes Paid **12**	2.0	•	2.6	3.4	2.9	2.4	2.1	2.3	1.6	1.6	•	1.7	•
Interest Paid **13**	3.4	•	0.5	0.4	0.7	0.4	0.4	1.5	0.3	1.2	•	2.0	•
Depreciation **14**	2.1	•	0.3	0.4	1.1	1.5	1.2	1.8	1.5	2.2	•	2.7	•
Amortization and Depletion **15**	1.2	•	0.0	0.0	0.1	0.1	0.2	0.2	0.6	0.8	•	1.4	•
Pensions and Other Deferred Comp. **16**	1.3	•	•	0.8	0.1	0.5	0.6	0.8	0.6	0.5	•	1.4	•
Employee Benefits **17**	2.1	•	1.9	1.4	1.2	2.5	1.9	2.3	2.2	3.1	•	1.7	•
Advertising **18**	0.6	•	1.6	0.2	1.7	0.8	0.6	0.8	1.8	0.5	•	0.6	•
Other Expenses **19**	12.3	•	12.8	12.4	14.6	11.8	8.4	9.3	11.5	13.6	•	11.6	•
Officers' Compensation **20**	1.2	•	11.1	6.4	5.1	3.2	3.7	2.6	1.9	1.7	•	1.0	•
Operating Margin **21**	3.3	•	18.5	7.8	5.5	9.6	9.5	8.6	8.4	5.2	•	5.5	•
Operating Margin Before Officers' Comp. **22**	4.5	•	29.6	14.2	10.6	12.8	13.3	11.2	10.3	6.9	•	6.5	•

Selected Average Balance Sheet ($ in Thousands)

Net Receivables 23	8561	55	205	693	2274	3497	7435	14148	32672	133530
Inventories 24	4745	105	66	633	749	3231	6644	11390	21218	82206
Net Property, Plant and Equipment 25	5375	2	65	194	972	1802	5262	6072	16809	86560
Total Assets 26	98821	277	628	2201	7119	14685	34074	69690	154349	1178316
Notes and Loans Payable 27	23407	58	150	533	1037	1712	7954	5172	23079	222467
All Other Liabilities 28	25625	26	186	699	1783	3876	8408	17590	40622	315174
Net Worth 29	49789	193	291	969	4298	9097	17712	46928	90648	640675

Selected Financial Ratios (Times to 1)

Current Ratio 30	1.2	9.7	2.3	1.9	2.3	2.5	2.5	1.3	2.2	1.3
Quick Ratio 31	0.7	5.7	1.9	1.2	1.6	1.5	1.3	1.4	1.3	0.9
Net Sales to Working Capital 32	12.9	3.9	5.7	5.3	4.3	4.0	3.6	3.5	3.5	5.9
Coverage Ratio 33	4.1	36.4	24.8	11.4	29.1	26.1	8.0	33.0	8.7	7.6
Total Asset Turnover 34	0.5	3.2	2.8	2.1	1.7	1.6	1.4	1.2	1.1	0.5
Inventory Turnover 35	5.9	2.7	12.7	3.7	9.0	4.3	3.9	4.3	4.9	4.1
Receivables Turnover 36	5.3		15.8	5.6	8.6	7.2	6.3	6.3	6.4	4.7
Total Liabilities to Net Worth 37	1.0	0.4	1.2	1.3	0.7	0.6	0.9	0.5	0.7	0.8
Current Assets to Working Capital 38	6.2	1.1	1.8	2.1	1.8	1.7	1.7	1.8	1.8	4.1
Current Liabilities to Working Capital 39	5.2	0.1	0.8	1.1	0.8	0.7	0.7	0.8	0.8	3.1
Working Capital to Net Sales 40	0.1	0.3	0.2	0.2	0.2	0.3	0.3	0.3	0.3	0.2
Inventory to Working Capital 41	1.3	0.5	0.2	0.7	0.4	0.5	0.5	0.5	0.5	0.8
Total Receipts to Cash Flow 42	5.2	3.6	5.9	6.8	5.1	6.0	5.6	5.2	5.0	5.1
Cost of Goods to Cash Flow 43	3.0	1.1	2.8	3.4	2.8	3.5	3.1	3.0	3.0	2.8
Cash Flow to Total Debt 44	0.2	2.9	0.9	0.6	0.8	0.7	0.5	0.7	0.5	0.2

Selected Financial Factors (in Percentages)

Debt Ratio 45	49.6	30.4	53.6	56.0	39.6	38.1	48.0	32.7	41.3	45.6
Return on Total Assets 46	6.8	60.4	24.6	17.2	18.1	18.3	16.8	13.0	11.4	7.8
Return on Equity Before Income Taxes 47	10.2	84.3	50.9	35.6	28.9	28.4	28.3	18.7	17.2	12.4
Return on Equity After Income Taxes 48	7.5	83.6	49.4	34.5	27.7	26.1	24.9	16.3	12.8	8.8
Profit Margin (Before Income Tax) 49	10.5	18.5	8.4	7.4	10.3	10.8	10.8	10.4	8.9	13.1
Profit Margin (After Income Tax) 50	7.6	18.3	8.1	7.2	9.8	9.9	9.5	9.1	6.6	9.3

Table I

Corporations with and without Net Income

ELECTRICAL LIGHTING EQUIPMENT AND HOUSEHOLD APPLIANCE

MONEY AMOUNTS AND SIZE OF ASSETS IN THOUSANDS OF DOLLARS

Item Description for Accounting Period 7/10 Through 6/11		Total	Zero Assets	Under 500	500 to 1,000	1,000 to 5,000	5,000 to 10,000	10,000 to 25,000	25,000 to 50,000	50,000 to 100,000	100,000 to 250,000	250,000 to 500,000	500,000 to 2,500,000	2,500,000 and over
Number of Enterprises	1	2002	640	751	69	318	66	95	11	16	17	7	7	5
Revenues ($ in Thousands)														
Net Sales	2	129891557	1213891	34317	30724	1212707	909578	2352864	561777	1364901	3515509	1945376	11940556	104809358
Interest	3	39777885	3	0	42	184	96	387	98	722	3751	1459	28707	39742437
Rents	4	9810741	0	0	0	0	0	4508	0	0	912	0	4322	9800999
Royalties	5	2432580	0	0	0	0	0	0	0	6	630	4431	23473	2404041
Other Portfolio Income	6	4605251	0	0	0	119	19573	8361	6	135	5067	566	67358	4504067
Other Receipts	7	26629037	1454	0	0	14421	18165	17384	2687	1543	23460	2829	111165	26435925
Total Receipts	8	213147051	1215348	34317	30766	1227431	947412	2383504	564568	1367307	3549329	1954661	12175581	187696827
Average Total Receipts	9	106467	1899	46	446	3860	14355	25090	51324	85457	208784	279237	1739369	37539365
Operating Costs/Operating Income (%)														
Cost of Operations	10	66.8	78.5	28.7	63.2	58.2	61.5	64.2	77.0	61.8	65.8	65.1	68.2	66.8
Salaries and Wages	11	11.7	6.3	31.8	7.7	19.6	11.5	12.7	5.7	7.9	8.7	5.5	6.5	12.5
Taxes Paid	12	0.7	1.1	6.4	0.1	4.9	1.7	1.9	1.6	1.4	1.5	1.3	1.3	0.5
Interest Paid	13	32.6	0.1	4.4	0.0	0.5	0.6	0.8	1.3	2.0	1.5	3.4	1.0	40.1
Depreciation	14	6.3	1.3	2.9	0.0	0.8	2.1	2.8	1.6	2.2	3.0	3.0	2.0	7.3
Amortization and Depletion	15	4.1	4.0	0.9	•	0.5	0.4	0.2	0.3	1.6	0.6	0.9	0.7	4.9
Pensions and Other Deferred Comp.	16	1.2	0.3	0.0	0.0	0.4	0.4	0.7	0.3	0.4	0.7	0.3	0.9	1.3
Employee Benefits	17	2.2	0.0	•	•	0.7	1.3	2.2	1.4	1.4	2.0	1.2	2.1	2.3
Advertising	18	1.7	0.1	1.0	0.2	0.4	1.2	0.9	0.7	1.1	1.5	5.3	2.6	1.7
Other Expenses	19	35.0	2.6	74.4	31.2	17.0	17.3	11.2	7.6	10.1	11.3	9.1	13.0	40.5
Officers' Compensation	20	0.4	0.7	7.5	8.5	2.2	1.9	1.8	1.9	1.8	1.5	1.5	0.3	0.3
Operating Margin	21	•	5.0	•	•	•	0.1	0.5	0.6	8.3	2.0	3.4	1.5	•
Operating Margin Before Officers' Comp.	22	•	5.7	•	•	2.0	2.0	2.3	2.5	10.1	3.5	4.8	1.8	•

Selected Average Balance Sheet ($ in Thousands)

Net Receivables 23	90784	0	6	128	572	1898	3255	7277	10458	34266	60620	228493	35653434
Inventories 24	5816	0	1	519	574	2831	4607	11137	12685	33152	64614	101505	1749731
Net Property, Plant and Equipment 25	21929	0	3	0	556	742	2992	3273	9384	28392	44965	168292	8245709
Total Assets 26	407509	0	10	887	2271	7599	15481	30052	70260	150054	339711	1508557	159225375
Notes and Loans Payable 27	274955	0	23	298	588	1219	3934	8822	20032	37161	140156	271019	109170544
All Other Liabilities 28	68643	0	7	135	1189	3299	4324	6046	17244	50527	97717	448292	26275604
Net Worth 29	63912	0	-21	454	494	3082	7223	15184	32984	62365	101838	789246	23779228

Selected Financial Ratios (Times to 1)

Current Ratio 30	0.8	•	0.4	4.9	1.4	2.1	2.2	2.2	1.7	2.0	1.8	1.9	0.8
Quick Ratio 31	0.7	•	0.3	2.2	0.7	1.2	1.1	1.0	0.8	0.9	0.9	1.2	0.7
Net Sales to Working Capital 32	•	•	•	0.8	8.1	4.1	4.2	4.6	5.5	4.8	4.1	6.0	•
Coverage Ratio 33	1.2	60.9	•	•	•	8.0	3.2	1.8	5.3	3.2	2.2	4.6	1.2
Total Asset Turnover 34	0.2	•	4.7	0.5	1.7	1.8	1.6	1.7	1.2	1.4	0.8	1.1	0.1
Inventory Turnover 35	7.5	•	25.2	0.5	3.9	3.0	3.5	3.5	4.2	4.1	2.8	11.5	8.0
Receivables Turnover 36	0.7	•	15.6	1.3	10.9	6.9	7.7	9.0	8.4	6.0	4.9	9.0	0.6
Total Liabilities to Net Worth 37	5.4	•	•	1.0	3.6	1.5	1.1	1.0	1.1	1.4	2.3	0.9	5.7
Current Assets to Working Capital 38	•	•	•	1.3	3.4	1.9	1.8	1.9	2.5	2.1	2.2	2.1	•
Current Liabilities to Working Capital 39	•	•	•	0.3	2.4	0.9	0.8	0.9	1.5	1.1	1.2	1.1	•
Working Capital to Net Sales 40	•	•	•	1.2	0.1	0.2	0.2	0.2	0.2	0.2	0.2	0.2	•
Inventory to Working Capital 41	•	•	•	0.0	1.7	0.7	0.8	0.9	0.9	0.8	0.8	0.5	•
Total Receipts to Cash Flow 42	3.0	13.3	38.3	5.6	9.9	5.2	10.2	13.6	5.8	8.4	9.1	6.7	2.6
Cost of Goods to Cash Flow 43	2.0	10.4	11.0	3.5	5.8	3.2	6.6	10.4	3.6	5.5	6.0	4.5	1.7
Cash Flow to Total Debt 44	0.1	0.0	0.2	0.2	0.6	0.3	0.3	0.3	0.4	0.3	0.1	0.4	0.1

Selected Financial Factors (in Percentages)

Debt Ratio 45	84.3	•	310.2	48.8	78.2	59.4	53.3	49.5	53.1	58.4	70.0	47.7	85.1
Return on Total Assets 46	6.4	•	•	•	•	8.9	4.3	4.1	12.7	6.5	6.1	5.1	6.4
Return on Equity Before Income Taxes 47	7.4	•	128.3	•	•	19.2	6.3	3.7	22.0	10.7	10.8	7.7	7.3
Return on Equity After Income Taxes 48	5.0	•	128.3	•	•	17.7	4.4	3.2	18.6	8.4	8.8	6.4	4.8
Profit Margin (Before Income Tax) 49	7.3	5.1	•	•	•	4.3	1.8	1.1	8.5	3.2	4.0	3.6	8.3
Profit Margin (After Income Tax) 50	4.9	5.1	•	•	•	4.0	1.3	0.9	7.2	2.5	3.2	2.9	5.5

Table II

Corporations with Net Income

ELECTRICAL LIGHTING EQUIPMENT AND HOUSEHOLD APPLIANCE

MONEY AMOUNTS AND SIZE OF ASSETS IN THOUSANDS OF DOLLARS

Item Description for Accounting Period 7/10 Through 6/11	Total	Zero Assets	Under 500	500 to 1,000	1,000 to 5,000	5,000 to 10,000	10,000 to 25,000	25,000 to 50,000	50,000 to 100,000	100,000 to 250,000	250,000 to 500,000	500,000 to 2,500,000	2,500,000 and over
Number of Enterprises 1	814	7	421	0	237	44	61	6	13	11	4	•	•
Revenues ($ in Thousands)													
Net Sales 2	115045461	1185396	7197	0	1002793	724686	1590537	400412	1277947	2698722	1599103	•	•
Interest 3	39770579	3	0	0	128	25	305	39	719	3467	1290	•	•
Rents 4	9797423	0	0	0	0	0	4508	0	0	891	0	•	•
Royalties 5	1903109	0	0	0	0	0	0	0	6	532	1070		•
Other Portfolio Income 6	4277892	0	0	0	0	19573	8257	6	135	4936	566	•	•
Other Receipts 7	26557509	1453	0	0	8914	15000	10801	2336	1136	7159	2769	•	•
Total Receipts 8	197351973	1186852	7197	0	1011835	759284	1614408	402793	1279943	2715707	1604798	•	•
Average Total Receipts 9	242447	169550	17	•	4269	17256	26466	67132	98457	246882	401200	•	•
Operating Costs/Operating Income (%)													
Cost of Operations 10	65.9	78.2	14.5	•	55.4	60.3	63.1	83.5	61.7	62.4	70.4	•	•
Salaries and Wages 11	12.5	6.4	0.3	•	20.6	9.2	11.6	4.0	8.1	8.8	3.6	•	•
Taxes Paid 12	0.7	1.2	0.4	•	5.3	1.4	1.5	1.4	1.4	1.5	1.1	•	•
Interest Paid 13	36.5	0.1	•	•	0.4	0.2	0.3	0.6	1.4	0.9	0.8	•	•
Depreciation 14	6.8	1.2	•	•	0.1	1.1	2.2	1.4	2.2	2.8	2.5	•	•
Amortization and Depletion 15	4.5	4.1	•	•	0.4	0.5	0.0	0.0	0.7	0.3	0.5	•	•
Pensions and Other Deferred Comp. 16	1.1	0.3	•	•	0.5	0.4	0.4	0.2	0.4	0.6	0.3	•	•
Employee Benefits 17	2.0	0.0	•	•	0.5	1.2	1.5	1.4	1.4	2.2	0.8	•	•
Advertising 18	1.8	0.1	4.3	•	0.3	0.3	1.2	0.6	1.2	1.6	5.0	•	•
Other Expenses 19	37.4	2.3	79.4	•	11.0	16.3	9.1	4.1	10.1	11.2	7.1	•	•
Officers' Compensation 20	0.4	0.7	•	•	1.9	1.8	1.6	1.3	1.8	1.2	1.4	•	•
Operating Margin 21	•	5.5	1.3	•	3.6	7.3	7.3	1.5	9.8	6.5	6.3	•	•
Operating Margin Before Officers' Comp. 22	•	6.1	1.3	•	5.5	9.1	9.0	2.8	11.6	7.7	7.8	•	•

Selected Average Balance Sheet ($ in Thousands)

Net Receivables 23	205743	0	0	•	460	2069	3409	10945	11686	40554	51667
Inventories 24	11905	0	0	•	629	2868	4974	16136	12696	32304	80035
Net Property, Plant and Equipment 25	51548	0	0	•	341	499	2732	4747	11061	29486	40844
Total Assets 26	951034	0	0	•	2113	7977	15594	33148	74008	162362	292765
Notes and Loans Payable 27	663397	0	10	•	516	1216	2300	8366	18713	30680	62773
All Other Liabilities 28	150874	0	-9	•	1011	2433	3121	6422	19802	53161	81220
Net Worth 29	136762	0	-1	•	586	4327	10173	18360	35493	78521	148772

Selected Financial Ratios (Times to 1)

Current Ratio 30	0.8	•	•	•	1.6	2.3	3.3	2.5	1.7	2.1	2.4
Quick Ratio 31	0.7	•	•	•	0.7	1.3	1.6	1.3	0.8	1.1	1.0
Net Sales to Working Capital 32	•	•	78.2	•	8.2	4.2	3.3	4.0	5.3	4.7	4.5
Coverage Ratio 33	1.2	64.4	•	•	11.9	52.6	31.7	4.5	8.2	9.1	9.1
Total Asset Turnover 34	0.1	•	78.2	•	2.0	2.1	1.7	2.0	1.3	1.5	1.4
Inventory Turnover 35	7.8	•	•	•	3.7	3.5	3.3	3.5	4.8	4.7	3.5
Receivables Turnover 36	0.7	•	•	•	13.7	7.3	7.7	7.7	10.3	6.0	•
Total Liabilities to Net Worth 37	6.0	•	•	•	2.6	0.8	0.5	0.8	1.1	1.1	1.0
Current Assets to Working Capital 38	•	•	•	1.0	2.8	1.7	1.4	1.7	2.4	1.9	1.7
Current Liabilities to Working Capital 39	•	•	•	•	1.8	0.7	0.4	0.7	1.4	0.9	0.7
Working Capital to Net Sales 40	•	•	•	0.0	0.1	0.2	0.3	0.3	0.2	0.2	0.2
Inventory to Working Capital 41	•	•	•	•	1.6	0.7	0.7	0.8	0.9	0.7	0.9
Total Receipts to Cash Flow 42	2.7	13.1	2.6	•	7.9	3.9	6.5	19.8	5.4	6.2	8.0
Cost of Goods to Cash Flow 43	1.8	10.2	0.4	•	4.4	2.4	4.1	16.5	3.3	3.8	5.6
Cash Flow to Total Debt 44	0.1	6.2	•	•	0.4	1.2	0.7	0.2	0.5	0.5	0.3

Selected Financial Factors (in Percentages)

Debt Ratio 45	85.6	487.0	•	•	72.3	45.8	34.8	44.6	52.0	51.6	49.2
Return on Total Assets 46	6.7	100.0	•	•	9.8	25.4	15.3	5.4	15.0	12.7	10.5
Return on Equity Before Income Taxes 47	9.0	•	•	•	32.2	45.9	22.6	7.6	27.5	23.4	18.4
Return on Equity After Income Taxes 48	6.2	•	•	•	28.4	44.3	20.6	6.7	23.7	20.6	16.0
Profit Margin (Before Income Tax) 49	8.7	5.6	1.3	1.3	4.5	12.1	8.8	2.1	9.9	7.5	6.9
Profit Margin (After Income Tax) 50	6.0	5.5	1.3	1.3	3.9	11.7	8.0	1.8	8.5	6.6	5.9

Table I

Corporations with and without Net Income

ELECTRICAL EQUIPMENT

MONEY AMOUNTS AND SIZE OF ASSETS IN THOUSANDS OF DOLLARS

Item Description for Accounting Period 7/10 Through 6/11	Total	Zero Assets	Under 500	500 to 1,000	1,000 to 5,000	5,000 to 10,000	10,000 to 25,000	25,000 to 50,000	50,000 to 100,000	100,000 to 250,000	250,000 to 500,000	500,000 to 2,500,000	2,500,000 and over
Number of Enterprises **1**	776	9	38	135	346	125	53	32	12	10	7	5	4
Revenues ($ in Thousands)													
Net Sales **2**	41168656	72687	17126	307242	1632022	1639380	1192264	1315809	1066877	1994115	2729136	3319743	26382253
Interest **3**	292804	8	0	0	558	32	102	1865	510	1014	2660	6987	279066
Rents **4**	54133	0	0	0	378	0	114	1986	165	311	0	0	51177
Royalties **5**	320045	2452	0	0	0	0	0	0	112	4833	12279	15180	285191
Other Portfolio Income **6**	410098	0	0	0	252	14	346	10733	187	4598	5811	11328	376826
Other Receipts **7**	482815	130	3741	1295	7540	5765	4124	9878	100	11844	7497	15377	415530
Total Receipts **8**	43228551	75277	20867	308537	1640750	1645191	1196950	1340271	1067951	2016715	2757383	3368615	27790043
Average Total Receipts **9**	55707	8364	549	2285	4742	13162	22584	41883	88996	201672	393912	673723	6947511
Operating Costs/Operating Income (%)													
Cost of Operations **10**	66.8	61.4	169.8	79.4	63.2	63.9	55.8	75.1	73.4	68.6	61.8	64.9	67.4
Salaries and Wages **11**	8.4	24.7	34.9	1.0	7.6	7.4	10.1	7.5	7.1	10.1	11.4	7.0	8.3
Taxes Paid **12**	1.9	1.1	6.5	1.9	2.8	2.1	1.7	1.9	1.1	1.5	2.0	1.0	2.0
Interest Paid **13**	2.6	19.8	10.6	0.3	1.1	0.5	0.7	1.9	0.7	1.5	0.6	3.8	3.1
Depreciation **14**	2.0	1.5	3.5	0.3	3.0	1.6	1.5	2.3	2.0	2.5	2.9	2.3	1.8
Amortization and Depletion **15**	1.2	2.3	1.5	•	0.1	0.1	0.1	0.9	0.3	1.0	0.6	6.2	0.8
Pensions and Other Deferred Comp. **16**	2.0	0.1	•	•	0.3	0.3	1.2	0.3	0.3	0.7	0.6	0.7	2.7
Employee Benefits **17**	1.9	1.9	5.0	1.9	1.2	2.9	2.8	2.6	0.8	1.7	1.7	2.1	1.8
Advertising **18**	0.5	2.5	0.1	0.1	0.4	0.2	0.5	0.3	0.8	0.7	2.5	0.6	0.5
Other Expenses **19**	10.0	18.2	179.2	11.9	11.9	9.3	13.7	7.8	6.8	5.9	15.0	8.9	9.7
Officers' Compensation **20**	1.4	0.4	0.3	2.5	7.0	6.2	2.2	1.4	1.5	0.8	1.3	0.6	0.9
Operating Margin **21**	1.4	•	•	0.8	1.4	5.4	9.7	•	5.1	5.0	0.0	1.8	0.9
Operating Margin Before Officers' Comp. **22**	2.8	•	•	3.3	8.4	11.6	11.9	•	6.6	5.8	1.3	1.8	2.5

Selected Average Balance Sheet ($ in Thousands)

Net Receivables 23	13709	0	3	428	482	1695	2932	8045	14536	34854	65256	88029	2092173
Inventories 24	5238	0	9	260	728	1205	3765	5686	13814	30594	55839	105803	463462
Net Property, Plant and Equipment 25	6818	0	103	0	473	1615	2152	4913	8882	30744	95620	86772	783075
Total Assets 26	79402	0	131	622	2123	8421	13642	34748	67222	182526	356188	1015818	11925090
Notes and Loans Payable 27	15793	0	3668	317	923	1696	3494	7171	7257	28286	77055	364076	2099335
All Other Liabilities 28	14102	0	15	229	400	1632	2326	8476	22641	59849	89829	155941	1974134
Net Worth 29	49506	0	-3552	76	800	5094	7822	19100	37324	94391	189305	495802	7851622

Selected Financial Ratios (Times to 1)

Current Ratio 30	1.4	•	1.4	1.4	2.8	1.9	2.7	2.2	2.3	1.7	2.0	2.4	1.1
Quick Ratio 31	0.9	•	0.8	1.0	1.4	1.2	1.6	1.3	1.2	0.9	1.1	1.2	0.8
Net Sales to Working Capital 32	8.6	•	41.7	13.9	4.6	5.0	3.6	4.0	3.8	5.1	4.0	4.2	19.5
Coverage Ratio 33	3.4	•	•	5.4	2.8	12.7	15.1	1.1	8.1	5.1	3.5	2.2	3.4
Total Asset Turnover 34	0.7	•	3.4	3.7	2.2	1.6	1.6	1.2	1.3	1.1	1.1	0.7	0.6
Inventory Turnover 35	6.8	•	87.8	7.0	4.1	7.0	3.3	5.4	4.7	4.5	4.3	4.1	9.6
Receivables Turnover 36	4.1	•	151.6	6.7	11.3	10.7	7.4	6.0	6.5	5.3	6.1	5.4	3.4
Total Liabilities to Net Worth 37	0.6	•	•	7.2	1.7	0.7	0.7	0.8	0.8	0.9	0.9	1.0	0.5
Current Assets to Working Capital 38	3.8	•	2.5	3.8	1.5	2.1	1.6	1.8	1.7	2.4	2.0	1.7	8.9
Current Liabilities to Working Capital 39	2.8	•	1.5	2.8	0.5	1.1	0.6	0.8	0.7	1.4	1.0	0.7	7.9
Working Capital to Net Sales 40	0.1	•	0.0	0.1	0.2	0.2	0.3	0.3	0.3	0.2	0.3	0.2	0.1
Inventory to Working Capital 41	0.9	•	1.2	1.0	0.7	0.6	0.6	0.6	0.7	0.8	0.5	0.6	1.4
Total Receipts to Cash Flow 42	7.7	•	•	11.9	8.8	8.0	4.6	16.4	9.1	9.6	6.8	9.9	7.3
Cost of Goods to Cash Flow 43	5.2	•	•	9.5	5.6	5.1	2.6	12.3	6.7	6.6	4.2	6.4	4.9
Cash Flow to Total Debt 44	0.2	•	•	0.3	0.4	0.5	0.8	0.2	0.3	0.2	0.3	0.1	0.2

Selected Financial Factors (in Percentages)

Debt Ratio 45	37.7	•	2813.7	87.8	62.3	39.5	42.7	45.0	44.5	48.3	46.9	51.2	34.2
Return on Total Assets 46	5.9	•	•	5.5	6.7	9.8	17.9	2.4	7.8	8.4	2.1	5.6	6.0
Return on Equity Before Income Taxes 47	6.7	•	36.7	36.8	11.5	14.9	29.2	0.3	12.3	13.1	2.8	6.3	6.4
Return on Equity After Income Taxes 48	4.4	•	36.7	29.4	7.8	14.9	27.1	•	11.0	11.1	0.6	3.8	4.1
Profit Margin (Before Income Tax) 49	6.2	•	•	1.2	1.9	5.8	10.1	0.1	5.2	6.2	1.4	4.7	7.6
Profit Margin (After Income Tax) 50	4.1	•	•	1.0	1.3	5.8	9.4	•	4.6	5.2	0.3	2.9	4.9

Table II
Corporations with Net Income

ELECTRICAL EQUIPMENT

MONEY AMOUNTS AND SIZE OF ASSETS IN THOUSANDS OF DOLLARS

Item Description for Accounting Period 7/10 Through 6/11

	Total	Zero Assets	Under 500	500 to 1,000	1,000 to 5,000	5,000 to 10,000	10,000 to 25,000	25,000 to 50,000	50,000 to 100,000	100,000 to 250,000	250,000 to 500,000	500,000 to 2,500,000	2,500,000 and over
Number of Enterprises 1	666	0	•	135	334	101	44	23	•	•	3	•	•
Revenues ($ in Thousands)													
Net Sales 2	30704571	0	•	307242	1631467	1444725	1099780	896773	•	•	1286015	•	•
Interest 3	282356	0	•	0	484	0	81	1773	•	•	908	•	•
Rents 4	45354	0	•	0	378	0	81	1897	•	•	0	•	•
Royalties 5	187455	0	•	0	0	0	0	0	•	•	3151	•	•
Other Portfolio Income 6	337830	0	•	0	252	14	346	6576	•	•	5811	•	•
Other Receipts 7	307781	0	•	1295	6200	5726	1426	8395	•	•	4981	•	•
Total Receipts 8	31865347	0	•	308537	1638781	1450465	1101714	915414	•	•	1300866	•	•
Average Total Receipts 9	47846	•	•	2285	4907	14361	25039	39801	•	•	433622	•	•
Operating Costs/Operating Income (%)													
Cost of Operations 10	64.7	•	•	79.4	63.2	60.6	55.1	71.2	•	•	56.3	•	•
Salaries and Wages 11	7.9	•	•	1.0	7.1	7.3	9.5	8.7	•	•	11.2	•	•
Taxes Paid 12	2.0	•	•	1.9	2.7	2.1	1.7	1.7	•	•	2.8	•	•
Interest Paid 13	2.4	•	•	0.3	1.1	0.2	0.4	1.3	•	•	0.5	•	•
Depreciation 14	2.1	•	•	0.3	2.9	1.6	1.5	2.6	•	•	2.9	•	•
Amortization and Depletion 15	1.1	•	•	•	0.0	0.0	0.1	1.2	•	•	0.3	•	•
Pensions and Other Deferred Comp. 16	1.4	•	•	•	0.3	0.2	1.3	0.4	•	•	3.3	•	•
Employee Benefits 17	1.7	•	•	1.9	1.1	3.1	3.0	2.1	•	•	2.3	•	•
Advertising 18	0.4	•	•	0.1	0.4	0.2	0.5	0.3	•	•	0.1	•	•
Other Expenses 19	9.8	•	•	11.9	10.7	8.9	13.1	8.4	•	•	10.8	•	•
Officers' Compensation 20	1.5	•	•	2.5	6.8	6.3	2.1	1.5	•	•	1.1	•	•
Operating Margin 21	4.9	•	•	0.8	3.5	9.4	11.9	0.6	•	•	8.4	•	•
Operating Margin Before Officers' Comp. 22	6.4	•	•	3.3	10.3	15.7	13.9	2.0	•	•	9.4	•	•

Selected Average Balance Sheet ($ in Thousands)

Net Receivables **23**	13125	•	•	428	498	1847	3002	8761	•	81193
Inventories **24**	4560	•	•	260	691	1277	3974	5600	•	33155
Net Property, Plant and Equipment **25**	5577	•	•	0	476	1531	2215	5043	•	99587
Total Assets **26**	70432	•	•	622	2141	8471	13169	35527	•	349548
Notes and Loans Payable **27**	10225	•	•	317	921	1603	2690	8025	•	88151
All Other Liabilities **28**	8497	•	•	229	409	1439	2086	9416	•	62709
Net Worth **29**	51710	•	•	76	812	5429	8392	18087	•	198688

Selected Financial Ratios (Times to 1)

Current Ratio **30**	1.4	•	•	1.4	2.9	2.1	3.6	1.9	•	3.0
Quick Ratio **31**	1.0	•	•	1.0	1.4	1.4	2.0	1.1	•	2.1
Net Sales to Working Capital **32**	7.4	•	•	13.9	4.6	4.5	3.3	4.3	•	3.3
Coverage Ratio **33**	5.0	•	•	5.4	4.8	45.4	30.1	3.4	•	18.9
Total Asset Turnover **34**	0.7	•	•	3.7	2.3	1.7	1.9	1.1	•	1.2
Inventory Turnover **35**	6.5	•	•	7.0	4.5	6.8	3.5	5.0	•	7.3
Receivables Turnover **36**	3.8	•	•	6.7	13.3	10.9	8.5	5.2	•	•
Total Liabilities to Net Worth **37**	0.4	•	•	7.2	1.6	0.6	0.6	1.0	•	0.8
Current Assets to Working Capital **38**	3.5	•	•	3.8	1.5	1.9	1.4	2.1	•	1.5
Current Liabilities to Working Capital **39**	2.5	•	•	2.8	0.5	0.9	0.4	1.1	•	0.5
Working Capital to Net Sales **40**	0.1	•	•	0.1	0.2	0.2	0.3	0.2	•	0.3
Inventory to Working Capital **41**	0.8	•	•	1.0	0.7	0.6	0.5	0.8	•	0.3
Total Receipts to Cash Flow **42**	6.2	•	•	11.9	8.1	6.1	4.4	10.2	•	5.2
Cost of Goods to Cash Flow **43**	4.0	•	•	9.5	5.1	3.7	2.4	7.3	•	3.0
Cash Flow to Total Debt **44**	0.4	•	•	0.3	0.5	0.8	1.2	0.2	•	0.5

Selected Financial Factors (in Percentages)

Debt Ratio **45**	26.6	•	•	87.8	62.1	35.9	36.3	49.1	•	43.2
Return on Total Assets **46**	8.0	•	•	5.5	11.5	17.0	23.6	4.8	•	12.6
Return on Equity Before Income Taxes **47**	8.7	•	•	36.8	23.9	25.9	35.8	6.7	•	21.0
Return on Equity After Income Taxes **48**	6.2	•	•	29.4	20.2	25.9	33.5	4.6	•	16.0
Profit Margin (Before Income Tax) **49**	9.8	•	•	1.2	4.0	9.8	12.0	3.1	•	9.7
Profit Margin (After Income Tax) **50**	7.0	•	•	1.0	3.4	9.8	11.3	2.1	•	7.4

Table I
Corporations with and without Net Income

OTHER ELECTRICAL EQUIPMENT AND COMPONENT

MONEY AMOUNTS AND SIZE OF ASSETS IN THOUSANDS OF DOLLARS

Item Description for Accounting Period 7/10 Through 6/11		Total	Zero Assets	Under 500	500 to 1,000	1,000 to 5,000	5,000 to 10,000	10,000 to 25,000	25,000 to 50,000	50,000 to 100,000	100,000 to 250,000	250,000 to 500,000	500,000 to 2,500,000	2,500,000 and over
Number of Enterprises	1	4018	853	984	697	770	270	228	87	50	43	17	15	4
Revenues ($ in Thousands)														
Net Sales	2	63355553	797464	760253	1163755	3843924	3294017	5909217	4193504	3771221	7000153	5563524	9339411	17719111
Interest	3	341263	194	152	8	664	757	2550	4105	5858	6604	59441	72548	188381
Rents	4	16640	69	0	162	312	103	2198	203	1298	278	951	1346	9720
Royalties	5	216983	0	1184	0	0	0	1147	1869	5694	16608	37391	47087	106003
Other Portfolio Income	6	963353	55808	1116	3	5054	8871	2294	7134	13619	33218	40557	280796	514883
Other Receipts	7	499077	26331	6215	200	21198	6855	39975	67877	18858	57814	33218	37938	182599
Total Receipts	8	65392869	879866	768920	1164128	3871152	3310603	5957381	4274692	3816548	7114675	5735082	9779126	18720697
Average Total Receipts	9	16275	1031	781	1670	5027	12261	26129	49134	76331	165458	337358	651942	4680174
Operating Costs/Operating Income (%)														
Cost of Operations	10	67.9	74.0	57.2	56.1	56.5	69.0	71.4	65.6	69.9	68.7	66.6	67.5	70.2
Salaries and Wages	11	9.0	8.9	18.4	9.3	11.7	8.0	7.9	10.0	8.2	9.6	9.4	9.3	8.0
Taxes Paid	12	1.6	1.8	1.7	3.3	2.1	2.0	2.2	1.7	2.2	1.7	1.1	1.4	1.3
Interest Paid	13	2.7	2.3	3.4	1.0	0.6	0.9	0.7	0.9	1.4	2.1	3.4	3.2	4.8
Depreciation	14	2.1	0.7	1.4	0.6	1.8	1.3	1.4	2.0	2.5	3.2	2.6	3.4	1.2
Amortization and Depletion	15	1.3	0.6	0.1	0.6	0.5	0.2	0.2	0.4	1.1	0.9	3.4	1.3	2.0
Pensions and Other Deferred Comp.	16	0.5	0.4	0.2	0.0	0.2	0.3	0.4	0.3	0.7	0.4	0.4	0.7	0.5
Employee Benefits	17	1.7	2.2	0.4	1.2	1.9	1.8	1.5	1.4	2.0	1.7	1.7	2.3	1.5
Advertising	18	1.3	0.1	3.2	0.2	0.6	0.4	0.5	1.0	0.4	0.7	0.8	0.8	2.7
Other Expenses	19	10.6	11.5	19.3	17.3	16.2	9.0	6.9	17.9	7.5	8.4	12.1	10.8	9.3
Officers' Compensation	20	1.6	3.2	1.5	6.1	5.6	3.0	2.4	2.3	1.7	1.8	0.6	1.1	0.2
Operating Margin	21	•	•	•	4.1	2.3	4.2	4.6	•	2.6	0.8	•	•	•
Operating Margin Before Officers' Comp.	22	1.4	•	•	10.1	7.2	7.9	7.0	•	4.2	2.5	•	•	•

Selected Average Balance Sheet ($ in Thousands)

Net Receivables 23	3337	0	32	190	680	1709	4313	7498	13705	31823	57618	98203	1529358
Inventories 24	1929	0	31	229	442	1966	3770	6954	12760	25565	35981	81751	412653
Net Property, Plant and Equipment 25	2068	0	7	26	406	1334	2560	4928	11487	28454	45237	167211	380752
Total Assets 26	23677	0	105	651	2455	6790	15178	33791	71341	156778	348042	1117730	12865699
Notes and Loans Payable 27	5025	0	684	244	439	2077	3712	7307	16029	49886	144763	300148	1764298
All Other Liabilities 28	7278	0	27	219	722	1482	4412	9687	17950	44046	102415	308510	4274611
Net Worth 29	11374	0	-605	187	1294	3231	7054	16797	37363	62846	100864	509072	6826791

Selected Financial Ratios (Times to 1)

Current Ratio 30	1.8	•	1.9	1.4	2.4	1.9	2.0	2.2	2.1	2.1	1.6	2.3	1.5
Quick Ratio 31	1.1	•	1.0	0.8	1.6	1.0	1.2	1.3	1.2	1.2	0.9	1.3	1.0
Net Sales to Working Capital 32	4.7	•	19.5	10.5	5.1	5.7	4.6	4.2	3.7	4.1	5.7	3.8	5.2
Coverage Ratio 33	2.3	3.1	•	5.1	6.1	6.4	9.1	•	3.7	2.8	1.3	2.2	2.1
Total Asset Turnover 34	0.7	•	7.3	2.6	2.0	1.8	1.7	1.4	1.1	1.0	0.9	0.6	0.3
Inventory Turnover 35	5.5	•	14.3	4.1	6.4	4.3	4.9	4.5	4.1	4.4	6.1	5.1	7.5
Receivables Turnover 36	4.4	•	17.3	7.4	9.9	8.9	6.5	6.1	5.5	5.2	6.3	7.0	2.4
Total Liabilities to Net Worth 37	1.1	•	•	2.5	0.9	1.1	1.2	1.0	0.9	1.5	2.5	1.2	0.9
Current Assets to Working Capital 38	2.2	•	2.2	3.4	1.7	2.1	2.0	1.9	1.9	2.0	2.6	1.8	3.0
Current Liabilities to Working Capital 39	1.2	•	1.2	2.4	0.7	1.1	1.0	0.9	0.9	1.0	1.6	0.8	2.0
Working Capital to Net Sales 40	0.2	•	0.1	0.1	0.2	0.2	0.2	0.2	0.3	0.2	0.2	0.3	0.2
Inventory to Working Capital 41	0.6	•	0.7	1.4	0.5	0.9	0.7	0.7	0.6	0.7	0.7	0.6	0.6
Total Receipts to Cash Flow 42	8.9	13.1	9.9	6.3	6.0	8.8	9.3	6.8	10.5	11.4	8.7	10.6	8.5
Cost of Goods to Cash Flow 43	6.0	9.7	5.7	3.6	3.4	6.0	6.6	4.5	7.4	7.8	5.8	7.1	6.0
Cash Flow to Total Debt 44	0.1	•	0.1	0.6	0.7	0.4	0.3	0.4	0.2	0.2	0.2	0.1	0.1

Selected Financial Factors (in Percentages)

Debt Ratio 45	52.0	•	674.9	71.3	47.3	52.4	53.5	50.3	47.6	59.9	71.0	54.5	46.9
Return on Total Assets 46	4.3	•	•	13.1	7.3	9.9	10.4	•	5.5	6.2	4.3	3.8	3.5
Return on Equity Before Income Taxes 47	5.1	•	7.1	36.8	11.6	17.6	19.8	•	7.7	9.9	3.6	4.5	3.4
Return on Equity After Income Taxes 48	3.3	•	8.7	34.9	9.5	15.7	18.2	•	5.8	6.5	•	3.1	2.0
Profit Margin (Before Income Tax) 49	3.7	4.7	•	4.1	3.0	4.7	5.4	•	3.8	3.8	1.1	3.7	5.3
Profit Margin (After Income Tax) 50	2.4	4.6	•	3.9	2.5	4.2	5.0	•	2.9	2.5	•	2.6	3.2

Table II

Corporations with Net Income

OTHER ELECTRICAL EQUIPMENT AND COMPONENT

MONEY AMOUNTS AND SIZE OF ASSETS IN THOUSANDS OF DOLLARS

Item Description for Accounting Period 7/10 Through 6/11	Total	Zero Assets	Under 500	500 to 1000	1,000 to 5,000	5,000 to 10,000	10,000 to 25,000	25,000 to 50,000	50,000 to 100,000	100,000 to 250,000	250,000 to 500,000	500,000 to 2,500,000	2,500,000 and over
Number of Enterprises **1**	2656	359	•	529	519	217	177	72	•	•	8	12	•
Revenues ($ in Thousands)													
Net Sales **2**	52247940	323863	•	934022	2998228	3046566	5071121	3702503	•	•	2540952	8069996	•
Interest **3**	239286	3	•	0	591	592	1396	1863	•	•	8902	62360	•
Rents **4**	14940	0	•	162	211	103	971	203	•	•	889	1346	•
Royalties **5**	165037	0	•	0	0	0	1082	1869	•	•	7228	47087	•
Other Portfolio Income **6**	917390	50598	•	0	892	1507	1970	6246	•	•	38206	274990	•
Other Receipts **7**	298960	13793	•	0	8066	6517	12765	58632	•	•	11656	22518	•
Total Receipts **8**	53883553	388257	•	934184	2998988	3055285	5089305	3771316	•	•	2607833	8478297	•
Average Total Receipts **9**	20287	1081	•	1766	5778	14080	28753	52379	•	•	325979	706525	•
Operating Costs/Operating Income (%)													
Cost of Operations **10**	68.0	65.9	•	57.2	58.2	70.5	71.7	65.8	•	•	62.9	67.2	•
Salaries and Wages **11**	8.1	11.5	•	6.7	10.0	6.7	6.6	8.9	•	•	7.0	8.1	•
Taxes Paid **12**	1.6	2.8	•	3.0	1.8	1.9	1.8	1.7	•	•	1.4	1.2	•
Interest Paid **13**	2.3	2.6	•	0.1	0.5	0.9	0.5	0.9	•	•	2.2	3.4	•
Depreciation **14**	1.8	1.0	•	0.3	1.4	1.2	1.1	1.8	•	•	2.8	3.2	•
Amortization and Depletion **15**	1.0	0.9	•	•	0.4	0.1	0.1	0.2	•	•	1.0	1.5	•
Pensions and Other Deferred Comp. **16**	0.5	0.6	•	•	0.2	0.2	0.4	0.3	•	•	0.6	0.7	•
Employee Benefits **17**	1.6	0.5	•	0.8	1.9	1.7	1.1	1.3	•	•	1.7	2.3	•
Advertising **18**	1.2	0.1	•	0.2	0.6	0.3	0.2	0.9	•	•	1.2	0.8	•
Other Expenses **19**	8.5	7.6	•	15.4	9.1	7.2	6.2	9.3	•	•	11.6	9.6	•
Officers' Compensation **20**	1.4	2.8	•	4.7	5.3	2.7	2.2	2.2	•	•	0.6	1.0	•
Operating Margin **21**	4.2	3.7	•	11.6	10.7	6.6	7.9	6.7	•	•	7.2	1.0	•
Operating Margin Before Officers' Comp. **22**	5.6	6.6	•	16.3	16.0	9.3	10.1	8.9	•	•	7.8	2.1	•

Selected Average Balance Sheet ($ in Thousands)

Net Receivables 23	4304	0	•	198	740	1912	4741	7956	•	73997	99101
Inventories 24	2100	0	•	225	457	2133	4011	6534	•	34479	69014
Net Property, Plant and Equipment 25	2214	0	•	7	451	1172	2247	4947	•	47076	162162
Total Assets 26	30337	0	•	642	2438	6532	15262	33053	•	339555	1246297
Notes and Loans Payable 27	5336	0	•	100	422	2313	3729	6996	•	114230	336101
All Other Liabilities 28	9470	0	•	185	672	1586	4458	9316	•	91636	352399
Net Worth 29	15532	0	•	358	1344	2633	7075	16740	•	133689	557797

Selected Financial Ratios (Times to 1)

Current Ratio 30	1.8	•	•	2.0	2.3	1.8	2.1	2.2	•	1.5	2.3
Quick Ratio 31	1.1	•	•	1.2	1.4	0.9	1.3	1.3	•	0.9	1.2
Net Sales to Working Capital 32	4.9	•	•	6.7	5.9	6.5	4.6	4.4	•	5.8	4.1
Coverage Ratio 33	4.6	10.2	•	131.0	22.4	8.6	16.5	11.2	•	5.8	3.0
Total Asset Turnover 34	0.6	•	•	2.7	2.4	2.1	1.9	1.6	•	0.9	0.5
Inventory Turnover 35	6.4	•	•	4.5	7.3	4.6	5.1	5.2	•	5.8	6.5
Receivables Turnover 36	4.4	•	•	7.0	10.5	9.3	6.7	7.2	•	5.3	9.1
Total Liabilities to Net Worth 37	1.0	•	•	0.8	0.8	1.5	1.2	1.0	•	1.5	1.2
Current Assets to Working Capital 38	2.3	•	•	2.0	1.8	2.3	1.9	1.8	•	3.0	1.8
Current Liabilities to Working Capital 39	1.3	•	•	1.0	0.8	1.3	0.9	0.8	•	2.0	0.8
Working Capital to Net Sales 40	0.2	•	•	0.2	0.2	0.2	0.2	0.2	•	0.2	0.2
Inventory to Working Capital 41	0.6	•	•	0.7	0.6	1.0	0.6	0.7	•	0.8	0.6
Total Receipts to Cash Flow 42	7.4	5.6	•	4.8	5.6	8.1	7.6	6.1	•	5.0	8.9
Cost of Goods to Cash Flow 43	5.0	3.7	•	2.7	3.3	5.7	5.5	4.0	•	3.2	6.0
Cash Flow to Total Debt 44	0.2	•	•	1.3	0.9	0.4	0.5	0.5	•	0.3	0.1

Selected Financial Factors (in Percentages)

Debt Ratio 45	48.8	•	•	44.3	44.9	59.7	53.6	49.4	•	60.6	55.2
Return on Total Assets 46	6.7	•	•	32.2	27.4	16.7	16.5	14.9	•	11.6	5.5
Return on Equity Before Income Taxes 47	10.1	•	•	57.5	47.4	36.5	33.5	26.7	•	24.4	8.3
Return on Equity After Income Taxes 48	8.1	•	•	56.1	44.5	33.6	31.4	22.1	•	16.3	6.7
Profit Margin (Before Income Tax) 49	8.0	23.6	•	11.6	11.1	6.9	8.3	8.7	•	10.3	6.9
Profit Margin (After Income Tax) 50	6.4	23.3	•	11.4	10.4	6.3	7.8	7.2	•	6.8	5.6

Table I

Corporations with and without Net Income

MOTOR VEHICLES AND PARTS

MONEY AMOUNTS AND SIZE OF ASSETS IN THOUSANDS OF DOLLARS

Item Description for Accounting Period 7/10 Through 6/11		Total	Zero Assets	Under 500	500 to 1,000	1,000 to 5,000	5,000 to 10,000	10,000 to 25,000	25,000 to 50,000	50,000 to 100,000	100,000 to 250,000	250,000 to 500,000	500,000 to 2,500,000	2,500,000 and over
Number of Enterprises	1	5585	499	2934	402	694	351	218	157	102	104	52	45	26
Revenues ($ in Thousands)														
Net Sales	2	539648988	2196661	1099474	913992	3411607	3522211	5938033	9182930	12067229	27098630	25233252	52642736	396342235
Interest	3	9340119	506	81	12	803	733	5911	2000	6542	22154	70020	405333	8826023
Rents	4	6194433	366	0	0	318	391	119	4214	3087	5048	11276	98287	6071327
Royalties	5	7185301	0	0	0	0	0	642	3261	5181	5036	36232	314918	6820031
Other Portfolio Income	6	10688893	23380	1297	0	5087	3439	5053	63037	9208	24844	34162	927918	9591469
Other Receipts	7	11249022	33886	22768	10950	44885	22355	66730	98941	89240	234241	368831	635265	9620927
Total Receipts	8	584306756	2254799	1123620	924954	3462700	3549129	6016488	9354383	12180487	27389953	25753773	55024457	437272012
Average Total Receipts	9	104621	4519	383	2301	4989	10111	27599	59582	119417	263365	495265	1222766	16818154
Operating Costs/Operating Income (%)														
Cost of Operations	10	81.1	86.7	62.3	62.1	71.7	77.5	75.3	78.1	81.9	83.9	81.9	81.9	81.1
Salaries and Wages	11	3.3	3.6	7.0	11.6	8.1	5.3	5.7	5.4	3.8	3.2	4.6	3.8	2.9
Taxes Paid	12	0.7	1.4	2.0	2.6	2.8	2.0	1.7	1.6	1.2	1.0	1.3	1.1	0.5
Interest Paid	13	2.7	1.0	0.6	1.2	1.6	1.8	1.2	0.9	1.0	0.9	1.5	2.6	3.0
Depreciation	14	5.6	2.0	1.4	1.2	1.8	2.0	3.2	3.3	3.5	3.4	3.2	3.6	6.4
Amortization and Depletion	15	0.9	0.5	0.3	0.2	0.1	0.2	0.3	0.1	0.4	0.3	0.4	0.7	1.1
Pensions and Other Deferred Comp.	16	1.1	0.1	0.2	0.1	0.2	0.2	0.3	0.3	0.3	0.3	0.5	1.1	1.2
Employee Benefits	17	1.5	0.8	1.0	1.0	0.7	1.2	1.4	1.6	1.6	1.3	1.6	1.7	1.5
Advertising	18	2.1	0.5	2.0	0.1	1.3	0.3	0.6	0.3	0.3	0.2	0.1	0.5	2.7
Other Expenses	19	9.5	9.1	20.9	17.1	11.1	8.4	9.0	7.0	5.3	4.4	7.1	6.9	10.5
Officers' Compensation	20	0.2	0.8	0.8	2.3	6.0	1.8	1.7	1.0	0.4	0.4	0.5	0.3	0.1
Operating Margin	21	•	•	1.5	0.6	•	•	•	0.3	0.3	0.6	•	•	•
Operating Margin Before Officers' Comp.	22	•	•	2.3	2.9	0.7	1.3	1.3	1.4	0.7	1.0	•	•	•

Selected Average Balance Sheet ($ in Thousands)

Net Receivables 23	39702	0	15	149	582	902	3158	8695	14347	32059	66874	224960	7709984
Inventories 24	6474	0	54	245	1055	2681	4465	8034	12304	24035	48452	111164	796845
Net Property, Plant and Equipment 25	20786	0	12	189	470	1540	4637	9312	23092	47557	87617	220832	3493931
Total Assets 26	146846	0	131	814	2726	6779	15946	35247	70664	154843	354419	1033381	27611995
Notes and Loans Payable 27	42925	0	67	253	1413	4361	6513	10544	23002	41495	107638	308198	7989249
All Other Liabilities 28	68902	0	79	510	1331	1979	4158	13536	25603	54639	128846	1245599	11872485
Net Worth 29	35019	0	-15	52	-19	438	5276	11168	22059	58709	117635	-520416	7750261

Selected Financial Ratios (Times to 1)

Current Ratio 30	1.4	•	1.4	1.0	1.8	2.3	1.7	1.3	1.2	1.3	1.4	1.3	1.4
Quick Ratio 31	1.0	•	0.6	0.4	0.7	1.0	0.8	0.8	0.7	0.7	0.8	0.9	1.0
Net Sales to Working Capital 32	4.6	•	12.1	233.3	5.7	3.5	6.6	10.4	17.9	13.6	10.0	11.6	3.8
Coverage Ratio 33	1.1	•	7.5	2.5	•	1.1	1.7	3.5	2.4	3.0	0.7	1.5	1.0
Total Asset Turnover 34	0.7	•	2.9	2.8	1.8	1.5	1.7	1.7	1.7	1.7	1.4	1.1	0.6
Inventory Turnover 35	12.1	•	4.3	5.8	3.3	2.9	4.6	5.7	7.9	9.1	8.2	8.6	15.5
Receivables Turnover 36	2.4	•	13.3	16.8	10.4	10.2	8.5	7.4	7.5	9.3	7.9	5.8	1.9
Total Liabilities to Net Worth 37	3.2	•	14.7	•	14.5	2.0	2.2	2.2	1.6	2.0	•	•	2.6
Current Assets to Working Capital 38	3.3	•	3.4	57.5	2.3	1.8	2.4	3.9	5.5	4.2	3.6	4.8	3.3
Current Liabilities to Working Capital 39	2.3	•	2.4	56.5	1.3	0.8	1.4	2.9	4.5	3.2	2.6	3.8	2.3
Working Capital to Net Sales 40	0.2	•	0.1	0.0	0.2	0.3	0.2	0.1	0.1	0.1	0.1	0.1	0.3
Inventory to Working Capital 41	0.3	•	1.9	30.8	1.3	1.0	1.1	1.5	1.8	1.4	1.1	1.2	0.2
Total Receipts to Cash Flow 42	12.4	38.3	5.0	7.7	29.1	17.7	13.1	15.1	18.4	19.5	21.4	19.9	11.1
Cost of Goods to Cash Flow 43	10.1	33.3	3.1	4.8	20.8	13.7	9.8	11.8	15.0	16.4	17.5	16.3	9.0
Cash Flow to Total Debt 44	0.1	•	0.5	0.4	0.1	0.1	0.2	0.2	0.1	0.1	0.1	0.0	0.1

Selected Financial Factors (in Percentages)

Debt Ratio 45	76.2	•	111.3	93.6	100.7	93.5	66.9	68.3	68.8	62.1	66.8	150.4	71.9
Return on Total Assets 46	1.9	•	12.3	8.3	•	3.0	3.6	5.2	4.2	4.4	1.4	4.5	1.6
Return on Equity Before Income Taxes 47	0.4	•	•	79.0	1002.8	6.0	4.4	11.8	7.9	7.7	•	•	•
Return on Equity After Income Taxes 48	•	•	•	49.6	1035.3	0.6	2.4	8.6	4.7	5.1	•	•	•
Profit Margin (Before Income Tax) 49	0.2	•	3.7	1.8	•	0.3	0.9	2.3	1.5	1.7	1.2	1.3	•
Profit Margin (After Income Tax) 50	•	•	3.7	1.1	•	0.0	0.5	1.7	0.9	1.2	•	0.3	•

Table II
Corporations with Net Income

MOTOR VEHICLES AND PARTS

MONEY AMOUNTS AND SIZE OF ASSETS IN THOUSANDS OF DOLLARS

Item Description for Accounting Period 7/10 Through 6/11	Total	Zero Assets	Under 500	500 to 1,000	1,000 to 5,000	5,000 to 10,000	10,000 to 25,000	25,000 to 50,000	50,000 to 100,000	100,000 to 250,000	250,000 to 500,000	500,000 to 2,500,000	2,500,000 and over
Number of Enterprises **1**	4431	399	•	•	406	171	152	102	68	79	28	27	16
Revenues ($ in Thousands)													
Net Sales **2**	286927928	1673238	•	•	2036380	2685976	4462668	6277860	9575000	21028812	16162511	36678849	184404588
Interest **3**	3095659	162	•	•	704	472	4969	1493	3015	18046	13326	281962	2771498
Rents **4**	2972367	362	•	•	91	90	0	2680	565	3745	1786	7404	2955644
Royalties **5**	1360072	0	•	•	0	0	100	243	4492	5036	810	266843	1082547
Other Portfolio Income **6**	6151775	2585	•	•	1305	2960	1624	55931	7739	22318	4975	848969	5203024
Other Receipts **7**	4199029	22540	•	•	29362	37570	30227	62585	50061	196067	248441	207938	3288781
Total Receipts **8**	304706830	1698887	•	•	2067842	2727068	4499588	6400792	9640872	21274024	16431849	38291965	199706082
Average Total Receipts **9**	68767	4258	•	•	5093	15948	29603	62753	141778	269291	586852	1418221	12481630
Operating Costs/Operating Income (%)													
Cost of Operations **10**	82.1	80.9	•	•	66.1	74.1	71.9	75.0	81.3	83.4	81.5	80.9	83.3
Salaries and Wages **11**	2.9	3.3	•	•	7.2	4.7	5.6	5.5	3.5	3.1	3.2	3.6	2.5
Taxes Paid **12**	0.8	1.2	•	•	2.4	1.9	1.8	1.7	1.2	1.1	1.3	1.1	0.6
Interest Paid **13**	1.8	1.0	•	•	1.1	0.7	1.0	0.8	0.8	0.6	0.8	2.2	2.1
Depreciation **14**	4.7	2.1	•	•	1.9	1.8	2.7	3.3	3.0	3.2	2.9	3.0	5.7
Amortization and Depletion **15**	0.2	0.5	•	•	0.0	0.2	0.2	0.0	0.2	0.2	0.2	0.3	0.2
Pensions and Other Deferred Comp. **16**	0.7	0.1	•	•	0.3	0.1	0.3	0.2	0.3	0.3	0.4	1.0	0.8
Employee Benefits **17**	1.2	1.0	•	•	0.7	1.1	1.6	1.5	1.6	1.2	1.7	1.6	1.0
Advertising **18**	2.1	0.5	•	•	1.3	0.2	0.6	0.4	0.3	0.3	0.1	0.2	3.1
Other Expenses **19**	5.0	6.0	•	•	8.5	8.6	7.5	6.4	4.0	3.9	6.0	4.8	4.8
Officers' Compensation **20**	0.3	0.9	•	•	7.0	1.8	1.7	1.2	0.4	0.3	0.5	0.3	0.1
Operating Margin **21**	•	2.8	•	•	3.4	4.8	5.2	4.0	3.3	2.4	1.5	1.0	•
Operating Margin Before Officers' Comp. **22**	•	3.7	•	•	10.3	6.6	6.9	5.2	3.7	2.7	2.0	1.3	•

Selected Average Balance Sheet ($ in Thousands)

Net Receivables 23	15162	0	822	1266	3349	9351	15932	32400	70312	232058	3324375
Inventories 24	3780	0	855	1397	3756	6750	10673	20587	49982	89628	533394
Net Property, Plant and Equipment 25	12932	0	640	1795	4519	9636	22593	44912	91320	216554	2591713
Total Assets 26	89196	0	2904	6827	16238	35532	71598	148852	347436	1043287	20724710
Notes and Loans Payable 27	17191	0	652	1334	5743	9110	21258	31598	77246	264502	3771204
All Other Liabilities 28	40062	0	899	1968	3758	10722	25108	50667	126203	436948	9615329
Net Worth 29	31942	0	1353	3525	6737	15700	25232	66587	143987	341836	7338177

Selected Financial Ratios (Times to 1)

Current Ratio 30	1.3		3.0	2.1	1.9	1.6	1.3	1.4	1.4	1.4	1.3
Quick Ratio 31	0.7		1.6	1.2	1.0	0.9	0.8	0.8	0.7	0.9	0.6
Net Sales to Working Capital 32	7.7		4.1	6.1	5.8	7.2	14.7	11.5	10.8	9.2	6.9
Coverage Ratio 33	3.7	5.5	5.4	9.9	6.9	8.7	6.2	6.8	5.1	4.1	3.3
Total Asset Turnover 34	0.7		1.7	2.3	1.8	1.7	2.0	1.8	1.7	1.3	0.6
Inventory Turnover 35	14.1		3.9	8.3	5.6	6.8	10.7	10.8	9.4	12.3	18.0
Receivables Turnover 36	4.7		8.3	11.1	10.5	8.8	10.3	10.7	10.6	8.5	3.6
Total Liabilities to Net Worth 37	1.8		1.1	0.9	1.4	1.3	1.8	1.2	1.4	2.1	1.8
Current Assets to Working Capital 38	4.4		1.5	1.9	2.1	2.7	4.0	3.5	3.6	3.4	4.9
Current Liabilities to Working Capital 39	3.4		0.5	0.9	1.1	1.7	3.0	2.5	2.6	2.4	3.9
Working Capital to Net Sales 40	0.1		0.2	0.2	0.2	0.1	0.1	0.1	0.1	0.1	0.1
Inventory to Working Capital 41	0.6		0.6	0.7	0.9	1.0	1.3	1.2	1.3	0.8	0.4
Total Receipts to Cash Flow 42	12.3	11.4	9.1	8.6	8.3	9.9	14.4	15.5	13.0	11.1	12.6
Cost of Goods to Cash Flow 43	10.1	9.3	6.0	6.4	6.0	7.4	11.7	13.0	10.6	9.0	10.5
Cash Flow to Total Debt 44	0.1		0.4	0.6	0.4	0.3	0.2	0.2	0.1	0.2	0.1

Selected Financial Factors (in Percentages)

Debt Ratio 45	64.2		53.4	48.4	58.5	55.8	64.8	55.3	58.6	67.2	64.6
Return on Total Assets 46	4.8		10.4	16.3	12.7	11.9	10.1	7.4	6.8	11.7	3.7
Return on Equity Before Income Taxes 47	9.8		18.2	28.4	26.3	23.8	24.1	14.2	13.1	27.0	7.3
Return on Equity After Income Taxes 48	8.6		17.5	27.1	24.0	20.2	19.9	11.2	10.8	21.2	6.7
Profit Margin (Before Income Tax) 49	4.8	4.3	4.9	6.4	6.0	6.1	4.3	3.6	3.3	6.8	4.7
Profit Margin (After Income Tax) 50	4.2	3.5	4.7	6.1	5.5	5.2	3.6	2.8	2.7	5.3	4.3

Table I

Corporations with and without Net Income

AEROSPACE PRODUCT AND PARTS

MONEY AMOUNTS AND SIZE OF ASSETS IN THOUSANDS OF DOLLARS

Item Description for Accounting Period 7/10 Through 6/11	Total	Zero Assets	Under 500	500 to 1,000	1,000 to 5,000	5,000 to 10,000	10,000 to 25,000	25,000 to 50,000	50,000 to 100,000	100,000 to 250,000	250,000 to 500,000	500,000 to 2,500,000	2,500,000 and over
Number of Enterprises **1**	1445	18	707	101	311	99	95	34	23	17	9	11	19
Revenues ($ in Thousands)													
Net Sales **2**	294788140	338974	235284	133079	1441482	1153814	2171918	1456312	1514022	2366843	2245325	15406189	266324898
Interest **3**	840734	67	14	0	969	492	1417	965	1854	1543	4287	50179	778948
Rents **4**	825344	0	0	0	0	0	326	361	786	0	389	9814	813669
Royalties **5**	1521098	0	0	0	0	0	0	0	0	2648	2859	3217	1512375
Other Portfolio Income **6**	2869787	4373	1	0	56	0	6392	543	10493	4365	172246	28867	2642451
Other Receipts **7**	3942087	9558	123	4	950	1834	9526	8584	5460	21923	6580	145379	3732163
Total Receipts **8**	304787190	352972	235422	133083	1443457	1156140	2189579	1466765	1532615	2397322	2431686	15643645	275804504
Average Total Receipts **9**	210925	19610	333	1318	4641	11678	23048	43140	66635	141019	270187	1422150	14516027
Operating Costs/Operating Income (%)													
Cost of Operations **10**	71.9	46.6	49.5	79.0	59.3	66.2	67.4	69.0	63.9	67.4	66.7	72.3	72.2
Salaries and Wages **11**	4.6	13.4	1.4	2.1	12.7	9.3	7.3	6.2	11.1	7.9	6.7	6.7	4.2
Taxes Paid **12**	1.5	1.3	1.7	2.9	2.8	2.8	2.5	2.1	2.5	1.6	2.0	1.6	1.4
Interest Paid **13**	1.6	9.1	1.0	0.6	0.8	0.9	1.8	1.3	2.0	3.7	4.4	1.2	1.6
Depreciation **14**	2.6	1.7	1.0	2.1	1.7	1.1	3.1	5.0	3.0	3.6	3.8	3.9	2.5
Amortization and Depletion **15**	0.7	3.3	•	•	0.2	0.0	0.3	0.4	0.5	1.4	1.8	0.7	0.7
Pensions and Other Deferred Comp. **16**	3.1	1.6	•	2.0	0.5	0.3	0.4	0.5	0.8	0.5	0.2	1.2	3.4
Employee Benefits **17**	2.6	1.3	0.7	1.0	1.4	2.3	2.7	2.6	2.0	2.3	2.1	3.5	2.6
Advertising **18**	0.3	0.0	0.4	•	0.2	0.1	0.3	0.2	0.5	0.1	0.2	0.1	0.3
Other Expenses **19**	10.5	19.3	13.6	23.4	8.3	10.4	10.1	7.8	13.3	7.9	12.5	5.6	10.7
Officers' Compensation **20**	0.3	0.9	10.8	9.6	4.4	2.0	2.9	1.8	2.1	0.8	1.5	0.5	0.2
Operating Margin **21**	0.5	1.4	19.9	•	7.7	4.7	1.0	3.1	•	2.7	•	2.7	0.3
Operating Margin Before Officers' Comp. **22**	0.8	2.3	30.7	•	12.1	6.6	4.0	4.9	•	3.5	•	3.2	0.5

Selected Average Balance Sheet ($ in Thousands)

Net Receivables **23**	26157	0	0	72	532	1028	3731	6912	10334	22567	36219	289539	1726355
Inventories **24**	35976	0	0	208	556	3365	5404	8522	15346	38138	64646	322160	2653601
Net Property, Plant and Equipment **25**	29163	0	6	23	415	664	3157	7239	13729	31714	54351	273743	1949343
Total Assets **26**	254527	0	92	699	2381	7211	17454	34462	67417	148059	325905	1403396	17943870
Notes and Loans Payable **27**	54393	0	60	525	561	2872	6532	10108	16599	53932	125736	320106	3743609
All Other Liabilities **28**	125397	0	1	87	525	3567	5428	7287	26505	64415	66322	538939	9035778
Net Worth **29**	74737	0	31	87	1295	773	5494	17067	24314	29712	133848	544351	5164482

Selected Financial Ratios (Times to 1)

Current Ratio **30**	1.3	•	31.4	3.6	2.9	2.8	2.1	2.3	1.6	1.4	2.6	1.6	1.3
Quick Ratio **31**	0.6	•	29.2	0.6	1.9	0.9	0.9	1.1	0.7	0.7	1.0	1.0	0.6
Net Sales to Working Capital **32**	10.0	•	11.9	4.0	3.9	3.4	3.9	3.4	4.7	6.2	2.6	5.4	11.4
Coverage Ratio **33**	4.0	1.6	22.0	•	10.7	6.6	2.0	3.9	0.8	2.1	2.5	4.4	4.1
Total Asset Turnover **34**	0.8	•	3.6	1.9	1.9	1.6	1.3	1.2	1.0	0.9	0.8	1.0	0.8
Inventory Turnover **35**	4.1	•	•	5.0	4.9	2.3	2.9	3.5	2.7	2.5	2.6	3.1	3.8
Receivables Turnover **36**	7.7	•	•	17.9	8.8	10.9	6.9	7.6	6.4	5.7	8.5	5.0	•
Total Liabilities to Net Worth **37**	2.4	•	2.0	7.0	0.8	8.3	2.2	1.0	1.8	4.0	1.4	1.6	2.5
Current Assets to Working Capital **38**	4.3	•	1.0	1.4	1.5	1.6	1.9	1.7	2.8	3.4	1.6	2.6	4.9
Current Liabilities to Working Capital **39**	3.3	•	0.0	0.4	0.5	0.6	0.9	0.7	1.8	2.4	0.6	1.6	3.9
Working Capital to Net Sales **40**	0.1	•	0.1	0.3	0.3	0.3	0.3	0.3	0.2	0.2	0.4	0.2	0.1
Inventory to Working Capital **41**	1.9	•	•	0.9	0.5	1.0	0.9	0.7	1.0	1.5	0.8	0.8	2.2
Total Receipts to Cash Flow **42**	8.3	5.2	3.7	•	7.9	8.3	10.9	10.6	9.6	10.5	10.7	12.2	8.0
Cost of Goods to Cash Flow **43**	5.9	2.4	1.8	•	4.7	5.5	7.3	7.3	6.2	7.1	7.2	8.9	5.8
Cash Flow to Total Debt **44**	0.1	•	1.5	•	0.5	0.2	0.2	0.7	0.2	0.2	0.1	0.1	0.1

Selected Financial Factors (in Percentages)

Debt Ratio **45**	70.6	•	66.1	87.6	45.6	89.3	68.5	50.5	63.9	79.9	58.9	61.2	71.2
Return on Total Assets **46**	5.1	•	75.5	•	16.8	9.3	4.7	6.4	1.6	7.2	8.3	5.5	5.0
Return on Equity Before Income Taxes **47**	13.1	•	212.7	•	28.1	73.4	7.6	9.5	•	18.7	12.1	10.9	13.2
Return on Equity After Income Taxes **48**	8.4	•	212.7	•	25.8	65.1	5.4	7.7	•	15.9	10.4	8.1	8.3
Profit Margin (Before Income Tax) **49**	4.8	5.5	20.0	•	7.8	4.9	1.8	3.8	•	4.0	6.5	4.2	4.9
Profit Margin (After Income Tax) **50**	3.1	3.4	20.0	•	7.2	4.3	1.3	3.1	•	3.4	5.6	3.2	3.0

Table II
Corporations with Net Income

AEROSPACE PRODUCT AND PARTS

Money Amounts and Size of Assets in Thousands of Dollars

Item Description for Accounting Period 7/10 Through 6/11	Total	Zero Assets	Under 500	500 to 1,000	1,000 to 5,000	5,000 to 10,000	10,000 to 25,000	25,000 to 50,000	50,000 to 100,000	100,000 to 250,000	250,000 to 500,000	500,000 to 2,500,000	2,500,000 and over
Number of Enterprises **1**	1009	10	456	•	311	70	64	22	10	10	4	•	•
Revenues ($ in Thousands)													
Net Sales **2**	250439245	256455	235284	•	1441482	1033684	1666630	1060460	677828	1448254	1184289	•	•
Interest **3**	366077	37	0	•	969	216	617	915	517	912	3111	•	•
Rents **4**	605361	0	0	•	0	0	290	229	263	0	60	•	•
Royalties **5**	780011	0	0		0	0	0	0	0	1059	18		
Other Portfolio Income **6**	2622436	4373	1	•	56	0	6355	67	9860	1283	168175	•	•
Other Receipts **7**	3423139	9544	123	•	950	1589	3099	7624	3440	16125	937	•	•
Total Receipts **8**	258236269	270409	235408	•	1443457	1035489	1676991	1069295	691908	1467633	1356590	•	•
Average Total Receipts **9**	255933	27041	516	•	4641	14793	26203	48604	69191	146763	339148	•	•
Operating Costs/Operating Income (%)													
Cost of Operations **10**	70.7	35.8	49.5	•	59.3	66.1	66.8	67.5	62.4	64.1	65.9	•	•
Salaries and Wages **11**	4.2	14.7	1.4	•	12.7	8.2	5.0	6.9	5.5	7.0	6.4	•	•
Taxes Paid **12**	1.5	1.2	1.6	•	2.8	2.8	2.6	2.3	1.9	1.2	1.8	•	•
Interest Paid **13**	1.4	11.9	1.0	•	0.8	0.9	1.2	1.3	1.2	3.2	3.5	•	•
Depreciation **14**	2.4	2.0	1.0	•	1.7	0.6	3.0	3.1	2.6	3.3	2.4	•	•
Amortization and Depletion **15**	0.7	4.4	•	•	0.2	0.0	0.3	0.4	0.2	0.7	1.1	•	•
Pensions and Other Deferred Comp. **16**	3.3	2.1	•	•	0.5	0.2	0.5	0.3	0.3	0.6	0.0	•	•
Employee Benefits **17**	2.6	1.2	0.7	•	1.4	2.3	2.9	1.8	1.8	1.9	2.5	•	•
Advertising **18**	0.3	0.0	0.4	•	0.2	0.0	0.1	0.3	0.3	0.1	0.2	•	•
Other Expenses **19**	10.5	23.0	13.4	•	8.3	9.8	7.7	7.3	12.8	7.5	14.9	•	•
Officers' Compensation **20**	0.3	1.1	10.8	•	4.4	1.2	3.3	2.0	2.7	1.0	1.5	•	•
Operating Margin **21**	2.2	2.6	20.2	•	7.7	7.7	6.5	7.1	8.1	9.4	•	•	•
Operating Margin Before Officers' Comp. **22**	2.5	3.7	31.0	•	12.1	8.9	9.9	9.1	10.8	10.4	1.3	•	•

Selected Average Balance Sheet ($ in Thousands)

Line Item									
Net Receivables 23	27071	●	0	●	532	4117	7869	12363	21744	40474
Inventories 24	43927	●	0	●	497	5321	8176	17389	41743	67442
Net Property, Plant and Equipment 25	33678	●	0	9	415	3661	7804	8597	25067	35141
Total Assets 26	268448	●	0	129	2381	17851	38686	67120	143163	311654
Notes and Loans Payable 27	51015	●	0	93	561	5448	9658	12285	25788	107272
All Other Liabilities 28	151526	●	0	1	525	3727	8246	17502	81870	69012
Net Worth 29	65907	●	0	35	1295	-689	20781	37333	35505	135371

Selected Financial Ratios (Times to 1)

Line Item									
Current Ratio 30	1.3	●	23.7	●	2.9	2.7	2.2	3.2	2.7	2.7	1.2	2.7
Quick Ratio 31	0.6	●	21.3	●	1.9	1.0	1.0	1.7	1.1	1.0	0.6	1.1
Net Sales to Working Capital 32	11.5	●	17.6	●	3.9	4.6	4.1	3.0	2.2	13.7	2.7
Coverage Ratio 33	5.5	1.7	22.3	10.7	10.0	6.8	7.3	7.3	9.2	4.4	5.2
Total Asset Turnover 34	0.9	●	4.0	1.9	2.1	1.5	1.2	1.0	1.0	1.0
Inventory Turnover 35	4.0	●	5.5	4.4	3.3	4.0	2.4	2.2	2.9
Receivables Turnover 36	8.3	●	●	8.8	15.7	7.1	7.3	4.6	4.9	14.6
Total Liabilities to Net Worth 37	3.1	2.7	0.8	●	1.1	0.9	0.8	3.0	1.3
Current Assets to Working Capital 38	4.8	1.0	1.5	1.6	1.8	1.4	1.6	7.0	1.6
Current Liabilities to Working Capital 39	3.8	0.0	0.5	0.6	0.8	0.4	0.6	6.0	0.6
Working Capital to Net Sales 40	0.1	0.1	0.3	0.2	0.2	0.3	0.4	0.1	0.4
Inventory to Working Capital 41	2.1	●	0.5	1.0	0.9	0.5	0.6	2.8	0.6
Total Receipts to Cash Flow 42	7.4	4.1	3.7	7.9	6.9	7.6	7.5	5.0	6.1	7.6
Cost of Goods to Cash Flow 43	5.2	1.5	1.8	4.7	4.5	5.1	5.1	3.1	3.9	5.0
Cash Flow to Total Debt 44	0.2	●	1.5	0.5	0.3	0.4	0.4	0.5	0.2	0.2

Selected Financial Factors (in Percentages)

Line Item									
Debt Ratio 45	75.4	●	73.3	●	45.6	109.7	51.4	46.3	44.4	75.2	56.6
Return on Total Assets 46	6.9	●	84.8	●	16.8	18.3	12.3	11.5	11.6	14.1	16.9
Return on Equity Before Income Taxes 47	23.2	●	303.0	●	28.1	●	21.5	18.5	18.6	43.7	31.4
Return on Equity After Income Taxes 48	15.5	●	303.0	●	25.8	●	19.5	16.2	15.1	39.7	27.7
Profit Margin (Before Income Tax) 49	6.1	8.1	20.3	7.8	7.9	7.2	8.0	10.2	10.7	14.4
Profit Margin (After Income Tax) 50	4.1	5.3	20.3	7.2	7.3	6.5	7.0	8.3	9.7	12.7

Table I

Corporations with and without Net Income

SHIP AND BOAT BUILDING

MONEY AMOUNTS AND SIZE OF ASSETS IN THOUSANDS OF DOLLARS

Item Description for Accounting Period 7/10 Through 6/11		Total	Zero Assets	Under 500	500 to 1,000	1,000 to 5,000	5,000 to 10,000	10,000 to 25,000	25,000 to 50,000	50,000 to 100,000	100,000 to 250,000	250,000 to 500,000	500,000 to 2,500,000	2,500,000 and over
Number of Enterprises	1	919	10	521	0	188	95	50	25	15	9	•	•	•
Revenues ($ in Thousands)														
Net Sales	2	38362167	155509	314726	0	1005489	1307924	1126470	1138793	1252754	1273661	•	•	•
Interest	3	19319	5	27	0	646	197	557	772	552	982	•	•	•
Rents	4	30520	0	0	0	0	128	0	2078	483	532	•	•	•
Royalties	5	606	0	0	0	0	0	0	0	190	0			
Other Portfolio Income	6	211550	5756	712	0	1385	119	98	3668	11655	318	•	•	•
Other Receipts	7	123205	4199	338	0	24512	5557	9667	15575	9633	21459	•	•	•
Total Receipts	8	38747367	165469	315803	0	1032032	1313925	1136792	1160886	1275267	1296952	•	•	•
Average Total Receipts	9	42163	16547	606	•	5490	13831	22736	46435	85018	144106	•	•	•
Operating Costs/Operating Income (%)														
Cost of Operations	10	73.5	71.6	52.8	•	68.4	65.4	80.3	68.6	79.9	82.6	•	•	•
Salaries and Wages	11	4.8	1.4	19.6	•	5.2	7.7	2.8	5.6	3.8	3.7	•	•	•
Taxes Paid	12	1.3	1.0	5.0	•	2.0	2.5	0.8	2.3	1.5	2.7	•	•	•
Interest Paid	13	0.7	9.8	0.1	•	1.1	0.8	0.8	0.9	1.5	0.6	•	•	•
Depreciation	14	1.7	2.1	3.3	•	1.6	1.7	5.1	2.2	4.6	3.4	•	•	•
Amortization and Depletion	15	0.8	3.7	0.0	•	0.0	•	0.1	0.4	0.3	0.0	•	•	•
Pensions and Other Deferred Comp.	16	1.1	•	0.6	•	•	0.3	0.2	0.5	0.7	1.2	•	•	•
Employee Benefits	17	1.9	2.4	5.5	•	1.4	2.1	0.8	2.4	1.2	3.0	•	•	•
Advertising	18	0.6	0.2	0.4	•	0.5	0.4	0.7	0.3	0.7	0.4	•	•	•
Other Expenses	19	5.6	28.4	19.5	•	15.3	10.8	8.7	14.8	4.4	3.4	•	•	•
Officers' Compensation	20	0.9	•	12.5	•	1.4	2.7	2.1	1.6	1.7	0.9	•	•	•
Operating Margin	21	7.1	•	•	•	3.1	5.6	•	0.4	•	•	•	•	•
Operating Margin Before Officers' Comp.	22	7.9	•	•	•	4.5	8.4	•	2.0	1.3	•	•	•	•

Selected Average Balance Sheet ($ in Thousands)

Net Receivables 23	3379	0	110	118	1655	3189	5239	8955	14734
Inventories 24	4837	0	47	677	1859	2943	4641	8322	24040
Net Property, Plant and Equipment 25	5260	0	138	887	2050	6155	9752	24581	40648
Total Assets 26	39437	0	334	2565	7635	16644	35156	71569	131702
Notes and Loans Payable 27	6444	0	114	939	1884	7468	12141	22436	49225
All Other Liabilities 28	15708	0	103	932	3219	6256	10428	20528	27512
Net Worth 29	17286	0	117	695	2532	2920	12586	28605	54965

Selected Financial Ratios (Times to 1)

Current Ratio 30	1.3	•	1.6	2.5	1.8	0.9	1.5	1.3	1.8
Quick Ratio 31	0.6	•	1.1	0.9	0.9	0.4	0.8	0.6	0.8
Net Sales to Working Capital 32	11.5	•	9.1	5.7	5.9	•	7.9	12.7	4.3
Coverage Ratio 33	12.3	•	•	6.2	8.4	•	3.8	1.9	0.8
Total Asset Turnover 34	1.1	•	1.8	2.1	1.8	1.4	1.3	1.2	1.1
Inventory Turnover 35	6.3	•	6.8	5.4	4.8	6.1	6.7	8.0	4.9
Receivables Turnover 36	12.9	•	•	32.2	10.2	6.9	11.7	9.8	7.0
Total Liabilities to Net Worth 37	1.3	•	1.9	2.7	2.0	4.7	1.8	1.5	1.4
Current Assets to Working Capital 38	4.0	•	2.7	1.6	2.2	•	2.9	4.4	2.2
Current Liabilities to Working Capital 39	3.0	•	1.7	0.6	1.2	•	1.9	3.4	1.2
Working Capital to Net Sales 40	0.1	•	0.1	0.2	0.2	•	0.1	0.1	0.2
Inventory to Working Capital 41	1.3	•	0.7	0.6	1.0	•	0.6	1.3	0.7
Total Receipts to Cash Flow 42	8.5	17.5	•	5.4	7.3	35.4	7.5	21.8	62.3
Cost of Goods to Cash Flow 43	6.3	12.5	•	3.7	4.8	28.4	5.1	17.4	51.5
Cash Flow to Total Debt 44	0.2	•	•	0.5	0.4	0.0	0.3	0.1	0.0

Selected Financial Factors (in Percentages)

Debt Ratio 45	56.2	•	65.1	72.9	66.8	82.5	64.2	60.0	58.3
Return on Total Assets 46	9.7	•	•	14.4	12.5	•	4.2	3.4	0.5
Return on Equity Before Income Taxes 47	20.4	•	•	44.5	33.1	•	8.6	4.1	•
Return on Equity After Income Taxes 48	13.4	•	•	44.2	30.7	•	6.3	3.3	•
Profit Margin (Before Income Tax) 49	8.4	•	•	5.8	6.1	•	2.4	1.4	•
Profit Margin (After Income Tax) 50	5.5	•	•	5.7	5.7	•	1.7	1.1	•

Table II

Corporations with Net Income

SHIP AND BOAT BUILDING

MONEY AMOUNTS AND SIZE OF ASSETS IN THOUSANDS OF DOLLARS

Item Description for Accounting Period 7/10 Through 6/11	Total	Zero Assets	Under 500	500 to 1,000	1,000 to 5,000	5,000 to 10,000	10,000 to 25,000	25,000 to 50,000	50,000 to 100,000	100,000 to 250,000	250,000 to 500,000	500,000 to 2,500,000	2,500,000 and over
Number of Enterprises 1	344	•	98	0	108	80	20	16	•	•	•	•	•
Revenues ($ in Thousands)													
Net Sales 2	36002318	•	45749	0	701894	1138044	725888	868668	•	•	•	•	•
Interest 3	18369	•	27	0	202	197	538	462	•	•	•	•	•
Rents 4	29750	•	0	0	0	128	0	1905	•	•	•	•	•
Royalties 5	417	•	0	0	0	0	0	0	•	•	•	•	•
Other Portfolio Income 6	207242	•	0	0	89	39	92	1796	•	•	•	•	•
Other Receipts 7	81297	•	1	0	5710	4666	8516	4118	•	•	•	•	•
Total Receipts 8	36339393	•	45777	0	707895	1143074	735034	876949	•	•	•	•	•
Average Total Receipts 9	105638	•	467	•	6555	14288	36752	54809	•	•	•	•	•
Operating Costs/Operating Income (%)													
Cost of Operations 10	73.1	•	50.1	•	64.0	62.2	76.6	67.6	•	•	•	•	•
Salaries and Wages 11	4.7	•	•	•	6.5	8.5	3.4	5.2	•	•	•	•	•
Taxes Paid 12	1.2	•	2.5	•	2.4	2.3	0.8	2.1	•	•	•	•	•
Interest Paid 13	0.7	•	•	•	0.9	0.6	0.7	0.2	•	•	•	•	•
Depreciation 14	1.5	•	2.7	•	1.7	1.8	2.3	2.0	•	•	•	•	•
Amortization and Depletion 15	0.9	•	0.0	•	•	•	0.1	0.1	•	•	•	•	•
Pensions and Other Deferred Comp. 16	1.2	•	0.3	•	•	0.2	0.3	0.7	•	•	•	•	•
Employee Benefits 17	1.9	•	2.5	•	1.1	2.4	1.2	1.8	•	•	•	•	•
Advertising 18	0.6	•	1.4	•	0.1	0.4	0.7	0.1	•	•	•	•	•
Other Expenses 19	5.0	•	22.6	•	9.3	11.0	5.4	14.5	•	•	•	•	•
Officers' Compensation 20	0.7	•	8.7	•	1.6	2.6	1.8	1.4	•	•	•	•	•
Operating Margin 21	8.6	•	9.2	•	12.5	8.0	6.6	4.3	•	•	•	•	•
Operating Margin Before Officers' Comp. 22	9.2	•	17.9	•	14.1	10.6	8.5	5.7	•	•	•	•	•

Selected Average Balance Sheet ($ in Thousands)

Net Receivables 23	8216	12	139	1527	4786	7057
Inventories 24	11174	80	419	1544	1428	686
Net Property, Plant and Equipment 25	11830	23	1322	2267	4383	8432
Total Assets 26	99400	248	3202	7837	16445	36494
Notes and Loans Payable 27	13971	0	1317	1716	4490	6529
All Other Liabilities 28	39704	38	301	2918	6034	12392
Net Worth 29	45725	210	1584	3203	5921	17572

Selected Financial Ratios (Times to 1)

Current Ratio 30	1.4	4.0	5.9	2.1	1.8	1.8
Quick Ratio 31	0.6	1.9	2.7	1.0	1.1	1.0
Net Sales to Working Capital 32	10.6	4.1	4.2	5.3	7.0	6.6
Coverage Ratio 33	15.7	•	16.3	14.8	12.1	34.7
Total Asset Turnover 34	1.1	1.9	2.0	1.8	2.2	1.5
Inventory Turnover 35	6.8	2.9	9.9	5.7	19.5	53.5
Receivables Turnover 36	13.7	76.3	•	10.7	8.1	11.7
Total Liabilities to Net Worth 37	1.2	0.2	1.0	1.4	1.8	1.1
Current Assets to Working Capital 38	3.6	1.3	1.2	1.9	2.2	2.3
Current Liabilities to Working Capital 39	2.6	0.3	0.2	0.9	1.2	1.3
Working Capital to Net Sales 40	0.1	0.2	0.2	0.2	0.1	0.2
Inventory to Working Capital 41	1.2	0.7	0.3	1.0	0.3	0.2
Total Receipts to Cash Flow 42	7.9	4.6	5.0	6.3	9.0	6.5
Cost of Goods to Cash Flow 43	5.8	2.3	3.2	3.9	6.9	4.4
Cash Flow to Total Debt 44	0.2	2.7	0.8	0.5	0.4	0.4

Selected Financial Factors (in Percentages)

Debt Ratio 45	54.0	15.2	50.5	59.1	64.0	51.8
Return on Total Assets 46	11.1	17.4	28.8	16.4	19.0	8.0
Return on Equity Before Income Taxes 47	22.6	20.6	54.6	37.3	48.4	16.2
Return on Equity After Income Taxes 48	15.5	17.5	54.5	35.1	46.3	13.6
Profit Margin (Before Income Tax) 49	9.9	9.3	13.3	8.4	7.9	5.2
Profit Margin (After Income Tax) 50	6.8	7.9	13.3	7.9	7.6	4.4

Table I

Corporations with and without Net Income

OTHER TRANSPORTATION EQUIPMENT AND RAILROAD ROLLING STOCK

MONEY AMOUNTS AND SIZE OF ASSETS IN THOUSANDS OF DOLLARS

Item Description for Accounting Period 7/10 Through 6/11	Total	Zero Assets	Under 500	500 to 1,000	1,000 to 5,000	5,000 to 10,000	10,000 to 25,000	25,000 to 50,000	50,000 to 100,000	100,000 to 250,000	250,000 to 500,000	500,000 to 2,500,000	2,500,000 and over
Number of Enterprises 1	1320	7	778	115	283	19	56	24	12	8	•	•	•
Revenues ($ in Thousands)													
Net Sales 2	27099412	135980	149877	72797	1612533	249058	1051813	987791	1598244	1498050	•	•	•
Interest 3	646154	21	0	96	6	141	267	489	1769	187	•	•	•
Rents 4	6424	0	0	197	27	0	0	0	1452	196	•	•	•
Royalties 5	87698	0	0	0	0	0	0	747	243	0	•	•	•
Other Portfolio Income 6	91331	77	5	497	1080	73	1960	2627	2741	2754	•	•	•
Other Receipts 7	503736	29426	112	10021	388	468	11598	12370	8675	10785	•	•	•
Total Receipts 8	28434755	165504	149994	83608	1614034	249740	1065638	1004024	1613124	1511972	•	•	•
Average Total Receipts 9	21541	23643	193	727	5703	13144	19029	41834	134427	188996	•	•	•
Operating Costs/Operating Income (%)													
Cost of Operations 10	67.5	73.5	75.9	72.4	80.9	74.5	64.9	72.7	76.6	73.8	•	•	•
Salaries and Wages 11	7.2	9.5	9.9	0.4	2.6	4.8	10.2	5.6	5.0	2.9	•	•	•
Taxes Paid 12	1.5	3.0	8.4	1.8	1.6	1.1	1.8	1.5	1.3	1.3	•	•	•
Interest Paid 13	3.5	0.6	2.8	2.0	0.4	2.9	0.9	1.3	0.6	1.5	•	•	•
Depreciation 14	5.6	4.6	5.3	13.1	0.9	1.5	1.6	2.7	1.7	3.1	•	•	•
Amortization and Depletion 15	0.7	1.8	1.3	0.0	0.2	0.3	0.0	1.1	0.2	0.3	•	•	•
Pensions and Other Deferred Comp. 16	0.8	0.9	•	•	0.1	0.0	0.2	0.2	0.4	0.2	•	•	•
Employee Benefits 17	1.9	2.4	0.8	0.3	0.5	0.7	1.0	1.2	0.9	3.0	•	•	•
Advertising 18	0.8	1.0	1.7	1.7	0.4	0.3	0.6	1.0	0.2	0.0	•	•	•
Other Expenses 19	11.3	6.4	28.0	18.5	5.5	9.4	12.0	8.6	4.4	3.9	•	•	•
Officers' Compensation 20	0.9	4.7	2.3	12.6	3.4	5.4	2.5	0.7	1.0	0.9	•	•	•
Operating Margin 21	•	•	•	•	3.7	•	4.2	3.5	7.7	9.0	•	•	•
Operating Margin Before Officers' Comp. 22	•	•	•	•	7.1	4.5	6.7	4.2	8.7	10.0	•	•	•

Selected Average Balance Sheet ($ in Thousands)

Net Receivables 23	7107	0	12	593	628	2629	5900	10676	20280
Inventories 24	2668	0	85	657	9642	2900	4124	15465	24173
Net Property, Plant and Equipment 25	8000	0	31	190	2848	3052	4333	12213	25260
Total Assets 26	27316	0	138	1843	7238	14315	29771	73892	149488
Notes and Loans Payable 27	9566	0	164	489	2082	2562	8421	21814	44186
All Other Liabilities 28	7008	0	14	409	1849	3480	6827	15234	31352
Net Worth 29	10742	0	-40	944	3308	8272	14523	36845	73949

Selected Financial Ratios (Times to 1)

Current Ratio 30	1.6	•	0.9	2.1	2.2	3.1	2.4	2.1	1.9
Quick Ratio 31	1.1	•	0.1	1.1	1.4	1.7	1.3	1.2	0.9
Net Sales to Working Capital 32	3.7	•	3.0	7.2	6.2	2.8	3.9	6.2	5.3
Coverage Ratio 33	2.0	21.6	•	11.3	0.8	7.4	5.1	16.8	7.8
Total Asset Turnover 34	0.8	•	1.4	3.1	1.8	1.3	1.4	1.8	1.3
Inventory Turnover 35	5.2	•	1.7	7.0	1.0	4.2	7.3	6.6	5.7
Receivables Turnover 36	3.2	•	158.4	11.3	3.6	7.7	8.7	11.9	9.4
Total Liabilities to Net Worth 37	1.5	•	•	1.0	1.2	0.7	1.0	1.0	1.0
Current Assets to Working Capital 38	2.7	•	1.4	1.9	1.8	1.5	1.7	1.9	2.1
Current Liabilities to Working Capital 39	1.7	•	0.4	0.9	0.8	0.5	0.7	0.9	1.1
Working Capital to Net Sales 40	0.3	•	0.3	0.1	0.2	0.4	0.3	0.2	0.2
Inventory to Working Capital 41	0.5	•	0.8	0.9	0.6	0.4	0.5	0.6	0.7
Total Receipts to Cash Flow 42	8.7	5.4	44.0	13.8	15.1	6.9	8.6	8.6	7.9
Cost of Goods to Cash Flow 43	5.9	4.0	31.8	11.1	11.2	4.5	6.2	6.6	5.8
Cash Flow to Total Debt 44	0.1	•	0.0	0.5	0.2	0.5	0.3	0.4	0.3

Selected Financial Factors (in Percentages)

Debt Ratio 45	60.7	129.2	213.3	48.8	54.3	42.2	51.2	50.1	50.5
Return on Total Assets 46	5.2	•	•	12.7	4.0	8.4	8.8	16.9	14.3
Return on Equity Before Income Taxes 47	6.5	173.7	7.6	22.6	•	12.6	14.6	31.8	25.3
Return on Equity After Income Taxes 48	4.2	173.7	10.5	20.1	•	12.2	12.9	26.6	22.6
Profit Margin (Before Income Tax) 49	3.4	13.4	•	3.7	•	5.5	5.1	8.8	10.0
Profit Margin (After Income Tax) 50	2.2	12.6	•	3.3	•	5.4	4.5	7.4	8.9

Table II
Corporations with Net Income

OTHER TRANSPORTATION EQUIPMENT AND RAILROAD ROLLING STOCK

MONEY AMOUNTS AND SIZE OF ASSETS IN THOUSANDS OF DOLLARS

Item Description for Accounting Period 7/10 Through 6/11	Total	Zero Assets	Under 500	500 to 1,000	1,000 to 5,000	5,000 to 10,000	10,000 to 25,000	25,000 to 50,000	50,000 to 100,000	100,000 to 250,000	250,000 to 500,000	500,000 to 2,500,000	2,500,000 and over
Number of Enterprises 1	397	•	•	57	234	14	42	19	•	•	•	7	0
Revenues ($ in Thousands)													
Net Sales 2	22530042	•	•	64325	1438213	238162	937536	910409	•	•	•	14062274	0
Interest 3	621081	•	•	0	0	140	91	407	•	•	•	616542	0
Rents 4	3762	•	•	197	0	0	0	0	•	•	•	2073	0
Royalties 5	78034	•	•	0	0	0	0	747	•	•	•	77098	0
Other Portfolio Income 6	37952	•	•	0	1080	73	1717	378	•	•	•	27165	0
Other Receipts 7	441714	•	•	247	387	76	12193	5454	•	•	•	369879	0
Total Receipts 8	23712585	•	•	64769	1439680	238451	951537	917395	•	•	•	15155031	0
Average Total Receipts 9	59729	•	•	1136	6152	17032	22656	48284	•	•	•	2165004	•
Operating Costs/Operating Income (%)													
Cost of Operations 10	68.4	•	•	50.6	82.6	74.3	66.4	72.2	•	•	•	64.9	•
Salaries and Wages 11	6.6	•	•	0.5	1.8	4.0	8.5	5.7	•	•	•	7.4	•
Taxes Paid 12	1.3	•	•	1.8	1.6	0.9	1.6	1.4	•	•	•	1.2	•
Interest Paid 13	2.7	•	•	2.3	0.2	1.0	0.4	1.0	•	•	•	4.0	•
Depreciation 14	4.2	•	•	2.7	0.7	1.5	0.9	2.4	•	•	•	5.6	•
Amortization and Depletion 15	0.7	•	•	•	0.2	0.2	0.0	0.9	•	•	•	0.9	•
Pensions and Other Deferred Comp. 16	0.8	•	•	•	0.1	0.0	0.1	0.1	•	•	•	1.1	•
Employee Benefits 17	1.9	•	•	0.2	0.4	0.7	0.9	0.9	•	•	•	2.4	•
Advertising 18	0.9	•	•	1.6	0.3	0.2	0.6	1.0	•	•	•	1.2	•
Other Expenses 19	10.3	•	•	13.8	3.4	6.1	9.9	8.1	•	•	•	13.3	•
Officers' Compensation 20	0.9	•	•	14.2	3.3	5.0	2.2	0.6	•	•	•	0.5	•
Operating Margin 21	1.4	•	•	12.1	5.4	6.1	8.3	5.7	•	•	•	•	•
Operating Margin Before Officers' Comp. 22	2.3	•	•	26.4	8.7	11.0	10.5	6.3	•	•	•	•	•

Selected Average Balance Sheet ($ in Thousands)

Net Receivables **23**	21717	0	705	818	3016	6796	1060942
Inventories **24**	5732	333	691	12059	2499	4175	202908
Net Property, Plant and Equipment **25**	15534	59	117	3708	1694	4404	777569
Total Assets **26**	66543	504	1812	7454	13644	29713	3041058
Notes and Loans Payable **27**	21309	74	391	2384	1298	6502	1076514
All Other Liabilities **28**	16059	159	419	1399	3418	7586	718960
Net Worth **29**	29174	271	1002	3672	8929	15625	1245583

Selected Financial Ratios (Times to 1)

Current Ratio **30**	1.5	2.1	2.3	2.9	3.4	2.5	1.4
Quick Ratio **31**	1.2	•	1.3	1.8	2.1	1.3	1.1
Net Sales to Working Capital **32**	4.1	6.4	6.9	7.4	3.0	3.9	4.0
Coverage Ratio **33**	3.4	6.6	24.4	7.0	24.5	7.5	2.4
Total Asset Turnover **34**	0.9	2.2	3.4	2.3	1.6	1.6	0.7
Inventory Turnover **35**	6.8	1.7	7.3	1.0	5.9	8.3	6.4
Receivables Turnover **36**	3.0	•	3.7	10.5	12.6	•	1.4
Total Liabilities to Net Worth **37**	1.3	0.9	0.8	1.0	0.5	0.9	1.4
Current Assets to Working Capital **38**	2.8	1.9	1.8	1.5	1.4	1.7	3.4
Current Liabilities to Working Capital **39**	1.8	0.9	0.8	0.5	0.4	0.7	2.4
Working Capital to Net Sales **40**	0.2	0.2	0.1	0.1	0.3	0.3	0.3
Inventory to Working Capital **41**	0.5	1.9	0.8	0.6	0.5	0.5	0.4
Total Receipts to Cash Flow **42**	7.1	4.7	14.5	9.7	6.0	7.9	6.6
Cost of Goods to Cash Flow **43**	4.9	2.4	12.0	7.2	4.0	5.7	4.3
Cash Flow to Total Debt **44**	0.2	1.0	0.5	0.5	0.8	0.4	0.2

Selected Financial Factors (in Percentages)

Debt Ratio **45**	56.2	46.2	44.7	50.7	34.6	47.4	59.0
Return on Total Assets **46**	8.0	33.9	19.6	16.4	16.8	12.0	6.2
Return on Equity Before Income Taxes **47**	12.9	53.4	33.9	28.6	24.6	19.9	8.7
Return on Equity After Income Taxes **48**	10.1	38.8	31.1	20.9	24.2	17.9	5.9
Profit Margin (Before Income Tax) **49**	6.6	12.8	5.5	6.2	9.8	6.5	5.4
Profit Margin (After Income Tax) **50**	5.2	9.3	5.1	4.5	9.7	5.8	3.6

Table I

Corporations with and without Net Income

FURNITURE AND RELATED PRODUCT MANUFACTURING

MONEY AMOUNTS AND SIZE OF ASSETS IN THOUSANDS OF DOLLARS

Item Description for Accounting Period 7/10 Through 6/11		Total	Zero Assets	Under 500	500 to 1,000	1,000 to 5,000	5,000 to 10,000	10,000 to 25,000	25,000 to 50,000	50,000 to 100,000	100,000 to 250,000	250,000 to 500,000	500,000 to 2,500,000	2,500,000 and over
Number of Enterprises	1	12685	2182	8279	803	992	145	166	52	29	17	5	15	0
Revenues ($ in Thousands)														
Net Sales	2	51305219	673797	4287054	1620482	5532218	2413890	4491834	3370819	3039076	3679860	2604574	19591615	0
Interest	3	37816	400	401	118	2726	829	514	1769	3237	6740	2977	18105	0
Rents	4	27341	708	0	0	1956	19	659	2474	477	7614	2209	11225	0
Royalties	5	61578	1316	0	0	0	0	0	779	366	239	0	58878	0
Other Portfolio Income	6	246615	2220	25372	1783	3234	8409	15860	1631	712	1106	1113	175275	0
Other Receipts	7	474534	214	11924	4326	13650	7485	21582	24220	18667	24039	4653	343774	0
Total Receipts	8	52153103	678655	4324751	1626709	5553784	2430632	4530449	3401692	3062535	3729498	2615526	20198872	0
Average Total Receipts	9	4111	311	522	2026	5599	16763	27292	65417	105605	219382	523105	1346591	•
Operating Costs/Operating Income (%)														
Cost of Operations	10	66.2	58.2	55.7	65.1	70.2	69.8	68.8	72.7	74.2	69.7	60.1	64.4	•
Salaries and Wages	11	8.9	16.4	13.7	3.1	9.1	6.9	7.8	7.8	6.5	7.9	11.4	8.8	•
Taxes Paid	12	2.1	1.7	2.6	2.2	2.7	1.6	1.9	2.1	1.6	1.9	1.8	2.1	•
Interest Paid	13	1.2	2.2	0.4	0.6	0.7	0.8	1.0	1.3	1.7	0.8	0.3	1.8	•
Depreciation	14	1.8	2.0	1.3	0.6	1.3	2.3	1.7	1.6	2.0	2.2	1.9	2.0	•
Amortization and Depletion	15	0.5	1.5	0.2	0.1	0.0	0.0	0.1	0.2	0.6	0.4	0.2	0.9	•
Pensions and Other Deferred Comp.	16	0.5	0.1	0.6	0.3	0.1	0.3	0.2	0.3	0.2	0.7	0.5	0.8	•
Employee Benefits	17	2.0	0.8	1.5	1.9	1.3	1.6	2.1	1.7	2.5	2.5	2.4	2.1	•
Advertising	18	2.3	1.4	1.0	0.2	0.8	1.5	1.6	1.2	0.9	1.1	4.3	3.8	•
Other Expenses	19	12.0	15.8	14.4	19.9	10.9	11.0	10.3	9.6	9.1	9.2	12.4	12.9	•
Officers' Compensation	20	1.8	0.7	7.3	4.8	2.4	1.7	2.2	1.3	1.3	1.0	0.6	0.6	•
Operating Margin	21	0.8	•	1.3	1.2	0.4	2.5	2.2	0.3	•	2.5	3.9	•	•
Operating Margin Before Officers' Comp.	22	2.6	•	8.6	6.0	2.8	4.2	4.4	1.6	0.8	3.6	4.5	0.4	•

Selected Average Balance Sheet ($ in Thousands)

	•	•	•	•	•	•	•	•	•	•	•	•
Net Receivables 23	445	0	29	253	578	1635	2867	8075	13614	25719	49048	161686
Inventories 24	383	0	27	91	529	1546	3208	8801	15604	31381	44594	107194
Net Property, Plant and Equipment 25	536	0	33	55	824	2022	3794	9868	13507	38326	71860	188622
Total Assets 26	2654	0	127	616	2388	6689	14830	34478	69569	146548	280652	1240679
Notes and Loans Payable 27	859	0	69	147	1287	2430	3448	12754	21441	41857	20249	394076
All Other Liabilities 28	778	0	48	283	680	1622	3803	9787	16185	32901	91755	380390
Net Worth 29	1017	0	11	186	421	2638	7579	11938	31943	71790	168648	466212

Selected Financial Ratios (Times to 1)

Current Ratio 30	1.6	•	1.2	1.9	1.5	1.8	2.1	1.4	2.2	2.8	2.1	1.4
Quick Ratio 31	0.9	•	0.7	1.5	0.9	1.0	1.1	0.7	1.0	1.5	1.3	0.7
Net Sales to Working Capital 32	8.5	•	38.5	8.0	11.2	9.3	5.5	12.0	4.9	4.7	7.1	9.4
Coverage Ratio 33	3.1	1.0	6.1	3.9	2.1	5.2	4.1	1.9	1.2	5.7	14.3	2.9
Total Asset Turnover 34	1.5	•	4.1	3.3	2.3	2.5	1.8	1.9	1.5	1.5	1.9	1.1
Inventory Turnover 35	7.0	•	10.7	14.4	7.4	7.5	5.8	5.4	5.0	4.8	7.0	7.8
Receivables Turnover 36	9.5	•	20.0	8.9	9.2	11.8	10.4	7.7	6.9	7.2	12.0	9.1
Total Liabilities to Net Worth 37	1.6	•	11.1	2.3	4.7	1.5	1.0	1.9	1.2	1.0	0.7	1.7
Current Assets to Working Capital 38	2.6	•	5.4	2.2	2.9	2.3	1.9	3.8	1.9	1.5	1.9	3.3
Current Liabilities to Working Capital 39	1.6	•	4.4	1.2	1.9	1.3	0.9	2.8	0.9	0.5	0.9	2.3
Working Capital to Net Sales 40	0.1	•	0.0	0.1	0.1	0.1	0.2	0.1	0.2	0.2	0.1	0.1
Inventory to Working Capital 41	0.8	•	1.4	0.4	1.0	0.8	0.7	1.5	0.8	0.6	0.6	0.8
Total Receipts to Cash Flow 42	8.7	7.6	8.1	6.5	12.8	9.0	9.2	11.3	13.3	9.7	7.4	7.6
Cost of Goods to Cash Flow 43	5.8	4.4	4.5	4.2	9.0	6.3	6.3	8.2	9.9	6.8	4.5	4.9
Cash Flow to Total Debt 44	0.3	•	0.5	0.7	0.2	0.5	0.4	0.3	0.2	0.3	0.6	0.2

Selected Financial Factors (in Percentages)

Debt Ratio 45	61.7	•	91.7	69.8	82.4	60.6	48.9	65.4	54.1	51.0	39.9	62.4
Return on Total Assets 46	5.8	•	10.7	7.1	3.6	9.8	7.4	4.7	2.9	6.9	8.6	5.4
Return on Equity Before Income Taxes 47	10.4	•	108.1	17.4	10.6	20.0	10.9	6.4	0.9	11.7	13.4	9.4
Return on Equity After Income Taxes 48	8.4	•	107.3	16.3	9.6	19.7	10.3	6.0	0.3	8.5	10.9	6.9
Profit Margin (Before Income Tax) 49	2.6	0.0	2.2	1.6	0.8	3.2	3.1	1.2	0.3	3.9	4.3	3.4
Profit Margin (After Income Tax) 50	2.1	0.0	2.2	1.5	0.7	3.1	2.9	1.1	0.1	2.8	3.5	2.5

Table II

Corporations with Net Income

FURNITURE AND RELATED PRODUCT MANUFACTURING

MONEY AMOUNTS AND SIZE OF ASSETS IN THOUSANDS OF DOLLARS

Item Description for Accounting Period 7/10 Through 6/11	Total	Zero Assets	Under 500	500 to 1,000	1,000 to 5,000	5,000 to 10,000	10,000 to 25,000	25,000 to 50,000	50,000 to 100,000	100,000 to 250,000	250,000 to 500,000	500,000 to 2,500,000	2,500,000 and over
Number of Enterprises 1	6848	781	4826	453	522	91	101	34	•	11	•	11	0
Revenues ($ in Thousands)													
Net Sales 2	35168913	297418	2084922	854757	3152247	1531456	3116875	2424591	•	2753474	•	14945427	0
Interest 3	20092	0	393	6	955	123	260	1405	•	223	•	12690	0
Rents 4	14154	0	0	0	603	0	97	857	•	285	•	9994	0
Royalties 5	35901	0	0	0	0	0	0	0	•	0	•	35535	0
Other Portfolio Income 6	200532	0	22763	62	2824	67	449	1174	•	844	•	171571	0
Other Receipts 7	389293	-22	8691	131	3870	1919	10187	8916	•	12614	•	329727	0
Total Receipts 8	35828885	297396	2116769	854956	3160499	1533565	3127868	2436943	•	2767440	•	15504944	0
Average Total Receipts 9	5232	381	439	1887	6055	16852	30969	71675	•	251585	•	1409540	•
Operating Costs/Operating Income (%)													
Cost of Operations 10	64.9	69.8	48.0	62.5	66.8	69.6	68.2	70.9	•	70.8	•	63.6	•
Salaries and Wages 11	8.6	6.8	10.9	3.3	8.4	8.2	6.9	8.1	•	7.8	•	8.9	•
Taxes Paid 12	1.9	0.6	2.8	2.5	2.2	0.9	1.5	2.1	•	1.7	•	1.9	•
Interest Paid 13	1.1	0.4	0.6	0.1	0.9	0.5	0.5	0.8	•	0.8	•	1.8	•
Depreciation 14	1.6	0.2	1.7	0.5	0.8	1.2	1.3	1.4	•	2.1	•	1.9	•
Amortization and Depletion 15	0.4	•	0.3	0.2	0.0	0.0	0.1	0.0	•	0.5	•	0.7	•
Pensions and Other Deferred Comp. 16	0.5	•	0.9	0.4	0.1	0.1	0.2	0.3	•	0.5	•	0.8	•
Employee Benefits 17	2.0	0.0	1.9	2.8	0.8	1.3	2.1	2.0	•	2.5	•	2.2	•
Advertising 18	2.3	1.5	0.3	0.3	1.1	1.4	2.0	0.9	•	0.9	•	3.6	•
Other Expenses 19	11.1	8.5	17.9	12.5	9.8	8.5	8.3	7.2	•	5.6	•	13.3	•
Officers' Compensation 20	1.7	0.1	9.0	6.0	2.1	2.1	2.4	1.2	•	1.1	•	0.5	•
Operating Margin 21	3.9	12.1	5.6	9.0	7.1	6.3	6.6	5.0	•	5.8	•	0.9	•
Operating Margin Before Officers' Comp. 22	5.6	12.2	14.6	15.0	9.1	8.4	9.0	6.3	•	6.9	•	1.4	•

Selected Average Balance Sheet ($ in Thousands)

	1	2	3	4	5	6	7	8	9	10	11
Net Receivables 23	588	0	27	205	683	1990	3274	9758	•	30579	165428
Inventories 24	412	0	8	97	502	1258	3058	7717	•	27577	100501
Net Property, Plant and Equipment 25	626	0	33	57	648	1694	2930	9033	•	37670	195156
Total Assets 26	3378	0	116	667	2433	6782	14644	35695	•	146260	1262469
Notes and Loans Payable 27	1062	0	83	14	869	1905	2538	9742	•	52637	435368
All Other Liabilities 28	1001	0	35	123	551	1945	3834	9181	•	32928	406073
Net Worth 29	1315	0	-2	529	1013	2932	8272	16772	•	60695	421028

Selected Financial Ratios (Times to 1)

	1	2	3	4	5	6	7	8	9	10	11
Current Ratio 30	1.7	•	1.2	4.5	2.4	2.0	2.3	1.8	•	2.9	1.3
Quick Ratio 31	0.9	•	0.7	3.7	1.5	1.2	1.3	1.0	•	1.6	0.6
Net Sales to Working Capital 32	8.0	•	39.5	4.1	6.3	6.9	5.5	7.1	•	5.0	12.1
Coverage Ratio 33	6.3	28.4	12.2	79.7	9.3	14.7	14.3	8.0	•	9.1	3.9
Total Asset Turnover 34	1.5	•	3.7	2.8	2.5	2.5	2.1	2.0	•	1.7	1.1
Inventory Turnover 35	8.1	•	25.1	12.1	8.0	9.3	6.9	6.5	•	6.4	8.6
Receivables Turnover 36	9.9	•	16.4	7.5	8.7	11.3	11.2	7.6	•	8.8	9.8
Total Liabilities to Net Worth 37	1.6	•	•	0.3	1.4	1.3	0.8	1.1	•	1.4	2.0
Current Assets to Working Capital 38	2.5	•	5.9	1.3	1.7	2.0	1.7	2.3	•	1.5	4.4
Current Liabilities to Working Capital 39	1.5	•	4.9	0.3	0.7	1.0	0.7	1.3	•	0.5	3.4
Working Capital to Net Sales 40	0.1	•	0.0	0.2	0.2	0.1	0.2	0.1	•	0.2	0.1
Inventory to Working Capital 41	0.7	•	0.9	0.2	0.5	0.7	0.6	0.8	•	0.6	1.1
Total Receipts to Cash Flow 42	7.1	5.0	5.1	6.5	7.3	8.2	7.5	8.7	•	10.0	6.5
Cost of Goods to Cash Flow 43	4.6	3.5	2.5	4.1	4.9	5.7	5.1	6.2	•	7.0	4.1
Cash Flow to Total Debt 44	0.4	•	0.7	2.1	0.6	0.5	0.6	0.4	•	0.3	0.2

Selected Financial Factors (in Percentages)

	1	2	3	4	5	6	7	8	9	10	11
Debt Ratio 45	61.1	•	101.7	20.6	58.4	56.8	43.5	53.0	•	58.5	66.7
Return on Total Assets 46	10.9	•	29.0	25.9	20.3	17.3	15.6	12.7	•	12.1	7.5
Return on Equity Before Income Taxes 47	23.6	•	•	32.2	43.6	37.2	25.7	23.6	•	25.9	16.9
Return on Equity After Income Taxes 48	20.8	•	•	31.5	42.8	36.8	24.8	23.1	•	20.1	13.2
Profit Margin (Before Income Tax) 49	6.0	12.1	7.2	9.0	7.3	6.5	6.9	5.5	•	6.3	5.2
Profit Margin (After Income Tax) 50	5.3	12.1	7.1	8.8	7.2	6.4	6.7	5.4	•	4.9	4.1

Table I

Corporations with and without Net Income

MEDICAL EQUIPMENT AND SUPPLIES

MONEY AMOUNTS AND SIZE OF ASSETS IN THOUSANDS OF DOLLARS

Item Description for Accounting Period 7/10 Through 6/11		Total	Zero Assets	Under 500	500 to 1,000	1,000 to 5,000	5,000 to 10,000	10,000 to 25,000	25,000 to 50,000	50,000 to 100,000	100,000 to 250,000	250,000 to 500,000	500,000 to 2,500,000	2,500,000 and over
Number of Enterprises	1	9239	1717	5506	452	971	129	183	85	63	47	28	41	17
Revenues ($ in Thousands)														
Net Sales	2	154873904	1561225	2060621	705582	5959881	1407617	3431508	3756145	4456020	5569021	6761405	34622646	84582233
Interest	3	1404159	3635	139	829	1731	1492	3261	3367	10875	169702	20139	106851	1082138
Rents	4	908232	57	0	0	0	455	340	0	1107	8009	2563	33702	861997
Royalties	5	3489395	4948	0	0	888	825	4422	29145	8980	37855	113942	136578	3151814
Other Portfolio Income	6	2620643	701791	417	11	1507	484	54406	12152	26483	42501	53237	354769	1372888
Other Receipts	7	3739963	37753	410	9857	35641	8672	53711	75692	105268	374158	69875	801989	2166933
Total Receipts	8	167036296	2309409	2061587	716279	5999648	1419545	3547648	3876501	4608733	6201246	7021161	36056535	93218003
Average Total Receipts	9	18079	1345	374	1585	6179	11004	19386	45606	73154	131941	250756	879428	5483412
Operating Costs/Operating Income (%)														
Cost of Operations	10	54.8	37.7	33.6	49.0	56.1	58.9	48.2	55.7	52.8	56.7	48.7	51.2	57.6
Salaries and Wages	11	16.5	23.9	14.8	6.5	10.2	13.1	19.3	15.2	13.8	12.7	18.2	14.7	18.0
Taxes Paid	12	1.6	3.8	3.5	4.0	2.4	3.1	3.0	2.1	1.9	1.5	1.9	1.6	1.3
Interest Paid	13	3.5	1.6	0.6	1.2	0.7	1.8	1.2	1.7	1.4	8.5	1.9	2.6	4.3
Depreciation	14	3.6	2.5	1.8	0.6	1.1	2.4	2.5	3.2	3.1	3.4	3.9	3.3	4.1
Amortization and Depletion	15	1.3	1.4	0.9	0.0	0.4	0.3	0.6	1.1	0.9	2.0	1.7	1.7	1.2
Pensions and Other Deferred Comp.	16	1.1	0.3	0.3	0.7	0.5	0.2	0.4	0.3	0.5	0.4	0.3	0.9	1.4
Employee Benefits	17	2.8	2.2	1.6	4.1	1.6	1.7	1.9	2.3	1.9	2.2	2.0	2.4	3.4
Advertising	18	1.0	0.7	0.5	0.8	1.0	1.6	1.6	1.8	1.6	1.2	1.3	0.8	0.9
Other Expenses	19	13.3	31.0	22.6	26.1	16.5	18.3	24.4	17.3	17.0	18.8	16.3	14.8	10.2
Officers' Compensation	20	1.5	14.8	17.0	9.4	5.1	4.9	6.0	1.8	1.8	1.6	1.6	1.1	0.4
Operating Margin	21	•	2.7	•	•	1.6	•	•	•	3.3	•	2.0	5.0	•
Operating Margin Before Officers' Comp.	22	0.5	19.7	7.0	6.7	1.3	•	•	•	5.1	•	3.7	6.1	•

Selected Average Balance Sheet ($ in Thousands)

Line Item													
Net Receivables **23**	3066	0	12	275	807	1707	3263	7049	11378	27690	40092	161261	952389
Inventories **24**	2236	0	11	68	508	1804	2950	6314	10031	15900	31372	102914	722660
Net Property, Plant and Equipment **25**	2619	0	18	80	251	920	1850	5770	9317	23321	31371	141077	854358
Total Assets **26**	27292	0	95	705	2251	7223	15936	35376	68898	160108	346203	1131613	10253641
Notes and Loans Payable **27**	8727	0	53	336	752	2036	3542	12495	13595	78263	60388	293493	3484029
All Other Liabilities **28**	8751	0	21	542	761	2208	3768	8360	17957	32044	67248	337679	3511755
Net Worth **29**	9814	0	21	-173	738	2978	8626	14520	37347	49802	218566	500441	3257856

Selected Financial Ratios (Times to 1)

Line Item												
Current Ratio **30**	1.9	•	0.9	1.8	2.1	2.8	2.1	2.3	2.3	3.4	1.9	1.7
Quick Ratio **31**	0.9	•	0.8	1.2	1.3	1.9	1.3	1.4	1.4	2.3	1.1	0.7
Net Sales to Working Capital **32**	4.1	23.6	•	7.5	3.9	2.4	4.2	3.5	3.2	2.4	4.0	4.2
Coverage Ratio **33**	3.4	18.1	5.5	0.2	4.3	•	1.3	5.8	1.3	4.2	5.1	3.2
Total Asset Turnover **34**	0.6	•	3.9	2.2	2.7	1.5	1.2	1.0	0.7	0.7	0.7	0.5
Inventory Turnover **35**	4.1	•	11.4	11.2	7.1	3.4	3.9	3.7	4.2	3.8	4.2	4.0
Receivables Turnover **36**	5.4	•	34.3	4.3	8.0	6.4	6.5	5.6	6.0	4.9	5.0	5.2
Total Liabilities to Net Worth **37**	1.8	•	3.4	2.1	1.4	0.8	1.4	0.8	2.2	0.6	1.3	2.1
Current Assets to Working Capital **38**	2.1	•	2.7	2.2	1.9	1.6	1.9	1.7	1.8	1.4	2.1	2.4
Current Liabilities to Working Capital **39**	1.1	•	1.7	1.2	0.9	0.6	0.9	0.7	0.8	0.4	1.1	1.4
Working Capital to Net Sales **40**	0.2	•	0.0	0.1	0.3	0.4	0.2	0.3	0.3	0.4	0.2	0.2
Inventory to Working Capital **41**	0.6	•	0.7	0.7	0.6	0.4	0.6	0.5	0.5	0.3	0.5	0.6
Total Receipts to Cash Flow **42**	5.8	1.8	5.1	4.7	7.0	8.3	6.5	4.8	5.3	5.0	4.5	6.9
Cost of Goods to Cash Flow **43**	3.2	0.7	1.7	2.3	4.1	4.6	3.6	2.5	3.0	2.4	2.3	4.0
Cash Flow to Total Debt **44**	0.2	•	1.0	0.4	0.3	0.3	0.3	0.5	0.2	0.4	0.3	0.1

Selected Financial Factors (in Percentages)

Line Item													
Debt Ratio **45**	64.0	•	77.5	124.5	67.2	58.8	45.9	59.0	45.8	68.9	36.9	55.8	68.2
Return on Total Assets **46**	7.2	•	13.2	0.7	8.0	•	•	2.9	8.4	8.1	5.7	9.9	6.6
Return on Income Before Taxes **47**	14.1	•	47.8	8.2	18.6	•	•	1.7	12.9	5.8	6.9	18.0	14.1
Return on Equity After Income Taxes **48**	9.5	•	47.6	10.7	16.5	•	•	•	9.2	3.0	4.4	13.4	9.3
Profit Margin (Before Income Tax) **49**	8.3	28.0	2.7	2.7	2.2	•	•	0.6	6.8	2.4	6.2	10.7	9.2
Profit Margin (After Income Tax) **50**	5.6	19.0	2.7	2.7	2.0	•	•	•	4.9	1.2	4.0	7.9	6.1

Table II
Corporations with Net Income

MEDICAL EQUIPMENT AND SUPPLIES

MONEY AMOUNTS AND SIZE OF ASSETS IN THOUSANDS OF DOLLARS

Item Description for Accounting Period 7/10 Through 6/11	Total	Zero Assets	Under 500	500 to 1,000	1,000 to 5,000	5,000 to 10,000	10,000 to 25,000	25,000 to 50,000	50,000 to 100,000	100,000 to 250,000	250,000 to 500,000	500,000 to 2,500,000	2,500,000 and over
Number of Enterprises **1**	5944	398	4165	•	731	83	86	49	49	30	20	35	•

Revenues ($ in Thousands)

Net Sales **2**	136627841	1058377	1603649	•	5128682	1087606	2497103	2883752	3827318	4425146	5423020	31509751	•
Interest **3**	1251171	915	0	•	742	1149	1031	994	8907	166772	18516	99617	•
Rents **4**	900849	57	0	•	0	401	259	0	1107	7968	1911	27148	•
Royalties **5**	2882849	1674	0	•	0	0	0	888	1124	36362	102557	87226	•
Other Portfolio Income **6**	2445727	693691	0	•	479	192	38438	8428	26054	21897	51873	349158	•
Other Receipts **7**	3126382	34745	16	•	8375	6686	35997	44462	94629	371881	49456	785085	•
Total Receipts **8**	147234819	1789459	1603665	•	5138278	1096034	2572828	2938524	3959139	5030026	5647333	32857985	•
Average Total Receipts **9**	24770	4496	385	•	7029	13205	29917	59970	80799	167668	282367	938800	•

Operating Costs/Operating Income (%)

Cost of Operations **10**	55.3	37.0	29.2	•	57.7	58.1	47.1	57.4	51.5	59.4	48.5	50.9	•
Salaries and Wages **11**	15.9	19.5	14.9	•	8.4	8.4	13.0	11.0	12.7	10.8	17.4	14.4	•
Taxes Paid **12**	1.6	4.4	3.6	•	2.3	2.1	2.3	2.0	1.8	1.4	2.1	1.6	•
Interest Paid **13**	3.1	1.3	0.2	•	0.5	1.2	0.3	0.9	1.1	9.3	1.4	2.3	•
Depreciation **14**	3.6	2.5	1.7	•	0.8	2.2	1.5	2.7	2.8	2.9	3.6	3.3	•
Amortization and Depletion **15**	1.0	1.8	1.0	•	0.1	0.0	0.2	0.7	0.8	1.5	1.3	1.5	•
Pensions and Other Deferred Comp. **16**	1.2	0.4	0.4	•	0.5	0.3	0.6	0.4	0.5	0.4	0.3	1.0	•
Employee Benefits **17**	2.8	2.4	1.4	•	1.6	1.3	1.3	1.9	1.7	1.9	2.0	2.2	•
Advertising **18**	1.0	0.6	0.4	•	0.9	0.9	1.3	1.9	1.7	1.0	1.3	0.8	•
Other Expenses **19**	11.2	29.0	21.2	•	13.8	11.0	15.1	12.1	15.7	16.1	15.2	14.7	•
Officers' Compensation **20**	1.2	8.8	17.4	•	4.7	3.7	5.3	1.5	1.6	1.3	1.6	1.0	•
Operating Margin **21**	2.1	•	8.4	•	8.8	10.8	12.0	7.6	8.0	•	5.4	6.4	•
Operating Margin Before Officers' Comp. **22**	3.3	1.1	25.9	•	13.5	14.5	17.3	9.1	9.6	•	7.0	7.4	•

Selected Average Balance Sheet ($ in Thousands)

Net Receivables 23	4061	0	12	•	886	2096	4625	8730	12252	32638	41310	168625
Inventories 24	2973	0	6	•	569	1479	3164	7147	10585	17740	32739	107263
Net Property, Plant and Equipment 25	3515	0	17	•	224	1050	1964	6529	9273	27547	33195	147773
Total Assets 26	33589	0	80	•	2292	7421	16147	35636	69419	169016	341638	1174685
Notes and Loans Payable 27	11274	0	27	•	647	1853	1589	8887	12276	91540	50972	297774
All Other Liabilities 28	11723	0	9	•	558	2385	4129	6715	17843	38601	54070	351739
Net Worth 29	10592	0	43	•	1087	3182	10428	20034	39300	38876	236595	525172

Selected Financial Ratios (Times to 1)

Current Ratio 30	1.9	2.0	•	2.7	2.4	2.8	2.5	2.6	2.5	4.0	2.0
Quick Ratio 31	1.0	1.6	•	1.7	1.5	1.8	1.6	1.4	1.5	2.7	1.2
Net Sales to Working Capital 32	4.3	26.9	•	5.8	4.2	3.6	4.5	3.5	3.4	2.4	3.9
Coverage Ratio 33	4.6	41.6	50.1	17.7	10.8	47.1	11.1	11.0	1.8	8.4	6.3
Total Asset Turnover 34	0.7	4.8	•	3.1	1.8	1.8	1.7	1.1	0.9	0.8	0.8
Inventory Turnover 35	4.3	18.6	•	7.1	5.1	4.3	4.7	3.8	4.9	4.0	4.3
Receivables Turnover 36	5.6	42.6	•	8.0	7.7	7.3	5.7	6.3	5.6	5.1	5.3
Total Liabilities to Net Worth 37	2.2	0.8	•	1.1	1.3	0.5	0.8	0.8	3.3	0.4	1.2
Current Assets to Working Capital 38	2.1	2.0	•	1.6	1.7	1.6	1.7	1.6	1.6	1.3	2.0
Current Liabilities to Working Capital 39	1.1	1.0	•	0.6	0.7	0.6	0.7	0.6	0.6	0.3	1.0
Working Capital to Net Sales 40	0.2	0.0	•	0.2	0.2	0.3	0.2	0.3	0.3	0.4	0.3
Inventory to Working Capital 41	0.6	0.4	•	0.5	0.6	0.5	0.5	0.5	0.5	0.3	0.5
Total Receipts to Cash Flow 42	5.5	4.0	1.1	5.3	5.2	3.8	5.2	4.1	4.6	4.4	4.3
Cost of Goods to Cash Flow 43	3.0	1.2	0.4	3.1	3.0	1.8	3.0	2.1	2.7	2.2	2.2
Cash Flow to Total Debt 44	0.2	2.6	•	1.1	0.6	1.3	0.7	0.6	0.2	0.6	0.3

Selected Financial Factors (in Percentages)

Debt Ratio 45	68.5	45.4	•	52.6	57.1	35.4	43.8	43.4	77.0	30.7	55.3
Return on Total Assets 46	9.9	41.9	•	29.1	22.6	27.6	17.1	14.2	14.9	9.0	11.2
Return on Equity Before Income Taxes 47	24.6	74.9	•	57.9	47.7	41.9	27.7	22.8	29.5	11.4	21.1
Return on Equity After Income Taxes 48	18.0	74.8	•	56.0	40.7	40.1	23.9	18.3	23.8	8.3	15.9
Profit Margin (Before Income Tax) 49	11.3	8.4	61.6	9.0	11.6	15.0	9.4	11.5	7.8	10.0	12.3
Profit Margin (After Income Tax) 50	8.3	8.4	48.2	8.7	9.9	14.4	8.1	9.2	6.3	7.2	9.3

Table I

Corporations with and without Net Income

OTHER MISCELLANEOUS MANUFACTURING

MONEY AMOUNTS AND SIZE OF ASSETS IN THOUSANDS OF DOLLARS

Item Description for Accounting Period 7/10 Through 6/11	Total	Zero Assets	Under 500	500 to 1,000	1,000 to 5,000	5,000 to 10,000	10,000 to 25,000	25,000 to 50,000	50,000 to 100,000	100,000 to 250,000	250,000 to 500,000	500,000 to 2,500,000	2,500,000 and over
Number of Enterprises **1**	19710	1212	14977	885	1639	447	284	118	63	43	23	15	4
Revenues ($ in Thousands)													
Net Sales **2**	74376339	2045272	5017466	1355662	8475182	5334179	6580778	5165348	5710829	6721216	7869771	10559183	9541454
Interest **3**	539689	1119	287	736	3430	1108	4517	2799	15191	19502	41656	45837	403505
Rents **4**	18686	54	0	0	1656	315	1728	205	354	5597	6074	2296	407
Royalties **5**	1031148	399	0	0	0	0	12913	492	11581	37790	55678	99684	812610
Other Portfolio Income **6**	671171	243106	0	16649	5143	32405	7025	9151	47971	3316	18475	271768	16161
Other Receipts **7**	1330912	75681	56817	10726	-52544	26299	67739	39597	32592	95297	182106	27446	769160
Total Receipts **8**	77967945	2365631	5074570	1383773	8432867	5394306	6674700	5217592	5818518	6882718	8173760	11006214	11543297
Average Total Receipts **9**	3956	1952	339	1564	5145	12068	23502	44217	92357	160063	355381	733748	2885824
Operating Costs/Operating Income (%)													
Cost of Operations **10**	59.5	66.5	46.3	59.5	65.6	64.8	68.5	62.7	62.1	63.6	61.1	52.9	50.2
Salaries and Wages **11**	10.8	14.1	14.6	9.5	7.9	9.0	8.3	9.8	10.0	9.2	11.3	11.4	14.8
Taxes Paid **12**	2.0	1.9	3.1	2.0	2.3	1.8	2.0	1.8	1.9	1.9	1.9	2.1	1.8
Interest Paid **13**	2.8	2.7	1.2	0.9	0.8	1.1	1.1	1.4	1.4	2.7	2.6	4.2	8.3
Depreciation **14**	2.7	1.3	1.3	1.2	1.6	2.5	2.2	2.1	2.9	3.0	2.7	3.8	4.4
Amortization and Depletion **15**	0.9	1.3	0.4	0.0	0.2	0.1	0.5	1.1	0.7	0.9	1.0	1.3	2.1
Pensions and Other Deferred Comp. **16**	0.7	0.2	0.3	0.2	0.5	0.3	0.4	0.5	0.8	0.5	1.1	1.6	0.9
Employee Benefits **17**	1.7	0.8	1.9	1.0	1.2	1.9	1.5	1.4	1.8	1.4	2.0	2.9	1.4
Advertising **18**	2.0	1.8	1.8	0.8	0.8	0.9	0.7	3.0	2.9	2.4	1.9	1.6	4.0
Other Expenses **19**	14.6	13.0	21.5	18.7	11.1	10.4	9.5	11.9	10.2	11.8	14.0	14.9	25.6
Officers' Compensation **20**	2.5	2.4	8.5	6.7	4.9	3.1	2.3	2.1	2.5	1.0	0.9	1.2	0.3
Operating Margin **21**	•	•	•	•	3.3	4.0	3.0	2.3	2.8	1.6	1.2	2.2	•
Operating Margin Before Officers' Comp. **22**	2.2	•	7.4	6.4	8.1	7.1	5.3	4.4	5.3	2.6	0.4	3.4	•

Selected Average Balance Sheet ($ in Thousands)

Net Receivables 23	569	0	24	120	663	1506	3791	6353	13956	25769	57889	130983	469243
Inventories 24	594	0	26	229	839	2041	4403	7427	13184	29042	52671	97759	486828
Net Property, Plant and Equipment 25	490	0	21	81	340	1671	2172	5424	13754	29280	56296	111877	405565
Total Assets 26	3692	0	105	656	2540	7159	15347	33615	69317	170926	360738	1240502	4077376
Notes and Loans Payable 27	1271	0	85	180	929	3209	4448	8618	21565	59992	117138	382891	1501692
All Other Liabilities 28	1232	0	39	168	771	1527	3743	12875	19542	36714	109372	469306	1665046
Net Worth 29	1189	0	-19	308	840	2423	7155	12122	28210	74220	134228	388304	910639

Selected Financial Ratios (Times to 1)

Current Ratio 30	1.7	•	1.2	2.5	2.0	1.4	2.0	1.8	2.0	2.1	2.0	2.1	1.2
Quick Ratio 31	0.9	•	0.7	1.3	1.0	0.6	1.1	0.9	1.1	1.1	0.9	1.1	0.5
Net Sales to Working Capital 32	5.3	•	26.2	6.0	5.3	10.0	4.5	4.6	4.7	3.9	4.2	3.5	8.4
Coverage Ratio 33	2.7	4.6	1.0	3.0	4.5	5.6	5.1	3.5	4.5	2.6	2.7	2.7	2.0
Total Asset Turnover 34	1.0	•	3.2	2.3	2.0	1.7	1.5	1.3	1.3	0.9	0.9	0.6	0.6
Inventory Turnover 35	3.8	•	6.0	4.0	4.0	3.8	3.6	3.7	4.3	3.4	4.0	3.8	2.5
Receivables Turnover 36	6.7	•	14.5	10.8	7.4	9.3	6.2	7.1	6.6	6.1	6.4	5.4	5.0
Total Liabilities to Net Worth 37	2.1	•	1.1	1.1	2.0	2.0	1.1	1.8	1.5	1.3	1.7	2.2	3.5
Current Assets to Working Capital 38	2.4	•	5.1	1.7	2.0	3.5	2.0	2.2	2.0	1.9	2.0	1.9	5.4
Current Liabilities to Working Capital 39	1.4	•	4.1	0.7	1.0	2.5	1.0	1.2	1.0	0.9	1.0	0.9	4.4
Working Capital to Net Sales 40	0.2	•	0.0	0.2	0.2	0.1	0.2	0.2	0.2	0.3	0.2	0.3	0.1
Inventory to Working Capital 41	0.8	•	2.0	0.7	0.8	1.7	0.8	0.8	0.7	0.7	0.8	0.5	1.8
Total Receipts to Cash Flow 42	6.5	9.3	6.1	5.7	9.4	8.4	9.4	7.7	7.8	7.3	6.8	5.7	3.6
Cost of Goods to Cash Flow 43	3.9	6.2	2.8	3.4	6.2	5.5	6.5	4.8	4.9	4.6	4.2	3.0	1.8
Cash Flow to Total Debt 44	0.2	•	0.4	0.8	0.3	0.3	0.3	0.3	0.3	0.2	0.2	0.1	0.2

Selected Financial Factors (in Percentages)

Debt Ratio 45	67.8	•	117.8	53.0	66.9	66.2	53.4	63.9	59.3	56.6	62.8	68.7	77.7
Return on Total Assets 46	7.9	•	4.1	6.0	7.2	10.3	8.5	6.2	8.0	6.3	6.8	6.3	9.7
Return on Equity Before Income Taxes 47	15.6	•	•	8.4	17.0	25.1	14.6	12.3	15.3	8.8	11.6	12.7	21.8
Return on Equity After Income Taxes 48	11.7	•	0.5	7.6	15.4	23.8	12.9	10.2	12.7	8.0	9.1	7.3	13.8
Profit Margin (Before Income Tax) 49	4.9	9.8	0.0	1.7	2.8	5.1	4.5	3.4	4.8	4.2	4.5	7.0	8.3
Profit Margin (After Income Tax) 50	3.7	7.3	•	1.5	2.5	4.8	4.0	2.8	4.0	3.8	3.6	4.0	5.3

Table II
Corporations with Net Income

OTHER MISCELLANEOUS MANUFACTURING

MONEY AMOUNTS AND SIZE OF ASSETS IN THOUSANDS OF DOLLARS

Item Description for Accounting Period 7/10 Through 6/11	Total	Zero Assets	Under 500	500 to 1,000	1,000 to 5,000	5,000 to 10,000	10,000 to 25,000	25,000 to 50,000	50,000 to 100,000	100,000 to 250,000	250,000 to 500,000	500,000 to 2,500,000	2,500,000 and over
Number of Enterprises **1**	9720	368	6821	•	1248	288	199	73	47	28	20	10	•
Revenues ($ in Thousands)													
Net Sales **2**	54955941	1598608	3046354	•	7573999	3702675	4642776	3802589	4732402	5003026	7239011	7349465	•
Interest **3**	182147	1054	242	•	1220	927	2791	962	12006	7469	41555	40059	•
Rents **4**	15655	43	0	•	1656	315	941	112	354	3467	6064	2296	•
Royalties **5**	973926	160	0	•	0	0	11715	0	3746	33830	48039	69412	•
Other Portfolio Income **6**	634234	237918	0	•	3886	31474	6421	7978	37540	2056	18450	264985	•
Other Receipts **7**	744070	52664	32216	•	19602	-8161	59077	25779	27440	83360	171462	19412	•
Total Receipts **8**	57505973	1890447	3078812	•	7600363	3727230	4723721	3837420	4813488	5133208	7524581	7745629	•
Average Total Receipts **9**	5916	5137	451	•	6090	12942	23737	52567	102415	183329	376229	774563	•
Operating Costs/Operating Income (%)													
Cost of Operations **10**	57.5	64.0	45.4	•	65.3	58.7	67.1	61.2	61.0	60.9	59.1	50.7	•
Salaries and Wages **11**	10.9	11.8	12.7	•	7.5	8.8	8.5	9.7	10.0	9.3	11.8	12.2	•
Taxes Paid **12**	2.1	2.0	2.3	•	2.3	1.9	2.0	1.8	1.8	1.8	1.9	2.3	•
Interest Paid **13**	2.0	3.0	1.0	•	0.6	0.9	0.8	0.9	1.0	1.9	2.7	2.4	•
Depreciation **14**	2.9	1.2	0.8	•	1.5	2.9	2.2	1.9	3.0	3.0	2.8	3.9	•
Amortization and Depletion **15**	0.7	0.7	0.4	•	0.1	0.1	0.2	0.3	0.4	0.7	0.8	1.5	•
Pensions and Other Deferred Comp. **16**	0.7	0.2	0.5	•	0.5	0.4	0.5	0.6	0.9	0.5	1.0	1.1	•
Employee Benefits **17**	1.8	0.7	1.6	•	1.0	1.9	1.8	1.6	1.9	1.5	2.0	2.7	•
Advertising **18**	1.9	2.0	1.7	•	0.8	0.9	0.5	1.7	2.1	2.3	2.0	1.0	•
Other Expenses **19**	12.6	10.7	15.6	•	10.3	11.0	7.7	11.3	9.4	10.4	14.3	14.3	•
Officers' Compensation **20**	2.3	1.6	8.3	•	4.6	3.2	2.0	2.2	2.7	0.8	0.9	1.0	•
Operating Margin **21**	4.7	2.1	9.8	•	5.7	9.3	6.7	6.8	5.9	6.8	0.5	6.8	•
Operating Margin Before Officers' Comp. **22**	7.0	3.7	18.1	•	10.2	12.6	8.7	9.1	8.6	7.6	1.4	7.7	•

Selected Average Balance Sheet ($ in Thousands)

Net Receivables 23	838	0	43	765	1756	3424	6611	13031	24797	61285	137168
Inventories 24	842	0	33	751	1400	4324	8495	12662	30780	44729	91360
Net Property, Plant and Equipment 25	751	0	24	318	1647	2359	5703	15222	34111	61000	121725
Total Assets 26	5111	0	140	2547	7039	15254	34150	68991	170569	356839	1222973
Notes and Loans Payable 27	1502	0	69	714	2128	3984	7036	19210	44679	114298	302920
All Other Liabilities 28	1526	0	43	773	1511	3176	10020	18340	34866	112304	468271
Net Worth 29	2083	0	27	1060	3400	8094	17094	31441	91024	130237	451782

Selected Financial Ratios (Times to 1)

Current Ratio 30	2.2	1.6	•	2.3	1.7	2.1	2.1	2.3	2.4	2.0	2.3
Quick Ratio 31	1.1	1.1	•	1.2	1.0	0.9	1.1	1.2	1.3	1.0	1.2
Net Sales to Working Capital 32	4.2	11.6	•	5.2	7.7	4.3	4.2	4.7	3.9	4.3	3.1
Coverage Ratio 33	5.9	11.9	7.9	11.6	12.8	9.6	11.4	8.7	6.2	3.1	6.3
Total Asset Turnover 34	1.1	3.2	•	2.4	1.8	1.5	1.5	1.5	1.0	1.0	0.6
Inventory Turnover 35	3.9	6.1	•	5.3	5.4	3.8	3.6	4.8	3.5	4.8	4.1
Receivables Turnover 36	6.9	10.9	•	9.2	8.6	7.6	6.8	8.0	7.2	7.5	5.7
Total Liabilities to Net Worth 37	1.5	4.1	•	1.4	1.1	1.0	0.9	1.2	0.9	1.7	1.7
Current Assets to Working Capital 38	1.9	2.6	•	1.8	2.4	1.9	1.9	1.8	1.7	2.0	1.8
Current Liabilities to Working Capital 39	0.9	1.6	•	0.8	1.4	0.9	0.9	0.8	0.7	1.0	0.8
Working Capital to Net Sales 40	0.2	0.1	•	0.2	0.1	0.2	0.2	0.2	0.3	0.2	0.3
Inventory to Working Capital 41	0.7	0.8	•	0.7	1.0	0.8	0.8	0.6	0.7	0.7	0.4
Total Receipts to Cash Flow 42	5.5	4.4	5.3	7.6	6.0	5.9	7.4	6.6	5.6	6.2	4.7
Cost of Goods to Cash Flow 43	3.2	2.0	3.4	4.9	3.5	3.6	5.0	4.0	3.4	3.7	2.4
Cash Flow to Total Debt 44	0.3	0.9	•	0.5	0.6	0.5	0.4	0.4	0.4	0.3	0.2

Selected Financial Factors (in Percentages)

Debt Ratio 45	59.3	80.4	•	58.4	51.7	49.9	46.9	54.4	46.6	63.5	63.1
Return on Total Assets 46	12.9	37.9	•	15.7	19.8	13.5	14.4	12.6	12.1	8.6	9.2
Return on Equity Before Income Taxes 47	26.3	177.0	•	34.4	37.8	24.1	24.7	24.5	19.0	16.0	21.1
Return on Equity After Income Taxes 48	21.7	175.0	•	32.8	36.3	21.7	22.5	21.4	18.0	13.1	14.1
Profit Margin (Before Income Tax) 49	9.7	10.9	20.6	6.0	10.0	7.9	8.6	7.7	9.7	5.8	13.0
Profit Margin (After Income Tax) 50	8.0	10.7	17.4	5.7	9.6	7.1	7.8	6.7	9.2	4.7	8.6

166

Table I

Corporations with and without Net Income

MOTOR VEHICLE AND MOTOR VEHICLE PARTS AND SUPPLIES

MONEY AMOUNTS AND SIZE OF ASSETS IN THOUSANDS OF DOLLARS

Item Description for Accounting Period 7/10 Through 6/11	Total	Zero Assets	Under 500	500 to 1,000	1,000 to 5,000	5,000 to 10,000	10,000 to 25,000	25,000 to 50,000	50,000 to 100,000	100,000 to 250,000	250,000 to 500,000	500,000 to 2,500,000	2,500,000 and over
Number of Enterprises **1**	19186	2145	11721	1976	2426	328	347	132	40	35	16	14	6
Revenues ($ in Thousands)													
Net Sales **2**	203928629	3170670	10834625	4266936	14879086	5235924	13050368	10194955	6242489	9279388	15124364	44594818	67055004
Interest **3**	2109089	3526	40	1422	9967	3806	8046	2304	2265	18484	3827	145840	1909562
Rents **4**	553570	9	0	1053	3096	563	2234	3560	5572	7824	760	35100	493799
Royalties **5**	51369	2369	0	0	0	0	0	0	27	129	10	10316	38517
Other Portfolio Income **6**	1524300	5777	795	5631	7878	12297	23007	15805	9107	47186	45482	394247	957090
Other Receipts **7**	1938477	-75877	40194	14507	134931	39771	107957	96349	33250	139676	60034	281622	1066064
Total Receipts **8**	210105434	3106474	10875654	4289549	15034958	5292361	13191612	10312973	6292710	9492687	15234477	45461943	71520036
Average Total Receipts **9**	10951	1448	928	2171	6197	16135	38016	78129	157318	271220	952155	3247282	11920006
Operating Costs/Operating Income (%)													
Cost of Operations **10**	80.7	81.5	86.1	76.0	77.4	77.9	80.0	77.9	80.7	78.9	86.2	87.9	75.7
Salaries and Wages **11**	4.4	4.2	4.3	7.6	6.1	6.4	7.2	7.5	6.2	6.1	3.5	3.0	3.5
Taxes Paid **12**	0.8	1.5	0.9	1.4	1.4	1.4	1.2	1.2	1.2	1.2	0.5	0.7	0.6
Interest Paid **13**	1.3	1.2	0.3	0.6	0.5	0.5	0.5	0.7	0.6	1.0	0.7	0.7	2.6
Depreciation **14**	4.7	0.4	0.3	0.8	0.5	0.6	1.0	1.0	1.4	1.6	0.7	1.5	12.2
Amortization and Depletion **15**	0.1	0.8	0.0	0.1	0.0	0.1	0.1	0.2	0.2	0.4	0.2	0.1	0.1
Pensions and Other Deferred Comp. **16**	0.3	0.2	0.0	0.1	0.1	0.1	0.1	0.2	0.1	0.2	0.2	0.1	0.5
Employee Benefits **17**	0.6	0.4	0.2	0.5	0.6	0.3	0.8	0.8	0.6	0.8	0.5	0.4	0.7
Advertising **18**	1.5	1.9	0.3	0.6	0.6	0.4	0.3	0.4	0.3	0.8	1.6	2.7	1.8
Other Expenses **19**	6.7	6.7	6.4	9.2	8.3	7.2	6.4	7.0	6.0	6.8	4.1	4.6	8.3
Officers' Compensation **20**	0.7	1.0	1.8	2.8	2.1	2.3	1.1	1.3	0.7	0.6	0.4	0.2	0.1
Operating Margin **21**	•	0.4	•	0.2	2.5	2.2	1.4	1.9	2.0	1.6	1.2	•	•
Operating Margin Before Officers' Comp. **22**	•	1.4	1.3	3.0	4.5	4.6	2.5	3.2	2.7	2.2	1.6	•	•

Selected Average Balance Sheet ($ in Thousands)

Item													
Net Receivables 23	2813	0	37	110	579	1779	4133	8166	15065	27100	71696	325576	6926999
Inventories 24	1343	0	39	287	798	3215	6054	14769	26615	41105	111820	442759	1202516
Net Property, Plant and Equipment 25	1719	0	8	112	185	653	1385	3583	13225	21183	40353	143202	4521297
Total Assets 26	7651	0	120	730	2149	7245	15458	35546	72452	155571	374103	1325599	15568280
Notes and Loans Payable 27	2680	0	55	261	553	1879	4715	11448	23739	52290	92713	407044	5867029
All Other Liabilities 28	3418	0	48	207	604	2729	5393	12472	25813	49506	169197	665885	7323562
Net Worth 29	1553	0	18	262	993	2638	5350	11626	22900	53775	112193	252670	2377688

Selected Financial Ratios (Times to 1)

Item													
Current Ratio 30	1.5	•	2.0	2.2	2.2	1.8	1.8	1.5	1.3	1.6	1.5	1.2	1.4
Quick Ratio 31	1.0	•	1.2	1.1	1.1	0.8	0.8	0.6	0.6	0.6	0.7	0.5	1.2
Net Sales to Working Capital 32	6.9	•	18.1	7.1	6.5	6.0	6.8	8.0	13.4	7.5	10.5	22.1	4.0
Coverage Ratio 33	2.0	•	0.5	2.3	8.7	7.8	5.6	5.6	5.8	5.4	3.7	1.2	1.1
Total Asset Turnover 34	1.4	•	7.7	3.0	2.9	2.2	2.4	2.2	2.2	1.7	2.5	2.4	0.7
Inventory Turnover 35	6.4	•	20.6	5.7	5.9	3.9	5.0	4.1	4.7	5.1	7.3	6.3	7.0
Receivables Turnover 36	3.8	•	28.4	21.5	10.2	9.3	10.1	9.9	11.6	10.4	14.0	9.3	1.6
Total Liabilities to Net Worth 37	3.9	•	5.8	1.8	1.2	1.7	1.9	2.1	2.2	1.9	2.3	4.2	5.5
Current Assets to Working Capital 38	3.2	•	2.0	1.8	1.8	2.3	2.3	2.9	4.4	2.7	2.8	6.3	3.3
Current Liabilities to Working Capital 39	2.2	•	1.0	0.8	0.8	1.3	1.3	1.9	3.4	1.7	1.8	5.3	2.3
Working Capital to Net Sales 40	0.1	•	0.1	0.1	0.2	0.2	0.1	0.1	0.1	0.1	0.1	0.0	0.2
Inventory to Working Capital 41	0.9	•	0.7	0.9	0.9	1.1	1.2	1.6	2.3	1.4	1.3	3.1	0.4
Total Receipts to Cash Flow 42	15.0	30.5	21.9	13.7	10.9	12.2	13.8	12.1	14.0	11.2	19.4	25.7	12.7
Cost of Goods to Cash Flow 43	12.1	24.9	18.9	10.4	8.4	9.5	11.1	9.4	11.3	8.8	16.7	22.6	9.6
Cash Flow to Total Debt 44	0.1	•	0.4	0.3	0.5	0.3	0.3	0.1	0.2	0.2	0.2	0.1	0.1

Selected Financial Factors (in Percentages)

Item													
Debt Ratio 45	79.7	•	85.2	64.1	53.8	63.6	65.4	67.3	68.4	65.4	70.0	80.9	84.7
Return on Total Assets 46	3.5	•	1.0	3.9	11.4	8.4	7.3	8.1	7.4	9.4	7.0	2.0	2.2
Return on Equity Before Income Taxes 47	8.5	•	•	6.1	21.8	20.1	17.3	20.2	19.3	22.2	17.2	1.8	1.8
Return on Equity After Income Taxes 48	6.2	•	•	5.9	20.1	17.8	15.0	18.5	17.8	17.0	14.1	•	0.2
Profit Margin (Before Income Tax) 49	1.2	•	•	0.7	3.5	3.3	2.5	3.0	2.8	4.5	2.0	0.1	0.4
Profit Margin (After Income Tax) 50	0.9	•	•	0.7	3.3	2.9	2.1	2.8	2.6	3.4	1.7	•	0.0

Table II
Corporations with Net Income

MOTOR VEHICLE AND MOTOR VEHICLE PARTS AND SUPPLIES

MONEY AMOUNTS AND SIZE OF ASSETS IN THOUSANDS OF DOLLARS

Item Description for Accounting Period 7/10 Through 6/11	Total	Zero Assets	Under 500	500 to 1,000	1,000 to 5,000	5,000 to 10,000	10,000 to 25,000	25,000 to 50,000	50,000 to 100,000	100,000 to 250,000	250,000 to 500,000	500,000 to 2,500,000	2,500,000 and over
Number of Enterprises 1	12494	937	7149	1593	2031	320	270	105	31	30	12	•	•
Revenues ($ in Thousands)													
Net Sales 2	155721736	1121600	7276743	3585723	13287276	5113257	10719690	8870541	4970284	8459696	12699389	•	•
Interest 3	1283218	56	15	939	9697	3696	6705	1401	1644	14597	2992	•	•
Rents 4	365822	7	0	0	2687	563	2234	441	259	1941	741	•	•
Royalties 5	50377	2350	0	0	0	0	0	0	0	129	0	•	•
Other Portfolio Income 6	1255956	5300	0	5631	6501	12297	22613	12126	8936	44891	45304	•	•
Other Receipts 7	1239869	23721	31515	7933	112789	39589	91074	78052	27292	129918	42726	•	•
Total Receipts 8	159916978	1153034	7308273	3600226	13418950	5169402	10842316	8962561	5008415	8651172	12791152	•	•
Average Total Receipts 9	12800	1231	1022	2260	6607	16154	40157	85358	161562	288372	1065929	•	•
Operating Costs/Operating Income (%)													
Cost of Operations 10	80.6	70.1	86.4	75.5	78.3	77.8	79.5	78.2	79.7	79.2	86.2	•	•
Salaries and Wages 11	4.8	8.4	3.0	7.1	5.5	6.2	7.0	7.0	6.3	6.1	3.2	•	•
Taxes Paid 12	0.9	1.4	0.6	1.3	1.3	1.4	1.2	1.1	1.1	1.2	0.5	•	•
Interest Paid 13	1.1	1.9	0.2	0.6	0.5	0.5	0.4	0.5	0.5	0.9	0.4	•	•
Depreciation 14	3.6	0.5	0.2	0.7	0.5	0.6	1.0	0.9	1.3	1.4	0.6	•	•
Amortization and Depletion 15	0.1	1.4	0.0	0.1	0.0	0.0	0.0	0.1	0.1	0.3	0.1	•	•
Pensions and Other Deferred Comp. 16	0.3	0.2	0.0	0.1	0.1	0.3	0.1	0.2	0.2	0.2	0.2	•	•
Employee Benefits 17	0.6	0.7	0.2	0.3	0.4	0.8	0.6	0.8	0.6	0.7	0.4	•	•
Advertising 18	1.1	0.3	0.2	0.4	0.6	0.4	0.3	0.3	0.3	0.6	1.2	•	•
Other Expenses 19	6.1	13.3	6.0	8.4	7.5	6.9	6.1	6.4	6.0	6.2	3.9	•	•
Officers' Compensation 20	0.7	2.2	1.4	2.7	1.9	2.4	1.1	1.3	0.7	0.6	0.4	•	•
Operating Margin 21	0.2	•	1.7	2.7	3.5	2.7	2.7	3.3	3.2	2.5	2.8	•	•
Operating Margin Before Officers' Comp. 22	0.9	1.8	3.1	5.4	5.4	5.1	3.7	4.6	3.9	3.1	3.2	•	•

Selected Average Balance Sheet ($ in Thousands)

Net Receivables 23	2808	0	42	101	604	1721	4155	8922	16526	27890	75435
Inventories 24	1300	0	26	225	727	3094	5905	14469	25934	40499	113036
Net Property, Plant and Equipment 25	1584	0	5	118	191	663	1401	3544	12258	17948	43688
Total Assets 26	8060	0	102	728	2199	7235	14976	35273	73115	156843	376996
Notes and Loans Payable 27	2641	0	40	201	563	1572	4059	9802	20061	53317	58215
All Other Liabilities 28	3401	0	28	188	592	2636	5232	11853	25191	46003	153110
Net Worth 29	2018	0	34	339	1045	3027	5685	13618	27862	57523	165671

Selected Financial Ratios (Times to 1)

Current Ratio 30	1.5	•	2.4	2.3	2.3	1.8	1.8	1.6	1.4	1.6	1.8
Quick Ratio 31	1.0	•	1.7	1.2	1.2	0.8	0.8	0.7	0.7	0.6	0.8
Net Sales to Working Capital 32	6.9	•	19.4	7.2	6.6	5.9	7.2	7.8	10.1	7.4	8.7
Coverage Ratio 33	3.7	2.3	9.5	6.6	10.7	9.3	9.6	9.7	8.4	7.2	9.7
Total Asset Turnover 34	1.5	•	9.9	3.1	3.0	2.2	2.7	2.4	2.2	1.8	2.8
Inventory Turnover 35	7.7	•	34.0	7.5	7.0	4.0	5.3	4.6	4.9	5.5	8.1
Receivables Turnover 36	6.2	•	31.9	30.8	11.1	9.8	10.3	10.2	11.3	13.1	15.9
Total Liabilities to Net Worth 37	3.0	•	2.0	1.1	1.1	1.4	1.6	1.6	1.6	1.7	1.3
Current Assets to Working Capital 38	2.9	•	1.7	1.8	1.8	2.2	2.3	2.6	3.3	2.6	2.2
Current Liabilities to Working Capital 39	1.9	•	0.7	0.8	0.8	1.2	1.3	1.6	2.3	1.6	1.2
Working Capital to Net Sales 40	0.1	•	0.1	0.1	0.2	0.2	0.1	0.1	0.1	0.1	0.1
Inventory to Working Capital 41	0.9	•	0.5	0.9	0.8	1.1	1.2	1.4	1.7	1.4	1.1
Total Receipts to Cash Flow 42	13.0	8.3	15.8	11.1	10.1	11.9	11.9	11.1	12.0	10.5	15.5
Cost of Goods to Cash Flow 43	10.5	5.8	13.7	8.4	7.9	9.2	9.4	8.7	9.6	8.3	13.4
Cash Flow to Total Debt 44	0.2	•	0.9	0.5	0.6	0.3	0.4	0.4	0.3	0.3	0.3

Selected Financial Factors (in Percentages)

Debt Ratio 45	75.0	•	67.0	53.4	52.5	58.2	62.0	61.4	61.9	63.3	56.1
Return on Total Assets 46	6.2	•	23.3	11.5	14.8	9.5	11.3	11.5	9.9	11.3	10.9
Return on Equity Before Income Taxes 47	18.0	•	63.2	20.9	28.2	20.2	26.7	26.7	22.9	26.5	22.3
Return on Equity After Income Taxes 48	15.3	•	62.4	20.7	26.3	18.1	23.9	24.8	21.2	20.8	19.5
Profit Margin (Before Income Tax) 49	2.9	2.4	2.1	3.1	4.5	3.8	3.8	4.3	4.0	5.4	3.5
Profit Margin (After Income Tax) 50	2.5	2.2	2.1	3.1	4.2	3.4	3.4	4.0	3.7	4.2	3.1

Table I
Corporations with and without Net Income

LUMBER AND OTHER CONSTRUCTION MATERIALS

MONEY AMOUNTS AND SIZE OF ASSETS IN THOUSANDS OF DOLLARS

Item Description for Accounting Period 7/10 Through 6/11	Total	Zero Assets	Under 500	500 to 1,000	1,000 to 5,000	5,000 to 10,000	10,000 to 25,000	25,000 to 50,000	50,000 to 100,000	100,000 to 250,000	250,000 to 500,000	500,000 to 2,500,000	2,500,000 and over
Number of Enterprises **1**	16413	1586	8064	1381	4119	732	384	85	38	12	7	5	0
Revenues ($ in Thousands)													
Net Sales **2**	91427702	458192	5488037	3411976	24508006	15135603	13818253	7686406	5445776	4034095	3599186	7842171	0
Interest **3**	64090	672	76	1978	15359	4053	10256	4449	7920	3251	11901	4175	0
Rents **4**	19341	0	128	472	5887	2891	2531	1475	102	1538	2688	1629	0
Royalties **5**	8578	0	0	0	0	29	0	40	642	41	7826	0	0
Other Portfolio Income **6**	103556	3550	235	641	32299	7481	14790	1829	2709	8533	23844	7644	0
Other Receipts **7**	510669	1417	25024	4787	178157	56724	85494	35971	28997	40917	33431	19752	0
Total Receipts **8**	92133936	463831	5513500	3419854	24739708	15206781	13931324	7730170	5486146	4088375	3678876	7875371	0
Average Total Receipts **9**	5613	292	684	2476	6006	20774	36279	90943	144372	340698	525554	1575074	•
Operating Costs/Operating Income (%)													
Cost of Operations **10**	78.8	77.9	69.1	67.9	75.2	84.5	80.7	82.8	79.6	83.2	78.8	81.0	•
Salaries and Wages **11**	7.2	5.1	5.8	7.3	8.3	5.8	7.8	6.6	7.9	5.7	9.8	6.9	•
Taxes Paid **12**	1.3	1.0	1.5	2.6	1.6	0.9	1.3	1.0	1.2	1.0	1.9	0.7	•
Interest Paid **13**	0.8	1.1	0.5	0.6	0.5	0.8	0.5	0.7	0.5	1.0	1.8	1.7	•
Depreciation **14**	1.0	3.0	0.6	1.9	0.8	0.6	1.1	0.8	1.2	1.3	2.0	1.2	•
Amortization and Depletion **15**	0.1	0.2	0.1	0.0	0.0	0.0	0.1	0.1	0.1	0.4	0.8	0.5	•
Pensions and Other Deferred Comp. **16**	0.2	•	0.1	0.1	0.3	0.1	0.2	0.1	0.2	0.2	0.1	0.2	•
Employee Benefits **17**	0.7	0.4	0.5	0.4	0.7	0.5	0.9	0.7	0.9	0.6	1.2	0.5	•
Advertising **18**	0.3	0.1	1.3	0.9	0.4	0.2	0.2	0.2	0.2	0.2	0.3	0.1	•
Other Expenses **19**	8.2	17.6	15.5	14.6	9.6	5.7	6.1	6.7	7.1	7.4	7.5	6.4	•
Officers' Compensation **20**	1.6	1.0	5.3	3.6	2.2	1.0	1.3	0.7	0.9	0.5	0.8	0.2	•
Operating Margin **21**	•	•	•	•	0.5	•	•	•	0.3	•	•	0.4	•
Operating Margin Before Officers' Comp. **22**	1.4	•	4.8	3.6	2.7	0.8	1.1	0.3	1.1	•	•	0.6	•

Selected Average Balance Sheet ($ in Thousands)

	•	•	•	•	•	•	•	•	•	•	•	•
Net Receivables 23	585	0	22	199	702	1910	4081	9115	16594	33840	79403	185118
Inventories 24	641	0	40	201	663	2968	4066	12506	21267	34130	42279	176639
Net Property, Plant and Equipment 25	378	0	12	149	359	829	2492	4682	10128	23316	104792	212884
Total Assets 26	2283	0	125	792	2242	7035	15112	37322	69304	151028	361845	1006932
Notes and Loans Payable 27	698	0	42	324	639	2257	3919	16864	15752	52675	85773	323272
All Other Liabilities 28	690	0	71	305	674	2497	3115	9054	17980	46794	116107	341204
Net Worth 29	895	0	12	163	930	2282	8078	11404	35571	51559	159966	342456

Selected Financial Ratios (Times to 1)

	•	•	•	•	•	•	•	•	•	•	•	•
Current Ratio 30	1.8	•	1.3	1.7	2.0	1.4	2.4	1.7	2.1	1.4	1.5	2.2
Quick Ratio 31	0.9	•	0.8	0.8	1.1	0.6	1.3	0.6	1.0	0.7	0.9	1.1
Net Sales to Working Capital 32	8.0	•	27.2	9.7	7.0	12.3	5.5	8.5	5.5	17.0	11.2	6.5
Coverage Ratio 33	1.7	•	1.0	1.3	3.8	1.3	2.2	1.2	3.2	0.9	•	1.5
Total Asset Turnover 34	2.4	•	5.5	3.1	2.7	2.9	2.4	2.4	2.1	2.2	1.4	1.6
Inventory Turnover 35	6.8	•	11.7	8.4	6.7	5.9	7.1	6.0	5.4	8.2	9.6	7.2
Receivables Turnover 36	9.3	•	27.6	14.8	8.1	10.3	9.5	9.9	8.8	10.3	6.8	7.1
Total Liabilities to Net Worth 37	1.6	•	9.7	3.9	1.4	2.1	0.9	2.3	0.9	1.9	1.3	1.9
Current Assets to Working Capital 38	2.2	•	3.9	2.4	2.0	3.4	1.7	2.5	1.9	3.7	3.2	1.8
Current Liabilities to Working Capital 39	1.2	•	2.9	1.4	1.0	2.4	0.7	1.5	0.9	2.7	2.2	0.8
Working Capital to Net Sales 40	0.1	•	0.0	0.1	0.1	0.1	0.2	0.1	0.2	0.1	0.1	0.2
Inventory to Working Capital 41	0.9	•	1.6	1.1	0.8	1.7	0.7	1.2	0.9	1.7	1.1	0.8
Total Receipts to Cash Flow 42	16.6	12.2	9.0	10.5	12.6	23.4	21.9	22.0	17.5	20.5	131.7	18.1
Cost of Goods to Cash Flow 43	13.1	9.5	6.2	7.1	9.5	19.7	17.7	18.2	13.9	17.0	103.9	14.7
Cash Flow to Total Debt 44	0.2	•	0.7	0.4	0.4	0.2	0.2	0.2	0.2	0.2	0.0	0.1

Selected Financial Factors (in Percentages)

	•	•	•	•	•	•	•	•	•	•	•	•
Debt Ratio 45	60.8	•	90.6	79.5	58.5	67.6	69.4	46.5	48.7	65.9	55.8	66.0
Return on Total Assets 46	3.2	•	2.8	2.7	5.2	3.2	2.1	2.7	3.1	2.1	•	4.0
Return on Equity Before Income Taxes 47	3.2	•	0.2	3.3	9.3	2.2	1.0	2.7	4.1	•	•	3.7
Return on Equity After Income Taxes 48	2.4	•	•	0.6	8.7	1.4	0.0	2.2	3.7	•	•	1.5
Profit Margin (Before Income Tax) 49	0.5	•	0.0	0.2	1.5	0.2	0.1	0.6	1.0	•	•	0.8
Profit Margin (After Income Tax) 50	0.4	•	•	0.0	1.4	0.2	0.0	0.5	0.9	•	•	0.3

Table II

Corporations with Net Income

LUMBER AND OTHER CONSTRUCTION MATERIALS

MONEY AMOUNTS AND SIZE OF ASSETS IN THOUSANDS OF DOLLARS

Item Description for Accounting Period 7/10 Through 6/11	Total	Zero Assets	Under 500	500 to 1,000	1,000 to 5,000	5,000 to 10,000	10,000 to 25,000	25,000 to 50,000	50,000 to 100,000	100,000 to 250,000	250,000 to 500,000	500,000 to 2,500,000	2,500,000 and over
Number of Enterprises **1**	10322	811	5141	1032	2521	482	251	51	•	7	•	0	0
Revenues ($ in Thousands)													
Net Sales **2**	62889728	326724	3702698	2161981	17753083	11668105	10374807	4900417	•	2920850	•	0	0
Interest **3**	23947	672	49	1721	11881	2656	2781	948	•	1278	•	0	0
Rents **4**	11361	0	0	472	3010	2422	2265	70	•	0	•	0	0
Royalties **5**	0	0	0	0	0	0	0	0	•	0	•	0	0
Other Portfolio Income **6**	54104	0	126	634	22248	5254	5974	841	•	8338	•	0	0
Other Receipts **7**	281310	85	16558	2534	72637	42278	69695	17520	•	30402	•	0	0
Total Receipts **8**	63260450	327481	3719431	2167342	17862859	11720715	10455522	4919796	•	2960868	•	0	0
Average Total Receipts **9**	6129	404	723	2100	7086	24317	41655	96467	•	422981	•	•	•
Operating Costs/Operating Income (%)													
Cost of Operations **10**	78.1	76.8	62.0	60.2	74.8	84.8	81.2	84.5	•	83.8	•	•	•
Salaries and Wages **11**	6.7	2.6	5.2	9.7	7.7	5.3	7.3	5.3	•	5.2	•	•	•
Taxes Paid **12**	1.2	0.6	1.2	3.7	1.4	0.7	1.1	0.8	•	0.8	•	•	•
Interest Paid **13**	0.5	0.0	0.4	0.7	0.4	0.4	0.4	0.5	•	0.9	•	•	•
Depreciation **14**	0.8	0.3	0.6	1.4	0.7	0.4	0.8	0.6	•	1.4	•	•	•
Amortization and Depletion **15**	0.1	0.2	0.0	0.0	0.0	0.0	0.1	0.1	•	0.5	•	•	•
Pensions and Other Deferred Comp. **16**	0.2	•	0.1	0.2	0.0	0.1	0.2	0.2	•	0.2	•	•	•
Employee Benefits **17**	0.6	0.1	0.6	0.3	0.3	0.5	0.8	0.7	•	0.4	•	•	•
Advertising **18**	0.4	0.0	1.8	1.2	0.4	0.1	0.2	0.1	•	0.2	•	•	•
Other Expenses **19**	7.2	15.9	18.2	15.2	7.9	4.5	5.1	5.2	•	6.0	•	•	•
Officers' Compensation **20**	1.6	0.6	5.5	4.7	2.1	1.1	1.2	0.4	•	0.6	•	•	•
Operating Margin **21**	2.6	2.7	4.3	2.9	3.8	2.0	1.5	1.5	•	0.6	•	•	•
Operating Margin Before Officers' Comp. **22**	4.2	3.3	9.8	7.6	5.9	3.1	2.8	2.0	•	0.6	•	•	•

Selected Average Balance Sheet ($ in Thousands)

Net Receivables 23	582	0	16	174	692	2102	4222	10037	37796
Inventories 24	611	0	23	189	579	3228	4154	14570	27052
Net Property, Plant and Equipment 25	313	0	15	163	280	702	1747	3286	24533
Total Assets 26	2173	0	119	804	2187	7117	14970	38756	140892
Notes and Loans Payable 27	605	0	27	283	537	1834	3777	15990	35145
All Other Liabilities 28	566	0	47	285	644	1587	2979	8893	39981
Net Worth 29	1001	0	46	236	1006	3695	8215	13873	65766

Selected Financial Ratios (Times to 1)

Current Ratio 30	2.1	•	1.8	1.8	2.1	2.2	2.7	1.6	1.7
Quick Ratio 31	1.1	•	1.1	0.8	1.2	1.0	1.4	0.6	0.9
Net Sales to Working Capital 32	7.2	•	18.4	7.7	7.8	7.4	5.4	8.0	12.3
Coverage Ratio 33	7.6	94.1	12.8	5.4	13.0	7.2	7.1	4.7	2.5
Total Asset Turnover 34	2.8	•	6.0	2.6	3.2	3.4	2.8	2.5	3.0
Inventory Turnover 35	7.8	•	19.1	6.7	9.1	6.4	8.1	5.6	12.9
Receivables Turnover 36	10.6	•	51.3	13.4	10.1	10.5	11.2	9.4	14.7
Total Liabilities to Net Worth 37	1.2	•	1.6	2.4	1.2	0.9	0.8	1.8	1.1
Current Assets to Working Capital 38	1.9	•	2.2	2.2	1.9	1.9	1.6	2.5	2.4
Current Liabilities to Working Capital 39	0.9	•	1.2	1.2	0.9	0.9	0.6	1.5	1.4
Working Capital to Net Sales 40	0.1	•	0.1	0.1	0.1	0.1	0.2	0.1	0.1
Inventory to Working Capital 41	0.8	•	0.8	1.0	0.7	0.9	0.6	1.3	1.1
Total Receipts to Cash Flow 42	12.3	6.0	5.6	7.0	10.2	17.3	18.0	18.7	19.3
Cost of Goods to Cash Flow 43	9.6	4.6	3.4	4.2	7.6	14.6	14.6	15.8	16.1
Cash Flow to Total Debt 44	0.4	•	1.8	0.5	0.6	0.4	0.3	0.2	0.3

Selected Financial Factors (in Percentages)

Debt Ratio 45	53.9	•	61.7	70.6	54.0	48.1	45.1	64.2	53.3
Return on Total Assets 46	10.2	•	31.3	10.0	15.5	9.6	7.4	6.0	6.8
Return on Equity Before Income Taxes 47	19.1	•	75.3	27.8	31.2	15.9	11.6	13.3	8.7
Return on Equity After Income Taxes 48	18.0	•	74.6	25.3	30.3	15.1	10.8	12.0	8.3
Profit Margin (Before Income Tax) 49	3.1	2.9	4.8	3.1	4.5	2.4	2.3	1.9	1.4
Profit Margin (After Income Tax) 50	3.0	2.8	4.7	2.9	4.3	2.3	2.1	1.7	1.3

Table I

Corporations with and without Net Income

PROFESSIONAL AND COMMERCIAL EQUIPMENT AND SUPPLIES

MONEY AMOUNTS AND SIZE OF ASSETS IN THOUSANDS OF DOLLARS

Item Description for Accounting Period 7/10 Through 6/11		Total	Zero Assets	Under 500	500 to 1,000	1,000 to 5,000	5,000 to 10,000	10,000 to 25,000	25,000 to 50,000	50,000 to 100,000	100,000 to 250,000	250,000 to 500,000	500,000 to 2,500,000	2,500,000 and over
Number of Enterprises	1	33897	2707	23056	2882	4002	508	404	133	86	59	27	21	11
Revenues ($ in Thousands)														
Net Sales	2	255083725	13191134	12135106	7766629	25303678	10123365	16671381	10956302	11334720	19378969	14077614	38444688	75700139
Interest	3	421250	7477	1563	1101	4141	9151	2802	9426	10432	11352	19687	73041	271077
Rents	4	399540	42277	6	0	2556	5115	1140	449	17160	2311	41819	39457	247249
Royalties	5	381328	0	4	0	263	409	22	174	3875	10523	91997	45474	228588
Other Portfolio Income	6	404230	21386	21702	23239	15748	2320	16946	32428	23088	25020	83658	73768	64926
Other Receipts	7	2137498	37942	44648	154600	56204	59814	98042	96054	66777	105664	203599	1051670	162486
Total Receipts	8	258827571	13300216	12203029	7945569	25382590	10200174	16790333	11094833	11456052	19533839	14518374	39728098	76674465
Average Total Receipts	9	7636	4913	529	2757	6342	20079	41560	83420	133210	331082	537718	1891814	6970406
Operating Costs/Operating Income (%)														
Cost of Operations	10	74.1	92.1	57.2	60.7	70.8	70.1	74.2	74.9	73.8	81.5	75.3	80.4	71.2
Salaries and Wages	11	10.9	3.3	9.9	11.5	9.6	11.2	9.3	9.8	9.3	6.8	10.0	8.1	16.2
Taxes Paid	12	1.1	0.4	1.9	1.8	1.4	1.2	1.2	1.3	1.5	0.8	1.1	0.8	1.0
Interest Paid	13	0.8	0.4	0.6	0.4	0.5	0.4	0.5	0.4	0.6	0.6	0.5	0.8	1.5
Depreciation	14	1.6	0.6	0.9	0.5	0.6	0.9	0.8	1.3	1.8	1.1	1.3	1.1	3.2
Amortization and Depletion	15	0.3	0.2	0.1	0.2	0.1	0.2	0.1	0.4	0.4	0.4	0.7	0.6	0.3
Pensions and Other Deferred Comp.	16	0.2	0.0	0.4	0.5	0.2	0.2	0.3	0.2	0.2	0.2	0.2	0.2	0.2
Employee Benefits	17	0.8	0.2	0.8	0.8	0.9	1.2	0.8	0.9	0.7	0.7	1.1	1.1	0.5
Advertising	18	0.9	0.0	1.1	1.2	0.5	0.5	0.9	1.0	0.8	0.7	1.4	0.9	1.0
Other Expenses	19	6.3	3.2	16.9	16.6	10.0	9.3	8.2	7.6	9.9	6.4	8.9	6.8	0.4
Officers' Compensation	20	1.3	0.2	7.2	4.4	3.3	2.7	1.8	1.1	0.7	0.5	0.7	0.4	0.3
Operating Margin	21	1.7	•	3.0	1.4	2.0	2.1	1.9	1.2	0.4	0.4	•	•	4.3
Operating Margin Before Officers' Comp.	22	3.0	•	10.2	5.8	5.3	4.8	3.7	2.3	1.0	0.9	•	•	4.6

Selected Average Balance Sheet ($ in Thousands)

Net Receivables 23	1086	0	28	213	637	2499	5414	12005	21426	48851	89549	244559	1424257
Inventories 24	557	0	26	166	547	1493	3980	7751	14106	27787	55110	167025	397221
Net Property, Plant and Equipment 25	350	0	9	53	276	691	1346	2575	6302	10329	25020	78554	518494
Total Assets 26	4815	0	111	729	2092	7137	15220	36190	69390	154945	355765	1188578	7810013
Notes and Loans Payable 27	1235	0	66	234	920	1678	4434	7675	15698	36302	56103	264378	1978961
All Other Liabilities 28	1879	0	69	217	983	3240	6940	15207	27726	66659	135357	407805	2957364
Net Worth 29	1701	0	-24	279	188	2220	3847	13307	25967	51984	164305	516396	2873688

Selected Financial Ratios (Times to 1)

Current Ratio 30	1.3	•	1.1	2.0	1.5	1.6	1.5	1.5	1.6	1.4	1.5	1.9	1.1
Quick Ratio 31	0.9	•	0.6	1.3	0.9	1.0	0.9	0.9	0.9	0.8	0.9	1.1	0.8
Net Sales to Working Capital 32	11.5	•	63.9	9.2	11.7	9.5	9.6	9.5	7.6	10.7	6.9	6.0	23.4
Coverage Ratio 33	5.5	1.4	6.8	10.3	5.2	7.8	6.1	7.8	3.5	3.0	5.3	3.8	6.1
Total Asset Turnover 34	1.6	•	4.7	3.7	3.0	2.8	2.7	2.3	1.9	2.1	1.5	1.5	0.9
Inventory Turnover 35	10.0	•	11.6	9.9	8.2	9.4	7.7	8.0	6.9	9.6	7.1	8.8	12.3
Receivables Turnover 36	7.6	•	22.9	12.4	9.9	8.1	8.0	6.3	6.8	7.0	5.6	7.0	6.3
Total Liabilities to Net Worth 37	1.8	•	•	1.6	10.1	2.2	3.0	1.7	1.7	2.0	1.2	1.3	1.7
Current Assets to Working Capital 38	3.9	•	10.6	2.0	3.1	2.7	2.8	2.9	2.7	3.3	2.8	2.1	10.9
Current Liabilities to Working Capital 39	2.9	•	9.6	1.0	2.1	1.7	1.8	1.9	1.7	2.3	1.8	1.1	9.9
Working Capital to Net Sales 40	0.1	•	0.0	0.1	0.1	0.1	0.1	0.1	0.1	0.1	0.1	0.2	0.0
Inventory to Working Capital 41	0.9	•	3.7	0.5	0.7	1.0	1.0	0.8	0.9	1.0	0.8	0.6	1.5
Total Receipts to Cash Flow 42	12.8	38.6	6.0	5.8	9.9	9.5	10.8	11.6	10.2	15.9	11.1	12.9	21.4
Cost of Goods to Cash Flow 43	9.5	35.5	3.4	3.5	7.0	6.7	8.0	8.7	7.5	12.9	8.3	10.3	15.3
Cash Flow to Total Debt 44	0.2	•	0.6	1.0	0.3	0.4	0.3	0.3	0.3	0.2	0.2	0.2	0.1

Selected Financial Factors (in Percentages)

Debt Ratio 45	64.7	•	121.5	61.8	91.0	68.9	74.7	63.2	62.6	66.5	53.8	56.6	63.2
Return on Total Assets 46	7.2	•	19.6	15.3	8.6	9.1	8.4	6.3	3.8	4.0	3.6	4.6	8.0
Return on Equity Before Income Taxes 47	16.6	•	•	36.1	77.7	25.6	28.0	15.0	7.3	8.0	6.3	7.8	18.1
Return on Equity After Income Taxes 48	11.6	•	•	34.8	73.9	23.3	23.4	12.0	4.1	4.7	3.2	4.3	11.9
Profit Margin (Before Income Tax) 49	3.8	0.2	3.5	3.7	2.3	2.9	2.6	2.4	1.4	1.3	2.0	2.2	7.6
Profit Margin (After Income Tax) 50	2.6	0.1	3.4	3.6	2.2	2.6	2.2	1.9	0.8	0.7	1.0	1.2	5.0

Table II
Corporations with Net Income

PROFESSIONAL AND COMMERCIAL EQUIPMENT AND SUPPLIES

MONEY AMOUNTS AND SIZE OF ASSETS IN THOUSANDS OF DOLLARS

Item Description for Accounting Period 7/10 Through 6/11		Total	Zero Assets	Under 500	500 to 1,000	1,000 to 5,000	5,000 to 10,000	10,000 to 25,000	25,000 to 50,000	50,000 to 100,000	100,000 to 250,000	250,000 to 500,000	500,000 to 2,500,000	2,500,000 and over
Number of Enterprises	1	22945	1998	15109	2121	2755	399	313	103	60	42	20	17	8
Revenues ($ in Thousands)														
Net Sales	2	207766057	12479007	9251417	5803882	19946216	7361123	14182407	9103332	8711106	14566279	12014705	34599501	59747081
Interest	3	366866	6437	1441	416	2934	2877	1976	7094	5686	10633	18797	70168	238406
Rents	4	289212	42277	0	0	1711	5115	419	449	16045	2308	41819	3740	175329
Royalties	5	324867	0	4	0	263	0	22	0	3875	9515	75912	21703	213575
Other Portfolio Income	6	303378	14010	19955	591	13912	799	15568	32108	9335	13676	83658	53065	46699
Other Receipts	7	1706941	33896	41667	153514	50814	46054	54898	92690	46191	80233	97761	879913	129311
Total Receipts	8	210757321	12575627	9314484	5958403	20015850	7415968	14255290	9235673	8792238	14682644	12332652	35628090	60550401
Average Total Receipts	9	9185	6294	616	2809	7265	18586	45544	89667	146537	349587	616633	2095770	7568800
Operating Costs/Operating Income (%)														
Cost of Operations	10	74.9	94.0	59.1	58.3	69.7	67.0	75.0	73.9	75.6	80.2	77.6	82.4	71.3
Salaries and Wages	11	11.0	2.1	8.4	11.6	9.2	12.4	8.5	9.7	8.0	6.4	8.1	7.3	18.9
Taxes Paid	12	1.0	0.3	1.7	1.6	1.4	1.4	1.1	1.4	1.0	0.8	1.0	0.7	1.0
Interest Paid	13	0.7	0.2	0.4	0.2	0.5	0.4	0.3	0.3	0.4	0.4	0.3	0.5	1.5
Depreciation	14	1.4	0.5	0.9	0.4	0.6	0.8	0.7	1.5	1.5	1.1	1.1	1.0	2.6
Amortization and Depletion	15	0.2	0.1	0.0	0.2	0.0	0.2	0.0	0.3	0.3	0.2	0.4	0.3	0.2
Pensions and Other Deferred Comp.	16	0.2	0.0	0.2	0.6	0.2	0.2	0.2	0.2	0.2	0.2	0.3	0.3	0.1
Employee Benefits	17	0.7	0.2	0.6	0.5	1.0	1.2	0.8	0.9	0.6	0.8	0.8	0.8	0.5
Advertising	18	0.8	0.0	0.6	1.4	0.6	0.5	0.6	1.0	0.7	0.7	1.2	1.0	0.8
Other Expenses	19	4.4	2.3	16.0	15.8	9.1	8.6	7.4	7.0	8.3	5.9	7.8	4.8	•
Officers' Compensation	20	1.2	0.2	5.3	3.9	3.4	3.1	1.8	1.2	0.7	0.4	0.5	0.3	0.3
Operating Margin	21	3.5	0.2	6.8	5.5	4.2	4.5	3.5	2.6	2.8	2.9	0.9	0.5	5.8
Operating Margin Before Officers' Comp.	22	4.7	0.4	12.1	9.3	7.6	7.6	5.3	3.8	3.4	3.3	1.4	0.8	6.2

Selected Average Balance Sheet ($ in Thousands)

Net Receivables 23	1314	0	23	189	645	2606	5448	12143	21307	50956	103081	253889	1730020
Inventories 24	607	0	22	168	530	1432	3880	8423	14190	30787	61835	176974	341841
Net Property, Plant and Equipment 25	422	0	8	49	353	660	1344	2974	5964	11625	26362	78420	598609
Total Assets 26	5661	0	111	719	2267	7001	15280	36230	68226	155957	358409	1141452	8991078
Notes and Loans Payable 27	1181	0	49	153	562	1245	3193	6940	12893	30933	47501	150684	2085410
All Other Liabilities 28	2316	C	40	213	1002	2862	5766	15077	26006	66503	146176	452643	3729375
Net Worth 29	2165	C	22	354	703	2894	6322	14213	29327	58521	164732	538126	3176293

Selected Financial Ratios (Times to 1)

Current Ratio 30	1.4	•	1.9	2.5	1.5	1.7	1.8	1.6	1.7	1.5	1.6	1.9	1.1
Quick Ratio 31	0.9	•	1.1	1.5	0.9	1.2	1.0	0.9	1.0	0.9	0.9	1.0	0.8
Net Sales to Working Capital 32	11.4	•	15.2	7.9	11.9	8.3	8.3	8.9	7.7	9.1	7.1	6.6	31.3
Coverage Ratio 33	8.9	6.6	21.2	36.3	10.2	15.6	13.2	13.3	9.5	10.9	12.3	7.6	7.3
Total Asset Turnover 34	1.6	•	5.5	3.8	3.2	2.6	3.0	2.4	2.1	2.2	1.7	1.8	0.8
Inventory Turnover 35	11.2	•	16.6	9.5	9.5	8.6	8.8	7.8	7.7	9.0	7.5	9.5	15.6
Receivables Turnover 36	7.9	•	34.8	13.7	10.8	7.1	8.7	6.6	7.7	6.9	6.1	7.8	6.0
Total Liabilities to Net Worth 37	1.6	•	4.1	1.0	2.2	1.4	1.4	1.5	1.3	1.7	1.2	1.1	1.8
Current Assets to Working Capital 38	3.8	•	2.1	1.7	2.8	2.5	2.3	2.7	2.5	2.9	2.8	2.1	15.8
Current Liabilities to Working Capital 39	2.8	•	1.1	0.7	1.8	1.5	1.3	1.7	1.5	1.9	1.8	1.1	14.8
Working Capital to Net Sales 40	0.1	•	0.1	0.1	0.1	0.1	0.1	0.1	0.1	0.1	0.1	0.2	0.0
Inventory to Working Capital 41	0.8	•	0.7	0.5	0.9	0.6	0.8	0.7	0.9	0.8	0.8	0.6	1.7
Total Receipts to Cash Flow 42	12.8	35.7	5.1	4.8	8.7	8.4	10.2	10.4	9.3	11.6	10.2	13.6	38.0
Cost of Goods to Cash Flow 43	9.5	33.5	3.0	2.8	6.1	5.7	7.7	7.7	7.1	9.3	7.9	11.2	27.1
Cash Flow to Total Debt 44	0.2	•	1.3	1.6	0.5	0.5	0.5	0.4	0.4	0.3	0.3	0.2	0.0

Selected Financial Factors (in Percentages)

Debt Ratio 45	61.8	•	80.5	50.8	69.0	58.7	58.6	60.8	57.0	62.5	54.0	52.9	64.7
Return on Total Assets 46	10.3	•	43.4	31.9	16.2	14.7	12.7	10.7	8.8	9.2	6.8	7.3	9.4
Return on Equity Before Income Taxes 47	23.9	•	212.0	62.9	47.0	33.4	28.5	25.2	18.3	22.3	13.5	13.4	22.9
Return on Equity After Income Taxes 48	18.1	•	208.3	61.6	45.5	31.0	24.9	21.5	14.4	18.2	9.4	9.1	15.1
Profit Margin (Before Income Tax) 49	5.7	1.0	7.5	8.1	4.6	5.2	4.0	4.1	3.7	3.8	3.7	3.5	9.7
Profit Margin (After Income Tax) 50	4.3	0.9	7.4	8.0	4.4	4.9	3.5	3.5	2.9	3.1	2.6	2.4	6.4

Table I
Corporations with and without Net Income

METAL AND MINERAL (EXCEPT PETROLEUM)

MONEY AMOUNTS AND SIZE OF ASSETS IN THOUSANDS OF DOLLARS

Item Description for Accounting Period 7/10 Through 6/11	Total	Zero Assets	Under 500	500 to 1,000	1,000 to 5,000	5,000 to 10,000	10,000 to 25,000	25,000 to 50,000	50,000 to 100,000	100,000 to 250,000	250,000 to 500,000	500,000 to 2,500,000	2,500,000 and over
Number of Enterprises 1	5498	480	2712	612	906	282	263	99	63	50	15	16	0
Revenues ($ in Thousands)													
Net Sales 2	100296501	1306952	1509985	1053945	7046831	7489783	9185649	9412643	9867986	15986556	8311507	29124665	0
Interest 3	76651	350	67	855	2570	2334	3137	3586	3615	24767	17258	18111	0
Rents 4	35920	85	0	1003	0	266	1065	2103	228	1878	13647	15644	0
Royalties 5	161	0	0	0	0	161	0	0	0	0	0	0	0
Other Portfolio Income 6	148445	1209	219	1410	2362	6	20426	1213	2462	59480	19735	39922	0
Other Receipts 7	761927	2832	311	19256	12999	16377	52456	19856	37982	418418	88351	93089	0
Total Receipts 8	101319605	1311428	1510582	1076469	7064762	7508927	9262733	9439401	9912273	16491099	8450498	29291431	0
Average Total Receipts 9	18428	2732	557	1759	7798	26627	35220	95347	157338	329822	563367	1830714	•
Operating Costs/Operating Income (%)													
Cost of Operations 10	87.5	82.3	66.1	71.5	85.1	91.9	85.3	89.9	88.8	90.9	88.1	86.4	•
Salaries and Wages 11	3.5	6.8	5.5	5.1	3.9	1.8	4.3	2.6	2.7	2.7	3.5	4.2	•
Taxes Paid 12	0.7	1.1	1.7	1.5	0.8	0.4	0.8	0.9	0.5	0.6	0.7	0.7	•
Interest Paid 13	0.8	0.5	0.3	0.3	0.2	0.3	0.4	0.5	0.5	0.4	1.7	1.4	•
Depreciation 14	0.7	0.7	0.2	0.6	0.4	0.2	0.7	0.7	0.5	0.6	1.0	1.0	•
Amortization and Depletion 15	0.2	0.0	0.0	0.0	0.0	0.0	0.1	0.0	0.1	0.0	0.3	0.5	•
Pensions and Other Deferred Comp. 16	0.2	0.0	0.1	0.0	0.0	0.1	0.1	0.0	0.1	0.2	0.3	0.2	•
Employee Benefits 17	0.6	0.5	0.2	1.1	0.4	0.3	0.5	0.4	0.3	0.4	0.6	1.0	•
Advertising 18	0.1	0.0	0.2	0.2	0.1	0.1	0.1	0.0	0.0	0.0	0.1	0.0	•
Other Expenses 19	3.7	5.4	6.2	9.5	4.6	2.5	4.2	2.7	2.7	4.1	4.9	3.3	•
Officers' Compensation 20	1.0	0.5	14.6	7.0	2.8	1.1	1.2	0.7	0.8	0.3	0.4	0.3	•
Operating Margin 21	1.0	2.1	4.8	3.3	1.2	1.5	2.2	1.6	2.9	•	•	0.8	•
Operating Margin Before Officers' Comp. 22	2.0	2.6	19.4	10.2	3.9	2.6	3.4	2.3	3.7	0.1	•	1.1	•

Selected Average Balance Sheet ($ in Thousands)

Net Receivables 23	2090	0	60	219	755	1600	4300	10606	21300	39682	77009	212105
Inventories 24	2505	0	32	137	641	3117	5950	12313	27340	49488	89695	238653
Net Property, Plant and Equipment 25	1152	0	20	85	93	264	1640	3561	4439	14959	48387	220730
Total Assets 26	8666	0	169	615	2580	6556	15517	34855	67990	160650	357776	1088194
Notes and Loans Payable 27	2463	0	145	130	365	1553	4191	8895	19624	41400	98885	345426
All Other Liabilities 28	3015	0	25	136	1346	2084	4135	13339	22149	52741	119285	399235
Net Worth 29	3189	0	-0	349	869	2919	7191	12621	26217	66509	139606	343533

Selected Financial Ratios (Times to 1)

Current Ratio 30	1.9	•	3.0	2.8	1.6	2.2	2.0	1.7	1.8	1.9	2.1	1.8
Quick Ratio 31	0.9	•	2.2	1.9	1.0	1.1	1.0	0.8	0.8	0.8	1.0	0.8
Net Sales to Working Capital 32	6.6	•	6.7	5.2	9.0	8.8	5.6	8.3	5.9	5.6	4.9	6.9
Coverage Ratio 33	3.6	5.9	16.3	20.3	8.1	7.3	8.8	5.0	8.3	8.8	1.1	2.0
Total Asset Turnover 34	2.1	•	3.3	2.8	3.0	4.1	2.3	2.7	2.3	2.0	1.5	1.7
Inventory Turnover 35	6.4	•	11.6	9.0	10.3	7.8	5.0	6.9	5.1	5.9	5.4	6.6
Receivables Turnover 36	9.8	•	10.0	8.3	12.2	13.3	7.7	11.2	9.5	8.9	7.5	10.2
Total Liabilities to Net Worth 37	1.7	•	•	0.8	2.0	1.2	1.2	1.8	1.6	1.4	1.6	2.2
Current Assets to Working Capital 38	2.1	•	1.5	1.5	2.6	1.8	2.0	2.5	2.2	2.1	1.9	2.2
Current Liabilities to Working Capital 39	1.1	•	0.5	0.5	1.6	0.8	1.0	1.5	1.2	1.1	0.9	1.2
Working Capital to Net Sales 40	0.2	•	0.1	0.2	0.1	0.1	0.2	0.1	0.2	0.2	0.2	0.1
Inventory to Working Capital 41	1.0	•	0.3	0.5	0.7	0.8	0.9	1.1	1.1	1.0	0.8	1.0
Total Receipts to Cash Flow 42	21.4	15.3	9.8	7.9	20.7	27.4	17.1	27.9	18.4	16.0	29.0	29.2
Cost of Goods to Cash Flow 43	18.8	12.6	6.4	5.7	17.6	25.2	14.5	25.0	16.3	14.6	25.6	25.2
Cash Flow to Total Debt 44	0.2	•	0.3	0.8	0.2	0.3	0.2	0.2	0.2	0.2	0.1	0.1

Selected Financial Factors (in Percentages)

Debt Ratio 45	63.2	•	100.2	43.2	66.3	55.5	53.7	63.8	61.4	58.6	61.0	68.4
Return on Total Assets 46	6.0	•	17.1	15.6	4.9	8.0	7.8	6.5	8.8	6.5	2.9	4.7
Return on Equity Before Income Taxes 47	11.7	•	•	26.1	12.7	15.6	14.9	14.2	20.1	13.9	0.5	7.4
Return on Equity After Income Taxes 48	9.1	•	•	25.9	12.3	14.5	13.3	12.6	16.4	10.2	•	4.2
Profit Margin (Before Income Tax) 49	2.1	2.4	4.9	5.3	1.4	1.7	3.1	1.9	3.4	2.9	0.1	1.4
Profit Margin (After Income Tax) 50	1.6	2.1	4.8	5.2	1.4	1.6	2.7	1.7	2.8	2.1	•	0.8

Table II

Corporations with Net Income

METAL AND MINERAL (EXCEPT PETROLEUM)

MONEY AMOUNTS AND SIZE OF ASSETS IN THOUSANDS OF DOLLARS

Item Description for Accounting Period 7/10 Through 6/11		Total	Zero Assets	Under 500	500 to 1,000	1,000 to 5,000	5,000 to 10,000	10,000 to 25,000	25,000 to 50,000	50,000 to 100,000	100,000 to 250,000	250,000 to 500,000	500,000 to 2,500,000	2,500,000 and over
Number of Enterprises	1	3455	440	1192	554	610	273	203	76	51	40	8	8	0
Revenues ($ in Thousands)														
Net Sales	2	75098034	1117057	1012066	941875	5981926	7378655	6993117	8107278	8479703	13899266	5259097	15927994	0
Interest	3	45305	350	38	855	588	2280	2364	2344	1870	17154	3938	13525	0
Rents	4	32008	85	0	1003	0	266	899	1581	228	1646	11556	14744	0
Royalties	5	0	0	0	0	0	0	0	0	0	0	0	0	0
Other Portfolio Income	6	141281	1209	219	1410	1248	5	20391	1120	1306	58868	19322	36181	0
Other Receipts	7	683900	1326	295	19256	7359	16364	42786	14855	33959	399324	80572	67805	0
Total Receipts	8	76000528	1120027	1012618	964399	5991121	7397570	7059557	8127178	8517066	14376258	5374485	16060249	0
Average Total Receipts	9	21997	2546	850	1741	9822	27097	34776	106937	167001	359406	671811	2007531	•
Operating Costs/Operating Income (%)														
Cost of Operations	10	87.0	82.5	52.7	72.6	86.6	92.0	82.7	89.5	89.2	90.7	88.8	84.0	•
Salaries and Wages	11	3.2	5.3	7.6	4.3	2.9	1.7	4.9	2.5	2.3	2.8	2.5	4.1	•
Taxes Paid	12	0.7	0.8	2.2	1.5	0.8	0.3	0.8	0.9	0.5	0.6	0.6	0.8	•
Interest Paid	13	0.5	0.6	0.4	0.3	0.1	0.3	0.4	0.4	0.4	0.3	0.6	0.9	•
Depreciation	14	0.6	0.8	0.2	0.6	0.2	0.1	0.7	0.6	0.4	0.5	1.0	1.1	•
Amortization and Depletion	15	0.2	0.0	0.0	0.0	0.0	0.0	0.1	0.0	0.0	0.0	0.2	0.6	•
Pensions and Other Deferred Comp.	16	0.2	0.0	0.2	0.0	0.0	0.1	0.2	0.1	0.1	0.1	0.2	0.3	•
Employee Benefits	17	0.5	0.4	0.3	0.9	0.6	0.2	0.6	0.3	0.3	0.4	0.4	0.9	•
Advertising	18	0.1	0.0	0.1	0.1	0.1	0.0	0.2	0.0	0.0	0.0	0.1	0.0	•
Other Expenses	19	3.6	5.6	5.7	9.3	4.0	2.3	4.4	2.6	2.1	3.8	4.5	3.9	•
Officers' Compensation	20	1.2	0.5	21.5	6.3	2.4	1.1	1.3	0.8	0.8	0.3	0.5	0.4	•
Operating Margin	21	2.3	3.5	8.9	4.2	2.1	1.8	3.8	2.2	4.0	0.2	0.4	2.9	•
Operating Margin Before Officers' Comp.	22	3.4	3.9	30.5	10.5	4.5	2.9	5.1	3.0	4.8	0.5	0.9	3.3	•

Selected Average Balance Sheet ($ in Thousands)

	•	•	•	•	•	•	•	•	•	•	•	•
Net Receivables 23	2465	0	87	221	878	1643	4620	11172	21913	40211	71398	277802
Inventories 24	2288	0	50	134	774	2106	5169	14111	24356	41984	50804	278536
Net Property, Plant and Equipment 25	1040	0	40	88	79	255	1550	3250	4354	14286	65722	187210
Total Assets 26	9364	0	258	609	2749	6502	15613	35011	69436	158852	341883	1224273
Notes and Loans Payable 27	1935	0	74	120	471	1600	3298	8504	18043	32247	41801	243309
All Other Liabilities 28	2936	0	20	129	1225	2133	4282	13118	21731	55726	141910	297266
Net Worth 29	4493	0	164	360	1053	2769	8033	13389	29662	70878	158172	683698

Selected Financial Ratios (Times to 1)

	•	•	•	•	•	•	•	•	•	•	•	•
Current Ratio 30	2.0	•	3.3	3.1	1.9	2.2	2.2	1.8	1.9	1.8	1.8	2.6
Quick Ratio 31	1.0	•	2.5	2.2	1.2	1.1	1.1	0.8	0.8	0.8	0.8	1.3
Net Sales to Working Capital 32	6.3	•	6.3	5.0	8.1	8.9	4.9	8.3	5.8	6.5	7.0	4.8
Coverage Ratio 33	8.3	7.5	22.2	26.3	18.0	8.4	13.2	6.8	12.5	11.5	5.2	5.2
Total Asset Turnover 34	2.3	•	3.3	2.8	3.6	4.2	2.2	3.0	2.4	2.2	1.9	1.6
Inventory Turnover 35	8.3	•	8.9	9.2	11.0	11.8	5.5	6.8	6.1	7.5	11.5	6.0
Receivables Turnover 36	11.1	•	9.4	•	14.1	19.4	8.1	•	10.2	11.2	11.7	•
Total Liabilities to Net Worth 37	1.1	•	0.6	0.7	1.6	1.3	0.9	1.6	1.3	1.2	1.2	0.8
Current Assets to Working Capital 38	2.0	•	1.4	1.5	2.1	1.8	1.9	2.3	2.1	2.3	2.2	1.6
Current Liabilities to Working Capital 39	1.0	•	0.4	0.5	1.1	0.8	0.9	1.3	1.1	1.3	1.2	0.6
Working Capital to Net Sales 40	0.2	•	0.2	0.2	0.1	0.1	0.2	0.1	0.2	0.2	0.1	0.2
Inventory to Working Capital 41	0.8	•	0.2	0.4	0.7	0.8	0.8	1.1	1.0	1.0	0.9	0.7
Total Receipts to Cash Flow 42	16.4	12.5	7.2	7.4	19.3	26.3	13.1	24.1	16.6	14.8	18.6	15.7
Cost of Goods to Cash Flow 43	14.3	10.4	3.8	5.4	16.7	24.2	10.8	21.6	14.8	13.4	16.5	13.2
Cash Flow to Total Debt 44	0.3	•	1.3	0.9	0.3	0.3	0.3	0.2	0.3	0.3	0.2	0.2

Selected Financial Factors (in Percentages)

	•	•	•	•	•	•	•	•	•	•	•	•
Debt Ratio 45	52.0	•	36.4	40.9	61.7	57.4	48.5	61.8	57.3	55.4	53.7	44.2
Return on Total Assets 46	9.3	•	31.0	18.6	8.4	9.7	11.3	8.7	11.5	8.7	6.3	7.7
Return on Equity Before Income Taxes 47	17.0	•	46.5	30.2	20.8	20.0	20.3	19.4	24.7	17.8	11.0	11.2
Return on Equity After Income Taxes 48	14.0	•	45.9	30.0	20.3	18.9	18.4	17.3	20.7	13.5	8.6	8.0
Profit Margin (Before Income Tax) 49	3.5	3.7	9.0	6.4	2.2	2.0	4.7	2.4	4.4	3.6	2.6	3.8
Profit Margin (After Income Tax) 50	2.9	3.3	8.9	6.4	2.2	1.9	4.3	2.2	3.7	2.8	2.1	2.7

Table I

Corporations with and without Net Income

ELECTRICAL GOODS

MONEY AMOUNTS AND SIZE OF ASSETS IN THOUSANDS OF DOLLARS

Item Description for Accounting Period 7/10 Through 6/11	Total	Zero Assets	Under 500	500 to 1,000	1,000 to 5,000	5,000 to 10,000	10,000 to 25,000	25,000 to 50,000	50,000 to 100,000	100,000 to 250,000	250,000 to 500,000	500,000 to 2,500,000	2,500,000 and over
Number of Enterprises **1**	27608	2908	15554	3610	3924	675	482	185	120	76	23	40	11
Revenues ($ in Thousands)													
Net Sales **2**	361903268	2349457	12358762	7876558	23800578	11677702	17863118	14765599	19166509	25636482	13313091	94735340	118360071
Interest **3**	357744	6034	1446	2783	5562	2880	6290	9303	13040	13371	19318	139039	138678
Rents **4**	151662	0	602	566	2225	2740	4313	5350	1783	2894	1864	51140	78184
Royalties **5**	1843850	0	0	1	0	0	148	0	15542	144252	31229	176754	1475924
Other Portfolio Income **6**	864775	2975	2151	5896	6555	2693	10040	2740	11227	284989	24529	350017	160964
Other Receipts **7**	3263932	104251	40682	60808	111358	118947	158922	98519	86340	149577	90891	432392	1811247
Total Receipts **8**	368385231	2462717	12403643	7946612	23926278	11804962	18042831	14881511	19294441	26231565	13480922	95584682	122025068
Average Total Receipts **9**	13343	847	797	2201	6097	17489	37433	80441	160787	345152	586127	2397117	11093188
Operating Costs/Operating Income (%)													
Cost of Operations **10**	82.6	80.6	66.7	69.5	73.0	75.3	81.5	79.4	82.1	81.1	83.9	87.7	84.5
Salaries and Wages **11**	6.1	11.4	9.2	7.7	9.0	7.8	7.4	7.4	6.6	7.0	7.2	4.5	5.2
Taxes Paid **12**	0.8	0.9	1.9	1.3	1.3	1.3	0.9	0.9	0.8	0.8	0.6	0.5	0.7
Interest Paid **13**	0.5	1.1	1.0	0.6	0.3	0.3	0.4	0.4	0.5	0.5	0.4	0.4	0.6
Depreciation **14**	0.8	0.5	0.4	0.7	0.5	0.7	0.5	0.5	0.8	0.6	1.0	0.7	1.2
Amortization and Depletion **15**	1.1	0.1	0.1	0.0	0.0	0.1	0.1	0.3	0.2	0.3	0.3	0.2	2.9
Pensions and Other Deferred Comp. **16**	0.2	0.2	0.2	0.5	0.3	0.3	0.2	0.4	0.3	0.2	0.2	0.2	0.2
Employee Benefits **17**	0.7	1.0	1.0	0.6	0.8	0.6	0.6	0.7	0.7	0.8	0.7	0.6	0.7
Advertising **18**	0.7	0.4	0.7	0.5	0.9	0.5	0.3	0.5	0.5	1.0	0.3	0.4	1.1
Other Expenses **19**	5.7	9.5	10.2	11.0	8.8	7.9	5.7	6.2	4.9	6.5	4.0	4.0	5.6
Officers' Compensation **20**	0.9	0.5	6.4	5.0	3.2	3.1	1.2	1.2	0.7	0.6	0.5	0.2	0.1
Operating Margin **21**	•	•	2.4	2.6	1.8	2.2	1.3	2.2	2.0	0.6	1.1	0.7	•
Operating Margin Before Officers' Comp. **22**	0.8	•	8.7	7.6	5.0	5.2	2.5	3.4	2.7	1.2	1.6	0.8	•

Selected Average Balance Sheet ($ in Thousands)

Net Receivables 23	1995	0	29	167	760	2475	5113	11752	23403	55363	92576	365058	1906754
Inventories 24	1031	0	23	212	689	2258	4083	10214	16225	34121	49988	162748	640994
Net Property, Plant and Equipment 25	542	0	9	132	146	635	1021	1882	5469	9295	19453	66080	732885
Total Assets 26	7114	0	109	707	2236	7339	14600	35106	68931	159699	346402	1156544	8204967
Notes and Loans Payable 27	1559	0	184	277	465	2360	2945	6130	12455	27921	29553	118774	2196762
All Other Liabilities 28	2893	0	44	251	899	2807	6822	15404	26164	64930	146689	497915	3213055
Net Worth 29	2662	0	-119	180	872	2173	4834	13571	30311	66849	170159	539854	2795149

Selected Financial Ratios (Times to 1)

Current Ratio 30	1.3	•	1.7	1.8	1.9	1.8	1.5	1.7	1.8	1.7	1.6	1.6	1.0
Quick Ratio 31	0.8	•	1.1	1.0	1.1	1.0	0.8	1.0	1.0	1.1	1.0	0.9	0.6
Net Sales to Working Capital 32	11.8	•	23.3	8.9	6.8	6.6	9.6	6.6	6.6	6.6	6.8	8.4	•
Coverage Ratio 33	4.7	•	3.8	7.2	8.2	10.6	6.7	8.8	6.6	8.4	7.6	5.9	1.7
Total Asset Turnover 34	1.8	•	7.3	3.1	2.7	2.4	2.5	2.3	2.3	2.1	1.7	2.0	1.3
Inventory Turnover 35	10.5	•	23.5	7.1	6.4	5.8	7.4	6.2	8.1	8.0	9.7	12.8	14.2
Receivables Turnover 36	7.1	•	25.8	13.9	8.7	7.0	7.5	6.6	7.4	6.5	6.5	7.5	6.0
Total Liabilities to Net Worth 37	1.7	•	•	2.9	1.6	2.4	2.0	1.6	1.3	1.4	1.0	1.1	1.9
Current Assets to Working Capital 38	3.9	•	2.5	2.2	2.1	2.3	3.0	2.4	2.3	2.4	2.6	2.8	•
Current Liabilities to Working Capital 39	2.9	•	1.5	1.2	1.1	1.3	2.0	1.4	1.3	1.4	1.6	1.8	•
Working Capital to Net Sales 40	0.1	•	0.0	0.1	0.1	0.2	0.1	0.2	0.2	0.2	0.1	0.1	•
Inventory to Working Capital 41	1.0	•	0.7	0.9	0.8	0.8	1.1	0.9	0.8	0.7	0.6	0.7	•
Total Receipts to Cash Flow 42	16.0	16.8	10.2	8.9	10.8	10.4	14.9	12.8	15.4	11.9	18.3	19.4	20.9
Cost of Goods to Cash Flow 43	13.2	13.5	6.8	6.2	7.9	7.8	12.2	10.2	12.7	9.6	15.4	17.1	17.7
Cash Flow to Total Debt 44	0.2	0.3	0.3	0.5	0.4	0.3	0.3	0.3	0.3	0.3	0.2	0.2	0.1

Selected Financial Factors (in Percentages)

Debt Ratio 45	62.6	•	209.3	74.6	61.0	70.4	66.9	61.3	56.0	58.1	50.9	53.3	65.9
Return on Total Assets 46	4.2	•	27.2	12.6	7.1	8.5	6.9	7.6	7.2	8.3	4.6	5.2	1.3
Return on Equity Before Income Taxes 47	8.9	•	•	42.7	15.9	25.9	17.6	17.3	13.9	17.5	8.1	9.3	1.5
Return on Equity After Income Taxes 48	6.9	•	•	41.3	13.9	23.0	15.0	15.0	12.0	12.4	6.4	6.9	0.6
Profit Margin (Before Income Tax) 49	1.8	•	2.7	3.5	2.3	3.2	2.3	2.9	2.6	2.6	2.4	2.1	0.4
Profit Margin (After Income Tax) 50	1.4	•	2.6	3.4	2.0	2.9	2.0	2.6	2.3	2.5	1.9	1.6	0.2

Table II
Corporations with Net Income

ELECTRICAL GOODS

MONEY AMOUNTS AND SIZE OF ASSETS IN THOUSANDS OF DOLLARS

Item Description for Accounting Period 7/10 Through 6/11	Total	Zero Assets	Under 500	500 to 1,000	1,000 to 5,000	5,000 to 10,000	10,000 to 25,000	25,000 to 50,000	50,000 to 100,000	100,000 to 250,000	250,000 to 500,000	500,000 to 2,500,000	2,500,000 and over
Number of Enterprises **1**	17607	1134	9531	2650	3036	499	393	154	93	62	17	31	7
Revenues ($ in Thousands)													
Net Sales **2**	294714519	1315167	9754289	6629265	20992817	9981155	15274077	13642114	15765116	22875673	12514357	91238799	74731689
Interest **3**	239211	455	319	2726	4957	2807	4449	8264	9765	9887	17229	131089	47263
Rents **4**	66042	0	602	566	528	205	3303	3114	1282	1232	1833	38052	15325
Royalties **5**	122919	0	0	1	0	0	0	0	15145	2841	31229	52870	20833
Other Portfolio Income **6**	655899	19	1016	5896	4825	2043	7974	1114	8887	282450	2915	280708	58051
Other Receipts **7**	1677101	11780	9657	47762	100345	110698	143984	80551	72802	137848	80946	281046	599687
Total Receipts **8**	297475691	1327421	9765883	6686216	21103472	10096908	15433787	13735157	15872997	23309931	12648509	92022564	75472848
Average Total Receipts **9**	16895	1171	1025	2523	6951	20234	39272	89189	170677	375967	744030	2968470	10781835
Operating Costs/Operating Income (%)													
Cost of Operations **10**	83.5	74.8	66.8	70.3	72.9	75.1	81.0	79.0	81.2	82.9	85.2	88.4	87.0
Salaries and Wages **11**	5.4	9.1	8.3	6.8	8.9	7.6	7.3	7.4	6.8	5.6	6.1	4.0	4.0
Taxes Paid **12**	0.7	0.7	1.4	1.2	1.2	1.2	0.9	0.9	0.9	0.7	0.6	0.4	0.6
Interest Paid **13**	0.4	0.2	0.1	0.6	0.3	0.3	0.4	0.4	0.3	0.4	0.4	0.4	0.4
Depreciation **14**	0.7	0.5	0.3	0.7	0.5	0.5	0.5	0.4	0.6	0.4	0.9	0.6	1.3
Amortization and Depletion **15**	0.2	•	0.0	0.0	0.0	0.1	0.1	0.2	0.1	0.2	0.3	0.2	0.2
Pensions and Other Deferred Comp. **16**	0.2	0.3	0.3	0.4	0.3	0.3	0.2	0.4	0.3	0.2	0.2	0.2	0.1
Employee Benefits **17**	0.6	0.8	0.6	0.6	0.8	0.6	0.6	0.7	0.7	0.6	0.6	0.5	0.7
Advertising **18**	0.5	0.1	0.6	0.5	0.9	0.5	0.3	0.5	0.4	0.7	0.2	0.4	0.6
Other Expenses **19**	5.0	9.1	9.1	10.1	7.9	7.1	5.1	5.8	4.7	5.7	3.5	3.4	4.5
Officers' Compensation **20**	0.9	0.6	6.2	4.8	3.0	3.1	1.3	1.1	0.7	0.6	0.4	0.1	0.1
Operating Margin **21**	1.9	3.7	6.4	4.2	3.4	3.5	2.5	3.1	3.1	2.0	1.8	1.4	0.5
Operating Margin Before Officers' Comp. **22**	2.8	4.3	12.6	9.0	6.3	6.6	3.8	4.3	3.9	2.6	2.2	1.6	0.6

Selected Average Balance Sheet ($ in Thousands)

Net Receivables 23	2334	0	24	177	841	2721	5443	12564	23783	58658	109707	443212	1565468
Inventories 24	1300	0	15	201	695	2083	3833	10206	16302	32896	58045	185294	766553
Net Property, Plant and Equipment 25	667	0	6	119	144	598	916	1882	5806	8252	23627	75666	885334
Total Assets 26	7222	0	99	699	2282	7405	14622	35045	69072	159708	343021	1224536	6067566
Notes and Loans Payable 27	1162	0	18	210	394	1610	2334	5855	11525	27851	34450	132191	1204513
All Other Liabilities 28	2899	0	42	238	912	2889	6861	14613	24982	63502	158105	533873	2192343
Net Worth 29	3161	0	39	251	976	2906	5427	14578	32565	68355	150466	558472	2670710

Selected Financial Ratios (Times to 1)

Current Ratio 30	1.6	•	2.0	2.1	1.9	1.8	1.6	1.9	1.8	1.8	1.7	1.6	1.4
Quick Ratio 31	1.0	•	1.5	1.2	1.1	1.1	0.9	1.1	1.1	1.1	1.1	1.0	0.9
Net Sales to Working Capital 32	8.9	•	24.5	8.9	7.4	7.3	8.5	6.2	6.7	6.5	7.2	9.3	11.9
Coverage Ratio 33	8.9	20.1	93.3	9.9	15.5	18.0	10.8	11.8	12.5	12.0	9.2	7.0	4.6
Total Asset Turnover 34	2.3	•	10.3	3.6	3.0	2.7	2.7	2.5	2.5	2.3	2.1	2.4	1.8
Inventory Turnover 35	10.8	•	45.0	8.7	7.2	7.2	8.2	6.9	8.4	9.3	10.8	14.0	12.1
Receivables Turnover 36	7.4	•	37.3	•	9.2	8.2	8.1	7.6	7.7	7.2	7.3	8.3	•
Total Liabilities to Net Worth 37	1.3	•	1.5	1.8	1.3	1.5	1.7	1.4	1.1	1.3	1.2	1.2	1.3
Current Assets to Working Capital 38	2.6	•	2.0	1.9	2.1	2.3	2.7	2.1	2.2	2.2	2.4	2.8	3.4
Current Liabilities to Working Capital 39	1.6	•	1.0	0.9	1.1	1.3	1.7	1.1	1.2	1.2	1.4	1.8	2.4
Working Capital to Net Sales 40	0.1	•	0.0	0.1	0.1	0.1	0.1	0.2	0.1	0.2	0.1	0.1	0.1
Inventory to Working Capital 41	0.8	•	0.4	0.7	0.8	0.7	1.0	0.8	0.8	0.7	0.6	0.8	0.9
Total Receipts to Cash Flow 42	14.7	8.9	7.8	8.2	10.0	9.8	13.4	12.1	13.5	11.5	17.6	19.6	19.4
Cost of Goods to Cash Flow 43	12.3	6.7	5.2	5.7	7.3	7.3	10.8	9.5	11.0	9.6	15.0	17.3	16.9
Cash Flow to Total Debt 44	0.3	•	2.2	0.7	0.5	0.5	0.3	0.4	0.3	0.4	0.2	0.2	0.2

Selected Financial Factors (in Percentages)

Debt Ratio 45	56.2	•	60.4	64.0	57.2	60.8	62.9	58.4	52.9	57.2	56.1	54.4	56.0
Return on Total Assets 46	7.7	•	68.0	20.0	12.6	13.3	10.5	10.6	10.2	11.3	7.0	7.0	3.3
Return on Equity Before Income Taxes 47	15.7	•	169.8	50.1	27.5	31.9	25.7	23.2	20.0	24.2	14.2	13.1	5.9
Return on Equity After Income Taxes 48	13.1	•	166.4	48.8	25.2	29.1	22.8	20.7	17.7	18.1	11.6	10.1	4.3
Profit Margin (Before Income Tax) 49	3.0	4.7	6.5	5.0	3.9	4.6	3.6	3.8	3.8	4.5	2.9	2.5	1.5
Profit Margin (After Income Tax) 50	2.5	3.8	6.4	4.9	3.6	4.2	3.2	3.4	3.4	3.4	2.4	1.9	1.1

Table I
Corporations with and without Net Income

HARDWARE, PLUMBING, HEATING EQUIPMENT, AND SUPPLIES

MONEY AMOUNTS AND SIZE OF ASSETS IN THOUSANDS OF DOLLARS

Item Description for Accounting Period 7/10 Through 6/11		Total	Zero Assets	Under 500	500 to 1,000	1,000 to 5,000	5,000 to 10,000	10,000 to 25,000	25,000 to 50,000	50,000 to 100,000	100,000 to 250,000	250,000 to 500,000	500,000 to 2,500,000	2,500,000 and over
Number of Enterprises	1	14429	2538	6375	1267	3155	559	356	97	46	24	6	6	0
Revenues ($ in Thousands)														
Net Sales	2	80730777	236717	3294988	2267707	16661354	9231111	11895141	7272774	6097313	5995266	3680604	14097801	0
Interest	3	71492	5	530	268	9906	4235	4812	6214	1934	2963	4796	35829	0
Rents	4	9227	0	0	0	3602	243	1305	1208	519	2212	65	73	0
Royalties	5	3399	0	0	0	0	0	0	0	0	0	0	3399	0
Other Portfolio Income	6	108345	0	8444	2929	9687	1124	19379	23025	4626	2837	22179	14118	0
Other Receipts	7	1243573	33	16423	7229	252074	429946	85796	45272	27356	70387	76719	232337	0
Total Receipts	8	82166813	236755	3320385	2278133	16936623	9666659	12006433	7348493	6131748	6073665	3784363	14383557	0
Average Total Receipts	9	5695	93	521	1798	5368	17293	33726	75758	133299	253069	630727	2397260	•
Operating Costs/Operating Income (%)														
Cost of Operations	10	71.5	29.2	63.1	66.8	71.3	70.6	74.5	73.8	73.7	75.8	75.9	68.4	•
Salaries and Wages	11	10.1	0.0	10.6	9.5	9.3	11.9	9.8	9.9	9.8	8.3	10.5	11.4	•
Taxes Paid	12	1.5	3.4	2.1	1.6	1.6	1.7	1.3	1.3	1.4	1.2	1.5	1.7	•
Interest Paid	13	0.8	0.2	0.8	0.6	0.4	0.8	0.5	0.6	0.5	0.7	0.8	2.1	•
Depreciation	14	0.9	0.5	0.9	0.6	0.5	1.2	0.5	0.6	1.0	1.1	2.2	1.2	•
Amortization and Depletion	15	0.2	•	0.2	0.0	0.1	0.0	0.1	0.1	0.2	0.1	0.5	0.4	•
Pensions and Other Deferred Comp.	16	0.4	•	0.5	0.4	0.3	0.4	0.3	0.7	0.3	0.2	0.4	0.5	•
Employee Benefits	17	1.0	•	0.9	0.4	0.9	1.1	0.9	1.0	1.1	0.8	1.5	1.3	•
Advertising	18	0.6	0.8	1.8	0.3	0.4	1.2	0.4	0.5	0.6	0.5	0.3	0.3	•
Other Expenses	19	8.9	37.1	14.3	11.8	9.7	9.4	7.3	7.3	7.8	8.3	6.8	9.0	•
Officers' Compensation	20	2.4	19.1	4.8	7.3	4.4	3.4	2.3	1.3	0.9	0.8	0.8	0.2	•
Operating Margin	21	1.6	9.6	0.1	0.7	1.1	•	2.1	3.0	2.8	2.1	•	3.5	•
Operating Margin Before Officers' Comp.	22	4.0	28.7	5.0	7.9	5.5	1.9	4.4	4.3	3.6	2.9	•	3.7	•

Selected Average Balance Sheet ($ in Thousands)

	•	•	•	•	•	•	•	•	•	•	•	•
Net Receivables 23	747	0	29	192	668	1971	4549	8856	17512	48464	64396	384380
Inventories 24	842	0	19	310	735	3155	5515	11922	25096	40418	96547	288434
Net Property, Plant and Equipment 25	298	0	12	57	153	728	1116	3814	9260	22435	73568	181410
Total Assets 26	2790	0	112	670	2190	7007	15283	33560	69033	159416	340063	1687952
Notes and Loans Payable 27	788	0	92	100	508	1958	3143	8771	17106	29786	70904	677454
All Other Liabilities 28	795	0	61	118	790	1907	4294	7651	16082	58943	110586	379513
Net Worth 29	1207	0	-41	452	892	3142	7845	17138	35845	70687	158573	630986

Selected Financial Ratios (Times to 1)

Current Ratio 30	2.1	•	1.0	3.2	2.1	2.3	2.1	2.5	2.3	1.9	1.9	2.4
Quick Ratio 31	1.1	•	0.6	1.8	1.1	1.0	1.0	1.2	1.0	1.0	0.7	1.4
Net Sales to Working Capital 32	5.3	•	453.8	5.1	5.5	4.7	5.2	4.8	4.5	4.7	6.6	5.1
Coverage Ratio 33	5.0	55.2	2.2	2.8	7.5	5.1	7.8	7.8	7.5	5.8	3.1	3.7
Total Asset Turnover 34	2.0	•	4.6	2.7	2.4	2.4	2.2	2.2	1.9	1.6	1.8	1.4
Inventory Turnover 35	4.8	•	16.9	3.9	5.1	3.7	4.5	4.6	3.9	4.7	4.8	5.6
Receivables Turnover 36	7.9	•	21.8	6.5	8.7	7.8	8.0	8.5	7.3	7.2	9.5	6.3
Total Liabilities to Net Worth 37	1.3	•	•	0.5	1.5	1.2	0.9	1.0	0.9	1.3	1.1	1.7
Current Assets to Working Capital 38	1.9	•	70.5	1.5	1.9	1.8	1.9	1.7	1.8	2.1	2.2	1.7
Current Liabilities to Working Capital 39	0.9	•	69.5	0.5	0.9	0.8	0.9	0.7	0.8	1.1	1.2	0.7
Working Capital to Net Sales 40	0.2	•	0.0	0.2	0.2	0.2	0.2	0.2	0.2	0.2	0.2	0.2
Inventory to Working Capital 41	0.8	•	23.2	0.6	0.8	0.9	0.9	0.8	0.9	0.9	1.1	0.6
Total Receipts to Cash Flow 42	10.3	2.4	8.3	9.7	9.9	10.1	12.9	11.7	11.3	10.2	16.8	8.8
Cost of Goods to Cash Flow 43	7.4	0.7	5.2	6.5	7.0	7.1	9.6	8.6	8.3	7.7	12.7	6.0
Cash Flow to Total Debt 44	0.3	•	0.4	0.8	0.4	0.4	0.3	0.4	0.4	0.3	0.2	0.3

Selected Financial Factors (in Percentages)

Debt Ratio 45	56.7	•	136.2	32.6	59.3	55.2	48.7	48.9	48.1	55.7	53.4	62.6
Return on Total Assets 46	8.5	•	7.7	4.7	7.5	9.4	7.7	10.2	7.5	6.4	4.2	10.8
Return on Equity Before Income Taxes 47	15.7	•	•	4.5	16.0	17.0	13.1	17.5	12.5	12.0	6.1	20.9
Return on Equity After Income Taxes 48	13.3	•	•	3.9	13.6	15.9	11.6	15.5	11.4	10.1	2.7	16.1
Profit Margin (Before Income Tax) 49	3.4	9.6	0.9	1.1	2.7	3.2	3.1	4.0	3.4	3.4	1.6	5.6
Profit Margin (After Income Tax) 50	2.9	9.6	0.8	1.0	2.3	3.0	2.7	3.5	3.1	2.9	0.7	4.3

Table II

Corporations with Net Income

HARDWARE, PLUMBING, HEATING EQUIPMENT, AND SUPPLIES

MONEY AMOUNTS AND SIZE OF ASSETS IN THOUSANDS OF DOLLARS

Item Description for Accounting Period 7/10 Through 6/11	Total	Zero Assets	Under 500	500 to 1,000	1,000 to 5,000	5,000 to 10,000	10,000 to 25,000	25,000 to 50,000	50,000 to 100,000	100,000 to 250,000	250,000 to 500,000	500,000 to 2,500,000	2,500,000 and over
Number of Enterprises **1**	8920	1297	3395	1009	2322	449	298	84	38	19	•	•	0
Revenues ($ in Thousands)													
Net Sales **2**	69343994	121517	2541389	1984063	13295998	7455754	10158629	6920926	5279020	4922364	•	•	0
Interest **3**	60516	0	56	51	7462	3974	3415	3154	1810	2657	•	•	0
Rents **4**	6768	0	0	0	2837	243	905	1208	519	982	•	•	0
Royalties **5**	3399	0	0	0	0	0	0	0	0	0	•	•	0
Other Portfolio Income **6**	78136	0	6196	288	8770	685	18184	22395	4587	2833	•	•	0
Other Receipts **7**	1178658	0	7434	7017	243238	406134	74705	45273	24488	69484	•	•	0
Total Receipts **8**	70671471	121517	2555075	1991419	13558305	7866790	10255838	6992956	5310424	4998320	•	•	0
Average Total Receipts **9**	7923	94	753	1974	5839	17521	34416	83249	139748	263069	•	•	•
Operating Costs/Operating Income (%)													
Cost of Operations **10**	71.2	9.1	60.9	66.6	70.8	69.1	73.3	73.5	73.9	77.4	•	•	•
Salaries and Wages **11**	10.2	•	10.5	9.9	9.2	12.6	10.0	9.8	9.4	8.0	•	•	•
Taxes Paid **12**	1.5	1.7	2.1	1.5	1.5	1.7	1.3	1.2	1.3	1.1	•	•	•
Interest Paid **13**	0.8	•	0.7	0.6	0.3	0.9	0.3	0.5	0.4	0.4	•	•	•
Depreciation **14**	0.8	0.0	0.7	0.4	0.4	1.3	0.5	0.5	1.0	1.1	•	•	•
Amortization and Depletion **15**	0.1	•	0.0	0.0	0.1	0.0	0.0	0.1	0.2	0.1	•	•	•
Pensions and Other Deferred Comp. **16**	0.4	•	0.6	0.5	0.4	0.5	0.4	0.7	0.3	0.2	•	•	•
Employee Benefits **17**	1.0	•	0.7	0.4	1.0	1.0	0.8	1.0	0.9	0.6	•	•	•
Advertising **18**	0.6	0.2	2.2	0.3	0.4	1.3	0.4	0.5	0.6	0.5	•	•	•
Other Expenses **19**	8.2	30.6	13.1	10.6	8.8	9.0	6.9	7.2	7.1	6.6	•	•	•
Officers' Compensation **20**	2.4	25.2	4.8	7.1	4.5	3.9	2.6	1.3	0.9	0.7	•	•	•
Operating Margin **21**	2.8	33.2	3.7	2.2	2.7	•	3.5	3.6	4.0	3.2	•	•	•
Operating Margin Before Officers' Comp. **22**	5.2	58.4	8.5	9.2	7.2	2.6	6.0	4.9	4.8	3.8	•	•	•

Selected Average Balance Sheet ($ in Thousands)

Net Receivables 23	1025	0	35	209	717	1916	4441	9838	17592	49122
Inventories 24	1048	0	15	272	722	3093	5178	12544	24030	36705
Net Property, Plant and Equipment 25	359	0	11	38	134	755	1026	3417	8728	20977
Total Assets 26	3645	0	116	679	2196	7083	14974	33816	69161	153556
Notes and Loans Payable 27	947	0	104	53	407	1894	2758	8123	15417	20590
All Other Liabilities 28	973	0	60	130	680	1880	3765	7660	15034	57532
Net Worth 29	1724	0	-48	496	1109	3310	8451	18033	38710	75435

Selected Financial Ratios (Times to 1)

Current Ratio 30	2.3	•	1.1	3.0	2.3	2.4	2.3	2.6	2.5	1.9
Quick Ratio 31	1.2	•	0.7	1.7	1.2	1.0	1.2	1.3	1.1	1.1
Net Sales to Working Capital 32	5.2	•	66.0	5.6	5.4	4.7	4.8	4.8	4.3	4.9
Coverage Ratio 33	7.2	•	7.1	5.5	14.8	6.0	14.0	10.6	12.3	12.5
Total Asset Turnover 34	2.1	•	6.5	2.9	2.6	2.3	2.3	2.4	2.0	1.7
Inventory Turnover 35	5.3	•	30.5	4.8	5.6	3.7	4.8	4.8	4.3	5.5
Receivables Turnover 36	9.0	•	31.6	8.0	9.2	8.6	8.6	8.8	7.9	7.7
Total Liabilities to Net Worth 37	1.1	•	•	0.4	1.0	1.1	0.8	0.9	0.8	1.0
Current Assets to Working Capital 38	1.8	•	7.9	1.5	1.8	1.7	1.8	1.6	1.7	2.1
Current Liabilities to Working Capital 39	0.8	•	6.9	0.5	0.8	0.7	0.8	0.6	0.7	1.1
Working Capital to Net Sales 40	0.2	•	0.0	0.2	0.2	0.2	0.2	0.2	0.2	0.2
Inventory to Working Capital 41	0.8	•	2.0	0.6	0.7	0.9	0.8	0.8	0.8	0.8
Total Receipts to Cash Flow 42	9.6	1.7	6.6	9.6	8.9	9.4	11.4	11.0	10.5	10.6
Cost of Goods to Cash Flow 43	6.8	0.2	4.0	6.4	6.3	6.5	8.3	8.1	7.8	8.2
Cash Flow to Total Debt 44	0.4	•	0.7	1.1	0.6	0.5	0.5	0.5	0.4	0.3

Selected Financial Factors (in Percentages)

Debt Ratio 45	52.7	141.7	26.9	49.5	53.3	43.6	46.7	44.0	50.9	
Return on Total Assets 46	11.8	•	31.6	8.9	13.0	12.1	10.9	12.6	10.1	8.6
Return on Equity Before Income Taxes 47	21.6	•	•	10.0	24.0	21.5	17.9	21.4	16.5	16.0
Return on Equity After Income Taxes 48	18.8	•	•	9.3	21.2	20.2	16.2	19.2	15.3	13.8
Profit Margin (Before Income Tax) 49	4.8	33.2	4.2	2.5	4.6	4.3	4.4	4.7	4.6	4.7
Profit Margin (After Income Tax) 50	4.2	33.2	4.1	2.4	4.1	4.0	4.0	4.2	4.3	4.0

Table I
Corporations with and without Net Income

MACHINERY, EQUIPMENT, AND SUPPLIES

MONEY AMOUNTS AND SIZE OF ASSETS IN THOUSANDS OF DOLLARS

Item Description for Accounting Period 7/10 Through 6/11	Total	Zero Assets	Under 500	500 to 1,000	1,000 to 5,000	5,000 to 10,000	10,000 to 25,000	25,000 to 50,000	50,000 to 100,000	100,000 to 250,000	250,000 to 500,000	500,000 to 2,500,000	2,500,000 and over
Number of Enterprises **1**	47373	2547	28929	4631	7892	1635	1076	349	160	93	31	24	5
Revenues ($ in Thousands)													
Net Sales **2**	249878786	6555403	14168310	7652628	45125392	24916705	33884053	20511695	17049879	18628509	11848333	21990027	27547851
Interest **3**	306291	8970	2006	3113	20650	8632	14827	16723	19169	20505	22173	31906	137617
Rents **4**	116131	118	3311	2916	8778	11476	20023	9360	7448	26616	9240	12457	4389
Royalties **5**	42311	0	0	13522	5447	0	13	28	6122	194	1140	11632	4213
Other Portfolio Income **6**	1168986	63422	8082	5398	134667	44352	131803	121171	203521	177542	112421	155506	11103
Other Receipts **7**	2043918	43704	154029	183686	265486	226665	272132	199732	259927	145109	98306	115867	79272
Total Receipts **8**	253556423	6671617	14335738	7861263	45560420	25207830	34322851	20858709	17546066	18998475	12091613	22317395	27784445
Average Total Receipts **9**	5352	2619	496	1698	5773	15418	31899	59767	109663	204285	390052	929891	5556889
Operating Costs/Operating Income (%)													
Cost of Operations **10**	75.0	93.5	63.2	69.3	71.8	74.0	76.7	79.1	77.0	72.9	71.6	68.9	85.8
Salaries and Wages **11**	7.5	1.5	5.8	8.2	8.9	8.2	7.9	6.6	7.7	8.1	8.6	8.7	4.7
Taxes Paid **12**	1.2	0.3	1.6	1.8	1.5	1.4	1.1	1.0	1.2	1.3	1.3	1.3	0.8
Interest Paid **13**	0.8	0.3	0.5	0.6	0.5	0.6	0.6	0.6	0.9	1.1	1.2	1.6	1.0
Depreciation **14**	1.7	0.4	0.5	1.2	0.9	1.1	1.4	2.3	2.8	3.1	4.5	3.2	0.7
Amortization and Depletion **15**	0.2	0.0	0.0	0.0	0.1	0.1	0.1	0.1	0.2	0.2	0.3	1.5	0.1
Pensions and Other Deferred Comp. **16**	0.4	0.0	1.3	0.2	0.4	0.3	0.3	0.3	0.3	0.4	0.3	0.7	0.6
Employee Benefits **17**	1.0	0.2	0.6	0.9	0.8	0.8	0.9	0.8	1.0	1.4	1.9	2.0	0.7
Advertising **18**	0.4	0.1	0.4	0.5	0.5	0.4	0.4	0.4	0.4	0.8	0.3	0.4	0.5
Other Expenses **19**	7.4	3.1	13.7	10.4	8.5	8.0	6.7	6.3	6.8	8.5	8.6	7.8	2.5
Officers' Compensation **20**	2.2	0.9	9.5	5.0	4.0	2.4	1.8	1.0	1.1	0.8	0.5	0.6	0.3
Operating Margin **21**	2.0	•	2.8	1.8	2.2	2.7	2.2	1.5	0.7	1.6	0.8	3.3	2.4
Operating Margin Before Officers' Comp. **22**	4.3	0.5	12.3	6.8	6.2	5.1	4.0	2.5	1.7	2.4	1.3	3.9	2.6

Selected Average Balance Sheet ($ in Thousands)

Net Receivables 23	685	0	31	171	598	1714	3678	6721	14772	31993	72924	161015	1091123
Inventories 24	896	0	33	226	825	3176	5716	14045	21037	47962	103491	181877	453430
Net Property, Plant and Equipment 25	398	0	18	71	195	767	1871	4856	10715	24489	62418	174540	282315
Total Assets 26	2939	0	126	692	2201	7062	14928	33892	67443	158037	335576	938062	3431177
Notes and Loans Payable 27	829	0	58	295	636	1890	4019	7708	17788	45781	100563	248144	982133
All Other Liabilities 28	1038	0	39	153	849	2179	5184	13559	22546	55554	100232	348162	1306481
Net Worth 29	1072	0	29	244	716	2993	5725	12625	27109	56702	134780	341756	1142562

Selected Financial Ratios (Times to 1)

Current Ratio 30	1.8	•	2.4	2.8	1.7	1.9	1.7	1.6	1.7	1.7	1.8	1.9	1.9
Quick Ratio 31	0.8	•	1.5	1.4	0.8	0.8	0.8	0.6	0.7	0.7	0.8	0.9	1.0
Net Sales to Working Capital 32	5.9	•	8.8	4.5	7.4	5.7	6.6	5.9	5.6	4.6	4.4	4.2	5.3
Coverage Ratio 33	5.5	5.3	9.4	8.1	6.8	7.8	7.2	5.9	4.8	4.4	3.3	4.0	4.4
Total Asset Turnover 34	1.8	•	3.9	2.4	2.6	2.2	2.1	1.7	1.6	1.3	1.1	1.0	1.6
Inventory Turnover 35	4.4	•	9.3	5.1	5.0	3.5	4.2	3.3	3.9	3.0	2.6	3.5	10.4
Receivables Turnover 36	8.3	•	17.7	8.8	9.9	10.0	9.3	8.9	8.4	6.7	5.7	6.5	5.2
Total Liabilities to Net Worth 37	1.7	•	3.3	1.8	2.1	1.4	1.6	1.7	1.5	1.8	1.5	1.7	2.0
Current Assets to Working Capital 38	2.3	•	1.7	1.5	2.4	2.2	2.5	2.7	2.5	2.4	2.3	2.2	2.1
Current Liabilities to Working Capital 39	1.3	•	0.7	0.5	1.4	1.2	1.5	1.7	1.5	1.4	1.3	1.2	1.1
Working Capital to Net Sales 40	0.2	•	0.1	0.2	0.1	0.2	0.2	0.2	0.2	0.2	0.2	0.2	0.2
Inventory to Working Capital 41	1.0	•	0.6	0.6	1.1	1.2	1.3	1.5	1.2	1.1	1.1	1.0	0.4
Total Receipts to Cash Flow 42	11.1	25.0	6.6	8.5	10.7	10.1	11.6	12.4	11.5	10.1	11.5	9.8	20.1
Cost of Goods to Cash Flow 43	8.3	23.4	4.2	5.9	7.7	7.5	8.9	9.8	8.8	7.4	8.2	6.8	17.3
Cash Flow to Total Debt 44	0.3	•	0.8	0.4	0.4	0.4	0.3	0.2	0.2	0.2	0.2	0.2	0.1

Selected Financial Factors (in Percentages)

Debt Ratio 45	63.5	•	76.6	64.8	67.5	57.6	61.6	62.7	59.8	64.1	59.8	63.6	66.7
Return on Total Assets 46	7.7	•	17.2	12.4	9.6	9.6	8.6	6.6	7.1	5.9	4.7	6.3	6.7
Return on Equity Before Income Taxes 47	17.3	•	65.6	31.0	25.2	19.7	19.3	14.7	14.0	12.8	8.1	13.0	15.6
Return on Equity After Income Taxes 48	14.0		64.7	30.4	23.1	17.6	17.2	12.6	11.7	9.2	6.2	6.9	9.6
Profit Margin (Before Income Tax) 49	3.5	1.3	3.9	4.6	3.2	3.9	3.5	3.2	3.6	3.6	2.9	4.8	3.2
Profit Margin (After Income Tax) 50	2.8	1.2	3.9	4.5	2.9	3.4	3.1	2.7	3.0	2.6	2.2	2.6	2.0

Table II

Corporations with Net Income

MACHINERY, EQUIPMENT, AND SUPPLIES

MONEY AMOUNTS AND SIZE OF ASSETS IN THOUSANDS OF DOLLARS

Item Description for Accounting Period 7/10 Through 6/11	Total	Zero Assets	Under 500	500 to 1,000	1,000 to 5,000	5,000 to 10,000	10,000 to 25,000	25,000 to 50,000	50,000 to 100,000	100,000 to 250,000	250,000 to 500,000	500,000 to 2,500,000	2,500,000 and over
Number of Enterprises 1	31926	1996	17823	2914	6387	1378	914	284	•	70	23	15	•
Revenues ($ in Thousands)													
Net Sales 2	201350781	6242909	10377046	5591247	39967085	22644948	30154746	17569905	•	15615786	9499767	16781820	•
Interest 3	262187	8586	1219	2197	17630	7070	13173	14242	•	14820	19383	18112	•
Rents 4	64847	8	0	2916	8437	10839	19287	7622	•	3234	2810	1104	•
Royalties 5	25369	0	0	13522	4868	0	13	0	•	105	1140	451	•
Other Portfolio Income 6	815812	61852	423	1965	100126	39227	85157	59324	•	138256	75488	95450	•
Other Receipts 7	1752624	40450	126407	177380	230030	196168	248151	187982	•	126217	83074	62097	•
Total Receipts 8	204271620	6353805	10505095	5789227	40328176	22898252	30520527	17839075	•	15898418	9681662	16959034	•
Average Total Receipts 9	6398	3183	589	1987	6314	16617	33392	62814	•	227120	420942	1130602	•
Operating Costs/Operating Income (%)													
Cost of Operations 10	73.6	94.1	60.8	68.9	71.5	73.6	76.2	79.4	•	73.5	72.1	68.0	•
Salaries and Wages 11	7.7	0.9	5.0	8.0	8.6	8.2	8.0	6.3	•	7.5	8.4	8.8	•
Taxes Paid 12	1.3	0.2	1.6	1.9	1.4	1.3	1.1	1.0	•	1.2	1.2	1.4	•
Interest Paid 13	0.6	0.3	0.4	0.6	0.5	0.5	0.5	0.5	•	0.9	1.1	1.1	•
Depreciation 14	1.4	0.3	0.4	0.9	0.7	1.0	1.2	1.6	•	2.4	3.3	2.4	•
Amortization and Depletion 15	0.1	0.0	0.0	0.0	0.1	0.1	0.1	0.1	•	0.1	0.3	0.7	•
Pensions and Other Deferred Comp. 16	0.5	0.0	1.8	0.1	0.4	0.3	0.3	0.3	•	0.4	0.4	0.9	•
Employee Benefits 17	1.0	0.1	0.6	0.8	0.8	0.8	0.8	0.7	•	1.2	1.8	1.7	•
Advertising 18	0.5	0.0	0.4	0.4	0.5	0.4	0.4	0.4	•	0.9	0.3	0.3	•
Other Expenses 19	7.1	2.1	12.0	9.2	8.1	7.7	6.3	5.7	•	8.0	8.0	6.2	•
Officers' Compensation 20	2.4	0.9	10.4	4.5	4.1	2.4	1.8	1.0	•	0.7	0.5	0.6	•
Operating Margin 21	4.0	0.9	6.7	4.7	3.3	3.7	3.3	3.1	•	3.2	2.4	7.9	•
Operating Margin Before Officers' Comp. 22	6.3	1.9	17.1	9.2	7.4	6.1	5.1	4.0	•	3.9	2.9	8.5	•

Selected Average Balance Sheet ($ in Thousands)

Net Receivables 23	816	0	29	202	642	1790	3659	6823	•	35017	82219	151245
Inventories 24	980	0	32	178	782	2927	5556	13202	•	43067	85529	214041
Net Property, Plant and Equipment 25	409	0	22	73	200	739	1720	4311	•	21845	49376	164990
Total Assets 26	3243	0	135	689	2187	7126	15041	33867	•	160980	333899	930670
Notes and Loans Payable 27	880	0	57	250	609	1816	3722	6844	•	42168	98872	279481
All Other Liabilities 28	1035	0	35	144	786	1938	5067	13666	•	57488	105051	266088
Net Worth 29	1328	0	43	295	793	3372	6251	13357	•	61324	134977	385102

Selected Financial Ratios (Times to 1)

Current Ratio 30	1.8	•	2.4	3.1	1.8	2.0	1.7	1.6	•	1.8	1.8	1.8
Quick Ratio 31	0.9	•	1.5	1.8	0.9	0.9	0.8	0.6	•	0.8	0.9	0.8
Net Sales to Working Capital 32	6.0	•	10.0	5.0	7.7	5.5	6.4	6.0	•	4.4	4.4	4.9
Coverage Ratio 33	9.7	11.4	20.2	15.8	9.6	10.6	10.3	9.8	•	6.5	4.9	8.8
Total Asset Turnover 34	1.9	•	4.3	2.8	2.9	2.3	2.2	1.8	•	1.4	1.2	1.2
Inventory Turnover 35	4.7	•	11.1	7.4	5.7	4.1	4.5	3.7	•	3.8	3.5	3.6
Receivables Turnover 36	8.8	•	20.9	8.9	10.9	11.1	10.4	10.3	•	8.1	6.2	8.7
Total Liabilities to Net Worth 37	1.4	•	2.1	1.3	1.8	1.1	1.4	1.5	•	1.6	1.5	1.4
Current Assets to Working Capital 38	2.3	•	1.7	1.5	2.3	2.0	2.4	2.6	•	2.2	2.3	2.3
Current Liabilities to Working Capital 39	1.3	•	0.7	0.5	1.3	1.0	1.4	1.6	•	1.2	1.3	1.3
Working Capital to Net Sales 40	0.2	•	0.1	0.2	0.1	0.2	0.2	0.2	•	0.2	0.2	0.2
Inventory to Working Capital 41	1.0	•	0.6	0.5	1.0	1.1	1.2	1.4	•	1.0	1.0	1.1
Total Receipts to Cash Flow 42	9.4	21.9	5.5	6.9	9.8	9.5	10.8	11.0	•	9.1	10.3	7.4
Cost of Goods to Cash Flow 43	6.9	20.6	3.4	4.7	7.0	7.0	8.2	8.8	•	6.7	7.4	5.1
Cash Flow to Total Debt 44	0.4	1.1	0.7	0.7	0.5	0.5	0.3	0.3	•	0.2	0.2	0.3

Selected Financial Factors (in Percentages)

Debt Ratio 45	59.1	•	68.0	57.2	63.8	52.7	58.4	60.6	•	61.9	60.2	58.6
Return on Total Assets 46	11.8	•	36.1	24.4	13.6	12.4	11.0	9.4	•	8.3	6.7	12.2
Return on Equity Before Income Taxes 47	25.8	•	107.3	53.5	33.5	23.7	23.8	21.4	•	18.5	13.4	26.1
Return on Equity After Income Taxes 48	21.8	•	106.4	52.8	31.2	21.5	21.6	18.9	•	14.2	10.8	17.5
Profit Margin (Before Income Tax) 49	5.4	2.7	8.0	8.2	4.2	4.9	4.5	4.6	•	5.1	4.4	9.0
Profit Margin (After Income Tax) 50	4.6	2.6	7.9	8.1	3.9	4.4	4.1	4.1	•	3.9	3.5	6.0

Table I
Corporations with and without Net Income

FURNITURE, SPORTS, TOYS, JEWELRY, OTHER DURABLE GOODS

MONEY AMOUNTS AND SIZE OF ASSETS IN THOUSANDS OF DOLLARS

Item Description for Accounting Period 7/10 Through 6/11		Total	Zero Assets	Under 500	500 to 1,000	1,000 to 5,000	5,000 to 10,000	10,000 to 25,000	25,000 to 50,000	50,000 to 100,000	100,000 to 250,000	250,000 to 500,000	500,000 to 2,500,000	2,500,000 and over
Number of Enterprises	1	70435	11776	42378	5242	8047	1633	878	240	145	59	24	9	4
Revenues ($ in Thousands)														
Net Sales	2	248867931	2076796	15303288	9652093	47948430	25797810	32024886	22773036	18827225	16261170	18586034	11863772	27753392
Interest	3	262221	5037	2285	2064	16885	9962	14708	10417	17121	11976	20645	6868	144253
Rents	4	73283	192	3619	0	7439	655	4095	2918	6061	5293	2176	29075	11760
Royalties	5	351092	0	0	0	3925	2769	14981	6109	47241	116023	84729	1179	74137
Other Portfolio Income	6	561113	6615	24999	5209	43874	23190	30111	19952	7952	20029	54253	40133	284796
Other Receipts	7	1544849	24522	87515	33507	316254	56826	193230	135009	189321	179567	195646	21986	111463
Total Receipts	8	251660489	2113162	15421706	9692873	48336807	25891212	32282011	22947441	19094921	16594058	18943483	11963013	28379801
Average Total Receipts	9	3573	179	364	1849	6007	15855	36768	95614	131689	281255	789312	1329224	7094950
Operating Costs/Operating Income (%)														
Cost of Operations	10	79.8	79.1	65.7	71.8	76.2	78.1	79.4	84.6	80.8	78.7	86.7	82.4	88.8
Salaries and Wages	11	5.4	4.6	7.1	6.7	6.7	6.1	5.8	4.2	5.1	5.8	3.6	5.1	3.3
Taxes Paid	12	1.0	2.2	1.5	1.5	1.1	1.1	1.1	0.7	1.0	1.0	0.5	0.9	0.7
Interest Paid	13	0.6	1.3	0.5	0.5	0.6	0.3	0.6	0.5	0.6	0.7	0.6	1.3	0.3
Depreciation	14	0.7	0.5	0.7	0.6	0.6	0.6	0.8	0.6	0.8	1.4	0.9	1.3	0.6
Amortization and Depletion	15	0.2	0.3	0.2	0.2	0.1	0.0	0.1	0.1	0.3	0.3	0.3	0.7	0.6
Pensions and Other Deferred Comp.	16	0.2	0.0	0.4	0.1	0.2	0.1	0.2	0.1	0.2	0.2	0.1	0.2	0.2
Employee Benefits	17	0.5	1.0	0.6	0.5	0.4	0.4	0.5	0.3	0.5	0.8	0.8	0.7	0.1
Advertising	18	1.1	0.3	1.0	0.8	0.5	0.4	1.0	1.0	1.3	2.3	1.3	0.8	2.0
Other Expenses	19	7.4	12.2	15.6	11.7	9.6	7.4	6.9	6.1	6.4	8.1	4.3	4.6	2.3
Officers' Compensation	20	2.0	3.7	6.4	3.8	2.9	2.8	1.8	0.8	0.9	0.6	0.5	0.7	0.3
Operating Margin	21	1.1	•	0.3	1.9	1.1	2.5	1.7	1.0	2.0	•	0.3	1.4	0.6
Operating Margin Before Officers' Comp.	22	3.1	•	6.7	5.7	4.1	5.3	3.5	1.9	2.9	0.6	0.8	2.0	0.9

Selected Average Balance Sheet ($ in Thousands)

Net Receivables 23	384	0	10	166	579	1890	4537	9409	18027	41109	101134	119639	806130
Inventories 24	449	0	46	275	844	2166	5256	11712	17897	35908	55467	171382	730979
Net Property, Plant and Equipment 25	128	0	10	92	154	431	1506	3302	5653	14022	32861	97975	179774
Total Assets 26	1564	0	103	700	2144	6922	15135	34927	67522	145778	325063	934027	4333940
Notes and Loans Payable 27	468	0	82	265	713	1451	4501	10651	20891	35969	78899	286043	970765
All Other Liabilities 28	573	0	24	349	881	2527	5662	13260	22331	48684	126442	232934	1730735
Net Worth 29	523	0	-3	86	549	2945	4972	11016	24301	61124	119721	415051	1632440

Selected Financial Ratios (Times to 1)

Current Ratio 30	1.7	•	2.6	1.4	1.7	1.8	1.6	1.6	1.7	1.8	1.5	2.3	1.5
Quick Ratio 31	0.8	•	1.1	0.7	0.8	0.9	0.8	0.7	0.8	1.0	0.8	0.9	0.6
Net Sales to Working Capital 32	7.6	•	7.5	11.4	7.8	6.2	8.0	9.2	6.4	6.2	10.4	5.9	7.5
Coverage Ratio 33	5.1	•	2.9	5.6	4.4	10.9	4.8	4.4	6.5	4.1	5.9	2.7	10.1
Total Asset Turnover 34	2.3	•	3.5	2.6	2.8	2.3	2.4	2.7	1.9	1.9	2.4	1.4	1.6
Inventory Turnover 35	6.3	•	5.2	4.8	5.4	5.7	5.5	6.9	5.9	6.0	12.1	6.3	8.4
Receivables Turnover 36	9.6	•	30.3	9.4	10.7	9.3	8.5	10.2	8.0	6.9	8.8	10.1	9.1
Total Liabilities to Net Worth 37	2.0	•	•	7.1	2.9	1.4	2.0	2.2	1.8	1.4	1.7	1.3	1.7
Current Assets to Working Capital 38	2.4	•	1.6	3.4	2.4	2.2	2.7	2.6	2.4	2.3	3.0	1.8	2.9
Current Liabilities to Working Capital 39	1.4	•	0.6	2.4	1.4	1.2	1.7	1.6	1.4	1.3	2.0	0.8	1.9
Working Capital to Net Sales 40	0.1	•	0.1	0.1	0.1	0.2	0.1	0.1	0.2	0.2	0.1	0.2	0.1
Inventory to Working Capital 41	1.0	•	0.9	1.6	1.1	1.0	1.2	1.2	1.0	0.8	0.9	0.8	0.8
Total Receipts to Cash Flow 42	13.1	16.1	8.2	9.7	11.6	11.8	13.5	15.2	11.7	11.9	18.6	19.7	23.4
Cost of Goods to Cash Flow 43	10.5	12.7	5.4	7.0	8.9	9.2	10.7	12.9	9.4	9.3	16.2	16.2	20.8
Cash Flow to Total Debt 44	0.3	•	0.4	0.3	0.3	0.3	0.3	0.3	0.3	0.3	0.2	0.1	0.1

Selected Financial Factors (in Percentages)

Debt Ratio 45	66.6	103.3	87.7	74.4	57.5	67.1	68.5	64.0	58.1	63.2	55.6	62.3
Return on Total Assets 46	6.6	5.6	7.5	7.0	7.2	7.5	6.3	7.9	5.1	8.2	5.1	5.6
Return on Equity Before Income Taxes 47	15.9	•	49.8	21.2	15.4	18.0	15.5	18.7	9.3	18.5	7.2	13.5
Return on Equity After Income Taxes 48	13.1	•	48.6	19.9	14.2	16.9	13.2	16.2	5.7	12.9	4.5	8.8
Profit Margin (Before Income Tax) 49	2.4	1.1	2.3	2.0	2.9	2.5	1.8	3.5	2.1	2.9	2.3	3.2
Profit Margin (After Income Tax) 50	1.9	0.9	1.8	1.8	2.6	2.3	1.5	3.0	1.3	2.0	1.4	2.1

Table II

Corporations with Net Income

FURNITURE, SPORTS, TOYS, JEWELRY, OTHER DURABLE GOODS

MONEY AMOUNTS AND SIZE OF ASSETS IN THOUSANDS OF DOLLARS

Item Description for Accounting Period 7/10 Through 6/11		Total	Zero Assets	Under 500	500 to 1,000	1,000 to 5,000	5,000 to 10,000	10,000 to 25,000	25,000 to 50,000	50,000 to 100,000	100,000 to 250,000	250,000 to 500,000	500,000 to 2,500,000	2,500,000 and over
Number of Enterprises	1	36176	4462	20069	•	5629	1304	726	187	•	43	19	•	4
Revenues ($ in Thousands)														
Net Sales	2	207740962	1154725	8431008	•	38078074	22736337	27841404	17243653	•	12426266	16740740	•	27755392
Interest	3	231358	4867	876	•	10373	7800	6632	9152	•	8454	20322	•	144253
Rents	4	60899	104	3402	•	1373	597	2783	2918	•	2006	2176	•	11760
Royalties	5	255105	0	0	•	3545	2769	14835	3158	•	25674	82573	•	74137
Other Portfolio Income	6	505800	6305	17212	•	26888	22285	28811	18522	•	19472	47690	•	284796
Other Receipts	7	1181462	37237	34614	•	166106	52960	149231	77735	•	154901	190346	•	111463
Total Receipts	8	209975586	1203238	8487112	•	38286359	22822748	28043696	17355138	•	12636773	17083847	•	28379801
Average Total Receipts	9	5804	270	423	•	6802	17502	38628	92808	•	293878	899150	•	7094950
Operating Costs/Operating Income (%)														
Cost of Operations	10	80.4	79.7	57.0	•	78.2	78.2	80.4	82.6	•	78.5	87.6	•	88.8
Salaries and Wages	11	4.8	1.2	7.4	•	4.9	5.7	5.3	4.4	•	5.0	3.4	•	3.3
Taxes Paid	12	0.9	1.0	1.5	•	1.0	1.1	1.1	0.7	•	0.9	0.5	•	0.7
Interest Paid	13	0.4	0.5	0.4	•	0.5	0.2	0.5	0.5	•	0.6	0.4	•	0.3
Depreciation	14	0.6	0.2	0.7	•	0.6	0.4	0.5	0.6	•	0.9	0.8	•	0.6
Amortization and Depletion	15	0.2	0.0	0.1	•	0.0	0.0	0.1	0.0	•	0.2	0.3	•	0.6
Pensions and Other Deferred Comp.	16	0.2	0.0	0.5	•	0.2	0.2	0.2	0.1	•	0.2	0.1	•	0.2
Employee Benefits	17	0.4	0.4	0.3	•	0.3	0.4	0.4	0.3	•	0.7	0.6	•	0.1
Advertising	18	1.0	0.3	0.6	•	0.4	0.4	1.0	1.1	•	2.0	1.2	•	2.0
Other Expenses	19	6.2	8.6	15.9	•	7.2	6.7	5.8	5.8	•	7.6	3.9	•	2.3
Officers' Compensation	20	1.8	2.9	7.8	•	2.9	2.9	1.8	0.9	•	0.6	0.3	•	0.3
Operating Margin	21	2.9	5.1	7.8	•	3.9	3.8	2.9	2.9	•	2.7	0.9	•	0.6
Operating Margin Before Officers' Comp.	22	4.8	8.0	15.6	•	6.8	6.7	4.7	3.7	•	3.3	1.2	•	0.9

Selected Average Balance Sheet ($ in Thousands)

	1	2	3	4	5	6	7	8	9	10
Net Receivables 23	618	0	13	619	2002	4730	10220	41580	88467	806130
Inventories 24	656	0	43	801	2039	5194	11730	35406	57322	730979
Net Property, Plant and Equipment 25	181	0	10	162	324	1213	2872	11486	36114	179774
Total Assets 26	2419	0	112	2171	6950	15212	34566	142974	311411	4333940
Notes and Loans Payable 27	590	0	53	589	1056	3806	9272	33169	66117	970765
All Other Liabilities 28	847	0	26	730	2458	5459	12800	48341	101141	1730735
Net Worth 29	982	0	33	851	3436	5947	12493	61464	144153	1632440

Selected Financial Ratios (Times to 1)

	1	2	3	4	5	6	7	8	9	10
Current Ratio 30	1.8		2.5	2.0	2.0	1.7	1.7	1.9	1.8	1.5
Quick Ratio 31	0.9		1.3	1.0	1.1	0.8	0.8	1.0	1.0	0.6
Net Sales to Working Capital 32	7.3		8.3	7.2	5.9	7.5	8.2	6.0	10.6	7.5
Coverage Ratio 33	10.4	18.1	23.3	10.6	19.5	8.6	8.0	8.0	11.3	10.1
Total Asset Turnover 34	2.4		3.7	3.1	2.5	2.5	2.7	2.0	2.8	1.6
Inventory Turnover 35	7.0		5.5	6.6	6.7	5.9	6.5	6.4	13.5	8.4
Receivables Turnover 36	10.3		29.7	11.6	10.8	9.0	9.6	7.2	13.1	9.1
Total Liabilities to Net Worth 37	1.5		2.4	1.5	1.0	1.6	1.8	1.3	1.2	1.7
Current Assets to Working Capital 38	2.3		1.7	2.0	2.0	2.5	2.5	2.1	2.3	2.9
Current Liabilities to Working Capital 39	1.3		0.7	1.0	1.0	1.5	1.5	1.1	1.3	1.9
Working Capital to Net Sales 40	0.1		0.1	0.1	0.2	0.1	0.1	0.2	0.1	0.1
Inventory to Working Capital 41	0.9		0.8	0.9	0.8	1.1	1.2	0.8	0.8	0.8
Total Receipts to Cash Flow 42	11.7	6.0	4.9	10.5	10.8	12.8	12.5	9.5	17.2	23.4
Cost of Goods to Cash Flow 43	9.4	4.8	2.8	8.2	8.5	10.3	10.3	7.5	15.0	20.8
Cash Flow to Total Debt 44	0.3		1.1	0.5	0.5	0.3	0.3	0.4	0.3	0.1

Selected Financial Factors (in Percentages)

	1	2	3	4	5	6	7	8	9	10
Debt Ratio 45	59.4		70.6	60.8	50.6	60.9	63.9	57.0	53.7	62.3
Return on Total Assets 46	10.8		33.1	15.3	11.1	10.3	10.7	10.1	11.4	5.6
Return on Equity Before Income Taxes 47	24.1		107.8	35.4	21.2	23.4	25.9	20.6	22.4	13.5
Return on Equity After Income Taxes 48	21.2		105.2	34.2	19.9	22.2	23.3	15.8	16.5	8.8
Profit Margin (Before Income Tax) 49	4.1	9.3	8.4	4.5	4.2	3.6	3.5	4.4	3.7	3.2
Profit Margin (After Income Tax) 50	3.6	8.7	8.2	4.3	3.9	3.4	3.2	3.4	2.7	2.1

Table I

Corporations with and without Net Income

PAPER AND PAPER PRODUCT

MONEY AMOUNTS AND SIZE OF ASSETS IN THOUSANDS OF DOLLARS

Item Description for Accounting Period 7/10 Through 6/11		Total	Zero Assets	Under 500	500 to 1,000	1,000 to 5,000	5,000 to 10,000	10,000 to 25,000	25,000 to 50,000	50,000 to 100,000	100,000 to 250,000	250,000 to 500,000	500,000 to 2,500,000	2,500,000 and over
Number of Enterprises	1	10164	2023	6269	622	923	98	131	55	19	14	5	5	0
Revenues ($ in Thousands)														
Net Sales	2	52645652	590917	2123374	1932074	6707091	2216930	6368415	6013091	3773814	6920930	4430755	11568260	0
Interest	3	19777	55	1428	165	2344	2278	1144	953	647	1507	2081	7174	0
Rents	4	12897	0	0	0	178	5290	262	979	1230	934	677	3346	0
Royalties	5	7047	0	0	0	0	0	0	0	0	0	0	7047	0
Other Portfolio Income	6	54520	0	22318	0	2022	169	10368	507	1319	311	555	16950	0
Other Receipts	7	243901	44	14508	323	33339	4550	30349	41425	23456	82159	6046	7708	0
Total Receipts	8	52983794	591016	2161628	1932562	6744974	2229217	6410538	6056955	3800466	7005841	4440114	11610485	0
Average Total Receipts	9	5213	292	345	3107	7308	22747	48935	110126	200025	500417	888023	2322097	•
Operating Costs/Operating Income (%)														
Cost of Operations	10	82.0	59.7	59.9	71.5	72.7	80.0	79.8	84.4	83.9	87.7	94.8	85.6	•
Salaries and Wages	11	5.9	5.5	6.6	8.4	8.9	7.1	6.4	5.8	5.5	4.8	1.4	5.6	•
Taxes Paid	12	0.8	0.7	1.7	1.0	1.2	1.2	0.8	0.8	0.8	0.5	0.2	0.7	•
Interest Paid	13	0.5	0.6	0.3	0.0	0.2	0.7	0.3	0.3	0.5	0.6	0.3	1.0	•
Depreciation	14	0.7	1.7	0.8	1.1	0.7	0.6	0.6	0.7	1.0	0.6	0.9	0.6	•
Amortization and Depletion	15	0.2	•	0.1	0.0	0.0	0.0	0.1	0.1	0.1	0.1	0.0	0.5	•
Pensions and Other Deferred Comp.	16	0.3	0.0	0.2	1.4	0.1	0.1	0.2	0.2	0.2	0.1	0.1	0.3	•
Employee Benefits	17	0.5	2.1	0.1	0.8	0.4	0.5	0.5	0.6	0.4	0.4	0.2	0.5	•
Advertising	18	0.3	0.4	1.1	0.4	0.2	0.1	1.1	0.2	0.1	0.1	0.0	0.1	•
Other Expenses	19	6.1	22.3	19.8	8.3	8.6	6.0	6.1	4.7	5.2	5.2	2.5	3.8	•
Officers' Compensation	20	1.2	4.9	5.7	3.2	2.2	1.7	1.5	1.0	0.9	0.4	0.2	0.2	•
Operating Margin	21	1.7	2.1	3.6	3.8	4.2	1.9	2.6	1.3	1.6	•	•	1.2	•
Operating Margin Before Officers' Comp.	22	2.9	7.0	9.3	7.0	6.3	3.6	4.1	2.3	2.4	0.0	•	1.4	•

Selected Average Balance Sheet ($ in Thousands)

Net Receivables 23	645	0	35	260	684	2782	5633	13679	22094	77184	200484	254934
Inventories 24	359	0	30	123	518	1470	3502	10146	21848	31048	38481	140173
Net Property, Plant and Equipment 25	188	0	12	109	192	1242	1241	3769	10565	17150	62275	69511
Total Assets 26	1702	0	134	732	2019	7303	15316	35753	72567	155712	337365	842083
Notes and Loans Payable 27	465	0	76	2	501	2410	2781	9521	19169	58365	81485	214043
All Other Liabilities 28	738	0	43	228	540	2161	5937	14890	24252	55941	212278	495815
Net Worth 29	499	0	15	502	977	2732	6598	11343	29147	41405	43603	132225

Selected Financial Ratios (Times to 1)

Current Ratio 30	1.4	•	2.0	2.7	2.1	1.9	1.7	1.5	1.8	1.7	1.2	0.9
Quick Ratio 31	0.9	•	1.2	2.2	1.2	1.2	1.1	0.8	0.9	1.1	0.9	0.5
Net Sales to Working Capital 32	14.0	•	7.0	8.1	8.5	8.6	9.4	12.9	8.1	9.9	19.6	•
Coverage Ratio 33	5.6	4.7	22.0	201.8	22.0	4.4	12.3	6.9	5.9	2.5	•	2.6
Total Asset Turnover 34	3.0	•	2.5	4.2	3.6	3.1	3.2	3.1	2.7	3.2	2.6	2.7
Inventory Turnover 35	11.8	•	6.8	18.1	10.2	12.3	11.1	9.1	7.6	14.0	21.8	14.1
Receivables Turnover 36	8.4	•	9.7	13.6	9.3	9.0	9.3	7.6	8.4	6.2	6.5	9.4
Total Liabilities to Net Worth 37	2.4	•	8.2	0.5	1.1	1.7	1.3	2.2	1.5	2.8	6.7	5.4
Current Assets to Working Capital 38	3.3	•	2.0	1.6	1.9	2.1	2.4	3.2	2.3	2.5	6.0	•
Current Liabilities to Working Capital 39	2.3	•	1.0	0.6	0.9	1.1	1.4	2.2	1.3	1.5	5.0	•
Working Capital to Net Sales 40	0.1	•	0.1	0.1	0.1	0.1	0.1	0.1	0.1	0.1	0.1	•
Inventory to Working Capital 41	1.0	•	0.7	0.3	0.7	0.6	0.7	1.2	0.9	0.6	1.1	•
Total Receipts to Cash Flow 42	15.4	5.7	5.3	10.1	9.7	14.9	12.8	17.9	17.3	22.4	60.1	25.4
Cost of Goods to Cash Flow 43	12.6	3.4	3.2	7.2	7.1	11.9	10.2	15.1	14.5	19.6	57.0	21.7
Cash Flow to Total Debt 44	0.3	•	0.5	1.3	0.7	0.3	0.4	0.3	0.3	0.2	0.1	0.1

Selected Financial Factors (in Percentages)

Debt Ratio 45	70.7	•	89.1	31.5	51.6	62.6	56.9	68.3	59.8	73.4	87.1	84.3
Return on Total Assets 46	8.5	•	14.2	16.3	17.8	9.9	11.4	7.2	7.5	4.6	•	7.0
Return on Equity Before Income Taxes 47	23.9	•	124.7	23.6	35.1	20.5	24.4	19.3	15.5	10.2	•	27.7
Return on Equity After Income Taxes 48	21.4	•	121.8	23.6	33.9	18.4	22.9	16.3	14.7	9.2	•	18.1
Profit Margin (Before Income Tax) 49	2.3	2.1	5.4	3.8	4.7	2.5	3.3	2.0	2.3	0.9	•	1.6
Profit Margin (After Income Tax) 50	2.1	2.1	5.2	3.8	4.6	2.2	3.1	1.7	2.2	0.8	•	1.0

Table II
Corporations with Net Income

PAPER AND PAPER PRODUCT

MONEY AMOUNTS AND SIZE OF ASSETS IN THOUSANDS OF DOLLARS

Item Description for Accounting Period 7/10 Through 6/11	Total	Zero Assets	Under 500	500 to 1,000	1,000 to 5,000	5,000 to 10,000	10,000 to 25,000	25,000 to 50,000	50,000 to 100,000	100,000 to 250,000	250,000 to 500,000	500,000 to 2,500,000	2,500,000 and over
Number of Enterprises **1**	6578	•	3362	563	763	70	112	49	19	8	•	•	0
Revenues ($ in Thousands)													
Net Sales **2**	42011579	•	1189109	1888808	5368569	1710291	5504806	5595749	3773814	4925783	•	•	0
Interest **3**	10662	•	1	42	2343	1059	1067	951	647	1048	•	•	0
Rents **4**	6200	•	0	0	20	2097	262	979	1230	934	•	•	0
Royalties **5**	22	•	0	0	0	0	0	0	0	0	•	•	0
Other Portfolio Income **6**	31365	•	2	0	1850	0	10368	507	1319	311	•	•	0
Other Receipts **7**	206468	•	977	323	33193	4208	28280	39070	23456	65915	•	•	0
Total Receipts **8**	42266296	•	1190089	1889173	5405975	1717655	5544783	5637256	3800466	4993991	•	•	0
Average Total Receipts **9**	6425	•	354	3356	7085	24538	49507	115046	200025	624249	•	•	•
Operating Costs/Operating Income (%)													
Cost of Operations **10**	81.5	•	50.8	71.4	71.7	78.4	80.1	84.3	83.9	86.1	•	•	•
Salaries and Wages **11**	5.7	•	6.6	8.6	8.4	7.9	5.7	5.8	5.5	5.7	•	•	•
Taxes Paid **12**	0.8	•	1.5	1.0	1.2	1.3	0.8	0.8	0.8	0.6	•	•	•
Interest Paid **13**	0.4	•	0.1	0.0	0.2	0.5	0.3	0.3	0.5	0.7	•	•	•
Depreciation **14**	0.6	•	1.3	1.0	0.6	0.4	0.7	0.5	1.0	0.5	•	•	•
Amortization and Depletion **15**	0.1	•	0.0	•	0.1	0.0	0.1	0.1	0.1	0.1	•	•	•
Pensions and Other Deferred Comp. **16**	0.3	•	0.3	0.6	0.5	0.1	0.3	0.2	0.2	0.1	•	•	•
Employee Benefits **17**	0.5	•	0.0	0.8	0.6	0.5	0.5	0.6	0.4	0.4	•	•	•
Advertising **18**	0.3	•	1.3	0.4	0.2	0.1	1.2	0.2	0.1	0.1	•	•	•
Other Expenses **19**	5.8	•	19.5	8.2	8.6	5.6	6.0	4.7	5.2	5.1	•	•	•
Officers' Compensation **20**	1.2	•	6.5	3.2	2.4	1.6	1.1	1.0	0.9	0.4	•	•	•
Operating Margin **21**	2.7	•	12.1	4.6	5.5	3.6	3.2	1.6	1.6	0.0	•	•	•
Operating Margin Before Officers' Comp. **22**	3.9	•	18.6	7.8	7.9	5.2	4.4	2.6	2.4	0.5	•	•	•

Selected Average Balance Sheet ($ in Thousands)

Net Receivables 23	759	•	34	283	650	2582	5734	14301	22094	92420
Inventories 24	439	•	26	115	491	1678	3297	10782	20946	38731
Net Property, Plant and Equipment 25	191	•	13	115	170	948	1333	2907	10565	17148
Total Assets 26	2023	•	134	752	1979	6880	15161	36305	72567	170376
Notes and Loans Payable 27	456	•	64	0	380	1776	2765	8071	19169	68394
All Other Liabilities 28	895	•	30	239	534	2013	6008	16094	24252	57634
Net Worth 29	671	•	39	513	1065	3091	6388	12140	29147	44349

Selected Financial Ratios (Times to 1)

Current Ratio 30	1.4	•	2.6	2.7	2.1	2.4	1.7	1.4	1.8	2.4
Quick Ratio 31	0.9	•	1.6	2.1	1.3	1.4	1.1	0.8	0.9	1.6
Net Sales to Working Capital 32	14.4	•	6.1	8.7	8.3	7.5	9.9	12.8	8.1	7.2
Coverage Ratio 33	8.9	•	193.3	259.3	33.5	9.9	14.7	9.5	5.9	3.1
Total Asset Turnover 34	3.2	•	2.6	4.5	3.6	3.6	3.2	3.1	2.7	3.6
Inventory Turnover 35	11.9	•	6.8	20.9	10.3	11.4	11.9	8.9	8.0	13.7
Receivables Turnover 36	8.8	•	10.4	14.1	8.9	9.4	10.0	7.9	10.2	•	2.8
Total Liabilities to Net Worth 37	2.0	•	2.4	0.5	0.9	1.2	1.4	2.0	1.5	2.8
Current Assets to Working Capital 38	3.3	•	1.6	1.6	1.9	1.7	2.5	3.3	2.3	1.7
Current Liabilities to Working Capital 39	2.3	•	0.6	0.6	0.9	0.7	1.5	2.3	1.3	0.7
Working Capital to Net Sales 40	0.1	•	0.2	0.1	0.1	0.1	0.1	0.1	0.1	0.1
Inventory to Working Capital 41	1.1	•	0.6	0.3	0.6	0.5	0.7	1.3	0.9	0.5
Total Receipts to Cash Flow 42	13.5	•	3.7	9.3	8.4	12.0	12.0	16.9	17.3	21.5
Cost of Goods to Cash Flow 43	11.0	•	1.9	6.7	6.0	9.4	9.6	14.3	14.5	18.5
Cash Flow to Total Debt 44	0.3	•	1.0	1.5	0.9	0.5	0.5	0.3	0.3	0.2

Selected Financial Factors (in Percentages)

Debt Ratio 45	66.8	•	70.5	31.8	46.2	55.1	57.9	66.6	59.8	74.0
Return on Total Assets 46	11.8	•	32.4	20.8	22.8	16.0	13.8	8.2	7.5	8.0
Return on Equity Before Income Taxes 47	31.6	•	109.4	30.4	41.1	32.0	30.5	21.9	15.5	20.8
Return on Equity After Income Taxes 48	28.8	•	107.4	30.4	39.7	29.3	28.7	18.7	14.7	19.2
Profit Margin (Before Income Tax) 49	3.3	•	12.2	4.7	6.2	4.0	4.0	2.3	2.3	1.5
Profit Margin (After Income Tax) 50	3.0	•	12.0	4.6	6.0	3.7	3.7	2.0	2.2	1.4

Table I
Corporations with and without Net Income

DRUGS AND DRUGGISTS' SUNDRIES

MONEY AMOUNTS AND SIZE OF ASSETS IN THOUSANDS OF DOLLARS

Item Description for Accounting Period 7/10 Through 6/11		Total	Zero Assets	Under 500	500 to 1,000	1,000 to 5,000	5,000 to 10,000	10,000 to 25,000	25,000 to 50,000	50,000 to 100,000	100,000 to 250,000	250,000 to 500,000	500,000 to 2,500,000	2,500,000 and over
Number of Enterprises	1	6538	1402	3001	592	918	269	146	73	47	36	11	21	22
Revenues ($ in Thousands)														
Net Sales	2	464150737	4946639	1361551	1109371	5423537	3906548	5599991	5846761	5467923	6636724	7926019	20255187	395671487
Interest	3	392086	6208	384	0	1021	1401	1711	5792	3350	4506	4766	207763	155183
Rents	4	49415	2573	0	838	6818	0	1753	0	101	1147	1195	5771	29218
Royalties	5	4117621	27004	0	0	25667	22	9277	929	47007	117419	2385	92631	3795279
Other Portfolio Income	6	748536	41740	884	17	1248	5753	13937	40496	142660	12325	1438	103354	384684
Other Receipts	7	5224153	2873	17563	9567	23816	62289	60393	34663	84314	144013	82323	1195789	3506551
Total Receipts	8	474682548	5027037	1380382	1119793	5482107	3976013	5686062	5928641	5745355	6916134	8018126	21860495	403542402
Average Total Receipts	9	72604	3586	460	1892	5972	14781	38946	81214	122242	192115	728921	1040976	18342836
Operating Costs/Operating Income (%)														
Cost of Operations	10	81.3	83.4	43.1	74.9	65.9	73.1	67.7	77.8	70.0	64.3	86.4	57.5	83.5
Salaries and Wages	11	3.7	4.4	7.8	5.9	7.7	7.3	9.1	5.8	9.2	11.0	4.1	9.8	3.0
Taxes Paid	12	0.5	0.5	1.2	1.5	1.4	0.8	1.2	0.7	1.0	1.4	0.5	1.3	0.4
Interest Paid	13	0.6	0.5	0.4	0.7	0.8	0.6	0.4	0.3	0.8	1.1	0.6	2.1	0.5
Depreciation	14	0.5	0.4	0.2	0.8	0.4	0.7	0.7	0.3	1.1	1.2	0.7	1.0	0.5
Amortization and Depletion	15	0.5	1.1	0.1	0.0	0.5	0.1	0.1	0.3	1.0	1.0	0.2	1.4	0.4
Pensions and Other Deferred Comp.	16	0.2	0.1	•	0.1	0.2	0.1	0.4	0.2	0.1	0.2	0.4	0.3	0.1
Employee Benefits	17	0.4	0.2	0.5	0.3	0.5	0.3	0.5	0.6	1.0	0.9	0.4	1.5	0.4
Advertising	18	0.9	1.7	1.9	0.4	1.0	0.6	0.9	1.8	3.9	2.6	0.9	1.9	0.7
Other Expenses	19	9.4	7.7	31.0	10.9	19.3	14.8	13.0	6.8	13.4	13.5	6.1	21.4	8.4
Officers' Compensation	20	0.4	2.9	5.1	4.4	4.9	1.3	2.4	1.5	1.0	1.0	0.3	0.7	0.2
Operating Margin	21	1.7	•	8.7	•	•	0.2	3.5	3.9	•	1.8	•	0.9	1.9
Operating Margin Before Officers' Comp.	22	2.1	0.1	13.7	4.4	2.2	1.5	5.9	5.5	4.4	2.8	•	1.6	2.1

Selected Average Balance Sheet ($ in Thousands)

Line Item													
Net Receivables 23	5640	0	2	125	666	2081	4932	11201	11798	26043	100145	139607	1298036
Inventories 24	4872	0	31	113	634	2114	4908	6338	12270	28722	77166	92208	1135041
Net Property, Plant and Equipment 25	2081	0	4	97	187	776	1656	779	5851	13147	34256	55284	480388
Total Assets 26	36534	0	51	772	2572	6714	16550	35628	72829	154031	359158	1018618	8852555
Notes and Loans Payable 27	7747	0	32	93	1086	2062	3362	4789	13453	63860	71308	198852	1828013
All Other Liabilities 28	15260	0	26	214	1374	2517	6660	14243	28641	45046	190470	278703	3849988
Net Worth 29	13527	-7	464	112	2135	6527	16596	30735	45125	97381		541063	3174554

Selected Financial Ratios (Times to 1)

Line Item													
Current Ratio 30	0.9	•	2.7	1.5	1.6	1.7	1.8	1.5	1.0	1.2	2.1	0.8	
Quick Ratio 31	0.5	•	1.4	0.9	0.8	1.0	1.2	0.8	0.5	0.7	1.2	0.5	
Net Sales to Working Capital 32	•	•	7.4	8.1	7.3	6.5	7.0	8.1	•	24.3	3.8	•	
Coverage Ratio 33	8.2	27.5	2.3	•	4.2	12.2	17.3	4.3	6.7	2.2	5.4	9.3	
Total Asset Turnover 34	1.9	•	2.4	2.3	2.2	2.3	2.2	1.6	1.2	2.0	0.9	2.0	
Inventory Turnover 35	11.8	6.4	12.4	6.1	5.0	5.3	9.8	6.6	4.1	8.1	6.0	13.2	
Receivables Turnover 36	13.6	131.7	16.8	10.0	8.0	8.2	8.0	10.8	6.3	6.6	7.5	15.1	
Total Liabilities to Net Worth 37	1.7	•	0.7	22.0	2.1	1.5	1.1	1.4	2.4	2.7	0.9	1.8	
Current Assets to Working Capital 38	•	•	1.6	2.8	2.7	2.4	2.2	3.0	•	6.8	1.9	•	
Current Liabilities to Working Capital 39	•	•	0.6	1.8	1.7	1.4	1.2	2.0	•	5.8	0.9	•	
Working Capital to Net Sales 40	•	•	0.1	0.1	0.1	0.2	0.1	0.1	•	0.0	0.3	•	
Inventory to Working Capital 41	•	•	0.6	0.8	1.2	0.9	0.5	1.0	•	2.0	0.4	•	
Total Receipts to Cash Flow 42	7.9	17.2	2.9	12.3	6.7	7.1	6.1	9.2	8.2	5.5	16.6	3.5	8.5
Cost of Goods to Cash Flow 43	6.5	14.3	1.2	9.2	4.4	5.2	4.1	7.1	5.8	3.5	14.3	2.0	7.1
Cash Flow to Total Debt 44	0.4	•	2.7	0.5	0.4	0.4	0.6	0.5	0.3	0.3	0.2	0.6	0.4

Selected Financial Factors (in Percentages)

Line Item													
Debt Ratio 45	63.0	•	114.7	95.7	68.2	60.6	53.4	57.8	70.7	72.9	46.9	64.1	
Return on Total Assets 46	9.1	93.5	4.0	39.8	5.6	12.7	12.9	5.6	8.5	2.7	10.7	9.2	
Return on Equity Before Income Taxes 47	21.6	•	3.8	13.5	29.5	26.0	10.2	24.8	5.4	16.3	22.8		
Return on Equity After Income Taxes 48	14.5	•	3.6	11.0	26.6	23.1	7.3	20.6	2.0	9.9	15.2		
Profit Margin (Before Income Tax) 49	4.1	10.1	•	0.9	2.0	5.4	2.7	6.1	0.7	9.2	4.0		
Profit Margin (After Income Tax) 50	2.8	10.1	0.9	1.6	2.0	4.8	1.9	5.0	0.3	5.6	2.7		

Table II
Corporations with Net Income

DRUGS AND DRUGGISTS' SUNDRIES

MONEY AMOUNTS AND SIZE OF ASSETS IN THOUSANDS OF DOLLARS

Item Description for Accounting Period 7/10 Through 6/11	Total	Zero Assets	Under 500	500 to 1,000	1,000 to 5,000	5,000 to 10,000	10,000 to 25,000	25,000 to 50,000	50,000 to 100,000	100,000 to 250,000	250,000 to 500,000	500,000 to 2,500,000	2,500,000 and over
Number of Enterprises **1**	3745	384	1995	352	237	114	•	•	29	28	7	15	•
Revenues ($ in Thousands)													
Net Sales **2**	453613357	3865893	1223265	811353	4361995	3593908	5045485	•	4335115	5918607	7018984	16777814	•
Interest **3**	227811	78	0	0	262	1217	1500	•	2504	2771	4346	55755	•
Rents **4**	39044	0	0	0	572	0	1753	•	93	1147	1195	5066	•
Royalties **5**	3984656	0	0	0	0	22	9263	•	31232	102040	1599	56411	•
Other Portfolio Income **6**	694761	35157	884	0	711	5753	13531	•	139859	1331	1438	72688	•
Other Receipts **7**	4861892	1727	15967	9539	5313	59444	43888	•	67377	142071	38376	941533	•
Total Receipts **8**	463421521	3902855	1240116	820892	4368853	3660344	5115420	•	4576180	6167967	7065938	17909267	•
Average Total Receipts **9**	123744	10164	622	2332	8738	15444	44872	•	157799	220285	1009420	1193951	•
Operating Costs/Operating Income (%)													
Cost of Operations **10**	81.8	91.3	39.7	78.2	70.3	74.5	67.9	•	75.1	67.3	90.1	54.4	•
Salaries and Wages **11**	3.5	1.6	7.6	4.4	7.2	5.4	8.7	•	7.4	11.2	2.9	9.7	•
Taxes Paid **12**	0.4	0.4	1.1	1.2	1.3	0.6	1.2	•	0.8	1.5	0.5	1.4	•
Interest Paid **13**	0.5	0.0	0.2	0.6	0.3	0.4	0.4	•	0.7	0.8	0.4	0.9	•
Depreciation **14**	0.5	0.1	0.2	0.2	0.4	0.6	0.7	•	0.6	1.1	0.6	1.0	•
Amortization and Depletion **15**	0.4	0.2	0.1	0.0	0.1	0.1	0.1	•	0.8	0.5	0.2	1.2	•
Pensions and Other Deferred Comp. **16**	0.2	0.0	•	•	0.2	0.1	0.4	•	0.1	0.2	0.4	0.3	•
Employee Benefits **17**	0.4	0.1	0.6	0.1	0.2	0.2	0.4	•	0.9	0.9	0.1	1.6	•
Advertising **18**	0.8	0.2	2.0	0.4	0.5	0.5	0.9	•	2.6	1.9	0.2	2.0	•
Other Expenses **19**	8.9	2.3	29.8	7.0	13.0	11.6	11.4	•	10.6	10.0	3.4	20.4	•
Officers' Compensation **20**	0.4	0.8	4.9	5.0	3.4	1.2	2.2	•	0.9	1.0	0.2	0.7	•
Operating Margin **21**	2.2	3.0	14.0	2.9	3.0	4.7	5.7	•	•	3.8	0.8	6.3	•
Operating Margin Before Officers' Comp. **22**	2.6	3.8	18.8	7.9	6.5	5.9	7.9	•	0.4	4.8	1.0	7.1	•

Selected Average Balance Sheet ($ in Thousands)

	•	•	•	•	•	•	•	•	•	•	•
Net Receivables 23	9330	0	0	154	933	2214	5651	15701	29214	123149	157516
Inventories 24	8199	0	26	142	944	2221	5749	15075	31713	71274	104821
Net Property, Plant and Equipment 25	3419	0	4	21	261	597	1877	4342	13932	44429	58267
Total Assets 26	58759	0	42	801	2935	6551	16771	71514	155312	367020	1101243
Notes and Loans Payable 27	11426	0	22	13	836	1643	2495	13676	45529	65770	172202
All Other Liabilities 28	25032	0	17	163	1806	2213	7029	30711	52055	203697	282267
Net Worth 29	22301	0	3	625	293	2696	7248	27128	57728	97553	646774

Selected Financial Ratios (Times to 1)

	•	•	•	•	•	•	•	•	•	•	•
Current Ratio 30	0.9	•	0.9	3.2	1.4	1.8	1.7	1.6	1.4	1.2	2.1
Quick Ratio 31	0.5	•	0.7	1.5	0.8	0.9	0.9	0.9	0.7	0.7	1.3
Net Sales to Working Capital 32	•	139.0	•	6.5	13.7	6.3	7.4	7.8	8.2	27.4	3.8
Coverage Ratio 33	10.4	70.5	8.0	11.9	18.5	18.5	8.1	11.5	4.6	•	15.7
Total Asset Turnover 34	2.1	14.8	2.9	3.0	2.3	2.6	2.1	1.4	2.7	1.4	1.0
Inventory Turnover 35	12.1	9.2	12.7	6.5	5.1	5.2	7.4	4.5	12.7	2.7	5.8
Receivables Turnover 36	13.8	1249.5	18.7	9.7	8.4	7.9	10.6	6.5	•	2.8	0.7
Total Liabilities to Net Worth 37	1.6	15.2	0.3	9.0	1.4	1.3	1.6	1.7	2.8	1.7	1.9
Current Assets to Working Capital 38	•	•	1.5	3.8	2.3	2.4	2.7	3.5	6.4	•	1.9
Current Liabilities to Working Capital 39	•	•	0.5	2.8	1.3	1.4	1.7	2.5	5.4	•	0.9
Working Capital to Net Sales 40	•	•	0.2	0.1	0.2	0.1	0.1	0.1	0.0	•	0.3
Inventory to Working Capital 41	•	•	0.6	1.5	1.0	1.0	0.9	1.2	1.9	•	0.4
Total Receipts to Cash Flow 42	7.9	17.4	10.8	7.4	6.3	6.0	8.4	5.9	22.7	•	3.1
Cost of Goods to Cash Flow 43	6.5	15.9	8.5	5.2	4.7	4.1	6.3	4.0	20.4	•	1.7
Cash Flow to Total Debt 44	0.4	6.2	1.2	0.4	0.6	0.8	0.4	0.4	0.2	•	0.8

Selected Financial Factors (in Percentages)

	•	•	•	•	•	•	•	•	•	•	•
Debt Ratio 45	62.0	93.8	22.0	90.0	58.9	56.8	62.1	62.8	73.4	•	41.3
Return on Total Assets 46	10.3	229.9	13.5	10.3	16.1	19.7	12.2	11.9	5.6	•	14.5
Return on Equity Before Income Taxes 47	24.6	3671.2	15.1	95.0	37.1	43.1	28.2	29.3	16.6	•	23.2
Return on Equity After Income Taxes 48	17.1	3670.4	14.8	82.8	34.8	39.8	22.8	25.1	11.3	•	15.7
Profit Margin (Before Income Tax) 49	4.5	3.9	15.4	4.1	3.2	6.6	7.1	5.1	8.0	1.6	13.4
Profit Margin (After Income Tax) 50	3.1	3.9	15.4	4.0	2.8	6.2	6.5	4.1	6.9	1.1	9.1

Table I
Corporations with and without Net Income

APPAREL, PIECE GOODS, AND NOTIONS

MONEY AMOUNTS AND SIZE OF ASSETS IN THOUSANDS OF DOLLARS

Item Description for Accounting Period 7/10 Through 6/11	Total	Zero Assets	Under 500	500 to 1,000	1,000 to 5,000	5,000 to 10,000	10,000 to 25,000	25,000 to 50,000	50,000 to 100,000	100,000 to 250,000	250,000 to 500,000	500,000 to 2,500,000	2,500,000 and over
Number of Enterprises **1**	19265	2192	12960	993	2300	359	245	103	46	31	18	13	5
Revenues ($ in Thousands)													
Net Sales **2**	101739462	1519917	5990641	2736651	11624400	7296641	9320416	7358522	6247337	6437324	8225088	12629682	22352842
Interest **3**	62404	380	1125	247	3096	460	1256	1231	2005	7011	9240	18947	17408
Rents **4**	39355	301	0	0	130	1850	231	1083	2597	18112	5577	1791	7683
Royalties **5**	1615662	94	0	0	0	2271	0	3637	26376	32080	137750	147472	1265981
Other Portfolio Income **6**	712273	11940	0	2	64094	3636	9333	10581	344	7885	6452	89958	508050
Other Receipts **7**	1293055	22771	1839	14990	22087	3506	110716	46253	39813	49380	57757	59930	864010
Total Receipts **8**	105462211	1555403	5993605	2751890	11713807	7308364	9441952	7421307	6318472	6551792	8441864	12947780	25015974
Average Total Receipts **9**	5474	710	462	2771	5093	20358	38539	72052	137358	211348	468992	995983	5003195
Operating Costs/Operating Income (%)													
Cost of Operations **10**	64.6	77.8	64.9	64.8	72.3	73.7	73.1	72.3	72.1	63.4	60.6	54.3	55.9
Salaries and Wages **11**	9.7	5.6	5.0	7.1	6.3	7.4	7.4	6.5	8.4	8.7	11.0	12.9	14.4
Taxes Paid **12**	2.6	2.0	1.5	2.2	2.2	3.4	2.7	2.1	2.1	2.6	2.2	2.7	3.0
Interest Paid **13**	0.9	1.4	0.3	0.1	0.7	0.5	0.7	0.4	0.6	2.0	1.4	1.1	0.9
Depreciation **14**	1.4	0.6	0.5	0.1	0.4	0.3	0.4	0.8	1.0	1.7	2.1	2.2	2.6
Amortization and Depletion **15**	0.3	0.1	0.0	0.0	0.0	0.2	0.2	0.1	0.2	0.5	0.9	0.4	0.4
Pensions and Other Deferred Comp. **16**	0.3	0.1	0.3	1.3	0.2	0.1	0.1	0.1	0.2	0.3	0.3	0.2	0.5
Employee Benefits **17**	0.7	0.2	0.3	0.5	0.5	0.9	0.4	0.4	0.7	0.8	1.0	0.9	0.8
Advertising **18**	2.4	1.0	0.3	1.5	0.9	0.8	0.9	1.0	1.5	3.0	1.9	3.1	5.3
Other Expenses **19**	14.0	17.0	17.9	10.0	12.9	8.6	8.4	8.7	10.8	13.6	14.6	14.3	20.4
Officers' Compensation **20**	2.0	1.5	6.7	5.9	2.7	1.9	2.2	2.4	1.6	1.5	1.1	0.9	1.1
Operating Margin **21**	1.3	•	2.3	6.6	0.7	2.3	3.4	5.2	1.0	1.8	3.0	7.1	•
Operating Margin Before Officers' Comp. **22**	3.3	•	8.9	12.4	3.5	4.1	5.6	7.6	2.6	3.3	4.1	8.0	•

Selected Average Balance Sheet ($ in Thousands)

Item												
Net Receivables 23	626	21	184	545	2222	4255	10100	14942	34575	54305	149156	557440
Inventories 24	684	24	433	533	2355	5588	11162	21028	39528	75810	146708	475816
Net Property, Plant and Equipment 25	321	5	27	75	760	784	2860	5709	17666	36184	105218	467219
Total Assets 26	4947	97	706	1966	6999	15479	34161	69712	155812	344228	968685	10436561
Notes and Loans Payable 27	927	67	178	555	2469	4435	8054	17792	67300	103432	155779	1189227
All Other Liabilities 28	981	37	345	770	3259	6649	12604	23775	39918	111010	219131	1005398
Net Worth 29	3039	-8	182	641	1271	4395	13502	28145	48594	129785	593775	8241937

Selected Financial Ratios (Times to 1)

Item													
Current Ratio 30	1.7	•	2.1	1.7	1.7	1.4	1.6	1.8	1.6	1.9	1.8	2.7	1.5
Quick Ratio 31	0.8	•	1.3	0.8	0.8	0.7	0.6	0.8	0.6	0.8	0.8	1.5	0.8
Net Sales to Working Capital 32	6.3	•	10.6	10.4	7.3	8.2	12.9	5.3	6.5	4.1	5.5	3.4	7.8
Coverage Ratio 33	7.7	•	8.4	53.6	3.1	7.7	5.4	15.5	4.5	2.8	5.9	10.1	12.3
Total Asset Turnover 34	1.1	•	4.8	3.9	2.6	2.5	2.9	2.1	1.9	1.3	1.3	1.0	0.4
Inventory Turnover 35	5.0	•	12.4	4.1	6.9	5.0	6.4	4.6	4.7	3.3	3.7	3.6	5.3
Receivables Turnover 36	9.3	•	22.8	12.9	10.1	9.9	9.7	8.3	8.3	6.6	9.1	7.1	9.8
Total Liabilities to Net Worth 37	0.6	•	•	2.9	2.1	2.5	4.5	1.5	1.5	2.2	1.7	0.6	0.3
Current Assets to Working Capital 38	2.3	•	1.9	2.4	2.4	2.7	3.7	2.2	2.6	2.1	2.2	1.6	3.2
Current Liabilities to Working Capital 39	1.3	•	0.9	1.4	1.4	1.7	2.7	1.2	1.6	1.1	1.2	0.6	2.2
Working Capital to Net Sales 40	0.2	•	0.1	0.1	0.1	0.1	0.1	0.2	0.2	0.2	0.2	0.3	0.1
Inventory to Working Capital 41	1.0	•	0.7	1.2	0.9	1.2	1.8	1.0	1.1	1.0	1.0	0.6	1.1
Total Receipts to Cash Flow 42	6.5	10.5	6.8	7.2	8.5	8.9	11.2	8.1	9.8	7.2	6.6	5.4	4.4
Cost of Goods to Cash Flow 43	4.2	8.1	4.4	4.7	6.2	6.5	8.2	5.8	7.0	4.6	4.0	2.9	2.4
Cash Flow to Total Debt 44	0.4	•	0.6	0.7	0.4	0.4	0.3	0.4	0.3	0.3	0.3	0.5	0.5

Selected Financial Factors (in Percentages)

Item													
Debt Ratio 45	38.6	•	108.1	74.2	67.4	81.8	71.6	60.5	59.6	68.8	62.3	38.7	21.0
Return on Total Assets 46	7.0	•	12.6	28.3	5.8	8.6	13.3	13.6	5.3	7.5	10.9	10.8	4.5
Return on Equity Before Income Taxes 47	10.0	•	•	107.6	11.9	38.7	40.8	32.2	10.2	15.5	24.1	15.9	5.3
Return on Equity After Income Taxes 48	7.3	•	•	107.2	11.1	36.3	38.3	29.8	8.2	10.6	15.8	10.8	3.4
Profit Margin (Before Income Tax) 49	5.7	•	2.3	7.1	1.5	2.4	4.7	6.1	2.1	3.6	6.8	9.7	9.8
Profit Margin (After Income Tax) 50	4.2	•	2.3	7.1	1.4	2.3	4.4	5.6	1.7	2.5	4.5	6.6	6.3

Table II
Corporations with Net Income

APPAREL, PIECE GOODS, AND NOTIONS

MONEY AMOUNTS AND SIZE OF ASSETS IN THOUSANDS OF DOLLARS

Item Description for Accounting Period 7/10 Through 6/11	Total	Zero Assets	Under 500	500 to 1,000	1,000 to 5,000	5,000 to 10,000	10,000 to 25,000	25,000 to 50,000	50,000 to 100,000	100,000 to 250,000	250,000 to 500,000	500,000 to 2,500,000	2,500,000 and over
Number of Enterprises 1	11664	425	8230	820	1517	285	202	100	32	26	14	•	•
Revenues ($ in Thousands)													
Net Sales 2	82182957	955513	5031620	2393382	8598897	5510684	8438510	7277164	4192225	5657404	6612597	•	•
Interest 3	49158	133	22	229	400	225	665	1230	1776	5898	8586	•	•
Rents 4	33194	301	0	0	121	1850	231	1083	1676	17959	5503	•	•
Royalties 5	1394088	0	0	0	0	0	0	3637	11093	20777	119578	•	•
Other Portfolio Income 6	701155	6619	0	2	63394	0	8996	10581	344	7803	5681	•	•
Other Receipts 7	1214863	13840	1813	28504	20927	-5407	100760	40255	33436	42728	50411	•	•
Total Receipts 8	85575415	976406	5033455	2422117	8683739	5507352	8549162	7333950	4240550	5752569	6802356	•	•
Average Total Receipts 9	7337	2297	612	2954	5724	19324	42323	73340	132517	221253	485883	•	•
Operating Costs/Operating Income (%)													
Cost of Operations 10	63.2	79.4	65.4	62.9	70.1	73.2	72.3	72.3	70.8	63.0	57.7	•	•
Salaries and Wages 11	9.9	2.3	3.9	7.2	7.1	6.7	7.3	6.5	8.3	8.7	11.5	•	•
Taxes Paid 12	2.3	1.7	1.1	2.3	2.0	2.3	2.9	2.1	1.9	2.7	2.3	•	•
Interest Paid 13	0.7	0.9	0.2	0.1	0.8	0.6	0.5	0.4	0.6	1.4	0.8	•	•
Depreciation 14	1.5	0.7	0.5	0.1	0.3	0.3	0.4	0.8	0.7	1.7	2.2	•	•
Amortization and Depletion 15	0.2	0.0	0.0	0.1	0.0	0.0	0.0	0.1	0.1	0.6	0.5	•	•
Pensions and Other Deferred Comp. 16	0.3	0.0	0.3	1.5	0.2	0.1	0.1	0.1	0.3	0.3	0.4	•	•
Employee Benefits 17	0.6	0.2	0.2	0.6	0.4	0.8	0.4	0.4	0.6	0.8	1.0	•	•
Advertising 18	2.4	0.4	0.2	1.7	1.1	0.6	1.0	0.9	1.1	2.7	2.1	•	•
Other Expenses 19	13.4	13.4	14.5	9.8	12.1	8.4	8.3	8.3	9.4	12.8	15.4	•	•
Officers' Compensation 20	2.2	0.2	6.5	5.6	3.1	1.8	2.3	2.4	1.8	1.5	1.2	•	•
Operating Margin 21	3.3	0.8	7.1	8.2	2.7	5.1	4.6	5.7	4.4	3.9	4.8	•	•
Operating Margin Before Officers' Comp. 22	5.4	1.0	13.6	13.8	5.9	7.0	6.9	8.2	6.2	5.4	6.0	•	•

Selected Average Balance Sheet ($ in Thousands)

Net Receivables 23	819	0	22	186	542	2626	4273	10362	16068	35946	58376
Inventories 24	884	0	23	373	613	2358	5642	10509	22358	37910	66550
Net Property, Plant and Equipment 25	445	0	7	31	70	762	835	2855	3522	17743	41631
Total Assets 26	6960	0	102	724	1970	7051	15428	34124	68874	156162	352434
Notes and Loans Payable 27	958	0	32	146	573	2384	4137	7169	17435	59063	50064
All Other Liabilities 28	1247	0	48	346	769	2393	6269	12732	21463	38215	111621
Net Worth 29	4755	0	22	232	628	2274	5022	14222	29975	58884	190748

Selected Financial Ratios (Times to 1)

Current Ratio 30	2.0	•	1.7	1.8	1.7	1.8	1.6	1.8	1.8	2.0	1.9
Quick Ratio 31	1.0	•	1.1	0.9	0.8	0.9	0.8	0.8	0.7	0.8	0.8
Net Sales to Working Capital 32	5.5	•	16.4	10.1	8.3	7.0	8.5	5.4	5.4	4.2	5.2
Coverage Ratio 33	13.2	4.5	34.9	73.7	5.5	10.1	11.9	16.4	9.6	5.2	12.9
Total Asset Turnover 34	1.0	•	6.0	4.0	2.9	2.7	2.7	2.1	1.9	1.4	1.3
Inventory Turnover 35	5.0	•	17.4	4.9	6.5	6.0	5.4	5.0	4.1	3.6	4.1
Receivables Turnover 36	9.7	•	28.8	16.7	10.5	7.9	11.6	9.3	7.0	6.9	11.5
Total Liabilities to Net Worth 37	0.5	•	3.6	2.1	2.1	2.1	2.1	1.4	1.3	1.7	0.8
Current Assets to Working Capital 38	2.0	•	2.4	2.3	2.4	2.7	2.2	2.2	2.3	2.0	2.1
Current Liabilities to Working Capital 39	1.0	•	1.4	1.3	1.4	1.2	1.7	1.2	1.3	1.0	1.1
Working Capital to Net Sales 40	0.2	•	0.1	0.1	0.1	0.1	0.1	0.2	0.2	0.2	0.2
Inventory to Working Capital 41	0.8	•	0.8	1.2	1.0	1.0	1.2	1.0	1.0	0.9	0.9
Total Receipts to Cash Flow 42	5.8	6.2	5.8	6.2	7.4	8.6	8.1	7.9	7.8	6.5	5.7
Cost of Goods to Cash Flow 43	3.7	4.9	3.8	3.9	5.2	6.3	5.9	5.7	5.5	4.1	3.3
Cash Flow to Total Debt 44	0.6	•	1.3	1.0	0.6	0.5	0.5	0.5	0.4	0.3	0.5

Selected Financial Factors (in Percentages)

Debt Ratio 45	31.7	•	78.5	68.0	68.1	67.7	67.4	58.3	56.5	62.3	45.9
Return on Total Assets 46	9.2	•	44.2	38.5	13.1	15.4	17.4	14.8	11.8	9.7	13.4
Return on Equity Before Income Taxes 47	12.4	•	199.6	118.6	33.7	43.2	49.0	33.4	24.3	20.8	22.8
Return on Equity After Income Taxes 48	9.6	9.6	197.3	118.2	32.4	41.5	46.3	31.1	21.5	16.0	15.5
Profit Margin (Before Income Tax) 49	8.4	3.0	7.1	9.4	3.7	5.1	5.9	6.5	5.6	5.6	9.2
Profit Margin (After Income Tax) 50	6.5	2.1	7.1	9.4	3.6	4.9	5.6	6.1	4.9	4.3	6.3

Table I

Corporations with and without Net Income

GROCERY AND RELATED PRODUCT

MONEY AMOUNTS AND SIZE OF ASSETS IN THOUSANDS OF DOLLARS

Item Description for Accounting Period 7/10 Through 6/11	Total	Zero Assets	Under 500	500 to 1,000	1,000 to 5,000	5,000 to 10,000	10,000 to 25,000	25,000 to 50,000	50,000 to 100,000	100,000 to 250,000	250,000 to 500,000	500,000 to 2,500,000	2,500,000 and over
Number of Enterprises 1	35132	4239	20638	3231	5160	771	661	207	131	54	15	19	6
Revenues ($ in Thousands)													
Net Sales 2	568770671	4890839	16076744	11681141	65510040	23356642	46533674	26535947	33804194	26322096	18817572	68680380	226561403
Interest 3	5376867	326	4284	1469	13071	10365	14644	6815	8218	13910	2173	52378	5249213
Rents 4	911909	0	1558	17407	12053	6233	9502	3047	3879	9123	1601	50691	796816
Royalties 5	453033	0	0	0	0	0	466	0	356	207	6480	3970	441553
Other Portfolio Income 6	5184393	23616	9319	7031	91760	3303	11077	14080	12978	12250	52705	112595	4833681
Other Receipts 7	4489154	46404	72540	37357	386781	198828	162298	310617	205796	305966	134421	812914	1815230
Total Receipts 8	585186027	4961185	16164445	11744405	66013705	23575371	46731661	26870506	34035421	26663552	19014952	69712928	239697896
Average Total Receipts 9	16657	1170	783	3635	12793	30578	70698	129809	259812	493769	1267663	3669101	39949649
Operating Costs/Operating Income (%)													
Cost of Operations 10	80.0	80.4	75.5	81.2	86.0	87.7	87.2	87.1	85.7	88.1	86.5	85.2	71.5
Salaries and Wages 11	6.1	7.0	5.1	5.9	3.8	3.5	4.0	4.4	4.8	3.8	3.5	5.3	8.6
Taxes Paid 12	1.1	1.1	1.3	1.1	0.9	0.7	0.7	0.7	0.7	0.6	0.5	0.8	1.6
Interest Paid 13	1.1	0.7	0.2	0.5	0.2	0.3	0.3	0.3	0.5	0.6	0.3	0.5	2.3
Depreciation 14	1.9	0.3	0.5	0.6	0.5	0.4	0.5	0.5	0.8	0.8	1.1	0.9	3.7
Amortization and Depletion 15	0.3	0.4	0.0	0.1	0.0	0.0	0.1	0.0	0.1	0.2	0.1	0.2	0.6
Pensions and Other Deferred Comp. 16	0.5	0.4	0.2	0.2	0.1	0.1	0.1	0.1	0.2	0.1	0.2	0.2	0.9
Employee Benefits 17	0.8	0.5	0.3	0.6	0.4	0.3	0.4	0.5	0.5	0.5	0.5	0.7	1.4
Advertising 18	0.7	0.1	0.2	0.3	0.2	0.2	0.4	0.2	0.6	0.8	1.4	0.6	1.0
Other Expenses 19	6.4	10.3	11.3	7.2	5.2	4.7	4.0	4.1	4.5	3.7	4.6	5.1	8.5
Officers' Compensation 20	0.7	1.5	4.5	2.7	1.8	0.9	1.0	0.9	0.8	0.6	0.3	0.2	0.2
Operating Margin 21	0.4	•	1.0	•	0.8	1.3	1.3	1.1	0.9	0.1	1.0	0.5	•
Operating Margin Before Officers' Comp. 22	1.1	•	5.5	2.4	2.6	2.2	2.3	2.0	1.7	0.7	1.3	0.6	•

Selected Average Balance Sheet ($ in Thousands)

Net Receivables **23**	1288	0	14	224	733	2556	5410	10753	18721	34303	73410	147917	4074936
Inventories **24**	902	0	17	119	462	1849	3517	9834	17799	45607	88728	205818	2125851
Net Property, Plant and Equipment **25**	3070	0	16	172	277	648	2248	4614	10973	23891	87532	203644	15782137
Total Assets **26**	21027	0	101	706	2067	7058	16102	33487	69295	151470	384824	998234	109780361
Notes and Loans Payable **27**	2933	0	53	393	586	1985	4150	7616	22197	61395	59147	322304	13095731
All Other Liabilities **28**	5379	0	24	287	712	2365	5758	12443	23827	41611	139864	371290	26854920
Net Worth **29**	12715	0	23	25	770	2707	6194	13428	23271	48464	185813	304640	69829710

Selected Financial Ratios (Times to 1)

Current Ratio **30**	1.1	•	2.4	1.4	1.9	1.6	1.7	1.5	1.6	2.0	0.9
Quick Ratio **31**	0.7	•	1.4	0.9	1.3	1.0	0.9	0.8	0.7	0.9	0.6
Net Sales to Working Capital **32**	52.5	•	23.9	29.0	16.8	15.9	12.0	15.6	12.5	12.2	22.1
Coverage Ratio **33**	3.9	•	8.8	1.5	9.2	7.2	9.7	4.4	3.3	9.2	5.3
Total Asset Turnover **34**	0.8	•	7.7	5.1	6.1	4.4	3.8	3.7	3.2	3.3	3.6
Inventory Turnover **35**	14.4	•	34.6	24.6	23.7	17.5	11.4	12.4	9.4	12.2	15.0
Receivables Turnover **36**	13.1	•	40.7	16.6	17.0	13.6	12.0	14.5	14.5	15.8	23.0
Total Liabilities to Net Worth **37**	0.7	•	3.3	27.3	1.7	1.6	1.5	2.0	2.1	1.1	2.3
Current Assets to Working Capital **38**	14.2	•	1.7	3.5	2.1	2.7	2.5	2.8	2.6	2.0	3.1
Current Liabilities to Working Capital **39**	13.2	•	0.7	2.5	1.1	1.7	1.5	1.8	1.6	1.0	2.1
Working Capital to Net Sales **40**	0.0	•	0.0	0.0	0.1	0.1	0.1	0.1	0.1	0.1	0.0
Inventory to Working Capital **41**	3.1	•	0.5	1.0	0.6	0.9	0.9	1.2	1.3	0.9	1.2
Total Receipts to Cash Flow **42**	12.7	14.1	9.5	16.1	19.4	16.8	18.6	19.4	23.9	18.4	18.1
Cost of Goods to Cash Flow **43**	10.2	11.3	7.2	13.1	16.7	14.7	16.2	16.6	21.1	15.9	15.4
Cash Flow to Total Debt **44**	0.2	•	1.1	0.3	0.5	0.4	0.3	0.3	0.2	0.3	0.3

Selected Financial Factors (in Percentages)

Debt Ratio **45**	39.5	•	76.9	96.5	62.8	61.6	61.5	59.9	66.4	68.0	51.7	69.5	36.4
Return on Total Assets **46**	3.4	•	13.8	4.1	11.0	10.6	8.8	10.1	7.7	6.4	7.5	8.8	2.8
Return on Equity Before Income Taxes **47**	4.2	•	53.2	37.0	26.2	24.6	19.7	22.5	17.9	13.9	13.9	23.4	3.1
Return on Equity After Income Taxes **48**	3.2	•	52.6	31.4	24.9	22.7	18.4	20.9	15.6	11.1	11.5	16.1	2.2
Profit Margin (Before Income Tax) **49**	3.3	•	1.6	0.3	1.6	2.2	1.7	2.4	1.6	1.4	2.1	2.0	5.8
Profit Margin (After Income Tax) **50**	2.5	•	1.6	0.2	1.5	2.0	1.6	2.2	1.4	1.1	1.7	1.4	4.0

Table II

Corporations with Net Income

GROCERY AND RELATED PRODUCT

MONEY AMOUNTS AND SIZE OF ASSETS IN THOUSANDS OF DOLLARS

Item Description for Accounting Period 7/10 Through 6/11		Total	Zero Assets	Under 500	500 to 1,000	1,000 to 5,000	5,000 to 10,000	10,000 to 25,000	25,000 to 50,000	50,000 to 100,000	100,000 to 250,000	250,000 to 500,000	500,000 to 2,500,000	2,500,000 and over
Number of Enterprises	1	23139	2200	13339	1871	4081	715	561	186	109	42	•	•	•
Revenues ($ in Thousands)														
Net Sales	2	491739073	3538449	11912103	7013880	53540869	22736989	42760038	24018423	28516877	22232092	•	•	•
Interest	3	5365499	301	3279	1405	12349	9904	14000	6399	6222	13202			•
Rents	4	902322	0	427	15915	11144	6178	9121	3039	3153	5845		•	•
Royalties	5	453023	0	0	0	0	0	466	0	346	207			•
Other Portfolio Income	6	5124760	23531	612	4617	77389	3265	10626	4939	11499	8363	•	•	•
Other Receipts	7	3609059	38275	56859	8315	254902	184894	151911	160829	186403	305670	•	•	•
Total Receipts	8	507193736	3600556	11973280	7044132	53896653	22941230	42946162	24193629	28724500	22565379	•	•	•
Average Total Receipts	9	21919	1637	898	3765	13207	32086	76553	130073	263528	537271	•	•	•
Operating Costs/Operating Income (%)														
Cost of Operations	10	79.1	87.2	75.2	83.7	85.8	87.6	87.3	86.8	85.5	88.7	•	•	•
Salaries and Wages	11	6.1	3.8	4.6	3.0	3.4	3.5	4.0	3.9	4.8	3.5	•	•	•
Taxes Paid	12	1.2	0.7	1.2	0.7	1.0	0.7	0.7	0.6	0.6	0.6	•	•	•
Interest Paid	13	1.2	0.0	0.2	0.4	0.2	0.3	0.3	0.3	0.4	0.5	•	•	•
Depreciation	14	2.0	0.1	0.4	0.3	0.5	0.4	0.4	0.5	0.7	0.8	•	•	•
Amortization and Depletion	15	0.3	0.0	0.0	0.1	0.1	0.0	0.1	0.0	0.1	0.1	•	•	•
Pensions and Other Deferred Comp.	16	0.5	0.5	0.2	0.2	0.1	0.1	0.1	0.1	0.2	0.1	•	•	•
Employee Benefits	17	0.9	0.2	0.2	0.6	0.4	0.3	0.4	0.5	0.5	0.5	•	•	•
Advertising	18	0.7	0.1	0.1	0.1	0.2	0.1	0.4	0.2	0.6	0.9	•	•	•
Other Expenses	19	6.5	4.8	9.6	5.4	5.0	4.6	3.7	3.9	4.3	3.3	•	•	•
Officers' Compensation	20	0.7	1.6	4.1	2.7	1.6	0.9	1.0	0.9	0.8	0.6	•	•	•
Operating Margin	21	0.9	1.2	4.3	2.7	1.8	1.5	1.7	2.1	1.5	0.5	•	•	•
Operating Margin Before Officers' Comp.	22	1.6	2.7	8.3	5.4	3.4	2.4	2.7	3.1	2.3	1.1	•	•	•

Selected Average Balance Sheet ($ in Thousands)

Net Receivables 23	1763	0	13	231	719	2631	5728	10174	18709	35195
Inventories 24	1187	0	14	97	427	1767	3715	9903	18589	48950
Net Property, Plant and Equipment 25	4497	0	13	117	294	639	1955	4581	10283	24223
Total Assets 26	30953	0	108	696	2059	7113	16253	33275	69048	150845
Notes and Loans Payable 27	4016	0	45	319	499	1976	3904	7577	21607	57906
All Other Liabilities 28	7822	0	17	271	613	2354	5901	12196	23087	42568
Net Worth 29	19114	0	46	107	947	2783	6448	13501	24354	50370

Selected Financial Ratios (Times to 1)

Current Ratio 30	1.1	•	3.2	1.7	2.1	1.7	1.6	1.7	1.6	1.6
Quick Ratio 31	0.7	•	2.0	1.2	1.5	1.0	1.0	0.8	0.8	0.7
Net Sales to Working Capital 32	65.8	•	22.9	19.2	15.6	13.1	15.7	12.6	14.5	12.7
Coverage Ratio 33	4.5	69.8	28.3	9.2	15.1	10.5	9.4	11.8	6.5	5.3
Total Asset Turnover 34	0.7	•	8.2	5.4	6.4	4.5	4.7	3.9	3.8	3.5
Inventory Turnover 35	14.2	•	49.5	32.3	26.4	15.8	17.9	11.3	12.0	9.6
Receivables Turnover 36	12.7	•	60.5	16.6	17.8	12.0	14.0	12.7	14.6	14.8
Total Liabilities to Net Worth 37	0.6	•	1.3	5.5	1.2	1.6	1.5	1.5	1.8	2.0
Current Assets to Working Capital 38	19.1	•	1.5	2.3	1.9	2.4	2.6	2.5	2.7	2.5
Current Liabilities to Working Capital 39	18.1	•	0.5	1.3	0.9	1.4	1.6	1.5	1.7	1.5
Working Capital to Net Sales 40	0.0	•	0.0	0.1	0.1	0.1	0.1	0.1	0.1	0.1
Inventory to Working Capital 41	3.9	•	0.3	0.6	0.5	0.8	0.9	1.0	1.2	1.3
Total Receipts to Cash Flow 42	11.6	17.9	8.1	13.6	17.1	16.5	20.7	17.6	17.6	22.3
Cost of Goods to Cash Flow 43	9.2	15.6	6.1	11.4	14.7	14.4	18.1	15.3	15.0	19.7
Cash Flow to Total Debt 44	0.2	•	1.8	0.5	0.7	0.4	0.4	0.4	0.3	0.2

Selected Financial Factors (in Percentages)

Debt Ratio 45	38.2	•	57.3	84.7	54.0	60.9	60.3	59.4	64.7	66.6
Return on Total Assets 46	3.7	•	41.0	18.9	16.7	11.9	11.2	12.1	10.0	8.6
Return on Equity Before Income Taxes 47	4.6	•	92.6	109.8	34.0	27.4	25.2	27.3	24.0	20.8
Return on Equity After Income Taxes 48	3.5	•	92.1	107.5	32.6	25.5	23.7	25.5	21.4	17.4
Profit Margin (Before Income Tax) 49	4.2	2.3	4.8	3.1	2.5	2.4	2.1	2.9	2.2	2.0
Profit Margin (After Income Tax) 50	3.2	2.4	4.8	3.1	2.4	2.2	2.0	2.7	2.0	1.7

Table I

Corporations with and without Net Income

FARM PRODUCT RAW MATERIAL

MONEY AMOUNTS AND SIZE OF ASSETS IN THOUSANDS OF DOLLARS

Item Description for Accounting Period 7/10 Through 6/11	Total	Zero Assets	Under 500	500 to 1,000	1,000 to 5,000	5,000 to 10,000	10,000 to 25,000	25,000 to 50,000	50,000 to 100,000	100,000 to 250,000	250,000 to 500,000	500,000 to 2,500,000	2,500,000 and over
Number of Enterprises 1	3947	118	1356	926	998	271	170	49	23	19	3	11	3
Revenues ($ in Thousands)													
Net Sales 2	166231943	70580	1661416	5211196	7911739	5751555	10900690	5978046	4416668	5734211	5198566	29940329	83456947
Interest 3	386067	96	4	2454	7607	4217	8894	2879	1921	3510	2702	35244	316540
Rents 4	65997	0	3	280	11504	961	2864	423	3271	2034	1273	2966	40419
Royalties 5	104640	0	0	0	0	462	1	0	3284	265	0	101	100527
Other Portfolio Income 6	594591	0	15	111	5067	51147	25412	1410	1889	9058	1964	98770	399747
Other Receipts 7	2502802	1049	55913	106517	113228	90818	68771	50063	22712	73112	20708	191839	1708072
Total Receipts 8	169886040	71725	1717351	5320558	8049145	5899160	11006632	6032821	4449745	5822190	5225213	30269249	86022252
Average Total Receipts 9	43042	608	1266	5746	8065	21768	64745	123119	193467	306431	1741738	2751750	28674084
Operating Costs/Operating Income (%)													
Cost of Operations 10	92.0	80.8	85.0	87.4	86.4	71.0	93.2	91.7	92.6	92.2	97.7	94.3	93.0
Salaries and Wages 11	2.4	0.5	1.6	2.5	2.7	17.9	1.8	3.1	2.4	2.3	0.4	1.2	1.9
Taxes Paid 12	0.4	0.2	0.5	0.6	0.7	1.3	0.3	0.4	0.3	0.4	0.1	0.2	0.4
Interest Paid 13	1.0	1.2	0.9	0.3	0.3	0.6	0.4	0.4	0.4	0.7	0.3	0.5	1.5
Depreciation 14	0.9	2.5	1.0	1.2	0.9	0.6	0.7	0.7	1.1	1.3	0.1	0.7	1.1
Amortization and Depletion 15	0.0	•	0.0	0.0	0.0	0.0	0.0	0.1	0.1	0.0	0.0	0.1	0.0
Pensions and Other Deferred Comp. 16	0.2	•	0.2	0.1	0.2	1.1	0.1	0.1	0.1	0.2	0.0	0.1	0.2
Employee Benefits 17	0.4	•	0.1	0.0	0.3	0.9	0.1	0.4	0.1	0.1	0.1	0.2	0.6
Advertising 18	0.1	0.9	0.3	0.1	0.1	0.1	0.0	0.0	0.1	0.0	0.0	0.1	0.1
Other Expenses 19	2.6	8.8	10.4	5.7	5.8	2.8	2.8	1.9	2.6	2.9	0.5	1.5	2.4
Officers' Compensation 20	0.6	0.0	3.1	1.4	1.7	2.6	0.7	0.5	0.3	0.6	0.1	0.3	0.4
Operating Margin 21	•	5.2	•	0.8	1.0	1.0	•	0.8	•	•	0.7	0.8	•
Operating Margin Before Officers' Comp. 22	•	5.2	0.2	2.2	2.6	3.6	0.5	1.3	0.2	0.8	0.8	1.1	•

Selected Average Balance Sheet ($ in Thousands)

Net Receivables 23	7668	0	39	104	555	920	3330	12193	22748	36790	80106	330349	7684376
Inventories 24	4038	0	7	66	577	1233	4134	14796	19415	47311	182620	247774	2971036
Net Property, Plant and Equipment 25	2333	0	33	159	369	958	3040	4383	10300	19711	7003	125112	1883387
Total Assets 26	28942	0	179	658	2327	7639	14806	37720	74810	158844	353165	1170472	28650242
Notes and Loans Payable 27	10268	0	201	232	554	1792	5400	11984	26094	55001	208273	473968	10004395
All Other Liabilities 28	9826	0	23	170	840	3616	5224	16308	22364	49369	68777	396972	9687997
Net Worth 29	8848	0	-45	256	933	2231	4182	9428	26352	54474	76114	299532	8957850

Selected Financial Ratios (Times to 1)

Current Ratio 30	1.4	•	3.5	2.4	1.7	1.8	1.4	1.3	1.6	1.3	1.3	1.3	1.4
Quick Ratio 31	0.8	•	3.3	1.7	0.8	0.7	0.6	0.7	0.7	0.5	0.5	0.5	0.9
Net Sales to Working Capital 32	8.6	•	15.1	24.7	10.8	9.2	19.9	17.4	8.7	10.4	26.4	15.7	6.1
Coverage Ratio 33	3.4	6.6	1.4	11.8	11.2	7.4	3.2	5.7	2.8	2.4	5.6	5.3	2.9
Total Asset Turnover 34	1.5	•	6.8	8.6	3.4	2.8	4.3	3.2	2.6	1.9	4.9	2.3	1.0
Inventory Turnover 35	9.6	•	155.5	74.8	11.9	12.2	14.5	7.6	9.2	5.9	9.3	10.4	8.7
Receivables Turnover 36	7.9	•	42.2	53.4	13.8	20.6	21.8	10.0	9.9	10.6	13.2	10.6	5.7
Total Liabilities to Net Worth 37	2.3	•	•	1.6	1.5	2.4	2.5	3.0	1.8	1.9	3.6	2.9	2.2
Current Assets to Working Capital 38	3.7	•	1.4	1.7	2.5	2.3	3.4	4.2	2.6	3.9	5.0	5.0	3.8
Current Liabilities to Working Capital 39	2.7	•	0.4	0.7	1.5	1.3	2.4	3.2	1.6	2.9	4.0	4.0	2.8
Working Capital to Net Sales 40	0.1	•	0.1	0.0	0.1	0.1	0.1	0.1	0.1	0.1	0.0	0.1	0.2
Inventory to Working Capital 41	1.0	•	0.0	0.3	0.8	0.5	1.5	1.7	1.2	2.0	1.8	2.0	0.8
Total Receipts to Cash Flow 42	30.1	8.5	10.1	13.3	15.3	16.7	36.7	35.5	36.6	34.0	61.0	35.8	34.5
Cost of Goods to Cash Flow 43	27.7	6.9	8.6	11.6	13.2	11.8	34.2	32.6	33.9	31.4	59.6	33.8	32.1
Cash Flow to Total Debt 44	0.1	•	0.5	1.1	0.4	0.2	0.2	0.1	0.1	0.1	0.1	0.1	0.0

Selected Financial Factors (in Percentages)

Debt Ratio 45	69.4	•	125.1	61.1	59.9	70.8	71.8	75.0	64.8	65.7	78.4	74.4	68.7
Return on Total Assets 46	4.9	•	8.6	26.7	10.1	11.5	5.0	6.6	2.7	3.1	7.9	6.4	4.2
Return on Equity Before Income Taxes 47	11.3	•	•	62.8	22.9	34.2	12.1	21.8	4.9	5.4	30.0	20.1	8.8
Return on Equity After Income Taxes 48	8.1	•	•	62.7	21.6	32.9	9.4	20.3	3.0	1.8	20.8	14.0	5.8
Profit Margin (Before Income Tax) 49	2.4	6.8	0.4	2.9	2.7	3.6	0.8	1.7	0.7	1.0	1.3	2.2	2.8
Profit Margin (After Income Tax) 50	1.7	6.6	0.3	2.8	2.5	3.5	0.6	1.6	0.4	0.3	0.9	1.5	1.9

Table II
Corporations with Net Income

FARM PRODUCT RAW MATERIAL

MONEY AMOUNTS AND SIZE OF ASSETS IN THOUSANDS OF DOLLARS

Item Description for Accounting Period 7/10 Through 6/11	Total	Zero Assets	Under 500	500 to 1,000	1,000 to 5,000	5,000 to 10,000	10,000 to 25,000	25,000 to 50,000	50,000 to 100,000	100,000 to 250,000	250,000 to 500,000	500,000 to 2,500,000	2,500,000 and over
Number of Enterprises **1**	2750	•	•	542	806	259	137	34	19	13	3	•	3
Revenues ($ in Thousands)													
Net Sales **2**	151259689	•	•	2955242	7087884	5391331	6639834	4030797	3762502	4063434	5198566	•	83456947
Interest **3**	377137	•	•	1169	3121	3937	7364	2781	1786	2978	2702	•	316540
Rents **4**	64354	•	•	280	11498	0	2643	423	3024	1984	1273	•	40419
Royalties **5**	104178	•	•	0	0	0	1	0	3284	265	0	•	100527
Other Portfolio Income **6**	592460	•	•	46	4983	51147	24035	1363	1853	8575	1964	•	399747
Other Receipts **7**	2440615	•	•	81226	97637	90150	69246	41678	16987	69390	20708	•	1708072
Total Receipts **8**	154833433	•	•	3037963	7205123	5536565	6743123	4077042	3789436	4146626	5225213	•	86022252
Average Total Receipts **9**	56305	•	•	5605	8939	21377	49220	119913	199444	318971	1741738	•	28674084
Operating Costs/Operating Income (%)													
Cost of Operations **10**	91.7	•	•	81.2	86.6	69.7	91.0	91.6	92.0	90.0	97.7	•	93.0
Salaries and Wages **11**	2.5	•	•	3.8	2.5	18.9	2.2	1.9	2.4	2.5	0.4	•	1.9
Taxes Paid **12**	0.4	•	•	0.9	0.6	1.4	0.4	0.3	0.3	0.4	0.1	•	0.4
Interest Paid **13**	1.0	•	•	0.3	0.2	0.4	0.4	0.3	0.3	0.4	0.3	•	1.5
Depreciation **14**	0.9	•	•	2.0	0.8	0.6	0.9	0.9	0.8	1.1	0.1	•	1.1
Amortization and Depletion **15**	0.0	•	•	0.0	0.0	0.0	0.0	0.0	0.0	0.0	0.0	•	0.0
Pensions and Other Deferred Comp. **16**	0.2	•	•	0.2	0.2	1.2	0.1	0.1	0.1	0.2	0.0	•	0.2
Employee Benefits **17**	0.4	•	•	0.0	0.3	0.9	0.2	0.3	0.1	0.1	0.1	•	0.6
Advertising **18**	0.1	•	•	0.1	0.1	0.1	0.0	0.0	0.1	0.0	0.0	•	0.1
Other Expenses **19**	2.5	•	•	5.6	5.5	2.7	3.2	2.3	2.5	3.4	0.5	•	2.4
Officers' Compensation **20**	0.6	•	•	2.2	1.7	2.7	0.9	0.6	0.3	0.5	0.1	•	0.4
Operating Margin **21**	•	•	•	3.8	1.5	1.4	0.6	1.6	1.0	1.3	0.7	•	•
Operating Margin Before Officers' Comp. **22**	0.2	•	•	6.0	3.1	4.1	1.5	2.2	1.3	1.8	0.8	•	•

Selected Average Balance Sheet ($ in Thousands)

Net Receivables 23	10632	•	95	609	845	3276	10928	24793	30032	80106	•	7684376
Inventories 24	5397	•	63	618	1018	4507	16691	17957	45884	117878	•	3656360
Net Property, Plant and Equipment 25	3080	•	209	408	969	3237	5606	8292	17721	7003	•	1883387
Total Assets 26	39798	•	705	2304	7592	15111	36163	71876	138590	353165	•	28650242
Notes and Loans Payable 27	13901	•	142	470	1631	4536	10110	25804	29391	208273	•	10004395
All Other Liabilities 28	13458	•	149	738	3546	5581	15172	21067	53764	68777	•	9687997
Net Worth 29	12440	•	415	1097	2415	4995	10881	25005	55434	76114	•	8957850

Selected Financial Ratios (Times to 1)

Current Ratio 30	1.4	•	2.7	1.8	1.9	1.5	1.4	1.8	1.3	1.3	•	1.4
Quick Ratio 31	0.8	•	2.1	0.8	0.8	0.6	0.7	0.9	0.5	0.5	•	0.9
Net Sales to Working Capital 32	8.1	•	20.4	10.8	8.6	13.8	13.8	8.2	14.3	26.4	•	6.1
Coverage Ratio 33	3.8	•	27.4	14.4	10.8	6.9	9.8	6.1	9.1	5.6	•	2.9
Total Asset Turnover 34	1.4	•	7.7	3.8	2.7	3.2	3.3	2.8	2.3	4.9	•	1.0
Inventory Turnover 35	9.3	•	69.8	12.3	14.3	9.8	6.5	10.1	6.1	14.4	•	7.1
Receivables Turnover 36	7.4	•	44.7	13.7	24.9	15.7	9.0	9.3	11.9	•	•	
Total Liabilities to Net Worth 37	2.2	•	0.7	1.1	2.1	2.0	2.3	1.9	1.5	3.6	•	2.2
Current Assets to Working Capital 38	3.7	•	1.6	2.2	2.1	3.2	3.3	2.3	4.3	5.0	•	3.8
Current Liabilities to Working Capital 39	2.7	•	0.6	1.2	1.1	2.2	2.3	1.3	3.3	4.0	•	2.8
Working Capital to Net Sales 40	0.1	•	0.0	0.1	0.1	0.1	0.1	0.1	0.1	0.0	•	0.2
Inventory to Working Capital 41	0.9	•	0.2	0.8	0.5	1.4	1.3	1.0	2.0	1.8	•	0.8
Total Receipts to Cash Flow 42	27.6	•	9.2	14.5	15.8	22.9	22.6	26.9	17.4	61.0	•	34.5
Cost of Goods to Cash Flow 43	25.3	•	7.4	12.5	11.0	20.9	20.7	24.7	15.7	59.6	•	32.1
Cash Flow to Total Debt 44	0.1	•	2.0	0.5	0.3	0.2	0.2	0.2	0.2	0.1	•	0.0

Selected Financial Factors (in Percentages)

Debt Ratio 45	68.7	•	41.2	52.4	68.2	66.9	69.9	65.2	60.0	78.4	•	68.7
Return on Total Assets 46	5.3	•	53.1	12.8	12.3	8.0	10.1	5.7	8.5	7.9	•	4.2
Return on Equity Before Income Taxes 47	12.4	•	87.1	25.0	35.1	20.6	30.3	13.6	18.9	30.0	•	8.8
Return on Equity After Income Taxes 48	9.1	•	86.9	23.6	33.9	17.9	28.3	11.2	14.0	20.8	•	5.8
Profit Margin (Before Income Tax) 49	2.8	•	6.6	3.1	4.1	2.1	2.8	1.7	3.4	1.3	•	2.8
Profit Margin (After Income Tax) 50	2.1	•	6.6	2.9	3.9	1.8	2.6	1.4	2.5	0.9	•	1.9

Table I
Corporations with and without Net Income

CHEMICAL AND ALLIED PRODUCTS

MONEY AMOUNTS AND SIZE OF ASSETS IN THOUSANDS OF DOLLARS

Item Description for Accounting Period 7/10 Through 6/11		Total	Zero Assets	Under 500	500 to 1,000	1,000 to 5,000	5,000 to 10,000	10,000 to 25,000	25,000 to 50,000	50,000 to 100,000	100,000 to 250,000	250,000 to 500,000	500,000 to 2,500,000	2,500,000 and over
Number of Enterprises	1	8088	1336	4045	633	1347	338	252	59	40	23	5	7	3
Revenues ($ in Thousands)														
Net Sales	2	80524244	1322627	3599954	994456	8854773	5868181	10742435	5722251	6739066	9039613	1493654	12078055	14069179
Interest	3	105116	745	149	482	1004	752	2909	1438	3696	5757	1195	21220	65768
Rents	4	13035	381	0	0	162	750	587	88	1478	390	5465	1577	2154
Royalties	5	4159	0	0	0	0	0	2	0	19	960	0	3178	0
Other Portfolio Income	6	254278	167	4489	2868	20445	20247	47069	27896	3812	19396	4015	74604	29270
Other Receipts	7	759368	-69330	26031	1659	38971	4598	4438	28805	76795	12267	-7124	288394	353867
Total Receipts	8	81660200	1254590	3630623	999465	8915355	5894528	10797440	5780478	6824866	9078383	1497205	12467028	14520238
Average Total Receipts	9	10096	939	898	1579	6619	17439	42847	97974	170622	394712	299441	1781004	4840079
Operating Costs/Operating Income (%)														
Cost of Operations	10	79.1	75.9	69.0	56.0	65.5	73.4	81.0	83.4	85.2	89.7	82.9	85.1	75.9
Salaries and Wages	11	5.9	7.3	6.3	10.5	10.1	7.7	5.3	5.2	4.5	2.1	3.4	4.0	7.6
Taxes Paid	12	1.0	1.5	1.0	2.2	1.5	1.1	0.9	1.2	0.8	0.4	0.6	1.1	0.7
Interest Paid	13	0.9	1.1	0.1	0.3	0.5	0.3	0.4	0.3	0.5	0.3	0.3	1.7	2.3
Depreciation	14	1.4	1.0	0.4	1.1	1.2	1.3	0.9	0.9	0.9	0.6	1.5	0.8	3.9
Amortization and Depletion	15	0.4	0.2	0.0	•	0.0	0.0	0.1	0.1	0.2	0.1	0.6	0.9	1.3
Pensions and Other Deferred Comp.	16	0.4	0.4	0.2	•	0.4	0.5	0.3	0.4	0.4	0.2	0.1	0.2	0.7
Employee Benefits	17	1.0	0.8	0.3	1.0	0.6	0.9	0.4	0.5	0.5	0.4	0.9	0.7	3.0
Advertising	18	0.2	0.1	0.6	0.3	0.3	0.1	0.2	0.2	0.1	0.1	0.1	0.1	0.0
Other Expenses	19	6.4	8.1	16.5	22.5	10.5	8.6	5.5	4.2	3.9	2.5	6.0	4.9	5.8
Officers' Compensation	20	1.5	0.7	3.4	4.0	3.9	2.8	1.5	0.9	0.8	0.8	0.1	0.4	0.8
Operating Margin	21	1.9	2.9	2.0	2.1	5.5	3.4	3.6	2.7	2.3	2.8	3.6	0.1	•
Operating Margin Before Officers' Comp.	22	3.4	3.6	5.4	6.1	9.4	6.2	5.1	3.7	3.1	3.6	3.7	0.5	•

Selected Average Balance Sheet ($ in Thousands)

Net Receivables 23	1273	0	44	192	651	2474	5824	13279	20550	46387	38544	196890	857338
Inventories 24	818	0	26	57	427	1834	3982	10090	14404	34435	35540	142967	377186
Net Property, Plant and Equipment 25	967	0	5	39	317	684	2439	4047	8998	22444	66520	105782	1437078
Total Assets 26	6085	0	141	647	2152	7213	16365	35644	71253	157638	298438	1172941	6831092
Notes and Loans Payable 27	1815	0	62	149	514	1122	4323	9843	15112	39161	51269	478343	2161284
All Other Liabilities 28	1922	0	51	123	850	2887	5157	12569	22344	55065	54631	314706	2154714
Net Worth 29	2347	0	28	375	787	3204	6885	13232	33797	63413	192538	379892	2515094

Selected Financial Ratios (Times to 1)

Current Ratio 30	1.6	•	2.0	4.6	1.8	1.6	1.8	1.5	1.6	1.5	1.5	1.5	1.5
Quick Ratio 31	0.9	•	1.4	3.8	1.1	1.0	1.1	0.9	0.9	0.8	0.7	0.8	0.7
Net Sales to Working Capital 32	8.3	•	14.4	3.5	10.3	8.5	7.1	9.6	9.3	11.5	8.1	11.6	5.1
Coverage Ratio 33	4.7	•	25.8	10.8	13.0	13.2	12.4	12.2	8.0	12.8	16.2	3.0	1.5
Total Asset Turnover 34	1.6	•	6.3	2.4	3.1	2.4	2.6	2.7	2.4	2.5	1.0	1.5	0.7
Inventory Turnover 35	9.6	•	23.3	15.5	10.1	6.9	8.7	8.0	10.0	10.2	7.0	10.3	9.4
Receivables Turnover 36	8.3	•	22.8	9.0	9.9	7.4	8.4	7.8	8.9	10.1	7.3	9.3	5.5
Total Liabilities to Net Worth 37	1.6	•	4.1	0.7	1.7	1.3	1.4	1.7	1.1	1.5	0.6	2.1	1.7
Current Assets to Working Capital 38	2.7	•	2.1	1.3	2.3	2.7	2.2	2.9	2.6	2.9	3.0	3.1	2.9
Current Liabilities to Working Capital 39	1.7	•	1.1	0.3	1.3	1.7	1.2	1.9	1.6	1.9	2.0	2.1	1.9
Working Capital to Net Sales 40	0.1	•	0.1	0.3	0.1	0.1	0.1	0.1	0.1	0.1	0.1	0.1	0.2
Inventory to Working Capital 41	0.7	•	0.5	0.2	0.7	1.0	0.8	1.1	0.9	1.1	1.1	1.0	0.4
Total Receipts to Cash Flow 42	12.3	23.4	5.6	4.4	6.9	9.2	11.6	16.1	15.9	19.2	11.7	13.6	26.8
Cost of Goods to Cash Flow 43	9.7	17.8	3.9	2.5	4.5	6.8	9.4	13.4	13.6	17.2	9.7	11.6	20.4
Cash Flow to Total Debt 44	0.2	•	1.4	1.3	0.7	0.5	0.4	0.3	0.3	0.2	0.2	0.2	0.0

Selected Financial Factors (in Percentages)

Debt Ratio 45	61.4	•	80.4	42.0	63.4	55.6	57.9	62.9	52.6	59.8	35.5	67.6	63.2
Return on Total Assets 46	7.0	•	18.9	7.0	20.4	10.0	11.7	11.1	9.7	9.0	4.2	7.5	2.3
Return on Equity Before Income Taxes 47	14.2	•	92.9	11.0	51.5	20.9	25.6	27.4	17.9	20.7	6.1	15.6	2.0
Return on Equity After Income Taxes 48	11.7	•	91.0	8.2	49.8	18.8	22.6	23.3	14.3	16.4	3.4	11.3	1.1
Profit Margin (Before Income Tax) 49	3.4	•	2.9	2.6	6.2	3.8	4.1	3.7	3.6	3.3	3.9	3.4	1.1
Profit Margin (After Income Tax) 50	2.8	•	2.8	2.0	6.0	3.5	3.6	3.2	2.9	2.6	2.2	2.5	0.6

Table II

Corporations with Net Income

CHEMICAL AND ALLIED PRODUCTS

MONEY AMOUNTS AND SIZE OF ASSETS IN THOUSANDS OF DOLLARS

Item Description for Accounting Period 7/10 Through 6/11	Total	Zero Assets	Under 500	500 to 1,000	1,000 to 5,000	5,000 to 10,000	10,000 to 25,000	25,000 to 50,000	50,000 to 100,000	100,000 to 250,000	250,000 to 500,000	500,000 to 2,500,000	2,500,000 and over
Number of Enterprises 1	4780	892	1831	446	1015	268	206	•	35	20	•	•	3
Revenues ($ in Thousands)													
Net Sales 2	73059292	1153422	1441286	994456	7906922	5269333	9890036	•	6302376	8792086	•	•	14069179
Interest 3	100641	745	145	482	438	731	1899	•	3576	5686	•	•	65768
Rents 4	12432	381	0	0	162	750	587	•	1307	316	•	•	2154
Royalties 5	979	0	0	0	0	0	0	•	19	960	•	•	0
Other Portfolio Income 6	201031	167	4034	2868	15541	20247	12866	•	3682	19396	•	•	29270
Other Receipts 7	860297	24206	14006	1659	30666	21309	45412	•	73608	12271	•	•	353867
Total Receipts 8	74234672	1178921	1459471	999465	7953729	5312370	9950800	•	6384568	8830715	•	•	14520238
Average Total Receipts 9	15530	1322	797	2241	7836	19822	48305	•	182416	441536	•	•	4840079
Operating Costs/Operating Income (%)													
Cost of Operations 10	79.4	79.8	58.3	56.0	66.1	73.1	81.3	•	85.0	90.0	•	•	75.9
Salaries and Wages 11	5.8	4.7	7.4	10.5	9.9	7.7	5.1	•	4.5	2.1	•	•	7.6
Taxes Paid 12	0.9	1.3	0.9	2.2	1.3	1.2	0.9	•	0.8	0.4	•	•	0.7
Interest Paid 13	0.8	1.3	0.1	0.3	0.4	0.2	0.3	•	0.4	0.3	•	•	2.3
Depreciation 14	1.4	0.6	0.2	0.3	1.1	1.2	0.6	•	0.8	0.6	•	•	3.9
Amortization and Depletion 15	0.4	0.3	0.0	0.0	0.0	0.0	0.1	•	0.2	0.1	•	•	1.3
Pensions and Other Deferred Comp. 16	0.4	0.4	•	•	0.4	0.5	0.3	•	0.4	0.2	•	•	0.7
Employee Benefits 17	1.0	0.8	0.0	1.0	0.5	1.0	0.4	•	0.5	0.4	•	•	3.0
Advertising 18	0.1	0.1	0.3	0.3	0.3	0.1	0.2	•	0.1	0.0	•	•	0.0
Other Expenses 19	5.9	6.8	20.0	22.5	9.8	8.0	5.2	•	3.7	2.2	•	•	5.8
Officers' Compensation 20	1.4	0.2	3.3	4.0	3.4	2.8	1.4	•	0.8	0.8	•	•	0.8
Operating Margin 21	2.5	3.9	9.4	2.1	6.9	4.3	4.2	•	2.9	2.9	•	•	•
Operating Margin Before Officers' Comp. 22	3.9	4.1	12.7	6.1	10.3	7.1	5.6	•	3.7	3.8	•	•	•

Selected Average Balance Sheet ($ in Thousands)

Net Receivables 23	2006	0	77	273	734	2824	6326	•	22008	51945	•	857338
Inventories 24	1166	0	51	80	436	1991	4197	•	14156	37502	•	392776
Net Property, Plant and Equipment 25	1474	0	3	56	329	781	2025	•	8698	14832	•	1437078
Total Assets 26	9124	0	214	650	2227	7253	16807	•	73245	157939	•	6831092
Notes and Loans Payable 27	2586	0	42	109	471	1016	3484	•	13741	38705	•	2161284
All Other Liabilities 28	2933	0	60	174	817	2904	5670	•	22984	57106	•	2154714
Net Worth 29	3605	0	112	366	939	3332	7653	•	36520	62128	•	2515094

Selected Financial Ratios (Times to 1)

Current Ratio 30	1.7	•	2.7	3.1	2.0	1.6	1.9	•	1.7	1.6	•	1.5
Quick Ratio 31	0.9	•	1.8	2.3	1.4	1.1	1.1	•	0.9	0.9	•	0.7
Net Sales to Working Capital 32	7.9	•	6.3	6.0	9.3	8.2	7.3	•	9.1	10.6	•	5.1
Coverage Ratio 33	6.0	5.8	86.4	10.8	18.3	28.1	18.1	•	11.0	13.1	•	1.5
Total Asset Turnover 34	1.7	•	3.7	3.4	3.5	2.7	2.9	•	2.5	2.8	•	0.7
Inventory Turnover 35	10.4	•	9.1	15.5	11.8	7.2	9.3	•	10.8	10.5	•	9.1
Receivables Turnover 36	8.8	•	12.0	9.0	10.5	7.2	8.9	•	9.1	10.2	•	10.9
Total Liabilities to Net Worth 37	1.5	•	0.9	0.8	1.4	1.2	1.2	•	1.0	1.5	•	1.7
Current Assets to Working Capital 38	2.5	•	1.6	1.5	2.0	2.5	2.1	•	2.5	2.7	•	2.9
Current Liabilities to Working Capital 39	1.5	•	0.6	0.5	1.0	1.5	1.1	•	1.5	1.7	•	1.9
Working Capital to Net Sales 40	0.1	•	0.2	0.2	0.1	0.1	0.1	•	0.1	0.1	•	0.2
Inventory to Working Capital 41	0.7	•	0.4	0.4	0.5	0.8	0.8	•	0.8	1.0	•	0.4
Total Receipts to Cash Flow 42	11.8	8.9	3.4	4.4	6.6	8.6	11.0	•	14.8	19.7	•	26.8
Cost of Goods to Cash Flow 43	9.4	7.1	2.0	2.5	4.3	6.3	9.0	•	12.6	17.8	•	20.4
Cash Flow to Total Debt 44	0.2	•	2.3	1.8	0.9	0.6	0.5	•	0.3	0.2	•	0.0

Selected Financial Factors (in Percentages)

Debt Ratio 45	60.5	•	47.7	43.7	57.8	54.1	54.5	•	50.1	60.7	•	63.2
Return on Total Assets 46	8.4	•	39.8	10.0	27.6	14.2	14.6	•	11.5	10.6	•	2.3
Return on Equity Before Income Taxes 47	17.7	•	75.1	16.0	61.8	29.9	30.3	•	21.0	24.8	•	2.0
Return on Equity After Income Taxes 48	15.0	•	74.1	12.0	59.8	27.5	27.0	•	17.2	19.8	•	1.1
Profit Margin (Before Income Tax) 49	4.2	6.1	10.7	2.6	7.5	5.1	4.8	•	4.3	3.5	•	1.1
Profit Margin (After Income Tax) 50	3.5	4.3	10.6	2.0	7.2	4.7	4.3	•	3.5	2.8	•	0.6

Table I

Corporations with and without Net Income

PETROLEUM AND PETROLEUM PRODUCTS

MONEY AMOUNTS AND SIZE OF ASSETS IN THOUSANDS OF DOLLARS

Item Description for Accounting Period 7/10 Through 6/11	Total	Zero Assets	Under 500	500 to 1,000	1,000 to 5,000	5,000 to 10,000	10,000 to 25,000	25,000 to 50,000	50,000 to 100,000	100,000 to 250,000	250,000 to 500,000	500,000 to 2,500,000	2,500,000 and over
Number of Enterprises 1	7719	952	2189	1076	2151	674	398	132	75	25	16	25	6
Revenues ($ in Thousands)													
Net Sales 2	522887659	39909247	1988233	4880930	49021109	37696373	46578314	37990830	31752687	31008012	48475613	104025424	89560886
Interest 3	269102	4068	2571	3501	11843	9437	10242	8248	3890	1046	11028	31133	172093
Rents 4	332089	232	0	483	17635	18584	43809	16948	11937	2160	25655	111819	82826
Royalties 5	46973	0	0	0	2029	64	373	0	485	0	1053	1209	41760
Other Portfolio Income 6	1116122	12153	15004	7289	60658	50087	14865	10495	18260	12092	58374	162186	694656
Other Receipts 7	2487927	35951	228	206115	206964	117490	127886	83730	97713	41762	97693	193312	1279090
Total Receipts 8	527139872	39961651	2006036	5098318	49320238	37892035	46775489	38110251	31884972	31065072	48669416	104525083	91831311
Average Total Receipts 9	68291	41977	916	4738	22929	56220	117526	288714	425133	1242603	3041838	4181003	15305218
Operating Costs/Operating Income (%)													
Cost of Operations 10	94.1	99.7	69.2	86.6	92.9	94.6	94.1	95.2	94.5	97.2	97.8	97.8	85.1
Salaries and Wages 11	1.3	0.3	20.0	1.6	2.2	1.6	1.8	1.4	1.6	0.5	0.7	0.5	1.6
Taxes Paid 12	0.4	0.0	0.9	2.3	0.4	0.3	0.3	0.3	0.3	0.5	0.1	0.1	0.8
Interest Paid 13	0.5	0.2	0.5	0.1	0.2	0.2	0.2	0.2	0.2	0.1	0.1	0.3	1.8
Depreciation 14	0.9	0.1	0.8	0.6	0.4	0.4	0.6	0.6	0.7	0.2	0.2	0.4	3.2
Amortization and Depletion 15	0.3	0.0	0.3	0.0	0.0	0.1	0.0	0.0	0.1	0.0	0.0	0.1	1.5
Pensions and Other Deferred Comp. 16	0.1	0.0	0.0	0.1	0.1	0.0	0.0	0.0	0.0	0.0	0.0	0.0	0.3
Employee Benefits 17	0.1	0.0	0.3	0.3	0.1	0.1	0.1	0.1	0.1	0.0	0.1	0.1	0.2
Advertising 18	0.0	0.0	0.2	0.1	0.1	0.1	0.1	0.0	0.1	0.0	0.0	0.0	0.0
Other Expenses 19	2.9	0.8	7.9	9.0	3.0	2.1	2.5	2.0	2.2	0.9	0.9	1.0	8.4
Officers' Compensation 20	0.3	0.0	3.1	2.3	0.6	0.4	0.3	0.2	0.3	0.1	0.2	0.1	0.2
Operating Margin 21	•	•	•	0.0	0.1	0.2	•	•	0.0	0.4	0.0	•	•
Operating Margin Before Officers' Comp. 22	•	•	•	0.7	0.7	0.5	0.3	0.1	0.3	0.5	0.3	•	•

Selected Average Balance Sheet ($ in Thousands)

Net Receivables 23	3458	0	27	252	903	2422	4842	11920	25112	58421	152034	214497	1358241
Inventories 24	1929	0	11	88	424	679	2196	3984	8240	39406	89352	167191	797260
Net Property, Plant and Equipment 25	9605	0	13	53	533	1714	4367	11798	14645	21361	45660	140635	10429372
Total Assets 26	21018	0	126	662	2478	7098	15909	35603	67196	156490	344435	988063	16823488
Notes and Loans Payable 27	7124	0	74	76	664	2018	3947	12476	17292	42226	124382	274080	6257711
All Other Liabilities 28	7140	0	26	229	1003	2358	5901	13194	29939	80772	136613	448993	4883171
Net Worth 29	6754	0	25	357	811	2722	6061	9933	19965	33492	83441	264990	5682606

Selected Financial Ratios (Times to 1)

Current Ratio 30	1.4	•	3.0	2.4	1.5	1.6	1.3	1.3	1.3	1.3	1.2	1.3	1.5
Quick Ratio 31	0.9	•	2.7	1.9	1.1	1.3	0.9	0.9	0.8	0.8	0.8	0.8	1.0
Net Sales to Working Capital 32	32.7	•	15.9	13.4	37.3	35.3	56.3	56.1	43.2	41.4	86.2	32.3	14.1
Coverage Ratio 33	1.3	•	•	21.5	5.5	4.8	1.8	3.4	3.6	5.9	3.5	1.6	0.7
Total Asset Turnover 34	3.2	•	7.2	6.8	9.2	7.9	8.1	7.4	6.3	7.9	8.8	4.2	0.9
Inventory Turnover 35	33.1	•	55.3	44.5	49.9	77.9	68.8	50.1	48.6	30.6	33.2	24.3	15.9
Receivables Turnover 36	21.9	•	19.3	19.7	26.3	24.4	26.4	27.0	19.9	22.1	19.4	22.8	12.9
Total Liabilities to Net Worth 37	2.1	•	4.0	0.9	2.1	1.6	2.6	1.6	2.4	3.7	3.1	2.7	2.0
Current Assets to Working Capital 38	3.6	•	1.5	1.7	2.8	4.5	3.9	4.4	3.9	7.2	4.3	3.1	•
Current Liabilities to Working Capital 39	2.6	•	0.5	0.7	1.8	3.5	2.9	3.4	2.9	6.2	3.3	2.1	•
Working Capital to Net Sales 40	0.0	•	0.1	0.1	0.0	0.0	0.0	0.0	0.0	0.0	0.0	0.0	0.1
Inventory to Working Capital 41	1.0	•	0.1	0.2	0.7	0.4	1.1	0.8	0.9	1.4	1.9	1.5	0.8
Total Receipts to Cash Flow 42	41.4	•	25.4	10.7	36.0	49.0	59.7	46.2	52.4	91.7	138.0	144.0	13.9
Cost of Goods to Cash Flow 43	39.0	•	17.6	9.2	33.4	46.3	56.9	43.5	49.5	89.1	135.0	140.7	11.8
Cash Flow to Total Debt 44	0.1	•	0.4	1.4	0.4	0.3	0.2	0.3	0.2	0.1	0.1	0.0	0.1

Selected Financial Factors (in Percentages)

Debt Ratio 45	67.9	•	79.9	46.1	67.3	61.7	72.1	61.9	70.3	78.6	75.8	73.2	66.2
Return on Total Assets 46	1.9	•	•	11.5	7.8	6.8	2.9	4.1	4.0	5.2	2.2	1.8	1.2
Return on Equity Before Income Taxes 47	1.2	•	•	20.3	19.6	14.2	4.7	7.6	9.7	20.1	6.5	2.6	•
Return on Equity After Income Taxes 48	•	•	•	19.5	18.9	13.2	6.7	4.0	8.4	16.6	3.8	1.9	•
Profit Margin (Before Income Tax) 49	0.1	•	1.6	0.7	0.7	0.4	0.2	0.4	0.5	0.5	0.2	0.2	•
Profit Margin (After Income Tax) 50	•	•	1.5	0.7	0.6	0.3	0.1	0.3	0.4	0.4	0.1	0.1	•

Table II

Corporations with Net Income

PETROLEUM AND PETROLEUM PRODUCTS

MONEY AMOUNTS AND SIZE OF ASSETS IN THOUSANDS OF DOLLARS

Item Description for Accounting Period 7/10 Through 6/11		Total	Zero Assets	Under 500	500 to 1,000	1,000 to 5,000	5,000 to 10,000	10,000 to 25,000	25,000 to 50,000	50,000 to 100,000	100,000 to 250,000	250,000 to 500,000	500,000 to 2,500,000	2,500,000 and over
Number of Enterprises	1	4685	468	930	660	1597	580	262	93	52	18	11	11	3
Revenues ($ in Thousands)														
Net Sales	2	353337110	7628946	1263731	3372721	41557080	34584338	31003268	30030064	24326337	22546743	27795053	54172380	75090448
Interest	3	108894	30	2435	3414	7417	8028	5400	7105	2662	820	3169	7759	60653
Rents	4	188174	0	0	133	13813	15272	25006	12359	4818	2160	25448	6567	82599
Royalties	5	45518	0	0	0	2029	64	30	0	485	0	809	342	41760
Other Portfolio Income	6	778612	11281	1	7289	59591	46045	12374	8471	16008	11525	55384	161770	388873
Other Receipts	7	1865582	11186	226	1530	179216	110911	75229	75759	95053	26850	64363	168361	1056900
Total Receipts	8	356357890	7651443	1266393	3385087	41819146	34764658	31121307	30133758	24445363	22588098	27944226	54517179	76721233
Average Total Receipts	9	76064	16349	1362	5129	26186	59939	118784	324019	470103	1254894	2540384	4956107	25573744
Operating Costs/Operating Income (%)														
Cost of Operations	10	94.2	99.0	58.2	83.1	93.5	95.1	93.8	95.6	94.4	96.7	96.8	97.4	90.3
Salaries and Wages	11	1.3	0.1	28.1	0.9	1.8	1.4	1.8	1.2	1.5	0.6	0.9	0.5	1.3
Taxes Paid	12	0.4	0.1	0.4	2.8	0.4	0.3	0.3	0.3	0.3	0.7	0.2	0.1	0.7
Interest Paid	13	0.4	0.0	0.2	0.1	0.1	0.1	0.1	0.2	0.1	0.1	0.1	0.2	1.3
Depreciation	14	0.7	0.0	0.8	0.8	0.3	0.3	0.5	0.5	0.6	0.2	0.3	0.3	2.0
Amortization and Depletion	15	0.1	0.0	0.2	0.0	0.1	0.0	0.0	0.0	0.1	0.0	0.0	0.1	0.2
Pensions and Other Deferred Comp.	16	0.1	0.0	0.1	0.2	0.0	0.1	0.1	0.0	0.0	0.0	0.0	0.0	0.3
Employee Benefits	17	0.1	0.0	0.1	0.4	0.1	0.1	0.1	0.1	0.1	0.0	0.2	0.1	0.2
Advertising	18	0.0	0.0	0.2	0.1	0.1	0.0	0.1	0.0	0.1	0.0	0.0	0.0	0.0
Other Expenses	19	2.2	0.4	7.6	6.2	2.7	1.8	2.3	1.7	2.2	0.9	1.2	0.9	3.6
Officers' Compensation	20	0.3	0.0	2.6	2.6	0.5	0.4	0.3	0.2	0.3	0.1	0.1	0.2	0.2
Operating Margin	21	0.2	0.2	1.5	2.8	0.3	0.3	0.6	0.1	0.3	0.6	0.1	0.2	•
Operating Margin Before Officers' Comp.	22	0.5	0.3	4.1	5.4	0.9	0.7	0.9	0.3	0.5	0.8	0.2	0.4	•

Selected Average Balance Sheet ($ in Thousands)

Net Receivables 23	3685	0	52	301	994	2623	5190	13790	24388	60760	155378	239102	1522018
Inventories 24	2332	0	18	106	452	639	2672	3854	9238	42319	86586	280754	1134741
Net Property, Plant and Equipment 25	9714	0	14	40	488	1061	3820	10245	14441	20191	59377	180812	12787845
Total Assets 26	20989	0	148	684	2648	6898	15829	34875	67450	162551	329351	1049005	20176818
Notes and Loans Payable 27	5628	0	40	120	616	1581	3275	12177	15230	37490	114786	364202	5208408
All Other Liabilities 28	7912	0	15	240	1041	2398	5959	13330	28520	91174	129298	446992	7192430
Net Worth 29	7449	0	94	324	991	2919	6595	9368	23699	33888	85267	237812	7775981

Selected Financial Ratios (Times to 1)

Current Ratio 30	1.5	•	7.0	2.3	1.7	1.7	1.4	1.4	1.3	1.4	1.2	1.4	1.5
Quick Ratio 31	0.9	•	6.3	1.9	1.2	1.4	0.9	1.0	1.0	0.8	0.9	0.7	1.0
Net Sales to Working Capital 32	29.2	•	14.9	15.0	33.9	30.5	42.2	62.8	39.5	33.3	68.2	28.9	16.2
Coverage Ratio 33	3.7	25.0	9.7	29.6	8.2	7.3	8.3	3.5	6.4	7.9	8.8	4.8	2.5
Total Asset Turnover 34	3.6	•	9.2	7.5	9.8	8.6	7.5	9.3	6.9	7.7	7.7	4.7	1.2
Inventory Turnover 35	30.5	•	44.5	40.1	53.8	88.7	41.5	80.1	47.8	28.6	28.2	17.1	19.9
Receivables Turnover 36	22.3	•	14.8	18.3	28.5	24.4	23.4	27.7	22.1	21.1	14.2	19.4	22.3
Total Liabilities to Net Worth 37	1.8	•	0.6	1.1	1.7	1.4	1.4	2.7	1.8	3.8	2.9	3.4	1.6
Current Assets to Working Capital 38	3.1	•	1.2	1.8	2.5	2.4	3.6	4.1	3.7	3.2	6.3	3.5	2.9
Current Liabilities to Working Capital 39	2.1	•	0.2	0.8	1.5	1.4	2.6	3.1	2.7	2.2	5.3	2.5	1.9
Working Capital to Net Sales 40	0.0	•	0.1	0.1	0.0	0.0	0.0	0.0	0.0	0.0	0.0	0.0	0.1
Inventory to Working Capital 41	0.9	•	0.1	0.2	0.6	0.4	1.0	0.8	0.8	1.3	1.2	1.5	0.9
Total Receipts to Cash Flow 42	37.8	135.9	14.0	12.7	34.7	47.8	37.3	55.7	44.6	72.0	75.2	71.3	20.5
Cost of Goods to Cash Flow 43	35.6	134.6	8.2	10.6	32.4	45.5	35.0	53.3	42.1	69.6	72.8	69.4	18.6
Cash Flow to Total Debt 44	0.1	•	1.8	1.1	0.5	0.3	0.3	0.2	0.2	0.1	0.1	0.1	0.1

Selected Financial Factors (in Percentages)

Debt Ratio 45	64.5	•	36.7	52.6	62.6	57.7	58.3	73.1	64.9	79.2	74.1	77.3	61.5
Return on Total Assets 46	5.3	•	17.3	24.8	10.8	8.7	8.3	5.7	6.3	7.3	5.6	5.1	4.1
Return on Equity Before Income Taxes 47	11.0	•	24.5	50.5	25.3	17.8	17.5	15.0	15.2	30.4	19.2	17.8	6.4
Return on Equity After Income Taxes 48	8.9	•	23.6	49.1	24.5	16.8	16.3	14.1	13.6	25.7	15.2	16.2	4.3
Profit Margin (Before Income Tax) 49	1.1	0.5	1.7	3.2	1.0	0.9	1.0	0.4	0.8	0.8	0.6	0.9	2.0
Profit Margin (After Income Tax) 50	0.9	0.4	1.6	3.1	0.9	0.8	0.9	0.4	0.7	0.7	0.5	0.8	1.3

Table I

Corporations with and without Net Income

BEER, WINE, AND DISTILLED ALCOHOLIC BEVERAGE

MONEY AMOUNTS AND SIZE OF ASSETS IN THOUSANDS OF DOLLARS

Item Description for Accounting Period 7/10 Through 6/11	Total	Zero Assets	Under 500	500 to 1,000	1,000 to 5,000	5,000 to 10,000	10,000 to 25,000	25,000 to 50,000	50,000 to 100,000	100,000 to 250,000	250,000 to 500,000	500,000 to 2,500,000	2,500,000 and over
Number of Enterprises 1	2677	680	117	242	813	381	248	76	63	36	8	10	3
Revenues ($ in Thousands)													
Net Sales 2	76556211	1663707	111660	1559035	6347200	7747087	10422943	5990483	8660318	9669678	5339775	8699705	10344619
Interest 3	54370	14512	0	151	2033	1385	315	2050	5908	2227	478	18015	7297
Rents 4	57676	2690	0	0	0	158	0	210	13264	13505	0	23767	4082
Royalties 5	49875	5477	0	0	0	0	0	0	996	36496	0	5810	1095
Other Portfolio Income 6	279974	33735	0	0	20126	23782	37261	34944	37802	21581	483	56085	14175
Other Receipts 7	1122682	107556	146	1753	35419	64981	84590	65456	156509	190583	56302	209985	149402
Total Receipts 8	78120788	1827677	111806	1560939	6404778	7837393	10545109	6093143	8874797	9934070	5397038	9013367	10520670
Average Total Receipts 9	29182	2688	956	6450	7878	20571	42521	80173	140870	275946	674630	901337	3506890
Operating Costs/Operating Income (%)													
Cost of Operations 10	74.6	52.7	2.3	75.4	75.5	74.4	74.2	75.1	75.7	74.6	79.8	71.8	77.4
Salaries and Wages 11	8.2	11.3	0.3	12.5	7.9	8.5	8.7	7.6	7.7	8.3	6.5	7.5	9.0
Taxes Paid 12	2.9	4.5	4.6	1.3	2.6	2.5	3.1	2.9	2.6	1.9	1.4	7.7	1.1
Interest Paid 13	1.1	10.1	0.0	0.1	0.2	0.5	0.5	0.4	0.9	0.6	0.6	1.3	2.6
Depreciation 14	0.7	1.1	0.7	0.3	0.7	0.9	0.5	0.6	1.1	0.6	0.4	1.4	0.5
Amortization and Depletion 15	2.3	33.1	0.2	0.1	0.1	0.3	0.7	0.7	1.2	0.7	1.2	1.7	6.3
Pensions and Other Deferred Comp. 16	0.4	1.1	0.0	0.1	0.3	0.6	0.3	0.3	0.3	0.4	0.2	0.4	0.5
Employee Benefits 17	0.8	0.4	0.0	0.8	0.5	0.9	1.0	0.9	0.9	0.9	0.5	0.5	1.1
Advertising 18	1.6	7.7	0.0	0.5	0.7	0.7	0.7	1.1	1.6	3.2	2.1	1.8	1.2
Other Expenses 19	6.0	11.2	7.1	1.8	7.3	5.4	5.4	6.6	5.4	6.0	7.1	7.1	4.5
Officers' Compensation 20	1.1	0.4	24.9	1.9	2.4	1.9	1.6	1.2	0.8	1.1	0.4	0.4	0.2
Operating Margin 21	0.2	•	59.8	5.2	1.7	3.6	3.2	2.6	1.7	1.8	•	•	•
Operating Margin Before Officers' Comp. 22	1.4	•	84.7	7.1	4.1	5.5	4.8	3.8	2.5	2.9	0.1	•	•

Selected Average Balance Sheet ($ in Thousands)

Net Receivables 23	2528	0	0	77	371	979	1701	4062	8457	30917	81123	101077	679278
Inventories 24	2972	0	51	206	753	1929	3086	6675	10254	31147	65464	122431	588821
Net Property, Plant and Equipment 25	1634	0	81	99	307	1310	2142	3311	9126	14603	30049	90413	188403
Total Assets 26	18713	0	115	821	2179	7321	15667	32216	69421	148864	318024	775487	6319209
Notes and Loans Payable 27	6258	0	2	338	414	1265	5047	8382	22567	41105	109286	247577	2571015
All Other Liabilities 28	3892	0	0	29	722	2185	2734	6250	13938	42303	98036	196222	897034
Net Worth 29	8563	0	113	454	1043	3872	7886	17583	32916	65456	110703	331688	2851160

Selected Financial Ratios (Times to 1)

Current Ratio 30	1.3	•	152.6	2.1	1.8	2.4	2.3	1.9	1.6	1.6	1.8	1.5	0.8
Quick Ratio 31	0.6	•	144.1	0.6	0.9	1.2	1.2	0.9	0.8	0.9	1.1	0.8	0.3
Net Sales to Working Capital 32	15.4	•	38.8	21.3	11.2	8.4	10.3	10.0	13.0	8.4	9.5	8.6	•
Coverage Ratio 33	3.1	•	1970.5	44.1	12.3	10.3	9.3	11.4	5.8	8.7	2.3	2.6	•
Total Asset Turnover 34	1.5	•	8.3	7.8	3.6	2.8	2.7	2.4	2.0	1.8	2.1	1.1	0.5
Inventory Turnover 35	7.2	•	0.4	23.6	7.8	7.8	10.1	8.9	10.2	6.4	8.1	5.1	4.5
Receivables Turnover 36	12.3	•	15951.4	70.6	19.8	20.7	23.4	18.2	14.6	10.5	8.5	8.9	6.4
Total Liabilities to Net Worth 37	1.2	•	0.0	0.8	1.1	0.9	1.0	0.8	1.1	1.3	1.9	1.3	1.2
Current Assets to Working Capital 38	4.0	•	1.0	1.9	2.2	1.7	1.8	2.2	2.5	2.6	2.2	2.9	•
Current Liabilities to Working Capital 39	3.0	•	0.0	0.9	1.2	0.7	0.8	1.2	1.5	1.6	1.2	1.9	•
Working Capital to Net Sales 40	0.1	•	0.0	0.0	0.1	0.1	0.1	0.1	0.1	0.1	0.1	0.1	•
Inventory to Working Capital 41	1.6	•	0.1	0.9	1.0	0.8	0.7	0.9	0.9	1.0	0.7	1.2	•
Total Receipts to Cash Flow 42	15.3	•	1.5	20.5	12.1	11.5	12.1	11.2	12.8	10.6	22.9	13.7	279.5
Cost of Goods to Cash Flow 43	11.5	•	0.0	15.4	9.1	8.5	9.0	8.4	9.7	7.9	18.3	9.9	216.4
Cash Flow to Total Debt 44	0.2		347.6	0.9	0.6	0.5	0.4	0.5	0.3	0.3	0.1	0.1	0.0

Selected Financial Factors (in Percentages)

Debt Ratio 45	54.2	•	1.6	44.7	52.1	47.1	49.7	45.4	52.6	56.0	65.2	57.2	54.9
Return on Total Assets 46	5.2	•	499.4	43.0	10.3	14.7	13.3	11.6	9.9	9.1	2.9	3.7	•
Return on Equity Before Income Taxes 47	7.6	•	507.1	76.0	19.7	25.1	23.5	19.3	17.4	18.3	4.7	5.3	•
Return on Equity After Income Taxes 48	6.6	•	507.1	75.3	18.0	23.1	22.6	18.1	16.8	16.3	2.4	3.4	•
Profit Margin (Before Income Tax) 49	2.3	•	60.0	5.4	2.6	4.8	4.4	4.3	4.2	4.5	0.8	2.0	•
Profit Margin (After Income Tax) 50	2.0	•	60.0	5.3	2.4	4.4	4.2	4.0	4.0	4.0	0.4	1.3	•

Table II

Corporations with Net Income

BEER, WINE, AND DISTILLED ALCOHOLIC BEVERAGE

MONEY AMOUNTS AND SIZE OF ASSETS IN THOUSANDS OF DOLLARS

Item Description for Accounting Period 7/10 Through 6/11	Total	Zero Assets	Under 500	500 to 1,000	1,000 to 5,000	5,000 to 10,000	10,000 to 25,000	25,000 to 50,000	50,000 to 100,000	100,000 to 250,000	250,000 to 500,000	500,000 to 2,500,000	2,500,000 and over
Number of Enterprises **1**	2128	402	•	184	680	364	216	64	56	31	•	•	0
Revenues ($ in Thousands)													
Net Sales **2**	69022284	834852	•	1559035	5523617	7460225	9204260	5160423	8174582	8770545	•	•	0
Interest **3**	31051	68	•	151	997	1333	299	1961	5699	2218	•	•	0
Rents **4**	49967	0	•	0	0	158	0	190	13264	12588	•	•	0
Royalties **5**	43303	0	•	0	0	0	0	0	996	36496	•	•	0
Other Portfolio Income **6**	212782	19408	•	0	17707	23782	32844	24944	26082	21576	•	•	0
Other Receipts **7**	862001	9137	•	1753	33911	63194	75087	68906	139062	179490	•	•	0
Total Receipts **8**	70221388	863465	•	1560939	5576232	7548692	9312490	5256424	8359685	9022913	•	•	0
Average Total Receipts **9**	32999	2148	•	8483	8200	20738	43113	82132	149280	291062	•	•	•
Operating Costs/Operating Income (%)													
Cost of Operations **10**	75.4	71.3	•	75.4	73.8	74.5	73.9	74.8	76.2	73.8	•	•	•
Salaries and Wages **11**	8.1	9.3	•	12.5	8.2	8.5	8.5	7.3	7.6	8.3	•	•	•
Taxes Paid **12**	3.0	5.8	•	1.3	2.8	2.4	3.0	3.2	2.6	2.0	•	•	•
Interest Paid **13**	0.6	0.1	•	0.1	0.2	0.5	0.5	0.4	0.8	0.5	•	•	•
Depreciation **14**	0.7	0.8	•	0.3	0.7	0.7	0.6	0.5	0.8	0.6	•	•	•
Amortization and Depletion **15**	0.8	1.0	•	0.1	0.1	0.3	0.7	0.6	1.1	0.6	•	•	•
Pensions and Other Deferred Comp. **16**	0.4	0.2	•	0.1	0.4	0.6	0.3	0.2	0.3	0.3	•	•	•
Employee Benefits **17**	0.8	•	•	0.8	0.5	0.8	1.0	1.1	0.9	0.9	•	•	•
Advertising **18**	1.3	0.4	•	0.5	0.7	0.7	0.7	1.0	1.7	3.3	•	•	•
Other Expenses **19**	5.2	6.4	•	1.8	7.3	5.1	5.1	6.0	5.0	6.1	•	•	•
Officers' Compensation **20**	1.1	0.7	•	1.9	2.6	1.9	1.5	1.1	0.7	1.2	•	•	•
Operating Margin **21**	2.6	4.0	•	5.2	2.8	3.9	4.1	3.8	2.3	2.4	•	•	•
Operating Margin Before Officers' Comp. **22**	3.8	4.8	•	7.2	5.4	5.8	5.7	5.0	3.0	3.6	•	•	•

Selected Average Balance Sheet ($ in Thousands)

Net Receivables 23	2563	0	•	54	316	927	1712	3266	8817	30610
Inventories 24	3398	0	•	146	747	1813	3123	7148	10195	30437
Net Property, Plant and Equipment 25	1613	0	•	131	351	1340	2369	3159	7679	15684
Total Assets 26	15579	0	•	801	2209	7339	15778	32448	69802	144907
Notes and Loans Payable 27	4373	0	•	159	446	1250	5015	7791	22516	34105
All Other Liabilities 28	4094	0	•	38	660	2201	2557	5652	13908	42528
Net Worth 29	7112	0	•	603	1103	3888	8206	19005	33378	68275

Selected Financial Ratios (Times to 1)

Current Ratio 30	1.9	•	•	6.4	1.9	2.4	2.3	2.0	1.7	1.6
Quick Ratio 31	0.9	•	•	2.3	1.0	1.2	1.2	0.9	0.9	0.9
Net Sales to Working Capital 32	8.8	•	•	21.2	11.5	8.6	11.0	9.7	13.4	9.5
Coverage Ratio 33	7.9	64.7	•	44.1	19.8	10.7	12.0	15.5	6.6	11.2
Total Asset Turnover 34	2.1	•	•	10.6	3.7	2.8	2.7	2.5	2.1	2.0
Inventory Turnover 35	7.2	•	•	43.8	8.0	8.4	10.1	8.4	10.9	6.9
Receivables Turnover 36	13.1	•	•	136.9	23.5	22.4	22.4	19.4	15.1	10.8
Total Liabilities to Net Worth 37	1.2	•	•	0.3	1.0	0.9	0.9	0.7	1.1	1.1
Current Assets to Working Capital 38	2.1	•	•	1.2	2.1	1.7	1.8	2.0	2.5	2.6
Current Liabilities to Working Capital 39	1.1	•	•	0.2	1.1	0.7	0.8	1.0	1.5	1.6
Working Capital to Net Sales 40	0.1	•	•	0.0	0.1	0.1	0.1	0.1	0.1	0.1
Inventory to Working Capital 41	0.9	•	•	0.3	1.0	0.8	0.7	0.9	0.9	1.0
Total Receipts to Cash Flow 42	12.4	7.9	•	20.4	10.9	11.2	11.0	10.3	12.6	9.7
Cost of Goods to Cash Flow 43	9.3	5.6	•	15.4	8.1	8.4	8.2	7.7	9.6	7.2
Cash Flow to Total Debt 44	0.3	•	•	2.1	0.7	0.5	0.5	0.6	0.3	0.4

Selected Financial Factors (in Percentages)

Debt Ratio 45	54.4	•	•	24.7	50.1	47.0	48.0	41.4	52.2	52.9
Return on Total Assets 46	10.4	•	•	58.1	14.5	15.6	15.6	15.1	11.4	11.2
Return on Equity Before Income Taxes 47	19.9	•	•	75.4	27.7	26.7	27.5	24.1	20.1	21.6
Return on Equity After Income Taxes 48	18.5	•	•	74.6	25.7	24.7	26.8	22.7	19.5	19.4
Profit Margin (Before Income Tax) 49	4.4	7.5	•	5.4	3.8	5.1	5.3	5.7	4.6	5.2
Profit Margin (After Income Tax) 50	4.1	7.2	•	5.3	3.5	4.7	5.2	5.4	4.5	4.7

Table I
Corporations with and without Net Income

MISCELLANEOUS NONDURABLE GOODS

MONEY AMOUNTS AND SIZE OF ASSETS IN THOUSANDS OF DOLLARS

Item Description for Accounting Period 7/10 Through 6/11	Total	Zero Assets	Under 500	500 to 1,000	1,000 to 5,000	5,000 to 10,000	10,000 to 25,000	25,000 to 50,000	50,000 to 100,000	100,000 to 250,000	250,000 to 500,000	500,000 to 2,500,000	2,500,000 and over
Number of Enterprises 1	30926	5597	18125	2615	3491	428	395	132	•	46	•	•	•	5
Revenues ($ in Thousands)													
Net Sales 2	172348927	992005	10308974	7279612	27331080	11307933	20298965	13041076	•	14041113	•	•	•	24825451
Interest 3	229942	555	1952	130	6946	12471	11724	4130	•	9500	•	•	•	166621
Rents 4	74651	31	0	4659	1080	1934	1643	3071	•	537	•	•	•	56538
Royalties 5	493163	452	2	0	0	0	22	1370	•	21872	•	•	•	462194
Other Portfolio Income 6	784155	24874	32687	73896	12242	2912	3734	8840	•	3920	•	•	•	606413
Other Receipts 7	3058855	9688	29428	205181	151817	204645	343383	155131	•	151537	•	•	•	1446991
Total Receipts 8	176989693	1027605	10373043	7563478	27503165	11529895	20659471	13213618	•	14228479	•	•	•	27564208
Average Total Receipts 9	5723	184	572	2892	7878	26939	52302	100103	•	309315	•	•	•	5512842
Operating Costs/Operating Income (%)													
Cost of Operations 10	80.1	67.7	80.4	81.2	83.5	85.6	82.3	82.5	•	77.7	•	•	•	67.4
Salaries and Wages 11	5.0	4.8	3.6	5.2	4.2	3.9	5.5	5.4	•	6.0	•	•	•	6.4
Taxes Paid 12	1.3	2.4	0.9	1.7	0.9	0.5	3.0	0.8	•	1.5	•	•	•	1.6
Interest Paid 13	0.6	1.7	0.2	0.3	0.3	0.2	0.4	0.4	•	0.8	•	•	•	1.6
Depreciation 14	0.9	1.2	0.4	0.6	0.6	0.4	0.6	0.7	•	1.2	•	•	•	1.6
Amortization and Depletion 15	0.3	0.3	0.1	0.0	0.0	0.0	0.1	0.1	•	0.4	•	•	•	1.2
Pensions and Other Deferred Comp. 16	0.2	0.1	0.2	0.0	0.2	0.1	0.2	0.2	•	0.2	•	•	•	0.5
Employee Benefits 17	0.5	0.5	0.3	0.5	0.3	0.1	0.5	0.6	•	0.5	•	•	•	0.7
Advertising 18	0.9	1.1	0.9	0.3	0.4	0.4	0.3	1.4	•	1.1	•	•	•	1.9
Other Expenses 19	7.3	20.3	8.5	8.5	6.4	6.4	5.4	5.8	•	6.4	•	•	•	13.2
Officers' Compensation 20	1.2	5.6	3.8	3.2	1.7	1.3	1.2	0.9	•	0.7	•	•	•	0.6
Operating Margin 21	1.6	•	0.8	•	1.4	1.0	0.6	1.3	•	3.5	•	•	•	3.3
Operating Margin Before Officers' Comp. 22	2.8	•	4.6	1.6	3.1	2.3	1.8	2.2	•	4.1	•	•	•	3.9

Selected Average Balance Sheet ($ in Thousands)

Net Receivables 23	485	0	12	235	549	1816	5270	8929	•	33010	•	463387
Inventories 24	500	0	28	307	569	1769	4352	10360	•	32476	•	622482
Net Property, Plant and Equipment 25	360	0	16	64	257	558	1730	4247	•	20192	•	872720
Total Assets 26	3004	0	97	700	2092	7437	15608	32921	•	14796	•	8400717
Notes and Loans Payable 27	883	0	42	190	556	2029	4841	9933	•	49582	•	2528099
All Other Liabilities 28	1013	0	35	194	842	2417	5454	12129	•	50718	•	2682611
Net Worth 29	1108	0	20	316	694	2991	5313	10859	•	48496	•	3190007

Selected Financial Ratios (Times to 1)

Current Ratio 30	1.4	•	1.7	3.2	1.7	1.7	1.6	1.5	•	1.6	•	1.2
Quick Ratio 31	0.6	•	0.9	1.6	1.0	1.1	0.9	0.8	•	0.8	•	0.3
Net Sales to Working Capital 32	11.4	•	22.3	7.0	12.1	10.5	11.7	11.4	•	9.0	•	9.8
Coverage Ratio 33	8.6	•	7.5	10.0	7.2	14.9	7.3	7.3	•	6.8	•	12.9
Total Asset Turnover 34	1.9	•	5.9	4.0	3.7	3.6	3.3	3.0	•	2.1	•	0.6
Inventory Turnover 35	8.9	•	16.6	7.4	11.5	12.8	9.7	7.9	•	7.3	•	5.4
Receivables Turnover 36	11.4	•	39.7	11.5	12.7	•	10.5	10.6	•	11.0	•	9.0
Total Liabilities to Net Worth 37	1.7	•	3.9	1.2	2.0	1.5	1.9	2.0	•	2.1	•	1.6
Current Assets to Working Capital 38	3.4	•	2.5	1.4	2.5	2.4	2.7	2.8	•	2.7	•	6.7
Current Liabilities to Working Capital 39	2.4	•	1.5	0.4	1.5	1.4	1.7	1.8	•	1.7	•	5.7
Working Capital to Net Sales 40	0.1	•	0.0	0.1	0.1	0.1	0.1	0.1	•	0.1	•	0.1
Inventory to Working Capital 41	1.1	•	1.1	0.7	0.9	0.7	1.0	1.2	•	1.1	•	1.5
Total Receipts to Cash Flow 42	10.1	7.9	13.3	13.5	14.1	11.9	15.3	13.9	•	10.1	•	4.0
Cost of Goods to Cash Flow 43	8.1	5.4	10.7	11.0	11.8	10.2	12.6	11.5	•	7.8	•	2.7
Cash Flow to Total Debt 44	0.3	•	0.6	0.5	0.4	0.5	0.3	0.3	•	0.3	•	0.2

Selected Financial Factors (in Percentages)

Debt Ratio 45	63.1	•	79.5	54.9	66.8	59.8	66.0	67.0	•	67.4	•	62.0
Return on Total Assets 46	10.3	•	9.7	10.6	9.0	11.5	9.0	9.3	•	11.7	•	12.0
Return on Equity Before Income Taxes 47	24.6	•	41.3	21.2	23.3	26.6	22.7	24.2	•	30.5	•	29.2
Return on Equity After Income Taxes 48	19.0	•	40.8	19.9	22.7	25.7	20.6	22.0	•	24.6	•	19.8
Profit Margin (Before Income Tax) 49	4.9	•	1.4	2.4	2.1	3.0	2.3	2.7	•	4.9	•	18.8
Profit Margin (After Income Tax) 50	3.8	•	1.4	2.3	2.0	2.9	2.1	2.4	•	3.9	•	12.7

Table II
Corporations with Net Income

MISCELLANEOUS NONDURABLE GOODS

MONEY AMOUNTS AND SIZE OF ASSETS IN THOUSANDS OF DOLLARS

Item Description for Accounting Period 7/10 Through 6/11		Total	Zero Assets	Under 500	500 to 1,000	1,000 to 5,000	5,000 to 10,000	10,000 to 25,000	25,000 to 50,000	50,000 to 100,000	100,000 to 250,000	250,000 to 500,000	500,000 to 2,500,000	2,500,000 and over
Number of Enterprises	1	18862	2678	10595	1943	2726	377	310	114	55	38	•	•	5
Revenues ($ in Thousands)														
Net Sales	2	155376995	567735	8373548	6584619	25931813	10591390	16390136	11801476	11264445	11514790	•	•	24825451
Interest	3	214036	11	1485	125	3965	9658	10016	3863	1274	9123	•	•	166621
Rents	4	70863	31	0	4659	593	1797	714	1517	1088	284	•	•	56538
Royalties	5	491971	0	0	0	0	0	22	650	514	21872	•	•	462194
Other Portfolio Income	6	741578	23922	64	69556	10730	2535	2450	8806	6874	3622	•	•	606413
Other Receipts	7	2712036	3765	27875	187075	66504	202229	238512	99013	81277	140657	•	•	1446991
Total Receipts	8	159607479	595464	8402972	6846034	26013605	10807609	16641850	11915325	11355472	11690348	•	•	27564208
Average Total Receipts	9	8462	222	793	3523	9543	28667	53683	104520	206463	307641	•	•	5512842
Operating Costs/Operating Income (%)														
Cost of Operations	10	79.9	62.0	81.4	82.7	83.4	85.7	80.9	82.6	86.1	77.5	•	•	67.4
Salaries and Wages	11	4.8	5.0	2.5	4.4	4.0	3.6	5.4	5.0	4.0	6.1	•	•	6.4
Taxes Paid	12	1.3	2.9	0.7	1.7	0.8	0.5	3.4	0.8	1.0	1.7	•	•	1.6
Interest Paid	13	0.6	1.5	0.2	0.2	0.2	0.2	0.4	0.3	0.5	0.8	•	•	1.6
Depreciation	14	0.9	0.8	0.3	0.5	0.6	0.3	0.4	0.7	0.7	1.1	•	•	1.6
Amortization and Depletion	15	0.3	0.0	0.1	0.0	0.0	0.0	0.1	0.1	0.1	0.4	•	•	1.2
Pensions and Other Deferred Comp.	16	0.2	0.1	0.1	0.0	0.2	0.1	0.2	0.2	0.2	0.2	•	•	0.5
Employee Benefits	17	0.5	0.3	0.2	0.4	0.3	0.2	0.5	0.5	0.3	0.5	•	•	0.7
Advertising	18	0.9	1.0	1.0	0.2	0.3	0.4	0.4	1.5	0.5	1.4	•	•	1.9
Other Expenses	19	6.9	14.8	6.9	7.2	5.7	6.1	5.2	5.1	3.9	5.1	•	•	13.2
Officers' Compensation	20	1.1	5.3	3.3	2.8	1.6	1.3	1.3	0.9	0.7	0.7	•	•	0.6
Operating Margin	21	2.6	6.3	3.4	•	2.8	1.7	2.0	2.3	2.0	4.6	•	•	3.3
Operating Margin Before Officers' Comp.	22	3.7	11.6	6.6	2.5	4.4	3.0	3.3	3.2	2.7	5.3	•	•	3.9

Selected Average Balance Sheet ($ in Thousands)

Item		C1	C2	C3	C4	C5	C6	C7	C8	C9	C10	C11	C12
23	Net Receivables	666	0	15	234	598	1857	5149	9007	19491	32844	•	463387
24	Inventories	684	0	29	234	606	1769	4469	9296	18033	35252	•	622482
25	Net Property, Plant and Equipment	510	0	10	42	221	560	1460	4658	8019	17657	•	872720
26	Total Assets	4407	0	113	689	2201	7504	15389	33489	67997	147988	•	8400717
27	Notes and Loans Payable	1192	0	47	166	409	1712	4156	8352	18454	48624	•	2528099
28	All Other Liabilities	1488	0	35	197	913	2211	5252	12239	21570	48394	•	2682611
29	Net Worth	1727	0	31	326	878	3581	5982	12897	27973	50971	•	3190007

Selected Financial Ratios (Times to 1)

Item		C1	C2	C3	C4	C5	C6	C7	C8	C9	C10	C11	C12
30	Current Ratio	1.4	•	1.9	3.4	1.7	2.0	1.8	1.5	1.7	1.7	•	1.2
31	Quick Ratio	0.6	•	0.9	1.8	1.0	1.3	1.0	0.8	0.9	0.8	•	0.3
32	Net Sales to Working Capital	11.2	•	20.4	8.4	12.2	8.8	9.8	12.2	10.4	8.3	•	9.8
33	Coverage Ratio	11.6	8.5	24.0	16.1	14.5	20.3	10.8	10.6	7.2	8.6	•	12.9
34	Total Asset Turnover	1.9	•	7.0	4.9	4.3	3.7	3.4	3.1	3.0	2.0	•	0.6
35	Inventory Turnover	9.6	•	22.5	12.0	13.1	13.6	9.6	9.2	9.8	6.7	•	5.4
36	Receivables Turnover	12.5	•	56.9	15.5	15.6	13.7	10.8	11.6	10.5	•	•	9.0
37	Total Liabilities to Net Worth	1.6	•	2.6	1.1	1.5	1.1	1.6	1.6	1.4	1.9	•	1.6
38	Current Assets to Working Capital	3.2	•	2.2	1.4	2.4	2.0	2.3	2.9	2.4	2.5	•	6.7
39	Current Liabilities to Working Capital	2.2	•	1.2	0.4	1.4	1.0	1.3	1.9	1.4	1.5	•	5.7
40	Working Capital to Net Sales	0.1	•	0.0	0.1	0.1	0.1	0.1	0.1	0.1	0.1	•	0.1
41	Inventory to Working Capital	1.0	•	1.0	0.6	0.8	0.5	0.9	1.2	0.9	1.0	•	1.5
42	Total Receipts to Cash Flow	9.4	5.3	11.9	13.0	13.3	11.2	13.2	13.4	16.7	9.9	•	4.0
43	Cost of Goods to Cash Flow	7.5	3.3	9.7	10.8	11.1	9.6	10.7	11.1	14.3	7.7	•	2.7
44	Cash Flow to Total Debt	0.3	0.8	0.8	0.7	0.5	0.6	0.4	0.4	0.3	0.3	•	0.2

Selected Financial Factors (in Percentages)

Item		C1	C2	C3	C4	C5	C6	C7	C8	C9	C10	C11	C12
45	Debt Ratio	60.8	•	72.3	52.8	60.1	52.3	61.1	61.5	58.9	65.6	•	62.0
46	Return on Total Assets	12.3	•	27.1	19.6	14.6	14.8	13.4	11.3	10.1	14.3	•	12.0
47	Return on Equity Before Income Taxes	28.8	•	94.0	39.0	34.1	29.4	31.4	26.5	21.1	36.6	•	29.2
48	Return on Equity After Income Taxes	22.8	•	93.5	37.3	33.4	28.6	28.9	24.3	18.7	29.9	•	19.8
49	Profit Margin (Before Income Tax)	6.0	11.2	3.7	3.7	3.1	3.8	3.5	3.3	2.9	6.2	•	18.8
50	Profit Margin (After Income Tax)	4.8	10.9	3.7	3.6	3.1	3.7	3.3	3.0	2.6	5.0	•	12.7

Table I

Corporations with and without Net Income

WHOLESALE ELECTRONIC MARKETS AND AGENTS AND BROKERS

MONEY AMOUNTS AND SIZE OF ASSETS IN THOUSANDS OF DOLLARS

Item Description for Accounting Period 7/10 Through 6/11	Total	Zero Assets	Under 500	500 to 1,000	1,000 to 5,000	5,000 to 10,000	10,000 to 25,000	25,000 to 50,000	50,000 to 100,000	100,000 to 250,000	250,000 to 500,000	500,000 to 2,500,000	2,500,000 and over
Number of Enterprises **1**	13871	3547	9929	218	169	0	0	3	•	0	•	•	0
Revenues ($ in Thousands)													
Net Sales **2**	5959371	208228	2441839	1710888	436306	0	0	20352	•	0	•	•	0
Interest **3**	5256	189	2494	1	1846	0	0	0	•	0	•	•	0
Rents **4**	4467	0	0	0	0	0	0	0	•	0	•	•	0
Royalties **5**	6160	0	0	0	0	0	0	0	•	0	•	•	0
Other Portfolio Income **6**	16228	0	189	4	12929	0	0	0	•	0	•	•	0
Other Receipts **7**	159061	6084	5806	124900	1335	0	0	1398	•	0	•	•	0
Total Receipts **8**	6150543	214501	2450328	1835793	452416	0	0	21750	•	0	•	•	0
Average Total Receipts **9**	443	60	247	8421	2677	•	•	7250	•	•	•	•	•
Operating Costs/Operating Income (%)													
Cost of Operations **10**	0.2	•	•	•	•	•	•	•	•	•	•	•	•
Salaries and Wages **11**	28.2	15.2	18.3	41.3	14.1	•	•	21.7	•	•	•	•	•
Taxes Paid **12**	3.6	2.6	3.1	2.8	2.4	•	•	2.2	•	•	•	•	•
Interest Paid **13**	1.0	1.6	1.6	0.0	1.5	•	•	8.4	•	•	•	•	•
Depreciation **14**	1.3	1.1	0.8	1.1	0.8	•	•	•	•	•	•	•	•
Amortization and Depletion **15**	0.6	•	0.9	•	0.2	•	•	0.3	•	•	•	•	•
Pensions and Other Deferred Comp. **16**	1.4	•	3.0	•	0.0	•	•	•	•	•	•	•	•
Employee Benefits **17**	2.0	0.1	2.8	0.9	0.8	•	•	•	•	•	•	•	•
Advertising **18**	0.4	0.0	0.2	0.0	1.4	•	•	•	•	•	•	•	•
Other Expenses **19**	30.1	53.5	30.2	18.3	78.5	•	•	7.4	•	•	•	•	•
Officers' Compensation **20**	21.7	11.2	22.5	39.5	5.3	•	•	56.3	•	•	•	•	•
Operating Margin **21**	9.4	14.7	16.6	•	•	•	•	3.6	•	•	•	•	•
Operating Margin Before Officers' Comp. **22**	31.1	25.9	39.2	35.5	0.4	•	•	59.9	•	•	•	•	•

Selected Average Balance Sheet ($ in Thousands)

Net Receivables 23	20	0	3	•	0	326	0
Inventories 24	2	0	0	•	0	342	121
Net Property, Plant and Equipment 25	47	0	6	•	158	89	0
Total Assets 26	215	0	55	•	696	2123	34034
Notes and Loans Payable 27	64	0	29	•	533	1119	4152
All Other Liabilities 28	54	0	14	•	62	876	31696
Net Worth 29	97	0	12	•	101	127	-1814

Selected Financial Ratios (Times to 1)

Current Ratio 30	1.5	•	1.4	0.8	3.9	•	0.7
Quick Ratio 31	1.0	•	1.3	0.7	1.8	•	0.0
Net Sales to Working Capital 32	12.7	•	28.2	•	2.8	•	•
Coverage Ratio 33	13.5	12.2	11.5	145.4	0.1	•	2.2
Total Asset Turnover 34	2.0	•	4.5	11.3	1.2	•	0.2
Inventory Turnover 35	0.5	•	•	•	•	•	•
Receivables Turnover 36	26.6	•	152.8	994.1	8.4	•	3.3
Total Liabilities to Net Worth 37	1.2	•	3.7	5.9	15.7	•	•
Current Assets to Working Capital 38	3.0	•	3.3	•	1.3	•	•
Current Liabilities to Working Capital 39	2.0	•	2.3	•	0.3	•	•
Working Capital to Net Sales 40	0.1	•	0.0	•	0.4	•	•
Inventory to Working Capital 41	0.1	•	•	•	0.4	•	•
Total Receipts to Cash Flow 42	2.6	1.5	2.3	5.3	1.4	•	5.9
Cost of Goods to Cash Flow 43	0.0	•	•	•	•	•	•
Cash Flow to Total Debt 44	1.4	•	2.5	2.5	0.9	•	0.0

Selected Financial Factors (in Percentages)

Debt Ratio 45	54.9	•	78.6	85.5	94.0	•	105.3
Return on Total Assets 46	27.2	•	83.8	37.1	0.3	•	3.8
Return on Equity Before Income Taxes 47	55.8	•	3578	254.6	•	•	
Return on Equity After Income Taxes 48	48.4	•	345.4	254.6	•	•	
Profit Margin (Before Income Tax) 49	12.6	17.7	17.0	3.3	•	10.5	
Profit Margin (After Income Tax) 50	10.9	17.7	16.4	3.3	•	10.5	

201

Table II
Corporations with Net Income

WHOLESALE ELECTRONIC MARKETS AND AGENTS AND BROKERS

MONEY AMOUNTS AND SIZE OF ASSETS IN THOUSANDS OF DOLLARS

Item Description for Accounting Period 7/10 Through 6/11	Total	Zero Assets	Under 500	500 to 1000	1,000 to 5,000	5,000 to 10,000	10,000 to 25,000	25,000 to 50,000	50,000 to 100,000	100,000 to 250,000	250,000 to 500,000	500,000 to 2,500,000	2,500,000 and over
Number of Enterprises **1**	9424	1702	7461	•	62	0	0	3	•	0	•	•	0
Revenues ($ in Thousands)													
Net Sales **2**	5708486	188059	2232377	•	415053	0	0	20352	•	0	•	•	0
Interest **3**	3646	149	2441	•	330	0	0	0	•	0	•	•	0
Rents **4**	4467	0	0	•	0	0	0	0	•	0	•	•	0
Royalties **5**	6160	0	0	•	0	0	0	0	•	0	•	•	0
Other Portfolio Income **6**	15855	0	189	•	12556	0	0	0	•	0	•	•	0
Other Receipts **7**	146777	0	706	•	234	0	0	1398	•	0	•	•	0
Total Receipts **8**	5885391	188208	2235713	•	428173	0	0	21750	•	0	•	•	0
Average Total Receipts **9**	625	111	300	•	6906	•	•	7250	•	•	•	•	•
Operating Costs/Operating Income (%)													
Cost of Operations **10**	0.2	•	•	•	•	•	•	•	•	•	•	•	•
Salaries and Wages **11**	27.9	13.8	16.7	•	11.8	•	•	21.7	•	•	•	•	•
Taxes Paid **12**	3.6	2.2	2.9	•	2.1	•	•	2.2	•	•	•	•	•
Interest Paid **13**	1.0	0.4	1.7	•	1.2	•	•	8.4	•	•	•	•	•
Depreciation **14**	1.1	1.2	0.8	•	0.8	•	•	•	•	•	•	•	•
Amortization and Depletion **15**	0.3	•	0.1	•	•	•	•	0.3	•	•	•	•	•
Pensions and Other Deferred Comp. **16**	1.5	•	3.3	•	0.0	•	•	•	•	•	•	•	•
Employee Benefits **17**	1.8	0.1	2.4	•	0.2	•	•	•	•	•	•	•	•
Advertising **18**	0.4	0.0	0.2	•	1.5	•	•	•	•	•	•	•	•
Other Expenses **19**	28.9	39.4	28.7	•	79.3	•	•	7.4	•	•	•	•	•
Officers' Compensation **20**	21.7	9.1	23.0	•	2.8	•	•	56.3	•	•	•	•	•
Operating Margin **21**	11.8	33.8	20.1	•	0.4	•	•	3.6	•	•	•	•	•
Operating Margin Before Officers' Comp. **22**	33.4	42.9	43.1	•	3.1	•	•	59.9	•	•	•	•	•

Selected Average Balance Sheet ($ in Thousands)

Net Receivables 23	28	0	2	•	773	0
Inventories 24	3	0	0	•	932	0
Net Property, Plant and Equipment 25	67	0	7	•	237	0
Total Assets 26	276	0	51	•	2611	34034
Notes and Loans Payable 27	76	0	35	•	721	4152
All Other Liabilities 28	67	0	18	•	756	31696
Net Worth 29	133	0	-2	•	1134	-1814

Selected Financial Ratios (Times to 1)

Current Ratio 30	1.4	•	1.3	•	3.0	0.7
Quick Ratio 31	0.9	•	1.2	•	1.1	0.0
Net Sales to Working Capital 32	15.4	79.0	42.1	•	4.4	•
Coverage Ratio 33	16.3	•	12.6	•	3.9	2.2
Total Asset Turnover 34	2.2	•	5.9	•	2.6	0.2
Inventory Turnover 35	0.5	•	•	•	•	•
Receivables Turnover 36	28.0	•	500.8	•	8.6	•
Total Liabilities to Net Worth 37	1.1	•	•	•	1.3	•
Current Assets to Working Capital 38	3.4	•	4.4	•	1.5	•
Current Liabilities to Working Capital 39	2.4	•	3.4	•	0.5	•
Working Capital to Net Sales 40	0.1	•	0.0	•	0.2	•
Inventory to Working Capital 41	0.2	•	•	•	0.6	•
Total Receipts to Cash Flow 42	2.5	1.5	2.2	•	1.3	5.9
Cost of Goods to Cash Flow 43	0.0	•	•	•	•	•
Cash Flow to Total Debt 44	1.7	•	2.6	•	3.6	0.0

Selected Financial Factors (in Percentages)

Debt Ratio 45	51.9	•	104.0	•	56.6	105.3
Return on Total Assets 46	34.8	•	129.2	•	12.2	3.8
Return on Equity Before Income Taxes 47	67.9	•	•	•	20.8	•
Return on Equity After Income Taxes 48	60.0	•	•	•	16.4	•
Profit Margin (Before Income Tax) 49	14.9	33.9	20.2	•	3.5	10.5
Profit Margin (After Income Tax) 50	13.1	33.9	19.6	•	2.8	10.5

Table I

Corporations with and without Net Income

NEW AND USED CAR DEALERS

MONEY AMOUNTS AND SIZE OF ASSETS IN THOUSANDS OF DOLLARS

Item Description for Accounting Period 7/10 Through 6/11	Total	Zero Assets	Under 500	500 to 1,000	1,000 to 5,000	5,000 to 10,000	10,000 to 25,000	25,000 to 50,000	50,000 to 100,000	100,000 to 250,000	250,000 to 500,000	500,000 to 2,500,000	2,500,000 and over
Number of Enterprises **1**	45606	4006	22043	3154	8465	4183	2950	595	142	48	10	6	3
Revenues ($ in Thousands)													
Net Sales **2**	545132509	757416	18442869	7222503	78980954	112490299	160370778	68164304	28171940	17626451	6053666	20050590	26800738
Interest **3**	794472	1078	8289	3666	114349	260404	121041	36993	38379	26174	5971	176078	2050
Rents **4**	272008	354	4816	1047	10483	7360	24664	20105	16935	25119	2893	153154	5078
Royalties **5**	2024	0	0	0	0	0	1605	33	0	0	0	387	0
Other Portfolio Income **6**	718026	38044	15264	26939	95961	64187	101830	127328	40595	31465	6934	161990	7486
Other Receipts **7**	10901254	19459	188181	36974	1095577	2344222	3591863	1484064	637318	397613	152246	436410	517330
Total Receipts **8**	557820293	816351	18659419	7291129	80297324	115166472	164211781	69832827	28905167	18106822	6221710	20978609	27332682
Average Total Receipts **9**	12231	204	847	2312	9486	27532	55665	117366	203558	377225	622171	3496435	9110894
Operating Costs/Operating Income (%)													
Cost of Operations **10**	87.2	89.4	82.9	81.3	87.5	88.0	87.9	87.7	87.2	86.4	81.3	84.2	86.2
Salaries and Wages **11**	5.2	2.2	2.9	4.5	4.9	5.0	5.3	5.2	5.4	5.6	6.8	6.6	6.5
Taxes Paid **12**	0.9	1.2	1.4	1.6	0.9	0.9	0.8	0.8	0.9	0.9	1.0	1.4	1.0
Interest Paid **13**	0.5	0.7	0.6	1.1	0.5	0.4	0.4	0.4	0.4	0.5	0.9	1.8	0.6
Depreciation **14**	0.5	0.5	0.3	0.5	0.3	0.3	0.4	0.8	0.9	0.8	1.1	0.7	0.5
Amortization and Depletion **15**	0.1	0.1	0.0	0.0	0.0	0.1	0.1	0.1	0.1	0.1	0.2	1.0	0.5
Pensions and Other Deferred Comp. **16**	0.0	0.0	0.1	0.0	0.0	0.0	0.0	0.1	0.0	0.1	0.1	0.0	0.1
Employee Benefits **17**	0.4	0.3	0.3	0.3	0.5	0.4	0.5	0.4	0.4	0.5	0.6	0.6	0.5
Advertising **18**	1.0	0.9	0.6	0.9	1.0	1.0	1.0	1.0	1.0	0.9	1.1	0.9	0.7
Other Expenses **19**	4.5	18.3	9.8	6.5	4.4	4.4	4.1	3.9	4.2	4.7	7.6	7.2	2.3
Officers' Compensation **20**	0.8	2.4	2.3	2.4	1.0	0.9	0.7	0.6	0.5	0.5	0.7	0.1	0.1
Operating Margin **21**	•	•	•	1.0	•	•	•	•	•	•	1.0	•	0.9
Operating Margin Before Officers' Comp. **22**	•	•	1.1	3.3	•	•	•	•	•	•	•	•	1.0

Selected Average Balance Sheet ($ in Thousands)

Net Receivables 23	424	0	20	135	321	1020	1700	3554	8360	23508	55882	108722	269441
Inventories 24	1610	0	85	332	1528	3976	6954	13631	25503	45121	70893	661883	1225683
Net Property, Plant and Equipment 25	448	0	24	60	152	410	1592	5254	11851	28649	79060	334094	1008927
Total Assets 26	3528	0	173	749	2517	6971	14742	33846	68355	145698	305C19	1558678	3848095
Notes and Loans Payable 27	2209	0	168	383	1552	4753	9902	21623	39675	82638	198843	745434	1562042
All Other Liabilities 28	457	0	49	108	375	701	1538	3546	9991	23032	46680	345014	533641
Net Worth 29	863	0	-43	258	590	1517	3302	8676	18689	40029	59495	468231	1752412

Selected Financial Ratios (Times to 1)

Current Ratio 30	1.4	•	1.8	2.9	1.6	1.4	1.3	1.3	1.2	1.3	1.0	1.2	1.3
Quick Ratio 31	0.4	•	0.5	1.2	0.4	0.4	0.4	0.4	0.4	0.5	0.4	0.3	0.3
Net Sales to Working Capital 32	17.1	•	14.0	5.9	11.1	16.4	20.6	18.9	21.9	17.2	•	26.0	24.8
Coverage Ratio 33	3.3	•	1.0	2.7	2.2	3.4	4.3	4.5	4.1	4.1	2.3	1.1	5.5
Total Asset Turnover 34	3.4	•	4.8	3.1	3.7	3.9	3.7	3.4	2.9	2.5	2.0	2.1	2.3
Inventory Turnover 35	6.5	•	8.1	5.6	5.3	6.0	6.9	7.4	6.8	7.0	6.9	4.2	6.3
Receivables Turnover 36	29.5	•	36.4	18.4	25.6	25.8	35.9	36.3	25.7	19.0	15.2	21.4	66.3
Total Liabilities to Net Worth 37	3.1	•	•	1.9	3.3	3.6	3.5	2.9	2.7	2.6	4.1	2.3	1.2
Current Assets to Working Capital 38	3.8	•	2.3	1.5	2.6	3.7	4.5	4.1	5.2	4.5	•	5.0	4.5
Current Liabilities to Working Capital 39	2.8	•	1.3	0.5	1.6	2.7	3.5	3.1	4.2	3.5	•	4.0	3.5
Working Capital to Net Sales 40	0.1	•	0.1	0.2	0.1	0.1	0.0	0.1	0.0	0.1	•	0.0	0.0
Inventory to Working Capital 41	2.5	•	1.6	0.8	1.8	2.5	3.1	2.6	3.3	2.4	•	3.6	3.4
Total Receipts to Cash Flow 42	24.6	•	15.0	17.3	28.1	25.3	25.8	24.2	23.1	22.4	22.9	22.9	25.1
Cost of Goods to Cash Flow 43	21.5	•	12.4	14.1	24.6	22.3	22.6	21.2	20.1	19.3	18.6	19.2	21.6
Cash Flow to Total Debt 44	0.2	•	0.3	0.3	0.2	0.2	0.2	0.2	0.2	0.2	0.1	0.1	0.2

Selected Financial Factors (in Percentages)

Debt Ratio 45	75.6	•	125.1	65.6	76.5	78.2	77.6	74.4	72.7	72.5	80.5	70.0	54.5
Return on Total Assets 46	5.5	•	2.8	9.2	4.1	5.1	6.0	6.5	5.3	5.6	4.3	4.5	8.2
Return on Equity Before Income Taxes 47	15.7	•	•	17.0	9.3	16.5	20.4	19.7	14.8	15.5	12.2	1.9	14.7
Return on Equity After Income Taxes 48	14.4	•	•	16.7	8.6	16.0	19.7	19.1	13.7	14.3	9.9	1.3	9.4
Profit Margin (Before Income Tax) 49	1.1	•	0.0	1.9	0.6	0.9	1.2	1.5	1.4	1.7	1.2	0.3	2.9
Profit Margin (After Income Tax) 50	1.0	•	0.0	1.9	0.5	0.9	1.2	1.4	1.3	1.6	1.0	0.2	1.9

Table II

Corporations with Net Income

NEW AND USED CAR DEALERS

MONEY AMOUNTS AND SIZE OF ASSETS IN THOUSANDS OF DOLLARS

Item Description for Accounting Period 7/10 Through 6/11		Total	Zero Assets	Under 500	500 to 1,000	1,000 to 5,000	5,000 to 10,000	10,000 to 25,000	25,000 to 50,000	50,000 to 100,000	100,000 to 250,000	250,000 to 500,000	500,000 to 2,500,000	2,500,000 and over
Number of Enterprises	1	25943	1181	10522	2436	5562	3138	2422	502	122	•	•	•	0
Revenues ($ in Thousands)														
Net Sales	2	439056634	401554	11892548	5661467	58502714	86621091	131577427	56096118	25440243	•	•	•	0
Interest	3	726935	75	1071	3384	93394	245463	108012	30040	36803	•	•	•	0
Rents	4	255290	354	4816	1047	4523	6878	21545	17553	12329	•	•	•	0
Royalties	5	2024	0	0	0	0	0	1605	33	0	•	•	•	0
Other Portfolio Income	6	569941	22217	11922	26724	78027	63680	76111	65303	25022	•	•	•	0
Other Receipts	7	8889596	9713	70416	28778	816374	1751449	3091545	1274258	571876	•	•	•	0
Total Receipts	8	449500420	433913	11980773	5721400	59495032	88688561	134876245	57483305	26086273	•	•	•	0
Average Total Receipts	9	17326	367	1139	2349	10697	28263	55688	114509	213822	•	•	•	•
Operating Costs/Operating Income (%)														
Cost of Operations	10	87.1	86.6	82.5	81.2	87.4	88.2	87.6	87.1	87.5	•	•	•	•
Salaries and Wages	11	5.2	1.1	2.3	3.6	4.7	4.7	5.3	5.4	5.3	•	•	•	•
Taxes Paid	12	0.9	0.8	1.4	1.6	0.8	0.8	0.8	0.8	0.8	•	•	•	•
Interest Paid	13	0.5	0.4	0.4	1.1	0.5	0.4	0.4	0.4	0.4	•	•	•	•
Depreciation	14	0.4	0.4	0.1	0.6	0.2	0.2	0.4	0.5	0.6	•	•	•	•
Amortization and Depletion	15	0.1	0.1	0.0	0.0	0.0	0.0	0.1	0.1	0.1	•	•	•	•
Pensions and Other Deferred Comp.	16	0.1	0.0	0.1	0.0	0.1	0.0	0.0	0.1	0.0	•	•	•	•
Employee Benefits	17	0.4	0.2	0.2	0.1	0.4	0.4	0.5	0.5	0.5	•	•	•	•
Advertising	18	0.9	0.2	0.6	0.8	0.9	0.9	1.0	1.1	1.0	•	•	•	•
Other Expenses	19	4.2	5.3	7.1	6.1	4.1	4.1	3.9	3.9	4.1	•	•	•	•
Officers' Compensation	20	0.8	1.7	2.1	2.2	1.0	0.9	0.7	0.6	0.5	•	•	•	•
Operating Margin	21	•	3.3	3.2	2.7	•	•	•	•	•	•	•	•	•
Operating Margin Before Officers' Comp.	22	0.2	4.9	5.2	4.9	1.0	0.2	•	0.1	•	•	•	•	•

Selected Average Balance Sheet ($ in Thousands)

Net Receivables 23	603	0	29	130	338	1101	1686	3644	8410
Inventories 24	2095	0	106	239	1531	3729	6680	13472	24164
Net Property, Plant and Equipment 25	643	0	27	75	146	391	1581	5088	11092
Total Assets 26	4937	0	224	737	2651	6905	14727	33743	68488
Notes and Loans Payable 27	2950	0	146	327	1512	4369	9741	21216	39653
All Other Liabilities 28	607	0	37	83	337	650	1543	3421	10170
Net Worth 29	1380	0	41	327	802	1886	3444	9106	18664

Selected Financial Ratios (Times to 1)

Current Ratio 30	1.4	•	2.5	5.5	1.7	1.4	1.3	1.3	1.2
Quick Ratio 31	0.4	•	0.8	2.6	0.4	0.4	0.4	0.5	0.4
Net Sales to Working Capital 32	16.2	•	10.2	5.1	11.3	14.8	19.4	17.9	23.3
Coverage Ratio 33	4.9	28.5	11.9	4.4	4.4	5.7	5.8	6.2	5.1
Total Asset Turnover 34	3.4	•	5.1	3.2	4.0	4.0	3.7	3.3	3.0
Inventory Turnover 35	7.0	•	8.8	7.9	6.0	6.5	7.1	7.2	7.6
Receivables Turnover 36	31.2	•	36.5	26.7	28.3	25.2	36.9	35.5	29.6
Total Liabilities to Net Worth 37	2.6	•	4.5	1.3	2.3	2.7	3.3	2.7	2.7
Current Assets to Working Capital 38	3.5	•	1.7	1.2	2.5	3.2	4.2	4.1	5.3
Current Liabilities to Working Capital 39	2.5	•	0.7	0.2	1.5	2.2	3.2	3.1	4.3
Working Capital to Net Sales 40	0.1	•	0.1	0.2	0.1	0.1	0.1	0.1	0.0
Inventory to Working Capital 41	2.4	•	1.1	0.6	1.8	2.2	2.9	2.6	3.4
Total Receipts to Cash Flow 42	21.9	9.5	11.1	13.4	23.1	22.3	23.4	21.5	22.2
Cost of Goods to Cash Flow 43	19.0	8.3	9.2	10.9	20.2	19.7	20.5	18.7	19.4
Cash Flow to Total Debt 44	0.2	•	0.6	0.4	0.2	0.2	0.2	0.2	0.2

Selected Financial Factors (in Percentages)

Debt Ratio 45	72.0	•	81.8	55.6	69.8	72.7	76.6	73.0	72.7
Return on Total Assets 46	8.0	•	21.7	15.4	8.6	8.1	7.6	8.0	6.4
Return on Equity Before Income Taxes 47	22.9	•	108.9	26.8	22.1	24.4	27.0	24.9	18.9
Return on Equity After Income Taxes 48	21.4	•	108.1	26.6	21.3	23.9	26.1	24.2	17.7
Profit Margin (Before Income Tax) 49	1.9	11.3	3.9	3.8	1.7	1.7	1.7	2.0	1.7
Profit Margin (After Income Tax) 50	1.7	11.2	3.9	3.7	1.6	1.6	1.7	2.0	1.6

Table I

Corporations with and without Net Income

OTHER MOTOR VEHICLE AND PARTS DEALERS

MONEY AMOUNTS AND SIZE OF ASSETS IN THOUSANDS OF DOLLARS

Item Description for Accounting Period 7/10 Through 6/11	Total	Zero Assets	Under 500	500 to 1,000	1,000 to 5,000	5,000 to 10,000	10,000 to 25,000	25,000 to 50,000	50,000 to 100,000	100,000 to 250,000	250,000 to 500,000	500,000 to 2,500,000	2,500,000 and over
Number of Enterprises 1	40638	3204	25110	5138	5922	816	273	105	40	17	6	5	3
Revenues ($ in Thousands)													
Net Sales 2	122527358	953274	13806134	8859968	30912698	11945506	8748424	7699963	6033289	4797657	2226253	7988435	18555755
Interest 3	98417	1597	4146	8166	15908	5220	8992	9862	8280	788	7369	22741	5347
Rents 4	76774	0	292	6073	23362	7503	2659	515	21807	1804	0	11897	862
Royalties 5	42930	0	0	0	339	1863	741	653	11	0	2210	31230	5884
Other Portfolio Income 6	197021	10350	2695	2328	48901	37567	23289	19403	9635	23138	12481	5914	1322
Other Receipts 7	1676294	109355	102838	142778	537426	103565	106668	42496	98445	24808	49200	263090	95625
Total Receipts 8	124618794	1074576	13916105	9019313	31538634	12101224	8890773	7772892	6171467	4848195	2297513	8323307	18664795
Average Total Receipts 9	3067	335	554	1755	5326	14830	32567	74028	154287	285188	382919	1664661	6221598
Operating Costs/Operating Income (%)													
Cost of Operations 10	68.5	92.0	69.0	67.3	73.9	77.5	76.5	77.3	76.2	69.5	65.0	56.7	48.3
Salaries and Wages 11	10.8	7.1	7.8	9.8	9.3	7.3	8.9	9.1	7.9	11.0	13.1	17.3	18.0
Taxes Paid 12	2.1	1.5	2.3	2.6	1.8	1.4	1.4	1.2	1.5	1.8	1.8	2.5	3.3
Interest Paid 13	1.0	1.3	0.5	1.4	1.1	1.1	1.0	0.8	0.9	0.7	1.0	2.0	1.0
Depreciation 14	1.6	2.2	0.7	0.8	0.8	1.3	2.1	1.1	2.1	3.0	6.0	2.2	2.6
Amortization and Depletion 15	0.1	0.1	0.1	0.1	0.1	0.1	0.1	0.1	0.1	0.2	0.5	0.6	0.1
Pensions and Other Deferred Comp. 16	0.2	0.1	0.0	0.0	0.2	0.1	0.1	0.1	0.3	0.4	0.4	0.3	0.2
Employee Benefits 17	0.8	0.5	0.3	1.0	0.6	0.5	0.8	0.9	1.0	1.2	2.2	1.3	1.4
Advertising 18	1.1	0.4	1.1	1.2	1.3	0.9	0.9	0.7	1.1	0.6	1.1	1.7	1.2
Other Expenses 19	10.7	15.9	13.8	12.0	9.1	8.2	7.9	7.5	8.4	8.5	11.3	15.8	13.6
Officers' Compensation 20	1.8	1.2	4.4	4.1	2.2	1.5	1.0	0.7	1.2	0.7	0.4	0.2	0.2
Operating Margin 21	1.2	•	•	•	•	0.1	•	0.4	•	2.5	•	•	10.0
Operating Margin Before Officers' Comp. 22	3.0	•	4.4	3.9	2.0	1.6	0.4	1.1	0.6	3.3	•	•	10.2

Selected Average Balance Sheet ($ in Thousands)

Net Receivables 23	150	0	13	70	194	572	1751	4559	10436	25831	29660	242059	199591
Inventories 24	697	0	60	381	1439	3640	7919	13074	26682	52273	103595	271518	1967532
Net Property, Plant and Equipment 25	298	0	17	96	301	1214	3360	5611	14379	34846	84534	229930	1364159
Total Assets 26	1477	0	124	695	2214	6963	15324	32858	70633	143718	290029	1264430	4533421
Notes and Loans Payable 27	569	0	61	360	832	3726	7502	16317	27644	48295	99973	363880	1217812
All Other Liabilities 28	469	0	32	153	678	1491	3211	7211	20342	41707	51917	432006	2201944
Net Worth 29	440	0	31	181	704	1746	4611	9330	22647	53716	138139	468544	1113665

Selected Financial Ratios (Times to 1)

Current Ratio 30	1.6	•	2.1	1.9	1.7	1.6	1.6	1.2	1.4	1.6	1.6	2.1	1.2
Quick Ratio 31	0.4	•	0.7	0.5	0.4	0.4	0.5	0.4	0.5	0.6	0.5	1.0	0.1
Net Sales to Working Capital 32	8.6	•	11.7	6.8	7.0	8.0	8.0	16.6	10.5	8.1	5.4	4.9	18.9
Coverage Ratio 33	3.8	•	2.5	2.2	2.7	2.2	2.0	2.7	3.0	6.5	1.4	2.7	11.7
Total Asset Turnover 34	2.0	•	4.4	2.5	2.4	2.1	2.1	2.2	2.1	2.0	1.3	1.3	1.4
Inventory Turnover 35	3.0	•	6.4	3.0	2.7	3.1	3.1	4.3	4.3	3.8	2.3	3.3	1.5
Receivables Turnover 36	20.4	•	45.8	24.2	25.9	27.1	17.7	18.4	16.1	10.9	11.0	6.6	32.5
Total Liabilities to Net Worth 37	2.4	•	3.1	2.8	2.1	3.0	2.3	2.5	2.1	1.7	1.1	1.7	3.1
Current Assets to Working Capital 38	2.8	•	1.9	2.1	2.3	2.7	2.5	5.2	3.3	2.6	2.6	1.9	7.2
Current Liabilities to Working Capital 39	1.8	•	0.9	1.1	1.3	1.7	1.5	4.2	2.3	1.6	1.6	0.9	6.2
Working Capital to Net Sales 40	0.1	•	0.1	0.1	0.1	0.1	0.1	0.1	0.1	0.1	0.2	0.2	0.1
Inventory to Working Capital 41	2.0	•	1.3	1.5	1.8	1.9	1.7	3.3	2.0	1.4	1.6	0.9	6.2
Total Receipts to Cash Flow 42	10.0	323.0	10.0	10.3	12.4	12.8	17.0	16.1	13.9	10.7	12.0	7.0	5.5
Cost of Goods to Cash Flow 43	6.9	297.1	6.9	6.9	9.2	10.0	13.0	12.4	10.6	7.4	7.8	4.0	2.6
Cash Flow to Total Debt 44	0.3	•	0.6	0.3	0.3	0.2	0.2	0.2	0.3	0.3	0.2	0.3	0.3

Selected Financial Factors (in Percentages)

Debt Ratio 45	70.2	•	75.3	73.9	68.2	74.9	69.9	71.6	67.9	62.6	52.4	62.9	75.4
Return on Total Assets 46	8.1	•	5.9	7.3	6.6	5.2	4.2	4.7	5.4	8.4	1.8	7.0	15.8
Return on Equity Before Income Taxes 47	20.1	•	14.2	15.1	13.0	11.4	7.1	10.4	11.2	18.9	1.0	11.9	58.8
Return on Equity After Income Taxes 48	15.2	•	13.4	14.4	12.2	10.7	5.6	9.2	10.0	17.8	0.8	8.7	38.7
Profit Margin (Before Income Tax) 49	2.9	•	0.8	1.6	1.8	1.4	1.0	1.3	1.7	3.6	0.4	3.5	10.6
Profit Margin (After Income Tax) 50	2.2	•	0.7	1.5	1.6	1.3	0.8	1.2	1.5	3.4	0.3	2.6	7.0

Table II
Corporations with Net Income

OTHER MOTOR VEHICLE AND PARTS DEALERS

Money Amounts and Size of Assets in Thousands of Dollars

Item Description for Accounting Period 7/10 Through 6/11	Total	Zero Assets	Under 500	500 to 1,000	1,000 to 5,000	5,000 to 10,000	10,000 to 25,000	25,000 to 50,000	50,000 to 100,000	100,000 to 250,000	250,000 to 500,000	500,000 to 2,500,000	2,500,000 and over
Number of Enterprises **1**	22734	1424	13344	3018	4059	542	218	73	28	•	•	•	3
Revenues ($ in Thousands)													
Net Sales **2**	96438883	569698	8549934	5930928	23058325	9184194	7599194	6552767	4288653	•	•	•	18555755
Interest **3**	56815	246	4076	6867	13698	3380	5998	6750	7878	•	•	•	5347
Rents **4**	43152	0	292	434	15337	433	2428	490	20507	•	•	•	862
Royalties **5**	8166	0	0	0	339	0	741	653	0	•	•	•	5884
Other Portfolio Income **6**	157232	8368	2199	963	26615	36519	17662	14331	7723	•	•	•	1322
Other Receipts **7**	1258058	71476	69343	18913	447334	75166	78698	18651	64181	•	•	•	95625
Total Receipts **8**	97962306	649788	8625844	5958105	23561648	9299692	7704721	6593642	4386942	•	•	•	18664795
Average Total Receipts **9**	4309	456	646	1974	5805	17158	35343	90324	156676	•	•	•	6221598
Operating Costs/Operating Income (%)													
Cost of Operations **10**	67.3	88.0	67.7	65.0	73.0	77.2	75.7	77.4	76.4	•	•	•	48.3
Salaries and Wages **11**	10.8	4.2	7.5	8.8	9.2	6.8	9.1	8.9	7.1	•	•	•	18.0
Taxes Paid **12**	2.0	1.1	2.0	2.6	1.8	1.3	1.4	1.1	1.5	•	•	•	3.3
Interest Paid **13**	0.8	0.6	0.4	0.6	0.8	0.8	0.9	0.5	0.8	•	•	•	1.0
Depreciation **14**	1.5	1.1	0.6	0.9	0.7	1.3	1.2	1.1	2.1	•	•	•	2.6
Amortization and Depletion **15**	0.1	•	0.1	0.1	0.0	0.0	0.1	0.0	0.1	•	•	•	0.1
Pensions and Other Deferred Comp. **16**	0.2	0.2	0.0	0.0	0.2	0.1	0.1	0.1	0.2	•	•	•	0.2
Employee Benefits **17**	0.8	0.0	0.3	0.9	0.6	0.4	0.7	0.8	0.9	•	•	•	1.4
Advertising **18**	1.1	0.3	1.3	1.2	1.3	0.8	1.0	0.7	1.0	•	•	•	1.2
Other Expenses **19**	10.4	10.0	12.7	11.3	9.0	8.1	7.4	6.9	7.9	•	•	•	13.6
Officers' Compensation **20**	1.6	1.9	4.3	4.1	2.3	1.5	1.1	0.7	1.2	•	•	•	0.2
Operating Margin **21**	3.2	•	3.2	4.4	1.1	1.7	1.2	1.6	0.6	•	•	•	10.0
Operating Margin Before Officers' Comp. **22**	4.9	•	7.5	8.5	3.4	3.2	2.2	2.3	1.9	•	•	•	10.2

Selected Average Balance Sheet ($ in Thousands)

Net Receivables 23	216	0	15	82	246	701	1921	4968	11172	199591
Inventories 24	855	0	53	344	1201	2786	7155	13498	24689	1967532
Net Property, Plant and Equipment 25	400	0	16	118	277	1025	2684	4165	16497	1364159
Total Assets 26	2016	0	133	677	2207	7089	15299	33553	72085	4533421
Notes and Loans Payable 27	680	0	35	303	782	2888	6708	13632	26300	1217812
All Other Liabilities 28	635	0	26	134	570	1849	3128	8543	18359	2201944
Net Worth 29	701	0	72	240	856	2351	5462	11378	27425	1113665

Selected Financial Ratios (Times to 1)

Current Ratio 30	1.6	•	3.1	1.9	1.9	1.7	1.8	1.4	1.6	1.2
Quick Ratio 31	0.4	•	1.3	0.6	0.5	0.5	0.5	0.5	0.6	0.1
Net Sales to Working Capital 32	8.2	•	10.3	8.2	6.5	7.5	7.1	12.5	8.6	18.9
Coverage Ratio 33	6.9	12.6	12.5	9.2	4.9	4.9	3.9	5.1	4.8	11.7
Total Asset Turnover 34	2.1	•	4.8	2.9	2.6	2.4	2.3	2.7	2.1	1.4
Inventory Turnover 35	3.3	•	8.1	3.7	3.5	4.7	3.7	5.1	4.7	1.5
Receivables Turnover 36	21.3	•	47.4	24.0	24.6	31.0	19.0	22.8	15.6	32.5
Total Liabilities to Net Worth 37	1.9	•	0.8	1.8	1.6	2.0	1.8	1.9	1.6	3.1
Current Assets to Working Capital 38	2.6	•	1.5	2.1	2.1	2.4	2.2	3.5	2.6	7.2
Current Liabilities to Working Capital 39	1.6	•	0.5	1.1	1.1	1.4	1.2	2.5	1.6	6.2
Working Capital to Net Sales 40	0.1	•	0.1	0.1	0.2	0.1	0.1	0.1	0.1	0.1
Inventory to Working Capital 41	1.8	•	0.9	1.3	1.5	1.6	1.5	2.3	1.5	6.2
Total Receipts to Cash Flow 42	8.5	8.0	8.2	7.7	10.3	10.5	13.9	14.8	12.1	5.5
Cost of Goods to Cash Flow 43	5.8	7.0	5.5	5.0	7.5	8.1	10.5	11.5	9.2	2.6
Cash Flow to Total Debt 44	0.4	•	1.3	0.6	0.4	0.3	0.3	0.3	0.3	0.3

Selected Financial Factors (in Percentages)

Debt Ratio 45	65.2	•	45.9	64.6	61.2	66.8	64.3	66.1	62.0	75.4
Return on Total Assets 46	11.8	•	21.3	15.8	10.4	9.0	7.8	7.4	7.9	15.8
Return on Equity Before Income Taxes 47	29.2	•	36.2	39.8	21.4	21.6	16.3	17.6	16.5	58.8
Return on Equity After Income Taxes 48	23.7	•	35.5	38.9	20.5	20.8	14.7	16.2	15.0	38.7
Profit Margin (Before Income Tax) 49	4.8	6.5	4.0	4.9	3.2	3.0	2.6	2.2	3.0	10.6
Profit Margin (After Income Tax) 50	3.9	5.6	4.0	4.7	3.1	2.9	2.3	2.1	2.7	7.0

Table I

Corporations with and without Net Income

FURNITURE AND HOME FURNISHINGS STORES

MONEY AMOUNTS AND SIZE OF ASSETS IN THOUSANDS OF DOLLARS

Item Description for Accounting Period 7/10 Through 6/11	Total	Zero Assets	Under 500	500 to 1,000	1,000 to 5,000	5,000 to 10,000	10,000 to 25,000	25,000 to 50,000	50,000 to 100,000	100,000 to 250,000	250,000 to 500,000	500,000 to 2,500,000	2,500,000 and over
Number of Enterprises 1	33641	3599	23102	3800	2635	279	144	31	21	12	9	9	0
Revenues ($ in Thousands)													
Net Sales 2	75664409	854480	11713110	6621204	12213692	4211160	5526779	2502115	2778678	2988398	5129696	21125098	0
Interest 3	229996	29	4563	28714	21846	10924	6729	3	104	20429	128883	7772	0
Rents 4	25389	0	3588	6	5683	301	4510	817	0	4021	2076	4388	0
Royalties 5	6199	0	0	0	0	0	22	0	658	0	0	5518	0
Other Portfolio Income 6	39085	11408	4822	5338	6746	737	1990	279	3299	2440	670	1354	0
Other Receipts 7	600690	5354	22454	28174	114547	31573	80431	47103	86017	48713	88961	47362	0
Total Receipts 8	76565768	871271	11748537	6683436	12362514	4254695	5620461	2550317	2868756	3064001	5350286	21191492	0
Average Total Receipts 9	2276	242	509	1759	4692	15250	39031	82268	136607	255333	594476	2354610	•
Operating Costs/Operating Income (%)													
Cost of Operations 10	57.3	67.9	61.2	64.9	59.8	53.0	61.8	58.2	51.3	56.4	54.7	51.9	•
Salaries and Wages 11	12.5	9.0	9.5	9.7	12.5	13.2	14.3	15.5	16.4	14.5	16.4	12.4	•
Taxes Paid 12	2.5	3.8	2.3	2.6	2.5	2.2	2.1	2.3	2.6	2.7	2.2	2.8	•
Interest Paid 13	0.7	1.1	0.7	0.6	0.8	0.9	0.6	0.9	0.7	0.7	0.7	0.7	•
Depreciation 14	1.6	2.3	0.6	1.1	0.9	2.1	0.8	0.9	2.6	2.6	2.1	2.5	•
Amortization and Depletion 15	0.2	0.6	0.1	0.1	0.1	0.1	0.0	0.2	0.3	0.2	0.1	0.3	•
Pensions and Other Deferred Comp. 16	0.1	•	0.1	0.1	0.1	0.1	0.2	0.2	0.1	0.1	0.2	0.1	•
Employee Benefits 17	1.0	0.2	0.7	0.9	0.4	0.7	0.9	1.8	1.3	1.2	1.3	1.3	•
Advertising 18	4.1	3.0	2.5	2.9	3.0	9.5	4.4	3.2	4.1	5.4	5.6	4.5	•
Other Expenses 19	16.4	29.3	16.9	14.3	16.2	17.4	13.4	17.4	20.0	19.7	19.4	15.2	•
Officers' Compensation 20	2.4	1.3	5.9	4.5	3.9	1.7	1.1	1.7	1.3	0.4	0.6	0.5	•
Operating Margin 21	1.2	•	•	•	•	•	0.4	•	•	•	•	7.8	•
Operating Margin Before Officers' Comp. 22	3.7	•	5.4	2.8	3.8	0.9	1.5	•	0.6	•	•	8.3	•

Selected Average Balance Sheet ($ in Thousands)

Net Receivables 23	223	0	107	23	385	850	2996	8084	5739	19728	97232	379764	•
Inventories 24	358	0	255	58	932	2912	6015	8909	24076	32388	121018	373445	•
Net Property, Plant and Equipment 25	294	0	153	26	368	1829	2314	7006	17531	55062	79998	545107	•
Total Assets 26	1215	0	688	140	2142	7496	14806	33618	72364	149676	353319	1956539	•
Notes and Loans Payable 27	321	0	212	79	862	3467	3795	10401	21059	43629	76672	267972	•
All Other Liabilities 28	506	0	177	56	778	3086	5837	9165	27262	55934	113189	973836	•
Net Worth 29	387	0	299	5	502	943	5174	14051	24043	50112	163458	714731	•

Selected Financial Ratios (Times to 1)

Current Ratio 30	1.5	•	1.5	2.3	1.7	0.9	1.8	1.5	1.6	1.4	2.0	1.4	•
Quick Ratio 31	0.7	•	0.7	1.1	0.7	0.3	0.7	0.6	0.5	0.6	0.9	0.7	•
Net Sales to Working Capital 32	8.3	•	14.4	6.6	7.2	•	7.7	12.2	9.3	11.0	4.7	6.8	•
Coverage Ratio 33	4.4	•	0.7	•	2.6	1.2	4.5	0.7	4.7	•	2.6	12.5	•
Total Asset Turnover 34	1.9	•	3.6	2.5	2.2	2.0	2.6	2.4	1.8	1.7	1.6	1.2	•
Inventory Turnover 35	3.6	•	5.4	4.4	3.0	2.7	3.9	5.3	2.8	4.3	2.6	3.3	•
Receivables Turnover 36	9.7	•	25.0	14.5	12.2	16.6	12.6	10.4	22.5	11.9	5.9	5.8	•
Total Liabilities to Net Worth 37	2.1	•	29.9	1.3	3.3	7.0	1.9	1.4	2.0	2.0	1.2	1.7	•
Current Assets to Working Capital 38	2.9	•	2.9	1.8	2.4	•	2.3	3.2	2.8	3.4	2.0	3.4	•
Current Liabilities to Working Capital 39	1.9	•	1.9	0.8	1.4	•	1.3	2.2	1.8	2.4	1.0	2.4	•
Working Capital to Net Sales 40	0.1	•	0.1	0.2	0.1	•	0.1	0.1	0.1	0.1	0.2	0.1	•
Inventory to Working Capital 41	1.3	•	1.5	0.9	1.4	•	1.2	1.5	1.8	1.6	1.0	1.1	•
Total Receipts to Cash Flow 42	8.4	33.9	9.8	11.9	9.0	12.5	11.7	9.5	6.8	9.8	8.2	6.1	•
Cost of Goods to Cash Flow 43	4.8	23.0	6.0	7.7	5.4	6.6	7.2	5.5	3.5	5.5	4.5	3.2	•
Cash Flow to Total Debt 44	0.3	•	0.4	0.4	0.3	0.2	0.3	0.4	0.4	0.3	0.4	0.3	•

Selected Financial Factors (in Percentages)

Debt Ratio 45	68.1	•	96.8	56.5	76.6	87.4	65.1	58.2	66.8	66.5	53.7	63.5	•
Return on Total Assets 46	5.8	•	1.6	•	4.2	2.1	7.0	1.5	6.1	•	2.9	10.5	•
Return on Equity Before Income Taxes 47	14.1	•	•	•	10.9	2.8	15.6	•	14.4	•	3.8	26.5	•
Return on Equity After Income Taxes 48	9.3	•	•	•	10.2	1.8	14.7	•	13.7	•	2.8	17.8	•
Profit Margin (Before Income Tax) 49	2.4	•	•	•	1.2	0.2	2.1	•	2.6	•	1.1	8.1	•
Profit Margin (After Income Tax) 50	1.6	•	•	•	1.1	0.1	2.0	•	2.5	•	0.8	5.4	•

Table II
Corporations with Net Income

FURNITURE AND HOME FURNISHINGS STORES

MONEY AMOUNTS AND SIZE OF ASSETS IN THOUSANDS OF DOLLARS

Item Description for Accounting Period 7/10 Through 6/11	Total	Zero Assets	Under 500	500 to 1,000	1,000 to 5,000	5,000 to 10,000	10,000 to 25,000	25,000 to 50,000	50,000 to 100,000	100,000 to 250,000	250,000 to 500,000	500,000 to 2,500,000	2,500,000 and over
Number of Enterprises **1**	17270	851	12411	1905	1818	120	112	18	14	7	•	•	0
Revenues ($ in Thousands)													
Net Sales **2**	55207145	131985	8079006	3532750	8498053	1726440	4644159	1448345	1906330	1574089	•	•	0
Interest **3**	158431	0	1266	11086	15657	9894	4122	0	6	8893	•	•	0
Rents **4**	20535	0	2730	0	5683	0	1721	0	0	4021	•	•	0
Royalties **5**	2323	0	0	0	0	0	0	0	0	0	•	•	0
Other Portfolio Income **6**	11293	0	2021	3106	461	494	1123	162	180	2294	•	•	0
Other Receipts **7**	374751	0	8015	17685	51324	22309	61562	42104	33497	21508	•	•	0
Total Receipts **8**	55774478	131985	8093038	3564627	8571178	1759137	4712687	1490611	1940013	1610805	•	•	0
Average Total Receipts **9**	3230	155	652	1871	4715	14659	42078	82812	138572	230115	•	•	•
Operating Costs/Operating Income (%)													
Cost of Operations **10**	56.3	57.4	59.9	64.7	58.7	53.4	60.1	57.9	49.1	56.7	•	•	•
Salaries and Wages **11**	11.8	•	8.7	8.0	11.3	11.5	13.8	13.3	16.2	13.5	•	•	•
Taxes Paid **12**	2.4	0.9	1.8	2.0	2.6	2.2	2.1	2.0	2.5	3.1	•	•	•
Interest Paid **13**	0.6	2.9	0.6	0.6	0.7	1.1	0.6	0.5	0.7	0.5	•	•	•
Depreciation **14**	1.6	•	0.5	0.8	1.0	0.7	0.7	0.8	3.0	2.6	•	•	•
Amortization and Depletion **15**	0.1	•	0.1	0.0	0.0	0.1	0.1	0.1	0.1	0.1	•	•	•
Pensions and Other Deferred Comp. **16**	0.1	•	0.1	0.1	0.1	0.1	0.2	0.3	0.2	0.2	•	•	•
Employee Benefits **17**	0.9	•	0.6	0.4	0.3	0.7	0.9	1.6	1.5	0.9	•	•	•
Advertising **18**	4.0	1.3	2.2	2.8	3.1	10.4	4.7	4.1	2.8	4.9	•	•	•
Other Expenses **19**	15.2	20.5	14.1	14.4	15.6	16.2	13.5	17.6	19.0	16.4	•	•	•
Officers' Compensation **20**	2.3	3.6	5.8	4.8	4.2	1.8	1.1	2.5	1.0	0.5	•	•	•
Operating Margin **21**	4.6	13.3	5.7	1.5	2.4	1.9	2.3	•	3.9	0.7	•	•	•
Operating Margin Before Officers' Comp. **22**	6.9	16.9	11.5	6.3	6.6	3.7	3.4	1.7	4.9	1.2	•	•	•

Selected Average Balance Sheet ($ in Thousands)

Net Receivables 23	348	0	27	126	346	666	2830	7549	7265	22336
Inventories 24	468	0	52	256	718	3975	5486	10735	22961	24387
Net Property, Plant and Equipment 25	439	0	20	152	391	1341	2399	6419	13856	48243
Total Assets 26	1791	0	146	718	2048	6707	14754	32972	72406	152447
Notes and Loans Payable 27	352	0	51	258	755	2384	2826	6693	21984	31291
All Other Liabilities 28	755	0	61	124	621	1998	5610	7743	27046	46005
Net Worth 29	684	0	34	336	672	2325	6318	18536	23376	75151

Selected Financial Ratios (Times to 1)

Current Ratio 30	1.6	•	1.5	2.6	2.0	1.5	1.8	1.8	1.7	1.7
Quick Ratio 31	0.7	•	0.7	1.1	0.7	0.4	0.7	0.8	0.6	0.8
Net Sales to Working Capital 32	7.2	5.7	18.2	6.2	6.2	8.4	8.1	8.7	8.4	6.1
Coverage Ratio 33	9.8	•	10.8	5.3	5.6	4.5	7.1	5.1	9.6	7.3
Total Asset Turnover 34	1.8	•	4.4	2.6	2.3	2.1	2.8	2.4	1.9	1.5
Inventory Turnover 35	3.8	•	7.4	4.7	3.8	1.9	4.5	4.3	2.9	5.2
Receivables Turnover 36	9.7	•	29.9	15.6	17.7	14.0	14.7	•	17.8	10.6
Total Liabilities to Net Worth 37	1.6	•	3.3	1.1	2.0	1.9	1.3	0.8	2.1	1.0
Current Assets to Working Capital 38	2.6	•	3.1	1.6	2.0	3.1	2.2	2.2	2.5	2.4
Current Liabilities to Working Capital 39	1.6	•	2.1	0.6	1.0	2.1	1.2	1.2	1.5	1.4
Working Capital to Net Sales 40	0.1	•	0.1	0.2	0.2	0.1	0.1	0.1	0.1	0.2
Inventory to Working Capital 41	1.2	•	1.5	0.9	1.2	2.1	1.2	1.2	1.5	1.0
Total Receipts to Cash Flow 42	6.9	3.7	6.9	8.7	7.4	9.0	9.5	7.1	5.9	7.9
Cost of Goods to Cash Flow 43	3.9	2.1	4.2	5.6	4.4	4.8	5.7	4.1	2.9	4.5
Cash Flow to Total Debt 44	0.4	•	0.8	0.6	0.5	0.4	0.5	0.8	0.5	0.4

Selected Financial Factors (in Percentages)

Debt Ratio 45	61.8	•	76.6	53.2	67.2	65.3	57.2	43.8	67.7	50.7
Return on Total Assets 46	11.2	•	28.9	7.6	9.2	10.6	12.2	6.6	12.1	5.0
Return on Equity Before Income Taxes 47	26.3	•	112.1	13.3	23.0	23.7	24.4	9.5	33.7	8.7
Return on Equity After Income Taxes 48	21.0	•	111.3	12.3	22.2	22.8	23.5	9.5	32.8	6.4
Profit Margin (Before Income Tax) 49	5.6	13.3	5.9	2.4	3.3	3.8	3.7	2.2	5.8	2.9
Profit Margin (After Income Tax) 50	4.5	13.3	5.8	2.2	3.2	3.7	3.6	2.2	5.6	2.1

Table I

Corporations with and without Net Income

ELECTRONICS AND APPLIANCE STORES

MONEY AMOUNTS AND SIZE OF ASSETS IN THOUSANDS OF DOLLARS

Item Description for Accounting Period 7/10 Through 6/11	Total	Zero Assets	Under 500	500 to 1,000	1,000 to 5,000	5,000 to 10,000	10,000 to 25,000	25,000 to 50,000	50,000 to 100,000	100,000 to 250,000	250,000 to 500,000	500,000 to 2,500,000	2,500,000 and over
Number of Enterprises 1	28085	4787	19541	1687	1779	142	87	17	18	12	4	10	0
Revenues ($ in Thousands)													
Net Sales 2	100079085	591322	8148414	3890811	9280600	2550767	3164443	1562937	3167762	4374703	2149486	61197841	0
Interest 3	175550	0	2634	1981	3978	138	1116	55	1646	11	305	163686	0
Rents 4	17273	0	436	2956	925	39	0	22	329	0	309	12257	0
Royalties 5	49790	0	828	0	0	0	0	0	0	0	0	48962	0
Other Portfolio Income 6	137665	0	4663	1507	2103	1842	167	778	79	850	5142	120535	0
Other Receipts 7	1183580	-31088	82970	12788	28521	47157	15775	3010	57312	45156	692	921285	0
Total Receipts 8	101642943	560234	8239945	3910043	9316127	2599943	3181501	1566802	3227128	4420720	2155934	62464566	0
Average Total Receipts 9	3619	117	422	2318	5237	18309	36569	92165	179285	368393	538984	6246457	•
Operating Costs/Operating Income (%)													
Cost of Operations 10	70.3	34.6	50.3	54.2	69.5	59.7	69.3	74.7	68.1	78.1	65.8	74.5	•
Salaries and Wages 11	10.2	4.9	16.2	17.8	12.1	17.8	14.0	7.7	14.2	10.2	13.3	8.0	•
Taxes Paid 12	1.6	1.8	2.6	2.4	1.9	1.8	1.3	1.0	1.3	1.1	1.8	1.4	•
Interest Paid 13	0.6	0.1	0.7	0.9	0.5	0.1	0.5	0.6	0.3	0.1	3.1	0.5	•
Depreciation 14	1.2	1.1	1.0	1.0	0.7	0.7	1.3	2.6	1.9	1.1	1.1	1.2	•
Amortization and Depletion 15	0.2	0.2	0.1	0.1	0.1	0.4	0.1	0.0	0.1	0.1	1.1	0.2	•
Pensions and Other Deferred Comp. 16	0.2	2.1	0.2	0.1	0.3	0.3	0.2	0.1	0.1	0.1	0.1	0.1	•
Employee Benefits 17	0.8	0.9	0.5	1.4	1.2	1.1	0.7	0.2	0.7	0.5	2.2	0.7	•
Advertising 18	1.7	1.1	2.3	0.6	1.1	2.2	0.8	1.3	1.0	1.0	0.3	2.0	•
Other Expenses 19	12.1	314.4	19.2	16.5	9.6	10.9	9.6	10.4	6.8	6.2	7.9	9.3	•
Officers' Compensation 20	1.5	5.9	6.8	4.9	3.2	2.0	1.4	1.0	5.7	1.0	0.9	0.1	•
Operating Margin 21	•	•	0.1	•	•	3.0	0.8	0.4	•	0.5	2.5	2.0	•
Operating Margin Before Officers' Comp. 22	1.3	•	6.9	4.9	2.9	5.0	2.1	1.4	5.5	1.5	3.3	2.1	•

Selected Average Balance Sheet ($ in Thousands)

Item													
Net Receivables 23	•	775676	69192	24532	18863	10378	5126	1384	501	59	9	0	380
Inventories 24	•	379297	26538	31524	16563	8170	2514	1759	534	169	33	0	348
Net Property, Plant and Equipment 25	•	412289	16966	21225	5708	5705	1042	550	216	140	14	0	203
Total Assets 26	•	3071877	360346	143666	72999	33315	14477	6508	1818	699	108		1583
Notes and Loans Payable 27	•	319394	130147	11000	10439	7467	3681	588	447	235	67	0	252
All Other Liabilities 28	•	1612107	180193	56980	33720	12621	7046	1800	782	350	69	0	802
Net Worth 29	•	1140376	50005	75686	28840	13226	3750	4120	589	113	-28	0	529

Selected Financial Ratios (Times to 1)

Item													
Current Ratio 30	•	1.1	1.1	1.3	1.5	1.9	1.5	1.9	1.6	1.4	0.9	•	1.2
Quick Ratio 31	•	0.6	0.6	0.6	0.9	1.2	0.9	1.1	0.9	0.7	0.4	•	0.6
Net Sales to Working Capital 32	•	33.1	29.7	18.4	10.8	8.6	10.0	8.4	10.8	17.0	•	•	23.7
Coverage Ratio 33	•	9.1	1.9	14.3	6.6	2.2	3.7	35.2	1.1	1.5	2.6	•	3.6
Total Asset Turnover 34	•	2.0	1.5	2.5	2.4	2.8	2.5	2.8	2.9	3.3	3.9	•	2.3
Inventory Turnover 35	•	12.0	13.3	9.0	7.2	8.4	10.0	6.1	6.8	7.4	6.3	•	7.2
Receivables Turnover 36	•	13.4	6.8	12.4	9.4	7.3	9.9	12.5	11.2	25.7	42.8	•	10.2
Total Liabilities to Net Worth 37	•	1.7	6.2	0.9	1.5	1.5	2.9	0.6	2.1	5.2	•	•	2.0
Current Assets to Working Capital 38	•	9.6	10.6	4.0	3.1	2.1	3.1	2.1	2.8	3.6	•	•	6.4
Current Liabilities to Working Capital 39	•	8.6	9.6	3.0	2.1	1.1	2.1	1.1	1.8	2.6	•	•	5.4
Working Capital to Net Sales 40	•	0.0	0.0	0.1	0.1	0.1	0.1	0.1	0.1	0.1	•	•	0.0
Inventory to Working Capital 41	•	3.7	0.6	1.7	0.9	0.7	0.9	0.8	1.2	1.4	•	•	2.4
Total Receipts to Cash Flow 42	•	9.9	12.0	17.5	15.0	10.1	11.4	8.4	14.5	7.5	7.0	•	10.6
Cost of Goods to Cash Flow 43	•	7.4	7.9	13.6	10.2	7.6	7.9	5.0	10.1	4.1	3.5	•	7.4
Cash Flow to Total Debt 44	•	0.3	0.1	0.3	0.3	0.5	0.3	0.9	0.3	0.5	0.4	•	0.3

Selected Financial Factors (in Percentages)

Item													
Debt Ratio 45	•	62.9	86.1	47.3	60.5	60.3	74.1	36.7	67.6	83.8	125.9	•	66.6
Return on Total Assets 46	•	9.6	8.7	4.3	4.6	3.4	4.6	13.9	1.5	4.3	7.6	•	4.6
Return on Equity Before Income Taxes 47	•	23.1	29.6	7.5	9.9	4.6	12.9	21.3	0.3	9.4	•	•	10.1
Return on Equity After Income Taxes 48	•	15.3	27.9	7.4	6.9	3.5	11.7	20.4	•	8.3	•	•	3.8
Profit Margin (Before Income Tax) 49	•	4.3	2.8	1.6	1.6	0.7	1.3	4.9	0.0	0.5	1.2	•	1.5
Profit Margin (After Income Tax) 50	•	2.8	2.6	1.5	1.1	0.5	1.2	4.7	•	0.4	1.2	•	0.6

Table II
Corporations with Net Income

ELECTRONICS AND APPLIANCE STORES

MONEY AMOUNTS AND SIZE OF ASSETS IN THOUSANDS OF DOLLARS

Item Description for Accounting Period 7/10 Through 6/11	Total	Zero Assets	Under 500	500 to 1,000	1,000 to 5,000	5,000 to 10,000	10,000 to 25,000	25,000 to 50,000	50,000 to 100,000	100,000 to 250,000	250,000 to 500,000	500,000 to 2,500,000	2,500,000 and over
Number of Enterprises 1	15721	2354	10646	1227	1264	130	59	•	12	7	4	•	0
Revenues ($ in Thousands)													
Net Sales 2	87408430	350934	5218507	3140075	6808986	2477815	2217251	•	2333479	2882458	2149486	•	0
Interest 3	160259	0	2552	585	3420	124	111	•	1308	11	305	•	0
Rents 4	15403	0	436	1253	758	39	0	•	329	0	309	•	0
Royalties 5	49790	0	828	0	0	0	0	•	0	0	0	•	0
Other Portfolio Income 6	135051	0	4663	603	1276	1842	167	•	15	148	5142	•	0
Other Receipts 7	1135851	0	58444	12196	19607	46063	8499	•	45545	49289	692	•	0
Total Receipts 8	88904784	350934	5285430	3154712	6834047	2525883	2226028	•	2380676	2931906	2155934	•	0
Average Total Receipts 9	5655	149	496	2571	5407	19430	37729	•	198390	418844	538984	•	•
Operating Costs/Operating Income (%)													
Cost of Operations 10	70.9	20.4	51.7	52.6	66.1	59.4	67.2	•	76.9	82.5	65.8	•	•
Salaries and Wages 11	9.5	4.2	13.0	17.8	13.1	17.5	14.4	•	10.0	8.0	13.3	•	•
Taxes Paid 12	1.5	1.5	2.3	2.4	2.0	1.7	1.5	•	1.0	0.9	1.8	•	•
Interest Paid 13	0.6	0.2	0.4	0.6	0.6	0.1	0.3	•	0.3	0.1	3.1	•	•
Depreciation 14	1.1	1.7	1.1	0.6	0.9	0.7	0.6	•	0.5	0.5	1.1	•	•
Amortization and Depletion 15	0.2	•	0.1	0.1	0.1	0.4	0.1	•	0.1	0.1	1.1	•	•
Pensions and Other Deferred Comp. 16	0.2	3.5	0.1	0.1	0.2	0.3	0.3	•	0.0	0.0	0.1	•	•
Employee Benefits 17	0.8	0.8	0.5	1.4	1.2	1.1	0.6	•	0.8	0.5	2.2	•	•
Advertising 18	1.8	0.3	2.5	0.3	1.3	2.0	1.0	•	0.9	0.4	0.3	•	•
Other Expenses 19	9.8	39.8	15.9	16.5	9.4	10.1	8.2	•	6.6	4.7	7.9	•	•
Officers' Compensation 20	1.2	6.6	7.1	5.1	3.1	2.0	1.4	•	1.2	0.9	0.9	•	•
Operating Margin 21	2.5	20.9	5.1	2.5	2.0	4.6	4.4	•	1.6	1.3	2.5	•	•
Operating Margin Before Officers' Comp. 22	3.7	27.4	12.3	7.6	5.1	6.6	5.8	•	2.8	2.2	3.3	•	•

Selected Average Balance Sheet ($ in Thousands)

	C1	C2	C3	C4	C5	C6	C7	C8	C9	C10	C11
Net Receivables 23	633	(D)	9	72	562	1249	5838	•	23217	33897	69192
Inventories 24	546	(D)	37	176	535	1407	2638	•	19679	36827	10409
Net Property, Plant and Equipment 25	322	(D)	14	144	239	533	956	•	4523	13747	16966
Total Assets 26	2528	(D)	111	715	1936	6473	14460	•	73524	156720	360346
Notes and Loans Payable 27	347	(D)	44	219	463	553	1903	•	10434	5334	130147
All Other Liabilities 28	1282	(D)	68	392	789	1461	8401	•	35238	64748	180193
Net Worth 29	899	(D)	-2	104	684	4459	4157	•	27852	86638	50005

Selected Financial Ratios (Times to 1)

	C1	C2	C3	C4	C5	C6	C7	C8	C9	C10	C11
Current Ratio 30	1.2	•	1.0	1.3	1.7	2.2	1.3	•	1.4	1.5	1.1
Quick Ratio 31	0.6	•	0.5	0.8	0.9	1.3	0.8	•	0.9	0.8	0.6
Net Sales to Working Capital 32	24.3	•	•	20.2	9.2	7.9	15.9	•	12.7	12.3	29.7
Coverage Ratio 33	8.8	128.1	16.5	6.5	5.3	45.5	16.3	•	14.5	34.9	1.9
Total Asset Turnover 34	2.2	•	4.4	3.6	2.8	2.9	2.6	•	2.6	2.6	1.5
Inventory Turnover 35	7.2	•	6.9	7.7	6.7	8.1	9.6	•	7.6	9.2	34.0
Receivables Turnover 36	9.8	•	49.7	25.0	10.4	17.6	9.2	•	8.9	•	6.2
Total Liabilities to Net Worth 37	1.8	•	•	5.9	1.8	0.5	2.5	•	1.6	0.8	6.2
Current Assets to Working Capital 38	6.6	•	•	3.9	2.5	1.8	4.9	•	3.4	2.9	10.6
Current Liabilities to Working Capital 39	5.6	•	•	2.9	1.5	0.8	3.9	•	2.4	1.9	9.6
Working Capital to Net Sales 40	0.0	•	•	0.0	0.1	0.1	0.1	•	0.1	0.1	0.0
Inventory to Working Capital 41	2.5	•	•	1.5	1.0	0.7	1.4	•	1.0	1.1	0.6
Total Receipts to Cash Flow 42	9.2	1.3	5.7	6.3	10.9	7.7	8.6	•	11.6	15.4	12.0
Cost of Goods to Cash Flow 43	6.5	0.4	3.0	3.3	7.2	4.6	5.8	•	8.9	12.7	7.9
Cash Flow to Total Debt 44	0.4	•	0.8	0.7	0.4	1.2	0.4	•	0.4	0.4	0.1

Selected Financial Factors (in Percentages)

	C1	C2	C3	C4	C5	C6	C7	C8	C9	C10	C11
Debt Ratio 45	64.4	•	101.5	85.5	64.7	31.1	71.3	•	62.1	44.7	86.1
Return on Total Assets 46	10.8	•	30.3	12.7	8.2	19.4	13.2	•	10.2	8.1	8.7
Return on Equity Before Income Taxes 47	27.0	•	•	74.1	18.9	27.5	43.1	•	25.1	14.3	29.6
Return on Equity After Income Taxes 48	20.4	•	•	72.4	17.5	26.6	41.5	•	20.4	14.1	27.9
Profit Margin (Before Income Tax) 49	4.4	20.3	6.4	3.0	2.4	6.4	4.8	•	3.6	3.0	2.8
Profit Margin (After Income Tax) 50	3.3	20.8	6.4	2.9	2.2	6.2	4.6	•	2.9	3.0	2.6

Table I

Corporations with and without Net Income

HOMES CENTERS; PAINT AND WALLPAPER STORES

MONEY AMOUNTS AND SIZE OF ASSETS IN THOUSANDS OF DOLLARS

Item Description for Accounting Period 7/10 Through 6/11	Total	Zero Assets	Under 500	500 to 1,000	1,000 to 5,000	5,000 to 10,000	10,000 to 25,000	25,000 to 50,000	50,000 to 100,000	100,000 to 250,000	250,000 to 500,000	500,000 to 2,500,000	2,500,000 and over
Number of Enterprises **1**	2629	427	1225	357	541	•	31	6	•	0	0	0	3
Revenues ($ in Thousands)													
Net Sales **2**	126940688	6316	2004147	251922	2834959	•	873590	553931	•	0	0	0	118922124
Interest **3**	78320	0	359	769	4067	•	189	280	•	0	0	0	70653
Rents **4**	362454	0	0	179	1243	•	0	0	•	0	0	0	357746
Royalties **5**	238152	0	0	0	0	•	0	0	•	0	0	0	238152
Other Portfolio Income **6**	52118	0	0	0	24653	•	554	32	•	0	0	0	26280
Other Receipts **7**	2494616	0	103	15089	11216	•	9400	2270	•	0	0	0	2446504
Total Receipts **8**	130166348	6316	2004609	267959	2876138	•	883733	556513	•	0	0	0	122061459
Average Total Receipts **9**	49512	15	1636	751	5316	•	28508	92752	•	•	•	•	40687153
Operating Costs/Operating Income (%)													
Cost of Operations **10**	65.9	332.0	62.8	65.8	68.6	•	66.8	70.4	•	•	•	•	65.7
Salaries and Wages **11**	13.4	8.4	11.0	6.6	13.2	•	14.7	12.2	•	•	•	•	13.4
Taxes Paid **12**	2.4	1.0	6.3	2.0	2.5	•	2.2	1.8	•	•	•	•	2.4
Interest Paid **13**	0.9	•	0.2	5.4	0.4	•	0.4	0.6	•	•	•	•	0.9
Depreciation **14**	2.4	0.0	0.3	3.1	0.6	•	1.3	2.1	•	•	•	•	2.5
Amortization and Depletion **15**	0.0	•	0.0	•	0.0	•	0.0	0.1	•	•	•	•	0.0
Pensions and Other Deferred Comp. **16**	0.2	•	0.0	0.1	0.3	•	0.3	0.0	•	•	•	•	0.2
Employee Benefits **17**	1.4	•	0.3	1.5	0.9	•	1.2	1.1	•	•	•	•	1.4
Advertising **18**	1.5	•	0.8	1.1	0.6	•	1.1	0.7	•	•	•	•	1.6
Other Expenses **19**	7.5	66.8	13.1	13.7	9.3	•	11.0	8.6	•	•	•	•	7.3
Officers' Compensation **20**	0.2	•	4.9	7.2	3.0	•	1.5	2.5	•	•	•	•	0.0
Operating Margin **21**	4.1	•	0.3	•	0.7	•	•	•	•	•	•	•	4.4
Operating Margin Before Officers' Comp. **22**	4.3	•	5.2	0.8	3.7	•	1.0	2.2	•	•	•	•	4.5

Selected Average Balance Sheet ($ in Thousands)

Net Receivables 23	1224	0	81	42	438	3280	8916	876647
Inventories 24	7522	0	150	169	637	5561	12792	6222564
Net Property, Plant and Equipment 25	15107	0	30	428	230	2569	10589	13018676
Total Assets 26	42686	0	287	707	2332	14008	36449	36340967
Notes and Loans Payable 27	16807	0	44	576	492	4754	10618	14431934
All Other Liabilities 28	12331	0	112	97	314	2316	8889	10595587
Net Worth 29	13547	0	131	35	1526	6939	16942	11313446

Selected Financial Ratios (Times to 1)

Current Ratio 30	1.2	•	2.1	1.6	4.8	2.0	2.8	1.2
Quick Ratio 31	0.2	•	0.8	0.5	2.5	1.0	1.2	0.1
Net Sales to Working Capital 32	18.4	•	12.3	8.3	3.5	5.8	6.5	21.8
Coverage Ratio 33	8.5	•	3.0	1.0	6.2	2.8	1.3	8.8
Total Asset Turnover 34	1.1	•	5.7	1.0	2.2	2.0	2.5	1.1
Inventory Turnover 35	4.2	•	6.9	2.7	5.6	3.4	5.1	4.2
Receivables Turnover 36	44.8	•	20.3	8.2	13.2	8.1	10.2	53.2
Total Liabilities to Net Worth 37	2.2	•	1.2	19.3	0.5	1.0	1.2	2.2
Current Assets to Working Capital 38	5.3	•	1.9	2.7	1.3	2.0	1.6	6.3
Current Liabilities to Working Capital 39	4.3	•	0.9	1.7	0.3	1.0	0.6	5.3
Working Capital to Net Sales 40	0.1	•	0.1	0.1	0.3	0.2	0.2	0.0
Inventory to Working Capital 41	2.9	•	1.1	1.9	0.5	1.0	0.8	3.5
Total Receipts to Cash Flow 42	8.6	•	11.1	8.0	12.4	12.7	17.2	8.4
Cost of Goods to Cash Flow 43	5.7	•	7.0	5.3	8.5	8.5	12.1	5.5
Cash Flow to Total Debt 44	0.2	•	0.9	0.1	0.5	0.3	0.3	0.2

Selected Financial Factors (in Percentages)

Debt Ratio 45	68.3	•	54.3	95.1	34.6	50.5	53.5	68.9
Return on Total Assets 46	8.5	•	2.7	5.3	5.7	2.2	2.0	8.7
Return on Equity Before Income Taxes 47	23.6	•	3.9	•	7.3	2.8	1.0	24.7
Return on Equity After Income Taxes 48	16.2	•	3.9	•	7.2	2.1	0.8	17.0
Profit Margin (Before Income Tax) 49	6.6	•	0.3	•	2.1	0.7	0.2	7.1
Profit Margin (After Income Tax) 50	4.6	•	0.3	•	2.1	0.5	0.2	4.8

Table II
Corporations with Net Income

HOMES CENTERS; PAINT AND WALLPAPER STORES

MONEY AMOUNTS AND SIZE OF ASSETS IN THOUSANDS OF DOLLARS

Item Description for Accounting Period 7/10 Through 6/11	Total	Zero Assets	Under 500	500 to 1,000	1,000 to 5,000	5,000 to 10,000	10,000 to 25,000	25,000 to 50,000	50,000 to 100,000	100,000 to 250,000	250,000 to 500,000	500,000 to 2,500,000	2,500,000 and over
Number of Enterprises 1	1292	0	•	299	291	20	20	•	0	0	0	0	3
Revenues ($ in Thousands)													
Net Sales 2	122568297	0	•	184844	1381746	377131	454995	•	0	0	0	0	118922124
Interest 3	72925	0	•	91	395	959	139	•	0	0	0	0	70653
Rents 4	358945	0	•	179	1021	0	0	•	0	0	0	0	357746
Royalties 5	238152	0	•	0	0	0	0	•	0	0	0	0	238152
Other Portfolio Income 6	30560	0	•	0	3801	43	414	•	0	0	0	0	26280
Other Receipts 7	2477979	0	•	14919	6567	1331	5169	•	0	0	0	0	2446504
Total Receipts 8	125746858	0	•	200033	1393530	379464	460717	•	0	0	0	0	122061459
Average Total Receipts 9	97327	•	•	669	4789	18973	23036	•	•	•	•	•	40687153
Operating Costs/Operating Income (%)													
Cost of Operations 10	65.8	•	•	63.9	69.1	64.1	66.4	•	•	•	•	•	65.7
Salaries and Wages 11	13.4	•	•	5.6	11.1	16.8	12.7	•	•	•	•	•	13.4
Taxes Paid 12	2.4	•	•	1.9	2.3	2.7	2.0	•	•	•	•	•	2.4
Interest Paid 13	0.9	•	•	6.2	0.4	0.6	0.3	•	•	•	•	•	0.9
Depreciation 14	2.4	•	•	3.4	0.3	0.8	1.4	•	•	•	•	•	2.5
Amortization and Depletion 15	0.0	•	•	•	0.0	•	0.1	•	•	•	•	•	0.0
Pensions and Other Deferred Comp. 16	0.2	•	•	•	0.1	0.0	0.6	•	•	•	•	•	0.2
Employee Benefits 17	1.4	•	•	0.7	1.0	1.1	1.1	•	•	•	•	•	1.4
Advertising 18	1.6	•	•	0.7	0.5	1.4	1.4	•	•	•	•	•	1.6
Other Expenses 19	7.4	•	•	16.4	6.5	9.2	8.5	•	•	•	•	•	7.3
Officers' Compensation 20	0.2	•	•	7.9	3.6	2.9	1.0	•	•	•	•	•	0.0
Operating Margin 21	4.4	•	•	5.1	4.5	0.6	4.5	•	•	•	•	•	4.4
Operating Margin Before Officers' Comp. 22	4.6	•	•	1.2	8.8	3.4	5.5	•	•	•	•	•	4.5

Selected Average Balance Sheet ($ in Thousands)

Net Receivables 23	2281	27	487	859	2168	876647
Inventories 24	14932	107	642	3267	5464	6222564
Net Property, Plant and Equipment 25	30518	487	171	992	2595	13018676
Total Assets 26	85627	700	1964	6628	13600	36340967
Notes and Loans Payable 27	33859	558	384	1234	2021	14431934
All Other Liabilities 28	24800	105	220	2160	1409	10595587
Net Worth 29	26968	37	1360	3234	10169	11313446

Selected Financial Ratios (Times to 1)

Current Ratio 30	1.2	1.4	7.4	1.5	3.5	1.2
Quick Ratio 31	0.1	0.4	3.8	0.5	1.7	0.1
Net Sales to Working Capital 32	19.7	12.5	3.5	11.4	3.5	21.8
Coverage Ratio 33	8.7	1.2	17.7	3.2	20.5	8.8
Total Asset Turnover 34	1.1	0.9	2.4	2.8	1.7	1.1
Inventory Turnover 35	4.2	3.7	5.1	3.7	2.8	4.2
Receivables Turnover 36	47.0	10.2	8.9	17.9	9.7	53.2
Total Liabilities to Net Worth 37	2.2	17.7	0.4	1.0	0.3	2.2
Current Assets to Working Capital 38	5.7	3.4	1.2	3.0	1.4	6.3
Current Liabilities to Working Capital 39	4.7	2.4	0.2	2.0	0.4	5.3
Working Capital to Net Sales 40	0.1	0.1	0.3	0.1	0.3	0.0
Inventory to Working Capital 41	3.1	2.3	0.5	1.9	0.7	3.5
Total Receipts to Cash Flow 42	8.4	6.0	9.3	16.6	9.2	8.4
Cost of Goods to Cash Flow 43	5.5	3.8	6.4	10.6	6.1	5.5
Cash Flow to Total Debt 44	0.2	0.2	0.8	0.3	0.7	0.2

Selected Financial Factors (in Percentages)

Debt Ratio 45	68.5	94.7	30.8	51.2	25.2	68.9
Return on Total Assets 46	8.7	6.8	15.3	5.0	10.1	8.7
Return on Equity Before Income Taxes 47	24.5	25.4	20.8	7.0	12.8	24.7
Return on Equity After Income Taxes 48	17.0	25.4	20.6	6.1	12.0	17.0
Profit Margin (Before Income Tax) 49	7.0	1.5	6.0	1.2	5.7	7.1
Profit Margin (After Income Tax) 50	4.8	1.5	5.9	1.1	5.4	4.8

Table I

Corporations with and without Net Income

HARDWARE STORES

MONEY AMOUNTS AND SIZE OF ASSETS IN THOUSANDS OF DOLLARS

Item Description for Accounting Period 7/10 Through 6/11	Total	Zero Assets	Under 500	500 to 1,000	1,000 to 5,000	5,000 to 10,000	10,000 to 25,000	25,000 to 50,000	50,000 to 100,000	100,000 to 250,000	250,000 to 500,000	500,000 to 2,500,000	2,500,000 and over
Number of Enterprises **1**	7838	87	2618	3029	1996	59	33	13	0	3	0	0	0
Revenues ($ in Thousands)													
Net Sales **2**	17731812	102889	1550529	4800162	6641717	481535	1082857	975789	0	2096335	0	0	0
Interest **3**	9688	0	550	3068	4684	511	188	687	0	1	0	0	0
Rents **4**	15008	0	22	6796	6053	0	29	1175	0	933	0	0	0
Royalties **5**	17	0	17	0	0	0	0	0	0	0	0	0	0
Other Portfolio Income **6**	26757	159	10119	4109	10577	0	643	1149	0	0	0	0	0
Other Receipts **7**	158058	1734	18812	46367	62817	3813	11344	3063	0	10106	0	0	0
Total Receipts **8**	17941340	104782	1580049	4860502	6725848	485859	1095061	981863	0	2107375	0	0	0
Average Total Receipts **9**	2289	1204	604	1605	3370	8235	33184	75528	•	702458	•	•	•
Operating Costs/Operating Income (%)													
Cost of Operations **10**	63.4	78.5	61.4	63.3	63.4	61.9	69.6	63.1	•	61.5	•	•	•
Salaries and Wages **11**	12.7	4.2	12.1	11.7	13.2	12.6	13.3	13.7	•	13.3	•	•	•
Taxes Paid **12**	2.5	2.6	2.6	2.4	2.8	2.3	1.9	2.8	•	2.0	•	•	•
Interest Paid **13**	0.9	0.3	0.7	0.9	0.8	0.2	0.5	1.2	•	1.8	•	•	•
Depreciation **14**	1.2	0.3	0.9	0.8	1.4	1.3	1.0	1.6	•	1.8	•	•	•
Amortization and Depletion **15**	0.1	•	0.0	0.0	0.0	0.1	0.1	0.4	•	0.1	•	•	•
Pensions and Other Deferred Comp. **16**	0.1	•	0.1	0.2	0.2	0.4	0.1	0.2	•	0.0	•	•	•
Employee Benefits **17**	1.2	0.3	1.8	0.8	1.1	1.7	1.3	1.4	•	1.3	•	•	•
Advertising **18**	1.8	1.0	1.2	1.8	1.4	1.1	1.0	1.3	•	4.1	•	•	•
Other Expenses **19**	11.2	13.6	14.0	12.7	11.6	8.1	9.0	10.7	•	6.5	•	•	•
Officers' Compensation **20**	3.7	1.2	9.3	4.5	3.4	5.8	1.3	1.1	•	0.5	•	•	•
Operating Margin **21**	1.2	•	•	0.7	0.6	4.5	1.1	2.6	•	7.1	•	•	•
Operating Margin Before Officers' Comp. **22**	4.9	5.2	5.2	5.2	4.0	10.3	2.4	3.7	•	7.6	•	•	•

Selected Average Balance Sheet ($ in Thousands)

	1	2	3	4	5	6	7	8	9	10
Net Receivables 23	92	0	18	66	163	500	2130	2450	•	7045
Inventories 24	518	0	156	378	795	1174	5849	13575	•	211527
Net Property, Plant and Equipment 25	226	0	39	66	320	3214	4553	10776	•	117393
Total Assets 26	1151	0	255	723	1766	6425	15333	37421	•	421708
Notes and Loans Payable 27	502	0	164	341	539	380	4760	16324	•	336335
All Other Liabilities 28	209	0	83	86	277	329	2444	7923	•	133086
Net Worth 29	440	0	8	295	950	5716	8129	13174	•	-47714

Selected Financial Ratios (Times to 1)

	1	2	3	4	5	6	7	8	9	10
Current Ratio 30	2.8	•	1.6	4.0	3.3	7.7	1.9	1.9	•	1.9
Quick Ratio 31	0.7	•	0.2	0.8	1.0	4.1	0.6	0.4	•	0.2
Net Sales to Working Capital 32	4.5	0.7	9.9	3.8	3.8	3.4	7.5	7.2	•	6.0
Coverage Ratio 33	3.5	•	•	3.1	3.3	36.1	5.5	3.8	•	5.2
Total Asset Turnover 34	2.0	•	2.3	2.2	1.9	1.3	2.1	2.0	•	1.7
Inventory Turnover 35	2.8	•	2.3	2.7	2.7	4.3	3.9	3.5	•	2.0
Receivables Turnover 36	24.9	•	27.0	27.2	20.2	•	15.3	37.7	•	•
Total Liabilities to Net Worth 37	1.6	•	30.0	1.4	0.9	0.1	0.9	1.8	•	1.8
Current Assets to Working Capital 38	1.5	•	2.6	1.3	1.4	1.2	2.1	2.1	•	2.1
Current Liabilities to Working Capital 39	0.5	•	1.6	0.3	0.4	0.2	1.1	1.1	•	1.1
Working Capital to Net Sales 40	0.2	•	0.1	0.3	0.3	0.3	0.1	0.1	•	0.2
Inventory to Working Capital 41	1.1	•	2.1	1.0	0.9	0.5	1.4	1.6	•	1.8
Total Receipts to Cash Flow 42	11.4	9.4	17.2	10.7	11.1	8.6	12.4	10.7	•	12.3
Cost of Goods to Cash Flow 43	7.2	7.4	10.6	6.8	7.1	5.3	8.6	6.8	•	7.6
Cash Flow to Total Debt 44	0.3	•	0.1	0.3	0.4	1.3	0.4	0.3	•	0.1

Selected Financial Factors (in Percentages)

	1	2	3	4	5	6	7	8	9	10
Debt Ratio 45	61.8	•	96.8	59.1	46.2	11.0	47.0	64.8	•	111.3
Return on Total Assets 46	6.5	•	•	6.3	5.0	7.1	5.7	8.7	•	15.6
Return on Equity Before Income Taxes 47	12.2	•	•	10.4	6.5	7.7	8.8	18.1	•	•
Return on Equity After Income Taxes 48	11.0	•	•	10.1	5.9	6.2	8.8	12.4	•	•
Profit Margin (Before Income Tax) 49	2.4	•	•	1.9	1.8	5.4	2.2	3.2	•	7.6
Profit Margin (After Income Tax) 50	2.1	•	•	1.7	1.7	4.3	2.2	2.2	•	7.2

Table II
Corporations with Net Income

HARDWARE STORES

MONEY AMOUNTS AND SIZE OF ASSETS IN THOUSANDS OF DOLLARS

Item Description for Accounting Period 7/10 Through 6/11	Total	Zero Assets	Under 500	500 to 1,000	1,000 to 5,000	5,000 to 10,000	10,000 to 25,000	25,000 to 50,000	50,000 to 100,000	100,000 to 250,000	250,000 to 500,000	500,000 to 2,500,000	2,500,000 and over
Number of Enterprises **1**	4082	57	785	1705	1444	49	30	•	0	•	0	0	0
Revenues ($ in Thousands)													
Net Sales **2**	13218837	68390	627219	3256623	5019954	347879	1034965	•	0	•	0	0	0
Interest **3**	5414	0	509	660	3369	267	10	•	0	•	0	0	0
Rents **4**	10384	0	0	6765	1821	0	0	•	0	•	0	0	0
Royalties **5**	0	0	0	0	0	0	0	•	0	•	0	0	0
Other Portfolio Income **6**	9900	159	184	624	8203	0	276	•	0	•	0	0	0
Other Receipts **7**	120636	17	18503	28210	47807	3048	10375	•	0	•	0	0	0
Total Receipts **8**	13365171	68566	646415	3292882	5081154	351194	1045626	•	0	•	0	0	0
Average Total Receipts **9**	3274	1203	823	1931	3519	7167	34854	•	•	•	•	•	•
Operating Costs/Operating Income (%)													
Cost of Operations **10**	63.2	76.5	60.1	63.8	62.6	63.0	69.3	•	•	•	•	•	•
Salaries and Wages **11**	12.3	2.2	11.5	11.2	12.5	10.1	13.4	•	•	•	•	•	•
Taxes Paid **12**	2.4	2.3	2.5	2.0	2.8	2.3	1.9	•	•	•	•	•	•
Interest Paid **13**	0.8	0.3	0.4	0.8	0.7	0.1	0.4	•	•	•	•	•	•
Depreciation **14**	1.1	0.1	1.1	0.5	1.4	1.2	0.8	•	•	•	•	•	•
Amortization and Depletion **15**	0.1	•	0.0	0.0	0.1	0.2	0.1	•	•	•	•	•	•
Pensions and Other Deferred Comp. **16**	0.2	•	0.1	0.2	0.2	0.5	0.1	•	•	•	•	•	•
Employee Benefits **17**	1.1	0.1	0.5	0.9	1.1	1.1	1.3	•	•	•	•	•	•
Advertising **18**	1.9	1.3	1.1	1.8	1.4	0.3	1.0	•	•	•	•	•	•
Other Expenses **19**	10.5	10.9	12.8	12.0	11.5	7.0	8.9	•	•	•	•	•	•
Officers' Compensation **20**	3.1	1.8	9.2	3.3	3.7	7.1	1.4	•	•	•	•	•	•
Operating Margin **21**	3.4	4.6	0.6	3.6	2.1	7.0	1.5	•	•	•	•	•	•
Operating Margin Before Officers' Comp. **22**	6.5	6.4	9.8	6.8	5.8	14.1	2.9	•	•	•	•	•	•

Selected Average Balance Sheet ($ in Thousands)

Net Receivables 23	111	0	22	70	131	464	2244
Inventories 24	699	0	208	446	806	1155	3886
Net Property, Plant and Equipment 25	309	0	10	49	316	3349	3943
Total Assets 26	1605	0	332	766	1825	6525	15077
Notes and Loans Payable 27	617	0	86	335	438	337	3632
All Other Liabilities 28	256	0	20	85	227	144	2600
Net Worth 29	732	0	226	346	1159	6044	8846

Selected Financial Ratios (Times to 1)

Current Ratio 30	3.5	•	8.0	6.2	4.5	18.7	1.8
Quick Ratio 31	0.9	•	1.3	1.2	1.4	9.9	0.6
Net Sales to Working Capital 32	4.2	•	4.2	3.7	3.5	2.8	8.0
Coverage Ratio 33	6.3	16.4	9.6	7.0	5.7	80.2	7.8
Total Asset Turnover 34	2.0	•	2.4	2.5	1.9	1.1	2.3
Inventory Turnover 35	2.9	•	2.3	2.7	2.7	3.9	6.2
Receivables Turnover 36	32.1	•	30.7	29.4	27.2	•	27.7
Total Liabilities to Net Worth 37	1.2	•	0.5	1.2	0.6	0.1	0.7
Current Assets to Working Capital 38	1.4	•	1.1	1.2	1.3	1.1	2.2
Current Liabilities to Working Capital 39	0.4	•	0.1	0.2	0.3	0.1	1.2
Working Capital to Net Sales 40	0.2	•	0.2	0.3	0.3	0.4	0.1
Inventory to Working Capital 41	1.0	•	0.9	0.9	0.8	0.5	1.4
Total Receipts to Cash Flow 42	9.7	7.9	10.4	8.3	9.6	7.5	12.1
Cost of Goods to Cash Flow 43	6.1	6.1	6.3	5.3	6.0	4.7	8.4
Cash Flow to Total Debt 44	0.4	•	0.7	0.5	0.5	2.0	0.5

Selected Financial Factors (in Percentages)

Debt Ratio 45	54.4	•	31.8	54.8	36.5	7.4	41.3
Return on Total Assets 46	10.7	•	9.8	13.6	7.6	8.8	6.6
Return on Equity Before Income Taxes 47	19.8	•	12.9	25.9	9.9	9.4	9.8
Return on Equity After Income Taxes 48	18.4	•	11.5	25.4	9.2	7.6	9.8
Profit Margin (Before Income Tax) 49	4.5	4.8	3.7	4.7	3.3	8.0	2.5
Profit Margin (After Income Tax) 50	4.2	4.0	3.3	4.6	3.1	6.4	2.5

Table I

Corporations with and without Net Income

OTHER BUILDING MATERIAL DEALERS

MONEY AMOUNTS AND SIZE OF ASSETS IN THOUSANDS OF DOLLARS

Item Description for Accounting Period 7/10 Through 6/11	Total	Zero Assets	Under 500	500 to 1,000	1,000 to 5,000	5,000 to 10,000	10,000 to 25,000	25,000 to 50,000	50,000 to 100,000	100,000 to 250,000	250,000 to 500,000	500,000 to 2,500,000	2,500,000 and over
Number of Enterprises 1	18321	1018	11400	2360	2849	484	140	39	16	5	6	3	0
Revenues ($ in Thousands)													
Net Sales 2	46262484	831157	5717441	4716415	13633426	6907842	3765786	2134915	1883989	1600012	2946139	2125362	0
Interest 3	382400	3298	607	5527	12971	2431	4562	3130	893	604	10654	337722	0
Rents 4	28460	7187	3672	282	4805	31	3060	4141	110	66	5106	0	0
Royalties 5	36938	0	3207	0	0	0	160	0	0	0	1374	32197	0
Other Portfolio Income 6	102611	4563	14033	1302	16734	11939	3240	4829	1995	102	36900	6974	0
Other Receipts 7	322540	4464	7976	41880	60687	51890	33298	35154	11089	2447	37475	36180	0
Total Receipts 8	47135433	850669	5746936	4765406	13728623	6974133	3810106	2182169	1898076	1603231	3037648	2538435	0
Average Total Receipts 9	2573	836	504	2019	4819	14409	27215	55953	118630	320646	506275	846145	•
Operating Costs/Operating Income (%)													
Cost of Operations 10	72.4	89.4	62.4	72.3	71.5	76.5	74.3	73.4	74.1	71.7	79.6	70.5	•
Salaries and Wages 11	10.0	2.5	9.2	7.2	9.4	11.1	10.6	12.8	12.1	9.4	10.7	14.2	•
Taxes Paid 12	2.0	0.5	3.0	2.1	1.9	1.8	1.9	2.1	1.8	1.6	1.5	1.6	•
Interest Paid 13	1.7	1.2	1.1	0.4	0.6	0.8	0.6	0.9	1.0	0.3	2.2	21.0	•
Depreciation 14	1.1	0.9	1.3	0.6	0.9	0.5	1.3	1.3	1.6	2.3	2.0	2.2	•
Amortization and Depletion 15	0.7	0.8	0.1	0.0	0.0	0.1	0.1	0.1	0.4	0.0	0.8	13.4	•
Pensions and Other Deferred Comp. 16	0.2	0.1	0.1	0.3	0.2	0.0	0.3	0.1	0.5	0.1	0.2	0.0	•
Employee Benefits 17	1.0	0.9	0.9	0.7	1.0	0.7	1.1	1.5	1.2	0.5	1.5	1.5	•
Advertising 18	0.8	0.3	1.6	1.4	0.6	0.4	0.7	0.6	0.5	3.3	0.2	0.4	•
Other Expenses 19	11.2	7.6	19.5	8.5	11.2	8.2	8.8	9.3	8.2	7.9	8.9	21.5	•
Officers' Compensation 20	2.4	0.5	4.1	4.9	3.0	1.5	1.3	1.0	1.1	0.8	0.5	1.1	•
Operating Margin 21	•	•	•	1.4	•	•	•	•	•	2.0	•	•	•
Operating Margin Before Officers' Comp. 22	•	•	0.8	6.3	2.7	•	0.2	•	•	2.8	•	•	•

Selected Average Balance Sheet ($ in Thousands)

Net Receivables 23	234	0	24	141	390	1596	3253	9020	14939	11823	53444	121481	•
Inventories 24	395	0	53	320	864	2482	5000	8166	13848	52640	68390	148618	•
Net Property, Plant and Equipment 25	267	0	31	60	315	1199	3228	7027	23004	47511	105360	319705	•
Total Assets 26	1613	0	147	736	2090	7423	14318	35589	74044	163522	384168	2962323	•
Notes and Loans Payable 27	783	0	100	203	670	2279	3596	8292	22054	39928	96591	2584418	•
All Other Liabilities 28	328	0	77	141	449	1124	3018	5617	12842	27936	57162	546071	•
Net Worth 29	502	0	-30	391	970	4020	7704	21680	39148	95659	230415	-168165	•

Selected Financial Ratios (Times to 1)

Current Ratio 30	2.1	•	1.1	3.3	2.8	2.3	2.3	2.4	2.3	2.3	2.3	1.2	•
Quick Ratio 31	1.0	•	0.4	1.7	1.3	1.0	1.1	1.3	1.2	0.8	1.2	0.5	•
Net Sales to Working Capital 32	5.5	•	46.9	4.5	4.7	4.6	4.7	4.3	5.4	6.3	4.8	8.4	•
Coverage Ratio 33	•	•	•	7.1	1.7	0.2	1.1	•	•	9.3	•	•	•
Total Asset Turnover 34	1.6	•	3.4	2.7	2.3	1.9	1.9	1.5	1.6	2.0	1.3	0.2	•
Inventory Turnover 35	4.6	•	5.9	4.5	4.0	4.4	4.0	4.9	6.4	4.4	5.7	3.4	•
Receivables Turnover 36	10.6	•	19.8	13.4	11.7	•	7.4	7.5	9.4	•	•	•	•
Total Liabilities to Net Worth 37	2.2	•	•	0.9	1.2	0.8	0.9	0.6	0.9	0.7	0.7	•	•
Current Assets to Working Capital 38	1.9	•	9.5	1.4	1.6	1.7	1.7	1.7	1.8	1.8	1.8	6.2	•
Current Liabilities to Working Capital 39	0.9	•	8.5	0.4	0.6	0.7	0.7	0.7	0.8	0.8	0.8	5.2	•
Working Capital to Net Sales 40	0.2	•	0.0	0.2	0.2	0.2	0.2	0.2	0.2	0.2	0.2	0.1	•
Inventory to Working Capital 41	0.9	•	4.9	0.7	0.8	0.8	0.8	0.6	0.8	1.0	0.7	1.8	•
Total Receipts to Cash Flow 42	16.7	24.5	9.9	11.9	12.5	20.0	17.4	19.0	27.1	12.5	156.1	•	•
Cost of Goods to Cash Flow 43	12.1	21.9	6.2	8.6	8.9	15.3	12.9	13.9	20.1	9.0	124.2	•	•
Cash Flow to Total Debt 44	0.1	•	0.3	0.5	0.3	0.2	0.2	0.2	0.1	0.4	0.0	•	•

Selected Financial Factors (in Percentages)

Debt Ratio 45	68.9	•	120.1	46.8	53.6	45.8	46.2	39.1	47.1	41.5	40.0	105.7	•
Return on Total Assets 46	•	•	•	7.8	2.2	0.2	1.3	•	•	4.9	•	•	•
Return on Equity Before Income Taxes 47	•	•	46.1	12.5	1.9	•	0.2	•	•	7.5	•	117.7	•
Return on Equity After Income Taxes 48	•	•	46.7	12.4	1.4	•	•	•	•	5.1	•	117.7	•
Profit Margin (Before Income Tax) 49	•	•	•	2.5	0.4	•	0.1	•	•	2.2	•	•	•
Profit Margin (After Income Tax) 50	•	•	•	2.4	0.3	•	•	•	•	1.5	•	•	•

Table II
Corporations with Net Income

OTHER BUILDING MATERIAL DEALERS

MONEY AMOUNTS AND SIZE OF ASSETS IN THOUSANDS OF DOLLARS

Item Description for Accounting Period 7/10 Through 6/11		Total	Zero Assets	Under 500	500 to 1,000	1,000 to 5,000	5,000 to 10,000	10,000 to 25,000	25,000 to 50,000	50,000 to 100,000	100,000 to 250,000	250,000 to 500,000	500,000 to 2,500,000	2,500,000 and over
Number of Enterprises	1	10025	9	6687	1414	1654	150	80	18	7	•	•	0	0
Revenues ($ in Thousands)														
Net Sales	2	26274179	609188	3274652	3670638	9001529	2818944	2520080	1101405	865174	•	•	0	0
Interest	3	24187	2727	13	3352	8852	1307	1531	1669	82	•	•	0	0
Rents	4	19304	7187	3672	212	4711	0	783	606	0	•	•	0	0
Royalties	5	3367	0	3207	0	0	0	160	0	0	•	•	0	0
Other Portfolio Income	6	60139	4563	5996	326	3303	8880	1440	1537	595	•	•	0	0
Other Receipts	7	151803	2359	7094	19156	28646	20170	18448	15090	3861	•	•	0	0
Total Receipts	8	26532979	626024	3294634	3693684	9047041	2849301	2542442	1120307	869712	•	•	0	0
Average Total Receipts	9	2647	69558	493	2612	5470	18995	31781	62239	124245	•	•	•	•
Operating Costs/Operating Income (%)														
Cost of Operations	10	71.9	96.3	58.0	70.7	71.4	82.0	74.4	71.8	72.6	•	•	•	•
Salaries and Wages	11	8.0	0.6	7.4	6.1	8.3	7.3	8.9	13.2	11.0	•	•	•	•
Taxes Paid	12	1.8	0.1	3.5	2.1	1.6	1.1	1.8	1.9	1.5	•	•	•	•
Interest Paid	13	0.5	1.5	1.2	0.2	0.4	0.7	0.5	0.3	0.6	•	•	•	•
Depreciation	14	1.0	1.0	1.7	0.6	0.8	0.3	1.0	1.0	1.4	•	•	•	•
Amortization and Depletion	15	0.1	1.0	0.0	0.0	0.0	0.2	0.1	0.1	0.0	•	•	•	•
Pensions and Other Deferred Comp.	16	0.2	0.0	0.1	0.3	0.2	0.1	0.3	0.1	0.2	•	•	•	•
Employee Benefits	17	0.8	0.1	1.0	0.8	0.7	0.6	1.2	1.4	1.1	•	•	•	•
Advertising	18	1.0	0.0	1.8	1.7	0.5	0.1	0.9	0.5	0.6	•	•	•	•
Other Expenses	19	9.1	0.8	17.0	7.6	9.4	5.7	8.4	7.6	7.1	•	•	•	•
Officers' Compensation	20	2.5	0.1	4.7	5.2	2.2	1.1	1.3	1.1	0.8	•	•	•	•
Operating Margin	21	2.9	•	3.6	4.7	4.4	0.9	1.3	1.0	3.0	•	•	•	•
Operating Margin Before Officers' Comp.	22	5.4	•	8.2	9.9	6.6	2.0	2.6	2.1	3.9	•	•	•	•

Selected Average Balance Sheet ($ in Thousands)

Net Receivables 23	214	0	22	167	419	2355	3704	6231	18068
Inventories 24	366	0	53	303	871	2424	5386	9039	16825
Net Property, Plant and Equipment 25	192	0	43	76	295	532	2661	8100	19097
Total Assets 26	1134	0	154	742	2192	8644	15042	38266	76179
Notes and Loans Payable 27	286	0	79	150	560	2219	3462	2906	17127
All Other Liabilities 28	217	0	47	116	412	1380	3409	4208	11139
Net Worth 29	631	0	28	475	1220	5045	8170	31153	47913

Selected Financial Ratios (Times to 1)

Current Ratio 30	2.8	•	1.6	4.6	3.4	3.9	2.3	4.0	2.5
Quick Ratio 31	1.3	•	0.5	2.5	1.6	1.7	1.2	1.8	1.3
Net Sales to Working Capital 32	5.1	•	13.3	5.4	4.4	4.1	4.9	3.4	4.2
Coverage Ratio 33	8.2	1.8	4.4	24.6	13.8	4.0	5.7	9.3	7.3
Total Asset Turnover 34	2.3	•	3.2	3.5	2.5	2.2	2.1	1.6	1.6
Inventory Turnover 35	5.2	•	5.3	6.1	4.5	6.4	4.4	4.9	5.3
Receivables Turnover 36	13.6	•	22.4	14.1	14.4	9.7	9.3	•	8.7
Total Liabilities to Net Worth 37	0.8	•	4.5	0.6	0.8	0.7	0.8	0.2	0.6
Current Assets to Working Capital 38	1.5	•	2.8	1.3	1.4	1.3	1.7	1.3	1.7
Current Liabilities to Working Capital 39	0.5	•	1.8	0.3	0.4	0.3	0.7	0.3	0.7
Working Capital to Net Sales 40	0.2	•	0.1	0.2	0.2	0.2	0.2	0.3	0.2
Inventory to Working Capital 41	0.8	•	1.3	0.6	0.7	0.7	0.8	0.5	0.7
Total Receipts to Cash Flow 42	9.8	48.7	6.4	9.4	8.7	16.2	13.3	12.1	13.7
Cost of Goods to Cash Flow 43	7.0	46.9	3.7	6.7	6.2	13.3	9.9	8.7	10.0
Cash Flow to Total Debt 44	0.5	•	0.6	1.0	0.6	0.3	0.3	0.7	0.3

Selected Financial Factors (in Percentages)

Debt Ratio 45	44.4	•	81.9	35.9	44.3	41.6	45.7	18.6	37.1
Return on Total Assets 46	10.3	•	17.2	19.5	13.0	5.7	5.6	4.8	6.6
Return on Equity Before Income Taxes 47	16.3	•	73.5	29.2	21.7	7.4	8.5	5.2	9.1
Return on Equity After Income Taxes 48	15.6	•	72.5	29.0	21.0	7.3	7.9	4.8	8.6
Profit Margin (Before Income Tax) 49	3.9	1.2	4.2	5.4	4.9	2.0	2.2	2.7	3.5
Profit Margin (After Income Tax) 50	3.8	1.2	4.1	5.3	4.7	1.9	2.0	2.4	3.3

Table I

Corporations with and without Net Income

LAWN AND GARDEN EQUIPMENT AND SUPPLIES STORES

MONEY AMOUNTS AND SIZE OF ASSETS IN THOUSANDS OF DOLLARS

Item Description for Accounting Period 7/10 Through 6/11		Total	Zero Assets	Under 500	500 to 1,000	1,000 to 5,000	5,000 to 10,000	10,000 to 25,000	25,000 to 50,000	50,000 to 100,000	100,000 to 250,000	250,000 to 500,000	500,000 to 2,500,000	2,500,000 and over
Number of Enterprises	1	8213	753	4694	1559	1089	•	32	14	•	0	0	0	0
Revenues ($ in Thousands)														
Net Sales	2	14665245	67742	2700511	2969090	5119252	•	1008432	1020419	•	0	0	0	0
Interest	3	10475	0	192	313	9243	•	0	414	•	0	0	0	0
Rents	4	2783	0	0	0	2704	•	0	75	•	0	0	0	0
Royalties	5	0	0	0	0	0	•	0	0	•	0	0	0	0
Other Portfolio Income	6	17196	0	2856	818	2032	•	2103	9137	•	0	0	0	0
Other Receipts	7	254530	0	186675	4015	28249	•	17770	4609	•	0	0	0	0
Total Receipts	8	14950229	67742	2890234	2974236	5161480	•	1028305	1034654	•	0	0	0	0
Average Total Receipts	9	1820	90	616	1908	4740	•	32135	73904	•	0	0	0	0
Operating Costs/Operating Income (%)														
Cost of Operations	10	69.1	51.5	71.5	66.5	73.2	•	64.8	70.7	•	•	•	•	•
Salaries and Wages	11	9.9	15.8	9.5	12.3	8.2	•	10.9	10.4	•	•	•	•	•
Taxes Paid	12	2.2	3.8	2.0	3.2	1.8	•	1.9	2.0	•	•	•	•	•
Interest Paid	13	0.8	0.8	1.0	0.5	1.0	•	0.7	0.6	•	•	•	•	•
Depreciation	14	1.4	0.3	1.5	0.8	1.8	•	1.0	2.5	•	•	•	•	•
Amortization and Depletion	15	0.0	•	0.0	0.0	0.0	•	0.1	0.1	•	•	•	•	•
Pensions and Other Deferred Comp.	16	0.1	•	0.0	0.1	0.1	•	0.5	0.2	•	•	•	•	•
Employee Benefits	17	0.8	•	0.4	0.7	0.9	•	1.0	0.3	•	•	•	•	•
Advertising	18	2.2	0.5	1.2	0.9	1.1	•	1.7	0.6	•	•	•	•	•
Other Expenses	19	11.8	31.5	15.6	10.0	9.6	•	14.8	8.6	•	•	•	•	•
Officers' Compensation	20	2.8	12.3	4.6	3.8	2.5	•	0.7	1.8	•	•	•	•	•
Operating Margin	21	•	•	•	1.0	1.8	•	1.8	2.2	•	•	•	•	•
Operating Margin Before Officers' Comp.	22	1.6	•	•	4.8	2.1	•	2.5	4.0	•	•	•	•	•

Selected Average Balance Sheet ($ in Thousands)

Net Receivables 23	72	0	15	70	232		1006	4308
Inventories 24	370	0	91	267	1103		7640	18226
Net Property, Plant and Equipment 25	184	0	47	171	642		1744	8207
Total Assets 26	768	0	160	736	2218		15357	36571
Notes and Loans Payable 27	345	0	102	198	1091		5906	15016
All Other Liabilities 28	204	0	84	128	377		4245	8149
Net Worth 29	219	0	-25	410	751		5207	13406

Selected Financial Ratios (Times to 1)

Current Ratio 30	1.6		1.2	3.6	1.6		1.5	1.6
Quick Ratio 31	0.5		0.3	1.6	0.4		0.2	0.4
Net Sales to Working Capital 32	9.2		34.0	4.7	8.4		9.7	8.6
Coverage Ratio 33	1.8		0.8	3.3	1.4		6.1	6.6
Total Asset Turnover 34	2.3		3.6	2.6	2.1		2.1	2.0
Inventory Turnover 35	3.3		4.5	4.7	3.1		2.7	2.8
Receivables Turnover 36	21.6		35.3	34.6	19.3		27.2	8.1
Total Liabilities to Net Worth 37	2.5			0.8	2.0		1.9	1.7
Current Assets to Working Capital 38	2.6		6.2	1.4	2.6		3.1	2.8
Current Liabilities to Working Capital 39	1.6		5.2	0.4	1.6		2.1	1.8
Working Capital to Net Sales 40	0.1		0.0	0.2	0.1		0.1	0.1
Inventory to Working Capital 41	1.8		4.5	0.7	1.8		2.7	1.8
Total Receipts to Cash Flow 42	10.6	10.2	9.0	12.3	13.7		6.4	10.5
Cost of Goods to Cash Flow 43	7.3	5.2	6.4	8.2	10.0		4.1	7.4
Cash Flow to Total Debt 44	0.3		0.3	0.5	0.2		0.5	0.3

Selected Financial Factors (in Percentages)

Debt Ratio 45	71.4		115.8	44.2	66.1		66.1	63.3
Return on Total Assets 46	3.5		2.8	4.4	3.1		9.2	8.4
Return on Equity Before Income Taxes 47	5.6		5.0	5.5	2.7		22.8	19.4
Return on Equity After Income Taxes 48	5.0		5.5	5.3	1.9		22.8	19.1
Profit Margin (Before Income Tax) 49	0.7		1.2	0.4			3.8	3.6
Profit Margin (After Income Tax) 50	0.6		1.1	0.3			3.8	3.5

Table II
Corporations with Net Income

LAWN AND GARDEN EQUIPMENT AND SUPPLIES STORES

MONEY AMOUNTS AND SIZE OF ASSETS IN THOUSANDS OF DOLLARS

Item Description for Accounting Period 7/10 Through 6/11	Total	Zero Assets	Under 500	500 to 1,000	1,000 to 5,000	5,000 to 10,000	10,000 to 25,000	25,000 to 50,000	50,000 to 100,000	100,000 to 250,000	250,000 to 500,000	500,000 to 2,500,000	2,500,000 and over
Number of Enterprises **1**	3118	251	•	615	643	9	29	•	0	0	0	0	0
Revenues ($ in Thousands)													
Net Sales **2**	8064883	5063	•	1643507	3009526	122657	934329	•	0	0	0	0	0
Interest **3**	8390	0	•	125	7746	71	0	•	0	0	0	0	0
Rents **4**	859	0	•	0	779	0	0	•	0	0	0	0	0
Royalties **5**	0	0		0	0	0	0	•	0	0	0	0	0
Other Portfolio Income **6**	16167	0	•	800	1273	42	2103	•	0	0	0	0	0
Other Receipts **7**	51841	0	•	240	22628	452	17761	•	0	0	0	0	0
Total Receipts **8**	8142140	5063	•	1644672	3041952	123222	954193	•	0	0	0	0	0
Average Total Receipts **9**	2611	20	•	2674	4731	13691	32903	•	•	•	•	•	•
Operating Costs/Operating Income (%)													
Cost of Operations **10**	71.4	27.9	•	64.5	75.8	85.7	67.9	•	•	•	•	•	•
Salaries and Wages **11**	8.4	•	•	12.8	6.7	4.8	9.1	•	•	•	•	•	•
Taxes Paid **12**	2.1	0.4	•	3.1	1.8	1.7	1.7	•	•	•	•	•	•
Interest Paid **13**	0.7	•	•	0.2	0.9	0.5	0.6	•	•	•	•	•	•
Depreciation **14**	1.4	•	•	0.8	1.4	0.9	1.0	•	•	•	•	•	•
Amortization and Depletion **15**	0.0	•	•	•	0.0	0.1	0.1	•	•	•	•	•	•
Pensions and Other Deferred Comp. **16**	0.2	•	•	0.1	0.2	•	0.5	•	•	•	•	•	•
Employee Benefits **17**	0.5	•	•	0.4	0.8	0.3	0.8	•	•	•	•	•	•
Advertising **18**	0.9	•	•	0.5	1.1	0.7	1.5	•	•	•	•	•	•
Other Expenses **19**	8.5	42.6	•	9.3	6.9	4.7	13.8	•	•	•	•	•	•
Officers' Compensation **20**	2.9	•	•	3.4	2.8	0.7	0.7	•	•	•	•	•	•
Operating Margin **21**	3.0	29.1	•	4.9	1.7	•	2.3	•	•	•	•	•	•
Operating Margin Before Officers' Comp. **22**	5.9	29.1	•	8.3	4.5	0.7	3.0	•	•	•	•	•	•

Selected Average Balance Sheet ($ in Thousands)

Item							
Net Receivables 23	110	0	•	115	247	455	870
Inventories 24	578	0	•	273	1321	4126	8296
Net Property, Plant and Equipment 25	213	0	•	122	496	885	1769
Total Assets 26	1023	0	•	785	2239	5965	14081
Notes and Loans Payable 27	376	0	•	139	929	1339	4590
All Other Liabilities 28	242	0	•	123	359	3338	3771
Net Worth 29	405	0	•	523	951	1288	5720

Selected Financial Ratios (Times to 1)

Item							
Current Ratio 30	1.8	•	•	4.3	1.8	1.4	1.9
Quick Ratio 31	0.6	•	•	2.8	0.5	0.2	0.2
Net Sales to Working Capital 32	7.6	•	•	5.3	6.3	9.1	6.4
Coverage Ratio 33	6.7	•	•	26.7	4.1	1.8	8.2
Total Asset Turnover 34	2.5	•	•	3.4	2.1	2.3	2.3
Inventory Turnover 35	3.2	•	•	6.3	2.7	2.8	2.6
Receivables Turnover 36	18.2	•	•	26.1	17.9	•	27.8
Total Liabilities to Net Worth 37	1.5	•	•	0.5	1.4	3.6	1.5
Current Assets to Working Capital 38	2.2	•	•	1.3	2.2	3.3	2.1
Current Liabilities to Working Capital 39	1.2	•	•	0.3	1.2	2.3	1.1
Working Capital to Net Sales 40	0.1	•	•	0.2	0.2	0.1	0.2
Inventory to Working Capital 41	1.5	•	•	0.5	1.5	2.7	1.8
Total Receipts to Cash Flow 42	10.0	1.5	•	8.7	13.7	21.5	6.5
Cost of Goods to Cash Flow 43	7.2	0.4	•	5.6	10.4	18.4	4.4
Cash Flow to Total Debt 44	0.4	•	•	1.2	0.3	0.1	0.6

Selected Financial Factors (in Percentages)

Item							
Debt Ratio 45	60.4	•	•	33.4	57.5	78.4	59.4
Return on Total Assets 46	11.8	•	•	17.6	7.6	2.0	11.6
Return on Equity Before Income Taxes 47	25.4	•	•	25.4	13.6	4.2	25.1
Return on Equity After Income Taxes 48	24.6	•	•	25.0	12.5	3.6	25.1
Profit Margin (Before Income Tax) 49	4.0	29.0	•	5.0	2.8	0.4	4.5
Profit Margin (After Income Tax) 50	3.8	29.0	•	4.9	2.5	0.3	4.5

Table I
Corporations with and without Net Income

FOOD AND BEVERAGE STORES

MONEY AMOUNTS AND SIZE OF ASSETS IN THOUSANDS OF DOLLARS

Item Description for Accounting Period 7/10 Through 6/11	Total	Zero Assets	Under 500	500 to 1,000	1,000 to 5,000	5,000 to 10,000	10,000 to 25,000	25,000 to 50,000	50,000 to 100,000	100,000 to 250,000	250,000 to 500,000	500,000 to 2,500,000	2,500,000 and over
Number of Enterprises 1	75350	8868	56880	4600	3975	616	206	65	49	40	12	26	12
Revenues ($ in Thousands)													
Net Sales 2	494524546	3298358	39136201	15239117	29093168	16621892	16023060	9376538	12683554	22067339	13176964	85002440	232805916
Interest 3	509921	25	2390	2177	6006	7632	998	2653	2268	2476	1747	64208	417343
Rents 4	564096	0	25	465	11685	27280	33707	10408	4576	25393	13567	98036	338953
Royalties 5	1769740	1098	0	0	282	580	2999	0	11405	9814	0	68598	1674965
Other Portfolio Income 6	310918	18729	63594	3254	55781	26415	4622	7865	1187	7489	3209	47572	71201
Other Receipts 7	5479020	31773	533358	119708	283542	340022	158375	67200	153440	184411	100419	1444753	2062015
Total Receipts 8	503158241	3349983	39735568	15364721	29450464	17023821	16223761	9464664	12856430	22296922	13295906	86725607	237370393
Average Total Receipts 9	6678	378	699	3340	7409	27636	78756	145610	262376	557423	1107992	3335600	19780866
Operating Costs/Operating Income (%)													
Cost of Operations 10	73.7	72.5	72.5	75.8	75.1	75.5	77.3	78.8	73.5	72.4	75.2	74.2	73.0
Salaries and Wages 11	9.8	7.6	7.5	8.2	9.0	9.7	9.0	8.2	10.4	11.5	10.9	10.6	10.0
Taxes Paid 12	1.6	2.3	2.3	1.4	1.5	1.5	1.4	1.6	1.7	1.8	1.5	1.5	1.5
Interest Paid 13	0.7	0.6	0.6	0.3	0.4	0.4	0.3	0.3	0.6	0.4	0.5	0.7	0.9
Depreciation 14	2.0	1.2	0.8	0.7	0.8	1.3	1.2	1.3	1.8	1.9	2.0	2.3	2.5
Amortization and Depletion 15	0.1	0.2	0.2	0.1	0.1	0.1	0.1	0.1	0.1	0.1	0.1	0.3	0.1
Pensions and Other Deferred Comp. 16	0.4	0.0	0.0	0.0	0.1	0.1	0.1	0.2	0.3	0.3	0.2	0.6	0.5
Employee Benefits 17	1.2	0.3	0.2	0.2	0.5	0.9	1.0	1.0	1.5	1.5	1.2	1.7	1.4
Advertising 18	0.7	0.6	0.5	0.3	1.1	1.0	0.9	0.7	0.8	0.8	0.7	0.8	0.6
Other Expenses 19	9.3	16.0	12.7	11.1	10.5	9.4	9.1	7.4	9.3	8.9	7.5	8.5	8.9
Officers' Compensation 20	0.5	2.2	3.1	1.5	0.9	1.1	0.5	0.5	0.4	0.3	0.3	0.1	0.0
Operating Margin 21	•	•	•	0.4	0.2	•	•	0.1	•	0.1	•	•	0.6
Operating Margin Before Officers' Comp. 22	0.5	•	2.9	1.9	1.1	0.2	•	0.6	0.0	0.4	0.2	•	0.6

Selected Average Balance Sheet ($ in Thousands)

Net Receivables	23	165	0	2	51	233	528	1404	3748	4789	7590	20881	46987	690266
Inventories	24	341	0	38	190	398	1403	3717	7722	11735	25636	51263	184417	993186
Net Property, Plant and Equipment	25	1015	0	33	174	621	2463	5180	14211	25401	70137	160012	576437	3906659
Total Assets	26	2369	0	122	690	1820	6812	15952	37630	68498	144134	323543	1172414	8978060
Notes and Loans Payable	27	636	0	73	270	752	2242	4682	13690	23408	34651	98080	299744	2063343
All Other Liabilities	28	1006	0	18	203	428	1863	5122	11513	25582	48121	105326	406511	4515796
Net Worth	29	727	0	31	217	639	2706	6147	12428	19508	61361	120137	466159	2398921

Selected Financial Ratios (Times to 1)

Current Ratio	30	1.0	•	3.0	1.9	1.8	1.3	1.4	1.5	1.2	1.2	1.1	0.9	
Quick Ratio	31	0.5	•	1.0	0.8	0.9	0.6	0.7	0.6	0.5	0.5	0.4	0.4	
Net Sales to Working Capital	32	275.3	•	16.6	17.6	20.1	38.1	35.1	25.9	48.4	67.2	61.8	89.0	
Coverage Ratio	33	3.5	•	5.7	4.8	4.7	5.1	2.4	4.5	2.7	4.3	2.1	3.8	
Total Asset Turnover	34	2.8	•	5.7	4.8	4.0	4.0	4.9	3.8	3.8	3.8	2.8	2.2	
Inventory Turnover	35	14.2	•	13.1	13.2	13.8	14.5	16.2	14.7	16.2	15.6	16.1	13.1	14.3
Receivables Turnover	36	39.8	•	325.3	56.6	30.2	45.1	46.4	46.4	54.1	69.5	55.8	65.6	28.8
Total Liabilities to Net Worth	37	2.3	•	3.0	2.2	1.8	1.5	1.6	2.0	2.5	1.3	1.7	2.7	
Current Assets to Working Capital	38	33.9	•	1.5	2.1	2.3	4.5	3.5	3.1	5.2	6.2	6.0	9.2	
Current Liabilities to Working Capital	39	32.9	•	0.5	1.1	1.3	3.5	2.5	2.1	4.2	5.2	5.0	8.2	
Working Capital to Net Sales	40	0.0	•	0.1	0.1	0.0	0.0	0.0	0.0	0.0	0.0	0.0	0.0	
Inventory to Working Capital	41	14.5	•	0.9	1.1	1.0	2.0	1.6	1.2	2.3	3.1	3.1	4.9	
Total Receipts to Cash Flow	42	13.0	17.5	11.7	11.9	11.8	12.0	15.6	18.6	14.9	15.1	18.4	15.3	12.0
Cost of Goods to Cash Flow	43	9.5	12.7	8.5	9.0	8.9	9.1	12.1	14.7	11.0	11.0	13.8	11.4	8.7
Cash Flow to Total Debt	44	0.3	•	0.6	0.6	0.5	0.5	0.5	0.3	0.4	0.3	0.3	0.2	

Selected Financial Factors (in Percentages)

Debt Ratio	45	69.3	•	74.7	68.6	64.9	60.3	61.5	67.0	71.5	57.4	62.9	60.2	73.3
Return on Total Assets	46	6.6	•	9.5	7.2	7.1	7.4	3.9	5.0	5.8	5.8	4.6	4.3	7.3
Return on Equity Before Income Taxes	47	15.5	•	30.9	18.2	15.9	15.0	6.0	11.8	12.9	10.4	7.7	5.6	20.2
Return on Equity After Income Taxes	48	10.7	•	30.0	17.0	14.8	13.5	5.5	10.6	10.8	9.1	5.8	3.4	12.7
Profit Margin (Before Income Tax)	49	1.7	•	1.4	1.2	1.4	1.5	0.5	1.0	1.0	1.0	0.8	0.8	2.5
Profit Margin (After Income Tax)	50	1.2	•	1.3	1.1	1.3	1.4	0.4	0.9	0.8	0.6	0.6	0.5	1.6

Table II
Corporations with Net Income

FOOD AND BEVERAGE STORES

MONEY AMOUNTS AND SIZE OF ASSETS IN THOUSANDS OF DOLLARS

Item Description for Accounting Period 7/10 Through 6/11	Total	Zero Assets	Under 500	500 to 1,000	1,000 to 5,000	5,000 to 10,000	10,000 to 25,000	25,000 to 50,000	50,000 to 100,000	100,000 to 250,000	250,000 to 500,000	500,000 to 2,500,000	2,500,000 and over
Number of Enterprises **1**	40264	2617	31783	2707	2406	463	141	47	35	•	•	17	9
Revenues ($ in Thousands)													
Net Sales **2**	384329475	1598786	24861394	11812800	21851012	13902411	10306919	7072393	9872726	•	•	58585241	196829156
Interest **3**	488682	0	1106	933	5869	7072	460	2572	2170	•	•	54355	410173
Rents **4**	397308	0	18	56	7547	17329	10845	4127	3855	•	•	81267	239813
Royalties **5**	1753012	0	0	0	65	0	2999	0	931	•	•	65336	1674965
Other Portfolio Income **6**	269973	18566	53913	1504	47584	25754	4195	4437	1186	•	•	41429	62093
Other Receipts **7**	4130137	5451	312684	105266	216032	324731	123600	45593	129891	•	•	1169536	1470210
Total Receipts **8**	391368587	1622803	25229115	11920559	22128109	14277297	10449018	7129122	10010759	•	•	59997164	200686410
Average Total Receipts **9**	9720	620	794	4404	9197	30836	74107	151683	286022	•	•	3529245	22298490
Operating Costs/Operating Income (%)													
Cost of Operations **10**	73.7	72.4	73.4	75.4	74.8	75.5	76.3	80.0	74.7	•	•	73.5	73.1
Salaries and Wages **11**	9.7	8.5	6.3	8.2	8.3	9.5	9.7	7.4	9.5	•	•	11.0	9.9
Taxes Paid **12**	1.6	2.3	2.3	1.3	1.4	1.5	1.4	1.4	1.6	•	•	1.6	1.5
Interest Paid **13**	0.6	1.0	0.3	0.2	0.3	0.3	0.3	0.2	0.4	•	•	0.6	0.7
Depreciation **14**	2.0	0.4	0.7	0.5	0.7	0.8	1.0	1.1	1.7	•	•	2.1	2.5
Amortization and Depletion **15**	0.1	0.0	0.2	0.2	0.1	0.1	0.1	0.1	0.1	•	•	0.2	0.1
Pensions and Other Deferred Comp. **16**	0.4	0.0	0.0	0.0	0.1	0.1	0.1	0.2	0.4	•	•	0.7	0.6
Employee Benefits **17**	1.3	0.3	0.2	0.2	0.4	1.0	0.7	0.8	1.4	•	•	2.0	1.4
Advertising **18**	0.6	0.8	0.3	0.3	1.0	1.0	1.0	0.7	0.8	•	•	0.7	0.5
Other Expenses **19**	8.7	12.2	10.9	10.1	10.3	8.9	8.9	6.2	8.6	•	•	7.9	8.5
Officers' Compensation **20**	0.4	1.6	2.9	1.6	0.9	1.1	0.5	0.5	0.4	•	•	0.2	0.0
Operating Margin **21**	1.0	0.6	2.4	2.0	1.7	0.1	0.1	1.3	0.4	•	•	•	1.2
Operating Margin Before Officers' Comp. **22**	1.4	2.2	5.4	3.6	2.6	1.2	0.6	1.8	0.8	•	•	•	1.3

Selected Average Balance Sheet ($ in Thousands)

Line Item											
Net Receivables 23	259	•	2	65	176	573	1665	2360	4892	52310	860544
Inventories 24	512	0	46	214	486	1570	3509	7579	12623	195067	1145369
Net Property, Plant and Equipment 25	1496	0	33	144	657	2173	4095	11674	24992	569309	4516702
Total Assets 26	3467	0	135	696	1849	6888	15568	36360	69805	1166947	10240258
Notes and Loans Payable 27	733	0	58	199	577	1496	3067	9768	21952	251444	1915388
All Other Liabilities 28	1566	0	17	121	440	1861	4537	9909	24168	411968	5428587
Net Worth 29	1169	0	60	376	832	3531	7964	16683	23685	503535	2896283

Selected Financial Ratios (Times to 1)

Line Item											
Current Ratio 30	1.0	•	3.8	3.3	1.9	1.5	1.8	1.8	1.3	1.1	0.8
Quick Ratio 31	0.5	•	1.4	1.7	0.9	0.7	0.9	0.7	0.6	0.5	0.4
Net Sales to Working Capital 32	•	•	14.6	14.3	21.4	25.1	20.0	19.9	41.9	107.7	•
Coverage Ratio 33	6.1	3.2	15.3	16.2	10.5	10.1	6.6	9.6	5.0	4.2	5.6
Total Asset Turnover 34	2.8	•	5.8	6.3	4.9	4.4	4.7	4.1	4.0	3.0	2.1
Inventory Turnover 35	13.7	•	12.5	15.4	14.0	14.4	15.9	15.9	16.7	13.0	14.0
Receivables Turnover 36	35.4	•	319.4	52.3	40.9	42.7	•	•	55.0	58.3	•
Total Liabilities to Net Worth 37	2.0	•	1.3	0.9	1.2	1.0	1.0	1.2	1.9	1.3	2.5
Current Assets to Working Capital 38	•	•	1.4	1.4	2.2	2.9	2.2	2.3	4.4	11.2	•
Current Liabilities to Working Capital 39	•	•	0.4	0.4	1.2	1.9	1.2	1.3	3.4	10.2	•
Working Capital to Net Sales 40	•	•	0.1	0.1	0.0	0.0	0.1	0.1	0.0	0.0	•
Inventory to Working Capital 41	•	•	0.8	0.7	1.0	1.2	1.0	1.0	2.0	5.7	•
Total Receipts to Cash Flow 42	11.6	11.9	10.3	10.4	9.9	10.7	13.5	17.0	14.1	13.5	11.0
Cost of Goods to Cash Flow 43	8.6	8.6	7.6	7.8	7.4	8.1	10.3	13.6	10.5	9.9	8.0
Cash Flow to Total Debt 44	0.4	•	1.0	1.3	0.9	0.8	0.7	0.5	0.4	0.4	0.3

Selected Financial Factors (in Percentages)

Line Item											
Debt Ratio 45	66.3	•	55.7	46.0	55.0	48.7	48.8	54.1	66.1	56.9	71.7
Return on Total Assets 46	9.2	•	24.2	19.4	16.4	13.5	8.1	9.7	8.8	7.8	8.2
Return on Equity Before Income Taxes 47	22.8	•	51.1	33.7	32.9	23.7	13.5	18.9	20.8	13.8	23.9
Return on Equity After Income Taxes 48	17.3	•	50.2	32.5	31.5	22.2	13.0	17.6	18.4	10.8	15.6
Profit Margin (Before Income Tax) 49	2.8	2.1	3.9	2.9	3.0	2.8	1.5	2.1	1.8	2.0	3.2
Profit Margin (After Income Tax) 50	2.1	2.1	3.8	2.8	2.9	2.6	1.4	1.9	1.5	1.6	2.1

Table I

Corporations with and without Net Income

BEER, WINE, AND LIQUOR STORES

MONEY AMOUNTS AND SIZE OF ASSETS IN THOUSANDS OF DOLLARS

Item Description for Accounting Period 7/10 Through 6/11	Total	Zero Assets	Under 500	500 to 1,000	1,000 to 5,000	5,000 to 10,000	10,000 to 25,000	25,000 to 50,000	50,000 to 100,000	100,000 to 250,000	250,000 to 500,000	500,000 to 2,500,000	2,500,000 and over
Number of Enterprises **1**	19451	1237	13863	3363	855	106	12	12	0	4	0	0	0
Revenues ($ in Thousands)													
Net Sales **2**	27030107	81889	10950793	5786381	4632692	1917066	672908	1163257	0	1825120	0	0	0
Interest **3**	9792	158	338	277	2094	6520	9	0	0	396	0	0	0
Rents **4**	4986	0	1234	183	842	813	1045	0	0	869	0	0	0
Royalties **5**	3826	0	0	0	0	3826	0	0	0	0	0	0	0
Other Portfolio Income **6**	69429	22609	20701	25525	54	0	0	23	0	516	0	0	0
Other Receipts **7**	464260	21696	253701	70960	40200	62956	1032	2171	0	11548	0	0	0
Total Receipts **8**	27582400	126352	11226767	5883326	4675882	1991181	674994	1165451	0	1838449	0	0	0
Average Total Receipts **9**	1418	102	810	1749	5469	18785	56250	97121	•	459612	•	•	•
Operating Costs/Operating Income (%)													
Cost of Operations **10**	77.5	82.9	76.5	78.7	76.4	82.2	75.3	78.2	•	77.1	•	•	•
Salaries and Wages **11**	5.8	3.1	5.5	5.2	5.5	6.2	8.8	7.5	•	7.7	•	•	•
Taxes Paid **12**	2.3	1.8	3.6	1.9	1.3	0.6	1.5	1.2	•	1.2	•	•	•
Interest Paid **13**	0.6	0.4	0.6	0.6	0.6	0.1	0.5	0.9	•	1.2	•	•	•
Depreciation **14**	0.7	1.8	0.6	0.8	0.4	0.8	0.7	0.7	•	1.4	•	•	•
Amortization and Depletion **15**	0.4	2.3	0.5	0.5	0.3	0.1	0.1	0.3	•	0.1	•	•	•
Pensions and Other Deferred Comp. **16**	0.0	•	0.0	0.0	0.1	0.0	0.0	0.0	•	0.1	•	•	•
Employee Benefits **17**	0.2	0.2	0.2	0.0	0.4	0.2	0.3	0.4	•	0.7	•	•	•
Advertising **18**	0.6	•	0.3	0.7	0.8	1.0	0.7	0.7	•	1.1	•	•	•
Other Expenses **19**	9.3	19.3	9.6	9.8	9.0	8.4	10.1	7.2	•	8.9	•	•	•
Officers' Compensation **20**	2.7	1.3	4.0	2.1	2.2	1.0	2.2	1.6	•	0.3	•	•	•
Operating Margin **21**	•	•	•	•	3.0	•	•	1.1	•	0.1	•	•	•
Operating Margin Before Officers' Comp. **22**	2.6	•	2.7	1.9	5.2	0.3	2.1	2.8	•	0.5	•	•	•

Selected Average Balance Sheet ($ in Thousands)

Net Receivables 23	18	0	1	4	60	1877	105	3840	•	5430
Inventories 24	204	0	99	290	839	2846	5211	20341	•	59099
Net Property, Plant and Equipment 25	76	0	31	79	437	676	1620	6270	•	64014
Total Assets 26	471	0	202	725	1935	7687	14446	43404	•	192725
Notes and Loans Payable 27	239	0	116	411	1032	1837	4173	17675	•	79924
All Other Liabilities 28	94	0	39	110	263	1951	8313	12741	•	59278
Net Worth 29	139	0	47	204	639	3899	1960	12988	•	53524

Selected Financial Ratios (Times to 1)

Current Ratio 30	2.6	•	3.1	3.8	2.5	2.4	1.0	2.3	•	1.5
Quick Ratio 31	0.7	•	0.7	1.0	0.6	1.1	0.2	0.3	•	0.2
Net Sales to Working Capital 32	7.3	•	9.4	5.1	7.1	4.6	•	5.2	•	15.1
Coverage Ratio 33	4.0	102.1	2.8	3.4	7.2	26.7	1.4	2.4	•	1.7
Total Asset Turnover 34	2.9	•	3.9	2.4	2.8	2.4	3.9	2.2	•	2.4
Inventory Turnover 35	5.3	•	6.1	4.7	4.9	5.2	8.1	3.7	•	6.0
Receivables Turnover 36	88.5	•	657.8	415.2	123.1	11.5	464.7	24.8	•	88.0
Total Liabilities to Net Worth 37	2.4	•	3.3	2.5	2.0	1.0	6.4	2.3	•	2.6
Current Assets to Working Capital 38	1.6	•	1.5	1.4	1.7	1.7	•	1.8	•	2.8
Current Liabilities to Working Capital 39	0.6	•	0.5	0.4	0.7	0.7	•	0.8	•	1.8
Working Capital to Net Sales 40	0.1	•	0.1	0.2	0.1	0.2	•	0.2	•	0.1
Inventory to Working Capital 41	1.1	•	1.1	1.0	1.1	0.8	•	1.1	•	2.2
Total Receipts to Cash Flow 42	13.9	4.1	15.0	14.6	10.4	11.2	20.9	19.8	•	19.2
Cost of Goods to Cash Flow 43	10.8	3.4	11.5	11.5	8.0	9.2	15.8	15.5	•	14.8
Cash Flow to Total Debt 44	0.3	•	0.3	0.2	0.4	0.4	0.2	0.2	•	0.2

Selected Financial Factors (in Percentages)

Debt Ratio 45	70.6	•	76.6	71.8	67.0	49.3	86.4	70.1	•	72.2
Return on Total Assets 46	7.6	•	6.9	5.0	12.6	7.7	2.6	5.1	•	4.9
Return on Equity Before Income Taxes 47	19.3	•	19.2	12.6	33.0	14.6	5.4	10.0	•	7.3
Return on Equity After Income Taxes 48	17.9	•	19.0	11.5	30.7	13.9	3.0	10.0	•	5.8
Profit Margin (Before Income Tax) 49	1.9	41.5	1.1	1.5	3.9	3.1	0.2	1.3	•	0.9
Profit Margin (After Income Tax) 50	1.8	31.5	1.1	1.4	3.6	3.0	0.1	1.3	•	0.7

Table II
Corporations with Net Income

BEER, WINE, AND LIQUOR STORES

MONEY AMOUNTS AND SIZE OF ASSETS IN THOUSANDS OF DOLLARS

Item Description for Accounting Period 7/10 Through 6/11	Total	Zero Assets	Under 500	500 to 1,000	1,000 to 5,000	5,000 to 10,000	10,000 to 25,000	25,000 to 50,000	50,000 to 100,000	100,000 to 250,000	250,000 to 500,000	500,000 to 2,500,000	2,500,000 and over
Number of Enterprises 1	11450	187	8666	1735	736	106	8	•	0	•	0	0	0
Revenues ($ in Thousands)													
Net Sales 2	20090178	29296	7409432	4089147	3834145	1917066	273722	•	0	•	0	0	0
Interest 3	7820	4	7	274	609	6520	9	•	0	•	0	0	0
Rents 4	3753	0	0	183	842	813	1045	•	0	•	0	0	0
Royalties 5	3826	0	0	0	0	3826	0	•	0	•	0	0	0
Other Portfolio Income 6	69404	22609	20701	25525	53	0	0	•	0	•	0	0	0
Other Receipts 7	314049	21696	128056	49375	39752	62956	240	•	0	•	0	0	0
Total Receipts 8	20489030	73605	7558196	4164504	3875401	1991181	275016	•	•	•	•	•	0
Average Total Receipts 9	1789	394	872	2400	5265	18785	34377	•	•	•	•	•	•
Operating Costs/Operating Income (%)													
Cost of Operations 10	77.2	99.3	76.2	76.9	77.0	82.2	72.7	•	•	•	•	•	•
Salaries and Wages 11	5.2	3.1	4.0	5.7	5.0	6.2	8.3	•	•	•	•	•	•
Taxes Paid 12	1.9	1.9	3.2	1.4	1.3	0.6	1.0	•	•	•	•	•	•
Interest Paid 13	0.5	0.3	0.3	0.5	0.6	0.1	0.1	•	•	•	•	•	•
Depreciation 14	0.6	0.1	0.5	0.5	0.8	0.8	0.8	•	•	•	•	•	•
Amortization and Depletion 15	0.2	1.7	0.4	0.1	0.3	0.1	0.0	•	•	•	•	•	•
Pensions and Other Deferred Comp. 16	0.0	•	0.0	0.0	0.1	0.0	0.1	•	•	•	•	•	•
Employee Benefits 17	0.3	•	0.2	0.0	0.3	0.2	0.6	•	•	•	•	•	•
Advertising 18	0.7	•	0.3	0.8	0.9	1.0	1.3	•	•	•	•	•	•
Other Expenses 19	8.9	20.3	9.1	9.6	8.5	8.4	8.1	•	•	•	•	•	•
Officers' Compensation 20	2.8	2.1	4.7	2.6	1.4	1.0	4.8	•	•	•	•	•	•
Operating Margin 21	1.6	•	1.1	1.6	4.1	•	2.1	•	•	•	•	•	•
Operating Margin Before Officers' Comp. 22	4.4	•	5.8	4.3	5.6	0.3	6.9	•	•	•	•	•	•

Selected Average Balance Sheet ($ in Thousands)

Net Receivables 23	26	0	1	4	67	1877	108
Inventories 24	248	0	107	289	815	2846	6033
Net Property, Plant and Equipment 25	87	0	23	47	502	676	1504
Total Assets 26	566	0	211	760	1888	7687	11819
Notes and Loans Payable 27	213	0	67	304	988	1837	549
All Other Liabilities 28	119	0	49	119	217	1951	4297
Net Worth 29	233	0	95	338	682	3899	6973

Selected Financial Ratios (Times to 1)

Current Ratio 30	2.8	•	3.7	3.7	2.5	2.4	2.0
Quick Ratio 31	0.8	•	1.0	1.3	0.8	1.1	0.5
Net Sales to Working Capital 32	7.2	•	8.6	6.2	7.3	4.6	7.8
Coverage Ratio 33	8.8	399.4	12.1	8.7	9.8	26.7	26.1
Total Asset Turnover 34	3.1	•	4.1	3.1	2.8	2.4	2.9
Inventory Turnover 35	5.5	•	6.1	6.3	4.9	5.2	4.1
Receivables Turnover 36	79.4	•	1279.0	738.4	106.2	11.5	•
Total Liabilities to Net Worth 37	1.4	•	1.2	1.3	1.8	1.0	0.7
Current Assets to Working Capital 38	1.6	•	1.4	1.4	1.7	1.7	2.0
Current Liabilities to Working Capital 39	0.6	•	0.4	0.4	0.7	0.7	1.0
Working Capital to Net Sales 40	0.1	•	0.1	0.2	0.1	0.2	0.1
Inventory to Working Capital 41	1.0	•	1.0	0.9	1.1	0.8	1.4
Total Receipts to Cash Flow 42	11.9	1.8	12.8	12.0	9.1	11.2	12.4
Cost of Goods to Cash Flow 43	9.2	1.7	9.8	9.2	7.0	9.2	9.0
Cash Flow to Total Debt 44	0.4	•	0.6	0.5	0.5	0.4	0.6

Selected Financial Factors (in Percentages)

Debt Ratio 45	58.7	•	54.7	55.6	63.9	49.3	41.0
Return on Total Assets 46	12.5	•	13.6	12.2	16.1	7.7	7.7
Return on Equity Before Income Taxes 47	26.8	•	27.6	24.3	39.9	14.6	12.5
Return on Equity After Income Taxes 48	25.4	•	27.4	22.9	37.5	13.9	11.5
Profit Margin (Before Income Tax) 49	3.6	122.4	3.1	3.5	5.2	3.1	2.6
Profit Margin (After Income Tax) 50	3.4	94.5	3.1	3.3	4.9	3.0	2.3

Table I
Corporations with and without Net Income

HEALTH AND PERSONAL CARE STORES

MONEY AMOUNTS AND SIZE OF ASSETS IN THOUSANDS OF DOLLARS

Item Description for Accounting Period 7/10 Through 6/11		Total	Zero Assets	Under 500	500 to 1,000	1,000 to 5,000	5,000 to 10,000	10,000 to 25,000	25,000 to 50,000	50,000 to 100,000	100,000 to 250,000	250,000 to 500,000	500,000 to 2,500,000	2,500,000 and over
Number of Enterprises	1	41920	4383	29918	3961	3372	134	87	23	15	10	7	5	4
Revenues ($ in Thousands)														
Net Sales	2	283623035	732587	24478806	13270574	21473907	3851808	3316212	1651475	3329757	4003055	3521576	7030396	196962881
Interest	3	54263	169	1188	2854	3153	3126	3163	902	325	3479	14004	3556	18344
Rents	4	137453	362	812	1451	1895	989	1568	1634	5	7879	7714	92	113052
Royalties	5	93988	58	0	13	0	0	0	0	15597	2103	0	47322	28895
Other Portfolio Income	6	125886	3472	13822	12348	1860	943	298	6128	4133	48500	11665	4083	18633
Other Receipts	7	5476753	4686	68917	42713	112785	11660	23639	61225	83821	52824	51635	23150	4939699
Total Receipts	8	289511378	741334	24563545	13329953	21593600	3868526	3344880	1721364	3433638	4117840	3606594	7108599	202081504
Average Total Receipts	9	6906	169	821	3365	6404	28870	38447	74842	228909	411784	515228	1421720	50520376
Operating Costs/Operating Income (%)														
Cost of Operations	10	71.9	59.9	70.0	73.7	69.3	76.8	65.4	56.3	75.4	70.0	60.3	64.5	73.0
Salaries and Wages	11	10.2	10.3	7.1	8.4	11.6	8.8	15.6	18.9	11.4	13.8	14.0	11.8	10.2
Taxes Paid	12	1.2	2.2	1.7	1.6	1.3	1.0	1.4	2.9	1.0	1.6	1.4	2.0	1.1
Interest Paid	13	0.6	0.3	0.2	0.2	0.5	0.3	0.5	0.9	1.0	0.3	2.2	1.3	0.7
Depreciation	14	1.2	1.2	0.6	0.3	0.8	0.8	2.1	1.6	1.2	1.1	2.1	2.1	1.3
Amortization and Depletion	15	0.3	0.0	0.1	0.1	0.2	0.1	0.3	0.3	0.6	0.2	1.2	0.9	0.3
Pensions and Other Deferred Comp.	16	0.3	0.0	0.2	0.6	0.3	0.2	0.3	0.3	0.2	0.3	0.1	0.2	0.3
Employee Benefits	17	0.6	0.7	0.2	0.4	0.6	1.1	1.4	0.7	0.9	1.8	1.1	1.0	0.5
Advertising	18	0.8	1.7	0.9	0.6	0.8	1.2	1.2	2.0	0.5	1.4	1.5	1.1	0.7
Other Expenses	19	10.5	30.7	11.0	7.0	8.9	6.5	8.8	16.6	15.5	9.8	15.6	12.4	10.5
Officers' Compensation	20	1.0	5.7	5.3	5.1	2.5	0.9	1.7	1.0	0.6	0.7	1.6	0.8	0.0
Operating Margin	21	1.5	•	2.7	1.9	3.1	2.3	1.2	•	•	•	•	1.8	1.4
Operating Margin Before Officers' Comp.	22	2.5	•	8.0	7.0	5.7	3.2	2.9	•	•	•	0.4	2.5	1.4

Selected Average Balance Sheet ($ in Thousands)

Net Receivables 23	594	0	12	91	328	2111	4295	5457	18969	14427	33210	111453	5272500
Inventories 24	688	0	63	304	479	1619	2752	7050	11519	36540	77294	146326	5429103
Net Property, Plant and Equipment 25	520	0	18	52	270	1031	2298	6233	11465	24504	44379	143058	4556556
Total Assets 26	3392	0	145	710	1756	6824	14748	34610	77885	161930	361493	1015190	28932518
Notes and Loans Payable 27	802	0	58	130	613	1885	4513	11790	34943	54481	149451	325301	6160000
All Other Liabilities 28	998	0	41	187	446	3510	5414	16697	33610	44379	93695	234288	8572096
Net Worth 29	1592	0	47	392	698	1428	4821	6123	9332	63071	118346	455601	14200422

Selected Financial Ratios (Times to 1)

Current Ratio 30	1.6	•	2.8	3.1	2.2	1.0	1.8	1.2	1.2	1.9	1.7	2.4	1.5
Quick Ratio 31	0.8	•	1.2	1.4	1.2	0.7	1.2	0.6	0.7	0.7	0.7	1.2	0.7
Net Sales to Working Capital 32	11.0	•	11.2	9.1	9.7	462.5	8.4	31.3	29.9	10.0	9.3	6.6	11.2
Coverage Ratio 33	6.5	•	16.3	12.3	8.0	10.9	5.2	4.1	•	7.4	1.5	3.1	6.8
Total Asset Turnover 34	2.0	•	5.6	4.7	3.6	4.2	2.6	2.1	2.9	2.5	1.4	1.4	1.7
Inventory Turnover 35	7.1	•	9.1	8.1	9.2	13.6	9.1	5.7	14.5	7.7	3.9	6.2	6.6
Receivables Turnover 36	11.1	•	68.0	33.0	18.3	11.6	8.7	14.4	11.6	21.1	12.5	15.5	9.1
Total Liabilities to Net Worth 37	1.1	•	2.1	0.8	1.5	3.8	2.1	4.7	7.3	1.6	2.1	1.2	1.0
Current Assets to Working Capital 38	2.6	•	1.6	1.5	1.8	76.9	2.2	7.5	5.9	2.2	2.3	1.7	2.9
Current Liabilities to Working Capital 39	1.6	•	0.6	0.5	0.8	75.9	1.2	6.5	4.9	1.2	1.3	0.7	1.9
Working Capital to Net Sales 40	0.1	•	0.1	0.1	0.1	0.0	0.1	0.0	0.0	0.1	0.1	0.2	0.1
Inventory to Working Capital 41	1.1	•	0.9	0.7	0.7	21.6	0.6	3.2	1.5	1.0	1.3	0.7	1.2
Total Receipts to Cash Flow 42	9.5	7.7	10.7	15.4	9.4	12.6	11.6	6.7	13.5	14.2	9.6	9.9	9.0
Cost of Goods to Cash Flow 43	6.8	4.6	7.5	11.3	6.5	9.7	7.6	3.8	10.2	10.0	5.8	6.4	6.6
Cash Flow to Total Debt 44	0.4	•	0.8	0.7	0.6	0.4	0.3	0.4	0.2	0.3	0.2	0.3	0.4

Selected Financial Factors (in Percentages)

Debt Ratio 45	53.1	•	67.9	44.7	60.3	79.1	67.3	82.3	88.0	61.1	67.3	55.1	50.9
Return on Total Assets 46	8.3	•	18.4	12.1	15.3	12.7	6.5	7.9	•	5.8	4.8	5.8	8.0
Return on Equity Before Income Taxes 47	15.0	•	53.8	20.2	33.6	55.2	16.1	33.7	•	12.9	5.2	8.7	13.9
Return on Equity After Income Taxes 48	10.4	•	53.1	19.2	32.7	46.1	15.5	28.9	•	12.1	2.9	5.4	8.8
Profit Margin (Before Income Tax) 49	3.5	•	3.1	2.4	3.7	2.7	2.0	2.9	•	2.0	1.2	2.8	4.0
Profit Margin (After Income Tax) 50	2.5	•	3.0	2.2	3.6	2.3	2.0	2.5	•	1.9	0.7	1.8	2.5

Table II

Corporations with Net Income

HEALTH AND PERSONAL CARE STORES

MONEY AMOUNTS AND SIZE OF ASSETS IN THOUSANDS OF DOLLARS

Item Description for Accounting Period 7/10 Through 6/11	Total	Zero Assets	Under 500	500 to 1,000	1,000 to 5,000	5,000 to 10,000	10,000 to 25,000	25,000 to 50,000	50,000 to 100,000	100,000 to 250,000	250,000 to 500,000	500,000 to 2,500,000	2,500,000 and over
Number of Enterprises 1	27304	1171	20008	3318	2649	66	53	15	5	•	•	5	0
Revenues ($ in Thousands)													
Net Sales 2	232126317	407494	21166813	10762812	16934250	1137056	2100497	1257388	1637161	•	•	•169490197	0
Interest 3	42769	9	885	2018	2054	701	2736	787	0	•	•	16872	0
Rents 4	95906	264	804	1153	1013	874	1525	1634	0	•	•	73047	0
Royalties 5	78333	0	0	13	0	0	0	0	0	•	•	76217	0
Other Portfolio Income 6	102590	3472	13801	11312	1373	943	27	38	2301	•	•	9388	0
Other Receipts 7	4596856	139	57550	19664	84592	2723	18653	59148	9670	•	•	4237265	0
Total Receipts 8	237042771	411378	21239853	10796972	17023282	1142297	2123438	1318995	1649132	•	•	•173902986	0
Average Total Receipts 9	8682	351	1062	3254	6426	17308	40065	87933	329826	•	•	34780597	•
Operating Costs/Operating Income (%)													
Cost of Operations 10	71.2	58.1	69.3	73.8	67.8	57.9	64.5	54.3	85.1	•	•	72.0	•
Salaries and Wages 11	10.0	8.3	6.7	7.9	11.1	12.7	15.2	19.6	6.3	•	•	10.1	•
Taxes Paid 12	1.1	2.2	1.6	1.5	1.3	1.8	1.6	3.0	0.6	•	•	1.0	•
Interest Paid 13	0.4	0.2	0.2	0.2	0.5	0.3	0.3	0.8	0.2	•	•	0.4	•
Depreciation 14	1.2	0.6	0.5	0.4	0.8	1.2	2.1	1.5	0.7	•	•	1.3	•
Amortization and Depletion 15	0.2	•	0.1	0.1	0.2	0.2	0.3	0.3	0.2	•	•	0.2	•
Pensions and Other Deferred Comp. 16	0.3	0.0	0.2	0.7	0.3	0.3	0.3	0.3	0.1	•	•	0.3	•
Employee Benefits 17	0.5	0.8	0.2	0.4	0.5	1.6	1.1	0.6	0.6	•	•	0.4	•
Advertising 18	0.7	1.0	0.8	0.7	0.9	2.4	0.2	1.7	0.2	•	•	0.6	•
Other Expenses 19	10.6	21.3	10.2	6.2	9.2	9.6	8.1	16.0	4.5	•	•	11.1	•
Officers' Compensation 20	1.0	1.4	5.0	5.0	2.5	0.8	1.8	1.0	0.4	•	•	0.1	•
Operating Margin 21	2.8	6.1	5.1	3.0	4.9	11.2	4.5	0.8	1.1	•	•	2.4	•
Operating Margin Before Officers' Comp. 22	3.8	7.6	10.1	8.0	7.5	12.0	6.3	1.8	1.5	•	•	2.5	•

Selected Average Balance Sheet ($ in Thousands)

Net Receivables 23	784	0	14	88	302	1186	5304	7494	29744	3833940 •
Inventories 24	874	0	73	260	512	2145	2505	7719	18094	1947257 •
Net Property, Plant and Equipment 25	686	0	19	52	276	629	1525	7506	9123	3325254 •
Total Assets 26	4419	0	172	701	1751	6734	14237	35803	77602	20982617 •
Notes and Loans Payable 27	811	0	59	136	573	653	2742	11460	15204	3481632 •
All Other Liabilities 28	1264	0	46	152	366	1662	5413	20285	41335	6054124 •
Net Worth 29	2344	0	68	414	811	4420	6081	4058	21063	11446861 •

Selected Financial Ratios (Times to 1)

Current Ratio 30	1.6	•	3.1	3.3	2.6	2.8	2.0	1.0	1.2	1.5 •
Quick Ratio 31	0.8	•	1.3	1.7	1.4	1.7	1.5	0.5	0.8	0.7 •
Net Sales to Working Capital 32	11.2	•	11.4	8.7	8.7	5.4	7.7	96.4	43.6	11.6 •
Coverage Ratio 33	13.3	41.4	29.6	17.5	13.1	43.3	20.6	8.2	9.4	13.3 •
Total Asset Turnover 34	1.9	•	6.1	4.6	3.7	2.6	2.8	2.3	4.2	1.6 •
Inventory Turnover 35	6.9	•	10.1	9.2	8.5	4.7	10.2	5.9	15.4	12.5 •
Receivables Turnover 36	10.2	•	76.1	32.4	18.6	9.5	7.2	•	10.7	17.4 •
Total Liabilities to Net Worth 37	0.9	•	1.5	0.7	1.2	0.5	1.3	7.8	2.7	0.8 •
Current Assets to Working Capital 38	2.7	•	1.5	1.4	1.6	1.6	2.0	21.9	7.3	3.1 •
Current Liabilities to Working Capital 39	1.7	•	0.5	0.4	0.6	0.6	1.0	20.9	6.3	2.1 •
Working Capital to Net Sales 40	0.1	•	0.1	0.1	0.1	0.2	0.1	0.0	0.0	0.1 •
Inventory to Working Capital 41	1.1	•	0.8	0.7	0.6	0.5	0.5	8.9	2.3	1.3 •
Total Receipts to Cash Flow 42	8.2	4.1	8.8	13.8	8.0	5.2	8.3	5.6	18.5	7.9 •
Cost of Goods to Cash Flow 43	5.8	2.4	6.1	10.2	5.4	3.0	5.4	3.0	15.8	5.7 •
Cash Flow to Total Debt 44	0.5	•	1.2	0.8	0.9	1.4	0.6	0.5	0.3	0.5 •

Selected Financial Factors (in Percentages)

Debt Ratio 45	47.0	•	60.8	41.0	53.7	34.4	57.3	88.7	72.9	45.4 •
Return on Total Assets 46	10.3	•	34.7	16.3	21.6	30.5	16.4	15.8	8.5	8.8 •
Return on Equity Before Income Taxes 47	17.9	•	85.6	26.0	43.0	45.4	36.5	122.3	27.9	14.9 •
Return on Equity After Income Taxes 48	13.2	•	84.8	24.9	42.0	39.4	35.7	111.1	27.1	9.7 •
Profit Margin (Before Income Tax) 49	4.9	7.1	5.5	3.3	5.5	11.7	5.6	5.9	1.8	5.0 •
Profit Margin (After Income Tax) 50	3.6	6.7	5.4	3.2	5.3	10.1	5.5	5.4	1.7	3.3 •

Table I

Corporations with and without Net Income

GASOLINE STATIONS

MONEY AMOUNTS AND SIZE OF ASSETS IN THOUSANDS OF DOLLARS

Item Description for Accounting Period 7/10 Through 6/11		Total	Zero Assets	Under 500	500 to 1,000	1,000 to 5,000	5,000 to 10,000	10,000 to 25,000	25,000 to 50,000	50,000 to 100,000	100,000 to 250,000	250,000 to 500,000	500,000 to 2,500,000	2,500,000 and over
Number of Enterprises	1	44275	3285	30143	5825	4320	370	188	73	37	17	5	13	0
Revenues ($ in Thousands)														
Net Sales	2	291512873	2203872	57216003	26352993	46183195	8663919	19091081	18584745	12471725	12131996	12453031	76160314	0
Interest	3	45291	0	1082	847	2472	800	897	4355	2554	193	144	31945	0
Rents	4	117062	0	9347	6957	7394	9568	12135	8157	8640	3847	91	50925	0
Royalties	5	16959	0	0	0	0	216	0	1	0	0	0	16742	0
Other Portfolio Income	6	204073	47942	26999	543	30477	27759	7796	12117	7080	5416	1344	36600	0
Other Receipts	7	1759009	20993	421824	106239	118529	79421	147975	69738	80797	82482	187845	443167	0
Total Receipts	8	29365267	2272807	57675255	26467579	46342067	8781683	19259884	18679113	12570796	12223934	12642455	76739693	0
Average Total Receipts	9	6633	692	1913	4544	10727	23734	102446	255878	339751	719055	2528491	5903053	•
Operating Costs/Operating Income (%)														
Cost of Operations	10	89.6	89.2	88.7	89.6	89.4	87.0	89.5	91.9	91.3	89.4	93.4	89.5	•
Salaries and Wages	11	3.1	3.9	2.4	2.7	3.4	5.1	3.4	2.8	2.7	3.7	2.1	3.4	•
Taxes Paid	12	0.8	1.1	1.2	0.9	1.0	1.0	0.8	0.6	0.7	0.7	0.4	0.6	•
Interest Paid	13	0.4	0.5	0.2	0.5	0.6	0.9	0.3	0.2	0.3	0.4	0.2	0.5	•
Depreciation	14	1.0	0.7	0.4	0.8	0.9	1.0	0.9	0.9	1.1	1.3	1.3	1.7	•
Amortization and Depletion	15	0.1	0.0	0.1	0.2	0.1	0.2	0.0	0.0	0.0	0.1	0.0	0.1	•
Pensions and Other Deferred Comp.	16	0.0	0.0	0.0	0.0	0.0	0.0	0.0	0.0	0.0	0.1	0.0	0.1	•
Employee Benefits	17	0.2	0.0	0.1	0.0	0.1	0.2	0.1	0.1	0.2	0.3	0.2	0.3	•
Advertising	18	0.1	0.0	0.0	0.0	0.1	0.1	0.2	0.1	0.1	0.1	0.1	0.2	•
Other Expenses	19	4.7	7.2	6.5	4.6	4.4	4.9	4.9	3.5	3.8	3.8	2.0	4.5	•
Officers' Compensation	20	0.4	1.1	1.0	0.7	0.5	0.6	0.3	0.2	0.2	0.1	0.1	0.1	•
Operating Margin	21	•	•	•	•	•	•	•	•	•	0.1	0.3	•	•
Operating Margin Before Officers' Comp.	22	•	•	0.4	0.7	0.2	•	•	•	•	0.2	0.3	•	•

Selected Average Balance Sheet ($ in Thousands)

	•	•	•	•	•	•	•	•	•	•	•	•
Net Receivables 23	82	0	10	27	101	497	1768	4033	5666	11571	33154	102467
Inventories 24	126	0	43	104	190	554	1792	3674	5558	19207	24108	108242
Net Property, Plant and Equipment 25	571	0	57	384	1074	3071	7542	15899	34374	83792	184962	721391
Total Assets 26	1114	0	177	728	1844	6582	15965	34458	65433	165190	335175	1301651
Notes and Loans Payable 27	468	0	98	477	1345	3904	6057	11695	24075	52865	66614	278889
All Other Liabilities 28	314	0	35	145	255	1107	4685	12326	18612	47784	122443	509675
Net Worth 29	331	0	44	106	245	1571	5223	10436	22746	64542	146118	513088

Selected Financial Ratios (Times to 1)

	•	•	•	•	•	•	•	•	•	•	•	•
Current Ratio 30	1.4	•	2.1	1.8	1.7	1.5	1.1	1.2	1.1	1.2	0.7	1.3
Quick Ratio 31	0.7	•	0.8	0.9	1.0	0.8	0.6	0.8	0.6	0.6	0.4	0.7
Net Sales to Working Capital 32	65.9	•	43.1	45.0	48.2	37.7	290.3	89.2	320.4	101.9	•	72.0
Coverage Ratio 33	1.7	•	2.3	1.8	0.9	1.4	2.6	1.6	2.0	3.2	12.5	1.1
Total Asset Turnover 34	5.9	•	10.8	6.2	5.8	3.6	6.4	7.4	5.2	4.3	7.4	4.5
Inventory Turnover 35	46.7	•	39.0	38.9	50.3	36.8	50.7	63.7	55.3	33.2	96.5	48.4
Receivables Turnover 36	81.5	•	222.3	146.4	124.1	50.8	72.8	72.2	68.8	62.9	78.4	49.3
Total Liabilities to Net Worth 37	2.4	•	3.1	5.9	6.5	3.2	2.1	2.3	1.9	1.6	1.3	1.5
Current Assets to Working Capital 38	3.7	•	1.9	2.3	2.4	3.1	15.9	5.1	20.8	6.7	•	4.9
Current Liabilities to Working Capital 39	2.7	•	0.9	1.3	1.4	2.1	14.9	4.1	19.8	5.7	•	3.9
Working Capital to Net Sales 40	0.0	•	0.0	0.0	0.0	0.0	0.0	0.0	0.0	0.0	•	0.0
Inventory to Working Capital 41	1.3	•	1.1	1.0	0.8	1.0	5.7	1.3	6.0	2.9	•	1.4
Total Receipts to Cash Flow 42	31.6	34.3	26.9	29.5	34.3	24.1	27.8	36.5	34.7	29.9	29.5	37.3
Cost of Goods to Cash Flow 43	28.3	30.6	23.8	26.5	30.7	21.0	24.8	33.6	31.7	26.7	27.5	33.4
Cash Flow to Total Debt 44	0.3	•	0.5	0.2	0.2	0.2	0.3	0.3	0.2	0.2	0.4	0.2

Selected Financial Factors (in Percentages)

	•		•	•	•	•	•	•	•	•	•	•
Debt Ratio 45	70.3		75.3	85.5	86.7	76.1	67.3	69.7	65.2	60.9	56.4	60.6
Return on Total Assets 46	4.0		5.1	5.6	3.0	4.8	4.9	2.7	3.4	5.2	14.7	2.4
Return on Equity Before Income Taxes 47	5.4		11.6	16.6	•	6.1	9.1	3.4	4.9	9.2	30.9	0.8
Return on Equity After Income Taxes 48	4.3		10.7	16.5	•	5.2	8.2	2.7	4.0	8.0	30.9	•
Profit Margin (Before Income Tax) 49	0.3		0.3	0.4	•	0.4	0.5	0.1	0.3	0.8	1.8	0.1
Profit Margin (After Income Tax) 50	0.2		0.2	0.4	•	0.3	0.4	0.1	0.3	0.7	1.8	•

Table II
Corporations with Net Income

GASOLINE STATIONS

MONEY AMOUNTS AND SIZE OF ASSETS IN THOUSANDS OF DOLLARS

Item Description for Accounting Period 7/10 Through 6/11	Total	Zero Assets	Under 500	500 to 1,000	1,000 to 5,000	5,000 to 10,000	10,000 to 25,000	25,000 to 50,000	50,000 to 100,000	100,000 to 250,000	250,000 to 500,000	500,000 to 2,500,000	2,500,000 and over
Number of Enterprises 1	25583	1171	17112	4159	2690	225	119	56	•	14	•	7	0
Revenues ($ in Thousands)													
Net Sales 2	188254391	374960	33182802	18693973	27125861	5237069	13888486	14877544	•	10939723	•	43645777	0
Interest 3	38382	0	694	18	1936	491	612	3154	•	193	•	29949	0
Rents 4	80126	0	9298	6928	7176	8949	10169	7892	•	3847	•	18388	0
Royalties 5	7710	0	0	0	0	216	0	1	•	0	•	7494	0
Other Portfolio Income 6	145124	46400	26811	93	16001	27537	5718	10469	•	4596	•	3350	0
Other Receipts 7	1382809	28138	302704	69116	71647	63062	123767	53001	•	80486	•	331187	0
Total Receipts 8	189908542	449498	33522309	18770128	27222621	5337324	14028752	14952061	•	11028845	•	44036145	0
Average Total Receipts 9	7423	384	1959	4513	10120	23721	117889	267001	•	787775	•	6290878	•
Operating Costs/Operating Income (%)													
Cost of Operations 10	89.2	83.9	87.5	89.1	89.7	84.0	88.8	92.0	•	89.7	•	88.2	•
Salaries and Wages 11	3.1	3.5	2.4	2.4	3.3	6.9	3.6	2.6	•	3.8	•	3.6	•
Taxes Paid 12	0.8	2.0	1.2	1.1	1.0	1.2	0.8	0.6	•	0.6	•	0.6	•
Interest Paid 13	0.3	2.6	0.2	0.6	0.5	0.7	0.2	0.2	•	0.3	•	0.4	•
Depreciation 14	1.0	1.2	0.3	0.8	0.7	1.1	1.0	0.8	•	1.2	•	1.7	•
Amortization and Depletion 15	0.1	0.0	0.1	0.2	0.1	0.1	0.0	0.0	•	0.1	•	0.1	•
Pensions and Other Deferred Comp. 16	0.0	•	•	0.0	0.1	0.0	0.0	0.0	•	0.1	•	0.1	•
Employee Benefits 17	0.2	0.0	0.1	0.0	0.1	0.1	0.2	0.1	•	0.3	•	0.3	•
Advertising 18	0.1	•	0.1	0.0	0.1	0.2	0.2	0.1	•	0.1	•	0.2	•
Other Expenses 19	4.4	14.3	6.6	4.5	3.4	5.0	5.0	3.3	•	3.5	•	4.5	•
Officers' Compensation 20	0.5	4.3	1.0	0.8	0.7	0.8	0.3	0.2	•	0.2	•	0.1	•
Operating Margin 21	0.3	•	0.5	0.5	0.7	•	•	0.0	•	0.2	•	0.3	•
Operating Margin Before Officers' Comp. 22	0.8	•	1.6	1.3	1.3	0.7	0.1	0.2	•	0.3	•	0.3	•

Selected Average Balance Sheet ($ in Thousands)

Line Item												
Net Receivables 23	90	0	12	31	93	218	1934	4296	•	12384	•	104995
Inventories 24	137	0	41	85	168	659	2146	3387	•	22241	•	121423
Net Property, Plant and Equipment 25	587	0	52	397	975	2961	7726	14879	•	83692	•	665506
Total Assets 26	1166	0	179	728	1724	6447	16939	33513	•	171586	•	1179913
Notes and Loans Payable 27	388	0	80	460	864	3468	5386	9626	•	53776	•	117978
All Other Liabilities 28	353	0	35	107	210	924	5330	12103	•	49023	•	606378
Net Worth 29	425	0	64	161	649	2056	6223	11784	•	68787	•	455557

Selected Financial Ratios (Times to 1)

Line Item												
Current Ratio 30	1.3	•	2.1	2.3	2.1	1.7	1.1	1.3	•	1.2	•	0.9
Quick Ratio 31	0.7	•	0.9	1.2	1.4	0.6	0.6	0.8	•	0.6	•	0.5
Net Sales to Working Capital 32	77.5	•	41.0	36.0	36.6	30.5	194.6	79.6	•	79.1	•	•
Coverage Ratio 33	4.6	4.1	9.5	2.7	3.2	3.6	5.0	3.7	•	3.9	•	4.2
Total Asset Turnover 34	6.3	•	10.8	6.2	5.9	3.6	6.9	7.9	•	4.6	•	5.3
Inventory Turnover 35	47.9	•	41.6	47.1	53.7	29.7	48.3	72.2	•	31.5	•	45.3
Receivables Turnover 36	84.2	•	249.2	132.7	131.0	123.5	77.1	74.8	•	64.1	•	48.9
Total Liabilities to Net Worth 37	1.7	•	1.8	3.5	1.7	2.1	1.7	1.8	•	1.5	•	1.6
Current Assets to Working Capital 38	4.0	•	1.9	1.8	1.9	2.5	10.6	4.4	•	5.2	•	•
Current Liabilities to Working Capital 39	3.0	•	0.9	0.8	0.9	1.5	9.6	3.4	•	4.2	•	•
Working Capital to Net Sales 40	0.0	•	0.0	0.0	0.0	0.0	0.0	0.0	•	0.0	•	•
Inventory to Working Capital 41	1.5	•	1.0	0.8	0.5	1.0	3.8	1.2	•	2.3	•	•
Total Receipts to Cash Flow 42	24.7	8.8	19.0	24.9	29.5	17.3	24.8	33.4	•	30.7	•	24.0
Cost of Goods to Cash Flow 43	22.0	7.3	16.7	22.2	26.5	14.6	22.1	30.8	•	27.5	•	21.1
Cash Flow to Total Debt 44	0.4	•	0.9	0.3	0.3	0.3	0.4	0.4	•	0.2	•	0.4

Selected Financial Factors (in Percentages)

Line Item												
Debt Ratio 45	63.6	•	64.1	77.9	62.4	68.1	63.3	64.8	•	59.9	•	61.4
Return on Total Assets 46	9.5	•	18.7	9.3	8.6	9.1	7.6	5.8	•	6.0	•	7.9
Return on Equity Before Income Taxes 47	20.4	•	46.7	26.6	15.8	20.7	16.6	12.1	•	11.1	•	15.7
Return on Equity After Income Taxes 48	18.9	•	45.6	26.5	15.6	19.5	15.5	11.3	•	9.8	•	12.6
Profit Margin (Before Income Tax) 49	1.2	8.0	1.6	1.0	1.0	1.8	0.9	0.5	•	1.0	•	1.1
Profit Margin (After Income Tax) 50	1.1	8.0	1.5	0.9	1.0	1.7	0.8	0.5	•	0.9	•	0.9

Table I
Corporations with and without Net Income

CLOTHING AND CLOTHING ACCESSORIES STORES

MONEY AMOUNTS AND SIZE OF ASSETS IN THOUSANDS OF DOLLARS

Item Description for Accounting Period 7/10 Through 6/11	Total	Zero Assets	Under 500	500 to 1,000	1,000 to 5,000	5,000 to 10,000	10,000 to 25,000	25,000 to 50,000	50,000 to 100,000	100,000 to 250,000	250,000 to 500,000	500,000 to 2,500,000	2,500,000 and over
Number of Enterprises 1	52664	12244	32569	4462	2784	290	163	39	30	19	22	32	9
Revenues ($ in Thousands)													
Net Sales 2	185651870	4671739	11311294	5069368	10486863	3114765	4103113	2863514	4518650	5838945	14419052	54252355	65002213
Interest 3	575146	24904	1013	2072	4866	1021	16614	1157	436	846	14151	81589	426476
Rents 4	109504	11	614	179	4318	0	8476	2812	56	2829	14401	42501	33307
Royalties 5	572029	5807	0	0	0	0	5687	0	171	17	72873	244758	242715
Other Portfolio Income 6	780743	3093	4109	3841	31506	446	392	3454	3298	491	5229	58076	666813
Other Receipts 7	2225898	24618	81024	75812	117646	28455	57856	17999	49552	78625	260140	566575	867591
Total Receipts 8	189915190	4730172	11398054	5151272	10645199	3144687	4192138	2888936	4572163	5921753	14785846	55245854	67239115
Average Total Receipts 9	3606	386	350	1154	3824	10844	25719	74075	152405	311671	672084	1726433	7471013
Operating Costs/Operating Income (%)													
Cost of Operations 10	52.8	53.1	52.9	60.7	60.2	57.4	57.6	58.3	55.0	48.9	53.2	50.1	52.7
Salaries and Wages 11	14.2	20.3	9.2	11.5	10.7	13.1	13.9	16.1	15.0	17.0	15.1	14.9	14.2
Taxes Paid 12	2.3	2.8	2.4	2.3	2.1	1.9	3.2	3.4	2.3	2.4	2.2	2.4	2.1
Interest Paid 13	0.8	0.7	0.6	0.5	0.7	0.7	0.6	0.5	1.0	1.3	0.4	0.8	1.0
Depreciation 14	2.7	2.4	0.7	0.8	0.8	1.2	1.8	1.8	2.3	3.4	3.3	3.5	2.8
Amortization and Depletion 15	0.2	0.0	0.1	0.0	0.2	0.1	0.2	0.1	0.4	0.2	0.1	0.3	0.3
Pensions and Other Deferred Comp. 16	0.3	0.2	0.2	0.1	0.2	0.2	0.1	0.2	0.1	0.1	0.0	0.2	0.4
Employee Benefits 17	1.2	0.9	0.4	0.7	0.5	0.5	0.8	0.9	1.2	1.3	1.2	1.6	1.3
Advertising 18	2.2	1.1	2.4	3.2	2.2	2.7	2.3	4.0	2.8	1.6	1.7	2.8	1.6
Other Expenses 19	19.0	26.5	25.9	15.4	16.1	21.3	20.0	18.6	19.5	24.5	21.9	20.5	15.3
Officers' Compensation 20	1.5	3.1	6.1	5.9	4.1	1.2	1.6	1.2	0.8	0.6	0.5	0.6	0.8
Operating Margin 21	2.8	•	•	•	2.3	•	•	•	•	•	0.4	2.2	7.3
Operating Margin Before Officers' Comp. 22	4.3	•	5.3	4.7	6.5	0.9	•	•	0.6	•	0.9	2.8	8.2

Selected Average Balance Sheet ($ in Thousands)

Net Receivables **23**	157	0	3	40	76	884	1285	3180	4001	15485	11131	49838	548253
Inventories **24**	563	0	77	401	963	2857	6035	15864	28178	63189	86196	279712	813944
Net Property, Plant and Equipment **25**	467	0	9	43	270	649	2873	5172	15269	40540	100597	286437	1098738
Total Assets **26**	2060	0	125	673	1889	6200	15397	36993	72003	165069	343289	1062699	4836153
Notes and Loans Payable **27**	480	0	77	221	572	1725	3152	9179	13235	63230	19659	173534	1252693
All Other Liabilities **28**	743	0	41	124	523	2100	6530	14064	41211	71645	122824	378836	1795623
Net Worth **29**	836	0	8	328	795	2375	5714	13750	17556	30194	200805	510329	1787837

Selected Financial Ratios (Times to 1)

Current Ratio **30**	1.8	•	2.3	3.8	2.5	1.8	1.6	1.9	1.3	1.8	2.1	2.0	1.6
Quick Ratio **31**	0.7	•	0.7	0.8	0.7	0.5	0.5	0.6	0.3	0.6	0.9	0.7	0.8
Net Sales to Working Capital **32**	6.7	•	5.9	2.7	4.4	4.6	6.2	5.2	15.5	7.3	6.4	6.2	8.7
Coverage Ratio **33**	7.4	•	0.9	1.8	6.8	1.9	1.2	•	2.2	1.0	8.0	6.0	12.0
Total Asset Turnover **34**	1.7	•	2.8	1.7	2.0	1.7	1.6	2.0	2.1	1.9	1.9	1.6	1.5
Inventory Turnover **35**	3.3	•	2.4	1.7	2.4	2.2	2.4	2.7	2.9	2.4	4.0	3.0	4.7
Receivables Turnover **36**	23.4	•	90.9	34.2	55.3	20.6	21.9	18.2	43.9	22.5	79.5	21.6	16.5
Total Liabilities to Net Worth **37**	1.5	•	15.4	1.1	1.4	1.6	1.7	1.7	3.1	4.5	0.7	1.1	1.7
Current Assets to Working Capital **38**	2.2	•	1.8	1.4	1.7	2.3	2.7	2.1	4.6	2.3	1.9	2.0	2.8
Current Liabilities to Working Capital **39**	1.2	•	0.8	0.4	0.7	1.3	1.7	1.1	3.6	1.3	0.9	1.0	1.8
Working Capital to Net Sales **40**	0.1	•	0.2	0.4	0.2	0.2	0.2	0.2	0.1	0.1	0.2	0.2	0.1
Inventory to Working Capital **41**	1.1	•	1.2	1.0	1.1	1.4	1.6	1.1	3.1	1.3	0.9	1.0	1.1
Total Receipts to Cash Flow **42**	6.8	28.5	6.7	11.0	8.0	8.6	9.2	17.7	9.8	9.1	7.9	7.6	5.2
Cost of Goods to Cash Flow **43**	3.6	15.1	3.6	6.7	4.8	5.0	5.3	10.3	5.4	4.4	4.2	3.8	2.7
Cash Flow to Total Debt **44**	0.4	•	0.4	0.3	0.4	0.3	0.3	0.2	0.3	0.3	0.6	0.4	0.5

Selected Financial Factors (in Percentages)

Debt Ratio **45**	59.4	•	93.9	51.3	57.9	61.7	62.9	62.8	75.6	81.7	41.5	52.0	63.0
Return on Total Assets **46**	10.6	•	1.5	1.5	9.0	2.4	1.1	•	4.3	2.4	6.6	8.0	18.3
Return on Equity Before Income Taxes **47**	22.6	•	•	1.4	18.3	3.0	0.5	•	9.5	9.8	9.8	14.0	45.4
Return on Equity After Income Taxes **48**	14.1	•	0.8	0.8	16.9	1.6	•	•	7.1	5.7	5.7	8.3	29.9
Profit Margin (Before Income Tax) **49**	5.3	•	0.4	0.4	3.9	0.7	0.1	•	1.1	3.0	3.0	4.2	11.2
Profit Margin (After Income Tax) **50**	3.3	•	0.2	0.2	3.6	0.3	•	•	0.8	1.7	1.7	2.5	7.4

Table II
Corporations with Net Income

CLOTHING AND CLOTHING ACCESSORIES STORES

MONEY AMOUNTS AND SIZE OF ASSETS IN THOUSANDS OF DOLLARS

Item Description for Accounting Period 7/10 Through 6/11	Total	Zero Assets	Under 500	500 to 1,000	1,000 to 5,000	5,000 to 10,000	10,000 to 25,000	25,000 to 50,000	50,000 to 100,000	100,000 to 250,000	250,000 to 500,000	500,000 to 2,500,000	2,500,000 and over
Number of Enterprises 1	28624	5412	17251	3372	2153	236	97	27	20	•	16	25	•
Revenues ($ in Thousands)													
Net Sales 2	154685543	1355794	7261913	4013037	8802088	2414891	2504712	2096234	3236401	•	10166943	44839450	•
Interest 3	493399	139	950	1647	2948	911	15881	1053	233	•	3593	39327	•
Rents 4	73326	0	614	104	4318	0	949	2812	56	•	214	30686	•
Royalties 5	407223	4280	0	0	0	0	0	0	171	•	24554	136960	•
Other Portfolio Income 6	767326	946	5	3262	31289	446	11	2531	3263	•	2715	56047	•
Other Receipts 7	1858690	-16378	54227	72169	104896	10434	82745	10698	39698	•	122240	440204	•
Total Receipts 8	158285507	1344781	7317709	4090219	8945539	2426682	2604298	2113328	3279822	•	10320259	45542674	•
Average Total Receipts 9	5530	248	424	1213	4155	10283	26848	78271	163991	•	645016	1821707	•
Operating Costs/Operating Income (%)													
Cost of Operations 10	52.3	41.4	50.7	59.4	61.2	64.5	54.7	53.8	55.7	•	52.6	49.3	•
Salaries and Wages 11	13.7	12.8	8.2	10.0	9.7	10.1	13.5	15.2	14.5	•	14.3	14.7	•
Taxes Paid 12	2.2	2.8	2.2	2.3	2.0	1.6	3.0	4.1	1.7	•	2.2	2.4	•
Interest Paid 13	0.7	0.5	0.4	0.6	0.6	0.5	0.4	0.5	1.0	•	0.3	0.6	•
Depreciation 14	2.7	2.7	0.6	0.7	0.7	0.7	1.4	1.3	2.0	•	3.4	3.6	•
Amortization and Depletion 15	0.2	0.0	0.1	0.0	0.1	0.0	0.3	0.1	0.4	•	0.1	0.2	•
Pensions and Other Deferred Comp. 16	0.3	•	0.2	0.1	0.2	0.3	0.2	0.3	0.1	•	0.0	0.2	•
Employee Benefits 17	1.1	0.8	0.1	0.7	0.5	0.3	0.6	0.9	1.1	•	1.0	1.1	•
Advertising 18	2.0	0.8	1.6	1.9	2.0	3.2	2.6	3.7	2.6	•	1.7	2.5	•
Other Expenses 19	17.8	25.1	24.3	15.7	15.7	14.2	18.3	16.9	18.1	•	18.9	20.2	•
Officers' Compensation 20	1.3	4.8	5.5	6.2	3.5	1.3	1.7	1.1	0.7	•	0.5	0.6	•
Operating Margin 21	5.6	8.4	6.0	2.4	4.0	3.3	3.3	2.1	2.2	•	5.0	4.4	•
Operating Margin Before Officers' Comp. 22	6.9	13.2	11.5	8.6	7.4	4.6	5.0	3.2	2.9	•	5.5	5.0	•

Selected Average Balance Sheet ($ in Thousands)

Item											
Net Receivables 23	239	0	3	48	77	936	1499	4011	2511	11138	50532
Inventories 24	767	0	81	384	861	2771	5637	15356	25562	88029	244140
Net Property, Plant and Equipment 25	735	0	8	42	273	477	2775	4455	13533	89900	316143
Total Assets 26	3149	0	141	680	1928	6327	15270	36971	72285	344582	1125761
Notes and Loans Payable 27	632	0	43	204	517	1874	2814	4245	11881	17983	153550
All Other Liabilities 28	1083	0	40	128	534	1294	5167	14467	33424	103632	376946
Net Worth 29	1434	0	57	348	878	3158	7289	18258	26980	222967	595265

Selected Financial Ratios (Times to 1)

Item											
Current Ratio 30	1.9	•	2.6	3.5	2.4	2.6	1.9	2.1	1.6	2.5	2.0
Quick Ratio 31	0.8	•	0.9	0.7	0.7	0.6	0.6	0.5	0.4	1.1	0.8
Net Sales to Working Capital 32	6.6	•	5.6	2.9	4.8	3.0	5.0	4.9	9.4	4.9	6.0
Coverage Ratio 33	12.2	17.0	19.9	8.8	10.1	8.0	17.4	6.3	4.8	27.1	10.8
Total Asset Turnover 34	1.7	•	3.0	1.7	2.1	1.6	1.7	2.1	2.2	1.8	1.6
Inventory Turnover 35	3.7	•	2.6	1.8	2.9	2.4	2.5	2.7	3.5	3.8	3.6
Receivables Turnover 36	25.6	•	82.7	32.5	70.0	19.2	20.6	25.1	77.7	78.7	31.5
Total Liabilities to Net Worth 37	1.2	•	1.5	1.0	1.2	1.0	1.1	1.0	1.7	0.5	0.9
Current Assets to Working Capital 38	2.1	•	1.6	1.4	1.7	1.6	2.1	1.9	2.6	1.7	2.0
Current Liabilities to Working Capital 39	1.1	•	0.6	0.4	0.7	0.6	1.1	0.9	1.6	0.7	1.0
Working Capital to Net Sales 40	0.2	•	0.2	0.3	0.2	0.3	0.2	0.2	0.2	0.2	0.2
Inventory to Working Capital 41	1.0	•	1.0	1.0	1.0	1.0	1.3	1.2	1.8	0.8	0.9
Total Receipts to Cash Flow 42	5.9	5.1	4.9	7.7	7.2	7.8	5.3	9.0	7.9	6.5	6.7
Cost of Goods to Cash Flow 43	3.1	2.1	2.5	4.6	4.4	5.0	2.9	4.8	4.4	3.4	3.3
Cash Flow to Total Debt 44	0.5	•	1.0	0.5	0.5	0.4	0.6	0.5	0.5	0.8	0.5

Selected Financial Factors (in Percentages)

Item											
Debt Ratio 45	54.5	•	59.2	48.8	54.5	50.1	52.3	50.6	62.7	35.3	47.1
Return on Total Assets 46	15.3	•	21.3	8.5	13.1	7.1	13.0	6.9	10.6	12.7	10.7
Return on Equity Before Income Taxes 47	30.8	•	49.7	14.8	26.0	12.4	25.7	11.7	22.5	18.8	18.4
Return on Equity After Income Taxes 48	21.8	•	49.1	14.1	24.5	11.1	23.5	9.1	20.1	13.8	12.2
Profit Margin (Before Income Tax) 49	8.2	7.6	6.8	4.3	5.6	3.8	7.3	2.8	3.7	6.6	6.1
Profit Margin (After Income Tax) 50	5.8	6.1	6.7	4.1	5.3	3.4	6.6	2.1	3.3	4.8	4.0

Table I
Corporations with and without Net Income

SPORTING GOODS, HOBBY, BOOK, AND MUSIC STORES

MONEY AMOUNTS AND SIZE OF ASSETS IN THOUSANDS OF DOLLARS

Item Description for Accounting Period 7/10 Through 6/11	Total	Zero Assets	Under 500	500 to 1,000	1,000 to 5,000	5,000 to 10,000	10,000 to 25,000	25,000 to 50,000	50,000 to 100,000	100,000 to 250,000	250,000 to 500,000	500,000 to 2,500,000	2,500,000 and over
Number of Enterprises **1**	26561	3421	19278	1796	1705	256	50	12	8	12	8	12	4
Revenues ($ in Thousands)													
Net Sales **2**	79736800	765110	6346191	2378013	6309801	2848185	1004403	555859	1292484	4255852	4542003	24759597	24675303
Interest **3**	314303	17	1397	1503	4603	2223	1428	185	56	9255	666	4786	288183
Rents **4**	43237	0	3172	0	3296	237	3135	0	0	2687	106	5480	25122
Royalties **5**	91810	0	0	32	3296	0	0	0	0	8183	5684	9930	67982
Other Portfolio Income **6**	58948	544	4887	31	1211	3928	1617	0	118	96	3491	22130	20895
Other Receipts **7**	1460358	94937	94914	3208	161408	18799	4590	5284	21660	54227	53196	355868	592268
Total Receipts **8**	81705456	860608	6450561	2382787	6480319	2873372	1015173	561328	1314318	4334300	4605146	25157791	25669753
Average Total Receipts **9**	3076	252	335	1327	3801	11224	20303	46777	164290	361192	575643	2096483	6417438
Operating Costs/Operating Income (%)													
Cost of Operations **10**	60.4	70.7	59.8	61.5	57.9	68.7	65.5	64.0	57.0	60.6	61.4	56.0	63.8
Salaries and Wages **11**	12.4	10.2	8.9	11.9	15.0	10.1	13.0	8.7	14.4	13.7	13.4	13.4	11.7
Taxes Paid **12**	2.3	2.1	3.0	2.0	2.4	2.7	1.9	1.6	2.7	1.8	2.0	2.4	2.0
Interest Paid **13**	2.0	0.2	0.8	1.1	0.9	0.4	0.6	1.0	1.9	1.0	1.1	2.7	2.4
Depreciation **14**	2.1	0.4	0.9	0.5	1.7	0.5	0.8	3.5	1.8	2.1	2.2	2.6	2.6
Amortization and Depletion **15**	0.2	0.0	0.0	0.3	0.1	0.1	0.2	0.8	0.3	0.5	0.4	0.3	0.2
Pensions and Other Deferred Comp. **16**	0.2	0.0	0.0	0.2	0.2	0.2	0.3	0.0	0.1	0.1	0.1	0.1	0.2
Employee Benefits **17**	0.8	0.3	0.6	0.9	0.8	0.4	0.7	1.0	1.3	1.1	0.4	0.7	0.9
Advertising **18**	2.6	1.4	1.7	1.7	1.8	1.8	1.9	4.9	2.0	3.1	2.7	2.8	2.8
Other Expenses **19**	16.7	16.5	20.6	16.6	14.7	14.5	14.0	13.5	18.6	17.4	14.7	17.1	16.5
Officers' Compensation **20**	1.4	1.0	5.2	3.8	4.6	1.1	2.4	1.3	0.5	0.7	0.6	0.4	0.6
Operating Margin **21**	•	•	•	•	•	•	•	•	•	•	0.9	1.4	•
Operating Margin Before Officers' Comp. **22**	0.4	3.6	•	3.2	4.5	0.6	1.0	1.0	•	•	1.5	1.8	1.8

Selected Average Balance Sheet ($ in Thousands)

Net Receivables 23	153	0	4	49	78	491	875	1649	15650	5030	18543	31986	717484
Inventories 24	668	0	74	524	949	3186	4744	13561	37440	84611	142187	644033	1182982
Net Property, Plant and Equipment 25	421	0	21	94	313	466	1308	6152	12508	35331	62921	280949	1353440
Total Assets 26	1782	0	123	728	1884	7222	13448	31094	75137	160063	353446	1143341	4619088
Notes and Loans Payable 27	740	0	88	419	452	1159	1087	10586	37565	47252	84582	556191	1935025
All Other Liabilities 28	710	0	35	125	589	1694	5256	6253	37381	72768	137099	537948	1866055
Net Worth 29	331	0	-1	184	844	4368	7105	14255	191	40043	131765	49201	818008

Selected Financial Ratios (Times to 1)

Current Ratio 30	1.7	•	2.3	3.1	2.3	2.5	1.4	2.5	1.5	1.8	1.4	1.5	1.5
Quick Ratio 31	0.5	•	0.5	0.8	0.7	0.9	0.5	0.8	0.5	0.3	0.3	0.3	0.7
Net Sales to Working Capital 32	7.3	•	6.1	3.5	4.7	3.9	10.3	3.9	8.5	7.1	9.0	9.5	8.0
Coverage Ratio 33	1.8	60.4	1.2	0.7	3.9	2.0	0.4	1.7	1.6	0.6	3.1	2.1	1.3
Total Asset Turnover 34	1.7	•	2.7	1.8	2.0	1.5	1.5	1.5	2.2	2.2	1.6	1.8	1.3
Inventory Turnover 35	2.7	•	2.6	1.6	2.3	2.4	2.8	2.2	2.5	2.5	2.5	1.8	3.3
Receivables Turnover 36	24.4	•	81.5	25.7	36.1	28.3	13.1	24.3	10.4	25.8	33.1	28.8	17.2
Total Liabilities to Net Worth 37	4.4	•	•	3.0	1.2	0.7	0.9	1.2	392.6	3.0	1.7	22.2	4.6
Current Assets to Working Capital 38	2.5	•	1.8	1.5	1.8	1.7	3.6	1.7	3.2	2.2	3.4	2.8	3.1
Current Liabilities to Working Capital 39	1.5	•	0.8	0.5	0.8	0.7	2.6	0.7	2.2	1.2	2.4	1.8	2.1
Working Capital to Net Sales 40	0.1	•	0.2	0.3	0.2	0.3	0.1	0.3	0.1	0.1	0.1	0.1	0.1
Inventory to Working Capital 41	1.6	•	1.3	1.1	1.2	1.0	2.0	1.1	2.0	1.8	2.4	2.0	1.5
Total Receipts to Cash Flow 42	9.7	5.5	8.4	10.3	8.8	12.4	11.1	8.9	9.6	12.6	9.3	9.3	10.2
Cost of Goods to Cash Flow 43	5.8	3.9	5.0	6.3	5.1	8.5	7.3	5.7	5.5	7.6	5.7	5.2	6.5
Cash Flow to Total Debt 44	0.2	•	0.3	0.2	0.4	0.3	0.3	0.3	0.2	0.2	0.3	0.2	0.2

Selected Financial Factors (in Percentages)

Debt Ratio 45	81.4	•	100.9	74.7	55.2	39.5	47.2	54.2	99.7	75.0	62.7	95.7	82.3
Return on Total Assets 46	5.9	•	2.4	1.4	6.9	1.3	0.3	2.4	6.6	1.3	5.6	10.3	4.2
Return on Equity Before Income Taxes 47	14.3	•	•	•	11.4	1.1	•	2.2	997.1	•	10.1	124.8	5.0
Return on Equity After Income Taxes 48	10.1	•	•	•	10.9	0.8	•	0.6	990.8	•	4.8	97.4	0.9
Profit Margin (Before Income Tax) 49	1.6	9.8	0.1	•	2.6	0.4	•	0.7	1.2	•	2.4	3.0	0.7
Profit Margin (After Income Tax) 50	1.1	9.8	0.1	•	2.5	0.3	•	0.2	1.2	•	1.1	2.3	0.1

Table II
Corporations with Net Income

SPORTING GOODS, HOBBY, BOOK, AND MUSIC STORES

MONEY AMOUNTS AND SIZE OF ASSETS IN THOUSANDS OF DOLLARS

Item Description for Accounting Period 7/10 Through 6/11	Total	Zero Assets	Under 500	500 to 1,000	1,000 to 5,000	5,000 to 10,000	10,000 to 25,000	25,000 to 50,000	50,000 to 100,000	100,000 to 250,000	250,000 to 500,000	500,000 to 2,500,000	2,500,000 and over
Number of Enterprises 1	11935	992	8527	948	1197	197	43	5	•	5	5	7	•
Revenues ($ in Thousands)													
Net Sales 2	55559977	532199	3374815	1319667	4922300	2041680	773537	210855	•	1821455	3357946	18422316	•
Interest 3	307082	0	207	1049	3568	2120	1389	185	•	9230	62	1507	•
Rents 4	28265	0	2163	0	3291	237	0	0	•	327	106	1829	•
Royalties 5	85272	0	0	32	0	0	0	0	•	8131	0	9318	•
Other Portfolio Income 6	37043	544	4857	25	412	3463	1617	0	•	0	3489	1623	•
Other Receipts 7	760188	95438	24376	4890	157869	11372	964	3477	•	35367	37994	162507	•
Total Receipts 8	56777827	628181	3406418	1325663	5087440	2058872	777507	214517	•	1874510	3399597	18599100	•
Average Total Receipts 9	4757	633	399	1398	4250	10451	18082	42903	•	374902	679919	2657014	•
Operating Costs/Operating Income (%)													
Cost of Operations 10	59.3	76.8	59.2	63.4	58.1	67.6	63.1	55.7	•	63.7	63.0	53.5	•
Salaries and Wages 11	12.4	10.4	8.4	9.9	15.5	10.2	12.3	8.9	•	13.2	12.8	13.9	•
Taxes Paid 12	2.3	1.8	2.7	1.8	2.1	3.1	1.8	1.9	•	2.0	1.8	2.7	•
Interest Paid 13	2.0	0.1	0.6	0.7	0.8	0.4	0.4	2.1	•	1.4	0.9	2.4	•
Depreciation 14	2.2	0.4	0.7	0.5	1.4	0.5	0.6	1.9	•	1.9	2.2	2.7	•
Amortization and Depletion 15	0.1	•	0.1	0.1	0.1	0.1	0.3	2.0	•	0.6	0.3	0.2	•
Pensions and Other Deferred Comp. 16	0.2	0.0	0.0	0.3	0.1	0.0	0.4	0.1	•	0.1	0.1	0.1	•
Employee Benefits 17	0.7	0.4	0.5	0.8	0.8	0.3	0.6	0.6	•	1.2	0.2	0.6	•
Advertising 18	2.8	1.2	1.6	1.8	1.5	2.0	1.9	1.4	•	1.9	2.5	3.1	•
Other Expenses 19	14.9	9.7	17.2	13.5	13.4	13.4	13.1	21.9	•	13.6	11.8	16.1	•
Officers' Compensation 20	1.2	0.9	3.8	4.2	4.6	0.9	2.6	1.5	•	1.1	0.6	0.4	•
Operating Margin 21	1.7	5.1	3.0	1.7	1.6	3.1	5.7	2.1	•	•	3.8	4.2	•
Operating Margin Before Officers' Comp. 22	2.9	9.0	7.3	6.2	2.5	5.7	7.3	3.6	•	0.5	4.4	4.7	•

Selected Average Balance Sheet ($ in Thousands)

Net Receivables 23	287	0	2	49	93	447	651	2310	•	6657	19815	34492
Inventories 24	1001	0	83	513	1016	2783	4089	21207	•	109162	147941	814458
Net Property, Plant and Equipment 25	718	0	9	63	281	265	985	2774	•	30428	80216	384995
Total Assets 26	2760	0	132	718	1934	7594	12084	38187	•	161268	351357	1327492
Notes and Loans Payable 27	1251	0	50	205	402	1322	892	16599	•	40366	84445	771517
All Other Liabilities 28	943	0	45	172	625	1552	4147	7106	•	69566	138707	512807
Net Worth 29	567	0	36	341	908	4721	7045	14482	•	51336	128205	43169

Selected Financial Ratios (Times to 1)

Current Ratio 30	1.9	•	2.5	2.8	2.6	2.7	1.8	3.5	•	2.3	1.7	1.7
Quick Ratio 31	0.7	•	0.6	0.7	0.9	1.0	0.7	1.1	•	0.2	0.3	0.4
Net Sales to Working Capital 32	6.0	•	5.8	3.5	4.4	3.6	6.0	2.3	•	5.1	7.7	8.8
Coverage Ratio 33	3.0	163.8	11.7	6.3	7.7	7.0	10.9	2.8	•	2.7	6.4	3.2
Total Asset Turnover 34	1.7	•	3.0	1.9	2.1	1.4	1.5	1.1	•	2.3	1.9	2.0
Inventory Turnover 35	2.8	•	2.8	1.7	2.3	2.5	2.8	1.1	•	2.1	2.9	1.7
Receivables Turnover 36	21.1	•	95.6	37.3	37.8	26.7	16.4	12.8	•	27.0	32.8	25.3
Total Liabilities to Net Worth 37	3.9	•	2.6	1.1	1.1	0.6	0.7	1.6	•	2.1	1.7	29.8
Current Assets to Working Capital 38	2.1	•	1.7	1.5	1.6	1.6	2.2	1.4	•	1.8	2.5	2.5
Current Liabilities to Working Capital 39	1.1	•	0.7	0.5	0.6	0.6	1.2	0.4	•	0.8	1.5	1.5
Working Capital to Net Sales 40	0.2	•	0.2	0.3	0.2	0.3	0.2	0.4	•	0.2	0.1	0.1
Inventory to Working Capital 41	1.2	•	1.3	1.1	1.0	1.0	1.3	0.9	•	1.6	1.9	1.8
Total Receipts to Cash Flow 42	8.4	4.4	6.5	8.0	7.7	10.5	8.4	4.1	•	11.7	8.1	7.9
Cost of Goods to Cash Flow 43	5.0	3.4	3.9	5.1	4.5	7.1	5.3	2.3	•	7.4	5.1	4.3
Cash Flow to Total Debt 44	0.3	•	0.6	0.5	0.5	0.3	0.4	0.4	•	0.3	0.4	0.3

Selected Financial Factors (in Percentages)

Debt Ratio 45	79.5	•	72.4	52.5	53.1	37.8	41.7	62.1	•	68.2	63.5	96.7
Return on Total Assets 46	10.2	•	20.0	8.1	12.3	3.8	5.8	6.5	•	8.4	11.3	15.0
Return on Equity Before Income Taxes 47	33.1	•	66.2	14.3	22.7	5.3	9.1	11.1	•	16.6	26.2	317.5
Return on Equity After Income Taxes 48	27.7	•	66.1	13.5	22.0	5.0	8.8	7.3	•	16.2	17.4	264.0
Profit Margin (Before Income Tax) 49	4.0	16.5	6.1	3.5	5.0	2.4	3.5	3.8	•	2.3	5.0	5.2
Profit Margin (After Income Tax) 50	3.4	16.5	6.1	3.3	4.8	2.3	3.5	2.5	•	2.3	3.3	4.3

GENERAL MERCHANDISE STORES

Table I

Corporations with and without Net Income

MONEY AMOUNTS AND SIZE OF ASSETS IN THOUSANDS OF DOLLARS

Item Description for Accounting Period 7/10 Through 6/11	Total	Zero Assets	Under 500	500 to 1,000	1,000 to 5,000	5,000 to 10,000	10,000 to 25,000	25,000 to 50,000	50,000 to 100,000	100,000 to 250,000	250,000 to 500,000	500,000 to 2,500,000	2,500,000 and over
Number of Enterprises **1**	11602	2159	8307	766	237	52	23	14	7	12	5	9	13
Revenues ($ in Thousands)													
Net Sales **2**	631239712	151646	3247900	1994420	1755126	1546780	858198	1143958	629754	4189066	3649279	36238802	575834784
Interest **3**	1288619	0	1835	1119	1990	87	1076	41	9619	800	4343	7752	1259958
Rents **4**	958203	0	0	0	0	525	0	7	7501	4348	701	18609	926510
Royalties **5**	2064973	0	0	0	26	0	0	0	0	0	13093	94377	1957478
Other Portfolio Income **6**	961595	0	243	116	728	0	1144	94	3	7679	1446	8765	941376
Other Receipts **7**	15931447	500895	14409	64458	13839	2659	3266	4515	13205	108679	16873	611969	14576680
Total Receipts **8**	652444549	652541	3264387	2060113	1771709	1550051	863684	1148615	660082	4310572	3685735	36980274	595496786
Average Total Receipts **9**	56236	302	393	2689	7476	29809	37551	82044	94297	359214	737147	4108919	45807445
Operating Costs/Operating Income (%)													
Cost of Operations **10**	73.2	64.8	60.1	85.6	62.9	60.2	70.1	71.0	60.6	65.0	68.3	70.8	73.6
Salaries and Wages **11**	11.0	15.9	7.0	4.1	11.3	17.9	12.1	10.0	17.0	11.8	11.5	10.6	11.1
Taxes Paid **12**	1.8	7.0	2.1	1.1	1.5	1.3	2.0	1.4	2.6	1.9	1.4	2.2	1.8
Interest Paid **13**	0.9	•	0.5	0.3	0.5	0.1	0.1	0.3	0.5	0.5	0.7	0.5	0.9
Depreciation **14**	2.4	0.9	0.9	0.3	0.5	0.5	0.5	0.8	1.8	2.2	1.7	2.3	2.4
Amortization and Depletion **15**	0.0	0.8	0.1	0.1	0.0	0.0	•	0.1	0.1	0.0	0.2	0.1	0.0
Pensions and Other Deferred Comp. **16**	0.6	•	0.1	0.0	0.7	0.0	0.1	0.1	0.4	0.2	0.0	0.3	0.6
Employee Benefits **17**	0.9	0.0	0.2	0.2	0.7	2.1	0.6	0.6	1.5	1.3	1.8	1.0	0.9
Advertising **18**	1.4	0.4	2.3	0.2	1.3	2.5	0.6	1.2	1.3	1.7	0.8	1.0	1.4
Other Expenses **19**	6.9	37.7	19.6	6.6	17.3	16.7	11.0	8.7	15.0	13.2	10.6	8.9	6.5
Officers' Compensation **20**	0.1	9.0	5.3	2.2	2.5	0.1	0.5	0.4	0.3	1.1	0.8	0.6	0.1
Operating Margin **21**	0.8	•	1.9	•	0.6	•	5.3	•	•	1.1	2.1	1.7	0.7
Operating Margin Before Officers' Comp. **22**	0.9	•	7.2	1.4	3.1	•	5.7	•	•	2.2	2.9	2.3	0.7

Selected Average Balance Sheet ($ in Thousands)

Net Receivables 23	1179	0	2	14	233	926	1947	442	14850	9957	36846	38128	981218
Inventories 24	5992	0	55	171	1003	3628	2109	21978	20948	55065	118379	579474	4734075
Net Property, Plant and Equipment 25	12632	0	27	117	221	1304	1009	3671	10100	42764	67053	481130	10830730
Total Assets 26	31236	0	137	621	2224	6046	13408	34205	62395	182879	345788	1517523	26241933
Notes and Loans Payable 27	8845	0	72	376	519	706	2987	9715	7864	52915	37123	220672	7577622
All Other Liabilities 28	10214	0	39	49	626	3879	69532	15440	15641	54044	114335	518716	8459404
Net Worth 29	12178	0	26	196	1079	1461	-59111	9050	38889	75919	194331	778136	10204907

Selected Financial Ratios (Times to 1)

Current Ratio 30	1.1	•	2.0	2.7	2.8	1.2	0.1	1.9	2.9	1.2	1.8	1.9	1.0
Quick Ratio 31	0.3	•	0.6	0.9	1.1	0.3	0.1	0.3	1.2	0.3	0.5	0.4	0.3
Net Sales to Working Capital 32	72.6	•	8.4	11.5	7.0	40.5	•	6.1	2.9	20.4	9.1	10.4	123.0
Coverage Ratio 33	5.8	•	5.8	8.7	3.9	•	35.7	18.6	9.2	9.1	5.4	8.2	5.6
Total Asset Turnover 34	1.7	•	2.9	4.2	3.3	4.9	2.8	2.4	1.4	1.9	2.1	2.7	1.7
Inventory Turnover 35	6.6	•	4.3	13.0	4.6	4.9	12.4	2.6	2.6	4.1	4.2	4.9	6.9
Receivables Turnover 36	43.7	•	437.5	85.2	36.3	29.5	31.1	109.0	7.1	34.8	20.6	118.1	42.4
Total Liabilities to Net Worth 37	1.6	•	4.3	2.2	1.1	3.1	•	2.8	0.6	1.4	0.8	1.0	1.6
Current Assets to Working Capital 38	13.0	•	2.0	1.6	1.6	6.3	•	2.1	1.5	5.0	2.3	2.2	21.5
Current Liabilities to Working Capital 39	12.0	•	1.0	0.6	0.6	5.3	•	1.1	0.5	4.0	1.3	1.2	20.5
Working Capital to Net Sales 40	0.0	•	0.1	0.1	0.1	0.0	•	0.2	0.3	0.0	0.1	0.1	0.0
Inventory to Working Capital 41	8.2	•	1.3	1.0	1.0	4.6	•	1.6	0.7	3.6	1.5	1.5	13.5
Total Receipts to Cash Flow 42	11.2	0.3	7.8	15.6	7.5	9.5	9.1	9.7	8.3	8.1	12.0	11.7	11.3
Cost of Goods to Cash Flow 43	8.2	0.2	4.7	13.3	4.7	5.7	6.4	6.9	5.0	5.3	8.2	8.3	8.3
Cash Flow to Total Debt 44	0.3	•	0.5	0.4	0.9	0.7	0.1	0.3	0.5	0.4	0.4	0.5	0.2

Selected Financial Factors (in Percentages)

Debt Ratio 45	61.0	•	81.1	68.5	51.5	75.8	540.9	73.5	37.7	58.5	43.8	48.7	61.1
Return on Total Assets 46	9.1	•	8.3	11.9	7.0	•	8.4	14.5	6.1	8.5	8.0	11.3	8.9
Return on Equity Before Income Taxes 47	19.3	•	36.2	33.5	10.7	•	•	51.9	8.8	18.3	11.7	19.4	18.8
Return on Equity After Income Taxes 48	12.8	•	33.6	32.0	9.4	•	•	50.8	8.5	14.2	9.3	12.6	12.3
Profit Margin (Before Income Tax) 49	4.3	293.8	2.4	2.5	1.6	•	•	5.7	3.8	4.0	3.1	3.7	4.3
Profit Margin (After Income Tax) 50	2.9	293.8	2.2	2.4	1.4	•	2.9	5.6	3.7	3.1	2.5	2.4	2.8

Table II

Corporations with Net Income

GENERAL MERCHANDISE STORES

MONEY AMOUNTS AND SIZE OF ASSETS IN THOUSANDS OF DOLLARS

Item Description for Accounting Period 7/10 Through 6/11	Total	Zero Assets	Under 500	500 to 1,000	1,000 to 5,000	5,000 to 10,000	10,000 to 25,000	25,000 to 50,000	50,000 to 100,000	100,000 to 250,000	250,000 to 500,000	500,000 to 2,500,000	2,500,000 and over
Number of Enterprises 1	5248	230	4104	608	193	45	15	•	•	•	•	•	13
Revenues ($ in Thousands)													
Net Sales 2	625340845	24807	2115992	1588238	1415030	1525684	858198	•	•	•	•	•	575834784
Interest 3	1273921	0	1833	319	243	3	0	•	•	•	•	•	1259958
Rents 4	956924	0	0	0	0	0	0	•	•	•	•	•	926510
Royalties 5	2064973	0	0	0	26	0	0	•	•	•	•	•	1957478
Other Portfolio Income 6	958832	0	243	110	548	0	1	•	•	•	•	•	941376
Other Receipts 7	15812226	500895	9955	60043	11449	257	2572	•	•	•	•	•	14576680
Total Receipts 8	646407721	525702	2128023	1648710	1427296	1525944	860771	•	•	•	•	•	595496786
Average Total Receipts 9	123172	2286	519	2712	7395	33910	57385	•	•	•	•	•	45807445
Operating Costs/Operating Income (%)													
Cost of Operations 10	73.3	36.6	55.7	86.6	62.7	59.9	70.1	•	•	•	•	•	73.6
Salaries and Wages 11	11.0	10.8	9.1	3.0	10.9	17.9	11.9	•	•	•	•	•	11.1
Taxes Paid 12	1.8	12.0	1.9	1.0	1.5	1.2	2.0	•	•	•	•	•	1.8
Interest Paid 13	0.9	•	0.6	0.3	0.5	•	0.1	•	•	•	•	•	0.9
Depreciation 14	2.4	0.5	0.6	0.3	0.3	0.2	0.5	•	•	•	•	•	2.4
Amortization and Depletion 15	0.0	•	0.0	0.1	0.0	•	•	•	•	•	•	•	0.0
Pensions and Other Deferred Comp. 16	0.6	•	0.1	0.0	0.8	0.0	0.1	•	•	•	•	•	0.6
Employee Benefits 17	0.9	•	0.1	0.1	0.8	2.1	0.4	•	•	•	•	•	0.9
Advertising 18	1.4	•	3.2	0.2	1.4	2.5	0.6	•	•	•	•	•	1.4
Other Expenses 19	6.7	37.5	15.7	6.1	16.5	15.7	9.9	•	•	•	•	•	6.5
Officers' Compensation 20	0.1	13.2	5.2	2.3	2.4	0.0	0.5	•	•	•	•	•	0.1
Operating Margin 21	0.8	•	7.7	0.1	2.1	0.4	3.9	•	•	•	•	•	0.7
Operating Margin Before Officers' Comp. 22	0.9	2.7	12.9	2.3	4.6	0.5	4.4	•	•	•	•	•	0.7

Selected Average Balance Sheet ($ in Thousands)

Net Receivables 23	2593	0	2	0	225	1061	2946	•	•	•	981218
Inventories 24	12162	0	44	150	900	3693	2752	•	•	•	4855843
Net Property, Plant and Equipment 25	27718	0	36	126	113	684	1542	•	•	•	10830730
Total Assets 26	68305	0	147	610	1861	5613	12792	•	•	•	26241933
Notes and Loans Payable 27	19266	0	59	340	502	0	320	•	•	•	7577622
All Other Liabilities 28	22073	0	53	19	561	1576	4875	•	•	•	8459404
Net Worth 29	26966	0	35	251	798	4037	7596	•	•	•	10204907

Selected Financial Ratios (Times to 1)

Current Ratio 30	1.1	•	1.6	2.9	2.9	3.2	2.3	•	•	•	1.0
Quick Ratio 31	0.3	•	0.8	1.0	1.0	0.8	1.4	•	•	•	0.3
Net Sales to Working Capital 32	68.6	•	13.9	13.1	7.1	10.0	9.0	•	•	•	123.0
Coverage Ratio 33	6.0	•	15.9	15.6	6.6	•	56.4	•	•	•	5.6
Total Asset Turnover 34	1.7	•	3.5	4.3	3.9	6.0	4.5	•	•	•	1.7
Inventory Turnover 35	7.2	•	6.5	15.0	5.1	5.5	14.6	•	•	•	6.7
Receivables Turnover 36	44.4	•	629.5	119.0	34.4	29.6	31.7	•	•	•	•
Total Liabilities to Net Worth 37	1.5	•	3.2	1.4	1.3	0.4	0.7	•	•	•	1.6
Current Assets to Working Capital 38	12.1	•	2.7	1.5	1.5	1.5	1.7	•	•	•	21.5
Current Liabilities to Working Capital 39	11.1	•	1.7	0.5	0.5	0.5	0.7	•	•	•	20.5
Working Capital to Net Sales 40	0.0	•	0.1	0.1	0.1	0.1	0.0	•	•	•	0.0
Inventory to Working Capital 41	7.7	•	1.4	1.0	1.0	1.1	0.6	•	•	•	13.5
Total Receipts to Cash Flow 42	11.1	0.0	5.9	13.6	6.7	8.4	9.0	•	•	•	11.3
Cost of Goods to Cash Flow 43	8.2	0.0	3.3	11.8	4.2	5.0	6.3	•	•	•	8.3
Cash Flow to Total Debt 44	0.3	•	0.8	0.5	1.0	2.6	1.2	•	•	•	0.2

Selected Financial Factors (in Percentages)

Debt Ratio 45	60.5	•	76.3	58.9	57.1	28.1	40.6	•	•	•	61.1
Return on Total Assets 46	9.2	•	31.0	17.7	13.9	2.7	19.1	•	•	•	8.9
Return on Equity Before Income Taxes 47	19.4	•	122.8	40.4	27.5	3.7	31.6	•	•	•	18.8
Return on Equity After Income Taxes 48	13.0	•	119.0	38.9	25.4	3.7	31.6	•	•	•	12.3
Profit Margin (Before Income Tax) 49	4.4	2008.6	8.3	3.9	3.0	0.4	4.2	•	•	•	4.3
Profit Margin (After Income Tax) 50	2.9	2008.6	8.0	2.8	2.8	0.4	4.2	•	•	•	2.8

Table I

Corporations with and without Net Income

MISCELLANEOUS STORE RETAILERS

MONEY AMOUNTS AND SIZE OF ASSETS IN THOUSANDS OF DOLLARS

Item Description for Accounting Period 7/10 Through 6/11	Total	Zero Assets	Under 500	500 to 1,000	1,000 to 5,000	5,000 to 10,000	10,000 to 25,000	25,000 to 50,000	50,000 to 100,000	100,000 to 250,000	250,000 to 500,000	500,000 to 2,500,000	2,500,000 and over
Number of Enterprises **1**	79129	14771	57495	3094	3265	218	187	41	24	17	6	8	3
Revenues ($ in Thousands)													
Net Sales **2**	100162279	1027803	21483405	6189050	11410087	2078091	5484944	2091754	2402767	3602482	2579039	11321014	30491844
Interest **3**	230826	153	1695	1996	19708	6229	2151	1750	1337	1711	6016	21281	166798
Rents **4**	42740	854	4452	1770	2955	3976	8899	1240	1	1036	4160	2328	11069
Royalties **5**	226057	0	8022	0	1291	55473	2799	7418	27000	0	1096	49740	73218
Other Portfolio Income **6**	252837	28843	12924	836	8039	7274	22780	773	2677	12730	13	51547	104398
Other Receipts **7**	1586107	49067	122622	30112	196293	32834	71734	55329	18050	36532	12418	909156	51962
Total Receipts **8**	102500846	1106720	21633120	6223764	11638373	2183877	5593307	2158264	2451832	3654491	2602742	12355066	30899289
Average Total Receipts **9**	1295	75	376	2012	3565	10018	29911	52641	102160	214970	433790	1544383	10299763
Operating Costs/Operating Income (%)													
Cost of Operations **10**	61.9	59.1	54.4	66.6	66.4	69.1	68.5	66.7	64.4	57.2	55.2	50.6	67.7
Salaries and Wages **11**	11.8	9.1	11.8	9.6	10.3	11.8	11.7	10.2	8.7	13.7	13.5	17.9	10.6
Taxes Paid **12**	2.2	2.7	2.6	2.1	2.7	1.6	1.8	1.6	1.3	2.1	2.4	3.2	1.4
Interest Paid **13**	1.3	2.1	0.7	0.9	1.0	1.5	0.7	1.1	1.1	2.7	2.5	2.7	1.1
Depreciation **14**	1.7	1.7	1.1	0.9	1.0	1.1	1.4	1.2	2.4	2.6	2.5	3.3	1.8
Amortization and Depletion **15**	0.2	0.6	0.2	0.1	0.1	0.4	0.1	0.4	0.2	0.2	0.6	0.4	0.3
Pensions and Other Deferred Comp. **16**	0.1	0.0	0.1	0.0	0.3	0.1	0.2	0.4	0.2	0.4	0.0	0.1	0.0
Employee Benefits **17**	1.0	0.2	0.7	0.7	0.5	0.3	0.6	1.0	1.0	1.4	1.9	1.6	1.2
Advertising **18**	1.8	2.4	1.3	1.0	0.6	1.6	0.6	0.7	5.4	1.7	3.0	2.2	2.5
Other Expenses **19**	16.2	36.1	21.8	14.1	13.1	15.8	10.6	12.9	13.3	16.5	18.3	20.4	12.8
Officers' Compensation **20**	2.2	3.7	5.5	3.9	3.5	2.3	2.1	1.2	1.4	1.1	0.6	0.8	0.1
Operating Margin **21**	•	•	•	0.0	0.4	•	1.7	2.6	0.6	0.5	•	•	0.6
Operating Margin Before Officers' Comp. **22**	2.0	•	5.3	3.9	3.9	•	3.8	3.8	2.1	1.5	0.2	•	0.7

Selected Average Balance Sheet ($ in Thousands)

	1	2	3	4	5	6	7	8	9	10	11	12	13
Net Receivables 23	115	0	9	88	304	1413	1816	6672	11685	33235	16453	124156	1493334
Inventories 24	193	0	42	327	788	4571	5870	11756	19226	41867	118624	203952	1051420
Net Property, Plant and Equipment 25	116	0	17	103	343	717	2714	4944	9486	38404	39355	273859	867597
Total Assets 26	708	0	100	693	2131	6880	14569	35643	65371	162969	312882	1264573	6397345
Notes and Loans Payable 27	269	0	67	333	575	3025	5386	13728	16039	89415	174272	593614	1520472
All Other Liabilities 28	231	0	27	249	482	1943	3828	10751	23526	68444	69602	370807	2562174
Net Worth 29	208	0	5	110	1074	1912	5354	11164	25806	5110	69009	300152	2314699

Selected Financial Ratios (Times to 1)

	1	2	3	4	5	6	7	8	9	10	11	12	13
Current Ratio 30	1.9	•	2.0	1.6	2.3	2.1	1.9	2.2	1.9	1.5	1.3	1.3	1.4
Quick Ratio 31	0.9	•	0.7	0.7	0.9	0.7	0.7	0.8	0.7	0.6	0.6	0.6	0.6
Net Sales to Working Capital 32	6.4	•	10.5	10.6	4.2	3.2	4.3	5.2	4.3	8.2	8.7	13.1	9.8
Coverage Ratio 33	2.7	•	1.8	1.7	3.4	0.7	6.3	6.0	6.3	3.3	1.7	1.2	3.5
Total Asset Turnover 34	1.8	•	3.7	2.9	1.6	1.4	1.4	2.0	1.4	1.5	1.3	1.4	1.1
Inventory Turnover 35	4.1	•	4.8	4.1	2.9	1.4	2.9	3.4	2.9	3.4	2.9	2.0	3.5
Receivables Turnover 36	12.0	•	40.8	19.8	12.0	6.0	13.6	13.6	7.6	7.8	8.8	12.8	13.9
Total Liabilities to Net Worth 37	2.4	•	17.5	5.3	1.0	2.6	1.9	1.7	2.2	1.5	30.9	3.5	3.2
Current Assets to Working Capital 38	2.2	•	2.0	2.7	1.8	1.9	1.8	1.8	2.2	3.1	4.3	4.9	3.6
Current Liabilities to Working Capital 39	1.2	•	1.0	1.7	0.8	0.9	0.8	0.8	1.2	2.1	3.3	3.9	2.6
Working Capital to Net Sales 40	0.2	•	0.1	0.1	0.2	0.3	0.2	0.2	0.2	0.1	0.1	0.1	0.1
Inventory to Working Capital 41	0.9	•	1.2	1.5	1.0	1.1	1.1	1.1	0.9	1.5	1.8	2.1	1.7
Total Receipts to Cash Flow 42	8.5	8.0	7.4	11.2	8.5	9.2	11.0	11.0	7.6	8.0	8.3	11.5	5.9
Cost of Goods to Cash Flow 43	5.3	4.7	4.0	7.5	5.6	6.4	7.5	5.1	5.1	4.8	6.4	3.0	7.0
Cash Flow to Total Debt 44	0.3	•	0.5	0.3	0.4	0.2	0.3	0.3	0.3	0.3	0.2	0.2	0.2

Selected Financial Factors (in Percentages)

	1	2	3	4	5	6	7	8	9	10	11	12	13
Debt Ratio 45	70.6	•	94.6	84.1	49.6	72.2	63.2	68.7	60.5	96.9	77.9	76.3	63.8
Return on Total Assets 46	6.2	•	4.7	4.2	5.6	1.4	8.9	10.0	5.8	6.0	4.1	10.5	5.1
Return on Equity Before Income Taxes 47	13.3	•	38.2	10.6	7.8	•	20.2	26.9	10.2	79.0	3.2	31.4	9.4
Return on Equity After Income Taxes 48	9.5	•	36.7	9.2	7.3	•	19.4	25.4	7.2	46.2	•	21.3	5.6
Profit Margin (Before Income Tax) 49	2.2	•	0.6	0.6	2.4	•	3.7	5.9	2.6	1.9	0.5	6.7	2.1
Profit Margin (After Income Tax) 50	1.6	•	0.5	0.5	2.2	•	3.5	5.6	1.9	1.1	•	4.5	1.3

Table II
Corporations with Net Income

MISCELLANEOUS STORE RETAILERS

MONEY AMOUNTS AND SIZE OF ASSETS IN THOUSANDS OF DOLLARS

Item Description for Accounting Period 7/10 Through 6/11	Total	Zero Assets	Under 500	500 to 1,000	1,000 to 5,000	5,000 to 10,000	10,000 to 25,000	25,000 to 50,000	50,000 to 100,000	100,000 to 250,000	250,000 to 500,000	500,000 to 2,500,000	2,500,000 and over
Number of Enterprises **1**	38766	4478	30317	1641	2024	105	128	32	16	12	•	•	0
Revenues ($ in Thousands)													
Net Sales **2**	68285335	443667	14535642	3492182	8545103	842337	4989633	1503590	1435399	3006734	•	•	0
Interest **3**	66078	129	668	1584	17221	4494	2151	252	1130	1574	•	•	0
Rents **4**	25870	854	822	289	2857	1039	5831	222	1	954	•	•	0
Royalties **5**	207190	0	0	0	0	55473	2799	0	27000	0	•	•	0
Other Portfolio Income **6**	233796	15168	12851	676	6655	7274	20445	733	2088	12356	•	•	0
Other Receipts **7**	1412883	27696	100015	20761	156440	14553	60050	49518	20103	31316	•	•	0
Total Receipts **8**	70231152	487514	14649998	3515492	8728276	925170	5080909	1554315	1485721	3052934	•	•	0
Average Total Receipts **9**	1812	109	483	2142	4312	8811	39695	48572	92858	254411	•	•	•
Operating Costs/Operating Income (%)													
Cost of Operations **10**	59.5	50.6	49.4	68.6	68.5	71.9	68.9	69.9	64.0	60.8	•	•	•
Salaries and Wages **11**	12.1	10.1	11.8	7.8	8.5	11.1	11.3	8.2	10.2	14.0	•	•	•
Taxes Paid **12**	2.2	2.5	2.7	1.6	2.5	1.5	1.7	1.5	1.7	2.0	•	•	•
Interest Paid **13**	1.1	1.3	0.6	0.6	0.9	0.8	0.5	0.6	1.0	1.2	•	•	•
Depreciation **14**	1.8	1.0	1.0	0.7	0.7	2.0	1.3	1.0	3.7	2.3	•	•	•
Amortization and Depletion **15**	0.2	0.4	0.1	0.0	0.1	0.1	0.0	0.0	0.2	0.1	•	•	•
Pensions and Other Deferred Comp. **16**	0.1	0.0	0.1	0.0	0.3	0.3	0.2	0.1	0.4	0.1	•	•	•
Employee Benefits **17**	1.0	0.1	0.8	0.6	0.4	0.1	0.5	0.7	1.2	1.1	•	•	•
Advertising **18**	1.5	2.0	1.2	0.6	0.6	1.5	0.5	0.6	2.6	1.5	•	•	•
Other Expenses **19**	15.7	23.9	21.6	12.2	11.8	13.3	9.9	10.1	10.9	13.9	•	•	•
Officers' Compensation **20**	2.4	5.8	5.8	4.8	3.0	3.2	2.1	1.4	1.9	1.0	•	•	•
Operating Margin **21**	2.4	2.2	4.9	2.3	2.8	•	3.1	5.8	2.3	2.1	•	•	•
Operating Margin Before Officers' Comp. **22**	4.7	8.0	10.7	7.1	5.8	•	5.2	7.2	4.1	3.1	•	•	•

Selected Average Balance Sheet ($ in Thousands)

Net Receivables 23	131	0	12	117	389	1247	2201	6591	11742	23228
Inventories 24	237	0	42	241	739	5328	5386	10869	19413	48762
Net Property, Plant and Equipment 25	159	0	21	71	261	847	2436	4387	11760	38225
Total Assets 26	913	0	118	661	2209	7082	14933	34420	62763	169294
Notes and Loans Payable 27	307	0	56	190	477	2997	4091	8791	15500	60786
All Other Liabilities 28	231	0	27	266	518	1872	4760	9942	23347	51073
Net Worth 29	375	0	35	204	1214	2214	6082	15687	23916	57435

Selected Financial Ratios (Times to 1)

Current Ratio 30	2.0	•	2.3	1.8	2.3	2.6	2.1	2.7	1.5	1.5
Quick Ratio 31	0.9	•	1.0	1.0	1.0	0.7	0.8	1.1	0.7	0.6
Net Sales to Working Capital 32	6.7	•	10.2	9.3	4.7	2.2	6.9	2.7	7.2	6.5
Coverage Ratio 33	5.7	10.6	10.3	5.7	6.7	5.9	10.5	15.7	6.6	4.1
Total Asset Turnover 34	1.9	•	4.1	3.2	1.9	1.1	2.6	1.4	1.4	1.5
Inventory Turnover 35	4.4	•	5.6	6.1	3.9	1.1	5.0	3.0	3.0	3.1
Receivables Turnover 36	15.1	•	44.8	15.1	11.3	4.6	16.2	•	7.9	13.8
Total Liabilities to Net Worth 37	1.4	•	2.4	2.2	0.8	2.2	1.5	1.2	1.6	1.9
Current Assets to Working Capital 38	2.0	•	1.7	2.2	1.8	1.6	1.9	1.6	3.1	2.8
Current Liabilities to Working Capital 39	1.0	•	0.7	1.2	0.8	0.6	0.9	0.6	2.1	1.8
Working Capital to Net Sales 40	0.2	•	0.1	0.1	0.2	0.4	0.1	0.4	0.1	0.2
Inventory to Working Capital 41	0.9	•	0.9	0.9	0.9	0.9	1.0	0.6	1.3	1.4
Total Receipts to Cash Flow 42	6.8	4.1	5.3	9.3	7.4	6.7	10.1	6.6	8.4	8.1
Cost of Goods to Cash Flow 43	4.0	2.1	2.6	6.4	5.1	4.8	7.0	4.6	5.4	5.0
Cash Flow to Total Debt 44	0.5	•	1.1	0.5	0.6	0.2	0.4	0.4	0.3	0.3

Selected Financial Factors (in Percentages)

Debt Ratio 45	58.9	•	70.4	69.1	45.0	68.7	59.3	54.4	61.9	66.1
Return on Total Assets 46	12.6	•	25.6	11.7	11.1	5.4	14.2	13.4	9.7	7.0
Return on Equity Before Income Taxes 47	25.3	•	78.1	31.2	17.1	14.3	31.6	27.6	21.6	15.7
Return on Equity After Income Taxes 48	21.0	•	77.7	29.8	16.5	13.1	30.6	26.2	16.7	11.5
Profit Margin (Before Income Tax) 49	5.4	12.1	5.7	3.0	4.9	3.9	4.9	9.2	5.8	3.6
Profit Margin (After Income Tax) 50	4.5	10.7	5.7	2.9	4.7	3.6	4.8	8.8	4.4	2.6

Table I
Corporations with and without Net Income

NONSTORE RETAILERS

MONEY AMOUNTS AND SIZE OF ASSETS IN THOUSANDS OF DOLLARS

Item Description for Accounting Period 7/10 Through 6/11	Total	Zero Assets	Under 500	500 to 1,000	1,000 to 5,000	5,000 to 10,000	10,000 to 25,000	25,000 to 50,000	50,000 to 100,000	100,000 to 250,000	250,000 to 500,000	500,000 to 2,500,000	2,500,000 and over
Number of Enterprises **1**	51149	12584	33203	2466	2233	277	179	75	56	34	17	13	11
Revenues ($ in Thousands)													
Net Sales **2**	190904059	2769692	15127572	9468339	20333888	4206134	8695867	5321474	9177138	10178613	13123601	17862190	74639550
Interest **3**	1033886	323	3285	3418	4891	3397	3041	1276	12841	26260	142053	83439	749661
Rents **4**	125134	0	3608	8309	3200	3407	1985	1511	8612	3792	5142	31120	54449
Royalties **5**	1679633	0	0	0	0	711	0	0	4530	245	0	81586	1592562
Other Portfolio Income **6**	1628453	237217	124233	3521	4327	22282	8783	25763	22803	6890	61955	361669	749006
Other Receipts **7**	2359121	-417747	15206	72718	90523	81559	94773	47295	117116	96923	217082	318729	1624949
Total Receipts **8**	197730286	2589485	15273904	9556305	20436829	4317490	8804449	5397319	9343040	10312723	13549833	18738733	79410177
Average Total Receipts **9**	3866	206	460	3875	9152	15587	49187	71964	166840	303315	797049	1441441	7219107
Operating Costs/Operating Income (%)													
Cost of Operations **10**	70.3	54.8	66.2	74.6	74.0	66.0	75.3	61.1	67.6	64.6	77.3	74.7	69.3
Salaries and Wages **11**	8.0	8.0	5.8	6.0	6.7	11.3	6.6	10.0	8.2	9.3	6.1	7.3	9.2
Taxes Paid **12**	1.0	1.7	1.2	1.8	1.2	1.8	1.2	1.5	1.1	1.1	0.9	0.9	0.8
Interest Paid **13**	1.6	1.8	0.4	0.2	0.5	1.0	0.4	0.3	0.9	0.7	1.6	1.0	2.8
Depreciation **14**	1.5	0.8	0.8	0.7	0.9	1.9	1.3	1.9	1.5	1.2	0.9	1.3	2.2
Amortization and Depletion **15**	0.4	1.4	0.2	0.0	0.2	0.3	0.2	0.4	0.6	0.6	0.3	0.5	0.6
Pensions and Other Deferred Comp. **16**	0.2	0.1	0.2	0.2	0.1	0.2	0.2	0.2	0.1	0.2	0.1	0.9	0.1
Employee Benefits **17**	0.8	0.2	0.4	0.6	0.5	0.9	0.6	1.2	0.9	0.7	0.7	0.8	0.9
Advertising **18**	2.4	4.5	1.2	3.1	2.0	1.6	3.5	3.5	2.4	3.8	3.0	2.8	2.1
Other Expenses **19**	13.6	27.2	16.7	8.5	9.9	15.2	10.0	16.2	15.9	14.6	9.5	11.5	15.0
Officers' Compensation **20**	1.4	3.3	5.2	3.8	1.9	3.3	1.1	1.4	0.6	1.5	0.6	0.3	0.5
Operating Margin **21**	•	•	1.4	0.4	2.1	•	•	2.5	0.2	1.8	•	•	•
Operating Margin Before Officers' Comp. **22**	0.2	•	6.6	4.2	4.0	•	0.6	3.9	0.9	3.3	•	•	•

Selected Average Balance Sheet ($ in Thousands)

Net Receivables 23	468	0	10	146	684	1524	2737	6974	14463	32967	74026	255256	1253380
Inventories 24	527	0	20	92	408	1532	2638	5654	11165	30454	58226	91860	1818021
Net Property, Plant and Equipment 25	223	0	11	101	422	1181	3084	4314	10383	12876	25290	68614	575299
Total Assets 26	2735		74	689	2368	7092	15600	33919	69624	150355	371431	1112242	8487196
Notes and Loans Payable 27	694	0	35	106	799	3114	4049	4920	19958	37473	130135	260294	2031430
All Other Liabilities 28	1045	0	24	226	894	2073	6063	13077	24406	54424	114758	412389	3355337
Net Worth 29	997	0	15	357	674	1904	5488	15923	25260	58458	126537	439559	3100429

Selected Financial Ratios (Times to 1)

Current Ratio 30	1.6	•	1.9	2.0	1.4	1.7	1.5	1.6	1.5	1.4	1.9	1.3	1.7
Quick Ratio 31	1.0	•	1.2	1.4	1.0	0.9	0.8	1.0	0.8	0.9	1.1	0.9	1.1
Net Sales to Working Capital 32	7.8	•	16.8	17.6	17.4	7.5	15.4	8.1	11.8	10.8	7.7	10.6	5.0
Coverage Ratio 33	2.8	•	6.4	7.5	6.6	0.1	2.8	13.9	3.5	5.6	2.5	5.0	2.4
Total Asset Turnover 34	1.4	•	6.1	5.6	3.8	2.1	3.1	2.1	2.4	2.0	2.1	1.2	0.8
Inventory Turnover 35	5.0	•	14.8	31.1	16.5	6.5	13.9	7.7	9.9	6.3	10.3	11.2	2.6
Receivables Turnover 36	4.0	•	46.2	24.5	13.3	9.6	18.2	10.2	12.7	9.8	11.9	6.3	1.9
Total Liabilities to Net Worth 37	1.7	•	3.8	0.9	2.5	2.7	1.8	1.1	1.8	1.6	1.9	1.5	1.7
Current Assets to Working Capital 38	2.6	•	2.1	2.0	3.3	2.4	3.2	2.6	2.9	3.4	2.2	4.1	2.4
Current Liabilities to Working Capital 39	1.6	•	1.1	1.0	2.3	1.4	2.2	1.6	1.9	2.4	1.2	3.1	1.4
Working Capital to Net Sales 40	0.1	•	0.1	0.1	0.1	0.1	0.1	0.1	0.1	0.1	0.1	0.1	0.2
Inventory to Working Capital 41	0.5	•	0.7	0.5	0.8	0.8	1.0	0.6	0.9	1.0	0.7	0.7	0.3
Total Receipts to Cash Flow 42	6.9	7.2	6.1	11.9	8.8	10.1	10.7	5.6	6.0	6.2	9.1	8.3	5.9
Cost of Goods to Cash Flow 43	4.9	4.0	4.0	8.8	6.6	6.7	8.1	3.4	4.1	4.0	7.0	6.2	4.1
Cash Flow to Total Debt 44	0.3	1.3	1.0	1.0	0.6	0.3	0.4	0.7	0.6	0.5	0.3	0.2	0.2

Selected Financial Factors (in Percentages)

Debt Ratio 45	63.6	•	79.3	48.2	71.5	73.1	64.8	53.1	63.7	61.1	65.9	60.5	63.5
Return on Total Assets 46	6.1	•	17.4	8.8	11.9	0.3	3.6	8.8	7.0	8.4	8.3	6.2	5.4
Return on Equity Before Income Taxes 47	10.7	•	70.9	14.7	35.4	•	6.6	17.4	13.8	17.8	14.6	12.5	8.6
Return on Equity After Income Taxes 48	8.7	•	70.6	14.1	34.1	•	4.5	15.3	11.5	13.9	10.4	10.7	6.7
Profit Margin (Before Income Tax) 49	2.9	•	2.4	1.4	2.6	•	0.7	3.9	2.1	3.5	2.4	4.0	3.9
Profit Margin (After Income Tax) 50	2.3	•	2.4	1.3	2.5	•	0.5	3.4	1.8	2.7	1.7	3.4	3.1

Table II
Corporations with Net Income

NONSTORE RETAILERS

Money Amounts and Size of Assets in Thousands of Dollars

Item Description for Accounting Period 7/10 Through 6/11	Total	Zero Assets	Under 500	500 to 1,000	1,000 to 5,000	5,000 to 10,000	10,000 to 25,000	25,000 to 50,000	50,000 to 100,000	100,000 to 250,000	250,000 to 500,000	500,000 to 2,500,000	2,500,000 and over
Number of Enterprises 1	24533	4940	15882	1592	1667	193	116	46	39	25	13	•	•
Revenues ($ in Thousands)													
Net Sales 2	157935132	782374	10017287	7213651	16881815	3399243	6984357	3944664	6585719	8363183	11318571	•	•
Interest 3	1015488	28	1216	1353	1806	3120	1834	828	11160	24629	137356	•	•
Rents 4	106515	0	237	8305	1269	2947	1829	589	2064	3673	444	•	•
Royalties 5	1678989	0	0	0	0	67	0	0	4530	245	0	•	•
Other Portfolio Income 6	1394643	20760	124149	3046	2191	21322	8638	19645	21171	1207	61955	•	•
Other Receipts 7	2413343	35050	11329	67271	43368	77375	85347	37809	56689	48513	32182	•	•
Total Receipts 8	164544110	838212	10154218	7293626	16930449	3504074	7082005	4003535	6681333	8441450	11550508	•	•
Average Total Receipts 9	6707	170	639	4581	10156	18156	61052	87033	171316	337658	888501	•	•
Operating Costs/Operating Income (%)													
Cost of Operations 10	70.6	31.3	66.6	79.1	76.4	66.7	78.2	57.9	67.3	63.4	80.7	•	•
Salaries and Wages 11	7.9	6.3	5.7	5.8	6.1	9.6	5.2	10.2	8.0	9.6	4.6	•	•
Taxes Paid 12	1.0	2.2	1.2	1.6	1.0	1.5	1.2	1.6	1.0	1.2	0.7	•	•
Interest Paid 13	1.3	0.4	0.4	0.2	0.3	0.6	0.2	0.3	0.6	0.7	1.0	•	•
Depreciation 14	1.5	0.3	0.7	0.7	0.7	1.6	1.0	1.5	1.2	1.1	0.7	•	•
Amortization and Depletion 15	0.4	0.0	0.3	0.0	0.1	0.2	0.1	0.1	0.3	0.3	0.1	•	•
Pensions and Other Deferred Comp. 16	0.2	0.3	0.2	0.2	0.1	0.1	0.2	0.2	0.1	0.2	0.1	•	•
Employee Benefits 17	0.8	0.1	0.3	0.5	0.5	0.9	0.6	1.3	0.8	0.7	0.5	•	•
Advertising 18	2.3	6.6	0.8	1.2	1.5	1.4	2.9	2.7	2.2	4.1	3.0	•	•
Other Expenses 19	12.9	36.2	13.4	6.2	7.3	10.8	7.3	17.4	14.4	13.8	6.3	•	•
Officers' Compensation 20	1.2	3.8	5.0	2.2	1.8	3.0	1.1	1.4	0.7	1.2	0.6	•	•
Operating Margin 21	0.0	12.5	5.6	2.3	4.1	3.5	1.9	5.3	3.4	3.9	1.7	•	•
Operating Margin Before Officers' Comp. 22	1.2	16.2	10.6	4.5	6.0	6.5	3.1	6.7	4.0	5.1	2.3	•	•

Selected Average Balance Sheet ($ in Thousands)

Net Receivables 23	869	0	16	155	782	1958	3304	6030	14379	35106	82828
Inventories 24	1021	0	28	108	416	2005	2771	6298	13072	32662	59893
Net Property, Plant and Equipment 25	389	0	14	105	356	1394	3079	5391	7830	13067	18179
Total Assets 26	4991	0	110	704	2410	7308	15689	33818	68139	150949	373893
Notes and Loans Payable 27	1087	0	36	84	732	2797	3753	4713	15481	35934	85200
All Other Liabilities 28	1933	0	25	188	875	1742	6965	10463	21388	56389	114383
Net Worth 29	1971	0	49	432	802	2770	4970	18642	31269	58626	174311

Selected Financial Ratios (Times to 1)

Current Ratio 30	1.7	•	2.7	2.6	1.5	1.8	1.3	2.1	1.7	1.4	1.9
Quick Ratio 31	1.1	•	1.8	1.8	1.1	0.9	0.7	1.2	0.9	0.9	1.2
Net Sales to Working Capital 32	7.0	•	12.0	15.7	16.3	7.5	28.1	7.2	9.6	11.4	7.7
Coverage Ratio 33	4.8	56.7	20.2	20.8	13.8	11.2	15.2	21.7	9.6	9.0	5.0
Total Asset Turnover 34	1.3	•	5.7	6.4	4.2	2.4	3.8	2.5	2.5	2.2	2.3
Inventory Turnover 35	4.4	•	15.1	33.3	18.6	5.9	17.0	7.9	8.7	6.5	11.7
Receivables Turnover 36	3.5	•	42.7	26.2	12.9	8.3	18.8	•	12.0	10.3	13.0
Total Liabilities to Net Worth 37	1.5	•	1.2	0.6	2.0	1.6	2.2	0.8	1.2	1.6	1.1
Current Assets to Working Capital 38	2.5	•	1.6	1.6	2.9	2.3	4.6	1.9	2.3	3.3	2.1
Current Liabilities to Working Capital 39	1.5	•	0.6	0.6	1.9	1.3	3.6	0.9	1.3	2.3	1.1
Working Capital to Net Sales 40	0.1	•	0.1	0.1	0.1	0.1	0.0	0.1	0.1	0.1	0.1
Inventory to Working Capital 41	0.4	•	0.5	0.4	0.7	0.9	1.6	0.5	0.8	1.0	0.7
Total Receipts to Cash Flow 42	6.4	1.9	5.6	12.2	9.4	6.7	10.6	4.6	5.5	5.9	10.8
Cost of Goods to Cash Flow 43	4.5	0.6	3.7	9.6	7.2	4.5	8.3	2.6	3.7	3.7	8.7
Cash Flow to Total Debt 44	0.3	•	1.9	1.4	0.7	0.6	0.5	1.2	0.8	0.6	0.4

Selected Financial Factors (in Percentages)

Debt Ratio 45	60.5	•	55.1	38.7	66.7	62.1	68.3	44.9	54.1	61.2	53.4
Return on Total Assets 46	7.9	•	42.2	23.2	20.0	17.3	13.7	18.2	13.7	13.0	11.2
Return on Equity Before Income Taxes 47	15.7	•	89.2	36.0	55.6	41.7	40.5	31.4	26.8	29.7	19.2
Return on Equity After Income Taxes 48	13.6	•	89.0	35.2	54.1	36.7	36.9	28.4	24.1	24.6	15.1
Profit Margin (Before Income Tax) 49	4.8	19.6	7.0	3.4	4.4	6.6	3.3	6.8	5.0	5.2	3.8
Profit Margin (After Income Tax) 50	4.2	18.9	7.0	3.4	4.3	5.8	3.0	6.2	4.5	4.3	3.0

Table I

Corporations with and without Net Income

AIR TRANSPORTATION

MONEY AMOUNTS AND SIZE OF ASSETS IN THOUSANDS OF DOLLARS

Item Description for Accounting Period 7/10 Through 6/11	Total	Zero Assets	Under 500	500 to 1,000	1,000 to 5,000	5,000 to 10,000	10,000 to 25,000	25,000 to 50,000	50,000 to 100,000	100,000 to 250,000	250,000 to 500,000	500,000 to 2,500,000	2,500,000 and over
Number of Enterprises **1**	7951	1420	4894	863	430	96	147	42	16	12	4	16	10
Revenues ($ in Thousands)													
Net Sales **2**	152066037	1822029	953063	362426	1401294	637801	3082763	1225223	1821799	2234240	1975841	13883520	122666036
Interest **3**	254074	250	108	5	4170	387	1454	913	271	290	381	32326	213518
Rents **4**	428744	0	0	1895	1359	0	0	3726	45	95	0	73921	347704
Royalties **5**	125	0	0	0	0	0	0	120	0	0	0	0	6
Other Portfolio Income **6**	581726	31192	14406	1079	85278	2435	12589	4337	11987	7856	1626	182528	226413
Other Receipts **7**	2872058	44176	28405	21261	5708	1244	41365	4850	9557	-54419	12381	113685	2643845
Total Receipts **8**	156202764	1897647	995982	386666	1497809	641867	3138171	1239169	1843659	2188062	1990229	14285980	126097522
Average Total Receipts **9**	19646	1336	204	448	3483	6686	21348	29504	115229	182338	497557	892874	12609752
Operating Costs/Operating Income (%)													
Cost of Operations **10**	27.7	2.6	71.1	19.0	75.6	69.3	68.6	60.6	32.8	42.5	12.1	24.2	26.0
Salaries and Wages **11**	16.9	19.9	2.6	26.1	3.9	5.3	7.3	10.3	17.7	11.7	15.0	14.2	17.9
Taxes Paid **12**	1.9	1.8	2.6	4.7	0.9	1.1	1.4	1.8	2.0	1.3	2.0	2.3	1.9
Interest Paid **13**	2.9	0.7	2.5	1.6	4.2	0.8	1.7	1.5	1.1	1.1	6.8	3.3	3.0
Depreciation **14**	5.3	5.3	5.7	37.5	11.1	8.8	6.3	5.7	3.9	4.4	5.5	7.9	4.9
Amortization and Depletion **15**	0.4	0.1	•	0.2	0.0	0.1	0.1	0.0	0.3	0.4	2.0	0.5	0.4
Pensions and Other Deferred Comp. **16**	1.8	0.9	0.1	0.7	0.0	0.1	0.1	0.2	0.1	0.2	0.2	0.7	2.1
Employee Benefits **17**	2.9	1.7	0.4	1.3	0.0	2.1	0.7	1.4	1.9	1.0	1.2	1.8	3.3
Advertising **18**	0.7	0.0	3.2	0.2	0.2	0.6	0.1	1.0	0.1	0.2	3.4	0.4	0.7
Other Expenses **19**	40.1	66.1	33.9	51.6	20.4	28.7	16.4	18.9	38.6	33.5	60.2	44.9	40.1
Officers' Compensation **20**	0.5	1.8	8.4	16.3	0.8	1.6	2.0	2.1	0.8	0.5	0.5	0.8	0.2
Operating Margin **21**	•	•	•	•	•	•	•	•	0.8	3.4	•	•	•
Operating Margin Before Officers' Comp. **22**	0.8	•	•	•	•	•	•	•	1.7	3.9	•	•	•

Selected Average Balance Sheet ($ in Thousands)

Net Receivables **23**	1034	0	10	75	176	1049	2672	3852	11687	26580	23342	66512
Inventories **24**	379	0	16	51	111	49	228	1096	2403	10276	9988	25535
Net Property, Plant and Equipment **25**	12612	0	38	553	1439	1614	7535	12224	27776	51477	138615	526503
Total Assets **26**	24350	0	79	761	2343	5912	15178	33171	69151	164783	364823	1036613
Notes and Loans Payable **27**	10225	0	166	582	1391	5386	10004	11737	27542	62803	340837	467687
All Other Liabilities **28**	12379	0	18	157	1209	1738	3322	7861	24890	62440	133926	318245
Net Worth **29**	1746	0	-105	22	-4780	3312	1852	13573	16718	39539	-109940	250681

Net Receivables **23**	571591
Inventories **24**	215066
Net Property, Plant and Equipment **25**	8717953
Total Assets **26**	16623333
Notes and Loans Payable **27**	6553042
All Other Liabilities **28**	8974388
Net Worth **29**	1095903

Selected Financial Ratios (Times to 1)

Current Ratio **30**	1.0	•	1.8	1.3	0.4	1.7	1.3	1.4	1.0	1.5	0.8	1.4	1.0
Quick Ratio **31**	0.7	•	1.0	0.7	0.2	1.4	1.0	1.0	0.8	0.7	0.6	1.0	0.7
Net Sales to Working Capital **32**	•	•	10.6	9.3	•	9.5	22.6	9.8	•	6.8	•	9.0	•
Coverage Ratio **33**	1.6	5.3	•	•	•	•	•	•	2.9	2.2	•	1.7	1.8
Total Asset Turnover **34**	0.8	•	2.5	0.6	1.4	1.1	1.4	0.9	1.6	1.1	1.4	0.8	0.7
Inventory Turnover **35**	14.0	•	8.6	1.6	22.2	93.3	63.1	16.1	15.5	7.7	6.0	8.2	14.8
Receivables Turnover **36**	19.9	•	19.6	4.8	7.4	4.4	7.8	7.7	5.6	9.2	12.8	14.2	24.8
Total Liabilities to Net Worth **37**	12.9	•	•	34.3	•	0.8	7.2	1.4	3.1	3.2	•	3.1	14.2
Current Assets to Working Capital **38**	•	•	2.3	4.2	•	2.5	4.6	3.5	•	3.2	•	3.3	•
Current Liabilities to Working Capital **39**	•	•	1.3	3.2	•	1.5	3.6	2.5	•	2.2	•	2.3	•
Working Capital to Net Sales **40**	•	•	0.1	0.1	•	0.1	0.0	0.1	•	0.1	•	0.1	•
Inventory to Working Capital **41**	•	•	0.9	1.5	•	0.1	0.2	0.3	•	0.5	•	0.3	•
Total Receipts to Cash Flow **42**	3.6	2.0	•	•	25.5	•	12.3	8.0	4.3	4.5	3.7	3.4	3.4
Cost of Goods to Cash Flow **43**	1.0	0.1	•	•	19.3	•	8.5	4.8	1.4	1.9	0.5	0.8	0.9
Cash Flow to Total Debt **44**	0.2	•	•	•	0.0	•	0.1	0.2	0.5	0.3	0.3	0.3	0.2

Selected Financial Factors (in Percentages)

Debt Ratio **45**	92.8	•	233.5	97.2	304.0	44.0	87.8	59.1	75.8	76.0	30.1	75.8	93.4
Return on Total Assets **46**	3.6	•	•	•	•	•	•	•	5.1	2.7	•	4.8	4.0
Return on Equity Before Income Taxes **47**	17.9	•	48.5	•	7.0	•	13.8	6.1	•	37.1	•	8.4	27.4
Return on Equity After Income Taxes **48**	15.0	•	48.5	•	7.8	•	6.7	6.1	•	37.2	•	5.4	25.3
Profit Margin (Before Income Tax) **49**	1.6	3.1	•	•	•	•	2.0	1.3	•	1.3	•	2.4	2.4
Profit Margin (After Income Tax) **50**	1.4	2.7	•	•	•	•	1.0	1.3	•	•	•	1.6	2.3

Table II
Corporations with Net Income

AIR TRANSPORTATION

MONEY AMOUNTS AND SIZE OF ASSETS IN THOUSANDS OF DOLLARS

Item Description for Accounting Period 7/10 Through 6/11	Total	Zero Assets	Under 500	500 to 1,000	1,000 to 5,000	5,000 to 10,000	10,000 to 25,000	25,000 to 50,000	50,000 to 100,000	100,000 to 250,000	250,000 to 500,000	500,000 to 2,500,000	2,500,000 and over
Number of Enterprises 1	1706	33	1336	63	177	10	46	10	10	•	0	0	9
Revenues ($ in Thousands)													
Net Sales 2	111855472	1053147	35118	2198	1001474	196888	2107721	288190	1630749	•	0	7916209	•
Interest 3	183128	8	0	0	3968	29	400	165	191	•	0	20808	•
Rents 4	355111	0	0	0	914	0	0	3726	45	•	0	61239	•
Royalties 5	6	0	0	0	0	0	0	0	0	•	0	0	•
Other Portfolio Income 6	403552	31192	14406	0	78593	149	3271	1196	11582	•	0	155240	•
Other Receipts 7	2992920	37559	90	0	5566	4	4032	2155	2095	•	0	96075	•
Total Receipts 8	115790189	1121906	49614	2198	1090515	197070	2115424	295432	1644662	•	0	8249571	•
Average Total Receipts 9	67872	33997	37	35	6161	19707	45987	29543	164466	•	•	916619	•
Operating Costs/Operating Income (%)													
Cost of Operations 10	28.6	4.6	10.6	•	79.2	75.5	68.6	47.7	35.2	•	•	38.3	•
Salaries and Wages 11	16.1	10.0	1.6	•	4.6	6.3	7.3	12.8	14.0	•	•	10.8	•
Taxes Paid 12	1.7	0.7	0.7	•	0.8	1.2	1.4	2.3	1.6	•	•	1.8	•
Interest Paid 13	2.8	0.2	•	•	0.6	0.1	0.7	3.3	1.1	•	•	2.8	•
Depreciation 14	4.6	5.4	3.1	12.9	0.7	0.8	1.7	10.1	2.2	•	•	5.7	•
Amortization and Depletion 15	0.3	0.1	•	•	0.0	•	0.0	0.0	0.1	•	•	0.7	•
Pensions and Other Deferred Comp. 16	2.0	0.1	0.3	•	0.0	0.0	0.1	0.5	0.1	•	•	0.9	•
Employee Benefits 17	2.9	0.3	•	•	0.0	1.3	0.6	3.4	1.6	•	•	2.2	•
Advertising 18	0.6	0.0	•	•	0.1	1.9	0.1	0.2	0.1	•	•	0.3	•
Other Expenses 19	39.4	72.9	19.1	4.8	11.3	6.2	12.2	8.4	39.2	•	•	32.4	•
Officers' Compensation 20	0.4	0.1	8.9	•	0.3	1.8	2.4	4.5	0.8	•	•	0.9	•
Operating Margin 21	0.5	5.6	55.8	82.3	2.5	5.0	4.9	6.8	4.0	•	•	3.1	•
Operating Margin Before Officers' Comp. 22	0.9	5.8	64.7	82.3	2.8	6.8	7.2	11.3	4.8	•	•	4.1	•

Selected Average Balance Sheet ($ in Thousands)

Net Receivables 23	3646	0	10	0	232	3664	5973	3127	13488	•	85534
Inventories 24	569	0	28	0	0	164	324	1628	2154	•	13919
Net Property, Plant and Equipment 25	41573	0	47	740	896	376	6237	18584	16919	•	417953
Total Assets 26	84258	0	80	758	2164	5344	14902	34666	64616	•	869206
Notes and Loans Payable 27	31703	0	207	0	1388	1878	4894	17030	27568	•	262590
All Other Liabilities 28	43039	0	5	20	157	3104	6192	3892	32087	•	304154
Net Worth 29	9516	0	-131	738	619	361	3816	13744	4961	•	302462

Selected Financial Ratios (Times to 1)

Current Ratio 30	1.0	•	6.9	0.9	2.6	1.5	1.2	3.2	1.2	•	1.2
Quick Ratio 31	0.7	•	6.9	0.9	1.2	1.4	1.1	1.0	1.0	•	0.9
Net Sales to Working Capital 32	•	73.4	0.9	•	12.2	11.9	30.0	2.7	24.9	•	19.9
Coverage Ratio 33	2.4	•	•	•	20.4	41.4	8.9	3.8	5.5	•	3.8
Total Asset Turnover 34	0.8	•	0.3	0.0	2.6	3.7	3.1	0.8	2.5	•	1.0
Inventory Turnover 35	32.9	•	0.1	•	•	90.3	97.1	8.4	26.7	•	24.2
Receivables Turnover 36	30.4	•	1.5	•	•	4.2	9.2	4.8	8.9	•	8.9
Total Liabilities to Net Worth 37	7.9	•	•	0.0	2.5	13.8	2.9	1.5	12.0	•	1.9
Current Assets to Working Capital 38	•	•	1.2	•	1.6	2.9	5.5	1.5	6.1	•	6.9
Current Liabilities to Working Capital 39	•	•	0.2	•	0.6	1.9	4.5	0.5	5.1	•	5.9
Working Capital to Net Sales 40	•	•	1.1	•	0.1	0.1	0.0	0.4	0.0	•	0.1
Inventory to Working Capital 41	•	•	•	•	•	0.1	0.4	0.2	0.3	•	0.3
Total Receipts to Cash Flow 42	3.2	1.4	0.9	1.1	4.8	11.3	7.9	6.4	3.8	•	3.8
Cost of Goods to Cash Flow 43	0.9	0.1	0.1	•	3.8	8.5	5.4	3.1	1.3	•	1.4
Cash Flow to Total Debt 44	0.3	•	0.1	1.6	0.8	0.3	0.5	0.2	0.7	•	0.4

Selected Financial Factors (in Percentages)

Debt Ratio 45	88.7	•	263.5	2.6	71.4	93.2	74.4	60.4	92.3	•	65.2
Return on Total Assets 46	5.4	•	31.8	3.8	31.3	19.2	18.1	10.5	14.9	•	10.8
Return on Equity Before Income Taxes 47	27.9	•	•	3.9	104.0	277.8	62.7	19.5	158.9	•	22.8
Return on Equity After Income Taxes 48	25.4	•	•	3.3	89.2	274.5	61.0	18.6	120.3	•	18.4
Profit Margin (Before Income Tax) 49	4.0	12.2	97.1	82.3	11.4	5.1	5.2	9.3	4.8	•	7.9
Profit Margin (After Income Tax) 50	3.7	11.6	97.0	70.0	9.8	5.0	5.1	8.9	3.7	•	6.3

Table I

Corporations with and without Net Income

RAIL TRANSPORTATION

MONEY AMOUNTS AND SIZE OF ASSETS IN THOUSANDS OF DOLLARS

Item Description for Accounting Period 7/10 Through 6/11	Total	Zero Assets	Under 500	500 to 1,000	1,000 to 5,000	5,000 to 10,000	10,000 to 25,000	25,000 to 50,000	50,000 to 100,000	100,000 to 250,000	250,000 to 500,000	500,000 to 2,500,000	2,500,000 and over
Number of Enterprises 1	228	12	101	18	22	14	13	15	9	8	3	5	7
Revenues ($ in Thousands)													
Net Sales 2	46971392	0	0	968	52688	252915	49617	361590	205830	406884	518085	1388781	43734032
Interest 3	188340	0	410	55	63	83	161	367	1115	1300	133	24922	159732
Rents 4	430607	0	31	0	1206	6	48	3610	2141	4433	2797	24970	391364
Royalties 5	57159	0	0	0	5	269	0	0	0	1526	0	0	55360
Other Portfolio Income 6	370504	0	0	0	7509	412	14170	3182	2144	13472	32167	5250	292198
Other Receipts 7	1096736	-6811	0	7883	2196	2698	2361	10256	5775	8918	8087	178995	876379
Total Receipts 8	49114738	-6811	441	8906	63667	256383	66357	379005	217005	436533	561269	1622918	45509065
Average Total Receipts 9	215416	-568	4	495	2894	18313	5104	25267	24112	54567	187090	324584	6501295
Operating Costs/Operating Income (%)													
Cost of Operations 10	14.9	•	•	•	9.2	0.0	21.5	23.5	4.5	31.5	35.1	•	15.0
Salaries and Wages 11	19.3	•	•	•	9.0	7.8	16.0	10.0	16.0	17.7	8.4	25.4	19.4
Taxes Paid 12	5.4	•	•	17.4	4.7	1.8	7.5	4.4	5.7	3.9	2.9	5.6	5.4
Interest Paid 13	5.7	•	•	121.4	0.3	0.8	5.3	1.8	0.8	3.7	14.9	11.6	5.5
Depreciation 14	14.0	•	•	•	16.9	1.2	5.3	7.8	15.7	14.2	11.7	15.6	14.1
Amortization and Depletion 15	0.2	•	•	107.1	•	•	0.1	0.0	0.1	0.1	0.1	0.9	0.1
Pensions and Other Deferred Comp. 16	0.7	•	•	•	•	•	•	0.2	0.9	1.5	0.1	0.3	0.8
Employee Benefits 17	5.7	•	•	•	0.9	1.2	4.2	1.0	3.7	4.3	0.2	7.5	5.8
Advertising 18	0.3	•	•	12.9	0.1	0.1	0.2	0.1	0.1	0.1	0.0	0.0	0.3
Other Expenses 19	27.8	•	•	3313.8	48.3	78.3	28.3	26.6	32.2	32.9	18.6	45.3	26.9
Officers' Compensation 20	0.5	•	•	•	4.8	0.1	1.8	1.9	2.8	1.4	0.6	1.4	0.5
Operating Margin 21	5.5	•	•	•	5.7	8.6	9.8	22.7	17.5	•	7.5	•	6.2
Operating Margin Before Officers' Comp. 22	6.1	•	•	•	10.4	8.8	11.7	24.7	20.3	8.1	•	•	6.6

Selected Average Balance Sheet ($ in Thousands)

Net Receivables 23	20759	0	2	0	95	1062	2648	3213	2379	8558	21794	135589	542875
Inventories 24	4993	0	0	0	0	59	145	672	655	412	12588	609	153654
Net Property, Plant and Equipment 25	505822	0	101	0	1357	2603	2482	17700	40266	103059	247101	656771	15677308
Total Assets 26	632632	0	309	881	2789	6262	13259	34007	66462	136556	408128	1436977	19037382
Notes and Loans Payable 27	138210	0	0	322	173	1494	4708	7188	14181	26278	95093	419543	4084498
All Other Liabilities 28	257022	0	4	1746	66	2833	1999	6301	15376	60866	134362	340618	7953736
Net Worth 29	237400	0	306	-1188	2551	1934	6552	20517	36905	49412	178673	676817	6999148

Selected Financial Ratios (Times to 1)

Current Ratio 30	0.8	•	58.4	0.0	8.1	0.5	2.8	2.8	2.2	1.0	1.0	1.5	0.8
Quick Ratio 31	0.7	•	58.4	0.0	7.2	0.5	2.7	2.4	1.8	0.7	0.7	1.3	0.6
Net Sales to Working Capital 32	•	•	•	•	4.8	•	1.2	3.6	3.1	•	•	4.4	•
Coverage Ratio 33	2.8	•	•	•	81.2	13.5	9.3	15.9	29.9	•	2.1	1.3	2.9
Total Asset Turnover 34	0.3	•	•	0.1	0.9	2.9	0.3	0.7	0.3	0.4	0.4	0.2	0.3
Inventory Turnover 35	6.1	•	•	•	1619.0	0.1	5.7	8.4	1.6	38.9	4.8	•	6.1
Receivables Turnover 36	9.0	•	•	•	4.4	23.4	1.4	4.2	8.3	7.1	4.9	2.2	10.3
Total Liabilities to Net Worth 37	1.7	•	0.0	•	0.1	2.2	1.0	0.7	0.8	1.8	1.3	1.1	1.7
Current Assets to Working Capital 38	•	•	1.0	•	1.1	•	1.6	1.6	1.8	•	•	3.1	•
Current Liabilities to Working Capital 39	•	•	0.0	•	0.1	•	0.6	0.6	0.8	•	•	2.1	•
Working Capital to Net Sales 40	•	•	•	•	0.2	•	0.8	0.3	0.3	•	•	0.2	•
Inventory to Working Capital 41	•	•	•	•	0.0	•	0.0	0.1	0.0	•	•	0.0	•
Total Receipts to Cash Flow 42	3.6	•	0.2	•	1.8	2.1	1.6	2.2	2.0	5.1	4.3	2.6	3.7
Cost of Goods to Cash Flow 43	0.5	•	•	•	0.2	0.0	0.3	0.5	0.1	1.6	1.5	•	0.6
Cash Flow to Total Debt 44	0.1	•	•	•	5.5	1.9	0.4	0.8	0.4	0.1	0.2	0.1	0.1

Selected Financial Factors (in Percentages)

Debt Ratio 45	62.5	•	1.2	234.8	8.5	69.1	50.6	39.7	44.5	63.8	56.2	52.9	63.2
Return on Total Assets 46	5.2	•	•	•	23.0	31.2	14.1	20.8	8.1	•	13.0	2.9	5.2
Return on Equity Before Income Taxes 47	8.8	•	•	120.1	24.9	93.4	25.4	32.3	14.2	•	15.3	1.4	9.2
Return on Equity After Income Taxes 48	5.5	•	•	120.1	16.8	88.6	16.3	28.5	9.7	•	11.7	0.4	5.7
Profit Margin (Before Income Tax) 49	10.2	•	•	•	26.5	10.0	43.6	27.5	22.9	•	15.8	3.4	10.3
Profit Margin (After Income Tax) 50	6.4	•	•	•	17.9	9.5	28.0	24.3	15.7	•	12.1	1.1	6.4

Table II
Corporations with Net Income

RAIL TRANSPORTATION

MONEY AMOUNTS AND SIZE OF ASSETS IN THOUSANDS OF DOLLARS

Item Description for Accounting Period 7/10 Through 6/11	Total	Zero Assets	Under 500	500 to 1,000	1,000 to 5,000	5,000 to 10,000	10,000 to 25,000	25,000 to 50,000	50,000 to 100,000	100,000 to 250,000	250,000 to 500,000	500,000 to 2,500,000	2,500,000 and over
Number of Enterprises **1**	82	0	0	0	22	14	9	15	•	•	0	•	•
Revenues ($ in Thousands)													
Net Sales **2**	43053778	0	0	0	52688	252915	49617	361590	•	•	0	•	•
Interest **3**	171906	0	0	0	63	83	161	367	•	•	0	•	•
Rents **4**	350126	0	0	0	1206	6	48	3610	•	•	0	•	•
Royalties **5**	55047	0	0	0	5	269	0	0	•	•	0	•	•
Other Portfolio Income **6**	326950	0	0	0	7509	412	14170	3182	•	•	0	•	•
Other Receipts **7**	444444	0	0	0	2196	2698	2361	10256	•	•	0	•	•
Total Receipts **8**	44402251	0	0	0	63667	256383	66357	379005	•	•	0	•	•
Average Total Receipts **9**	541491	•	•	•	2894	18313	7373	25267	•	•	•	•	•
Operating Costs/Operating Income (%)													
Cost of Operations **10**	15.4	•	•	•	9.2	0.0	21.5	23.5	•	•	•	•	•
Salaries and Wages **11**	17.5	•	•	•	9.0	7.8	16.0	10.0	•	•	•	•	•
Taxes Paid **12**	5.1	•	•	•	4.7	1.8	7.5	4.4	•	•	•	•	•
Interest Paid **13**	5.4	•	•	•	0.3	0.8	4.8	1.8	•	•	•	•	•
Depreciation **14**	14.3	•	•	•	16.9	1.2	5.3	7.8	•	•	•	•	•
Amortization and Depletion **15**	0.2	•	•	•	•	•	0.1	0.0	•	•	•	•	•
Pensions and Other Deferred Comp. **16**	0.7	•	•	•	•	•	•	0.2	•	•	•	•	•
Employee Benefits **17**	5.8	•	•	•	0.9	1.2	4.2	1.0	•	•	•	•	•
Advertising **18**	0.0	•	•	•	0.1	0.1	0.2	0.1	•	•	•	•	•
Other Expenses **19**	25.8	•	•	•	48.3	78.3	25.8	26.6	•	•	•	•	•
Officers' Compensation **20**	0.5	•	•	•	4.8	0.1	1.8	1.9	•	•	•	•	•
Operating Margin **21**	9.3	•	•	•	5.7	8.6	12.8	22.7	•	•	•	•	•
Operating Margin Before Officers' Comp. **22**	9.8	•	•	•	10.4	8.8	14.6	24.7	•	•	•	•	•

Selected Average Balance Sheet ($ in Thousands)

Net Receivables 23	54545	95	1062	3825	3213
Inventories 24	11675	0	59	209	592
Net Property, Plant and Equipment 25	1248483	1357	2603	3585	17700
Total Assets 26	1554555	2789	6262	13434	34007
Notes and Loans Payable 27	340415	173	1494	6800	7188
All Other Liabilities 28	656761	66	2833	1059	6301
Net Worth 29	557378	2551	1934	5575	20517

Selected Financial Ratios (Times to 1)

Current Ratio 30	0.8	8.1	0.5	2.9	2.8
Quick Ratio 31	0.7	7.2	0.5	2.8	2.4
Net Sales to Working Capital 32	•	4.8	•	1.2	3.6
Coverage Ratio 33	3.3	81.2	13.5	10.6	15.9
Total Asset Turnover 34	0.3	0.9	2.9	0.4	0.7
Inventory Turnover 35	6.9	1619.0	0.1	5.7	9.6
Receivables Turnover 36	8.9	23.4		1.4	4.4
Total Liabilities to Net Worth 37	1.8	0.1	2.2	1.4	0.7
Current Assets to Working Capital 38	•	1.1	•	1.5	1.6
Current Liabilities to Working Capital 39	•	0.1	•	0.5	0.6
Working Capital to Net Sales 40	•	0.2	•	0.9	0.3
Inventory to Working Capital 41	•	0.0	•	0.0	0.1
Total Receipts to Cash Flow 42	3.6	1.8	2.1	1.5	2.2
Cost of Goods to Cash Flow 43	0.6	0.2	0.0	0.3	0.5
Cash Flow to Total Debt 44	0.1	5.5	1.9	0.5	0.8

Selected Financial Factors (in Percentages)

Debt Ratio 45	64.1	8.5	69.1	58.5	39.7
Return on Total Assets 46	6.1	23.0	31.2	21.1	20.8
Return on Equity Before Income Taxes 47	11.8	24.9	93.4	46.1	32.3
Return on Equity After Income Taxes 48	7.9	16.8	88.6	30.7	28.5
Profit Margin (Before Income Tax) 49	12.5	26.5	10.0	46.6	27.5
Profit Margin (After Income Tax) 50	8.3	17.9	9.5	31.0	24.3

240

Table I
Corporations with and without Net Income

WATER TRANSPORTATION

MONEY AMOUNTS AND SIZE OF ASSETS IN THOUSANDS OF DOLLARS

Item Description for Accounting Period 7/10 Through 6/11		Total	Zero Assets	Under 500	500 to 1,000	1,000 to 5,000	5,000 to 10,000	10,000 to 25,000	25,000 to 50,000	50,000 to 100,000	100,000 to 250,000	250,000 to 500,000	500,000 to 2,500,000	2,500,000 and over
Number of Enterprises	1	3719	469	1426	523	929	184	80	32	26	22	15	13	0
Revenues ($ in Thousands)														
Net Sales	2	28351132	1685160	1026698	646531	3001433	733490	1809482	808290	1158092	1610523	1947305	13924128	0
Interest	3	146988	9	1	213	298	82	977	604	915	3818	4233	135839	0
Rents	4	106159	35	0	0	0	0	419	1037	55	979	5542	98093	0
Royalties	5	474	464	0	0	0	0	0	0	0	0	9	1	0
Other Portfolio Income	6	213725	10250	0	0	34661	2679	161	1542	19508	34768	7773	102383	0
Other Receipts	7	567585	289134	133919	2733	9381	5102	13789	11642	-50665	2148	436552	-286150	0
Total Receipts	8	29386063	1985052	1160618	649477	3045773	741353	1824828	823115	1127905	1652236	2401414	13974294	0
Average Total Receipts	9	7902	4233	814	1242	3279	4029	22810	25722	43381	75102	160094	1074946	•
Operating Costs/Operating Income (%)														
Cost of Operations	10	40.7	38.2	34.0	3.6	27.6	58.5	48.4	48.8	46.4	34.1	39.1	44.2	•
Salaries and Wages	11	9.8	11.6	12.5	24.4	12.4	19.7	10.9	15.6	10.0	11.9	8.8	7.0	•
Taxes Paid	12	1.7	1.7	2.1	2.4	1.8	2.3	2.2	3.3	2.4	2.0	1.9	1.3	•
Interest Paid	13	2.5	2.8	0.1	0.9	1.9	1.8	1.4	3.0	2.8	4.2	3.9	2.6	•
Depreciation	14	8.8	5.8	0.5	4.9	5.5	5.0	7.9	8.8	14.6	14.6	20.8	8.1	•
Amortization and Depletion	15	0.3	1.2	•	•	0.1	0.0	0.1	0.1	0.6	0.3	0.2	0.3	•
Pensions and Other Deferred Comp.	16	0.6	0.1	1.1	•	0.1	0.1	0.3	1.2	0.4	0.5	0.5	0.8	•
Employee Benefits	17	2.2	1.4	0.5	1.7	1.0	1.6	1.9	3.7	1.3	3.8	2.2	2.6	•
Advertising	18	0.3	1.2	0.3	0.5	0.2	0.1	0.4	0.2	0.6	0.1	0.8	0.1	•
Other Expenses	19	35.2	58.1	49.3	55.1	44.9	7.9	26.6	15.2	19.0	29.6	45.0	32.8	•
Officers' Compensation	20	1.5	0.1	7.7	5.7	2.6	3.5	1.5	2.0	1.3	0.8	0.9	0.9	•
Operating Margin	21	•	•	•	0.8	2.0	•	•	•	0.7	•	•	•	•
Operating Margin Before Officers' Comp.	22	•	•	•	6.5	4.6	3.0	•	0.2	2.0	•	•	0.2	•

Selected Average Balance Sheet ($ in Thousands)

Item												
Net Receivables 23	1213	10	3	225	1588	3460	2251	8008	8909	51454	190029	•
Inventories 24	112	18	0	11	0	133	284	222	742	1936	23929	•
Net Property, Plant and Equipment 25	5297	10	187	1227	2880	7018	15927	44558	107856	175203	822199	•
Total Assets 26	9921	141	686	2161	7133	15977	34626	74386	152990	361795	1530870	•
Notes and Loans Payable 27	4327	114	571	1763	2719	7549	14758	27102	73019	102004	659581	•
All Other Liabilities 28	1945	22	170	301	907	4405	9471	15437	17805	70244	320332	•
Net Worth 29	3649	5	-55	98	3507	4022	10396	31848	62165	189547	550957	•

Selected Financial Ratios (Times to 1)

Item												
Current Ratio 30	1.2	2.6	1.4	1.0	1.6	1.2	1.3	1.4	1.0	1.7	1.1	•
Quick Ratio 31	0.9	1.6	1.4	0.9	1.1	0.9	0.8	0.9	0.8	1.5	0.8	•
Net Sales to Working Capital 32	18.4	16.0	15.3	126.7	3.2	19.6	14.0	8.2	110.8	3.9	37.1	•
Coverage Ratio 33	1.0	36.9	2.4	2.8	1.3	0.5	1.0	0.4	1.1	0.8	0.9	•
Total Asset Turnover 34	0.8	5.1	1.8	1.5	0.6	1.4	0.7	0.6	0.5	0.4	0.7	•
Inventory Turnover 35	27.6	13.6	84.0	•	82.5	43.4	93.1	33.6	26.2	19.8		•
Receivables Turnover 36	6.5	87.4	15.4	304.0	2.2	6.4	11.7	7.2	6.9	3.1	5.7	•
Total Liabilities to Net Worth 37	1.7	28.8	21.1	•	1.0	3.0	2.3	1.3	1.5	0.9	1.8	•
Current Assets to Working Capital 38	6.1	1.6	24.6	3.4	2.6	5.7	4.4	3.5	36.6	2.4	13.2	•
Current Liabilities to Working Capital 39	5.1	0.6	23.6	2.4	1.6	4.7	3.4	2.5	35.6	1.4	12.2	•
Working Capital to Net Sales 40	0.1	0.1	0.0	0.1	0.3	0.1	0.1	0.1	0.0	0.3	0.0	•
Inventory to Working Capital 41	0.3	0.5	0.3	•	•	0.1	0.2	0.1	1.2	0.1	0.7	•
Total Receipts to Cash Flow 42	3.7	2.1	2.9	2.5	12.1	7.2	9.9	10.9	4.3	2.6	4.0	•
Cost of Goods to Cash Flow 43	1.5	0.7	0.8	0.1	7.1	3.5	4.8	5.1	1.5	1.0	1.8	•
Cash Flow to Total Debt 44	0.3	2.5	0.5	0.7	0.1	0.3	0.1	0.1	0.2	0.3	0.3	•

Selected Financial Factors (in Percentages)

Item												
Debt Ratio 45	63.2	96.6	108.0	95.5	50.8	74.8	70.0	57.2	59.4	47.6	64.0	•
Return on Total Assets 46	2.0	26.1	3.9	8.0	1.3	1.0	2.2	0.7	2.3	1.1	1.7	•
Return on Equity Before Income Taxes 47	0.2	757.7	•	113.6	0.6	•	0.0	•	0.7	•	•	•
Return on Equity After Income Taxes 48	•	757.7	•	109.0	0.5	•	•	•	•	•	•	•
Profit Margin (Before Income Tax) 49	0.1	5.0	1.3	3.4	0.5	0.0	0.0	•	0.6	•	0.6	•
Profit Margin (After Income Tax) 50	•	5.0	0.9	3.3	0.5	•	•	•	•	•	•	•

Table II
Corporations with Net Income

WATER TRANSPORTATION

MONEY AMOUNTS AND SIZE OF ASSETS IN THOUSANDS OF DOLLARS

Item Description for Accounting Period 7/10 Through 6/11	Total	Zero Assets	Under 500	500 to 1,000	1,000 to 5,000	5,000 to 10,000	10,000 to 25,000	25,000 to 50,000	50,000 to 100,000	100,000 to 250,000	250,000 to 500,000	500,000 to 2,500,000	2,500,000 and over
Number of Enterprises 1	2307	25	1325	387	386	98	40	16	•	10	6	•	0
Revenues ($ in Thousands)													
Net Sales 2	20392982	801031	943936	451254	2158360	692000	1342792	417620	•	793016	836365	•	0
Interest 3	103045	0	1	2	23	82	971	260	•	3789	292	•	0
Rents 4	99410	35	0	0	0	0	248	0	•	979	0	•	0
Royalties 5	464	464	0	0	0	0	0	0	•	0	0	•	0
Other Portfolio Income 6	109312	766	0	0	34316	2679	161	865	•	3945	1893	•	0
Other Receipts 7	202202	389	130603	0	3714	5102	13377	7469	•	7058	409850	•	0
Total Receipts 8	20907415	802685	1074540	451256	2196413	699863	1357549	426214	•	808787	1248400	•	0
Average Total Receipts 9	9063	32107	811	1166	5690	7141	33939	26638	•	80879	208067	•	•
Operating Costs/Operating Income (%)													
Cost of Operations 10	44.1	20.3	37.0	0.4	27.7	60.6	57.1	68.2	•	34.7	44.6	•	•
Salaries and Wages 11	6.9	3.8	10.2	17.7	7.0	18.6	8.5	2.8	•	8.5	6.0	•	•
Taxes Paid 12	1.5	0.4	1.7	1.2	1.6	2.1	1.9	2.9	•	2.2	0.9	•	•
Interest Paid 13	1.3	0.2	•	1.0	0.8	1.9	0.7	1.6	•	3.3	1.6	•	•
Depreciation 14	4.9	0.9	0.5	4.5	3.1	5.1	1.9	5.7	•	10.4	19.1	•	•
Amortization and Depletion 15	0.1	0.0	•	0.0	0.0	0.0	0.1	0.0	•	0.3	0.0	•	•
Pensions and Other Deferred Comp. 16	0.6	0.1	1.2	•	0.1	0.1	0.3	0.3	•	0.6	0.5	•	•
Employee Benefits 17	1.6	0.5	•	1.4	1.1	1.6	1.2	1.5	•	3.6	1.5	•	•
Advertising 18	0.2	2.3	0.3	0.0	0.2	0.1	0.5	0.1	•	0.1	0.0	•	•
Other Expenses 19	35.4	66.7	49.0	59.8	49.6	8.0	19.9	9.9	•	29.5	63.1	•	•
Officers' Compensation 20	1.1	0.2	6.3	•	1.5	1.6	1.5	1.9	•	1.1	0.6	•	•
Operating Margin 21	2.4	4.4	•	14.0	7.4	0.4	6.4	4.9	•	5.7	•	•	•
Operating Margin Before Officers' Comp. 22	3.5	4.5	0.0	14.0	8.9	2.0	7.9	6.8	•	6.8	•	•	•

Selected Average Balance Sheet ($ in Thousands)

Net Receivables 23	1259	0	0	0	195	587	4827	3418	10411	78403
Inventories 24	106	0	26	0	7	0	208	469	1218	435
Net Property, Plant and Equipment 25	3885	0	11	149	858	5105	3589	17451	101526	155696
Total Assets 26	7481	0	130	717	2079	7346	15133	33470	148432	329511
Notes and Loans Payable 27	2132	0	104	498	773	2994	3103	7757	57812	59903
All Other Liabilities 28	1702	0	1	30	314	881	5497	6359	23509	48296
Net Worth 29	3646	0	25	190	992	3471	6532	19353	67111	221312

Selected Financial Ratios (Times to 1)

Current Ratio 30	1.3	•	20.5	7.7	2.5	0.5	1.6	2.2	1.2	1.7
Quick Ratio 31	1.0	•	11.6	7.5	2.2	0.4	1.2	1.6	0.9	1.5
Net Sales to Working Capital 32	14.5	•	12.3	4.4	12.7	•	9.4	4.2	18.4	3.2
Coverage Ratio 33	4.9	26.7	•	14.6	13.0	1.8	11.1	5.4	3.3	7.9
Total Asset Turnover 34	1.2	•	5.5	1.6	2.7	1.0	2.2	0.8	0.5	0.4
Inventory Turnover 35	36.8	•	10.0	•	227.6	•	92.0	37.9	22.6	142.8
Receivables Turnover 36	7.3	•	•	45125.4	55.9	3.1	8.6	9.4	6.2	2.0
Total Liabilities to Net Worth 37	1.1	•	4.3	2.8	1.1	1.1	1.3	0.7	1.2	0.5
Current Assets to Working Capital 38	4.1	•	1.1	1.1	1.7	•	2.7	1.8	6.8	2.5
Current Liabilities to Working Capital 39	3.1	•	0.1	0.1	0.7	•	1.7	0.8	5.8	1.5
Working Capital to Net Sales 40	0.1	•	0.1	0.2	0.1	•	0.1	0.2	0.1	0.3
Inventory to Working Capital 41	0.1	•	0.5	•	0.0	•	0.1	0.1	0.3	0.0
Total Receipts to Cash Flow 42	3.1	1.5	1.9	1.7	2.3	10.6	6.9	7.5	3.1	1.5
Cost of Goods to Cash Flow 43	1.4	0.3	0.7	0.0	0.6	6.4	4.0	5.1	1.1	0.7
Cash Flow to Total Debt 44	0.7	•	3.5	1.3	2.2	0.2	0.6	0.2	0.3	0.9

Selected Financial Factors (in Percentages)

Debt Ratio 45	51.3	•	81.1	73.5	52.3	52.7	56.8	42.2	54.8	32.8
Return on Total Assets 46	7.5	•	41.6	24.5	26.7	3.3	18.2	6.6	5.9	5.5
Return on Equity Before Income Taxes 47	12.2	•	220.3	86.1	51.6	3.2	38.3	9.3	9.1	7.1
Return on Equity After Income Taxes 48	10.4	•	220.3	83.2	50.5	3.1	35.4	6.3	7.2	6.5
Profit Margin (Before Income Tax) 49	5.0	4.6	7.6	14.0	9.1	1.6	7.5	6.9	7.7	11.3
Profit Margin (After Income Tax) 50	4.3	2.5	7.6	13.5	9.0	1.5	6.9	4.7	6.1	10.3

Table I
Corporations with and without Net Income

TRUCK TRANSPORTATION

MONEY AMOUNTS AND SIZE OF ASSETS IN THOUSANDS OF DOLLARS

Item Description for Accounting Period 7/10 Through 6/11	Total	Zero Assets	Under 500	500 to 1,000	1,000 to 5,000	5,000 to 10,000	10,000 to 25,000	25,000 to 50,000	50,000 to 100,000	100,000 to 250,000	250,000 to 500,000	500,000 to 2,500,000	2,500,000 and over
Number of Enterprises **1**	107274	27011	68894	4174	5691	858	350	140	67	41	26	21	0
Revenues ($ in Thousands)													
Net Sales **2**	208929247	4386481	40042868	12866668	40045723	17367342	12724341	11442089	7963255	10376163	14515578	37198740	0
Interest **3**	458436	10923	2577	4867	9704	2706	5723	2847	4885	13924	36496	363784	0
Rents **4**	344821	0	4674	1352	29273	8586	5531	20446	7863	40375	72808	153912	0
Royalties **5**	12330	0	0	0	80	0	5	2	1740	0	1114	9389	0
Other Portfolio Income **6**	1261816	80072	187882	80091	270905	79682	42770	87557	45359	48682	93663	245153	0
Other Receipts **7**	3211041	144683	656343	128954	237496	249407	68874	107779	47912	178621	335306	1055666	0
Total Receipts **8**	214217691	4622159	40894344	13081932	40593181	17707723	12847244	11660720	8071014	10657765	15054965	39026644	0
Average Total Receipts **9**	1997	171	594	3134	7133	20638	36706	83291	120463	259945	579037	1858412	•
Operating Costs/Operating Income (%)													
Cost of Operations **10**	32.5	21.3	24.3	41.3	41.1	46.3	36.7	40.4	24.8	26.5	39.8	20.4	•
Salaries and Wages **11**	16.8	6.8	11.7	14.9	13.5	14.9	16.5	14.7	23.0	21.6	17.6	26.1	•
Taxes Paid **12**	3.5	2.6	2.9	2.7	3.3	2.7	3.5	3.3	4.5	3.7	3.1	4.9	•
Interest Paid **13**	1.3	0.7	0.7	0.7	0.8	0.8	0.9	0.9	1.9	1.8	1.9	2.8	•
Depreciation **14**	4.5	3.8	3.5	3.6	3.9	3.9	4.8	5.0	6.1	5.7	5.9	5.5	•
Amortization and Depletion **15**	0.2	0.3	0.0	0.0	0.1	0.0	0.1	0.1	0.2	0.4	0.4	0.3	•
Pensions and Other Deferred Comp. **16**	0.3	0.3	0.1	0.1	0.2	0.2	0.2	0.2	0.2	0.3	0.3	0.9	•
Employee Benefits **17**	2.3	0.4	1.1	1.4	1.7	1.7	2.2	1.7	3.2	2.7	2.4	5.0	•
Advertising **18**	0.3	0.1	0.4	0.8	0.3	0.2	0.2	0.2	0.1	0.2	0.2	0.2	•
Other Expenses **19**	35.3	56.3	40.0	31.0	31.8	28.0	33.1	32.8	36.3	38.4	31.8	38.3	•
Officers' Compensation **20**	3.9	6.8	14.5	2.9	1.9	1.2	1.5	1.2	0.8	0.5	0.3	•	•
Operating Margin **21**	•	0.6	0.8	0.6	1.4	0.2	0.2	•	0.8	0.4	0.9	•	•
Operating Margin Before Officers' Comp. **22**	3.1	7.4	15.4	3.5	3.3	1.4	1.6	0.8	•	•	•	•	•

Selected Average Balance Sheet ($ in Thousands)

Net Receivables 23	176	0	10	124	555	2461	4650	8613	13752	29720	67688	266652
Inventories 24	10	0	1	24	26	141	422	545	1440	1320	4179	8108
Net Property, Plant and Equipment 25	337	0	31	278	772	2660	5981	15015	31187	72459	163247	606242
Total Assets 26	889	0	72	708	2080	6926	15662	33284	67336	149120	355484	1187195
Notes and Loans Payable 27	330	0	60	456	1020	3096	6235	12613	30540	63905	120409	434559
All Other Liabilities 28	316	0	15	257	476	1952	4020	7172	16563	38321	109822	927983
Net Worth 29	243	0	-3	-5	584	1878	5406	13499	20232	46894	125253	524653

Selected Financial Ratios (Times to 1)

Current Ratio 30	1.1	•	1.4	0.7	1.5	1.3	1.3	1.3	1.1	1.1	1.3	0.9
Quick Ratio 31	0.8	•	1.1	0.6	1.2	1.0	1.0	1.1	0.8	0.8	1.0	0.4
Net Sales to Working Capital 32	57.1	10.1	70.0	•	20.8	20.9	24.1	23.8	43.9	44.1	21.9	•
Coverage Ratio 33	2.4	•	5.1	4.0	4.5	3.7	2.2	2.7	1.2	1.5	1.0	1.1
Total Asset Turnover 34	2.2	•	8.1	4.4	3.4	2.9	2.3	2.5	1.8	1.7	1.6	0.9
Inventory Turnover 35	63.1	•	242.8	53.0	112.5	66.4	31.6	60.5	20.4	50.8	53.1	44.5
Receivables Turnover 36	10.5	•	55.0	25.3	13.2	9.3	8.1	9.8	9.5	8.5	9.7	8.4
Total Liabilities to Net Worth 37	2.7	•	•	•	2.6	2.7	1.9	1.5	2.3	2.2	1.8	2.6
Current Assets to Working Capital 38	10.5	•	3.7	•	3.1	4.0	4.7	4.0	9.6	8.4	4.6	•
Current Liabilities to Working Capital 39	9.5	•	2.7	•	2.1	3.0	3.7	3.0	8.6	7.4	3.6	•
Working Capital to Net Sales 40	0.0	•	0.0	•	0.0	0.0	0.0	0.0	0.0	0.0	0.0	•
Inventory to Working Capital 41	0.3	•	0.1	•	0.1	0.2	0.2	0.2	0.6	0.2	0.2	•
Total Receipts to Cash Flow 42	3.4	1.8	2.8	3.9	3.7	4.5	4.2	4.7	3.5	3.3	4.4	3.0
Cost of Goods to Cash Flow 43	1.1	0.4	0.7	1.6	1.5	2.1	1.5	1.9	0.9	0.9	1.7	0.6
Cash Flow to Total Debt 44	0.9	•	2.7	1.1	1.3	0.9	0.8	0.9	0.7	0.8	0.6	0.4

Selected Financial Factors (in Percentages)

Debt Ratio 45	72.7	•	104.6	100.7	71.9	72.9	65.5	59.4	70.0	68.6	64.8	72.2
Return on Total Assets 46	6.8	•	29.7	13.0	11.9	8.5	4.8	6.0	4.1	4.7	3.1	2.8
Return on Equity Before Income Taxes 47	14.4	•	•	•	32.8	22.9	7.7	9.4	2.3	5.1	0.3	0.8
Return on Equity After Income Taxes 48	12.4	•	•	•	31.4	21.6	6.9	8.4	1.5	4.1	•	•
Profit Margin (Before Income Tax) 49	1.8	6.0	3.0	2.2	2.7	2.1	1.1	1.6	0.4	1.0	0.1	0.2
Profit Margin (After Income Tax) 50	1.5	5.8	2.9	2.1	2.6	2.0	1.0	1.4	0.3	0.8	•	•

Table II

Corporations with Net Income

TRUCK TRANSPORTATION

MONEY AMOUNTS AND SIZE OF ASSETS IN THOUSANDS OF DOLLARS

Item Description for Accounting Period 7/10 Through 6/11	Total	Zero Assets	Under 500	500 to 1,000	1,000 to 5,000	5,000 to 10,000	10,000 to 25,000	25,000 to 50,000	50,000 to 100,000	100,000 to 250,000	250,000 to 500,000	500,000 to 2,500,000	2,500,000 and over
Number of Enterprises **1**	67572	16677	42855	2674	4354	636	196	95	34	23	12	15	0
Revenues ($ in Thousands)													
Net Sales **2**	13876851	2950170	29688832	7242854	33556352	12413229	7483575	8236129	4172570	6008934	5987920	21025286	0
Interest **3**	56355	10923	1933	1771	6576	2340	4905	2207	3231	3607	8602	10259	0
Rents **4**	178234	0	0	1352	20865	5730	3872	20379	6864	32151	11239	75782	0
Royalties **5**	82	0	0	0	80	0	0	2	0	0	0	0	0
Other Portfolio Income **6**	904284	67820	146069	76741	241336	51851	30803	55994	22349	24247	45025	142049	0
Other Receipts **7**	2879562	98539	581394	122988	207726	232600	54399	93523	36559	158664	266739	1026431	0
Total Receipts **8**	142782368	3127452	30416228	7445706	34032935	12705750	7577554	8408234	4241573	6227603	6319525	22279807	0
Average Total Receipts **9**	2113	188	710	2784	7816	19978	38661	88508	124752	270765	526627	1485320	•
Operating Costs/Operating Income (%)													
Cost of Operations **10**	31.0	7.8	25.1	41.0	39.2	40.3	34.6	46.4	28.6	33.4	20.3	16.3	•
Salaries and Wages **11**	15.6	7.2	9.3	12.9	14.0	15.6	18.8	13.0	20.0	19.8	24.5	24.5	•
Taxes Paid **12**	3.4	2.7	2.6	2.7	3.2	2.8	3.2	3.2	3.9	3.6	4.7	4.9	•
Interest Paid **13**	0.7	0.6	0.6	0.9	0.7	0.7	1.0	0.7	0.9	1.2	0.8	0.7	•
Depreciation **14**	4.3	4.0	3.0	4.6	3.9	3.7	3.7	3.8	5.0	4.5	7.0	6.7	•
Amortization and Depletion **15**	0.1	0.1	0.0	0.0	0.1	0.0	0.2	0.2	0.1	0.1	0.1	0.1	•
Pensions and Other Deferred Comp. **16**	0.2	0.5	0.1	0.0	0.2	0.2	0.2	0.1	0.2	0.2	0.2	0.2	•
Employee Benefits **17**	2.0	0.2	1.0	1.5	1.9	2.1	2.1	1.3	2.4	2.4	3.3	4.0	•
Advertising **18**	0.3	0.2	0.2	1.1	0.3	0.2	0.3	0.2	0.1	0.2	0.1	0.1	•
Other Expenses **19**	35.5	64.8	36.2	27.5	32.4	31.6	31.7	28.7	35.4	34.0	39.2	43.8	•
Officers' Compensation **20**	5.1	5.2	18.4	3.9	1.9	1.2	1.9	1.3	0.8	0.6	0.6	0.3	•
Operating Margin **21**	1.7	6.8	3.4	3.9	2.2	1.5	2.4	1.0	2.7	0.1	•	•	•
Operating Margin Before Officers' Comp. **22**	6.9	11.9	21.8	7.8	4.1	2.7	4.3	2.3	3.5	0.6	•	•	•

Selected Average Balance Sheet ($ in Thousands)

	C1	C2	C3	C4	C5	C6	C7	C8	C9	C10	C11	C12	
Net Receivables 23	178	0	12	61	613	1989	4214	9103	14946	30959	59484	253820	•
Inventories 24	10	0	1	16	27	97	614	480	2030	1793	6657	4616	•
Net Property, Plant and Equipment 25	329	0	33	292	736	2705	5704	14307	30339	69514	195456	508565	•
Total Assets 26	756	0	83	725	2117	6839	15728	33578	66644	146638	356816	1056312	•
Notes and Loans Payable 27	265	0	59	373	947	2632	6089	11070	22854	47410	53124	258352	•
All Other Liabilities 28	197	0	12	233	497	1705	3269	7387	15898	37479	89576	340248	•
Net Worth 29	294	0	13	120	673	2503	6370	15121	27892	61749	214116	457713	•

Selected Financial Ratios (Times to 1)

	C1	C2	C3	C4	C5	C6	C7	C8	C9	C10	C11	C12	
Current Ratio 30	1.5	•	1.9	0.6	1.6	1.5	1.6	1.4	1.4	1.2	1.8	1.7	•
Quick Ratio 31	1.2	•	1.6	0.5	1.3	1.3	1.2	1.2	1.0	0.8	1.3	1.5	•
Net Sales to Working Capital 32	19.3	•	39.9	•	17.8	17.3	14.3	19.7	14.6	31.5	9.5	9.5	•
Coverage Ratio 33	7.2	21.2	10.9	8.8	5.9	6.2	4.7	5.2	6.1	4.2	7.4	6.9	•
Total Asset Turnover 34	2.7	•	8.3	3.7	3.6	2.9	2.4	2.6	1.8	1.8	1.4	1.3	•
Inventory Turnover 35	63.9	•	279.3	67.8	113.0	81.1	21.5	83.9	17.3	48.6	15.2	49.5	•
Receivables Turnover 36	13.2	•	75.1	30.8	16.1	12.4	8.3	11.2	8.7	8.4	8.5	6.4	•
Total Liabilities to Net Worth 37	1.6	•	5.4	5.1	2.1	1.7	1.5	1.2	1.4	1.4	0.7	1.3	•
Current Assets to Working Capital 38	2.9	•	2.1	•	2.7	3.2	2.7	3.3	3.5	6.4	2.3	2.4	•
Current Liabilities to Working Capital 39	1.9	•	1.1	•	1.7	2.2	1.7	2.3	2.5	5.4	1.3	1.4	•
Working Capital to Net Sales 40	0.1	•	0.0	•	0.1	0.1	0.1	0.1	0.1	0.0	0.1	0.1	•
Inventory to Working Capital 41	0.1	•	0.1	•	0.1	0.2	0.1	0.1	0.3	0.2	0.2	0.0	•
Total Receipts to Cash Flow 42	3.1	1.4	2.8	3.8	3.5	3.7	4.3	4.7	3.2	3.6	3.6	2.3	•
Cost of Goods to Cash Flow 43	1.0	0.1	0.7	1.6	1.4	1.5	1.5	2.2	0.9	1.2	0.7	0.4	•
Cash Flow to Total Debt 44	1.4	•	3.5	1.2	1.5	1.2	1.0	1.0	1.0	0.8	1.0	1.0	•

Selected Financial Factors (in Percentages)

	C1	C2	C3	C4	C5	C6	C7	C8	C9	C10	C11	C12	
Debt Ratio 45	61.1	•	84.4	83.5	68.2	63.4	59.5	55.0	58.1	57.9	40.0	56.7	•
Return on Total Assets 46	14.6	•	53.9	28.1	15.8	13.1	11.3	9.9	9.6	8.7	7.8	6.7	•
Return on Equity Before Income Taxes 47	32.3	•	313.5	151.3	41.3	29.9	21.9	17.8	19.1	15.7	11.2	13.3	•
Return on Equity After Income Taxes 48	29.7	•	308.2	145.9	39.7	28.6	20.7	16.5	18.0	14.3	8.9	9.2	•
Profit Margin (Before Income Tax) 49	4.6	12.8	5.9	6.7	3.6	3.8	3.6	3.1	4.3	3.7	4.8	4.3	•
Profit Margin (After Income Tax) 50	4.2	12.5	5.8	6.4	3.5	3.7	3.4	2.9	4.1	3.4	3.8	3.0	•

Table I

Corporations with and without Net Income

TRANSIT AND GROUND PASSENGER TRANSPORTATION

MONEY AMOUNTS AND SIZE OF ASSETS IN THOUSANDS OF DOLLARS

Item Description for Accounting Period 7/10 Through 6/11	Total	Zero Assets	Under 500	500 to 1,000	1,000 to 5,000	5,000 to 10,000	10,000 to 25,000	25,000 to 50,000	50,000 to 100,000	100,000 to 250,000	250,000 to 500,000	500,000 to 2,500,000	2,500,000 and over
Number of Enterprises **1**	31031	8031	18591	2309	1871	101	92	12	11	9	0	0	4
Revenues ($ in Thousands)													
Net Sales **2**	23395056	611280	3898294	770960	5694991	1240830	1853440	653077	823042	2330534	0	0	5518608
Interest **3**	145492	47	97	38	1743	155	404	364	288	1792	0	0	140565
Rents **4**	15197	0	39	0	1049	1259	329	0	174	866	0	0	11480
Royalties **5**	1535	0	0	0	0	0	0	0	0	0	0	0	1535
Other Portfolio Income **6**	178548	30236	20531	7581	14353	12166	46691	18333	1269	9593	0	0	17795
Other Receipts **7**	306240	0	91406	20970	63046	19550	41292	1595	2611	-12987	0	0	78758
Total Receipts **8**	24042068	641563	4010367	799549	5775182	1273960	1942156	673369	827384	2329798	0	0	5768741
Average Total Receipts **9**	775	80	216	346	3087	12613	21110	56114	75217	258866	•	•	1442185
Operating Costs/Operating Income (%)													
Cost of Operations **10**	29.1	28.6	7.9	34.2	38.8	28.9	43.3	44.3	55.0	32.7	•	•	21.3
Salaries and Wages **11**	24.8	7.4	35.5	16.1	15.7	12.5	14.0	21.4	9.2	25.9	•	•	38.6
Taxes Paid **12**	4.5	4.0	4.9	3.0	3.6	4.8	3.6	5.6	4.1	5.0	•	•	5.6
Interest Paid **13**	2.9	0.8	1.7	9.2	1.7	1.5	1.8	0.6	2.1	3.9	•	•	5.0
Depreciation **14**	5.5	3.5	3.4	6.1	5.7	5.7	12.6	5.7	8.1	5.5	•	•	4.1
Amortization and Depletion **15**	0.7	•	0.3	2.9	0.5	0.0	0.0	0.0	0.3	0.5	•	•	1.7
Pensions and Other Deferred Comp. **16**	0.4	•	0.1	0.0	0.4	0.3	0.7	0.8	0.6	0.5	•	•	0.4
Employee Benefits **17**	2.2	1.4	0.4	1.9	1.2	1.9	2.8	1.7	3.1	5.3	•	•	3.1
Advertising **18**	0.5	0.4	0.8	0.4	0.8	0.3	0.4	0.2	0.3	0.6	•	•	0.2
Other Expenses **19**	25.7	38.6	37.2	23.2	23.7	36.3	22.4	13.1	13.8	20.7	•	•	22.6
Officers' Compensation **20**	2.9	10.5	5.8	6.5	4.2	4.2	1.5	0.5	1.4	0.4	•	•	0.1
Operating Margin **21**	0.6	4.9	1.8	•	3.6	3.7	•	6.0	2.1	•	•	•	•
Operating Margin Before Officers' Comp. **22**	3.6	15.3	7.6	2.8	7.7	7.9	•	6.5	3.6	•	•	•	•

Selected Average Balance Sheet ($ in Thousands)

Net Receivables 23	58	0	1	3	328	586	1543	5462	10956	38127	108296
Inventories 24	4	0	0	0	4	58	89	351	2272	1021	13623
Net Property, Plant and Equipment 25	190	0	20	95	575	1675	8821	14569	24248	61609	562378
Total Assets 26	600	0	78	756	1715	6229	15346	31299	62996	196567	1834608
Notes and Loans Payable 27	339	0	50	613	981	3123	6730	6940	31463	137784	934816
All Other Liabilities 28	127	0	12	40	265	1134	2122	8013	7116	57193	533803
Net Worth 29	134	0	17	103	468	1972	6494	16346	24418	1590	365988

Selected Financial Ratios (Times to 1)

Current Ratio 30	1.2	•	2.1	0.7	1.7	1.0	1.3	1.7	1.4	•	0.7
Quick Ratio 31	0.8	•	1.1	0.2	1.4	0.6	1.0	1.3	1.0	•	0.5
Net Sales to Working Capital 32	35.3	•	27.2	•	11.4	•	20.2	9.7	7.4	11.5	•
Coverage Ratio 33	2.2	13.8	3.7	1.0	3.9	5.1	1.9	15.7	2.3	0.8	1.4
Total Asset Turnover 34	1.3	•	2.7	0.4	1.8	2.0	1.3	1.7	1.2	1.3	0.8
Inventory Turnover 35	55.5	•	110.0	759.1	269.3	61.5	97.8	68.6	18.1	83.0	21.6
Receivables Turnover 36	12.6	•	98.1	93.2	10.5	8.9	16.3	7.9	7.6	8.4	10.9
Total Liabilities to Net Worth 37	3.5	•	3.7	6.3	2.7	2.2	1.4	0.9	1.6	122.6	4.0
Current Assets to Working Capital 38	6.5	•	1.9	•	2.4	•	4.5	2.4	2.4	3.2	•
Current Liabilities to Working Capital 39	5.5	•	0.9	•	1.4	•	3.5	1.4	1.4	2.2	•
Working Capital to Net Sales 40	0.0	•	0.0	•	0.1	•	0.0	0.1	0.1	0.1	•
Inventory to Working Capital 41	0.2	•	0.0	•	0.0	•	0.1	0.1	0.2	0.1	•
Total Receipts to Cash Flow 42	4.6	2.5	2.8	7.8	4.9	4.7	5.0	6.0	8.5	8.1	5.2
Cost of Goods to Cash Flow 43	1.3	0.7	0.2	2.6	1.9	1.4	2.2	2.7	4.7	2.6	1.1
Cash Flow to Total Debt 44	0.4	•	1.2	0.1	0.5	0.6	0.5	0.6	0.2	0.2	0.2

Selected Financial Factors (in Percentages)

Debt Ratio 45	77.6	•	78.5	86.3	72.7	68.3	57.7	47.8	61.2	99.2	80.1
Return on Total Assets 46	7.9	•	17.1	4.1	11.9	15.6	4.4	17.0	5.6	4.1	5.1
Return on Equity Before Income Taxes 47	19.1	•	58.1	0.1	32.3	39.7	4.9	30.5	8.1	•	6.7
Return on Equity After Income Taxes 48	17.5	•	56.9	•	30.7	39.1	3.9	29.6	7.5	•	6.5
Profit Margin (Before Income Tax) 49	3.4	9.8	4.7	0.0	5.0	6.4	1.6	9.2	2.7	•	1.8
Profit Margin (After Income Tax) 50	3.1	8.7	4.6	•	4.7	6.3	1.3	8.9	2.4	•	1.7

Table II
Corporations with Net Income

TRANSIT AND GROUND PASSENGER TRANSPORTATION

MONEY AMOUNTS AND SIZE OF ASSETS IN THOUSANDS OF DOLLARS

Item Description for Accounting Period 7/10 Through 6/11	Total	Zero Assets	Under 500	500 to 1,000	1,000 to 5,000	5,000 to 10,000	10,000 to 25,000	25,000 to 50,000	50,000 to 100,000	100,000 to 250,000	250,000 to 500,000	500,000 to 2,500,000	2,500,000 and over
Number of Enterprises 1	19402	3155	13128	1442	1510	86	58	•	7	3	•	•	•
Revenues ($ in Thousands)													
Net Sales 2	18894714	412941	3504079	438404	5451363	1074823	1332119	•	470758	900795	•	•	•
Interest 3	142644	47	6	0	1248	97	126	•	278	1148	•	•	•
Rents 4	13931	0	39	0	1049	1259	77	•	174	0	•	•	•
Royalties 5	1535	0	0	0	0	0	0		0	0			
Other Portfolio Income 6	147822	30236	20490	236	12833	12162	28662		589	5954	•	•	•
Other Receipts 7	263278	0	88929	19457	55582	19246	38845		1164	-12218	•	•	•
Total Receipts 8	19463924	443224	3613543	458097	5522075	1107587	1399829		472963	895679	•	•	•
Average Total Receipts 9	1003	140	275	318	3657	12879	24135	•	67566	298560	•	•	•
Operating Costs/Operating Income (%)													
Cost of Operations 10	26.5	21.4	8.7	31.1	40.2	22.1	37.7	•	54.9	11.7	•	•	•
Salaries and Wages 11	26.7	9.1	37.4	16.9	14.8	13.2	15.9	•	9.5	44.2	•	•	•
Taxes Paid 12	4.6	4.5	5.1	2.7	3.6	4.9	3.4	•	4.6	4.7	•	•	•
Interest Paid 13	2.5	0.4	1.3	8.7	1.3	1.3	1.0	•	1.2	1.2	•	•	•
Depreciation 14	4.8	3.7	3.2	3.5	5.5	6.2	9.6	•	7.2	1.4	•	•	•
Amortization and Depletion 15	0.5	•	0.0	0.4	0.2	0.0	0.1	•	0.0	0.1	•	•	•
Pensions and Other Deferred Comp. 16	0.4	•	0.1	•	0.4	0.3	0.9	•	0.6	0.1	•	•	•
Employee Benefits 17	2.0	1.7	0.5	1.3	1.2	1.8	3.3	•	3.7	3.7	•	•	•
Advertising 18	0.6	0.5	0.7	0.2	0.9	0.2	0.4	•	0.2	0.8	•	•	•
Other Expenses 19	25.3	31.1	34.1	18.9	23.1	40.2	25.1	•	10.4	22.7	•	•	•
Officers' Compensation 20	3.2	15.5	5.1	9.5	4.2	4.5	1.6	•	1.3	0.5	•	•	•
Operating Margin 21	3.1	12.0	3.7	6.8	4.6	5.3	0.9	•	6.2	8.8	•	•	•
Operating Margin Before Officers' Comp. 22	6.2	27.5	8.9	16.4	8.8	9.8	2.5	•	7.5	9.3	•	•	•

Selected Average Balance Sheet ($ in Thousands)

Net Receivables 23	69	0	2	0	402	433	1721	•	11894	27585
Inventories 24	5	0	0	1	12	74	•	•	3493	2497
Net Property, Plant and Equipment 25	221	0	23	102	617	1674	7818	•	23301	25824
Total Assets 26	708	0	80	738	1792	6154	15105	•	66203	204047
Notes and Loans Payable 27	362	0	40	555	856	3048	4824	•	31523	17661
All Other Liabilities 28	145	0	14	37	303	911	2688	•	5007	88013
Net Worth 29	202	0	26	146	633	2194	7593	•	29673	98374

Selected Financial Ratios (Times to 1)

Current Ratio 30	1.2	•	2.4	0.4	1.8	0.9	1.4	•	2.0	1.6
Quick Ratio 31	0.8	•	1.1	0.1	1.5	0.5	1.1	•	1.6	1.0
Net Sales to Working Capital 32	42.4	•	23.5	•	10.5	•	17.8	•	4.6	11.1
Coverage Ratio 33	3.4	49.0	6.4	2.3	5.5	7.6	6.9	•	6.4	8.2
Total Asset Turnover 34	1.4	•	3.3	0.4	2.0	2.0	1.5	•	1.0	1.5
Inventory Turnover 35	53.5	•	200.4	478.9	1102.1	223.3	116.5	•	10.6	14.1
Receivables Turnover 36	15.2	•	156.3	103.1	12.1	8.7	17.5	•	5.8	•
Total Liabilities to Net Worth 37	2.5	•	2.1	4.1	1.8	1.8	1.0	•	1.2	1.1
Current Assets to Working Capital 38	7.1	•	1.7	•	2.2	•	3.8	•	2.0	2.8
Current Liabilities to Working Capital 39	6.1	•	0.7	•	1.2	•	2.8	•	1.0	1.8
Working Capital to Net Sales 40	0.0	•	0.0	•	0.1	•	0.1	•	0.2	0.1
Inventory to Working Capital 41	0.2	•	0.0	•	0.0	•	0.1	•	0.2	0.1
Total Receipts to Cash Flow 42	4.2	2.4	2.9	4.3	4.9	4.2	3.7	•	7.8	4.0
Cost of Goods to Cash Flow 43	1.1	0.5	0.3	1.3	2.0	0.9	1.4	•	4.3	0.5
Cash Flow to Total Debt 44	0.5	•	1.7	0.1	0.6	0.8	0.8	•	0.2	0.7

Selected Financial Factors (in Percentages)

Debt Ratio 45	71.5	•	67.4	80.2	64.7	64.3	49.7	•	55.2	51.8
Return on Total Assets 46	11.8	•	27.1	8.3	14.5	19.4	10.7	•	8.1	14.9
Return on Equity Before Income Taxes 47	29.5	•	70.0	23.6	33.7	47.2	18.2	•	15.2	27.1
Return on Equity After Income Taxes 48	27.8	•	68.9	23.1	32.2	46.6	16.8	•	14.4	18.0
Profit Margin (Before Income Tax) 49	6.1	19.4	6.9	11.3	5.9	8.3	6.0	•	6.7	8.9
Profit Margin (After Income Tax) 50	5.8	17.7	6.7	11.1	5.6	8.2	5.6	•	6.3	5.9

Table I

Corporations with and without Net Income

PIPELINE TRANSPORTATION

MONEY AMOUNTS AND SIZE OF ASSETS IN THOUSANDS OF DOLLARS

Item Description for Accounting Period 7/10 Through 6/11	Total	Zero Assets	Under 500	500 to 1,000	1,000 to 5,000	5,000 to 10,000	10,000 to 25,000	25,000 to 50,000	50,000 to 100,000	100,000 to 250,000	250,000 to 500,000	500,000 to 2,500,000	2,500,000 and over
Number of Enterprises **1**	250	9	0	0	133	63	15	7	5	5	3	6	4
Revenues ($ in Thousands)													
Net Sales **2**	14567323	114175	0	0	450466	172687	160717	258548	310906	341665	249854	3163013	9345291
Interest **3**	81504	28	0	0	281	1	62	21	143	54	2868	861	77185
Rents **4**	48739	0	0	0	0	0	1849	4776	213	7531	934	9727	23709
Royalties **5**	321	0	0	0	239	0	0	0	0	0	17	0	65
Other Portfolio Income **6**	1471580	16317	0	0	0	0	0	0	6	79	271	746	1454162
Other Receipts **7**	665523	15515	0	0	22264	-9064	10628	402	447	12577	46366	42225	524163
Total Receipts **8**	16834990	146035	0	0	473250	163624	173256	263747	311715	361906	300310	3216572	11424575
Average Total Receipts **9**	67340	16226	•	•	3558	2597	11550	37678	62343	72381	100103	536095	2856144
Operating Costs/Operating Income (%)													
Cost of Operations **10**	47.2	70.5	•	•	39.7	28.6	22.6	23.0	12.5	25.1	14.8	38.1	54.6
Salaries and Wages **11**	5.9	1.4	•	•	23.3	6.9	3.8	2.4	26.5	6.0	0.5	5.2	4.9
Taxes Paid **12**	3.1	2.4	•	•	2.9	1.6	3.5	6.2	6.8	2.8	4.4	3.6	2.7
Interest Paid **13**	11.5	•	•	•	0.4	0.9	1.3	0.5	0.7	3.1	4.6	8.6	14.7
Depreciation **14**	11.3	18.2	•	•	0.2	17.8	4.6	8.9	6.4	9.2	25.6	12.0	11.4
Amortization and Depletion **15**	2.5	0.6	•	•	0.3	•	0.0	•	0.0	0.1	0.5	1.0	3.5
Pensions and Other Deferred Comp. **16**	0.4	•	•	•	•	0.0	•	•	1.4	0.3	0.1	0.7	0.3
Employee Benefits **17**	1.0	0.2	•	•	•	3.7	0.6	0.6	6.5	1.5	1.2	0.6	0.9
Advertising **18**	0.0	•	•	•	0.8	•	•	•	0.0	•	0.0	0.0	0.0
Other Expenses **19**	23.5	14.9	•	•	41.7	35.9	27.2	19.3	20.5	47.9	51.2	19.3	22.4
Officers' Compensation **20**	0.5	•	•	•	2.3	0.7	0.1	•	0.2	0.2	0.2	0.4	0.4
Operating Margin **21**	•	•	•	•	•	3.8	36.3	39.1	18.4	3.8	•	10.5	•
Operating Margin Before Officers' Comp. **22**	•	•	•	•	•	4.5	36.4	39.1	18.6	4.0	•	10.9	•

Selected Average Balance Sheet ($ in Thousands)

Item											
Net Receivables 23	9226	0	264	1063	1003	2845	6160	11049	16572	70492	402678
Inventories 24	3056	0	198	264	254	500	887	673	480	25189	138509
Net Property, Plant and Equipment 25	89627	0	46	1358	9717	28677	41459	81758	153945	669589	4218289
Total Assets 26	159732	0	1618	7068	14984	36470	70119	149138	343632	1037487	7610103
Notes and Loans Payable 27	86289	0	652	3125	0	4880	9301	39492	78135	524619	4407082
All Other Liabilities 28	34464	0	105	822	2166	10423	24720	56641	76557	284773	1524904
Net Worth 29	38980	0	862	3121	12818	21167	36098	53005	188899	228095	1678116

Selected Financial Ratios (Times to 1)

Item											
Current Ratio 30	1.3	•	3.0	3.0	3.5	1.2	2.0	0.8	1.3	1.0	1.3
Quick Ratio 31	0.7	•	2.2	2.3	3.0	0.9	1.8	0.6	0.8	0.7	0.6
Net Sales to Working Capital 32	12.2	•	6.3	2.2	4.1	27.7	5.4	•	2.6	•	11.0
Coverage Ratio 33	1.8	•	•	•	34.2	86.6	26.7	4.2	4.7	2.4	1.4
Total Asset Turnover 34	0.4	•	2.1	0.4	0.7	1.0	0.9	0.5	0.2	0.5	0.3
Inventory Turnover 35	9.0	•	6.8	3.0	9.5	17.0	8.7	25.5	25.7	8.0	9.2
Receivables Turnover 36	5.0	•	13.2	4.2	6.9	12.1	7.3	1.4	10.1	6.5	4.7
Total Liabilities to Net Worth 37	3.1	•	0.9	1.3	0.2	0.7	0.9	1.8	0.8	3.5	3.5
Current Assets to Working Capital 38	5.0	•	1.5	1.5	1.4	5.5	2.0	•	4.5	•	4.6
Current Liabilities to Working Capital 39	4.0	•	0.5	0.5	0.4	4.5	1.0	•	3.5	•	3.6
Working Capital to Net Sales 40	0.1	•	0.2	0.5	0.2	0.0	0.2	0.2	0.4	•	0.1
Inventory to Working Capital 41	0.6	•	0.4	0.3	0.1	0.3	0.1	•	0.0	•	0.5
Total Receipts to Cash Flow 42	3.8	5.6	3.6	3.7	1.5	1.8	3.1	1.8	1.6	3.5	4.6
Cost of Goods to Cash Flow 43	1.8	4.0	1.4	1.1	0.3	0.4	0.4	0.4	0.2	1.3	2.5
Cash Flow to Total Debt 44	0.1	•	1.3	0.2	3.3	1.4	0.6	0.4	0.3	0.2	0.1

Selected Financial Factors (in Percentages)

Item											
Debt Ratio 45	75.6	•	46.7	55.8	14.5	42.0	48.5	64.5	45.0	78.0	77.9
Return on Total Assets 46	7.4	•	•	•	32.5	42.1	17.2	5.8	5.2	10.6	6.5
Return on Equity Before Income Taxes 47	13.3	•	•	•	36.9	71.8	32.2	12.5	7.5	28.2	9.0
Return on Equity After Income Taxes 48	9.6	•	•	•	25.9	46.7	24.6	8.9	3.3	16.2	8.1
Profit Margin (Before Income Tax) 49	8.9	19.7	•	•	44.1	41.1	18.7	9.7	17.1	12.2	6.5
Profit Margin (After Income Tax) 50	6.4	9.5	•	•	31.0	26.8	14.3	6.9	7.6	7.0	5.8

Table II
Corporations with Net Income

PIPELINE TRANSPORTATION

MONEY AMOUNTS AND SIZE OF ASSETS IN THOUSANDS OF DOLLARS

Item Description for Accounting Period 7/10 Through 6/11	Total	Zero Assets	Under 500	500 to 1,000	1,000 to 5,000	5,000 to 10,000	10,000 to 25,000	25,000 to 50,000	50,000 to 100,000	100,000 to 250,000	250,000 to 500,000	500,000 to 2,500,000	2,500,000 and over
Number of Enterprises **1**	76	•	0	0	25	7	11	7	5	5	0	•	•
Revenues ($ in Thousands)													
Net Sales **2**	11314892	•	0	0	878	50117	150117	258548	310906	541126	0	•	•
Interest **3**	76201	•	0	0	281	1	41	21	143	341	0	•	•
Rents **4**	35984	•	0	0	0	0	1849	4776	213	5594	0	•	•
Royalties **5**	239	•	0	0	239	0	0	0	0	0	0	•	•
Other Portfolio Income **6**	1469941	•	0	0	0	0	0	0	6	79	0	•	•
Other Receipts **7**	676120	•	0	0	22263	11267	10629	402	447	58654	0	•	•
Total Receipts **8**	13573377	•	0	0	23661	61385	162636	263747	311715	605794	0	•	•
Average Total Receipts **9**	178597	•	•	•	946	8769	14785	37678	62343	121159	•	•	•
Operating Costs/Operating Income (%)													
Cost of Operations **10**	46.1	•	•	•	21.1	43.2	19.3	23.0	12.5	21.2	•	•	•
Salaries and Wages **11**	5.5	•	•	•	20.3	0.9	4.1	2.4	26.5	2.9	•	•	•
Taxes Paid **12**	3.3	•	•	•	52.6	1.9	3.7	6.2	6.8	3.3	•	•	•
Interest Paid **13**	9.8	•	•	•	0.7	•	1.4	0.5	0.7	3.4	•	•	•
Depreciation **14**	11.7	•	•	•	0.8	6.1	3.6	8.9	6.4	11.4	•	•	•
Amortization and Depletion **15**	2.9	•	•	•	19.1	•	0.0	•	0.0	0.1	•	•	•
Pensions and Other Deferred Comp. **16**	0.5	•	•	•	•	0.0	•	•	0.0	0.3	•	•	•
Employee Benefits **17**	1.0	•	•	•	•	4.6	0.6	0.6	6.5	1.2	•	•	•
Advertising **18**	0.0	•	•	•	•	•	•	•	0.0	0.0	•	•	•
Other Expenses **19**	24.5	•	•	•	17.7	2.2	28.0	19.3	20.5	47.2	•	•	•
Officers' Compensation **20**	0.5	•	•	•	•	2.3	0.1	•	0.2	0.1	•	•	•
Operating Margin **21**	•	•	•	•	•	38.8	39.3	39.1	18.4	8.9	•	•	•
Operating Margin Before Officers' Comp. **22**	•	•	•	•	•	41.1	39.3	39.1	18.6	9.0	•	•	•

Selected Average Balance Sheet ($ in Thousands)

Net Receivables 23	24860	9	628	1243	2845	6160	17494
Inventories 24	6800	520	66	302	445	1100	363
Net Property, Plant and Equipment 25	252554	0	1039	10682	28677	41459	124934
Total Assets 26	394197	3737	8124	15865	36470	70119	191293
Notes and Loans Payable 27	202057	17	0	0	4880	9301	68018
All Other Liabilities 28	93741	0	1138	2267	10423	24720	52960
Net Worth 29	98399	3720	6986	13598	21167	36098	70315

Selected Financial Ratios (Times to 1)

Current Ratio 30	1.2	71.7	3.3	1.2	2.0	0.8	
Quick Ratio 31	0.6	66.5	3.0	0.9	1.8	0.6	
Net Sales to Working Capital 32	16.6	0.0	2.1	5.0	27.7	5.4	•
Coverage Ratio 33	2.4	3751.0	•	34.5	86.6	26.7	7.0
Total Asset Turnover 34	0.4	0.0	0.9	0.9	1.0	0.9	0.6
Inventory Turnover 35	10.1	0.0	46.8	8.7	19.1	7.0	63.4
Receivables Turnover 36	5.0	0.1	12.5	•	•	•	1.7
Total Liabilities to Net Worth 37	3.0	0.0	0.2	0.2	0.7	0.9	
Current Assets to Working Capital 38	6.7	1.0	1.4	5.5	2.0		
Current Liabilities to Working Capital 39	5.7	0.0	0.4	4.5	1.0		
Working Capital to Net Sales 40	0.1	21.8	0.5	0.2	0.0	0.2	
Inventory to Working Capital 41	0.5	•	0.0	0.1	0.3	0.1	
Total Receipts to Cash Flow 42	3.1	0.0	1.6	1.4	1.8	3.1	1.5
Cost of Goods to Cash Flow 43	1.5	0.0	0.7	0.3	0.4	0.4	0.3
Cash Flow to Total Debt 44	0.2	52.2	4.0	4.3	1.4	0.6	0.6

Selected Financial Factors (in Percentages)

Debt Ratio 45	75.0	0.5	14.0	14.3	42.0	48.5	63.2
Return on Total Assets 46	9.1	24.1	54.0	42.2	42.1	17.2	13.7
Return on Equity Before Income Taxes 47	21.4	24.2	62.8	47.8	71.8	32.2	32.1
Return on Equity After Income Taxes 48	16.6	17.4	55.7	33.7	46.7	24.6	22.6
Profit Margin (Before Income Tax) 49	14.1	2562.6	61.3	47.6	41.1	18.7	20.8
Profit Margin (After Income Tax) 50	11.0	1842.8	54.4	33.6	26.8	14.3	14.7

Table I
Corporations with and without Net Income

OTHER TRANSPORTATION AND SUPPORT ACTIVITIES

MONEY AMOUNTS AND SIZE OF ASSETS IN THOUSANDS OF DOLLARS

Item Description for Accounting Period 7/10 Through 6/11	Total	Zero Assets	Under 500	500 to 1,000	1,000 to 5,000	5,000 to 10,000	10,000 to 25,000	25,000 to 50,000	50,000 to 100,000	100,000 to 250,000	250,000 to 500,000	500,000 to 2,500,000	2,500,000 and over
Number of Enterprises 1	41912	7509	28331	2486	2724	349	287	70	62	46	22	22	4
Revenues ($ in Thousands)													
Net Sales 2	215803555	935602	22959323	5847788	19081419	5984112	11662218	6089850	8232673	7766010	7773707	13791475	105679379
Interest 3	810583	45	2633	1102	8614	1402	5925	2534	7440	8756	26309	116210	629616
Rents 4	252903	40	0	56	0	5404	4990	4	6139	74548	13668	46524	101530
Royalties 5	1927500	0	0	9	0	0	7719	0	23	1588	0	0	1918161
Other Portfolio Income 6	958175	133015	55963	15372	14659	5805	94331	4269	15871	10397	99631	347914	160944
Other Receipts 7	2533798	23627	108118	35788	101131	39658	35535	112884	216631	93034	182741	260827	1323825
Total Receipts 8	222286514	1092329	23126037	5900115	19205823	6036381	11810718	6209541	8478777	7954333	8096056	14562950	109813455
Average Total Receipts 9	5304	145	816	2373	7051	17296	41152	88708	136754	172920	368003	661952	27453364
Operating Costs/Operating Income (%)													
Cost of Operations 10	40.0	22.3	58.6	42.6	62.3	62.0	63.8	75.3	59.2	63.8	46.5	44.1	21.8
Salaries and Wages 11	17.1	14.4	6.3	13.0	15.0	13.4	11.9	7.8	13.5	9.6	19.3	18.3	21.9
Taxes Paid 12	2.7	2.4	1.6	7.9	1.9	3.7	1.9	2.1	2.5	1.7	2.2	2.7	3.0
Interest Paid 13	1.2	0.8	0.4	1.1	0.5	0.6	0.7	0.6	0.9	1.5	1.4	5.2	1.1
Depreciation 14	3.4	2.3	0.9	3.0	1.8	1.3	1.8	1.4	2.3	3.9	3.3	3.5	4.8
Amortization and Depletion 15	0.4	0.0	0.0	0.0	0.2	0.1	0.1	0.2	0.5	1.0	1.2	2.3	0.2
Pensions and Other Deferred Comp. 16	2.4	•	0.2	0.4	0.2	0.5	0.5	0.2	0.3	0.3	0.4	0.6	4.5
Employee Benefits 17	3.7	0.6	0.4	0.8	0.9	1.4	1.5	0.9	1.8	2.0	2.8	5.3	5.8
Advertising 18	0.3	0.3	0.2	0.4	0.3	0.1	0.1	0.0	0.1	0.3	0.2	0.2	0.5
Other Expenses 19	28.0	55.8	25.6	24.1	12.4	12.5	15.2	8.8	19.3	17.5	23.6	20.2	37.5
Officers' Compensation 20	1.3	4.1	3.7	5.0	2.7	2.0	1.6	1.6	0.7	1.0	1.3	0.6	0.3
Operating Margin 21	•	•	2.0	1.7	1.8	2.4	0.9	1.0	•	•	•	•	•
Operating Margin Before Officers' Comp. 22	0.8	1.0	5.8	6.7	4.5	4.4	2.5	2.6	•	•	•	•	•

Selected Average Balance Sheet ($ in Thousands)

Net Receivables 23	822	0	12	131	722	2598	5661	10626	21661	32959	63320	141215	5294609
Inventories 24	42	0	2	17	67	36	205	547	2851	4685	5437	16924	125040
Net Property, Plant and Equipment 25	1032	0	32	241	564	1712	4421	7873	18308	37905	63795	178564	7396986
Total Assets 26	3711	0	92	699	2188	7101	15144	34285	69816	150564	347733	1174291	22817903
Notes and Loans Payable 27	1038	0	48	404	934	1878	4833	10526	23388	43290	107792	414437	5214506
All Other Liabilities 28	1589	0	36	285	719	2458	5858	15001	22119	52731	107052	343498	11405213
Net Worth 29	1085	0	8	9	534	2766	4453	8759	24309	54544	132888	416356	6198184

Selected Financial Ratios (Times to 1)

Current Ratio 30	1.2	•	1.4	1.1	1.5	1.7	1.3	1.1	1.4	1.3	1.6	1.5	1.1
Quick Ratio 31	1.0	•	1.3	0.8	1.2	1.5	1.1	0.9	1.1	1.0	1.0	1.1	1.0
Net Sales to Working Capital 32	23.0	•	63.1	54.6	17.6	10.8	21.2	41.3	13.0	10.8	6.6	6.2	58.0
Coverage Ratio 33	3.2	17.9	8.8	3.4	5.7	6.7	4.3	5.6	3.1	0.9	2.6	1.6	3.4
Total Asset Turnover 34	1.4	•	8.8	3.4	3.2	2.4	2.7	2.5	1.9	1.1	1.0	0.5	1.2
Inventory Turnover 35	48.9	•	278.4	57.9	65.6	294.4	126.2	119.8	27.6	23.0	30.2	16.3	46.2
Receivables Turnover 36	7.7	•	63.0	12.7	9.8	5.6	8.7	8.1	7.2	5.4	6.7	4.5	6.9
Total Liabilities to Net Worth 37	2.4	•	10.5	74.8	3.1	1.6	2.4	2.9	1.9	1.8	1.6	1.8	2.7
Current Assets to Working Capital 38	5.9	•	3.3	8.2	3.2	2.5	4.9	8.6	3.6	3.9	2.7	3.0	16.4
Current Liabilities to Working Capital 39	4.9	•	2.3	7.2	2.2	1.5	3.9	7.6	2.6	2.9	1.7	2.0	15.4
Working Capital to Net Sales 40	0.0	•	0.0	0.0	0.1	0.1	0.0	0.0	0.1	0.1	0.2	0.2	0.0
Inventory to Working Capital 41	0.2	•	0.1	0.4	0.1	0.0	0.1	0.2	0.3	0.4	0.2	0.1	0.3
Total Receipts to Cash Flow 42	4.1	2.0	4.5	4.2	8.5	8.0	7.3	10.5	5.6	8.3	5.1	5.5	3.1
Cost of Goods to Cash Flow 43	1.6	0.5	2.6	1.8	5.3	5.0	4.6	7.9	3.3	5.3	2.4	2.4	0.7
Cash Flow to Total Debt 44	0.5	•	2.2	0.8	0.5	0.5	0.5	0.3	0.5	0.2	0.3	0.1	0.5

Selected Financial Factors (in Percentages)

Debt Ratio 45	70.8	•	91.3	98.7	75.6	61.1	70.6	74.5	65.2	63.8	61.8	64.5	72.8
Return on Total Assets 46	5.3	•	27.1	12.4	9.5	9.2	7.7	9.1	5.4	1.5	3.6	4.6	4.4
Return on Equity Before Income Taxes 47	12.3	•	277.4	661.4	32.1	20.2	20.3	29.1	10.3	•	5.8	5.1	11.4
Return on Equity After Income Taxes 48	8.2	•	268.5	638.1	29.7	18.3	17.5	25.0	7.8	•	3.3	0.5	6.9
Profit Margin (Before Income Tax) 49	2.6	13.6	2.7	2.6	2.4	3.3	2.2	2.9	1.9	•	2.2	3.4	2.7
Profit Margin (After Income Tax) 50	1.7	8.3	2.7	2.5	2.3	3.0	1.9	2.5	1.4	•	1.2	0.3	1.6

249

Table II
Corporations with Net Income

OTHER TRANSPORTATION AND SUPPORT ACTIVITIES

MONEY AMOUNTS AND SIZE OF ASSETS IN THOUSANDS OF DOLLARS

Item Description for Accounting Period 7/10 Through 6/11	Total	Zero Assets	Under 500	500 to 1,000	1,000 to 5,000	5,000 to 10,000	10,000 to 25,000	25,000 to 50,000	50,000 to 100,000	100,000 to 250,000	250,000 to 500,000	500,000 to 2,500,000	2,500,000 and over
Number of Enterprises **1**	23591	2500	17138	1723	1654	238	183	59	43	26	15	13	0
Revenues ($ in Thousands)													
Net Sales **2**	178352785	374100	18211863	5046632	15063627	5379362	7991580	5788978	6198091	4677101	5381626	104239825	0
Interest **3**	624049	22	57	523	7986	1203	2984	2397	6817	3884	10728	587448	0
Rents **4**	174107	40	0	56	0	3918	3751	0	5583	47488	11840	101431	0
Royalties **5**	1904021	0	0	9	0	0	0	0	23	1173	0	1902816	0
Other Portfolio Income **6**	900922	131442	43834	14572	14504	2790	90994	2085	13309	6668	94950	485770	0
Other Receipts **7**	1138002	985	93698	31484	75272	29462	17513	128060	148015	52686	159043	401789	0
Total Receipts **8**	183093886	506589	18349452	5093276	15161389	5416735	8106822	5921520	6371838	4789000	5658187	107719079	0
Average Total Receipts **9**	7761	203	1071	2956	9166	22759	44300	100365	148182	184192	377212	8286083	•
Operating Costs/Operating Income (%)													
Cost of Operations **10**	37.4	14.0	58.9	42.3	60.8	63.2	56.3	77.3	57.5	67.1	42.7	22.3	•
Salaries and Wages **11**	17.7	11.9	4.9	13.6	16.1	11.8	14.6	7.4	13.0	8.6	19.2	22.1	•
Taxes Paid **12**	2.7	2.2	1.3	8.7	1.9	3.7	2.1	2.0	2.2	1.6	2.3	3.0	•
Interest Paid **13**	0.8	0.8	0.2	1.0	0.3	0.5	0.5	0.7	0.7	1.1	1.9	1.0	•
Depreciation **14**	3.6	4.8	0.8	2.4	1.4	0.9	1.7	1.2	1.7	4.3	3.7	5.0	•
Amortization and Depletion **15**	0.2	0.0	0.0	0.0	0.1	0.1	0.1	0.2	0.3	0.7	0.8	0.2	•
Pensions and Other Deferred Comp. **16**	2.8	•	0.2	0.5	0.2	0.5	0.6	0.2	0.3	0.3	0.5	4.6	•
Employee Benefits **17**	3.9	0.7	0.3	0.7	0.8	1.2	1.9	0.8	1.5	2.3	3.1	5.9	•
Advertising **18**	0.3	0.0	0.2	0.4	0.2	0.1	0.1	0.0	0.1	0.2	0.2	0.5	•
Other Expenses **19**	27.6	49.0	25.7	22.7	12.4	12.2	16.3	7.5	20.9	11.3	23.1	34.4	•
Officers' Compensation **20**	1.1	5.9	3.0	4.5	2.5	2.2	1.6	1.6	0.7	0.8	1.6	0.3	•
Operating Margin **21**	1.8	10.8	4.5	3.2	3.3	3.7	4.3	1.0	1.1	1.6	0.9	0.8	•
Operating Margin Before Officers' Comp. **22**	2.9	16.7	7.5	7.7	5.8	5.9	5.9	2.7	1.8	2.5	2.5	1.1	•

Selected Average Balance Sheet ($ in Thousands)

Net Receivables 23	1253	0	13	152	827	3323	6286	11714	23528	33661	61087	1713779	•
Inventories 24	45	0	1	14	56	15	212	372	2582	5245	7247	38328	•
Net Property, Plant and Equipment 25	1603	0	37	224	435	1684	3882	7075	16350	44420	80184	2422673	•
Total Assets 26	4830	0	103	696	2215	7542	15249	34689	70261	151345	350187	6805371	•
Notes and Loans Payable 27	1239	0	46	287	633	1796	3890	12027	19529	38504	101149	1669191	•
All Other Liabilities 28	1929	0	34	227	792	2219	6061	16331	22740	56434	104019	2816606	•
Net Worth 29	1662	0	23	182	790	3526	5298	6331	27992	56407	145019	2319574	•

Selected Financial Ratios (Times to 1)

Current Ratio 30	1.2	•	2.0	1.3	1.6	2.0	1.4	1.1	1.4	1.4	1.7	1.2	•
Quick Ratio 31	1.1	•	1.8	1.2	1.3	1.9	1.2	0.9	1.2	1.1	1.1	1.0	•
Net Sales to Working Capital 32	19.8	•	43.3	35.0	17.6	9.4	16.9	67.9	13.0	9.9	6.4	22.5	•
Coverage Ratio 33	6.4	59.9	23.8	5.3	13.8	10.2	13.6	6.1	6.8	4.7	4.4	5.2	•
Total Asset Turnover 34	1.6	•	10.3	4.2	4.1	3.0	2.9	2.8	2.1	1.2	1.0	1.2	•
Inventory Turnover 35	63.1	•	465.2	90.3	99.3	964.3	116.1	204.0	32.1	23.0	21.1	46.7	•
Receivables Turnover 36	7.8	•	88.2	19.1	11.8	6.5	8.2	9.0	7.2	5.7	7.8	6.4	•
Total Liabilities to Net Worth 37	1.9	•	3.4	2.8	1.8	1.1	1.9	4.5	1.5	1.7	1.4	1.9	•
Current Assets to Working Capital 38	5.1	•	2.0	4.0	2.8	2.0	3.8	13.0	3.4	3.5	2.5	7.0	•
Current Liabilities to Working Capital 39	4.1	•	1.0	3.0	1.8	1.0	2.8	12.0	2.4	2.5	1.5	6.0	•
Working Capital to Net Sales 40	0.1	•	0.0	0.0	0.1	0.1	0.1	0.0	0.1	0.1	0.2	0.0	•
Inventory to Working Capital 41	0.1	•	0.0	0.1	0.1	0.0	0.1	0.4	0.3	0.4	0.2	0.1	•
Total Receipts to Cash Flow 42	3.8	2.0	3.8	4.0	7.7	7.4	5.4	11.6	4.6	9.3	4.2	3.2	•
Cost of Goods to Cash Flow 43	1.4	0.3	2.3	1.7	4.7	4.7	3.0	8.9	2.7	6.2	1.8	0.7	•
Cash Flow to Total Debt 44	0.6	•	3.5	1.4	0.8	0.8	0.8	0.3	0.7	0.2	0.4	0.6	•

Selected Financial Factors (in Percentages)

Debt Ratio 45	65.6	•	77.4	73.8	64.3	53.2	65.3	81.7	60.2	62.7	58.6	65.9	•
Return on Total Assets 46	8.4	•	56.6	21.5	17.5	14.8	17.8	11.2	9.5	6.0	8.4	6.2	•
Return on Equity Before Income Taxes 47	20.5	•	240.0	66.6	45.6	28.5	47.4	51.5	20.4	12.8	15.6	14.7	•
Return on Equity After Income Taxes 48	15.8	•	234.9	64.9	42.9	26.3	43.7	44.7	17.2	10.2	12.2	9.7	•
Profit Margin (Before Income Tax) 49	4.5	46.2	5.3	4.1	4.0	4.4	5.7	3.3	4.0	4.0	6.3	4.3	•
Profit Margin (After Income Tax) 50	3.5	33.2	5.2	4.0	3.7	4.1	5.3	2.9	3.3	3.2	4.9	2.8	•

Table I
Corporations with and without Net Income

WAREHOUSING AND STORAGE

MONEY AMOUNTS AND SIZE OF ASSETS IN THOUSANDS OF DOLLARS

Item Description for Accounting Period 7/10 Through 6/11	Total	Zero Assets	Under 500	500 to 1,000	1,000 to 5,000	5,000 to 10,000	10,000 to 25,000	25,000 to 50,000	50,000 to 100,000	100,000 to 250,000	250,000 to 500,000	500,000 to 2,500,000	2,500,000 and over
Number of Enterprises **1**	5452	941	2098	957	898	255	211	49	17	13	4	9	0
Revenues ($ in Thousands)													
Net Sales **2**	24338151	350914	452309	1195410	3441508	2746355	4455595	1400673	1591544	1328606	614281	6760956	0
Interest **3**	79469	1022	1	2381	1572	706	8135	662	475	465	8876	55174	0
Rents **4**	19569	836	0	0	1816	718	1022	2645	233	4123	7294	882	0
Royalties **5**	30023	0	0	0	0	0	0	0	0	4	30020	0	0
Other Portfolio Income **6**	172250	81506	8	665	2564	557	22656	27174	919	9224	1487	25491	0
Other Receipts **7**	543001	48987	6349	1882	37972	33103	104496	42328	18996	93810	120731	34344	0
Total Receipts **8**	25182463	483265	458667	1200338	3485432	2781439	4591904	1473482	1612167	1436228	752673	6906867	0
Average Total Receipts **9**	4619	514	219	1254	3881	10908	21763	30071	94833	110479	188168	767430	•
Operating Costs/Operating Income (%)													
Cost of Operations **10**	39.1	24.1	22.5	3.7	60.5	55.8	49.5	50.2	59.7	21.0	0.8	22.8	•
Salaries and Wages **11**	17.5	24.6	30.7	28.2	10.8	7.6	16.9	14.2	9.0	33.3	24.8	21.2	•
Taxes Paid **12**	3.3	3.3	4.2	3.0	2.5	2.2	3.2	3.2	2.7	4.3	6.1	3.9	•
Interest Paid **13**	3.0	3.5	1.0	1.3	1.6	1.7	1.1	2.4	1.2	1.8	5.3	6.3	•
Depreciation **14**	4.6	5.0	0.9	2.5	2.7	2.1	4.0	6.9	3.9	6.3	13.7	6.0	•
Amortization and Depletion **15**	0.7	0.2	•	0.0	0.1	0.0	0.2	0.2	0.6	0.6	0.1	2.2	•
Pensions and Other Deferred Comp. **16**	0.4	0.6	•	0.4	0.2	0.6	0.2	0.3	0.7	1.2	1.8	0.4	•
Employee Benefits **17**	2.1	0.5	0.1	1.9	1.6	1.1	1.4	1.2	3.0	5.5	5.1	2.5	•
Advertising **18**	0.3	0.2	0.1	1.1	0.3	0.1	0.1	0.1	0.1	0.1	0.1	0.4	•
Other Expenses **19**	27.4	44.6	59.2	55.4	16.9	24.1	20.2	22.5	16.3	29.6	45.9	32.3	•
Officers' Compensation **20**	1.4	0.4	1.4	1.9	3.1	2.0	1.9	0.9	0.9	1.0	0.4	0.2	•
Operating Margin **21**	0.2	•	•	0.4	•	2.7	1.4	•	1.9	•	•	1.8	•
Operating Margin Before Officers' Comp. **22**	1.6	•	•	2.4	2.8	4.7	3.3	•	2.8	•	•	2.0	•

Selected Average Balance Sheet ($ in Thousands)

Net Receivables 23	566	0	21	155	401	1062	2217	3538	12169	23206	13843	117337
Inventories 24	140	0	1	17	205	237	667	1362	3222	12995	44	7690
Net Property, Plant and Equipment 25	1877	0	75	288	1173	2811	6623	19033	32284	57337	244128	381383
Total Assets 26	5653	0	152	664	2208	7062	15600	35422	71189	142652	390039	1825816
Notes and Loans Payable 27	2305	0	104	600	1081	3408	5397	17139	17145	30642	85756	769125
All Other Liabilities 28	1231	0	3	261	614	963	2725	5083	23211	35918	135729	381404
Net Worth 29	2117	0	45	-198	514	2692	7478	13201	30832	76092	168555	675286

Selected Financial Ratios (Times to 1)

Current Ratio 30	1.2	•	1.6	1.1	1.1	1.2	2.0	1.7	0.9	1.5	0.7	1.0
Quick Ratio 31	0.9	•	1.0	0.9	0.7	0.9	1.2	1.2	0.6	1.0	0.5	0.8
Net Sales to Working Capital 32	18.4	•	10.1	41.9	69.5	23.3	6.7	6.3	•	6.3	•	126.1
Coverage Ratio 33	2.3	9.9	•	1.7	1.6	3.4	5.1	2.6	3.7	2.8	4.6	1.6
Total Asset Turnover 34	0.8	•	1.4	1.9	1.7	1.5	1.4	0.8	1.3	0.7	0.4	0.4
Inventory Turnover 35	12.5	•	91.8	2.6	11.3	25.4	15.7	10.5	17.3	1.7	26.0	22.2
Receivables Turnover 36	8.2	•	9.0	8.7	11.2	13.4	11.0	10.4	8.1	3.5	15.3	6.1
Total Liabilities to Net Worth 37	1.7	•	2.4	•	3.3	1.6	1.1	1.7	1.3	0.9	1.3	1.7
Current Assets to Working Capital 38	5.0	•	2.6	9.7	15.4	6.2	2.0	2.4	•	3.0	•	32.0
Current Liabilities to Working Capital 39	4.0	•	1.6	8.7	14.4	5.2	1.0	1.4	•	2.0	•	31.0
Working Capital to Net Sales 40	0.1	•	0.1	0.0	0.0	0.0	0.1	0.2	•	0.2	•	0.0
Inventory to Working Capital 41	0.7	•	•	0.8	3.8	0.8	0.2	0.6	•	0.8	•	2.1
Total Receipts to Cash Flow 42	4.8	2.2	8.0	2.7	8.2	8.1	6.3	5.3	7.0	4.3	1.7	3.8
Cost of Goods to Cash Flow 43	1.9	0.5	1.8	0.1	5.0	4.5	3.1	2.7	4.2	0.9	0.0	0.9
Cash Flow to Total Debt 44	0.3	•	0.3	0.5	0.3	0.3	0.4	0.2	0.3	0.4	0.4	0.2

Selected Financial Factors (in Percentages)

Debt Ratio 45	62.5	•	70.3	129.8	76.7	61.9	52.1	62.7	56.7	46.7	56.8	63.0
Return on Total Assets 46	5.3	•	•	4.0	4.4	8.6	7.4	4.9	5.8	3.7	9.5	4.3
Return on Equity Before Income Taxes 47	7.8	•	•	•	7.0	15.8	12.4	8.1	9.7	4.5	17.1	4.5
Return on Equity After Income Taxes 48	5.5	•	•	•	4.4	14.7	10.4	5.7	7.6	3.9	13.5	2.4
Profit Margin (Before Income Tax) 49	3.7	30.7	•	0.9	0.9	4.0	4.4	3.7	3.2	3.3	18.7	4.0
Profit Margin (After Income Tax) 50	2.6	20.9	•	0.8	0.6	3.7	3.7	2.6	2.5	2.9	14.8	2.2

Table II
Corporations with Net Income

WAREHOUSING AND STORAGE

MONEY AMOUNTS AND SIZE OF ASSETS IN THOUSANDS OF DOLLARS

Item Description for Accounting Period 7/10 Through 6/11	Total	Zero Assets	Under 500	500 to 1000	1,000 to 5,000	5,000 to 10,000	10,000 to 25,000	25,000 to 50,000	50,000 to 100,000	100,000 to 250,000	250,000 to 500,000	500,000 to 2,500,000	2,500,000 and over
Number of Enterprises 1	2461	•	651	689	563	142	144	•	13	9	•	5	0
Revenues ($ in Thousands)													
Net Sales 2	17675247	•	147121	705669	1466087	2380840	3518067	•	1492388	1250166	•	511846	0
Interest 3	25022	•	1	2339	1527	664	7493	•	358	385	•	2171	0
Rents 4	17868	•	0	0	1816	109	1022	•	233	3862	•	874	0
Royalties 5	30023	•	0	0	0	0	0	•	0	0	•	30020	0
Other Portfolio Income 6	164247	•	0	629	2505	400	22010	•	747	8826	•	20943	0
Other Receipts 7	465991	•	-1	1582	29866	26753	74195	•	18982	93018	•	11708	0
Total Receipts 8	18378398	•	147121	710219	1501801	2408766	3622787	•	1512708	1356257	•	5177562	0
Average Total Receipts 9	7468	•	226	1031	2667	16963	25158	•	116362	150695	•	1035512	•
Operating Costs/Operating Income (%)													
Cost of Operations 10	37.0	•	0.1	0.7	37.1	55.9	53.9	•	62.5	21.0	•	21.2	•
Salaries and Wages 11	18.4	•	44.0	24.8	14.3	7.3	16.0	•	8.5	34.0	•	23.9	•
Taxes Paid 12	3.3	•	2.5	2.4	3.4	2.0	2.8	•	2.5	4.4	•	4.1	•
Interest Paid 13	2.5	•	0.0	1.4	2.3	1.0	1.0	•	0.7	1.8	•	5.0	•
Depreciation 14	4.1	•	2.0	3.4	3.6	1.2	2.4	•	3.4	4.2	•	5.8	•
Amortization and Depletion 15	0.6	•	•	0.0	0.2	0.0	0.1	•	0.3	0.4	•	1.8	•
Pensions and Other Deferred Comp. 16	0.5	•	•	0.4	0.3	0.4	0.1	•	0.7	1.3	•	0.4	•
Employee Benefits 17	2.3	•	0.0	1.0	2.5	1.1	1.1	•	3.0	5.6	•	2.6	•
Advertising 18	0.3	•	0.0	1.9	0.1	0.1	0.1	•	0.0	0.1	•	0.4	•
Other Expenses 19	25.6	•	42.2	55.8	26.8	22.3	17.0	•	14.7	30.0	•	27.5	•
Officers' Compensation 20	1.2	•	0.1	3.2	2.5	2.2	1.6	•	0.9	0.8	•	0.3	•
Operating Margin 21	4.2	•	9.0	4.9	7.0	6.5	3.9	•	2.9	•	•	6.9	•
Operating Margin Before Officers' Comp. 22	5.5	•	9.1	8.1	9.5	8.7	5.5	•	3.7	•	•	7.2	•

Selected Average Balance Sheet ($ in Thousands)

Item											
Net Receivables 23	859	•	0	97	275	1231	2488	•	14723	25051	155707
Inventories 24	198	•	0	1	69	269	808	•	6670	18434	10733
Net Property, Plant and Equipment 25	2873	•	210	307	1202	3233	6059	•	34848	63288	475011
Total Assets 26	7500	•	254	650	2041	7675	15311	•	70458	152031	1731510
Notes and Loans Payable 27	3070	•	212	439	1099	2524	5611	•	13490	40530	837248
All Other Liabilities 28	1636	•	2	44	217	1217	3063	•	28616	21937	390441
Net Worth 29	2795	•	40	167	726	3934	6637	•	28353	89564	503822

Selected Financial Ratios (Times to 1)

Item											
Current Ratio 30	1.5	•	0.4	3.9	2.5	2.5	2.1	•	0.9	1.6	1.2
Quick Ratio 31	1.1	•	0.0	3.5	2.0	2.0	1.2	•	0.5	1.0	0.9
Net Sales to Working Capital 32	10.8	•	•	6.1	6.9	7.2	6.5	•	6.8	6.5	25.3
Coverage Ratio 33	4.3	•	1470.9	5.0	5.2	8.5	7.5	•	6.8	3.8	2.7
Total Asset Turnover 34	1.0	•	0.9	1.6	1.3	2.2	1.6	•	1.6	0.9	0.6
Inventory Turnover 35	13.4	•	•	6.1	14.0	34.9	16.3	•	10.8	1.6	20.2
Receivables Turnover 36	8.3	•	8.2	8.0	8.9	16.5	•	•	•	•	6.3
Total Liabilities to Net Worth 37	1.7	•	5.4	2.9	1.8	1.0	1.3	•	1.5	0.7	2.4
Current Assets to Working Capital 38	3.0	•	•	1.3	1.7	1.7	1.9	•	•	2.7	6.8
Current Liabilities to Working Capital 39	2.0	•	•	0.3	0.7	0.7	0.9	•	•	1.7	5.8
Working Capital to Net Sales 40	0.1	•	•	0.2	0.1	0.1	0.2	•	•	0.2	0.0
Inventory to Working Capital 41	0.4	•	•	0.0	0.1	0.2	0.2	•	•	0.9	0.5
Total Receipts to Cash Flow 42	4.3	•	3.0	2.5	3.9	7.4	6.2	•	7.0	4.0	3.8
Cost of Goods to Cash Flow 43	1.6	•	0.0	0.0	1.4	4.1	3.3	•	4.4	0.8	0.8
Cash Flow to Total Debt 44	0.4	•	0.3	0.8	0.5	0.6	0.5	•	0.4	0.6	0.2

Selected Financial Factors (in Percentages)

Item											
Debt Ratio 45	62.7	•	84.3	74.3	64.4	48.7	56.7	•	59.8	41.1	70.9
Return on Total Assets 46	10.3	•	8.0	10.9	14.9	19.0	12.5	•	8.0	6.1	7.9
Return on Equity Before Income Taxes 47	21.2	•	51.0	34.0	33.8	32.7	25.0	•	17.0	7.7	16.9
Return on Equity After Income Taxes 48	17.3	•	40.9	33.5	30.9	31.3	21.7	•	14.1	7.0	11.9
Profit Margin (Before Income Tax) 49	8.2	•	9.0	5.6	9.4	7.7	6.8	•	4.2	5.0	8.3
Profit Margin (After Income Tax) 50	6.7	•	7.2	5.5	8.6	7.3	5.9	•	3.5	4.5	5.9

INFORMATION
511110

Table I
Corporations with and without Net Income

NEWSPAPER PUBLISHERS

MONEY AMOUNTS AND SIZE OF ASSETS IN THOUSANDS OF DOLLARS

Item Description for Accounting Period 7/10 Through 6/11		Total	Zero Assets	Under 500	500 to 1,000	1,000 to 5,000	5,000 to 10,000	10,000 to 25,000	25,000 to 50,000	50,000 to 100,000	100,000 to 250,000	250,000 to 500,000	500,000 to 2,500,000	2,500,000 and over
Number of Enterprises	1	5259	644	3583	482	324	45	86	38	22	13	10	8	5
Revenues ($ in Thousands)														
Net Sales	2	27151453	97690	1542400	575963	2263593	313841	1306427	1205372	1164465	1637740	2540896	3580692	10922374
Interest	3	61514	30	488	6	238	3140	3361	1997	1170	19906	7291	12664	11225
Rents	4	65252	0	0	0	0	494	1586	4805	413	9998	12503	9488	25963
Royalties	5	23798	0	0	0	0	0	109	2392	0	358	109	494	20335
Other Portfolio Income	6	114660	8	0	501	5	195	9077	6882	8334	3523	23276	11505	51352
Other Receipts	7	1305488	-3696	2316	3	54301	3688	11078	62544	16150	17798	22481	179926	938902
Total Receipts	8	28722165	94032	1545204	576473	2318137	321358	1331638	1283992	1190532	1689323	2606556	3794769	11970151
Average Total Receipts	9	5462	146	431	1196	7155	7141	15484	33789	54115	129948	260656	474346	2394030
Operating Costs/Operating Income (%)														
Cost of Operations	10	29.3	10.2	41.6	54.7	59.3	23.0	32.7	24.1	28.0	17.5	26.3	17.5	27.1
Salaries and Wages	11	24.2	7.3	22.7	5.7	16.7	26.5	26.6	28.3	29.6	28.5	23.9	28.2	23.9
Taxes Paid	12	3.5	1.7	3.3	4.2	2.4	3.3	4.4	4.2	3.7	4.2	3.6	3.7	3.4
Interest Paid	13	6.2	0.7	0.4	0.3	1.6	1.3	2.0	2.1	2.2	3.9	3.6	8.9	9.8
Depreciation	14	3.6	0.5	1.8	0.4	2.0	1.3	3.9	3.5	5.2	5.6	4.5	3.9	3.7
Amortization and Depletion	15	4.9	•	0.5	2.4	0.0	1.5	1.0	2.5	1.9	3.3	6.0	10.7	5.9
Pensions and Other Deferred Comp.	16	1.9	0.3	0.1	0.1	0.1	0.5	1.7	0.7	1.9	1.6	2.0	0.7	3.3
Employee Benefits	17	3.5	0.4	1.0	5.1	1.6	1.1	3.8	4.7	4.2	4.3	3.7	3.6	3.8
Advertising	18	1.5	0.2	0.9	1.0	0.7	3.4	0.8	1.7	1.8	1.6	1.4	1.1	2.0
Other Expenses	19	24.3	57.2	24.7	25.3	15.7	26.7	24.6	31.5	23.7	28.9	28.5	33.6	20.1
Officers' Compensation	20	1.4	0.0	3.7	5.9	2.0	1.3	3.6	2.2	3.0	1.5	1.2	1.0	0.4
Operating Margin	21	•	21.5	•	•	•	10.3	•	•	•	•	•	•	•
Operating Margin Before Officers' Comp.	22	•	21.5	2.7	0.9	•	11.6	•	•	•	0.7	•	•	•

Selected Average Balance Sheet ($ in Thousands)

Net Receivables	23	725	0	32	187	940	1119	1632	4881	6097	15336	37784	55862	354238
Inventories	24	77	0	1	7	186	66	262	679	809	2349	3818	7875	27458
Net Property, Plant and Equipment	25	1777	0	27	64	804	1232	4319	10820	23758	56407	91555	172974	912612
Total Assets	26	8704	0	93	535	3302	7216	15597	34781	64076	186063	342591	826161	5452248
Notes and Loans Payable	27	2774	0	192	284	1681	1595	3677	12222	28356	56188	116978	577113	1044766
All Other Liabilities	28	5043	0	46	981	1181	1651	3929	6364	15251	107084	101395	176189	4139670
Net Worth	29	887	0	-144	-731	440	3970	7991	16195	20469	22791	124218	72859	267812

Selected Financial Ratios (Times to 1)

Current Ratio	30	1.4	•	1.3	0.2	0.9	4.1	2.1	1.5	1.5	1.0	1.3	1.0	2.0
Quick Ratio	31	1.1	•	1.2	0.2	0.7	3.0	1.5	1.2	1.0	0.9	1.1	0.8	1.4
Net Sales to Working Capital	32	10.0	•	41.3	•	•	3.1	5.0	8.6	7.4	•	13.3	120.7	5.0
Coverage Ratio	33	1.2	25.8	•	•	1.2	10.8	1.0	1.4	0.8	1.6	0.4	0.2	1.6
Total Asset Turnover	34	0.6	•	4.6	2.2	2.1	1.0	1.0	0.9	0.8	0.7	0.7	0.5	0.4
Inventory Turnover	35	19.6	•	140.0	100.2	22.3	24.3	19.0	11.3	18.3	9.4	17.5	10.0	21.6
Receivables Turnover	36	6.0	•	13.4	6.2	7.4	8.7	9.1	5.6	8.6	8.3	5.8	3.7	5.9
Total Liabilities to Net Worth	37	8.8	•	4.7	•	6.5	0.8	1.0	1.1	2.1	7.2	1.8	10.3	19.4
Current Assets to Working Capital	38	3.2	•	•	•	•	1.3	1.9	3.1	2.9	•	4.0	26.1	2.0
Current Liabilities to Working Capital	39	2.2	•	3.7	•	•	0.3	0.9	2.1	1.9	•	3.0	25.1	1.0
Working Capital to Net Sales	40	0.1	•	0.0	•	•	0.3	0.2	0.1	0.1	•	0.1	0.0	0.2
Inventory to Working Capital	41	0.2	•	0.1	•	•	0.0	0.1	0.1	0.1	•	0.2	2.0	0.1
Total Receipts to Cash Flow	42	4.4	1.4	5.1	5.9	7.1	2.7	5.4	3.4	5.9	3.6	4.4	4.2	4.3
Cost of Goods to Cash Flow	43	1.3	0.1	2.1	3.2	4.2	0.6	1.8	0.8	1.6	0.6	1.2	0.7	1.2
Cash Flow to Total Debt	44	0.1	•	0.4	0.2	0.3	0.8	0.4	0.5	0.2	0.2	0.3	0.1	0.1

Selected Financial Factors (in Percentages)

Debt Ratio	45	89.8	•	254.7	236.7	86.7	45.0	48.8	53.4	68.1	87.8	63.7	91.2	95.1
Return on Total Assets	46	4.4	•	•	•	4.1	13.5	•	2.7	•	4.2	1.0	1.1	6.4
Return on Equity Before Income Taxes	47	7.7	•	2.3	8.1	5.2	22.3	•	1.6	•	12.5	•	•	50.0
Return on Equity After Income Taxes	48	1.5	•	2.5	8.1	5.1	17.9	•	0.4	•	8.6	•	•	34.6
Profit Margin (Before Income Tax)	49	1.3	17.7	•	•	0.3	12.7	•	0.8	•	2.3	•	•	6.1
Profit Margin (After Income Tax)	50	0.3	17.5	•	•	0.3	10.2	•	0.2	•	1.6	•	•	4.2

253

Table II
Corporations with Net Income

NEWSPAPER PUBLISHERS

MONEY AMOUNTS AND SIZE OF ASSETS IN THOUSANDS OF DOLLARS

Item Description for Accounting Period 7/10 Through 6/11	Total	Zero Assets	Under 500	500 to 1,000	1,000 to 5,000	5,000 to 10,000	10,000 to 25,000	25,000 to 50,000	50,000 to 100,000	100,000 to 250,000	250,000 to 500,000	500,000 to 2,500,000	2,500,000 and over
Number of Enterprises **1**	2076	363	1139	263	181	30	46	21	15	7	5	•	•
Revenues ($ in Thousands)													
Net Sales **2**	15973430	61609	525043	514598	1550237	268981	811680	424243	706278	1106844	1181858	•	•
Interest **3**	35918	0	488	6	236	2689	1432	1139	1140	1194	4926	•	•
Rents **4**	55661	0	0	0	0	135	779	3420	413	9364	9550	•	•
Royalties **5**	21080	0	0	0	0	0	0	0	0	345	106	•	•
Other Portfolio Income **6**	83367	8	0	501	0	109	1296	4385	2323	869	16123	•	•
Other Receipts **7**	714114	0	388	2	49375	3651	9586	53289	17317	15420	8668	•	•
Total Receipts **8**	16883570	61617	525919	515107	1599848	275565	824773	486476	727471	1134036	1221231	•	•
Average Total Receipts **9**	8133	170	462	1959	8839	9186	17930	23166	48498	162005	244246	•	•
Operating Costs/Operating Income (%)													
Cost of Operations **10**	34.2	1.8	46.7	56.0	79.1	23.9	32.9	32.1	27.8	14.2	22.0	•	•
Salaries and Wages **11**	21.1	5.2	18.0	5.3	4.9	24.7	24.7	24.3	26.8	28.5	27.5	•	•
Taxes Paid **12**	3.4	1.2	2.0	4.0	1.1	3.0	4.1	4.1	3.5	4.5	3.3	•	•
Interest Paid **13**	3.9	•	0.0	0.3	1.1	1.5	0.8	2.4	2.2	1.7	3.5	•	•
Depreciation **14**	3.3	0.7	1.3	0.3	1.4	1.1	3.2	3.2	4.1	5.2	4.9	•	•
Amortization and Depletion **15**	3.3	•	•	1.3	0.0	1.6	0.4	3.5	1.7	3.5	7.3	•	•
Pensions and Other Deferred Comp. **16**	2.2	0.5	0.4	0.1	0.1	0.4	0.6	0.7	1.5	1.0	1.6	•	•
Employee Benefits **17**	4.0	0.6	2.2	5.1	0.8	0.9	2.8	3.9	3.6	3.9	3.0	•	•
Advertising **18**	1.5	0.3	0.9	0.1	1.0	3.6	0.5	0.8	0.6	1.2	0.9	•	•
Other Expenses **19**	19.1	28.3	18.5	13.6	8.5	25.7	22.5	29.3	19.2	30.4	24.6	•	•
Officers' Compensation **20**	1.3	0.0	2.8	4.8	2.3	0.8	2.8	2.7	3.3	1.5	0.4	•	•
Operating Margin **21**	2.7	61.4	7.2	9.2	•	12.7	4.7	•	5.7	4.4	1.2	•	•
Operating Margin Before Officers' Comp. **22**	4.0	61.4	10.0	14.0	1.9	13.5	7.5	•	9.0	5.9	1.6	•	•

Selected Average Balance Sheet ($ in Thousands)

	•	•	•	•	•	•	•	•	•	•
Net Receivables 23	1099	0	53	178	1274	1337	1694	3751	5781	18761	30617
Inventories 24	119	0	0	12	291	87	267	852	595	3075	3275
Net Property, Plant and Equipment 25	2678	0	26	84	187	837	4452	5907	19059	67181	97065
Total Assets 26	15098	0	122	528	3255	6853	16405	31468	64106	207559	359088
Notes and Loans Payable 27	4239	0	1	213	1501	2365	3718	9890	17775	42952	133664
All Other Liabilities 28	4087	0	70	9	1379	1569	2372	3595	12905	45675	91213
Net Worth 29	6772	0	50	306	375	2920	10316	17983	33426	118933	134211

Selected Financial Ratios (Times to 1)

	•	•	•	•	•	•	•	•	•	•
Current Ratio 30	1.6	•	2.9	27.0	1.0	4.4	3.0	2.0	1.9	1.8	1.1
Quick Ratio 31	1.1	•	2.8	24.9	0.8	2.9	2.1	1.4	1.2	1.6	1.0
Net Sales to Working Capital 32	8.8	•	9.2	8.0	184.4	3.7	3.8	3.6	4.5	5.7	38.6
Coverage Ratio 33	3.1	•	1133.2	28.8	3.5	11.1	8.3	4.2	4.8	5.0	2.3
Total Asset Turnover 34	0.5	•	3.8	3.7	2.6	1.3	1.1	0.6	0.7	0.8	0.7
Inventory Turnover 35	22.2	•	5767.2	91.8	23.3	24.6	21.8	7.6	22.0	7.3	15.9
Receivables Turnover 36	7.4	•	8.2	11.3	6.9	10.1	9.7	3.3	9.3	•	6.8
Total Liabilities to Net Worth 37	1.2	•	1.4	0.7	7.7	1.3	0.6	0.7	0.9	0.7	1.7
Current Assets to Working Capital 38	2.6	•	1.5	1.0	41.1	1.3	1.5	2.0	2.1	2.3	10.4
Current Liabilities to Working Capital 39	1.6	•	0.5	0.0	40.1	0.3	0.5	1.0	1.1	1.3	9.4
Working Capital to Net Sales 40	0.1	•	0.1	0.1	0.0	0.3	0.3	0.3	0.2	0.2	0.0
Inventory to Working Capital 41	0.2	•	0.0	0.1	9.2	0.0	0.1	0.1	0.1	0.1	0.4
Total Receipts to Cash Flow 42	4.1	1.1	4.4	5.0	11.1	2.5	3.8	2.9	4.0	3.0	3.9
Cost of Goods to Cash Flow 43	1.4	0.0	2.0	2.8	8.8	0.6	1.3	0.9	1.1	0.4	0.9
Cash Flow to Total Debt 44	0.2	•	1.5	1.8	0.3	0.9	0.8	0.5	0.4	0.6	0.3

Selected Financial Factors (in Percentages)

	•	•	•	•	•	•	•	•	•	•
Debt Ratio 45	55.1	•	58.8	42.1	88.5	57.4	37.1	42.9	47.9	42.7	62.6
Return on Total Assets 46	6.3	•	27.7	35.7	10.3	21.7	7.6	6.4	8.0	6.5	5.3
Return on Equity Before Income Taxes 47	9.5	•	67.2	59.5	63.8	46.4	10.6	8.5	12.1	9.1	8.0
Return on Equity After Income Taxes 48	7.5	61.4	64.7	59.3	63.8	37.5	9.6	6.5	10.2	7.7	6.6
Profit Margin (Before Income Tax) 49	8.4	61.0	7.3	9.3	2.8	15.1	6.2	7.6	8.6	6.9	4.5
Profit Margin (After Income Tax) 50	6.6		7.1	9.3	2.8	12.2	5.6	5.8	7.2	5.8	3.8

Table I

Corporations with and without Net Income

PERIODICAL PUBLISHERS

MONEY AMOUNTS AND SIZE OF ASSETS IN THOUSANDS OF DOLLARS

Item Description for Accounting Period 7/10 Through 6/11		Total	Zero Assets	Under 500	500 to 1,000	1,000 to 5,000	5,000 to 10,000	10,000 to 25,000	25,000 to 50,000	50,000 to 100,000	100,000 to 250,000	250,000 to 500,000	500,000 to 2,500,000	2,500,000 and over
Number of Enterprises	1	8218	1162	5995	272	626	20	63	26	15	21	6	8	4
Revenues ($ in Thousands)														
Net Sales	2	25653931	100928	1712760	286942	2946992	298402	1535242	1031860	1035344	2198754	1187971	3797063	9521674
Interest	3	174226	73	62	0	1672	103	604	503	2019	3043	2942	12973	150231
Rents	4	133135	9	0	0	0	0	127	0	445	4535	2443	3164	122413
Royalties	5	335750	0	0	0	0	1776	0	1230	13159	114089	7167	15267	183061
Other Portfolio Income	6	972619	62	0	0	1633	0	8584	2942	2214	71024	10925	120082	755153
Other Receipts	7	1364200	4926	10023	1940	36422	21564	8468	14178	24735	150889	5543	10978	1074533
Total Receipts	8	28633861	105998	1722845	288882	2986719	321845	1553025	1050713	1077916	2542334	1216991	3959527	11807065
Average Total Receipts	9	3484	91	287	1062	4771	16092	24651	40412	71861	121064	202832	494941	2951766
Operating Costs/Operating Income (%)														
Cost of Operations	10	31.5	32.8	19.5	42.4	53.1	25.9	51.1	34.2	26.5	36.2	25.2	32.7	23.2
Salaries and Wages	11	21.5	1.6	14.2	12.5	9.6	35.3	14.1	23.5	22.3	18.8	28.8	17.8	28.6
Taxes Paid	12	2.7	2.2	2.0	1.2	3.7	2.5	1.9	2.5	1.9	2.5	3.2	2.1	3.0
Interest Paid	13	6.4	1.8	0.1	0.3	1.6	0.5	1.1	0.7	4.4	6.2	6.4	7.3	10.8
Depreciation	14	2.4	2.3	1.4	0.2	1.0	0.6	2.3	2.2	1.6	4.0	1.6	1.8	3.3
Amortization and Depletion	15	3.8	2.1	0.0	4.0	1.0	3.4	1.1	1.9	3.1	5.4	7.5	6.3	4.2
Pensions and Other Deferred Comp.	16	1.3	•	0.0	0.1	2.2	0.4	0.2	0.3	0.6	0.6	1.1	0.4	2.2
Employee Benefits	17	3.2	0.1	3.6	3.1	1.6	4.3	2.0	2.5	3.5	2.5	4.9	1.5	4.4
Advertising	18	1.9	0.2	5.0	0.1	2.1	4.9	2.6	0.7	2.0	4.1	1.0	1.2	1.1
Other Expenses	19	29.8	39.1	34.3	27.0	19.9	26.6	20.2	30.2	30.7	31.7	21.3	28.7	34.7
Officers' Compensation	20	2.9	0.9	12.9	5.7	5.1	1.4	2.1	1.4	1.3	2.5	2.4	1.4	1.7
Operating Margin	21	•	16.9	7.1	3.4	•	•	1.3	•	2.1	•	•	•	•
Operating Margin Before Officers' Comp.	22	•	17.8	19.9	9.1	4.1	•	3.4	1.4	3.5	•	•	0.1	•

Selected Average Balance Sheet ($ in Thousands)

	1	2	3	4	5	6	7	8	9	10	11	12	13
Net Receivables 23	1188	0	13	136	636	1688	3418	6666	10974	18746	26782	78412	1869578
Inventories 24	71	0	6	7	58	757	1396	1085	1631	2772	5416	9397	47763
Net Property, Plant and Equipment 25	389	0	15	8	195	115	3245	6329	4204	14570	31558	38200	435848
Total Assets 26	7117	0	76	721	2134	6710	16635	36564	68484	165413	397842	966228	9937763
Notes and Loans Payable 27	2600	0	106	23	398	2997	3781	7062	33381	85589	206524	387230	3340642
All Other Liabilities 28	3006	0	51	156	1766	7932	9930	12774	30454	62391	120422	274825	4360922
Net Worth 29	1511	0	-80	543	-30	-4218	2925	16728	4649	17433	70896	304174	2236200

Selected Financial Ratios (Times to 1)

	1	2	3	4	5	6	7	8	9	10	11	12	13
Current Ratio 30	1.0	•	0.7	1.3	1.6	0.5	2.0	1.4	1.1	0.6	1.4	0.9	1.0
Quick Ratio 31	0.8	•	0.5	1.2	1.2	0.3	1.5	0.9	0.6	0.5	1.2	0.6	0.8
Net Sales to Working Capital 32	672.1	•	•	19.8	8.1	•	9.4	4.2	18.3	•	6.3	•	•
Coverage Ratio 33	1.7	12.9	81.9	14.4	1.2	5.2	3.2	3.6	2.4	1.3	0.7	1.5	1.7
Total Asset Turnover 34	0.4	•	3.8	1.5	2.2	2.2	1.5	1.1	1.0	0.6	0.5	0.5	0.2
Inventory Turnover 35	13.9	•	10.1	60.3	43.0	5.1	8.9	12.5	11.2	13.7	9.2	16.5	11.6
Receivables Turnover 36	3.7	•	20.0	12.0	7.5	5.7	8.0	6.9	5.9	5.7	6.3	6.1	2.1
Total Liabilities to Net Worth 37	3.7	•	•	0.3	•	•	4.7	1.2	13.7	8.5	4.6	2.2	3.4
Current Assets to Working Capital 38	431.4	•	•	4.1	2.6	•	3.3	2.0	8.0	•	3.6	•	•
Current Liabilities to Working Capital 39	430.4	•	•	3.1	1.6	•	2.3	1.0	7.0	•	2.6	•	•
Working Capital to Net Sales 40	0.0	•	•	0.1	0.1	•	0.1	0.2	0.1	•	0.2	•	•
Inventory to Working Capital 41	14.8	•	•	0.3	0.1	•	0.5	0.1	0.4	•	0.1	•	•
Total Receipts to Cash Flow 42	3.5	1.8	2.6	3.6	5.9	4.1	5.2	3.5	2.9	4.0	6.2	4.0	2.9
Cost of Goods to Cash Flow 43	1.1	0.6	0.5	1.5	3.2	1.1	2.6	1.2	0.8	1.4	1.6	1.3	0.7
Cash Flow to Total Debt 44	0.2	•	0.7	1.6	0.4	0.3	0.3	0.6	0.4	0.2	0.1	0.2	0.1

Selected Financial Factors (in Percentages)

	1	2	3	4	5	6	7	8	9	10	11	12	13
Debt Ratio 45	78.8	•	205.9	24.8	101.4	162.9	82.4	54.3	93.2	89.5	82.2	68.5	77.5
Return on Total Assets 46	4.8	•	29.2	6.5	4.3	5.6	5.2	2.6	10.8	5.0	2.4	5.5	4.3
Return on Equity Before Income Taxes 47	9.2	•	•	8.0	•	•	20.3	4.1	93.2	10.2	•	5.9	7.6
Return on Equity After Income Taxes 48	6.6	•	•	6.6	•	•	19.0	1.4	65.2	2.5	•	0.8	6.3
Profit Margin (Before Income Tax) 49	4.5	21.9	7.7	4.1	0.4	2.0	2.4	1.7	6.3	1.7	•	3.8	7.2
Profit Margin (After Income Tax) 50	3.2	20.5	7.7	3.4	0.3	2.0	2.3	0.6	4.4	0.4	•	0.5	5.9

Table II

Corporations with Net Income

PERIODICAL PUBLISHERS

MONEY AMOUNTS AND SIZE OF ASSETS IN THOUSANDS OF DOLLARS

Item Description for Accounting Period 7/10 Through 6/11	Total	Zero Assets	Under 500	500 to 1,000	1,000 to 5,000	5,000 to 10,000	10,000 to 25,000	25,000 to 50,000	50,000 to 100,000	100,000 to 250,000	250,000 to 500,000	500,000 to 2,500,000	2,500,000 and over
Number of Enterprises **1**	5103	453	4037	272	239	10	52	•	9	13	0	•	0
Revenues ($ in Thousands)													
Net Sales **2**	14224145	75697	1072195	286942	1308980	110975	1189927	•	703506	1809365	•	•	0
Interest **3**	115885	71	3	0	414	74	565	•	1996	3830	0	0	0
Rents **4**	106369	0	0	0	0	0	127	•	445	3641	0	0	0
Royalties **5**	132794	0	0	0	0	1776	0	•	13159	3860	0	0	0
Other Portfolio Income **6**	961604	62	0	0	1393	0	7317	•	1055	79466	0	0	0
Other Receipts **7**	1369770	4913	5139	1940	32959	21441	7431	•	19585	129831	0	0	0
Total Receipts **8**	16910567	80743	1077337	288882	1343746	134266	1205367	•	739746	2029993	0	0	0
Average Total Receipts **9**	3314	178	267	1062	5622	13427	23180	•	82194	156153	•	•	•
Operating Costs/Operating Income (%)													
Cost of Operations **10**	29.5	20.9	8.7	42.4	39.9	•	55.0	•	21.5	28.3	•	•	•
Salaries and Wages **11**	21.0	•	5.2	12.5	18.3	44.9	11.4	•	21.1	21.8	•	•	•
Taxes Paid **12**	2.8	1.3	1.5	1.2	3.2	2.9	1.7	•	2.2	2.9	•	•	•
Interest Paid **13**	2.2	0.1	•	0.3	2.1	•	1.1	•	1.6	2.1	•	•	•
Depreciation **14**	2.3	1.8	1.4	0.2	1.3	1.2	2.7	•	1.9	2.7	•	•	•
Amortization and Depletion **15**	3.0	•	0.0	4.0	0.3	•	1.0	•	1.8	3.4	•	•	•
Pensions and Other Deferred Comp. **16**	1.4	•	0.0	0.1	0.3	0.8	0.2	•	0.8	1.3	•	•	•
Employee Benefits **17**	3.2	•	1.5	3.1	0.8	6.8	2.2	•	4.4	3.0	•	•	•
Advertising **18**	1.5	•	3.3	0.1	0.6	0.2	1.3	•	2.2	3.6	•	•	•
Other Expenses **19**	32.3	44.5	40.4	27.0	20.5	54.9	14.7	•	29.4	27.2	•	•	•
Officers' Compensation **20**	4.2	•	18.6	5.7	7.2	1.9	2.3	•	1.4	2.5	•	•	•
Operating Margin **21**	•	31.4	19.3	3.4	5.4	•	6.3	•	11.7	1.1	•	•	•
Operating Margin Before Officers' Comp. **22**	0.9	31.4	37.9	9.1	12.6	•	8.6	•	13.0	3.6	•	•	•

Selected Average Balance Sheet ($ in Thousands)

Net Receivables 23	492	0	7	136	633	989	3646	12812	17594
Inventories 24	61	0	6	7	30	1233	1369	1848	3577
Net Property, Plant and Equipment 25	473	0	14	8	441	153	3728	5884	23030
Total Assets 26	6600	0	58	721	2401	5120	17067	75241	196234
Notes and Loans Payable 27	623	0	96	23	180	2171	3281	16512	41591
All Other Liabilities 28	2738	0	29	156	3018	9926	8407	37913	86518
Net Worth 29	3239	0	-67	543	-797	-6977	5380	20817	68125

Selected Financial Ratios (Times to 1)

Current Ratio 30	1.5	•	1.3	1.3	2.1	0.2	1.9	1.1	1.2
Quick Ratio 31	1.0	•	1.0	1.2	1.5	0.2	1.1	0.6	1.0
Net Sales to Working Capital 32	5.7	•	31.8	19.8	6.6	•	5.3	19.8	11.8
Coverage Ratio 33	8.4	288.2	•	14.4	4.9	•	7.9	11.6	7.4
Total Asset Turnover 34	0.4	•	4.6	1.5	2.3	2.2	1.3	1.0	0.7
Inventory Turnover 35	13.5	•	4.1	60.3	74.0	•	9.2	9.1	11.0
Receivables Turnover 36	6.3	•	77.9	12.0	5.8	6.1	7.5	6.0	8.3
Total Liabilities to Net Worth 37	1.0	•	0.3	•	•	•	2.2	2.6	1.9
Current Assets to Working Capital 38	2.9	•	4.5	4.1	1.9	•	2.1	9.5	7.0
Current Liabilities to Working Capital 39	1.9	•	3.5	3.1	0.9	•	1.1	8.5	6.0
Working Capital to Net Sales 40	0.2	•	0.0	0.1	0.2	•	0.2	0.1	0.1
Inventory to Working Capital 41	0.1	•	1.0	0.3	0.0	•	0.3	0.5	0.4
Total Receipts to Cash Flow 42	2.4	1.3	1.8	3.6	4.0	1.8	5.0	2.3	3.0
Cost of Goods to Cash Flow 43	0.7	0.3	0.2	1.5	1.6	•	2.7	0.5	0.8
Cash Flow to Total Debt 44	0.3	•	1.2	1.6	0.4	0.5	0.4	0.6	0.4

Selected Financial Factors (in Percentages)

Debt Ratio 45	50.9	•	215.2	24.8	133.2	236.3	68.5	72.3	65.3
Return on Total Assets 46	7.6	•	89.9	6.5	23.2	15.8	11.6	19.4	11.1
Return on Equity Before Income Taxes 47	13.7	•	•	8.0	•	•	32.3	63.9	27.6
Return on Equity After Income Taxes 48	11.7	•	•	6.6	•	•	31.4	53.5	22.6
Profit Margin (Before Income Tax) 49	15.9	33.0	19.7	4.1	8.1	7.3	7.6	17.0	13.5
Profit Margin (After Income Tax) 50	13.6	33.1	19.7	3.4	8.0	7.2	7.4	14.3	11.0

Table I

Corporations with and without Net Income

Book Publishers

MONEY AMOUNTS AND SIZE OF ASSETS IN THOUSANDS OF DOLLARS

Item Description for Accounting Period 7/10 Through 6/11	Total	Zero Assets	Under 500	500 to 1,000	1,000 to 5,000	5,000 to 10,000	10,000 to 25,000	25,000 to 50,000	50,000 to 100,000	100,000 to 250,000	250,000 to 500,000	500,000 to 2,500,000	2,500,000 and over
Number of Enterprises **1**	4519	1239	2457	524	167	51	29	19	10	12	0	5	6
Revenues ($ in Thousands)													
Net Sales **2**	27917342	85505	207310	777168	677755	365987	779477	527523	646390	1641278	0	3840439	18368510
Interest **3**	215478	126	117	2080	1595	0	494	1091	763	5614	0	26405	177195
Rents **4**	22520	0	0	0	92	0	0	1355	1009	42	0	5660	14363
Royalties **5**	354906	3139	0	0	2572	0	0	5600	7731	12490	0	111314	212060
Other Portfolio Income **6**	1460371	9793	0	0	2835	346	99	7	319	1452	0	34752	1410767
Other Receipts **7**	772154	5901	19907	1769	7283	5139	2365	13679	4032	180005	0	177937	354137
Total Receipts **8**	30742771	104464	227334	781017	692132	371472	782435	549255	660244	1840881	0	4196507	20537032
Average Total Receipts **9**	6803	84	93	1490	4145	7284	26981	28908	66024	153407	•	839301	3422839
Operating Costs/Operating Income (%)													
Cost of Operations **10**	33.5	44.3	53.1	44.4	32.0	43.0	41.9	41.7	35.2	42.4	•	45.7	28.6
Salaries and Wages **11**	21.7	13.6	28.0	6.0	9.3	15.7	20.3	19.5	20.1	14.9	•	23.4	23.4
Taxes Paid **12**	2.5	2.5	2.0	1.6	1.6	1.7	2.7	1.9	2.3	1.9	•	2.7	2.5
Interest Paid **13**	6.5	3.7	0.6	2.2	0.2	1.0	3.5	0.4	1.7	5.2	•	3.5	8.2
Depreciation **14**	3.7	0.2	0.4	1.0	0.4	0.8	1.3	1.3	3.3	1.2	•	3.2	4.6
Amortization and Depletion **15**	5.1	0.9	0.7	0.0	0.0	0.1	0.2	2.3	2.9	5.4	•	3.3	6.4
Pensions and Other Deferred Comp. **16**	1.7	0.9	•	5.7	2.3	0.3	0.6	1.2	0.8	0.5	•	0.7	1.9
Employee Benefits **17**	2.4	6.1	0.3	0.8	0.7	1.6	2.8	3.0	2.0	1.5	•	2.8	2.6
Advertising **18**	1.6	3.9	9.7	0.0	1.6	2.1	1.1	3.3	4.2	2.4	•	3.5	1.0
Other Expenses **19**	20.4	28.5	13.1	23.4	35.2	20.4	15.4	18.6	21.8	33.9	•	17.4	19.4
Officers' Compensation **20**	1.4	1.8	4.7	10.8	8.1	3.1	4.1	3.8	2.8	2.0	•	1.0	0.4
Operating Margin **21**	•	•	•	4.1	8.6	10.2	6.3	3.0	2.9	•	•	•	0.9
Operating Margin Before Officers' Comp. **22**	1.0	•	•	14.9	16.6	13.4	10.4	6.8	5.6	•	•	•	1.4

Selected Average Balance Sheet ($ in Thousands)

Item													
Net Receivables **23**	1467	0	9	73	400	1181	3727	3105	14022	28800	•	401104	630515
Inventories **24**	680	0	18	195	1000	1609	2319	8454	9441	18913	•	77943	289817
Net Property, Plant and Equipment **25**	475	0	13	205	104	536	2068	2068	7080	9244	•	89538	206053
Total Assets **26**	11675		64	608	2973	6652	16095	33823	64085	195450	•	1539351	6609251
Notes and Loans Payable **27**	5375	0	75	1172	344	1083	4914	2668	14662	87203	•	515347	3235729
All Other Liabilities **28**	3615	0	14	274	703	1844	8620	11326	25352	53987	•	747835	1806787
Net Worth **29**	2685	0	-25	-839	1925	3725	2561	19828	24071	54260	•	276169	1566735

Selected Financial Ratios (Times to 1)

Item													
Current Ratio **30**	1.1		•	1.0	3.7	2.1	1.5	2.8	1.6	1.3	•	1.0	1.1
Quick Ratio **31**	0.7		•	0.8	2.4	1.0	1.1	0.7	0.8	0.7	•	0.8	0.6
Net Sales to Working Capital **32**	15.5		•	113.8	2.2	3.5	8.4	2.0	4.4	7.4	•	28.1	36.0
Coverage Ratio **33**	2.6	5.2	•	3.1	47.2	13.3	2.9	17.8	4.0	1.1	•	1.7	2.6
Total Asset Turnover **34**	0.5		•	1.3	1.4	1.1	1.7	0.8	1.0	0.7	•	0.5	0.5
Inventory Turnover **35**	3.0		•	2.4	1.3	1.9	4.9	1.4	2.4	3.1	•	4.5	3.0
Receivables Turnover **36**	4.7		•	9.7	19.3	7.2	5.7	8.3	4.8	5.0	•	2.5	5.2
Total Liabilities to Net Worth **37**	3.3		•	•	0.5	0.8	5.3	0.7	1.7	2.6	•	4.6	3.2
Current Assets to Working Capital **38**	9.1		•	22.4	1.4	1.9	2.9	1.6	2.6	4.1	•	22.0	20.6
Current Liabilities to Working Capital **39**	8.1		•	21.4	0.4	0.9	1.9	0.6	1.6	3.1	•	21.0	19.6
Working Capital to Net Sales **40**	0.1		•	0.0	0.5	0.3	0.1	0.5	0.2	0.1	•	0.0	0.0
Inventory to Working Capital **41**	1.6		•	15.0	0.5	0.8	0.6	0.6	0.6	1.1	•	2.8	3.2
Total Receipts to Cash Flow **42**	4.6	3.3	10.9	4.8	2.4	3.4	5.1	4.5	4.2	3.1	•	6.7	4.7
Cost of Goods to Cash Flow **43**	1.5	1.5	5.8	2.1	0.8	1.5	1.9	1.9	1.5	1.3	•	3.1	1.3
Cash Flow to Total Debt **44**	0.1		•	0.2	1.6	0.7	0.4	0.4	0.3		•	0.1	0.1

Selected Financial Factors (in Percentages)

Item													
Debt Ratio **45**	77.0	•	139.1	237.9	35.2	44.0	84.1	41.4	62.4	72.2	•	82.1	76.3
Return on Total Assets **46**	8.7	•	•	16.5	14.9	13.6	17.0	6.2	6.8	4.2	•	3.0	9.9
Return on Equity Before Income Taxes **47**	23.0	9.3	•	9.3	22.5	22.5	69.8	9.9	13.6	6.8	•	6.8	25.6
Return on Equity After Income Taxes **48**	16.3	10.0	•		20.7	22.3	60.6	8.3	10.4		•	3.7	18.0
Profit Margin (Before Income Tax) **49**	10.0	15.7	•	4.6	10.7	11.7	6.6	7.1	5.1		•	2.5	13.1
Profit Margin (After Income Tax) **50**	7.1	10.9	•	4.6	9.8	11.6	5.8	5.9	3.9		•	1.3	9.2

Table II

Corporations with Net Income

BOOK PUBLISHERS

MONEY AMOUNTS AND SIZE OF ASSETS IN THOUSANDS OF DOLLARS

Item Description for Accounting Period 7/10 Through 6/11	Total	Zero Assets	Under 500	500 to 1,000	1,000 to 5,000	5,000 to 10,000	10,000 to 25,000	25,000 to 50,000	50,000 to 100,000	100,000 to 250,000	250,000 to 500,000	500,000 to 2,500,000	2,500,000 and over
Number of Enterprises **1**	2145	542	1049	324	147	29	21	14	•	5	•	0	•
Revenues ($ in Thousands)													
Net Sales **2**	22233518	76920	57316	769140	641586	295501	626162	428107	•	770696	•	0	•
Interest **3**	146398	123	117	2080	646	0	22	562	•	5112	•	0	•
Rents **4**	20959	0	0	0	92	0	0	756	•	0	•	0	•
Royalties **5**	253758	1250	0	0	368	0	0	5012	•	8528	•	0	•
Other Portfolio Income **6**	1450033	9793	0	0	72	0	99	0	•	356	•	0	•
Other Receipts **7**	369858	5654	14997	1410	399	4034	2175	13339	•	107860	•	0	•
Total Receipts **8**	24474524	93740	72430	772630	643163	299535	628458	447776	•	892552	•	0	•
Average Total Receipts **9**	11410	173	69	2385	4375	10329	29927	31984	•	178510	•	•	•
Operating Costs/Operating Income (%)													
Cost of Operations **10**	30.9	42.9	2.1	44.2	28.2	38.3	35.7	42.4	•	36.9	•	•	•
Salaries and Wages **11**	23.1	13.3	54.4	5.7	8.3	14.6	22.1	18.9	•	18.5	•	•	•
Taxes Paid **12**	2.6	2.7	3.4	1.5	1.5	1.4	2.6	1.9	•	2.6	•	•	•
Interest Paid **13**	4.0	4.2	•	0.3	0.2	0.7	0.7	0.1	•	1.1	•	•	•
Depreciation **14**	4.2	0.2	1.0	1.0	0.3	0.5	1.4	1.1	•	0.7	•	•	•
Amortization and Depletion **15**	2.7	0.8	2.0	0.0	0.0	•	0.0	2.8	•	0.9	•	•	•
Pensions and Other Deferred Comp. **16**	1.9	1.0	•	5.8	2.4	0.3	0.7	0.7	•	0.9	•	•	•
Employee Benefits **17**	2.6	6.3	0.7	0.6	0.7	1.5	2.8	2.8	•	1.4	•	•	•
Advertising **18**	1.3	3.7	12.2	0.0	1.4	1.0	1.0	3.5	•	2.6	•	•	•
Other Expenses **19**	20.6	25.1	10.8	22.7	35.0	21.6	15.9	16.6	•	36.5	•	•	•
Officers' Compensation **20**	1.5	2.0	8.4	10.9	7.4	3.1	4.9	3.8	•	3.5	•	•	•
Operating Margin **21**	4.7	•	5.0	7.3	14.5	16.9	12.1	5.5	•	•	•	•	•
Operating Margin Before Officers' Comp. **22**	6.2	•	13.4	18.2	21.9	20.0	17.0	9.3	•	•	•	•	•

Selected Average Balance Sheet ($ in Thousands)

Net Receivables 23	38770	3114	3566	1500	411	105	1	0	2062
Inventories 24	15424	6090	1989	1860	1107	1	25	0	1028
Net Property, Plant and Equipment 25	7192	501	2688	275	112	331	0	0	793
Total Assets 26	160527	35190	15990	5561	2944	597	64	0	15512
Notes and Loans Payable 27	18378	1016	2798	1315	131	195	36	0	5908
All Other Liabilities 28	56314	12232	6001	2549	508	154	0	0	5138
Net Worth 29	85835	21942	7190	1696	2305	248	28	0	4466

Selected Financial Ratios (Times to 1)

Current Ratio 30	1.5	3.3	1.7	1.8	4.6	0.9	30.3	•	1.1
Quick Ratio 31	0.9	0.9	1.2	0.9	2.8	0.8	25.5	•	0.6
Net Sales to Working Capital 32	5.3	1.9	7.1	4.6	2.2	•	2.7	5.7	15.2
Coverage Ratio 33	10.3	169.8	18.6	25.9	86.1	29.4	•	•	4.8
Total Asset Turnover 34	1.0	0.9	1.9	1.8	1.5	4.0	0.9	•	0.7
Inventory Turnover 35	3.7	2.1	5.4	2.1	1.1	909.5	0.0	•	3.1
Receivables Turnover 36	5.1	12.9	7.3	6.8	7.0	20.9	16.6	•	5.1
Total Liabilities to Net Worth 37	0.9	0.6	1.2	2.3	0.3	1.4	1.3	•	2.5
Current Assets to Working Capital 38	3.1	1.4	2.4	2.3	1.3	1.0	•	•	8.2
Current Liabilities to Working Capital 39	2.1	0.4	1.4	1.3	0.3	0.0	•	•	7.2
Working Capital to Net Sales 40	0.2	0.5	0.1	0.2	0.4	0.4	•	•	0.1
Inventory to Working Capital 41	0.6	0.4	0.4	0.9	0.5	0.1	•	•	1.3
Total Receipts to Cash Flow 42	2.3	4.3	3.8	2.7	2.2	4.3	2.4	3.4	3.9
Cost of Goods to Cash Flow 43	0.9	1.8	1.4	1.0	0.6	1.9	0.1	1.4	1.2
Cash Flow to Total Debt 44	0.9	0.5	0.9	1.0	3.1	1.6	0.6	•	0.2

Selected Financial Factors (in Percentages)

Debt Ratio 45	46.5	37.6	55.0	69.5	21.7	58.4	56.6	•	71.2
Return on Total Assets 46	10.9	8.8	24.5	34.8	22.1	31.9	26.9	•	12.8
Return on Equity Before Income Taxes 47	18.4	14.1	51.5	109.7	27.9	74.2	61.9	•	35.2
Return on Equity After Income Taxes 48	12.8	12.1	46.9	108.9	26.3	74.1	60.5	•	26.7
Profit Margin (Before Income Tax) 49	10.2	10.1	12.4	18.3	14.7	7.7	31.4	19.7	15.2
Profit Margin (After Income Tax) 50	7.1	8.7	11.3	18.1	13.9	7.7	30.7	14.3	11.5

258

Table I

Corporations with and without Net Income

DATABASE, DIRECTORY, AND OTHER PUBLISHERS

MONEY AMOUNTS AND SIZE OF ASSETS IN THOUSANDS OF DOLLARS

Item Description for Accounting Period 7/10 Through 6/11	Total	Zero Assets	Under 500	500 to 1,000	1,000 to 5,000	5,000 to 10,000	10,000 to 25,000	25,000 to 50,000	50,000 to 100,000	100,000 to 250,000	250,000 to 500,000	500,000 to 2,500,000	2,500,000 and over
Number of Enterprises **1**	4458	1134	2700	328	206	12	42	8	7	8	0	6	5
Revenues ($ in Thousands)													
Net Sales **2**	19059545	270166	1388821	253544	1308071	75292	910175	285097	359934	881205	0	3702880	9624361
Interest **3**	117164	196	40	258	460	32	497	260	1574	3084	0	3105	107657
Rents **4**	68386	0	0	0	61	0	1395	0	622	279	0	1232	64797
Royalties **5**	84069	0	0	0	2106	0	0	0	1	245	0	30571	51147
Other Portfolio Income **6**	251856	0	291	3	15492	0	202	557	1233	20957	0	63552	149568
Other Receipts **7**	1838201	-4519	42	992	19827	15	7666	5318	6820	12586	0	214016	1575438
Total Receipts **8**	21419221	265843	1389194	254797	1346017	75339	919935	291232	370184	918356	0	4015356	11572968
Average Total Receipts **9**	4805	234	515	777	6534	6278	21903	36404	52883	114794	•	669226	2314594
Operating Costs/Operating Income (%)													
Cost of Operations **10**	30.1	20.5	60.5	32.8	39.4	61.0	45.0	25.3	15.6	31.6	•	28.5	24.1
Salaries and Wages **11**	20.6	43.2	17.3	31.2	28.4	26.0	15.8	22.8	26.5	18.3	•	31.9	15.2
Taxes Paid **12**	2.9	3.5	2.6	5.3	2.3	0.9	2.6	2.2	2.7	2.1	•	2.9	3.0
Interest Paid **13**	7.7	1.3	0.3	7.5	0.0	4.7	2.3	0.7	4.7	4.5	•	6.9	11.5
Depreciation **14**	2.1	2.4	0.2	8.6	2.1	0.8	1.9	2.5	2.9	2.0	•	2.6	2.0
Amortization and Depletion **15**	6.4	2.0	•	0.0	0.0	4.5	1.5	2.5	2.9	4.8	•	6.0	9.6
Pensions and Other Deferred Comp. **16**	0.7	0.7	•	•	0.2	•	0.3	0.5	1.0	0.5	•	0.7	1.0
Employee Benefits **17**	2.3	2.1	•	4.0	0.4	0.2	1.7	1.7	3.7	3.3	•	4.1	2.0
Advertising **18**	3.0	1.7	1.5	0.0	0.9	0.2	6.6	5.0	7.5	3.0	•	0.5	4.1
Other Expenses **19**	38.6	29.6	17.3	22.4	9.9	12.5	14.9	23.5	28.3	33.9	•	22.8	56.1
Officers' Compensation **20**	2.8	2.1	3.4	16.6	17.9	6.6	2.8	5.3	2.8	1.0	•	1.9	0.7
Operating Margin **21**	•	•	•	•	•	•	4.4	8.1	1.6	•	•	•	•
Operating Margin Before Officers' Comp. **22**	•	•	0.3	•	16.5	•	7.3	13.3	4.3	•	•	•	•

Selected Average Balance Sheet ($ in Thousands)

Item												
Net Receivables 23	756	0	43	24	907	830	1854	6850	13796	17100	160209	344626
Inventories 24	208	0	26	0	3	405	103	379	1580	1660	24944	134560
Net Property, Plant and Equipment 25	395	0	1	246	361	81	1769	2074	10865	6472	74131	188133
Total Assets 26	6898	0	78	615	2516	7162	16095	33597	71867	169726	981217	4207828
Notes and Loans Payable 27	3625	0	12	424	372	2630	5923	4956	17815	127276	627895	2136106
All Other Liabilities 28	2292	0	118	665	1069	2980	5032	12474	16741	49809	369001	1276638
Net Worth 29	981	0	-51	-473	1074	1551	5140	16166	37312	-7360	-15679	795084

Selected Financial Ratios (Times to 1)

Item												
Current Ratio 30	1.0	•	0.6	0.3	1.4	0.8	1.3	1.4	1.9	0.9	0.6	1.2
Quick Ratio 31	0.5	•	0.4	0.2	1.0	0.7	1.1	1.7	0.5	•	0.4	0.6
Net Sales to Working Capital 32	•	•	•	•	11.0	14.4	8.1	4.3	•	•	•	8.8
Coverage Ratio 33	0.5	•	•	•	3.4	66.0	20.5	1.9	1.8	1.0	•	0.3
Total Asset Turnover 34	0.6	6.6	1.3	2.5	1.3	0.9	1.1	0.7	•	0.6	•	0.5
Inventory Turnover 35	6.2	12.1	•	972.2	95.0	23.8	5.1	5.1	21.0	•	7.0	3.4
Receivables Turnover 36	4.4	19.4	33.6	4.8	12.6	2.7	5.1	2.8	5.4	•	3.0	4.3
Total Liabilities to Net Worth 37	6.0	•	•	1.3	2.1	3.6	1.1	0.9	•	•	•	4.3
Current Assets to Working Capital 38	•	•	•	3.5	3.5	•	4.7	2.2	•	•	•	5.2
Current Liabilities to Working Capital 39	•	•	•	2.5	2.5	•	3.7	1.2	•	•	•	4.2
Working Capital to Net Sales 40	•	•	•	0.1	0.1	•	0.1	0.2	•	•	•	0.1
Inventory to Working Capital 41	•	•	•	0.0	0.1	•	0.0	0.0	•	•	•	0.6
Total Receipts to Cash Flow 42	3.9	6.8	9.2	12.1	5.8	•	3.3	3.5	•	•	5.3	2.9
Cost of Goods to Cash Flow 43	1.2	1.4	5.6	4.8	2.6	•	0.8	0.5	•	•	1.5	0.7
Cash Flow to Total Debt 44	0.2	•	0.4	0.4	0.3	•	0.6	0.4	•	•	0.1	0.2

Selected Financial Factors (in Percentages)

Item												
Debt Ratio 45	85.8	165.5	177.0	57.3	68.1	78.3	51.9	48.1	104.3	101.6	81.1	
Return on Total Assets 46	2.2	•	•	3.6	10.5	•	15.2	6.5	5.2	4.4	1.5	
Return on Equity Before Income Taxes 47	•	30.9	45.9	8.4	23.1	•	30.1	6.1	•	•	•	
Return on Equity After Income Taxes 48	•	30.9	45.9	4.8	17.7	•	23.1	1.7	•	71.2	•	
Profit Margin (Before Income Tax) 49	•	•	1.4	5.5	4.4	13.6	3.6	•	•	0.0	•	
Profit Margin (After Income Tax) 50	•	•	0.8	4.2	1.3	10.5	3.5	•	•	•	•	

259

Table II
Corporations with Net Income

DATABASE, DIRECTORY, AND OTHER PUBLISHERS

MONEY AMOUNTS AND SIZE OF ASSETS IN THOUSANDS OF DOLLARS

Item Description for Accounting Period 7/10 Through 6/11	Total	Zero Assets	Under 500	500 to 1,000	1,000 to 5,000	5,000 to 10,000	10,000 to 25,000	25,000 to 50,000	50,000 to 100,000	100,000 to 250,000	250,000 to 500,000	500,000 to 2,500,000	2,500,000 and over
Number of Enterprises **1**	2117	428	1455	62	120	0	32	•	•	4	0	6	0
Revenues ($ in Thousands)													
Net Sales **2**	11715523	224382	105168	68783	316914	0	799963	•	•	541523	0	9143195	0
Interest **3**	21659	28	40	258	328	0	476	•	•	2458	0	16385	0
Rents **4**	67485	0	0	0	61	0	1395	•	•	0	0	66028	0
Royalties **5**	67031	0	0	0	2102	0	0	•	•	0	0	64929	0
Other Portfolio Income **6**	86753	0	291	0	15492	0	202	•	•	1305	0	67673	0
Other Receipts **7**	239704	15	42	957	189	0	7586	•	•	7185	0	217717	0
Total Receipts **8**	12198155	224425	105541	69998	335086	0	809622	•	•	552471	0	9575927	0
Average Total Receipts **9**	5762	524	73	1129	2792	•	25301	•	•	138118	•	1595988	•
Operating Costs/Operating Income (%)													
Cost of Operations **10**	28.5	12.7	19.8	70.7	31.1	•	48.5	•	•	45.8	•	26.4	•
Salaries and Wages **11**	23.3	47.8	3.0	7.3	28.9	•	14.3	•	•	12.9	•	24.3	•
Taxes Paid **12**	3.4	4.3	0.3	4.6	4.3	•	2.6	•	•	1.1	•	3.6	•
Interest Paid **13**	4.0	1.5	3.0	0.3	0.1	•	1.3	•	•	1.4	•	4.8	•
Depreciation **14**	2.4	2.9	0.1	•	2.3	•	2.0	•	•	1.1	•	2.6	•
Amortization and Depletion **15**	1.5	2.4	•	0.2	0.2	•	0.4	•	•	2.3	•	1.5	•
Pensions and Other Deferred Comp. **16**	1.0	0.8	•	•	0.6	•	0.2	•	•	0.7	•	1.2	•
Employee Benefits **17**	2.5	2.6	•	1.2	1.1	•	1.5	•	•	2.8	•	2.7	•
Advertising **18**	3.4	2.1	2.2	•	0.3	•	4.7	•	•	1.7	•	3.3	•
Other Expenses **19**	24.6	19.8	30.8	6.3	18.6	•	13.9	•	•	19.2	•	26.3	•
Officers' Compensation **20**	1.3	•	4.0	6.2	6.1	•	1.8	•	•	0.5	•	1.1	•
Operating Margin **21**	4.1	3.2	36.9	3.1	6.5	•	8.8	•	•	10.5	•	2.2	•
Operating Margin Before Officers' Comp. **22**	5.4	3.2	40.8	9.3	12.5	•	10.6	•	•	11.0	•	3.3	•

Selected Average Balance Sheet ($ in Thousands)

Net Receivables 23	784	0	7	129	493	2065	20980	217995
Inventories 24	359	0	32	0	2	135	1300	107255
Net Property, Plant and Equipment 25	575	0	0	0	265	2089	7946	177116
Total Assets 26	6273		25	830	2155	15400	127256	1905482
Notes and Loans Payable 27	2193	0	10	0	160	3916	62605	693419
All Other Liabilities 28	2170	0	15	238	574	5090	20302	685598
Net Worth 29	1910	0	-1	592	1421	6395	44350	526465

Selected Financial Ratios (Times to 1)

Current Ratio 30	1.2	0.8	0.6	1.9	1.6		5.5	1.1
Quick Ratio 31	0.8	0.5	0.6	1.7	1.2		3.2	0.7
Net Sales to Working Capital 32	13.2			4.7	8.0		2.3	22.4
Coverage Ratio 33	3.2	3.1	13.5	16.4	228.5	8.6	9.6	2.6
Total Asset Turnover 34	0.9		2.9	1.3	1.2	1.6	1.1	0.8
Inventory Turnover 35	4.4	0.4	17.2	331.3	90.0		47.7	3.7
Receivables Turnover 36	4.2		5.7	1.5	17.3			2.6
Total Liabilities to Net Worth 37	2.3		0.4	0.5	1.4		1.9	2.6
Current Assets to Working Capital 38	5.2			2.1	2.6		1.2	9.0
Current Liabilities to Working Capital 39	4.2			1.1	1.6		0.2	8.0
Working Capital to Net Sales 40	0.1			0.2	0.1		0.4	0.0
Inventory to Working Capital 41	0.7			0.0	0.1		0.0	1.6
Total Receipts to Cash Flow 42	4.1	5.5	11.0	4.2	4.8		3.3	4.2
Cost of Goods to Cash Flow 43	1.2	0.7	7.8	1.3	2.3		1.5	1.1
Cash Flow to Total Debt 44	0.3	1.8	0.4	0.9	0.6		0.5	0.3

Selected Financial Factors (in Percentages)

Debt Ratio 45	69.5		103.3	28.7	34.0	58.5	65.1	72.4
Return on Total Assets 46	11.2		116.4	6.9	15.0	18.4	14.6	9.9
Return on Equity Before Income Taxes 47	25.4			9.1	22.7	39.1	37.4	22.0
Return on Equity After Income Taxes 48	19.7			9.1	18.0	33.4	37.3	15.9
Profit Margin (Before Income Tax) 49	8.8	3.3	37.2	4.9	12.2	10.0	12.3	7.6
Profit Margin (After Income Tax) 50	6.8	3.2	37.2	4.9	9.7	8.5	12.2	5.5

Table I

Corporations with and without Net Income

SOFTWARE PUBLISHERS

MONEY AMOUNTS AND SIZE OF ASSETS IN THOUSANDS OF DOLLARS

Item Description for Accounting Period 7/10 Through 6/11		Total	Zero Assets	Under 500	500 to 1,000	1,000 to 5,000	5,000 to 10,000	10,000 to 25,000	25,000 to 50,000	50,000 to 100,000	100,000 to 250,000	250,000 to 500,000	500,000 to 2,500,000	2,500,000 and over
Number of Enterprises	1	7626	343	5679	416	602	194	146	69	46	43	27	44	17
Revenues ($ in Thousands)														
Net Sales	2	123656990	2288567	2177934	543058	1928901	1568191	2322566	2298832	1980823	3648248	5143577	17909467	81846826
Interest	3	833085	3893	84	594	1262	1951	4277	5351	11620	22552	38284	65748	677469
Rents	4	193737	56	0	0	49	268	0	4	0	500	508	26259	166093
Royalties	5	8755514	71513	0	4458	3458	262	0	289	50122	216642	65736	1599745	6743290
Other Portfolio Income	6	2846909	15935	22699	206	18077	8439	44880	1518	2267	10089	50147	280031	2392624
Other Receipts	7	21661040	227902	5609	10972	-4115	29543	49261	37007	156192	123853	106002	271961	20646849
Total Receipts	8	157947275	2607866	2206326	559288	1947632	1608654	2420984	2343001	2201024	4021884	5404254	20153211	112473151
Average Total Receipts	9	20712	7603	389	1344	3235	8292	16582	33957	47848	93532	200158	458028	6616068
Operating Costs/Operating Income (%)														
Cost of Operations	10	27.7	42.4	3.7	17.3	15.9	11.3	18.8	23.9	27.3	15.1	26.9	16.0	32.1
Salaries and Wages	11	33.7	47.0	39.6	39.0	43.6	51.8	40.4	31.6	34.2	37.4	29.0	39.4	31.4
Taxes Paid	12	3.2	4.8	5.6	3.6	5.1	4.5	4.5	3.4	3.5	3.4	3.9	2.8	3.0
Interest Paid	13	2.4	1.8	1.4	0.7	2.4	1.0	1.8	0.9	2.4	1.8	2.3	3.1	2.4
Depreciation	14	3.9	2.8	0.7	1.4	1.8	3.0	2.8	2.2	2.4	3.6	2.8	2.9	4.5
Amortization and Depletion	15	1.9	1.7	1.0	1.0	2.1	0.2	1.2	0.9	3.5	3.2	2.7	3.4	1.5
Pensions and Other Deferred Comp.	16	0.3	0.7	•	0.4	0.7	0.4	0.6	0.3	0.5	0.4	0.3	0.9	0.2
Employee Benefits	17	3.5	1.5	1.8	0.6	4.8	3.2	3.6	2.9	3.7	3.0	3.1	4.1	3.4
Advertising	18	4.5	2.1	3.2	1.1	2.5	2.6	3.1	1.6	2.4	3.4	2.1	2.3	5.6
Other Expenses	19	29.4	27.5	34.1	39.7	29.7	27.0	31.3	33.0	22.3	34.3	22.0	31.8	29.0
Officers' Compensation	20	2.0	7.1	15.2	9.2	9.0	5.7	4.0	2.8	3.7	4.3	3.6	2.6	0.8
Operating Margin	21	•	•	•	•	•	•	•	•	•	•	1.2	•	•
Operating Margin Before Officers' Comp.	22	•	8.9	•	•	•	•	•	•	•	4.8	•	•	•

Selected Average Balance Sheet ($ in Thousands)

Net Receivables 23	4150	0	13	254	414	1021	3122	8609	7766	18580	46576	144339	1247276
Inventories 24	257	0	0	1	64	53	229	184	578	573	3065	5801	86755
Net Property, Plant and Equipment 25	2035	0	6	22	257	640	918	2533	2673	6709	13483	54620	688782
Total Assets 26	40214	0	45	698	1950	7769	15142	32444	72080	161527	360855	1093552	13580702
Notes and Loans Payable 27	5464	0	61	275	719	865	2596	6628	9338	27918	65772	196259	1631282
All Other Liabilities 28	18140	0	102	921	3776	5142	10000	19749	32729	54081	152030	345407	6361881
Net Worth 29	16609	0	-118	-498	-2545	1762	2547	6067	30012	79528	143053	551886	5587540

Selected Financial Ratios (Times to 1)

Current Ratio 30	0.7	•	0.6	0.8	0.3	1.2	1.2	1.3	1.2	1.3	1.4	1.5	0.6
Quick Ratio 31	0.5	•	0.6	0.7	0.3	1.0	1.0	1.1	0.8	1.0	1.1	1.3	0.4
Net Sales to Working Capital 32	•	•	•	•	•	9.9	13.2	7.7	9.8	5.4	4.2	3.2	•
Coverage Ratio 33	9.0	•	•	•	•	•	•	•	3.3	1.3	3.9	3.3	12.8
Total Asset Turnover 34	0.4	•	8.5	1.9	1.6	1.0	1.1	1.0	0.6	0.5	0.5	0.4	0.4
Inventory Turnover 35	17.5	•	173.4	292.8	8.0	17.1	13.0	43.2	20.3	22.4	16.7	11.2	17.8
Receivables Turnover 36	4.0	•	34.5	5.8	5.5	7.7	4.0	3.7	4.9	3.8	3.8	3.0	4.1
Total Liabilities to Net Worth 37	1.4	•	•	•	•	3.4	4.9	4.3	1.4	1.0	1.5	1.0	1.4
Current Assets to Working Capital 38	•	•	•	•	•	5.9	7.6	4.4	7.0	4.0	3.3	2.9	•
Current Liabilities to Working Capital 39	•	•	•	•	•	4.9	6.6	3.4	6.0	3.0	2.3	1.9	•
Working Capital to Net Sales 40	•	•	•	•	•	0.1	0.1	0.1	0.1	0.2	0.2	0.3	•
Inventory to Working Capital 41	•	•	•	•	•	0.1	0.2	0.0	0.1	0.0	0.1	0.0	•
Total Receipts to Cash Flow 42	2.5	•	4.1	4.1	12.4	6.8	5.6	3.6	4.1	3.2	4.0	3.2	2.1
Cost of Goods to Cash Flow 43	0.7	•	0.2	0.7	2.0	0.8	1.1	0.8	1.1	0.5	1.1	0.5	0.7
Cash Flow to Total Debt 44	0.3	•	0.6	0.3	0.1	0.2	0.2	0.4	0.3	0.3	0.2	0.2	0.3

Selected Financial Factors (in Percentages)

Debt Ratio 45	58.7	•	360.3	171.4	230.5	77.3	83.2	81.3	58.4	50.8	60.4	49.5	58.9
Return on Total Assets 46	8.6	•	•	•	•	•	•	•	4.7	1.2	4.7	3.8	10.9
Return on Equity Before Income Taxes 47	18.6	•	16.2	28.8	21.0	•	•	•	7.8	0.5	8.7	5.3	24.4
Return on Equity After Income Taxes 48	11.9	•	16.2	29.2	22.1	•	•	•	6.1	•	5.1	3.2	16.3
Profit Margin (Before Income Tax) 49	19.0	•	•	•	•	•	•	•	5.5	0.5	6.6	7.1	28.3
Profit Margin (After Income Tax) 50	12.2	•	•	•	•	•	•	•	4.2	•	3.8	4.4	19.0

Table II
Corporations with Net Income

SOFTWARE PUBLISHERS

MONEY AMOUNTS AND SIZE OF ASSETS IN THOUSANDS OF DOLLARS

Item Description for Accounting Period 7/10 Through 6/11	Total	Zero Assets	Under 500	500 to 1,000	1,000 to 5,000	5,000 to 10,000	10,000 to 25,000	25,000 to 50,000	50,000 to 100,000	100,000 to 250,000	250,000 to 500,000	500,000 to 2,500,000	2,500,000 and over
Number of Enterprises 1	3483	3	2832	177	162	100	55	44	26	25	•	25	•
Revenues ($ in Thousands)													
Net Sales 2	106128470	1389186	1708506	462774	699445	1016977	1013360	1526805	1261350	2236404	•	11605271	•
Interest 3	735347	938	6	587	880	995	2063	4469	4225	11226	•	37288	•
Rents 4	178923	56	0	0	0	268	0	4	0	73	•	12088	•
Royalties 5	8324809	44022	0	0	0	0	0	289	34160	75568	•	1388105	•
Other Portfolio Income 6	268004	15928	13387	206	17853	315	44575	746	2254	8782	•	183957	•
Other Receipts 7	21233103	1670	3818	10585	498	23774	42473	31414	145394	31452	•	246425	•
Total Receipts 8	139283656	1451800	1725717	474152	718676	1042329	1102471	1563727	1447383	2363505	•	13473134	•
Average Total Receipts 9	39990	483933	609	2679	4436	10423	20045	35539	55669	94540	•	538925	•
Operating Costs/Operating Income (%)													
Cost of Operations 10	28.5	52.5	1.6	9.8	14.8	7.8	20.7	22.5	19.0	20.7	•	14.6	•
Salaries and Wages 11	32.2	13.2	36.7	35.9	31.9	45.3	31.0	26.6	35.8	32.6	•	39.0	•
Taxes Paid 12	3.2	4.3	4.9	3.4	4.2	4.1	3.5	3.4	4.0	3.4	•	3.0	•
Interest Paid 13	2.3	0.5	0.6	0.0	1.5	1.1	0.7	0.7	1.5	1.7	•	2.8	•
Depreciation 14	4.0	0.9	0.5	1.3	0.6	2.0	2.6	2.2	3.0	2.4	•	2.7	•
Amortization and Depletion 15	1.6	0.2	0.0	1.2	2.0	0.0	0.9	0.8	2.1	2.6	•	2.9	•
Pensions and Other Deferred Comp. 16	0.4	0.8	•	0.4	0.2	0.5	0.9	0.3	0.6	0.4	•	1.3	•
Employee Benefits 17	3.4	0.3	2.0	0.2	3.4	2.3	3.1	2.5	3.8	2.8	•	4.2	•
Advertising 18	4.6	0.5	3.3	0.9	1.3	1.3	3.7	1.7	2.4	2.0	•	1.9	•
Other Expenses 19	28.5	20.3	28.9	29.5	18.4	20.6	22.4	30.3	18.8	23.1	•	29.9	•
Officers' Compensation 20	1.5	0.0	12.9	10.3	10.9	4.6	4.6	2.3	4.4	2.7	•	1.8	•
Operating Margin 21	•	6.4	8.6	7.2	10.8	10.3	5.8	6.7	4.7	5.7	•	•	•
Operating Margin Before Officers' Comp. 22	•	6.4	21.5	17.5	21.7	14.9	10.5	9.0	9.1	8.3	•	•	•

Selected Average Balance Sheet ($ in Thousands)

Net Receivables 23	7877	0	7	276	431	1148	3366	9471	7542	21430	160509	•
Inventories 24	459	0	0	2	194	71	210	212	478	784	2143	•
Net Property, Plant and Equipment 25	3926	0	3	28	210	746	713	3158	3727	5784	62153	•
Total Assets 26	77780	0	44	704	2375	8156	15118	32705	70062	163724	1104923	•
Notes and Loans Payable 27	10173	0	60	122	472	489	1528	2989	9625	27815	201891	•
All Other Liabilities 28	35774	0	141	1096	10267	4529	8078	16155	34884	47707	382214	•
Net Worth 29	31833	0	-157	-513	-8364	3139	5512	13561	25554	88203	520918	•

Selected Financial Ratios (Times to 1)

Current Ratio 30	0.6	•	0.7	0.8	0.2	1.3	1.8	1.2	1.3	1.8	1.3	•
Quick Ratio 31	0.4	•	0.7	0.7	0.1	1.2	1.6	1.1	0.9	1.4	1.1	•
Net Sales to Working Capital 32	•	•	•	•	•	9.1	4.3	10.6	7.5	2.9	5.2	•
Coverage Ratio 33	12.0	23.3	16.7	286.3	10.0	12.3	22.0	13.8	13.9	7.9	7.2	•
Total Asset Turnover 34	0.4	•	13.6	3.7	1.8	1.2	1.2	1.1	0.7	0.5	0.4	•
Inventory Turnover 35	18.9	•	•	142.0	3.3	11.1	18.1	36.8	19.2	23.6	31.6	•
Receivables Turnover 36	4.1	•	123.8	8.5	3.5	7.2	3.6	4.1	5.4	•	3.0	•
Total Liabilities to Net Worth 37	1.4	•	•	•	1.6	1.7	1.4	1.7	0.9	1.1	•	•
Current Assets to Working Capital 38	•	•	•	•	•	4.3	2.3	5.8	4.8	2.2	4.0	•
Current Liabilities to Working Capital 39	•	•	•	•	3.3	3.3	1.3	4.8	3.8	1.2	3.0	•
Working Capital to Net Sales 40	•	•	•	•	•	0.1	0.2	0.1	0.1	0.3	0.2	•
Inventory to Working Capital 41	•	•	•	•	•	0.1	0.0	0.1	0.0	0.0	0.0	•
Total Receipts to Cash Flow 42	2.2	3.3	2.8	2.9	3.8	3.4	3.3	2.8	2.9	3.2	2.7	•
Cost of Goods to Cash Flow 43	0.6	1.7	0.0	0.3	0.6	0.3	0.7	0.6	0.5	0.7	0.4	•
Cash Flow to Total Debt 44	0.3	•	1.1	0.7	0.1	0.6	0.6	0.6	0.4	0.4	0.3	•

Selected Financial Factors (in Percentages)

Debt Ratio 45	59.1	•	453.9	172.8	452.2	61.5	63.5	58.5	63.5	46.1	52.9	•
Return on Total Assets 46	10.9	•	139.5	35.8	27.3	17.3	18.7	10.6	14.6	7.2	8.4	•
Return on Equity Before Income Taxes 47	24.4	•	•	•	41.4	48.9	23.6	37.1	•	15.4	•	•
Return on Equity After Income Taxes 48	16.8	•	•	•	35.4	41.7	20.9	33.4	8.9	11.6	•	•
Profit Margin (Before Income Tax) 49	25.5	11.5	9.6	13.5	12.8	14.6	9.2	19.5	11.4	•	17.3	•
Profit Margin (After Income Tax) 50	17.5	7.7	9.6	11.0	10.9	12.5	8.2	17.6	8.8	•	13.0	•

Table I

Corporations with and without Net Income

MOTION PICTURE AND VIDEO INDUSTRIES (EXCEPT VIDEO RENTAL)

MONEY AMOUNTS AND SIZE OF ASSETS IN THOUSANDS OF DOLLARS

Item Description for Accounting Period 7/10 Through 6/11	Total	Zero Assets	Under 500	500 to 1,000	1,000 to 5,000	5,000 to 10,000	10,000 to 25,000	25,000 to 50,000	50,000 to 100,000	100,000 to 250,000	250,000 to 500,000	500,000 to 2,500,000	2,500,000 and over
Number of Enterprises **1**	30292	4821	23397	794	866	195	121	34	17	16	10	10	9
Revenues ($ in Thousands)													
Net Sales **2**	96730122	677191	5271002	1453439	1745739	1087013	3056058	816555	1107867	1438649	1620453	6448923	72007232
Interest **3**	506017	2077	2058	61	3385	146	1323	1436	1505	10228	13883	45557	424357
Rents **4**	328763	0	0	0	0	0	0	2762	302	94	7375	21551	296680
Royalties **5**	1990288	464050	4924	94	0	0	0	6	5619	22265	3519	20023	1469788
Other Portfolio Income **6**	1544435	12540	8701	0	1601	18051	737	19839	281	2300	195	165158	1315030
Other Receipts **7**	4102033	276294	114989	15096	128209	9230	35340	70859	71342	61318	55794	723230	2540335
Total Receipts **8**	105201658	1432152	5401674	1468690	1878934	1114440	3093458	911457	1186916	1534854	1701219	7424442	78053422
Average Total Receipts **9**	3473	297	231	1850	2170	5715	25566	26808	69819	95928	170122	742444	8672602
Operating Costs/Operating Income (%)													
Cost of Operations **10**	21.8	22.5	18.7	17.2	29.4	42.0	45.2	45.4	54.8	23.8	38.2	20.2	19.5
Salaries and Wages **11**	10.9	1.9	5.0	18.9	14.5	11.6	9.6	11.2	8.8	7.1	8.8	13.0	11.1
Taxes Paid **12**	3.3	1.8	2.3	3.5	2.6	2.1	2.2	10.7	2.2	1.8	2.1	4.6	3.3
Interest Paid **13**	5.3	12.0	0.4	0.8	0.8	2.2	1.2	2.6	2.1	5.4	3.9	5.4	6.1
Depreciation **14**	6.4	20.1	2.0	2.1	3.3	4.8	11.0	7.6	5.4	3.6	12.5	5.8	6.6
Amortization and Depletion **15**	13.0	0.3	0.0	3.7	0.9	0.1	0.9	7.4	5.1	9.9	8.7	6.8	16.1
Pensions and Other Deferred Comp. **16**	0.6	8.7	2.1	1.4	0.7	0.2	0.1	0.1	0.2	0.1	0.1	0.5	0.5
Employee Benefits **17**	1.4	0.5	1.6	1.6	1.1	0.5	0.8	1.2	0.8	0.5	1.2	1.0	1.5
Advertising **18**	5.9	3.2	0.6	1.6	0.3	0.7	0.7	1.1	1.0	0.3	0.1	3.2	7.5
Other Expenses **19**	28.9	137.9	29.0	29.2	36.6	26.4	15.6	27.8	25.6	39.5	25.4	41.3	27.1
Officers' Compensation **20**	3.8	3.1	30.1	18.0	14.4	6.3	11.6	3.3	3.1	22.3	1.1	2.5	0.8
Operating Margin **21**	•	•	8.2	2.1	•	3.2	1.1	•	•	•	•	•	•
Operating Margin Before Officers' Comp. **22**	2.6	•	38.3	20.0	9.8	9.4	12.7	•	•	8.1	•	•	0.7

Selected Average Balance Sheet ($ in Thousands)

Net Receivables 23	885	0	3	33	211	928	3539	6661	9079	15962	96738	109702	2580875
Inventories 24	252	0	1	27	9	171	685	572	3815	6451	4417	14380	788964
Net Property, Plant and Equipment 25	563	0	9	331	368	1803	4145	8557	18646	17012	73038	380754	1109124
Total Assets 26	7822	53	744	1730	6928	16525	33729	71921	161170	325431	1399199	23120776	
Notes and Loans Payable 27	2564	0	157	508	1193	2626	6758	15445	22116	90905	118840	618179	6833902
All Other Liabilities 28	2294	0	32	208	522	2083	7501	12505	22376	52229	183093	513187	6467242
Net Worth 29	2964	0	-137	29	15	2219	2266	5779	27429	18036	23498	267833	9819632

Selected Financial Ratios (Times to 1)

Current Ratio 30	1.2	•	0.9	2.0	2.1	2.0	1.1	1.1	1.6	1.2	1.1	0.8	1.3
Quick Ratio 31	0.9	•	0.8	1.6	1.6	1.4	0.9	0.7	1.2	0.9	0.7	0.5	0.9
Net Sales to Working Capital 32	8.2	•	•	11.1	4.2	2.6	22.5	29.2	6.0	12.0	13.5	•	6.4
Coverage Ratio 33	2.5	1.0	25.9	5.0	4.5	3.6	3.0	•	0.1	•	1.7	3.0	2.5
Total Asset Turnover 34	0.4	•	4.3	2.5	1.2	0.8	1.5	0.7	0.9	0.6	0.5	0.5	0.3
Inventory Turnover 35	2.8	•	41.9	11.8	62.5	13.7	16.7	19.1	9.4	3.3	14.0	9.0	2.0
Receivables Turnover 36	5.3	•	71.0	52.7	15.6	7.6	7.7	4.9	6.4	6.1	2.8	5.9	4.7
Total Liabilities to Net Worth 37	1.6	•	•	24.6	116.2	2.1	6.3	4.8	1.6	7.9	12.8	4.2	1.4
Current Assets to Working Capital 38	5.3	•	•	2.0	1.9	2.0	7.9	19.1	2.6	6.0	15.7	•	4.7
Current Liabilities to Working Capital 39	4.3	•	•	1.0	0.9	1.0	6.9	18.1	1.6	5.0	14.7	•	3.7
Working Capital to Net Sales 40	0.1	•	•	0.1	0.2	0.4	0.0	0.0	0.2	0.1	0.1	•	0.2
Inventory to Working Capital 41	0.9	•	•	0.2	0.0	0.1	0.6	1.0	0.1	0.9	0.5	•	0.9
Total Receipts to Cash Flow 42	3.5	0.8	3.0	4.2	3.6	4.4	10.2	7.5	8.2	4.3	4.9	4.9	3.4
Cost of Goods to Cash Flow 43	0.8	0.2	0.6	0.7	1.1	1.9	4.6	4.5	4.5	1.0	1.9	1.0	0.7
Cash Flow to Total Debt 44	0.2	•	0.4	0.6	0.3	0.3	0.2	0.1	0.2	0.1	0.1	0.1	0.2

Selected Financial Factors (in Percentages)

Debt Ratio 45	62.1	•	360.2	96.1	99.1	68.0	86.3	82.9	61.9	88.8	92.8	80.9	57.5
Return on Total Assets 46	5.5	•	47.5	9.6	4.4	6.4	5.3	•	0.2	•	3.4	7.5	5.2
Return on Equity Before Income Taxes 47	8.8	•	•	196.2	402.5	14.3	25.5	•	•	•	20.0	26.0	7.4
Return on Equity After Income Taxes 48	5.3	•	•	196.2	352.1	14.3	24.0	•	•	•	9.0	17.1	4.2
Profit Margin (Before Income Tax) 49	8.1	•	10.7	3.1	2.9	5.7	2.3	•	•	•	2.9	10.8	9.1
Profit Margin (After Income Tax) 50	5.0	•	10.5	3.1	2.6	5.7	2.2	•	•	•	1.3	7.1	5.2

Table II
Corporations with Net Income

MOTION PICTURE AND VIDEO INDUSTRIES (EXCEPT VIDEO RENTAL)

MONEY AMOUNTS AND SIZE OF ASSETS IN THOUSANDS OF DOLLARS

Item Description for Accounting Period 7/10 Through 6/11	Total	Zero Assets	Under 500	500 to 1,000	1,000 to 5,000	5,000 to 10,000	10,000 to 25,000	25,000 to 50,000	50,000 to 100,000	100,000 to 250,000	250,000 to 500,000	500,000 to 2,500,000	2,500,000 and over
Number of Enterprises **1**	16260	2204	13259	180	425	82	67	•	8	•	5	•	•
Revenues ($ in Thousands)													
Net Sales **2**	81995359	278227	3576034	449876	1532666	567839	2126531	•	662332	•	951867	•	•
Interest **3**	294522	415	2027	10	2522	0	1266	•	1177	•	12554	•	•
Rents **4**	303427	0	0	0	0	0	0	•	302	•	3255	•	•
Royalties **5**	884975	77	0	0	0	0	0	•	0	•	37	•	•
Other Portfolio Income **6**	1338476	10830	6916	0	1175	17269	709	•	200	•	6	•	•
Other Receipts **7**	3366119	79693	67011	15102	124429	885	12584	•	4155	•	40306	•	•
Total Receipts **8**	88482878	369242	3651988	464988	1660792	585993	2141090	•	668166	•	1008025	•	•
Average Total Receipts **9**	5442	168	275	2583	3908	7146	31957	•	83521	•	201605	•	•
Operating Costs/Operating Income (%)													
Cost of Operations **10**	19.7	48.4	13.9	12.5	30.3	38.0	43.5	•	55.3	•	39.0	•	•
Salaries and Wages **11**	10.7	3.6	5.2	8.2	12.0	9.7	7.9	•	7.6	•	5.5	•	•
Taxes Paid **12**	3.3	1.8	2.1	4.1	2.1	1.8	1.3	•	2.3	•	1.2	•	•
Interest Paid **13**	4.3	0.4	0.5	0.1	0.6	0.8	0.7	•	1.2	•	1.7	•	•
Depreciation **14**	6.2	1.7	1.6	1.4	2.7	3.3	13.8	•	2.7	•	13.2	•	•
Amortization and Depletion **15**	14.2	•	0.0	0.0	0.0	0.0	0.0	•	0.8	•	12.1	•	•
Pensions and Other Deferred Comp. **16**	0.5	•	1.3	1.3	0.8	0.3	0.1	•	0.2	•	0.1	•	•
Employee Benefits **17**	1.3	0.7	0.9	0.8	1.2	0.6	0.5	•	0.7	•	1.2	•	•
Advertising **18**	6.6	0.1	0.6	0.0	0.3	0.0	0.5	•	0.7	•	0.1	•	•
Other Expenses **19**	25.3	21.8	26.4	9.3	28.9	16.8	7.8	•	18.6	•	22.3	•	•
Officers' Compensation **20**	3.5	6.8	29.6	41.7	14.8	10.3	15.5	•	3.7	•	0.9	•	•
Operating Margin **21**	4.3	14.7	18.0	20.5	6.3	18.4	8.3	•	6.2	•	2.6	•	•
Operating Margin Before Officers' Comp. **22**	7.8	21.5	47.6	62.2	21.1	28.7	23.8	•	9.9	•	3.5	•	•

Selected Average Balance Sheet ($ in Thousands)

Net Receivables 23	1482	0	4	53	223	822	4134	6695	96258
Inventories 24	447	0	1	1	1	1	327	347	8147
Net Property, Plant and Equipment 25	662	0	11	88	259	1223	3039	18991	21499
Total Assets 26	12727	0	62	663	1559	7454	15121	78806	315206
Notes and Loans Payable 27	4023	0	69	25	322	950	3755	14396	82070
All Other Liabilities 28	3511	0	16	88	374	1182	6168	28029	178601
Net Worth 29	5193	0	-23	551	863	5322	5198	36381	54535

Selected Financial Ratios (Times to 1)

Current Ratio 30	1.3	•	2.0	7.8	2.9	4.6	1.4	1.3	1.2
Quick Ratio 31	0.9	•	2.0	7.7	2.5	4.5	1.2	0.9	0.6
Net Sales to Working Capital 32	7.4	•	14.8	5.0	4.6	1.5	10.5	16.6	5.9
Coverage Ratio 33	4.0	124.7	44.5	349.5	25.7	26.6	13.4	7.0	6.0
Total Asset Turnover 34	0.4	•	4.3	3.8	2.3	0.9	2.1	1.1	0.6
Inventory Turnover 35	2.2	•	46.9	372.2	777.9	4450.3	42.2	132.1	9.1
Receivables Turnover 36	5.2	•	67.3	44.9	26.3	7.6	7.9	7.9	3.7
Total Liabilities to Net Worth 37	1.5	•	•	0.2	0.8	0.4	1.9	1.2	4.8
Current Assets to Working Capital 38	4.8	•	2.0	1.1	1.5	1.3	3.2	4.3	6.6
Current Liabilities to Working Capital 39	3.8	•	1.0	0.1	0.5	0.3	2.2	3.3	5.6
Working Capital to Net Sales 40	0.1	•	0.1	0.2	0.2	0.7	0.1	0.1	0.2
Inventory to Working Capital 41	0.9	•	0.0	•	0.0	•	0.1	0.1	0.3
Total Receipts to Cash Flow 42	3.2	1.6	2.4	3.3	3.1	2.8	6.9	6.8	3.6
Cost of Goods to Cash Flow 43	0.6	0.8	0.3	0.4	0.9	1.1	3.0	3.8	1.4
Cash Flow to Total Debt 44	0.2	•	1.3	6.8	1.7	1.2	0.5	0.3	0.2

Selected Financial Factors (in Percentages)

Debt Ratio 45	59.2	•	136.4	17.0	44.6	28.6	65.6	53.8	82.7
Return on Total Assets 46	6.8	•	89.2	90.2	35.2	20.8	20.3	8.6	6.2
Return on Equity Before Income Taxes 47	12.5	•	•	108.3	61.2	28.1	54.6	16.0	29.7
Return on Equity After Income Taxes 48	8.9	•	•	108.3	59.4	28.1	53.4	13.8	20.2
Profit Margin (Before Income Tax) 49	12.9	47.3	20.1	23.9	14.6	21.6	8.9	7.0	8.5
Profit Margin (After Income Tax) 50	9.2	43.6	19.9	23.9	14.2	21.6	8.8	6.1	5.8

Table I

Corporations with and without Net Income

SOUND RECORDING INDUSTRIES

MONEY AMOUNTS AND SIZE OF ASSETS IN THOUSANDS OF DOLLARS

Item Description for Accounting Period 7/10 Through 6/11	Total	Zero Assets	Under 500	500 to 1,000	1,000 to 5,000	5,000 to 10,000	10,000 to 25,000	25,000 to 50,000	50,000 to 100,000	100,000 to 250,000	250,000 to 500,000	500,000 to 2,500,000	2,500,000 and over
Number of Enterprises **1**	6572	2012	4162	163	152	46	12	13	3	6	0	3	0
Revenues ($ in Thousands)													
Net Sales **2**	6312373	5593	668929	567701	45048	126292	151515	115002	189156	314065	0	4129070	0
Interest **3**	48901	0	0	2	0	0	284	1666	965	439	0	45546	0
Rents **4**	368	9	0	0	0	0	0	333	0	0	0	26	0
Royalties **5**	2155235	0	0	0	18901	0	0	76684	43	45201	0	2014406	0
Other Portfolio Income **6**	176283	0	694	0	0	0	0	2170	18	2	0	173400	0
Other Receipts **7**	740725	26	95	-1	-4351	0	0	13106	27439	9282	0	695128	0
Total Receipts **8**	9433885	5628	669718	567702	59598	126292	151799	208961	217621	368989	0	7057576	0
Average Total Receipts **9**	1435	3	161	3483	392	2745	12650	16074	72540	61498	•	2352525	•
Operating Costs/Operating Income (%)													
Cost of Operations **10**	37.2	24.4	32.2	39.6	8.0	49.6	2.6	37.2	47.8	57.7	•	36.8	•
Salaries and Wages **11**	13.4	•	3.1	18.7	3.3	9.2	12.1	25.8	13.5	10.4	•	14.6	•
Taxes Paid **12**	3.5	3.2	2.0	2.0	1.3	2.9	1.8	8.9	3.6	2.5	•	4.0	•
Interest Paid **13**	6.8	•	0.1	0.9	0.0	0.5	0.0	2.1	3.2	8.2	•	9.5	•
Depreciation **14**	5.0	•	0.7	1.7	1.1	1.1	1.3	3.0	1.1	1.2	•	7.0	•
Amortization and Depletion **15**	5.5	•	•	0.0	•	•	3.1	18.1	4.1	16.3	•	6.3	•
Pensions and Other Deferred Comp. **16**	0.8	•	1.2	0.3	•	•	•	1.0	0.6	0.3	•	0.9	•
Employee Benefits **17**	1.4	•	4.8	0.1	0.2	•	0.6	4.0	1.3	0.9	•	1.1	•
Advertising **18**	3.2	•	0.3	0.1	•	0.3	6.4	0.6	0.4	5.9	•	4.2	•
Other Expenses **19**	69.4	78.3	26.2	30.2	94.0	20.6	87.3	60.1	18.2	23.4	•	88.5	•
Officers' Compensation **20**	3.4	10.3	20.6	1.7	1.2	•	5.9	12.1	1.4	4.1	•	0.6	•
Operating Margin **21**	•	•	8.7	4.7	•	15.9	•	•	4.6	•	•	•	•
Operating Margin Before Officers' Comp. **22**	•	•	29.3	6.4	•	15.9	•	•	6.1	•	•	•	•

Selected Average Balance Sheet ($ in Thousands)

	1	2	3	4	5	6	7	8	9	10	11
Net Receivables 23	685	0	3	0	0	854	418	227	3884	9718	1458327
Inventories 24	59	0	0	6	256	852	0	112	67	6720	88548
Net Property, Plant and Equipment 25	79	0	8	313	0	1908	226	3825	1674	2425	92305
Total Assets 26	4306	0	36	571	1644	5996	17102	32588	77687	162333	8565405
Notes and Loans Payable 27	793	0	243	146	1168	1196	0	9029	49192	73396	1078728
All Other Liabilities 28	1665	0	2	335	31	989	6745	8515	50842	40894	3413895
Net Worth 29	1848	0	-210	89	445	3811	10357	15044	-22348	48043	4072783

Selected Financial Ratios (Times to 1)

	1	2	3	4	5	6	7	8	9	10	11
Current Ratio 30	0.6	•	7.5	0.2	3.7	4.1	1.7	0.9	1.0	0.6	0.6
Quick Ratio 31	0.5	•	7.2	0.1	3.1	1.9	1.6	0.5	0.9	0.4	0.5
Net Sales to Working Capital 32	•	•	6.9	•	0.3	0.9	2.7	•	46.4	•	•
Coverage Ratio 33	1.1	•	95.8	6.3	2191.4	35.5	8.1	8.1	7.1	•	0.9
Total Asset Turnover 34	0.2	•	4.5	6.1	0.2	0.5	0.7	0.3	0.8	0.3	0.2
Inventory Turnover 35	6.1	•	•	221.5	0.1	1.6	29.4	29.4	449.0	4.5	5.7
Receivables Turnover 36	1.5	•	63.5	•	1.4	3.1	59.5	8.3	17.8	6.4	1.0
Total Liabilities to Net Worth 37	1.3	•	•	5.4	2.7	0.6	0.7	1.2	•	2.4	1.1
Current Assets to Working Capital 38	•	•	1.2	•	1.4	1.3	2.4	•	38.7	•	•
Current Liabilities to Working Capital 39	•	•	0.2	•	0.4	0.3	1.4	•	37.7	•	•
Working Capital to Net Sales 40	•	•	0.1	•	3.1	1.1	0.4	•	0.0	•	•
Inventory to Working Capital 41	•	•	•	•	•	0.2	•	•	•	•	•
Total Receipts to Cash Flow 42	1.5	2.9	4.0	4.4	0.9	3.0	1.5	1.6	2.9	13.6	1.2
Cost of Goods to Cash Flow 43	0.6	0.7	1.3	1.7	0.1	1.5	0.0	0.6	1.4	7.9	0.4
Cash Flow to Total Debt 44	0.3	•	0.2	1.6	0.3	0.4	1.2	0.3	0.2	0.0	0.3

Selected Financial Factors (in Percentages)

	1	2	3	4	5	6	7	8	9	10	11
Debt Ratio 45	57.1	•	689.2	84.4	72.9	36.4	39.4	53.8	128.8	70.4	52.5
Return on Total Assets 46	1.7	•	40.1	34.1	4.4	7.5	•	4.6	18.6	•	1.4
Return on Equity Before Income Taxes 47	0.5	•	•	184.3	16.2	11.5	•	8.7	•	•	•
Return on Equity After Income Taxes 48	0.4	•	•	182.2	14.3	11.5	•	6.6	•	•	•
Profit Margin (Before Income Tax) 49	1.0	•	8.8	4.7	24.3	15.9	•	14.7	19.6	•	•
Profit Margin (After Income Tax) 50	0.7	•	8.8	•	21.4	15.9	•	11.2	12.9	•	•

Table II

Corporations with Net Income

SOUND RECORDING INDUSTRIES

MONEY AMOUNTS AND SIZE OF ASSETS IN THOUSANDS OF DOLLARS

Item Description for Accounting Period 7/10 Through 6/11	Total	Zero Assets	Under 500	500 to 1,000	1,000 to 5,000	5,000 to 10,000	10,000 to 25,000	25,000 to 50,000	50,000 to 100,000	100,000 to 250,000	250,000 to 500,000	500,000 to 2,500,000	2,500,000 and over
Number of Enterprises **1**	2892	294	2333	163	41	46	0	•	0	0	0	•	•

Revenues ($ in Thousands)

Item Description for Accounting Period 7/10 Through 6/11	Total	Zero Assets	Under 500	500 to 1,000	1,000 to 5,000	5,000 to 10,000	10,000 to 25,000	25,000 to 50,000	50,000 to 100,000	100,000 to 250,000	250,000 to 500,000	500,000 to 2,500,000	2,500,000 and over
Net Sales **2**	3934383	4520	595298	567701	45048	126292	0	•	•	•	0	•	•
Interest **3**	46829	0	0	2	0	0	0	•	0	0	0	•	•
Rents **4**	368	9	0	0	0	0	0	•	0	0	0	•	•
Royalties **5**	772266	0	0	0	18901	0	0	•	•	•	•	•	•
Other Portfolio Income **6**	63994	0	694	0	0	0	0	•	•	•	0	•	•
Other Receipts **7**	371829	-9	95	-1	88	0	0	•	•	•	0	•	•
Total Receipts **8**	5189669	4520	596087	567702	64037	126292	0	•	•	•	0	•	•
Average Total Receipts **9**	1794	15	256	3483	1562	2745	•	•	•	•	•	•	•

Operating Costs/Operating Income (%)

Item Description for Accounting Period 7/10 Through 6/11	Total	Zero Assets	Under 500	500 to 1,000	1,000 to 5,000	5,000 to 10,000	10,000 to 25,000	25,000 to 50,000	50,000 to 100,000	100,000 to 250,000	250,000 to 500,000	500,000 to 2,500,000	2,500,000 and over
Cost of Operations **10**	38.7	9.8	34.7	39.6	•	49.6	•	•	•	•	•	•	•
Salaries and Wages **11**	13.5	•	3.5	18.7	3.3	9.2	•	•	•	•	•	•	•
Taxes Paid **12**	3.5	0.4	1.5	2.0	1.3	2.9	•	•	•	•	•	•	•
Interest Paid **13**	5.2	•	0.0	0.9	•	0.5	•	•	•	•	•	•	•
Depreciation **14**	7.5	•	0.3	1.7	•	1.1	•	•	•	•	•	•	•
Amortization and Depletion **15**	4.1	•	•	0.0	•	•	•	•	•	•	•	•	•
Pensions and Other Deferred Comp. **16**	0.3	•	1.3	0.3	•	•	•	•	•	•	•	•	•
Employee Benefits **17**	0.8	•	2.4	0.1	0.2	•	•	•	•	•	•	•	•
Advertising **18**	1.6	•	0.3	0.1	•	0.3	•	•	•	•	•	•	•
Other Expenses **19**	43.6	68.0	15.1	30.2	89.3	20.6	•	•	•	•	•	•	•
Officers' Compensation **20**	4.3	•	19.4	1.7	1.2	•	•	•	•	•	•	•	•
Operating Margin **21**	•	21.8	21.6	4.7	4.8	15.9	•	•	•	•	•	•	•
Operating Margin Before Officers' Comp. **22**	•	21.8	41.0	6.4	6.0	15.9	•	•	•	•	•	•	•

Selected Average Balance Sheet ($ in Thousands)

Net Receivables 23	1348	0	5	0	0	854
Inventories 24	48	0	0	9	947	852
Net Property, Plant and Equipment 25	145	0	4	313	0	1908
Total Assets 26	3074	0	49	571	2260	5996
Notes and Loans Payable 27	1264	0	3	146	1141	1196
All Other Liabilities 28	1788	0	4	335	69	989
Net Worth 29	22	0	43	89	1050	3811

Selected Financial Ratios (Times to 1)

Current Ratio 30	1.0	•	9.9	0.2	0.7	4.1
Quick Ratio 31	0.9	•	9.9	0.1	0.0	1.9
Net Sales to Working Capital 32	27.3	•	6.3	•	•	0.9
Coverage Ratio 33	2.8	•	881.1	6.3	•	35.5
Total Asset Turnover 34	0.4	•	5.2	6.1	0.5	0.5
Inventory Turnover 35	10.8	•	•	148.1	•	1.6
Receivables Turnover 36	1.1	•	56.5	•	1.9	3.1
Total Liabilities to Net Worth 37	141.9	•	0.2	5.4	1.2	0.6
Current Assets to Working Capital 38	36.5	•	1.1	•	•	1.3
Current Liabilities to Working Capital 39	35.5	•	0.1	•	•	0.3
Working Capital to Net Sales 40	0.0	•	0.2	•	•	1.1
Inventory to Working Capital 41	0.7	•	•	•	•	0.2
Total Receipts to Cash Flow 42	2.1	1.8	3.1	4.4	0.8	3.0
Cost of Goods to Cash Flow 43	0.8	0.2	1.1	1.7	•	1.5
Cash Flow to Total Debt 44	0.2	•	12.1	1.6	1.2	0.4

Selected Financial Factors (in Percentages)

Debt Ratio 45	99.3	•	13.6	84.4	53.5	36.4
Return on Total Assets 46	6.5	•	112.4	34.1	22.8	7.5
Return on Equity Before Income Taxes 47	605.4	•	129.9	184.3	49.1	11.5
Return on Equity After Income Taxes 48	575.7	•	129.9	182.2	46.1	11.5
Profit Margin (Before Income Tax) 49	9.6	21.8	21.7	4.7	46.9	15.9
Profit Margin (After Income Tax) 50	9.1	21.8	21.7	4.6	44.0	15.9

Table I

Corporations with and without Net Income

BROADCASTING (EXCEPT INTERNET)

MONEY AMOUNTS AND SIZE OF ASSETS IN THOUSANDS OF DOLLARS

Item Description for Accounting Period 7/10 Through 6/11		Total	Zero Assets	Under 500	500 to 1,000	1,000 to 5,000	5,000 to 10,000	10,000 to 25,000	25,000 to 50,000	50,000 to 100,000	100,000 to 250,000	250,000 to 500,000	500,000 to 2,500,000	2,500,000 and over
Number of Enterprises	1	6501	578	4301	549	663	136	124	41	34	19	22	23	11
Revenues ($ in Thousands)														
Net Sales	2	94317738	66018	703765	469180	1314290	994640	2141772	699855	1248936	1589056	6574610	7066469	71449147
Interest	3	1986949	117	55	1002	1343	2407	2606	1518	1367	11683	16623	205389	1742838
Rents	4	374407	0	0	0	6661	315	1078	3071	1077	3508	30967	15276	312454
Royalties	5	5125039	0	0	0	0	3336	0	712	3421	28407	66601	6962	5015598
Other Portfolio Income	6	1062177	0	27128	0	18857	2901	3810	2231	6657	37218	20098	185023	758253
Other Receipts	7	4588612	5237	13512	2555	22813	12685	93288	3198	34008	19081	115593	151005	4115642
Total Receipts	8	107454922	71372	744460	472737	1363964	1016284	2242554	710585	1295466	1688953	6824492	7630124	83393932
Average Total Receipts	9	16529	123	173	861	2057	7473	18085	17331	38102	88892	310204	331745	7581267
Operating Costs/Operating Income (%)														
Cost of Operations	10	12.1	18.1	11.2	21.0	6.4	23.1	38.2	10.2	15.0	16.5	49.0	4.3	8.5
Salaries and Wages	11	15.4	17.4	12.3	28.3	35.7	23.3	18.9	25.6	21.8	19.5	13.2	23.9	13.9
Taxes Paid	12	2.4	4.0	24.6	6.3	5.6	2.7	4.0	3.1	3.1	3.3	2.2	3.5	1.9
Interest Paid	13	7.9	13.3	3.6	3.0	2.8	1.8	3.8	6.3	9.5	7.8	5.1	14.6	7.8
Depreciation	14	5.0	5.9	2.4	2.2	3.9	4.9	4.6	7.6	5.2	5.0	5.9	5.7	4.9
Amortization and Depletion	15	10.1	11.9	0.6	0.3	2.1	1.5	5.6	9.1	9.4	8.7	5.4	13.2	10.9
Pensions and Other Deferred Comp.	16	1.3	•	2.0	•	0.2	0.3	0.5	0.5	0.4	0.2	0.7	0.9	1.5
Employee Benefits	17	3.3	2.8	2.7	1.4	2.0	2.4	1.1	1.3	1.4	1.6	1.8	1.8	3.8
Advertising	18	3.3	0.9	0.4	1.0	1.6	2.6	1.4	1.8	1.9	3.4	1.0	1.4	3.9
Other Expenses	19	46.2	266.7	32.8	39.9	37.9	34.6	21.1	38.7	35.3	33.0	19.3	42.9	50.6
Officers' Compensation	20	1.7	10.1	22.0	6.0	7.1	4.8	1.5	1.7	3.0	1.9	1.3	1.1	1.4
Operating Margin	21	•	•	•	•	•	•	•	•	•	•	•	•	•
Operating Margin Before Officers' Comp.	22	•	•	7.4	•	1.7	2.8	0.8	•	•	1.1	•	•	•

Selected Average Balance Sheet ($ in Thousands)

Net Receivables 23	2408	0	5	89	439	790	2042	3916	6579	20434	45367	85850	1016986
Inventories 24	209	0	0	6	14	19	20	68	290	5573	1903	567	106071
Net Property, Plant and Equipment 25	4957	0	7	117	567	1404	2729	6224	11005	23817	78195	102667	2369217
Total Assets 26	41677	0	30	668	2143	6768	15271	38318	70217	150403	345456	1093423	20603908
Notes and Loans Payable 27	14706	0	98	1075	1368	10871	7473	28066	43668	91511	210093	510016	6414038
All Other Liabilities 28	14576	0	36	226	565	-13460	6131	7613	22028	21816	103440	289893	7705013
Net Worth 29	12395	0	-103	-633	211	9357	1667	2638	4522	37076	31923	293514	6484857

Selected Financial Ratios (Times to 1)

Current Ratio 30	0.8	•	5.1	1.4	0.8	1.6	1.2	1.3	1.4	2.3	1.6	1.5	0.7
Quick Ratio 31	0.5	•	5.1	1.0	0.6	1.4	1.1	0.9	1.1	1.6	1.3	1.3	0.4
Net Sales to Working Capital 32	•	•	11.7	11.0	•	7.8	12.7	10.7	8.0	2.6	8.9	6.3	•
Coverage Ratio 33	1.7	•	•	•	0.4	1.1	2.0	0.3	0.8	1.7	0.8	0.6	2.1
Total Asset Turnover 34	0.3	•	5.4	1.3	0.9	1.1	1.1	0.4	0.5	0.6	0.9	0.3	0.3
Inventory Turnover 35	8.4	•	29.3	8.9	•	90.7	327.4	25.7	19.0	2.5	76.9	23.5	5.2
Receivables Turnover 36	5.7	•	20.6	5.6	4.3	9.0	9.4	5.4	4.7	3.6	7.8	3.9	5.8
Total Liabilities to Net Worth 37	2.4	•	•	•	9.2	•	8.2	13.5	14.5	3.1	9.8	2.7	2.2
Current Assets to Working Capital 38	•	•	1.2	3.7	•	2.8	5.1	4.9	3.7	1.7	2.8	3.1	•
Current Liabilities to Working Capital 39	•	•	0.2	2.7	•	1.8	4.1	3.9	2.7	0.7	1.8	2.1	•
Working Capital to Net Sales 40	•	•	0.1	0.1	•	0.1	0.1	0.1	0.1	0.4	0.1	0.2	•
Inventory to Working Capital 41	•	•	•	0.1	•	0.0	0.0	0.1	0.1	0.2	0.1	0.0	•
Total Receipts to Cash Flow 42	2.1	•	5.8	4.1	3.4	3.3	4.3	3.5	3.4	3.1	6.5	3.3	1.8
Cost of Goods to Cash Flow 43	0.3	•	0.6	0.9	0.2	0.8	1.6	0.4	0.5	0.5	3.2	0.1	0.2
Cash Flow to Total Debt 44	0.2	•	0.2	0.2	0.3	•	0.3	0.1	0.2	0.2	0.1	0.1	0.2

Selected Financial Factors (in Percentages)

Debt Ratio 45	70.3	•	442.1	194.8	90.2	•	89.1	93.1	93.6	75.3	90.8	73.2	68.5
Return on Total Assets 46	4.8	•	•	•	1.1	2.1	8.7	0.9	3.8	7.3	3.5	2.6	5.1
Return on Equity Before Income Taxes 47	6.8	•	14.0	11.8	•	0.1	39.8	•	12.2	•	•	•	8.5
Return on Equity After Income Taxes 48	3.5	•	14.0	12.0	•	•	33.8	•	6.6	•	•	•	5.1
Profit Margin (Before Income Tax) 49	5.8	•	•	•	0.1	3.8	•	5.4	•	•	•	•	8.5
Profit Margin (After Income Tax) 50	3.0	•	•	•	•	3.3	•	2.9	•	•	•	•	5.1

Table II
Corporations with Net Income

BROADCASTING (EXCEPT INTERNET)

MONEY AMOUNTS AND SIZE OF ASSETS IN THOUSANDS OF DOLLARS

Item Description for Accounting Period 7/10 Through 6/11	Total	Zero Assets	Under 500	500 to 1,000	1,000 to 5,000	5,000 to 10,000	10,000 to 25,000	25,000 to 50,000	50,000 to 100,000	100,000 to 250,000	250,000 to 500,000	500,000 to 2,500,000	2,500,000 and over
Number of Enterprises 1	2099	22	1086	•	421	83	80	21	18	10	11	11	•
Revenues ($ in Thousands)													
Net Sales 2	75921710	19573	305215	•	1032190	840583	1660797	535102	830105	1153034	4619044	3253562	•
Interest 3	1851943	112	0	•	12	1527	441	402	1123	11191	15113	94067	•
Rents 4	311592	0	0	•	1239	315	807	2191	848	3236	14418	5720	•
Royalties 5	4874648	0	0	•	0	0	0	0	3421	28407	65097	6955	•
Other Portfolio Income 6	831819	0	0	•	17097	0	3788	1685	5863	35633	16992	33285	•
Other Receipts 7	4189640	5234	6194	•	38315	11913	88848	2012	30674	11776	77280	37706	•
Total Receipts 8	87981352	24919	311409	•	1088853	854338	1754681	541392	872034	1243277	4807944	3431295	•
Average Total Receipts 9	41916	1133	287	•	2586	10293	21934	25781	48446	124328	437086	311936	•
Operating Costs/Operating Income (%)													
Cost of Operations 10	12.6	61.0	•	•	4.5	22.9	47.5	11.1	22.2	20.5	57.8	8.8	•
Salaries and Wages 11	13.8	7.1	7.3	•	34.0	23.4	17.0	26.3	22.3	18.0	9.9	17.4	•
Taxes Paid 12	2.0	2.9	51.8	•	5.8	2.9	2.7	2.9	3.2	2.9	1.6	3.0	•
Interest Paid 13	5.5	•	0.4	•	1.3	1.4	3.2	3.4	3.2	6.1	2.4	13.0	•
Depreciation 14	4.5	7.4	0.5	•	0.9	5.2	3.5	5.1	4.2	3.8	5.0	6.1	•
Amortization and Depletion 15	9.4	•	•	•	1.3	1.3	1.2	5.2	5.9	7.7	1.9	8.1	•
Pensions and Other Deferred Comp. 16	1.5	•	•	•	0.3	0.3	0.4	0.2	0.6	0.3	0.6	1.4	•
Employee Benefits 17	3.6	2.0	1.6	•	1.9	2.3	1.0	1.3	1.5	1.4	1.6	1.7	•
Advertising 18	3.6	2.6	0.3	•	1.3	0.4	1.2	1.8	1.6	4.1	0.7	1.0	•
Other Expenses 19	46.9	10.7	30.7	•	33.5	29.9	14.9	35.0	27.8	29.4	17.4	29.0	•
Officers' Compensation 20	1.7	4.6	0.0	•	8.1	5.1	1.4	1.8	3.5	2.1	0.7	1.0	•
Operating Margin 21	•	1.6	7.6	•	7.1	4.9	6.1	5.9	3.9	3.8	0.5	9.6	•
Operating Margin Before Officers' Comp. 22	•	6.3	7.6	•	15.1	10.0	7.5	7.7	7.4	5.9	1.2	10.6	•

Selected Average Balance Sheet ($ in Thousands)

Net Receivables **23**	5996	0	10	•	556	850	2508	6017	7571	19971	58031	112183
Inventories **24**	616	0	0	•	14	22	31	64	315	10560	3509	990
Net Property, Plant and Equipment **25**	11020	0	1	•	205	1912	2379	7605	10497	21773	83525	103667
Total Assets **26**	96983	0	19	•	2054	6779	15101	34864	72985	156618	361590	1080219
Notes and Loans Payable **27**	21511	0	4	•	915	2191	6892	20220	26093	109470	162768	431188
All Other Liabilities **28**	34507	0	1	•	533	1296	5304	6797	18914	17202	138789	359523
Net Worth **29**	40966	0	14	•	607	3292	2906	7847	27979	29947	60033	289509

Selected Financial Ratios (Times to 1)

Current Ratio **30**	1.0	•	24.0	1.0	1.6	2.1	1.9	1.6	2.6	1.5	1.4
Quick Ratio **31**	0.5	•	23.9	0.7	1.4	1.9	1.5	1.2	1.4	1.3	1.2
Net Sales to Working Capital **32**	•	•	17.8	•	12.4	4.9	4.7	5.9	2.6	9.7	5.4
Coverage Ratio **33**	3.1	•	28.3	10.6	5.7	4.6	3.1	3.9	2.9	2.9	2.2
Total Asset Turnover **34**	0.4	•	14.8	1.2	1.5	1.4	0.7	0.6	0.7	1.2	0.3
Inventory Turnover **35**	7.4	•	•	7.8	104.5	323.1	44.4	32.4	2.2	69.2	26.4
Receivables Turnover **36**	5.7	•	13.2	4.2	11.6	9.7	5.7	5.4	5.8	11.9	3.6
Total Liabilities to Net Worth **37**	1.4	•	0.3	2.4	1.1	4.2	3.4	1.6	4.2	5.0	2.7
Current Assets to Working Capital **38**	•	•	1.0	•	2.8	1.9	2.1	2.7	1.6	2.9	3.6
Current Liabilities to Working Capital **39**	•	•	0.0	•	1.8	0.9	1.1	1.7	0.6	1.9	2.6
Working Capital to Net Sales **40**	•	•	0.1	•	0.1	0.2	0.2	0.2	0.4	0.1	0.2
Inventory to Working Capital **41**	•	•	•	•	0.0	0.0	0.0	0.1	0.2	0.1	0.0
Total Receipts to Cash Flow **42**	1.8	2.8	3.2	2.5	3.2	4.0	2.8	3.0	2.9	5.1	2.4
Cost of Goods to Cash Flow **43**	0.2	1.7	•	0.1	0.7	1.9	0.3	0.7	0.6	2.9	0.2
Cash Flow to Total Debt **44**	0.3	•	19.5	0.7	0.9	0.4	0.3	0.3	0.3	0.3	0.2

Selected Financial Factors (in Percentages)

Debt Ratio **45**	57.8	•	23.6	70.5	51.4	80.8	77.5	61.7	80.9	83.4	73.2
Return on Total Assets **46**	6.3	•	147.8	16.5	11.9	20.4	7.7	7.8	13.0	8.0	7.7
Return on Equity Before Income Taxes **47**	10.1	•	186.7	50.8	20.2	82.7	23.0	15.1	44.7	31.7	15.4
Return on Equity After Income Taxes **48**	7.0	•	186.6	48.7	16.1	77.5	21.3	13.7	31.6	24.3	12.1
Profit Margin (Before Income Tax) **49**	11.4	29.0	9.6	12.6	6.6	11.6	7.1	9.2	11.6	4.5	15.0
Profit Margin (After Income Tax) **50**	7.9	20.1	9.6	12.0	5.2	10.8	6.6	8.3	8.2	3.5	11.8

Table I

Corporations with and without Net Income

TELECOMMUNICATIONS (WIRED, WIRELESS, SATELLITE, INTERNET PROVIDERS)

MONEY AMOUNTS AND SIZE OF ASSETS IN THOUSANDS OF DOLLARS

Item Description for Accounting Period 7/10 Through 6/11	Total	Zero Assets	Under 500	500 to 1,000	1,000 to 5,000	5,000 to 10,000	10,000 to 25,000	25,000 to 50,000	50,000 to 100,000	100,000 to 250,000	250,000 to 500,000	500,000 to 2,500,000	2,500,000 and over
1 Number of Enterprises	18110	4112	10474	961	1311	388	374	164	128	87	36	43	31
Revenues ($ in Thousands)													
2 Net Sales	408238119	2080245	4972273	4349813	7541663	4248945	4292872	4724754	5788355	9022545	10332839	20359237	330524578
3 Interest	11769430	3767	1388	1926	9812	8839	18446	9877	26951	39584	55563	226480	11366797
4 Rents	8704820	276	0	0	3135	3409	23015	6076	8898	20390	11498	28601	8599522
5 Royalties	4669456	0	2	13705	0	1185	309	277	150	907		18060	4634862
6 Other Portfolio Income	13144357	433999	551	9587	50078	5315	127714	64401	124536	60594	202735	48288	12016557
7 Other Receipts	21446893	29264	80882	8977	93532	60684	188507	218149	179673	294234	386851	708589	19197553
8 Total Receipts	467973075	2547551	5055096	4384008	7698220	4328377	4650863	5023534	6128563	9437347	10990393	21389255	386339869
9 Average Total Receipts	25841	620	483	4562	5872	11156	12435	30631	47879	108475	305289	497425	12462576
Operating Costs/Operating Income (%)													
10 Cost of Operations	22.8	40.9	35.3	77.6	61.7	54.0	38.5	43.0	41.3	42.0	50.1	43.9	17.0
11 Salaries and Wages	13.8	22.0	16.8	7.9	13.1	14.8	14.1	11.9	10.7	9.9	15.9	14.7	13.9
12 Taxes Paid	2.8	3.3	2.3	1.2	1.9	2.0	2.7	2.2	2.0	2.9	1.7	2.6	2.9
13 Interest Paid	7.7	4.3	1.3	1.4	1.5	0.8	2.5	1.9	2.5	3.7	4.3	6.1	8.7
14 Depreciation	13.1	9.3	1.4	1.5	1.7	5.4	11.4	8.2	11.4	9.8	8.6	13.7	14.1
15 Amortization and Depletion	1.9	1.1	0.4	0.3	0.5	0.4	1.1	1.3	1.5	1.8	1.5	3.1	2.0
16 Pensions and Other Deferred Comp.	0.7	0.7	1.0	0.0	0.1	0.2	0.4	0.2	0.1	0.2	0.4	0.6	0.8
17 Employee Benefits	3.1	2.3	1.7	0.6	1.2	0.8	1.7	1.2	1.1	1.1	2.1	1.9	3.5
18 Advertising	1.9	1.5	0.8	0.4	0.7	1.4	1.2	5.2	1.1	2.7	0.7	1.4	1.9
19 Other Expenses	40.9	38.7	24.5	9.4	21.7	19.9	35.8	24.4	31.8	27.2	18.4	20.3	45.0
20 Officers' Compensation	0.6	5.4	10.8	1.7	2.9	1.9	2.7	1.5	1.3	0.9	0.9	1.0	0.2
21 Operating Margin	•	•	3.6	•	•	•	•	•	•	•	•	•	•
22 Operating Margin Before Officers' Comp.	•	•	14.4	•	0.4	•	•	0.5	•	•	•	•	•

Selected Average Balance Sheet ($ in Thousands)

Item													
Net Receivables 23	7599	0	16	186	508	1269	1846	3602	6810	16855	49097	97404	4081927
Inventories 24	472	0	10	24	125	182	317	1097	989	3293	6611	12171	216534
Net Property, Plant and Equipment 25	15514	0	12	208	469	2055	5811	11767	27027	55320	92421	297156	8088373
Total Assets 26	73371	0	89	754	2079	6925	16050	35273	71318	157967	333868	986380	39755191
Notes and Loans Payable 27	25422	0	69	1520	1168	2938	4691	13532	17443	50626	114881	381535	13689835
All Other Liabilities 28	24041	0	108	444	1264	2543	3982	11633	19946	41131	101554	241854	13148329
Net Worth 29	23908	0	-88	-1210	-353	1444	7377	10108	33929	66210	122433	362990	12917028

Selected Financial Ratios (Times to 1)

Item													
Current Ratio 30	0.8	•	0.5	1.2	1.1	1.4	1.8	1.5	1.5	1.5	1.7	1.2	0.7
Quick Ratio 31	0.6	•	0.3	1.0	0.8	1.4	1.0	1.1	1.0	1.0	1.3	1.0	0.6
Net Sales to Working Capital 32	•	•	•	58.3	69.5	9.8	4.3	6.5	5.8	6.8	6.0	11.7	•
Coverage Ratio 33	1.7	•	5.0	0.2	1.6	•	4.0	1.5	1.6	1.4	0.3	•	1.8
Total Asset Turnover 34	0.3	•	5.3	6.0	2.8	1.6	0.7	0.8	0.6	0.7	0.8	0.5	0.3
Inventory Turnover 35	10.9	•	17.1	143.5	28.4	32.4	13.9	11.3	18.9	13.2	21.7	17.1	8.4
Receivables Turnover 36	3.0	•	27.1	34.6	10.2	9.5	6.0	7.6	7.0	5.5	5.1	4.6	2.7
Total Liabilities to Net Worth 37	2.1	•	•	3.8	2.5	1.2	2.5	1.1	1.4	1.8	1.7	•	2.1
Current Assets to Working Capital 38	•	•	6.7	13.4	3.5	2.2	3.2	2.9	3.2	2.5	5.3	•	•
Current Liabilities to Working Capital 39	•	•	5.7	12.4	2.5	1.2	2.2	1.9	2.2	1.5	4.3	•	•
Working Capital to Net Sales 40	•	•	0.0	0.0	0.1	0.2	0.2	0.2	0.1	0.2	0.1	0.2	•
Inventory to Working Capital 41	•	•	0.4	1.1	0.2	0.1	0.2	0.1	0.2	0.2	0.1	0.3	•
Total Receipts to Cash Flow 42	2.5	4.2	15.0	8.8	5.8	4.1	4.1	4.2	4.0	6.8	8.5	•	2.2
Cost of Goods to Cash Flow 43	0.6	1.5	11.6	5.4	3.2	1.6	1.7	1.8	1.7	3.4	3.7	•	0.4
Cash Flow to Total Debt 44	0.2	0.6	0.2	0.3	0.3	0.3	0.3	0.3	0.2	0.2	0.1	•	0.2

Selected Financial Factors (in Percentages)

Item													
Debt Ratio 45	67.4	•	198.3	260.4	117.0	79.1	54.0	71.3	52.4	58.1	63.9	63.2	67.5
Return on Total Assets 46	4.1	35.2	1.8	•	2.0	•	6.1	2.4	3.8	5.1	0.9	•	4.2
Return on Equity Before Income Taxes 47	5.2	•	•	4.1	81.6	3.7	15.9	1.6	3.4	4.0	•	•	5.7
Return on Equity After Income Taxes 48	3.4	5.3	5.3	•	85.5	5.3	10.7	•	0.6	1.4	•	•	4.0
Profit Margin (Before Income Tax) 49	5.5	•	•	0.5	•	•	5.6	1.2	2.2	1.7	•	•	7.0
Profit Margin (After Income Tax) 50	3.6	5.2	•	•	•	•	3.7	0.4	0.6	•	•	•	4.8

Table II
Corporations with Net Income

TELECOMMUNICATIONS (WIRED, WIRELESS, SATELLITE, INTERNET PROVIDERS)

MONEY AMOUNTS AND SIZE OF ASSETS IN THOUSANDS OF DOLLARS

Item Description for Accounting Period 7/10 Through 6/11		Total	Zero Assets	Under 500	500 to 1,000	1,000 to 5,000	5,000 to 10,000	10,000 to 25,000	25,000 to 50,000	50,000 to 100,000	100,000 to 250,000	250,000 to 500,000	500,000 to 2,500,000	2,500,000 and over
Number of Enterprises	1	8923	1136	5779	535	752	211	205	117	69	61	20	18	20
Revenues ($ in Thousands)														
Net Sales	2	298382487	754200	291189	3889915	4708212	2484925	1975576	3555702	3883620	6363201	6040255	10029978	251785715
Interest	3	7173088	349	1252	189	7123	5850	11135	8084	19925	30640	22124	128287	6938131
Rents	4	6625570	105	0	0	1496	1099	2876	3791	4332	19875	5712	10542	6575743
Royalties	5	4558426	0	2	0	0	0	58	277	150	0	907	75	4556957
Other Portfolio Income	6	12398935	416015	220	9587	43604	3394	115136	62443	112209	35056	189502	39434	11372336
Other Receipts	7	15153983	6249	75997	6761	33925	45312	120889	195004	125478	245926	378036	537800	13382603
Total Receipts	8	344292489	1176918	2988660	3906452	4794360	2540580	2225670	3825301	4145714	6694698	6636536	10746116	294611485
Average Total Receipts	9	38585	1036	517	7302	6375	12041	10857	32695	60083	109749	331827	597006	14730574
Operating Costs/Operating Income (%)														
Cost of Operations	10	23.6	26.3	33.4	83.9	58.0	55.0	29.1	41.0	44.5	41.5	47.8	47.1	19.0
Salaries and Wages	11	12.7	20.7	15.7	5.3	7.8	10.8	10.6	10.4	9.6	8.7	16.0	14.8	13.0
Taxes Paid	12	2.7	3.6	2.1	0.8	1.9	1.7	2.7	2.2	1.9	2.7	1.8	2.6	2.8
Interest Paid	13	7.3	3.2	1.1	0.9	0.3	0.4	1.3	1.6	1.7	2.0	3.9	3.2	8.3
Depreciation	14	11.9	10.3	1.0	0.5	1.7	4.1	11.7	6.8	8.6	9.6	7.8	7.5	12.9
Amortization and Depletion	15	2.0	0.6	0.5	•	0.1	0.1	0.6	1.0	0.9	1.6	0.9	2.8	2.2
Pensions and Other Deferred Comp.	16	0.5	1.5	0.9	0.0	0.1	0.1	0.6	0.2	0.2	0.2	0.5	0.7	0.6
Employee Benefits	17	2.6	2.9	1.4	0.1	1.1	0.7	1.4	1.1	1.0	1.3	2.4	1.7	2.8
Advertising	18	1.6	1.2	1.0	0.2	0.7	1.8	0.6	6.7	1.1	0.6	0.9	1.9	1.6
Other Expenses	19	38.5	41.5	22.9	5.8	19.2	18.5	35.8	22.9	25.7	26.7	18.4	14.5	42.0
Officers' Compensation	20	0.4	3.9	7.2	1.3	2.5	1.6	2.1	1.3	1.3	0.7	1.1	0.5	0.2
Operating Margin	21	•	•	12.8	1.1	6.6	5.2	3.5	4.9	3.5	4.5	•	2.7	•
Operating Margin Before Officers' Comp.	22	•	•	20.1	2.4	9.1	6.8	5.6	6.2	4.9	5.2	•	3.3	•

Selected Average Balance Sheet ($ in Thousands)

Net Receivables 23	12293	0	18	225	407	858	1957	3828	7143	19087	57524	146438	5134218
Inventories 24	730	0	4	35	140	153	295	1128	1182	3594	9071	11777	272679
Net Property, Plant and Equipment 25	20576	0	13	69	514	2082	5295	11293	26715	53314	97673	163273	8513168
Total Assets 26	100791	0	97	772	1971	7186	16176	33859	69741	157554	340749	986779	42455090
Notes and Loans Payable 27	37887	0	41	2109	403	1027	2490	14357	13759	38541	97119	257528	16205813
All Other Liabilities 28	29268	0	159	523	758	1875	3403	9936	17444	40478	95660	226900	12373479
Net Worth 29	33635	0	-102	-1859	810	4284	10282	9566	38538	78534	147970	502351	13875799

Selected Financial Ratios (Times to 1)

Current Ratio 30	0.8	•	0.4	1.1	1.6	2.1	2.9	1.6	1.7	1.6	1.7	1.8	0.8
Quick Ratio 31	0.7	•	0.3	1.0	1.1	1.7	2.3	1.1	1.3	1.2	1.4	1.5	0.7
Net Sales to Working Capital 32	•	•	•	83.5	16.5	5.9	2.2	6.2	5.3	5.5	6.2	3.9	•
Coverage Ratio 33	2.6	13.7	14.8	2.7	28.0	18.4	13.7	8.8	7.2	5.8	3.2	4.1	2.4
Total Asset Turnover 34	0.3	•	5.2	9.4	3.2	1.6	0.6	0.9	0.8	0.7	0.9	0.6	0.3
Inventory Turnover 35	10.8	•	46.1	174.9	25.9	42.3	9.5	11.1	21.2	12.0	15.9	22.3	8.8
Receivables Turnover 36	2.7	•	20.3	43.2	12.9	13.0	4.5	8.3	8.5	5.5	4.6	3.9	2.4
Total Liabilities to Net Worth 37	2.0	•	•	•	1.4	0.7	0.6	2.5	0.8	1.0	1.3	1.0	2.1
Current Assets to Working Capital 38	•	•	•	7.7	2.7	1.9	1.5	2.8	2.3	2.6	2.5	2.2	•
Current Liabilities to Working Capital 39	•	•	•	6.7	1.7	0.9	0.5	1.8	1.3	1.6	1.5	1.2	•
Working Capital to Net Sales 40	•	•	•	0.0	0.1	0.2	0.5	0.2	0.2	0.2	0.2	0.3	•
Inventory to Working Capital 41	•	•	•	0.5	0.2	0.1	0.1	0.2	0.1	0.2	0.2	0.1	•
Total Receipts to Cash Flow 42	2.3	11.5	3.0	15.7	4.1	4.3	2.4	3.3	3.8	3.1	4.8	4.6	2.1
Cost of Goods to Cash Flow 43	0.5	3.0	1.0	13.2	2.4	2.4	0.7	1.3	1.7	1.3	2.3	2.2	0.4
Cash Flow to Total Debt 44	0.2	•	0.8	0.2	1.3	0.9	0.7	0.4	0.5	0.4	0.3	0.2	0.2

Selected Financial Factors (in Percentages)

Debt Ratio 45	66.6	•	•	340.8	58.9	40.4	36.4	71.7	44.7	50.2	56.6	49.1	67.3
Return on Total Assets 46	6.3	•	86.0	23.5	27.6	13.5	10.5	12.9	10.1	7.8	10.9	7.5	6.0
Return on Equity Before Income Taxes 47	11.6	•	•	•	64.8	21.3	15.3	40.6	15.8	12.9	17.2	11.1	10.8
Return on Equity After Income Taxes 48	9.0	•	•	•	61.8	18.4	12.6	32.9	12.6	9.5	13.3	8.3	8.3
Profit Margin (Before Income Tax) 49	11.7	40.5	15.5	1.6	8.4	7.8	16.3	12.8	10.8	9.7	8.4	10.0	12.0
Profit Margin (After Income Tax) 50	9.0	40.0	15.4	1.2	8.0	6.7	13.5	10.4	8.6	7.1	6.5	7.5	9.1

Table I

Corporations with and without Net Income

DATA PROCESSING, HOSTING AND RELATED SERVICES

MONEY AMOUNTS AND SIZE OF ASSETS IN THOUSANDS OF DOLLARS

Item Description for Accounting Period 7/10 Through 6/11	Total	Zero Assets	Under 500	500 to 1,000	1,000 to 5,000	5,000 to 10,000	10,000 to 25,000	25,000 to 50,000	50,000 to 100,000	100,000 to 250,000	250,000 to 500,000	500,000 to 2,500,000	2,500,000 and over
Number of Enterprises 1	8865	1864	5831	449	478	77	70	27	22	18	8	14	6
Revenues ($ in Thousands)													
Net Sales 2	29900004	464172	1950941	388725	1869019	842774	1079598	817394	1525497	1716674	885817	5870710	12488683
Interest 3	63483	67	96	166	657	384	1426	1050	911	4979	1105	7701	44941
Rents 4	37309	0	0	0	0	67	33	0	1336	0	0	26924	8949
Royalties 5	315632	0	0	0	0	0	7	0	300	562	8229	160895	145639
Other Portfolio Income 6	128734	10459	1077	1263	205	389	974	7043	8866	125	8224	11644	78466
Other Receipts 7	372579	5552	4402	6931	5480	15190	4259	4391	13325	9189	131221	67667	104971
Total Receipts 8	30817741	480250	1956516	397085	1875361	858804	1086297	829878	1550235	1731529	1034596	6145541	12871649
Average Total Receipts 9	3476	258	336	884	3923	11153	15519	30736	70465	96196	129324	438967	2145275
Operating Costs/Operating Income (%)													
Cost of Operations 10	23.6	22.3	39.5	30.2	34.0	11.4	36.8	27.2	38.9	20.4	25.9	24.9	16.7
Salaries and Wages 11	24.9	24.7	12.6	33.0	20.4	24.9	26.8	30.9	23.0	34.1	32.6	23.2	25.9
Taxes Paid 12	2.7	2.7	2.8	4.4	2.2	2.5	3.2	3.1	3.0	3.1	4.3	3.7	1.9
Interest Paid 13	5.7	2.1	0.7	2.7	1.3	2.2	1.4	5.2	2.5	4.9	2.5	7.2	8.1
Depreciation 14	8.9	3.4	0.6	1.7	3.0	4.0	3.8	6.8	5.7	7.4	5.8	9.9	12.9
Amortization and Depletion 15	2.4	2.1	0.1	1.1	2.5	0.6	1.7	3.2	1.9	2.8	7.0	3.6	2.2
Pensions and Other Deferred Comp. 16	0.5	0.2	0.3	0.1	1.5	0.7	0.4	3.2	0.3	0.5	0.2	0.3	0.3
Employee Benefits 17	2.1	4.0	1.0	5.0	1.6	1.9	2.3	2.4	2.0	3.2	3.1	2.6	1.7
Advertising 18	1.7	0.1	0.5	0.7	1.0	2.6	2.7	2.6	2.0	1.4	5.1	4.2	0.5
Other Expenses 19	28.8	42.4	34.1	30.8	24.6	43.2	28.6	31.0	22.6	31.8	27.5	18.4	32.1
Officers' Compensation 20	3.0	26.0	7.3	12.4	11.3	5.9	4.4	4.2	2.5	3.2	3.1	1.6	0.3
Operating Margin 21	•	0.5	•	•	8.0	•	•	•	•	•	•	0.5	•
Operating Margin Before Officers' Comp. 22	•	7.8	•	•	8.0	5.9	•	•	•	•	•	2.2	•

Selected Average Balance Sheet ($ in Thousands)

Net Receivables 23	489	20	76	238	875	2316	3939	15797	17523	40893	48608	344674
Inventories 24	13	0	3	55	79	186	154	247	557	92	3478	0
Net Property, Plant and Equipment 25	1357	6	159	258	1466	1380	5185	9642	27093	22071	137978	1440129
Total Assets 26	6756	79	550	1937	7262	14918	33862	69806	142606	365263	914358	5986137
Notes and Loans Payable 27	2694	101	327	904	2721	2251	8693	17636	55429	55025	411417	2421372
All Other Liabilities 28	1584	61	486	758	2227	6601	14597	20078	46149	103977	234290	1116298
Net Worth 29	2478	-83	-263	275	2314	6066	10572	32092	41028	206261	268651	2448466

Selected Financial Ratios (Times to 1)

Current Ratio 30	1.3	0.9	0.5	1.4	1.7	1.4	2.0	1.8	1.1	1.1	1.1	1.3
Quick Ratio 31	1.0	0.6	0.4	1.0	1.6	1.3	1.6	1.6	0.7	1.0	0.8	1.2
Net Sales to Working Capital 32	11.9	•	•	13.6	7.3	6.0	3.3	5.0	34.8	9.7	38.3	9.0
Coverage Ratio 33	0.8	2.2	•	•	1.8	•	•	•	•	0.9	1.8	1.1
Total Asset Turnover 34	0.5	4.2	1.6	2.0	1.5	1.0	0.9	1.0	0.7	0.3	0.5	0.3
Inventory Turnover 35	60.7	2149.1	76.7	24.2	15.9	30.6	53.5	109.2	34.9	310.1	30.0	•
Receivables Turnover 36	7.2	20.1	15.6	13.2	10.7	7.7	4.3	5.6	5.2	2.7	3.9	12.1
Total Liabilities to Net Worth 37	1.7	•	•	6.0	2.1	1.5	2.2	1.2	2.5	0.8	2.4	1.4
Current Assets to Working Capital 38	4.9	•	•	3.7	2.5	3.4	2.0	2.3	16.2	8.9	13.3	4.0
Current Liabilities to Working Capital 39	3.9	•	•	2.7	1.5	2.4	1.0	1.3	15.2	7.9	12.3	3.0
Working Capital to Net Sales 40	0.1	•	•	0.1	0.1	0.2	0.3	0.2	0.0	0.1	0.0	0.1
Inventory to Working Capital 41	0.0	•	•	0.2	•	0.1	0.0	0.0	0.3	0.0	0.3	•
Total Receipts to Cash Flow 42	4.7	3.4	49.9	5.9	2.4	7.3	15.1	6.2	8.0	4.2	4.8	4.1
Cost of Goods to Cash Flow 43	1.1	1.4	15.1	2.0	0.3	2.7	4.1	2.4	1.6	1.1	1.2	0.7
Cash Flow to Total Debt 44	0.2	0.6	0.0	0.4	0.9	0.2	0.1	0.3	0.1	0.2	0.1	0.1

Selected Financial Factors (in Percentages)

Debt Ratio 45	63.3	204.7	147.9	85.8	68.1	59.3	68.8	54.0	71.2	43.5	70.6	59.1
Return on Total Assets 46	2.3	6.2	•	•	6.2	•	•	•	•	0.7	5.8	3.0
Return on Equity Before Income Taxes 47	•	•	65.4	•	8.9	•	•	•	•	•	8.5	0.6
Return on Equity After Income Taxes 48	•	•	65.4	•	•	•	•	•	•	•	4.3	•
Profit Margin (Before Income Tax) 49	•	0.8	0.8	•	1.9	•	•	•	•	•	5.5	•
Profit Margin (After Income Tax) 50	•	0.8	•	•	•	•	•	•	•	•	2.7	•

Table II
Corporations with Net Income

DATA PROCESSING, HOSTING AND RELATED SERVICES

MONEY AMOUNTS AND SIZE OF ASSETS IN THOUSANDS OF DOLLARS

Item Description for Accounting Period 7/10 Through 6/11	Total	Zero Assets	Under 500	500 to 1,000	1,000 to 5,000	5,000 to 10,000	10,000 to 25,000	25,000 to 50,000	50,000 to 100,000	100,000 to 250,000	250,000 to 500,000	500,000 to 2,500,000	2,500,000 and over
Number of Enterprises **1**	5068	850	3630	126	330	62	31	8	8	9	4	10	0
Revenues ($ in Thousands)													
Net Sales **2**	17069191	160917	1121546	213815	1384637	800808	664631	268863	621098	684602	562762	10585711	0
Interest **3**	14687	15	1	0	567	271	1118	121	104	2173	941	9376	0
Rents **4**	31938	0	0	0	0	0	0	0	1336	0	0	30602	0
Royalties **5**	261464	0	0	0	0	0	7	0	0	562	0	260895	0
Other Portfolio Income **6**	89987	10459	1077	1189	0	359	903	0	8397	123	7906	59572	0
Other Receipts **7**	287112	1037	0	6469	2709	14658	222	1501	9391	3251	24307	223570	0
Total Receipts **8**	17754379	172428	1122624	221473	1387913	816096	666881	270285	640326	690711	595916	1169726	0
Average Total Receipts **9**	3503	203	309	1758	4206	13163	21512	33786	80041	76746	148979	1116973	•
Operating Costs/Operating Income (%)													
Cost of Operations **10**	20.4	37.5	19.8	16.5	43.6	11.7	39.9	13.0	23.4	21.4	29.6	16.2	•
Salaries and Wages **11**	22.7	8.1	10.2	35.4	15.4	19.2	18.0	21.2	28.9	25.5	22.5	25.0	•
Taxes Paid **12**	1.9	2.9	2.5	3.1	1.6	2.0	2.8	2.6	3.9	2.2	3.0	1.6	•
Interest Paid **13**	3.3	2.8	0.6	0.8	0.4	2.2	0.3	0.8	2.1	4.9	0.7	4.4	•
Depreciation **14**	4.7	6.9	0.5	0.8	1.8	3.7	3.4	4.1	4.7	6.3	3.6	5.7	•
Amortization and Depletion **15**	2.0	2.6	•	0.2	0.2	0.5	1.0	2.8	1.3	3.7	1.8	2.6	•
Pensions and Other Deferred Comp. **16**	0.5	0.1	0.5	•	1.9	0.7	0.6	3.5	0.4	0.9	0.1	0.3	•
Employee Benefits **17**	1.9	0.1	1.4	3.4	0.6	1.5	2.2	3.6	1.5	0.8	1.7	2.2	•
Advertising **18**	2.0	0.0	0.2	•	0.4	2.2	1.7	0.3	0.3	1.2	5.6	2.4	•
Other Expenses **19**	27.9	27.3	42.2	23.5	13.8	39.2	22.5	27.4	24.0	22.2	23.8	28.6	•
Officers' Compensation **20**	2.8	3.4	9.2	3.8	12.5	5.3	3.0	6.2	2.7	1.4	2.4	0.7	•
Operating Margin **21**	9.9	8.3	12.9	12.8	7.8	11.8	4.8	14.6	6.8	9.5	5.2	10.3	•
Operating Margin Before Officers' Comp. **22**	12.7	11.7	22.1	16.6	20.2	17.1	7.8	20.8	9.5	10.9	7.6	11.1	•

Selected Average Balance Sheet ($ in Thousands)

	•	•	•	•	•	•	•	•	•	•	•	•
Net Receivables 23	493	0	18	115	209	913	3543	4373	10153	9412	61924	173312
Inventories 24	16	0	0	2	37	71	288	400	271	195	142	4818
Net Property, Plant and Equipment 25	520	0	3	40	163	1690	2009	2488	10416	21443	14253	204366
Total Assets 26	5956	0	78	552	1450	7225	15646	31972	67570	132773	315518	2516516
Notes and Loans Payable 27	2339	0	95	304	446	2830	2322	5105	24178	43162	4152	1044015
All Other Liabilities 28	1234	0	38	842	634	2393	7099	8526	23372	26932	140963	436819
Net Worth 29	2383	0	-55	-594	371	2002	6224	18340	20020	62679	170403	1035682

Selected Financial Ratios (Times to 1)

Current Ratio 30	1.4	•	1.1	0.9	1.7	1.3	1.7	1.9	1.6	1.3	0.9	1.5
Quick Ratio 31	1.2	•	0.6	0.9	1.2	1.2	1.6	1.3	1.4	1.0	0.8	1.3
Net Sales to Working Capital 32	8.4	•	40.0	•	9.5	20.9	5.1	4.9	8.0	9.7	•	6.9
Coverage Ratio 33	5.3	6.6	21.7	21.4	21.1	7.3	18.7	19.9	5.9	3.1	16.7	4.7
Total Asset Turnover 34	0.6	•	4.0	3.1	2.9	1.8	1.4	1.1	1.1	0.6	0.4	0.4
Inventory Turnover 35	42.7	•	2300.6	135.1	49.9	21.3	29.7	10.9	67.0	83.4	292.1	35.6
Receivables Turnover 36	6.2	•	26.4	18.0	18.4	13.6	7.7	2.9	8.1	4.8	1.9	5.7
Total Liabilities to Net Worth 37	1.5	•	•	•	2.9	2.6	1.5	0.7	2.4	1.1	0.9	1.4
Current Assets to Working Capital 38	3.4	•	8.3	•	2.5	4.9	2.5	2.2	2.6	4.2	•	3.0
Current Liabilities to Working Capital 39	2.4	•	7.3	•	1.5	3.9	1.5	1.2	1.6	3.2	•	2.0
Working Capital to Net Sales 40	0.1	•	0.0	•	0.1	0.0	0.2	0.2	0.1	0.1	0.4	0.1
Inventory to Working Capital 41	0.0	•	•	•	0.2	0.0	0.0	0.1	0.0	0.0	•	0.0
Total Receipts to Cash Flow 42	2.7	3.2	2.0	3.5	5.2	2.0	4.1	2.5	3.4	3.4	3.2	2.6
Cost of Goods to Cash Flow 43	0.6	1.2	0.4	0.6	2.2	0.2	1.6	0.3	0.8	0.7	0.9	0.4
Cash Flow to Total Debt 44	0.3	•	1.2	0.4	0.8	1.3	0.6	1.0	0.5	0.3	0.3	0.3

Selected Financial Factors (in Percentages)

Debt Ratio 45	60.0	•	170.2	207.7	74.4	72.3	60.2	42.6	70.4	52.8	46.0	58.8
Return on Total Assets 46	9.8	•	53.9	52.8	24.3	28.4	7.4	16.8	14.2	8.7	5.2	8.6
Return on Equity Before Income Taxes 47	19.9	•	•	•	90.5	88.5	17.6	27.9	39.9	12.6	9.1	16.5
Return on Equity After Income Taxes 48	14.5	•	•	•	84.8	74.2	14.7	23.3	32.6	9.9	8.3	10.9
Profit Margin (Before Income Tax) 49	14.1	15.7	13.0	16.3	8.0	13.7	5.1	15.2	10.3	10.4	11.1	16.2
Profit Margin (After Income Tax) 50	10.3	15.7	13.0	16.3	7.5	11.5	4.3	12.7	8.4	8.2	10.1	10.6

Table I

Corporations with and without Net Income

OTHER INFORMATION SERVICES, INTERNET PUBLISHING, WEB PORTALS

MONEY AMOUNTS AND SIZE OF ASSETS IN THOUSANDS OF DOLLARS

Item Description for Accounting Period 7/10 Through 6/11	Total	Zero Assets	Under 500	500 to 1,000	1,000 to 5,000	5,000 to 10,000	10,000 to 25,000	25,000 to 50,000	50,000 to 100,000	100,000 to 250,000	250,000 to 500,000	500,000 to 2,500,000	2,500,000 and over
Number of Enterprises **1**	22329	5810	14575	564	898	256	113	38	20	25	9	16	5
Revenues ($ in Thousands)													
Net Sales **2**	63483524	1208334	3536416	819571	4077615	4190948	2277734	794034	1437068	2448532	2185627	8974353	31533293
Interest **3**	423943	498	727	145	3545	1715	1860	1821	2913	5354	3685	76609	325072
Rents **4**	96209	1823	0	0	457	55	135	0	0	0	3642	4199	85897
Royalties **5**	1471625	0	40	0	21	521	0	0	3386	10629	3101	664881	789046
Other Portfolio Income **6**	651392	43725	77420	8	51021	6602	11273	5023	99	2020	17854	263303	173044
Other Receipts **7**	3097182	30576	43288	42505	38623	29840	4812	58660	210159	13650	-1070	209733	2416406
Total Receipts **8**	69223875	1284956	3657891	862229	4171282	4229681	2295814	859538	1653625	2480185	2212839	10193078	35322758
Average Total Receipts **9**	3100	221	251	1529	4645	16522	20317	22619	82681	99207	245871	637067	7064552
Operating Costs/Operating Income (%)													
Cost of Operations **10**	26.6	14.8	30.5	11.5	53.5	47.1	38.3	14.8	46.7	14.8	16.6	30.7	19.9
Salaries and Wages **11**	23.0	36.8	12.2	32.1	24.6	20.6	24.7	42.9	17.6	24.4	21.9	26.9	22.1
Taxes Paid **12**	2.9	2.4	2.1	2.6	2.5	3.2	3.9	4.0	6.6	2.6	2.9	2.5	2.9
Interest Paid **13**	3.0	0.7	1.2	0.8	0.7	0.5	1.0	4.0	1.9	0.7	1.7	5.0	3.8
Depreciation **14**	4.6	2.8	1.1	0.4	1.0	1.9	3.4	4.7	2.3	5.1	4.0	2.7	6.7
Amortization and Depletion **15**	1.8	2.0	0.7	0.3	1.4	1.2	1.6	4.5	2.1	1.5	3.2	5.1	0.9
Pensions and Other Deferred Comp. **16**	0.7	0.4	0.5	0.3	0.0	0.6	0.1	0.1	0.1	0.7	3.5	1.0	0.6
Employee Benefits **17**	1.9	3.9	1.0	4.9	1.4	2.5	2.1	3.8	1.7	2.6	1.9	2.5	1.7
Advertising **18**	2.8	3.4	4.3	3.6	2.1	5.8	5.6	5.6	2.4	10.8	6.9	2.2	1.4
Other Expenses **19**	31.2	44.4	35.7	36.0	22.2	18.2	25.7	36.7	24.4	32.3	25.3	27.1	35.0
Officers' Compensation **20**	2.6	13.6	11.6	11.3	5.8	3.3	3.6	4.0	1.8	1.9	2.4	2.7	0.5
Operating Margin **21**	•	•	•	•	•	•	•	•	•	2.7	9.6	•	4.7
Operating Margin Before Officers' Comp. **22**	1.5	•	10.8	7.6	•	•	•	•	•	4.6	12.0	•	5.1

Selected Average Balance Sheet ($ in Thousands)

Net Receivables **23**	616	0	12	101	179	1971	3063	3803	15469	12664	41246	88052	1994697
Inventories **24**	26	0	0	10	10	4	92	170	1263	128	831	28377	9928
Net Property, Plant and Equipment **25**	545	0	8	21	186	749	1229	2081	5872	11735	27585	74291	1922825
Total Assets **26**	5298	0	47	670	1973	7280	13969	33939	66924	169593	391012	1038062	17004211
Notes and Loans Payable **27**	1069	0	102	120	518	1052	3791	6376	39417	10363	127135	316564	2730462
All Other Liabilities **28**	1285	0	31	250	875	3057	6955	15610	22730	61579	74830	379392	3283034
Net Worth **29**	2943	0	-87	301	580	3170	3223	11953	4776	97650	189047	342106	10990715

Selected Financial Ratios (Times to 1)

Current Ratio **30**	1.8	•	0.7	1.4	1.4	1.4	1.5	1.6	1.8	1.2	1.6	0.8	2.2
Quick Ratio **31**	1.0	•	0.6	1.2	1.3	1.1	1.4	1.4	1.6	1.1	1.3	0.4	1.1
Net Sales to Working Capital **32**	3.0	•	•	15.0	12.7	10.7	5.7	3.5	4.3	7.5	5.4	•	1.6
Coverage Ratio **33**	3.9	•	3.2	2.8	•	•	•	•	5.0	7.0	7.5	2.2	5.7
Total Asset Turnover **34**	0.5	•	5.2	2.2	2.3	2.2	1.4	0.6	1.1	0.6	0.6	0.5	0.4
Inventory Turnover **35**	29.3	•	185.6	16.8	241.8	1905.6	83.4	18.2	26.6	113.4	48.4	6.1	126.3
Receivables Turnover **36**	4.9	•	26.5	18.4	21.5	9.1	8.5	5.3	5.8	9.7	5.3	7.5	3.3
Total Liabilities to Net Worth **37**	0.8	•	•	1.2	2.4	1.3	3.3	1.8	13.0	0.7	1.1	2.0	0.5
Current Assets to Working Capital **38**	2.3	•	•	3.8	3.3	3.3	2.9	2.8	2.2	5.6	2.8	•	1.9
Current Liabilities to Working Capital **39**	1.3	•	•	2.8	2.3	2.3	1.9	1.8	1.2	4.6	1.8	•	0.9
Working Capital to Net Sales **40**	0.3	•	•	0.1	0.1	0.1	0.2	0.3	0.2	0.1	0.2	•	0.6
Inventory to Working Capital **41**	0.0	•	•	0.2	0.1	0.0	0.0	0.0	0.1	0.0	0.0	•	0.0
Total Receipts to Cash Flow **42**	2.8	5.1	2.9	2.9	18.0	8.9	7.4	6.1	3.3	3.1	3.1	3.6	2.0
Cost of Goods to Cash Flow **43**	0.7	0.7	1.0	0.3	9.6	4.2	2.8	0.9	1.6	0.5	0.5	1.1	0.4
Cash Flow to Total Debt **44**	0.4	0.6	1.4	0.2	0.4	0.3	0.3	0.2	0.3	0.4	0.4	0.2	0.5

Selected Financial Factors (in Percentages)

Debt Ratio **45**	44.4	•	285.5	55.1	70.6	56.4	76.9	64.8	92.9	42.4	51.7	67.0	35.4
Return on Total Assets **46**	6.3	•	19.6	5.1	•	•	•	•	10.1	2.9	8.0	5.9	8.2
Return on Equity Before Income Taxes **47**	8.5	•	•	7.4	•	•	•	•	112.6	4.3	14.3	9.7	10.5
Return on Equity After Income Taxes **48**	4.6	•	•	3.1	•	•	•	•	59.8	1.4	9.6	5.6	6.6
Profit Margin (Before Income Tax) **49**	8.8	•	2.6	1.5	•	•	•	•	7.5	4.3	11.1	5.9	18.2
Profit Margin (After Income Tax) **50**	4.7	•	2.5	0.6	•	•	•	•	4.0	1.4	7.4	3.4	11.6

Table II
Corporations with Net Income

OTHER INFORMATION SERVICES, INTERNET PUBLISHING, WEB PORTALS

MONEY AMOUNTS AND SIZE OF ASSETS IN THOUSANDS OF DOLLARS

Item Description for Accounting Period 7/10 Through 6/11		Total	Zero Assets	Under 500	500 to 1,000	1,000 to 5,000	5,000 to 10,000	10,000 to 25,000	25,000 to 50,000	50,000 to 100,000	100,000 to 250,000	250,000 to 500,000	500,000 to 2,500,000	2,500,000 and over
Number of Enterprises	1	11925	3441	7707	•	320	121	35	18	11	16	6	11	•
Revenues ($ in Thousands)														
Net Sales	2	50055408	208210	2217912	•	2668747	3096700	949152	403271	996882	1614313	1819612	6388745	•
Interest	3	340835	98	527	•	2250	215	464	1075	1711	3085	2746	69096	•
Rents	4	81345	0	0	•	63	0	120	0	0	0	0	1852	•
Royalties	5	859468	0	0	•	0	0	0	0	124	10394	696	59208	•
Other Portfolio Income	6	531560	26733	77420	•	49826	130	8365	5018	99	282	13554	235886	•
Other Receipts	7	2915433	30554	42522	•	12621	24506	3736	57452	206023	8085	-1207	141141	•
Total Receipts	8	54784049	265595	2338381	•	2753507	3121551	961837	466816	1204839	1636159	1835401	6895928	•
Average Total Receipts	9	4594	77	303	•	8605	25798	27481	25934	109531	102260	305900	626903	•
Operating Costs/Operating Income (%)														
Cost of Operations	10	25.0	23.2	14.1	•	48.8	51.2	26.3	8.1	56.9	16.6	10.4	25.1	•
Salaries and Wages	11	21.5	6.2	13.7	•	21.5	14.9	17.2	38.5	14.8	24.7	23.3	23.3	•
Taxes Paid	12	2.8	2.1	2.5	•	2.0	3.1	2.8	3.7	1.5	2.7	2.9	2.5	•
Interest Paid	13	2.7	1.4	0.5	•	0.3	0.0	0.3	1.3	0.7	0.4	0.1	2.9	•
Depreciation	14	4.7	0.7	1.1	•	0.4	1.4	2.5	3.3	1.2	2.9	3.8	2.5	•
Amortization and Depletion	15	1.4	0.2	0.3	•	1.3	0.0	0.4	1.3	1.6	1.4	3.2	4.8	•
Pensions and Other Deferred Comp.	16	0.7	0.7	0.5	•	0.0	0.8	0.2	0.1	0.2	0.8	4.2	0.8	•
Employee Benefits	17	1.8	2.3	1.2	•	0.9	2.3	1.5	3.1	1.3	2.1	2.2	2.2	•
Advertising	18	2.4	0.1	1.6	•	1.8	6.9	5.6	5.9	0.8	9.7	8.0	2.0	•
Other Expenses	19	27.7	25.3	34.2	•	14.0	12.2	25.0	33.5	20.5	23.1	26.0	27.8	•
Officers' Compensation	20	2.1	10.5	14.8	•	5.1	2.4	2.7	4.0	1.3	2.0	2.3	2.5	•
Operating Margin	21	7.3	27.3	15.5	•	4.0	4.8	15.6	•	•	13.6	13.5	3.6	•
Operating Margin Before Officers' Comp.	22	9.4	37.8	30.3	•	9.0	7.1	18.3	1.2	0.5	15.6	15.8	6.1	•

Selected Average Balance Sheet ($ in Thousands)

	•	•	•	•	•	•	•	•	•	•	•	•	•
Net Receivables 23	742	0	17	•	195	1948	3826	3976	16390	15766	46150	94167	•
Inventories 24	27	0	0	•	1	2	4	192	1223	233	226	22495	•
Net Property, Plant and Equipment 25	888	0	6	•	174	835	1011	1528	7542	9184	33555	73023	•
Total Assets 26	7203	0	54	•	1583	7380	14094	32055	67111	177085	390102	1104243	•
Notes and Loans Payable 27	1340	0	43	•	410	156	4504	1783	26259	8949	2916	290476	•
All Other Liabilities 28	1686	0	31	•	881	2564	7629	12176	24438	55797	74415	433610	•
Net Worth 29	4177	0	-20	•	292	4659	1961	18096	16413	112339	312771	380157	•

Selected Financial Ratios (Times to 1)

	•		•		•	•	•	•	•	•	•	•	•
Current Ratio 30	1.9	•	0.9	•	1.8	2.5	1.8	1.2	1.6	1.4	2.2	0.8	•
Quick Ratio 31	1.0	•	0.8	•	1.7	1.7	1.7	1.0	1.4	1.3	1.9	0.4	•
Net Sales to Working Capital 32	2.7	•	•	•	25.2	7.1	6.5	11.0	6.2	4.8	3.9	•	•
Coverage Ratio 33	7.7	39.4	44.2	•	23.2	119.7	67.4	10.7	27.8	40.3	278.2	5.3	•
Total Asset Turnover 34	0.6	•	5.3	•	5.3	3.5	1.9	0.7	1.4	0.6	0.8	0.5	•
Inventory Turnover 35	38.8	•	•	•	3842.2	7616.2	1771.6	9.4	42.2	71.7	139.8	6.5	•
Receivables Turnover 36	6.0	20.1	•	•	45.4	11.3	10.1	4.9	6.5	8.5	5.2	7.0	•
Total Liabilities to Net Worth 37	0.7	•	•	•	4.4	0.6	6.2	0.8	3.1	0.6	0.2	1.9	•
Current Assets to Working Capital 38	2.1	•	•	•	2.2	1.7	2.3	6.2	2.5	3.6	1.8	•	•
Current Liabilities to Working Capital 39	1.1	•	•	•	1.2	0.7	1.3	5.2	1.5	2.6	0.8	•	•
Working Capital to Net Sales 40	0.4	•	•	•	0.0	0.1	0.2	0.1	0.2	0.2	0.3	•	•
Inventory to Working Capital 41	0.0	•	•	•	0.0	0.0	0.0	0.1	0.1	0.0	•	•	•
Total Receipts to Cash Flow 42	2.4	1.5	2.2	•	5.8	6.4	2.5	2.3	2.6	2.8	2.7	2.9	•
Cost of Goods to Cash Flow 43	0.6	0.4	0.3	•	2.8	3.3	0.7	0.2	1.5	0.5	0.3	0.7	•
Cash Flow to Total Debt 44	0.6	•	1.8	•	1.1	1.5	0.9	0.7	0.7	0.5	1.4	0.3	•

Selected Financial Factors (in Percentages)

Debt Ratio 45	42.0	•	137.5	•	81.5	36.9	86.1	43.5	75.5	36.6	19.8	65.6	•
Return on Total Assets 46	12.0	•	114.5	•	35.5	19.6	33.1	10.0	28.1	8.9	11.5	8.0	•
Return on Equity Before Income Taxes 47	18.0	•	•	•	183.7	30.7	234.0	16.1	110.9	13.7	14.3	18.9	•
Return on Equity After Income Taxes 48	12.8	•	•	•	175.6	30.1	199.4	15.1	82.9	9.8	10.0	13.6	•
Profit Margin (Before Income Tax) 49	17.9	54.9	21.0	•	6.4	5.6	16.9	13.0	20.1	15.3	14.8	12.4	•
Profit Margin (After Income Tax) 50	12.8	52.5	20.8	•	6.1	5.5	14.4	12.2	15.0	10.9	10.3	8.9	•

Table I

Corporations with and without Net Income

CREDIT INTERMEDIATION

MONEY AMOUNTS AND SIZE OF ASSETS IN THOUSANDS OF DOLLARS

Item Description for Accounting Period 7/10 Through 6/11		Total	Zero Assets	Under 500	500 to 1,000	1,000 to 5,000	5,000 to 10,000	10,000 to 25,000	25,000 to 50,000	50,000 to 100,000	100,000 to 250,000	250,000 to 500,000	500,000 to 2,500,000	2,500,000 and over
Number of Enterprises	1	43184	9827	21156	3371	3900	1037	835	590	686	877	404	374	127
Revenues ($ in Thousands)														
Net Sales	2	466120381	48346975	4072733	1386171	3980620	2899430	5228388	5943781	7056488	13887319	15989412	33893212	323435852
Interest	3	269834180	26871933	12974	60454	305434	106158	239202	478417	1613315	5162902	4933847	14862890	215186654
Rents	4	987808	138070	887	0	4655	383	3106	4148	4825	21154	33387	89443	687749
Royalties	5	770015	28364	0	54	0	0	0	223	229	9724	6	9063	722352
Other Portfolio Income	6	15389179	1722641	3152	1068	9399	20091	32687	101480	114366	527812	472306	1910441	10473738
Other Receipts	7	179139199	19585967	4055720	1324595	3661132	2772798	4953393	5359513	5323753	8165727	10549866	17021375	96365359
Total Receipts	8	466120381	48346975	4072733	1386171	3980620	2899430	5228388	5943781	7056488	13887319	15989412	33893212	323435852
Average Total Receipts	9	10794	4920	193	411	1021	2796	6262	10074	10286	15835	39578	90624	2546739
Operating Costs/Operating Income (%)														
Cost of Operations	10	0.5	0.0	0.0	•	0.2	•	2.4	2.2	0.2	1.0	3.4	0.1	0.4
Salaries and Wages	11	8.5	8.8	19.4	15.9	19.9	23.8	28.4	23.2	21.0	19.0	19.6	14.9	5.5
Taxes Paid	12	1.4	3.3	3.8	3.0	3.4	3.2	3.4	2.6	2.6	2.7	2.3	2.1	0.8
Interest Paid	13	37.1	28.0	1.3	5.4	6.3	6.7	8.1	7.9	12.1	16.3	13.5	16.9	45.4
Depreciation	14	3.8	1.1	1.2	2.3	1.3	1.5	1.4	1.7	1.8	2.9	2.1	2.3	4.7
Amortization and Depletion	15	1.0	0.4	0.2	1.9	0.6	0.1	0.7	0.4	0.6	0.6	1.2	1.6	1.1
Pensions and Other Deferred Comp.	16	0.4	0.4	0.3	0.8	0.1	0.3	0.3	0.5	0.5	0.8	0.7	0.9	0.3
Employee Benefits	17	0.9	0.8	1.3	0.9	2.6	1.5	1.3	1.6	1.6	2.0	1.7	1.8	0.7
Advertising	18	1.5	0.1	4.7	1.8	3.3	3.1	4.3	1.9	0.9	1.3	1.8	1.6	1.5
Other Expenses	19	49.3	42.1	46.2	67.9	62.7	62.1	46.7	51.8	56.5	54.4	49.0	49.7	49.7
Officers' Compensation	20	1.1	1.3	14.6	8.9	6.1	4.7	6.5	3.9	4.4	4.5	2.6	1.9	0.3
Operating Margin	21	•	13.8	7.0	•	•	•	•	2.4	•	•	2.1	6.3	•
Operating Margin Before Officers' Comp.	22	•	15.0	21.7	0.1	•	•	3.4	6.3	2.2	4.7	4.7	8.2	•

Selected Average Balance Sheet ($ in Thousands)

Net Receivables 23	18423	0	•	13	•	122	759	2701	7100	14757	29547	64941	97749	221629	4526681
Inventories 24	•	•	•	•	•	•	•	•	•	•	•	•	•	•	•
Net Property, Plant and Equipment 25	1416	•	0	16	120	152	378	479	889	1489	3400	6334	14575	366117
Total Assets 26	192537	98	16	120	685	2169	6963	16021	36569	73147	159903	349996	984096	59524595
Notes and Loans Payable 27	148423	0	55	424	1210	4189	8372	12130	20770	50869	173740	49389799
All Other Liabilities 28	37782	0	26	404	2299	2567	7936	30166	58946	130075	274028	703575	8387739
Net Worth 29	6331	0	17	-142	-1340	207	-287	-5726	3318	9057	25099	106781	1747057

Selected Financial Ratios (Times to 1)

Current Ratio 30	0.7	•	2.8	1.7	0.8	1.4	1.0	1.2	1.0	0.9	0.8	0.6	0.5	0.7
Quick Ratio 31	0.6	•	2.3	1.1	0.6	1.2	0.9	1.0	0.8	0.8	0.7	0.6	0.5	0.6
Net Sales to Working Capital 32	•	1.5	5.3	2.7	•	2.1	3.3	10.5	•	•	•	•	•	•
Coverage Ratio 33	0.8	1.5	6.4	•	•	0.6	0.6	1.3	0.8	0.6	1.1	1.3	0.8
Total Asset Turnover 34	0.1	•	2.0	0.6	0.5	0.4	0.4	0.3	0.1	0.1	0.1	0.1	0.0
Inventory Turnover 35	•	•	•	•	•	•	•	•	•	•	•	•	•	•
Receivables Turnover 36	•	•	•	•	•	•	•	•	21.0	16.7	12.9	8.2	33.1
Total Liabilities to Net Worth 37	29.4	•	4.9	•	32.6	•	•	25.1	21.0	•	•	•	•	•
Current Assets to Working Capital 38	1.5	•	•	2.5	•	3.2	5.7	•	•	•	•	•	•	•
Current Liabilities to Working Capital 39	0.5	•	•	1.5	•	2.2	4.7	24.1	•	•	•	•	•	•
Working Capital to Net Sales 40	0.2	•	•	0.4	•	0.5	0.3	0.1	0.0	0.0	•	•	•	•
Inventory to Working Capital 41	•	•	•	•	•	•	•	•	•	•	•	•	•	•
Total Receipts to Cash Flow 42	2.5	2.0	2.2	2.1	2.7	2.4	3.0	2.9	2.4	3.1	2.9	2.2	2.6
Cost of Goods to Cash Flow 43	0.0	0.0	0.0	0.0	0.0	0.1	0.1	0.1	0.0	0.0	0.1	0.0	0.0
Cash Flow to Total Debt 44	0.0	•	1.1	0.2	0.1	0.2	0.1	0.1	0.1	0.0	0.0	0.0	0.0

Selected Financial Factors (in Percentages)

Debt Ratio 45	96.7	•	83.0	120.7	161.8	97.0	101.8	115.7	95.5	94.3	92.8	89.1	97.1
Return on Total Assets 46	1.7	•	16.4	•	•	1.9	2.8	1.3	1.0	1.7	2.1	1.5
Return on Equity Before Income Taxes 47	•	•	80.9	25.6	5.0	70.2	•	•	•	3.1	5.0	•
Return on Equity After Income Taxes 48	•	•	78.5	26.5	5.3	87.0	•	•	•	•	2.1	•
Profit Margin (Before Income Tax) 49	•	12.6	7.0	•	•	2.2	•	•	•	2.0	5.9	•
Profit Margin (After Income Tax) 50	•	10.0	6.8	•	•	1.2	•	•	•	•	2.4	•

Table II

Corporations with Net Income

CREDIT INTERMEDIATION

MONEY AMOUNTS AND SIZE OF ASSETS IN THOUSANDS OF DOLLARS

Item Description for Accounting Period 7/10 Through 6/11		Total	Zero Assets	Under 500	500 to 1,000	1,000 to 5,000	5,000 to 10,000	10,000 to 25,000	25,000 to 50,000	50,000 to 100,000	100,000 to 250,000	250,000 to 500,000	500,000 to 2,500,000	2,500,000 and over
Number of Enterprises	1	22148	3164	11327	1935	2476	562	601	390	449	598	296	265	85
Revenues ($ in Thousands)														
Net Sales	2	226458025	41917467	2991867	789483	2469216	2163061	3633738	3787943	4534786	9662824	11124581	22876469	120505591
Interest	3	94555863	23484966	8847	26228	118825	47438	102218	288057	948020	3505320	3393400	11064212	51568331
Rents	4	646909	72954	887	0	4079	200	2341	786	3161	10098	22099	54752	475551
Royalties	5	740763	38	0	0	0	0	0	58	24	9591	6	9063	721985
Other Portfolio Income	6	6225135	1370232	583	780	3198	16789	19949	91496	85897	405102	364924	1653948	2212240
Other Receipts	7	124289355	16989277	2981550	762475	2343114	2098634	3509230	3407546	3497684	5732713	7344152	10094494	65528484
Total Receipts	8	226458025	41917467	2991867	789483	2469216	2163061	3633738	3787943	4534786	9662824	11124581	22876469	120506591
Average Total Receipts	9	10225	13248	264	408	997	3849	6046	9713	10100	16159	37583	86326	1417725
Operating Costs/Operating Income (%)														
Cost of Operations	10	0.1	0.0	0.0	•	0.2	•	2.0	0.8	0.3	0.1	0.5	0.2	0.1
Salaries and Wages	11	12.5	7.9	16.0	12.6	21.7	25.5	28.4	28.4	25.2	20.7	23.0	16.6	9.8
Taxes Paid	12	2.3	3.5	2.7	2.8	3.7	3.4	3.5	3.4	2.9	3.0	2.6	2.4	1.7
Interest Paid	13	17.8	28.6	0.5	4.1	4.3	4.3	7.3	7.6	11.3	13.8	13.3	17.9	16.7
Depreciation	14	1.6	1.0	0.9	3.5	1.1	1.0	0.9	1.2	1.9	2.9	2.4	2.6	1.4
Amortization and Depletion	15	1.1	0.3	0.3	0.1	0.2	0.0	0.4	0.2	0.6	0.7	0.8	1.6	1.4
Pensions and Other Deferred Comp.	16	0.6	0.4	0.3	1.3	0.1	0.4	0.3	0.7	0.6	0.8	0.8	1.0	0.6
Employee Benefits	17	1.3	0.8	0.8	0.5	1.2	1.6	1.3	1.5	1.9	2.0	1.9	2.0	1.2
Advertising	18	2.6	0.1	2.7	1.9	3.7	3.9	2.1	2.8	1.1	1.5	1.6	2.0	3.8
Other Expenses	19	39.5	30.5	43.4	41.5	36.7	30.0	30.7	31.2	32.0	31.1	34.3	31.1	46.2
Officers' Compensation	20	1.8	1.3	12.8	11.4	8.1	4.8	8.0	4.9	5.1	4.9	3.0	2.1	0.6
Operating Margin	21	18.8	25.5	19.7	20.4	19.0	25.0	15.3	17.4	16.9	18.6	15.8	20.4	16.5
Operating Margin Before Officers' Comp.	22	20.6	26.8	32.5	31.8	27.1	29.9	23.3	22.3	22.0	23.5	18.8	22.5	17.1

Selected Average Balance Sheet ($ in Thousands)

Net Receivables 23	21066	•	11	114	895	3068	8370	16112	30017	65232	96783	235370	3617314
Inventories 24	•	•	•	•	•	•	•	•	•	•	•	•	•
Net Property, Plant and Equipment 25	851	0	21	127	168	354	296	896	1330	3176	6680	15380	101888
Total Assets 26	89669	0	117	703	2177	6997	16145	37267	73563	160998	350595	1030179	16984290
Notes and Loans Payable 27	26086	0	27	223	1129	3865	7700	11005	12018	19752	39908	129968	5878467
All Other Liabilities 28	51478	0	13	83	323	1642	4580	18635	49900	124200	262364	694970	9053805
Net Worth 29	12105	0	77	397	725	1490	3865	7627	11644	17045	48323	205241	2052018

Selected Financial Ratios (Times to 1)

Current Ratio 30	0.7	•	5.6	3.0	3.0	1.5	1.5	1.1	0.9	0.8	0.6	0.6	0.7
Quick Ratio 31	0.6	•	4.2	1.7	2.6	1.2	1.4	1.0	0.8	0.7	0.6	0.5	0.6
Net Sales to Working Capital 32	•	•	5.3	1.3	0.9	2.5	1.5	4.6	•	•	•	•	•
Coverage Ratio 33	2.0	1.9	38.1	6.0	5.5	6.8	3.1	3.3	2.4	2.3	2.2	2.1	2.0
Total Asset Turnover 34	0.1	•	2.3	0.6	0.5	0.6	0.4	0.3	0.1	0.1	0.1	0.1	0.1
Inventory Turnover 35	•	•	•	•	•	•	•	•	•	•	•	•	•
Receivables Turnover 36	•	•	•	•	•	•	•	•	•	•	•	•	•
Total Liabilities to Net Worth 37	6.4	•	0.5	0.8	2.0	3.7	3.2	3.9	5.3	8.4	6.3	4.0	7.3
Current Assets to Working Capital 38	•	•	1.2	1.5	1.5	3.2	2.8	12.3	•	•	•	•	•
Current Liabilities to Working Capital 39	•	•	0.2	0.5	0.5	2.2	1.8	11.3	•	•	•	•	•
Working Capital to Net Sales 40	•	•	0.2	0.8	1.1	0.4	0.7	0.2	•	•	•	•	•
Inventory to Working Capital 41	•	•	•	•	0.0	•	0.0	0.0	•	•	•	•	•
Total Receipts to Cash Flow 42	1.8	2.0	1.8	2.0	2.0	2.1	2.4	2.2	2.2	2.2	2.2	2.1	1.7
Cost of Goods to Cash Flow 43	0.0	0.0	0.0	0.0	0.0	•	0.0	0.0	0.0	0.0	0.0	0.0	0.0
Cash Flow to Total Debt 44	0.1	•	3.8	0.7	0.3	0.3	0.2	0.1	0.1	0.1	0.1	0.0	0.1

Selected Financial Factors (in Percentages)

Debt Ratio 45	86.5	•	34.3	43.6	66.7	78.7	76.1	79.5	84.2	89.4	86.2	80.1	87.9
Return on Total Assets 46	4.2	•	46.0	14.2	10.7	16.1	8.4	6.5	3.8	3.1	3.1	3.2	2.8
Return on Equity Before Income Taxes 47	15.7	•	68.1	21.0	26.2	64.6	23.9	21.9	13.9	16.6	12.3	8.4	11.5
Return on Equity After Income Taxes 48	12.1	•	67.1	20.4	25.3	62.6	22.1	20.0	12.2	13.9	9.4	6.2	7.9
Profit Margin (Before Income Tax) 49	18.6	24.9	19.7	20.4	19.0	25.0	15.2	17.2	16.0	17.5	15.8	20.0	16.6
Profit Margin (After Income Tax) 50	14.4	21.9	19.5	19.8	18.4	24.2	14.1	15.7	14.0	14.6	12.1	14.7	11.4

Table I

Corporations with and without Net Income

COMMERCIAL BANKING

MONEY AMOUNTS AND SIZE OF ASSETS IN THOUSANDS OF DOLLARS

Item Description for Accounting Period 7/10 Through 6/11	Total	Zero Assets	Under 500	500 to 1,000	1,000 to 5,000	5,000 to 10,000	10,000 to 25,000	25,000 to 50,000	50,000 to 100,000	100,000 to 250,000	250,000 to 500,000	500,000 to 2,500,000	2,500,000 and over
Number of Enterprises **1**	1622	216	•	•	•	21	96	166	360	477	140	73	16
Revenues ($ in Thousands)													
Net Sales **2**	71403799	46288709	•	•	•	326778	569724	482849	2493573	5198869	3423860	7655039	3970810
Interest **3**	36708796	26266756	•	•	•	45220	126108	196179	875889	2499694	1499002	2254809	2870890
Rents **4**	280650	126110	•	•	•	76	432	200	1105	5966	11906	13267	121587
Royalties **5**	28616	28364	•	•	•	0	0	0	24	159	6	0	64
Other Portfolio Income **6**	2496296	1697848	•	•	•	2166	15921	13298	75387	200381	150412	127022	213151
Other Receipts **7**	31889441	18169631	•	•	•	279316	427263	273172	1541168	2492669	1762534	5259941	765118
Total Receipts **8**	71403799	46288709	•	•	•	326778	569724	482849	2493573	5198869	3423860	7655039	3970810
Average Total Receipts **9**	44022	214300	•	•	•	15561	5935	2909	6927	10899	24456	104864	248176
Operating Costs/Operating Income (%)													
Cost of Operations **10**	0.0	•	•	•	•	•	•	•	•	0.0	0.5	•	•
Salaries and Wages **11**	9.0	8.5	•	•	•	4.7	5.5	11.3	10.1	12.5	13.1	7.8	10.8
Taxes Paid **12**	2.8	3.3	•	•	•	0.3	0.8	2.2	1.7	2.3	2.0	1.2	2.8
Interest Paid **13**	24.0	28.7	•	•	•	9.1	9.0	15.1	14.2	18.2	16.6	12.0	21.6
Depreciation **14**	1.4	1.1	•	•	•	0.6	0.8	1.8	1.8	2.0	1.9	1.1	4.7
Amortization and Depletion **15**	0.4	0.2	•	•	•	0.3	0.0	0.6	0.3	0.7	0.4	0.7	1.3
Pensions and Other Deferred Comp. **16**	0.4	0.4	•	•	•	0.0	0.1	0.7	0.4	0.6	0.5	0.4	0.7
Employee Benefits **17**	1.0	0.8	•	•	•	0.6	1.3	2.6	1.8	2.0	1.6	1.0	2.0
Advertising **18**	0.2	0.1	•	•	•	0.1	0.2	0.8	0.5	0.6	0.5	0.3	0.8
Other Expenses **19**	51.2	41.1	•	•	•	202.9	108.3	72.4	86.6	67.9	60.6	73.1	30.2
Officers' Compensation **20**	2.1	1.2	•	•	•	0.7	2.2	8.5	5.0	5.6	4.3	2.0	4.8
Operating Margin **21**	7.5	14.6	•	•	•	•	•	•	•	•	•	0.7	20.4
Operating Margin Before Officers' Comp. **22**	9.6	15.8	•	•	•	•	•	•	•	•	2.3	2.6	25.1

Selected Average Balance Sheet ($ in Thousands)

Net Receivables 23	107021	0	854	7623	20759	40751	92927	189288	407610	3383095
Inventories 24	•	•	•	•	•	•	•	•	•	•
Net Property, Plant and Equipment 25	2590	0	30	144	529	1296	2783	5243	11734	44573
Total Assets 26	197476	•	7002	17684	38947	73431	157817	340732	965173	5749498
Notes and Loans Payable 27	8169	0	0	71	389	1408	5605	12872	40158	329010
All Other Liabilities 28	181419	0	48374	31044	37399	73275	147966	321703	883163	4603604
Net Worth 29	7888	0	-41372	-13430	1160	-1251	4245	6156	41852	816884

Selected Financial Ratios (Times to 1)

Current Ratio 30	0.9	•	0.4	0.9	1.0	1.0	1.0	0.9	0.8	1.0
Quick Ratio 31	0.9	•	0.4	0.9	1.0	0.9	0.9	0.9	0.8	0.9
Net Sales to Working Capital 32	•	•	•	•	2.1	•	•	•	•	•
Coverage Ratio 33	1.3	1.5	•	•	•	0.2	0.2	0.8	1.0	1.9
Total Asset Turnover 34	0.2	•	2.2	0.3	0.1	0.1	0.1	0.1	0.1	0.0
Inventory Turnover 35	•	•	•	•	•	•	•	•	•	•
Receivables Turnover 36	•	•	•	•	•	•	•	•	•	•
Total Liabilities to Net Worth 37	24.0	•	•	•	32.6	36.2	54.3	22.1	•	6.0
Current Assets to Working Capital 38	•	•	•	•	24.6	•	•	•	•	•
Current Liabilities to Working Capital 39	•	•	•	•	23.6	•	•	•	•	•
Working Capital to Net Sales 40	•	•	•	•	0.5	•	•	•	•	•
Inventory to Working Capital 41	•	•	•	•	•	•	•	•	•	•
Total Receipts to Cash Flow 42	2.2	2.0	4.2	3.0	2.7	2.5	3.1	3.9	1.9	2.2
Cost of Goods to Cash Flow 43	0.0	•	•	•	0.0	•	0.0	0.0	•	•
Cash Flow to Total Debt 44	0.1	•	0.1	0.1	0.0	0.0	0.0	0.0	0.1	0.0

Selected Financial Factors (in Percentages)

Debt Ratio 45	96.0	•	690.9	175.9	97.0	101.7	97.3	98.2	95.7	85.8
Return on Total Assets 46	6.7	•	•	•	•	•	0.3	0.9	1.3	1.7
Return on Equity Before Income Taxes 47	34.7	•	44.9	12.6	•	132.1	•	•	•	5.7
Return on Equity After Income Taxes 48	20.7	•	44.9	12.7	•	136.3	•	•	•	3.5
Profit Margin (Before Income Tax) 49	6.2	13.4	•	•	•	•	•	•	•	18.8
Profit Margin (After Income Tax) 50	3.7	10.7	•	•	•	•	•	•	•	11.4

Table II
Corporations with Net Income

COMMERCIAL BANKING

MONEY AMOUNTS AND SIZE OF ASSETS IN THOUSANDS OF DOLLARS

Item Description for Accounting Period 7/10 Through 6/11		Total	Zero Assets	Under 500	500 to 1,000	1,000 to 5,000	5,000 to 10,000	10,000 to 25,000	25,000 to 50,000	50,000 to 100,000	100,000 to 250,000	250,000 to 500,000	500,000 to 2,500,000	2,500,000 and over
Number of Enterprises	1	974	113	0	4	0	0	70	105	216	308	97	48	13
Revenues ($ in Thousands)														
Net Sales	2	52497849	40734717	0	7566	0	0	86104	216422	864752	2774865	1798814	2542406	3472204
Interest	3	29907809	22902289	0	0	0	0	48017	92994	397684	1563689	956468	1425682	2520986
Rents	4	201712	61112	0	0	0	0	70	103	660	3221	9520	5439	121587
Royalties	5	156	38	0	0	0	0	0	0	24	26	6	0	64
Other Portfolio Income	6	1921726	1346047	0	399	0	0	12081	9174	53141	150579	91114	102768	156420
Other Receipts	7	20466446	16425231	0	7167	0	0	25936	114151	413243	1057350	741706	1008517	673147
Total Receipts	8	52497849	40734717	0	7566	0	0	86104	216422	864752	2774865	1798814	2542406	3472204
Average Total Receipts	9	53899	360484	•	1892	•	•	1230	2061	4003	9009	18544	52967	267093
Operating Costs/Operating Income (%)														
Cost of Operations	10	0.0	•	•	•	•	•	•	•	•	0.0	1.0	•	•
Salaries and Wages	11	9.0	7.6	•	8.8	•	•	13.3	12.7	14.0	14.8	16.7	14.7	11.2
Taxes Paid	12	3.4	3.6	•	4.8	•	•	2.7	3.0	2.9	3.0	2.8	2.4	3.1
Interest Paid	13	26.9	28.9	•	15.8	•	•	18.6	18.5	19.6	20.0	20.1	24.3	16.7
Depreciation	14	1.5	1.0	•	0.6	•	•	2.6	1.7	2.3	2.5	2.6	2.1	5.1
Amortization and Depletion	15	0.3	0.2	•	•	•	•	0.1	0.4	0.3	0.9	0.6	0.6	1.4
Pensions and Other Deferred Comp.	16	0.4	0.4	•	0.4	•	•	0.5	1.0	0.8	0.7	0.7	0.7	0.5
Employee Benefits	17	1.1	0.8	•	1.5	•	•	4.8	3.8	3.4	2.5	2.4	1.7	1.9
Advertising	18	0.2	0.1	•	0.5	•	•	0.8	1.0	0.7	0.8	0.8	0.5	0.8
Other Expenses	19	29.6	30.4	•	43.4	•	•	30.7	25.3	26.3	28.4	25.5	28.5	26.1
Officers' Compensation	20	2.2	1.2	•	12.6	•	•	13.4	13.1	9.3	7.4	5.9	3.7	4.7
Operating Margin	21	25.2	25.9	•	11.6	•	•	12.6	19.5	20.3	18.9	21.0	20.7	28.4
Operating Margin Before Officers' Comp.	22	27.4	27.1	•	24.2	•	•	26.0	32.6	29.6	26.3	26.9	24.5	33.2

Selected Average Balance Sheet ($ in Thousands)

Net Receivables **23**	135749	0	35	9430	21738	41916	93994	203003	419369	3957843
Inventories **24**	•	•	•	•	•	•	•	•	•	•
Net Property, Plant and Equipment **25**	2881	0	0	179	410	1105	2735	5164	11108	48853
Total Assets **26**	235877	0	1011	18238	39592	73825	158819	345064	939520	6221217
Notes and Loans Payable **27**	8148	0	0	97	396	1423	4140	12823	34990	260154
All Other Liabilities **28**	200659	0	467	15937	33935	63742	137145	294274	805847	5194373
Net Worth **29**	27070	0	543	2205	5260	8660	17534	37967	98682	766689

Selected Financial Ratios (Times to 1)

Current Ratio **30**	1.0	•	•	1.1	1.1	1.0	1.0	1.0	0.9	1.0
Quick Ratio **31**	0.9	•	•	1.0	1.1	1.0	0.9	0.9	0.9	1.0
Net Sales to Working Capital **32**	•	•	•	1.1	0.8	1.7	•	•	•	10.3
Coverage Ratio **33**	1.9	1.9	•	1.6	1.9	1.8	1.8	1.9	1.7	2.6
Total Asset Turnover **34**	0.2	•	•	0.1	0.1	0.1	0.1	0.1	0.1	0.0
Inventory Turnover **35**	•	•	•	•	•	•	•	•	•	•
Receivables Turnover **36**	•	•	•	•	•	•	•	•	•	•
Total Liabilities to Net Worth **37**	7.7	•	•	7.3	6.5	7.5	8.1	8.1	8.5	7.1
Current Assets to Working Capital **38**	•	•	•	15.4	13.7	28.9	•	•	•	200.4
Current Liabilities to Working Capital **39**	8.2	•	•	14.4	12.7	27.9	•	•	•	199.4
Working Capital to Net Sales **40**	0.0	•	•	0.9	1.3	0.6	•	•	•	0.1
Inventory to Working Capital **41**	•	•	•	•	•	•	•	•	•	0.0
Total Receipts to Cash Flow **42**	2.0	2.0	•	3.4	2.4	2.3	2.3	2.3	2.2	2.0
Cost of Goods to Cash Flow **43**	0.0	•	•	0.0	•	0.0	0.0	0.0	•	•
Cash Flow to Total Debt **44**	0.1	•	•	0.0	0.0	0.0	0.0	0.0	0.0	0.0

Selected Financial Factors (in Percentages)

Debt Ratio **45**	88.5	•	•	87.9	86.7	88.3	89.0	89.0	89.5	87.7
Return on Total Assets **46**	11.7	•	•	2.0	1.8	2.0	2.1	2.1	2.4	1.9
Return on Equity Before Income Taxes **47**	48.0	•	•	5.9	6.3	7.7	8.4	9.2	9.7	9.3
Return on Equity After Income Taxes **48**	41.2	•	•	5.2	5.4	6.7	7.0	7.5	7.5	6.3
Profit Margin (Before Income Tax) **49**	24.1	25.2	•	10.6	16.0	16.6	16.4	18.8	18.1	26.7
Profit Margin (After Income Tax) **50**	20.7	22.2	•	9.3	13.7	14.4	13.7	15.3	14.0	18.2

Table I

Corporations with and without Net Income

SAVINGS INSTITUTIONS AND OTHER DEPOSITORY CREDIT

MONEY AMOUNTS AND SIZE OF ASSETS IN THOUSANDS OF DOLLARS

Item Description for Accounting Period 7/10 Through 6/11		Total	Zero Assets	Under 500	500 to 1,000	1,000 to 5,000	5,000 to 10,000	10,000 to 25,000	25,000 to 50,000	50,000 to 100,000	100,000 to 250,000	250,000 to 500,000	500,000 to 2,500,000	2,500,000 and over
Number of Enterprises	1	1473	418	•	•	•	4	24	102	153	259	199	223	55
Revenues ($ in Thousands)														
Net Sales	2	62268779	204246	•	•	•	3525	33984	1165858	715340	2509914	4268281	12077062	41151012
Interest	3	43042316	163208	•	•	•	3354	14921	157988	483607	1848586	3039213	8923594	28395508
Rents	4	443317	1634	•	•	•	0	139	618	1956	10240	11915	61433	355342
Royalties	5	1977	0	•	•	•	0	0	14	0	0	0	1304	659
Other Portfolio Income	6	2702321	2077	•	•	•	0	1733	7309	17431	138834	153660	700915	1679240
Other Receipts	7	16078848	37327	•	•	•	171	17191	999929	212346	512254	1063493	2389816	10720263
Total Receipts	8	62268779	204246	•	•	•	3525	33984	1165858	715340	2509914	4268281	12077062	41151012
Average Total Receipts	9	42273	489	•	•	•	881	1416	11430	4675	9691	21449	54157	748200
Operating Costs/Operating Income (%)														
Cost of Operations	10	0.0	•	•	•	•	•	•	•	•	1.1	•	0.0	0.0
Salaries and Wages	11	12.9	14.9	•	•	•	14.0	8.7	2.6	12.3	16.4	15.5	17.2	11.5
Taxes Paid	12	2.5	2.9	•	•	•	1.0	1.2	0.8	4.0	3.1	2.7	2.7	2.4
Interest Paid	13	26.1	28.5	•	•	•	56.1	14.7	5.2	25.2	27.6	24.3	25.6	27.0
Depreciation	14	2.1	2.0	•	•	•	0.0	1.6	0.4	2.1	4.6	2.3	2.5	1.9
Amortization and Depletion	15	1.2	1.0	•	•	•	•	•	0.1	0.1	0.5	0.2	0.4	1.6
Pensions and Other Deferred Comp.	16	1.0	0.7	•	•	•	•	0.5	0.3	1.5	1.8	1.7	1.8	0.7
Employee Benefits	17	2.0	4.9	•	•	•	•	2.0	0.6	2.5	2.7	2.8	2.7	1.7
Advertising	18	1.1	1.0	•	•	•	0.0	0.5	0.2	0.8	1.1	1.2	1.2	1.1
Other Expenses	19	42.6	36.5	•	•	•	33.9	283.2	89.1	45.4	59.4	41.1	43.1	39.7
Officers' Compensation	20	1.6	3.7	•	•	•	0.3	2.0	1.7	6.5	5.2	3.7	2.5	0.8
Operating Margin	21	6.8	3.7	•	•	•	•	•	•	•	•	4.5	0.3	11.6
Operating Margin Before Officers' Comp.	22	8.4	7.5	•	•	•	•	•	0.7	6.0	8.2	•	2.8	12.4

Selected Average Balance Sheet ($ in Thousands)

Item												
Net Receivables 23	45197	0	•	•	0	1058	1568	6076	16561	25711	56800	788815
Inventories 24	•	•	•	•	•	•	•	•	•	•	•	•
Net Property, Plant and Equipment 25	7267	0	•	•	2	215	522	1472	3443	6404	14746	90269
Total Assets 26	731565	0	•	•	8706	15344	37621	75572	165574	357489	978229	13264548
Notes and Loans Payable 27	97200	0	•	•	2197	6995	5306	4013	10839	30120	75707	211896
All Other Liabilities 28	576977	0	•	•	6174	19914	87893	67202	137940	298140	805193	10007637
Net Worth 29	57388	0	•	•	336	-11566	-55578	4357	16795	29229	97330	1145015

Selected Financial Ratios (Times to 1)

Item												
Current Ratio 30	0.3	•	•	•	0.1	0.5	0.3	0.3	0.3	0.3	0.3	0.3
Quick Ratio 31	0.2	•	•	•	0.1	0.5	0.3	0.3	0.3	0.3	0.2	0.2
Net Sales to Working Capital 32	•	•	•	•	•	•	•	•	•	•	•	•
Coverage Ratio 33	1.2	•	•	1.1	0.9	•	0.8	0.9	0.1	1.1	1.0	1.4
Total Asset Turnover 34	0.1	•	•	•	0.1	0.1	0.1	0.1	0.1	0.1	0.1	0.1
Inventory Turnover 35	•	•	•	•	•	•	•	•	•	•	•	•
Receivables Turnover 36	•	•	•	•	•	•	•	•	•	•	•	•
Total Liabilities to Net Worth 37	11.7	•	•	•	24.9	16.3	8.9	11.2	•	9.1	•	10.6
Current Assets to Working Capital 38	•	•	•	•	•	•	•	•	•	•	•	•
Current Liabilities to Working Capital 39	•	•	•	•	•	•	•	•	•	•	•	•
Working Capital to Net Sales 40	•	•	•	•	•	•	•	•	•	•	•	•
Inventory to Working Capital 41	•	•	•	•	•	•	•	•	•	•	•	•
Total Receipts to Cash Flow 42	2.5	•	2.8	•	3.6	7.1	3.8	10.7	3.1	3.1	•	2.2
Cost of Goods to Cash Flow 43	0.0	•	•	•	0.0	0.0	0.0	0.0	0.1	•	0.0	0.0
Cash Flow to Total Debt 44	0.0	•	•	•	0.0	0.0	0.0	•	•	•	0.0	0.0

Selected Financial Factors (in Percentages)

Item												
Debt Ratio 45	92.2	•	•	•	96.1	175.4	247.7	94.2	89.9	91.8	90.1	91.4
Return on Total Assets 46	1.9	•	•	•	5.1	•	1.3	1.5	0.2	1.7	1.4	2.1
Return on Equity Before Income Taxes 47	4.4	•	•	•	26.2	26.2	•	•	0.2	2.4	•	7.1
Return on Equity After Income Taxes 48	1.2	•	•	•	26.3	•	0.2	•	0.3	•	•	3.8
Profit Margin (Before Income Tax) 49	5.9	•	•	3.5	•	•	•	•	3.2	•	•	10.8
Profit Margin (After Income Tax) 50	1.6	•	•	•	•	•	•	•	0.4	•	•	5.7

Table II
Corporations with Net Income

SAVINGS INSTITUTIONS AND OTHER DEPOSITORY CREDIT

MONEY AMOUNTS AND SIZE OF ASSETS IN THOUSANDS OF DOLLARS

Item Description for Accounting Period 7/10 Through 6/11		Total	Zero Assets	Under 500	500 to 1,000	1,000 to 5,000	5,000 to 10,000	10,000 to 25,000	25,000 to 50,000	50,000 to 100,000	100,000 to 250,000	250,000 to 500,000	500,000 to 2,500,000	2,500,000 and over
Number of Enterprises	1	775	9	0	0	29	0	9	64	106	195	155	164	44
Revenues ($ in Thousands)														
Net Sales	2	49954020	175657	0	0	35566	0	7500	135012	404288	1790330	2826654	8640606	35938407
Interest	3	36467580	152217	0	0	58	0	7183	104925	340614	1379362	2287214	6616565	25579441
Rents	4	357014	1516	0	0	0	0	0	383	918	4076	8068	42303	299751
Royalties	5	1977	0	0	0	0	0	0	14	0	0	0	1304	659
Other Portfolio Income	6	1950358	1468	0	0	0	0	15	3684	12785	99369	116512	512591	1203933
Other Receipts	7	11177091	20456	0	0	35508	0	302	26006	49971	307523	414860	1467843	8854623
Total Receipts	8	49954020	175657	0	0	35566	0	7500	135012	404288	1790330	2826654	8640606	35938407
Average Total Receipts	9	64457	19517	•	•	1226	•	833	2110	3814	9181	18236	52687	816782
Operating Costs/Operating Income (%)														
Cost of Operations	10	0.0	0.0	•	•	•	•	•	•	•	•	•	0.0	0.0
Salaries and Wages	11	12.6	14.8	•	•	30.1	•	17.2	12.5	13.0	15.2	16.3	17.9	10.8
Taxes Paid	12	2.5	2.7	•	•	2.0	•	3.3	5.0	3.3	3.1	3.2	2.9	2.2
Interest Paid	13	26.9	29.3	•	•	•	•	35.2	24.4	29.8	25.3	27.4	25.0	27.4
Depreciation	14	2.3	1.7	•	•	0.9	•	1.2	2.2	2.3	5.3	2.8	2.8	1.9
Amortization and Depletion	15	1.3	0.4	•	•	•	•	•	0.0	0.1	0.5	0.2	0.4	1.7
Pensions and Other Deferred Comp.	16	1.1	0.5	•	•	•	•	0.9	2.0	1.8	1.9	2.1	2.0	0.7
Employee Benefits	17	2.0	5.4	•	•	3.5	•	2.2	3.2	3.1	2.8	3.2	3.0	1.6
Advertising	18	1.2	1.1	•	•	•	•	0.7	0.8	0.9	1.1	1.1	1.4	1.2
Other Expenses	19	28.4	30.0	•	•	48.8	•	19.6	17.7	22.4	23.7	23.9	25.9	29.7
Officers' Compensation	20	1.5	2.2	•	•	•	•	7.8	9.7	7.8	5.8	4.6	2.8	0.7
Operating Margin	21	20.3	11.8	•	•	14.7	•	12.1	22.5	15.5	15.3	15.2	15.9	22.1
Operating Margin Before Officers' Comp.	22	21.8	14.0	•	•	14.7	•	19.8	32.1	23.4	21.0	19.8	18.7	22.8

Selected Average Balance Sheet ($ in Thousands)

Net Receivables **23**	69284	110	1061	1625	6242	18704	23210	55675	830472
Inventories **24**	0	•	•	•	•	•	•	•	•
Net Property, Plant and Equipment **25**	10617	27	76	520	1271	3083	6563	15459	88749
Total Assets **26**	1183190	2021	15999	37362	75726	166366	355154	976394	14971196
Notes and Loans Payable **27**	162206	0	1430	1235	4216	9772	26640	63593	2470610
All Other Liabilities **28**	887954	189	12380	30659	60777	135808	286211	798040	10861801
Net Worth **29**	133030	1832	2189	5468	10733	20786	42303	114762	1638785

Selected Financial Ratios (Times to 1)

Current Ratio **30**	0.3	34.0	0.3	0.3	0.3	0.3	0.3	0.3	0.2
Quick Ratio **31**	0.2	33.9	0.3	0.3	0.3	0.3	0.3	0.2	0.2
Net Sales to Working Capital **32**	•	0.6	•	•	•	•	•	•	•
Coverage Ratio **33**	1.7	1.4	1.3	1.9	1.5	1.5	1.5	1.6	1.8
Total Asset Turnover **34**	0.1	0.6	0.1	0.1	0.1	0.1	0.1	0.1	0.1
Inventory Turnover **35**	•	•	•	•	•	•	•	•	•
Receivables Turnover **36**	•	•	•	•	•	•	•	•	•
Total Liabilities to Net Worth **37**	7.9	0.1	6.3	5.8	6.1	7.0	7.4	7.5	8.1
Current Assets to Working Capital **38**	•	1.0	•	•	•	•	•	•	•
Current Liabilities to Working Capital **39**	•	0.0	•	•	•	•	•	•	•
Working Capital to Net Sales **40**	•	1.6	•	•	•	•	•	•	•
Inventory to Working Capital **41**	•	•	•	•	•	•	•	•	•
Total Receipts to Cash Flow **42**	2.2	2.1	3.3	2.7	2.8	2.8	2.8	2.6	2.1
Cost of Goods to Cash Flow **43**	0.0	•	•	•	•	•	•	0.0	0.0
Cash Flow to Total Debt **44**	0.0	3.1	0.0	0.0	0.0	0.0	0.0	0.0	0.0

Selected Financial Factors (in Percentages)

Debt Ratio **45**	88.8	9.4	86.3	85.4	85.8	87.5	88.1	88.2	89.1
Return on Total Assets **46**	2.5	8.9	2.5	2.6	2.2	2.2	2.1	2.2	2.7
Return on Equity Before Income Taxes **47**	9.4	9.8	4.5	8.5	4.9	6.1	5.9	6.8	10.6
Return on Equity After Income Taxes **48**	6.8	9.8	3.4	6.8	3.5	4.4	4.1	4.7	7.7
Profit Margin (Before Income Tax) **49**	19.4	11.6	14.7	11.9	22.1	13.9	13.7	14.9	21.3
Profit Margin (After Income Tax) **50**	14.0	7.4	14.7	9.0	17.7	9.8	10.0	10.2	15.5

Table I

Corporations with and without Net Income

CREDIT CARD ISSUING AND OTHER CONSUMER CREDIT

MONEY AMOUNTS AND SIZE OF ASSETS IN THOUSANDS OF DOLLARS

Item Description for Accounting Period 7/10 Through 6/11		Total	Zero Assets	Under 500	500 to 1,000	1,000 to 5,000	5,000 to 10,000	10,000 to 25,000	25,000 to 50,000	50,000 to 100,000	100,000 to 250,000	250,000 to 500,000	500,000 to 2,500,000	2,500,000 and over
Number of Enterprises	1	7474	1425	2945	1215	1093	237	302	84	53	54	22	29	15
Revenues ($ in Thousands)														
Net Sales	2	99473978	715358	210611	169650	862866	507085	1529003	948698	1063586	2335938	4517216	5189021	81424947
Interest	3	28737404	331495	1639	4850	100398	25255	25318	44481	146329	544629	216486	2219824	25076700
Rents	4	26523	6687	0	0	3	134	1066	310	72	729	3515	6107	7900
Royalties	5	465983	0	0	0	0	0	0	0	0	9498	0	0	456486
Other Portfolio Income	6	4129987	21496	173	655	2250	16485	3613	2280	9278	61842	9772	64718	3937426
Other Receipts	7	66114081	355680	208799	164145	760215	465211	1499006	901627	907907	1719240	4287443	2898372	51946435
Total Receipts	8	99473978	715358	210611	169650	862866	507085	1529003	948698	1063586	2335938	4517216	5189021	81424947
Average Total Receipts	9	13309	502	72	140	789	2140	5063	11294	20068	43258	205328	178932	5428330
Operating Costs/Operating Income (%)														
Cost of Operations	10	0.9	•	•	•	•	•	0.6	•	•	0.3	0.1	0.5	1.1
Salaries and Wages	11	9.1	19.1	23.2	8.3	21.0	14.5	20.8	17.4	21.3	18.0	26.1	12.6	6.9
Taxes Paid	12	1.2	0.9	2.3	1.9	3.7	3.2	2.4	2.8	2.7	2.4	1.9	1.9	1.0
Interest Paid	13	20.0	11.3	4.6	4.5	12.1	13.0	13.4	9.1	13.4	12.3	5.3	17.0	21.9
Depreciation	14	13.5	1.0	2.3	1.4	2.3	0.8	0.7	1.7	2.4	4.1	1.7	2.0	16.1
Amortization and Depletion	15	1.2	12.6	0.3	5.0	0.4	0.3	0.6	1.0	0.5	0.5	0.5	2.2	1.1
Pensions and Other Deferred Comp.	16	0.5	0.1	0.4	0.0	0.2	0.3	0.4	0.2	0.9	0.3	0.2	0.3	0.6
Employee Benefits	17	0.8	1.2	0.2	0.5	1.5	0.9	1.3	1.0	1.4	1.3	1.3	1.3	0.7
Advertising	18	3.3	0.5	4.6	2.9	1.9	0.6	1.7	2.3	1.5	1.8	2.2	0.8	3.6
Other Expenses	19	47.5	45.2	42.9	69.2	50.4	60.1	44.1	48.4	35.5	47.0	62.6	43.0	47.0
Officers' Compensation	20	0.8	5.5	13.1	6.6	12.5	8.9	10.4	3.0	3.9	2.7	1.0	1.0	0.2
Operating Margin	21	1.2	2.5	6.0	•	•	•	3.7	13.2	16.6	9.2	•	17.6	•
Operating Margin Before Officers' Comp.	22	2.0	8.0	19.1	6.2	6.5	6.4	14.0	16.1	20.5	12.0	18.6	•	0.1

Selected Average Balance Sheet ($ in Thousands)

Line Item													
Net Receivables 23	49486	0	47	203	1557	4172	11945	25271	44038	82397	185597	607639	22171052
Inventories 24	•	•	•	•	•	•	•	•	•	•	•	•	•
Net Property, Plant and Equipment 25	4811	0	8	14	41	75	251	1652	2171	3195	9405	7656	2328138
Total Assets 26	107610	0	121	668	2338	6722	16321	36044	69768	159987	357115	931532	49586254
Notes and Loans Payable 27	49648	145	377	983	4833	9776	23139	37538	88682	204251	599408		22294069
All Other Liabilities 28	43490	-8	92	368	1043	3826	5051	16454	30226	79861	178964		20885071
Net Worth 29	14472	-16	199	987	846	2719	7854	15777	41079	73003	153160		6407114

Selected Financial Ratios (Times to 1)

Line Item													
Current Ratio 30	1.5	•	16.3	4.7	3.8	2.3	2.2	2.4	2.1	2.0	1.9	2.0	1.5
Quick Ratio 31	1.5	•	13.4	2.4	3.5	1.8	2.1	2.1	1.9	1.7	1.7	2.0	1.4
Net Sales to Working Capital 32	0.6	•	0.9	0.4	0.5	0.6	0.7	0.6	0.7	0.8	1.7	0.5	0.6
Coverage Ratio 33	1.1	1.2	2.3	0.9	0.5	0.8	1.3	2.4	2.2	1.8	0.5	2.0	1.0
Total Asset Turnover 34	0.1	•	0.6	0.2	0.3	0.3	0.3	0.3	0.3	0.3	0.6	0.2	0.1
Inventory Turnover 35	•	•	•	•	•	•	•	•	•	•	•	•	•
Receivables Turnover 36	•	•	•	•	•	•	•	•	•	•	•	•	•
Total Liabilities to Net Worth 37	6.4	•	•	2.4	1.4	1.4	5.0	3.6	3.4	2.9	3.9	5.1	6.7
Current Assets to Working Capital 38	2.9	•	1.1	1.3	1.4	1.8	1.7	1.9	2.0	2.2	2.0	2.0	3.0
Current Liabilities to Working Capital 39	1.9	•	0.1	0.3	0.4	0.8	0.7	0.9	0.9	1.0	1.2	1.0	2.0
Working Capital to Net Sales 40	1.6	•	1.1	2.8	1.8	1.5	1.6	1.4	1.3	0.6	1.3	2.0	1.7
Inventory to Working Capital 41	0.0	•	0.0	0.0	0.0	0.0	0.0	0.0	0.0	0.0	0.0	0.0	0.0
Total Receipts to Cash Flow 42	2.2	2.2	2.3	1.6	2.8	1.9	2.3	1.7	2.1	2.1	2.4	1.7	2.2
Cost of Goods to Cash Flow 43	0.0	•	•	•	•	•	0.0	•	0.0	0.0	0.0	0.0	0.0
Cash Flow to Total Debt 44	0.1	0.2	0.2	0.2	0.2	0.2	0.2	0.2	0.3	0.6	0.3	0.1	0.1

Selected Financial Factors (in Percentages)

Line Item													
Debt Ratio 45	86.6	113.2	70.2	57.8	87.4	83.3	78.2	77.4	74.3	79.6	83.6	87.1	
Return on Total Assets 46	2.7	6.3	0.9	2.1	3.3	5.3	7.0	8.6	5.8	1.4	6.6	2.4	
Return on Equity Before Income Taxes 47	1.4	•	•	•	6.8	18.9	21.2	9.7	20.4	0.3			
Return on Equity After Income Taxes 48	•	•	•	•	•	5.1	17.8	18.3	7.5	12.7	•		
Profit Margin (Before Income Tax) 49	1.6	2.7	6.0	•	•	3.7	13.2	16.6	9.2	17.4	0.3		
Profit Margin (After Income Tax) 50	•	0.1	5.8	•	•	2.7	12.4	14.4	7.1	10.9	•		

Table II
Corporations with Net Income

CREDIT CARD ISSUING AND OTHER CONSUMER CREDIT

MONEY AMOUNTS AND SIZE OF ASSETS IN THOUSANDS OF DOLLARS

Item Description for Accounting Period 7/10 Through 6/11	Total	Zero Assets	Under 500	500 to 1,000	1,000 to 5,000	5,000 to 10,000	10,000 to 25,000	25,000 to 50,000	50,000 to 100,000	100,000 to 250,000	250,000 to 500,000	500,000 to 2,500,000	2,500,000 and over
Number of Enterprises **1**	3470	391	1074	650	803	125	248	59	38	38	17	16	9
Revenues ($ in Thousands)													
Net Sales **2**	64015776	596356	178876	146767	660859	357435	1487451	898681	964316	1836543	4063141	3794720	49030631
Interest **3**	17778476	321814	1134	3532	45160	24471	9065	27507	136765	382142	87106	1399682	15340098
Rents **4**	20238	6687	0	0	3	134	887	101	72	729	3515	305	7806
Royalties **5**	465983	0	0	0	0	0	0	0	0	9498	0	0	456486
Other Portfolio Income **6**	458249	21496	0	14	1255	16485	1193	1277	9151	61574	3343	13709	328753
Other Receipts **7**	45292830	246359	177742	143221	614441	316345	1476306	869796	818328	1382600	3969177	2381024	32897488
Total Receipts **8**	64015776	596356	178876	146767	660859	357435	1487451	898681	964316	1836543	4063141	3794720	49030631
Average Total Receipts **9**	18448	1525	167	226	823	2859	5998	15232	25377	48330	239008	237170	5447848
Operating Costs/Operating Income (%)													
Cost of Operations **10**	0.2	•	•	•	•	•	0.6	•	•	•	0.1	0.7	0.2
Salaries and Wages **11**	10.3	21.5	22.0	2.8	17.4	11.9	18.1	17.1	20.8	15.3	27.7	13.7	7.5
Taxes Paid **12**	1.3	0.8	0.8	1.4	3.2	3.1	2.3	2.8	2.7	2.3	2.0	2.2	1.0
Interest Paid **13**	10.7	11.3	0.0	4.7	8.5	8.5	9.5	6.6	10.6	7.7	5.0	10.7	11.6
Depreciation **14**	0.7	1.1	0.2	0.4	1.2	0.3	0.6	1.6	2.5	3.1	1.6	1.5	0.5
Amortization and Depletion **15**	1.4	10.4	0.0	•	0.0	0.1	0.6	0.0	0.3	0.5	0.5	2.3	1.5
Pensions and Other Deferred Comp. **16**	0.5	0.2	•	0.0	0.2	0.4	0.4	0.3	0.9	0.4	0.2	0.3	0.6
Employee Benefits **17**	0.8	0.6	0.0	0.0	1.4	1.1	0.9	1.0	1.4	1.3	1.3	1.4	0.7
Advertising **18**	4.7	0.6	5.0	2.4	1.2	0.5	1.7	2.3	1.1	1.9	2.1	0.8	5.6
Other Expenses **19**	57.8	38.7	26.4	64.4	38.3	32.5	38.3	44.6	34.3	41.8	48.9	35.1	63.0
Officers' Compensation **20**	1.0	5.7	9.7	4.0	13.1	10.3	9.2	2.9	3.6	3.1	0.8	0.9	0.2
Operating Margin **21**	10.6	9.3	35.9	20.0	15.4	31.3	17.9	20.7	21.8	22.7	9.8	30.5	7.7
Operating Margin Before Officers' Comp. **22**	11.5	14.9	45.5	23.9	28.5	41.6	27.1	23.7	25.4	25.8	10.7	31.4	7.9

Selected Average Balance Sheet ($ in Thousands)

Net Receivables 23	47821	0	28	117	1807	2568	12834	28548	50551	94056	179656	658003	15568480
Inventories 24	•	•	•	•	•	•	•	•	•	•	•	•	•
Net Property, Plant and Equipment 25	773	0	2	9	35	86	254	2044	1988	3465	11693	12353	205231
Total Assets 26	116300	0	122	692	2399	6291	16471	37541	71353	161598	359999	962985	40398819
Notes and Loans Payable 27	40536	0	12	156	1041	3546	9473	24708	36451	80456	177390	304256	13681593
All Other Liabilities 28	57428	0	4	166	251	675	2891	5595	14087	28710	86154	245412	21201414
Net Worth 29	18336	0	106	371	1107	2071	4107	7238	20815	52433	96455	413318	5515812

Selected Financial Ratios (Times to 1)

Current Ratio 30	1.6	•	17.6	4.9	4.8	1.5	2.8	2.5	2.5	2.6	2.0	2.7	1.5
Quick Ratio 31	1.5	•	11.5	1.3	4.5	0.9	2.6	2.3	2.3	2.3	1.8	2.6	1.4
Net Sales to Working Capital 32	0.8	•	3.5	0.5	0.5	1.6	0.6	0.7	0.7	0.6	1.9	0.5	0.8
Coverage Ratio 33	2.0	1.8	2470.0	5.2	2.8	4.7	2.9	4.1	3.1	4.0	3.0	3.8	1.7
Total Asset Turnover 34	0.2	•	1.4	0.3	0.3	0.5	0.4	0.4	0.4	0.3	0.7	0.2	0.1
Inventory Turnover 35	•	•	•	•	•	•	•	•	•	•	•	•	•
Receivables Turnover 36	•	•	•	•	•	•	•	•	•	•	•	•	•
Total Liabilities to Net Worth 37	5.3	•	0.2	0.9	1.2	2.0	3.0	4.2	2.4	2.1	2.7	1.3	6.3
Current Assets to Working Capital 38	2.7	•	1.1	1.3	1.3	2.9	1.5	1.6	1.7	1.6	2.1	1.6	3.0
Current Liabilities to Working Capital 39	1.7	•	0.1	0.3	0.3	1.9	0.5	0.6	0.7	0.6	1.1	0.6	2.0
Working Capital to Net Sales 40	1.3	•	0.3	2.2	2.1	0.6	1.6	1.3	1.4	1.6	0.5	2.0	1.2
Inventory to Working Capital 41	0.0	•	•	•	•	•	0.0	0.0	•	0.0	0.0	0.0	0.0
Total Receipts to Cash Flow 42	1.5	2.2	1.7	1.3	2.0	1.7	1.9	1.6	1.9	1.7	1.9	1.6	1.4
Cost of Goods to Cash Flow 43	0.0	•	•	•	•	•	•	•	•	•	0.0	0.0	0.0
Cash Flow to Total Debt 44	0.1	•	6.1	0.6	0.3	0.4	0.3	0.3	0.3	0.3	0.5	0.3	0.1

Selected Financial Factors (in Percentages)

Debt Ratio 45	84.2	•	13.2	46.5	53.8	67.1	75.1	80.7	70.8	67.6	73.2	57.1	86.3
Return on Total Assets 46	3.4	•	49.2	8.1	8.2	18.1	10.0	11.1	11.5	9.1	9.8	10.1	2.6
Return on Equity Before Income Taxes 47	10.6	•	56.6	12.2	11.4	43.2	26.1	43.7	26.6	20.9	24.3	17.4	7.5
Return on Equity After Income Taxes 48	7.7	•	56.2	11.6	10.9	37.9	24.7	42.0	23.5	18.4	19.5	12.3	5.0
Profit Margin (Before Income Tax) 49	10.5	9.4	35.9	20.0	15.4	31.3	17.9	20.7	21.8	22.7	9.8	30.3	7.6
Profit Margin (After Income Tax) 50	7.7	6.3	35.6	19.0	14.7	27.4	16.9	20.0	19.3	20.0	21.4	7.9	5.1

FINANCE AND INSURANCE
522292

Table I

Corporations with and without Net Income

REAL ESTATE CREDIT INCL. MORTGAGE BANKERS AND ORIGINATORS

MONEY AMOUNTS AND SIZE OF ASSETS IN THOUSANDS OF DOLLARS

Item Description for Accounting Period 7/10 Through 6/11	Total	Zero Assets	Under 500	500 to 1,000	1,000 to 5,000	5,000 to 10,000	10,000 to 25,000	25,000 to 50,000	50,000 to 100,000	100,000 to 250,000	250,000 to 500,000	500,000 to 2,500,000	2,500,000 and over
Number of Enterprises 1	8683	1821	•	•	979	227	194	116	47	44	16	7	5
Revenues ($ in Thousands)													
Net Sales 2	16816420	520653	•	•	771888	549066	1562371	1857025	1230230	1785863	1264510	1886669	4047177
Interest 3	1960953	1302	•	•	61262	17265	36085	26439	33565	99008	59572	112958	1504038
Rents 4	44830	0	•	•	3711	172	247	2844	252	3320	4654	0	29291
Royalties 5	63	0	•	•	0	0	0	0	0	63	0	0	0
Other Portfolio Income 6	1633477	0	•	•	2712	0	766	77613	5944	124644	3614	970664	445826
Other Receipts 7	13177097	519351	•	•	704203	531629	1525273	1750129	1190469	1558828	1196670	803047	2068022
Total Receipts 8	16816420	520653	•	•	771888	549066	1562371	1857025	1230230	1785863	1264510	1886669	4047177
Average Total Receipts 9	1937	286	•	•	788	2419	8053	16009	26175	40588	79032	269524	809435
Operating Costs/Operating Income (%)													
Cost of Operations 10	0.8	0.5	•	•	•	•	•	•	•	•	2.8	•	2.2
Salaries and Wages 11	27.2	14.2	•	•	34.8	30.0	46.5	36.0	44.8	39.9	32.9	19.0	9.3
Taxes Paid 12	3.1	1.8	•	•	4.7	3.9	5.2	3.3	3.9	4.1	3.3	2.4	1.2
Interest Paid 13	11.7	0.3	•	•	7.4	6.2	5.6	7.6	5.5	12.5	7.7	5.1	27.9
Depreciation 14	1.2	2.1	•	•	1.3	1.8	0.8	0.9	0.9	1.4	0.8	1.8	1.2
Amortization and Depletion 15	0.8	•	•	•	0.3	0.0	0.1	0.3	0.0	0.2	2.7	0.0	2.0
Pensions and Other Deferred Comp. 16	0.3	0.9	•	•	0.1	0.1	0.2	0.6	0.2	0.7	0.4	0.2	0.1
Employee Benefits 17	1.3	0.0	•	•	0.7	1.5	1.2	2.2	1.5	1.5	1.4	1.3	1.0
Advertising 18	2.4	0.1	•	•	10.4	5.6	2.9	2.4	1.8	1.7	1.6	5.9	0.1
Other Expenses 19	49.0	99.2	•	•	44.3	33.6	32.8	36.7	29.5	33.4	40.4	38.9	75.1
Officers' Compensation 20	3.4	0.0	•	•	5.3	7.3	4.4	3.9	3.9	5.9	1.9	0.8	0.2
Operating Margin 21	•	•	•	•	•	10.0	0.2	6.2	8.0	•	4.1	24.6	•
Operating Margin Before Officers' Comp. 22	2.3	•	•	•	•	17.3	4.6	10.1	11.9	4.4	6.0	25.4	•

Selected Average Balance Sheet ($ in Thousands)

Net Receivables 23	1374	0	519	2035	2672	9721	12665	14091	29466	204015	1233628
Inventories 24	•	•	•	•	•	•	•	•	•	•	•
Net Property, Plant and Equipment 25	196	0	297	464	488	994	1766	7624	4454	8688	103681
Total Assets 26	8809	0	2611	7418	14983	33557	69577	157102	314793	914180	8638798
Notes and Loans Payable 27	4351	0	1209	3960	7949	19592	42222	117550	211841	648818	3264510
All Other Liabilities 28	3411	0	324	2548	7312	11121	15456	98700	115768	365439	3297606
Net Worth 29	1047	0	1079	910	-278	2844	11899	-59147	-12816	-100076	2076682

Selected Financial Ratios (Times to 1)

Current Ratio 30	0.7	•	1.2	0.6	0.5	1.2	0.6	0.5	0.3	0.5	0.9
Quick Ratio 31	0.6	•	1.0	0.6	0.4	0.8	0.4	0.4	0.2	0.5	0.9
Net Sales to Working Capital 32	•	•	3.6	•	•	6.4	•	•	•	•	•
Coverage Ratio 33	0.9	•	•	2.6	1.0	1.8	2.4	0.9	1.5	5.8	0.3
Total Asset Turnover 34	0.2	•	0.3	0.3	0.5	0.5	0.4	0.3	0.3	0.3	0.1
Inventory Turnover 35	•	•	•	•	•	•	•	•	•	•	•
Receivables Turnover 36	•	•	•	•	•	•	•	•	•	•	•
Total Liabilities to Net Worth 37	7.4	•	1.4	7.2	7.2	10.8	4.8	7.4	3.2	•	3.2
Current Assets to Working Capital 38	5.4	•	5.4	•	•	7.4	•	•	•	•	•
Current Liabilities to Working Capital 39	4.4	•	4.4	•	•	6.4	•	•	•	•	•
Working Capital to Net Sales 40	•	•	•	•	•	0.2	•	•	•	•	•
Inventory to Working Capital 41	•	•	•	•	•	•	•	•	•	•	•
Total Receipts to Cash Flow 42	2.3	1.5	3.5	2.8	3.6	2.6	3.2	3.8	2.4	1.6	1.9
Cost of Goods to Cash Flow 43	0.0	0.0	•	•	•	•	•	•	0.1	•	0.0
Cash Flow to Total Debt 44	0.1	•	0.1	0.1	0.1	0.2	0.1	0.0	0.1	0.2	0.1

Selected Financial Factors (in Percentages)

Debt Ratio 45	88.1	•	58.7	87.7	101.9	91.5	82.9	137.6	104.1	110.9	76.0
Return on Total Assets 46	2.3	•	3.1	5.3	6.6	5.0	2.8	3.0	•	8.7	0.7
Return on Equity Before Income Taxes 47	•	•	26.6	•	34.9	17.4	•	•	•	•	•
Return on Equity After Income Taxes 48	•	•	22.9	26.5	31.7	16.0	1.5	•	•	•	•
Profit Margin (Before Income Tax) 49	10.0	•	6.2	7.9	•	•	•	•	4.1	•	24.6
Profit Margin (After Income Tax) 50	10.0	•	5.6	7.3	•	•	•	•	3.2	•	24.2

Table II

Corporations with Net Income

REAL ESTATE CREDIT INCL. MORTGAGE BANKERS AND ORIGINATORS

MONEY AMOUNTS AND SIZE OF ASSETS IN THOUSANDS OF DOLLARS

Item Description for Accounting Period 7/10 Through 6/11	Total	Zero Assets	Under 500	500 to 1,000	1,000 to 5,000	5,000 to 10,000	10,000 to 25,000	25,000 to 50,000	50,000 to 100,000	100,000 to 250,000	250,000 to 500,000	500,000 to 2,500,000	2,500,000 and over
Number of Enterprises **1**	4373	8	3147	140	594	186	146	76	37	24	10	7	0
Revenues ($ in Thousands)													
Net Sales **2**	10399561	23550	777847	92730	588941	541024	1166465	1392629	1103839	1532296	909104	2271136	0
Interest **3**	672156	0	5037	2047	2147	11445	19995	20560	20795	29947	16663	543520	0
Rents **4**	5462	0	339	0	3275	66	179	70	252	1284	0	0	0
Royalties **5**	63	0	0	0	0	0	0	0	0	63	0	0	0
Other Portfolio Income **6**	1156485	0	583	0	888	0	759	76809	5057	91908	2614	977867	0
Other Receipts **7**	8565395	23550	771888	90683	582631	529513	1145532	1295190	1077735	1409094	889827	749749	0
Total Receipts **8**	10399561	23550	777847	92730	588941	541024	1166465	1392629	1103839	1532296	909104	2271136	0
Average Total Receipts **9**	2378	2944	247	662	991	2909	7989	18324	29833	63846	90910	324448	•
Operating Costs/Operating Income (%)													
Cost of Operations **10**	•	•	•	•	•	•	•	•	•	•	•	•	•
Salaries and Wages **11**	32.9	34.4	14.2	35.1	35.4	28.4	44.5	38.6	46.8	41.3	36.9	16.0	•
Taxes Paid **12**	3.3	2.3	1.2	4.0	4.3	3.7	4.7	3.7	3.7	3.9	3.7	2.1	•
Interest Paid **13**	8.2	•	0.4	2.4	4.3	4.6	5.7	5.7	5.0	5.5	8.0	19.5	•
Depreciation **14**	0.9	0.6	0.6	0.9	1.4	1.0	0.6	0.8	0.8	1.0	0.5	1.4	•
Amortization and Depletion **15**	0.1	•	0.0	•	0.4	0.0	0.1	0.3	0.0	0.1	0.0	0.0	•
Pensions and Other Deferred Comp. **16**	0.3	20.8	•	1.3	0.1	0.1	0.1	0.7	0.2	0.4	0.5	0.2	•
Employee Benefits **17**	1.2	•	•	•	0.6	1.4	1.3	1.9	1.5	1.3	1.5	1.1	•
Advertising **18**	3.6	•	2.1	0.3	11.2	5.7	3.2	2.8	1.9	1.9	1.9	4.9	•
Other Expenses **19**	27.2	35.1	57.4	30.0	27.3	24.4	23.4	27.8	23.5	21.3	24.3	25.7	•
Officers' Compensation **20**	3.8	•	3.2	23.4	4.8	6.2	4.8	4.1	4.1	6.3	2.4	0.7	•
Operating Margin **21**	18.4	6.8	20.8	2.7	10.2	24.5	11.7	13.6	12.5	17.0	20.4	28.3	•
Operating Margin Before Officers' Comp. **22**	22.2	6.8	24.0	26.0	15.0	30.7	16.4	17.6	16.6	23.3	22.8	29.0	•

Selected Average Balance Sheet ($ in Thousands)

Net Receivables 23	1518	0	0	53	325	2323	2562	10487	14698	9554	10494	565206
Inventories 24	•	•	•	•	•	•	•	•	•	•	•	•
Net Property, Plant and Equipment 25	171	0	7	21	423	397	346	1178	1281	5880	1604	7766
Total Assets 26	8374	0	91	802	2487	7264	15373	34917	71690	152523	313694	2720671
Notes and Loans Payable 27	3091	0	8	54	1092	3039	8328	17043	44006	128715	145217	513079
All Other Liabilities 28	2175	0	2	62	397	2218	3317	9586	16870	131460	131900	362306
Net Worth 29	3108	0	81	685	998	2007	3729	8289	10814	-107652	36578	1845287

Selected Financial Ratios (Times to 1)

Current Ratio 30	0.8	•	5.8	5.9	1.3	0.8	0.7	1.1	0.6	0.3	0.2	1.8
Quick Ratio 31	0.7	•	5.5	4.5	1.0	0.7	0.5	0.8	0.5	0.3	0.1	1.7
Net Sales to Working Capital 32	•	•	6.7	1.3	4.1	•	•	16.1	•	•	•	1.0
Coverage Ratio 33	3.2	•	53.0	2.1	3.4	6.4	3.1	3.4	3.5	4.1	3.5	2.5
Total Asset Turnover 34	0.3	•	2.7	0.8	0.4	0.4	0.5	0.5	0.4	0.4	0.3	0.1
Inventory Turnover 35	•	•	•	•	•	•	•	•	•	•	•	•
Receivables Turnover 36	•	•	•	•	•	•	•	•	•	•	•	•
Total Liabilities to Net Worth 37	1.7	•	0.1	0.2	1.5	3.1	3.1	3.2	5.6	7.6	•	0.5
Current Assets to Working Capital 38	•	•	1.2	1.2	4.2	•	•	16.7	•	•	•	2.2
Current Liabilities to Working Capital 39	•	•	0.2	0.2	3.2	•	•	15.7	•	•	•	1.2
Working Capital to Net Sales 40	•	•	0.1	0.8	0.2	•	•	0.1	•	•	•	1.0
Inventory to Working Capital 41	•	•	•	•	•	•	•	•	•	•	•	•
Total Receipts to Cash Flow 42	2.4	2.8	1.4	4.2	3.1	2.3	3.2	2.8	3.1	2.8	2.4	1.9
Cost of Goods to Cash Flow 43	•	•	•	•	•	•	•	•	•	•	•	•
Cash Flow to Total Debt 44	0.2	•	17.3	1.4	0.2	0.2	0.2	0.2	0.2	0.1	0.1	0.2

Selected Financial Factors (in Percentages)

Debt Ratio 45	62.9	•	10.9	14.5	59.9	72.4	75.7	76.3	84.9	170.6	88.3	32.2
Return on Total Assets 46	7.5	•	57.6	4.2	5.7	11.6	9.0	10.1	7.3	9.4	8.2	5.7
Return on Equity Before Income Taxes 47	14.0	•	63.5	2.6	10.1	35.5	25.0	29.9	34.6	50.6	•	5.0
Return on Equity After Income Taxes 48	13.2	•	63.3	2.3	9.5	35.4	22.3	28.3	32.6	47.6	•	4.6
Profit Margin (Before Income Tax) 49	18.4	6.8	20.8	2.7	10.2	24.5	11.7	13.5	12.5	20.4	•	28.3
Profit Margin (After Income Tax) 50	17.3	4.5	20.8	2.4	9.6	24.5	10.4	12.8	11.8	16.2	19.1	26.1

Table I

Corporations with and without Net Income

INTL. TRADE, SECONDARY FINANCING, OTHER NONDEPOSITORY CREDIT

MONEY AMOUNTS AND SIZE OF ASSETS IN THOUSANDS OF DOLLARS

Item Description for Accounting Period 7/10 Through 6/11		Total	Zero Assets	Under 500	500 to 1,000	1,000 to 5,000	5,000 to 10,000	10,000 to 25,000	25,000 to 50,000	50,000 to 100,000	100,000 to 250,000	250,000 to 500,000	500,000 to 2,500,000	2,500,000 and over
Number of Enterprises	1	6790	1821	2751	746	909	280	113	54	30	21	12	26	25
Revenues ($ in Thousands)														
Net Sales	2	169592527	220800	559350	352124	424731	614072	575372	404054	291582	423120	445934	2445303	162836085
Interest	3	157297812	109154	289	23538	71487	5662	11133	47537	55148	159880	73610	1102820	155637553
Rents	4	52482	3640	0	0	801	0	0	57	345	8	1380	6706	39545
Royalties	5	8029	0	0	54	0	0	0	209	0	5	0	7759	2
Other Portfolio Income	6	3650411	1220	2	368	2129	1052	3197	357	659	1618	202	32734	3606873
Other Receipts	7	8583793	106786	559059	328164	350314	607358	561042	355894	235430	261609	370742	1295284	3552112
Total Receipts	8	169592527	220800	559350	352124	424731	614072	575372	404054	291582	423120	445934	2445303	162836085
Average Total Receipts	9	24977	121	203	472	467	2193	5092	7482	9719	20149	37161	94050	6513443
Operating Costs/Operating Income (%)														
Cost of Operations	10	0.0	•	•	•	1.4	•	8.9	•	•	•	•	0.2	•
Salaries and Wages	11	2.0	5.6	34.8	11.0	22.9	27.2	24.5	19.2	15.7	14.9	6.8	15.2	1.3
Taxes Paid	12	0.2	3.1	5.4	4.8	4.7	3.8	3.4	2.6	1.9	2.1	2.8	2.3	0.1
Interest Paid	13	67.4	43.0	0.0	3.7	6.1	7.7	7.0	12.2	18.9	17.5	25.2	16.2	69.6
Depreciation	14	0.3	0.4	1.5	6.3	1.1	2.0	5.2	1.4	0.9	1.4	2.4	3.5	0.2
Amortization and Depletion	15	0.8	1.7	0.3	0.2	2.7	0.1	0.9	0.4	0.7	0.7	0.8	2.4	0.8
Pensions and Other Deferred Comp.	16	0.1	0.1	•	2.5	0.2	0.4	0.2	0.5	0.6	0.4	0.2	0.2	0.1
Employee Benefits	17	0.3	0.1	0.7	0.8	3.3	2.6	1.5	0.5	0.7	1.3	1.0	0.9	0.2
Advertising	18	0.2	0.3	15.9	1.8	2.3	5.3	2.3	1.5	0.5	0.6	0.6	3.1	0.0
Other Expenses	19	54.0	44.1	33.4	29.1	49.8	41.6	30.5	31.4	44.0	37.9	45.5	44.8	54.5
Officers' Compensation	20	0.3	7.9	12.1	15.5	5.8	4.0	9.0	4.4	6.6	2.8	0.9	1.8	0.1
Operating Margin	21	•	•	•	24.2	•	5.3	6.7	25.9	9.6	19.6	13.9	9.5	•
Operating Margin Before Officers' Comp.	22	•	1.7	8.0	39.7	5.5	9.3	15.7	30.3	16.2	22.4	14.8	11.2	•

Selected Average Balance Sheet ($ in Thousands)

Net Receivables 23	22812	0	33	208	598	3390	6160	18866	45251	110845	162701	636655	5169961
Inventories 24	•	•	•	•	•	•	•	•	•	•	•	•	•
Net Property, Plant and Equipment 25	572	0	35	148	161	487	1532	612	619	2218	5297	13143	108722
Total Assets 26	865037	0	135	670	1696	6965	16279	35341	74582	157121	358323	1178527	233000485
Notes and Loans Payable 27	850691	0	60	262	1653	3954	14220	15496	38314	91564	280478	696842	229848917
All Other Liabilities 28	11931	0	3	57	241	788	1374	6145	15892	34888	40932	189210	2936556
Net Worth 29	2415	0	72	351	-199	2223	685	13700	20376	30669	36912	292475	215012

Selected Financial Ratios (Times to 1)

Current Ratio 30	0.7	•	29.5	5.0	1.4	2.9	1.4	1.7	2.1	1.5	1.0	1.7	0.7
Quick Ratio 31	0.6	•	16.0	3.9	1.1	2.5	1.0	1.3	1.7	1.3	0.6	1.3	0.6
Net Sales to Working Capital 32	•	•	2.2	1.2	1.7	0.6	1.6	0.7	0.3	0.5	•	0.3	•
Coverage Ratio 33	0.6	0.9	•	7.5	1.0	1.7	2.0	3.1	1.5	2.1	1.6	1.6	0.6
Total Asset Turnover 34	0.0	•	1.5	0.7	•	0.3	0.3	0.2	0.1	0.1	0.1	0.1	0.0
Inventory Turnover 35	•	•	•	•	•	•	•	•	•	•	•	•	•
Receivables Turnover 36	•	•	•	•	•	•	•	•	•	•	•	•	•
Total Liabilities to Net Worth 37	357.2	•	0.9	•	2.1	22.8	2.1	1.6	2.7	4.1	8.7	3.0	1082.7
Current Assets to Working Capital 38	•	•	1.0	1.3	3.8	1.5	3.6	2.5	1.9	3.1	2.5	2.5	•
Current Liabilities to Working Capital 39	•	•	0.0	0.3	2.8	0.5	2.6	1.5	0.9	2.1	1.5	1.5	•
Working Capital to Net Sales 40	•	•	0.5	0.8	0.6	1.7	0.6	1.4	3.3	2.1	3.5	•	•
Inventory to Working Capital 41	•	•	•	•	0.0	0.0	0.0	•	•	0.0	0.0	•	•
Total Receipts to Cash Flow 42	3.6	3.1	4.7	2.2	2.6	2.5	3.3	1.9	2.0	1.8	2.0	3.7	•
Cost of Goods to Cash Flow 43	0.0	•	•	•	0.0	0.3	•	•	•	0.0	0.0	•	•
Cash Flow to Total Debt 44	0.0	•	0.7	0.7	0.1	0.2	0.1	0.2	0.1	0.1	0.1	0.0	0.0

Selected Financial Factors (in Percentages)

Debt Ratio 45	99.7	•	46.7	47.6	111.7	68.1	95.8	61.2	72.7	80.5	89.7	75.2	99.9
Return on Total Assets 46	1.2	•	•	19.6	1.6	4.1	4.3	8.1	3.7	4.8	4.1	2.1	1.2
Return on Equity Before Income Taxes 47	•	•	•	32.5	0.6	5.2	5.2	14.2	4.5	12.9	14.0	3.1	•
Return on Equity After Income Taxes 48	•	•	•	31.5	•	4.2	5.2	11.9	3.5	9.3	7.2	1.7	•
Profit Margin (Before Income Tax) 49	•	•	•	24.2	5.3	6.7	•	25.9	9.5	19.6	13.9	9.6	•
Profit Margin (After Income Tax) 50	•	•	•	23.4	5.3	6.3	•	21.7	7.3	14.2	7.1	5.1	•

Table II

Corporations with Net Income

INTL. TRADE, SECONDARY FINANCING, OTHER NONDEPOSITORY CREDIT

MONEY AMOUNTS AND SIZE OF ASSETS IN THOUSANDS OF DOLLARS

Item Description for Accounting Period 7/10 Through 6/11	Total	Zero Assets	Under 500	500 to 1,000	1,000 to 5,000	5,000 to 10,000	10,000 to 25,000	25,000 to 50,000	50,000 to 100,000	100,000 to 250,000	250,000 to 500,000	500,000 to 2,500,000	2,500,000 and over
Number of Enterprises 1	3952	793	1781	•	458	147	68	51	20	17	7	20	•
Revenues ($ in Thousands)													
Net Sales 2	12757288	223335	336085	•	343672	528472	400112	393555	171280	389870	324835	2138623	•
Interest 3	7827141	108629	204	•	66891	3063	6227	37644	34802	144287	29585	930262	•
Rents 4	50900	3640	0	•	801	0	0	12	164	8	980	6706	•
Royalties 5	7807	0	0	•	0	0	0	43	0	5	0	7759	•
Other Portfolio Income 6	55380	1220	0	•	538	101	0	129	485	1618	196	32639	•
Other Receipts 7	4816060	109846	335881	•	275442	525308	393885	355727	135829	243952	294074	1161257	•
Total Receipts 8	12757288	223335	336085	•	343672	528472	400112	393555	171280	389870	324835	2138623	•
Average Total Receipts 9	3228	282	189	•	750	3595	5884	7717	8564	22934	46405	106931	•
Operating Costs/Operating Income (%)													
Cost of Operations 10	0.1	•	•	•	1.8	•	•	•	•	•	•	0.3	•
Salaries and Wages 11	11.0	4.0	33.1	•	22.4	25.9	21.9	19.6	14.9	15.4	9.1	15.8	•
Taxes Paid 12	1.8	2.5	6.9	•	4.5	4.0	3.3	2.5	1.7	2.0	3.8	2.4	•
Interest Paid 13	27.6	42.2	0.1	•	2.5	7.0	5.1	12.0	12.6	15.9	5.5	11.1	•
Depreciation 14	1.7	0.3	1.2	•	0.8	1.9	1.6	1.4	0.6	1.5	3.2	4.0	•
Amortization and Depletion 15	1.0	1.0	0.2	•	0.2	0.1	0.2	0.4	0.3	0.7	1.1	2.4	•
Pensions and Other Deferred Comp. 16	0.5	0.1	•	•	0.2	0.5	0.3	0.5	0.7	0.4	0.2	0.2	•
Employee Benefits 17	1.0	•	0.7	•	3.1	2.7	1.6	0.5	0.8	1.3	1.3	0.9	•
Advertising 18	1.3	•	2.9	•	2.2	5.3	2.5	1.5	0.7	1.4	0.9	3.5	•
Other Expenses 19	30.8	21.3	28.2	•	36.0	27.7	28.4	28.6	34.2	35.8	45.1	37.5	•
Officers' Compensation 20	2.8	7.8	14.7	•	5.6	3.4	11.2	4.2	8.4	2.6	1.2	1.7	•
Operating Margin 21	20.2	20.8	11.9	•	20.8	21.5	23.9	28.8	25.1	22.8	28.6	20.1	•
Operating Margin Before Officers' Comp. 22	23.1	28.6	26.7	•	26.4	25.0	35.1	33.0	33.5	25.5	29.8	21.8	•

Selected Average Balance Sheet ($ in Thousands)

Net Receivables 23	23445	0	•	819	4916	8628	18496	49202	110840	190257	734643
Inventories 24	•	•	•	•	•	•	•	•	•	•	•
Net Property, Plant and Equipment 25	288	0	•	122	515	443	646	404	1903	8971	16959
Total Assets 26	72661	189	•	1691	7792	15750	34680	73774	163148	342362	1143156
Notes and Loans Payable 27	64137	52	•	1653	4062	9007	15524	35094	100490	173422	519999
All Other Liabilities 28	3270	4	•	237	1236	1125	6480	18172	26940	50762	199586
Net Worth 29	5254	133	•	-199	2495	5619	12676	20508	35718	118178	423570

Selected Financial Ratios (Times to 1)

Current Ratio 30	2.1	36.9	•	7.1	2.2	2.1	1.6	1.8	1.7	1.2	2.1
Quick Ratio 31	2.0	19.3	•	5.3	2.0	1.6	1.2	1.5	1.5	0.9	2.1
Net Sales to Working Capital 32	0.2	1.4	•	0.6	1.0	0.9	0.7	0.3	0.4	1.2	0.3
Coverage Ratio 33	1.7	202.6	1.5	9.4	4.1	5.7	3.4	3.0	2.4	6.2	2.8
Total Asset Turnover 34	0.0	1.0	•	0.4	0.5	0.4	0.2	0.1	0.1	0.1	0.1
Inventory Turnover 35	•	•	•	•	•	•	•	•	•	•	•
Receivables Turnover 36	•	•	•	•	•	•	•	•	•	•	•
Total Liabilities to Net Worth 37	12.8	0.4	•	•	2.1	1.8	1.7	2.6	3.6	1.9	1.7
Current Assets to Working Capital 38	1.9	1.0	•	1.2	1.8	1.9	2.5	2.2	2.5	6.6	1.9
Current Liabilities to Working Capital 39	0.9	0.0	•	0.2	0.8	0.9	1.5	1.2	1.5	5.6	0.9
Working Capital to Net Sales 40	5.3	0.7	•	1.8	1.0	1.2	1.3	3.3	2.3	0.8	3.9
Inventory to Working Capital 41	0.0	•	•	0.0	0.0	0.0	0.0	0.0	0.1	0.1	0.0
Total Receipts to Cash Flow 42	2.1	2.6	•	2.2	2.4	2.2	1.9	1.8	1.8	1.5	1.9
Cost of Goods to Cash Flow 43	0.0	•	•	0.0	•	•	•	•	•	•	0.0
Cash Flow to Total Debt 44	0.0	1.0	•	0.2	0.3	0.2	0.1	0.1	0.1	0.1	0.1

Selected Financial Factors (in Percentages)

Debt Ratio 45	92.8	29.5	•	111.8	68.0	64.3	63.4	72.2	78.1	65.5	62.9
Return on Total Assets 46	2.1	•	•	10.3	13.2	10.8	9.1	4.4	5.4	4.6	2.9
Return on Equity Before Income Taxes 47	12.5	16.9	•	•	31.0	25.1	17.5	10.4	14.7	11.2	5.1
Return on Equity After Income Taxes 48	9.3	14.9	•	•	31.0	24.5	14.9	8.9	10.9	7.6	3.8
Profit Margin (Before Income Tax) 49	20.3	11.9	20.8	20.8	21.5	23.9	28.8	25.0	22.8	28.6	20.3
Profit Margin (After Income Tax) 50	15.1	10.5	18.5	18.9	21.5	23.4	24.5	21.2	17.1	19.3	15.2

Table I

Corporations with and without Net Income

ACTIVITIES RELATED TO CREDIT INTERMEDIATION

MONEY AMOUNTS AND SIZE OF ASSETS IN THOUSANDS OF DOLLARS

Item Description for Accounting Period 7/10 Through 6/11		Total	Zero Assets	Under 500	500 to 1,000	1,000 to 5,000	5,000 to 10,000	10,000 to 25,000	25,000 to 50,000	50,000 to 100,000	100,000 to 250,000	250,000 to 500,000	500,000 to 2,500,000	2,500,000 and over
Number of Enterprises	1	17142	4127	10518	1102	844	268	107	69	43	22	15	16	11
Revenues ($ in Thousands)														
Net Sales	2	46564879	397209	2236358	289635	1088196	898904	957935	1085298	1262177	1633616	2069611	4640119	30005821
Interest	3	2086900	17	2504	326	16524	9403	25636	5793	18776	11106	45965	248884	1701964
Rents	4	140006	0	548	0	101	0	1221	118	1096	891	16	1929	134084
Royalties	5	265348	0	0	0	0	0	0	0	206	0	0	0	265142
Other Portfolio Income	6	776687	0	1284	0	526	388	7454	621	5665	491	154646	14389	591222
Other Receipts	7	43295938	397192	2232022	289309	1071045	889113	923624	1078766	1236434	1621128	1868984	4374917	27313409
Total Receipts	8	46564879	397209	2236358	289635	1088196	898904	957935	1085298	1262177	1633616	2069611	4640119	30005821
Average Total Receipts	9	2716	96	213	263	1289	3354	8953	15729	29353	74255	137974	290007	2727802
Operating Costs/Operating Income (%)														
Cost of Operations	10	2.8	1.7	0.0	•	•	•	6.6	11.9	1.2	6.7	23.5	0.3	1.6
Salaries and Wages	11	17.5	19.1	17.4	20.1	20.1	29.8	27.6	35.1	25.0	23.2	19.3	21.2	14.7
Taxes Paid	12	2.4	3.1	3.7	3.6	4.1	3.6	3.5	3.6	2.5	2.7	1.8	2.2	2.1
Interest Paid	13	7.3	0.4	0.7	6.3	3.4	1.7	3.5	5.2	4.3	2.7	4.8	7.5	8.9
Depreciation	14	2.5	1.5	1.4	1.9	1.2	1.7	1.6	4.4	2.1	3.1	4.0	3.5	2.4
Amortization and Depletion	15	2.1	0.5	0.3	3.5	0.5	0.1	1.9	0.4	2.2	1.2	5.6	5.6	1.7
Pensions and Other Defered Comp.	16	0.6	•	0.5	•	0.1	0.4	0.1	0.7	0.3	0.6	0.1	0.6	0.7
Employee Benefits	17	2.0	0.8	1.7	1.8	6.1	1.4	0.9	2.1	1.2	2.3	1.2	2.0	2.0
Advertising	18	4.3	1.8	3.1	2.3	2.2	2.6	14.3	3.4	0.8	2.2	4.5	3.1	4.7
Other Expenses	19	42.7	73.5	43.2	63.1	39.4	43.6	37.9	38.9	50.2	41.3	22.4	42.9	43.6
Officers' Compensation	20	2.0	0.6	17.6	9.0	6.6	2.7	5.0	4.9	2.5	1.4	2.0	1.7	0.4
Operating Margin	21	13.8	10.5	10.5	•	16.2	12.5	•	•	7.6	12.6	10.8	9.4	17.0
Operating Margin Before Officers' Comp.	22	15.7	28.1	28.1	•	22.8	15.1	1.9	•	10.1	14.0	12.9	11.2	17.5

Selected Average Balance Sheet ($ in Thousands)

Net Receivables 23	1092	0	2	3	230	1428	3265	12052	8902	42766	91108	304027	853741
Inventories 24	•	•	•	•	•	•	•	•	•	•	•	•	•
Net Property, Plant and Equipment 25	275	0	18	248	133	493	351	1394	2633	9441	13913	42593	241851
Total Assets 26	9464	0	87	693	1918	6758	15293	35429	69206	146413	357498	962100	11461958
Notes and Loans Payable 27	3970	0	34	461	1134	4415	6674	21704	28411	38670	100426	320140	4920864
All Other Liabilities 28	3018	0	27	49	452	2146	4110	8386	39558	48268	149235	402534	3453383
Net Worth 29	2475	0	26	183	333	197	4509	5339	1238	59475	107837	239426	3087710

Selected Financial Ratios (Times to 1)

Current Ratio 30	1.3	1.6	1.4	1.8	1.2	1.3	1.0	0.8	1.6	1.1	1.8	1.2
Quick Ratio 31	0.8	1.4	1.0	1.3	1.0	0.8	0.9	0.7	1.4	1.0	1.7	0.7
Net Sales to Working Capital 32	4.0	13.4	4.9	2.0	8.6	4.8	•	•	2.2	6.6	1.4	4.6
Coverage Ratio 33	3.1	16.3	•	5.7	8.4	0.1	•	2.8	5.7	4.1	2.4	3.2
Total Asset Turnover 34	0.3	2.4	0.4	0.7	0.5	0.6	0.4	0.4	0.5	0.4	0.3	0.2
Inventory Turnover 35	•	•	•	•	•	•	•	•	•	•	•	•
Receivables Turnover 36	•	•	•	•	•	•	•	•	•	•	•	•
Total Liabilities to Net Worth 37	2.8	2.3	2.8	4.8	33.3	2.4	5.6	54.9	1.5	2.3	3.0	2.7
Current Assets to Working Capital 38	4.9	2.8	3.8	2.3	7.0	4.2	•	•	2.6	7.9	2.2	5.9
Current Liabilities to Working Capital 39	3.9	1.8	2.8	1.3	6.0	3.2	•	•	1.6	6.9	1.2	4.9
Working Capital to Net Sales 40	0.3	0.1	0.2	0.5	0.1	0.2	•	•	0.4	0.2	0.7	0.2
Inventory to Working Capital 41	0.0	•	•	•	0.0	0.0	•	•	0.0	0.0	0.0	0.0
Total Receipts to Cash Flow 42	1.9	2.2	3.6	2.0	2.0	3.3	4.3	1.8	2.1	3.3	2.3	1.7
Cost of Goods to Cash Flow 43	0.1	0.0	•	•	•	0.2	0.5	0.0	0.1	0.8	0.0	0.0
Cash Flow to Total Debt 44	0.2	1.6	0.1	0.4	0.3	0.3	0.1	0.2	0.4	0.2	0.0	0.2

Selected Financial Factors (in Percentages)

Debt Ratio 45	73.8	70.1	73.6	82.7	97.1	70.5	84.9	98.2	59.4	69.8	75.1	73.1
Return on Total Assets 46	6.6	27.2	•	13.2	7.0	0.2	•	5.0	7.8	7.5	5.5	6.8
Return on Equity Before Income Taxes 47	17.2	85.5	•	62.8	212.2	•	•	179.7	15.7	18.7	13.1	17.3
Return on Equity After Income Taxes 48	11.1	84.5	•	62.1	208.3	•	•	147.1	11.5	12.4	7.9	10.8
Profit Margin (Before Income Tax) 49	15.7	10.5	•	16.2	12.4	•	•	7.6	12.6	14.6	10.8	19.6
Profit Margin (After Income Tax) 50	10.1	10.3	•	16.0	12.2	•	•	6.2	9.2	9.7	6.5	12.3

Table II
Corporations with Net Income

ACTIVITIES RELATED TO CREDIT INTERMEDIATION

MONEY AMOUNTS AND SIZE OF ASSETS IN THOUSANDS OF DOLLARS

Item Description for Accounting Period 7/10 Through 6/11	Total	Zero Assets	Under 500	500 to 1,000	1,000 to 5,000	5,000 to 10,000	10,000 to 25,000	25,000 to 50,000	50,000 to 100,000	100,000 to 250,000	250,000 to 500,000	500,000 to 2,500,000	2,500,000 and over
Number of Enterprises **1**	8604	1850	5325	•	592	104	60	35	32	16	10	10	•
Revenues ($ in Thousands)													
Net Sales **2**	36833529	163851	1699058	•	840178	736130	486107	751644	1026311	1338920	1202032	3488979	•
Interest **3**	1902700	17	2472	•	4569	8458	11731	4427	17360	5893	16365	148501	•
Rents **4**	11583	0	548	•	0	0	1206	118	1096	781	16	0	•
Royalties **5**	264777	0	0	•	0	0	0	0	0	0	0	0	•
Other Portfolio Income **6**	682940	0	0	•	519	203	5898	422	5274	55	151145	14375	•
Other Receipts **7**	33971529	163834	1696038	•	835090	727469	467272	746677	1002581	1332191	1034506	3326103	•
Total Receipts **8**	36833529	163851	1699058	•	840178	736130	486107	751644	1026311	1338920	1202032	3488979	•
Average Total Receipts **9**	4281	89	319	•	1419	7078	8102	21476	32072	83682	120203	348898	•
Operating Costs/Operating Income (%)													
Cost of Operations **10**	0.5	0.9	0.0	•	•	•	13.0	4.1	1.5	0.8	2.5	0.2	•
Salaries and Wages **11**	16.2	17.4	12.7	•	14.9	29.6	29.3	34.9	22.2	25.3	25.4	19.0	•
Taxes Paid **12**	2.5	3.3	2.8	•	3.4	2.9	4.3	3.9	2.5	2.8	2.1	1.8	•
Interest Paid **13**	4.1	0.0	0.7	•	1.8	0.2	3.7	3.8	4.4	2.6	4.4	6.3	•
Depreciation **14**	2.3	2.6	1.1	•	0.8	0.7	1.8	0.9	2.1	3.0	5.3	3.2	•
Amortization and Depletion **15**	1.4	1.3	0.4	•	0.3	0.0	0.5	0.2	2.0	1.1	4.0	5.4	•
Pensions and Other Deferred Comp. **16**	0.6	•	0.5	•	0.1	0.4	0.2	0.8	0.3	0.4	0.1	0.8	•
Employee Benefits **17**	1.3	1.2	1.2	•	0.5	1.2	1.5	0.8	1.3	1.8	0.9	1.7	•
Advertising **18**	4.6	0.6	2.6	•	1.1	3.1	0.5	4.7	0.8	2.6	2.2	3.2	•
Other Expenses **19**	43.0	57.7	41.7	•	41.7	34.7	27.5	26.7	47.0	42.0	27.6	41.3	•
Officers' Compensation **20**	1.9	0.3	17.1	•	7.8	2.2	8.1	6.0	2.6	0.5	2.9	1.8	•
Operating Margin **21**	21.5	14.7	19.1	•	27.6	24.8	9.6	13.2	13.3	17.1	22.7	15.4	•
Operating Margin Before Officers' Comp. **22**	23.4	15.0	36.2	•	35.4	27.0	17.7	19.2	15.9	17.6	25.6	17.2	•

Selected Average Balance Sheet ($ in Thousands)

	1	2	3	4	5	6	7	8	9	10	11
Net Receivables 23	1793	0	0	326	2390	3614	13506	9793	45231	86790	393532
Inventories 24	•	•	•	•	•	•	•	•	•	•	•
Net Property, Plant and Equipment 25	377	0	28	137	374	352	856	2896	9388	18139	41620
Total Assets 26	13009	0	106	1950	6245	14703	38523	69286	146516	360259	1045637
Notes and Loans Payable 27	4238	0	33	935	5449	7176	17897	28951	48526	75795	347325
All Other Liabilities 28	4046	0	24	422	2347	4134	10090	20994	52790	161361	415352
Net Worth 29	4725	0	49	593	-1551	3393	10536	19340	45200	123103	282960

Selected Financial Ratios (Times to 1)

	1	2	3	4	5	6	7	8	9	10	11
Current Ratio 30	1.3	•	2.7	2.1	2.2	1.1	1.1	0.8	1.4	1.2	2.0
Quick Ratio 31	0.9	•	2.5	1.9	1.8	0.9	0.8	0.7	1.3	1.0	1.9
Net Sales to Working Capital 32	3.4	•	11.3	1.8	2.5	10.4	13.0	•	3.1	4.7	1.3
Coverage Ratio 33	6.7	6023.8	26.8	15.9	133.4	4.4	3.6	4.0	7.4	7.7	3.7
Total Asset Turnover 34	0.3	•	3.0	0.7	1.1	0.6	0.6	0.5	0.6	0.3	0.3
Inventory Turnover 35	•	•	•	•	•	•	•	•	•	•	•
Receivables Turnover 36	•	•	•	•	•	•	•	•	•	•	•
Total Liabilities to Net Worth 37	1.8	•	1.2	2.3	3.3	2.7	2.6	•	2.2	1.9	2.7
Current Assets to Working Capital 38	4.3	•	1.6	1.9	1.8	11.4	12.5	•	3.4	6.4	2.0
Current Liabilities to Working Capital 39	3.3	•	0.6	0.9	0.8	10.4	11.5	•	2.4	5.4	1.0
Working Capital to Net Sales 40	0.3	•	0.1	0.6	0.4	0.1	0.1	•	0.3	0.2	0.8
Inventory to Working Capital 41	0.0	•	0.0	0.0	0.0	0.0	0.0	•	0.0	0.0	0.0
Total Receipts to Cash Flow 42	1.6	1.8	1.6	1.5	3.1	2.7	1.7	•	1.9	2.1	2.0
Cost of Goods to Cash Flow 43	0.0	0.0	•	0.0	0.4	0.1	0.0	•	0.0	0.1	0.0
Cash Flow to Total Debt 44	0.3	•	3.1	0.7	0.5	0.2	0.3	•	0.4	0.4	0.2

Selected Financial Factors (in Percentages)

	1	2	3	4	5	6	7	8	9	10	11
Debt Ratio 45	63.7	•	53.8	69.6	124.8	76.9	72.6	72.1	69.2	65.8	72.9
Return on Total Assets 46	9.0	•	59.5	21.4	28.3	7.3	9.5	8.2	11.3	11.2	7.8
Return on Equity Before Income Taxes 47	21.2	•	124.1	66.1	•	22.8	26.7	22.0	31.6	28.6	21.2
Return on Equity After Income Taxes 48	14.8	•	123.0	65.5	•	18.8	24.0	19.2	24.0	20.2	14.2
Profit Margin (Before Income Tax) 49	23.4	14.7	19.1	27.6	24.8	13.1	13.3	17.1	29.3	20.2	17.2
Profit Margin (After Income Tax) 50	16.3	14.5	18.9	27.4	24.5	11.8	11.6	12.9	20.7	•	11.5

Table I

Corporations with and without Net Income

INVESTMENT BANKING AND SECURITIES DEALING

MONEY AMOUNTS AND SIZE OF ASSETS IN THOUSANDS OF DOLLARS

Item Description for Accounting Period 7/10 Through 6/11		Total	Zero Assets	Under 500	500 to 1,000	1,000 to 5,000	5,000 to 10,000	10,000 to 25,000	25,000 to 50,000	50,000 to 100,000	100,000 to 250,000	250,000 to 500,000	500,000 to 2,500,000	2,500,000 and over
Number of Enterprises	1	3793	957	2008	453	204	28	45	35	17	13	3	17	14
Revenues ($ in Thousands)														
Net Sales	2	103815596	939004	265452	44418	284659	46812	199813	377808	443520	239223	446564	1869942	98658382
Interest	3	37417001	305346	1214	432	8586	2327	7243	7456	622	50667	28680	309306	36695121
Rents	4	230263	0	0	0	5061	0	0	6	0	3	0	7033	218160
Royalties	5	64316	21	0	3116	125	0	0	0	0	8279	0	2779	49996
Other Portfolio Income	6	5180699	191866	2628	9729	7597	2255	9399	16370	8423	38990	3098	245397	4644947
Other Receipts	7	60923317	441771	261610	31141	263290	42230	183171	353976	434475	141284	414786	1305427	57050158
Total Receipts	8	103815596	939004	265452	44418	284659	46812	199813	377808	443520	239223	446564	1869942	98658382
Average Total Receipts	9	27370	981	132	98	1395	1672	4440	10795	26089	18402	148855	109997	7047027
Operating Costs/Operating Income (%)														
Cost of Operations	10	10.7	1.3	•	•	•	•	•	•	•	•	•	1.1	11.2
Salaries and Wages	11	23.6	10.5	6.5	24.3	6.6	18.9	10.0	34.8	49.8	24.5	37.8	33.6	23.4
Taxes Paid	12	1.6	3.2	3.4	3.4	3.2	3.6	2.6	3.2	2.9	3.8	2.9	3.6	1.5
Interest Paid	13	27.3	9.9	15.6	•	4.6	7.1	2.2	1.9	0.5	11.7	0.5	14.4	28.2
Depreciation	14	1.1	0.2	0.5	0.9	0.2	2.6	0.2	0.9	0.9	1.4	2.2	1.6	1.1
Amortization and Depletion	15	0.6	•	0.6	•	•	•	1.4	0.3	0.1	0.6	0.5	3.7	0.6
Pensions and Other Deferred Comp.	16	0.6	0.4	1.6	•	0.1	0.8	0.2	0.4	1.0	0.5	0.1	4.0	0.5
Employee Benefits	17	0.6	0.3	0.5	2.9	1.8	2.7	0.9	1.1	0.9	1.4	1.6	1.7	0.6
Advertising	18	0.2	0.0	3.7	•	0.1	0.2	0.1	1.2	0.3	0.3	6.2	0.1	0.1
Other Expenses	19	25.8	32.8	38.6	104.2	56.4	25.7	35.9	74.1	34.3	37.7	39.6	63.9	24.5
Officers' Compensation	20	1.1	6.4	23.6	6.1	6.2	80.9	16.5	1.6	9.2	5.5	2.4	2.4	0.8
Operating Margin	21	6.9	35.1	5.5	•	20.9	•	30.1	•	0.1	12.6	6.1	•	7.5
Operating Margin Before Officers' Comp.	22	8.0	41.4	29.0	•	27.1	38.3	46.5	•	9.3	18.1	8.5	•	8.3

Selected Average Balance Sheet ($ in Thousands)

Line Item	Values
Net Receivables **23**	222062, •, 0, 0, 4, •, 29, 2536, 585, 4018, 8226, 22225, 113312, 254828, 59780934
Inventories **24**	•, •, •, •, •, •, •, •, •, •, •, •, •, •, •
Net Property, Plant and Equipment **25**	2332, 0, 78, 0, 3, 40, 80, 75, 379, 568, 1549, 4257, 15826, •, 607435
Total Assets **26**	994614, 78, 713, 2330, 7160, 16008, 37188, 70065, 160527, 346443, 999041, 267720858
Notes and Loans Payable **27**	188357, 20, 237, 352, 3092, 1856, 7726, 9922, 46485, 6235, 95442, 50811689
All Other Liabilities **28**	701164, 11, 7, 216, 738, 3031, 6340, 10882, 39194, 93003, 604982, 189129189
Net Worth **29**	105093, 46, 469, 1762, 3330, 11121, 23122, 49260, 74848, 247205, 298617, 27779980

Selected Financial Ratios (Times to 1)

Line Item	Values
Current Ratio **30**	1.1, 1.5, •, 51.2, 2.3, 3.2, 2.7, 1.5, 1.2, 3.2, 1.1
Quick Ratio **31**	0.6, 1.1, 9.7, 1.5, 1.9, 2.9, 1.1, 0.7, 0.8, 0.6
Net Sales to Working Capital **32**	0.8, 9.6, 0.3, 3.8, 0.9, 1.0, 2.9, 1.4, 0.8, 1.1, 0.8
Coverage Ratio **33**	1.6, 1.3, 4.5, 5.5, 13.9, •, 1.8, 12.2, 1.6
Total Asset Turnover **34**	0.0, 1.7, •, 0.1, 0.6, 0.3, 0.3, 0.4, 0.1, 0.4, 0.1, 0.0
Inventory Turnover **35**	•, •, •, •, •, •, •, •, •, •, •
Receivables Turnover **36**	•, •, •, •, •, •, •, •, •, •, •
Total Liabilities to Net Worth **37**	8.5, 0.7, 0.5, 0.3, 1.2, 0.4, 0.6, 0.4, 1.1, 0.4, 2.3, 8.6
Current Assets to Working Capital **38**	17.5, 3.0, 1.0, 1.8, 1.2, 1.4, 1.6, 2.8, 5.8, 1.5, 5.8, 17.9
Current Liabilities to Working Capital **39**	16.5, 2.0, 0.0, 0.8, 0.2, 0.4, 0.6, 1.8, 4.8, 0.5, 4.8, 16.9
Working Capital to Net Sales **40**	1.2, 0.1, 3.4, 0.3, 2.3, 1.1, 1.0, 0.3, 0.7, 1.2, 0.9, 1.2
Inventory to Working Capital **41**	0.0, •, •, •, •, •, •, •, •, •, 0.0, 0.0
Total Receipts to Cash Flow **42**	3.6, 2.5, 4.1, 1.4, 1.6, 2.0, 1.6, 3.3, 2.7, 2.4, 15.4, 3.6
Cost of Goods to Cash Flow **43**	0.4, 0.0, •, •, •, •, •, •, •, •, 0.2, 0.4
Cash Flow to Total Debt **44**	0.0, 1.7, 0.1, 1.8, 0.6, 0.4, 0.4, 0.1, 0.6, 0.5, 0.0, 0.0

Selected Financial Factors (in Percentages)

Line Item	Values
Debt Ratio **45**	89.4, 40.4, 34.3, 53.5, 30.5, 37.8, 29.7, 53.4, 28.6, 70.1, 89.6
Return on Total Assets **46**	1.2, 35.5, 15.1, 8.6, •, •, 2.4, 2.9, 1.2
Return on Equity Before Income Taxes **47**	4.0, 15.1, 16.3, 11.5, 2.3, 3.7, 4.1
Return on Equity After Income Taxes **48**	2.6, 14.2, 16.2, 10.2, 1.4, 0.8, 2.8
Profit Margin (Before Income Tax) **49**	15.2, 34.8, 5.3, 20.6, 28.9, 9.3, 6.1, 16.2
Profit Margin (After Income Tax) **50**	10.0, 25.5, 5.0, 20.5, 25.4, 5.7, 1.4, 10.9

Table II
Corporations with Net Income

INVESTMENT BANKING AND SECURITIES DEALING

MONEY AMOUNTS AND SIZE OF ASSETS IN THOUSANDS OF DOLLARS

Item Description for Accounting Period 7/10 Through 6/11		Total	Zero Assets	Under 500	500 to 1,000	1,000 to 5,000	5,000 to 10,000	10,000 to 25,000	25,000 to 50,000	50,000 to 100,000	100,000 to 250,000	250,000 to 500,000	500,000 to 2,500,000	2,500,000 and over
Number of Enterprises	1	1850	216	1263	107	172	13	20	24	9	9	0	9	8
Revenues ($ in Thousands)														
Net Sales	2	99340163	915594	292281	8759	91253	50920	155927	345475	339380	419458	0	1408142	95312974
Interest	3	35272579	297816	1214	301	2099	653	1879	7281	592	50528	0	156193	34754023
Rents	4	220919	0	0	0	5061	0	0	6	0	3	0	0	215849
Royalties	5	54651	21	0	3116	125	0	0	0	0	0	0	1394	49996
Other Portfolio Income	6	5098013	189004	2628	17	6678	2060	9337	16350	6870	38442	0	197752	4628874
Other Receipts	7	58694001	428753	288439	5325	77290	48207	144711	321838	331918	330485	0	1052803	55664232
Total Receipts	8	99340163	915594	292281	8759	91253	50920	155927	345475	339380	419458	0	1408142	95312974
Average Total Receipts	9	53697	4239	231	82	531	3917	7796	14395	37709	46606	•	156460	11914122
Operating Costs/Operating Income (%)														
Cost of Operations	10	11.1	1.4	•	•	•	•	•	•	•	•	•	•	11.6
Salaries and Wages	11	23.9	10.1	5.9	•	2.6	6.2	7.5	35.2	44.0	18.9	•	35.0	23.9
Taxes Paid	12	1.5	3.2	2.9	0.5	2.0	3.2	2.1	3.1	2.1	2.8	•	3.4	1.5
Interest Paid	13	27.3	8.5	14.2	•	0.7	0.0	0.1	1.7	0.4	2.9	•	9.5	28.2
Depreciation	14	1.1	0.2	0.5	•	0.3	1.7	0.1	0.7	0.7	1.6	•	1.4	1.1
Amortization and Depletion	15	0.6	•	0.6	•	•	•	1.7	0.3	0.0	0.4	•	4.3	0.6
Pensions and Other Deferred Comp.	16	0.5	0.4	1.4	•	0.2	0.7	0.2	0.4	0.9	0.4	•	1.2	0.5
Employee Benefits	17	0.6	0.3	0.4	•	0.1	2.5	0.0	1.2	0.4	1.2	•	1.6	0.6
Advertising	18	0.2	0.0	2.9	•	0.0	0.2	0.0	1.3	0.3	6.7	•	0.1	0.1
Other Expenses	19	21.3	31.2	32.0	52.2	8.5	15.1	30.7	36.5	31.4	36.9	•	27.6	20.9
Officers' Compensation	20	1.0	6.5	21.4	•	2.3	61.2	12.0	1.6	8.9	4.3	•	2.7	0.8
Operating Margin	21	10.8	38.1	17.8	47.3	83.2	9.2	45.4	18.0	10.8	23.9	•	13.1	10.3
Operating Margin Before Officers' Comp.	22	11.8	44.6	39.2	47.3	85.5	70.4	57.5	19.7	19.7	28.1	•	15.8	11.1

Selected Average Balance Sheet ($ in Thousands)

Line	Item													
23	Net Receivables	350176	•	0	0	2	4	164	653	5603	386	53754	•	292560	80569340
24	Inventories	•	•	•	•	•	•	•	•	•	•	•	•	•	•
25	Net Property, Plant and Equipment	4632	•	1	0	41	151	92	286	377	2499	•	20863	1042242
26	Total Assets	1825102	103	778	2368	7371	16289	36768	66231	179112	•	1134489	420261867
27	Notes and Loans Payable	321280	28	0	367	0	28	6640	9075	26597	•	41593	74176887
28	All Other Liabilities	1277088	18	0	149	1568	5274	7646	9386	54558	•	764415	294350036
29	Net Worth	226734	58	778	1852	5803	10987	22483	47770	97957	•	328481	51734943

Selected Financial Ratios (Times to 1)

Line	Item												
30	Current Ratio	1.0	•	1.0	2.3	2.1	2.1	3.7	1.4	2.0	•	1.0	1.0
31	Quick Ratio	0.5	•	0.6	1.2	2.0	1.7	2.0	0.9	1.7	•	0.7	0.5
32	Net Sales to Working Capital	2.1	•	186.8	1.8	2.3	1.7	1.0	7.8	0.8	•	13.4	2.0
33	Coverage Ratio	1.7	5.4	2.2	112.8	234.2	476.7	11.5	26.2	8.5	•	2.3	1.7
34	Total Asset Turnover	0.0	•	2.2	0.2	0.5	0.5	0.4	0.6	0.3	•	0.1	0.0
35	Inventory Turnover	•	•	•	•	•	•	•	•	•	•	•	•
36	Receivables Turnover	•	•	•	•	•	•	•	•	•	•	•	•
37	Total Liabilities to Net Worth	7.0	•	0.8	0.3	0.3	0.5	0.6	0.4	0.8	•	2.5	7.1
38	Current Assets to Working Capital	38.7	•	37.2	1.8	1.9	1.9	1.4	3.8	2.0	•	52.3	39.5
39	Current Liabilities to Working Capital	37.7	•	36.2	0.8	0.9	0.9	0.4	2.8	1.0	•	51.3	38.5
40	Working Capital to Net Sales	0.5	•	0.0	0.6	0.4	0.6	1.1	0.1	1.2	•	0.1	0.5
41	Inventory to Working Capital	0.0	•	•	•	•	•	•	•	•	•	0.0	0.0
42	Total Receipts to Cash Flow	3.5	1.5	2.2	1.1	5.5	1.4	2.0	2.6	1.9	•	2.8	3.7
43	Cost of Goods to Cash Flow	0.4	0.0	•	•	•	•	•	•	•	•	•	0.4
44	Cash Flow to Total Debt	0.0	•	2.4	448.1	0.9	0.5	1.1	0.5	0.8	•	0.1	0.0

Selected Financial Factors (in Percentages)

Line	Item												
45	Debt Ratio	87.6	•	43.8	0.0	21.8	21.3	32.5	38.9	27.9	45.3	71.0	87.7
46	Return on Total Assets	1.4	•	71.5	5.0	18.8	4.4	7.7	21.1	5.7	6.5	3.1	1.3
47	Return on Equity Before Income Taxes	4.6	•	70.7	5.0	23.8	5.6	11.4	31.2	7.6	10.4	6.0	4.4
48	Return on Equity After Income Taxes	3.3	•	69.5	4.1	23.7	5.0	9.5	28.1	7.5	7.1	4.0	3.2
49	Profit Margin (Before Income Tax)	19.4	37.8	17.7	47.3	83.0	8.2	17.9	43.9	9.7	22.0	12.7	19.3
50	Profit Margin (After Income Tax)	13.9	28.2	17.4	38.7	82.6	7.4	14.8	39.5	9.5	14.9	8.3	13.8

Table I

Corporations with and without Net Income

SECURITIES BROKERAGE

MONEY AMOUNTS AND SIZE OF ASSETS IN THOUSANDS OF DOLLARS

Item Description for Accounting Period 7/10 Through 6/11	Total	Zero Assets	Under 500	500 to 1,000	1,000 to 5,000	5,000 to 10,000	10,000 to 25,000	25,000 to 50,000	50,000 to 100,000	100,000 to 250,000	250,000 to 500,000	500,000 to 2,500,000	2,500,000 and over
Number of Enterprises **1**	6883	866	4700	448	566	86	77	45	26	15	9	19	27
Revenues ($ in Thousands)													
Net Sales **2**	97863892	223686	1737343	1374995	2059354	357972	2044494	1048659	1214137	1361448	1810119	4943098	79688588
Interest **3**	35420436	31117	3592	6315	2176	3189	8387	2188	9352	13187	6697	230339	35103896
Rents **4**	183253	0	0	0	0	1492	613	2	1362	0	490	83	179211
Royalties **5**	20228	0	0	0	0	0	0	0	0	2	0	16902	3323
Other Portfolio Income **6**	1547921	1806	2587	3656	14441	6491	6190	36242	54566	20032	4385	50111	1347413
Other Receipts **7**	60692054	190763	1731164	1365024	2042737	346800	2029304	1010227	1148857	1328227	1798547	4645663	43054745
Total Receipts **8**	97863892	223686	1737343	1374995	2059354	357972	2044494	1048659	1214137	1361448	1810119	4943098	79688588
Average Total Receipts **9**	14218	258	370	3069	3638	4162	26552	23304	46698	90763	201124	260163	2951429
Operating Costs/Operating Income (%)													
Cost of Operations **10**	0.0	•	•	•	•	0.2	•	•	•	•	•	0.1	0.0
Salaries and Wages **11**	23.6	21.8	18.7	39.2	40.6	27.3	21.7	45.4	36.8	30.2	34.7	44.9	20.8
Taxes Paid **12**	2.3	3.7	4.1	2.0	3.5	3.1	2.4	3.2	3.4	2.6	2.5	3.2	2.1
Interest Paid **13**	22.3	8.2	0.9	0.0	0.3	1.4	0.9	1.0	0.8	1.6	0.5	4.4	26.9
Depreciation **14**	1.0	0.1	0.7	0.1	0.2	1.3	0.7	0.9	0.6	1.4	1.8	1.5	1.0
Amortization and Depletion **15**	0.8	0.5	0.0	•	0.0	0.0	0.1	0.3	1.6	0.3	0.3	1.9	0.8
Pensions and Other Deferred Comp. **16**	0.6	0.4	2.2	0.2	0.4	0.3	0.2	0.7	0.3	0.1	1.0	2.5	0.4
Employee Benefits **17**	1.3	1.0	0.8	2.6	1.9	2.7	1.9	1.4	1.4	1.4	1.9	2.2	1.1
Advertising **18**	0.8	2.5	1.3	0.1	0.1	0.2	0.5	0.2	1.1	0.6	0.7	0.7	0.8
Other Expenses **19**	32.8	39.3	35.7	35.3	37.1	53.8	65.2	37.1	36.9	54.0	48.6	30.6	30.9
Officers' Compensation **20**	4.8	4.0	25.3	10.6	12.6	11.1	4.4	7.2	8.7	2.2	1.4	1.5	4.3
Operating Margin **21**	9.9	18.5	10.4	10.0	3.3	•	2.0	2.5	8.4	5.6	6.6	6.5	10.8
Operating Margin Before Officers' Comp. **22**	14.7	22.5	35.6	20.6	15.9	9.7	6.4	9.7	17.1	7.8	8.0	8.0	15.0

Selected Average Balance Sheet ($ in Thousands)

Line Item												
Net Receivables **23**	46077	0	221	90	261	1742	1624	10296	14928	135397	254870	11489415
Inventories **24**	•	•	•	•	•	•	•	•	•	•	•	•
Net Property, Plant and Equipment **25**	578	10	15	67	330	814	678	1430	4231	10960	13675	122262
Total Assets **26**	252910	86	713	2359	7943	15165	35962	69686	154170	371475	1381857	63019519
Notes and Loans Payable **27**	36655	56	3	109	575	1642	2906	7556	26474	66070	132752	9183459
All Other Liabilities **28**	200187	16	203	745	2454	6250	15539	23534	87275	133979	889223	50218062
Net Worth **29**	16067	14	507	1505	4914	7273	17517	38597	40421	171426	359881	3617998

Selected Financial Ratios (Times to 1)

Line Item												
Current Ratio **30**	1.1	•	1.3	3.1	2.8	10.4	1.4	1.8	1.0	2.5	0.9	1.1
Quick Ratio **31**	0.4	•	0.9	2.7	1.5	9.1	0.9	1.3	0.6	2.2	0.7	0.4
Net Sales to Working Capital **32**	0.8	•	56.5	7.3	4.1	0.9	4.2	2.7	53.1	1.2	•	0.7
Coverage Ratio **33**	1.4	3.3	12.8	4.3	11.7	3.0	3.3	10.5	4.2	13.9	2.5	1.4
Total Asset Turnover **34**	0.1	•	4.3	1.5	0.5	1.8	0.6	0.7	0.6	0.5	0.2	0.0
Inventory Turnover **35**	•	•	•	•	•	•	•	•	•	•	•	•
Receivables Turnover **36**	•	•	•	•	•	•	•	•	•	•	•	•
Total Liabilities to Net Worth **37**	14.7	5.1	0.4	0.6	1.1	0.8	1.1	2.8	1.2	2.8	16.4	•
Current Assets to Working Capital **38**	10.6	4.8	1.5	1.5	1.1	1.9	3.4	2.2	55.4	1.7	•	10.6
Current Liabilities to Working Capital **39**	9.6	3.8	0.5	0.5	0.1	0.9	2.4	1.2	54.4	0.7	•	9.6
Working Capital to Net Sales **40**	1.2	•	0.0	0.1	0.2	1.1	0.2	0.4	0.0	0.9	•	1.5
Inventory to Working Capital **41**	0.0	•	•	•	•	•	•	•	•	•	•	•
Total Receipts to Cash Flow **42**	2.6	2.1	3.0	2.4	2.8	2.1	1.6	2.9	2.4	1.8	1.9	3.0
Cost of Goods to Cash Flow **43**	0.0	•	•	•	0.0	•	•	•	•	•	•	0.0
Cash Flow to Total Debt **44**	0.0	1.7	6.2	1.5	0.7	2.2	0.4	0.6	0.0	0.5	0.5	0.1

Selected Financial Factors (in Percentages)

Line Item												
Debt Ratio **45**	93.6	83.7	28.9	36.2	38.1	52.0	51.3	44.6	73.8	53.9	74.0	94.3
Return on Total Assets **46**	1.8	•	48.2	42.9	5.6	4.5	2.1	5.9	3.9	3.8	2.1	1.8
Return on Equity Before Income Taxes **47**	8.7	•	272.4	60.3	8.0	6.3	3.0	9.6	9.6	11.3	4.7	8.8
Return on Equity After Income Taxes **48**	7.1	•	269.3	58.7	6.8	3.9	0.0	7.9	9.3	6.1	2.8	7.2
Profit Margin (Before Income Tax) **49**	9.8	18.5	10.4	10.0	3.3	1.7	8.0	5.0	6.1	6.5	6.5	10.7
Profit Margin (After Income Tax) **50**	8.0	13.2	10.3	9.7	2.8	1.1	6.6	4.2	5.2	3.8	6.5	8.8

Table II
Corporations with Net Income

SECURITIES BROKERAGE

MONEY AMOUNTS AND SIZE OF ASSETS IN THOUSANDS OF DOLLARS

Item Description for Accounting Period 7/10 Through 6/11		Total	Zero Assets	Under 500	500 to 1,000	1,000 to 5,000	5,000 to 10,000	10,000 to 25,000	25,000 to 50,000	50,000 to 100,000	100,000 to 250,000	250,000 to 500,000	500,000 to 2,500,000	2,500,000 and over
Number of Enterprises	1	5116	383	3691	•	480	52	39	28	17	10	•	14	20
Revenues ($ in Thousands)														
Net Sales	2	75578421	128244	1404809	•	1804888	160678	1251802	676165	887761	1135281	•	3646971	61946061
Interest	3	27037518	30667	71	•	1848	145	7407	1753	7954	11288	•	198202	26765573
Rents	4	89042	0	0	•	0	1492	0	2	1362	0	•	0	85695
Royalties	5	4187	0	0	•	0	0	0	0	0	2	•	889	3296
Other Portfolio Income	6	670397	810	0	•	14441	5388	748	25011	49583	19544	•	31464	519995
Other Receipts	7	47777277	96767	1404738	•	1788599	153653	1243647	649399	828862	1104447	•	3416416	34571502
Total Receipts	8	75578421	128244	1404809	•	1804888	160678	1251802	676165	887761	1135281	•	3646971	61946061
Average Total Receipts	9	14773	335	381	•	3760	3090	32097	24149	52221	113528	•	260498	3097303
Operating Costs/Operating Income (%)														
Cost of Operations	10	0.0	•	•	•	•	0.4	•	•	•	•	•	0.2	0.0
Salaries and Wages	11	25.4	7.8	17.0	•	43.6	20.7	15.8	35.0	44.1	28.8	•	44.8	23.0
Taxes Paid	12	2.1	4.7	3.7	•	3.8	4.5	1.9	3.1	3.6	2.1	•	3.5	1.9
Interest Paid	13	21.7	13.6	0.4	•	0.3	0.1	0.2	0.4	0.6	1.3	•	4.1	26.2
Depreciation	14	1.1	0.1	0.8	•	0.2	0.8	0.3	0.7	0.7	1.2	•	1.4	1.2
Amortization and Depletion	15	0.7	•	0.0	•	•	0.1	0.0	0.0	1.5	0.3	•	1.2	0.7
Pensions and Other Deferred Comp.	16	0.5	0.1	1.8	•	0.5	0.6	0.3	1.0	0.3	0.1	•	0.4	0.5
Employee Benefits	17	1.2	0.1	0.4	•	2.0	1.9	1.1	1.1	1.7	1.3	•	2.2	1.1
Advertising	18	1.0	4.4	1.0	•	0.1	0.1	0.2	0.1	0.9	0.8	•	0.9	1.0
Other Expenses	19	28.7	18.9	32.0	•	27.5	15.4	68.1	33.2	21.5	53.0	•	28.1	27.5
Officers' Compensation	20	2.3	•	23.5	•	14.3	23.8	3.6	8.3	10.2	1.8	•	1.0	1.1
Operating Margin	21	15.2	50.2	19.3	•	7.7	31.6	8.4	17.1	14.9	9.3	•	12.2	15.8
Operating Margin Before Officers' Comp.	22	17.5	50.2	42.8	•	22.0	55.4	12.0	25.4	25.1	11.1	•	13.2	16.9

Selected Average Balance Sheet ($ in Thousands)

Net Receivables 23	55208	0	•	106	1819	263	1639	10794	20482	•	323017	13828253
Inventories 24	•	•	•	•	•	•	•	•	•	•	•	•
Net Property, Plant and Equipment 25	588	11	•	73	810	352	726	1824	5294	•	9234	127713
Total Assets 26	228046	86	•	2028	15757	8702	36468	67511	161612	•	1375158	56924735
Notes and Loans Payable 27	33036	59	•	127	776	19	1319	7389	28716	•	70251	8360967
All Other Liabilities 28	180929	8	•	823	5386	3595	13050	25878	87499	•	983910	45409384
Net Worth 29	14081	19	•	1077	9595	5087	22099	34245	45398	•	320996	3154384

Selected Financial Ratios (Times to 1)

Current Ratio 30	1.3	1.5	•	2.8	2.2	10.7	1.4	2.0	1.0	•	0.9	1.3
Quick Ratio 31	0.7	0.9	•	1.4	1.6	10.6	0.9	1.3	0.6	•	0.7	0.7
Net Sales to Working Capital 32	0.4	46.3	•	4.0	5.3	0.7	4.4	2.3	•	•	•	0.3
Coverage Ratio 33	1.7	51.3	4.7	24.4	45.1	230.9	43.4	23.4	7.7	•	3.9	1.6
Total Asset Turnover 34	0.1	4.4	•	1.9	2.0	0.4	0.7	0.8	0.7	•	0.2	0.1
Inventory Turnover 35	•	•	•	•	•	•	•	•	•	•	•	•
Receivables Turnover 36	•	•	•	•	•	•	•	•	•	•	•	•
Total Liabilities to Net Worth 37	15.2	3.5	•	0.9	0.6	0.7	0.7	1.0	2.6	•	3.3	17.0
Current Assets to Working Capital 38	4.5	3.1	•	1.6	1.9	1.1	3.5	2.0	•	•	•	4.5
Current Liabilities to Working Capital 39	3.5	2.1	•	0.6	0.9	0.1	2.5	1.0	•	•	•	3.5
Working Capital to Net Sales 40	2.4	0.0	•	0.2	0.2	1.5	0.2	0.4	•	•	0.4	2.9
Inventory to Working Capital 41	0.0	•	•	•	•	•	•	•	•	•	•	0.0
Total Receipts to Cash Flow 42	2.5	2.7	1.5	3.3	1.3	2.4	2.2	3.0	1.7	•	2.8	2.5
Cost of Goods to Cash Flow 43	0.0	•	•	•	0.0	0.0	•	•	•	•	0.0	0.0
Cash Flow to Total Debt 44	0.0	2.1	•	1.2	3.9	0.4	0.8	0.5	0.6	•	0.1	0.0

Selected Financial Factors (in Percentages)

Debt Ratio 45	93.8	77.8	•	46.9	39.1	41.5	39.4	49.3	71.9	•	76.7	94.5
Return on Total Assets 46	2.4	87.3	•	14.8	17.6	10.5	11.3	11.6	6.9	•	3.1	2.3
Return on Equity Before Income Taxes 47	15.9	385.2	•	26.7	28.2	17.9	18.3	21.8	21.5	•	9.8	15.5
Return on Equity After Income Taxes 48	13.4	382.3	•	24.8	24.6	14.7	14.4	18.9	18.9	•	6.9	13.1
Profit Margin (Before Income Tax) 49	15.1	50.2	19.3	7.6	8.4	29.5	16.7	14.3	8.6	•	12.1	15.8
Profit Margin (After Income Tax) 50	12.8	41.0	19.1	7.1	7.4	24.2	13.2	12.4	7.6	•	8.5	13.3

Table I
Corporations with and without Net Income

COMMODITY CONTRACTS DEALING AND BROKERAGE

MONEY AMOUNTS AND SIZE OF ASSETS IN THOUSANDS OF DOLLARS

Item Description for Accounting Period 7/10 Through 6/11	Total	Zero Assets	Under 500	500 to 1,000	1,000 to 5,000	5,000 to 10,000	10,000 to 25,000	25,000 to 50,000	50,000 to 100,000	100,000 to 250,000	250,000 to 500,000	500,000 to 2,500,000	2,500,000 and over
Number of Enterprises 1	2609	999	870	404	177	46	67	9	13	3	7	6	8
Revenues ($ in Thousands)													
Net Sales 2	6030812	101153	86646	40458	87292	58493	250387	96455	130750	77874	261092	589590	4250623
Interest 3	708227	7635	20	4	173	30	122	1687	2657	0	16338	11970	667591
Rents 4	104014	0	0	0	0	0	0	0	18	183	198	0	103616
Royalties 5	1126	0	0	0	0	0	0	0	0	0	1050	0	76
Other Portfolio Income 6	382057	0	656	0	6	0	1515	0	21037	0	48988	1888	307967
Other Receipts 7	4835388	93518	85970	40454	87113	58463	248750	94768	107038	77691	194518	575732	3171373
Total Receipts 8	6030812	101153	86646	40458	87292	58493	250387	96455	130750	77874	261092	589590	4250623
Average Total Receipts 9	2312	101	100	100	493	1272	3737	10717	10058	25958	37299	98265	531328
Operating Costs/Operating Income (%)													
Cost of Operations 10	0.5	0.1	•	•	•	•	•	•	•	•	•	•	0.7
Salaries and Wages 11	20.4	14.3	14.0	4.7	23.4	8.9	32.6	73.6	40.7	11.0	20.7	7.5	20.3
Taxes Paid 12	2.2	0.6	2.1	2.5	6.2	3.2	5.9	6.5	5.1	1.1	2.1	0.9	2.0
Interest Paid 13	9.6	10.6	4.9	0.6	22.0	•	3.4	5.9	2.4	5.9	3.0	5.4	11.4
Depreciation 14	2.5	0.6	0.6	16.0	4.6	0.2	1.3	2.6	1.0	0.1	1.0	0.2	3.1
Amortization and Depletion 15	1.9	•	•	•	12.6	•	0.4	•	1.1	•	5.7	0.5	1.9
Pensions and Other Deferred Comp. 16	0.3	0.3	•	•	0.2	1.9	0.4	0.1	1.3	0.4	0.4	0.7	0.2
Employee Benefits 17	1.7	0.1	5.2	1.0	1.5	0.9	1.8	5.5	3.1	1.1	2.9	0.8	1.6
Advertising 18	0.7	1.0	1.1	1.6	0.3	•	2.7	•	1.1	•	0.5	0.2	0.7
Other Expenses 19	55.9	59.8	49.8	63.9	38.8	3.5	45.2	51.2	52.4	16.1	36.7	78.7	56.5
Officers' Compensation 20	2.7	0.5	23.0	22.2	1.6	1.6	6.4	7.6	9.3	19.0	7.7	1.6	1.2
Operating Margin 21	1.5	12.3	•	•	•	79.8	•	•	•	45.2	19.4	3.5	0.4
Operating Margin Before Officers' Comp. 22	4.2	12.8	22.3	9.8	•	81.3	6.3	•	•	64.3	27.1	5.1	1.6

Selected Average Balance Sheet ($ in Thousands)

Net Receivables 23	8236	0	0	39	609	482	2278	2898	19959	30121	53023	194967	2408913
Inventories 24	•	•	•	•	•	•	•	•	•	•	•	•	•
Net Property, Plant and Equipment 25	221	0	1	82	37	19	414	1711	584	575	1182	806	58563
Total Assets 26	47845	0	54	704	2062	5867	16472	28447	73647	145657	350239	606136	14377401
Notes and Loans Payable 27	3897	0	31	254	437	0	2678	13414	15913	55773	13371	166306	1024295
All Other Liabilities 28	41103	0	0	63	1695	332	8857	14101	27684	14674	207672	464453	12691537
Net Worth 29	2845	0	23	387	-70	5536	4936	932	30050	75210	129196	-24622	661569

Selected Financial Ratios (Times to 1)

Current Ratio 30	1.3	•	2.5	1.2	1.2	17.2	1.8	1.3	1.3	0.8	1.1	1.3	1.3
Quick Ratio 31	0.7	•	1.8	0.9	1.2	3.4	0.9	1.2	0.8	0.6	0.7	0.9	0.7
Net Sales to Working Capital 32	0.3	•	22.5	4.4	2.3	0.2	0.8	4.2	0.9	•	3.2	1.1	0.2
Coverage Ratio 33	1.2	2.2	0.8	•	0.6	1.0	1.0	•	•	8.7	7.6	1.6	1.0
Total Asset Turnover 34	0.0	•	1.9	0.1	0.2	0.2	0.2	0.4	0.1	0.2	0.1	0.2	0.0
Inventory Turnover 35	•	•	•	•	•	•	•	•	•	•	•	•	•
Receivables Turnover 36	•	•	•	•	•	•	•	•	•	•	•	•	•
Total Liabilities to Net Worth 37	15.8	•	1.4	0.8	•	0.1	2.3	29.5	1.5	0.9	1.7	•	20.7
Current Assets to Working Capital 38	4.9	•	1.7	7.3	5.2	1.1	2.2	4.9	4.0	•	20.0	5.0	4.9
Current Liabilities to Working Capital 39	3.9	•	0.7	6.3	4.2	0.1	1.2	3.9	3.0	•	19.0	4.0	3.9
Working Capital to Net Sales 40	3.3	•	0.0	0.2	0.4	4.2	1.2	0.2	1.1	•	0.3	0.9	4.4
Inventory to Working Capital 41	0.0	•	•	•	•	•	•	•	•	•	•	•	0.0
Total Receipts to Cash Flow 42	2.2	1.5	2.4	2.0	8.2	1.2	3.2	•	8.8	1.7	3.0	1.2	2.3
Cost of Goods to Cash Flow 43	0.0	0.0	•	•	•	•	•	•	•	•	•	•	0.0
Cash Flow to Total Debt 44	0.0	•	1.3	0.2	0.0	3.1	0.1	0.0	0.0	0.2	0.1	0.1	0.0

Selected Financial Factors (in Percentages)

Debt Ratio 45	94.1	•	57.9	45.0	103.4	5.7	70.0	96.7	59.2	48.4	63.1	104.1	95.4
Return on Total Assets 46	0.5	•	7.8	•	3.0	17.3	0.7	•	•	9.1	2.4	1.4	0.4
Return on Equity Before Income Taxes 47	1.3	•	•	•	67.0	18.3	•	•	•	15.6	5.6	•	0.3
Return on Equity After Income Taxes 48	0.2	•	•	•	69.5	15.3	•	•	•	14.9	4.1	•	•
Profit Margin (Before Income Tax) 49	1.5	12.3	•	•	•	79.8	•	•	•	45.2	19.4	3.5	0.4
Profit Margin (After Income Tax) 50	0.2	12.3	•	•	•	66.6	•	•	•	43.2	14.0	3.4	•

Table II

Corporations with Net Income

COMMODITY CONTRACTS DEALING AND BROKERAGE

MONEY AMOUNTS AND SIZE OF ASSETS IN THOUSANDS OF DOLLARS

Item Description for Accounting Period 7/10 Through 6/11	Total	Zero Assets	Under 500	500 to 1,000	1,000 to 5,000	5,000 to 10,000	10,000 to 25,000	25,000 to 50,000	50,000 to 100,000	100,000 to 250,000	250,000 to 500,000	500,000 to 2,500,000	2,500,000 and over
Number of Enterprises **1**	1857	761	732	•	57	10	42	6	10	0	•	3	3
Revenues ($ in Thousands)													
Net Sales **2**	3482760	41835	89016	•	66052	58493	242188	161360	229786	0	•	526484	1836364
Interest **3**	216378	0	0	•	145	30	15	1687	2537	0	•	8473	188759
Rents **4**	86008	0	0	•	0	0	0	0	201	0	•	0	85627
Royalties **5**	1126	0	0	•	0	0	0	0	0	0	•	0	76
Other Portfolio Income **6**	356397	0	0	•	6	0	1446	0	21037	0	•	0	284952
Other Receipts **7**	2822851	41835	89016	•	65901	58463	240727	159673	206011	0	•	518011	1276950
Total Receipts **8**	3482760	41835	89016	•	66052	58493	242188	161360	229786	0	•	526484	1836364
Average Total Receipts **9**	1875	55	122	•	1159	5849	5766	26893	22979	•	•	175495	612121
Operating Costs/Operating Income (%)													
Cost of Operations **10**	0.8	•	•	•	•	•	•	•	•	•	•	•	1.5
Salaries and Wages **11**	17.4	•	13.6	•	2.2	8.9	23.0	44.0	21.3	•	•	5.6	19.0
Taxes Paid **12**	2.6	1.0	1.9	•	0.4	3.2	5.1	3.9	2.1	•	•	0.6	2.9
Interest Paid **13**	10.3	3.9	4.8	•	21.3	•	3.1	3.5	1.4	•	•	3.6	16.2
Depreciation **14**	2.7	•	0.3	•	0.1	0.2	1.1	1.6	0.4	•	•	0.2	4.6
Amortization and Depletion **15**	0.7	•	•	•	16.6	•	•	•	0.4	•	•	0.3	0.5
Pensions and Other Deferred Comp. **16**	0.3	•	•	•	0.2	1.9	0.4	0.1	0.8	•	•	0.2	0.2
Employee Benefits **17**	1.2	•	4.7	•	0.2	0.9	1.7	3.3	1.0	•	•	0.5	1.2
Advertising **18**	1.0	2.4	1.1	•	•	•	2.2	•	0.6	•	•	0.3	1.3
Other Expenses **19**	43.3	43.5	43.9	•	7.9	3.3	27.0	30.3	27.3	•	•	81.4	42.0
Officers' Compensation **20**	2.7	•	22.2	•	•	1.6	4.7	4.6	9.6	•	•	0.6	0.2
Operating Margin **21**	17.1	49.2	7.5	•	51.2	79.9	31.7	8.8	35.1	•	•	6.9	10.5
Operating Margin Before Officers' Comp. **22**	19.8	49.2	29.7	•	51.2	81.5	36.3	13.4	44.7	•	•	7.6	10.7

Selected Average Balance Sheet ($ in Thousands)

Net Receivables 23	3499	•	0	0	•	422	2216	3444	2946	19648	•	27959	1875532
Inventories 24	•	•	•	•	•	•	•	•	•	•	•	•	•
Net Property, Plant and Equipment 25	229	•	0	1	•	1	87	547	2567	759	•	1008	123009
Total Assets 26	19767	•	0	3	•	1529	6949	15624	26915	88837	•	643022	10198726
Notes and Loans Payable 27	2615	•	0	4	•	2	0	4001	20121	25398	•	200559	1217840
All Other Liabilities 28	15404	•	0	0	•	1484	1526	6826	21108	28373	•	572429	8222705
Net Worth 29	1747	•	0	-1	•	44	5423	4797	-14314	35066	•	-129967	758181

Selected Financial Ratios (Times to 1)

Current Ratio 30	1.0	•	•	0.4	•	1.9	4.0	1.3	1.2	1.1	•	1.5	0.9
Quick Ratio 31	0.7	•	•	0.0	•	1.9	3.3	0.8	1.1	0.8	•	0.9	0.6
Net Sales to Working Capital 32	•	13.8	•	•	•	3.8	1.3	3.0	11.3	5.6	•	1.1	•
Coverage Ratio 33	2.7	13.8	•	2.6	•	3.4	11.3	3.5	25.9	•	•	2.9	1.6
Total Asset Turnover 34	0.1	•	48.5	•	•	0.8	0.8	0.4	1.0	0.3	•	0.3	0.1
Inventory Turnover 35	•	•	•	•	•	•	•	•	•	•	•	•	•
Receivables Turnover 36	•	•	•	•	•	•	•	•	•	•	•	•	•
Total Liabilities to Net Worth 37	10.3	•	•	33.9	•	2.3	1.3	4.6	7.3	1.5	•	2.9	12.5
Current Assets to Working Capital 38	•	•	•	2.1	•	1.3	4.6	3.6	6.3	10.8	9.8	1.9	2.9
Current Liabilities to Working Capital 39	•	•	•	1.1	•	0.3	3.6	0.3	0.3	9.8	•	1.9	•
Working Capital to Net Sales 40	•	•	•	0.3	•	0.8	0.3	0.8	0.1	0.2	•	0.9	•
Inventory to Working Capital 41	•	•	•	•	•	•	•	•	•	•	•	•	•
Total Receipts to Cash Flow 42	1.8	1.2	•	2.2	•	1.7	1.2	2.2	3.0	1.9	•	1.1	2.0
Cost of Goods to Cash Flow 43	0.0	•	•	•	•	•	•	•	•	•	•	•	0.0
Cash Flow to Total Debt 44	0.1	15.3	•	0.5	•	3.1	0.2	0.2	0.3	0.2	•	0.2	0.0

Selected Financial Factors (in Percentages)

Debt Ratio 45	91.2	•	•	141.0	•	97.1	22.0	69.3	153.2	60.5	•	120.2	92.6
Return on Total Assets 46	2.6	•	•	594.1	•	54.9	67.3	12.8	12.3	9.4	•	2.9	1.6
Return on Equity Before Income Taxes 47	18.4	•	•	1354.7	•	86.2	38.1	23.0	•	•	•	•	8.5
Return on Equity After Income Taxes 48	15.9	•	•	1342.1	•	72.0	37.0	19.7	•	•	•	•	6.5
Profit Margin (Before Income Tax) 49	17.1	49.2	49.2	7.5	•	51.2	79.9	31.7	8.8	35.1	•	6.9	10.5
Profit Margin (After Income Tax) 50	14.8	49.2	49.2	7.5	•	50.7	66.7	30.8	8.8	30.1	•	6.8	8.1

Table I
Corporations with and without Net Income

SECURITIES & COMMODITY EXCHANGES, OTHER FINANCIAL INVESTMENT

MONEY AMOUNTS AND SIZE OF ASSETS IN THOUSANDS OF DOLLARS

Item Description for Accounting Period 7/10 Through 6/11	Total	Zero Assets	Under 500	500 to 1,000	1,000 to 5,000	5,000 to 10,000	10,000 to 25,000	25,000 to 50,000	50,000 to 100,000	100,000 to 250,000	250,000 to 500,000	500,000 to 2,500,000	2,500,000 and over
Number of Enterprises **1**	46011	6300	33271	2330	2349	702	468	221	136	99	48	50	38
Revenues ($ in Thousands)													
Net Sales **2**	114730451	2372557	8213028	1513693	5549200	4601953	3323316	3857658	3740228	6118791	5536545	10290244	59613237
Interest **3**	4141124	97836	29385	6534	20949	15829	45085	115515	72059	137985	123069	250361	3226517
Rents **4**	164162	1	1400	0	2210	95	1616	2818	804	13802	2726	37427	101263
Royalties **5**	75579	1	0	104	4055	12205	8693	353	667	3776	2013	114	43598
Other Portfolio Income **6**	2385145	85013	4462	1127	77971	95997	115521	200210	53113	165340	252825	320707	1012862
Other Receipts **7**	107964441	2189706	8177781	1505928	5444015	4477827	3152401	3538762	3613585	5797888	5155912	9681635	55228997
Total Receipts **8**	114730451	2372557	8213028	1513693	5549200	4601953	3323316	3857658	3740228	6118791	5536545	10290244	59613237
Average Total Receipts **9**	2494	377	247	650	2362	6555	7101	17455	27502	61806	115345	205805	1568769
Operating Costs/Operating Income (%)													
Cost of Operations **10**	1.5	0.4	0.1	•	0.5	•	0.6	2.5	1.1	•	0.1	0.8	2.4
Salaries and Wages **11**	24.9	7.6	17.9	18.3	23.0	42.1	31.8	37.5	24.7	29.8	11.6	20.0	25.9
Taxes Paid **12**	3.5	1.9	3.0	2.6	2.6	7.7	2.8	3.6	2.5	2.5	2.1	2.3	3.9
Interest Paid **13**	5.5	1.4	0.7	1.3	0.7	1.3	1.5	4.2	2.6	4.8	4.1	5.7	7.8
Depreciation **14**	1.9	1.0	0.6	1.0	0.6	1.2	1.8	2.4	1.3	2.1	1.7	1.7	2.4
Amortization and Depletion **15**	2.2	3.1	0.1	0.1	0.4	0.6	0.9	0.5	1.8	1.9	4.7	4.7	2.4
Pensions and Other Deferred Comp. **16**	1.6	1.3	4.2	3.5	0.9	0.4	1.0	0.7	1.1	1.2	0.2	0.6	1.9
Employee Benefits **17**	1.9	0.9	2.7	1.9	1.7	1.5	3.0	1.9	1.4	1.9	1.2	1.4	2.0
Advertising **18**	1.2	0.2	1.5	1.6	0.2	0.4	0.6	0.4	0.8	1.4	0.2	0.9	1.6
Other Expenses **19**	34.4	72.0	31.7	29.0	34.5	22.6	27.9	28.0	36.7	40.1	33.4	55.3	30.8
Officers' Compensation **20**	7.2	5.5	23.3	27.3	16.5	16.0	10.2	10.2	16.2	9.4	1.7	6.3	2.4
Operating Margin **21**	14.3	4.8	14.1	13.5	18.4	6.3	18.1	8.1	9.8	4.9	38.9	0.2	16.6
Operating Margin Before Officers' Comp. **22**	21.5	10.3	37.4	40.8	34.9	22.3	28.3	18.3	26.0	14.2	40.7	6.5	19.1

Selected Average Balance Sheet ($ in Thousands)

Item													
Net Receivables 23	1119	•	0	2	92	297	428	1824	3686	7666	17794	97637	1053115
Inventories 24	•	•	•	•	•	•	•	•	•	•	•	•	•
Net Property, Plant and Equipment 25	348	•	0	11	30	197	596	988	2538	3739	8572	22394	285772
Total Assets 26	16256	•	58	713	2403	7442	15411	34949	71014	159155	360711	1029197	16430947
Notes and Loans Payable 27	3304	0	24	407	680	2143	6514	15307	57154	102292	299030	•	3059746
All Other Liabilities 28	7588	0	27	114	455	1553	2637	8307	15962	58563	66538	287324	8348178
Net Worth 29	5364	0	8	191	1268	3747	8750	20127	39745	43438	191881	442843	5023023

Selected Financial Ratios (Times to 1)

Item													
Current Ratio 30	0.9	•	1.4	3.6	3.0	1.2	1.7	2.0	1.6	0.9	1.1	1.1	0.9
Quick Ratio 31	0.6	•	1.2	3.2	2.0	0.8	1.3	1.5	1.1	0.7	0.6	0.7	0.5
Net Sales to Working Capital 32	•	•	22.4	2.8	20.4	3.0	2.6	3.2	•	•	15.6	9.0	•
Coverage Ratio 33	3.7	4.7	20.3	11.0	26.9	5.8	2.9	13.4	4.7	2.0	10.4	1.0	3.2
Total Asset Turnover 34	0.2	•	4.2	0.9	1.0	0.9	0.5	0.5	0.4	0.4	0.3	0.2	0.1
Inventory Turnover 35	•	•	•	•	•	•	•	•	•	•	•	•	•
Receivables Turnover 36	•	•	•	•	•	•	•	•	•	•	•	•	•
Total Liabilities to Net Worth 37	2.0	•	6.7	2.7	0.9	0.7	0.7	0.8	0.8	2.7	0.9	1.3	2.3
Current Assets to Working Capital 38	•	•	3.3	1.4	1.5	2.4	2.4	2.0	2.8	12.5	13.2	•	•
Current Liabilities to Working Capital 39	•	•	2.3	0.4	0.5	1.4	1.4	1.0	1.8	11.5	12.2	•	•
Working Capital to Net Sales 40	•	•	0.0	0.4	0.4	0.3	0.3	0.4	0.3	0.1	0.1	•	•
Inventory to Working Capital 41	•	•	•	•	•	•	0.0	•	0.0	•	•	•	•
Total Receipts to Cash Flow 42	2.3	•	2.2	2.5	2.6	2.2	3.4	4.3	2.5	2.4	1.5	1.9	2.3
Cost of Goods to Cash Flow 43	0.0	•	0.0	0.0	•	0.0	0.1	•	0.0	0.0	0.0	0.0	0.1
Cash Flow to Total Debt 44	0.1	•	2.0	0.5	1.0	0.4	0.3	0.4	0.2	0.5	0.2	•	0.1

Selected Financial Factors (in Percentages)

Item													
Debt Ratio 45	67.0	•	87.0	73.2	47.2	49.7	42.4	43.2	44.0	72.7	46.8	57.0	69.4
Return on Total Assets 46	3.1	•	62.7	13.5	18.8	6.7	6.1	9.0	4.8	3.7	13.8	1.1	2.4
Return on Equity Before Income Taxes 47	6.8	•	458.6	45.6	34.3	11.0	6.9	14.7	6.7	6.8	23.4	•	5.4
Return on Equity After Income Taxes 48	5.0	•	456.5	45.4	32.0	9.3	5.0	13.3	5.7	3.3	21.8	•	3.6
Profit Margin (Before Income Tax) 49	14.7	5.2	14.1	13.4	18.4	6.3	8.0	18.1	9.7	4.8	39.0	•	17.4
Profit Margin (After Income Tax) 50	10.7	3.2	14.0	13.3	17.2	5.3	5.8	16.4	8.3	2.3	36.2	•	11.6

Table II

Corporations with Net Income

SECURITIES & COMMODITY EXCHANGES, OTHER FINANCIAL INVESTMENT

MONEY AMOUNTS AND SIZE OF ASSETS IN THOUSANDS OF DOLLARS

Item Description for Accounting Period 7/10 Through 6/11		Total	Zero Assets	Under 500	500 to 1,000	1,000 to 5,000	5,000 to 10,000	10,000 to 25,000	25,000 to 50,000	50,000 to 100,000	100,000 to 250,000	250,000 to 500,000	500,000 to 2,500,000	2,500,000 and over
Number of Enterprises	1	27996	2409	21535	1536	1593	365	246	123	58	47	28	30	26
Revenues ($ in Thousands)														
Net Sales	2	96344369	2031921	6785981	1337354	4807901	3744108	2672531	2952754	2877552	4618590	4692345	7758131	52065202
Interest	3	3471662	73498	213	4645	12727	11044	24070	94932	28342	32580	78348	105028	3006232
Rents	4	135069	1	1400	0	111	0	1455	409	144	6493	2693	21231	101131
Royalties	5	54768	1	0	0	4055	12205	8693	3	485	119	2000	114	27092
Other Portfolio Income	6	1890141	61912	1069	1071	75878	89908	94021	160827	31023	143813	204276	101060	925283
Other Receipts	7	90792729	1896509	6783299	1331638	4715130	3630951	2544292	2696583	2817558	4435585	4405028	7530698	48005464
Total Receipts	8	96344369	2031921	6785981	1337354	4807901	3744108	2672531	2952754	2877552	4618590	4692345	7758131	52065202
Average Total Receipts	9	3441	843	315	871	3018	10258	10864	24006	49613	98268	167584	258604	2002508
Operating Costs/Operating Income (%)														
Cost of Operations	10	0.1	0.4	0.2	•	•	•	0.7	•	1.4	•	•	0.2	0.0
Salaries and Wages	11	23.4	4.1	16.7	18.0	20.9	39.1	26.1	35.2	19.1	29.7	7.4	17.9	25.4
Taxes Paid	12	3.6	1.3	2.6	2.6	2.4	8.4	2.8	3.0	2.3	2.5	2.1	2.4	4.1
Interest Paid	13	4.4	0.3	0.3	0.2	0.5	0.8	1.0	2.9	1.1	2.8	2.4	4.4	6.5
Depreciation	14	1.8	0.2	0.5	0.8	0.6	0.9	1.1	1.2	0.9	1.2	1.3	1.4	2.5
Amortization and Depletion	15	1.5	3.4	0.0	0.0	0.4	0.1	0.5	0.5	0.7	1.2	1.3	3.0	1.8
Pensions and Other Deferred Comp.	16	1.7	1.1	4.3	2.2	0.9	0.4	1.2	0.7	1.1	1.3	0.2	0.7	2.1
Employee Benefits	17	1.8	0.9	2.5	1.9	1.6	0.9	2.2	1.7	1.0	1.2	0.9	1.4	2.0
Advertising	18	1.3	0.0	1.6	1.7	0.2	0.4	0.6	0.2	0.2	1.8	0.2	1.2	1.8
Other Expenses	19	29.4	65.8	29.5	18.2	28.5	17.0	20.0	21.2	32.4	24.1	29.4	38.5	29.1
Officers' Compensation	20	6.6	2.7	19.1	30.2	15.8	15.0	11.0	8.4	17.3	11.2	1.6	5.8	2.3
Operating Margin	21	24.5	19.7	22.7	24.2	28.2	17.1	32.8	24.9	22.5	22.9	53.4	23.2	22.5
Operating Margin Before Officers' Comp.	22	31.1	22.4	41.8	54.4	44.0	32.1	43.8	33.3	39.8	34.1	54.9	29.0	24.8

Selected Average Balance Sheet ($ in Thousands)

Item													
Net Receivables 23	1629	0	2	32	385	285	1838	3226	10120	16774	9420	113615	1496325
Inventories 24	•	•	•	•	•	•	•	•	•	•	•	•	•
Net Property, Plant and Equipment 25	462	0	13	43	218	697	795	1385	2868	6807	6406	24273	392983
Total Assets 26	20672	0	68	734	2503	7415	15530	35144	71426	158792	362301	1113484	19467030
Notes and Loans Payable 27	3705	0	3	264	631	1978	3265	3650	14786	38949	81356	314813	3302368
All Other Liabilities 28	10649	0	28	146	386	1830	3093	7858	13041	62560	81236	270840	10777200
Net Worth 29	6318	0	37	323	1485	3606	9172	23636	43600	57283	199709	527831	5387462

Selected Financial Ratios (Times to 1)

Item													
Current Ratio 30	1.0	•	3.1	3.5	4.0	1.2	2.2	1.6	2.1	1.3	0.9	1.4	0.9
Quick Ratio 31	0.6	•	2.5	3.2	2.7	0.7	1.7	1.3	1.6	0.9	0.5	0.9	0.6
Net Sales to Working Capital 32	•	•	10.2	3.5	2.7	29.7	3.5	4.3	3.4	5.9	•	2.3	•
Coverage Ratio 33	6.7	57.8	83.3	114.6	56.3	22.9	33.6	9.5	21.5	9.1	23.6	6.2	4.6
Total Asset Turnover 34	0.2	•	4.6	1.2	1.2	1.4	0.7	0.7	0.7	0.6	0.5	0.2	0.1
Inventory Turnover 35	•	•	•	•	•	•	•	•	•	•	•	•	•
Receivables Turnover 36	•	•	•	•	•	•	•	•	•	•	•	•	•
Total Liabilities to Net Worth 37	2.3	•	0.8	1.3	0.7	1.1	0.7	0.5	0.6	1.8	0.8	1.1	2.6
Current Assets to Working Capital 38	•	•	1.5	1.4	1.3	6.3	1.8	2.6	1.9	4.0	•	3.6	•
Current Liabilities to Working Capital 39	•	•	0.5	0.4	0.3	5.3	0.8	1.6	0.9	3.0	•	2.6	•
Working Capital to Net Sales 40	•	0.1	0.1	0.3	0.4	0.0	0.3	0.2	0.3	0.2	0.4	0.4	•
Inventory to Working Capital 41	•	•	•	•	•	•	•	•	•	0.0	0.0	0.0	•
Total Receipts to Cash Flow 42	2.0	1.9	2.1	2.6	1.9	3.4	2.1	2.4	1.9	2.3	1.3	1.7	2.1
Cost of Goods to Cash Flow 43	0.0	0.0	0.0	•	•	•	0.0	•	0.0	•	•	0.0	0.0
Cash Flow to Total Debt 44	0.1	•	4.8	0.8	1.6	0.8	0.8	0.9	0.9	0.4	0.8	0.3	0.1

Selected Financial Factors (in Percentages)

Item													
Debt Ratio 45	69.4	•	45.6	55.9	40.6	51.4	40.9	32.7	39.0	63.9	44.9	52.6	72.3
Return on Total Assets 46	4.9	•	105.8	28.9	34.6	24.7	23.8	19.0	16.4	15.9	25.8	6.3	3.1
Return on Equity Before Income Taxes 47	13.6	•	192.0	65.0	57.3	48.5	39.1	25.2	25.6	39.3	44.8	11.1	8.7
Return on Equity After Income Taxes 48	11.0	•	191.3	64.7	54.4	45.2	36.6	22.3	23.5	33.7	42.1	8.2	6.3
Profit Margin (Before Income Tax) 49	25.0	19.7	22.7	24.1	28.2	17.1	33.0	24.8	22.5	22.9	53.4	22.7	23.5
Profit Margin (After Income Tax) 50	20.3	17.6	22.6	24.0	26.8	15.9	30.9	22.0	20.7	19.6	50.2	16.8	16.9

Table I

Corporations with and without Net Income

LIFE INSURANCE

MONEY AMOUNTS AND SIZE OF ASSETS IN THOUSANDS OF DOLLARS

Item Description for Accounting Period 7/10 Through 6/11		Total	Zero Assets	Under 500	500 to 1,000	1,000 to 5,000	5,000 to 10,000	10,000 to 25,000	25,000 to 50,000	50,000 to 100,000	100,000 to 250,000	250,000 to 500,000	500,000 to 2,500,000	2,500,000 and over
Number of Enterprises	1	796	45	154	67	108	51	67	54	23	33	37	66	91
Revenues ($ in Thousands)														
Net Sales	2	967309095	4733846	22362	24156	102402	81645	1079981	922788	590512	1303160	4432370	23524785	930491090
Interest	3	167426812	695592	298	601	5682	12041	27909	59706	62676	182422	572828	3042066	162764990
Rents	4	7692763	4643	0	0	52	299	1381	4350	7288	4372	9289	30122	7630968
Royalties	5	18071	0	0	0	0	0	0	0	19	870	28	269	16885
Other Portfolio Income	6	42465563	43711	39	246	3508	2934	9555	8717	6706	21558	424334	188459	41755793
Other Receipts	7	749705886	3989900	22025	23309	93160	66371	1041136	850015	513823	1093938	3425891	20263869	718322454
Total Receipts	8	967309095	4733846	22362	24156	102402	81645	1079981	922788	590512	1303160	4432370	23524785	930491090
Average Total Receipts	9	1215212	105197	145	361	948	1601	16119	17089	25674	39490	119794	356436	10225177
Operating Costs/Operating Income (%)														
Cost of Operations	10	52.1	66.1	37.0	17.6	26.7	24.3	20.2	40.3	38.0	46.3	41.3	54.8	52.1
Salaries and Wages	11	2.2	1.0	•	•	•	•	0.1	0.7	3.3	0.3	0.8	0.8	2.2
Taxes Paid	12	0.8	0.4	1.1	0.7	1.0	3.3	0.9	1.9	1.8	1.8	1.4	0.8	0.8
Interest Paid	13	3.5	1.0	0.1	0.3	0.0	0.0	0.1	0.6	0.1	0.3	1.0	0.3	3.6
Depreciation	14	0.7	0.4	•	0.0	0.2	0.3	0.1	0.5	0.7	0.3	0.3	0.3	0.7
Amortization and Depletion	15	1.3	0.5	0.5	0.6	1.3	2.2	1.3	1.8	1.9	4.8	2.4	1.4	1.3
Pensions and Other Deferred Comp.	16	0.6	0.9	•	0.0	0.0	0.3	0.2	1.2	1.3	0.6	0.5	0.5	0.6
Employee Benefits	17	0.3	0.4	•	0.3	0.1	0.1	0.1	0.6	1.0	0.2	0.2	0.2	0.3
Advertising	18	0.2	1.2	•	•	0.6	0.1	0.0	0.1	1.0	0.1	0.6	0.5	0.2
Other Expenses	19	35.3	29.7	46.5	52.8	57.4	55.2	27.5	51.8	45.0	66.7	39.9	38.1	35.1
Officers' Compensation	20	0.1	•	•	•	0.2	0.2	•	0.2	0.1	0.0	0.3	0.1	0.1
Operating Margin	21	3.1	•	14.8	28.0	13.0	13.6	49.5	0.3	5.7	•	11.2	2.1	3.1
Operating Margin Before Officers' Comp.	22	3.2	•	14.8	28.0	13.0	13.7	49.5	0.5	5.9	•	11.5	2.2	3.1

Selected Average Balance Sheet ($ in Thousands)

Net Receivables 23	91831	6	10	120	45	937	1480	440	3926	2721	10376	791345
Inventories 24	•	•	•	•	•	•	•	•	•	•	•	•
Net Property, Plant and Equipment 25	67480	0	0	13	99	103	350	1586	396	1821	3250	586270
Total Assets 26	7993018	176	762	2737	6963	16315	37097	71509	158526	366958	1255230	68739765
Notes and Loans Payable 27	202364	0	0	0	0	20	225	238	105	1822	8616	1762897
All Other Liabilities 28	6735978	174	325	1657	3301	9500	25736	50884	140061	363519	1067499	5790899
Net Worth 29	1054676	2	436	1080	3662	6796	11135	20387	18360	1617	179114	9067869

Selected Financial Ratios (Times to 1)

Current Ratio 30	0.4	7.1	12.2	3.4	5.1	1.9	2.5	1.2	1.2	1.1	0.8	0.4
Quick Ratio 31	0.3	5.3	8.1	2.8	4.0	1.4	2.0	0.9	0.9	0.7	0.6	0.3
Net Sales to Working Capital 32	•	1.1	0.7	0.8	0.6	4.3	1.7	8.1	5.3	12.5	•	•
Coverage Ratio 33	1.9	128.0	99.5	3272.8	10714.0	596.5	1.2	52.2	•	11.6	7.6	1.9
Total Asset Turnover 34	0.2	0.8	0.5	0.3	0.2	1.0	0.5	0.4	0.2	0.3	0.3	0.1
Inventory Turnover 35	•	•	•	•	•	•	•	•	•	•	•	•
Receivables Turnover 36	•	•	•	•	•	•	•	•	•	•	•	•
Total Liabilities to Net Worth 37	6.6	71.8	0.7	1.5	0.9	1.4	2.3	2.5	7.6	225.9	6.0	6.6
Current Assets to Working Capital 38	•	1.2	1.1	1.4	1.2	2.1	1.7	6.8	7.4	13.7	•	•
Current Liabilities to Working Capital 39	•	0.2	0.1	0.4	0.2	1.1	0.7	5.8	6.4	12.7	•	•
Working Capital to Net Sales 40	•	0.9	1.4	1.3	1.7	0.2	0.6	0.1	0.2	0.1	•	•
Inventory to Working Capital 41	•	•	•	•	•	•	•	•	•	•	•	•
Total Receipts to Cash Flow 42	2.8	3.8	1.6	1.2	1.5	1.3	2.0	2.1	2.3	2.0	2.5	2.8
Cost of Goods to Cash Flow 43	1.4	2.5	0.6	0.2	0.4	0.4	0.3	0.8	0.8	1.1	0.8	1.4
Cash Flow to Total Debt 44	0.1	0.5	0.9	0.4	0.3	1.3	0.3	0.2	0.1	0.2	0.1	0.1

Selected Financial Factors (in Percentages)

Debt Ratio 45	86.8	98.6	42.7	60.5	47.4	58.3	70.0	71.5	88.4	99.6	85.7	86.8
Return on Total Assets 46	1.0	12.3	13.3	4.4	3.0	49.0	0.3	2.1	2.1	3.9	0.7	1.0
Return on Equity Before Income Taxes 47	3.6	885.0	22.9	11.2	5.7	117.3	0.2	7.1	7.1	817.7	4.0	3.5
Return on Equity After Income Taxes 48	2.5	827.3	19.9	9.1	4.2	99.4	•	4.8	4.8	696.6	1.2	2.5
Profit Margin (Before Income Tax) 49	3.1	14.8	27.7	12.8	13.1	49.5	0.1	5.7	5.7	11.0	2.0	3.1
Profit Margin (After Income Tax) 50	2.2	13.8	24.1	10.3	9.7	41.9	•	3.8	3.8	9.4	0.6	2.2

Table II
Corporations with Net Income

LIFE INSURANCE

MONEY AMOUNTS AND SIZE OF ASSETS IN THOUSANDS OF DOLLARS

Item Description for Accounting Period 7/10 Through 6/11		Total	Zero Assets	Under 500	500 to 1,000	1,000 to 5,000	5,000 to 10,000	10,000 to 25,000	25,000 to 50,000	50,000 to 100,000	100,000 to 250,000	250,000 to 500,000	500,000 to 2,500,000	2,500,000 and over
Number of Enterprises	1	582	26	111	59	75	39	53	36	20	20	29	47	66
Revenues ($ in Thousands)														
Net Sales	2	784182550	1435311	19710	19695	62972	54992	1038824	655361	606978	748943	3584756	20255552	755669455
Interest	3	139783794	134960	253	554	3790	8437	25420	42145	66232	116108	385372	2456030	136544494
Rents	4	7155776	3779	0	0	0	172	865	2138	5322	3955	8599	28016	7102878
Royalties	5	12449	0	0	0	52	0	0	0	19	0	28	266	12136
Other Portfolio Income	6	38591137	37342	39	160	2649	2445	7421	6963	7414	15899	414607	159232	37936966
Other Receipts	7	598633394	1259230	19418	18981	56481	43938	1005118	604115	527991	612981	2776150	17612008	574102981
Total Receipts	8	784182550	1435311	19710	19695	62972	54992	1038824	655361	606978	748943	3584756	20255552	755699455
Average Total Receipts	9	1347393	55204	178	334	840	1410	19600	18204	30349	37447	123612	430969	11449992
Operating Costs/Operating Income (%)														
Cost of Operations	10	48.3	69.7	32.4	17.9	17.8	22.5	17.9	42.4	41.3	49.9	43.1	54.6	48.2
Salaries and Wages	11	2.5	3.3	•	•	•	•	0.1	0.2	3.2	0.6	1.0	0.8	2.5
Taxes Paid	12	0.8	0.3	1.1	0.8	0.6	2.7	0.8	2.0	1.6	1.7	1.6	0.8	0.8
Interest Paid	13	3.9	2.9	0.1	0.3	0.0	0.0	0.1	0.7	0.1	0.2	0.3	0.3	4.0
Depreciation	14	0.8	1.2	•	0.0	0.0	0.2	0.1	0.3	0.6	0.1	0.4	0.3	0.8
Amortization and Depletion	15	1.2	1.5	0.3	0.7	0.7	1.2	1.3	1.8	1.8	4.6	2.6	1.4	1.2
Pensions and Other Deferred Comp.	16	0.5	1.3	•	0.0	0.0	0.4	0.3	1.2	0.9	0.4	0.6	0.5	0.5
Employee Benefits	17	0.3	0.4	•	•	•	0.1	0.2	0.5	1.0	0.1	0.3	0.2	0.3
Advertising	18	0.2	0.0	•	•	0.0	0.4	0.0	0.2	0.9	0.1	0.6	0.4	0.2
Other Expenses	19	36.7	18.0	43.0	42.9	55.1	33.9	26.0	41.9	41.2	34.1	32.7	35.3	36.9
Officers' Compensation	20	0.1	•	•	•	•	0.2	•	0.3	0.1	•	0.4	0.1	0.1
Operating Margin	21	4.5	1.5	23.1	37.3	25.8	38.4	53.3	8.6	7.3	8.2	16.5	5.4	4.4
Operating Margin Before Officers' Comp.	22	4.6	1.5	23.1	37.3	25.8	38.6	53.3	8.8	7.5	8.2	16.9	5.5	4.5

Selected Average Balance Sheet ($ in Thousands)

Item													
Net Receivables 23	118505	0	8	11	161	56	1172	2191	599	5585	3088	13803	1029443
Inventories 24	•	•	•	•	•	•	•	•	•	•	•	•	•
Net Property, Plant and Equipment 25	90516	0	0	0	1	93	77	481	772	270	2318	3054	794296
Total Assets 26	8340189	181	758	2416	6913	17114	36659	83333	149237	364128	1326942		72328340
Notes and Loans Payable 27	239312	0	0	0	0	0	25	281	273	173	2324	9812	2101981
All Other Liabilities 28	6900050	188	326	1189	3114	9717	23102	62933	130968	289866	1059588		59881015
Net Worth 29	1200827	-7	432	1227	3799	7372	13276	20127	18095	71937	257542		10345344

Selected Financial Ratios (Times to 1)

Item													
Current Ratio 30	0.4	•	7.0	12.7	6.3	7.3	2.8	2.2	1.2	1.3	1.2	0.9	0.4
Quick Ratio 31	0.3	•	4.9	8.7	5.1	5.8	2.2	1.6	0.9	1.2	0.9	0.7	0.3
Net Sales to Working Capital 32	•	•	1.3	0.7	0.6	0.5	3.6	2.3	6.1	2.5	5.2	•	•
Coverage Ratio 33	2.2	1.5	176.2	109.8	4010.2	20877.0	618.3	13.0	109.0	38.3	55.3	18.3	2.1
Total Asset Turnover 34	0.2	1.0	0.4	0.3	0.2	1.1	0.5	0.4	0.3	0.3	0.3	0.3	0.2
Inventory Turnover 35	•	•	•	•	•	•	•	•	•	•	•	•	•
Receivables Turnover 36	•	•	•	•	•	•	•	•	•	•	•	•	•
Total Liabilities to Net Worth 37	5.9	•	•	0.8	1.0	0.8	1.3	1.8	3.1	7.2	4.1	4.2	6.0
Current Assets to Working Capital 38	•	•	1.2	1.1	1.2	1.2	1.6	1.8	5.3	3.9	5.8	•	•
Current Liabilities to Working Capital 39	•	•	0.2	0.1	0.2	0.2	0.6	0.8	4.3	2.9	4.8	•	•
Working Capital to Net Sales 40	•	•	0.8	1.5	1.7	2.1	0.3	0.4	0.2	0.4	0.2	•	•
Inventory to Working Capital 41	•	•	•	•	•	•	•	•	•	•	•	•	•
Total Receipts to Cash Flow 42	2.6	6.0	1.5	1.3	1.3	1.4	1.3	2.0	2.2	2.5	2.2	2.5	2.6
Cost of Goods to Cash Flow 43	1.2	4.2	0.5	0.2	0.2	0.3	0.2	0.9	0.9	1.2	0.9	1.4	1.2
Cash Flow to Total Debt 44	0.1	•	0.6	0.8	0.5	0.3	1.6	0.4	0.2	0.1	0.2	0.2	0.1

Selected Financial Factors (in Percentages)

Item													
Debt Ratio 45	85.6	•	103.6	43.0	49.2	45.0	56.9	63.8	75.8	87.9	80.2	80.6	85.7
Return on Total Assets 46	1.4	•	22.8	16.4	8.9	7.7	61.1	4.5	2.7	2.0	5.6	1.8	1.3
Return on Equity Before Income Taxes 47	5.2	•	28.6	17.4	14.1	141.7	11.0	16.5	28.1	8.8	4.9		
Return on Equity After Income Taxes 48	3.9	•	25.1	14.9	12.2	120.8	8.2	12.0	24.6	6.0	3.7		
Profit Margin (Before Income Tax) 49	4.6	1.5	23.1	37.0	25.5	38.0	53.3	8.3	7.3	8.0	16.3	5.3	4.5
Profit Margin (After Income Tax) 50	3.5	1.4	22.0	32.5	21.8	32.9	45.4	6.3	5.5	5.8	14.3	3.6	3.4

Table I

Corporations with and without Net Income

LIFE INSURANCE, STOCK COMPANIES (FORM 1120L)

MONEY AMOUNTS AND SIZE OF ASSETS IN THOUSANDS OF DOLLARS

Item Description for Accounting Period 7/10 Through 6/11	Total	Zero Assets	Under 500	500 to 1,000	1,000 to 5,000	5,000 to 10,000	10,000 to 25,000	25,000 to 50,000	50,000 to 100,000	100,000 to 250,000	250,000 to 500,000	500,000 to 2,500,000	2,500,000 and over
Number of Enterprises **1**	741	39	149	65	98	51	67	49	23	30	32	56	83
Revenues ($ in Thousands)													
Net Sales **2**	853404612	4710376	22316	24034	84595	81645	1079981	858231	590512	1181902	3926462	20698841	820145717
Interest **3**	143787434	688891	282	551	4184	12041	27909	52165	62676	156371	494306	2289922	139998136
Rents **4**	7214906	4643	0	0	0	299	1381	3022	7288	4074	6381	24367	7163451
Royalties **5**	12267	0	0	0	0	0	0	0	19	0	28	263	11958
Other Portfolio Income **6**	39114932	43443	39	179	2718	2934	9555	8356	6706	18681	420385	172597	38429338
Other Receipts **7**	663275073	3973399	21995	23304	77693	66371	1041136	794688	513823	1002776	3005362	18211692	634542834
Total Receipts **8**	853404612	4710376	22316	24034	84595	81645	1079981	858231	590512	1181902	3926462	20698841	820145717
Average Total Receipts **9**	1151693	120779	150	370	863	1601	16119	17515	25674	39397	122702	369622	9881274
Operating Costs/Operating Income (%)													
Cost of Operations **10**	52.5	66.1	37.0	17.6	29.8	24.3	20.2	38.1	38.0	46.0	39.9	56.2	52.5
Salaries and Wages **11**	2.4	1.0	•	•	•	•	0.1	0.7	3.3	0.4	0.9	0.9	2.4
Taxes Paid **12**	0.8	0.4	1.1	0.7	0.6	3.3	0.9	1.8	1.8	1.8	1.3	0.7	0.8
Interest Paid **13**	3.8	1.0	0.1	0.0	0.0	0.0	0.1	0.6	0.1	0.3	1.2	0.2	3.9
Depreciation **14**	0.8	0.4	•	0.0	0.1	0.3	0.1	0.4	0.7	0.3	0.3	0.3	0.8
Amortization and Depletion **15**	1.2	0.5	0.5	0.6	1.1	2.2	1.3	1.9	1.9	4.9	2.2	1.3	1.2
Pensions and Other Deferred Comp. **16**	0.5	0.9	•	0.0	0.0	0.3	0.2	1.0	1.3	0.5	0.6	0.4	0.5
Employee Benefits **17**	0.3	0.4	•	0.0	0.0	0.1	0.1	0.6	1.0	0.2	0.2	0.2	0.3
Advertising **18**	0.3	1.2	•	•	0.1	0.6	0.0	0.2	1.0	0.1	0.7	0.5	0.2
Other Expenses **19**	34.3	29.7	46.2	52.9	52.9	55.2	27.5	53.9	45.0	68.8	40.0	37.2	34.2
Officers' Compensation **20**	0.1	•	•	•	•	0.2	•	0.2	0.1	0.0	0.3	0.1	0.1
Operating Margin **21**	3.0	•	15.0	28.1	15.3	13.6	49.5	0.6	5.7	•	12.5	1.9	3.0
Operating Margin Before Officers' Comp. **22**	3.1	•	15.0	28.1	15.3	13.7	49.5	0.8	5.9	•	12.8	2.0	3.1

Selected Average Balance Sheet ($ in Thousands)

Item												
Net Receivables 23	95815	6	10	130	45	937	1628	440	4230	2444	12039	842776
Inventories 24	•	•	•	•	•	•	•	•	•	•	•	•
Net Property, Plant and Equipment 25	69647	0	0	4	99	103	365	1586	325	2034	3411	617784
Total Assets 26	7677251	174	750	2482	6963	16315	36246	71509	154833	370750	1203840	67466654
Notes and Loans Payable 27	216201	0	0	0	0	20	248	238	116	2106	10052	1922319
All Other Liabilities 28	6425684	171	330	1375	3301	9500	23805	50884	136216	373908	1018741	56445873
Net Worth 29	1035366	3	420	1108	3662	6796	12193	20387	18501	-5264	175047	9098462

Selected Financial Ratios (Times to 1)

Item												
Current Ratio 30	0.4	6.9	12.1	4.2	5.1	1.9	2.3	1.2	1.1	1.1	0.9	0.3
Quick Ratio 31	0.2	5.0	8.1	3.4	4.0	1.4	1.8	0.9	0.8	0.7	0.6	0.2
Net Sales to Working Capital 32	•	1.1	0.7	0.7	0.6	4.3	1.9	8.1	14.6	10.0	•	•
Coverage Ratio 33	1.8	129.7	3344.5	3183.8	10714.0	596.5	1.6	52.2	11.6	8.2	1.8	•
Total Asset Turnover 34	0.2	0.9	0.5	0.3	0.2	1.0	0.5	0.4	0.3	0.3	0.3	0.1
Inventory Turnover 35	•	•	•	•	•	•	•	•	•	•	•	•
Receivables Turnover 36	6.4	•	•	•	•	•	•	•	•	•	5.9	6.4
Total Liabilities to Net Worth 37	6.4	68.4	0.8	1.2	0.9	1.4	2.0	2.5	7.4	6.8	5.9	6.4
Current Assets to Working Capital 38	•	1.2	1.1	1.3	1.2	2.1	1.8	6.8	20.3	10.8	•	•
Current Liabilities to Working Capital 39	•	0.2	0.1	0.3	0.2	1.1	0.8	5.8	19.3	9.8	•	•
Working Capital to Net Sales 40	•	0.9	1.4	1.5	1.7	0.2	0.5	0.1	0.1	0.1	0.3	0.1
Inventory to Working Capital 41	•	•	•	•	•	•	•	•	•	•	•	•
Total Receipts to Cash Flow 42	2.8	1.6	1.2	1.5	1.5	1.3	1.9	2.1	2.3	2.0	2.6	2.9
Cost of Goods to Cash Flow 43	1.5	0.6	0.2	0.5	0.4	0.3	0.7	0.8	1.1	0.8	1.5	1.5
Cash Flow to Total Debt 44	0.1	0.5	0.9	0.4	0.3	1.3	0.4	0.2	0.1	0.2	0.1	0.1

Selected Financial Factors (in Percentages)

Item												
Debt Ratio 45	86.5	98.6	44.0	55.4	47.4	58.3	66.4	71.5	88.1	101.4	85.5	86.5
Return on Total Assets 46	1.0	13.0	13.7	5.2	3.0	0.5	•	2.1	•	4.5	0.6	1.0
Return on Equity Before Income Taxes 47	3.4	897.3	24.5	11.7	5.7	117.3	0.5	7.1	•	•	3.7	3.3
Return on Equity After Income Taxes 48	2.4	839.7	21.2	9.6	4.2	99.4	•	4.8	•	•	0.8	2.4
Profit Margin (Before Income Tax) 49	3.1	15.0	27.8	15.0	13.1	49.5	0.4	5.7	12.3	•	1.8	3.1
Profit Margin (After Income Tax) 50	2.2	14.0	24.1	12.4	9.7	41.9	•	3.8	10.6	0.4	0.4	2.2

Table II
Corporations with Net Income

LIFE INSURANCE, STOCK COMPANIES (FORM 1120L)

MONEY AMOUNTS AND SIZE OF ASSETS IN THOUSANDS OF DOLLARS

Item Description for Accounting Period 7/10 Through 6/11	Total	Zero Assets	Under 500	500 to 1,000	1,000 to 5,000	5,000 to 10,000	10,000 to 25,000	25,000 to 50,000	50,000 to 100,000	100,000 to 250,000	250,000 to 500,000	500,000 to 2,500,000	2,500,000 and over
Number of Enterprises 1	554	26	111	56	73	39	50	36	17	20	•	•	•
Revenues ($ in Thousands)													
Net Sales 2	675153988	1435311	19710	19573	62086	54992	1014763	655361	496048	748943	•	•	•
Interest 3	116991949	134960	253	504	3244	8437	23459	42145	47953	116108	•	•	•
Rents 4	6679676	3779	0	0	0	172	865	2138	3875	3955	•	•	•
Royalties 5	12254	0	0	0	0	0	0	0	19	0	•	•	•
Other Portfolio Income 6	35278403	37342	39	93	2517	2445	6744	6963	5114	15899	•	•	•
Other Receipts 7	516191706	1259230	19418	18976	56325	43938	983695	604115	439087	612981	•	•	•
Total Receipts 8	675153988	1435311	19710	19573	62086	54992	1014763	655361	496048	748943	•	•	•
Average Total Receipts 9	1218690	55204	178	350	850	1410	20295	18204	29179	37447	•	•	•
Operating Costs/Operating Income (%)													
Cost of Operations 10	48.3	69.7	32.4	17.9	17.9	22.5	17.8	42.4	39.1	49.9	•	•	•
Salaries and Wages 11	2.7	3.3	•	•	•	•	0.1	0.2	4.0	0.6	•	•	•
Taxes Paid 12	0.9	0.3	1.1	0.8	0.6	2.7	0.7	2.0	1.6	1.7	•	•	•
Interest Paid 13	4.4	2.9	0.1	0.0	0.0	0.0	0.1	0.7	0.1	0.2	•	•	•
Depreciation 14	0.9	1.2	•	0.0	0.0	0.2	0.1	0.3	0.5	0.1	•	•	•
Amortization and Depletion 15	1.1	1.5	0.3	0.7	0.7	1.2	1.3	1.8	1.6	4.6	•	•	•
Pensions and Other Deferred Comp. 16	0.5	1.3	•	•	0.0	0.4	0.2	1.2	0.7	0.4	•	•	•
Employee Benefits 17	0.4	0.4	•	•	0.1	0.1	0.1	0.5	1.1	0.1	•	•	•
Advertising 18	0.3	0.0	•	•	0.0	0.4	0.0	0.2	1.1	0.1	•	•	•
Other Expenses 19	35.9	18.0	43.0	43.0	54.8	33.9	25.4	41.9	41.6	34.1	•	•	•
Officers' Compensation 20	0.1	•	•	•	•	0.2	•	0.3	0.2	•	•	•	•
Operating Margin 21	4.7	1.5	23.1	37.5	25.9	38.4	54.3	8.6	8.4	8.2	•	•	•
Operating Margin Before Officers' Comp. 22	4.7	1.5	23.1	37.5	25.9	38.6	54.3	8.8	8.6	8.2	•	•	•

Selected Average Balance Sheet ($ in Thousands)

Item										
Net Receivables 23	120733	0	8	12	165	56	1235	2191	579	5985
Inventories 24	•	•	•	•	•	•	•	•	•	•
Net Property, Plant and Equipment 25	91322	0	0	0	1	93	60	481	812	270
Total Assets 26	7588593	•	181	758	2364	6913	16932	36659	74157	149237
Notes and Loans Payable 27	249835	•	0	0	0	0	27	281	322	173
All Other Liabilities 28	6203265	•	188	337	1104	3114	9421	23102	52092	130968
Net Worth 29	1136493	•	-7	421	1260	3799	7484	13276	21743	18095

Selected Financial Ratios (Times to 1)

Item										
Current Ratio 30	0.4	•	7.0	12.7	6.7	7.3	2.7	2.2	1.0	1.3
Quick Ratio 31	0.3	•	4.9	8.7	5.4	5.8	2.1	1.6	0.7	1.2
Net Sales to Working Capital 32	•	•	1.3	0.7	0.6	0.5	3.8	2.3	•	2.5
Coverage Ratio 33	2.1	1.5	176.2	7276.0	3968.5	208877.0	615.4	13.0	107.1	38.3
Total Asset Turnover 34	0.2	•	1.0	0.5	0.4	0.2	1.2	0.5	0.4	0.3
Inventory Turnover 35	•	•	•	•	•	•	•	•	•	•
Receivables Turnover 36	•	•	•	•	•	•	•	•	•	•
Total Liabilities to Net Worth 37	5.7	•	•	0.8	0.9	0.8	1.3	1.8	2.4	7.2
Current Assets to Working Capital 38	•	•	1.2	1.1	1.2	1.3	1.6	1.8	1.8	3.9
Current Liabilities to Working Capital 39	•	•	0.2	0.1	0.2	0.2	0.6	0.8	•	2.9
Working Capital to Net Sales 40	•	•	0.8	1.5	1.7	2.1	•	•	•	0.4
Inventory to Working Capital 41	•	•	•	•	•	•	•	•	•	•
Total Receipts to Cash Flow 42	2.6	6.0	1.5	1.2	1.3	1.4	1.3	2.0	2.1	2.5
Cost of Goods to Cash Flow 43	1.3	4.2	0.5	0.2	0.2	0.3	0.2	0.9	0.8	1.2
Cash Flow to Total Debt 44	0.1	•	0.6	0.8	0.6	0.3	0.3	0.4	0.3	0.1

Selected Financial Factors (in Percentages)

Item										
Debt Ratio 45	85.0	•	103.6	44.5	46.7	45.0	55.8	63.8	70.7	87.9
Return on Total Assets 46	1.5	•	22.8	17.1	9.2	7.7	65.2	4.5	3.3	2.0
Return on Equity Before Income Taxes 47	5.1	•	•	30.9	17.2	14.1	147.3	11.4	11.2	16.5
Return on Equity After Income Taxes 48	3.9	•	•	27.1	14.8	12.2	125.5	8.6	8.3	12.0
Profit Margin (Before Income Tax) 49	4.7	1.5	23.1	37.2	25.6	38.0	54.3	8.3	8.3	8.0
Profit Margin (After Income Tax) 50	3.6	1.4	22.0	32.6	21.9	32.9	46.3	6.3	6.2	5.8

Table I
Corporations with and without Net Income

LIFE INSURANCE, MUTUAL COMPANIES (FORM 1120L)

MONEY AMOUNTS AND SIZE OF ASSETS IN THOUSANDS OF DOLLARS

Item Description for Accounting Period 7/10 Through 6/11	Total	Zero Assets	Under 500	500 to 1,000	1,000 to 5,000	5,000 to 10,000	10,000 to 25,000	25,000 to 50,000	50,000 to 100,000	100,000 to 250,000	250,000 to 500,000	500,000 to 2,500,000	2,500,000 and over
Number of Enterprises 1	55	6	5	3	10	0	0	5	0	3	5	10	8
Revenues ($ in Thousands)													
Net Sales 2	113904483	23470	46	122	17807	0	0	64557	0	121258	505908	2825944	110345373
Interest 3	23639377	6701	17	50	1499	0	0	7541	0	26051	78522	752143	22766854
Rents 4	477857	0	0	0	52	0	0	1328	0	298	2908	5755	467517
Royalties 5	5804	0	0	0	0	0	0	0	0	870	0	6	4928
Other Portfolio Income 6	3350631	269	0	67	791	0	0	361	0	2876	3949	15863	3326455
Other Receipts 7	86430814	16500	29	5	15465	0	0	55327	0	91163	420529	2052177	83779619
Total Receipts 8	113904483	23470	46	122	17807	0	0	64557	0	121258	505908	2825944	110345373
Average Total Receipts 9	2070991	3912	9	41	1781	•	•	12911	•	40419	101182	282594	13793172
Operating Costs/Operating Income (%)													
Cost of Operations 10	48.9	58.5	41.3	4.9	12.3	•	•	69.7	•	49.5	52.5	44.4	48.9
Salaries and Wages 11	0.8	•	•	•	•	•	•	•	•	•	0.0	0.5	0.8
Taxes Paid 12	0.7	2.9	2.2	2.5	2.6	•	•	2.3	•	1.8	2.5	1.7	0.6
Interest Paid 13	0.8	1.5	•	54.1	•	•	•	•	•	0.0	0.1	0.7	0.8
Depreciation 14	0.2	0.5	•	•	0.6	•	•	2.1	•	0.2	0.5	0.3	0.2
Amortization and Depletion 15	1.6	3.8	•	•	2.1	•	•	1.5	•	3.1	3.6	2.4	1.6
Pensions and Other Deferred Comp. 16	0.6	0.7	•	•	0.0	•	•	2.9	•	1.7	0.2	1.1	0.6
Employee Benefits 17	0.2	0.0	•	•	1.5	•	•	1.3	•	1.1	0.5	0.2	0.2
Advertising 18	0.2	0.0	•	•	0.1	•	•	0.0	•	0.1	0.0	0.5	0.2
Other Expenses 19	42.4	39.8	154.3	27.9	78.7	•	•	23.6	•	46.5	39.0	44.4	42.4
Officers' Compensation 20	0.1	•	•	•	•	•	•	•	•	•	•	•	0.1
Operating Margin 21	3.5	•	•	9.8	2.2	•	•	•	•	•	1.0	3.9	3.5
Operating Margin Before Officers' Comp. 22	3.6	•	•	9.8	2.2	•	•	2.1	•	•	1.0	3.9	3.6

Selected Average Balance Sheet ($ in Thousands)

Net Receivables **23**	38148	0	0	20	•	32	•	896	4497	1059	257752
Inventories **24**	•	•	•	•	•	•	•	•	•	•	•
Net Property, Plant and Equipment **25**	38286	0	0	106	•	200	•	1111	459	2349	259317
Total Assets **26**	12247260	255	760	5230	•	45436	•	195460	342687	1543013	81948289
Notes and Loans Payable **27**	15943	0	0	0	•	0	•	0	0	580	108887
All Other Liabilities **28**	10916488	255	124	4424	•	44668	•	178509	297033	1340542	73088937
Net Worth **29**	1314829	0	636	806	•	767	•	16951	45654	201891	8750466

Selected Financial Ratios (Times to 1)

Current Ratio **30**	0.9	•	16.4	1.3	•	8.6	•	12.8	0.9	0.6	0.9
Quick Ratio **31**	0.7	•	•	1.0	•	8.1	•	10.5	0.7	0.5	0.7
Net Sales to Working Capital **32**	•	0.0	0.4	3.7	•	0.7	•	0.7	•	•	•
Coverage Ratio **33**	5.3	•	1.2	•	•	•	•	•	7.6	6.2	5.3
Total Asset Turnover **34**	0.2	0.0	0.1	0.3	•	0.3	•	0.2	0.3	0.2	0.2
Inventory Turnover **35**	•	•	•	•	•	•	•	•	•	•	•
Receivables Turnover **36**	•	•	•	•	•	•	•	•	•	•	•
Total Liabilities to Net Worth **37**	8.3	•	0.2	5.5	•	58.2	•	10.5	6.5	6.6	8.4
Current Assets to Working Capital **38**	•	1.0	1.1	4.2	•	1.1	•	1.1	•	•	•
Current Liabilities to Working Capital **39**	•	•	0.1	3.2	•	0.1	•	0.1	•	•	•
Working Capital to Net Sales **40**	•	21.7	2.3	0.3	•	1.4	•	1.4	•	•	•
Inventory to Working Capital **41**	•	•	•	•	•	•	•	•	•	•	•
Total Receipts to Cash Flow **42**	2.3	4.0	2.1	1.3	•	5.1	•	2.6	2.6	2.1	2.3
Cost of Goods to Cash Flow **43**	1.1	2.3	0.9	0.2	•	3.6	•	1.3	1.3	0.9	1.1
Cash Flow to Total Debt **44**	0.1	0.0	•	0.3	•	0.1	•	0.1	0.1	0.1	0.1

Selected Financial Factors (in Percentages)

Debt Ratio **45**	89.3	100.0	16.4	84.6	•	98.3	•	91.3	86.7	86.9	89.3
Return on Total Assets **46**	0.7	•	3.4	0.7	•	•	•	•	0.3	0.8	0.7
Return on Equity Before Income Taxes **47**	5.6	•	0.6	4.4	•	•	•	•	2.0	5.4	5.6
Return on Equity After Income Taxes **48**	3.6	•	0.6	1.6	•	•	•	•	0.5	3.2	3.6
Profit Margin (Before Income Tax) **49**	3.5	•	9.8	2.0	•	•	•	•	0.9	3.9	3.6
Profit Margin (After Income Tax) **50**	2.3	•	9.8	0.7	•	•	•	•	0.2	0.2	2.3

Table II
Corporations with Net Income

LIFE INSURANCE, MUTUAL COMPANIES (FORM 1120L)

MONEY AMOUNTS AND SIZE OF ASSETS IN THOUSANDS OF DOLLARS

Item Description for Accounting Period 7/10 Through 6/11	Total	Zero Assets	Under 500	500 to 1000	1,000 to 5,000	5,000 to 10,000	10,000 to 25,000	25,000 to 50,000	50,000 to 100,000	100,000 to 250,000	250,000 to 500,000	500,000 to 2,500,000	2,500,000 and over
Number of Enterprises 1	28	0	0	3	3	0	3	0	3	0	•	•	•
Revenues ($ in Thousands)													
Net Sales 2	109028562	0	0	122	886	0	24062	0	110930	0	•	•	•
Interest 3	22791845	0	0	50	546	0	1960	0	18278	0	•	•	•
Rents 4	476100	0	0	0	52	0	0	0	1447	0	•	•	•
Royalties 5	195	0	0	0	0	0	0	0	0	0	•	•	•
Other Portfolio Income 6	3312733	0	0	67	131	0	676	0	2300	0	•	•	•
Other Receipts 7	82447689	0	0	5	157	0	21426	0	88905	0	•	•	•
Total Receipts 8	109028562	0	0	122	886	0	24062	0	110930	0	•	•	•
Average Total Receipts 9	3893877	•	•	41	295	•	8021	•	36977	•	•	•	•
Operating Costs/Operating Income (%)													
Cost of Operations 10	48.7	•	•	4.9	8.6	•	22.3	•	50.9	•	•	•	•
Salaries and Wages 11	0.8	•	•	•	•	•	•	•	•	•	•	•	•
Taxes Paid 12	0.7	•	•	2.5	•	•	2.8	•	1.6	•	•	•	•
Interest Paid 13	0.8	•	•	54.1	•	•	•	•	0.0	•	•	•	•
Depreciation 14	0.2	•	•	•	•	•	0.6	•	1.2	•	•	•	•
Amortization and Depletion 15	1.6	•	•	•	1.4	•	2.3	•	2.5	•	•	•	•
Pensions and Other Deferred Comp. 16	0.6	•	•	•	•	•	5.2	•	1.4	•	•	•	•
Employee Benefits 17	0.2	•	•	•	•	•	2.7	•	0.2	•	•	•	•
Advertising 18	0.2	•	•	•	•	•	0.1	•	0.1	•	•	•	•
Other Expenses 19	42.3	•	•	27.9	71.2	•	53.1	•	39.5	•	•	•	•
Officers' Compensation 20	0.1	•	•	•	•	•	•	•	•	•	•	•	•
Operating Margin 21	3.8	•	•	9.8	18.8	•	10.8	•	2.5	•	•	•	•
Operating Margin Before Officers' Comp. 22	3.9	•	•	9.8	18.8	•	10.8	•	2.5	•	•	•	•

Selected Average Balance Sheet ($ in Thousands)

	1	2	3	4	5	6	7
Net Receivables 23	74421	•	0	0	121	•	710
Inventories 24	•	•	•	•	•	•	•
Net Property, Plant and Equipment 25	74559	•	0	0	356	•	546
Total Assets 26	23191286	•	760	2862	20158	•	135332
Notes and Loans Payable 27	31119	•	0	0	0	•	0
All Other Liabilities 28	20686449	•	124	2862	14654	•	124366
Net Worth 29	2473718	•	636	0	5505	•	10966

Selected Financial Ratios (Times to 1)

	1	2	3	4	5	6	7
Current Ratio 30	0.9	•	16.4	•	7.3	•	11.5
Quick Ratio 31	0.7	•	•	•	6.1	•	9.3
Net Sales to Working Capital 32	•	•	0.4	•	1.1	•	0.9
Coverage Ratio 33	5.5	•	1.2	•	147.5	•	•
Total Asset Turnover 34	0.2	•	0.1	0.1	0.4	•	0.3
Inventory Turnover 35	•	•	•	•	•	•	•
Receivables Turnover 36	•	•	•	•	•	•	•
Total Liabilities to Net Worth 37	8.4	•	0.2	•	2.7	•	11.3
Current Assets to Working Capital 38	•	•	1.1	•	1.2	•	1.1
Current Liabilities to Working Capital 39	•	•	0.1	•	0.2	•	0.1
Working Capital to Net Sales 40	•	•	2.3	•	0.9	•	1.1
Inventory to Working Capital 41	•	•	•	•	•	•	•
Total Receipts to Cash Flow 42	2.3	•	•	1.3	1.6	•	2.6
Cost of Goods to Cash Flow 43	1.1	•	•	0.1	0.4	•	1.3
Cash Flow to Total Debt 44	0.1	•	•	0.1	0.3	•	0.1

Selected Financial Factors (in Percentages)

	1	2	3	4	5	6	7
Debt Ratio 45	89.3	•	16.4	100.0	72.7	•	91.9
Return on Total Assets 46	0.8	•	3.4	1.9	4.3	•	0.7
Return on Equity Before Income Taxes 47	6.0	•	0.6	•	15.8	•	8.5
Return on Equity After Income Taxes 48	3.9	•	0.6	•	13.3	•	8.0
Profit Margin (Before Income Tax) 49	3.8	•	9.8	18.7	10.8	•	2.5
Profit Margin (After Income Tax) 50	2.5	•	9.8	17.6	9.1	•	2.4

Table I

Corporations with and without Net Income

MUTUAL PROPERTY AND CASUALTY COMPANIES (FORM 1120-PC)

MONEY AMOUNTS AND SIZE OF ASSETS IN THOUSANDS OF DOLLARS

Item Description for Accounting Period 7/10 Through 6/11		Total	Zero Assets	Under 500	500 to 1,000	1,000 to 5,000	5,000 to 10,000	10,000 to 25,000	25,000 to 50,000	50,000 to 100,000	100,000 to 250,000	250,000 to 500,000	500,000 to 2,500,000	2,500,000 and over
Number of Enterprises	1	1418	12	84	0	528	135	221	125	89	70	59	65	30
Revenues ($ in Thousands)														
Net Sales	2	266751376	7874	1393	0	477646	405829	1124560	2058059	2213404	5266730	10077375	39986424	205132081
Interest	3	14318912	433	65	0	29429	17039	68628	86203	147939	243672	434343	1537360	11753800
Rents	4	421806	9	82	0	980	564	1888	1820	2895	5962	18217	47350	342038
Royalties	5	1037	0	0	0	0	0	1	0	1	7	6	281	741
Other Portfolio Income	6	8527542	452	224	0	7650	9990	35957	42492	88380	178045	316542	1138737	6709076
Other Receipts	7	243482079	6980	1022	0	439587	378236	1018086	1927544	1974189	4839044	9308267	37262696	186326426
Total Receipts	8	266751376	7874	1393	0	477646	405829	1124560	2058059	2213404	5266730	10077375	39986424	205132081
Average Total Receipts	9	18118	656	17	•	905	3006	5089	16464	24870	75239	170803	615176	6837736
Operating Costs/Operating Income (%)														
Cost of Operations	10	59.6	85.2	93.8	•	60.0	52.0	59.6	64.4	47.4	55.9	59.7	66.5	58.4
Salaries and Wages	11	13.8	11.3	•	•	12.3	12.6	9.0	10.2	18.9	17.2	14.0	13.6	13.8
Taxes Paid	12	2.3	12.1	0.6	•	2.5	2.6	2.6	2.3	3.4	2.5	2.3	1.9	2.3
Interest Paid	13	0.6	•	•	•	0.1	7.3	0.2	0.2	0.4	0.2	0.2	0.2	0.7
Depreciation	14	1.1	0.2	0.7	•	0.5	0.4	0.5	0.8	1.1	1.5	1.4	1.2	1.1
Amortization and Depletion	15	0.3	•	•	•	0.0	0.2	1.5	0.0	0.0	0.0	0.1	0.1	0.3
Pensions and Other Deferred Comp.	16	0.9	0.6	•	•	0.1	0.4	0.3	0.2	0.2	0.4	0.6	0.6	1.0
Employee Benefits	17	1.4	0.5	•	•	1.9	0.7	1.0	1.0	1.6	2.6	2.0	1.5	1.3
Advertising	18	0.9	0.0	•	•	0.4	0.2	0.2	0.5	0.6	0.7	0.4	0.5	1.0
Other Expenses	19	14.2	15.0	•	•	22.4	22.2	30.2	18.4	20.2	14.9	13.7	8.8	15.0
Officers' Compensation	20	0.2	0.9	3.0	•	2.2	1.8	1.0	0.9	1.3	0.6	0.7	0.4	0.1
Operating Margin	21	4.9	•	43.1	•	•	•	•	1.0	4.8	3.3	4.9	4.8	5.0
Operating Margin Before Officers' Comp.	22	5.1	•	46.2	•	•	1.4	•	1.9	6.1	4.0	5.6	5.1	5.2

Selected Average Balance Sheet ($ in Thousands)

Net Receivables 23	39557	0	2	75	353	866	2605	5584	15202	36850	106000	1495423
Inventories 24	•	•	•	•	•	•	•	•	•	•	•	•
Net Property, Plant and Equipment 25	5356	0	2	57	98	142	323	1068	2893	5760	24066	175941
Total Assets 26	495174	0	177	2656	7320	15888	34934	71106	164631	347397	1141080	19311789
Notes and Loans Payable 27	9149	0	17	5	27	190	47	93	913	1310	6566	411389
All Other Liabilities 28	285959	0	68	999	3642	10568	25402	42200	98249	204608	668075	11094151
Net Worth 29	200066	0	92	1652	3651	5131	9485	28814	65469	141479	466439	7806249

Selected Financial Ratios (Times to 1)

Current Ratio 30	1.0	•	2.0	•	1.8	1.7	1.0	0.8	1.0	1.0	1.0	0.9	1.0
Quick Ratio 31	0.9	•	2.0	•	1.6	1.5	0.8	0.7	0.9	1.0	0.8	0.9	0.9
Net Sales to Working Capital 32	•	•	0.2	•	1.2	1.3	56.6	•	23.7	•	•	•	•
Coverage Ratio 33	6.6	•	•	•	0.7	•	3.2	9.5	12.5	18.8	9.5	17.6	5.9
Total Asset Turnover 34	0.4	•	0.1	•	0.3	0.4	0.5	0.3	0.5	0.5	0.3	0.5	0.4
Inventory Turnover 35	•	•	•	•	•	•	•	•	•	•	•	•	•
Receivables Turnover 36	•	•	•	•	•	•	•	•	•	•	•	•	•
Total Liabilities to Net Worth 37	1.5	•	0.9	•	0.6	1.0	2.1	2.7	1.5	1.5	1.5	1.4	1.5
Current Assets to Working Capital 38	•	•	2.0	•	2.2	2.4	89.9	•	89.9	27.2	•	•	•
Current Liabilities to Working Capital 39	•	•	1.0	•	1.2	1.4	88.9	•	88.9	26.2	•	•	•
Working Capital to Net Sales 40	•	•	4.1	•	0.8	0.8	0.0	•	0.0	0.0	•	•	•
Inventory to Working Capital 41	•	•	•	•	•	•	•	•	•	•	•	•	•
Total Receipts to Cash Flow 42	5.8	•	•	•	5.2	4.8	4.5	5.6	4.5	6.0	6.2	8.6	5.5
Cost of Goods to Cash Flow 43	3.5	•	•	•	3.1	2.5	2.7	3.6	2.1	3.6	3.5	5.7	3.2
Cash Flow to Total Debt 44	0.1	•	•	•	0.2	0.2	0.1	0.1	0.1	0.1	0.1	0.1	0.1

Selected Financial Factors (in Percentages)

Debt Ratio 45	59.6	•	48.2	37.8	50.1	59.5	72.8	67.7	59.5	60.2	59.3	59.1	59.6
Return on Total Assets 46	1.5	•	3.7	•	2.2	1.4	0.3	•	1.4	1.0	1.9	2.0	1.5
Return on Equity Before Income Taxes 47	3.1	•	7.2	•	•	3.1	0.6	•	3.1	2.3	4.3	4.7	3.0
Return on Equity After Income Taxes 48	1.9	•	7.1	•	•	1.7	•	•	1.7	0.7	2.8	2.8	1.9
Profit Margin (Before Income Tax) 49	3.3	•	39.8	•	•	3.6	0.4	•	3.6	2.0	3.6	3.6	3.4
Profit Margin (After Income Tax) 50	2.0	•	39.1	•	•	1.9	•	•	1.9	0.6	2.3	2.1	2.1

Table II

Corporations with Net Income

MUTUAL PROPERTY AND CASUALTY COMPANIES (FORM 1120-PC)

MONEY AMOUNTS AND SIZE OF ASSETS IN THOUSANDS OF DOLLARS

Item Description for Accounting Period 7/10 Through 6/11	#	Total	Zero Assets	Under 500	500 to 1,000	1,000 to 5,000	5,000 to 10,000	10,000 to 25,000	25,000 to 50,000	50,000 to 100,000	100,000 to 250,000	250,000 to 500,000	500,000 to 2,500,000	2,500,000 and over
Number of Enterprises	1	857	•	42	0	348	81	105	57	58	39	•	•	27
Revenues ($ in Thousands)														
Net Sales	2	225928798	•	1329	0	198710	245393	594077	743074	1500152	3505893	•	•	181142564
Interest	3	13161597	•	48	0	20007	10235	31768	42176	90300	143442	•	•	11354090
Rents	4	392967	•	82	0	315	350	743	453	1502	2861	•	•	337405
Royalties	5	1024	•	0	0	0	0	0	0	1	1	•	•	741
Other Portfolio Income	6	7926957	•	177	0	5057	7285	16369	18330	72718	123529	•	•	6542454
Other Receipts	7	204446253	•	1022	0	173331	227523	545197	682115	1335631	3236060	•	•	162907874
Total Receipts	8	225928798	•	1329	0	198710	245393	594077	743074	1500152	3505893	•	•	181142564
Average Total Receipts	9	263628	•	32	•	571	3030	5658	13036	25865	89895	•	•	6708984
Operating Costs/Operating Income (%)														
Cost of Operations	10	56.9	•	36.6	•	35.9	44.1	48.0	49.1	43.8	53.8	•	•	55.5
Salaries and Wages	11	15.0	•	•	•	14.2	15.4	10.1	10.0	19.6	17.7	•	•	15.4
Taxes Paid	12	2.5	•	0.6	•	3.2	1.4	2.6	2.3	3.4	2.5	•	•	2.6
Interest Paid	13	0.7	•	•	•	0.1	0.0	0.2	0.0	0.1	0.1	•	•	0.8
Depreciation	14	1.1	•	0.8	•	0.8	0.4	0.6	0.7	1.0	1.8	•	•	1.1
Amortization and Depletion	15	0.3	•	•	•	0.0	0.0	0.0	0.0	0.0	0.0	•	•	0.3
Pensions and Other Deferred Comp.	16	1.0	•	•	•	0.1	0.5	0.2	0.2	0.3	0.1	•	•	1.1
Employee Benefits	17	1.5	•	•	•	1.0	0.7	1.3	1.7	1.5	2.9	•	•	1.4
Advertising	18	1.0	•	•	•	0.5	0.3	0.2	0.9	0.5	0.9	•	•	1.2
Other Expenses	19	13.8	•	9.3	•	19.4	17.4	23.4	18.9	17.7	11.7	•	•	14.8
Officers' Compensation	20	0.2	•	3.2	•	2.8	1.1	1.0	1.3	1.3	0.6	•	•	0.1
Operating Margin	21	6.1	•	49.6	•	22.1	18.7	12.4	14.8	10.8	7.7	•	•	5.7
Operating Margin Before Officers' Comp.	22	6.3	•	52.7	•	25.0	19.9	13.4	16.1	12.1	8.4	•	•	5.8

Selected Average Balance Sheet ($ in Thousands)

Net Receivables 23	58786	33	252	894	2172	5379	15032	1581642
Inventories 24	•	•	•	•	•	•	•	•
Net Property, Plant and Equipment 25	7956	61	73	171	242	966	2877	191536
Total Assets 26	750980	2538	7065	16471	35168	69712	168006	20601464
Notes and Loans Payable 27	14368	3	2	93	16	42	726	441626
All Other Liabilities 28	433340	626	2542	10354	23468	40396	88876	11932463
Net Worth 29	303272	1909	4521	6025	11684	29274	78403	8227374

Selected Financial Ratios (Times to 1)

Current Ratio 30	1.0	3.7	2.7	2.6	1.1	0.9	1.1	1.0
Quick Ratio 31	0.9	3.7	2.5	2.2	0.9	0.7	0.9	0.9
Net Sales to Working Capital 32	•	0.2	0.6	1.0	6.6	•	9.5	8.8
Coverage Ratio 33	7.5	•	282.9	368.5	54.6	297.7	115.7	47.0
Total Asset Turnover 34	0.4	0.1	0.2	0.4	0.3	0.4	0.4	0.5
Inventory Turnover 35	•	•	•	•	•	•	•	•
Receivables Turnover 36	•	•	•	•	•	•	•	•
Total Liabilities to Net Worth 37	1.5	0.5	0.3	0.6	1.7	2.0	1.4	1.5
Current Assets to Working Capital 38	•	1.4	1.6	1.6	12.6	•	14.7	9.2
Current Liabilities to Working Capital 39	•	0.4	0.6	0.6	11.6	•	13.7	8.2
Working Capital to Net Sales 40	•	4.6	1.7	1.0	0.2	•	0.1	0.1
Inventory to Working Capital 41	•	•	•	•	•	•	•	•
Total Receipts to Cash Flow 42	5.6	1.9	2.5	2.8	2.9	3.1	3.9	5.4
Cost of Goods to Cash Flow 43	3.2	0.7	0.9	1.2	1.4	1.5	1.7	3.0
Cash Flow to Total Debt 44	0.1	0.2	0.4	0.4	0.2	0.2	0.2	0.1

Selected Financial Factors (in Percentages)

Debt Ratio 45	59.6	32.2	24.8	36.0	63.4	66.8	58.0	53.3	60.1
Return on Total Assets 46	1.8	5.5	4.8	7.4	4.0	5.1	3.5	3.5	1.5
Return on Equity Before Income Taxes 47	3.8	8.1	6.3	11.5	10.7	15.4	8.4	7.3	3.2
Return on Equity After Income Taxes 48	2.6	8.0	5.0	8.5	8.4	12.7	6.2	4.9	2.1
Profit Margin (Before Income Tax) 49	4.4	49.6	21.1	17.2	11.4	13.8	9.5	6.3	3.9
Profit Margin (After Income Tax) 50	2.9	48.9	16.7	12.7	8.9	11.4	7.0	4.3	2.6

Table I
Corporations with and without Net Income

STOCK PROPERTY AND CASUALTY COMPANIES (FORM 1120-PC)

MONEY AMOUNTS AND SIZE OF ASSETS IN THOUSANDS OF DOLLARS

Item Description for Accounting Period 7/10 Through 6/11	Total	Zero Assets	Under 500	500 to 1,000	1,000 to 5,000	5,000 to 10,000	10,000 to 25,000	25,000 to 50,000	50,000 to 100,000	100,000 to 250,000	250,000 to 500,000	500,000 to 2,500,000	2,500,000 and over
Number of Enterprises **1**	6826	191	2594	934	1768	371	275	181	133	126	65	108	79
Revenues ($ in Thousands)													
Net Sales **2**	688558747	2207746	85696	59949	528504	571165	2237811	5051483	6733787	17157793	16423755	80546257	553984802
Interest **3**	35893567	30389	10925	9323	43694	34582	61874	81912	131452	327022	496250	2311203	32354942
Rents **4**	1012685	3453	160	0	1222	2693	1219	1407	2033	13526	16498	58673	911800
Royalties **5**	24326	0	0	0	701	204	0	0	366	1053	6859	4036	11109
Other Portfolio Income **6**	15198135	38594	4397	4541	22477	21497	24625	42182	89656	207366	171286	1299274	13272243
Other Receipts **7**	633460034	2135310	70214	46085	460410	512189	2150093	4925982	6510280	16608826	15732862	76873071	507434708
Total Receipts **8**	688558747	2207746	85696	59949	528504	571165	2237811	5051483	6733787	17157793	16423755	80546257	553984802
Average Total Receipts **9**	100438	11559	33	64	299	1540	8137	27909	50630	136173	252673	745799	7012466
Operating Costs/Operating Income (%)													
Cost of Operations **10**	63.5	74.9	79.9	57.1	78.8	52.0	64.8	69.7	66.4	65.1	59.6	63.1	63.4
Salaries and Wages **11**	11.3	7.8	3.1	•	12.0	11.9	11.5	11.7	10.8	11.3	10.7	12.0	11.3
Taxes Paid **12**	2.0	1.1	0.9	0.4	1.7	3.8	1.8	1.5	2.1	2.3	1.8	2.3	2.0
Interest Paid **13**	1.4	0.6	2.8	0.1	0.5	0.2	0.2	0.3	0.1	0.5	0.3	0.8	1.6
Depreciation **14**	0.8	0.4	0.0	•	0.3	1.0	0.4	0.3	0.6	0.7	0.7	0.8	0.8
Amortization and Depletion **15**	0.3	3.5	0.2	0.4	0.1	0.0	0.2	0.0	0.2	0.2	0.1	0.3	0.3
Pensions and Other Deferred Comp. **16**	0.4	0.2	•	0.0	0.0	0.2	0.0	0.1	0.1	0.1	0.2	0.5	0.4
Employee Benefits **17**	1.0	0.7	0.0	•	0.5	1.0	0.5	0.8	1.0	0.5	1.0	1.7	1.0
Advertising **18**	0.6	0.1	•	•	0.1	0.4	0.5	0.7	0.6	0.3	1.8	0.3	0.7
Other Expenses **19**	12.6	13.9	23.1	17.8	18.0	27.9	18.6	13.4	15.1	15.8	21.6	13.5	12.0
Officers' Compensation **20**	0.3	2.9	•	•	0.3	0.9	0.9	0.5	0.5	0.5	0.4	0.4	0.3
Operating Margin **21**	5.7	•	•	24.3	•	0.6	0.6	0.9	2.5	2.7	1.8	4.1	6.3
Operating Margin Before Officers' Comp. **22**	6.0	•	•	24.3	•	1.4	1.5	1.4	3.0	3.2	2.1	4.6	6.6

Selected Average Balance Sheet ($ in Thousands)

Line Item													
Net Receivables **23**	17105	0	4	23	100	272	1299	2541	6496	12220	29557	120967	1243632
Inventories **24**	•	0	•	•	•	•	•	•	•	•	•	•	•
Net Property, Plant and Equipment **25**	3674	•	0	0	13	66	108	251	367	2324	5979	23109	275092
Total Assets **26**	273705	•	226	741	2307	7000	15788	36483	69687	156548	344081	1214508	21099838
Notes and Loans Payable **27**	23005	•	2	0	19	137	350	1223	1257	7444	13311	76088	1853619
All Other Liabilities **28**	149709	•	187	520	1912	4349	13222	26704	55814	99011	254914	712526	11317176
Net Worth **29**	100992	•	37	221	376	2514	2216	8556	12616	50093	75857	425893	7929043

Selected Financial Ratios (Times to 1)

Line Item													
Current Ratio **30**	0.7	•	0.9	0.8	1.4	1.1	1.0	1.0	1.1	1.0	0.8	1.0	0.7
Quick Ratio **31**	0.6	•	0.7	0.7	1.1	0.9	0.9	0.8	0.9	0.8	0.8	0.9	0.6
Net Sales to Working Capital **32**	•	•	•	0.8	3.3	24.3	•	9.5	•	•	•	•	•
Coverage Ratio **33**	4.3	•	471.0	0.8	2.5	2.8	19.4	6.2	5.4	5.6	4.2	•	•
Total Asset Turnover **34**	0.4	•	0.1	0.1	0.2	0.5	0.8	0.7	0.9	0.7	0.7	0.6	0.3
Inventory Turnover **35**	•	•	•	•	•	•	•	•	•	•	•	•	•
Receivables Turnover **36**	•	•	•	•	•	•	•	•	•	•	•	•	•
Total Liabilities to Net Worth **37**	1.7	•	5.1	2.4	5.1	1.8	6.1	3.3	4.5	2.1	3.5	1.9	1.7
Current Assets to Working Capital **38**	•	•	•	3.9	7.9	30.7	8.9	•	•	•	•	•	•
Current Liabilities to Working Capital **39**	•	•	2.9	6.9	29.7	7.9	•	•	•	•	•	•	•
Working Capital to Net Sales **40**	•	•	1.2	0.3	0.0	0.1	•	•	•	•	•	•	•
Inventory to Working Capital **41**	•	•	•	0.0	0.0	•	•	•	•	•	•	•	•
Total Receipts to Cash Flow **42**	6.0	19.5	10.6	2.8	31.9	3.7	5.5	7.4	6.3	5.8	4.5	6.3	6.0
Cost of Goods to Cash Flow **43**	3.8	14.6	8.5	1.6	25.2	1.9	3.6	5.2	4.2	3.8	2.7	4.0	3.8
Cash Flow to Total Debt **44**	0.1	0.0	0.0	0.0	0.1	0.1	0.1	0.1	0.2	0.2	0.1	0.1	0.1

Selected Financial Factors (in Percentages)

Line Item													
Debt Ratio **45**	63.1	•	83.6	70.2	83.7	64.1	86.0	76.5	81.9	68.0	78.0	64.9	62.4
Return on Total Assets **46**	2.3	•	2.1	•	•	0.2	0.5	1.6	2.5	1.3	2.7	•	2.3
Return on Equity Before Income Taxes **47**	4.8	•	7.1	•	•	0.9	1.4	8.5	6.4	4.7	6.3	•	4.7
Return on Equity After Income Taxes **48**	2.9	•	5.7	•	•	•	2.9	2.6	0.5	3.5	•	•	2.9
Profit Margin (Before Income Tax) **49**	4.8	•	24.3	•	•	0.2	0.4	2.1	2.4	1.4	3.6	•	5.3
Profit Margin (After Income Tax) **50**	2.9	•	19.6	•	•	•	0.4	0.7	0.9	0.1	2.0	•	3.3

Table II

Corporations with Net Income

STOCK PROPERTY AND CASUALTY COMPANIES (FORM 1120-PC)

MONEY AMOUNTS AND SIZE OF ASSETS IN THOUSANDS OF DOLLARS

Item Description for Accounting Period 7/10 Through 6/11	Total	Zero Assets	Under 500	500 to 1,000	1,000 to 5,000	5,000 to 10,000	10,000 to 25,000	25,000 to 50,000	50,000 to 100,000	100,000 to 250,000	250,000 to 500,000	500,000 to 2,500,000	2,500,000 and over
Number of Enterprises **1**	5003	103	1806	788	1409	251	172	113	90	88	45	78	61
Revenues ($ in Thousands)													
Net Sales **2**	621443500	197948	23551	58561	245207	299451	1182773	4079219	4905617	12271950	11096138	65241204	521841881
Interest **3**	32274610	10469	10405	9029	39755	24567	42762	51600	84519	239012	343210	1743457	29675826
Rents **4**	934229	0	160	0	514	2689	1101	915	1841	10358	9019	46151	861481
Royalties **5**	18874	0	0	0	701	204	0	0	0	3	6859	14	11095
Other Portfolio Income **6**	12488933	19966	4045	4502	20451	17725	17606	29628	73793	165859	129871	946458	11059028
Other Receipts **7**	575726854	167513	8941	45030	183786	254266	1121304	3997076	4745464	11856718	10607179	62505124	480234451
Total Receipts **8**	621443500	197948	23551	58561	245207	299451	1182773	4079219	4905617	12271950	11096138	65241204	521841881
Average Total Receipts **9**	124214	1922	13	74	174	1193	6877	36099	54507	139454	246581	836426	8554785
Operating Costs/Operating Income (%)													
Cost of Operations **10**	63.1	6.3	15.2	58.1	18.5	37.1	52.0	69.1	62.9	67.1	57.5	63.0	63.2
Salaries and Wages **11**	10.9	9.4	0.5	•	17.2	8.3	13.4	11.0	9.8	9.6	10.3	11.3	10.9
Taxes Paid **12**	2.0	1.7	0.6	0.3	1.9	1.3	2.0	1.4	2.1	2.4	1.8	2.3	2.0
Interest Paid **13**	1.2	1.2	9.7	0.1	0.4	0.2	0.1	0.1	0.1	0.3	0.2	0.6	1.4
Depreciation **14**	0.8	1.3	•	•	0.4	0.4	0.2	0.3	0.7	0.7	0.8	0.8	0.8
Amortization and Depletion **15**	0.3	0.6	•	0.0	0.1	0.0	0.1	0.0	0.2	0.1	0.1	0.3	0.3
Pensions and Other Deferred Comp. **16**	0.3	0.8	•	•	•	0.3	0.1	0.1	0.1	0.1	0.2	0.4	0.3
Employee Benefits **17**	1.0	1.1	•	•	0.2	0.4	0.4	0.9	1.0	0.5	0.7	1.9	0.9
Advertising **18**	0.6	0.4	•	•	0.1	0.1	0.3	0.8	0.6	0.2	1.2	0.3	0.7
Other Expenses **19**	12.0	15.0	15.8	14.6	23.4	21.8	16.8	8.9	15.1	12.0	20.1	11.8	11.8
Officers' Compensation **20**	0.3	6.4	•	•	0.3	1.3	1.0	0.4	0.4	0.5	0.5	0.4	0.3
Operating Margin **21**	7.3	55.9	58.3	26.9	37.6	28.8	13.5	6.9	7.0	6.6	6.5	7.0	7.4
Operating Margin Before Officers' Comp. **22**	7.6	62.3	58.3	26.9	37.8	30.1	14.5	7.3	7.4	7.1	7.0	7.4	7.6

Selected Average Balance Sheet ($ in Thousands)

Net Receivables 23	20757	0	5	20	85	254	1237	2367	5741	12986	29481	125171	1482149
Inventories 24	•	•	•	•	•	•	•	•	•	•	•	•	•
Net Property, Plant and Equipment 25	4697	0	0	0	11	96	87	239	319	1935	6003	24556	344827
Total Assets 26	325694	•	259	739	2327	7065	15812	36783	68667	156198	336628	1262004	24310773
Notes and Loans Payable 27	26563	0	0	0	21	170	213	524	1173	5416	8503	80056	2057652
All Other Liabilities 28	174619	•	184	537	1039	3804	8902	21214	41735	87253	198767	690924	12987629
Net Worth 29	124511	•	75	201	1267	3091	6698	15046	25759	63529	129358	491024	9265492

Selected Financial Ratios (Times to 1)

Current Ratio 30	0.7	•	0.9	0.7	1.3	1.1	1.2	1.3	1.3	1.1	1.0	1.0	0.7
Quick Ratio 31	0.6	•	0.8	0.5	1.1	0.8	1.0	1.2	1.1	1.0	0.9	0.9	0.6
Net Sales to Working Capital 32	•	•	•	0.5	5.0	4.1	6.0	5.6	20.1	59.2	•	•	•
Coverage Ratio 33	6.2	41.6	6.8	508.8	84.7	155.0	146.1	46.9	52.3	20.2	27.7	12.4	5.6
Total Asset Turnover 34	0.4	•	0.1	0.1	0.1	0.2	0.4	1.0	0.8	0.9	0.7	0.7	0.4
Inventory Turnover 35	•	•	•	•	•	•	•	•	•	•	•	•	•
Receivables Turnover 36	•	•	•	•	•	•	•	•	•	•	•	•	•
Total Liabilities to Net Worth 37	1.6	•	2.5	2.7	0.8	1.3	1.4	1.4	1.7	1.5	1.6	1.6	1.6
Current Assets to Working Capital 38	•	•	•	4.1	13.9	5.9	4.0	4.8	12.6	40.4	•	•	•
Current Liabilities to Working Capital 39	•	•	•	3.1	12.9	4.9	3.0	3.8	11.6	39.4	•	•	•
Working Capital to Net Sales 40	•	•	•	1.9	0.2	0.2	0.2	0.2	0.0	0.0	0.1	•	•
Inventory to Working Capital 41	•	•	•	•	•	•	•	•	•	•	•	•	•
Total Receipts to Cash Flow 42	5.6	•	1.5	1.5	2.8	1.8	2.0	3.4	4.9	5.8	3.9	5.8	5.6
Cost of Goods to Cash Flow 43	3.5	0.1	0.2	1.6	0.3	0.8	1.8	4.6	3.1	3.9	2.3	3.7	3.5
Cash Flow to Total Debt 44	0.1	•	0.0	0.0	0.1	0.1	0.2	0.3	0.3	0.0	0.3	0.2	0.1

Selected Financial Factors (in Percentages)

Debt Ratio 45	61.8	•	71.1	72.7	45.6	56.3	57.6	59.1	62.5	59.3	61.6	61.1	61.9
Return on Total Assets 46	2.9	•	3.3	2.7	2.8	4.7	5.7	6.5	5.4	5.8	4.6	4.6	2.8
Return on Equity Before Income Taxes 47	6.5	•	9.8	9.9	5.0	10.7	13.3	15.6	14.1	13.5	11.6	11.0	5.9
Return on Equity After Income Taxes 48	4.4	•	8.6	8.2	4.0	8.1	9.7	10.5	10.0	9.1	8.2	7.6	4.0
Profit Margin (Before Income Tax) 49	6.5	49.1	56.3	26.9	36.5	27.6	13.0	6.5	6.6	6.2	6.1	6.4	6.4
Profit Margin (After Income Tax) 50	4.4	32.9	49.4	22.1	29.2	21.1	9.4	4.4	4.7	4.2	4.3	4.5	4.4

Table I
Corporations with and without Net Income

INSURANCE AGENCIES AND BROKERAGES

MONEY AMOUNTS AND SIZE OF ASSETS IN THOUSANDS OF DOLLARS

Item Description for Accounting Period 7/10 Through 6/11		Total	Zero Assets	Under 500	500 to 1,000	1,000 to 5,000	5,000 to 10,000	10,000 to 25,000	25,000 to 50,000	50,000 to 100,000	100,000 to 250,000	250,000 to 500,000	500,000 to 2,500,000	2,500,000 and over
Number of Enterprises	1	93814	17335	66264	5404	3970	451	216	85	41	26	8	9	6
Revenues ($ in Thousands)														
Net Sales	2	70819258	1684133	20845377	4901549	9343212	4605838	3631415	2022601	2268485	2167200	1338756	4681342	13329350
Interest	3	307505	5294	10384	3816	12554	5945	13562	8357	9955	22448	8903	41146	165140
Rents	4	58946	3720	4676	47	4939	12093	9990	1675	1344	2144	0	9728	8591
Royalties	5	32284	0	0	2	3052	4	0	0	40	0	0	0	29187
Other Portfolio Income	6	589407	60245	21870	12343	29160	42048	19923	8372	8220	9898	5001	84103	288223
Other Receipts	7	69831116	1614874	20808447	4885341	9293507	4545748	3587940	2004197	2248926	2132710	1324852	4546365	12838209
Total Receipts	8	70819258	1684133	20845377	4901549	9343212	4605838	3631415	2022601	2268485	2167200	1338756	4681342	13329350
Average Total Receipts	9	755	97	315	907	2353	10213	16812	23795	55329	83354	167344	520149	2221558
Operating Costs/Operating Income (%)														
Cost of Operations	10	1.6	•	•	•	4.5	0.1	2.9	1.2	14.3	7.2	3.6	1.3	0.0
Salaries and Wages	11	32.9	22.7	26.6	24.9	32.7	39.4	35.8	30.7	32.4	30.0	21.2	35.8	45.0
Taxes Paid	12	3.5	3.2	3.5	3.9	3.5	3.3	3.2	3.6	3.0	3.3	2.2	3.2	3.8
Interest Paid	13	2.8	3.5	0.9	1.5	1.3	1.3	1.3	1.2	1.1	4.0	3.5	4.2	7.9
Depreciation	14	1.2	2.3	0.8	1.3	0.7	1.1	1.1	1.1	1.4	1.4	1.0	1.9	1.8
Amortization and Depletion	15	1.8	4.2	0.8	2.0	1.5	1.0	1.0	1.3	1.4	3.3	1.3	5.5	2.6
Pensions and Other Deferred Comp.	16	1.5	0.4	1.1	1.3	1.0	0.5	1.4	0.9	1.3	0.7	0.3	0.9	3.5
Employee Benefits	17	2.3	1.9	1.6	2.8	2.8	2.4	2.4	2.6	2.6	2.2	1.9	2.7	3.0
Advertising	18	1.5	3.2	2.4	1.1	0.8	2.0	1.1	0.7	2.5	3.3	1.8	0.5	0.4
Other Expenses	19	31.9	43.3	31.8	31.5	28.7	30.9	33.7	40.7	29.5	37.9	46.7	35.4	28.2
Officers' Compensation	20	11.1	11.2	17.4	18.0	13.8	10.1	10.2	9.5	5.4	4.2	2.7	2.3	3.9
Operating Margin	21	7.8	4.1	13.1	11.7	8.8	7.8	6.0	6.5	5.3	2.5	13.7	6.4	•
Operating Margin Before Officers' Comp.	22	19.0	15.3	30.5	29.7	22.6	18.0	16.1	16.0	10.7	6.7	16.4	8.7	3.7

Selected Average Balance Sheet ($ in Thousands)

Item												
Net Receivables **23**	271	0	45	286	941	2904	9790	10088	23071	57656	173059	3142780
Inventories **24**	•	•	•	•	•	•	•	•	•	•	•	•
Net Property, Plant and Equipment **25**	48	14	100	103	981	914	1380	3146	4754	8735	32861	202889
Total Assets **26**	1304	81	699	2018	6795	14313	34186	66048	169824	346777	1321626	12382692
Notes and Loans Payable **27**	264	49	298	525	2113	3427	8025	12370	56091	83394	315178	1665415
All Other Liabilities **28**	508	18	141	884	2689	7636	19883	34978	64424	176156	470420	4807552
Net Worth **29**	532	13	260	609	1992	3251	6278	18700	49309	87227	536028	5909725

Selected Financial Ratios (Times to 1)

Item												
Current Ratio **30**	1.1	1.2	1.7	1.4	1.4	1.2	1.2	1.1	0.9	1.2	1.0	1.0
Quick Ratio **31**	1.0	1.1	1.5	1.2	1.2	1.0	1.1	0.8	0.8	1.0	0.8	0.9
Net Sales to Working Capital **32**	16.6	48.7	9.4	7.2	10.1	11.4	6.1	17.5	•	6.6	•	15.8
Coverage Ratio **33**	3.9	15.2	9.0	7.8	6.9	5.7	6.4	5.9	1.6	4.9	2.5	1.3
Total Asset Turnover **34**	0.6	2.2	3.9	1.3	1.5	1.2	0.7	0.8	0.5	0.5	0.4	0.2
Inventory Turnover **35**	•	•	•	•	•	•	•	•	•	•	•	•
Receivables Turnover **36**	•	•	•	•	•	•	•	•	•	•	•	•
Total Liabilities to Net Worth **37**	1.5	5.0	1.7	2.3	2.4	3.4	4.4	2.5	2.4	3.0	1.5	1.1
Current Assets to Working Capital **38**	11.0	5.1	2.5	3.7	3.6	6.3	5.6	12.0	•	6.9	•	29.8
Current Liabilities to Working Capital **39**	10.0	4.1	1.5	2.7	2.6	5.3	4.6	11.0	•	5.9	•	28.8
Working Capital to Net Sales **40**	0.1	0.0	0.1	0.1	0.1	0.1	0.2	0.1	•	0.2	•	0.1
Inventory to Working Capital **41**	0.0	•	•	•	•	0.0	0.0	•	•	•	•	•
Total Receipts to Cash Flow **42**	3.0	2.9	2.7	3.1	3.1	2.8	2.3	3.2	2.8	1.8	2.7	4.3
Cost of Goods to Cash Flow **43**	0.0	•	•	0.1	0.0	0.1	0.0	0.5	0.2	0.1	0.0	0.0
Cash Flow to Total Debt **44**	0.3	1.8	0.8	0.5	0.7	0.5	0.4	0.4	0.3	0.4	0.2	0.1

Selected Financial Factors (in Percentages)

Item												
Debt Ratio **45**	59.2	83.3	62.7	69.8	70.7	77.3	81.6	71.7	71.0	74.8	59.4	52.3
Return on Total Assets **46**	6.4	54.7	17.0	11.7	13.7	8.5	5.3	5.3	3.2	8.2	4.2	1.8
Return on Equity Before Income Taxes **47**	11.7	306.8	40.7	33.7	40.1	30.8	24.6	15.4	4.1	25.8	6.3	0.9
Return on Equity After Income Taxes **48**	10.7	302.9	40.3	32.9	38.2	28.0	20.1	13.1	3.0	19.4	4.3	0.3
Profit Margin (Before Income Tax) **49**	8.3	13.1	11.7	8.7	7.8	5.9	6.5	5.2	2.4	13.5	6.5	2.3
Profit Margin (After Income Tax) **50**	7.6	13.0	11.6	8.5	7.5	5.4	5.3	4.4	1.8	10.1	4.4	0.8

Table II
Corporations with Net Income

INSURANCE AGENCIES AND BROKERAGES

MONEY AMOUNTS AND SIZE OF ASSETS IN THOUSANDS OF DOLLARS

Item Description for Accounting Period 7/10 Through 6/11	Total	Zero Assets	Under 500	500 to 1,000	1,000 to 5,000	5,000 to 10,000	10,000 to 25,000	25,000 to 50,000	50,000 to 100,000	100,000 to 250,000	250,000 to 500,000	500,000 to 2,500,000	2,500,000 and over
Number of Enterprises **1**	69288	10699	51308	3665	2946	376	159	71	30	15	•	•	•
Revenues ($ in Thousands)													
Net Sales **2**	55352301	929114	17020401	4320841	8055371	4123862	2896776	1732819	1870180	1373873			•
Interest **3**	192563	1503	9076	3008	9645	4397	4852	3418	8864	11368	•	•	•
Rents **4**	46787	3720	2778	47	4136	9948	7139	1675	1341	2144	•	•	•
Royalties **5**	31518	0	0	2	3052	2	0	0	40	0			•
Other Portfolio Income **6**	486429	45811	21678	12093	17941	39344	4744	7800	7949	6907	•	•	•
Other Receipts **7**	54595004	878080	16986869	4305691	8020597	4070171	2880041	1719926	1851986	1353454	•	•	•
Total Receipts **8**	55352301	929114	17020401	4320841	8055371	4123862	2896776	1732819	1870180	1373873	•	•	•
Average Total Receipts **9**	799	87	332	1179	2734	10968	18219	24406	62339	91592			•
Operating Costs/Operating Income (%)													
Cost of Operations **10**	1.7	•	•	•	4.8	0.1	1.5	1.0	17.0	5.2			•
Salaries and Wages **11**	30.5	13.4	24.0	23.3	31.5	39.4	31.4	33.1	29.8	27.8	•	•	•
Taxes Paid **12**	3.3	3.3	3.5	3.6	3.1	3.1	3.2	3.7	3.0	3.0	•	•	•
Interest Paid **13**	2.4	0.4	0.8	1.2	1.1	1.3	0.8	1.2	0.8	2.7	•	•	•
Depreciation **14**	1.1	0.9	0.8	1.1	0.6	0.9	0.9	1.2	1.4	1.5	•	•	•
Amortization and Depletion **15**	1.7	7.3	0.6	1.5	1.6	0.8	0.7	1.3	0.8	2.0	•	•	•
Pensions and Other Deferred Comp. **16**	1.3	0.6	1.1	1.4	1.1	0.4	1.4	1.1	1.5	1.0	•	•	•
Employee Benefits **17**	2.2	1.1	1.5	2.5	2.8	2.4	2.2	2.7	2.5	2.0	•	•	•
Advertising **18**	1.3	1.6	2.3	1.0	0.6	0.9	0.6	0.7	1.0	4.3	•	•	•
Other Expenses **19**	29.5	31.1	28.9	30.8	26.0	31.3	35.1	33.6	28.2	36.1	•	•	•
Officers' Compensation **20**	11.9	13.5	17.7	17.9	13.1	10.0	11.9	10.3	5.5	3.8	•	•	•
Operating Margin **21**	13.1	26.8	18.9	15.6	13.7	9.4	10.3	10.2	8.4	10.6	•	•	•
Operating Margin Before Officers' Comp. **22**	25.0	40.3	36.6	33.5	26.9	19.4	22.2	20.5	13.9	14.4	•	•	•

Selected Average Balance Sheet ($ in Thousands)

Net Receivables 23	244	0	4	45	265	907	3123	10579	10131	18560
Inventories 24	•	•	•	•	114	1062	958	1578	3546	4948
Net Property, Plant and Equipment 25	46	0	14	81	•	•	•	•	•	•
Total Assets 26	1022	14	78	715	2028	6858	14348	33778	66544	172247
Notes and Loans Payable 27	229	0	37	245	494	2040	2799	7210	11969	52293
All Other Liabilities 28	475	0	17	145	958	2750	7381	20582	36001	52889
Net Worth 29	318	0	24	324	576	2069	4167	5987	18574	67065

Selected Financial Ratios (Times to 1)

Current Ratio 30	1.1	•	1.5	1.7	1.3	1.3	1.3	1.2	1.1	1.1
Quick Ratio 31	1.0	•	1.4	1.5	1.2	1.2	1.1	1.1	0.8	0.9
Net Sales to Working Capital 32	20.1	•	30.6	10.7	8.9	11.9	7.3	6.1	12.9	12.1
Coverage Ratio 33	6.7	76.2	24.7	14.1	14.0	8.1	13.9	9.4	11.3	4.9
Total Asset Turnover 34	0.8	•	4.3	1.6	1.3	1.6	1.3	0.7	0.9	0.5
Inventory Turnover 35	•	•	•	•	•	•	•	•	•	•
Receivables Turnover 36	•	•	•	•	•	•	•	•	•	•
Total Liabilities to Net Worth 37	2.2	•	2.2	1.2	2.5	2.3	2.4	4.6	2.6	1.6
Current Assets to Working Capital 38	11.5	•	3.1	2.5	4.0	3.9	4.0	5.7	8.9	8.5
Current Liabilities to Working Capital 39	10.5	•	2.1	1.5	3.0	2.9	3.0	4.7	7.9	7.5
Working Capital to Net Sales 40	0.0	•	0.0	0.1	0.1	0.1	0.1	0.2	0.1	0.1
Inventory to Working Capital 41	0.0	•	•	•	•	•	0.0	0.0	0.0	0.0
Total Receipts to Cash Flow 42	2.7	2.1	2.5	2.5	2.9	2.9	2.4	2.5	3.0	2.4
Cost of Goods to Cash Flow 43	0.0	•	•	•	0.1	0.0	0.0	0.0	0.5	0.1
Cash Flow to Total Debt 44	0.4	•	2.5	1.2	0.7	0.8	0.7	0.4	0.4	0.4

Selected Financial Factors (in Percentages)

Debt Ratio 45	68.9	•	69.0	54.7	71.6	69.8	71.0	82.3	72.1	61.1
Return on Total Assets 46	12.4	•	83.9	27.7	19.9	17.2	14.1	8.2	8.6	7.0
Return on Equity Before Income Taxes 47	34.0	•	259.6	56.9	65.3	49.9	45.1	41.4	28.0	14.3
Return on Equity After Income Taxes 48	31.7	•	256.8	56.4	64.0	47.8	42.1	35.9	24.8	12.9
Profit Margin (Before Income Tax) 49	13.5	26.8	18.9	15.6	13.7	9.4	10.3	10.2	8.3	10.4
Profit Margin (After Income Tax) 50	12.6	25.1	18.7	15.5	13.5	9.0	9.6	8.8	7.4	9.5

Table I
Corporations with and without Net Income

OTHER INSURANCE RELATED ACTIVITIES

MONEY AMOUNTS AND SIZE OF ASSETS IN THOUSANDS OF DOLLARS

Item Description for Accounting Period 7/10 Through 6/11		Total	Zero Assets	Under 500	500 to 1,000	1,000 to 5,000	5,000 to 10,000	10,000 to 25,000	25,000 to 50,000	50,000 to 100,000	100,000 to 250,000	250,000 to 500,000	500,000 to 2,500,000	2,500,000 and over
Number of Enterprises	1	14345	2928	9558	1012	450	136	114	42	45	30	10	15	5
Revenues ($ in Thousands)														
Net Sales	2	47658150	299427	1572455	788512	3267472	1131496	1048156	1726892	2421779	4595125	2712365	7041833	21052637
Interest	3	874998	958	2090	2873	4919	5523	6386	4942	15359	38992	11181	115315	666460
Rents	4	103837	839	0	0	9104	719	120	2814	3947	1644	15393	3046	66210
Royalties	5	15891	2	0	0	0	0	11	0	0	0	0	15779	99
Other Portfolio Income	6	374325	1468	2857	0	9300	3953	3650	23552	14557	170876	12627	56411	75072
Other Receipts	7	46289099	296160	1567508	785639	3244149	1121301	1037989	1695584	2387916	4383613	2673164	6851282	20244796
Total Receipts	8	47658150	299427	1572455	788512	3267472	1131496	1048156	1726892	2421779	4595125	2712365	7041833	21052637
Average Total Receipts	9	3322	102	165	779	7261	8320	9194	41116	53817	153171	271236	469456	4210527
Operating Costs/Operating Income (%)														
Cost of Operations	10	11.4	•	•	•	•	•	0.1	4.2	13.6	4.1	12.6	18.3	15.3
Salaries and Wages	11	16.5	31.5	16.5	19.5	21.2	26.7	35.1	29.6	25.8	16.8	15.2	21.9	10.1
Taxes Paid	12	2.2	3.1	4.1	2.9	2.3	2.6	3.9	3.2	4.5	2.3	3.3	2.4	1.2
Interest Paid	13	2.2	4.3	1.3	2.3	0.2	0.9	0.8	0.4	2.4	1.0	2.8	4.3	2.2
Depreciation	14	1.3	1.9	1.9	0.8	1.2	1.3	1.7	1.2	2.3	1.3	1.8	1.9	1.0
Amortization and Depletion	15	0.9	1.7	0.0	1.5	0.1	0.3	0.4	0.4	1.9	0.7	2.7	2.0	0.5
Pensions and Other Deferred Comp.	16	0.9	0.5	0.0	15.9	1.0	0.2	0.3	1.0	0.5	0.4	0.2	1.2	0.5
Employee Benefits	17	2.0	1.5	1.5	1.5	2.2	2.8	4.4	2.9	7.5	1.4	1.6	3.2	1.1
Advertising	18	0.6	1.4	2.6	1.7	1.5	0.4	0.8	2.1	0.8	0.2	0.3	0.8	0.2
Other Expenses	19	50.1	52.6	40.0	34.4	62.4	50.2	40.1	40.1	35.2	66.6	54.9	33.5	53.9
Officers' Compensation	20	2.7	3.2	18.8	12.4	5.5	2.7	3.3	5.0	3.3	1.5	0.8	3.3	0.7
Operating Margin	21	9.2	•	13.4	7.1	2.5	11.8	9.1	10.0	2.4	3.7	3.8	7.2	13.3
Operating Margin Before Officers' Comp.	22	11.9	1.5	32.1	19.6	7.9	14.5	12.4	15.0	5.7	5.2	4.6	10.5	14.0

Selected Average Balance Sheet ($ in Thousands)

Net Receivables 23	660	•	8	130	479	1159	3023	8873	8925	19094	93736	218740	596768
Inventories 24	•	•	•	•	•	•	•	•	•	•	•	•	•
Net Property, Plant and Equipment 25	169	•	10	15	295	639	880	1689	5897	8757	14987	38198	133389
Total Assets 26	5600	0	39	700	2657	6897	15135	34974	69069	169202	363427	970525	9509154
Notes and Loans Payable 27	1659	0	29	326	287	1256	1859	2586	20019	33715	88925	411238	2719842
All Other Liabilities 28	1993	0	-1	179	2056	5789	6972	13838	29650	76754	174176	286081	3130489
Net Worth 29	1949	0	11	196	313	-148	6305	18549	19400	58733	100326	273206	3658823

Selected Financial Ratios (Times to 1)

Current Ratio 30	1.0	•	1.5	1.5	1.3	1.1	2.2	1.6	1.2	1.6	0.8	1.0	0.9
Quick Ratio 31	0.8	•	1.3	1.1	1.0	0.7	2.0	1.2	0.9	1.0	0.8	0.9	0.6
Net Sales to Working Capital 32	492.2	•	28.2	5.1	15.9	14.5	1.9	4.9	11.3	5.8	•	43.7	•
Coverage Ratio 33	5.3	0.6	11.7	4.0	12.0	14.1	12.7	26.8	2.0	4.5	2.2	2.7	7.1
Total Asset Turnover 34	0.6	•	4.2	1.1	2.7	1.2	0.6	1.2	0.8	0.9	0.7	0.5	0.4
Inventory Turnover 35	•	•	•	•	•	•	•	•	•	•	•	•	•
Receivables Turnover 36	•	•	•	•	•	•	•	•	•	•	•	•	•
Total Liabilities to Net Worth 37	1.9	•	2.5	2.6	7.5	•	1.4	0.9	2.6	1.9	2.6	2.6	1.6
Current Assets to Working Capital 38	325.6	•	3.2	2.9	4.2	9.7	1.8	2.6	7.0	2.8	•	34.2	•
Current Liabilities to Working Capital 39	324.6	•	2.2	1.9	3.2	8.7	0.8	1.6	6.0	1.8	•	33.2	•
Working Capital to Net Sales 40	0.0	•	0.0	0.2	0.1	0.1	0.5	0.2	0.1	0.2	0.0	0.0	•
Inventory to Working Capital 41	1.5	•	•	•	•	•	•	•	0.0	0.0	0.0	0.0	•
Total Receipts to Cash Flow 42	1.8	2.4	2.1	2.6	1.6	1.7	2.2	2.2	2.9	1.5	1.8	2.6	1.5
Cost of Goods to Cash Flow 43	0.2	•	•	•	•	•	0.0	0.1	0.4	0.1	0.2	0.5	0.2
Cash Flow to Total Debt 44	0.5	•	2.8	0.6	1.9	0.7	0.5	1.2	0.4	0.9	0.6	0.3	0.5

Selected Financial Factors (in Percentages)

Debt Ratio 45	65.2	•	71.3	72.1	88.2	102.1	58.3	47.0	71.9	65.3	72.4	71.8	61.5
Return on Total Assets 46	6.8	•	61.2	10.6	7.0	15.3	5.9	12.0	3.7	4.2	4.7	5.7	6.9
Return on Equity Before Income Taxes 47	15.8	•	194.8	28.5	54.5	•	13.0	21.8	6.5	9.4	9.2	12.9	15.4
Return on Equity After Income Taxes 48	10.8	•	193.2	28.3	42.5	•	11.6	19.1	1.1	7.1	6.7	7.9	10.1
Profit Margin (Before Income Tax) 49	9.2	•	13.4	7.1	2.4	11.8	8.9	9.8	2.3	3.6	3.4	7.5	13.4
Profit Margin (After Income Tax) 50	6.4	•	13.3	7.1	1.8	10.3	7.9	8.6	0.4	2.7	2.5	4.6	8.7

Table II
Corporations with Net Income

OTHER INSURANCE RELATED ACTIVITIES

MONEY AMOUNTS AND SIZE OF ASSETS IN THOUSANDS OF DOLLARS

Item Description for Accounting Period 7/10 Through 6/11	Total	Zero Assets	Under 500	500 to 1,000	1,000 to 5,000	5,000 to 10,000	10,000 to 25,000	25,000 to 50,000	50,000 to 100,000	100,000 to 250,000	250,000 to 500,000	500,000 to 2,500,000	2,500,000 and over
Number of Enterprises **1**	9380	•	6645	550	317	79	63	32	30	20	•	•	8
Revenues ($ in Thousands)													
Net Sales **2**	41570306	•	1225139	462668	2553701	949692	735738	1572803	1669956	3572324	•	5580969	•
Interest **3**	794905	•	1160	0	4021	2351	5105	4340	11482	29081	•	75596	•
Rents **4**	83703	•	0	0	9104	0	0	2814	2340	1185	•	1211	•
Royalties **5**	15098	•	0	0	0	0	0	0	0	0	•	14998	•
Other Portfolio Income **6**	346406	•	2857	0	7761	2637	2732	20971	12242	167330	•	50335	•
Other Receipts **7**	40330194	•	1221122	462668	2532815	944704	727901	1544678	1643892	3374728	•	5438829	•
Total Receipts **8**	41570306	•	1225139	462668	2553701	949692	735738	1572803	1669956	3572324	•	5580969	•
Average Total Receipts **9**	4432	•	184	841	8056	12021	11678	49150	55665	178616	•	697621	•
Operating Costs/Operating Income (%)													
Cost of Operations **10**	12.1	•	•	•	•	•	0.2	•	7.7	4.2	•	22.2	•
Salaries and Wages **11**	15.6	•	19.0	18.1	23.4	28.3	35.2	30.8	23.6	16.6	•	21.2	•
Taxes Paid **12**	2.1	•	4.3	2.7	2.6	2.8	3.7	3.4	4.6	2.1	•	2.3	•
Interest Paid **13**	1.9	•	0.6	2.3	0.2	0.3	0.7	0.4	0.6	1.0	•	4.1	•
Depreciation **14**	1.2	•	0.9	0.9	1.4	0.8	2.1	1.2	1.5	1.2	•	1.8	•
Amortization and Depletion **15**	0.7	•	0.0	2.6	0.2	0.3	0.1	0.4	0.6	0.9	•	1.5	•
Pensions and Other Deferred Comp. **16**	0.9	•	0.0	26.8	1.2	0.2	0.2	1.1	0.3	0.5	•	1.3	•
Employee Benefits **17**	2.0	•	1.1	1.3	2.6	3.0	4.3	3.0	9.6	1.4	•	3.2	•
Advertising **18**	0.6	•	2.0	2.4	1.9	0.2	0.4	2.2	0.4	0.2	•	0.9	•
Other Expenses **19**	48.5	•	29.6	11.5	55.8	45.4	30.6	40.6	36.5	63.4	•	27.3	•
Officers' Compensation **20**	2.5	•	20.8	13.6	6.2	2.8	3.6	5.5	2.6	1.7	•	2.4	•
Operating Margin **21**	12.0	•	21.7	17.9	4.5	16.0	18.9	11.4	11.9	6.8	•	11.8	•
Operating Margin Before Officers' Comp. **22**	14.5	•	42.5	31.4	10.7	18.8	22.5	16.9	14.5	8.6	•	14.2	•

Selected Average Balance Sheet ($ in Thousands)

Net Receivables **23**	891	•	•	10	193	464	990	2993	7228	9022	23912	•	366583
Inventories **24**	•	•	•	•	•	•	•	•	•	•	•	•	•
Net Property, Plant and Equipment **25**	178	•	•	10	19	370	331	1108	2068	3760	8710	•	37750
Total Assets **26**	6987	•	•	42	698	2743	7063	16126	34867	69307	165623	•	1138634
Notes and Loans Payable **27**	2180	•	•	19	398	360	676	1868	3114	12124	27914	•	649161
All Other Liabilities **28**	2440	•	•	-8	208	1812	4252	8574	14949	30897	74557	•	216085
Net Worth **29**	2367	•	•	31	92	571	2135	5683	16804	26285	63151	•	273388

Selected Financial Ratios (Times to 1)

Current Ratio **30**	1.0	•	•	2.1	1.0	1.2	3.5	2.6	1.5	1.2	1.3	•	1.0
Quick Ratio **31**	0.8	•	•	1.9	1.0	0.9	1.9	2.4	1.1	0.9	0.9	•	0.9
Net Sales to Working Capital **32**	•	•	•	16.6	•	22.3	2.7	1.7	7.0	8.0	9.8	•	•
Coverage Ratio **33**	7.4	•	•	40.1	8.7	20.4	65.0	28.5	29.7	19.5	8.0	•	4.0
Total Asset Turnover **34**	0.6	•	•	4.4	1.2	2.9	1.7	0.7	1.4	0.8	1.1	•	0.6
Inventory Turnover **35**	•	•	•	•	•	•	•	•	•	•	•	•	•
Receivables Turnover **36**	•	•	•	•	•	•	•	•	•	•	•	•	•
Total Liabilities to Net Worth **37**	2.0	•	•	0.4	6.6	3.8	2.3	1.8	1.1	1.6	1.6	•	3.2
Current Assets to Working Capital **38**	•	•	•	1.9	•	5.2	1.4	1.6	3.1	5.1	3.9	•	•
Current Liabilities to Working Capital **39**	•	•	•	0.9	•	4.2	0.4	0.6	2.1	4.1	2.9	•	•
Working Capital to Net Sales **40**	•	•	•	0.1	0.0	0.0	0.4	0.6	0.1	0.1	0.1	•	•
Inventory to Working Capital **41**	•	•	•	•	•	•	•	•	•	0.0	0.0	•	•
Total Receipts to Cash Flow **42**	1.7	•	•	2.1	3.7	1.8	1.7	2.2	2.1	2.2	1.5	•	2.8
Cost of Goods to Cash Flow **43**	0.2	•	•	•	•	•	•	0.0	•	0.2	0.1	•	0.6
Cash Flow to Total Debt **44**	0.6	•	•	7.7	0.4	2.1	1.4	0.5	1.3	0.6	1.2	•	0.3

Selected Financial Factors (in Percentages)

Debt Ratio **45**	66.1	•	•	26.6	86.9	79.2	69.8	64.8	51.8	62.1	61.9	•	76.0
Return on Total Assets **46**	8.9	•	•	97.0	24.3	13.6	27.7	14.0	16.7	10.0	8.3	•	10.0
Return on Equity Before Income Taxes **47**	22.6	•	•	128.8	163.8	62.2	90.2	38.3	33.4	25.1	19.2	•	31.2
Return on Equity After Income Taxes **48**	16.4	•	•	128.0	163.0	52.9	80.5	35.4	29.5	19.1	16.0	•	21.7
Profit Margin (Before Income Tax) **49**	12.1	•	•	21.7	17.9	4.4	16.0	18.6	11.4	11.8	6.8	•	12.2
Profit Margin (After Income Tax) **50**	8.8	•	•	21.6	17.8	3.7	14.3	17.2	10.1	9.0	5.6	•	8.5

Table I

Corporations with and without Net Income

OPEN-END INVESTMENT FUNDS (FORM 1120-RIC)

MONEY AMOUNTS AND SIZE OF ASSETS IN THOUSANDS OF DOLLARS

Item Description for Accounting Period 7/10 Through 6/11		Total	Zero Assets	Under 500	500 to 1,000	1,000 to 5,000	5,000 to 10,000	10,000 to 25,000	25,000 to 50,000	50,000 to 100,000	100,000 to 250,000	250,000 to 500,000	500,000 to 2,500,000	2,500,000 and over
Number of Enterprises	1	13256	1016	68	75	776	715	1179	1093	1190	2000	1550	2545	1050
Revenues ($ in Thousands)														
Net Sales	2	352717269	2535284	301	3126	106393	175960	585709	1113564	2424651	9432077	16636004	79619625	240084577
Interest	3	136683415	1154110	6	293	27792	45607	136357	272104	615053	2555001	5490598	26454674	99931820
Rents	4	0	0	0	0	0	0	0	0	0	0	0	0	0
Royalties	5	0	0	0	0	0	0	0	0	0	0	0	0	0
Other Portfolio Income	6	53007902	566466	52	258	36892	65422	174895	351680	728667	2592682	4199286	16877400	27414202
Other Receipts	7	163025952	814708	243	2575	41709	64931	274457	489780	1080931	4284394	6946120	36287551	112738555
Total Receipts	8	352717269	2535284	301	3126	106393	175960	585709	1113564	2424651	9432077	16636004	79619625	240084577
Average Total Receipts	9	26608	2495	4	42	137	246	497	1019	2038	4716	10733	31285	228652
Operating Costs/Operating Income (%)														
Cost of Operations	10	•	•	•	•	•	•	•	•	•	•	•	•	•
Salaries and Wages	11	0.0	0.0	10.3	•	0.0	0.0	0.2	0.2	0.1	0.1	0.1	0.1	0.0
Taxes Paid	12	0.3	0.4	1.0	0.8	0.5	0.6	0.4	0.6	0.5	0.5	0.5	0.4	0.3
Interest Paid	13	0.3	0.2	•	•	0.0	0.0	0.3	0.5	0.5	0.3	0.6	0.4	0.2
Depreciation	14	0.0	•	•	•	0.0	•	0.0	0.0	0.0	0.0	0.0	0.0	0.0
Amortization and Depletion	15	0.0	0.3	7.3	4.6	2.3	1.5	1.2	0.6	0.1	0.0	0.0	0.0	0.0
Pensions and Other Deferred Comp.	16	•	•	•	•	•	•	•	•	•	•	•	•	•
Employee Benefits	17	•	•	•	•	•	•	•	•	•	•	•	•	•
Advertising	18	0.0	•	•	•	•	•	0.0	0.0	•	0.0	0.0	•	0.0
Other Expenses	19	21.6	22.2	353.2	44.5	13.1	14.1	29.9	28.8	28.3	26.2	24.1	23.9	20.3
Officers' Compensation	20	0.0	•	•	•	•	•	0.5	0.1	0.1	0.0	0.0	0.0	0.0
Operating Margin	21	77.8	76.9	•	50.1	84.1	83.8	67.4	69.1	70.3	72.9	74.6	75.2	79.2
Operating Margin Before Officers' Comp.	22	77.8	76.9	•	50.1	84.1	83.8	67.9	69.2	70.5	72.9	74.7	75.2	79.2

Selected Average Balance Sheet ($ in Thousands)

Net Receivables 23	10738	0	9	1	11	62	174	370	912	2012	4327	14219	89213
Inventories 24	•	•	•	•	•	•	•	•	•	•	•	•	•
Net Property, Plant and Equipment 25	2	0	0	0	0	0	0	0	0	0	•	2	27
Total Assets 26	1093521	0	219	852	2945	7573	16343	35785	72511	165941	359943	1113222	10114599
Notes and Loans Payable 27	1343	0	1	0	0	0	22	68	168	435	1647	2421	7544
All Other Liabilities 28	48454	0	20	23	64	163	481	1006	3535	7379	19445	59417	419193
Net Worth 29	1043724	0	198	828	2881	7410	15840	34711	68808	158127	338850	1051384	9687862

Selected Financial Ratios (Times to 1)

Current Ratio 30	3.6	•	0.8	2.7	1.6	4.3	6.2	4.5	3.8	4.3	3.3	3.0	3.8
Quick Ratio 31	3.3	•	0.5	0.7	0.3	2.3	4.8	2.9	3.9	3.4	2.9	2.7	3.5
Net Sales to Working Capital 32	0.2	•	•	1.2	3.8	0.5	0.3	0.2	0.2	0.2	0.2	0.3	0.2
Coverage Ratio 33	252.7	332.6	•	2039.3	3157.0	184.9	100.4	100.0	188.5	90.6	169.5	337.9	
Total Asset Turnover 34	0.0	0.0	0.0	0.0	0.0	0.0	0.0	0.0	0.0	0.0	0.0	0.0	0.0
Inventory Turnover 35	•	•	•	•	•	•	•	•	•	•	•	•	•
Receivables Turnover 36	•	•	•	•	•	•	•	•	•	•	•	•	•
Total Liabilities to Net Worth 37	0.0	0.1	•	0.0	0.0	0.0	0.0	0.0	0.1	0.0	0.1	0.1	0.0
Current Assets to Working Capital 38	1.4	•	1.6	2.7	1.3	1.2	1.3	1.4	1.3	1.4	1.5	1.4	
Current Liabilities to Working Capital 39	0.4	•	0.6	1.7	0.3	0.2	0.3	0.4	0.3	0.4	0.5	0.4	
Working Capital to Net Sales 40	4.7	•	0.9	0.3	2.2	3.5	4.0	4.3	5.1	4.1	3.8	5.1	
Inventory to Working Capital 41	•	•	•	•	•	•	•	•	•	•	•	•	•
Total Receipts to Cash Flow 42	1.1	1.1	1.2	1.6	1.2	1.3	1.2	1.1	1.1	1.1	1.1	1.1	
Cost of Goods to Cash Flow 43	•	•	•	•	•	•	•	•	•	•	•	•	•
Cash Flow to Total Debt 44	0.5	•	1.5	0.1	1.2	0.8	1.7	0.5	0.5	0.5	0.5	0.5	

Selected Financial Factors (in Percentages)

Debt Ratio 45	4.6	•	9.6	2.7	2.2	2.2	3.1	3.0	5.1	4.7	5.9	5.6	4.2
Return on Total Assets 46	1.7	•	2.5	3.0	2.0	1.7	1.6	1.4	1.5	1.5	1.7	1.7	1.7
Return on Equity Before Income Taxes 47	1.8	•	2.5	3.1	2.1	1.7	1.6	1.5	1.6	1.6	1.8	1.8	1.8
Return on Equity After Income Taxes 48	1.8	•	2.5	3.1	2.1	1.7	1.6	1.5	1.6	1.6	1.8	1.8	1.8
Profit Margin (Before Income Tax) 49	69.5	62.3	50.1	65.1	62.8	55.3	54.6	51.0	53.7	57.5	60.3	74.3	
Profit Margin (After Income Tax) 50	69.5	62.3	50.1	65.1	62.8	55.3	54.6	51.0	53.7	57.5	60.3	74.3	

Table II
Corporations with Net Income

OPEN-END INVESTMENT FUNDS (FORM 1120-RIC)

MONEY AMOUNTS AND SIZE OF ASSETS IN THOUSANDS OF DOLLARS

Item Description for Accounting Period 7/10 Through 6/11	Total	Zero Assets	Under 500	500 to 1,000	1,000 to 5,000	5,000 to 10,000	10,000 to 25,000	25,000 to 50,000	50,000 to 100,000	100,000 to 250,000	250,000 to 500,000	500,000 to 2,500,000	2,500,000 and over
Number of Enterprises **1**	10877	707	48	68	592	565	885	836	950	1663	1338	2237	989
Revenues ($ in Thousands)													
Net Sales **2**	343513894	2398985	205	3071	91655	152501	507627	1010861	2199803	8780540	15766878	75917120	236684646
Interest **3**	135763786	1138703	5	293	27576	45370	131670	252033	599634	2536507	5473691	26308684	99249620
Rents **4**	0	0	0	0	0	0	0	0	0	0	0	0	0
Royalties **5**	0	0	0	0	0	0	0	0	0	0	0	0	0
Other Portfolio Income **6**	49289629	512970	52	258	24190	44311	137496	292316	596528	2259900	3774323	15101702	26545582
Other Receipts **7**	158460479	747312	148	2520	39889	62820	238461	466512	1003641	3984133	6518864	34506734	110889444
Total Receipts **8**	343513894	2398985	205	3071	91655	152501	507627	1010861	2199803	8780540	15766878	75917120	236684646
Average Total Receipts **9**	31582	3393	4	45	155	270	574	1209	2316	5280	11784	33937	239317
Operating Costs/Operating Income (%)													
Cost of Operations **10**	•	•	•	•	•	•	•	•	•	•	•	•	•
Salaries and Wages **11**	0.0	0.0	1.0	•	0.0	0.0	0.1	0.1	0.1	0.1	0.1	0.1	0.0
Taxes Paid **12**	0.3	0.3	1.0	0.8	0.1	0.3	0.0	0.6	0.5	0.5	0.4	0.4	0.2
Interest Paid **13**	0.2	0.2	•	•	0.0	0.0	0.0	0.0	0.5	0.3	0.7	0.4	0.1
Depreciation **14**	0.0	•	•	•	0.0	0.0	•	0.0	0.0	0.0	0.0	0.0	0.0
Amortization and Depletion **15**	0.0	0.2	2.9	4.7	2.6	1.7	1.4	0.7	0.1	0.0	0.0	0.0	0.0
Pensions and Other Deferred Comp. **16**	•	•	•	•	•	•	•	•	•	•	•	•	•
Employee Benefits **17**	•	•	•	•	•	•	•	•	•	•	•	•	•
Advertising **18**	0.0	•	•	•	0.0	•	•	•	•	0.0	0.0	0.0	0.0
Other Expenses **19**	19.8	18.8	35.1	43.0	9.8	12.5	18.0	21.7	22.9	22.0	21.0	21.1	19.3
Officers' Compensation **20**	0.0	•	•	•	•	0.0	0.0	0.0	0.1	0.0	0.0	0.0	0.0
Operating Margin **21**	79.6	80.4	60.5	51.5	87.5	85.5	80.2	76.9	75.8	77.2	77.8	78.1	80.3
Operating Margin Before Officers' Comp. **22**	79.6	80.4	60.5	51.5	87.5	85.5	80.2	76.9	75.8	77.2	77.8	78.1	80.3

Selected Average Balance Sheet ($ in Thousands)

	Total	1	2	3	4	5	6	7	8	9	10	11	12
Net Receivables **23**	12232	0	13	1	13	74	187	245	914	1924	4020	14374	92038
Inventories **24**	•	•	•	•	•	•	•	•	•	•	•	•	•
Net Property, Plant and Equipment **25**	1	0	0	0	0	0	0	0	0	0	0	2	6
Total Assets **26**	1259484	0	219	857	2896	7519	16354	35546	72759	166314	360955	1120360	10428998
Notes and Loans Payable **27**	1383	2	2	0	0	0	0	2	188	522	1907	2692	5474
All Other Liabilities **28**	55873	0	22	23	62	147	514	814	3442	6981	19720	60295	435111
Net Worth **29**	1202228	0	195	835	2834	7372	15840	34729	69128	158811	339328	1057373	9988412

Selected Financial Ratios (Times to 1)

	Total	1	2	3	4	5	6	7	8	9	10	11	12
Current Ratio **30**	3.6	•	0.9	2.9	1.9	4.8	4.4	6.2	3.5	4.4	3.3	3.5	3.7
Quick Ratio **31**	3.3	•	0.6	0.7	0.4	2.1	2.8	4.5	3.1	3.9	2.9	2.7	3.5
Net Sales to Working Capital **32**	0.2	•	•	1.1	2.7	0.5	0.3	0.3	0.3	0.2	0.3	0.3	0.2
Coverage Ratio **33**	339.2	415.8	•	•	72652.0	3817.1	2375.8	3682.0	116.0	219.0	96.7	177.5	577.4
Total Asset Turnover **34**	0.0	•	0.0	0.1	0.1	0.0	0.0	0.0	0.0	0.0	0.0	0.0	0.0
Inventory Turnover **35**	•	•	•	•	•	•	•	•	•	•	•	•	•
Receivables Turnover **36**	•	•	•	•	•	•	•	•	•	•	•	•	•
Total Liabilities to Net Worth **37**	0.0	•	0.1	0.0	0.0	0.0	0.0	0.0	0.1	0.0	0.1	0.1	0.0
Current Assets to Working Capital **38**	1.4	•	•	1.5	2.1	1.3	1.3	1.2	1.4	1.3	1.4	1.5	1.4
Current Liabilities to Working Capital **39**	0.4	•	•	0.5	1.1	0.3	0.3	0.2	0.4	0.3	0.4	0.5	0.4
Working Capital to Net Sales **40**	4.6	•	•	0.9	0.4	2.0	3.0	3.2	3.4	4.4	3.8	3.6	5.0
Inventory to Working Capital **41**	•	•	•	•	•	•	•	•	•	•	•	•	•
Total Receipts to Cash Flow **42**	1.1	1.1	1.4	1.2	1.3	1.3	1.3	1.2	1.1	1.1	1.1	1.1	1.1
Cost of Goods to Cash Flow **43**	•	•	•	•	•	•	•	•	•	•	•	•	•
Cash Flow to Total Debt **44**	0.5	•	0.1	1.7	2.0	1.5	0.9	1.2	0.6	0.6	0.5	0.5	0.5

Selected Financial Factors (in Percentages)

	Total	1	2	3	4	5	6	7	8	9	10	11	12
Debt Ratio **45**	4.5	•	11.0	2.7	2.1	2.0	3.1	2.3	5.0	4.5	6.0	5.6	4.2
Return on Total Assets **46**	1.8	•	1.2	2.7	4.2	2.7	2.6	2.3	1.9	1.9	2.1	2.0	1.7
Return on Equity Before Income Taxes **47**	1.9	•	1.3	2.8	4.3	2.7	2.6	2.3	2.0	2.0	2.2	2.1	1.8
Return on Equity After Income Taxes **48**	1.9	•	1.3	2.8	4.3	2.7	2.6	2.3	2.0	2.0	2.2	2.1	1.8
Profit Margin (Before Income Tax) **49**	72.1	67.2	60.0	51.5	79.3	75.1	73.0	66.6	60.4	60.4	62.4	64.7	75.7
Profit Margin (After Income Tax) **50**	72.1	67.1	60.0	51.5	79.3	75.1	73.0	66.6	60.4	60.4	62.4	64.7	75.7

Table I
Corporations with and without Net Income

OTHER FINANCIAL VEHICLES

MONEY AMOUNTS AND SIZE OF ASSETS IN THOUSANDS OF DOLLARS

Item Description for Accounting Period 7/10 Through 6/11	Total	Zero Assets	Under 500	500 to 1,000	1,000 to 5,000	5,000 to 10,000	10,000 to 25,000	25,000 to 50,000	50,000 to 100,000	100,000 to 250,000	250,000 to 500,000	500,000 to 2,500,000	2,500,000 and over
Number of Enterprises 1	9172	3240	3856	245	780	221	199	112	120	104	83	135	78
Revenues ($ in Thousands)													
Net Sales 2	37332566	1769295	195152	41932	187271	168386	611401	367807	1482569	1240219	2676463	6513139	22078932
Interest 3	28286535	1063877	8909	1303	106364	14891	278026	112604	525996	801355	1548609	4776980	19047621
Rents 4	1303750	135727	1164	0	950	0	5358	49901	108015	170054	97616	467792	267173
Royalties 5	23886	10817	0	68	0	7987	0	1654	2977	0	309	73	0
Other Portfolio Income 6	2217192	234467	2912	3851	16359	14002	54795	27867	152278	102756	822147	189976	595781
Other Receipts 7	5501203	324407	182167	36710	63598	131506	273222	175781	693303	166054	207782	1078318	2168357
Total Receipts 8	37332566	1769295	195152	41932	187271	168386	611401	367807	1482569	1240219	2676463	6513139	22078932
Average Total Receipts 9	4070	546	51	171	240	762	3072	3284	12355	11925	32247	48245	283063
Operating Costs/Operating Income (%)													
Cost of Operations 10	0.2	•	13.3	•	•	•	•	•	2.9	•	•	•	•
Salaries and Wages 11	1.1	0.0	24.2	•	2.4	19.6	17.2	1.6	2.5	0.3	0.3	0.8	0.5
Taxes Paid 12	0.6	0.2	2.4	0.0	1.4	4.0	0.8	0.8	2.7	1.1	0.5	1.0	0.3
Interest Paid 13	18.8	21.8	5.9	11.9	14.9	4.2	38.4	22.3	17.6	29.1	32.6	22.4	14.9
Depreciation 14	0.7	0.0	3.2	0.8	0.1	1.4	0.6	0.2	3.3	0.7	0.3	1.6	0.3
Amortization and Depletion 15	0.5	0.2	0.8	3.7	5.1	7.6	0.2	0.4	0.4	0.4	0.6	0.5	0.4
Pensions and Other Deferred Comp. 16	0.0	0.0	•	•	0.4	0.4	1.4	0.1	0.2	•	0.0	0.0	0.0
Employee Benefits 17	0.6	•	1.4	•	0.2	1.8	4.1	0.2	0.2	•	0.0	0.0	0.8
Advertising 18	0.0	0.0	0.9	•	0.1	0.1	0.3	0.1	0.1	0.0	0.0	0.1	0.0
Other Expenses 19	46.2	85.6	60.8	96.7	119.4	34.7	58.7	93.4	61.3	62.2	27.7	36.1	44.4
Officers' Compensation 20	0.3	0.0	0.8	•	1.0	10.1	1.1	2.9	0.6	0.2	0.1	0.1	0.3
Operating Margin 21	31.0	•	•	•	•	16.1	•	•	8.1	5.9	37.9	37.5	38.0
Operating Margin Before Officers' Comp. 22	31.4	•	•	•	26.2	•	•	•	8.7	6.0	38.0	37.6	38.3

Selected Average Balance Sheet ($ in Thousands)

	1	2	3	4	5	6	7	8	9	10	11	12	13
Net Receivables 23	9500	0	8	0	249	331	548	1813	2791	5354	23264	96391	906237
Inventories 24	•	•	•	•	•	•	•	•	•	•	•	•	•
Net Property, Plant and Equipment 25	1032	0	2	13	0	462	1082	491	2446	944	3288	41160	36675
Total Assets 26	93603	0	125	737	1969	7051	16381	35159	71619	165573	352694	1196892	8088514
Notes and Loans Payable 27	25598	0	35	496	918	2160	4482	9793	14500	36175	63321	421772	2098120
All Other Liabilities 28	15283	0	42	63	1091	1419	3864	4409	7226	21209	49142	160921	1393468
Net Worth 29	52722	0	48	179	-39	3471	8035	20956	49893	108189	240231	614199	4596925

Selected Financial Ratios (Times to 1)

	1	2	3	4	5	6	7	8	9	10	11	12	13
Current Ratio 30	1.1	•	2.7	2.7	167.9	1.2	1.5	2.6	2.4	2.0	1.8	0.9	1.1
Quick Ratio 31	0.9	•	2.7	2.7	51.7	0.7	1.2	1.3	1.9	1.5	1.6	0.7	0.9
Net Sales to Working Capital 32	1.9	•	1.6	1.6	0.4	2.2	2.3	0.7	1.7	0.9	1.1	•	1.3
Coverage Ratio 33	2.6	0.4	•	•	•	4.8	0.4	0.0	1.5	1.2	2.2	2.7	3.5
Total Asset Turnover 34	0.0	•	0.4	0.4	0.2	0.1	0.2	0.1	0.2	0.1	0.1	0.0	0.0
Inventory Turnover 35	•	•	•	•	•	•	•	•	•	•	•	•	•
Receivables Turnover 36	•	•	•	•	•	•	•	•	•	•	•	•	•
Total Liabilities to Net Worth 37	0.8	•	1.6	1.6	3.1	1.0	1.0	0.7	0.4	0.5	0.5	0.9	0.8
Current Assets to Working Capital 38	9.8	•	1.6	1.6	1.0	5.9	2.9	1.6	1.7	2.0	2.2	2.2	8.7
Current Liabilities to Working Capital 39	8.8	•	0.6	0.6	0.0	4.9	1.9	0.6	0.7	1.0	1.2	•	7.7
Working Capital to Net Sales 40	0.5	•	0.6	0.6	2.5	0.5	0.4	1.5	0.6	1.2	0.9	•	0.8
Inventory to Working Capital 41	0.0	•	•	•	•	•	•	0.0	0.0	•	•	•	•
Total Receipts to Cash Flow 42	1.4	1.6	2.8	2.8	1.3	2.6	4.7	1.9	1.9	1.7	2.8	1.4	1.3
Cost of Goods to Cash Flow 43	0.0	•	0.4	0.4	•	0.4	•	•	0.1	•	•	•	•
Cash Flow to Total Debt 44	0.1	•	0.2	0.2	0.2	0.1	0.1	0.1	0.3	0.1	0.1	0.1	0.1

Selected Financial Factors (in Percentages)

	1	2	3	4	5	6	7	8	9	10	11	12	13
Debt Ratio 45	43.7	•	61.8	75.8	102.0	50.8	50.9	40.4	30.3	34.7	31.9	48.7	43.2
Return on Total Assets 46	2.2	•	•	•	2.2	2.8	0.0	4.4	2.5	6.4	2.4	•	1.9
Return on Equity Before Income Taxes 47	2.4	•	•	•	274.5	3.5	•	2.0	0.6	5.1	2.9	•	2.3
Return on Equity After Income Taxes 48	2.2	•	•	•	380.3	2.2	•	1.0	0.3	4.1	2.7	•	2.3
Profit Margin (Before Income Tax) 49	30.8	•	•	•	•	16.0	•	8.1	5.4	37.9	37.3	•	38.0
Profit Margin (After Income Tax) 50	28.4	•	•	•	•	10.0	•	3.9	2.5	30.5	34.8	•	37.1

Table II
Corporations with Net Income

OTHER FINANCIAL VEHICLES

MONEY AMOUNTS AND SIZE OF ASSETS IN THOUSANDS OF DOLLARS

Item Description for Accounting Period 7/10 Through 6/11	Total	Zero Assets	Under 500	500 to 1,000	1,000 to 5,000	5,000 to 10,000	10,000 to 25,000	25,000 to 50,000	50,000 to 100,000	100,000 to 250,000	250,000 to 500,000	500,000 to 2,500,000	2,500,000 and over
Number of Enterprises 1	3007	1066	1038	57	315	54	80	55	70	60	55	93	63
Revenues ($ in Thousands)													
Net Sales 2	28780799	1268793	168068	26034	159505	155198	319526	260586	712004	754475	1914816	5045821	17995973
Interest 3	22464528	918134	1731	10	87414	11213	198299	78174	184376	482536	813729	3807619	15881292
Rents 4	482342	266	1164	0	950	0	0	0	11443	38635	97602	277157	55124
Royalties 5	5008	27	0	68	0	0	0	1616	2977	0	247	73	0
Other Portfolio Income 6	1797749	168162	2912	3036	16337	13038	38673	21073	139241	95021	818428	142330	339494
Other Receipts 7	4031172	182204	162261	22920	54804	130947	82554	159723	373967	138283	184810	818642	1720063
Total Receipts 8	28780799	1268793	168068	26034	159505	155198	319526	260586	712004	754475	1914816	5045821	17995973
Average Total Receipts 9	9571	1190	162	457	506	2874	3994	4738	10171	12575	34815	54256	285650
Operating Costs/Operating Income (%)													
Cost of Operations 10	0.2	•	12.4	•	•	•	•	•	6.0	•	•	•	•
Salaries and Wages 11	0.8	0.1	20.6	•	2.7	18.2	4.4	1.9	4.0	0.3	0.4	0.7	0.3
Taxes Paid 12	0.4	0.2	2.6	0.0	1.2	3.9	0.7	0.8	3.2	1.5	0.3	0.8	0.1
Interest Paid 13	14.8	18.0	1.2	19.2	1.6	3.0	56.2	13.5	8.0	16.8	10.9	18.5	13.8
Depreciation 14	0.4	0.0	2.9	•	0.1	0.6	0.5	0.3	0.6	1.1	0.4	1.2	0.1
Amortization and Depletion 15	0.3	0.2	1.0	2.3	0.0	0.5	0.3	0.1	0.7	0.3	0.7	0.4	0.2
Pensions and Other Deferred Comp. 16	0.0	0.0	•	•	•	0.5	•	0.0	0.3	•	0.0	0.0	0.0
Employee Benefits 17	0.0	0.0	1.4	•	0.3	1.7	0.7	0.2	0.4	•	0.0	0.0	0.0
Advertising 18	0.0	0.0	1.0	•	0.1	•	0.6	0.1	0.3	0.0	0.0	0.1	0.0
Other Expenses 19	21.4	20.3	26.1	4.7	9.8	18.1	4.6	15.6	13.5	22.6	17.0	17.0	23.9
Officers' Compensation 20	0.4	0.0	0.9	•	0.7	10.2	0.6	3.4	1.3	0.0	0.2	0.2	0.3
Operating Margin 21	61.3	61.2	29.8	73.7	83.6	43.4	31.4	64.1	61.8	57.4	70.1	61.1	61.3
Operating Margin Before Officers' Comp. 22	61.6	61.2	30.8	73.7	84.3	53.6	32.0	67.6	63.0	57.4	70.2	61.3	61.6

Selected Average Balance Sheet ($ in Thousands)

Net Receivables 23	26203	12	0	0	143	15	1862	4165	384	32208	99508	1068730
Inventories 24	•	•	•	•	•	•	•	•	•	•	•	•
Net Property, Plant and Equipment 25	1752	6	0	1	78	1409	68	2132	121	548	41926	16748
Total Assets 26	218575	287	726	1959	6791	17148	37061	72650	164205	351272	1159446	8102125
Notes and Loans Payable 27	53372	21	1468	629	2738	3014	6317	7890	23045	37567	257693	2087037
All Other Liabilities 28	39228	46	258	1689	590	3197	4777	5614	9729	33816	153558	1582479
Net Worth 29	125975	220	-1000	-358	3463	10937	25966	59146	131431	279889	748195	4432610

Selected Financial Ratios (Times to 1)

Current Ratio 30	1.3	•	2.1	2.0	2.0	0.8	4.6	4.1	4.2	3.7	1.7	1.2
Quick Ratio 31	1.0	•	2.1	2.0	1.9	0.6	2.3	3.4	3.1	3.2	1.2	0.9
Net Sales to Working Capital 32	0.9	3.2	0.7	2.2	5.2	•	0.7	0.9	1.0	0.7	0.5	1.0
Coverage Ratio 33	5.1	25.8	4.8	54.5	15.7	1.6	5.8	8.8	4.4	7.4	4.3	5.4
Total Asset Turnover 34	0.0	0.6	0.6	0.3	0.4	0.2	0.1	0.1	0.1	0.1	0.0	0.0
Inventory Turnover 35	•	•	•	•	•	•	•	•	•	•	•	•
Receivables Turnover 36	•	•	•	•	•	•	•	•	•	•	•	•
Total Liabilities to Net Worth 37	0.7	0.3	0.3	•	1.0	0.6	0.4	0.2	0.2	0.3	0.5	0.8
Current Assets to Working Capital 38	4.8	1.9	1.9	1.0	2.0	2.0	1.3	1.3	1.3	1.4	2.5	7.0
Current Liabilities to Working Capital 39	3.8	0.9	0.9	•	1.0	1.0	0.3	0.3	0.3	0.4	1.5	6.0
Working Capital to Net Sales 40	1.2	•	0.3	1.5	0.5	0.2	1.5	1.2	1.0	1.5	2.1	1.0
Inventory to Working Capital 41	0.0	•	•	•	•	•	•	0.0	•	•	•	•
Total Receipts to Cash Flow 42	1.3	1.4	2.2	1.5	1.1	2.1	1.4	1.8	1.4	2.2	1.3	1.2
Cost of Goods to Cash Flow 43	0.0	•	0.3	•	•	•	•	0.1	•	•	•	•
Cash Flow to Total Debt 44	0.1	0.2	0.2	0.2	0.4	0.2	0.3	0.4	0.3	0.2	0.1	0.1

Selected Financial Factors (in Percentages)

Debt Ratio 45	42.4	•	237.7	118.3	49.0	36.2	29.9	18.6	20.0	20.3	35.5	45.3
Return on Total Assets 46	3.3	17.5	58.4	21.9	19.6	20.4	9.9	9.8	5.7	8.0	3.7	2.6
Return on Equity Before Income Taxes 47	4.6	21.9	36.0	•	36.0	11.5	11.7	10.6	5.5	8.7	4.4	3.9
Return on Equity After Income Taxes 48	4.4	20.9	•	•	30.7	9.6	10.7	9.1	5.0	7.4	4.2	3.9
Profit Margin (Before Income Tax) 49	61.0	29.8	73.7	83.3	43.4	31.4	64.1	61.7	57.4	70.1	60.9	61.3
Profit Margin (After Income Tax) 50	57.9	28.5	73.7	62.9	36.9	26.3	58.8	53.1	52.7	59.8	57.7	60.1

Table I
Corporations with and without Net Income

LESSORS OF BUILDINGS

MONEY AMOUNTS AND SIZE OF ASSETS IN THOUSANDS OF DOLLARS

Item Description for Accounting Period 7/10 Through 6/11	Total	Zero Assets	Under 500	500 to 1,000	1,000 to 5,000	5,000 to 10,000	10,000 to 25,000	25,000 to 50,000	50,000 to 100,000	100,000 to 250,000	250,000 to 500,000	500,000 to 2,500,000	2,500,000 and over
Number of Enterprises **1**	225390	26700	111954	38726	39786	4566	2250	587	327	205	98	129	62
Revenues ($ in Thousands)													
Net Sales **2**	96663804	20584310	2711168	2831662	6094047	2088618	2995699	2309006	3643246	3459397	4646523	13969234	31330893
Interest **3**	2959843	85593	16121	28292	54664	28702	36036	24139	62253	85082	120669	665552	1752741
Rents **4**	3601814	1024515	26775	43131	217455	108393	224791	237340	664088	1354633	2010479	7960457	22146556
Royalties **5**	29606	0	49	431	14940	4909	24	27	362	338	69	8456	0
Other Portfolio Income **6**	21466410	16898632	135425	124878	237758	67628	181054	34577	376248	198361	67091	598608	2546148
Other Receipts **7**	36189331	2575570	2532798	2634930	5569230	1878986	2553794	2012923	2540295	1820983	2448215	4736161	4885448
Total Receipts **8**	96663804	20584310	2711168	2831662	6094047	2088618	2995699	2309006	3643246	3459397	4646523	13969234	31330893
Average Total Receipts **9**	429	771	24	73	153	457	1331	3934	11141	16875	47414	108289	505337
Operating Costs/Operating Income (%)													
Cost of Operations **10**	4.4	0.7	9.2	9.5	20.9	4.4	14.0	9.3	7.9	11.4	13.7	1.1	0.2
Salaries and Wages **11**	5.2	0.4	5.5	11.0	6.6	13.1	8.6	14.1	11.6	3.6	5.4	9.4	3.6
Taxes Paid **12**	6.4	2.2	13.2	10.2	14.6	10.6	8.9	8.4	7.5	8.7	6.3	7.3	5.3
Interest Paid **13**	12.1	3.3	8.3	7.3	11.3	15.4	14.1	13.8	13.0	19.6	13.0	16.2	15.2
Depreciation **14**	10.2	2.1	8.7	8.7	10.4	12.7	11.4	10.8	10.4	14.6	9.0	13.1	13.8
Amortization and Depletion **15**	1.0	0.2	0.2	0.7	0.4	0.7	1.0	0.8	1.0	1.5	1.6	1.5	1.4
Pensions and Other Deferred Comp. **16**	0.1	0.0	•	0.3	0.5	1.1	0.3	0.4	0.3	0.1	0.1	0.1	•
Employee Benefits **17**	0.5	0.0	0.4	1.4	0.7	2.2	1.3	0.9	1.7	0.4	0.5	0.9	0.0
Advertising **18**	0.3	0.0	0.4	1.0	0.3	1.2	0.4	0.6	1.4	0.4	0.6	0.2	0.2
Other Expenses **19**	28.6	9.1	54.0	35.3	31.0	32.6	35.3	44.0	38.9	36.8	42.8	43.1	25.3
Officers' Compensation **20**	1.3	0.1	3.7	6.5	4.1	8.2	3.9	2.5	1.4	1.0	0.5	1.0	0.4
Operating Margin **21**	30.0	82.0	•	8.0	•	•	0.8	•	5.0	2.0	6.6	6.0	34.5
Operating Margin Before Officers' Comp. **22**	31.3	82.0	0.1	14.6	3.2	6.0	4.6	•	6.4	2.9	7.1	7.0	34.9

Selected Average Balance Sheet ($ in Thousands)

	1	2	3	4	5	6	7	8	9	10	11	12	13
Net Receivables 23	66	0	4	20	48	160	443	634	2401	2742	9185	27473	61440
Inventories 24	•	•	•	•	•	•	•	•	•	•	•	•	•
Net Property, Plant and Equipment 25	2304	0	148	484	1474	4678	9690	20877	39369	92094	184296	654826	3800017
Total Assets 26	3682	0	195	711	2116	6849	15061	34441	68835	152626	353612	1200896	5931262
Notes and Loans Payable 27	1733	0	138	473	1446	4786	9633	19487	34377	78375	163407	490350	2220567
All Other Liabilities 28	272	0	7	49	175	500	1547	2760	5392	13917	25194	116802	355552
Net Worth 29	1678	0	49	189	494	1564	3882	12194	29066	60333	165011	593744	3355143

Selected Financial Ratios (Times to 1)

	1	2	3	4	5	6	7	8	9	10	11	12	13
Current Ratio 30	1.4	•	2.3	2.2	1.9	2.1	1.7	2.1	2.2	1.4	1.4	1.1	0.9
Quick Ratio 31	0.9	•	2.0	1.4	1.2	1.3	1.2	1.3	1.5	0.9	1.0	0.8	0.7
Net Sales to Working Capital 32	5.2	•	1.7	1.2	1.0	1.0	1.6	1.6	2.2	3.3	6.0	12.7	•
Coverage Ratio 33	3.5	26.0	0.6	2.1	0.9	0.8	1.0	0.6	1.4	1.1	1.5	1.4	3.3
Total Asset Turnover 34	0.1	•	0.1	0.1	0.1	0.1	0.1	0.1	0.2	0.1	0.1	0.1	0.1
Inventory Turnover 35	•	•	•	•	•	•	•	•	•	•	•	•	•
Receivables Turnover 36	•	•	•	•	•	•	•	•	•	•	•	•	•
Total Liabilities to Net Worth 37	1.2	•	3.0	2.8	3.3	3.4	2.9	1.8	1.4	1.5	1.1	1.0	0.8
Current Assets to Working Capital 38	3.8	•	1.8	1.8	2.1	1.9	2.4	1.9	1.9	3.2	3.6	10.8	•
Current Liabilities to Working Capital 39	2.8	•	0.8	0.8	1.1	0.9	1.4	0.9	0.9	2.2	2.6	9.8	•
Working Capital to Net Sales 40	0.2	•	0.6	0.9	1.0	1.0	0.6	0.6	0.4	0.3	0.2	0.1	•
Inventory to Working Capital 41	0.0	•	•	0.0	0.0	0.0	0.0	0.0	0.0	0.1	0.0	0.0	•
Total Receipts to Cash Flow 42	3.3	14.6	3.4	3.6	5.2	5.1	4.3	3.5	4.4	3.5	3.4	2.8	2.1
Cost of Goods to Cash Flow 43	0.1	0.1	0.3	0.3	1.1	0.2	0.6	0.3	0.3	0.4	0.5	0.0	0.0
Cash Flow to Total Debt 44	0.1	0.0	0.0	0.0	0.0	0.0	0.0	0.1	0.1	0.1	0.1	0.1	0.1

Selected Financial Factors (in Percentages)

	1	2	3	4	5	6	7	8	9	10	11	12	13
Debt Ratio 45	54.4	•	74.8	73.5	76.6	77.2	74.2	64.6	57.8	60.5	53.3	50.6	43.4
Return on Total Assets 46	4.9	•	0.6	1.6	0.7	0.9	1.3	0.9	2.9	2.4	2.6	2.0	4.2
Return on Equity Before Income Taxes 47	7.7	•	•	3.1	•	•	0.1	•	1.8	0.5	1.9	1.1	5.2
Return on Equity After Income Taxes 48	7.5	•	•	2.6	•	•	•	•	0.7	•	1.8	1.1	5.2
Profit Margin (Before Income Tax) 49	29.9	81.9	•	8.0	•	•	0.4	•	4.8	1.8	6.5	6.0	34.5
Profit Margin (After Income Tax) 50	29.2	81.3	•	6.7	•	•	•	•	1.8	•	6.3	5.8	34.5

Table II

Corporations with Net Income

LESSORS OF BUILDINGS

MONEY AMOUNTS AND SIZE OF ASSETS IN THOUSANDS OF DOLLARS

Item Description for Accounting Period 7/10 Through 6/11	Total	Zero Assets	Under 500	500 to 1,000	1,000 to 5,000	5,000 to 10,000	10,000 to 25,000	25,000 to 50,000	50,000 to 100,000	100,000 to 250,000	250,000 to 500,000	500,000 to 2,500,000	2,500,000 and over
Number of Enterprises **1**	43386	3700	20726	8600	7879	1209	663	207	128	92	53	75	55
Revenues ($ in Thousands)													
Net Sales **2**	78114461	19629009	1926558	2286369	3873060	1217680	1687546	1644046	1836620	1979051	3229083	9987080	28818358
Interest **3**	2609453	74922	12253	25099	36975	22144	14630	17905	44270	64985	90272	515825	1690174
Rents **4**	29645461	869662	24639	42845	121724	37624	154944	85342	389375	694793	1628199	5556872	20039442
Royalties **5**	7892	0	0	0	4637	2641	24	2	359	227	0	0	0
Other Portfolio Income **6**	21152313	16874210	132218	123014	214262	46055	172625	24301	344965	179769	56895	439437	2544561
Other Receipts **7**	24699342	1810215	1757448	2095411	3495462	1109216	1345323	1516496	1057651	1039277	1453717	3474946	4544181
Total Receipts **8**	78114461	19629009	1926558	2286369	3873060	1217680	1687546	1644046	1836620	1979051	3229083	9987080	28818358
Average Total Receipts **9**	1800	5305	93	266	492	1007	2545	7942	14349	21511	60926	133161	523970
Operating Costs/Operating Income (%)													
Cost of Operations **10**	3.4	0.0	12.5	11.3	23.1	2.3	5.3	10.0	8.1	6.5	18.9	0.3	0.2
Salaries and Wages **11**	4.5	0.3	4.9	10.9	5.6	11.7	6.6	15.1	6.8	3.6	3.0	10.7	3.5
Taxes Paid **12**	5.1	1.4	8.7	7.9	9.0	9.1	8.5	7.9	8.7	8.7	5.5	7.2	5.0
Interest Paid **13**	9.7	2.1	5.7	4.7	7.0	8.9	9.8	8.1	10.5	14.5	9.5	13.2	14.5
Depreciation **14**	8.7	1.2	4.2	5.1	6.5	8.0	9.8	6.9	8.2	13.6	7.5	12.1	13.3
Amortization and Depletion **15**	0.8	0.2	0.0	0.3	0.3	0.3	0.7	0.6	1.0	1.3	0.8	1.2	1.2
Pensions and Other Deferred Comp. **16**	0.1	0.0	•	0.4	0.5	1.0	0.3	0.3	0.2	0.1	0.0	0.1	•
Employee Benefits **17**	0.3	0.0	0.2	1.2	0.4	0.9	1.1	0.9	0.5	0.3	0.2	1.1	0.0
Advertising **18**	0.2	0.0	0.4	1.1	0.3	1.7	0.2	0.4	0.3	0.4	0.4	0.2	0.2
Other Expenses **19**	19.8	4.2	34.4	31.2	20.8	23.6	25.8	34.8	26.5	22.0	32.4	25.2	23.1
Officers' Compensation **20**	1.1	0.0	3.4	7.2	4.7	10.6	3.3	1.7	1.7	0.9	0.7	0.7	0.4
Operating Margin **21**	46.3	90.6	25.7	18.7	21.8	21.8	28.6	13.2	27.6	28.1	21.2	27.9	38.6
Operating Margin Before Officers' Comp. **22**	47.4	90.6	29.0	25.9	26.4	32.4	31.8	15.0	29.3	29.0	21.9	28.6	39.0

Selected Average Balance Sheet ($ in Thousands)

	1	2	3	4	5	6	7	8	9	10	11	12	13	14
Net Receivables 23	195	•	0	8	23	71	245	309	740	3630	3139	8005	30694	62223
Inventories 24	•	•	•	•	•	•	•	•	•	•	•	•	•	•
Net Property, Plant and Equipment 25	7192	•	0	114	417	1252	4546	8913	20552	38693	97889	193617	716457	3683845
Total Assets 26	11975	•	0	190	726	2066	7125	15453	35196	70240	153745	361196	1283318	5971075
Notes and Loans Payable 27	4499	•	0	129	360	1049	3961	8085	15481	30661	67423	136493	449979	2121971
All Other Liabilities 28	835	•	0	12	92	171	477	1003	3172	6115	11711	16731	125380	360244
Net Worth 29	6640	•	0	49	274	847	2687	6366	16544	33465	74611	207971	707959	3488861

Selected Financial Ratios (Times to 1)

	1	2	3	4	5	6	7	8	9	10	11	12	13	14
Current Ratio 30	1.3	•	4.2	2.1	2.9	2.9	1.8	1.7	2.7	1.4	2.1	1.1	1.0	
Quick Ratio 31	1.0	•	3.9	1.4	2.1	2.1	1.3	1.2	2.2	1.2	1.3	0.9	0.8	
Net Sales to Working Capital 32	8.4	•	2.5	3.1	1.8	1.2	2.4	3.7	2.1	4.5	3.7	9.9	96.9	
Coverage Ratio 33	5.8	43.9	5.5	5.0	4.1	3.4	3.9	2.6	3.6	2.9	3.2	3.1	3.7	
Total Asset Turnover 34	0.2	•	0.5	0.4	0.2	0.1	0.2	0.2	0.2	0.1	0.2	0.1	0.1	
Inventory Turnover 35	•	•	•	•	•	•	•	•	•	•	•	•	•	
Receivables Turnover 36	•	•	•	•	•	•	•	•	•	•	•	•	•	
Total Liabilities to Net Worth 37	0.8	•	2.9	1.6	1.4	1.7	1.4	1.1	1.1	1.1	0.7	0.8	0.7	
Current Assets to Working Capital 38	4.0	•	1.3	1.9	1.5	1.5	2.3	2.4	1.6	3.3	1.9	7.8	51.5	
Current Liabilities to Working Capital 39	3.0	•	0.3	0.9	0.5	0.5	1.3	1.4	0.6	2.3	0.9	6.8	50.5	
Working Capital to Net Sales 40	0.1	•	0.4	0.3	0.6	0.8	0.4	0.3	0.5	0.2	0.3	0.1	0.0	
Inventory to Working Capital 41	0.0	•	•	0.0	0.0	0.0	0.0	0.0	0.0	0.0	0.0	0.1	0.0	
Total Receipts to Cash Flow 42	2.8	11.2	2.3	3.0	3.0	2.7	2.5	2.4	3.1	2.6	2.5	2.3	2.1	
Cost of Goods to Cash Flow 43	0.1	0.0	0.3	0.3	0.7	0.1	0.1	0.2	0.2	0.2	0.5	0.0	0.0	
Cash Flow to Total Debt 44	0.1	•	0.3	0.2	0.1	0.1	0.1	0.2	0.1	0.1	0.2	0.1	0.1	

Selected Financial Factors (in Percentages)

	1	2	3	4	5	6	7	8	9	10	11	12	13
Debt Ratio 45	44.5	•	74.2	62.2	59.0	62.3	58.8	53.0	52.4	51.5	42.4	44.8	41.6
Return on Total Assets 46	8.4	•	15.3	8.6	6.8	4.3	6.3	4.8	7.7	5.9	5.2	4.3	4.7
Return on Equity Before Income Taxes 47	12.5	•	48.4	18.2	12.6	8.1	11.3	6.3	11.8	8.0	6.2	5.2	5.8
Return on Equity After Income Taxes 48	12.3	•	43.4	16.6	11.0	6.8	9.5	5.2	9.2	7.1	6.1	5.2	5.8
Profit Margin (Before Income Tax) 49	46.3	90.6	25.6	18.7	21.6	21.7	28.2	13.1	27.4	27.9	21.2	27.9	38.6
Profit Margin (After Income Tax) 50	45.4	89.9	23.0	17.1	18.9	18.3	23.7	10.8	21.4	24.6	20.8	27.6	38.6

Table I
Corporations with and without Net Income

LESSORS OF MINIWAREHOUSES, SELF-STORAGE, OTHER REAL ESTATE

MONEY AMOUNTS AND SIZE OF ASSETS IN THOUSANDS OF DOLLARS

Item Description for Accounting Period 7/10 Through 6/11		Total	Zero Assets	Under 500	500 to 1,000	1,000 to 5,000	5,000 to 10,000	10,000 to 25,000	25,000 to 50,000	50,000 to 100,000	100,000 to 250,000	250,000 to 500,000	500,000 to 2,500,000	2,500,000 and over
Number of Enterprises	1	85712	12466	47691	10080	12135	1482	1007	324	181	187	79	67	15
Revenues ($ in Thousands)														
Net Sales	2	27964545	1970896	3518292	911307	1863570	747380	1207927	1046982	1575613	2925377	2693398	5030689	4473116
Interest	3	1202633	71748	10699	12148	47776	32353	44297	196769	53640	114605	152715	249785	216098
Rents	4	9527676	323689	3146	29791	20984	82790	303538	302550	626003	1274378	1267614	3257684	2035508
Royalties	5	111066	4187	4174	8764	33660	7423	22273	5031	318	6499	18737	0	0
Other Portfolio Income	6	3904575	660333	83532	10079	181791	16816	106952	103762	189251	405921	538407	712146	895583
Other Receipts	7	13218595	910939	3416741	850525	1579359	607998	730867	438870	706401	1123974	715925	811074	1325927
Total Receipts	8	27964545	1970896	3518292	911307	1863570	747380	1207927	1046982	1575613	2925377	2693398	5030689	4473116
Average Total Receipts	9	326	158	74	90	154	504	1200	3231	8705	15644	34094	75085	298208
Operating Costs/Operating Income (%)														
Cost of Operations	10	1.3	0.9	•	•	4.0	0.0	1.4	0.7	0.0	0.7	7.4	0.3	0.0
Salaries and Wages	11	7.7	1.1	29.6	6.7	12.0	7.5	6.7	4.7	7.8	4.4	2.9	1.2	5.4
Taxes Paid	12	6.0	3.0	6.5	10.5	8.5	9.8	7.3	6.0	5.1	5.4	2.8	6.8	5.9
Interest Paid	13	13.5	16.2	2.4	6.4	11.9	21.2	17.8	31.4	14.0	13.0	14.1	14.8	15.0
Depreciation	14	8.9	4.9	3.0	5.0	14.1	14.4	8.6	9.1	6.4	11.7	5.9	12.6	9.7
Amortization and Depletion	15	1.5	0.8	0.5	0.2	1.0	1.0	2.2	1.1	0.7	1.4	0.8	1.7	3.8
Pensions and Other Deferred Comp.	16	0.2	0.0	0.7	1.0	0.2	0.2	0.8	0.2	0.2	0.3	0.0	•	0.0
Employee Benefits	17	0.6	0.1	2.5	0.2	1.0	0.7	0.8	0.6	0.4	0.4	0.2	•	0.1
Advertising	18	0.6	0.3	2.2	0.5	0.5	0.5	0.3	0.7	0.6	0.2	0.3	0.2	0.7
Other Expenses	19	57.0	66.9	44.1	59.5	46.7	68.4	83.3	74.5	78.9	68.9	66.4	56.1	33.4
Officers' Compensation	20	2.8	0.2	10.3	5.2	5.4	5.5	2.3	2.2	1.6	1.2	1.0	0.5	1.3
Operating Margin	21	•	5.5	•	4.8	•	•	•	•	•	•	•	5.8	24.6
Operating Margin Before Officers' Comp.	22	2.6	5.7	8.6	10.0	•	•	•	•	•	•	•	6.3	25.9

Selected Average Balance Sheet ($ in Thousands)

Item													
Net Receivables 23	72	•	6	9	105	283	808	516	2580	5487	9865	6634	27037
Inventories 24	•	•	•	•	•	•	•	•	•	•	•	•	•
Net Property, Plant and Equipment 25	1300	0	71	379	1048	3066	5393	11872	23902	52302	116479	368038	1979000
Total Assets 26	3135	0	151	669	2056	7026	15898	34641	70575	155799	369166	900733	4048350
Notes and Loans Payable 27	1074	0	65	293	1170	3500	7144	13810	23457	43522	109554	211942	1315698
All Other Liabilities 28	275	0	26	59	221	606	2233	3639	7190	14771	20427	45306	399953
Net Worth 29	1786	0	60	317	665	2920	6521	17192	39928	97507	239185	643485	2332699

Selected Financial Ratios (Times to 1)

Ratio													
Current Ratio 30	1.6	•	1.2	2.5	2.1	2.4	2.0	2.0	2.0	1.7	2.9	1.6	0.6
Quick Ratio 31	1.1	•	1.0	1.7	1.4	0.9	1.1	0.8	1.4	1.0	2.3	1.3	0.6
Net Sales to Working Capital 32	2.7	•	17.8	1.3	0.8	0.6	0.7	1.1	1.7	2.0	1.7	4.6	•
Coverage Ratio 33	1.0	1.3	0.2	1.7	0.5	•	0.0	0.0	•	0.4	0.9	1.4	2.6
Total Asset Turnover 34	0.1	•	0.5	0.1	0.1	0.1	0.1	0.1	0.1	0.1	0.1	0.1	0.1
Inventory Turnover 35	•	•	•	•	•	•	•	•	•	•	•	•	•
Receivables Turnover 36	•	•	•	•	•	•	•	•	•	•	•	•	•
Total Liabilities to Net Worth 37	0.8	•	1.5	1.1	2.1	1.4	1.4	1.0	0.8	0.6	0.5	0.4	0.7
Current Assets to Working Capital 38	2.7	•	7.2	1.7	1.9	1.7	2.0	2.0	2.0	2.5	1.5	2.7	•
Current Liabilities to Working Capital 39	1.7	•	6.2	0.7	0.9	0.7	1.0	1.0	1.0	1.5	0.5	1.7	•
Working Capital to Net Sales 40	0.4	•	0.1	0.8	1.2	1.8	1.3	0.9	0.6	0.5	0.6	0.2	•
Inventory to Working Capital 41	0.0	•	•	0.0	0.0	0.0	0.0	0.0	0.1	0.0	0.0	0.0	•
Total Receipts to Cash Flow 42	3.1	3.3	4.4	1.9	4.1	3.7	4.0	3.6	3.0	3.3	3.2	2.3	3.5
Cost of Goods to Cash Flow 43	0.0	0.0	•	0.2	0.0	0.0	0.1	0.0	0.0	0.0	0.2	0.0	0.0
Cash Flow to Total Debt 44	0.1	•	0.2	0.1	0.0	0.0	0.0	0.1	0.1	0.1	0.1	0.1	0.1

Selected Financial Factors (in Percentages)

Factor													
Debt Ratio 45	43.0	•	60.1	52.6	67.6	58.4	59.0	50.4	43.4	37.4	35.2	28.6	42.4
Return on Total Assets 46	1.4	•	0.3	1.5	0.5	•	0.0	•	•	0.5	1.1	1.7	2.9
Return on Equity Before Income Taxes 47	•	•	•	1.3	•	•	•	•	•	•	•	0.7	3.1
Return on Equity After Income Taxes 48	•	•	•	0.9	•	•	•	•	•	•	•	0.6	3.1
Profit Margin (Before Income Tax) 49	•	5.3	4.7	•	•	•	•	•	•	•	•	5.9	24.6
Profit Margin (After Income Tax) 50	•	3.7	3.2	•	•	•	•	•	•	•	•	5.1	24.5

LESSORS OF MINIWAREHOUSES, SELF-STORAGE, OTHER REAL ESTATE

Table II
Corporations with Net Income

MONEY AMOUNTS AND SIZE OF ASSETS IN THOUSANDS OF DOLLARS

Item Description for Accounting Period 7/10 Through 6/11	Total	Zero Assets	Under 500	500 to 1,000	1,000 to 5,000	5,000 to 10,000	10,000 to 25,000	25,000 to 50,000	50,000 to 100,000	100,000 to 250,000	250,000 to 500,000	500,000 to 2,500,000	2,500,000 and over
Number of Enterprises 1	21515	3166	11426	2953	2779	563	•	106	62	86	36	33	•

Revenues ($ in Thousands)

Item Description for Accounting Period 7/10 Through 6/11	Total	Zero Assets	Under 500	500 to 1,000	1,000 to 5,000	5,000 to 10,000	10,000 to 25,000	25,000 to 50,000	50,000 to 100,000	100,000 to 250,000	250,000 to 500,000	500,000 to 2,500,000	2,500,000 and over
Net Sales 2	18381610	1412166	2406937	793937	1042607	429178	•	524509	1028302	2145482	1633384	2776710	•
Interest 3	639002	7215	9051	7765	22177	15834	•	21230	29571	64348	68277	154871	•
Rents 4	5855506	230570	2966	2456	3778	288	•	136482	288350	850454	880841	1664447	•
Royalties 5	87864	12	4171	8764	33660	7423	•	4745	318	6499	0	0	•
Other Portfolio Income 6	3358119	624335	79948	9851	122433	12372	•	72907	173089	355588	414168	594817	•
Other Receipts 7	8438119	550034	2310801	765101	860559	393261	•	289145	536974	868593	270098	362575	•
Total Receipts 8	18381610	1412166	2406937	793937	1042607	429178	•	524509	1028302	2145482	1633384	2776710	•
Average Total Receipts 9	854	446	211	269	375	762	•	4948	16586	24947	45372	84143	•

Operating Costs/Operating Income (%)

Item Description for Accounting Period 7/10 Through 6/11	Total	Zero Assets	Under 500	500 to 1,000	1,000 to 5,000	5,000 to 10,000	10,000 to 25,000	25,000 to 50,000	50,000 to 100,000	100,000 to 250,000	250,000 to 500,000	500,000 to 2,500,000	2,500,000 and over
Cost of Operations 10	0.1	0.0	•	•	0.0	•	•	1.2	0.0	0.2	•	•	•
Salaries and Wages 11	6.3	0.9	18.1	7.5	10.3	3.5	•	4.2	9.0	5.0	1.2	1.6	•
Taxes Paid 12	5.4	2.4	5.7	6.9	7.3	8.5	•	5.7	4.0	4.9	1.8	7.1	•
Interest Paid 13	8.2	8.0	0.8	3.7	6.9	14.0	•	9.3	5.1	8.2	7.9	12.9	•
Depreciation 14	6.1	3.8	1.1	3.2	6.7	8.5	•	8.7	3.8	9.1	3.8	12.2	•
Amortization and Depletion 15	1.0	0.7	0.5	0.2	1.5	0.8	•	0.7	0.6	1.3	0.6	1.6	•
Pensions and Other Deferred Comp. 16	0.2	•	0.9	1.2	0.0	0.1	•	0.1	0.2	0.3	0.0	•	•
Employee Benefits 17	0.4	0.1	1.7	0.1	0.3	0.5	•	0.4	0.3	0.4	0.0	•	•
Advertising 18	0.8	0.4	3.1	0.5	0.2	0.7	•	0.5	0.5	0.2	0.1	0.1	•
Other Expenses 19	31.9	24.1	38.0	52.5	22.2	36.3	•	34.7	38.9	37.8	40.2	24.1	•
Officers' Compensation 20	2.6	0.2	9.6	5.9	4.0	3.8	•	2.8	1.3	1.2	0.2	0.9	•
Operating Margin 21	37.0	59.3	20.5	18.3	40.5	23.2	•	31.7	36.3	31.4	44.1	39.5	•
Operating Margin Before Officers' Comp. 22	39.6	59.6	30.1	24.2	44.5	27.0	•	34.5	37.6	32.6	44.3	40.4	•

Selected Average Balance Sheet ($ in Thousands)

	•	•	•	•	•	•	•	•	•	•	•
Net Receivables 23	106	0	8	29	126	143	191	2988	4284	3156	10662
Inventories 24	•	•	•	•	•	•	•	•	•	•	•
Net Property, Plant and Equipment 25	2376	0	49	288	1117	3041	11086	24064	61429	108994	439728
Total Assets 26	5790	0	144	639	2144	6607	35528	73220	160672	383741	945114
Notes and Loans Payable 27	1489	0	50	230	1042	2302	11791	13603	38095	109511	182345
All Other Liabilities 28	379	0	23	80	270	482	2123	5766	14957	18902	51342
Net Worth 29	3922	0	72	329	832	3823	21614	53851	107620	255328	711428

Selected Financial Ratios (Times to 1)

	•	•	•	•	•	•	•	•	•	•	•
Current Ratio 30	2.1	•	1.9	1.9	2.7	3.5	5.5	3.4	1.4	2.9	1.8
Quick Ratio 31	1.6	•	1.6	1.7	2.0	1.9	2.7	3.0	0.9	2.1	1.6
Net Sales to Working Capital 32	2.8	•	7.4	3.6	1.5	0.9	0.8	2.2	5.3	1.9	3.1
Coverage Ratio 33	5.5	8.4	26.5	5.9	6.9	2.6	4.4	8.2	4.8	6.5	4.1
Total Asset Turnover 34	0.1	•	1.5	0.4	0.2	0.1	0.1	0.2	0.2	0.1	0.1
Inventory Turnover 35	•	•	•	•	•	•	•	•	•	•	•
Receivables Turnover 36	•	•	•	•	•	•	•	•	•	•	•
Total Liabilities to Net Worth 37	0.5	•	1.0	0.9	1.6	0.7	0.6	0.4	0.5	0.5	0.3
Current Assets to Working Capital 38	1.9	•	2.1	2.1	1.6	1.4	1.2	1.4	3.8	1.5	2.2
Current Liabilities to Working Capital 39	0.9	•	1.1	1.1	0.6	0.4	0.2	0.4	2.8	0.5	1.2
Working Capital to Net Sales 40	0.4	•	0.1	0.3	0.7	1.1	1.3	0.5	0.2	0.5	0.3
Inventory to Working Capital 41	0.0	•	•	0.0	0.0	0.0	0.0	0.0	0.0	•	•
Total Receipts to Cash Flow 42	2.1	2.5	2.5	1.5	2.1	2.0	1.9	1.7	2.1	2.1	2.1
Cost of Goods to Cash Flow 43	0.0	0.0	•	•	•	•	0.0	0.0	0.0	•	•
Cash Flow to Total Debt 44	0.2	1.2	1.2	0.6	0.1	0.1	0.2	0.5	0.2	0.2	0.2

Selected Financial Factors (in Percentages)

	•	•	•	•	•	•	•	•	•	•	•
Debt Ratio 45	32.3	•	50.2	48.5	61.2	42.1	39.2	26.5	33.0	33.5	24.7
Return on Total Assets 46	6.7	•	31.0	9.2	8.3	4.2	5.7	9.4	6.2	6.2	4.7
Return on Equity Before Income Taxes 47	8.1	•	59.8	14.9	18.2	4.5	7.2	11.2	7.3	7.8	4.7
Return on Equity After Income Taxes 48	7.5	•	57.3	13.5	15.8	3.6	6.6	9.6	6.6	7.0	4.5
Profit Margin (Before Income Tax) 49	37.0	59.3	20.4	18.2	40.4	22.4	31.6	36.3	31.4	44.1	39.5
Profit Margin (After Income Tax) 50	34.6	57.1	19.6	16.5	34.9	18.1	28.9	31.2	28.4	39.2	38.1

Table I

Corporations with and without Net Income

OFFICES OF REAL ESTATE AGENTS AND BROKERS

MONEY AMOUNTS AND SIZE OF ASSETS IN THOUSANDS OF DOLLARS

Item Description for Accounting Period 7/10 Through 6/11	Total	Zero Assets	Under 500	500 to 1,000	1,000 to 5,000	5,000 to 10,000	10,000 to 25,000	25,000 to 50,000	50,000 to 100,000	100,000 to 250,000	250,000 to 500,000	500,000 to 2,500,000	2,500,000 and over
Number of Enterprises **1**	128548	31875	90829	3203	2217	250	120	16	11	13	5	8	0
Revenues ($ in Thousands)													
Net Sales **2**	40018795	2946276	18091676	3367622	3054778	822046	1828695	371371	382055	711387	1496739	6946151	0
Interest **3**	247889	183	11506	2229	13693	5942	6836	5541	2757	9140	38921	151140	0
Rents **4**	264349	26825	32104	13486	26769	38384	4231	23231	14948	18995	17181	48195	0
Royalties **5**	501014	29	124	496	4	272	65	0	0	0	519	499504	0
Other Portfolio Income **6**	185553	21364	13356	4417	2107	5733	2887	6612	77	13279	42749	72972	0
Other Receipts **7**	38819990	2897875	18034586	3346994	3012205	771715	1814676	335987	364273	669973	1397369	6174340	0
Total Receipts **8**	40018795	2946276	18091676	3367622	3054778	822046	1828695	371371	382055	711387	1496739	6946151	0
Average Total Receipts **9**	311	92	199	1051	1378	3288	15239	23211	34732	54722	299348	868269	•
Operating Costs/Operating Income (%)													
Cost of Operations **10**	0.3	•	•	•	•	•	1.2	•	16.5	0.1	•	0.4	•
Salaries and Wages **11**	36.4	47.5	27.7	49.8	36.6	40.2	56.9	41.7	29.4	36.0	5.9	48.8	•
Taxes Paid **12**	2.5	2.3	2.2	2.0	2.0	4.4	2.0	4.9	4.2	3.7	1.0	3.8	•
Interest Paid **13**	3.3	0.9	0.7	1.1	1.8	4.9	3.0	1.1	2.7	4.9	1.5	13.0	•
Depreciation **14**	1.4	0.7	1.2	1.1	1.4	2.7	1.6	3.9	2.1	4.0	0.6	2.0	•
Amortization and Depletion **15**	1.0	0.0	0.1	0.5	0.1	12.3	0.2	0.5	0.5	2.1	1.4	3.3	•
Pensions and Other Deferred Comp. **16**	0.5	0.0	0.8	1.2	0.0	0.3	0.1	0.2	0.7	0.6	0.0	0.1	•
Employee Benefits **17**	1.1	0.7	0.6	0.6	0.6	0.2	1.3	3.2	1.6	1.4	0.3	2.9	•
Advertising **18**	3.6	4.6	3.9	4.6	4.0	0.6	4.8	10.1	3.3	2.6	0.5	2.4	•
Other Expenses **19**	37.4	30.8	40.5	24.7	53.4	29.7	18.5	36.6	22.3	59.2	92.7	23.9	•
Officers' Compensation **20**	7.4	4.5	11.9	10.3	2.0	3.1	4.9	5.9	3.4	5.2	0.7	0.8	•
Operating Margin **21**	5.1	8.0	10.4	4.0	•	1.7	5.4	•	13.4	•	•	•	•
Operating Margin Before Officers' Comp. **22**	12.4	12.5	22.3	14.3	0.2	4.8	10.3	•	16.7	•	•	•	•

Selected Average Balance Sheet ($ in Thousands)

	•	•	•	•	•	•	•	•	•	•	•	•
Net Receivables **23**	22	•	3	32	177	319	714	3266	1708	16586	32971	191449
Inventories **24**	•	•	•	•	•	•	•	•	•	•	•	•
Net Property, Plant and Equipment **25**	64	0	18	286	654	2609	4641	12569	13487	42864	31354	242730
Total Assets **26**	319	0	66	694	1960	6908	16405	37626	65627	141500	393332	2450101
Notes and Loans Payable **27**	180	0	45	373	1138	4064	10715	13778	20975	44110	126164	1423094
All Other Liabilities **28**	89	0	15	94	294	1782	3105	7682	6360	32349	102519	888462
Net Worth **29**	50	0	6	228	528	1063	2585	16166	38292	65041	164649	138545

Selected Financial Ratios (Times to 1)

	•	•	•	•	•	•	•	•	•	•	•	•
Current Ratio **30**	1.2	•	1.3	1.4	2.6	2.4	1.0	2.3	1.5	1.5	1.7	0.8
Quick Ratio **31**	0.8	•	1.1	0.7	1.6	0.8	0.6	1.4	1.2	1.0	1.5	0.5
Net Sales to Working Capital **32**	23.9	•	30.2	14.3	3.3	2.2	85.5	2.4	5.4	2.8	8.8	0.9
Coverage Ratio **33**	2.5	9.5	16.5	4.8	0.0	1.3	2.8	•	6.0	•	•	0.9
Total Asset Turnover **34**	1.0	•	3.0	1.5	0.7	0.5	0.9	0.6	0.5	0.4	0.8	0.4
Inventory Turnover **35**	•	•	•	•	•	•	•	•	•	•	•	•
Receivables Turnover **36**	•	•	•	•	•	•	•	•	•	•	•	•
Total Liabilities to Net Worth **37**	5.3	•	9.8	2.0	2.7	5.5	5.3	1.3	0.7	1.2	1.4	16.7
Current Assets to Working Capital **38**	6.8	•	4.4	3.4	1.6	1.7	24.7	1.7	2.9	2.9	2.4	•
Current Liabilities to Working Capital **39**	5.8	•	3.4	2.4	0.6	0.7	23.7	0.7	1.9	1.9	1.4	•
Working Capital to Net Sales **40**	0.0	•	0.0	0.1	0.3	0.5	0.0	0.4	0.2	0.4	0.1	•
Inventory to Working Capital **41**	0.0	•	•	•	•	•	0.1	•	0.1	0.1	0.1	•
Total Receipts to Cash Flow **42**	3.0	3.0	2.3	4.3	2.2	3.9	5.9	5.8	4.2	3.9	15.5	6.5
Cost of Goods to Cash Flow **43**	0.0	•	•	•	0.1	•	0.1	0.7	0.7	0.0	0.0	0.0
Cash Flow to Total Debt **44**	0.4	•	1.5	0.5	0.4	0.1	0.2	0.4	0.3	0.2	0.1	0.1

Selected Financial Factors (in Percentages)

	•	•	•	•	•	•	•	•	•	•	•	•
Debt Ratio **45**	84.2	•	90.8	67.2	73.1	84.6	84.2	57.0	41.7	54.0	58.1	94.3
Return on Total Assets **46**	8.1	•	33.4	7.7	0.0	3.1	7.8	•	8.5	•	•	4.1
Return on Equity Before Income Taxes **47**	31.2	•	340.0	18.7	•	5.2	31.8	•	12.1	•	•	•
Return on Equity After Income Taxes **48**	29.3	•	337.2	18.6	•	4.4	30.7	•	11.6	•	•	•
Profit Margin (Before Income Tax) **49**	5.1	8.0	10.4	4.0	•	1.7	5.4	•	13.4	•	•	•
Profit Margin (After Income Tax) **50**	4.7	7.8	10.3	4.0	•	1.4	5.2	•	12.8	•	•	•

Table II

Corporations with Net Income

OFFICES OF REAL ESTATE AGENTS AND BROKERS

MONEY AMOUNTS AND SIZE OF ASSETS IN THOUSANDS OF DOLLARS

Item Description for Accounting Period 7/10 Through 6/11		Total	Zero Assets	Under 500	500 to 1,000	1,000 to 5,000	5,000 to 10,000	10,000 to 25,000	25,000 to 50,000	50,000 to 100,000	100,000 to 250,000	250,000 to 500,000	500,000 to 2,500,000	2,500,000 and over
Number of Enterprises	1	77291	14525	59845	1721	1044	76	50	•	6	•	0	4	0
Revenues ($ in Thousands)														
Net Sales	2	28641824	2553092	13384022	3005709	1835112	713766	1485803	•	277200	•	0	4593787	0
Interest	3	171580	114	2014	806	4680	4457	5783	•	1899	•	0	121478	0
Rents	4	158246	9396	18149	850	11530	26360	4030	•	14805	•	0	30785	0
Royalties	5	32619	0	124	0	0	272	65	•	0	•	0	32157	0
Other Portfolio Income	6	119876	21364	13306	1429	538	1196	2763	•	49	•	0	69597	0
Other Receipts	7	28159503	2522218	13350429	3002624	1818364	681481	1473162	•	260447	•	0	4339770	0
Total Receipts	8	28641824	2553092	13384022	3005709	1835112	713766	1485803	•	277200	•	0	4593787	0
Average Total Receipts	9	371	176	224	1746	1758	9392	29716	•	46200	•	•	1148447	•
Operating Costs/Operating Income (%)														
Cost of Operations	10	0.1	•	•	•	•	•	•	•	0.0	•	•	0.4	•
Salaries and Wages	11	38.7	50.6	23.2	50.9	53.5	41.4	56.3	•	35.1	•	•	57.7	•
Taxes Paid	12	2.4	1.7	2.1	1.9	1.8	3.3	1.7	•	4.6	•	•	3.9	•
Interest Paid	13	1.7	0.2	0.7	0.5	0.4	1.5	2.2	•	2.3	•	•	6.1	•
Depreciation	14	1.1	0.5	0.9	0.5	1.2	1.4	1.4	•	2.4	•	•	1.7	•
Amortization and Depletion	15	0.7	0.0	0.2	0.5	0.0	14.0	0.2	•	0.6	•	•	0.7	•
Pensions and Other Deferred Comp.	16	0.7	0.0	1.0	1.4	0.0	0.3	0.1	•	1.0	•	•	0.1	•
Employee Benefits	17	1.0	0.8	0.6	0.6	0.6	0.1	1.1	•	1.8	•	•	3.0	•
Advertising	18	3.7	4.6	4.3	3.4	5.9	0.3	5.5	•	3.2	•	•	0.6	•
Other Expenses	19	27.7	21.4	36.4	20.6	22.7	26.4	14.8	•	24.2	•	•	16.9	•
Officers' Compensation	20	8.4	3.8	13.2	10.7	2.6	1.5	5.1	•	4.1	•	•	1.0	•
Operating Margin	21	13.8	16.5	17.5	9.1	11.3	9.8	11.7	•	20.5	•	•	7.9	•
Operating Margin Before Officers' Comp.	22	22.2	20.3	30.7	19.8	13.8	11.3	16.7	•	24.6	•	•	8.9	•

Selected Average Balance Sheet ($ in Thousands)

	1	2	3	4	5	6	7	8
Net Receivables 23	22	2	23	68	784	806	1158	293774
Inventories 24	0	0	•	•	•	•	•	•
Net Property, Plant and Equipment 25	52	18	299	450	1908	4270	18778	254954
Total Assets 26	275	72	666	1942	7557	17166	69709	2389848
Notes and Loans Payable 27	108	42	261	549	2680	7158	20144	886534
All Other Liabilities 28	84	14	82	356	2624	4739	9082	1009118
Net Worth 29	83	16	323	1037	2253	5269	40483	494197

Selected Financial Ratios (Times to 1)

	1	2	3	4	5	6	7	8
Current Ratio 30	1.1	1.5	1.1	2.5	4.5	1.1	1.7	0.7
Quick Ratio 31	0.8	1.3	0.7	1.9	2.6	0.9	1.6	0.5
Net Sales to Working Capital 32	48.4	19.5	107.7	4.6	3.6	54.3	5.3	•
Coverage Ratio 33	9.2	24.4	20.5	28.9	7.6	6.4	9.9	2.3
Total Asset Turnover 34	1.3	3.1	2.6	0.9	1.2	1.7	0.7	0.5
Inventory Turnover 35	•	73.3	•	•	•	•	•	•
Receivables Turnover 36	•	•	•	•	•	•	•	•
Total Liabilities to Net Worth 37	2.3	3.6	1.1	0.9	2.4	2.3	0.7	3.8
Current Assets to Working Capital 38	11.3	2.8	14.1	1.7	1.3	8.9	2.5	•
Current Liabilities to Working Capital 39	10.3	1.8	13.1	0.7	0.3	7.9	1.5	•
Working Capital to Net Sales 40	0.0	0.1	0.0	0.2	0.3	0.0	0.2	•
Inventory to Working Capital 41	0.0	•	•	•	•	•	0.0	•
Total Receipts to Cash Flow 42	2.8	2.1	3.9	3.5	3.2	4.9	3.2	5.1
Cost of Goods to Cash Flow 43	0.0	3.0	•	•	•	0.0	0.0	0.0
Cash Flow to Total Debt 44	0.7	1.9	1.3	0.6	0.5	0.5	0.5	0.1

Selected Financial Factors (in Percentages)

	1	2	3	4	5	6	7	8
Debt Ratio 45	69.9	78.1	51.5	46.6	70.2	69.3	41.9	79.3
Return on Total Assets 46	20.9	56.7	25.2	10.6	14.0	23.9	15.1	6.7
Return on Equity Before Income Taxes 47	61.9	248.5	49.4	19.1	40.8	65.6	23.4	18.4
Return on Equity After Income Taxes 48	59.9	246.9	49.3	18.7	39.6	64.3	22.5	14.1
Profit Margin (Before Income Tax) 49	13.8	17.5	9.1	11.3	9.8	11.6	20.5	7.9
Profit Margin (After Income Tax) 50	13.4	17.4	9.1	11.0	9.5	11.4	19.7	6.1

Table I

Corporations with and without Net Income

OTHER REAL ESTATE ACTIVITIES

MONEY AMOUNTS AND SIZE OF ASSETS IN THOUSANDS OF DOLLARS

Item Description for Accounting Period 7/10 Through 6/11	Total	Zero Assets	Under 500	500 to 1,000	1,000 to 5,000	5,000 to 10,000	10,000 to 25,000	25,000 to 50,000	50,000 to 100,000	100,000 to 250,000	250,000 to 500,000	500,000 to 2,500,000	2,500,000 and over
Number of Enterprises 1	157121	35165	100953	8324	9984	1211	930	280	161	73	27	12	0
Revenues ($ in Thousands)													
Net Sales 2	49495155	2196891	18420631	4230698	8288578	2326562	2041982	1471574	1237632	1912445	2522381	4845781	0
Interest 3	1231797	58585	16716	7720	44029	26136	45210	35837	54886	71733	102196	768747	0
Rents 4	1654240	80142	160013	162072	110570	169314	142058	126891	207654	116745	286780	92001	0
Royalties 5	394216	1	2054	0	0	780	10398	543	3503	6	40739	336192	0
Other Portfolio Income 6	1318590	371470	83111	54025	129899	56328	51635	17931	85570	82536	30643	355442	0
Other Receipts 7	44896312	1686693	18158737	4006881	8004080	2074004	1792681	1290372	886019	1641425	2062023	3293399	0
Total Receipts 8	49495155	2196891	18420631	4230698	8288578	2326562	2041982	1471574	1237632	1912445	2522381	4845781	0
Average Total Receipts 9	315	62	182	508	830	1921	2196	5256	7687	26198	93422	403815	•
Operating Costs/Operating Income (%)													
Cost of Operations 10	0.6	0.8	•	•	•	•	2.4	3.6	11.2	0.3	0.1	0.8	•
Salaries and Wages 11	32.7	17.1	27.8	55.2	46.1	32.5	27.6	24.3	13.9	38.6	31.2	24.5	•
Taxes Paid 12	4.1	3.9	3.5	5.1	5.5	4.2	6.0	6.1	5.4	4.1	2.9	2.2	•
Interest Paid 13	4.7	8.4	0.7	1.6	2.5	5.9	10.6	8.8	14.9	14.2	8.9	11.6	•
Depreciation 14	2.4	2.5	1.1	0.9	2.7	2.5	3.8	3.7	7.5	4.5	5.0	3.3	•
Amortization and Depletion 15	0.5	0.9	0.1	0.1	0.5	0.2	0.3	0.9	1.2	1.4	1.1	1.3	•
Pensions and Other Deferred Comp. 16	0.7	0.2	1.0	0.2	0.6	0.2	0.7	0.3	1.1	0.6	0.1	0.9	•
Employee Benefits 17	2.6	1.7	1.5	9.4	1.9	3.1	1.9	1.9	1.2	2.8	2.2	2.5	•
Advertising 18	1.1	0.8	1.2	0.2	0.7	2.5	0.7	1.2	0.7	0.8	1.6	1.5	•
Other Expenses 19	41.3	67.5	41.2	23.2	33.1	40.7	45.2	47.9	58.4	37.9	54.6	46.2	•
Officers' Compensation 20	8.5	7.0	14.7	5.9	6.6	8.0	4.7	6.5	3.0	4.7	0.6	1.2	•
Operating Margin 21	0.9	•	7.3	•	•	0.2	•	•	•	•	•	4.1	•
Operating Margin Before Officers' Comp. 22	9.4	•	22.0	4.2	6.2	8.2	0.7	1.3	•	•	•	5.2	•

Selected Average Balance Sheet ($ in Thousands)

Net Receivables 23	85	0	2	•	46	192	690	863	2471	3100	12522	34605	509560
Inventories 24	•	•	•	•	•	•	•	•	•	•	•	•	•
Net Property, Plant and Equipment 25	225	0	24	•	293	706	2820	4670	9664	25372	41414	107038	245184
Total Assets 26	785	82	693	2142	7287	14643	33829	70120	151811	333119	2059070
Notes and Loans Payable 27	389	0	45	562	1083	3979	8034	14430	29708	80538	161877	813738
All Other Liabilities 28	165	0	16	126	356	1143	2362	6638	12414	26369	74862	704424
Net Worth 29	230	0	21	5	704	2165	4248	12761	27998	44904	96380	540908

Selected Financial Ratios (Times to 1)

Current Ratio 30	2.3	•	1.8	2.4	2.6	2.8	1.8	2.3	1.7	2.3	1.7	2.8
Quick Ratio 31	1.3	•	1.2	1.4	1.6	1.8	0.9	1.1	0.8	1.2	1.1	1.4
Net Sales to Working Capital 32	1.9	•	11.6	3.6	1.7	1.3	1.1	0.8	1.2	1.1	2.4	0.5
Coverage Ratio 33	1.2	•	11.7	•	0.8	1.0	0.6	0.4	•	0.3	0.1	1.4
Total Asset Turnover 34	0.4	•	2.2	0.7	0.4	0.3	0.1	0.2	0.1	0.2	0.3	0.2
Inventory Turnover 35	•	•	•	•	•	•	•	•	•	•	•	•
Receivables Turnover 36	•	•	•	•	•	2.4	2.4	•	•	•	•	2.8
Total Liabilities to Net Worth 37	2.4	•	2.9	134.4	2.0	1.5	2.4	1.7	1.5	2.4	2.5	2.8
Current Assets to Working Capital 38	1.8	•	2.3	1.7	1.6	0.5	2.3	1.8	2.5	1.8	2.4	1.6
Current Liabilities to Working Capital 39	0.8	•	1.3	0.7	0.6	0.5	1.3	0.8	1.5	0.8	1.4	0.6
Working Capital to Net Sales 40	0.5	•	0.1	0.3	0.6	0.8	0.9	1.2	0.8	0.9	0.4	1.8
Inventory to Working Capital 41	0.0	•	0.0	•	0.0	0.0	0.0	0.0	0.0	0.1	0.0	0.0
Total Receipts to Cash Flow 42	3.0	3.4	2.4	6.3	3.7	3.2	3.2	3.2	8.5	5.6	2.7	2.3
Cost of Goods to Cash Flow 43	0.0	0.0	•	•	•	•	0.1	0.1	0.9	0.0	0.0	0.0
Cash Flow to Total Debt 44	0.2	•	1.2	0.1	0.2	0.1	0.1	0.1	0.0	0.0	0.1	0.1

Selected Financial Factors (in Percentages)

Debt Ratio 45	70.7	•	74.4	99.3	67.1	70.3	71.0	62.3	60.1	70.4	71.1	73.7
Return on Total Assets 46	2.2	•	17.9	•	0.8	1.6	1.0	0.5	•	0.7	0.2	3.2
Return on Equity Before Income Taxes 47	1.2	•	63.8	•	0.1	•	•	•	•	•	•	3.3
Return on Equity After Income Taxes 48	0.0	•	63.0	•	•	•	•	•	•	•	•	1.9
Profit Margin (Before Income Tax) 49	0.8	•	7.3	•	0.1	•	•	•	•	•	•	4.5
Profit Margin (After Income Tax) 50	0.0	•	7.2	•	•	•	•	•	•	•	•	2.6

Table II
Corporations with Net Income

OTHER REAL ESTATE ACTIVITIES

MONEY AMOUNTS AND SIZE OF ASSETS IN THOUSANDS OF DOLLARS

Item Description for Accounting Period 7/10 Through 6/11	Total	Zero Assets	Under 500	500 to 1,000	1,000 to 5,000	5,000 to 10,000	10,000 to 25,000	25,000 to 50,000	50,000 to 100,000	100,000 to 250,000	250,000 to 500,000	500,000 to 2,500,000	2,500,000 and over
Number of Enterprises **1**	73379	12079	54136	2735	3494	449	300	•	60	•	7	4	0

Revenues ($ in Thousands)

Net Sales **2**	35461553	1690196	13706215	3227872	5507261	1743844	1065833	•	697459	•	1391296	4334769	0
Interest **3**	944812	52607	8662	4921	25568	18851	28244	•	28860	•	43959	673477	0
Rents **4**	799935	17691	53396	136454	64892	158983	72728	•	111888	•	0	70345	0
Royalties **5**	392115	0	0	0	0	780	10398	•	3457	•	40739	336192	0
Other Portfolio Income **6**	1202067	325177	76273	46417	121467	47895	47555	•	79825	•	12138	354883	0
Other Receipts **7**	32112624	1294721	13567884	3040080	5295334	1517335	906908	•	473429	•	1294460	2899872	0
Total Receipts **8**	35461553	1690196	13706215	3227872	5507261	1743844	1065833	•	697459	•	1391296	4334769	0
Average Total Receipts **9**	483	140	253	1180	1576	3884	3553	•	11624	•	198757	1083692	•

Operating Costs/Operating Income (%)

Cost of Operations **10**	0.2	0.1	•	•	•	•	0.3	•	4.7	•	0.2	0.4	•
Salaries and Wages **11**	30.4	16.3	22.4	61.6	41.6	29.4	17.9	•	14.0	•	38.9	25.6	•
Taxes Paid **12**	3.5	3.3	2.9	5.1	4.9	3.7	4.6	•	4.7	•	1.1	2.1	•
Interest Paid **13**	3.0	6.9	0.6	0.8	1.0	2.7	6.9	•	8.0	•	1.3	11.6	•
Depreciation **14**	1.5	1.0	0.9	0.5	1.2	1.9	3.2	•	6.2	•	1.6	2.8	•
Amortization and Depletion **15**	0.4	1.1	0.1	0.0	0.1	0.1	0.2	•	1.4	•	0.9	1.2	•
Pensions and Other Deferred Comp. **16**	0.7	0.2	1.1	0.1	0.7	0.2	0.4	•	0.3	•	0.1	0.8	•
Employee Benefits **17**	2.5	1.4	0.8	11.5	2.2	3.0	2.0	•	1.5	•	1.5	2.3	•
Advertising **18**	1.0	0.7	1.4	0.2	0.8	0.7	0.3	•	0.4	•	0.9	1.6	•
Other Expenses **19**	32.5	23.9	37.7	9.5	26.1	33.3	30.0	•	25.1	•	45.0	44.5	•
Officers' Compensation **20**	7.7	5.9	13.8	4.4	5.0	8.6	5.7	•	2.8	•	0.0	0.4	•
Operating Margin **21**	16.6	39.0	18.4	6.3	16.3	16.5	28.5	•	30.9	•	8.3	6.7	•
Operating Margin Before Officers' Comp. **22**	24.3	45.0	32.2	10.7	21.2	25.1	34.2	•	33.7	•	8.4	7.1	•

Selected Average Balance Sheet ($ in Thousands)

	Item										
23	Net Receivables	93	0	2	20	213	575	1188	4382	59952	923813
24	Inventories		0	16	218	521	2645	3966	21430	26354	436983
25	Net Property, Plant and Equipment	146									
26	Total Assets	711		80	678	2128	7003	14697	70592	310610	4307424
27	Notes and Loans Payable	299		24	398	850	2554	6910	23362	120473	2075830
28	All Other Liabilities	128		14	133	330	1331	1928	14139	58794	855745
29	Net Worth	284		43	147	948	3118	5859	33091	131344	1375848

Selected Financial Ratios (Times to 1)

	Item										
30	Current Ratio	3.2		2.2	2.9	2.5	1.9		2.1	1.4	7.1
31	Quick Ratio	1.8		1.6	1.9	1.7	1.0		1.2	1.1	2.9
32	Net Sales to Working Capital	2.2	11.5	5.3	2.2	3.1	1.3		1.0	7.1	0.5
33	Coverage Ratio	6.4	6.6	30.3	9.3	16.5	7.1	5.1	0.2	4.9	7.3	1.6
34	Total Asset Turnover	0.7		3.2	1.7	0.7	0.6	0.2		0.2	0.6	0.3
35	Inventory Turnover										
36	Receivables Turnover										
37	Total Liabilities to Net Worth	1.5		0.9	1.2	1.2	1.5		1.1	1.4	2.1
38	Current Assets to Working Capital	1.5		1.9	1.5	1.6	2.1		2.0	3.5	1.2
39	Current Liabilities to Working Capital	0.5		0.9	0.5	0.6	1.1		1.0	2.5	0.2
40	Working Capital to Net Sales	0.5		0.1	0.4	0.3	0.8		1.0	0.1	1.9
41	Inventory to Working Capital	0.0			0.0	0.0	0.0		0.0		0.0
42	Total Receipts to Cash Flow	2.4	2.0	2.7	2.3	2.0		2.5	2.2	2.3
43	Cost of Goods to Cash Flow	0.0	0.0		0.0	0.0	0.0		0.1	0.0	0.0
44	Cash Flow to Total Debt	0.5		3.3	0.2	0.5	0.4	0.2		0.1	0.5	0.2

Selected Financial Factors (in Percentages)

	Item										
45	Debt Ratio	60.0		47.0	78.3	55.4	55.5	60.1		53.1	57.7	68.1
46	Return on Total Assets	13.3		59.9	12.2	12.7	10.6	8.5		6.4	6.3	4.7
47	Return on Equity Before Income Taxes	28.2		109.3	50.5	26.8	20.5	17.2		10.8	12.9	5.6
48	Return on Equity After Income Taxes	26.2		108.6	49.1	25.4	19.2	15.3		9.3	8.7	3.9
49	Profit Margin (Before Income Tax)	16.6	39.0	18.4	6.3	16.1	16.5	28.3	30.7	18.4	8.5	7.1
50	Profit Margin (After Income Tax)	15.4	34.1	18.3	6.1	15.3	15.4	25.3	26.5		5.7	5.0

Table I

Corporations with and without Net Income

AUTOMOTIVE EQUIPMENT RENTAL AND LEASING

MONEY AMOUNTS AND SIZE OF ASSETS IN THOUSANDS OF DOLLARS

Item Description for Accounting Period 7/10 Through 6/11	Total	Zero Assets	Under 500	500 to 1,000	1,000 to 5,000	5,000 to 10,000	10,000 to 25,000	25,000 to 50,000	50,000 to 100,000	100,000 to 250,000	250,000 to 500,000	500,000 to 2,500,000	2,500,000 and over
Number of Enterprises **1**	7147	1123	3654	1117	783	189	182	52	24	13	0	3	7
Revenues ($ in Thousands)													
Net Sales **2**	48182151	376363	701342	625352	1447642	609044	2423365	1559069	1080765	1270155	0	1810611	36278442
Interest **3**	371544	100	6	0	3635	137	964	822	851	4123	0	8025	352881
Rents **4**	164404	0	0	0	3353	6	2183	487	915	0	0	0	157460
Royalties **5**	135663	0	0	0	125	0	0	0	0	0	0	0	135538
Other Portfolio Income **6**	3052897	12068	22224	29708	96732	121581	167916	89230	139168	53419	0	3166	2317687
Other Receipts **7**	44457643	364195	679112	595644	1343797	487320	2252302	1468530	939831	1212613	0	1799420	33314876
Total Receipts **8**	48182151	376363	701342	625352	1447642	609044	2423365	1559069	1080765	1270155	0	1810611	36278442
Average Total Receipts **9**	6742	335	192	560	1849	3222	13315	29982	45032	97704	•	603537	5182635
Operating Costs/Operating Income (%)													
Cost of Operations **10**	17.0	40.9	16.1	8.6	28.0	24.5	40.3	45.7	31.6	20.3	•	0.7	13.9
Salaries and Wages **11**	12.6	16.9	6.6	14.9	5.7	6.0	7.7	6.9	7.8	5.9	•	5.1	14.3
Taxes Paid **12**	3.4	2.9	2.2	2.6	1.7	4.4	2.6	1.9	2.1	2.4	•	0.5	3.8
Interest Paid **13**	5.2	4.7	1.8	3.4	5.9	5.6	2.9	3.0	3.8	3.8	•	3.5	5.7
Depreciation **14**	34.0	11.7	7.2	16.6	28.0	20.8	24.6	26.5	37.5	40.2	•	83.7	33.7
Amortization and Depletion **15**	0.3	0.9	0.0	0.8	0.1	0.0	0.1	0.1	0.1	0.2	•	0.2	0.4
Pensions and Other Deferred Comp. **16**	0.6	0.0	0.2	1.0	0.0	0.1	0.1	0.2	0.1	0.1	•	0.1	0.7
Employee Benefits **17**	1.4	0.2	1.8	0.3	0.7	0.3	0.6	0.5	1.1	0.8	•	0.4	1.7
Advertising **18**	1.3	0.1	0.3	3.5	0.5	0.3	0.9	0.3	0.5	0.3	•	0.1	1.5
Other Expenses **19**	25.3	20.1	54.5	44.6	30.9	18.0	15.7	12.1	16.7	31.2	•	3.6	26.7
Officers' Compensation **20**	0.9	0.1	3.2	4.5	1.9	8.9	1.6	0.8	1.4	1.2	•	0.2	0.7
Operating Margin **21**	•	1.5	6.0	•	•	11.0	2.9	2.1	•	•	•	2.0	•
Operating Margin Before Officers' Comp. **22**	•	1.6	9.2	3.6	•	19.9	4.6	2.9	•	•	•	2.2	•

Selected Average Balance Sheet ($ in Thousands)

Net Receivables 23	1117	0	10	78	105	1187	2571	4072	4285	8900	72326	919260
Inventories 24	•	•	•	•	•	•	•	•	•	•	•	•
Net Property, Plant and Equipment 25	5926	0	18	441	1552	3874	8774	21133	37692	118637	661287	4674613
Total Assets 26	10457	0	60	754	2340	6361	15721	35909	63197	172835	1290295	8325613
Notes and Loans Payable 27	6123	0	60	318	1829	2804	9109	23339	39904	97596	1194622	4648834
All Other Liabilities 28	2455	0	5	85	185	629	1878	4029	7233	34184	256654	2175303
Net Worth 29	1880	0	-5	351	327	2929	4734	8541	16060	41055	-160981	1501476

Selected Financial Ratios (Times to 1)

Current Ratio 30	0.7	•	1.4	1.6	1.7	3.2	1.3	0.8	0.9	0.5	0.1	0.8
Quick Ratio 31	0.5	•	1.0	1.3	0.7	2.8	1.1	0.4	0.6	0.3	0.1	0.6
Net Sales to Working Capital 32	•	27.2	6.0	8.2	2.5	9.4	•	•	•	•	1.6	•
Coverage Ratio 33	0.6	1.3	4.4	0.7	3.0	2.0	•	•	•	•	0.5	0.6
Total Asset Turnover 34	0.6	3.2	3.2	0.7	0.5	0.8	•	•	•	•	•	•
Inventory Turnover 35	•	•	•	•	•	•	•	•	•	•	•	•
Receivables Turnover 36	•	•	•	•	•	•	•	•	•	•	•	4.5
Total Liabilities to Net Worth 37	4.6	•	1.2	6.2	1.2	2.3	3.2	3.2	2.9	•	•	•
Current Assets to Working Capital 38	•	3.8	2.7	2.5	1.5	3.9	2.5	•	•	•	•	•
Current Liabilities to Working Capital 39	•	2.8	1.7	1.5	0.5	2.9	1.5	•	•	•	•	•
Working Capital to Net Sales 40	•	0.0	0.2	0.1	0.4	0.1	0.4	0.3	•	•	•	•
Inventory to Working Capital 41	•	•	•	0.3	0.0	0.4	0.4	•	•	•	•	•
Total Receipts to Cash Flow 42	6.7	6.8	2.1	4.4	8.3	5.7	8.0	10.8	14.9	5.8	19.4	6.6
Cost of Goods to Cash Flow 43	1.2	2.8	0.3	0.4	2.3	1.4	3.2	4.9	4.7	1.2	0.1	0.9
Cash Flow to Total Debt 44	0.1	•	1.4	0.3	0.1	0.2	0.2	0.1	0.1	0.1	0.0	0.1

Selected Financial Factors (in Percentages)

Debt Ratio 45	82.0	107.7	53.5	86.0	54.0	69.9	76.2	74.6	76.2	•	112.5	82.0
Return on Total Assets 46	2.0	24.9	1.9	1.9	8.4	4.9	4.3	0.8	•	•	2.6	1.7
Return on Equity Before Income Taxes 47	•	•	•	•	12.1	8.1	7.3	•	•	•	•	•
Return on Equity After Income Taxes 48	•	•	•	•	11.7	7.6	6.6	•	•	•	•	•
Profit Margin (Before Income Tax) 49	1.5	6.0	•	•	11.0	2.9	2.1	•	•	•	2.0	•
Profit Margin (After Income Tax) 50	1.2	5.8	•	•	10.6	2.7	1.9	•	•	•	1.5	•

Table II

Corporations with Net Income

AUTOMOTIVE EQUIPMENT RENTAL AND LEASING

MONEY AMOUNTS AND SIZE OF ASSETS IN THOUSANDS OF DOLLARS

Item Description for Accounting Period 7/10 Through 6/11		Total	Zero Assets	Under 500	500 to 1,000	1,000 to 5,000	5,000 to 10,000	10,000 to 25,000	25,000 to 50,000	50,000 to 100,000	100,000 to 250,000	250,000 to 500,000	500,000 to 2,500,000	2,500,000 and over
Number of Enterprises	1	3565	3	2075	858	334	123	115	38	10	6	0	•	•
Revenues ($ in Thousands)														
Net Sales	2	12353688	176070	701336	279819	724400	369734	1878924	1186945	499408	552147			•
Interest	3	285157	99	0	0	1803	137	77	230	737	1340	0	•	•
Rents	4	104504	0	0	0	3353	6	2183	0	915	0	0	•	•
Royalties	5	125	0	0	0	125	0	0	0	0	0	0		
Other Portfolio Income	6	688508	9955	22224	0	68687	96255	100666	27298	84739	28798	0	•	•
Other Receipts	7	11275394	166016	679112	279819	650432	273336	1775998	1159417	413017	522009	0	•	•
Total Receipts	8	12353688	176070	701336	279819	724400	369734	1878924	1186945	499408	552147	0	•	•
Average Total Receipts	9	3465	58690	338	326	2169	3006	16338	31235	49941	92024			
Operating Costs/Operating Income (%)														
Cost of Operations	10	25.7	54.4	16.1	5.7	17.6	5.9	48.5	55.5	27.1	36.0		•	•
Salaries and Wages	11	8.1	3.4	6.6	10.2	6.7	5.1	6.3	6.2	7.8	5.6		•	•
Taxes Paid	12	2.5	2.1	2.2	1.8	2.3	4.5	2.6	1.6	2.1	4.0		•	•
Interest Paid	13	4.7	3.2	1.3	4.0	3.2	5.2	2.4	2.3	2.9	4.9		•	•
Depreciation	14	26.8	17.3	7.2	22.7	17.6	23.8	14.6	15.5	36.3	24.5		•	•
Amortization and Depletion	15	0.2	0.1	0.0	1.6	0.1	0.1	0.1	0.1	0.0	0.2		•	•
Pensions and Other Deferred Comp.	16	0.1	0.1	0.2	•		0.0	0.1	0.2	0.2	0.1		•	•
Employee Benefits	17	1.0	0.3	1.8	•	0.8	0.2	0.4	0.2	1.6	1.1		•	•
Advertising	18	0.5	0.2	0.3	2.5	0.6	0.3	0.9	0.3	0.3	0.2		•	•
Other Expenses	19	23.0	8.1	54.4	33.9	42.4	21.4	12.6	11.2	14.4	16.0		•	•
Officers' Compensation	20	1.4	0.3	3.2	5.9	2.6	11.4	1.6	0.5	2.1	1.4		•	•
Operating Margin	21	6.1	10.7	6.7	11.7	6.1	22.2	9.9	6.4	5.2	6.1		•	•
Operating Margin Before Officers' Comp.	22	7.5	10.9	9.9	17.6	8.7	33.6	11.5	6.9	7.3	7.5		•	•

Selected Average Balance Sheet ($ in Thousands)

Net Receivables 23	1126	0	10	65	104	1544	1959	4828	3487	9561
Inventories 24	•	•	•	•	•	•	•	•	•	•
Net Property, Plant and Equipment 25	2358	0	26	414	1150	3404	7525	18260	46149	89612
Total Assets 26	5530	•	71	747	1783	6200	15880	34661	62808	153350
Notes and Loans Payable 27	3468	0	23	230	927	2535	7789	20698	37610	93823
All Other Liabilities 28	1012	0	5	12	96	543	2135	4081	6192	26576
Net Worth 29	1050	0	43	505	759	3122	5955	9882	19006	32951

Selected Financial Ratios (Times to 1)

Current Ratio 30	1.1	•	3.2	24.1	2.7	5.9	1.5	0.9	0.9	0.7
Quick Ratio 31	0.9	•	3.1	18.4	2.2	5.5	1.1	0.4	0.6	0.6
Net Sales to Working Capital 32	23.0	•	18.7	1.3	8.0	1.7	8.3	3.8	•	•
Coverage Ratio 33	2.3	4.4	5.9	4.0	2.9	5.3	5.2	5.2	2.8	2.2
Total Asset Turnover 34	0.6	•	4.8	0.4	1.2	0.5	1.0	0.9	0.8	0.6
Inventory Turnover 35	•	•	•	•	•	•	•	•	•	•
Receivables Turnover 36	•	•	•	•	•	•	•	•	•	•
Total Liabilities to Net Worth 37	4.3	•	0.6	0.5	1.3	1.0	1.7	2.5	2.3	3.7
Current Assets to Working Capital 38	14.3	•	1.4	1.0	1.6	1.2	3.1	•	•	•
Current Liabilities to Working Capital 39	13.3	•	0.4	0.0	0.6	0.2	2.1	•	•	•
Working Capital to Net Sales 40	0.0	•	0.1	0.8	0.1	0.6	0.1	•	•	•
Inventory to Working Capital 41	0.4	•	•	0.0	0.0	0.0	0.4	•	•	•
Total Receipts to Cash Flow 42	5.4	6.7	2.1	4.2	4.6	3.6	6.2	7.3	8.3	6.0
Cost of Goods to Cash Flow 43	1.4	3.6	0.3	0.2	0.8	0.2	3.0	4.0	2.2	2.2
Cash Flow to Total Debt 44	0.1	•	5.9	0.3	0.5	0.3	0.3	0.2	0.1	0.1

Selected Financial Factors (in Percentages)

Debt Ratio 45	81.0	•	39.4	32.4	57.4	49.6	62.5	71.5	69.7	78.5
Return on Total Assets 46	6.8	•	38.3	6.9	11.3	13.2	12.5	7.9	6.5	6.6
Return on Equity Before Income Taxes 47	20.2	•	52.6	7.6	17.3	21.3	27.0	20.3	13.7	16.9
Return on Equity After Income Taxes 48	18.3	•	50.9	7.6	15.9	20.8	26.3	19.4	13.7	14.6
Profit Margin (Before Income Tax) 49	6.1	10.7	6.7	11.7	6.1	22.2	9.8	6.4	5.2	6.1
Profit Margin (After Income Tax) 50	5.6	10.0	6.4	11.7	5.6	21.6	9.6	6.1	5.2	5.2

Table I

Corporations with and without Net Income

OTHER CONSUMER GOODS AND GENERAL RENTAL CENTERS

MONEY AMOUNTS AND SIZE OF ASSETS IN THOUSANDS OF DOLLARS

Item Description for Accounting Period 7/10 Through 6/11	Total	Zero Assets	Under 500	500 to 1,000	1,000 to 5,000	5,000 to 10,000	10,000 to 25,000	25,000 to 50,000	50,000 to 100,000	100,000 to 250,000	250,000 to 500,000	500,000 to 2,500,000	2,500,000 and over
Number of Enterprises **1**	11038	1271	8233	708	636	133	24	23	0	6	0	4	0
Revenues ($ in Thousands)													
Net Sales **2**	18349420	591422	3052745	724409	1035807	1244637	562489	990524	0	983174	0	9164214	0
Interest **3**	17499	35	1189	205	668	0	49	350	0	1857	0	13146	0
Rents **4**	9205	0	1003	0	1290	0	0	2149	0	4764	0	0	0
Royalties **5**	84718	0	0	0	0	0	0	0	0	0	0	84718	0
Other Portfolio Income **6**	98986	212	12424	7977	5764	60	15646	5175	0	4792	0	46935	0
Other Receipts **7**	18139012	591175	3038129	716227	1028085	1244577	546794	982850	0	971761	0	9019415	0
Total Receipts **8**	18349420	591422	3052745	724409	1035807	1244637	562489	990524	0	983174	0	9164214	0
Average Total Receipts **9**	1662	465	371	1023	1629	9358	23437	43066	•	163862	•	2291054	•
Operating Costs/Operating Income (%)													
Cost of Operations **10**	27.6	37.1	23.7	34.4	22.5	33.3	25.9	32.3	•	23.0	•	27.7	•
Salaries and Wages **11**	18.9	20.7	17.8	18.5	23.1	14.9	22.3	14.9	•	16.9	•	19.7	•
Taxes Paid **12**	3.3	4.3	4.3	3.0	4.9	3.1	2.9	2.8	•	3.9	•	2.8	•
Interest Paid **13**	2.0	1.7	1.4	1.2	5.0	0.5	2.3	2.7	•	6.0	•	1.6	•
Depreciation **14**	16.7	12.4	7.7	15.6	12.1	18.1	15.0	21.2	•	16.4	•	20.0	•
Amortization and Depletion **15**	1.1	•	0.2	•	0.3	0.1	0.2	0.8	•	11.9	•	0.7	•
Pensions and Other Deferred Comp. **16**	0.1	0.0	0.0	•	0.4	0.3	0.1	0.0	•	0.1	•	0.2	•
Employee Benefits **17**	1.7	2.4	1.2	0.7	1.3	1.8	1.2	1.3	•	1.2	•	2.1	•
Advertising **18**	3.5	7.8	1.9	2.3	1.7	1.7	1.2	3.3	•	2.5	•	4.5	•
Other Expenses **19**	25.8	120.4	35.9	20.2	21.2	13.8	21.4	20.9	•	22.5	•	20.0	•
Officers' Compensation **20**	2.3	0.7	4.6	4.1	4.9	3.4	1.9	1.2	•	1.1	•	1.3	•
Operating Margin **21**	•	•	1.3	•	2.5	9.0	5.7	•	•	•	•	•	•
Operating Margin Before Officers' Comp. **22**	•	•	5.9	4.0	7.4	12.4	7.7	•	•	•	•	0.8	•

Selected Average Balance Sheet ($ in Thousands)

Item														
Net Receivables 23	58	•	0	8	•	0	152	337	4698	2237	•	6309	•	58590
Inventories 24	•	•	•	•	•	•	•	•	•	•	•	•	•	•
Net Property, Plant and Equipment 25	484	•	0	62	•	397	985	2303	5334	21725	•	94982	•	605509
Total Assets 26	1221	•	0	130	•	706	1621	6526	14804	40550	•	193446	•	1890546
Notes and Loans Payable 27	539	•	0	98	•	568	1295	1307	8092	19755	•	113541	•	602004
All Other Liabilities 28	483	•	0	19	•	42	237	2405	2535	7630	•	38569	•	1051162
Net Worth 29	199	•	0	12	•	96	89	2814	4177	13165	•	41335	•	237379

Selected Financial Ratios (Times to 1)

Item														
Current Ratio 30	0.7	•	1.5	4.9	•	1.8	2.9	2.2	1.0	•	0.6	•	0.4	
Quick Ratio 31	0.4	•	0.9	2.2	•	1.3	0.6	1.8	0.6	•	0.5	•	0.2	
Net Sales to Working Capital 32	•	23.9	5.0	•	8.7	3.8	5.3	181.2	•	0.1	•	0.7		
Coverage Ratio 33	1.9	0.9	1.5	•	17.6	3.5	0.5	•	0.1	•	0.7			
Total Asset Turnover 34	1.4	2.9	1.4	1.0	1.4	1.6	1.1	•	0.8	•	1.2			
Inventory Turnover 35	•	•	•	•	•	•	•	•	•	•	•	•	•	•
Receivables Turnover 36	•	•	•	•	•	•	•	•	•	•	•	•	•	•
Total Liabilities to Net Worth 37	5.1	9.7	6.3	17.3	1.3	2.3	2.5	2.1	•	3.7	•	7.0		
Current Assets to Working Capital 38	•	2.9	1.3	•	1.5	2.3	1.9	33.9						
Current Liabilities to Working Capital 39	•	1.9	0.3	•	0.5	1.3	0.9	32.9						
Working Capital to Net Sales 40	•	0.0	0.2	•	0.2	0.3	0.6	0.2	0.0					
Inventory to Working Capital 41	•	0.9	0.6	•	0.5	0.6	0.5	0.2	4.5					
Total Receipts to Cash Flow 42	7.4	4.1	9.2	•	6.2	9.2	5.4	5.0	12.6	9.2				
Cost of Goods to Cash Flow 43	2.1	1.0	3.2	•	1.4	1.8	1.3	2.4	2.9	2.5				
Cash Flow to Total Debt 44	0.2	0.8	0.2	•	0.2	0.5	0.4	0.2	0.1	0.2				

Selected Financial Factors (in Percentages)

Item														
Debt Ratio 45	83.7	90.7	86.4	94.5	56.9	71.8	67.5	78.6	87.4					
Return on Total Assets 46	•	7.6	1.6	•	7.6	13.7	12.5	0.5	1.3					
Return on Equity Before Income Taxes 47	•	38.7	•	46.2	30.0	31.6	31.6							
Return on Equity After Income Taxes 48	•	38.4	•	42.6	30.0	30.0	31.6							
Profit Margin (Before Income Tax) 49	•	1.3	•	2.5	9.0	5.6	5.6							
Profit Margin (After Income Tax) 50	•	1.3	•	2.3	9.0	5.6	5.6							

Table II
Corporations with Net Income

OTHER CONSUMER GOODS AND GENERAL RENTAL CENTERS

MONEY AMOUNTS AND SIZE OF ASSETS IN THOUSANDS OF DOLLARS

Item Description for Accounting Period 7/10 Through 6/11	Total	Zero Assets	Under 500	500 to 1,000	1,000 to 5,000	5,000 to 10,000	10,000 to 25,000	25,000 to 50,000	50,000 to 100,000	100,000 to 250,000	250,000 to 500,000	500,000 to 2,500,000	2,500,000 and over
1 Number of Enterprises	5996	8	5073	446	314	127	•	10	0	0	•	•	•

Revenues ($ in Thousands)

	Total	Zero Assets	Under 500	500 to 1,000	1,000 to 5,000	5,000 to 10,000	10,000 to 25,000	25,000 to 50,000	50,000 to 100,000	100,000 to 250,000	250,000 to 500,000	500,000 to 2,500,000	2,500,000 and over
2 Net Sales	10693839	2317	2157697	675693	807185	1245034	•	356706	0	0	•	•	•
3 Interest	12871	0	10	205	319	0	•	186	0	0	•	•	•
4 Rents	8202	0	0	0	1290	0	•	2149	0	0	•	•	•
5 Royalties	5547	0	0	0	0	0	•	0	0	0	•	•	•
6 Other Portfolio Income	77920	0	11052	7977	5764	60	•	4744	0	0	•	•	•
7 Other Receipts	10589299	2317	2146635	667511	799812	1244974	•	349627	0	0	•	•	•
8 Total Receipts	10693839	2317	2157697	675693	807185	1245034	•	356706	0	0	•	•	•
9 Average Total Receipts	1783	290	425	1515	2571	9803	•	35671	0	0	•	•	•

Operating Costs/Operating Income (%)

	Total	Zero Assets	Under 500	500 to 1,000	1,000 to 5,000	5,000 to 10,000	10,000 to 25,000	25,000 to 50,000	50,000 to 100,000	100,000 to 250,000	250,000 to 500,000	500,000 to 2,500,000	2,500,000 and over
10 Cost of Operations	25.9	•	21.7	32.0	28.4	33.3	•	52.4	•	•	•	•	•
11 Salaries and Wages	18.8	•	17.2	19.6	23.3	14.9	•	13.8	•	•	•	•	•
12 Taxes Paid	3.5	6.9	4.4	3.2	4.6	3.1	•	1.9	•	•	•	•	•
13 Interest Paid	1.3	•	1.5	1.1	3.6	0.5	•	1.8	•	•	•	•	•
14 Depreciation	15.0	30.5	6.7	13.7	10.0	18.1	•	5.4	•	•	•	•	•
15 Amortization and Depletion	1.5	•	0.3	•	0.4	0.1	•	0.6	•	•	•	•	•
16 Pensions and Other Deferred Comp.	0.2	•	0.0	•	0.4	0.3	•	0.0	•	•	•	•	•
17 Employee Benefits	1.4	•	1.0	0.8	1.5	1.8	•	0.9	•	•	•	•	•
18 Advertising	4.0	•	2.2	2.4	1.5	1.7	•	1.0	•	•	•	•	•
19 Other Expenses	20.7	17.6	37.0	20.3	15.9	13.4	•	16.8	•	•	•	•	•
20 Officers' Compensation	3.1	•	3.5	4.4	5.7	3.4	•	1.9	•	•	•	•	•
21 Operating Margin	4.7	45.0	4.6	2.5	4.7	9.4	•	3.5	•	•	•	•	•
22 Operating Margin Before Officers' Comp.	7.8	45.0	8.1	7.0	10.4	12.8	•	5.4	•	•	•	•	•

Selected Average Balance Sheet ($ in Thousands)

Item							
Net Receivables 23	60	0	1	0	134	353	4363
Inventories 24							
Net Property, Plant and Equipment 25	472	0	55	360	1123	2412	10775
Total Assets 26	1419	118	777	1966	6465		40639
Notes and Loans Payable 27	499	0	111	368	1179	1359	11587
All Other Liabilities 28	416	0	18	66	312	1230	4102
Net Worth 29	504	0	-11	343	475	3876	24950

Selected Financial Ratios (Times to 1)

Item							
Current Ratio 30	0.9		1.5	5.0	1.1	2.9	3.1
Quick Ratio 31	0.5		0.8	2.7	0.7	0.6	1.8
Net Sales to Working Capital 32			32.5	5.7	47.3	3.8	3.8
Coverage Ratio 33	4.6		4.0	3.4	2.3	18.2	2.9
Total Asset Turnover 34	1.3		3.6	1.9	1.3	1.5	0.9
Inventory Turnover 35							
Receivables Turnover 36							
Total Liabilities to Net Worth 37	1.8			1.3	3.1	0.7	0.6
Current Assets to Working Capital 38			3.2	1.3	9.0	1.5	1.5
Current Liabilities to Working Capital 39			2.2	0.3	8.0	0.5	0.5
Working Capital to Net Sales 40			0.0	0.2	0.0	0.3	0.3
Inventory to Working Capital 41			1.2	0.5	2.7	0.6	0.2
Total Receipts to Cash Flow 42	5.5	2.0	3.6	7.2	6.8	5.4	5.4
Cost of Goods to Cash Flow 43	1.4		0.8	2.3	1.9	1.8	2.8
Cash Flow to Total Debt 44	0.4		0.9	0.5	0.3	0.7	0.4

Selected Financial Factors (in Percentages)

Item							
Debt Ratio 45	64.5		109.5	55.9	75.8	40.1	38.6
Return on Total Assets 46	7.6		22.2	7.0	10.9	15.0	4.7
Return on Equity Before Income Taxes 47	16.8			11.2	25.6	23.7	4.9
Return on Equity After Income Taxes 48	15.1			10.9	24.3	23.7	4.4
Profit Margin (Before Income Tax) 49	4.7	45.0	4.6	2.5	4.7	9.4	3.5
Profit Margin (After Income Tax) 50	4.3	33.1	4.6	2.5	4.5	9.4	3.1

COMMERCIAL AND INDUSTRIAL MACHINERY AND EQUIPMENT RENTAL

Table I
Corporations with and without Net Income

MONEY AMOUNTS AND SIZE OF ASSETS IN THOUSANDS OF DOLLARS

Item Description for Accounting Period 7/10 Through 6/11	Total	Zero Assets	Under 500	500 to 1,000	1,000 to 5,000	5,000 to 10,000	10,000 to 25,000	25,000 to 50,000	50,000 to 100,000	100,000 to 250,000	250,000 to 500,000	500,000 to 2,500,000	2,500,000 and over
Number of Enterprises 1	24827	2127	15118	2914	3481	524	361	147	59	41	20	28	7
Revenues ($ in Thousands)													
Net Sales 2	44640580	1386160	4540818	1377977	5029733	2531255	3404351	2480128	2233660	2599325	3019367	8445333	7592472
Interest 3	955254	12449	2421	2632	4421	6554	9972	19820	27543	123007	84873	219847	441716
Rents 4	108620	369	0	1176	5878	1025	856	55	741	10624	6541	81354	0
Royalties 5	8913	0	0	0	0	0	1439	0	0	1490	0	2071	3913
Other Portfolio Income 6	2384229	374132	167641	40496	225127	55321	159388	92935	68000	161765	137662	482716	419047
Other Receipts 7	41183564	999210	4370756	1333673	4794307	2468355	3232696	2367318	2137376	2302439	2790291	7659345	6727796
Total Receipts 8	44640580	1386160	4540818	1377977	5029733	2531255	3404351	2480128	2233660	2599325	3019367	8445333	7592472
Average Total Receipts 9	1798	652	300	473	1445	4831	9430	16872	37859	63398	150968	301619	1084639
Operating Costs/Operating Income (%)													
Cost of Operations 10	28.3	29.1	41.6	15.6	31.0	46.6	38.4	40.9	33.5	27.6	39.5	17.9	11.8
Salaries and Wages 11	11.0	5.9	11.0	15.7	10.8	6.7	10.4	10.8	10.5	10.9	9.6	13.9	10.3
Taxes Paid 12	2.3	1.3	3.0	3.7	2.8	3.8	2.4	2.2	1.8	1.6	1.6	2.0	2.0
Interest Paid 13	7.8	6.3	2.3	4.4	3.0	4.1	3.5	3.8	6.1	11.1	8.2	11.6	14.8
Depreciation 14	26.4	18.1	11.0	14.2	16.1	19.0	20.2	23.3	23.9	28.8	25.3	36.3	41.9
Amortization and Depletion 15	1.0	1.2	0.0	0.5	1.0	0.1	0.4	0.4	0.6	1.9	1.1	1.3	1.9
Pensions and Other Deferred Comp. 16	0.4	0.1	0.7	0.6	0.3	0.3	0.2	0.4	0.4	0.7	0.5	0.3	0.6
Employee Benefits 17	1.3	0.6	1.5	1.9	0.8	0.9	1.1	1.2	1.4	1.1	1.3	2.3	1.0
Advertising 18	0.3	0.5	0.3	0.5	0.4	0.3	0.3	0.4	0.5	0.3	0.3	0.3	0.1
Other Expenses 19	20.8	20.8	17.5	33.6	25.0	15.8	19.9	17.7	19.9	18.1	14.1	19.7	25.7
Officers' Compensation 20	2.7	0.3	9.4	5.8	3.5	4.8	2.5	1.8	2.1	3.1	1.2	0.8	0.5
Operating Margin 21	•	15.9	1.9	3.5	5.3	•	0.8	•	•	•	•	•	•
Operating Margin Before Officers' Comp. 22	0.3	16.1	11.3	9.3	8.8	2.2	3.3	•	1.3	•	•	•	•

Selected Average Balance Sheet ($ in Thousands)

Line Item													
Net Receivables 23	788	•	6	93	283	914	1687	4279	10959	24969	89283	97684	1473149
Inventories 24	•	•	•	•	•	•	•	•	•	•	•	•	•
Net Property, Plant and Equipment 25	2008	0	60	297	1033	3084	6751	17461	28450	74399	165198	534870	2121276
Total Assets 26	4218	0	125	678	2010	6794	14656	34804	70863	155127	360729	1114087	4418841
Notes and Loans Payable 27	2484	0	131	326	1317	3598	6144	15970	33182	69539	220622	599244	3099765
All Other Liabilities 28	876	0	30	108	343	1442	2410	4810	16773	25617	63575	305114	799050
Net Worth 29	859	0	-35	243	351	1753	6103	14023	20908	59970	76531	209729	520025

Selected Financial Ratios (Times to 1)

Line Item													
Current Ratio 30	1.6	•	0.9	2.4	1.7	1.5	1.3	1.5	1.6	1.9	2.0	0.9	2.5
Quick Ratio 31	1.2	•	0.7	2.0	1.4	0.7	0.8	0.9	0.9	1.3	1.6	0.6	2.4
Net Sales to Working Capital 32	3.9	•	•	3.4	5.2	5.0	8.0	5.0	3.5	3.1	2.2	•	1.1
Coverage Ratio 33	0.7	3.5	1.9	1.8	2.8	0.4	1.2	0.2	0.9	0.6	0.7	0.5	0.3
Total Asset Turnover 34	0.4	2.4	2.4	0.7	0.7	0.7	0.6	0.5	0.5	0.4	0.4	0.3	0.2
Inventory Turnover 35	•	•	•	•	•	•	•	•	•	•	•	•	•
Receivables Turnover 36	•	•	•	•	•	•	•	•	•	•	•	•	•
Total Liabilities to Net Worth 37	3.9	•	1.8	4.7	2.9	1.5	1.4	1.5	2.4	1.6	3.7	4.3	7.5
Current Assets to Working Capital 38	2.8	•	1.7	2.5	3.0	4.3	3.0	2.6	2.1	2.0	1.6	1.1	1.7
Current Liabilities to Working Capital 39	1.8	•	0.7	1.5	2.0	3.3	2.0	1.6	1.1	1.0	1.1	1.0	0.7
Working Capital to Net Sales 40	0.3	•	0.3	0.3	0.2	0.2	0.1	0.2	0.3	0.3	0.3	0.4	0.9
Inventory to Working Capital 41	0.2	•	0.1	0.2	0.2	0.1	0.7	0.2	0.5	0.4	0.3	0.3	0.0
Total Receipts to Cash Flow 42	11.9	3.9	7.4	4.8	18.4	8.9	11.0	9.8	16.7	11.6	•	•	68.0
Cost of Goods to Cash Flow 43	3.4	1.1	3.1	0.7	8.6	3.4	4.5	3.3	4.6	4.6	•	•	12.2
Cash Flow to Total Debt 44	0.0	•	0.3	0.2	0.1	0.2	0.1	0.1	0.3	0.1	0.0	0.0	0.0

Selected Financial Factors (in Percentages)

Line Item													
Debt Ratio 45	79.6	•	128.0	64.1	82.6	74.2	58.4	59.7	70.5	61.3	78.8	81.2	88.2
Return on Total Assets 46	2.3	•	10.1	5.5	5.9	1.1	2.8	0.4	2.8	2.4	•	•	1.0
Return on Equity Before Income Taxes 47	•	•	6.7	21.7	1.2	•	•	•	•	•	•	•	•
Return on Equity After Income Taxes 48	•	•	5.6	20.2	0.9	•	•	•	•	•	•	•	•
Profit Margin (Before Income Tax) 49	15.9	1.9	3.5	5.3	0.8	•	•	•	•	•	•	•	•
Profit Margin (After Income Tax) 50	15.4	1.6	2.9	4.9	0.6	•	•	•	•	•	•	•	•

Table II
Corporations with Net Income

COMMERCIAL AND INDUSTRIAL MACHINERY AND EQUIPMENT RENTAL

MONEY AMOUNTS AND SIZE OF ASSETS IN THOUSANDS OF DOLLARS

Item Description for Accounting Period 7/10 Through 6/11	Total	Zero Assets	Under 500	500 to 1,000	1,000 to 5,000	5,000 to 10,000	10,000 to 25,000	25,000 to 50,000	50,000 to 100,000	100,000 to 250,000	250,000 to 500,000	500,000 to 2,500,000	2,500,000 and over
Number of Enterprises **1**	11485	1196	6620	1405	1817	125	•	64	25	20	•	10	•
Revenues ($ in Thousands)													
Net Sales **2**	21529895	763329	3766433	812743	3192872	1711328	•	1456326	1295700	1544164	•	3780417	•
Interest **3**	168305	12290	1297	831	3148	5060	•	6479	16003	31442	•	67739	•
Rents **4**	16211	0	0	0	184	1025	•	0	10	8586	•	0	•
Royalties **5**	5000	0	0	0	0	0	•	0	0	1490	•	2071	•
Other Portfolio Income **6**	1508489	349417	165407	37088	187322	41817	•	55849	48107	147590	•	331618	•
Other Receipts **7**	19831890	401622	3599729	774824	3002218	1663426	•	1393998	1231580	1355056	•	3378989	•
Total Receipts **8**	21529895	763329	3766433	812743	3192872	1711328	•	1456326	1295700	1544164	•	3780417	•
Average Total Receipts **9**	1875	638	569	578	1757	13691	•	22755	51828	77208	•	378042	•
Operating Costs/Operating Income (%)													
Cost of Operations **10**	32.3	16.4	45.3	13.2	26.0	54.9	•	41.5	32.7	29.5	•	10.1	•
Salaries and Wages **11**	9.0	6.2	10.0	6.7	10.3	5.5	•	10.8	8.1	11.2	•	8.9	•
Taxes Paid **12**	2.3	1.5	2.8	2.5	2.7	4.3	•	2.2	1.7	1.8	•	1.7	•
Interest Paid **13**	3.8	5.2	0.8	2.8	2.2	1.5	•	2.7	5.8	5.0	•	7.6	•
Depreciation **14**	14.6	9.0	2.8	15.8	15.4	8.6	•	14.8	19.2	18.7	•	22.9	•
Amortization and Depletion **15**	0.3	1.9	0.0	•	0.1	0.0	•	0.1	0.3	0.4	•	0.5	•
Pensions and Other Deferred Comp. **16**	0.5	0.1	0.8	0.2	0.3	0.2	•	0.2	0.6	1.1	•	0.3	•
Employee Benefits **17**	1.2	0.7	1.7	1.3	0.9	0.9	•	0.7	1.4	1.2	•	1.5	•
Advertising **18**	0.3	0.1	0.2	0.3	0.5	0.2	•	0.4	0.5	0.3	•	0.2	•
Other Expenses **19**	19.1	20.7	16.4	19.2	25.1	13.6	•	15.7	18.1	15.4	•	28.6	•
Officers' Compensation **20**	3.4	0.4	8.4	3.8	3.1	3.6	•	1.6	2.2	4.7	•	0.6	•
Operating Margin **21**	13.3	37.8	10.8	34.2	13.5	6.7	•	9.1	9.2	10.8	•	17.2	•
Operating Margin Before Officers' Comp. **22**	16.7	38.2	19.2	38.0	16.6	10.3	•	10.8	11.4	15.4	•	17.7	•

Selected Average Balance Sheet ($ in Thousands)

Item										
Net Receivables 23	344	0	13	63	258	1819	6032	13906	35897	82420
Inventories 24	•	•	•	•	•	•	•	•	•	•
Net Property, Plant and Equipment 25	1247	0	64	345	855	2829	9704	31978	64196	658450
Total Assets 26	2792	0	159	719	1984	6793	33580	77517	153310	1341425
Notes and Loans Payable 27	1208	0	67	219	891	4419	14256	40072	55113	565731
All Other Liabilities 28	562	0	37	30	246	694	5811	18799	26084	340801
Net Worth 29	1021	0	55	470	847	1679	13513	18646	72113	434892

Selected Financial Ratios (Times to 1)

Item										
Current Ratio 30	1.4	1.0	2.8	2.0	1.6	1.7	1.6	2.1	1.0	
Quick Ratio 31	1.0	0.8	2.1	1.5	1.3	0.8	0.9	1.4	0.6	
Net Sales to Working Capital 32	6.9	3.6	4.7	13.2	4.0	4.5	2.4			
Coverage Ratio 33	4.6	8.3	15.0	13.2	7.1	5.4	4.4	2.6	3.5	3.3
Total Asset Turnover 34	0.7	3.6	0.8	0.9	2.0	0.7	0.7	0.5	0.3	
Inventory Turnover 35	•	•	•	•	•	•	•	•	•	•
Receivables Turnover 36	•	•	•	•	•	•	•	•	•	•
Total Liabilities to Net Worth 37	1.7	1.9	0.5	1.3	3.0	1.5	3.2	1.1	2.1	
Current Assets to Working Capital 38	3.2	1.6	2.0	2.7	2.5	2.8	1.9			
Current Liabilities to Working Capital 39	2.2	0.6	1.0	1.7	1.5	1.8	0.9			
Working Capital to Net Sales 40	0.1	0.3	0.2	0.1	0.3	0.2	0.4			
Inventory to Working Capital 41	0.4	0.0	0.2	0.1	0.6	0.3	0.2			
Total Receipts to Cash Flow 42	4.6	2.3	4.7	2.2	3.7	8.6	4.8	5.0	4.8	5.2
Cost of Goods to Cash Flow 43	1.5	0.4	2.1	0.3	1.0	4.7	2.0	1.6	1.4	0.5
Cash Flow to Total Debt 44	0.2	1.2	1.1	0.4	0.3	0.2	0.2	0.2	0.1	

Selected Financial Factors (in Percentages)

Item										
Debt Ratio 45	63.4	65.6	34.6	57.3	75.3	59.8	75.9	53.0	67.6	
Return on Total Assets 46	11.5	41.5	29.7	13.9	16.6	8.0	10.0	8.6	7.0	
Return on Income Before Taxes 47	24.6	112.4	42.0	28.0	54.8	15.4	25.6	13.0	14.9	
Return on Equity After Income Taxes 48	21.9	108.0	40.8	26.8	49.6	13.6	23.7	11.9	10.5	
Profit Margin (Before Income Tax) 49	13.4	37.8	10.8	34.2	13.5	6.7	9.1	9.2	12.2	17.2
Profit Margin (After Income Tax) 50	11.9	37.0	10.4	33.2	12.9	6.1	8.1	8.5	11.1	12.0

Table I

Corporations with and without Net Income

LESSORS OF NONFINAN. INTANGIBLE ASSETS (EX. COPYRIGHTED WORKS)

MONEY AMOUNTS AND SIZE OF ASSETS IN THOUSANDS OF DOLLARS

Item Description for Accounting Period 7/10 Through 6/11	Total	Zero Assets	Under 500	500 to 1,000	1,000 to 5,000	5,000 to 10,000	10,000 to 25,000	25,000 to 50,000	50,000 to 100,000	100,000 to 250,000	250,000 to 500,000	500,000 to 2,500,000	2,500,000 and over
Number of Enterprises 1	2936	407	1987	363	79	40	26	3	9	11	0	10	0
Revenues ($ in Thousands)													
Net Sales 2	7182413	166065	639748	191889	75619	340601	363112	123882	142312	880539	0	4258645	0
Interest 3	67188	1296	0	0	476	2083	49	25	5995	16554	0	40711	0
Rents 4	5273	0	0	0	0	168	0	0	327	4624	0	154	0
Royalties 5	2737808	60000	29901	0	0	111596	522	0	19979	466955	0	2048856	0
Other Portfolio Income 6	79456	13983	0	0	12903	4	16940	0	662	3	0	34961	0
Other Receipts 7	4292688	90786	609847	191889	62240	226750	345601	123857	115349	392403	0	2133963	0
Total Receipts 8	7182413	166065	639748	191889	75619	340601	363112	123882	142312	880539	0	4258645	0
Average Total Receipts 9	2446	408	322	529	957	8515	13966	41294	15812	80049	•	425864	•
Operating Costs/Operating Income (%)													
Cost of Operations 10	7.0	3.4	0.1	•	21.4	3.2	7.2	10.4	5.5	6.9	•	8.6	•
Salaries and Wages 11	16.3	0.6	1.0	34.2	19.2	16.2	24.1	2.5	26.6	8.9	•	19.2	•
Taxes Paid 12	3.5	1.5	16.4	4.4	4.8	1.8	2.0	1.3	3.8	1.6	•	2.3	•
Interest Paid 13	6.2	2.7	0.1	4.3	1.7	0.6	3.1	0.1	6.3	5.6	•	8.5	•
Depreciation 14	2.6	0.9	0.0	0.6	15.6	1.4	2.5	0.1	4.5	1.9	•	3.2	•
Amortization and Depletion 15	3.9	5.3	0.1	2.1	4.4	0.9	0.9	1.1	6.4	1.9	•	5.3	•
Pensions and Other Deferred Comp. 16	0.5	0.3	•	0.0	•	1.2	2.9	0.6	2.3	0.0	•	0.4	•
Employee Benefits 17	1.3	0.6	•	1.4	3.5	1.1	1.5	0.1	2.4	0.6	•	1.6	•
Advertising 18	2.7	0.1	17.5	•	0.3	0.6	3.9	•	1.7	2.0	•	1.1	•
Other Expenses 19	26.0	32.0	45.8	47.9	•	31.2	25.3	14.8	48.5	20.2	•	22.8	•
Officers' Compensation 20	4.1	0.4	0.5	11.8	54.4	9.3	6.0	6.9	7.6	3.6	•	2.9	•
Operating Margin 21	25.8	52.2	18.5	•	•	32.4	20.5	62.0	•	46.8	•	24.1	•
Operating Margin Before Officers' Comp. 22	29.9	52.6	19.0	5.0	34.0	41.7	26.5	68.9	•	50.4	•	26.9	•

Selected Average Balance Sheet ($ in Thousands)

Net Receivables 23	393	0	2	0	187	771	1620	2422	2978	10349	•	91616
Inventories 24	•	•	•	•	•	•	•	•	•	•	•	•
Net Property, Plant and Equipment 25	375	0	13	9	112	238	1935	81	1862	10823	•	86584
Total Assets 26	8371	0	71	721	1980	7377	15394	27368	75308	173218	•	2065761
Notes and Loans Payable 27	2398	0	47	504	745	994	6024	2427	12262	61382	•	571454
All Other Liabilities 28	1663	0	106	78	400	2892	2846	6968	21518	40984	•	375810
Net Worth 29	4310	-82	0	139	835	3491	6525	17973	41529	70852	•	1118497

Selected Financial Ratios (Times to 1)

Current Ratio 30	1.4	•	0.6	83.6	1.0	1.1	1.5	2.4	1.6	1.5	•	1.4
Quick Ratio 31	0.8	•	0.2	67.0	0.8	0.7	0.9	2.0	0.8	1.0	•	0.8
Net Sales to Working Capital 32	4.3	•	•	1.9	•	26.7	6.9	3.5	2.0	4.4	•	3.3
Coverage Ratio 33	5.2	20.4	299.8	•	•	53.3	7.6	483.7	•	9.5	•	3.8
Total Asset Turnover 34	0.3	•	4.5	0.7	0.5	1.2	0.9	1.5	0.2	0.5	•	0.2
Inventory Turnover 35	•	•	•	•	•	•	•	•	•	•	•	•
Receivables Turnover 36	•	•	•	•	•	•	•	•	•	•	•	•
Total Liabilities to Net Worth 37	0.9	•	4.2	1.4	1.1	1.4	0.5	0.8	1.4	•	•	0.8
Current Assets to Working Capital 38	3.6	•	•	1.0	•	9.3	3.2	1.7	2.8	3.0	•	3.6
Current Liabilities to Working Capital 39	2.6	•	•	0.0	•	8.3	2.2	0.7	1.8	2.0	•	2.6
Working Capital to Net Sales 40	0.2	•	•	0.5	•	0.0	0.1	0.3	0.5	0.2	•	0.3
Inventory to Working Capital 41	0.0	•	•	•	•	0.0	0.1	•	0.0	0.0	•	0.0
Total Receipts to Cash Flow 42	2.1	1.2	1.6	3.0	•	1.6	2.3	1.3	3.7	1.5	•	2.4
Cost of Goods to Cash Flow 43	0.1	0.0	0.0	•	•	0.1	0.2	0.1	0.2	0.1	•	0.2
Cash Flow to Total Debt 44	0.3	•	1.3	0.3	•	1.3	0.7	3.4	0.1	0.5	•	0.2

Selected Financial Factors (in Percentages)

Debt Ratio 45	48.5	•	215.8	80.7	57.8	52.7	57.6	34.3	44.9	59.1	•	45.9
Return on Total Assets 46	9.4	•	84.1	•	•	38.1	21.4	93.7	•	24.4	•	6.7
Return on Equity Before Income Taxes 47	14.7	•	•	79.1	•	43.7	•	142.4	53.4	•	•	9.2
Return on Equity After Income Taxes 48	10.2	•	•	67.2	•	43.7	•	119.7	36.5	•	•	5.9
Profit Margin (Before Income Tax) 49	25.9	52.2	18.5	32.4	•	20.4	62.0	47.3	•	•	•	24.1
Profit Margin (After Income Tax) 50	17.9	29.6	18.5	27.6	•	20.4	52.1	32.3	•	•	•	15.5

Table II

Corporations with Net Income

LESSORS OF NONFINAN. INTANGIBLE ASSETS (EX. COPYRIGHTED WORKS)

MONEY AMOUNTS AND SIZE OF ASSETS IN THOUSANDS OF DOLLARS

Item Description for Accounting Period 7/10 Through 6/11	Total	Zero Assets	Under 500	500 to 1,000	1,000 to 5,000	5,000 to 10,000	10,000 to 25,000	25,000 to 50,000	50,000 to 100,000	100,000 to 250,000	250,000 to 500,000	500,000 to 2,500,000	2,500,000 and over
Number of Enterprises 1	1877	407	1339	0	54	31	•	3	6	8	0	•	0

Revenues ($ in Thousands)

Item Description for Accounting Period 7/10 Through 6/11	Total	Zero Assets	Under 500	500 to 1,000	1,000 to 5,000	5,000 to 10,000	10,000 to 25,000	25,000 to 50,000	50,000 to 100,000	100,000 to 250,000	250,000 to 500,000	500,000 to 2,500,000	2,500,000 and over
Net Sales 2	6079616	166065	597061	0	54370	308729	•	123882	110964	873417	0	•	0
Interest 3	37782	1296	0	0	466	1648	•	25	1832	16514	0	•	0
Rents 4	5270	0	0	0	0	168	•	0	327	4621	0	•	0
Royalties 5	2627239	60000	0	0	0	111489	•	0	19380	461710	0	•	0
Other Portfolio Income 6	62942	13983	0	0	12833	4	•	0	600	3	0	•	0
Other Receipts 7	3346383	90786	597061	0	41071	195420	•	123857	88825	390569	0	•	0
Total Receipts 8	6079616	166065	597061	0	54370	308729	•	123882	110964	873417	0	•	0
Average Total Receipts 9	3239	408	446	•	1007	9959	•	41294	18494	109177	•	•	•

Operating Costs/Operating Income (%)

Item Description for Accounting Period 7/10 Through 6/11	Total	Zero Assets	Under 500	500 to 1,000	1,000 to 5,000	5,000 to 10,000	10,000 to 25,000	25,000 to 50,000	50,000 to 100,000	100,000 to 250,000	250,000 to 500,000	500,000 to 2,500,000	2,500,000 and over
Cost of Operations 10	6.4	3.4	0.1	•	15.4	0.4	•	10.4	3.7	6.9	•	•	•
Salaries and Wages 11	14.4	0.6	1.1	•	23.3	16.6	•	2.5	22.5	8.9	•	•	•
Taxes Paid 12	3.7	1.5	17.5	•	5.6	1.9	•	1.3	3.7	1.6	•	•	•
Interest Paid 13	5.9	2.7	0.1	•	0.9	0.4	•	0.1	8.0	5.6	•	•	•
Depreciation 14	2.3	0.9	0.0	•	0.7	1.3	•	0.1	5.1	1.9	•	•	•
Amortization and Depletion 15	3.0	5.3	0.2	•	1.6	0.1	•	1.1	1.7	0.9	•	•	•
Pensions and Other Deferred Comp. 16	0.6	0.3	•	•	•	1.3	•	0.6	2.9	0.0	•	•	•
Employee Benefits 17	1.3	0.6	•	•	4.5	1.2	•	0.1	2.3	0.6	•	•	•
Advertising 18	3.0	0.1	18.0	•	0.4	0.7	•	•	1.2	2.0	•	•	•
Other Expenses 19	23.1	32.0	40.0	•	68.4	30.1	•	14.8	34.6	20.1	•	•	•
Officers' Compensation 20	3.1	0.4	0.5	•	68.4	9.2	•	6.9	4.8	3.6	•	•	•
Operating Margin 21	33.1	52.2	22.5	•	26.6	36.8	•	62.0	9.6	47.8	•	•	•
Operating Margin Before Officers' Comp. 22	36.2	52.6	23.0	•	94.9	46.0	•	68.9	14.4	51.4	•	•	•

Selected Average Balance Sheet ($ in Thousands)

Net Receivables 23	474	0	1	206	855	2422	3065	11989
Inventories 24	•	•	•	•	•	•	•	•
Net Property, Plant and Equipment 25	529	0	73	67	281	81	2472	14001
Total Assets 26	10677	0		1622	6922	27368	77211	180488
Notes and Loans Payable 27	3194	0	70	631	559	2427	18310	80447
All Other Liabilities 28	2084	0	153	138	2604	6968	26789	43910
Net Worth 29	5400	0	-150	852	3759	17973	32112	56131

Selected Financial Ratios (Times to 1)

Current Ratio 30	1.4	•	0.5	1.1	1.3	2.4	0.8	1.4
Quick Ratio 31	0.8	•	0.2	0.9	0.9	2.0	0.8	1.0
Net Sales to Working Capital 32	4.2	•	•	24.9	14.3	3.5	•	5.1
Coverage Ratio 33	6.6	20.4	339.8	31.8	97.0	483.7	2.1	9.6
Total Asset Turnover 34	0.3	•	6.1	0.6	1.4	1.5	0.2	0.6
Inventory Turnover 35	•	•	•	•	•	•	•	•
Receivables Turnover 36	•	•	•	•	•	•	•	•
Total Liabilities to Net Worth 37	1.0	•	0.9	0.9	0.8	0.5	1.4	2.2
Current Assets to Working Capital 38	3.5	•	•	19.3	4.5	1.7	•	3.3
Current Liabilities to Working Capital 39	2.5	•	•	18.3	3.5	0.7	•	2.3
Working Capital to Net Sales 40	0.2	•	•	0.0	0.1	0.3	•	0.2
Inventory to Working Capital 41	0.0	•	•	0.0	0.0	•	•	0.0
Total Receipts to Cash Flow 42	1.9	1.2	1.6	•	1.5	1.3	2.4	1.5
Cost of Goods to Cash Flow 43	0.1	0.0	0.0	0.0	0.0	0.1	0.1	0.1
Cash Flow to Total Debt 44	0.3	•	1.2	•	2.0	3.4	0.2	0.6

Selected Financial Factors (in Percentages)

Debt Ratio 45	49.4	•	305.2	47.4	45.7	34.3	58.4	68.9
Return on Total Assets 46	11.8	•	137.3	17.0	53.5	93.7	4.1	32.6
Return on Equity Before Income Taxes 47	19.8	•	•	31.4	97.6	142.4	5.3	93.9
Return on Equity After Income Taxes 48	14.2	•	•	22.7	83.4	119.7	3.7	64.5
Profit Margin (Before Income Tax) 49	33.1	52.2	22.5	26.6	36.8	62.0	9.1	48.3
Profit Margin (After Income Tax) 50	23.7	29.6	22.5	19.2	31.5	52.1	6.5	33.2

Table I

Corporations with and without Net Income

LEGAL SERVICES

MONEY AMOUNTS AND SIZE OF ASSETS IN THOUSANDS OF DOLLARS

Item Description for Accounting Period 7/10 Through 6/11	Total	Zero Assets	Under 500	500 to 1,000	1,000 to 5,000	5,000 to 10,000	10,000 to 25,000	25,000 to 50,000	50,000 to 100,000	100,000 to 250,000	250,000 to 500,000	500,000 to 2,500,000	2,500,000 and over
Number of Enterprises 1	118043	22006	88849	3610	3182	207	124	45	13	3	3	0	0
Revenues ($ in Thousands)													
Net Sales 2	97943966	2951533	46253294	10168158	17007646	4642223	5622568	5393509	2191217	874110	2839709	0	0
Interest 3	36935	452	5962	15219	3869	3170	749	2403	3486	498	1127	0	0
Rents 4	28051	70	5101	1684	720	3731	2363	12955	1086	340	0	0	0
Royalties 5	2612	0	1696	799	0	0	8	41	68	0	0	0	0
Other Portfolio Income 6	64067	1497	49855	1431	2166	273	938	2660	4405	805	36	0	0
Other Receipts 7	3170131	251789	1673213	486319	184791	62860	234453	125889	17762	11243	121812	0	0
Total Receipts 8	101245762	3205341	47989121	10673610	17199192	4712257	5861079	5537457	2218024	886996	2962684	0	0
Average Total Receipts 9	858	146	540	2957	5405	22765	47267	123055	170617	295665	987561	•	•
Operating Costs/Operating Income (%)													
Cost of Operations 10	5.1	1.7	3.7	9.8	6.6	0.2	3.0	0.0	3.5	10.4	27.0	•	•
Salaries and Wages 11	32.2	16.0	25.6	32.6	33.5	46.3	50.3	57.6	51.2	34.5	24.0	•	•
Taxes Paid 12	3.6	3.6	3.8	3.6	3.6	3.7	3.5	3.6	2.9	3.3	1.3	•	•
Interest Paid 13	0.5	0.6	0.4	0.3	0.5	0.6	0.4	0.4	1.0	0.5	2.3	•	•
Depreciation 14	0.9	0.5	0.7	1.0	0.6	1.4	1.3	1.4	1.1	1.3	2.4	•	•
Amortization and Depletion 15	0.1	0.0	0.0	0.0	0.0	0.0	0.0	0.0	0.2	0.7	3.3	•	•
Pensions and Other Deferred Comp. 16	1.9	0.5	2.0	1.8	1.6	2.3	2.4	2.7	2.5	0.1	0.3	•	•
Employee Benefits 17	2.2	1.5	2.0	2.8	2.4	2.3	2.7	3.0	2.5	1.8	1.9	•	•
Advertising 18	2.0	1.6	2.0	1.5	3.4	1.1	1.7	0.5	1.7	0.1	0.5	•	•
Other Expenses 19	26.3	43.9	28.2	22.5	23.9	20.8	22.3	20.2	34.1	39.3	22.6	•	•
Officers' Compensation 20	19.1	22.2	23.5	21.6	16.5	22.0	9.1	11.5	2.2	0.6	0.3	•	•
Operating Margin 21	6.2	7.9	8.2	2.5	7.4	•	3.4	•	•	7.5	14.0	•	•
Operating Margin Before Officers' Comp. 22	25.3	30.1	31.7	24.1	23.8	21.2	12.5	10.5	•	8.1	14.3	•	•

Selected Average Balance Sheet ($ in Thousands)

Net Receivables 23	17	0	4	40	156	121	1409	2890	5758	8269	167096
Inventories 24	1	0	0	0	7	0	250	215	857	5	0
Net Property, Plant and Equipment 25	29	0	11	76	283	1233	2483	9046	9647	18712	56436
Total Assets 26	212	0	75	694	1847	7857	15704	32971	66620	135135	1230721
Notes and Loans Payable 27	78	0	36	293	593	2473	4939	8304	18904	22924	416501
All Other Liabilities 28	95	0	35	293	782	5257	5748	13016	19761	77458	555706
Net Worth 29	40	0	5	108	473	127	5017	11651	27956	34753	258514

Selected Financial Ratios (Times to 1)

Current Ratio 30	1.2	•	1.3	1.1	1.3	1.1	1.5	1.3	1.4	1.3	1.1
Quick Ratio 31	0.8	•	0.9	0.8	0.8	0.5	0.8	0.8	0.9	1.1	0.4
Net Sales to Working Capital 32	33.0	•	49.0	56.3	19.1	62.4	13.9	26.5	22.1	21.3	21.9
Coverage Ratio 33	21.1	30.0	34.3	22.9	18.0	2.3	19.0	5.8	•	18.9	8.9
Total Asset Turnover 34	3.9	•	6.9	4.1	2.9	2.9	2.9	3.6	2.5	2.2	0.8
Inventory Turnover 35	72.7	•	418.9	1922.3	52.0	•	5.4	0.0	6.9	5688.5	•
Receivables Turnover 36	55.0	•	144.4	117.3	42.1	•	30.7	37.6	22.7	70.5	•
Total Liabilities to Net Worth 37	4.3	•	14.6	5.4	2.9	60.7	2.1	1.8	1.4	2.9	3.8
Current Assets to Working Capital 38	5.1	•	4.7	8.1	4.3	15.5	3.1	4.1	3.7	3.9	13.6
Current Liabilities to Working Capital 39	4.1	•	3.7	7.1	3.3	14.5	2.1	3.1	2.7	2.9	12.6
Working Capital to Net Sales 40	0.0	•	0.0	0.0	0.1	0.0	0.1	0.0	0.0	0.0	0.0
Inventory to Working Capital 41	0.0	•	0.0	0.0	0.0	•	0.1	0.0	•	0.0	•
Total Receipts to Cash Flow 42	3.4	1.9	3.1	4.3	3.7	6.6	4.2	7.2	3.9	2.2	2.6
Cost of Goods to Cash Flow 43	0.2	0.0	0.1	0.4	0.2	0.0	0.1	0.0	0.1	0.2	0.7
Cash Flow to Total Debt 44	1.4	•	2.4	1.1	1.0	0.4	1.0	0.8	1.1	1.3	0.4

Selected Financial Factors (in Percentages)

Debt Ratio 45	81.1	•	93.6	84.4	74.4	98.4	68.1	64.7	58.0	74.3	79.0
Return on Total Assets 46	39.1	•	85.2	31.8	26.0	3.9	23.3	7.6	•	20.3	15.9
Return on Equity Before Income Taxes 47	197.1	•	1293.0	194.9	95.9	136.6	69.0	17.8	•	74.7	67.2
Return on Equity After Income Taxes 48	190.9	•	1286.4	190.7	94.5	83.9	67.1	15.1	•	38.0	50.1
Profit Margin (Before Income Tax) 49	9.5	16.5	12.0	7.5	8.5	0.8	7.6	1.7	•	8.9	18.4
Profit Margin (After Income Tax) 50	9.2	16.1	11.9	7.3	8.4	0.5	7.4	1.5	•	4.5	13.7

Table II

Corporations with Net Income

LEGAL SERVICES

MONEY AMOUNTS AND SIZE OF ASSETS IN THOUSANDS OF DOLLARS

Item Description for Accounting Period 7/10 Through 6/11	Total	Zero Assets	Under 500	500 to 1,000	1,000 to 5,000	5,000 to 10,000	10,000 to 25,000	25,000 to 50,000	50,000 to 100,000	100,000 to 250,000	250,000 to 500,000	500,000 to 2,500,000	2,500,000 and over
Number of Enterprises **1**	84882	14417	65041	2901	2251	121	112	•	8	0	0	0	0
Revenues ($ in Thousands)													
Net Sales **2**	78522571	2060587	36932939	8017791	13342178	3836574	5491599	•	2211942	0	0	0	0
Interest **3**	25786	1	3954	10440	3393	2459	654	•	1562	0	0	0	0
Rents **4**	17192	0	3996	179	720	1046	0	•	475	0	0	0	0
Royalties **5**	117	0	0	0	0	0	8	•	68	0	0	0	0
Other Portfolio Income **6**	61351	1431	49624	202	2166	92	938	•	4371	0	0	0	0
Other Receipts **7**	2796928	42573	1551975	478739	175357	58384	232853	•	10370	0	0	0	0
Total Receipts **8**	81423945	2104592	38542488	8507351	13523814	3898555	5726052	•	2228788	0	0	0	0
Average Total Receipts **9**	959	146	593	2933	6008	32219	51125	•	278598	•	•	•	•
Operating Costs/Operating Income (%)													
Cost of Operations **10**	4.2	2.4	1.5	12.4	5.3	0.1	3.1	•	0.0	•	•	•	•
Salaries and Wages **11**	31.5	13.1	26.5	29.7	30.9	46.7	50.7	•	42.2	•	•	•	•
Taxes Paid **12**	3.4	2.6	3.7	3.4	3.3	3.5	3.5	•	2.9	•	•	•	•
Interest Paid **13**	0.4	0.8	0.4	0.2	0.4	0.3	0.4	•	0.2	•	•	•	•
Depreciation **14**	0.9	0.4	0.8	0.9	0.5	0.9	1.3	•	0.9	•	•	•	•
Amortization and Depletion **15**	0.1	0.0	0.0	0.0	0.0	0.0	0.0	•	0.2	•	•	•	•
Pensions and Other Deferred Comp. **16**	1.8	0.2	1.8	1.9	1.7	2.4	2.4	•	2.0	•	•	•	•
Employee Benefits **17**	2.1	1.2	1.8	2.1	2.3	2.6	2.7	•	2.2	•	•	•	•
Advertising **18**	1.9	1.4	1.7	1.7	3.9	1.3	1.8	•	1.0	•	•	•	•
Other Expenses **19**	25.6	39.5	27.9	22.2	22.7	18.8	22.1	•	39.6	•	•	•	•
Officers' Compensation **20**	18.3	14.4	21.8	21.4	17.9	20.9	8.6	•	2.2	•	•	•	•
Operating Margin **21**	9.6	24.1	12.0	4.0	10.9	2.6	3.6	•	6.6	•	•	•	•
Operating Margin Before Officers' Comp. **22**	27.9	38.5	33.9	25.4	28.8	23.4	12.2	•	8.8	•	•	•	•

Selected Average Balance Sheet ($ in Thousands)

Net Receivables 23	21	0	6	49	216	38	1528	4397
Inventories 24	1	0	0	0	10	51	276	1380
Net Property, Plant and Equipment 25	28	0	12	80	224	1032	2327	18002
Total Assets 26	230	0	82	697	1908	7603	15928	69153
Notes and Loans Payable 27	77	0	35	211	566	2741	4267	9247
All Other Liabilities 28	100	0	34	276	904	3917	5842	25489
Net Worth 29	53	0	13	210	438	945	5819	34416

Selected Financial Ratios (Times to 1)

Current Ratio 30	1.4	•	1.4	1.3	1.4	1.2	1.6	1.8
Quick Ratio 31	0.8	•	1.1	1.0	0.9	0.4	0.9	1.3
Net Sales to Working Capital 32	24.1	•	33.4	25.1	15.2	30.5	12.9	18.4
Coverage Ratio 33	31.4	35.0	46.1	42.1	29.0	14.5	22.8	35.0
Total Asset Turnover 34	4.0	•	6.9	4.0	3.1	4.2	3.1	4.0
Inventory Turnover 35	47.8	•	141.1	1919.9	32.7	0.6	5.4	0.0
Receivables Turnover 36	51.4	•	128.3	98.7	42.6	129.3	33.1	29.9
Total Liabilities to Net Worth 37	3.3	•	5.4	2.3	3.4	7.0	1.7	1.0
Current Assets to Working Capital 38	3.9	•	3.3	4.0	3.6	5.0	2.7	2.3
Current Liabilities to Working Capital 39	2.9	•	2.3	3.0	2.6	4.0	1.7	1.3
Working Capital to Net Sales 40	0.0	•	0.0	0.0	0.1	0.0	0.1	0.1
Inventory to Working Capital 41	0.0	•	0.0	•	0.0	•	0.1	0.0
Total Receipts to Cash Flow 42	3.1	1.7	2.7	3.7	3.3	5.8	4.2	2.4
Cost of Goods to Cash Flow 43	0.1	0.0	0.0	0.5	0.2	0.0	0.1	0.0
Cash Flow to Total Debt 44	1.7	•	3.1	1.5	1.2	0.8	1.2	3.3

Selected Financial Factors (in Percentages)

Debt Ratio 45	77.0	•	84.5	69.9	77.0	87.6	63.5	50.2
Return on Total Assets 46	55.3	•	116.0	41.2	39.6	18.8	25.6	30.4
Return on Equity Before Income Taxes 47	232.7	•	732.0	133.7	166.2	140.9	66.9	59.3
Return on Equity After Income Taxes 48	226.2	•	728.6	131.1	164.1	128.7	65.2	43.0
Profit Margin (Before Income Tax) 49	13.3	26.3	16.4	10.2	12.3	4.2	7.9	7.4
Profit Margin (After Income Tax) 50	12.9	25.7	16.3	9.9	12.1	3.8	7.7	5.4

Table I

Corporations with and without Net Income

ACCOUNTING, TAX PREPARATION, BOOKKEEPING, AND PAYROLL SERVICES

MONEY AMOUNTS AND SIZE OF ASSETS IN THOUSANDS OF DOLLARS

Item Description for Accounting Period 7/10 Through 6/11		Total	Zero Assets	Under 500	500 to 1,000	1,000 to 5,000	5,000 to 10,000	10,000 to 25,000	25,000 to 50,000	50,000 to 100,000	100,000 to 250,000	250,000 to 500,000	500,000 to 2,500,000	2,500,000 and over
Number of Enterprises	1	85839	18589	65268	1256	546	69	65	19	10	6	7	0	3
Revenues ($ in Thousands)														
Net Sales	2	60223356	1409300	21178107	4681312	4193898	458827	1301281	3506980	662107	535911	10494749	0	11800884
Interest	3	709314	30	4570	4216	3390	1050	3874	4685	158	4539	6955	0	675848
Rents	4	91378	0	3251	13385	0	0	6502	0	244	410	0	0	67586
Royalties	5	318668	0	2455	0	0	0	0	0	0	0	61505	0	254708
Other Portfolio Income	6	140323	3270	14892	208	1358	2595	506	0	2747	3089	4	0	111656
Other Receipts	7	1350954	52062	464629	17005	16871	30076	56017	51370	-189	3445	50816	0	608850
Total Receipts	8	62833993	1464662	21667904	4716126	4215517	492548	1368180	3563035	665067	547394	10614029	0	13519532
Average Total Receipts	9	732	79	332	3755	7721	7138	21049	187528	66507	91232	1516290	•	4506511
Operating Costs/Operating Income (%)														
Cost of Operations	10	24.1	0.2	4.4	0.3	48.9	•	19.3	72.3	30.0	5.8	78.9	•	1.8
Salaries and Wages	11	25.7	12.2	31.9	40.6	20.5	38.7	34.5	3.5	28.1	38.0	2.7	•	37.2
Taxes Paid	12	4.6	3.3	4.1	4.4	6.2	3.5	3.8	6.6	1.8	3.5	5.1	•	4.6
Interest Paid	13	1.2	1.9	0.6	0.6	0.7	0.1	0.9	0.3	2.2	4.3	0.6	•	3.0
Depreciation	14	1.3	1.6	0.7	0.8	1.9	0.7	2.9	0.1	1.5	1.5	0.2	•	3.6
Amortization and Depletion	15	0.7	1.4	0.3	0.3	0.4	0.1	0.4	0.0	0.9	2.5	0.3	•	2.1
Pensions and Other Deferred Comp.	16	1.1	0.4	1.4	2.4	0.4	1.5	0.7	0.1	0.1	0.1	0.4	•	1.6
Employee Benefits	17	2.5	2.5	2.1	2.6	1.8	1.9	2.3	0.9	1.5	2.5	4.5	•	2.5
Advertising	18	0.7	2.1	0.7	0.5	0.5	0.5	0.6	0.0	0.4	0.8	0.0	•	1.8
Other Expenses	19	24.9	56.0	26.4	24.2	13.0	22.7	22.6	15.9	31.2	32.3	8.6	•	39.9
Officers' Compensation	20	9.6	13.8	19.9	19.3	3.6	15.5	13.6	0.2	0.6	2.7	0.1	•	0.3
Operating Margin	21	3.5	4.4	7.6	3.9	2.3	14.7	•	0.1	1.8	5.9	•	•	1.8
Operating Margin Before Officers' Comp.	22	13.1	18.2	27.5	23.2	5.8	30.2	11.9	0.4	2.4	8.6	•	•	2.1

Selected Average Balance Sheet ($ in Thousands)

Net Receivables **23**	74	0	6	86	169	2988	1271	6901	22826	13946	91150	• 1475611
Inventories **24**	0	0	0	4	1	0	173	81	334	178	1	• 5195
Net Property, Plant and Equipment **25**	29	0	13	199	249	307	1908	1171	1866	6164	9688	• 317349
Total Assets **26**	1038	56	750	2405	8175	16651	36698	69875	154312	396950		• 25497838
Notes and Loans Payable **27**	116	26	336	1027	410	3183	10191	10953	46504	116383		• 1878055
All Other Liabilities **28**	716	17	280	860	1370	9979	23937	46654	74379	164353		• 18772677
Net Worth **29**	206	13	134	518	6395	3490	2570	12268	33429	116214		• 4847107

Selected Financial Ratios (Times to 1)

Current Ratio **30**	0.7	•	1.5	1.0	0.8	5.9	1.2	1.4	1.2	0.9	1.0	• 0.6
Quick Ratio **31**	0.3	•	1.4	0.8	0.7	5.9	0.4	0.8	0.9	0.4	0.6	• 0.2
Net Sales to Working Capital **32**	•	•	33.3	734.8	•	1.1	13.4	21.5	9.9	•	•	•
Coverage Ratio **33**	7.9	5.4	17.0	8.9	223.7	4.8	4.9	7.3	2.1	2.9	0.7	• 6.6
Total Asset Turnover **34**	0.7	•	5.8	5.0	3.2	0.8	1.2	5.0	0.9	0.6	3.8	• 0.2
Inventory Turnover **35**	371.9	1224.5	3.3	3546.8	•	22.4	1655.0	59.4	29.1	2070045.8		• 13.4
Receivables Turnover **36**	9.9	63.2	49.1	24.8	•	10.3	28.4	4.2	6.5	•		• 2.8
Total Liabilities to Net Worth **37**	4.0	3.3	4.6	3.6	0.3	3.8	13.3	4.7	3.6	2.4		• 4.3
Current Assets to Working Capital **38**	•	2.8	63.1	•	1.2	6.9	3.3	6.6	•	•		•
Current Liabilities to Working Capital **39**	•	1.8	62.1	•	0.2	5.9	2.3	5.6	•	•		•
Working Capital to Net Sales **40**	•	0.0	0.0	•	0.9	0.1	0.0	0.1	•	•		•
Inventory to Working Capital **41**	•	0.0	•	•	•	0.0	0.0	0.0	•	•		•
Total Receipts to Cash Flow **42**	3.6	1.9	3.3	4.3	7.9	2.5	5.2	5.8	3.3	2.8	12.5	• 2.1
Cost of Goods to Cash Flow **43**	0.9	0.0	0.1	0.0	3.9	•	1.0	4.2	1.0	0.2	9.9	• 0.0
Cash Flow to Total Debt **44**	0.2	•	2.3	1.4	0.5	1.5	0.3	0.9	0.3	0.3	0.4	• 0.1

Selected Financial Factors (in Percentages)

Debt Ratio **45**	80.1	•	76.7	82.2	78.5	21.8	79.0	93.0	82.4	78.3	70.7	• 81.0
Return on Total Assets **46**	6.1	•	61.4	26.0	11.1	18.0	5.3	10.1	4.2	7.1	1.6	• 3.1
Return on Equity Before Income Taxes **47**	27.0	•	247.8	129.7	41.1	23.0	20.0	124.2	12.3	21.4	•	• 13.7
Return on Equity After Income Taxes **48**	22.8	•	246.2	122.9	40.9	21.9	19.7	114.0	9.7	15.3	•	• 8.9
Profit Margin (Before Income Tax) **49**	7.9	8.3	9.9	4.6	2.8	22.1	3.5	1.7	2.3	8.0	•	• 16.9
Profit Margin (After Income Tax) **50**	6.7	8.2	9.8	4.4	2.8	21.1	3.4	1.6	1.8	5.7	•	• 11.0

Table II
Corporations with Net Income

ACCOUNTING, TAX PREPARATION, BOOKKEEPING, AND PAYROLL SERVICES

MONEY AMOUNTS AND SIZE OF ASSETS IN THOUSANDS OF DOLLARS

Item Description for Accounting Period 7/10 Through 6/11	Total	Zero Assets	Under 500	500 to 1,000	1,000 to 5,000	5,000 to 10,000	10,000 to 25,000	25,000 to 50,000	50,000 to 100,000	100,000 to 250,000	250,000 to 500,000	500,000 to 2,500,000	2,500,000 and over
Number of Enterprises 1	59682	11520	46587	933	499	64	44	•	7	•	•	0	0
Revenues ($ in Thousands)													
Net Sales 2	52350236	1002826	16807839	3905909	4025020	456765	1037623	•	314951	•	•	0	0
Interest 3	691289	0	3272	3922	2543	1050	182	•	153	•	•	0	0
Rents 4	91378	0	3251	13385	0	0	6502	•	244	•	•	0	0
Royalties 5	254508	0	0	0	0	0	0	•	0	•	•	0	0
Other Portfolio Income 6	134626	1983	14682	62	25	2595	506	•	32	•	•	0	0
Other Receipts 7	1283738	51215	457373	15535	16404	30076	55222	•	240	•	•	0	0
Total Receipts 8	54805775	1056024	17286417	3938813	4043992	490486	1100035	•	315620	•	•	0	0
Average Total Receipts 9	918	92	371	4222	8104	7664	25001	•	45089	•	•	•	•
Operating Costs/Operating Income (%)													
Cost of Operations 10	26.8	0.2	5.2	0.3	50.1	•	15.3	•	1.7	•	•	•	•
Salaries and Wages 11	24.5	8.7	30.5	42.8	20.0	38.8	36.4	•	39.1	•	•	•	•
Taxes Paid 12	4.6	2.9	3.8	4.4	6.3	3.5	3.9	•	2.2	•	•	•	•
Interest Paid 13	0.7	1.8	0.7	0.6	0.7	0.1	0.5	•	2.3	•	•	•	•
Depreciation 14	1.2	1.8	0.6	0.8	0.7	0.7	2.3	•	0.9	•	•	•	•
Amortization and Depletion 15	0.7	0.6	0.4	0.3	0.4	0.1	0.2	•	0.2	•	•	•	•
Pensions and Other Deferred Comp. 16	1.0	0.2	1.4	1.5	0.4	1.5	0.6	•	0.0	•	•	•	•
Employee Benefits 17	2.5	1.7	2.0	2.3	1.7	1.9	2.2	•	0.6	•	•	•	•
Advertising 18	0.7	1.1	0.6	0.5	0.5	0.5	0.6	•	0.6	•	•	•	•
Other Expenses 19	23.7	25.2	25.3	25.3	11.7	22.6	22.1	•	44.0	•	•	•	•
Officers' Compensation 20	8.3	12.8	19.0	16.2	2.7	15.5	13.9	•	0.9	•	•	•	•
Operating Margin 21	5.3	17.3	10.5	5.0	4.9	14.8	2.1	•	7.6	•	•	•	•
Operating Margin Before Officers' Comp. 22	13.6	30.1	29.5	21.2	7.6	30.3	15.9	•	8.5	•	•	•	•

Selected Average Balance Sheet ($ in Thousands)

Net Receivables 23	66	0	8	70	162	3107	1322	21711
Inventories 24	0	0	0	0	1	0	1	0
Net Property, Plant and Equipment 25	34	0	15	156	250	331	1855	481
Total Assets 26	1278	0	68	764	2470	8153	16610	71903
Notes and Loans Payable 27	80	0	27	372	930	442	3077	5449
All Other Liabilities 28	932	0	20	280	804	816	9777	52339
Net Worth 29	267	0	21	112	736	6894	3756	14115

Selected Financial Ratios (Times to 1)

Current Ratio 30	0.7	•	1.6	1.2	0.8	11.3	1.3	1.0
Quick Ratio 31	0.3	•	1.5	1.0	0.7	11.2	0.3	0.7
Net Sales to Working Capital 32	•	•	27.2	77.9	•	1.1	9.8	263.3
Coverage Ratio 33	16.4	13.9	20.2	10.8	8.8	225.2	18.6	4.4
Total Asset Turnover 34	0.7	•	5.3	5.5	3.3	0.9	1.4	0.6
Inventory Turnover 35	849.8	•	2252.3	148.4	3490.5	•	4680.7	•
Receivables Turnover 36	14.5	•	52.3	56.5	39.2	3.6	9.5	•
Total Liabilities to Net Worth 37	3.8	•	2.2	5.8	2.4	0.2	3.4	4.1
Current Assets to Working Capital 38	•	•	2.6	5.8	•	1.1	4.7	284.1
Current Liabilities to Working Capital 39	•	•	1.6	4.8	•	0.1	3.7	283.1
Working Capital to Net Sales 40	•	•	0.0	0.0	•	0.9	0.1	0.0
Inventory to Working Capital 41	•	•	0.0	•	•	•	0.0	•
Total Receipts to Cash Flow 42	3.4	1.6	3.0	3.9	7.1	2.5	4.3	2.0
Cost of Goods to Cash Flow 43	0.9	0.0	0.2	0.0	3.6	•	0.7	0.0
Cash Flow to Total Debt 44	0.3	•	2.5	1.6	0.7	2.3	0.4	0.4

Selected Financial Factors (in Percentages)

Debt Ratio 45	79.1	•	69.0	85.3	70.2	15.4	77.4	80.4
Return on Total Assets 46	7.4	•	74.0	35.0	20.0	19.5	12.1	6.3
Return on Equity Before Income Taxes 47	33.2	•	227.0	217.0	59.4	23.0	50.7	24.9
Return on Equity After Income Taxes 48	28.5	•	225.6	206.2	59.3	21.9	50.4	21.6
Profit Margin (Before Income Tax) 49	10.1	22.6	13.3	5.8	5.4	22.2	8.1	7.8
Profit Margin (After Income Tax) 50	8.7	22.4	13.2	5.5	5.4	21.2	8.0	6.8

Table I

Corporations with and without Net Income

ARCHITECTURAL, ENGINEERING, AND RELATED SERVICES

MONEY AMOUNTS AND SIZE OF ASSETS IN THOUSANDS OF DOLLARS

Item Description for Accounting Period 7/10 Through 6/11	Total	Zero Assets	Under 500	500 to 1,000	1,000 to 5,000	5,000 to 10,000	10,000 to 25,000	25,000 to 50,000	50,000 to 100,000	100,000 to 250,000	250,000 to 500,000	500,000 to 2,500,000	2,500,000 and over
Number of Enterprises 1	101276	16532	75511	3937	3880	635	458	121	69	61	30	31	10
Revenues ($ in Thousands)													
Net Sales 2	220894499	2337401	54205734	9338076	21807144	9736085	13725476	7448582	6552632	11905348	12279994	26005852	45552177
Interest 3	330809	2021	2653	5519	8796	5695	15520	5197	11795	13709	82097	89467	88338
Rents 4	192404	716	257	11759	6401	9987	509	9691	4180	8552	43169	7946	89237
Royalties 5	116353	34	0	1100	2096	1135	0	684	4273	8216	10726	47324	40765
Other Portfolio Income 6	883824	142687	3304	2286	99200	54225	16418	11192	33851	35256	60786	105661	318955
Other Receipts 7	2223123	35656	178655	122266	318243	138093	167236	99604	53750	146084	146617	260731	556191
Total Receipts 8	224641012	2518515	54390603	9481006	22241880	9945220	13925159	7574950	6660481	12117165	12623389	26516981	46645663
Average Total Receipts 9	2218	152	720	2408	5732	15662	30404	62603	96529	198642	420780	855386	4664566
Operating Costs/Operating Income (%)													
Cost of Operations 10	46.6	23.0	35.2	26.3	34.4	31.7	34.2	37.9	53.4	47.9	51.3	51.8	74.1
Salaries and Wages 11	18.6	19.9	18.2	19.5	24.1	29.0	26.2	25.2	17.6	19.0	17.4	15.4	12.6
Taxes Paid 12	2.8	2.5	3.2	3.4	3.7	3.9	3.8	3.3	2.9	2.7	2.5	2.0	1.7
Interest Paid 13	0.8	3.1	0.4	0.5	0.5	0.5	0.5	0.4	0.8	0.7	1.8	2.2	0.5
Depreciation 14	1.6	3.3	0.7	1.1	1.5	1.7	2.0	1.9	2.0	1.9	3.6	2.5	1.2
Amortization and Depletion 15	0.4	0.1	0.0	0.1	0.1	0.3	0.2	0.4	0.7	0.5	0.9	1.2	0.7
Pensions and Other Deferred Comp. 16	1.0	0.9	0.8	1.7	1.2	1.3	1.4	1.3	1.0	1.1	1.4	0.6	0.9
Employee Benefits 17	2.4	2.1	1.7	2.0	2.1	3.1	3.2	2.9	2.3	3.0	2.9	2.0	2.7
Advertising 18	0.3	0.6	0.4	0.1	0.4	0.3	0.3	0.4	0.3	0.2	0.2	0.2	0.0
Other Expenses 19	16.9	32.9	20.6	28.8	19.9	21.6	21.0	21.1	16.7	18.4	14.7	18.8	3.8
Officers' Compensation 20	6.3	8.1	15.4	10.3	7.9	5.5	4.7	3.3	2.6	2.3	1.7	1.3	0.8
Operating Margin 21	2.5	3.4	3.4	6.0	4.1	1.2	2.6	2.1	•	2.3	1.6	2.1	1.0
Operating Margin Before Officers' Comp. 22	8.8	11.5	18.7	16.4	12.0	6.7	7.3	5.3	2.3	4.7	3.3	3.3	1.7

Selected Average Balance Sheet ($ in Thousands)

Net Receivables 23	320	7	201	689	2115	5436	11263	21269	39558	86857	239311	931386
Inventories 24	39	1	16	147	425	618	1467	1942	6068	9699	18167	116636
Net Property, Plant and Equipment 25	140	19	109	481	1322	2384	5244	7496	17635	30831	92132	246024
Total Assets 26	1361	65	663	2384	7199	15263	36108	67062	153941	357177	980632	5001163
Notes and Loans Payable 27	317	57	293	664	1770	2905	7562	16187	38161	77846	270428	650423
All Other Liabilities 28	510	19	201	648	2087	5325	14183	27968	61936	129253	372571	2029823
Net Worth 29	534	-11	169	1072	3343	7034	14363	22906	53844	150078	337633	2320916

Selected Financial Ratios (Times to 1)

Current Ratio 30	1.5	•	1.2	1.8	2.0	1.9	1.6	1.6	1.3	1.5	1.5	1.4
Quick Ratio 31	1.1	•	1.0	1.5	1.6	1.5	1.3	1.3	0.9	1.2	1.2	0.8
Net Sales to Working Capital 32	9.3	•	123.9	12.2	6.3	6.2	7.0	5.9	9.7	7.3	5.7	7.2
Coverage Ratio 33	6.4	4.6	9.9	17.1	7.6	9.5	10.0	2.7	7.4	3.6	2.9	8.8
Total Asset Turnover 34	1.6	•	11.1	3.6	2.1	2.0	1.7	1.4	1.3	1.1	0.9	0.9
Inventory Turnover 35	26.1	•	335.1	39.6	11.4	16.6	15.9	26.1	15.4	21.6	23.9	28.9
Receivables Turnover 36	7.2	•	93.6	12.6	6.2	5.7	5.3	4.7	5.1	5.4	4.0	5.3
Total Liabilities to Net Worth 37	1.5	•	•	2.9	1.2	1.2	1.5	1.9	1.9	1.4	1.9	1.2
Current Assets to Working Capital 38	3.0	•	5.8	2.3	2.0	2.1	2.7	2.6	4.0	2.9	2.9	3.8
Current Liabilities to Working Capital 39	2.0	•	4.8	1.3	1.0	1.1	1.7	1.6	3.0	1.9	1.9	2.8
Working Capital to Net Sales 40	0.1	•	0.0	0.1	0.2	0.2	0.1	0.2	0.1	0.1	0.2	0.1
Inventory to Working Capital 41	0.2	•	0.1	0.1	0.1	0.1	0.2	0.1	0.3	0.2	0.2	0.1
Total Receipts to Cash Flow 42	5.9	2.9	4.9	3.1	5.0	4.8	4.8	7.0	5.4	6.5	5.1	38.7
Cost of Goods to Cash Flow 43	2.8	0.7	1.7	0.8	1.6	1.6	1.8	3.7	2.6	3.4	2.6	28.7
Cash Flow to Total Debt 44	0.4	•	1.9	1.6	0.9	0.8	0.6	0.3	0.4	0.3		0.0

Selected Financial Factors (in Percentages)

Debt Ratio 45	60.7	•	116.8	74.6	53.6	53.9	60.2	65.8	65.0	58.0	65.6	53.6
Return on Total Assets 46	8.2	•	45.8	28.7	8.2	9.0	7.4	3.1	6.9	7.4	5.3	3.9
Return on Equity Before Income Taxes 47	17.5	•	•	106.4	15.4	17.5	16.7	5.7	17.1	12.7	10.0	7.5
Return on Equity After Income Taxes 48	14.5	•	•	102.0	12.4	14.6	12.4	2.1	12.8	7.9	7.4	5.2
Profit Margin (Before Income Tax) 49	4.3	11.2	3.7	7.6	3.4	4.1	3.9	1.4	4.7	4.7	4.0	3.8
Profit Margin (After Income Tax) 50	3.6	9.5	3.7	7.3	2.7	3.4	2.9	0.5	3.5	2.9	3.0	2.6

ARCHITECTURAL, ENGINEERING, AND RELATED SERVICES

Table II
Corporations with Net Income

MONEY AMOUNTS AND SIZE OF ASSETS IN THOUSANDS OF DOLLARS

Item Description for Accounting Period 7/10 Through 6/11	Total	Zero Assets	Under 500	500 to 1,000	1,000 to 5,000	5,000 to 10,000	10,000 to 25,000	25,000 to 50,000	50,000 to 100,000	100,000 to 250,000	250,000 to 500,000	500,000 to 2,500,000	2,500,000 and over
Number of Enterprises **1**	66136	9729	49808	2689	2910	429	327	93	49	50	•	22	•
Revenues ($ in Thousands)													
Net Sales **2**	185793543	1888066	44252359	6657027	17297042	6886623	10395834	6481280	5175387	10313127	•	21420318	•
Interest **3**	222003	1105	1553	3194	3650	2982	7299	3746	9627	9142	•	71103	•
Rents **4**	156591	85	257	1599	6008	2964	260	9666	2950	6821	•	7151	•
Royalties **5**	82473	5	0	0	2096	40	0	11	259	8204	•	43606	•
Other Portfolio Income **6**	614175	23403	1102	1293	8346	49604	12338	10066	33584	34706	•	94876	•
Other Receipts **7**	1919295	30123	101222	88913	270745	132718	152849	85626	37492	144787	•	257831	•
Total Receipts **8**	18788080	1942787	44356493	6752026	17587887	7074931	10568580	6590395	5259299	10516787	•	21894885	•
Average Total Receipts **9**	2855	200	891	2511	6044	16492	32320	70864	107333	210336	•	995222	•
Operating Costs/Operating Income (%)													
Cost of Operations **10**	48.6	24.6	37.9	21.6	34.6	34.7	36.5	37.0	50.1	45.9	•	52.0	•
Salaries and Wages **11**	17.4	9.2	16.6	18.3	21.8	24.6	24.0	24.5	17.9	19.3	•	16.2	•
Taxes Paid **12**	2.7	1.8	3.0	3.2	3.6	3.7	3.9	3.3	2.9	2.8	•	2.0	•
Interest Paid **13**	0.5	1.6	0.3	0.4	0.3	0.3	0.3	0.4	0.7	0.6	•	1.4	•
Depreciation **14**	1.2	3.2	0.5	0.9	1.3	1.4	1.8	1.8	1.5	1.5	•	1.5	•
Amortization and Depletion **15**	0.3	0.0	0.0	0.1	0.1	0.0	0.1	0.2	0.3	0.4	•	0.9	•
Pensions and Other Deferred Comp. **16**	1.1	1.1	0.8	1.9	1.4	1.5	1.5	1.4	1.1	1.2	•	0.7	•
Employee Benefits **17**	2.2	1.6	1.3	1.5	2.1	3.1	3.1	3.0	2.3	3.1	•	1.9	•
Advertising **18**	0.2	0.5	0.3	0.1	0.4	0.3	0.3	0.3	0.3	0.2	•	0.2	•
Other Expenses **19**	14.8	28.1	18.2	30.5	17.3	16.9	17.8	20.1	16.0	18.8	•	17.8	•
Officers' Compensation **20**	6.1	6.9	15.3	10.4	8.5	6.2	4.7	3.4	2.5	2.6	•	1.4	•
Operating Margin **21**	4.9	21.5	5.7	11.1	8.6	7.2	6.0	4.7	4.3	3.6	•	4.1	•
Operating Margin Before Officers' Comp. **22**	11.1	28.3	21.0	21.5	17.2	13.4	10.7	8.1	6.9	6.1	•	5.4	•

Selected Average Balance Sheet ($ in Thousands)

Net Receivables 23	412	0	7	202	725	2364	6098	12507	24123	37514	•	278643
Inventories 24	46	0	0	170	421	530	1076	1844	6328		•	13093
Net Property, Plant and Equipment 25	145	0	20	110	476	809	2146	5422	5603	15417	•	60045
Total Assets 26	1629	0	69	678	2350	7403	15582	36620	66634	154676	•	993159
Notes and Loans Payable 27	283	0	49	249	376	995	2552	6351	13388	35635	•	224755
All Other Liabilities 28	646	0	18	188	594	2126	5023	15085	29357	58905	•	434215
Net Worth 29	699	0	2	241	1381	4282	8007	15184	23889	60137	•	334189

Selected Financial Ratios (Times to 1)

Current Ratio 30	1.5	•	1.4	2.1	2.4	2.1	2.0	1.7	1.6	1.4	•	1.4
Quick Ratio 31	1.1	•	1.3	1.9	1.9	1.7	1.7	1.4	1.3	0.9	•	1.1
Net Sales to Working Capital 32	8.8	•	75.6	10.0	6.3	5.4	5.7	6.6	6.1	9.1	•	6.9
Coverage Ratio 33	14.7	16.4	19.9	34.1	32.4	33.1	27.6	19.0	9.2	11.7	•	5.7
Total Asset Turnover 34	1.7	•	12.9	3.6	2.5	2.2	2.0	1.9	1.6	1.3	•	1.0
Inventory Turnover 35	29.6	•	1315.5	121.3	12.1	13.2	21.9	23.9	28.7	15.0	•	38.7
Receivables Turnover 36	7.2	•	134.9	13.1	7.5	5.6	5.5	5.9	4.6	5.5	•	4.2
Total Liabilities to Net Worth 37	1.3	•	33.2	1.8	0.7	0.7	0.9	1.4	1.8	1.6	•	2.0
Current Assets to Working Capital 38	2.9	•	3.4	1.9	1.7	1.9	2.0	2.4	2.7	3.7	•	3.4
Current Liabilities to Working Capital 39	1.9	•	2.4	0.9	0.7	0.9	1.0	1.4	1.7	2.7	•	2.4
Working Capital to Net Sales 40	0.1	•	0.0	0.1	0.2	0.2	0.2	0.2	0.2	0.1	•	0.1
Inventory to Working Capital 41	0.1	•	0.0	0.0	0.2	0.1	0.1	0.1	0.1	0.3	•	0.1
Total Receipts to Cash Flow 42	5.6	2.1	4.7	2.5	4.2	4.5	4.6	4.4	5.3	4.9	•	4.8
Cost of Goods to Cash Flow 43	2.7	0.5	1.8	0.5	1.5	1.5	1.7	1.6	2.7	2.3	•	2.5
Cash Flow to Total Debt 44	0.5	•	2.8	2.3	1.5	1.2	0.9	0.7	0.5	0.4	•	0.3

Selected Financial Factors (in Percentages)

Debt Ratio 45	57.1	•	97.1	64.5	41.2	42.2	48.6	58.5	64.1	61.1	•	66.4
Return on Total Assets 46	12.4	•	80.5	47.0	26.9	22.2	16.4	12.9	10.8	9.1	•	7.5
Return on Equity Before Income Taxes 47	26.9	•	2611.2	128.7	44.4	37.2	30.7	29.5	26.9	21.4	•	18.3
Return on Equity After Income Taxes 48	23.3	•	2590.1	124.2	42.5	33.7	27.0	24.2	22.0	16.7	•	14.6
Profit Margin (Before Income Tax) 49	6.7	24.4	5.9	12.5	10.3	9.9	7.7	6.4	6.1	6.2	•	6.3
Profit Margin (After Income Tax) 50	5.8	22.3	5.9	12.1	9.9	9.0	6.8	5.3	5.0	4.9	•	5.0

Table I
Corporations with and without Net Income

SPECIALIZED DESIGN SERVICES

MONEY AMOUNTS AND SIZE OF ASSETS IN THOUSANDS OF DOLLARS

Item Description for Accounting Period 7/10 Through 6/11	Total	Zero Assets	Under 500	500 to 1,000	1,000 to 5,000	5,000 to 10,000	10,000 to 25,000	25,000 to 50,000	50,000 to 100,000	100,000 to 250,000	250,000 to 500,000	500,000 to 2,500,000	2,500,000 and over
Number of Enterprises 1	38698	8580	29255	477	288	62	19	15	0	3	0	0	0
Revenues ($ in Thousands)													
Net Sales 2	15516095	590525	10263199	626852	1287521	421142	396068	644473	0	1286314	0	0	0
Interest 3	3670	1	2168	230	679	65	0	330	0	197	0	0	0
Rents 4	73	0	73	0	1	0	0	0	0	0	0	0	0
Royalties 5	0	0	0	0	0	0	0	0	0	0	0	0	0
Other Portfolio Income 6	13927	2910	8947	0	491	1	124	1454	0	0	0	0	0
Other Receipts 7	108953	9909	85596	-184	5968	2931	2378	824	0	1530	0	0	0
Total Receipts 8	15642718	603345	10359983	626898	1294660	424139	398570	647081	0	1288041	0	0	0
Average Total Receipts 9	404	70	354	1314	4495	6841	20977	43139	•	429347	•	•	•
Operating Costs/Operating Income (%)													
Cost of Operations 10	37.3	21.3	39.7	55.1	34.0	61.0	63.7	44.7	•	0.2	•	•	•
Salaries and Wages 11	13.8	2.6	10.9	11.9	19.5	9.7	13.0	16.9	•	36.7	•	•	•
Taxes Paid 12	2.5	3.8	2.3	2.7	2.2	2.5	1.2	2.0	•	3.7	•	•	•
Interest Paid 13	0.5	0.2	0.5	0.9	0.3	0.3	0.2	0.4	•	1.0	•	•	•
Depreciation 14	1.2	3.6	0.8	0.5	1.2	1.6	0.3	2.7	•	3.0	•	•	•
Amortization and Depletion 15	0.1	0.0	0.1	0.3	0.2	0.3	•	0.9	•	0.3	•	•	•
Pensions and Other Deferred Comp. 16	0.4	0.7	0.4	0.1	0.8	0.3	0.4	0.6	•	0.3	•	•	•
Employee Benefits 17	1.2	0.1	0.8	0.0	1.7	1.8	0.7	2.5	•	4.7	•	•	•
Advertising 18	0.8	0.5	0.8	2.3	1.4	0.4	0.7	0.1	•	0.2	•	•	•
Other Expenses 19	28.4	49.3	26.2	28.7	31.0	11.2	12.1	18.8	•	49.1	•	•	•
Officers' Compensation 20	8.2	15.2	9.5	6.7	7.8	5.4	1.5	3.2	•	1.3	•	•	•
Operating Margin 21	5.7	2.7	8.1	•	0.0	5.6	6.4	7.3	•	•	•	•	•
Operating Margin Before Officers' Comp. 22	13.8	17.9	17.5	•	7.8	11.1	7.8	10.5	•	0.8	•	•	•

Selected Average Balance Sheet ($ in Thousands)

Net Receivables 23	18	0	7	242	158	561	3670	7408	41607
Inventories 24	14	0	4	234	145	762	3188	5033	25907
Net Property, Plant and Equipment 25	37	0	14	74	207	342	913	3177	281458
Total Assets 26	142	0	66	698	1564	8638	14043	32492	498673
Notes and Loans Payable 27	60	0	48	929	852	510	2580	2410	37931
All Other Liabilities 28	67	0	19	395	449	6623	3285	17310	327089
Net Worth 29	15	0	-1	-626	262	1505	8178	12773	133653

Selected Financial Ratios (Times to 1)

Current Ratio 30	1.5	•	1.7	1.6	0.9	1.2	2.6	1.5	1.3
Quick Ratio 31	1.1	•	1.5	1.1	0.6	0.7	2.0	0.8	0.7
Net Sales to Working Capital 32	17.7	•	23.0	6.0	•	15.6	4.3	5.0	14.2
Coverage Ratio 33	13.5	22.5	18.6	•	2.9	25.1	45.5	19.3	0.6
Total Asset Turnover 34	2.8	•	5.3	1.9	2.9	0.8	1.5	1.3	0.9
Inventory Turnover 35	11.0	•	36.6	3.1	10.4	5.4	4.2	3.8	0.0
Receivables Turnover 36	20.5	•	40.4	6.4	18.4	9.1	5.9	6.7	10.3
Total Liabilities to Net Worth 37	8.3	•	•	•	5.0	4.7	0.7	1.5	2.7
Current Assets to Working Capital 38	3.0	•	2.4	2.8	•	5.7	1.6	2.8	4.8
Current Liabilities to Working Capital 39	2.0	•	1.4	1.8	•	4.7	0.6	1.8	3.8
Working Capital to Net Sales 40	0.1	•	0.0	0.2	•	0.1	0.2	0.2	0.1
Inventory to Working Capital 41	0.5	•	0.2	0.8	•	1.6	0.1	1.0	0.8
Total Receipts to Cash Flow 42	3.4	2.0	3.4	15.3	3.5	6.7	5.9	4.6	2.4
Cost of Goods to Cash Flow 43	1.3	0.4	1.3	8.4	1.2	4.1	3.8	2.1	0.0
Cash Flow to Total Debt 44	0.9	•	1.6	0.1	1.0	0.1	0.6	0.5	0.5

Selected Financial Factors (in Percentages)

Debt Ratio 45	89.2	•	101.3	189.6	83.3	82.6	41.8	60.7	73.2
Return on Total Assets 46	19.7	•	50.6	•	2.5	5.2	10.6	10.7	0.5
Return on Equity Before Income Taxes 47	169.1	•	•	19.2	9.8	28.7	17.7	25.9	•
Return on Equity After Income Taxes 48	166.7	•	•	19.3	9.3	24.2	17.7	23.8	•
Profit Margin (Before Income Tax) 49	6.5	4.8	9.0	•	0.6	6.4	7.0	7.7	•
Profit Margin (After Income Tax) 50	6.4	4.5	9.0	•	0.5	5.4	7.0	7.1	•

Table II

Corporations with Net Income

SPECIALIZED DESIGN SERVICES

MONEY AMOUNTS AND SIZE OF ASSETS IN THOUSANDS OF DOLLARS

Item Description for Accounting Period 7/10 Through 6/11	Total	Zero Assets	Under 500	500 to 1,000	1,000 to 5,000	5,000 to 10,000	10,000 to 25,000	25,000 to 50,000	50,000 to 100,000	100,000 to 250,000	250,000 to 500,000	500,000 to 2,500,000	2,500,000 and over
Number of Enterprises 1	25240	4890	19856	306	147	•	14	•	0	0	0	0	0
Revenues ($ in Thousands)													
Net Sales 2	13178149	341425	9050207	442968	1006942	•	396068	•	0	0	0	0	0
Interest 3	2183	0	1783	228	129	•	0	•	0	0	0	0	0
Rents 4	1	0	0	0	1	•	0	•	0	0	0	0	0
Royalties 5	0	0	0	0	0	•	0	•	0	0	0	0	0
Other Portfolio Income 6	872	0	445	0	334	•	0	•	0	0	0	0	•
Other Receipts 7	100645	9909	81613	6	2388	•	2381	•	0	0	0	0	0
Total Receipts 8	13281850	351334	9134048	443202	1009794	•	398449	•	0	0	0	0	•
Average Total Receipts 9	526	72	460	1448	6869	•	28461	•					
Operating Costs/Operating Income (%)													
Cost of Operations 10	35.8	4.7	38.6	58.7	37.2	•	63.7	•	•	•	•	•	•
Salaries and Wages 11	12.8	1.3	9.6	5.9	15.4	•	12.4	•	•	•	•	•	•
Taxes Paid 12	2.3	5.3	2.1	2.7	1.8	•	1.1	•	•	•	•	•	•
Interest Paid 13	0.4	0.1	0.4	0.7	0.1	•	0.1	•	•	•	•	•	•
Depreciation 14	0.9	1.6	0.7	0.3	0.5	•	0.3	•	•	•	•	•	•
Amortization and Depletion 15	0.1	•	0.0	0.4	0.1	•	•	•	•	•	•	•	•
Pensions and Other Deferred Comp. 16	0.4	1.2	0.4	0.1	0.4	•	0.4	•	•	•	•	•	•
Employee Benefits 17	1.2	•	0.6	0.1	1.5	•	0.7	•	•	•	•	•	•
Advertising 18	0.7	0.8	0.8	0.0	1.6	•	0.7	•	•	•	•	•	•
Other Expenses 19	27.7	43.8	26.4	19.5	32.1	•	11.9	•	•	•	•	•	•
Officers' Compensation 20	7.8	18.1	9.0	9.5	6.3	•	1.2	•	•	•	•	•	•
Operating Margin 21	9.9	23.1	11.4	2.0	3.0	•	7.6	•	•	•	•	•	•
Operating Margin Before Officers' Comp. 22	17.7	41.2	20.4	11.5	9.4	•	8.7	•	•	•	•	•	•

Selected Average Balance Sheet ($ in Thousands)

Net Receivables 23	18	0	6	313	178	4042
Inventories 24	12	0	3	76	267	4321
Net Property, Plant and Equipment 25	23	0	16	22	115	1232
Total Assets 26	124	0	76	638	1498	13657
Notes and Loans Payable 27	44	0	43	54	879	3501
All Other Liabilities 28	35	0	17	255	395	3785
Net Worth 29	44	0	16	328	225	6371

Selected Financial Ratios (Times to 1)

Current Ratio 30	1.9	•	2.5	2.4	0.6	2.2
Quick Ratio 31	1.4	•	2.2	2.3	0.3	1.8
Net Sales to Working Capital 32	15.5	•	17.9	4.1	•	6.0
Coverage Ratio 33	26.7	323.0	33.1	3.9	31.5	60.8
Total Asset Turnover 34	4.2	•	6.0	2.3	4.6	2.1
Inventory Turnover 35	15.1	•	53.8	11.2	9.6	4.2
Receivables Turnover 36	25.7	•	54.7	5.6	19.1	8.7
Total Liabilities to Net Worth 37	1.8	•	3.8	0.9	5.7	1.1
Current Assets to Working Capital 38	2.1	•	1.7	1.7	•	1.8
Current Liabilities to Working Capital 39	1.1	•	0.7	0.7	•	0.8
Working Capital to Net Sales 40	0.1	•	0.1	0.2	•	0.2
Inventory to Working Capital 41	0.3	•	0.1	0.0	•	0.2
Total Receipts to Cash Flow 42	3.0	1.5	3.0	6.3	2.9	5.6
Cost of Goods to Cash Flow 43	1.1	0.1	1.2	3.7	1.1	3.6
Cash Flow to Total Debt 44	2.2	•	2.5	0.7	1.9	0.7

Selected Financial Factors (in Percentages)

Debt Ratio 45	64.2	•	79.1	48.6	85.0	53.4
Return on Total Assets 46	46.5	•	76.2	6.2	15.7	17.2
Return on Equity Before Income Taxes 47	125.1	•	353.1	9.0	100.9	36.2
Return on Equity After Income Taxes 48	123.8	•	352.0	8.8	99.8	36.2
Profit Margin (Before Income Tax) 49	10.6	26.0	12.3	2.0	3.3	8.2
Profit Margin (After Income Tax) 50	10.5	25.5	12.2	2.0	3.3	8.2

338

Table I

Corporations with and without Net Income

COMPUTER SYSTEMS DESIGN AND RELATED SERVICES

MONEY AMOUNTS AND SIZE OF ASSETS IN THOUSANDS OF DOLLARS

Item Description for Accounting Period 7/10 Through 6/11	Total	Zero Assets	Under 500	500 to 1,000	1,000 to 5,000	5,000 to 10,000	10,000 to 25,000	25,000 to 50,000	50,000 to 100,000	100,000 to 250,000	250,000 to 500,000	500,000 to 2,500,000	2,500,000 and over
Number of Enterprises **1**	142528	31201	99739	3987	5373	811	783	277	163	103	33	46	11
Revenues ($ in Thousands)													
Net Sales **2**	234271284	11276509	35874038	7087993	29687691	12217129	19234907	11363309	13150963	12990952	7623619	36401619	37362556
Interest **3**	765264	14394	5857	5777	25446	8953	14630	17307	20254	35303	25570	111314	480459
Rents **4**	75945	2	33005	17	2199	308	3152	1234	8519	9707	2916	11756	3130
Royalties **5**	972246	2289	11	1165	16159	9	20043	57092	70737	38663	113821	146122	506135
Other Portfolio Income **6**	2245100	257333	54287	46830	130856	18013	190026	91554	64013	68260	33535	818894	471499
Other Receipts **7**	2887944	113175	326605	29943	368871	129861	152665	117487	315388	226667	191108	362603	553572
Total Receipts **8**	241217783	11663702	36293803	7171725	30231222	12374273	19615423	11647983	13629874	13369552	7990569	37852308	39377351
Average Total Receipts **9**	1692	374	364	1799	5627	15258	25052	42050	83619	129801	242138	822876	3579759
Operating Costs/Operating Income (%)													
Cost of Operations **10**	30.4	21.2	26.8	25.0	37.4	47.7	38.4	39.8	42.2	38.1	31.1	37.6	5.8
Salaries and Wages **11**	25.1	34.8	19.0	30.2	27.7	21.4	25.9	25.0	23.7	25.3	29.3	18.7	32.0
Taxes Paid **12**	3.6	3.9	3.2	3.7	3.3	2.5	3.2	2.8	2.9	2.5	2.5	2.2	7.1
Interest Paid **13**	1.8	1.4	0.5	1.1	0.8	0.4	0.7	1.0	0.9	1.1	1.9	2.9	4.9
Depreciation **14**	1.8	1.1	0.8	1.3	1.2	1.0	1.6	2.0	1.8	2.2	2.6	2.3	2.8
Amortization and Depletion **15**	1.3	1.0	0.2	0.4	0.4	0.4	1.2	1.2	1.2	1.6	3.0	2.4	2.1
Pensions and Other Deferred Comp. **16**	0.8	0.3	1.1	0.5	0.5	0.8	0.7	0.3	0.3	0.4	0.5	0.9	1.2
Employee Benefits **17**	2.5	1.4	1.4	2.1	2.4	2.2	2.3	2.6	1.8	2.3	2.6	3.2	4.0
Advertising **18**	0.9	0.5	0.5	0.6	0.9	0.9	1.9	1.6	0.8	3.1	0.7	0.4	0.3
Other Expenses **19**	26.8	28.0	29.3	31.1	20.5	17.9	21.9	23.4	22.8	20.9	25.7	24.7	40.2
Officers' Compensation **20**	4.7	6.3	14.7	7.2	6.2	4.1	3.1	2.8	2.1	1.9	1.9	0.9	0.6
Operating Margin **21**	0.4	0.1	2.7	•	•	0.5	•	•	•	0.6	•	3.7	•
Operating Margin Before Officers' Comp. **22**	5.0	6.4	17.4	4.0	4.9	4.6	2.3	0.3	1.6	2.5	0.0	4.6	•

Selected Average Balance Sheet ($ in Thousands)

Item													
Net Receivables 23	426	0	11	186	744	2625	4950	9474	16994	31497	53753	163272	2811601
Inventories 24	13	0	2	25	44	180	333	622	869	1152	4484	6689	5710
Net Property, Plant and Equipment 25	94	0	9	51	180	364	1072	1951	3656	5667	17615	75988	400973
Total Assets 26	1649	60	727	2213	7114	15378	34208	69799	160728	328388	1116341	8799794	
Notes and Loans Payable 27	452	44	451	880	1092	3213	6999	12616	26381	76038	258295	2632478	
All Other Liabilities 28	632	27	315	874	3379	7633	17348	29021	56959	121007	320183	3515500	
Net Worth 29	565	-11	-40	459	2643	4531	9861	28162	77387	131343	537862	2651816	

Selected Financial Ratios (Times to 1)

Item													
Current Ratio 30	1.2	•	1.3	1.4	1.7	1.6	1.4	1.3	1.4	1.4	1.3	1.6	0.9
Quick Ratio 31	1.0	•	1.1	1.2	1.4	1.4	1.2	1.1	1.1	1.1	1.0	1.3	0.9
Net Sales to Working Capital 32	12.7	•	12.0	8.7	7.2	7.7	9.1	6.8	5.7	8.6	6.2		
Coverage Ratio 33	3.0	3.6	•	1.5	5.3	2.7	1.2	4.7	4.3	2.8	3.7	2.2	
Total Asset Turnover 34	1.0	•	2.4	2.5	2.1	1.6	1.2	1.2	0.8	0.7	0.7	0.4	
Inventory Turnover 35	37.7	•	17.6	47.1	40.1	28.3	26.3	39.2	41.7	16.0	44.4	34.2	
Receivables Turnover 36	4.0	•	10.8	7.0	6.0	5.2	4.3	5.0	4.3	4.1	5.4	1.2	
Total Liabilities to Net Worth 37	1.9	•	•	3.8	1.7	2.4	2.5	1.5	1.1	1.5	1.1	2.3	
Current Assets to Working Capital 38	5.7	4.4	3.5	2.5	2.6	3.4	4.5	3.2	3.3	4.9	2.7		
Current Liabilities to Working Capital 39	4.7	3.4	2.5	1.5	1.6	2.4	3.5	2.2	2.3	3.9	1.7		
Working Capital to Net Sales 40	0.1	0.0	0.1	0.1	0.1	0.1	0.1	0.2	0.2	0.1	0.2	•	
Inventory to Working Capital 41	0.1	0.2	0.2	0.1	0.1	0.1	0.1	0.1	0.1	0.1	0.1	•	
Total Receipts to Cash Flow 42	3.8	3.4	4.1	5.6	5.8	4.9	5.0	4.3	4.6	4.2	3.7	2.5	
Cost of Goods to Cash Flow 43	1.2	0.8	0.9	1.0	2.1	2.8	1.9	1.9	1.8	1.8	1.3	1.4	0.1
Cash Flow to Total Debt 44	0.4	•	1.5	0.6	0.6	0.5	0.3	0.3	0.5	0.3	0.3	0.4	0.2

Selected Financial Factors (in Percentages)

Item													
Debt Ratio 45	65.8	•	117.5	105.5	79.3	62.8	70.5	71.2	59.7	51.9	60.0	51.8	69.9
Return on Total Assets 46	5.4	25.8	3.2	4.7	3.0	1.5	4.9	3.8	3.9	7.7	4.2		
Return on Equity Before Income Taxes 47	10.6	•	89.1	5.5	10.2	6.3	0.8	9.6	6.1	6.3	11.6	7.6	
Return on Equity After Income Taxes 48	7.4	•	97.3	1.7	5.7	2.1	•	6.6	4.6	3.7	8.3	4.8	
Profit Margin (Before Income Tax) 49	3.6	3.9	•	0.5	1.8	1.2	0.2	3.3	3.7	3.6	7.9	5.9	
Profit Margin (After Income Tax) 50	2.5	3.8	•	0.1	1.0	0.4	•	2.3	2.8	2.1	5.7	3.8	

Table II

Corporations with Net Income

COMPUTER SYSTEMS DESIGN AND RELATED SERVICES

MONEY AMOUNTS AND SIZE OF ASSETS IN THOUSANDS OF DOLLARS

Item Description for Accounting Period 7/10 Through 6/11		Total	Zero Assets	Under 500	500 to 1,000	1,000 to 5,000	5,000 to 10,000	10,000 to 25,000	25,000 to 50,000	50,000 to 100,000	100,000 to 250,000	250,000 to 500,000	500,000 to 2,500,000	2,500,000 and over
Number of Enterprises	1	82633	16354	59187	2279	3438	521	461	•	102	72	22	37	•
Revenues ($ in Thousands)														
Net Sales	2	187272543	9065372	26097545	4949719	24160149	9619207	13943153	•	10588640	10461710	4430887	32271457	•
Interest	3	263264	5408	4563	3256	11661	4062	6628	•	8590	21758	19536	102550	•
Rents	4	38674	2	1157	17	1793	277	578	•	7733	9482	2573	10941	•
Royalties	5	765681	1563	0	1089	0	9	363	•	65386	25971	87798	146122	•
Other Portfolio Income	6	2096236	247961	53630	34922	99131	1362	185717	•	49131	66926	27637	818481	•
Other Receipts	7	2116808	87186	373638	29996	161103	112933	86235	•	291017	109492	52130	360708	•
Total Receipts	8	192553206	9407492	26530533	5018999	24433837	9737850	14222674	•	11010497	10695339	4620561	33710259	•
Average Total Receipts	9	2330	575	448	2202	7107	18691	30852	•	107946	148546	210026	911088	•
Operating Costs/Operating Income (%)														
Cost of Operations	10	29.2	21.4	23.4	25.5	38.8	51.7	41.3	•	46.2	38.6	15.8	35.7	•
Salaries and Wages	11	24.1	32.7	19.0	28.0	24.1	17.8	21.3	•	20.7	24.1	33.8	19.2	•
Taxes Paid	12	3.6	3.9	3.0	3.7	3.0	2.3	3.0	•	2.7	2.3	3.1	2.1	•
Interest Paid	13	1.4	0.3	0.2	0.7	0.5	0.2	0.4	•	0.5	1.0	1.6	2.5	•
Depreciation	14	1.6	0.5	0.7	1.0	0.8	0.7	1.2	•	1.6	2.1	2.4	2.3	•
Amortization and Depletion	15	1.0	0.5	0.0	0.1	0.2	0.1	0.7	•	0.6	1.2	3.3	1.9	•
Pensions and Other Deferred Comp.	16	0.8	0.2	1.0	0.3	0.6	0.9	0.9	•	0.2	0.3	0.6	0.8	•
Employee Benefits	17	2.5	1.3	1.3	1.6	2.2	2.0	1.9	•	1.5	2.1	3.0	3.1	•
Advertising	18	0.6	0.3	0.4	0.5	0.6	0.6	0.9	•	0.6	2.5	0.8	0.5	•
Other Expenses	19	24.6	23.9	25.5	25.3	16.0	11.0	18.1	•	19.6	19.0	29.0	26.1	•
Officers' Compensation	20	4.2	4.8	14.7	5.7	5.8	3.9	2.9	•	1.8	1.4	2.6	0.9	•
Operating Margin	21	6.3	10.0	10.6	7.5	7.7	8.7	7.4	•	3.8	5.3	4.0	4.9	•
Operating Margin Before Officers' Comp.	22	10.5	14.8	25.3	13.2	13.4	12.6	10.3	•	5.6	6.7	6.5	5.8	•

Selected Average Balance Sheet ($ in Thousands)

Net Receivables 23	540	0	9	235	848	3009	5818	•	19691	30289	49282	178288
Inventories 24	15	0	3	31	46	145	271	•	1181	840	3180	7408
Net Property, Plant and Equipment 25	131	0	10	65	168	379	982	•	3952	6622	12900	85531
Total Assets 26	2142	0	71	681	2224	6999	15516	•	70163	160620	334303	1137568
Notes and Loans Payable 27	467	0	27	207	745	757	2832	•	8039	24784	55530	219353
All Other Liabilities 28	861	0	14	244	722	3074	7292	•	29982	58183	104324	342034
Net Worth 29	814	0	29	230	758	3168	5392	•	32142	77652	174450	576180

Selected Financial Ratios (Times to 1)

Current Ratio 30	1.3	•	2.6	2.0	2.1	1.9	1.5	•	1.5	1.4	1.4	1.7
Quick Ratio 31	1.1	•	2.2	1.8	1.8	1.7	1.3	•	1.1	1.0	1.1	1.4
Net Sales to Working Capital 32	11.7	•	14.2	8.6	7.6	6.9	8.4	•	7.5	7.0	6.0	5.6
Coverage Ratio 33	7.5	50.5	51.4	13.9	20.4	40.7	23.8	•	18.4	8.5	6.6	4.8
Total Asset Turnover 34	1.1	•	6.3	3.2	3.2	2.6	1.9	•	1.5	0.9	0.6	0.8
Inventory Turnover 35	43.4	•	34.6	17.8	59.5	65.9	46.1	•	40.6	66.9	10.0	42.0
Receivables Turnover 36	4.1	•	48.8	10.4	7.4	7.4	5.6	•	•	5.4	3.3	5.4
Total Liabilities to Net Worth 37	1.6	•	1.4	2.0	1.9	1.2	1.9	•	1.2	1.1	0.9	1.0
Current Assets to Working Capital 38	4.8	•	1.6	2.0	1.9	2.1	3.1	•	3.0	3.5	3.5	2.5
Current Liabilities to Working Capital 39	3.8	•	0.6	1.0	0.9	1.1	2.1	•	2.0	2.5	1.5	
Working Capital to Net Sales 40	0.1	•	0.1	0.1	0.1	0.1	0.1	•	0.1	0.1	0.2	0.2
Inventory to Working Capital 41	0.1	•	0.1	0.0	0.0	0.1	0.1	•	0.1	0.1	0.1	0.0
Total Receipts to Cash Flow 42	3.3	2.9	2.9	3.3	4.6	5.3	4.1	•	4.0	4.2	3.2	3.3
Cost of Goods to Cash Flow 43	1.0	0.6	0.7	0.8	1.8	2.7	1.7	•	1.8	1.6	0.5	1.2
Cash Flow to Total Debt 44	0.5	•	3.7	1.4	1.1	0.9	0.7	•	0.7	0.4	0.4	0.5

Selected Financial Factors (in Percentages)

Debt Ratio 45	62.0	•	58.6	66.2	65.9	54.7	65.2	•	54.2	51.7	47.8	49.3
Return on Total Assets 46	11.5	•	78.3	30.5	29.2	26.8	19.2	•	12.5	8.0	6.5	9.3
Return on Equity Before Income Taxes 47	26.2	•	185.2	83.6	81.6	57.7	52.9	•	25.8	14.5	10.5	14.4
Return on Equity After Income Taxes 48	22.4	•	183.4	81.1	78.0	51.9	46.9	•	21.6	12.4	7.6	10.7
Profit Margin (Before Income Tax) 49	9.4	13.9	12.3	8.9	8.8	9.9	9.4	•	8.0	7.8	9.1	9.5
Profit Margin (After Income Tax) 50	8.0	12.1	12.2	8.6	8.4	8.9	8.4	•	6.7	6.6	6.6	7.1

Table I
Corporations with and without Net Income

MANAGEMENT, SCIENTIFIC, AND TECHNICAL CONSULTING SERVICES

MONEY AMOUNTS AND SIZE OF ASSETS IN THOUSANDS OF DOLLARS

Item Description for Accounting Period 7/10 Through 6/11	Total	Zero Assets	Under 500	500 to 1,000	1,000 to 5,000	5,000 to 10,000	10,000 to 25,000	25,000 to 50,000	50,000 to 100,000	100,000 to 250,000	250,000 to 500,000	500,000 to 2,500,000	2,500,000 and over
1 Number of Enterprises	227489	51280	162935	5983	5577	752	525	195	105	79	30	22	5
Revenues ($ in Thousands)													
2 Net Sales	196570250	6229113	49167002	19197184	23241126	8145720	12570785	7064369	6954311	9571730	8482814	17600763	28345332
3 Interest	295267	1335	9597	11853	20836	29554	14093	19361	21382	14795	33487	97395	21580
4 Rents	52791	303	2018	1170	3041	550	426	813	3185	16531	956	5994	17806
5 Royalties	191810	223	473	0	4	1563	1177	1442	8833	65831	40620	29450	42195
6 Other Portfolio Income	752977	31804	18847	21963	143454	13264	17572	33954	58671	53098	116352	137381	106615
7 Other Receipts	4232076	154327	780035	463181	399274	418446	331458	354680	202245	295217	180919	383317	268977
8 Total Receipts	202095171	6417105	49977972	19695351	23807735	8609097	12935511	7474619	7248627	10017202	8855148	18254300	28802505
9 Average Total Receipts	888	125	307	3292	4269	11448	24639	38331	69035	126800	295172	829741	5760501
Operating Costs/Operating Income (%)													
10 Cost of Operations	28.3	12.9	19.6	56.6	29.5	34.4	46.0	35.1	19.1	26.3	25.3	30.2	17.7
11 Salaries and Wages	25.5	24.0	18.3	16.1	22.7	27.0	21.5	24.9	38.8	29.6	31.7	25.9	41.5
12 Taxes Paid	3.0	3.4	3.0	1.7	2.9	3.3	2.9	2.7	3.6	2.9	3.2	3.4	3.8
13 Interest Paid	0.8	0.9	0.4	0.2	0.5	1.2	0.7	1.2	1.3	1.5	1.2	2.0	1.0
14 Depreciation	1.3	1.1	0.9	0.8	0.7	1.0	1.3	2.4	1.5	2.9	1.9	1.8	1.4
15 Amortization and Depletion	0.5	1.0	0.1	0.1	0.2	0.2	0.5	1.1	0.6	1.4	1.0	2.3	0.4
16 Pensions and Other Defered Comp.	1.5	2.0	1.4	0.7	1.3	1.2	0.7	0.9	1.0	1.1	1.0	1.4	3.1
17 Employee Benefits	1.9	3.8	1.7	0.6	1.7	1.9	2.0	2.3	2.1	2.8	2.3	2.4	1.6
18 Advertising	0.9	0.9	1.8	0.2	0.3	0.3	0.4	0.3	0.4	0.9	0.2	2.4	0.1
19 Other Expenses	24.3	35.7	28.1	15.1	25.3	20.9	17.7	20.2	28.7	28.2	26.0	24.1	23.0
20 Officers' Compensation	7.5	10.7	16.1	6.6	9.1	8.7	4.5	2.9	2.9	2.5	1.2	4.0	0.3
21 Operating Margin	4.5	3.7	8.7	1.2	5.7	0.0	1.7	6.1	2.9	•	5.1	0.2	6.1
22 Operating Margin Before Officers' Comp.	12.0	14.4	24.8	7.8	14.8	8.7	6.2	9.0	2.8	2.5	6.3	4.2	6.4

Selected Average Balance Sheet ($ in Thousands)

Net Receivables 23	125	0	4	108	559	2153	3891	8147	14039	34445	71731	244394	1414386
Inventories 24	10	0	1	22	24	68	308	540	1436	865	2337	44518	64457
Net Property, Plant and Equipment 25	50	0	10	175	284	684	1677	4368	6048	14801	24051	49937	237644
Total Assets 26	530	0	53	692	2180	7274	15346	35940	70252	157726	340032	1080838	4250819
Notes and Loans Payable 27	162	0	52	311	707	2167	4015	10710	18385	35401	58805	276677	828234
All Other Liabilities 28	182	0	15	161	586	2865	5645	12196	24028	50837	105221	390884	1796453
Net Worth 29	186	0	-14	220	887	2243	5686	13034	27839	71487	176006	413277	1626083

Selected Financial Ratios (Times to 1)

Current Ratio 30	1.6	•	1.8	2.0	2.2	1.4	1.5	1.5	1.4	1.6	1.7	1.4	1.7
Quick Ratio 31	1.3	•	1.5	1.6	1.8	1.2	1.1	1.1	1.0	1.2	1.3	1.0	1.6
Net Sales to Working Capital 32	8.3	•	22.3	17.8	5.7	9.5	9.3	6.2	7.5	4.3	4.6	5.7	5.8
Coverage Ratio 33	9.8	8.2	25.6	16.1	17.8	5.9	7.5	11.4	4.1	4.0	9.5	3.4	9.0
Total Asset Turnover 34	1.6	•	5.7	4.6	1.9	1.5	1.6	1.0	0.9	0.8	0.8	0.7	1.3
Inventory Turnover 35	24.0	•	67.4	84.3	51.8	54.4	35.8	23.6	8.8	36.8	30.6	5.4	15.6
Receivables Turnover 36	6.7	•	65.4	23.7	8.5	5.5	6.6	4.7	4.8	3.5	4.1	3.3	3.4
Total Liabilities to Net Worth 37	1.9	•	•	2.2	1.5	2.2	1.7	1.8	1.5	1.2	0.9	1.6	1.6
Current Assets to Working Capital 38	2.6	•	2.3	2.0	1.8	3.7	3.2	3.1	3.6	2.8	2.5	3.3	2.4
Current Liabilities to Working Capital 39	1.6	•	1.3	1.0	0.8	2.7	2.2	2.1	2.6	1.8	1.5	2.3	1.4
Working Capital to Net Sales 40	0.1	•	0.0	0.1	0.2	0.1	0.1	0.2	0.1	0.2	0.2	0.2	0.2
Inventory to Working Capital 41	0.1	•	0.1	0.1	0.0	0.0	0.1	0.1	0.1	0.0	0.0	0.3	0.1
Total Receipts to Cash Flow 42	3.6	2.5	2.9	6.3	3.6	4.2	5.4	3.5	3.5	3.4	3.2	4.1	3.6
Cost of Goods to Cash Flow 43	1.0	0.3	0.6	3.6	1.1	1.4	2.5	1.2	0.7	0.9	0.8	1.2	0.6
Cash Flow to Total Debt 44	0.7	•	1.6	1.1	0.9	0.5	0.5	0.5	0.4	0.4	0.5	0.3	0.6

Selected Financial Factors (in Percentages)

Debt Ratio 45	65.0	•	126.7	68.3	59.3	69.2	62.9	63.7	60.4	54.7	48.2	61.8	61.7
Return on Total Assets 46	13.5	61.0	•	18.7	16.3	10.2	8.3	13.2	5.2	4.8	9.2	5.2	11.7
Return on Equity Before Income Taxes 47	34.7	•	•	55.1	37.7	27.3	19.5	33.3	9.8	7.9	15.9	9.6	27.1
Return on Equity After Income Taxes 48	30.5	•	•	53.4	36.2	25.9	17.4	30.9	6.7	6.2	12.5	6.2	18.5
Profit Margin (Before Income Tax) 49	7.4	6.7	10.3	3.8	8.0	5.7	4.6	12.0	4.1	4.7	9.9	5.0	7.8
Profit Margin (After Income Tax) 50	6.6	5.4	10.3	3.7	7.7	5.4	4.1	11.1	2.8	3.6	7.8	3.2	5.3

Table II

Corporations with Net Income

MANAGEMENT, SCIENTIFIC, AND TECHNICAL CONSULTING SERVICES

MONEY AMOUNTS AND SIZE OF ASSETS IN THOUSANDS OF DOLLARS

Item Description for Accounting Period 7/10 Through 6/11		Total	Zero Assets	Under 500	500 to 1,000	1,000 to 5,000	5,000 to 10,000	10,000 to 25,000	25,000 to 50,000	50,000 to 100,000	100,000 to 250,000	250,000 to 500,000	500,000 to 2,500,000	2,500,000 and over
Number of Enterprises	1	138348	25132	104548	3796	3661	597	329	115	73	53	22	16	5
Revenues ($ in Thousands)														
Net Sales	2	164144631	3800921	40820133	17764850	17709677	7470869	10191772	5259886	6194991	7070741	7036213	12479247	28345332
Interest	3	234455	295	4651	8196	14618	22432	8653	11406	11468	9965	25677	95512	21580
Rents	4	43695	0	40	1170	999	228	167	312	3003	16006	956	3009	17806
Royalties	5	176984	0	13	0	4	16	340	854	8833	56202	40620	27907	42195
Other Portfolio Income	6	690953	29432	13660	19251	140338	8513	11752	26606	56191	45175	107789	125630	106615
Other Receipts	7	3490808	194092	480583	450938	351639	124680	297450	325298	190123	254339	164056	388635	268977
Total Receipts	8	168781526	4024740	41319080	18244405	18217275	7626738	10510134	5624362	6464609	7452428	7375311	13119940	28802505
Average Total Receipts	9	1220	160	395	4806	4976	12775	31946	48907	88556	140612	335241	819996	5760501
Operating Costs/Operating Income (%)														
Cost of Operations	10	27.7	12.2	16.6	59.3	31.0	33.4	46.4	36.1	18.3	25.5	23.6	27.1	17.7
Salaries and Wages	11	25.1	14.6	17.1	15.6	19.0	24.9	21.4	21.6	40.0	27.8	31.5	31.1	41.5
Taxes Paid	12	2.9	3.1	2.7	1.5	2.7	3.0	2.9	2.7	3.7	2.9	3.1	3.7	3.8
Interest Paid	13	0.6	0.6	0.3	0.1	0.4	0.9	0.4	0.6	1.0	1.4	1.2	0.9	1.0
Depreciation	14	1.0	0.9	0.8	0.3	0.6	0.7	1.1	1.8	1.3	2.2	2.1	1.5	1.4
Amortization and Depletion	15	0.4	0.1	0.0	0.0	0.1	0.0	0.2	0.4	0.5	1.2	0.9	1.5	0.4
Pensions and Other Deferred Comp.	16	1.4	0.6	1.1	0.7	1.4	1.1	0.8	1.1	1.1	0.8	0.9	1.4	3.1
Employee Benefits	17	1.6	1.4	1.4	0.4	1.5	1.6	1.9	2.2	2.0	2.8	2.3	2.4	1.6
Advertising	18	0.6	1.0	1.6	0.2	0.2	0.2	0.3	0.2	0.4	1.0	0.1	0.3	0.1
Other Expenses	19	22.6	32.2	27.9	13.1	22.5	17.5	13.7	14.3	25.1	28.5	25.8	22.9	23.0
Officers' Compensation	20	7.3	11.7	15.6	5.9	9.8	8.6	4.8	2.8	3.0	1.7	1.2	5.5	0.3
Operating Margin	21	8.7	21.5	14.9	2.8	10.8	7.9	6.1	16.2	3.6	4.1	7.4	1.6	6.1
Operating Margin Before Officers' Comp.	22	16.1	33.2	30.5	8.7	20.5	16.5	10.9	19.1	6.6	5.8	8.6	7.0	6.4

Selected Average Balance Sheet ($ in Thousands)

Item												
Net Receivables 23	165	0	107	442	2210	5028	10319	15211	37320	69480	276364	1414386
Inventories 24	13	0	23	17	51	286	351	711	944	3378	56228	61031
Net Property, Plant and Equipment 25	54	0	103	249	552	1477	4408	5849	15513	30049	43135	237644
Total Assets 26	648	59	680	2105	7345	15705	36035	69787	161297	352396	1050008	4250819
Notes and Loans Payable 27	137	0	217	518	1560	3341	8861	15448	31636	62526	144172	828284
All Other Liabilities 28	224	0	192	472	2500	5417	12431	26462	57314	105534	396217	1796453
Net Worth 29	288	0	270	1115	3285	6947	14742	27877	72348	184335	509619	1626083

Selected Financial Ratios (Times to 1)

Item													
Current Ratio 30	1.7	•	2.5	2.2	2.5	1.6	1.9	1.7	1.4	1.5	1.5	1.6	1.7
Quick Ratio 31	1.4	•	2.3	1.8	2.1	1.4	1.5	1.3	1.0	1.2	1.1	1.3	1.6
Net Sales to Working Capital 32	7.9	•	17.7	19.7	5.9	7.8	6.8	5.2	9.4	4.8	5.9	4.4	5.8
Coverage Ratio 33	19.7	50.8	51.3	46.2	33.9	11.5	22.0	40.1	9.0	7.8	11.6	10.2	9.0
Total Asset Turnover 34	1.8	•	6.6	6.9	2.3	1.7	2.0	1.3	1.2	0.8	0.9	0.7	1.3
Inventory Turnover 35	25.7	•	97.3	121.0	89.7	82.2	50.2	47.1	21.8	36.1	22.3	3.8	16.4
Receivables Turnover 36	7.2	•	76.1	36.1	11.8	7.1	7.5	4.9	6.3	3.5	•	2.9	•
Total Liabilities to Net Worth 37	1.3	•	1.5	1.5	0.9	1.2	1.3	1.4	1.5	1.2	0.9	1.1	1.6
Current Assets to Working Capital 38	2.3	•	1.7	1.8	1.6	2.8	2.2	2.5	3.7	3.1	2.7	2.9	2.4
Current Liabilities to Working Capital 39	1.3	•	0.7	0.8	0.6	1.8	1.2	1.5	2.7	2.1	1.7	1.9	1.4
Working Capital to Net Sales 40	0.1	•	0.1	0.1	0.2	0.1	0.1	0.2	0.1	0.2	0.2	0.2	0.2
Inventory to Working Capital 41	0.1	•	0.0	0.1	0.0	0.0	0.1	0.1	0.1	0.0	0.1	0.3	0.1
Total Receipts to Cash Flow 42	3.3	1.7	2.5	6.1	3.4	4.0	5.2	2.9	3.4	2.9	2.9	3.9	3.6
Cost of Goods to Cash Flow 43	0.9	0.2	0.4	3.6	1.1	1.3	2.4	1.0	0.6	0.7	0.7	1.0	0.6
Cash Flow to Total Debt 44	1.0	4.5	1.9	1.4	0.8	0.7	0.7	0.6	0.6	0.5	0.6	0.4	0.6

Selected Financial Factors (in Percentages)

Item													
Debt Ratio 45	55.6	•	59.4	60.3	55.3	47.0	55.8	59.1	60.1	55.1	47.7	51.5	61.7
Return on Total Assets 46	22.5	•	107.9	38.8	18.6	31.9	19.0	30.2	10.9	9.1	12.6	6.8	11.7
Return on Equity Before Income Taxes 47	48.2	•	260.5	95.6	58.5	38.0	40.9	71.9	24.2	17.7	22.0	12.6	27.1
Return on Equity After Income Taxes 48	43.8	•	258.8	93.3	56.7	36.7	38.2	68.3	19.8	15.1	17.6	8.8	18.5
Profit Margin (Before Income Tax) 49	11.7	27.4	16.1	5.5	13.5	10.0	9.2	23.2	8.0	9.6	12.7	8.2	7.8
Profit Margin (After Income Tax) 50	10.6	25.2	16.0	5.4	13.1	9.6	8.6	22.0	6.5	8.2	10.1	5.7	5.3

SCIENTIFIC RESEARCH AND DEVELOPMENT SERVICES

Table I
Corporations with and without Net Income

MONEY AMOUNTS AND SIZE OF ASSETS IN THOUSANDS OF DOLLARS

Item Description for Accounting Period 7/10 Through 6/11		Total	Zero Assets	Under 500	500 to 1,000	1,000 to 5,000	5,000 to 10,000	10,000 to 25,000	25,000 to 50,000	50,000 to 100,000	100,000 to 250,000	250,000 to 500,000	500,000 to 2,500,000	2,500,000 and over
Number of Enterprises	1	17549	4042	9165	1037	1919	617	400	137	105	68	31	25	3
Revenues ($ in Thousands)														
Net Sales	2	44402296	771015	2301790	1618839	4954021	2897947	2556648	2693306	2396569	4074648	3903300	13555593	2296620
Interest	3	259458	5583	877	705	8547	9468	20588	23880	16569	23439	41061	80570	28173
Rents	4	18246	30	123	0	2857	3007	1317	158	1715	5215	2236	1583	6
Royalties	5	1924113	89044	72	211	45596	6247	9310	116263	71669	199814	90280	796583	499024
Other Portfolio Income	6	1029896	226397	46101	209	44447	105432	90469	11952	78561	16192	180975	219820	9339
Other Receipts	7	5960189	159616	70254	86832	303691	181066	138904	198325	491101	424224	600403	1360063	1945709
Total Receipts	8	53212198	1251685	2419217	1706796	5359159	3203167	2817236	3043884	3056184	4743532	4818255	16014212	4778871
Average Total Receipts	9	3032	310	264	1646	2793	5192	7043	22218	29107	69758	155428	640568	1592957
Operating Costs/Operating Income (%)														
Cost of Operations	10	27.4	21.8	20.1	0.7	29.6	36.5	31.3	26.3	17.8	25.4	27.0	27.2	52.0
Salaries and Wages	11	32.5	64.1	29.7	28.7	31.6	40.8	42.4	36.1	45.2	29.2	35.5	26.2	28.2
Taxes Paid	12	3.7	5.7	3.4	3.6	4.0	5.1	5.8	4.5	6.4	3.4	3.0	2.5	3.3
Interest Paid	13	3.1	3.3	1.8	2.3	1.7	3.5	3.8	4.3	4.2	2.2	4.6	2.9	4.1
Depreciation	14	4.2	3.6	1.9	2.3	3.2	5.9	7.2	5.9	5.1	4.6	5.2	3.6	2.7
Amortization and Depletion	15	3.0	8.4	2.4	1.2	0.8	2.7	4.7	3.2	9.4	3.3	2.8	2.2	2.8
Pensions and Other Deferred Comp.	16	1.5	0.3	1.1	3.3	0.9	1.6	0.8	1.1	0.3	0.8	0.5	2.8	•
Employee Benefits	17	3.8	4.4	3.2	1.4	4.2	4.7	5.3	3.7	5.7	2.9	4.1	3.5	3.0
Advertising	18	1.8	1.6	3.8	0.2	1.8	1.0	1.6	1.4	2.0	1.8	0.7	2.1	2.2
Other Expenses	19	47.7	69.7	46.8	57.7	44.2	47.7	73.6	58.9	74.2	52.1	45.7	37.3	28.2
Officers' Compensation	20	5.7	11.0	13.0	6.4	12.3	9.3	10.2	5.8	7.8	4.2	2.6	1.9	1.1
Operating Margin	21	•	•	•	•	•	•	•	•	•	•	•	•	•
Operating Margin Before Officers' Comp.	22	•	•	•	•	•	•	•	•	•	•	•	•	•

Selected Average Balance Sheet ($ in Thousands)

Item	1	2	3	4	5	6	7	8	9	10	11	12	13
Net Receivables 23	482	0	4	137	342	747	1215	4308	5320	12892	21417	126934	271990
Inventories 24	179	0	1	9	137	310	489	861	1438	3691	10961	47079	291152
Net Property, Plant and Equipment 25	576	0	16	53	323	1275	1940	4439	5878	12675	40621	155037	168052
Total Assets 26	5303	0	78	668	2233	7046	15358	36541	69321	147496	352070	1101901	5367159
Notes and Loans Payable 27	1499	0	110	359	999	4616	3160	7821	14652	12756	93722	308881	1595122
All Other Liabilities 28	1607	0	33	217	698	2301	4732	12052	29116	45685	111072	300888	1414707
Net Worth 29	2197	0	-65	92	536	128	7466	16669	25553	89055	147276	492133	2357330

Selected Financial Ratios (Times to 1)

Item	1	2	3	4	5	6	7	8	9	10	11	12	13
Current Ratio 30	2.0	•	0.7	1.5	1.7	1.8	2.4	1.9	2.1	2.7	2.3	1.7	2.0
Quick Ratio 31	1.3	•	0.6	1.4	1.4	1.4	1.9	1.4	1.5	1.9	1.3	1.1	0.5
Net Sales to Working Capital 32	1.9	•	•	11.6	4.4	2.4	1.1	1.8	1.0	1.1	1.2	3.1	0.8
Coverage Ratio 33	•	•	•	•	•	•	•	•	•	•	•	3.5	20.5
Total Asset Turnover 34	0.5	•	3.2	2.3	1.2	0.7	0.4	0.5	0.3	0.4	0.4	0.5	0.1
Inventory Turnover 35	3.8	•	39.2	1.2	5.6	5.5	4.1	6.0	2.8	4.1	3.1	3.1	1.4
Receivables Turnover 36	5.4	•	36.7	14.3	6.3	7.3	4.8	5.2	4.8	4.6	5.1	4.3	5.6
Total Liabilities to Net Worth 37	1.4	•	•	6.2	3.2	53.9	1.1	1.2	1.7	0.7	1.4	1.2	1.3
Current Assets to Working Capital 38	2.0	•	•	3.2	2.4	2.2	1.7	2.1	1.9	1.6	1.8	2.5	2.0
Current Liabilities to Working Capital 39	1.0	•	•	2.2	1.4	1.2	0.7	1.1	0.9	0.6	0.8	1.5	1.0
Working Capital to Net Sales 40	0.5	•	•	0.1	0.2	0.4	0.9	0.6	1.0	0.9	0.9	0.3	1.3
Inventory to Working Capital 41	0.1	•	•	0.0	0.2	0.2	0.1	0.1	0.1	0.1	0.1	0.2	0.3
Total Receipts to Cash Flow 42	3.8	•	9.6	8.5	2.1	8.9	•	7.7	7.9	3.0	3.7	2.5	1.0
Cost of Goods to Cash Flow 43	1.0	•	2.1	1.7	0.0	2.6	•	2.0	1.4	0.8	1.0	0.7	0.5
Cash Flow to Total Debt 44	0.2	•	1.3	0.2	•	•	0.1	0.1	0.3	0.3	0.2	0.4	0.3

Selected Financial Factors (in Percentages)

Item	1	2	3	4	5	6	7	8	9	10	11	12	13
Debt Ratio 45	58.6	•	183.9	86.2	76.0	98.2	54.4	51.4	63.1	39.6	58.2	55.3	56.1
Return on Total Assets 46	•	•	•	•	•	•	•	•	•	•	•	5.0	12.1
Return on Equity Before Income Taxes 47	•	•	85.0	•	•	•	•	•	•	•	•	8.0	26.2
Return on Equity After Income Taxes 48	•	•	85.8	•	•	•	•	•	•	•	•	4.5	15.1
Profit Margin (Before Income Tax) 49	•	•	•	•	•	•	•	•	•	•	•	7.2	80.6
Profit Margin (After Income Tax) 50	•	•	•	•	•	•	•	•	•	•	•	4.1	46.6

SCIENTIFIC RESEARCH AND DEVELOPMENT SERVICES

Table II
Corporations with Net Income

MONEY AMOUNTS AND SIZE OF ASSETS IN THOUSANDS OF DOLLARS

Item Description for Accounting Period 7/10 Through 6/11	Total	Zero Assets	Under 500	500 to 1,000	1,000 to 5,000	5,000 to 10,000	10,000 to 25,000	25,000 to 50,000	50,000 to 100,000	100,000 to 250,000	250,000 to 500,000	500,000 to 2,500,000	2,500,000 and over
Number of Enterprises 1	6649	463	4404	695	726	155	84	44	22	31	8	18	0
Revenues ($ in Thousands)													
Net Sales 2	30817641	286599	1347140	1529225	3085837	1925455	1572343	1782233	1132672	2980283	1604084	13571771	0
Interest 3	116079	688	346	179	2575	3849	7710	15494	1695	11146	14192	58205	0
Rents 4	10105	0	123	0	2455	1159	114	0	0	3200	1466	1588	0
Royalties 5	1462367	0	0	209	45596	0	7191	93603	44433	111606	652	1159078	0
Other Portfolio Income 6	925423	175830	45209	0	41500	102636	85925	11091	58067	4834	178757	221577	0
Other Receipts 7	4761619	52935	42893	75944	204605	65614	19512	158364	173249	408560	546182	3013757	0
Total Receipts 8	38093234	516052	1435711	1605557	3382568	2098713	1692795	2060785	1410116	3519629	2345333	18025976	0
Average Total Receipts 9	5729	1115	326	2310	4659	13540	20152	46836	64096	113536	293167	1001443	•
Operating Costs/Operating Income (%)													
Cost of Operations 10	27.5	15.9	5.1	•	28.5	30.7	28.8	27.3	17.9	30.6	11.2	34.4	•
Salaries and Wages 11	23.1	31.4	28.0	25.5	19.4	22.7	19.8	25.8	25.1	22.9	26.4	22.6	•
Taxes Paid 12	2.8	3.6	1.5	3.3	2.9	3.1	3.7	3.3	3.2	2.8	2.0	2.6	•
Interest Paid 13	1.9	2.6	0.5	1.4	0.5	0.6	0.6	1.8	0.7	2.4	2.9	2.5	•
Depreciation 14	2.7	1.1	1.9	1.4	1.3	1.8	3.8	3.2	2.1	2.7	4.5	3.0	•
Amortization and Depletion 15	1.4	0.6	0.3	•	0.2	0.3	0.9	0.9	3.4	1.8	1.4	1.9	•
Pensions and Other Deferred Comp. 16	1.0	•	1.6	3.4	0.8	1.9	0.9	1.2	0.3	0.9	0.7	0.8	•
Employee Benefits 17	2.8	1.9	2.7	1.2	2.0	2.7	3.8	2.4	1.6	2.4	2.6	3.3	•
Advertising 18	1.5	0.8	5.6	0.1	0.9	0.4	0.4	1.3	0.3	2.1	0.7	1.8	•
Other Expenses 19	30.8	41.2	35.6	46.1	24.6	21.8	24.3	32.4	34.8	28.9	43.2	30.3	•
Officers' Compensation 20	3.5	1.7	10.8	5.7	10.1	5.3	3.1	3.0	2.2	3.0	2.0	1.4	•
Operating Margin 21	1.0	•	6.4	11.9	8.9	8.7	9.9	•	8.3	•	2.4	•	•
Operating Margin Before Officers' Comp. 22	4.5	1.0	17.3	17.5	19.0	14.0	13.0	0.4	10.5	2.3	4.4	•	•

Selected Average Balance Sheet ($ in Thousands)

Net Receivables 23	•	767	0	3	157	505	1744	2880	6619	9777	20440	13934	158267
Inventories 24	•	307	0	3	179	582	333	1155	1982	4838	19256		76682
Net Property, Plant and Equipment 25	•	756	0	17	51	270	823	3160	4735	5109	15418	48231	174752
Total Assets 26	•	7132	0	62	662	2167	6750	15996	37357	69206	154973	359427	1770814
Notes and Loans Payable 27	•	1697	0	18	70	504	1612	1948	6914	9216	19710	84975	476534
All Other Liabilities 28	•	2158	0	8	69	438	2268	3813	11549	32749	52557	141768	515561
Net Worth 29	•	3277	0	36	523	1225	2870	10235	18894	27241	82706	132683	778719

Selected Financial Ratios (Times to 1)

Current Ratio 30	•	2.0	•	3.1	5.1	3.0	2.1	3.0	1.9	2.2	2.3	2.8	1.8
Quick Ratio 31	•	1.3	•	2.9	4.9	2.5	1.4	2.3	1.6	1.7	1.7	1.9	0.9
Net Sales to Working Capital 32	•	2.7	•	12.6	7.0	4.2	5.0	2.8	3.7	2.1	2.0	1.3	2.4
Coverage Ratio 33	•	14.6	31.7	25.7	12.8	38.2	29.1	32.0	8.2	46.1	8.2	17.6	12.8
Total Asset Turnover 34	•	0.6	•	4.9	3.3	2.0	1.8	1.2	1.1	0.7	0.6	0.6	0.4
Inventory Turnover 35	•	4.2	•	6.0	•	6.8	6.5	16.2	9.6	4.6	6.1	1.2	3.4
Receivables Turnover 36	•	6.3	37.2	37.2	17.0	6.1	8.4	5.5	6.8	5.7	4.6	6.0	5.8
Total Liabilities to Net Worth 37	•	1.2	0.7	0.7	0.3	0.8	1.4	0.6	1.0	1.5	0.9	1.7	1.3
Current Assets to Working Capital 38	•	2.0	•	1.5	1.2	1.5	1.9	1.5	2.1	1.8	1.8	1.5	2.2
Current Liabilities to Working Capital 39	•	1.0	•	0.5	0.2	0.5	0.9	0.5	1.1	0.8	0.8	0.5	1.2
Working Capital to Net Sales 40	•	0.4	•	0.1	0.1	0.2	0.2	0.4	0.3	0.5	0.5	0.8	0.4
Inventory to Working Capital 41	•	0.2	•	0.1	•	0.1	0.4	0.1	0.1	0.1	0.1	0.2	0.3
Total Receipts to Cash Flow 42	•	2.0	1.5	2.7	1.8	2.6	3.3	3.1	2.5	1.7	2.4	1.3	1.8
Cost of Goods to Cash Flow 43	•	0.6	0.2	0.1	•	0.7	1.0	0.9	0.7	0.3	0.7	0.1	0.6
Cash Flow to Total Debt 44	•	0.6	•	4.4	9.0	1.7	1.0	1.0	0.9	0.7	0.6	0.7	0.4

Selected Financial Factors (in Percentages)

Debt Ratio 45	•	54.0	•	42.1	21.0	43.5	57.5	36.0	49.4	60.6	46.6	63.1	56.0
Return on Total Assets 46	•	17.6	•	66.3	60.8	37.3	33.6	21.2	16.0	25.0	12.3	28.8	13.7
Return on Equity Before Income Taxes 47	•	35.6	•	110.0	71.0	64.3	76.4	32.1	27.8	62.1	20.2	73.5	28.6
Return on Equity After Income Taxes 48	•	29.1	•	106.9	70.7	62.0	70.2	29.1	22.4	53.8	19.0	72.0	20.1
Profit Margin (Before Income Tax) 49	•	25.2	79.4	13.0	16.9	18.5	17.6	17.5	13.0	32.8	17.4	48.7	29.6
Profit Margin (After Income Tax) 50	•	20.6	77.6	12.6	16.8	17.9	16.2	15.9	10.5	28.5	16.3	47.7	20.7

Table I

Corporations with and without Net Income

ADVERTISING AND RELATED SERVICES

MONEY AMOUNTS AND SIZE OF ASSETS IN THOUSANDS OF DOLLARS

Item Description for Accounting Period 7/10 Through 6/11	Total	Zero Assets	Under 500	500 to 1,000	1,000 to 5,000	5,000 to 10,000	10,000 to 25,000	25,000 to 50,000	50,000 to 100,000	100,000 to 250,000	250,000 to 500,000	500,000 to 2,500,000	2,500,000 and over
Number of Enterprises 1	50808	10117	37073	899	1980	433	151	71	32	28	9	10	5
Revenues ($ in Thousands)													
Net Sales 2	87244871	1569689	21170989	1481219	10568355	7780642	4981455	3723787	2600786	5857520	2081631	6616788	18812009
Interest 3	985581	310	5742	1304	4218	4556	1560	7682	3533	5499	1058	10726	939393
Rents 4	141838	28	1696	64	654	0	0	664	53	976	322	12252	125130
Royalties 5	43023	0	0	0	0	0	0	35040	2	23	646	4746	2566
Other Portfolio Income 6	551620	56421	11836	0	12232	4359	470	2163	22697	11495	1514	12778	415657
Other Receipts 7	1843902	4672	38699	4581	160444	53348	24196	39056	39634	19710	96653	830461	532446
Total Receipts 8	90810835	1631120	21228962	1487168	10745903	7842905	5007681	3808392	2666705	5895223	2197854	7471721	20827201
Average Total Receipts 9	1787	161	573	1654	5427	18113	33163	53639	83335	210544	244206	747172	4165440
Operating Costs/Operating Income (%)													
Cost of Operations 10	43.4	44.3	55.4	28.3	53.2	59.8	67.0	49.8	59.6	59.8	43.0	39.6	5.2
Salaries and Wages 11	19.8	13.1	8.8	16.8	15.0	10.2	12.9	16.1	17.7	14.0	22.7	25.4	42.2
Taxes Paid 12	2.3	1.8	1.5	2.9	2.3	1.0	1.3	1.9	1.8	1.4	1.9	3.5	4.0
Interest Paid 13	3.9	2.1	0.4	1.2	0.5	0.1	0.3	1.2	1.5	1.3	3.5	11.6	11.6
Depreciation 14	1.5	2.0	0.8	2.3	0.9	0.5	0.7	1.4	1.8	1.1	1.8	3.1	2.6
Amortization and Depletion 15	1.2	1.2	0.1	0.1	0.4	0.1	0.4	0.7	1.4	1.5	3.2	2.8	3.0
Pensions and Other Deferred Comp. 16	0.5	0.1	0.3	1.1	0.5	0.5	0.2	0.4	0.1	0.5	0.6	0.2	1.1
Employee Benefits 17	1.2	1.5	0.6	0.9	1.2	0.5	1.0	1.2	0.8	1.0	1.1	2.6	2.0
Advertising 18	3.7	0.9	3.3	6.0	7.4	10.3	1.1	11.4	1.2	1.1	0.8	3.6	0.2
Other Expenses 19	18.9	29.0	18.8	27.7	13.8	10.7	9.6	14.4	14.7	14.3	26.4	14.0	30.0
Officers' Compensation 20	3.9	4.0	6.2	8.3	5.3	3.3	3.0	2.8	1.5	1.2	1.0	1.5	3.4
Operating Margin 21	•	•	3.8	4.3	•	3.0	2.7	•	•	2.7	•	•	•
Operating Margin Before Officers' Comp. 22	3.5	3.9	10.0	12.6	4.8	6.4	5.7	1.7	•	3.8	•	•	•

Selected Average Balance Sheet ($ in Thousands)

Net Receivables 23	341	0	13	121	604	2311	6246	9818	22000	36038	53262	184569	1774149
Inventories 24	33	0	1	38	129	294	90	664	881	3575	3467	11132	174670
Net Property, Plant and Equipment 25	133	0	16	320	311	665	1433	5618	4182	8316	24406	105771	540561
Total Assets 26	2139	0	69	744	2450	7467	15854	37262	70791	155839	312343	1304286	13972121
Notes and Loans Payable 27	460	0	80	515	886	1306	1404	8700	14134	33020	79602	447978	2046523
All Other Liabilities 28	961	0	28	237	1295	3197	10354	15410	31698	76308	105522	452899	6466530
Net Worth 29	718	0	-40	-8	268	2964	4096	13152	24958	46511	127219	403408	5459069

Selected Financial Ratios (Times to 1)

Current Ratio 30	0.9	•	1.0	1.0	1.6	1.8	1.2	1.4	1.5	1.1	1.3	1.1	0.7
Quick Ratio 31	0.7	•	1.0	0.8	1.3	1.6	1.1	1.1	1.2	0.8	0.9	0.8	0.5
Net Sales to Working Capital 32	•	•	322.7	134.5	8.4	7.9	17.0	8.8	5.3	50.6	9.6	16.0	•
Coverage Ratio 33	2.0	2.8	12.0	5.0	3.7	28.3	12.8	2.0	1.3	3.4	0.9	1.4	1.5
Total Asset Turnover 34	0.8	•	8.3	2.2	2.2	2.4	2.1	1.4	1.1	1.3	0.7	0.5	0.3
Inventory Turnover 35	22.6	•	222.0	12.4	22.0	36.5	245.9	39.3	54.9	35.0	28.7	23.5	1.1
Receivables Turnover 36	4.9	•	47.3	9.1	8.1	9.3	5.5	6.1	4.0	5.7	5.8	3.9	1.9
Total Liabilities to Net Worth 37	2.0	•	•	8.1	8.1	1.5	2.9	1.8	1.8	2.4	1.5	2.2	1.6
Current Assets to Working Capital 38	•	•	21.4	27.1	2.6	2.3	5.9	3.5	3.1	17.6	4.2	8.4	•
Current Liabilities to Working Capital 39	•	•	20.4	26.1	1.6	1.3	4.9	2.5	2.1	16.6	3.2	7.4	•
Working Capital to Net Sales 40	•	•	0.0	0.0	0.1	0.1	0.1	0.1	0.2	0.0	0.1	0.1	•
Inventory to Working Capital 41	•	•	0.7	4.5	0.3	0.2	0.1	0.1	0.0	0.8	0.3	0.3	•
Total Receipts to Cash Flow 42	5.4	3.6	5.1	3.8	8.7	8.2	10.0	7.6	7.8	6.3	4.2	6.3	3.6
Cost of Goods to Cash Flow 43	2.3	1.6	2.8	1.1	4.6	4.9	6.7	3.8	4.7	3.8	1.8	2.5	0.2
Cash Flow to Total Debt 44	0.2	1.0	0.6	0.3	0.5	0.3	0.3	0.2	0.3	0.3	0.1	0.1	

Selected Financial Factors (in Percentages)

Debt Ratio 45	66.5	•	158.0	101.1	89.0	60.3	74.2	64.7	64.7	70.2	59.3	69.1	60.9
Return on Total Assets 46	6.2	•	37.0	13.0	3.7	9.5	7.3	3.3	2.3	6.2	2.4	8.5	4.9
Return on Equity Before Income Taxes 47	9.2	•	•	•	24.7	23.0	26.1	4.7	1.5	14.7	•	8.4	4.4
Return on Equity After Income Taxes 48	7.3	•	•	•	23.4	22.4	25.1	3.9	•	11.5	•	1.8	3.3
Profit Margin (Before Income Tax) 49	3.9	3.9	4.1	4.7	1.2	3.8	3.2	1.2	0.4	3.3	•	5.1	6.4
Profit Margin (After Income Tax) 50	3.1	3.8	4.0	4.2	1.2	3.7	3.1	1.0	•	2.6	•	1.1	4.8

Table II
Corporations with Net Income

ADVERTISING AND RELATED SERVICES

MONEY AMOUNTS AND SIZE OF ASSETS IN THOUSANDS OF DOLLARS

Item Description for Accounting Period 7/10 Through 6/11	Total	Zero Assets	Under 500	500 to 1,000	1,000 to 5,000	5,000 to 10,000	10,000 to 25,000	25,000 to 50,000	50,000 to 100,000	100,000 to 250,000	250,000 to 500,000	500,000 to 2,500,000	2,500,000 and over
Number of Enterprises **1**	25126	4472	18196	540	1455	270	98	36	22	•	6	7	•
Revenues ($ in Thousands)													
Net Sales **2**	64357389	1271484	12032269	927404	7569912	5411218	3982521	2642159	1955775	•	1211002	4792674	•
Interest **3**	964056	13	2491	932	3266	1912	915	729	1029	•	973	8078	•
Rents **4**	138645	28	0	20	123	0	0	208	53	•	12250	322	•
Royalties **5**	42907	0	0	0	0	0	0	35040	2	•	4746	646	•
Other Portfolio Income **6**	531249	56421	6743	0	10713	3358	354	1804	22685	•	1107	1547	•
Other Receipts **7**	1710348	4521	20624	4501	169046	52610	15963	12072	20090	•	92012	768065	•
Total Receipts **8**	67744594	1332467	12062127	932857	7753060	5469098	3999753	2692012	1999634	•	1322090	5571332	•
Average Total Receipts **9**	2696	298	663	1728	5329	20256	40814	74778	90892	•	220348	795905	•
Operating Costs/Operating Income (%)													
Cost of Operations **10**	38.3	48.2	45.4	16.9	53.6	60.5	69.6	45.2	57.9	•	25.8	34.6	•
Salaries and Wages **11**	22.0	13.1	9.2	14.0	14.1	8.9	9.7	14.1	18.3	•	29.5	28.8	•
Taxes Paid **12**	2.4	1.5	1.6	3.1	2.1	0.9	1.1	1.9	1.5	•	2.5	3.8	•
Interest Paid **13**	4.0	2.3	0.3	1.3	0.4	0.1	0.1	0.4	0.8	•	2.2	7.0	•
Depreciation **14**	1.2	2.1	0.4	2.6	0.7	0.3	0.4	0.9	1.4	•	2.5	2.9	•
Amortization and Depletion **15**	1.0	1.3	0.0	0.1	0.4	0.0	0.1	0.4	0.5	•	1.2	2.1	•
Pensions and Other Deferred Comp. **16**	0.6	0.1	0.3	0.1	0.7	0.6	0.3	0.5	0.2	•	0.4	0.3	•
Employee Benefits **17**	1.3	1.2	0.8	0.8	1.0	0.4	0.8	1.1	0.5	•	1.4	2.9	•
Advertising **18**	2.6	0.7	2.9	2.1	2.5	9.5	1.1	15.6	0.8	•	1.1	1.9	•
Other Expenses **19**	19.6	21.6	22.9	33.5	12.7	9.3	7.6	12.7	10.9	•	35.3	13.0	•
Officers' Compensation **20**	3.9	3.3	6.1	10.4	6.2	3.4	2.8	2.9	1.2	•	1.2	1.7	•
Operating Margin **21**	3.0	4.6	10.1	15.1	5.6	6.2	6.2	4.1	6.0	•	•	1.1	•
Operating Margin Before Officers' Comp. **22**	6.9	7.9	16.2	25.5	11.9	9.6	9.1	7.1	7.2	•	•	2.8	•

Selected Average Balance Sheet ($ in Thousands)

Net Receivables 23	578	0	142	569	2473	6167	10790	26098	37933	205880
Inventories 24	51	0	43	132	435	73	1165	1197	10167	48198
Net Property, Plant and Equipment 25	144	0	278	252	870	1103	6230	3513	18303	66206
Total Assets 26	3642	0	799	2361	7549	14723	37101	68809	292164	1265859
Notes and Loans Payable 27	643	0	500	369	502	1156	6930	8599	88914	557342
All Other Liabilities 28	1683	0	293	1260	2981	10226	15231	37880	99241	355545
Net Worth 29	1316	-45	7	731	4066	3341	14940	22331	104008	352972

Selected Financial Ratios (Times to 1)

Current Ratio 30	0.9	•	1.3	1.1	1.7	2.1	1.2	1.6	1.3	1.3
Quick Ratio 31	0.7	•	1.2	0.9	1.4	1.8	1.1	1.3	0.9	1.1
Net Sales to Working Capital 32	•	•	79.3	65.7	8.3	6.6	27.2	8.7	10.0	9.8
Coverage Ratio 33	3.1	5.2	39.2	12.9	21.3	108.8	53.4	15.0	3.9	3.5
Total Asset Turnover 34	0.7	•	9.7	2.1	2.2	2.7	2.8	2.0	0.7	0.5
Inventory Turnover 35	19.1	•	349.9	6.7	21.1	27.9	387.6	28.5	5.1	4.9
Receivables Turnover 36	4.9	•	61.8	8.7	7.9	9.3	6.5	7.3	10.6	1.0
Total Liabilities to Net Worth 37	1.8	•	113.8	2.2	0.9	3.4	1.5	1.8	2.6	
Current Assets to Working Capital 38	•	•	4.8	16.2	2.4	1.9	7.6	2.8	3.9	5.0
Current Liabilities to Working Capital 39	•	•	3.8	15.2	1.4	0.9	6.6	1.8	2.9	4.0
Working Capital to Net Sales 40	•	•	0.0	0.0	0.1	0.2	0.0	0.1	0.1	0.1
Inventory to Working Capital 41	•	•	0.1	2.7	0.3	0.2	0.0	0.1	0.5	0.2
Total Receipts to Cash Flow 42	4.2	3.8	3.3	2.4	5.7	7.2	8.2	5.9	2.6	3.7
Cost of Goods to Cash Flow 43	1.6	1.8	1.5	0.4	3.1	4.3	5.7	2.7	0.7	1.3
Cash Flow to Total Debt 44	0.3	•	1.8	0.9	0.6	0.8	0.4	0.6	0.4	0.2

Selected Financial Factors (in Percentages)

Debt Ratio 45	63.9	•	166.0	99.1	69.0	46.1	77.3	59.7	67.5	72.1
Return on Total Assets 46	8.8	•	102.6	36.5	18.6	19.3	18.9	12.8	11.6	13.1
Return on Equity Before Income Taxes 47	16.6	•	•	3868.8	57.3	35.5	81.5	29.7	32.8	33.6
Return on Equity After Income Taxes 48	14.5	•	•	3663.3	56.7	34.8	79.5	28.2	29.6	22.9
Profit Margin (Before Income Tax) 49	8.5	9.4	10.4	15.7	8.1	7.2	6.7	6.0	8.2	17.3
Profit Margin (After Income Tax) 50	7.5	9.3	10.2	14.9	8.0	7.1	6.5	5.7	7.4	11.8

Table I

Corporations with and without Net Income

OTHER PROFESSIONAL, SCIENTIFIC, AND TECHNICAL SERVICES

MONEY AMOUNTS AND SIZE OF ASSETS IN THOUSANDS OF DOLLARS

Item Description for Accounting Period 7/10 Through 6/11		Total	Zero Assets	Under 500	500 to 1,000	1,000 to 5,000	5,000 to 10,000	10,000 to 25,000	25,000 to 50,000	50,000 to 100,000	100,000 to 250,000	250,000 to 500,000	500,000 to 2,500,000	2,500,000 and over
Number of Enterprises	1	97334	17512	73456	3381	2421	160	213	76	51	35	13	12	3
Revenues ($ in Thousands)														
Net Sales	2	88657882	4475973	33211171	5796801	8029483	1551596	5101567	3542686	3456446	6699666	3596187	9811639	3484667
Interest	3	68683	9710	3657	2693	6859	1926	5732	5503	3403	6528	2522	17280	2870
Rents	4	38035	20	622	0	2300	0	2373	102	589	21	17208	14800	0
Royalties	5	713581	0	0	0	0	0	32166	0	0	7099	29642	231305	413369
Other Portfolio Income	6	254001	36029	5213	5089	8815	532	4337	11567	5432	129702	3665	2272	41348
Other Receipts	7	1213207	64146	216400	113070	169040	10758	130468	36840	54953	238197	19314	131701	28320
Total Receipts	8	90945389	4585878	33437063	5917653	8216497	1564812	5276643	3596698	3520823	6981213	3668538	10208997	3970574
Average Total Receipts	9	934	262	455	1750	3394	9780	24773	47325	69036	199463	282195	850750	1323525
Operating Costs/Operating Income (%)														
Cost of Operations	10	28.0	6.9	20.5	26.9	48.4	35.9	49.5	42.9	35.4	52.9	24.4	19.5	3.7
Salaries and Wages	11	20.7	16.5	20.2	21.5	17.6	17.7	17.2	20.7	21.2	17.4	19.1	27.6	30.6
Taxes Paid	12	2.9	2.4	3.3	3.6	2.3	2.9	2.6	2.6	2.5	1.9	2.9	3.5	2.3
Interest Paid	13	1.7	4.0	0.6	1.1	1.1	0.6	0.7	1.7	1.8	1.6	1.6	2.8	12.0
Depreciation	14	1.8	1.7	1.3	0.9	2.0	1.6	1.7	1.8	2.5	3.6	1.4	1.8	3.6
Amortization and Depletion	15	1.0	1.3	0.3	0.3	0.4	1.5	0.4	1.3	1.1	1.5	1.4	2.1	4.6
Pensions and Other Deferred Comp.	16	0.9	0.4	0.8	1.5	0.9	0.5	0.4	0.9	0.8	0.3	0.8	1.8	1.1
Employee Benefits	17	1.9	1.5	1.1	1.2	1.0	8.0	1.4	2.2	2.0	1.0	3.4	5.1	2.8
Advertising	18	1.0	0.8	1.0	3.5	0.6	1.8	0.5	0.7	0.9	0.7	0.5	0.5	0.2
Other Expenses	19	30.1	57.9	29.3	26.3	18.5	29.9	22.9	25.7	22.5	19.9	39.1	36.0	49.9
Officers' Compensation	20	6.7	6.8	12.0	6.6	7.2	4.2	3.6	1.7	1.9	1.8	1.6	1.1	1.6
Operating Margin	21	3.4	•	9.5	6.7	•	•	•	•	7.6	•	3.6	•	•
Operating Margin Before Officers' Comp.	22	10.1	6.7	21.5	13.3	7.2	•	2.8	•	9.5	•	5.3	•	•

Selected Average Balance Sheet ($ in Thousands)

Net Receivables 23	105	0	8	76	534	1630	3598	9604	13110	30403	91264	172557	441179
Inventories 24	11	0	3	9	37	707	593	594	1175	6421	3150	7518	6967
Net Property, Plant and Equipment 25	66	0	21	166	292	357	1853	4181	7897	14972	19762	92699	178821
Total Assets 26	772	0	92	693	2172	7111	14551	35353	71539	159887	338373	1202964	8590735
Notes and Loans Payable 27	219	0	49	338	611	3129	3357	12334	19320	51436	54469	374187	1640172
All Other Liabilities 28	306	0	29	138	871	1627	4968	14919	18214	53433	123883	420866	4400710
Net Worth 29	247	0	15	216	690	2355	6226	8100	34005	55018	160022	407911	2549852

Selected Financial Ratios (Times to 1)

Current Ratio 30	1.2	•	1.5	1.2	1.5	2.6	1.8	1.1	1.6	1.0	2.0	1.2	0.7
Quick Ratio 31	0.9	•	1.2	1.1	1.3	2.1	1.3	1.0	1.2	0.8	1.6	0.8	0.4
Net Sales to Working Capital 32	18.0	•	30.2	38.0	8.2	3.9	6.0	20.6	5.9	72.7	3.2	13.2	•
Coverage Ratio 33	4.6	1.6	18.0	9.4	3.0	•	4.5	1.0	6.3	3.0	4.6	1.8	1.7
Total Asset Turnover 34	1.2	•	4.9	2.5	1.5	1.4	1.6	1.3	0.9	1.2	0.8	0.7	0.1
Inventory Turnover 35	22.9	•	27.3	51.9	42.9	4.9	20.0	33.7	20.4	15.5	21.4	21.2	6.2
Receivables Turnover 36	9.8	•	64.1	17.1	6.7	3.0	6.1	5.5	4.3	7.6	3.8	5.6	5.3
Total Liabilities to Net Worth 37	2.1	•	5.4	2.2	2.1	2.0	1.3	3.4	1.1	1.9	1.1	1.9	2.4
Current Assets to Working Capital 38	5.1	•	3.0	5.3	3.1	1.6	2.3	8.1	2.7	26.0	2.0	6.4	•
Current Liabilities to Working Capital 39	4.1	•	2.0	4.3	2.1	0.6	1.3	7.1	1.7	25.0	1.0	5.4	•
Working Capital to Net Sales 40	0.1	•	0.0	0.0	0.1	0.3	0.2	0.0	0.2	0.0	0.3	0.1	•
Inventory to Working Capital 41	0.2	•	0.2	0.1	0.1	0.1	0.2	0.2	0.2	2.2	0.1	0.1	•
Total Receipts to Cash Flow 42	3.2	1.8	3.0	3.3	5.8	4.3	4.6	4.7	3.4	5.2	2.4	2.8	2.1
Cost of Goods to Cash Flow 43	0.9	0.1	0.6	0.9	2.8	1.6	2.3	2.0	1.2	2.7	0.6	0.5	0.1
Cash Flow to Total Debt 44	0.5	•	1.9	1.1	0.4	0.5	0.6	0.4	0.5	0.3	0.7	0.4	0.1

Selected Financial Factors (in Percentages)

Debt Ratio 45	68.0	•	84.3	68.8	68.2	66.9	57.2	77.1	52.5	65.6	52.7	66.1	70.3
Return on Total Assets 46	9.4	•	52.9	24.4	5.2	•	5.5	2.1	10.7	5.7	5.9	3.5	2.7
Return on Equity Before Income Taxes 47	22.9	•	317.7	69.7	11.0	•	10.0	•	19.0	11.2	9.8	4.7	3.7
Return on Equity After Income Taxes 48	21.0	•	314.2	68.7	10.3	•	6.8	•	16.7	7.7	7.7	2.3	2.9
Profit Margin (Before Income Tax) 49	6.2	2.4	10.2	8.8	2.3	•	2.6	•	9.5	3.3	5.7	2.4	8.0
Profit Margin (After Income Tax) 50	5.7	2.0	10.1	8.7	2.1	•	1.8	•	8.4	2.3	4.5	1.2	6.5

Table II
Corporations with Net Income

OTHER PROFESSIONAL, SCIENTIFIC, AND TECHNICAL SERVICES

MONEY AMOUNTS AND SIZE OF ASSETS IN THOUSANDS OF DOLLARS

Item Description for Accounting Period 7/10 Through 6/11	Total	Zero Assets	Under 500	500 to 1,000	1,000 to 5,000	5,000 to 10,000	10,000 to 25,000	25,000 to 50,000	50,000 to 100,000	100,000 to 250,000	250,000 to 500,000	500,000 to 2,500,000	2,500,000 and over
Number of Enterprises **1**	63552	8639	51182	2407	1007	•	155	39	34	22	•	9	0
Revenues ($ in Thousands)													
Net Sales **2**	67742827	3245662	28303381	5059419	4481513	•	4135204	2168044	2787056	3064301	•	10322905	0
Interest **3**	44545	7952	1825	2673	3510	•	3792	1724	2570	3214	•	13135	0
Rents **4**	32221	0	0	0	1695	•	0	0	530	21	•	12767	0
Royalties **5**	713581	0	0	0	0	•	32166	0	0	7099	•	644673	0
Other Portfolio Income **6**	228494	33994	1844	4152	5461	•	4337	353	5327	129595	•	42841	0
Other Receipts **7**	1041351	53398	179225	110174	115345	•	51895	37975	43086	121105	•	300230	0
Total Receipts **8**	69803019	3341006	28486275	5176418	4607524	•	4227394	2208096	2838569	3325335	•	11336551	0
Average Total Receipts **9**	1098	387	557	2151	4575	•	27274	56618	83487	151152	•	1259617	•
Operating Costs/Operating Income (%)													
Cost of Operations **10**	25.0	5.7	21.3	28.7	44.2	•	45.6	47.5	35.4	22.5	•	16.9	•
Salaries and Wages **11**	19.1	8.0	18.9	19.8	16.1	•	16.7	15.5	19.2	28.3	•	23.5	•
Taxes Paid **12**	3.0	2.1	3.2	3.6	2.1	•	2.5	2.3	2.3	3.1	•	3.2	•
Interest Paid **13**	1.5	0.3	0.5	1.0	0.3	•	0.5	0.2	1.5	2.2	•	5.5	•
Depreciation **14**	1.7	1.3	1.0	0.8	1.8	•	1.5	0.7	1.9	6.2	•	2.7	•
Amortization and Depletion **15**	0.8	0.3	0.2	0.3	0.2	•	0.2	0.8	0.8	1.3	•	3.0	•
Pensions and Other Deferred Comp. **16**	0.8	0.1	0.8	1.2	0.7	•	0.5	0.9	0.6	0.5	•	1.2	•
Employee Benefits **17**	1.4	1.2	1.1	1.1	0.8	•	1.2	1.1	1.8	1.3	•	2.0	•
Advertising **18**	1.0	0.6	1.0	3.9	0.4	•	0.5	0.8	1.0	1.2	•	0.5	•
Other Expenses **19**	30.6	64.5	27.6	23.3	16.1	•	20.9	20.7	20.7	27.2	•	44.6	•
Officers' Compensation **20**	6.6	5.8	11.6	6.1	5.3	•	3.4	1.8	1.8	1.8	•	1.2	•
Operating Margin **21**	8.5	10.0	12.7	10.2	12.1	•	6.3	7.7	12.9	4.4	•	•	•
Operating Margin Before Officers' Comp. **22**	15.1	15.9	24.3	16.3	17.3	•	9.8	9.6	14.7	6.3	•	•	•

Selected Average Balance Sheet ($ in Thousands)

Item	Line											
Net Receivables	23	89	0	8	74	428	•	3711	8809	14849	20734	215245
Inventories	24	9	0	4	8	43	•	493	393	1105	1241	11695
Net Property, Plant and Equipment	25	71	0	22	187	312	•	2041	2744	6726	16372	145011
Total Assets	26	825	0	99	699	2239	•	14556	34088	71004	160828	3286856
Notes and Loans Payable	27	196	0	47	313	272	•	3175	3448	18406	42053	673610
All Other Liabilities	28	338	0	33	113	887	•	4514	15971	18096	51723	1576513
Net Worth	29	291	0	19	274	1080	•	6867	14668	34502	67052	1036733

Selected Financial Ratios (Times to 1)

Item	Line											
Current Ratio	30	1.3	•	1.5	1.2	2.1	•	1.9	1.4	1.6	1.2	0.9
Quick Ratio	31	1.0	•	1.3	1.0	1.9	•	1.4	1.2	1.3	0.9	0.6
Net Sales to Working Capital	32	18.3	•	31.2	61.7	5.9	•	5.8	10.8	7.0	14.6	•
Coverage Ratio	33	9.1	43.8	26.9	13.5	51.5	•	16.5	43.9	10.7	7.1	2.4
Total Asset Turnover	34	1.3	•	5.6	3.0	2.0	•	1.8	1.6	1.2	0.9	0.3
Inventory Turnover	35	29.7	•	29.3	71.1	46.0	•	24.6	67.2	26.3	25.3	16.5
Receivables Turnover	36	12.5	•	75.6	20.1	10.7	•	7.0	6.2	5.5	6.8	•
Total Liabilities to Net Worth	37	1.8	•	4.3	1.6	1.1	•	1.1	1.3	1.1	1.4	2.2
Current Assets to Working Capital	38	4.4	•	3.0	6.6	1.9	•	2.1	3.7	2.6	6.2	•
Current Liabilities to Working Capital	39	3.4	•	2.0	5.6	0.9	•	1.1	2.7	1.6	5.2	•
Working Capital to Net Sales	40	0.1	•	0.0	0.0	0.2	•	0.2	0.1	0.1	0.1	•
Inventory to Working Capital	41	0.2	•	0.2	0.2	0.0	•	0.1	0.0	0.2	0.2	•
Total Receipts to Cash Flow	42	2.7	1.3	2.9	3.2	3.6	•	3.9	3.5	3.0	3.0	2.1
Cost of Goods to Cash Flow	43	0.7	0.1	0.6	0.9	1.6	•	1.8	1.7	1.1	0.7	0.4
Cash Flow to Total Debt	44	0.7	•	2.3	1.6	1.1	•	0.9	0.8	0.7	0.5	0.2

Selected Financial Factors (in Percentages)

Item	Line											
Debt Ratio	45	64.7	•	81.0	60.8	51.8	•	52.8	57.0	51.4	58.3	68.5
Return on Total Assets	46	17.2	•	77.5	40.7	30.2	•	16.5	17.4	18.9	13.3	4.7
Return on Equity Before Income Taxes	47	43.4	•	393.2	96.2	61.4	•	32.9	39.5	35.2	27.3	8.6
Return on Equity After Income Taxes	48	40.9	•	389.2	95.0	60.4	•	29.0	35.0	31.8	22.8	6.8
Profit Margin (Before Income Tax)	49	11.9	13.0	13.4	12.5	14.9	•	8.5	10.4	14.8	13.2	7.8
Profit Margin (After Income Tax)	50	11.2	12.5	13.3	12.4	14.6	•	7.5	9.2	13.4	11.0	6.1

Table I

Corporations with and without Net Income

OFFICES OF BANK HOLDING COMPANIES

MONEY AMOUNTS AND SIZE OF ASSETS IN THOUSANDS OF DOLLARS

Item Description for Accounting Period 7/10 Through 6/11	Total	Zero Assets	Under 500	500 to 1,000	1,000 to 5,000	5,000 to 10,000	10,000 to 25,000	25,000 to 50,000	50,000 to 100,000	100,000 to 250,000	250,000 to 500,000	500,000 to 2,500,000	2,500,000 and over
Number of Enterprises **1**	5418	51	425	4	188	25	163	473	853	1523	845	707	163
Revenues ($ in Thousands)													
Net Sales **2**	183509134	263948	2774	6652	391791	30203	35527	258746	959405	3585238	3566016	8370120	166038716
Interest **3**	419387823	665957	8726	2728	49450	169351	133188	390368	1336712	6268284	8579188	23470365	378313505
Rents **4**	16542562	4002	0	92	400	467	280	2431	7796	26741	46804	200144	16253404
Royalties **5**	264017	174	0	0	0	0	9	6	140	438	195	4847	258209
Other Portfolio Income **6**	36130168	87921	2613	9	1333	4660	11475	66894	188878	770339	899960	2223288	31872800
Other Receipts **7**	129759669	170672	78494	17326	355737	371187	685968	1541688	1425821	5220331	3847704	7813912	108230826
Total Receipts **8**	785593373	1192674	92607	26807	798711	575868	866447	2260133	3918752	15871371	16939867	42082676	700967460
Average Total Receipts **9**	144997	23386	218	6702	4248	23035	5316	4778	4594	10421	20047	59523	4300414
Operating Costs/Operating Income (%)													
Cost of Operations **10**	1.7	•	•	•	•	•	•	•	0.2	0.0	0.0	0.0	1.9
Salaries and Wages **11**	71.1	97.4	290.6	41.4	7.3	165.0	102.7	53.8	54.1	63.3	77.2	89.1	70.4
Taxes Paid **12**	8.0	14.1	12.0	6.9	0.9	18.9	15.5	12.3	11.2	11.5	13.6	14.1	7.4
Interest Paid **13**	66.7	99.2	331.8	70.5	8.0	227.8	156.6	87.9	80.7	88.8	106.3	106.8	63.2
Depreciation **14**	16.6	6.7	15.8	5.2	0.6	23.9	10.4	8.9	9.3	10.6	12.7	15.4	17.0
Amortization and Depletion **15**	5.2	1.5	3.1	0.1	0.0	18.5	8.3	1.1	1.3	1.3	1.8	2.8	5.6
Pensions and Other Deferred Comp. **16**	4.6	4.0	•	0.0	0.4	1.6	2.5	3.7	3.4	3.7	4.2	4.9	4.6
Employee Benefits **17**	7.4	8.8	9.2	4.7	1.0	19.5	18.7	13.8	12.1	11.3	11.8	11.2	7.0
Advertising **18**	5.1	2.3	7.6	0.5	0.1	6.3	3.9	3.2	3.1	3.6	3.6	4.7	5.2
Other Expenses **19**	215.9	314.7	5395.9	607.0	174.0	2050.1	3057.5	745.9	190.0	206.5	196.3	209.2	215.1
Officers' Compensation **20**	5.0	10.4	25.2	7.3	1.3	10.5	63.0	44.4	36.7	29.5	27.6	20.3	3.0
Operating Margin **21**	•	•	•	•	•	•	•	•	•	•	•	•	•
Operating Margin Before Officers' Comp. **22**	•	•	•	•	•	•	•	•	•	•	•	•	•

Selected Average Balance Sheet ($ in Thousands)

Net Receivables 23	1051354	0	0	16	690	10	7777	20216	43671	98542	206709	562359	30218951
Inventories 24	3	0	0	0	0	0	0	0	0	0	0	2	98
Net Property, Plant and Equipment 25	21270	0	0	216	176	230	712	1359	3379	6959	19651	544445	544445
Total Assets 26	2719504	0	11	718	2404	7180	18219	37902	74059	162715	346694	1004294	82200958
Notes and Loans Payable 27	473254	0	36	206	758	2113	1186	1476	2832	7417	17487	56016	15306110
All Other Liabilities 28	1783966	0	31	12948	3921	31348	33859	34842	66324	144136	303107	861672	52150442
Net Worth 29	462284	0	-56	-12437	-2276	-26280	-16826	1584	4904	11162	26100	86606	14744405

(Note: row 25 values read left to right: 21270, 0, 0, 216, 176, 230, 712, 1359, 3379, 6959, 19651, 544445)

Selected Financial Ratios (Times to 1)

Current Ratio 30	0.9	•	0.0	0.1	0.5	0.1	0.6	1.0	1.0	1.0	0.9	0.9	0.9
Quick Ratio 31	0.8	•	0.0	0.1	0.5	0.1	0.6	1.0	1.0	1.0	0.9	0.9	0.8
Net Sales to Working Capital 32	•	•	•	•	•	•	•	1.4	•	•	•	•	•
Coverage Ratio 33	1.3	•	•	2.3	2.2	0.2	0.0	0.9	0.9	1.0	1.0	1.1	1.4
Total Asset Turnover 34	0.0	•	0.6	•	0.9	•	0.0	0.0	0.0	0.0	0.0	0.0	0.0
Inventory Turnover 35	165.6	•	•	•	4.7	•	•	8.2	0.3	5.1	0.0	•	193.3
Receivables Turnover 36	55.5	•	80.1	•	•	243.6	•	•	•	•	•	•	•
Total Liabilities to Net Worth 37	4.9	•	•	•	22.9	•	•	14.1	13.6	12.3	10.6	•	4.6
Current Assets to Working Capital 38	•	•	•	•	81.4	•	•	•	•	•	•	•	•
Current Liabilities to Working Capital 39	•	•	•	•	80.4	•	•	•	•	•	•	•	•
Working Capital to Net Sales 40	•	•	•	•	0.7	•	•	•	•	•	•	•	•
Inventory to Working Capital 41	•	•	•	•	0.0	•	•	•	•	•	•	•	•
Total Receipts to Cash Flow 42	0.5	0.6	0.1	0.4	0.7	0.1	0.3	0.7	0.6	0.5	0.5	0.5	0.5
Cost of Goods to Cash Flow 43	0.0	•	•	•	0.0	•	0.0	0.0	0.0	0.0	0.0	0.0	0.0
Cash Flow to Total Debt 44	0.0	1.3	0.3	0.3	0.7	0.1	0.1	0.3	0.0	0.0	0.0	0.0	0.0

Selected Financial Factors (in Percentages)

Debt Ratio 45	83.0	•	606.1	•	1832.8	194.7	192.4	95.8	93.4	93.1	92.5	91.4	82.1
Return on Total Assets 46	1.1	•	•	•	15.6	•	•	•	1.1	1.3	1.4	1.4	1.1
Return on Equity Before Income Taxes 47	1.5	•	319.8	45.6	29.4	13.1	466.0	29.4	•	•	0.8	1.5	1.6
Return on Equity After Income Taxes 48	0.8	•	319.8	45.6	29.4	13.2	466.0	29.4	•	•	•	•	0.9
Profit Margin (Before Income Tax) 49	20.7	•	•	9.9	•	•	•	•	•	•	4.7	11.1	23.0
Profit Margin (After Income Tax) 50	11.2	•	9.9	•	•	•	•	•	•	•	•	•	13.6

Table II

Corporations with Net Income

OFFICES OF BANK HOLDING COMPANIES

MONEY AMOUNTS AND SIZE OF ASSETS IN THOUSANDS OF DOLLARS

Item Description for Accounting Period 7/10 Through 6/11	Total	Zero Assets	Under 500	500 to 1,000	1,000 to 5,000	5,000 to 10,000	10,000 to 25,000	25,000 to 50,000	50,000 to 100,000	100,000 to 250,000	250,000 to 500,000	500,000 to 2,500,000	2,500,000 and over
Number of Enterprises **1**	3412	19	0	0	39	0	106	330	626	1098	592	488	113
Revenues ($ in Thousands)													
Net Sales **2**	125424228	64523	0	0	389365	0	22811	174801	715147	2757408	2846255	6144985	112308934
Interest **3**	311226606	189792	0	0	69957	0	61030	225945	899069	4054432	5654709	15637916	284433756
Rents **4**	10746536	2461	0	0	191	0	148	503	4552	15314	27444	137211	10558714
Royalties **5**	47822	174	0	0	0	0	9	6	11	220	194	1207	46003
Other Portfolio Income **6**	28350326	15025	0	0	2859	0	8078	51251	143054	582775	666218	1573104	25307961
Other Receipts **7**	91521003	62754	0	0	43943	0	22985	993090	770711	2723409	2355501	5235014	79313592
Total Receipts **8**	567316521	334729	0	0	506315	0	115061	1445596	2532544	10133558	11550321	28729437	511968960
Average Total Receipts **9**	166271	17617	•	•	12982	•	1085	4381	4046	9229	19511	58872	4530699
Operating Costs/Operating Income (%)													
Cost of Operations **10**	1.0	•	•	•	•	•	•	•	0.2	0.0	0.0	0.0	1.1
Salaries and Wages **11**	70.6	138.8	•	•	7.5	•	61.8	50.0	48.7	56.1	66.0	82.4	70.8
Taxes Paid **12**	9.3	21.6	•	•	0.9	•	16.1	12.0	10.9	11.0	12.2	13.8	9.0
Interest Paid **13**	66.7	53.1	•	•	8.5	•	91.4	74.6	73.4	77.2	87.0	90.2	64.8
Depreciation **14**	16.8	12.3	•	•	0.8	•	8.1	7.2	8.5	9.6	11.4	14.4	17.4
Amortization and Depletion **15**	5.4	3.9	•	•	0.0	•	0.8	0.8	1.0	1.1	1.6	2.6	5.8
Pensions and Other Deferred Comp. **16**	3.8	6.7	•	•	0.1	•	3.5	4.0	3.6	4.0	4.3	5.4	3.7
Employee Benefits **17**	8.7	13.7	•	•	0.8	•	21.9	14.6	11.9	10.7	10.9	10.9	8.5
Advertising **18**	5.8	4.7	•	•	0.3	•	3.1	3.4	3.1	3.7	3.4	4.6	6.0
Other Expenses **19**	208.8	172.8	•	•	26.7	•	124.1	528.4	85.1	92.9	101.6	137.6	219.3
Officers' Compensation **20**	6.0	13.3	•	•	1.1	•	82.7	46.9	35.9	29.1	25.6	21.3	3.9
Operating Margin **21**	•	•	•	•	53.4	•	•	•	•	•	•	•	•
Operating Margin Before Officers' Comp. **22**	•	•	•	•	54.5	•	•	•	•	•	•	•	•

Selected Average Balance Sheet ($ in Thousands)

Line Item	1	2	3	4	5	6	7	8	9	10	11
Net Receivables 23	1286697	•	2028	•	10766	21082	43840	98654	210495	564060	34033875
Inventories 24	3	•	0	•	0	0	0	1	0	3	60
Net Property, Plant and Equipment 25	22228	•	1156	•	172	449	1219	3147	6689	18575	516704
Total Assets 26	2636875	•	4165	•	20037	38034	73544	161582	347420	993471	71400344
Notes and Loans Payable 27	430655	•	1653	•	783	1179	2092	6543	14488	50621	12629066
All Other Liabilities 28	1900846	•	1884	•	19665	32322	63503	138646	299599	847717	50352457
Net Worth 29	305374	•	628	•	-412	4533	7949	16393	33332	95133	8418821

Selected Financial Ratios (Times to 1)

Line Item	1	2	3	4	5	6	7	8	9	10	11
Current Ratio 30	1.0	•	1.2	•	1.0	1.0	1.0	1.0	1.0	0.9	1.0
Quick Ratio 31	0.8	•	1.1	•	1.0	1.0	1.0	1.0	0.9	0.9	0.8
Net Sales to Working Capital 32	•	•	23.4	•	0.3	1.9	0.7	1.8	1.8	•	•
Coverage Ratio 33	1.8	2.3	10.9	•	1.9	1.9	1.8	1.8	1.8	1.8	1.7
Total Asset Turnover 34	0.0	•	2.4	•	0.0	0.0	0.0	0.0	0.0	0.0	0.0
Inventory Turnover 35	132.0	•	•	•	•	•	8.2	0.1	5.7	0.0	183.7
Receivables Turnover 36	0.0	•	6.8	•	0.0	0.0	0.0	0.0	0.0	0.0	0.0
Total Liabilities to Net Worth 37	7.6	•	5.6	•	7.4	8.3	8.9	9.4	9.4	•	7.5
Current Assets to Working Capital 38	•	•	5.9	•	24.5	29.2	41.6	•	•	•	•
Current Liabilities to Working Capital 39	•	•	4.9	•	23.5	28.2	40.6	•	•	•	•
Working Capital to Net Sales 40	•	•	0.0	•	3.2	2.2	1.4	•	•	•	•
Inventory to Working Capital 41	•	•	•	•	•	•	0.0	•	•	•	•
Total Receipts to Cash Flow 42	0.4	•	1.0	•	0.5	0.5	0.7	0.6	0.6	0.5	0.4
Cost of Goods to Cash Flow 43	0.0	•	•	•	•	•	0.0	0.0	0.0	0.0	0.0
Cash Flow to Total Debt 44	0.0	•	2.9	•	0.0	0.0	0.0	0.0	0.0	0.0	0.0

Selected Financial Factors (in Percentages)

Line Item	1	2	3	4	5	6	7	8	9	10	11
Debt Ratio 45	88.4	•	84.9	•	102.1	88.1	89.2	89.9	90.4	90.4	88.2
Return on Total Assets 46	1.6	•	220.3	•	1.8	2.0	2.0	2.1	2.1	2.0	1.6
Return on Equity Before Income Taxes 47	6.0	•	1326.4	•	8.2	8.2	9.0	9.6	9.3	•	5.7
Return on Equity After Income Taxes 48	4.4	•	1326.0	•	7.5	7.2	7.7	7.8	7.1	•	4.1
Profit Margin (Before Income Tax) 49	50.1	67.3	83.4	•	79.0	70.5	57.2	58.6	66.8	70.6	48.1
Profit Margin (After Income Tax) 50	36.5	64.3	83.4	•	67.9	64.1	50.4	50.0	54.0	53.7	34.4

Table I

Corporations with and without Net Income

OFFICES OF OTHER HOLDING COMPANIES

MONEY AMOUNTS AND SIZE OF ASSETS IN THOUSANDS OF DOLLARS

Item Description for Accounting Period 7/10 Through 6/11	Total	Zero Assets	Under 500	500 to 1,000	1,000 to 5,000	5,000 to 10,000	10,000 to 25,000	25,000 to 50,000	50,000 to 100,000	100,000 to 250,000	250,000 to 500,000	500,000 to 2,500,000	2,500,000 and over
Number of Enterprises 1	44912	11203	21541	2636	5297	1465	1260	658	367	279	101	85	20
Revenues ($ in Thousands)													
Net Sales 2	1201546	6364	2057	24	11439	19291	22466	40009	38220	69570	105964		879506
Interest 3	4336969	361031	30453	10580	65872	79190	78372	119046	150054	251669	352239	1111272	1727190
Rents 4	221291	78857	14087	1378	9429	12699	8986	11707	53197	25760	346	4809	35
Royalties 5	141884	15795	890	23379	4398	7332	13892	4271	8399	26790	16554	15400	4784
Other Portfolio Income 6	8816022	954601	141691	133728	354423	290002	340484	360249	639255	1107691	650950	1187546	2655401
Other Receipts 7	22699437	3895321	216541	206361	1123089	925029	707599	996088	656745	2013847	357178	5410971	6190668
Total Receipts 8	37417149	5311969	405719	375450	1568650	1333543	1171799	1531370	1545870	3495327	1383903	7835962	11457584
Average Total Receipts 9	833	474	19	142	296	910	930	2327	4212	12528	13702	92188	572879
Operating Costs/Operating Income (%)													
Cost of Operations 10	16.4	•	•	•	5.0	•	•	86.9	1.4	63.9	24.8	36.0	8.8
Salaries and Wages 11	64.0	119.7	313.3	140037.5	460.4	77.0	170.1	625.3	324.9	52.9	329.7	87.9	13.7
Taxes Paid 12	100.8	1872.6	1323.8	19841.7	272.2	155.2	181.0	94.6	98.6	131.3	284.1	133.6	71.6
Interest Paid 13	723.8	114487.4	4372.1	86262.5	575.5	568.9	505.0	483.0	590.0	796.9	5790.9	1796.2	489.5
Depreciation 14	15.8	129.4	216.7	2520.8	171.0	72.2	58.9	49.8	87.8	30.2	116.2	12.3	3.9
Amortization and Depletion 15	141.0	11620.1	415.3	2245.8	91.5	51.6	438.5	61.9	106.1	106.6	933.9	479.6	13.3
Pensions and Other Deferred Comp. 16	8.5	0.0	59.5	50.0	21.2	17.6	23.9	0.9	2.0	1.9	42.1	5.1	8.9
Employee Benefits 17	10.1	7.3	1059.2	5279.2	134.6	24.4	27.8	48.4	17.6	6.4	37.9	7.4	3.4
Advertising 18	3.8	10.2	0.3	441.7	4.9	0.3	0.3	1.3	2.2	50.1	1.4	3.6	0.5
Other Expenses 19	1036.2	50541.8	27729.7	492925.0	5295.1	3489.1	3477.3	1783.4	2061.2	1731.8	16404.9	1518.5	123.0
Officers' Compensation 20	36.7	43.6	2835.6	41958.3	614.9	126.8	126.9	57.2	84.3	44.2	167.0	46.1	11.4
Operating Margin 21	•											•	•
Operating Margin Before Officers' Comp. 22	•											•	•

Selected Average Balance Sheet ($ in Thousands)

Net Receivables 23	477	0	7	20	85	219	530	1172	3082	5176	15290	14862	680845
Inventories 24	7	0	0	0	2	2	11	0	39	701	11	546	1768
Net Property, Plant and Equipment 25	96	0	0	25	61	462	226	1154	1063	3174	1265	7640	7116
Total Assets 26	10120	117	717	2209	7011	16083	34805	70896	153414	346167		1093536	9412432
Notes and Loans Payable 27	2826	60	143	670	1750	5825	5785	10941	27052	67035		323131	3110170
All Other Liabilities 28	2027	46	24	274	1205	2810	25918	9649	18046	37587		148514	2059948
Net Worth 29	5267	11	550	1264	4057	7448	3102	50306	108316	241545		621890	4242314

Selected Financial Ratios (Times to 1)

Current Ratio 30	1.4	•	1.1	3.8	3.3	1.4	2.1	1.2	3.1	1.6	2.0	1.7	0.9
Quick Ratio 31	0.8	•	0.8	2.6	1.8	1.0	1.1	0.8	1.8	1.1	1.2	0.8	0.6
Net Sales to Working Capital 32	0.1	•	0.0	0.0	0.0	0.0	0.0	0.0	0.0	0.0	0.0	0.0	•
Coverage Ratio 33	3.2	3.0	•	11.2	11.6	5.2	2.1	1.4	2.3	3.8	0.8	2.9	3.6
Total Asset Turnover 34	0.0	•	0.0	0.0	0.0	0.0	0.0	0.0	0.0	0.0	0.0	0.0	0.0
Inventory Turnover 35	0.6	•	•	•	0.1	•	•	1103.6	0.0	0.2	1.5	0.8	2.2
Receivables Turnover 36	0.1	•	0.0	0.0	0.0	0.1	0.1	0.0	0.0	0.0	0.0	0.1	0.1
Total Liabilities to Net Worth 37	0.9	•	9.3	0.3	0.7	0.7	10.2	1.2	0.4	0.4	0.4	0.8	1.2
Current Assets to Working Capital 38	3.7	•	11.4	1.4	1.4	3.4	1.9	6.7	1.5	2.8	2.0	2.3	•
Current Liabilities to Working Capital 39	2.7	•	10.4	0.4	0.4	2.4	0.9	5.7	0.5	1.8	1.0	1.3	•
Working Capital to Net Sales 40	15.4	•	45.8	186.4	30.0	25.0	57.4	25.0	82.4	32.4	439.1	55.1	•
Inventory to Working Capital 41	0.0	•	0.0	•	0.0	0.0	•	0.0	0.0	0.1	0.0	0.0	•
Total Receipts to Cash Flow 42	0.1	0.0	0.0	0.0	0.0	0.0	0.1	0.0	0.1	0.0	0.0	0.0	0.1
Cost of Goods to Cash Flow 43	0.0	•	•	0.0	0.0	0.0	0.1	•	0.0	0.0	0.0	0.0	0.0
Cash Flow to Total Debt 44	0.1	•	0.5	0.2	0.2	0.2	0.0	0.0	0.1	0.1	0.1	0.1	0.1

Selected Financial Factors (in Percentages)

Debt Ratio 45	48.0	•	90.3	23.3	42.8	42.1	53.7	91.1	29.0	29.4	30.2	43.1	54.9
Return on Total Assets 46	6.1	•	•	12.2	6.6	5.5	0.8	1.7	2.0	4.9	0.9	6.0	8.1
Return on Equity Before Income Taxes 47	8.1	•	•	14.5	10.5	7.7	0.5	10.1	1.6	5.1	•	7.0	13.0
Return on Equity After Income Taxes 48	4.9	•	•	12.9	8.8	6.1	•	0.7	0.4	3.2	•	5.6	8.5
Profit Margin (Before Income Tax) 49	1600.1	23105.9	878000.0	6125.6	2378.6	224.8	514.6	762.5	2234.2	514.6	•	3499.1	1252.2
Profit Margin (After Income Tax) 50	973.3	3280.9	776933.3	5136.5	1893.4	•	34.8	205.1	1385.6	224.8	•	2801.2	817.3

Table II

Corporations with Net Income

OFFICES OF OTHER HOLDING COMPANIES

MONEY AMOUNTS AND SIZE OF ASSETS IN THOUSANDS OF DOLLARS

Item Description for Accounting Period 7/10 Through 6/11	Total	Zero Assets	Under 500	500 to 1000	1,000 to 5,000	5,000 to 10,000	10,000 to 25,000	25,000 to 50,000	50,000 to 100,000	100,000 to 250,000	250,000 to 500,000	500,000 to 2,500,000	2,500,000 and over
Number of Enterprises 1	13653	2531	5467	1227	2507	728	526	279	159	123	41	52	13
Revenues ($ in Thousands)													
Net Sales 2	1048168	4623	0	24	6993	13267	15375	37807	14849	66047	2138	49684	837362
Interest 3	2674704	155070	10777	5080	46879	53292	42132	66957	86909	160917	163948	891214	991528
Rents 4	107245	13480	291	175	8328	10015	6961	8516	43446	13795	51	2087	0
Royalties 5	119372	14806	818	23361	3076	6515	12626	2877	7845	26498	4800	11587	4564
Other Portfolio Income 6	8302518	908330	99568	99243	322509	280421	290910	302629	594923	1047550	599562	1113723	2643150
Other Receipts 7	24704292	4102181	339607	219026	1197712	989987	940188	1165250	1075822	2073634	1017727	5476687	6106471
Total Receipts 8	36956299	5198490	451061	346909	1585497	1353597	1308192	1584036	1823794	3388441	1788226	7544982	10583075
Average Total Receipts 9	2707	2054	83	283	632	1859	2487	5678	11470	27548	43615	145096	814083
Operating Costs/Operating Income (%)													
Cost of Operations 10	17.8	•	•	•	8.1	•	•	91.8	3.5	66.0	66.2	57.4	9.2
Salaries and Wages 11	31.3	26.9	•	•	552.6	56.1	51.9	4.8	659.8	13.2	743.2	81.8	12.7
Taxes Paid 12	103.7	2325.8	•	8916.7	344.1	135.9	214.1	80.6	173.3	110.4	629.7	256.3	75.0
Interest Paid 13	556.4	9012.6	•	38654.2	501.8	515.3	165.6	175.5	449.2	246.0	8225.4	2632.8	417.2
Depreciation 14	11.3	146.5	•	1412.5	69.7	39.9	67.8	37.0	144.2	9.4	265.9	18.2	4.1
Amortization and Depletion 15	120.1	15070.2	•	33.3	64.9	59.0	168.3	38.6	148.3	26.3	356.5	918.1	0.6
Pensions and Other Deferred Comp. 16	8.7	•	•	•	3.0	21.2	7.8	0.9	3.1	1.4	65.3	8.9	9.3
Employee Benefits 17	5.9	0.5	•	266.7	18.5	32.5	2.9	1.5	13.9	0.8	104.0	2.6	3.5
Advertising 18	4.1	13.6	•	441.7	7.2	0.2	0.4	0.1	0.1	52.1	3.5	7.4	0.4
Other Expenses 19	363.0	18019.0	•	86000.0	1968.8	1788.5	806.9	458.8	1196.0	658.2	9862.6	1185.3	100.1
Officers' Compensation 20	23.0	2.8	•	5175.0	540.9	131.8	104.2	35.5	40.0	22.9	368.6	35.9	11.6
Operating Margin 21	•	•	•	•	•	•	•	•	•	•	•	•	•
Operating Margin Before Officers' Comp. 22	•	•	•	•	•	•	•	•	•	•	•	•	•

Selected Average Balance Sheet ($ in Thousands)

Line item													
Net Receivables **23**	1183	0	6	20	27	304	433	939	2401	6695	27348	11310	953584
Inventories **24**	9	0	0	0	3	4	17	0	60	267	14	543	2719
Net Property, Plant and Equipment **25**	100	0	0	0	36	191	223	952	702	3387	23	1745	10726
Total Assets **26**	21219	156	776	2061	7037	16628	34463	72119	153932	357239		1167500	11807486
Notes and Loans Payable **27**	6221	27	162	278	1449	4576	8229	19418	55977	409556			4122521
All Other Liabilities **28**	2251	80	32	215	684	952	3651	10612	19447	39832		125073	1191726
Net Worth **29**	12747	49	582	1568	4904	14379	26236	53278	115067	261429		632872	6493238

Selected Financial Ratios (Times to 1)

Line item												
Current Ratio **30**	1.8	•	0.9	4.4	3.0	2.0	2.2	2.6	1.9	1.8	2.6	1.5
Quick Ratio **31**	1.2	•	0.8	2.6	1.3	1.4	1.3	1.4	1.4	1.1	1.4	1.0
Net Sales to Working Capital **32**	0.1	•	•	0.0	0.0	0.0	0.0	0.0	0.0	0.0	0.0	0.1
Coverage Ratio **33**	6.4	10.9	34.5	38.5	15.6	43.6	19.6	22.7	18.0	9.6	5.0	4.2
Total Asset Turnover **34**	0.0	•	0.0	0.0	0.0	0.0	0.0	0.0	0.0	0.0	0.0	0.0
Inventory Turnover **35**	1.5	•	•	0.1	•	•	•	0.1	1.3	2.5	1.0	2.2
Receivables Turnover **36**	0.1	•	•	0.0	0.1	0.1	0.2	0.1	0.1	0.0	0.1	0.1
Total Liabilities to Net Worth **37**	0.7	2.2	•	0.3	0.4	0.2	0.3	0.3	0.3	0.4	0.8	0.8
Current Assets to Working Capital **38**	2.2	•	1.3	1.5	2.0	1.3	1.8	1.6	2.1	2.3	1.6	3.1
Current Liabilities to Working Capital **39**	1.2	•	0.3	0.5	1.0	0.3	0.8	0.6	1.1	1.3	0.6	2.1
Working Capital to Net Sales **40**	18.9	•	8316.1	125.5	29.5	75.5	25.7	84.8	23.7	595.9	118.0	7.6
Inventory to Working Capital **41**	0.0	•	•	•	0.0	•	0.0	0.0	0.0	0.0	0.0	0.0
Total Receipts to Cash Flow **42**	0.0	0.0	•	0.0	0.0	0.0	0.0	0.0	0.0	0.0	0.0	0.1
Cost of Goods to Cash Flow **43**	0.0	•	•	0.0	•	0.0	•	0.0	0.0	0.0	0.0	0.0
Cash Flow to Total Debt **44**	0.2	0.6	1.1	1.0	0.6	0.8	0.5	0.4	0.5	0.3	0.2	0.1

Selected Financial Factors (in Percentages)

Line item												
Debt Ratio **45**	39.9	•	68.5	25.0	23.9	23.9	13.5	30.3	26.1	25.2	26.8	45.0
Return on Total Assets **46**	13.0	•	45.2	33.6	26.1	20.8	12.7	13.6	13.2	15.4	11.5	9.7
Return on Equity Before Income Taxes **47**	18.2	•	141.9	43.5	33.4	28.0	14.3	16.9	17.1	19.5	14.0	13.4
Return on Equity After Income Taxes **48**	13.9	•	133.3	40.1	30.6	25.3	12.1	14.3	14.6	15.3	11.4	8.9
Profit Margin (Before Income Tax) **49**	3023.7	894437.4	1294945.8	18803.5	7523.1	7058.2	3272.1	9737.0	4173.2	70425.7	10465.3	1352.5
Profit Margin (After Income Tax) **50**	2307.8	62147.2	1193879.2	17186.5	6817.6	5936.1	2764.5	8305.3	3279.6	57272.4	9024.7	895.8

Table I

Corporations with and without Net Income

EMPLOYMENT SERVICES

MONEY AMOUNTS AND SIZE OF ASSETS IN THOUSANDS OF DOLLARS

Item Description for Accounting Period 7/10 Through 6/11	Total	Zero Assets	Under 500	500 to 1,000	1,000 to 5,000	5,000 to 10,000	10,000 to 25,000	25,000 to 50,000	50,000 to 100,000	100,000 to 250,000	250,000 to 500,000	500,000 to 2,500,000	2,500,000 and over
Number of Enterprises **1**	24717	5806	15957	1272	1302	162	124	36	14	15	13	15	0
Revenues ($ in Thousands)													
Net Sales **2**	138249070	1014034	27120537	7949964	16681870	4628185	7732033	5250269	3200266	12455406	8023049	44193457	0
Interest **3**	164288	20	958	2631	5454	101	1363	1041	1815	13181	2845	134878	0
Rents **4**	10558	0	3408	0	1979	59	0	0	0	2546	73	2493	0
Royalties **5**	281639	0	0	0	9223	0	0	0	185	0	49910	222321	0
Other Portfolio Income **6**	472089	616	0	10640	1901	341	41408	10383	611	2388	501	403303	0
Other Receipts **7**	1760370	9524	74464	2518	39127	11239	16977	8419	5298	3814	141134	1447853	0
Total Receipts **8**	140938014	1024194	27199367	7965753	16739554	4639925	7791781	5270112	3208175	12477335	8217512	46404305	0
Average Total Receipts **9**	5702	176	1705	6262	12857	28642	62837	146392	229155	831822	632116	3093620	•
Operating Costs/Operating Income (%)													
Cost of Operations **10**	51.7	27.8	28.6	63.8	54.8	56.8	51.6	44.7	64.7	52.0	58.7	60.9	•
Salaries and Wages **11**	27.1	37.9	44.0	18.8	22.5	17.1	25.6	37.9	19.2	35.3	17.5	19.9	•
Taxes Paid **12**	5.3	5.9	3.3	5.0	5.6	3.6	6.1	5.2	6.6	7.1	5.2	6.1	•
Interest Paid **13**	0.5	2.8	0.1	0.1	0.3	0.6	0.8	0.7	0.4	0.4	0.7	0.7	•
Depreciation **14**	0.4	0.7	0.1	0.1	0.2	0.2	0.3	0.2	0.2	0.1	0.7	0.7	•
Amortization and Depletion **15**	0.5	2.4	0.1	0.1	0.1	0.1	0.4	0.5	0.2	0.6	1.5	0.7	•
Pensions and Other Deferred Comp. **16**	0.2	0.0	0.3	0.6	0.3	0.0	0.1	0.1	0.1	0.1	0.2	0.2	•
Employee Benefits **17**	2.4	2.3	1.5	0.7	3.7	2.1	2.4	1.5	2.6	1.7	1.8	3.1	•
Advertising **18**	0.4	1.2	0.3	0.1	0.6	0.2	1.7	0.1	0.2	0.1	0.4	0.2	•
Other Expenses **19**	10.2	20.0	17.2	8.0	9.0	13.8	10.0	8.6	5.2	2.6	11.7	8.6	•
Officers' Compensation **20**	1.5	5.3	4.0	1.6	1.8	1.7	1.5	0.9	0.4	0.2	1.1	0.4	•
Operating Margin **21**	•	0.5	1.2	1.2	3.7	•	•	•	0.3	•	0.5	1.5	•
Operating Margin Before Officers' Comp. **22**	1.4	4.5	2.7	3.0	5.5	0.8	0.5	0.7	1.5	0.1	0.4	1.5	•

Selected Average Balance Sheet ($ in Thousands)

Line item													
Net Receivables 23	435	0	17	232	628	2922	5665	10083	28886	70265	83643	352089	•
Inventories 24	1	0	0	0	2	2	69	41	18	299	103	987	•
Net Property, Plant and Equipment 25	160	0	11	30	242	390	785	1441	2059	7984	15253	191010	•
Total Assets 26	1757	0	90	662	1927	6158	14690	35391	64591	163608	354536	1772126	•
Notes and Loans Payable 27	431	0	41	250	666	2255	4631	12518	18925	44579	66027	374931	•
All Other Liabilities 28	575	0	27	187	937	1752	6235	13253	26468	90423	98682	518810	•
Net Worth 29	751	0	22	226	324	2150	3824	9620	19198	28606	189827	878385	•

Selected Financial Ratios (Times to 1)

Line item													
Current Ratio 30	1.2	•	1.8	1.2	1.5	1.5	1.4	1.3	1.1	2.0	1.3		
Quick Ratio 31	1.1	•	1.6	1.1	1.3	1.3	1.1	1.2	0.9	1.6	1.1		
Net Sales to Working Capital 32	29.1	•	39.1	51.7	17.7	16.9	24.0	25.1	72.7	8.0	23.8		
Coverage Ratio 33	5.3	•	11.5	5.9	8.2	1.3	1.0	2.4	1.4	5.3	7.3		
Total Asset Turnover 34	3.2	•	9.4	6.6	4.6	4.2	4.1	3.5	5.1	1.7	1.7		
Inventory Turnover 35	1969.3	53572.7	•	4649.4	7229.7	465.1	1588.5	8103.3	1444.4	3507.2	1818.7		
Receivables Turnover 36	12.0	83.6	32.6	20.4	10.5	10.5	15.2	7.0	13.7	7.0	10.3		
Total Liabilities to Net Worth 37	1.3	•	3.2	1.9	4.9	1.9	2.7	2.4	4.7	0.9	1.0		
Current Assets to Working Capital 38	3.9	•	6.1	2.3	5.1	3.1	3.8	4.6	8.5	2.0	4.6		
Current Liabilities to Working Capital 39	2.9	•	5.1	1.3	4.1	2.1	2.8	3.6	7.5	1.0	3.6		
Working Capital to Net Sales 40	0.0	•	0.0	0.0	0.0	0.1	0.0	0.0	0.0	0.1	0.0		
Inventory to Working Capital 41	0.0	•	0.0	•	0.0	0.0	0.0	•	0.0	0.0	0.0		
Total Receipts to Cash Flow 42	9.5	11.0	6.0	11.4	11.5	6.2	12.2	13.4	20.1	44.4	7.8	9.5	
Cost of Goods to Cash Flow 43	4.9	3.1	1.7	7.3	6.3	3.5	6.3	6.0	13.0	23.1	4.6	5.8	
Cash Flow to Total Debt 44	0.6	•	4.1	1.3	0.7	1.1	0.5	0.4	0.3	0.1	0.5	0.3	

Selected Financial Factors (in Percentages)

Line item													
Debt Ratio 45	57.3	•	76.0	65.9	83.2	65.1	74.0	72.8	70.3	82.5	46.5	50.4	
Return on Total Assets 46	8.0	•	17.6	12.6	12.5	21.1	4.5	2.9	3.3	2.6	6.3	8.0	
Return on Equity Before Income Taxes 47	15.2	•	63.5	33.8	61.8	53.0	3.7	0.0	6.5	4.6	9.5	13.9	
Return on Equity After Income Taxes 48	11.6	•	61.7	32.7	60.6	52.4	1.1	•	2.7	0.4	7.2	9.7	
Profit Margin (Before Income Tax) 49	2.0	•	0.8	1.2	1.6	4.0	0.2	0.0	0.5	0.2	2.9	4.1	
Profit Margin (After Income Tax) 50	1.6	•	0.8	1.2	1.5	3.9	0.1	•	0.2	0.0	2.2	2.9	

Table II
Corporations with Net Income

EMPLOYMENT SERVICES

MONEY AMOUNTS AND SIZE OF ASSETS IN THOUSANDS OF DOLLARS

Item Description for Accounting Period 7/10 Through 6/11		Total	Zero Assets	Under 500	500 to 1,000	1,000 to 5,000	5,000 to 10,000	10,000 to 25,000	25,000 to 50,000	50,000 to 100,000	100,000 to 250,000	250,000 to 500,000	500,000 to 2,500,000	2,500,000 and over
Number of Enterprises	1	10685	1875	7103	580	834	•	80	21	10	8	•	12	0
Revenues ($ in Thousands)														
Net Sales	2	107105832	316971	23171661	3380615	9948411	•	5005763	3822003	2444559	6924721	•	40117969	0
Interest	3	135856	0	12	536	5186	•	389	985	205	3053	•	123164	0
Rents	4	6809	0	3408	0	427	•	0	0	0	747	•	2227	0
Royalties	5	272257	0	0	0	0	•	0	0	185	0	•	222162	0
Other Portfolio Income	6	447297	616	0	42	1860	•	31537	8556	611	280	•	403303	0
Other Receipts	7	1488435	8746	11614	1605	30826	•	11055	4183	4171	2486	•	1262602	0
Total Receipts	8	109456486	326333	23186695	3382798	9986710	•	5048744	3835727	2449731	6931287	•	42131427	0
Average Total Receipts	9	10244	174	3264	5832	11974	•	63109	182654	244973	866411	•	3510952	•
Operating Costs/Operating Income (%)														
Cost of Operations	10	50.9	5.4	30.1	38.9	41.2	•	55.2	52.5	73.9	65.7	•	59.2	•
Salaries and Wages	11	27.1	32.3	43.6	37.4	32.3	•	22.5	30.8	8.9	20.9	•	21.1	•
Taxes Paid	12	5.2	5.0	3.1	7.7	4.4	•	6.9	4.6	6.1	7.2	•	5.9	•
Interest Paid	13	0.4	0.6	0.0	0.2	0.4	•	0.8	0.1	0.3	0.3	•	0.6	•
Depreciation	14	0.4	0.0	0.1	0.2	0.2	•	0.2	0.2	0.3	0.2	•	0.7	•
Amortization and Depletion	15	0.4	0.4	0.1	0.1	0.0	•	0.3	0.2	0.1	0.4	•	0.6	•
Pensions and Other Deferred Comp.	16	0.2	•	0.2	0.4	0.4	•	0.1	0.1	0.1	0.1	•	0.2	•
Employee Benefits	17	2.3	0.1	1.5	0.5	3.0	•	3.1	1.7	1.9	1.0	•	3.2	•
Advertising	18	0.2	2.8	0.2	0.1	0.2	•	0.3	0.1	0.1	0.1	•	0.2	•
Other Expenses	19	10.5	27.8	15.7	7.4	13.1	•	7.4	7.6	6.0	2.7	•	8.8	•
Officers' Compensation	20	1.4	13.2	3.3	2.7	1.8	•	1.6	0.8	0.5	0.2	•	0.4	•
Operating Margin	21	1.0	12.5	2.2	4.5	3.0	•	1.6	1.3	1.9	1.0	•	1.0	•
Operating Margin Before Officers' Comp.	22	2.5	25.7	5.5	7.2	4.8	•	3.2	2.1	2.3	1.2	•	•	•

Selected Average Balance Sheet ($ in Thousands)

	1	2	3	4	5	6	7	8	9	10	11
Net Receivables 23	741	0	13	310	536	•	6185	10638	31976	80127	338646
Inventories 24	1	0	0	0	1	•	1	58	0	87	652
Net Property, Plant and Equipment 25	329	0	14	66	288	•	679	1937	2544	5174	232609
Total Assets 26	3326	112	706	1794	14087	•		37081	60801	185248	1992814
Notes and Loans Payable 27	699	40	83	638	4161	•		10096	19554	41737	375209
All Other Liabilities 28	1011	42	160	733	4569	•		11792	21489	107092	560522
Net Worth 29	1616	30	463	424	5357	•		15193	19758	36419	1057083

Selected Financial Ratios (Times to 1)

	1	2	3	4	5	6	7	8	9	10	11
Current Ratio 30	1.4	•	1.0	2.8	1.8	•			1.8	1.2	1.3
Quick Ratio 31	1.2	•	0.9	2.7	1.5	•		1.6	1.7	1.0	1.1
Net Sales to Working Capital 32	26.4	•	•	19.1	24.3	•		13.5	11.9	45.6	27.8
Coverage Ratio 33	9.5	25.3	45.8	31.4	9.8	•		4.7	8.2	4.4	8.7
Total Asset Turnover 34	3.0	•	29.2	8.3	6.6	•		4.4	4.0	4.7	1.7
Inventory Turnover 35	5194.0	48042.4	•	5081.0	•		64273.9	1641.9		6536.3	3033.1
Receivables Turnover 36	13.8	205.2	29.5	22.4	•		11.4	10.5		14.4	14.7
Total Liabilities to Net Worth 37	1.1	2.7	0.5	3.2	•		1.6	2.1		4.1	0.9
Current Assets to Working Capital 38	3.4	•	1.6	2.3	•		2.2	2.3		5.9	4.8
Current Liabilities to Working Capital 39	2.4	•	0.6	1.3	•		1.2	1.3		4.9	3.8
Working Capital to Net Sales 40	0.0	•	0.1	0.0	•		0.1	0.1		0.0	0.0
Inventory to Working Capital 41	0.0	•	•	0.0	•		0.0	0.0		•	0.0
Total Receipts to Cash Flow 42	8.2	2.7	6.0	9.4	7.4	•		12.4	14.0	30.5	8.9
Cost of Goods to Cash Flow 43	4.2	0.1	1.8	3.7	3.0	•		6.8	10.4	20.0	5.2
Cash Flow to Total Debt 44	0.7	•	6.7	2.5	1.2	•		0.6	0.4	0.2	0.4

Selected Financial Factors (in Percentages)

	1	2	3	4	5	6	7	8	9	10	11
Debt Ratio 45	51.4	•	72.9	34.5	76.4	•	62.0	59.0	67.5	80.3	47.0
Return on Total Assets 46	11.7	•	66.2	39.1	24.8	•	15.6	8.7	9.6	6.6	8.8
Return on Equity Before Income Taxes 47	21.6	•	239.3	57.8	94.2	•	32.2	19.4	26.0	25.9	14.7
Return on Equity After Income Taxes 48	17.7	•	236.4	56.7	92.9	•	29.3	17.9	20.7	19.8	10.4
Profit Margin (Before Income Tax) 49	3.5	15.5	2.2	4.6	3.3	•	2.8	1.6	2.1	1.1	4.7
Profit Margin (After Income Tax) 50	2.9	15.4	2.2	4.5	3.3	•	2.5	1.5	1.7	0.8	3.3

Table I

Corporations with and without Net Income

TRAVEL ARRANGEMENT AND RESERVATION SERVICES

MONEY AMOUNTS AND SIZE OF ASSETS IN THOUSANDS OF DOLLARS

Item Description for Accounting Period 7/10 Through 6/11	Total	Zero Assets	Under 500	500 to 1,000	1,000 to 5,000	5,000 to 10,000	10,000 to 25,000	25,000 to 50,000	50,000 to 100,000	100,000 to 250,000	250,000 to 500,000	500,000 to 2,500,000	2,500,000 and over
Number of Enterprises 1	17504	2694	13224	574	813	34	71	33	20	18	12	11	0
Revenues ($ in Thousands)													
Net Sales 2	35272309	368468	8491769	1758991	3504122	1011879	2054262	1585141	1871850	2181774	3651936	8792116	0
Interest 3	151138	38	182	861	1091	209	1667	1561	9783	7632	23112	105002	0
Rents 4	38633	0	3	0	42	11	362	154	372	4325	4461	28904	0
Royalties 5	128722	0	0	0	0	0	0	1	538	0	0	128182	0
Other Portfolio Income 6	160392	8100	130	724	64332	650	3551	9471	24784	11399	27403	9849	0
Other Receipts 7	1138031	5970	22728	2522	34665	18348	37226	82701	136593	164594	251813	380873	0
Total Receipts 8	36889225	382576	8514812	1763098	3604252	1031097	2097068	1679029	2043920	2369724	3958725	9444926	0
Average Total Receipts 9	2107	142	644	3072	4433	30326	29536	50880	102196	131651	329894	858630	•
Operating Costs/Operating Income (%)													
Cost of Operations 10	48.0	49.9	79.2	49.9	56.6	64.8	44.3	66.9	45.0	34.9	49.4	12.9	•
Salaries and Wages 11	14.6	4.2	5.5	13.7	10.7	15.2	24.3	11.7	19.4	19.4	14.4	21.7	•
Taxes Paid 12	1.9	0.5	0.7	1.9	1.7	1.8	2.1	1.9	2.0	2.7	1.5	2.9	•
Interest Paid 13	1.5	0.9	0.1	0.3	0.5	0.0	0.1	0.2	1.5	0.5	1.4	4.7	•
Depreciation 14	1.2	0.8	0.1	0.9	1.6	0.6	1.0	0.6	1.5	2.7	1.4	1.8	•
Amortization and Depletion 15	0.7	1.4	0.0	0.0	0.4	0.1	0.3	0.4	0.9	0.9	0.7	1.6	•
Pensions and Other Deferred Comp. 16	0.7	0.0	0.2	0.2	0.2	0.1	0.3	0.2	0.3	1.7	1.2	1.4	•
Employee Benefits 17	1.4	0.6	0.7	0.9	0.4	1.5	1.7	0.9	2.0	2.1	1.7	2.3	•
Advertising 18	3.2	0.6	0.5	0.5	1.4	1.9	3.5	3.0	2.1	1.9	1.5	8.6	•
Other Expenses 19	26.3	40.5	9.7	28.1	22.3	8.6	16.0	14.6	29.8	37.0	31.3	43.9	•
Officers' Compensation 20	1.7	0.5	2.7	2.4	2.8	3.3	2.0	1.2	1.6	1.2	0.5	0.8	•
Operating Margin 21	•	0.3	0.5	1.1	1.4	2.3	4.1	•	•	•	•	•	•
Operating Margin Before Officers' Comp. 22	0.5	0.8	3.2	3.5	4.1	5.6	6.1	•	•	•	•	•	•

Selected Average Balance Sheet ($ in Thousands)

Net Receivables 23	243	0	5	71	521	1332	2832	7870	8759	32965	30269	189051
Inventories 24	9	0	1	0	65	75	230	46	1079	342	1434	2438
Net Property, Plant and Equipment 25	117	0	5	126	174	366	1045	1625	9424	22723	18763	73354
Total Assets 26	1799	66	641	1755	8146	15429	36470	70773	155058	352740	1619511	
Notes and Loans Payable 27	505	0	35	184	144	46	568	626	22613	14352	82915	580903
All Other Liabilities 28	763	0	28	255	1169	5402	10452	24980	34553	69663	134451	598400
Net Worth 29	531	0	3	202	442	2698	4408	10863	13607	71043	135374	440208

Selected Financial Ratios (Times to 1)

Current Ratio 30	1.0	•	2.4	1.4	1.5	1.2	1.1	0.7	1.1	1.2	0.9	0.8
Quick Ratio 31	0.7	•	2.1	1.3	1.2	1.0	0.7	0.6	0.8	0.9	0.5	0.6
Net Sales to Working Capital 32	•	•	19.8	26.7	9.5	26.6	21.6	•	21.7	11.7	•	•
Coverage Ratio 33	3.3	5.4	8.7	6.0	9.7	151.2	77.7	23.0	3.1	7.6	4.7	2.1
Total Asset Turnover 34	1.1	•	9.8	4.8	2.5	3.7	1.9	1.3	1.3	0.8	0.9	0.5
Inventory Turnover 35	111.9	1003.0	•	•	37.8	257.7	55.8	697.3	39.0	123.8	104.7	42.3
Receivables Turnover 36	10.3	•	120.3	61.0	10.4	18.1	12.0	7.4	12.1	3.3	10.8	6.2
Total Liabilities to Net Worth 37	2.4	•	24.1	2.2	3.0	2.0	2.5	2.4	4.2	1.2	1.6	2.7
Current Assets to Working Capital 38	•	•	1.7	3.4	3.1	5.5	7.8	•	7.8	6.5	•	•
Current Liabilities to Working Capital 39	•	•	0.7	2.4	2.1	4.5	6.8	•	6.8	5.5	•	•
Working Capital to Net Sales 40	•	•	0.1	0.0	0.1	0.0	0.0	•	0.0	0.1	•	•
Inventory to Working Capital 41	•	•	0.0	•	0.1	0.1	0.3	•	0.2	0.0	•	•
Total Receipts to Cash Flow 42	3.7	2.4	11.7	3.6	4.2	9.3	5.1	5.9	3.3	2.7	3.2	2.2
Cost of Goods to Cash Flow 43	1.8	1.2	9.3	1.8	2.4	6.0	2.2	3.9	1.5	0.9	1.6	0.3
Cash Flow to Total Debt 44	0.4	0.9	0.9	1.9	0.8	0.6	0.5	0.3	0.5	0.5	0.4	0.3

Selected Financial Factors (in Percentages)

Debt Ratio 45	70.5	•	96.0	68.5	74.8	66.9	71.4	70.2	80.8	54.2	61.6	72.8
Return on Total Assets 46	5.6	•	8.3	7.7	11.6	15.3	11.8	5.6	6.1	3.2	5.6	4.7
Return on Equity Before Income Taxes 47	13.4	•	184.9	20.4	41.4	45.8	40.7	17.8	21.3	6.0	11.4	9.0
Return on Equity After Income Taxes 48	10.4	•	163.9	20.0	38.0	36.3	38.5	15.6	15.6	3.7	8.1	6.3
Profit Margin (Before Income Tax) 49	3.5	4.1	0.8	1.3	4.2	4.2	6.2	4.0	3.1	3.5	5.1	5.0
Profit Margin (After Income Tax) 50	2.7	3.4	0.7	1.3	3.9	3.3	5.9	3.5	2.3	2.2	3.6	3.5

TRAVEL ARRANGEMENT AND RESERVATION SERVICES

Table II

Corporations with Net Income

MONEY AMOUNTS AND SIZE OF ASSETS IN THOUSANDS OF DOLLARS

Item Description for Accounting Period 7/10 Through 6/11	Total	Zero Assets	Under 500	500 to 1,000	1,000 to 5,000	5,000 to 10,000	10,000 to 25,000	25,000 to 50,000	50,000 to 100,000	100,000 to 250,000	250,000 to 500,000	500,000 to 2,500,000	2,500,000 and over
Number of Enterprises 1	8493	801	6363	452	724	•	66	23	9	13	•	7	0
Revenues ($ in Thousands)													
Net Sales 2	27809434	171169	4911175	1550493	3072192	•	2052194	1453030	1068251	1781194	•	7330813	0
Interest 3	112043	11	115	775	1027	•	1667	794	4493	4368	•	75592	0
Rents 4	17073	0	3	0	0	•	362	11	255	4114	•	7856	0
Royalties 5	128183	0	0	0	0	•	0	1	0	0	•	128182	0
Other Portfolio Income 6	126498	8100	130	724	63972	•	3551	3406	3175	10657	•	4732	0
Other Receipts 7	692039	5808	18656	2522	27783	•	37226	22294	96505	152737	•	64296	0
Total Receipts 8	28885270	185088	4930079	1554514	3164974	•	2095000	1479536	1172679	1953070	•	7611471	0
Average Total Receipts 9	3401	231	775	3439	4372	•	31742	64328	130298	150236	•	1087353	•
Operating Costs/Operating Income (%)													
Cost of Operations 10	45.4	3.4	76.7	56.6	56.8	•	44.4	68.3	31.5	36.3	•	13.3	•
Salaries and Wages 11	14.2	7.4	5.1	12.0	10.4	•	24.3	9.9	21.8	19.2	•	18.2	•
Taxes Paid 12	1.8	0.5	0.7	1.4	1.6	•	2.1	1.8	2.4	2.5	•	2.7	•
Interest Paid 13	1.7	1.9	0.1	0.1	0.3	•	0.1	0.1	1.1	0.4	•	5.5	•
Depreciation 14	1.1	1.5	0.2	0.5	1.0	•	1.0	0.5	1.2	2.2	•	1.8	•
Amortization and Depletion 15	0.7	1.7	0.1	•	0.4	•	0.3	0.4	0.1	1.0	•	1.8	•
Pensions and Other Deferred Comp. 16	0.6	0.1	0.1	0.3	0.2	•	0.3	0.2	0.1	1.0	•	0.8	•
Employee Benefits 17	1.4	1.3	0.9	0.3	0.4	•	1.7	0.8	2.0	2.0	•	1.8	•
Advertising 18	3.4	0.3	0.4	0.2	1.4	•	3.5	2.9	1.5	1.5	•	8.8	•
Other Expenses 19	26.3	70.1	8.6	24.3	21.2	•	16.0	10.4	37.2	35.7	•	42.0	•
Officers' Compensation 20	1.6	0.8	2.5	2.5	2.8	•	2.0	1.3	1.5	1.2	•	0.6	•
Operating Margin 21	1.8	11.2	4.6	1.9	3.4	•	4.2	3.5	•	•	•	2.6	•
Operating Margin Before Officers' Comp. 22	3.4	12.0	7.1	4.4	6.3	•	6.3	4.8	0.8	•	•	3.2	•

Selected Average Balance Sheet ($ in Thousands)

	1	2	3	4	5	6	7	8	9	10	11	12	13
Net Receivables **23**	318	0	3	71	547	•	2628	10447	8574	33303	•	137727	•
Inventories **24**	13	0	1	0	68	•	212	33	244	443	•	2714	•
Net Property, Plant and Equipment **25**	161	0	6	65	122	•	1124	1745	11565	15000	•	82622	•
Total Assets **26**	2945		86	623	1764	•	15254	33935	69493	151518	•	2111131	•
Notes and Loans Payable **27**	863	0	20	139	84	•	556	705	10448	8574	•	903542	•
All Other Liabilities **28**	1161	0	35	283	1228	•	9917	29908	34454	73503	•	621924	•
Net Worth **29**	921	0	31	201	452	•	4780	3323	24591	69441	•	585665	•

Selected Financial Ratios (Times to 1)

	1	2	3	4	5	6	7	8	9	10	11	12	13
Current Ratio **30**	1.0	•	2.8	1.3	1.5	•	1.2	0.8	1.2	1.1	•	0.7	•
Quick Ratio **31**	0.7	•	2.6	1.2	1.2	•	0.8	0.6	0.9	0.9	•	0.5	•
Net Sales to Working Capital **32**	•	•	17.8	34.2	9.2	•	21.8	•	16.5	16.5	•	•	•
Coverage Ratio **33**	4.5	11.3	68.2	19.8	22.8	•	80.0	102.5	9.5	18.9	•	2.2	•
Total Asset Turnover **34**	1.1	•	8.9	5.5	2.4	•	2.0	1.9	1.7	0.9	•	0.5	•
Inventory Turnover **35**	113.7	•	611.2	•	35.3	•	65.2	1321.1	153.0	112.3	•	51.4	•
Receivables Turnover **36**	12.4	•	140.1	89.3	10.7	•	14.0	7.5	18.7	3.7	•	10.8	•
Total Liabilities to Net Worth **37**	2.2	•	1.8	2.1	2.9	•	2.2	9.2	1.8	1.2	•	2.6	•
Current Assets to Working Capital **38**	•	•	1.5	4.0	3.1	•	6.9	•	5.1	8.6	•	•	•
Current Liabilities to Working Capital **39**	•	•	0.5	3.0	2.1	•	5.9	•	4.1	7.6	•	•	•
Working Capital to Net Sales **40**	•	•	0.1	0.0	0.1	•	0.0	•	0.1	0.1	•	•	•
Inventory to Working Capital **41**	•	•	0.0	•	0.2	•	0.3	•	0.0	0.1	•	•	•
Total Receipts to Cash Flow **42**	3.4	1.1	8.2	3.9	4.0	•	5.0	6.9	2.3	2.5	•	2.2	•
Cost of Goods to Cash Flow **43**	1.5	0.0	6.3	2.2	2.3	•	2.2	4.7	0.7	0.9	•	0.3	•
Cash Flow to Total Debt **44**	0.5	•	1.7	2.1	0.8	•	0.6	0.3	1.2	0.7	•	0.3	•

Selected Financial Factors (in Percentages)

	1	2	3	4	5	6	7	8	9	10	11	12	13
Debt Ratio **45**	68.7	•	64.3	67.7	74.4	•	68.7	90.2	64.6	54.2	•	72.3	•
Return on Total Assets **46**	8.5	•	45.5	12.3	16.3	•	13.1	9.7	17.2	6.4	•	6.0	•
Return on Equity Before Income Taxes **47**	21.0	•	125.5	36.2	60.8	•	41.2	98.4	43.6	13.2	•	11.6	•
Return on Equity After Income Taxes **48**	17.5	•	121.8	35.8	57.1	•	39.0	87.9	36.6	10.0	•	8.5	•
Profit Margin (Before Income Tax) **49**	5.9	19.3	5.0	2.1	6.5	•	6.3	5.2	9.0	6.7	•	6.5	•
Profit Margin (After Income Tax) **50**	4.9	17.6	4.9	2.1	6.1	•	6.0	4.6	7.6	5.1	•	4.7	•

OTHER ADMINISTRATIVE AND SUPPORT SERVICES

Table I

Corporations with and without Net Income

MONEY AMOUNTS AND SIZE OF ASSETS IN THOUSANDS OF DOLLARS

Item Description for Accounting Period 7/10 Through 6/11	Total	Zero Assets	Under 500	500 to 1,000	1,000 to 5,000	5,000 to 10,000	10,000 to 25,000	25,000 to 50,000	50,000 to 100,000	100,000 to 250,000	250,000 to 500,000	500,000 to 2,500,000	2,500,000 and over
Number of Enterprises 1	215463	50134	151508	6962	5380	790	304	155	97	52	35	38	8
Revenues ($ in Thousands)													
Net Sales 2	212828415	4174473	57130480	12773896	32720506	9781404	10242645	7439708	7833061	7645217	10951096	34372176	17763754
Interest 3	408390	10687	9479	5518	11572	2450	6817	8341	16074	18152	8792	201643	108864
Rents 4	87357	375	880	6063	6181	505	1628	2806	8357	1225	4424	44833	10081
Royalties 5	272235	0	0	0	2	0	0	5647	337	853	6964	150502	107930
Other Portfolio Income 6	1247710	26294	132798	29357	53981	76969	5438	16633	61681	51584	62423	354622	375933
Other Receipts 7	4228149	331165	228467	73593	368803	378408	147870	201888	484956	162028	373588	1122326	355054
Total Receipts 8	219072256	4542994	57502104	12888427	33161045	10239736	10404398	7675023	8404466	7879059	11407287	36246102	18721616
Average Total Receipts 9	1017	91	380	1851	6164	12962	34225	49516	86644	151520	325922	953845	2340202
Operating Costs/Operating Income (%)													
Cost of Operations 10	36.3	20.8	31.5	41.5	53.4	37.5	41.0	41.8	41.9	27.1	40.6	31.0	23.0
Salaries and Wages 11	21.5	17.3	19.1	19.5	13.4	27.6	22.6	21.4	25.3	20.4	23.9	30.6	22.1
Taxes Paid 12	3.6	3.7	3.4	3.7	3.4	3.5	4.1	3.7	3.6	3.0	3.5	4.5	2.5
Interest Paid 13	2.2	2.1	0.7	1.0	0.6	0.9	0.7	1.2	2.1	2.5	3.2	2.9	10.2
Depreciation 14	2.1	2.7	1.7	1.8	1.4	2.0	1.7	2.3	2.7	2.5	2.8	2.4	3.5
Amortization and Depletion 15	1.1	1.7	0.1	0.1	0.2	0.2	0.5	1.1	1.4	1.7	2.2	1.4	5.5
Pensions and Other Deferred Comp. 16	0.5	0.1	0.6	0.4	0.2	0.5	0.4	0.4	0.3	0.3	0.5	0.8	0.8
Employee Benefits 17	2.2	0.9	1.1	1.3	1.9	2.8	2.2	3.1	2.9	2.9	2.9	3.5	2.6
Advertising 18	1.3	3.5	1.5	0.9	1.3	1.1	2.3	2.0	2.4	1.2	1.5	0.4	1.4
Other Expenses 19	23.6	41.1	26.4	18.7	17.8	21.5	20.5	21.1	19.5	37.0	19.0	23.8	27.2
Officers' Compensation 20	4.0	10.1	8.0	6.4	4.2	3.9	1.9	2.0	2.1	1.4	1.1	0.7	0.4
Operating Margin 21	1.7	•	5.9	4.8	2.3	•	1.9	•	•	•	•	•	0.9
Operating Margin Before Officers' Comp. 22	5.7	6.1	13.9	11.2	6.5	2.6	3.8	1.8	1.4	1.4	•	•	1.3

Selected Average Balance Sheet ($ in Thousands)

Net Receivables 23	111	0	10	111	503	1471	4343	6912	18462	21139	65851	198233	330882
Inventories 24	10	0	2	35	62	109	636	1031	1994	2305	3016	7168	18692
Net Property, Plant and Equipment 25	114	0	20	182	530	1471	2683	5084	9580	18759	53853	116734	788290
Total Assets 26	700	0	69	665	2089	6435	15563	36614	69941	153497	354035	980295	5575711
Notes and Loans Payable 27	327	0	47	333	967	2130	4492	11397	22772	62894	147055	344354	3419880
All Other Liabilities 28	172	0	19	135	655	2190	5066	1116	24855	43989	85927	217567	1102084
Net Worth 29	201	0	4	197	467	2116	6005	14101	22314	46614	121053	418373	1053747

Selected Financial Ratios (Times to 1)

Current Ratio 30	1.5	•	1.3	2.0	1.4	1.4	1.4	1.5	1.4	1.2	1.7	1.5	1.6
Quick Ratio 31	1.1	•	1.1	1.4	1.1	0.9	1.1	1.1	1.1	0.8	1.3	1.2	0.9
Net Sales to Working Capital 32	12.8	•	46.1	10.1	18.0	10.9	15.1	8.1	8.3	17.6	5.6	8.5	7.4
Coverage Ratio 33	3.2	3.3	10.7	6.5	7.0	4.7	5.7	3.5	2.5	2.2	1.9	2.3	1.8
Total Asset Turnover 34	1.4	•	5.4	2.8	2.9	1.9	2.2	1.3	1.2	1.0	0.9	0.9	0.4
Inventory Turnover 35	35.2	•	53.5	21.8	52.6	42.6	21.7	19.5	17.0	17.3	42.2	39.2	27.3
Receivables Turnover 36	9.4	•	39.4	18.9	12.0	8.9	7.5	6.8	4.7	6.2	5.2	4.9	7.5
Total Liabilities to Net Worth 37	2.5	•	17.8	2.4	3.5	2.0	1.6	1.6	2.1	2.3	1.9	1.3	4.3
Current Assets to Working Capital 38	3.1	•	4.1	2.0	3.5	3.4	3.6	3.0	3.4	6.5	2.4	2.8	2.6
Current Liabilities to Working Capital 39	2.1	•	3.1	1.0	2.5	2.4	2.6	2.0	2.4	5.5	1.4	1.8	1.6
Working Capital to Net Sales 40	0.1	•	0.0	0.1	0.1	0.1	0.1	0.1	0.1	0.1	0.2	0.1	0.1
Inventory to Working Capital 41	0.1	•	0.3	0.2	0.2	0.1	0.2	0.2	0.2	0.3	0.0	0.1	0.1
Total Receipts to Cash Flow 42	4.2	2.6	3.5	5.0	5.6	5.1	4.8	4.9	5.5	2.7	6.0	4.2	3.4
Cost of Goods to Cash Flow 43	1.5	0.5	1.1	2.1	3.0	1.9	2.0	2.1	2.3	0.7	2.4	1.3	0.8
Cash Flow to Total Debt 44	0.5	•	1.6	0.8	0.7	0.6	0.7	0.4	0.3	0.5	0.2	0.4	0.1

Selected Financial Factors (in Percentages)

Debt Ratio 45	71.3	•	94.7	70.4	77.6	67.1	61.4	61.5	68.1	69.6	65.8	57.3	81.1
Return on Total Assets 46	9.8	•	39.2	18.5	12.3	8.3	9.2	5.4	5.9	5.3	5.4	6.3	7.1
Return on Equity Before Income Taxes 47	23.7	•	669.3	53.0	47.3	19.9	19.6	9.9	11.1	9.6	7.6	8.4	16.3
Return on Equity After Income Taxes 48	20.6	•	656.1	51.9	45.8	18.5	18.3	8.5	9.2	7.0	5.3	5.5	10.7
Profit Margin (Before Income Tax) 49	4.8	4.8	6.5	5.7	3.6	3.4	3.5	2.9	3.1	3.0	2.9	3.9	7.7
Profit Margin (After Income Tax) 50	4.2	4.0	6.4	5.6	3.5	3.2	3.3	2.5	2.5	2.2	2.0	2.6	5.1

OTHER ADMINISTRATIVE AND SUPPORT SERVICES

Table II

Corporations with Net Income

MONEY AMOUNTS AND SIZE OF ASSETS IN THOUSANDS OF DOLLARS

Item Description for Accounting Period 7/10 Through 6/11	Total	Zero Assets	Under 500	500 to 1,000	1,000 to 5,000	5,000 to 10,000	10,000 to 25,000	25,000 to 50,000	50,000 to 100,000	100,000 to 250,000	250,000 to 500,000	500,000 to 2,500,000	2,500,000 and over
Number of Enterprises **1**	133907	29864	95008	4639	3475	•	200	93	56	34	21	22	•
Revenues ($ in Thousands)													
Net Sales **2**	151510643	3019093	41065182	9664147	21365582	•	7350236	5308560	5546413	5911857	8423284	24841521	•
Interest **3**	303656	8592	5514	4078	8468	•	4140	4712	13554	17484	5804	120654	•
Rents **4**	39938	295	325	4897	4848	•	1561	1568	6810	1216	3085	8597	•
Royalties **5**	249751	0	0	0	0	•	0	6	0	853	0	140962	•
Other Portfolio Income **6**	1165014	25952	124308	28199	45121	•	4971	14486	54346	51256	58127	320579	•
Other Receipts **7**	3482313	306427	211967	66090	332123	•	136574	185656	330488	163859	345132	876794	•
Total Receipts **8**	156751315	3360359	41407296	9767411	21756142	•	7497482	5514988	5951611	6146525	8835432	26309107	•
Average Total Receipts **9**	1171	113	436	2105	6261	•	37487	59301	106279	180780	420735	1195868	•
Operating Costs/Operating Income (%)													
Cost of Operations **10**	34.7	16.7	31.9	43.5	51.4	•	40.6	42.3	41.9	24.4	37.0	31.5	•
Salaries and Wages **11**	21.8	17.0	18.2	15.9	15.0	•	24.5	20.2	26.1	19.2	27.0	32.9	•
Taxes Paid **12**	3.6	3.8	3.2	3.4	3.3	•	3.8	3.9	3.8	2.7	4.0	5.0	•
Interest Paid **13**	2.0	1.6	0.6	0.8	0.5	•	0.5	0.7	1.5	2.1	1.8	2.1	•
Depreciation **14**	2.0	2.6	1.5	1.6	1.1	•	1.5	1.7	1.9	2.4	3.0	2.3	•
Amortization and Depletion **15**	1.1	0.4	0.1	0.1	0.2	•	0.3	0.9	0.7	1.1	1.9	1.3	•
Pensions and Other Deferred Comp. **16**	0.5	0.0	0.4	0.5	0.3	•	0.4	0.6	0.4	0.3	0.7	0.9	•
Employee Benefits **17**	2.0	0.8	1.0	1.1	1.2	•	1.9	3.3	2.8	2.9	3.0	3.3	•
Advertising **18**	1.2	0.9	1.4	0.9	1.5	•	0.5	1.3	1.5	1.4	1.1	0.4	•
Other Expenses **19**	21.6	35.7	23.4	18.1	14.5	•	17.5	19.3	17.8	39.8	16.5	19.7	•
Officers' Compensation **20**	4.0	9.9	7.6	6.1	5.0	•	2.1	2.2	1.9	1.2	1.2	0.6	•
Operating Margin **21**	5.5	10.8	10.6	7.9	6.1	•	6.4	3.8	•	2.5	2.9	0.1	•
Operating Margin Before Officers' Comp. **22**	9.6	20.7	18.2	13.9	11.1	•	8.5	5.9	1.6	3.8	4.1	0.6	•

Selected Average Balance Sheet ($ in Thousands)

Net Receivables 23	126	0	8	127	596	•	4602	8474	22137	23539	93831	234048	•
Inventories 24	10	0	2	38	66	•	548	1398	2184	2529	2607	4571	•
Net Property, Plant and Equipment 25	127	0	20	175	426	•	2660	3224	8373	23856	56754	137990	•
Total Assets 26	774	0	74	673	2147	•	14867	35596	70424	156246	351251	1018325	•
Notes and Loans Payable 27	336	0	33	226	712	•	2976	9983	22176	57755	113982	376174	•
All Other Liabilities 28	189	0	16	147	613	•	4618	10681	26163	44240	94869	244860	•
Net Worth 29	248	0	25	300	822	•	7273	14931	22086	54252	142400	397292	•

Selected Financial Ratios (Times to 1)

Current Ratio 30	1.6	1.7	1.9	1.9	•	1.7	1.9	1.5	1.2	1.8	1.5	•
Quick Ratio 31	1.2	1.4	1.4	1.6	•	1.4	1.4	1.2	0.8	1.5	1.3	•
Net Sales to Working Capital 32	10.8	27.8	11.0	9.8	•	11.1	5.7	8.0	16.6	5.7	8.8	•
Coverage Ratio 33	5.6	20.0	12.5	17.9	•	19.1	12.0	5.7	4.1	5.4	4.1	•
Total Asset Turnover 34	1.5	15.0	5.8	3.1	2.9	•	2.5	1.6	1.4	1.1	1.1	1.1	•
Inventory Turnover 35	38.4	61.4	23.8	47.7	•	27.2	17.3	19.0	16.8	56.9	77.9	•
Receivables Turnover 36	9.4	51.6	18.9	10.2	•	7.6	7.2	4.6	7.2	4.7	5.0	•
Total Liabilities to Net Worth 37	2.1	1.9	1.2	1.6	•	1.0	1.4	2.2	1.9	1.5	1.6	•
Current Assets to Working Capital 38	2.5	2.4	2.1	2.1	•	2.5	2.1	3.2	5.5	2.2	2.8	•
Current Liabilities to Working Capital 39	1.5	1.4	1.1	1.1	•	1.5	1.1	2.2	4.5	1.2	1.8	•
Working Capital to Net Sales 40	0.1	0.0	0.1	0.1	•	0.1	0.2	0.1	0.1	0.2	0.1	•
Inventory to Working Capital 41	0.1	0.2	0.2	0.1	•	0.1	0.1	0.2	0.3	0.0	0.0	•
Total Receipts to Cash Flow 42	3.8	3.3	4.4	5.2	•	4.4	4.1	4.8	2.3	5.4	4.4	•
Cost of Goods to Cash Flow 43	1.3	1.0	1.9	2.7	•	1.8	1.7	2.0	0.6	2.0	1.4	•
Cash Flow to Total Debt 44	0.6	2.7	1.3	0.9	•	1.1	0.7	0.4	0.7	0.4	0.4	•

Selected Financial Factors (in Percentages)

Debt Ratio 45	67.9	66.0	55.3	61.7	•	51.1	58.1	68.6	65.3	59.5	61.0	•
Return on Total Assets 46	16.5	70.5	30.0	24.1	•	21.9	13.4	12.0	9.5	10.9	9.7	•
Return on Equity Before Income Taxes 47	42.3	197.0	61.9	59.3	•	42.5	29.3	31.7	20.7	22.0	18.7	•
Return on Equity After Income Taxes 48	38.1	193.9	60.8	58.0	•	40.8	27.1	28.3	17.3	18.8	13.4	•
Profit Margin (Before Income Tax) 49	9.3	22.1	11.5	8.9	7.9	•	8.4	7.7	7.1	6.4	7.8	6.6	•
Profit Margin (After Income Tax) 50	8.4	20.9	11.3	8.8	7.8	•	8.1	7.1	6.3	5.4	6.7	4.7	•

Table I

Corporations with and without Net Income

WASTE MANAGEMENT AND REMEDIATION SERVICES

MONEY AMOUNTS AND SIZE OF ASSETS IN THOUSANDS OF DOLLARS

Item Description for Accounting Period 7/10 Through 6/11	Total	Zero Assets	Under 500	500 to 1,000	1,000 to 5,000	5,000 to 10,000	10,000 to 25,000	25,000 to 50,000	50,000 to 100,000	100,000 to 250,000	250,000 to 500,000	500,000 to 2,500,000	2,500,000 and over
Number of Enterprises 1	16475	1662	11126	722	2235	409	174	60	31	28	9	12	7
Revenues ($ in Thousands)													
Net Sales 2	77882128	785765	6780285	2264808	12027514	4695229	4575978	2169144	2233766	4498265	2300554	6644164	28906656
Interest 3	477867	321	604	167	3628	733	4010	2684	1049	6297	425	38864	419086
Rents 4	76520	0	0	879	37	491	901	288	727	3761	12	4819	64606
Royalties 5	29704	10158	0	5	0	0	0	0	514	231	0	17464	1332
Other Portfolio Income 6	698136	1834	148262	15350	44352	1218	6600	3965	5933	27975	30059	113107	299480
Other Receipts 7	818947	2115	8767	2162	36331	38082	11493	20689	70471	54713	34280	55297	484545
Total Receipts 8	79983302	800193	6937918	2283371	12111862	4735753	4598982	2196770	2312460	4591242	2365330	6873715	30175705
Average Total Receipts 9	4855	481	624	3163	5419	11579	26431	36613	74595	163973	262814	572810	4310815
Operating Costs/Operating Income (%)													
Cost of Operations 10	39.3	33.3	33.2	45.9	45.7	62.2	49.7	50.6	57.8	58.0	25.7	23.9	31.9
Salaries and Wages 11	15.4	17.6	13.9	10.2	11.8	6.7	12.0	8.2	7.6	9.3	16.5	19.2	20.7
Taxes Paid 12	3.0	4.2	4.7	2.2	2.7	2.1	2.1	1.8	2.2	2.2	2.8	3.1	3.3
Interest Paid 13	3.1	3.8	0.7	0.8	0.8	1.3	0.9	1.6	2.8	2.2	4.9	4.3	5.4
Depreciation 14	5.9	8.0	2.7	4.6	3.9	3.7	5.4	5.9	6.3	4.2	7.3	6.9	7.8
Amortization and Depletion 15	1.8	2.8	0.1	0.0	0.0	0.2	0.2	0.5	0.7	1.2	2.6	3.5	3.5
Pensions and Other Deferred Comp. 16	0.5	0.2	0.5	0.3	0.6	0.7	0.7	0.2	0.4	0.3	0.2	1.1	0.3
Employee Benefits 17	1.6	2.6	1.6	0.4	1.1	0.9	1.8	1.2	1.9	1.9	1.4	3.0	1.7
Advertising 18	0.4	0.4	1.3	0.3	0.4	0.4	0.5	0.2	0.2	0.1	0.2	0.4	0.3
Other Expenses 19	23.1	25.1	30.4	24.5	25.1	17.5	17.4	22.6	18.8	15.6	38.9	30.9	20.7
Officers' Compensation 20	2.1	3.1	7.6	4.0	3.1	3.4	3.1	1.5	1.3	1.4	0.7	1.2	0.3
Operating Margin 21	3.7	•	3.3	6.8	4.7	0.9	6.2	5.7	0.2	3.6	•	2.6	4.2
Operating Margin Before Officers' Comp. 22	5.8	1.9	11.0	10.7	7.8	4.3	9.3	7.2	1.4	5.0	•	3.7	4.4

Selected Average Balance Sheet ($ in Thousands)

Net Receivables 23	547	0	14	52	460	1843	2868	7474	14403	25225	37018	92346	498314
Inventories 24	52	0	1	72	43	286	579	391	1574	2170	564	7916	34600
Net Property, Plant and Equipment 25	2100	0	37	407	914	2074	6403	12766	24738	37726	122196	329804	3175854
Total Assets 26	5600	0	119	781	2054	6934	16119	35818	71728	163035	330528	1022001	7994492
Notes and Loans Payable 27	2107	0	80	453	885	3466	5615	16201	26859	65662	183141	355051	2797074
All Other Liabilities 28	1552	0	18	23	235	1083	4968	12185	20825	41524	77349	228377	2506261
Net Worth 29	1941	0	22	305	934	2384	5536	7433	24044	55848	70038	438573	2691158

Selected Financial Ratios (Times to 1)

Current Ratio 30	1.3	•	2.5	8.5	1.3	2.9	1.8	1.3	1.7	1.3	0.7	1.3	1.0
Quick Ratio 31	0.9	•	2.2	6.3	1.1	1.8	1.5	1.1	1.5	0.9	0.6	1.1	0.7
Net Sales to Working Capital 32	19.4	•	16.9	9.8	25.3	4.4	7.5	11.9	6.9	16.1	•	14.2	156.1
Coverage Ratio 33	3.0	1.2	9.5	10.4	7.8	2.4	8.2	5.3	2.3	3.5	1.4	2.4	2.6
Total Asset Turnover 34	0.8	•	5.1	4.0	2.6	1.7	1.6	1.0	1.0	1.0	0.8	0.5	0.5
Inventory Turnover 35	35.9	•	183.1	20.0	56.6	24.9	22.6	46.7	26.5	42.9	116.4	16.7	38.1
Receivables Turnover 36	9.2	•	46.8	23.2	11.9	5.9	9.2	6.7	5.8	8.0	7.3	6.9	8.5
Total Liabilities to Net Worth 37	1.9	•	4.5	1.6	1.2	1.9	1.9	3.8	2.0	1.9	3.7	1.3	2.0
Current Assets to Working Capital 38	4.7	•	1.7	1.1	4.3	1.5	2.2	4.4	2.4	4.9	•	4.1	40.6
Current Liabilities to Working Capital 39	3.7	•	0.7	0.1	3.3	0.5	1.2	3.4	1.4	3.9	•	3.1	39.6
Working Capital to Net Sales 40	0.1	•	0.1	0.1	0.0	0.2	0.1	0.1	0.1	0.1	•	0.1	0.0
Inventory to Working Capital 41	0.2	•	0.0	0.2	0.2	0.1	0.2	0.1	0.1	0.3	•	0.2	1.5
Total Receipts to Cash Flow 42	4.2	5.6	3.5	3.3	3.9	7.3	5.1	4.0	5.4	5.8	2.9	3.2	4.3
Cost of Goods to Cash Flow 43	1.6	1.9	1.2	1.5	1.8	4.6	2.5	2.0	3.1	3.4	0.7	0.8	1.4
Cash Flow to Total Debt 44	0.3	•	1.8	2.0	1.2	0.3	0.5	0.3	0.3	0.3	0.3	0.3	0.2

Selected Financial Factors (in Percentages)

Debt Ratio 45	65.3	•	81.9	60.9	54.5	65.6	65.7	79.2	66.5	65.7	78.8	57.1	66.3
Return on Total Assets 46	8.1	•	32.3	33.8	16.3	5.1	12.4	8.6	6.5	7.8	5.1	5.6	7.3
Return on Equity Before Income Taxes 47	15.7	•	159.5	78.2	31.3	8.6	31.6	33.6	11.0	16.3	6.3	7.6	13.2
Return on Equity After Income Taxes 48	12.3	•	159.1	77.7	30.5	7.3	28.9	31.8	9.7	10.4	4.7	5.7	9.0
Profit Margin (Before Income Tax) 49	6.4	0.6	5.7	7.6	5.4	1.8	6.7	6.9	3.7	5.7	1.7	6.0	8.6
Profit Margin (After Income Tax) 50	5.1	•	5.6	7.6	5.3	1.5	6.1	6.5	3.2	3.6	1.3	4.5	5.9

Table II
Corporations with Net Income

WASTE MANAGEMENT AND REMEDIATION SERVICES

MONEY AMOUNTS AND SIZE OF ASSETS IN THOUSANDS OF DOLLARS

Item Description for Accounting Period 7/10 Through 6/11	Total	Zero Assets	Under 500	500 to 1,000	1,000 to 5,000	5,000 to 10,000	10,000 to 25,000	25,000 to 50,000	50,000 to 100,000	100,000 to 250,000	250,000 to 500,000	500,000 to 2,500,000	2,500,000 and over
Number of Enterprises **1**	11196	1283	7198	536	1751	194	137	41	17	19	•	8	•
Revenues ($ in Thousands)													
Net Sales **2**	67287059	569881	5503340	1734474	10611960	3629168	3967541	1543280	1564337	3787398	•	5678016	•
Interest **3**	450018	294	506	167	3280	489	3152	1007	781	2213	•	31819	•
Rents **4**	74419	0	0	879	37	90	901	8	170	3761	•	4819	•
Royalties **5**	29175	10144	0	5	0	0	0	0	0	231	•	17464	•
Other Portfolio Income **6**	638667	1834	118047	927	42378	117	6584	3886	3592	25066	•	110814	•
Other Receipts **7**	710471	1564	8234	1908	19018	15752	7123	20221	68698	59280	•	49130	•
Total Receipts **8**	69189809	583717	5630127	1738360	10676673	3645616	3985301	1568402	1637578	3877949	•	5892062	•
Average Total Receipts **9**	6180	455	782	3243	6097	18792	29090	38254	96328	204103	•	736508	•
Operating Costs/Operating Income (%)													
Cost of Operations **10**	38.3	23.7	34.5	42.9	43.3	69.2	49.5	44.2	67.2	59.7	•	24.8	•
Salaries and Wages **11**	15.6	18.7	11.6	7.6	11.9	3.6	11.0	7.7	5.0	8.5	•	19.4	•
Taxes Paid **12**	2.9	4.5	4.6	1.9	2.5	1.6	1.9	1.8	1.8	2.1	•	3.2	•
Interest Paid **13**	2.9	4.3	0.6	0.8	0.7	0.4	0.8	1.1	1.0	1.6	•	3.5	•
Depreciation **14**	5.6	9.4	1.7	3.2	3.6	1.8	4.8	6.2	3.4	3.8	•	6.4	•
Amortization and Depletion **15**	1.8	2.5	0.1	0.0	0.0	0.0	0.2	0.4	0.4	0.9	•	2.8	•
Pensions and Other Deferred Comp. **16**	0.5	0.3	0.6	0.0	0.0	0.8	0.6	0.2	0.4	0.3	•	1.2	•
Employee Benefits **17**	1.6	3.1	1.7	0.1	1.1	0.6	1.4	1.0	1.5	1.7	•	3.2	•
Advertising **18**	0.4	0.5	1.3	0.4	0.3	0.2	0.2	0.2	0.1	0.1	•	0.3	•
Other Expenses **19**	22.6	25.8	28.6	27.6	25.8	10.7	17.1	23.6	13.7	14.1	•	30.0	•
Officers' Compensation **20**	2.0	3.9	7.7	3.3	3.4	3.3	3.1	1.5	1.0	1.4	•	1.2	•
Operating Margin **21**	5.9	3.5	6.9	12.1	6.7	7.7	9.4	12.2	4.4	5.7	•	3.9	•
Operating Margin Before Officers' Comp. **22**	7.9	7.4	14.6	15.4	10.0	11.0	12.5	13.7	5.4	7.2	•	5.1	•

Selected Average Balance Sheet ($ in Thousands)

	•	•	•	•	•	•	•	•	•	•	•
Net Receivables 23	664	0	18	69	498	1895	2870	8466	20349	27830	121927
Inventories 24	60	0	1	0	38	504	630	151	2747	2229	8664
Net Property, Plant and Equipment 25	2568	0	33	442	963	1884	6190	12021	16558	36799	357220
Total Assets 26	6561	0	117	837	2177	6875	15894	35460	71902	165247	1150427
Notes and Loans Payable 27	2328	0	74	536	801	1459	4915	13173	14596	56473	404587
All Other Liabilities 28	1758	0	10	16	193	880	3602	13190	23278	37577	262889
Net Worth 29	2476	0	33	286	1183	4536	7377	9096	34028	71197	482950

Selected Financial Ratios (Times to 1)

Current Ratio 30	1.2	•	4.2	12.5	1.3	3.1	2.0	2.2	2.1	1.3	1.3
Quick Ratio 31	1.0	•	3.8	11.1	1.1	2.2	1.7	1.8	1.8	1.0	1.1
Net Sales to Working Capital 32	26.5	•	14.8	9.2	23.2	6.7	7.1	4.8	5.2	19.0	14.0
Coverage Ratio 33	4.0	2.4	16.1	15.6	11.6	20.3	12.8	13.3	9.8	6.0	3.2
Total Asset Turnover 34	0.9	•	6.6	3.9	2.8	2.7	1.8	1.1	1.3	1.2	0.6
Inventory Turnover 35	38.4	•	190.2	35435.4	68.4	25.7	22.8	110.7	22.5	53.4	20.3
Receivables Turnover 36	9.9	•	45.5	21.2	13.9	9.0	11.3	7.0	5.6	8.5	7.3
Total Liabilities to Net Worth 37	1.7	•	2.6	1.9	0.8	0.5	1.2	2.9	1.1	1.3	1.4
Current Assets to Working Capital 38	5.5	•	1.3	1.1	3.9	1.5	2.0	1.9	1.9	4.9	4.1
Current Liabilities to Working Capital 39	4.5	•	0.3	0.1	2.9	0.5	1.0	0.9	0.9	3.9	3.1
Working Capital to Net Sales 40	0.0	•	0.1	0.1	0.0	0.1	0.1	0.2	0.2	0.1	0.1
Inventory to Working Capital 41	0.3	•	0.0	0.0	0.2	0.2	0.2	0.0	0.1	0.3	0.2
Total Receipts to Cash Flow 42	3.8	4.1	3.2	2.6	3.6	7.0	4.4	3.1	5.2	5.3	3.1
Cost of Goods to Cash Flow 43	1.5	1.0	1.1	1.1	1.6	4.8	2.2	1.4	3.5	3.2	0.8
Cash Flow to Total Debt 44	0.4	•	2.8	2.3	1.7	1.1	0.8	0.5	0.5	0.4	0.3

Selected Financial Factors (in Percentages)

Debt Ratio 45	62.3	•	72.0	65.8	45.6	34.0	53.6	74.3	52.7	56.9	58.0
Return on Total Assets 46	10.7	•	64.3	50.8	22.2	23.4	19.3	15.7	12.9	11.8	6.9
Return on Equity Before Income Taxes 47	21.3	•	215.4	139.0	37.2	33.8	38.4	56.5	24.5	22.8	11.3
Return on Equity After Income Taxes 48	17.4	•	214.9	138.2	36.5	32.3	35.8	54.4	22.9	16.0	8.7
Profit Margin (Before Income Tax) 49	8.8	5.9	9.2	12.3	7.3	8.2	9.8	13.7	9.1	8.1	7.7
Profit Margin (After Income Tax) 50	7.2	4.2	9.2	12.2	7.1	7.8	9.1	13.2	8.5	5.7	5.9

EDUCATIONAL SERVICES

Table I
Corporations with and without Net Income

MONEY AMOUNTS AND SIZE OF ASSETS IN THOUSANDS OF DOLLARS

Item Description for Accounting Period 7/10 Through 6/11	Total	Zero Assets	Under 500	500 to 1,000	1,000 to 5,000	5,000 to 10,000	10,000 to 25,000	25,000 to 50,000	50,000 to 100,000	100,000 to 250,000	250,000 to 500,000	500,000 to 2,500,000	2,500,000 and over
Number of Enterprises **1**	59620	16341	39768	1113	1830	239	166	57	38	•	16	•	10
Revenues ($ in Thousands)													
Net Sales **2**	63705946	1655357	9100927	2501730	6697282	2100885	3133461	3120789	3068518	•	4449115	•	9555880
Interest **3**	115433	779	897	709	3127	3359	1717	6957	5458	•	3026	•	12464
Rents **4**	35082	0	168	12	1859	446	491	3331	728	•	3408	•	2833
Royalties **5**	124368	0	0	0	1653	0	7203	2344	24	•	28376	•	72847
Other Portfolio Income **6**	194429	110582	1645	3555	15695	997	7213	690	3840	•	3358	•	6760
Other Receipts **7**	751139	39390	88842	31378	54531	16606	168034	41976	50542	•	54549	•	137368
Total Receipts **8**	64926397	1806108	9192479	2537384	6774147	2122293	3331819	3176087	3129110	•	4541832	•	9788152
Average Total Receipts **9**	1089	111	231	2280	3702	8880	19989	55721	82345	•	283864	•	978815
Operating Costs/Operating Income (%)													
Cost of Operations **10**	11.6	32.1	10.3	35.8	12.1	6.0	13.7	21.9	9.1	•	2.1	•	13.7
Salaries and Wages **11**	29.9	8.8	25.9	26.5	29.5	38.2	32.8	30.0	31.8	•	31.5	•	26.4
Taxes Paid **12**	3.4	1.6	4.0	3.5	4.0	4.4	3.9	3.3	4.2	•	5.0	•	2.8
Interest Paid **13**	1.4	0.7	0.9	0.3	0.6	0.7	0.9	1.6	1.7	•	1.9	•	1.1
Depreciation **14**	3.2	2.5	1.3	0.6	2.0	1.6	2.9	2.5	5.0	•	4.1	•	4.3
Amortization and Depletion **15**	1.0	3.7	0.2	0.0	0.2	0.2	0.6	0.8	1.4	•	1.1	•	1.8
Pensions and Other Deferred Comp. **16**	0.4	0.0	0.5	0.6	0.4	0.5	0.3	0.3	0.5	•	0.5	•	0.5
Employee Benefits **17**	2.4	0.8	1.9	2.3	1.0	2.8	1.8	2.5	2.5	•	3.0	•	4.2
Advertising **18**	5.9	1.9	2.2	0.6	2.1	3.1	6.2	6.5	5.9	•	8.1	•	9.6
Other Expenses **19**	29.1	51.8	39.8	17.7	34.1	34.8	32.2	22.1	27.5	•	27.1	•	23.5
Officers' Compensation **20**	3.4	4.5	9.0	10.0	6.6	4.5	3.3	1.4	1.8	•	1.3	•	0.6
Operating Margin **21**	8.4	•	4.0	2.0	7.5	3.2	1.4	7.2	8.6	•	14.3	•	11.4
Operating Margin Before Officers' Comp. **22**	11.9	•	13.1	12.0	14.1	7.7	4.7	8.5	10.4	•	15.5	•	12.0

Selected Average Balance Sheet ($ in Thousands)

	•	•	•	•	•	•	•	•	•	•	•
Net Receivables 23	102	0	5	160	390	2124	3742	5311	10186	40936	87264
Inventories 24	9	0	2	8	48	80	213	1517	784	2047	6679
Net Property, Plant and Equipment 25	166	0	13	234	600	1216	3183	7089	16558	79377	137759
Total Assets 26	958	0	59	652	1996	6341	15966	34708	67106	349572	990348
Notes and Loans Payable 27	258	0	38	199	683	1010	2702	14880	17059	79748	114213
All Other Liabilities 28	309	0	29	196	648	3999	6656	12651	22083	117880	389724
Net Worth 29	391	0	-8	258	665	1332	6609	7176	27964	151944	486412

Selected Financial Ratios (Times to 1)

Current Ratio 30	1.3	•	1.1	1.7	1.6	1.2	1.5	1.5	1.2	1.4	
Quick Ratio 31	1.0	•	0.9	1.4	1.3	1.1	1.2	1.1	1.0	1.0	
Net Sales to Working Capital 32	12.1	•	57.4	13.7	8.1	12.9	6.1	9.6	18.8	14.9	13.4
Coverage Ratio 33	8.2	1.8	6.5	14.1	15.9	7.3	9.1	6.6	7.2	13.3	
Total Asset Turnover 34	1.1	•	3.9	3.4	1.8	1.4	1.2	1.6	0.8	1.0	
Inventory Turnover 35	13.2	•	11.6	102.0	9.2	6.6	12.2	7.9	2.9	19.6	
Receivables Turnover 36	11.3	•	44.2	20.0	9.2	5.8	6.6	9.7	6.6	12.8	
Total Liabilities to Net Worth 37	1.4	•	•	1.5	2.0	3.8	1.4	1.4	1.3	1.0	
Current Assets to Working Capital 38	3.9	7.7	2.4	2.6	5.2	3.0	3.2	5.5	5.8	3.9	
Current Liabilities to Working Capital 39	2.9	6.7	1.4	1.6	4.2	2.0	2.2	4.5	4.8	2.9	
Working Capital to Net Sales 40	0.1	0.0	0.1	0.1	0.1	0.2	0.1	0.1	0.1	0.1	
Inventory to Working Capital 41	0.1	0.4	0.1	0.1	0.0	0.1	0.3	0.2	0.1	0.2	
Total Receipts to Cash Flow 42	3.1	2.4	3.0	6.5	2.9	3.1	3.1	4.0	3.3	2.7	3.2
Cost of Goods to Cash Flow 43	0.4	0.8	0.3	2.3	0.4	0.2	0.4	0.9	0.3	0.1	0.4
Cash Flow to Total Debt 44	0.6	•	1.1	0.9	0.9	0.6	0.7	0.5	0.6	0.5	0.6

Selected Financial Factors (in Percentages)

Debt Ratio 45	59.1	•	113.1	60.5	66.7	79.0	58.6	79.3	58.3	56.5	50.9
Return on Total Assets 46	13.2	•	23.1	12.7	16.9	6.8	9.8	16.6	14.9	14.5	14.5
Return on Equity Before Income Taxes 47	28.4	•	•	29.9	47.4	27.8	21.0	68.1	30.7	29.8	27.3
Return on Equity After Income Taxes 48	21.0	•	•	28.5	45.6	26.2	19.9	61.9	24.5	19.5	17.6
Profit Margin (Before Income Tax) 49	10.4	0.5	5.0	3.4	8.6	4.2	7.4	8.9	10.6	16.3	13.9
Profit Margin (After Income Tax) 50	7.7	0.1	4.8	3.3	8.3	4.0	7.0	8.5	10.6	14.5	8.9

Table II
Corporations with Net Income

EDUCATIONAL SERVICES

MONEY AMOUNTS AND SIZE OF ASSETS IN THOUSANDS OF DOLLARS

Item Description for Accounting Period 7/10 Through 6/11		Total	Zero Assets	Under 500	500 to 1,000	1,000 to 5,000	5,000 to 10,000	10,000 to 25,000	25,000 to 50,000	50,000 to 100,000	100,000 to 250,000	250,000 to 500,000	500,000 to 2,500,000	2,500,000 and over
Number of Enterprises	1	32535	9052	20917	851	1294	182	114	47	29	26	11	•	•
Revenues ($ in Thousands)														
Net Sales	2	54515522	1460175	6344297	1924040	5443144	1796935	2413312	2937456	2604428	4683659	4171753	•	•
Interest	3	56366	544	662	209	2915	3017	809	6853	2385	7053	2028	•	•
Rents	4	30793	0	18	12	1859	446	491	3331	399	7650	3390	•	•
Royalties	5	93113	0	0	0	0	0	7203	2344	24	2599	2820	•	•
Other Portfolio Income	6	193671	110582	1645	3555	15695	997	7156	690	3673	4162	3358	•	•
Other Receipts	7	633163	14287	74801	4429	45847	7576	157980	43665	21815	53184	47664	•	•
Total Receipts	8	55522628	1585588	6421423	1932245	5509460	1808971	2586951	2994339	2632724	4758307	4231013	•	•
Average Total Receipts	9	1707	175	307	2271	4258	9939	22693	63709	90784	183012	384638	•	•
Operating Costs/Operating Income (%)														
Cost of Operations	10	11.1	33.6	12.0	43.5	10.9	3.3	13.9	21.5	10.0	15.7	1.4	•	•
Salaries and Wages	11	28.3	6.9	19.5	16.8	27.0	38.8	28.1	29.7	30.2	30.0	31.8	•	•
Taxes Paid	12	3.2	1.4	3.2	2.8	3.7	4.9	3.8	3.3	4.2	3.4	5.1	•	•
Interest Paid	13	1.0	0.7	0.6	0.1	0.4	0.6	0.6	1.5	1.4	1.1	1.3	•	•
Depreciation	14	3.1	2.2	1.2	0.6	1.5	1.6	2.8	2.2	4.7	3.0	4.3	•	•
Amortization and Depletion	15	0.7	0.1	0.2	0.0	0.1	0.0	0.2	0.4	1.1	1.3	0.6	•	•
Pensions and Other Deferred Comp.	16	0.4	0.0	0.4	0.8	0.5	0.6	0.4	0.3	0.6	0.2	0.5	•	•
Employee Benefits	17	2.3	0.7	1.3	1.3	1.0	1.6	1.5	2.4	2.3	1.9	3.0	•	•
Advertising	18	6.3	1.9	2.2	0.6	2.1	2.5	7.4	6.7	5.7	6.1	8.1	•	•
Other Expenses	19	27.8	46.9	37.7	17.3	33.4	31.4	32.3	21.6	24.6	24.5	25.8	•	•
Officers' Compensation	20	3.4	4.3	10.3	11.3	7.7	5.1	3.1	1.3	1.7	1.6	1.1	•	•
Operating Margin	21	12.4	1.3	11.4	4.8	11.7	9.6	6.0	9.1	13.5	11.2	17.1	•	•
Operating Margin Before Officers' Comp.	22	15.8	5.5	21.7	16.1	19.4	14.7	9.1	10.4	15.1	12.9	18.2	•	•

Selected Average Balance Sheet ($ in Thousands)

	1	2	3	4	5	6	7	8	9	10	11	12
Net Receivables **23**	143	0	3	178	416	1582	4594	5749	11309	20370	47170	•
Inventories **24**	12	0	3	5	36	104	184	1810	893	863	1015	•
Net Property, Plant and Equipment **25**	258	0	18	232	570	1432	3060	7372	17554	34746	107728	•
Total Assets **26**	1311	0	70	659	2068	6481	15324	34960	68228	150111	366205	•
Notes and Loans Payable **27**	298	0	38	126	520	754	2077	16657	15432	27195	73882	•
All Other Liabilities **28**	437	0	16	135	727	3568	6532	12324	21763	48212	138201	•
Net Worth **29**	576	0	16	398	821	2159	6715	5979	31033	74704	154121	•

Selected Financial Ratios (Times to 1)

	1	2	3	4	5	6	7	8	9	10	11	12
Current Ratio **30**	1.4	•	1.9	1.8	1.5	1.6	1.6	1.2	1.2	1.3	1.2	•
Quick Ratio **31**	1.0	•	1.6	1.4	1.4	1.4	1.2	1.0	1.0	1.1	1.0	•
Net Sales to Working Capital **32**	11.1	•	18.5	13.2	6.9	9.7	5.2	8.7	20.3	15.7	14.8	•
Coverage Ratio **33**	15.4	14.6	22.0	67.5	37.6	18.9	22.1	8.6	11.5	13.0	15.8	•
Total Asset Turnover **34**	1.3	•	4.3	3.4	2.0	1.5	1.4	1.8	1.3	1.2	1.0	•
Inventory Turnover **35**	15.6	•	13.8	192.4	12.6	3.1	16.0	7.4	10.1	32.8	5.2	•
Receivables Turnover **36**	12.5	•	73.6	17.2	10.2	8.2	6.2	11.0	9.7	10.0	•	•
Total Liabilities to Net Worth **37**	1.3	•	3.5	0.7	1.5	2.0	1.3	4.8	1.2	1.0	1.4	•
Current Assets to Working Capital **38**	3.5	•	2.1	2.3	2.2	3.0	2.6	2.8	5.6	4.6	5.3	•
Current Liabilities to Working Capital **39**	2.5	•	1.1	1.3	1.2	2.0	1.6	1.8	4.6	3.6	4.3	•
Working Capital to Net Sales **40**	0.1	•	0.1	0.1	0.1	0.1	0.2	0.1	0.0	0.1	0.1	•
Inventory to Working Capital **41**	0.1	•	0.1	0.0	0.0	0.0	0.1	0.2	0.1	0.1	0.0	•
Total Receipts to Cash Flow **42**	2.9	2.1	2.6	5.9	2.6	2.9	2.6	3.7	3.1	3.2	2.6	•
Cost of Goods to Cash Flow **43**	0.3	0.7	0.3	2.6	0.3	0.1	0.4	0.8	0.3	0.5	0.0	•
Cash Flow to Total Debt **44**	0.8	•	2.1	1.5	1.3	0.8	0.9	0.6	0.8	0.8	0.7	•

Selected Financial Factors (in Percentages)

	1	2	3	4	5	6	7	8	9	10	11	12
Debt Ratio **45**	56.0	•	77.7	39.6	60.3	66.7	56.2	82.9	54.5	50.2	57.9	•
Return on Total Assets **46**	19.5	•	57.1	18.3	27.0	16.5	19.3	22.3	21.0	16.7	20.4	•
Return on Equity Before Income Taxes **47**	41.6	•	244.2	29.8	66.1	46.9	42.0	115.4	42.2	31.0	45.5	•
Return on Equity After Income Taxes **48**	32.5	•	239.0	28.6	64.0	45.6	40.4	106.3	34.9	26.4	30.7	•
Profit Margin (Before Income Tax) **49**	14.3	9.9	12.6	5.2	12.9	10.2	13.3	11.0	14.6	12.9	18.5	•
Profit Margin (After Income Tax) **50**	11.2	9.3	12.3	5.0	12.5	10.0	12.8	10.2	12.1	10.9	12.5	•

Table I

Corporations with and without Net Income

OFFICES OF PHYSICIANS

MONEY AMOUNTS AND SIZE OF ASSETS IN THOUSANDS OF DOLLARS

Item Description for Accounting Period 7/10 Through 6/11		Total	Zero Assets	Under 500	500 to 1,000	1,000 to 5,000	5,000 to 10,000	10,000 to 25,000	25,000 to 50,000	50,000 to 100,000	100,000 to 250,000	250,000 to 500,000	500,000 to 2,500,000	2,500,000 and over
Number of Enterprises	1	152167	17596	124011	5417	4491	362	181	48	35	17	3	5	0
Revenues ($ in Thousands)														
Net Sales	2	249014734	2089201	135469030	20983527	48489505	8826527	9233168	4791691	3764558	3509876	661254	11196396	0
Interest	3	103643	57	17447	3558	7870	4717	4182	3617	5750	8163	1133	47150	0
Rents	4	179017	39	101144	7497	14461	8997	2774	16964	6586	15317	1309	3928	0
Royalties	5	13695	0	0	0	0	0	265	0	0	0	0	13430	0
Other Portfolio Income	6	569772	35668	94671	2181	181856	177640	17520	35395	5900	6459	479	12004	0
Other Receipts	7	7859757	341933	4074955	427598	1696635	89432	417732	99821	337438	42476	9467	322269	0
Total Receipts	8	257740618	2466898	139757247	21424361	50390327	9107313	9675641	4947488	4120232	3582291	673642	11595177	0
Average Total Receipts	9	1694	140	1127	3955	11220	25158	53457	103073	117721	210723	224547	2319035	•
Operating Costs/Operating Income (%)														
Cost of Operations	10	4.4	8.2	2.1	10.5	5.5	3.1	14.8	4.0	11.5	11.4	8.2	4.0	•
Salaries and Wages	11	32.0	8.5	29.5	25.1	32.3	41.0	40.6	50.7	43.8	49.4	42.6	45.8	•
Taxes Paid	12	3.1	3.2	3.2	2.9	2.9	3.3	3.2	2.9	3.2	3.2	3.9	2.9	•
Interest Paid	13	0.4	0.7	0.3	0.3	0.5	0.5	0.6	0.8	0.9	1.4	5.3	1.4	•
Depreciation	14	1.2	0.9	0.8	1.1	1.6	2.7	1.6	1.6	2.4	2.2	6.9	0.8	•
Amortization and Depletion	15	0.1	0.1	0.0	0.0	0.0	0.1	0.1	0.3	0.5	0.5	2.7	0.6	•
Pensions and Other Deferred Comp.	16	3.6	2.3	3.7	3.1	3.1	1.8	3.2	5.1	1.8	2.2	2.7	7.8	•
Employee Benefits	17	2.3	1.5	1.9	1.6	2.3	2.7	2.8	3.9	3.7	3.8	4.8	6.0	•
Advertising	18	0.5	0.6	0.5	0.6	0.5	0.6	0.3	0.2	1.0	0.2	0.7	0.1	•
Other Expenses	19	30.9	46.4	28.3	30.6	34.7	39.5	33.5	34.7	37.7	25.4	32.0	32.0	•
Officers' Compensation	20	19.4	25.2	26.1	16.0	16.8	7.1	2.5	1.2	1.1	0.6	3.2	0.5	•
Operating Margin	21	2.0	2.1	3.6	8.2	•	•	•	•	•	•	•	•	•
Operating Margin Before Officers' Comp.	22	21.5	27.3	29.6	24.2	16.5	4.7	•	•	•	•	•	•	•

Selected Average Balance Sheet ($ in Thousands)

Item													
Net Receivables 23	28	•	0	3	54	184	1421	2892	6147	11458	29871	29310	100576
Inventories 24	2	•	0	0	5	6	35	104	318	316	647	1104	20355
Net Property, Plant and Equipment 25	71	•	0	25	186	641	2068	4117	10749	15905	33388	54561	83997
Total Assets 26	290	•	0	93	685	1758	6968	14573	37705	70131	155039	353683	1566955
Notes and Loans Payable 27	123	•	0	57	255	867	2937	8075	12887	20101	51295	126880	264096
All Other Liabilities 28	132	•	0	33	173	779	2666	5720	10715	21290	54169	39242	1464934
Net Worth 29	34	•	0	3	258	112	1366	777	14103	28740	49575	187562	-162075

Selected Financial Ratios (Times to 1)

Item													
Current Ratio 30	1.1	•	1.2	1.5	0.8	1.3	0.9	1.0	1.1	0.9	1.4	1.4	
Quick Ratio 31	0.9	•	1.1	1.2	0.7	1.1	0.7	0.7	0.7	0.8	1.1	1.1	
Net Sales to Working Capital 32	135.9	•	128.3	32.8	•	37.2	•	250.0	37.1	•	16.0	23.1	
Coverage Ratio 33	13.6	28.0	26.0	33.1	8.2	2.8	3.8	•	2.8	2.2	•	2.1	
Total Asset Turnover 34	5.6	•	11.8	5.7	6.1	3.5	3.5	2.6	1.5	1.3	0.6	1.4	
Inventory Turnover 35	39.9	•	57.4	77.7	104.0	21.6	72.5	12.5	39.2	36.5	16.3	4.4	
Receivables Turnover 36	58.6	•	494.4	76.4	50.4	22.1	18.5	16.5	7.9	7.2	7.2	22.8	
Total Liabilities to Net Worth 37	7.5	•	27.7	1.7	14.6	4.1	17.8	1.7	1.4	2.1	0.9	•	
Current Assets to Working Capital 38	9.7	•	5.8	3.1	•	4.8	•	38.2	10.0	3.5	3.5	3.7	
Current Liabilities to Working Capital 39	8.7	•	4.8	2.1	•	3.8	•	37.2	9.0	2.5	2.5	2.7	
Working Capital to Net Sales 40	0.0	•	0.0	0.0	•	0.0	•	0.0	0.0	0.1	0.1	0.0	
Inventory to Working Capital 41	0.2	•	0.0	0.0	•	0.1	•	0.5	0.1	0.1	0.1	0.2	
Total Receipts to Cash Flow 42	3.2	1.7	3.3	2.9	3.1	3.4	3.4	3.5	2.9	4.3	6.5	3.5	
Cost of Goods to Cash Flow 43	0.1	0.1	0.1	0.3	0.2	0.1	0.5	0.1	0.3	0.5	0.5	0.1	
Cash Flow to Total Debt 44	2.0	•	3.7	3.2	2.1	1.3	1.1	1.2	0.9	0.5	0.2	0.4	

Selected Financial Factors (in Percentages)

Item													
Debt Ratio 45	88.2	•	96.5	62.4	93.6	80.4	94.7	62.6	59.0	68.0	47.0	110.3	
Return on Total Assets 46	33.8	•	82.7	60.3	24.9	4.4	7.4	•	4.1	4.1	4.2	4.2	
Return on Equity Before Income Taxes 47	264.7	•	2284.3	155.6	341.4	14.5	101.8	•	6.4	7.0	•	•	
Return on Equity After Income Taxes 48	258.7	•	2266.1	154.0	337.5	10.6	93.0	•	5.6	2.4	•	•	
Profit Margin (Before Income Tax) 49	5.5	20.2	6.8	10.3	3.6	0.8	1.6	1.6	1.7	1.7	•	1.5	
Profit Margin (After Income Tax) 50	5.4	19.9	6.7	10.2	3.5	0.6	1.4	1.4	1.5	0.6	•	0.6	

Table II

Corporations with Net Income

OFFICES OF PHYSICIANS

MONEY AMOUNTS AND SIZE OF ASSETS IN THOUSANDS OF DOLLARS

Item Description for Accounting Period 7/10 Through 6/11		Total	Zero Assets	Under 500	500 to 1,000	1,000 to 5,000	5,000 to 10,000	10,000 to 25,000	25,000 to 50,000	50,000 to 100,000	100,000 to 250,000	250,000 to 500,000	500,000 to 2,500,000	2,500,000 and over
Number of Enterprises	1	104743	10721	85795	4593	3263	195	124	21	19	13	0	0	0
Revenues ($ in Thousands)														
Net Sales	2	165634206	1828727	91393904	17306305	34393848	5500110	6182449	2572713	2344407	4411742	0	0	0
Interest	3	64646	0	11961	706	5982	3770	2171	2406	3002	34650	0	0	0
Rents	4	88440	0	55640	6971	4403	203	2059	13453	2673	3038	0	0	0
Royalties	5	265	0	0	0	0	0	265	0	0	0	0	0	0
Other Portfolio Income	6	506219	35666	77071	2174	168325	177450	8707	31454	2746	2624	0	0	0
Other Receipts	7	5722447	231995	3380723	406310	793822	65457	294539	30393	275468	243743	0	0	0
Total Receipts	8	172016223	2096388	94919299	17722466	35366380	5746990	6490190	2650419	2628296	4395797	0	0	0
Average Total Receipts	9	1642	196	1106	3859	10839	29472	52340	126210	138331	338138	•	•	•
Operating Costs/Operating Income (%)														
Cost of Operations	10	5.0	8.6	2.3	10.2	6.6	3.7	11.4	•	12.4	17.9	•	•	•
Salaries and Wages	11	28.9	9.4	26.1	23.1	30.6	42.6	42.9	57.3	45.2	43.2	•	•	•
Taxes Paid	12	3.0	3.7	3.1	2.7	2.9	3.3	3.4	3.1	3.3	2.9	•	•	•
Interest Paid	13	0.3	0.8	0.3	0.3	0.3	0.4	0.5	0.4	0.8	1.8	•	•	•
Depreciation	14	1.0	0.4	0.7	0.9	1.5	2.5	1.6	1.2	2.1	1.8	•	•	•
Amortization and Depletion	15	0.1	0.1	0.0	0.1	0.0	0.1	0.1	0.3	0.4	1.1	•	•	•
Pensions and Other Deferred Comp.	16	3.1	2.5	3.1	3.2	2.9	2.3	4.2	6.1	2.0	1.6	•	•	•
Employee Benefits	17	1.8	1.6	1.6	1.3	2.2	2.4	2.3	4.2	4.2	3.2	•	•	•
Advertising	18	0.5	0.4	0.4	0.6	0.5	0.9	0.4	0.2	0.5	0.2	•	•	•
Other Expenses	19	30.0	38.7	29.3	31.6	31.3	32.5	30.3	27.1	34.4	21.3	•	•	•
Officers' Compensation	20	19.9	23.5	25.7	14.8	16.9	7.5	2.5	0.9	1.0	1.1	•	•	•
Operating Margin	21	6.3	10.4	7.4	11.1	4.3	1.8	0.4	•	•	4.0	•	•	•
Operating Margin Before Officers' Comp.	22	26.2	34.0	33.1	25.9	21.1	9.3	2.9	0.0	•	5.0	•	•	•

Selected Average Balance Sheet ($ in Thousands)

Net Receivables	23	22	0	3	57	131	1053	2567	3698	11038	43990
Inventories	24	2	0	0	6	2	38	107	288	359	4540
Net Property, Plant and Equipment	25	66	0	25	190	594	1862	3447	11443	20280	38242
Total Assets	26	245		98	683	1676	7000	13892	37246	71198	263761
Notes and Loans Payable	27	89	0	40	212	581	3242	5219	17079	16710	82112
All Other Liabilities	28	59	0	28	150	437	1799	3992	8751	20346	16899
Net Worth	29	98	0	31	322	658	1959	4681	11416	34141	164750

Selected Financial Ratios (Times to 1)

Current Ratio	30	1.5	•	1.5	1.9	1.2	1.6	1.1	0.9	1.6	1.6
Quick Ratio	31	1.2	•	1.4	1.4	1.1	1.3	0.8	0.7	0.9	1.2
Net Sales to Working Capital	32	44.9	56.0	21.9	84.6	22.8	170.5	•		11.8	9.6
Coverage Ratio	33	30.5	33.8	44.8	47.7	21.9	16.4	11.7	6.4	7.8	7.2
Total Asset Turnover	34	6.4	•	10.8	5.5	6.3	4.0	3.6	3.3	1.7	1.2
Inventory Turnover	35	38.8	•	58.2	63.1	357.9	27.5	53.1	•	42.7	12.5
Receivables Turnover	36	71.7	•	405.1	88.2	62.9	34.6	26.1	23.7	9.6	8.0
Total Liabilities to Net Worth	37	1.5	•	2.2	1.1	1.5	2.6	2.0	2.3	1.1	0.6
Current Assets to Working Capital	38	3.2	•	2.8	2.2	5.3	2.7	19.2	•	2.8	2.6
Current Liabilities to Working Capital	39	2.2	•	1.8	1.2	4.3	1.7	18.2	•	1.8	1.6
Working Capital to Net Sales	40	0.0	•	0.0	0.0	0.0	0.0	0.0	•	0.1	0.1
Inventory to Working Capital	41	0.1	•	0.0	0.0	0.0	0.0	0.5	•	0.0	0.2
Total Receipts to Cash Flow	42	2.9	1.7	2.8	2.5	3.1	3.2	3.2	4.1	2.8	3.5
Cost of Goods to Cash Flow	43	0.1	0.2	0.1	0.3	0.2	0.1	0.4	•	0.3	0.6
Cash Flow to Total Debt	44	3.7	•	5.5	4.1	3.3	1.8	1.7	1.2	1.2	0.9

Selected Financial Factors (in Percentages)

Debt Ratio	45	60.1	•	68.8	52.9	60.8	72.0	66.3	69.3	52.0	37.5
Return on Total Assets	46	67.8	•	124.8	76.2	46.7	26.8	21.3	8.5	11.3	15.1
Return on Equity Before Income Taxes	47	164.4	•	390.6	158.5	113.6	90.0	57.7	23.3	20.5	20.8
Return on Equity After Income Taxes	48	161.3	•	387.9	157.0	112.7	85.0	55.6	19.7	19.3	14.1
Profit Margin (Before Income Tax)	49	10.2	25.1	11.3	13.5	7.1	6.3	5.4	2.2	5.7	10.8
Profit Margin (After Income Tax)	50	10.0	24.8	11.2	13.4	7.0	5.9	5.2	1.8	5.3	7.3

Table I

Corporations with and without Net Income

OFFICES OF DENTISTS

MONEY AMOUNTS AND SIZE OF ASSETS IN THOUSANDS OF DOLLARS

Item Description for Accounting Period 7/10 Through 6/11	Total	Zero Assets	Under 500	500 to 1,000	1,000 to 5,000	5,000 to 10,000	10,000 to 25,000	25,000 to 50,000	50,000 to 100,000	100,000 to 250,000	250,000 to 500,000	500,000 to 2,500,000	2,500,000 and over
Number of Enterprises **1**	74514	4434	62316	6406	1322	18	4	3	4	5	3	0	0
Revenues ($ in Thousands)													
Net Sales **2**	62729804	2954996	44388857	9820243	3081797	393877	131245	171702	166601	862596	757890	0	0
Interest **3**	6870	1215	3742	1196	274	142	110	6	12	38	135	0	0
Rents **4**	778	0	778	0	0	0	0	0	0	0	0	0	0
Royalties **5**	0	0	0	0	0	0	0	0	0	0	0	0	0
Other Portfolio Income **6**	78372	7771	62185	14	7952	0	0	447	0	3	0	0	0
Other Receipts **7**	1317656	-20352	1152808	155807	15845	245	1191	235	8679	2870	328	0	0
Total Receipts **8**	64133480	2943630	45608370	9977260	3105868	394264	132546	172390	175292	865507	758353	0	0
Average Total Receipts **9**	861	664	732	1557	2349	21904	33136	57463	43823	173101	252784	•	
Operating Costs/Operating Income (%)													
Cost of Operations **10**	5.5	1.1	5.6	5.0	10.1	•	•	28.9	7.6	12.8	0.1	•	
Salaries and Wages **11**	25.1	44.6	22.9	24.5	29.9	34.6	64.3	26.0	53.4	32.7	39.5	•	
Taxes Paid **12**	3.8	5.1	3.8	3.6	3.6	2.6	4.4	3.3	2.3	3.2	4.2	•	
Interest Paid **13**	1.2	0.7	0.9	2.1	1.6	0.1	•	1.0	2.9	4.4	3.1	•	
Depreciation **14**	2.0	1.5	1.9	1.9	2.8	0.6	0.4	2.2	2.2	3.8	4.9	•	
Amortization and Depletion **15**	0.6	0.5	0.3	1.1	1.2	•	•	0.4	0.4	3.4	4.4	•	
Pensions and Other Deferred Comp. **16**	2.0	0.9	2.2	1.9	0.8	0.4	14.6	0.1	•	1.9	0.2	•	
Employee Benefits **17**	1.2	1.2	1.2	1.4	0.9	0.9	6.2	1.8	0.9	1.0	1.0	•	
Advertising **18**	1.5	4.8	1.4	1.1	1.2	3.9	0.2	1.7	2.1	1.6	2.6	•	
Other Expenses **19**	31.1	38.8	30.8	28.7	31.3	52.7	8.9	22.9	33.7	33.8	36.3	•	
Officers' Compensation **20**	18.2	3.2	20.8	18.8	5.8	4.8	1.0	2.4	0.3	1.0	0.9	•	
Operating Margin **21**	7.7	•	8.1	9.9	10.8	•	0.0	9.5	•	0.2	2.5	•	
Operating Margin Before Officers' Comp. **22**	25.9	1.0	28.9	28.7	16.6	4.2	1.1	11.9	•	1.2	3.5	•	

Selected Average Balance Sheet ($ in Thousands)

Net Receivables 23	12	0	3	48	44	5033	3432	5402	11779	7543	58287
Inventories 24	1	0	1	2	0	316	0	933	1624	1743	423
Net Property, Plant and Equipment 25	74	0	51	175	624	316	342	2363	7560	22025	64525
Total Assets 26	241	0	137	684	1582	5765	13206	34350	63223	172717	521493
Notes and Loans Payable 27	155	0	97	484	858	264	0	3688	34503	90423	220410
All Other Liabilities 28	43	0	26	97	173	4561	8234	34152	23339	35025	89224
Net Worth 29	43	0	15	103	551	941	4973	-3491	5381	47270	211859

Selected Financial Ratios (Times to 1)

Current Ratio 30	1.4	•	1.2	1.7	2.3	1.1	0.9	0.5	2.4	1.1	1.8
Quick Ratio 31	1.2	•	1.1	1.4	2.1	1.0	0.9	0.4	1.2	0.4	1.4
Net Sales to Working Capital 32	42.4	•	88.9	17.0	14.0	34.0	•	•	2.5	74.7	5.2
Coverage Ratio 33	9.2	•	12.5	6.5	8.0	•	•	11.1	0.8	1.1	1.8
Total Asset Turnover 34	3.5	•	5.2	2.2	1.5	3.8	2.5	1.7	0.7	1.0	0.5
Inventory Turnover 35	46.2	•	58.8	32.4	11959.9	•	•	17.7	2.0	12.7	0.9
Receivables Turnover 36	69.6	•	237.9	31.7	79.7	5.5	6.7	21.2	2.6	30.1	4.4
Total Liabilities to Net Worth 37	4.6	•	8.3	5.7	1.9	5.1	1.7	•	10.7	2.7	1.5
Current Assets to Working Capital 38	3.6	•	5.4	2.4	1.8	8.5	•	•	1.7	12.4	2.2
Current Liabilities to Working Capital 39	2.6	•	4.4	1.4	0.8	7.5	•	•	0.7	11.4	1.2
Working Capital to Net Sales 40	0.0	•	0.0	0.1	0.1	0.0	•	•	0.4	0.0	0.2
Inventory to Working Capital 41	0.0	•	0.1	0.0	•	•	•	•	0.1	0.6	•
Total Receipts to Cash Flow 42	2.9	3.5	2.9	2.9	2.8	2.0	10.4	3.3	4.0	3.6	3.2
Cost of Goods to Cash Flow 43	0.2	0.0	0.2	0.1	0.3	0.3	•	1.0	0.3	0.5	0.0
Cash Flow to Total Debt 44	1.5	•	2.0	0.9	0.8	2.3	0.4	0.5	0.2	0.4	0.3

Selected Financial Factors (in Percentages)

Debt Ratio 45	82.0	•	89.2	85.0	65.2	83.7	62.3	110.2	91.5	72.6	59.4
Return on Total Assets 46	39.1	•	61.2	30.4	19.5	2.5	2.5	18.1	1.5	5.0	2.8
Return on Equity Before Income Taxes 47	194.2	•	523.9	171.4	48.9	6.7	6.7	•	•	2.1	3.1
Return on Equity After Income Taxes 48	192.5	•	521.5	169.5	48.1	6.7	6.7	•	•	0.8	2.0
Profit Margin (Before Income Tax) 49	10.0	•	10.9	11.5	11.6	1.0	1.0	9.9	•	0.6	2.6
Profit Margin (After Income Tax) 50	9.9	•	10.8	11.3	11.4	1.0	1.0	9.0	•	0.2	1.7

Table II

Corporations with Net Income

OFFICES OF DENTISTS

MONEY AMOUNTS AND SIZE OF ASSETS IN THOUSANDS OF DOLLARS

Item Description for Accounting Period 7/10 Through 6/11		Total	Zero Assets	Under 500	500 to 1,000	1,000 to 5,000	5,000 to 10,000	10,000 to 25,000	25,000 to 50,000	50,000 to 100,000	100,000 to 250,000	250,000 to 500,000	500,000 to 2,500,000	2,500,000 and over
Number of Enterprises	1	55603	1703	47070	5597	1220	0	•	0	0	•	0	0	0
Revenues ($ in Thousands)														
Net Sales	2	50456618	2171854	34499912	9057672	2849150	0	•	0	0	•	0	0	0
Interest	3	2688	496	1429	253	274	0	•	0	0	•	0	0	0
Rents	4	778	0	778	0	0	0	•	0	0	•	0	0	0
Royalties	5	0	0	0	0	0	0	•	0	0	•	0	0	0
Other Portfolio Income	6	58245	4567	45691	0	7952	0	•	0	0	•	0	0	0
Other Receipts	7	941833	15829	751118	154492	15844	0	•	0	0	•	0	0	0
Total Receipts	8	51460162	2192746	35298928	9212417	2873220	0	•	0	0	•	0	0	0
Average Total Receipts	9	925	1288	750	1646	2355	•	•	•	•	•	•	•	•
Operating Costs/Operating Income (%)														
Cost of Operations	10	6.1	0.3	6.2	5.3	10.9	•	•	•	•	•	•	•	•
Salaries and Wages	11	24.0	46.5	21.4	23.8	30.5	•	•	•	•	•	•	•	•
Taxes Paid	12	3.7	4.3	3.7	3.5	3.7	•	•	•	•	•	•	•	•
Interest Paid	13	1.2	0.1	0.9	2.0	1.5	•	•	•	•	•	•	•	•
Depreciation	14	1.8	0.4	1.8	1.6	2.8	•	•	•	•	•	•	•	•
Amortization and Depletion	15	0.6	•	0.4	1.2	0.7	•	•	•	•	•	•	•	•
Pensions and Other Deferred Comp.	16	1.9	1.2	2.0	2.0	0.9	•	•	•	•	•	•	•	•
Employee Benefits	17	1.1	1.6	1.1	1.4	1.0	•	•	•	•	•	•	•	•
Advertising	18	1.6	5.8	1.4	1.1	1.3	•	•	•	•	•	•	•	•
Other Expenses	19	29.2	35.6	29.2	27.3	28.2	•	•	•	•	•	•	•	•
Officers' Compensation	20	17.2	2.8	19.5	18.7	6.2	•	•	•	•	•	•	•	•
Operating Margin	21	11.5	1.4	12.4	12.1	12.4	•	•	•	•	•	•	•	•
Operating Margin Before Officers' Comp.	22	28.7	4.2	31.9	30.8	18.6	•	•	•	•	•	•	•	•

Selected Average Balance Sheet ($ in Thousands)

Net Receivables 23	12	0	3	46	46
Inventories 24	1	0	1	2	0
Net Property, Plant and Equipment 25	77	0	50	157	667
Total Assets 26	256	0	146	679	1552
Notes and Loans Payable 27	152	0	90	460	745
All Other Liabilities 28	36	0	21	83	184
Net Worth 29	67	0	35	136	622

Selected Financial Ratios (Times to 1)

Current Ratio 30	1.8	•	1.6	2.6	2.3
Quick Ratio 31	1.6	•	1.5	2.2	2.2
Net Sales to Working Capital 32	25.0	•	41.4	11.4	13.1
Coverage Ratio 33	12.4	36.8	17.3	7.8	9.7
Total Asset Turnover 34	3.6	•	5.0	2.4	1.5
Inventory Turnover 35	60.8	•	83.6	35.1	1734.0
Receivables Turnover 36	76.4	•	217.6	34.9	76.4
Total Liabilities to Net Worth 37	2.8	•	3.1	4.0	1.5
Current Assets to Working Capital 38	2.2	•	2.7	1.6	1.8
Current Liabilities to Working Capital 39	1.2	•	1.7	0.6	0.8
Working Capital to Net Sales 40	0.0	•	0.0	0.1	0.1
Inventory to Working Capital 41	0.0	•	0.0	0.0	•
Total Receipts to Cash Flow 42	2.8	3.2	2.7	2.9	2.9
Cost of Goods to Cash Flow 43	0.2	0.0	0.2	0.2	0.3
Cash Flow to Total Debt 44	1.7	•	2.4	1.0	0.9

Selected Financial Factors (in Percentages)

Debt Ratio 45	73.7	•	75.8	79.9	59.9
Return on Total Assets 46	52.1	•	78.1	37.8	22.2
Return on Equity Before Income Taxes 47	182.1	•	304.2	163.9	49.6
Return on Equity After Income Taxes 48	180.6	•	302.9	162.3	48.9
Profit Margin (Before Income Tax) 49	13.5	2.4	14.7	13.8	13.2
Profit Margin (After Income Tax) 50	13.4	2.2	14.6	13.7	13.0

Table I

Corporations with and without Net Income

OFFICES OF OTHER HEALTH PRACTITIONERS

MONEY AMOUNTS AND SIZE OF ASSETS IN THOUSANDS OF DOLLARS

Item Description for Accounting Period 7/10 Through 6/11	Total	Zero Assets	Under 500	500 to 1,000	1,000 to 5,000	5,000 to 10,000	10,000 to 25,000	25,000 to 50,000	50,000 to 100,000	100,000 to 250,000	250,000 to 500,000	500,000 to 2,500,000	2,500,000 and over
Number of Enterprises 1	109768	18774	87305	2402	1129	41	56	26	18	11	6	0	0	0
Revenues ($ in Thousands)														
Net Sales 2	64598259	2517668	37057537	3822817	4601603	1273720	1835108	1395952	1624495	3527758	6941601	0	0	0
Interest 3	86428	80	1150	332	366	41	2475	1926	2125	11813	66121	0	0	0
Rents 4	27448	0	3380	0	16	1272	640	4687	5310	1639	10503	0	0	0
Royalties 5	141	0	91	0	0	0	0	0	0	0	49	0	0	0
Other Portfolio Income 6	102118	59149	26772	873	0	0	90	3200	1263	6516	4258	0	0	0
Other Receipts 7	1428741	-94342	156030	3183	19698	25884	69357	29285	541003	193762	484880	0	0	0
Total Receipts 8	66243135	2482555	37244960	3827205	4621683	1300917	1907670	1435050	2174196	3741488	7507412	0	0	0
Average Total Receipts 9	603	132	427	1593	4094	31730	34066	55194	120789	340135	1251235	•	•	•
Operating Costs/Operating Income (%)														
Cost of Operations 10	15.6	10.5	11.9	14.5	17.1	16.8	40.5	34.7	12.9	55.2	7.3	•	•	•
Salaries and Wages 11	20.0	15.4	18.3	27.7	24.5	43.0	30.4	33.1	25.3	18.2	13.9	•	•	•
Taxes Paid 12	2.8	3.0	3.1	3.9	2.5	3.6	2.8	3.4	2.5	1.4	1.6	•	•	•
Interest Paid 13	0.7	0.4	0.5	1.3	0.7	0.7	0.6	1.2	1.5	0.3	1.8	•	•	•
Depreciation 14	1.1	0.8	1.0	1.4	1.3	0.8	1.9	1.3	2.0	1.0	0.9	•	•	•
Amortization and Depletion 15	0.5	0.2	0.1	1.3	0.4	0.1	0.2	0.1	1.3	0.4	2.0	•	•	•
Pensions and Other Deferred Comp. 16	0.7	0.6	0.9	0.8	1.0	0.8	0.2	0.9	0.5	0.1	0.4	•	•	•
Employee Benefits 17	1.8	3.4	1.2	2.0	0.9	2.1	2.6	3.0	2.9	8.2	1.3	•	•	•
Advertising 18	1.3	0.4	1.7	1.1	1.0	0.4	1.6	0.1	0.6	0.4	1.1	•	•	•
Other Expenses 19	40.7	41.7	39.1	23.4	36.0	30.5	20.6	21.4	85.3	19.9	72.4	•	•	•
Officers' Compensation 20	9.5	13.4	13.2	12.2	6.9	1.6	1.6	1.6	0.5	0.2	0.3	•	•	•
Operating Margin 21	5.2	10.2	9.1	10.4	7.7	•	•	•	•	•	•	•	•	•
Operating Margin Before Officers' Comp. 22	14.7	23.7	22.3	22.6	14.5	1.3	•	0.8	•	•	•	•	•	•

Selected Average Balance Sheet ($ in Thousands)

Net Receivables 23	23	0	5	35	268	2217	2339	11241	8357	24758	132617
Inventories 24	4	0	2	16	30	31	388	470	1195	1033	10298
Net Property, Plant and Equipment 25	33	0	21	128	387	1484	2259	4235	15209	8956	48337
Total Assets 26	165	0	69	653	1397	7799	15687	35331	72261	146833	648071
Notes and Loans Payable 27	66	0	37	309	478	6665	4667	12749	20947	16049	219170
All Other Liabilities 28	45	0	15	69	245	4035	6530	12955	20584	64353	220410
Net Worth 29	54	0	18	276	674	-2901	4490	9626	30730	66431	208492

Selected Financial Ratios (Times to 1)

Current Ratio 30	1.5	•	1.7	3.7	2.0	0.8	0.9	1.5	1.2	1.0	1.5
Quick Ratio 31	1.2	•	1.5	3.4	1.4	0.7	0.5	1.1	0.7	0.8	1.2
Net Sales to Working Capital 32	24.4	•	30.6	7.5	12.1	•	•	7.9	27.0	•	15.1
Coverage Ratio 33	11.4	21.1	19.2	9.4	13.1	3.6	2.8	2.8	0.2	3.3	4.0
Total Asset Turnover 34	3.6	•	6.1	2.4	2.9	4.0	2.1	1.5	1.2	2.2	1.8
Inventory Turnover 35	25.9	•	23.5	14.4	23.0	169.7	34.2	39.6	9.8	171.4	8.1
Receivables Turnover 36	27.0	•	87.8	34.3	16.0	12.7	17.1	4.7	9.8	12.1	11.4
Total Liabilities to Net Worth 37	2.1	•	2.8	1.4	1.1	•	2.5	2.7	1.4	1.2	2.1
Current Assets to Working Capital 38	3.0	•	2.3	1.4	2.0	•	•	3.0	7.6	•	3.1
Current Liabilities to Working Capital 39	2.0	•	1.3	0.4	1.0	•	•	2.0	6.6	•	2.1
Working Capital to Net Sales 40	0.0	•	0.0	0.1	0.1	•	•	0.1	0.0	•	0.1
Inventory to Working Capital 41	0.1	•	0.1	0.1	0.1	•	•	0.1	0.4	•	0.1
Total Receipts to Cash Flow 42	2.4	2.5	2.5	3.7	2.5	3.8	5.6	5.0	1.2	5.4	1.3
Cost of Goods to Cash Flow 43	0.4	0.3	0.3	0.5	0.4	0.6	2.3	1.7	0.2	3.0	0.1
Cash Flow to Total Debt 44	2.2	•	3.4	1.2	2.2	0.8	0.5	0.4	1.7	0.7	2.0

Selected Financial Factors (in Percentages)

Debt Ratio 45	67.3	•	73.8	57.8	51.8	137.2	71.4	72.8	57.5	54.8	67.8
Return on Total Assets 46	30.3	•	62.0	28.7	25.6	9.7	3.3	4.8	0.4	2.4	12.7
Return on Equity Before Income Taxes 47	84.4	•	223.9	60.8	49.1	•	7.4	11.3	•	3.8	29.5
Return on Equity After Income Taxes 48	81.1	•	223.1	59.2	47.2	•	2.6	7.3	•	2.1	20.1
Profit Margin (Before Income Tax) 49	7.7	8.8	9.6	10.5	8.1	1.8	1.0	2.0	•	0.8	5.3
Profit Margin (After Income Tax) 50	7.4	8.8	9.6	10.3	7.8	1.7	0.4	1.3	•	0.4	3.6

Table II

Corporations with Net Income

OFFICES OF OTHER HEALTH PRACTITIONERS

MONEY AMOUNTS AND SIZE OF ASSETS IN THOUSANDS OF DOLLARS

Item Description for Accounting Period 7/10 Through 6/11	Total	Zero Assets	Under 500	500 to 1,000	1,000 to 5,000	5,000 to 10,000	10,000 to 25,000	25,000 to 50,000	50,000 to 100,000	100,000 to 250,000	250,000 to 500,000	500,000 to 2,500,000	2,500,000 and over
Number of Enterprises **1**	84609	12772	68384	2325	1027	30	38	13	8	7	6	0	0
Revenues ($ in Thousands)													
Net Sales **2**	52669773	1561792	30310828	3756409	3627849	1060190	1470475	1081973	581366	2277289	6941601	0	0
Interest **3**	82746	32	954	156	12	22	2440	94	1273	11643	66121	0	0
Rents **4**	19539	0	3380	0	0	1272	85	3779	70	450	10503	0	0
Royalties **5**	141	0	91	0	0	0	0	0	0	0	49	0	0
Other Portfolio Income **6**	52980	11891	26765	88	0	0	53	2293	1255	6379	4258	0	0
Other Receipts **7**	1467812	3946	130968	3183	19237	23607	60136	12336	540615	188902	484880	0	0
Total Receipts **8**	54292991	1577661	30472986	3759836	3647098	1085091	1533189	1100475	1124579	2484663	7507412	0	0
Average Total Receipts **9**	642	124	446	1617	3551	36170	40347	84652	140572	354952	1251235	•	•
Operating Costs/Operating Income (%)													
Cost of Operations **10**	15.0	4.4	11.6	14.2	15.1	5.5	49.2	44.4	3.8	65.0	7.3	•	•
Salaries and Wages **11**	19.5	12.7	17.5	28.0	28.7	47.4	25.1	27.2	37.5	13.7	13.9	•	•
Taxes Paid **12**	2.8	2.7	3.0	3.9	3.0	4.2	2.9	2.8	3.6	1.0	1.6	•	•
Interest Paid **13**	0.7	0.2	0.5	1.2	0.7	0.8	0.6	0.4	2.0	0.5	1.8	•	•
Depreciation **14**	1.1	1.0	1.0	1.3	1.5	1.0	1.8	1.5	3.1	0.9	0.9	•	•
Amortization and Depletion **15**	0.5	0.0	0.2	1.3	0.5	0.0	0.3	0.0	2.2	0.4	2.0	•	•
Pensions and Other Deferred Comp. **16**	0.8	1.0	0.9	0.8	1.3	0.8	0.1	1.0	0.2	0.1	0.4	•	•
Employee Benefits **17**	1.3	0.7	0.9	2.1	0.9	2.0	1.9	2.9	3.5	4.8	1.3	•	•
Advertising **18**	1.4	0.3	1.8	1.1	1.3	0.3	1.8	0.1	0.1	0.3	1.1	•	•
Other Expenses **19**	39.4	33.0	37.7	22.7	27.7	32.4	11.9	14.1	132.8	20.3	72.4	•	•
Officers' Compensation **20**	9.6	18.0	13.0	12.3	8.4	1.6	1.6	1.9	0.7	0.3	0.3	•	•
Operating Margin **21**	7.8	26.0	12.1	11.2	10.8	4.0	2.8	3.8	•	•	•	•	•
Operating Margin Before Officers' Comp. **22**	17.5	44.0	25.0	23.5	19.2	5.6	4.4	5.6	•	•	•	•	•

Selected Average Balance Sheet ($ in Thousands)

Net Receivables 23	23	0	3	33	249	2913	1773	15712	12120	27809	132617
Inventories 24	4	0	2	17	33	42	528	755	510	157	10339
Net Property, Plant and Equipment 25	34	0	22	131	394	2014	2723	4835	13522	7431	48337
Total Assets 26	174	0	73	657	1367	7863	15277	32082	72079	156083	648071
Notes and Loans Payable 27	64	0	32	315	492	6322	3845	6623	24056	10542	219170
All Other Liabilities 28	41	0	12	59	228	2050	4674	10994	20455	62389	220410
Net Worth 29	68	0	29	283	647	-510	6758	14465	27568	83153	208492

Selected Financial Ratios (Times to 1)

Current Ratio 30	1.7	•	2.1	4.2	1.9	1.3	1.0	1.7	1.4	1.0	1.5
Quick Ratio 31	1.4	•	1.8	3.9	1.4	1.2	0.8	1.5	0.7	0.9	1.2
Net Sales to Working Capital 32	19.2	•	24.7	7.4	11.7	26.8	173.7	8.5	8.7	•	15.1
Coverage Ratio 33	15.6	116.5	26.7	10.1	16.3	9.0	12.0	16.0	2.9	4.8	4.0
Total Asset Turnover 34	3.6	•	6.1	2.5	2.6	4.5	2.5	2.6	1.0	2.1	1.8
Inventory Turnover 35	23.6	•	21.7	13.8	15.9	46.6	36.0	49.0	5.5	1344.7	8.1
Receivables Turnover 36	28.1	•	105.6	35.8	14.9	11.2	24.3	•	4.6	•	•
Total Liabilities to Net Worth 37	1.5	•	1.5	1.3	1.1	1.3	1.2	1.6	0.9	•	2.1
Current Assets to Working Capital 38	2.4	•	1.9	2.1	1.3	4.1	24.9	2.4	3.8	•	3.1
Current Liabilities to Working Capital 39	1.4	•	0.9	0.3	0.3	3.1	23.9	1.4	2.8	•	2.1
Working Capital to Net Sales 40	0.1	•	0.0	0.1	0.1	0.0	0.0	0.1	0.1	•	0.1
Inventory to Working Capital 41	0.1	•	0.1	0.1	0.1	0.0	2.5	0.1	0.0	•	0.1
Total Receipts to Cash Flow 42	2.3	1.9	2.4	3.6	3.0	3.2	6.7	5.7	0.8	5.1	1.3
Cost of Goods to Cash Flow 43	0.3	0.1	0.3	0.5	0.5	0.2	3.3	2.5	0.0	3.3	0.1
Cash Flow to Total Debt 44	2.6	•	4.3	1.2	1.6	1.3	0.7	0.8	2.2	0.9	2.0

Selected Financial Factors (in Percentages)

Debt Ratio 45	60.7	•	60.3	57.0	52.7	106.5	55.8	54.9	61.8	46.7	67.8
Return on Total Assets 46	41.7	•	79.3	30.9	31.2	32.3	19.5	15.1	5.8	4.9	12.7
Return on Equity Before Income Taxes 47	99.2	•	192.3	64.8	61.9	•	40.4	31.5	10.0	7.3	29.5
Return on Equity After Income Taxes 48	95.8	•	191.7	63.1	59.9	•	35.7	26.1	9.0	5.3	20.1
Profit Margin (Before Income Tax) 49	10.9	27.0	12.6	11.3	11.3	6.4	7.1	5.5	3.8	1.9	5.3
Profit Margin (After Income Tax) 50	10.5	26.9	12.6	11.0	11.0	6.2	6.2	4.5	3.4	1.3	3.6

Table I

Corporations with and without Net Income

OUTPATIENT CARE CENTERS

MONEY AMOUNTS AND SIZE OF ASSETS IN THOUSANDS OF DOLLARS

Item Description for Accounting Period 7/10 Through 6/11	Total	Zero Assets	Under 500	500 to 1,000	1,000 to 5,000	5,000 to 10,000	10,000 to 25,000	25,000 to 50,000	50,000 to 100,000	100,000 to 250,000	250,000 to 500,000	500,000 to 2,500,000	2,500,000 and over
Number of Enterprises 1	8240	1326	5723	176	852	70	41	13	10	11	6	9	3
Revenues ($ in Thousands)													
Net Sales 2	34504869	672230	1963316	499063	6387336	1022349	1730544	1352118	2167021	1692552	1776057	1906830	13335453
Interest 3	90099	326	0	368	4459	9181	595	3407	1248	2792	11742	43617	12365
Rents 4	17753	321	0	0	310	216	669	0	122	1153	4335	6124	4504
Royalties 5	0	0	0	0	0	0	0	0	0	0	0	0	0
Other Portfolio Income 6	56296	23	292	0	246	0	1978	171	1062	552	4189	23502	24280
Other Receipts 7	2700955	21103	282	971	8029	-679	5634	40466	36655	212943	83039	161592	680919
Total Receipts 8	37369972	694003	1963890	500402	6400380	1031067	1739420	1396162	2206108	1909992	1879362	3591665	14057521
Average Total Receipts 9	4535	523	343	2843	7512	14730	42425	107397	220611	173636	313227	399074	4685840
Operating Costs/Operating Income (%)													
Cost of Operations 10	27.4	8.0	6.0	8.6	10.5	2.4	32.5	66.1	27.5	18.8	65.4	6.4	36.7
Salaries and Wages 11	21.3	25.2	23.5	30.2	29.2	7.8	19.7	13.7	4.3	26.4	12.9	48.4	18.1
Taxes Paid 12	2.9	2.9	3.5	3.9	2.7	1.4	1.5	1.8	0.6	2.5	2.7	4.5	3.4
Interest Paid 13	3.4	4.8	0.4	0.2	0.4	1.2	0.8	0.9	0.7	3.9	2.2	16.6	4.9
Depreciation 14	2.6	3.0	1.8	3.0	1.0	0.6	2.0	0.9	0.6	3.1	1.2	6.0	3.8
Amortization and Depletion 15	1.6	4.4	•	•	0.1	0.3	0.4	0.1	0.4	1.8	0.9	6.9	2.4
Pensions and Other Deferred Comp. 16	0.7	0.2	0.6	0.2	2.2	0.1	0.5	0.3	0.0	0.7	0.3	0.3	0.3
Employee Benefits 17	3.6	3.0	1.1	2.4	2.9	1.1	1.7	1.5	0.4	2.3	0.9	4.8	5.9
Advertising 18	0.4	0.2	0.9	5.0	0.3	0.5	0.3	0.7	0.4	0.7	0.1	0.8	0.1
Other Expenses 19	37.0	53.2	45.3	30.1	42.9	83.6	38.3	12.9	64.4	48.5	18.3	93.9	19.6
Officers' Compensation 20	1.9	5.2	8.1	4.7	4.8	0.3	1.3	0.5	0.3	1.1	0.9	1.2	0.2
Operating Margin 21	•	•	8.8	11.8	3.0	0.8	1.1	0.5	0.5	•	•	•	4.7
Operating Margin Before Officers' Comp. 22	•	•	16.9	16.5	7.8	1.1	2.4	1.0	0.8	•	•	•	4.9

Selected Average Balance Sheet ($ in Thousands)

Net Receivables 23 595	0	6	2	476	1763	3559	11389	5104	25732	34310	71851	953485
Inventories 24 56	0	2	80	27	228	8	147	677	839	415	1252	122392
Net Property, Plant and Equipment 25 526	0	11	252	453	910	2878	2758	16292	25644	14518	49360	830679
Total Assets 26 6527	0	46	720	1758	7821	13782	35972	77392	162102	386211	1063047	11955956
Notes and Loans Payable 27 3656	0	73	190	832	1817	3774	10086	19375	61045	119847	502515	7480378
All Other Liabilities 28 1400	0	10	78	523	3206	6452	17852	34611	34715	61022	314614	2126148
Net Worth 29 1470	0	-37	452	403	2798	3555	8035	23406	66342	205342	245917	2349430

Selected Financial Ratios (Times to 1)

Current Ratio 30 1.2	•	0.4	5.5	1.2	1.4	1.1	1.6	1.0	1.3	2.3	0.7	1.2
Quick Ratio 31 0.8	•	0.3	1.7	0.8	1.0	1.4	0.6	•	1.2	1.2	0.6	0.9
Net Sales to Working Capital 32 21.2	•	•	7.4	46.8	9.1	45.3	10.1	1312.6	13.2	5.1	•	10.1
Coverage Ratio 33 2.6	•	25.5	71.5	8.6	2.4	5.2	3.1	4.4	1.8	1.0	0.9	3.1
Total Asset Turnover 34 0.6	•	7.4	3.9	4.3	1.9	3.1	2.9	2.8	0.9	0.8	0.2	0.4
Inventory Turnover 35 20.4	•	9.9	3.0	29.1	1.5	1645.4	468.2	87.9	34.5	466.3	10.8	13.3
Receivables Turnover 36 7.7	•	68.8	8.4	15.4	8.5	15.7	14.6	34.2	9.1	7.1	3.0	5.3
Total Liabilities to Net Worth 37 3.4	•	•	0.6	3.4	1.8	2.9	3.5	2.3	1.4	0.9	3.3	4.1
Current Assets to Working Capital 38 7.0	•	•	1.2	6.8	3.5	8.4	2.7	208.1	4.1	1.7	•	5.1
Current Liabilities to Working Capital 39 6.0	•	•	0.2	5.8	2.5	7.4	1.7	207.1	3.1	0.7	•	4.1
Working Capital to Net Sales 40 0.0	•	•	0.0	0.0	0.1	0.0	0.1	0.0	0.1	0.2	•	0.1
Inventory to Working Capital 41 0.3	•	•	0.0	0.0	0.3	0.0	0.0	3.8	0.1	0.0	•	0.3
Total Receipts to Cash Flow 42 2.7	2.6	2.5	2.8	2.3	1.2	2.7	6.9	1.5	2.0	6.2	1.2	4.3
Cost of Goods to Cash Flow 43 0.7	0.2	0.1	0.2	0.2	0.0	0.9	4.5	0.4	0.4	4.0	0.1	1.6
Cash Flow to Total Debt 44 0.3	•	1.7	3.8	2.4	1.5	1.5	0.5	2.7	0.8	0.3	0.2	0.1

Selected Financial Factors (in Percentages)

Debt Ratio 45 77.5	•	180.1	37.2	77.1	64.2	74.2	77.7	69.8	59.1	46.8	76.9	80.3
Return on Total Assets 46 5.7	•	68.4	48.2	15.5	5.3	7.2	13.4	8.1	6.6	1.7	2.9	5.6
Return on Equity Before Income Taxes 47 15.7	•	•	75.7	59.6	8.6	18.9	48.6	20.7	7.2	0.1	•	19.1
Return on Equity After Income Taxes 48 11.3	•	•	75.5	56.9	0.9	18.2	33.5	13.0	5.8	•	•	13.4
Profit Margin (Before Income Tax) 49 5.5	•	8.9	12.1	3.2	1.7	1.6	3.8	2.2	3.1	0.1	•	10.1
Profit Margin (After Income Tax) 50 4.0	•	8.8	12.0	3.1	0.2	1.5	2.6	1.4	2.5	•	•	7.1

Table II
Corporations with Net Income

OUTPATIENT CARE CENTERS

MONEY AMOUNTS AND SIZE OF ASSETS IN THOUSANDS OF DOLLARS

Item Description for Accounting Period 7/10 Through 6/11	Total	Zero Assets	Under 500	500 to 1,000	1,000 to 5,000	5,000 to 10,000	10,000 to 25,000	25,000 to 50,000	50,000 to 100,000	100,000 to 250,000	250,000 to 500,000	500,000 to 2,500,000	2,500,000 and over
Number of Enterprises 1	4329	639	2638	121	803	61	•	10	6	•	0	4	3
Revenues ($ in Thousands)													
Net Sales 2	29845687	99419	1401162	399696	5351336	986177	•	1277214	1868089	•	0	1202196	13335453
Interest 3	42368	0	0	199	3714	9033	•	2562	637	•	0	5235	12365
Rents 4	8348	320	0	0	310	182	•	0	122	•	0	1757	4504
Royalties 5	0	0	0	0	0	0	•	0	0	•	0	0	0
Other Portfolio Income 6	41318	0	292	0	0	0	•	171	1062	•	0	12687	24280
Other Receipts 7	1257455	12534	0	909	8014	3033	•	9449	22008	•	0	288431	680919
Total Receipts 8	31195176	112273	1401454	400804	5363374	998425	•	1289396	1891918	•	0	1510306	14057521
Average Total Receipts 9	7206	176	531	3312	6679	16368	•	128940	315320	•	•	377576	4685840
Operating Costs/Operating Income (%)													
Cost of Operations 10	30.4	•	7.3	10.7	12.5	2.3	•	69.5	27.5	•	•	2.0	36.7
Salaries and Wages 11	18.4	10.5	21.0	23.0	24.5	6.9	•	11.7	3.7	•	•	37.7	18.1
Taxes Paid 12	2.8	2.5	3.1	2.6	2.7	1.4	•	1.6	0.5	•	•	4.3	3.4
Interest Paid 13	3.0	0.6	0.4	0.1	0.5	1.2	•	0.3	0.2	•	•	11.0	4.9
Depreciation 14	2.4	0.1	0.6	3.3	0.8	0.6	•	0.7	0.3	•	•	4.4	3.8
Amortization and Depletion 15	1.5	•	•	•	0.1	0.3	•	0.0	0.1	•	•	7.3	2.4
Pensions and Other Deferred Comp. 16	0.6	0.1	0.9	0.2	1.8	0.1	•	0.4	0.0	•	•	0.3	0.3
Employee Benefits 17	3.7	•	1.5	1.1	2.9	0.7	•	1.4	0.3	•	•	3.5	5.9
Advertising 18	0.4	0.8	0.6	6.2	0.3	0.5	•	0.4	0.2	•	•	1.2	0.1
Other Expenses 19	31.1	77.3	29.2	32.2	43.6	81.6	•	9.0	65.2	•	•	43.0	19.6
Officers' Compensation 20	1.9	8.1	10.4	4.7	5.5	0.3	•	0.4	0.2	•	•	1.5	0.2
Operating Margin 21	3.9	0.0	25.1	15.9	4.7	4.3	•	4.6	1.9	•	•	•	4.7
Operating Margin Before Officers' Comp. 22	5.7	8.1	35.5	20.6	10.2	4.7	•	5.0	2.1	•	•	•	4.9

Selected Average Balance Sheet ($ in Thousands)

Net Receivables 23	950	0	12	2	501	1906	14070	5358	28427	953485
Inventories 24	95	0	5	2	26	19	122	141	3	122392
Net Property, Plant and Equipment 25	899	0	13	261	460	975	2125	18301	67783	880679
Total Assets 26	10718	0	62	794	1762	7763	36333	74184	1298742	11955956
Notes and Loans Payable 27	6045	0	28	130	715	1816	4552	12130	503173	7480378
All Other Liabilities 28	2284	0	1	68	537	2965	19823	33985	471167	2126148
Net Worth 29	2389	0	33	596	510	2981	11958	28069	324402	2349430

Selected Financial Ratios (Times to 1)

Current Ratio 30	1.3	•	1.4	7.4	1.3	1.5	1.8	1.3	0.8	1.2
Quick Ratio 31	0.9	•	1.2	0.8	0.9	1.1	1.7	0.6	0.5	0.9
Net Sales to Working Capital 32	14.4	•	50.6	7.2	23.8	8.6	8.6	31.8	•	10.1
Coverage Ratio 33	3.8	21.0	70.8	139.8	11.6	5.7	23.0	21.7	1.9	3.1
Total Asset Turnover 34	0.6	•	8.6	4.2	3.8	2.1	3.5	4.2	0.2	0.4
Inventory Turnover 35	22.1	•	8.5	180.1	32.4	19.3	724.9	607.9	2175.2	13.3
Receivables Turnover 36	8.3	•	91.5	299.2	20.2	•	•	•	5.4	5.3
Total Liabilities to Net Worth 37	3.5	•	0.9	0.3	2.5	1.6	2.0	1.6	3.0	4.1
Current Assets to Working Capital 38	4.7	•	3.7	1.2	4.0	3.1	2.2	4.6	•	5.1
Current Liabilities to Working Capital 39	3.7	•	2.7	0.2	3.0	2.1	1.2	3.6	•	4.1
Working Capital to Net Sales 40	0.1	•	0.0	0.1	0.0	0.1	0.1	0.0	•	0.1
Inventory to Working Capital 41	0.2	•	0.4	0.0	0.1	0.0	0.0	0.0	•	0.3
Total Receipts to Cash Flow 42	2.9	1.4	2.2	2.4	2.2	1.2	7.6	1.5	2.2	4.3
Cost of Goods to Cash Flow 43	0.9	•	0.2	0.3	0.3	0.0	5.3	0.4	0.0	1.6
Cash Flow to Total Debt 44	0.3	•	8.3	6.8	2.4	2.9	0.7	4.6	0.1	0.1

Selected Financial Factors (in Percentages)

Debt Ratio 45	77.7	•	46.4	25.0	71.1	61.6	67.1	62.2	75.0	80.3
Return on Total Assets 46	7.3	•	219.0	67.6	20.4	14.1	20.2	13.8	4.7	5.6
Return on Equity Before Income Taxes 47	24.2	•	402.7	89.5	64.5	30.3	58.8	34.9	8.8	19.1
Return on Equity After Income Taxes 48	19.1	•	402.2	89.3	62.2	22.0	45.6	24.1	6.0	13.4
Profit Margin (Before Income Tax) 49	8.4	13.0	25.1	16.1	4.9	5.6	5.5	3.1	9.5	10.1
Profit Margin (After Income Tax) 50	6.6	13.0	25.1	16.1	4.8	4.1	4.3	2.2	6.5	7.1

Table I
Corporations with and without Net Income

MISC. HEALTH CARE AND SOCIAL ASSISTANCE

MONEY AMOUNTS AND SIZE OF ASSETS IN THOUSANDS OF DOLLARS

Item Description for Accounting Period 7/10 Through 6/11	Total	Zero Assets	Under 500	500 to 1,000	1,000 to 5,000	5,000 to 10,000	10,000 to 25,000	25,000 to 50,000	50,000 to 100,000	100,000 to 250,000	250,000 to 500,000	500,000 to 2,500,000	2,500,000 and over
Number of Enterprises 1	68453	13988	48826	3170	1864	260	141	74	49	40	20	19	0
Revenues ($ in Thousands)													
Net Sales 2	111929275	4229281	30050261	6685238	8560545	3860555	5421445	4309019	4858421	6405995	9006335	28542180	0
Interest 3	141823	280	1217	381	2016	1741	2730	7378	3494	11706	6768	104113	0
Rents 4	33016	0	2681	0	5042	1296	4439	257	1520	10273	7143	364	0
Royalties 5	84859	0	0	0	0	0	581	0	26950	30994	3060	23275	0
Other Portfolio Income 6	234840	34828	22503	7358	7280	30569	2871	14980	6190	19354	13248	75662	0
Other Receipts 7	2528174	-4881	1213524	21903	304998	109588	24100	48985	45408	39279	182570	542696	0
Total Receipts 8	114951987	4259508	31290186	6714880	8879881	4003749	5456166	4380619	4941983	6517601	9219124	29288290	0
Average Total Receipts 9	1679	305	641	2118	4764	15399	38696	59198	100857	162940	460956	1541489	•
Operating Costs/Operating Income (%)													
Cost of Operations 10	14.5	1.4	7.2	12.9	13.6	15.0	29.2	25.0	26.5	24.1	7.3	18.6	•
Salaries and Wages 11	34.5	47.3	39.5	36.2	39.9	42.1	17.6	31.8	27.2	27.8	38.2	29.7	•
Taxes Paid 12	4.1	2.0	4.8	4.3	4.9	3.7	2.6	4.2	3.2	4.3	4.0	3.8	•
Interest Paid 13	1.8	0.6	0.4	0.7	0.8	0.6	1.4	1.2	1.7	2.7	4.0	3.6	•
Depreciation 14	2.2	1.4	0.9	1.7	1.5	1.4	1.4	3.4	1.8	3.2	3.8	3.5	•
Amortization and Depletion 15	0.8	0.7	0.1	0.5	0.1	0.5	0.5	0.6	1.4	1.7	1.2	1.6	•
Pensions and Other Deferred Comp. 16	0.4	0.1	0.4	0.2	0.6	0.6	0.2	0.5	0.2	0.3	0.2	0.4	•
Employee Benefits 17	3.0	0.6	1.6	1.4	1.7	4.0	13.2	3.1	2.4	2.5	2.2	4.1	•
Advertising 18	0.5	0.2	0.6	0.4	0.4	0.6	0.5	0.4	0.4	0.8	0.4	0.5	•
Other Expenses 19	31.1	44.2	31.7	30.9	30.4	25.1	27.9	28.2	34.1	30.8	39.4	27.6	•
Officers' Compensation 20	4.6	3.0	11.2	4.7	5.4	5.6	1.7	1.6	2.5	1.2	0.8	0.7	•
Operating Margin 21	2.4	•	1.5	6.1	0.7	0.8	3.8	•	•	0.6	•	6.1	•
Operating Margin Before Officers' Comp. 22	6.9	1.5	12.7	10.8	6.1	6.5	5.6	1.6	1.2	1.8	•	6.8	•

Selected Average Balance Sheet ($ in Thousands)

	•	•	•	•	•	•	•	•	•	•	•	•
Net Receivables 23	149	0	8	112	316	1610	3703	9303	16227	27218	73423	205448
Inventories 24	10	0	0	4	9	355	376	430	974	2013	6022	11245
Net Property, Plant and Equipment 25	174	0	29	212	888	1321	2394	8036	6178	21886	63606	234605
Total Assets 26	1056	0	84	727	2236	7116	15955	36491	70895	155464	377888	1984953
Notes and Loans Payable 27	459	0	48	342	1029	1698	7141	11568	29494	58554	200068	840407
All Other Liabilities 28	258	0	21	264	310	1941	5082	12203	21453	39792	97946	447976
Net Worth 29	339	0	14	121	897	3477	3732	12719	19948	57118	79874	696570

Selected Financial Ratios (Times to 1)

	•	•	•	•	•	•	•	•	•	•	•	•
Current Ratio 30	1.6	•	1.8	1.2	2.5	2.0	1.5	1.3	1.4	1.3	2.2	1.5
Quick Ratio 31	1.2	•	1.5	1.0	2.1	1.6	1.1	1.1	1.1	1.1	1.6	1.1
Net Sales to Working Capital 32	13.7	•	36.4	34.8	7.8	7.7	14.7	14.0	12.6	11.8	6.0	11.6
Coverage Ratio 33	3.8	•	16.9	9.8	6.4	9.1	4.3	2.4	1.2	1.8	1.2	3.4
Total Asset Turnover 34	1.5	•	7.4	2.9	2.1	2.1	2.4	1.6	1.4	1.0	1.2	0.8
Inventory Turnover 35	23.6	•	117.6	62.0	69.9	6.3	29.8	33.9	26.9	19.2	5.4	24.8
Receivables Turnover 36	11.7	•	88.5	18.3	16.2	8.6	12.5	6.6	5.9	5.9	6.6	8.2
Total Liabilities to Net Worth 37	2.1	•	4.9	5.0	1.5	1.0	3.3	1.9	2.6	1.7	3.7	1.8
Current Assets to Working Capital 38	2.7	•	2.3	5.7	1.6	2.0	3.2	4.2	3.8	4.0	1.8	3.2
Current Liabilities to Working Capital 39	1.7	•	1.3	4.7	0.6	1.0	2.2	3.2	2.8	3.0	0.8	2.2
Working Capital to Net Sales 40	0.1	•	0.0	0.0	0.1	0.1	0.1	0.1	0.1	0.1	0.2	0.1
Inventory to Working Capital 41	0.1	•	0.0	0.1	0.0	0.2	0.1	0.1	0.1	0.1	0.1	0.1
Total Receipts to Cash Flow 42	3.2	2.7	3.3	3.2	3.4	3.9	3.4	4.1	3.1	3.4	2.8	3.2
Cost of Goods to Cash Flow 43	0.5	0.0	0.2	0.4	0.5	0.6	1.0	1.0	0.8	0.8	0.2	0.6
Cash Flow to Total Debt 44	0.7	•	2.7	1.1	1.0	0.9	0.6	0.6	0.6	0.5	0.5	0.4

Selected Financial Factors (in Percentages)

	•	•	•	•	•	•	•	•	•	•	•	•
Debt Ratio 45	67.9	•	83.0	83.3	59.9	51.1	76.6	65.1	71.9	63.3	78.9	64.9
Return on Total Assets 46	10.6	•	43.9	21.1	10.7	10.6	14.0	4.4	3.0	5.2	5.7	9.3
Return on Equity Before Income Taxes 47	24.4	•	243.8	113.4	22.5	19.4	46.0	7.3	1.9	6.4	4.2	18.7
Return on Equity After Income Taxes 48	19.2	•	238.8	111.9	21.3	17.5	42.0	5.6	•	2.1	•	12.1
Profit Margin (Before Income Tax) 49	5.1	•	5.6	6.5	4.4	4.5	4.5	1.6	0.4	2.3	0.8	8.7
Profit Margin (After Income Tax) 50	4.0	•	5.5	6.4	4.2	4.1	4.1	1.2	0.7	•	0.5	5.6

Table II
Corporations with Net Income

MISC. HEALTH CARE AND SOCIAL ASSISTANCE

MONEY AMOUNTS AND SIZE OF ASSETS IN THOUSANDS OF DOLLARS

Item Description for Accounting Period 7/10 Through 6/11		Total	Zero Assets	Under 500	500 to 1,000	1,000 to 5,000	5,000 to 10,000	10,000 to 25,000	25,000 to 50,000	50,000 to 100,000	100,000 to 250,000	250,000 to 500,000	500,000 to 2,500,000	2,500,000 and over
Number of Enterprises	1	42822	5757	32808	2488	1372	188	92	41	27	27	9	12	0
Revenues ($ in Thousands)														
Net Sales	2	87265443	1938722	23804979	6144210	7142367	3100311	3828768	2736020	2867466	5111443	6070079	24521079	0
Interest	3	116748	0	1213	357	1170	1671	2355	3371	907	7352	1924	96428	0
Rents	4	19789	0	2681	0	4974	1296	2442	0	716	708	6630	341	0
Royalties	5	48035	0	0	0	0	0	45	0	26190	21796	0	3	0
Other Portfolio Income	6	117279	10151	549	7358	2220	187	697	13068	5432	2898	4914	69806	0
Other Receipts	7	2018776	4478	1142347	21471	210142	95219	13231	23376	3836	19954	116840	367881	0
Total Receipts	8	89586070	1953351	24951769	6173396	7360873	3198684	3847538	2775835	2904547	5164151	6200387	25055538	0
Average Total Receipts	9	2092	339	761	2481	5365	17014	41821	67703	107576	191265	688932	2087962	•
Operating Costs/Operating Income (%)														
Cost of Operations	10	14.7	0.7	6.7	13.1	15.1	13.1	38.0	23.6	24.9	24.3	3.3	19.0	•
Salaries and Wages	11	33.8	39.1	38.7	34.3	36.8	39.6	20.3	32.3	33.0	27.0	39.9	29.1	•
Taxes Paid	12	4.0	1.0	4.6	4.3	4.7	3.4	3.0	4.1	4.1	4.5	3.9	3.7	•
Interest Paid	13	1.4	0.2	0.3	0.6	0.8	0.4	1.1	0.9	1.6	1.5	1.3	3.0	•
Depreciation	14	1.8	0.4	0.9	1.3	1.2	1.4	1.3	3.4	1.6	2.1	1.7	3.2	•
Amortization and Depletion	15	0.6	•	0.1	0.3	0.1	0.2	0.5	0.5	1.2	1.5	0.7	1.3	•
Pensions and Other Deferred Comp.	16	0.4	0.1	0.4	0.2	0.6	0.5	0.2	0.7	0.3	0.3	0.2	0.4	•
Employee Benefits	17	2.4	0.2	1.5	1.5	1.2	3.8	1.2	2.7	2.9	2.0	1.8	4.2	•
Advertising	18	0.5	0.2	0.7	0.5	0.3	0.5	0.4	0.4	0.4	0.5	0.1	0.5	•
Other Expenses	19	29.4	49.7	30.0	30.0	28.9	25.8	22.5	24.4	24.2	29.5	43.2	26.6	•
Officers' Compensation	20	4.6	2.1	11.6	5.1	4.9	3.6	2.0	1.7	1.1	1.1	0.4	0.7	•
Operating Margin	21	6.4	6.4	4.5	8.9	5.4	7.7	9.5	5.5	4.6	5.8	3.4	8.4	•
Operating Margin Before Officers' Comp.	22	11.0	8.5	16.2	14.0	10.3	11.3	11.5	7.2	5.8	6.9	3.8	9.1	•

Selected Average Balance Sheet ($ in Thousands)

Net Receivables 23	177	10	0	132	307	1673	2943	10148	16120	30862	109659	271855
Inventories 24	10	0	0	5	6	254	535	399	1004	1988	6203	10599
Net Property, Plant and Equipment 25	177	0	29	230	832	1136	1858	8052	5830	12491	40390	281036
Total Assets 26	1216	0	85	728	2279	7130	16485	36250	69364	159723	389153	2525381
Notes and Loans Payable 27	459	0	28	298	890	1858	6879	11763	26896	38347	129898	1032613
All Other Liabilities 28	304	0	19	276	294	1645	4374	10554	18880	43645	130710	607141
Net Worth 29	453	0	38	154	1096	3626	5232	13932	23588	77731	128544	885627

Selected Financial Ratios (Times to 1)

Current Ratio 30	1.6	•	2.0	1.4	3.2	2.0	1.6	1.5	1.3	1.6	1.8	1.3
Quick Ratio 31	1.3	•	1.7	1.2	2.7	1.6	1.1	1.2	1.0	1.3	1.6	1.0
Net Sales to Working Capital 32	14.9	•	33.6	25.6	7.1	8.6	13.7	10.6	14.8	8.7	9.0	15.8
Coverage Ratio 33	7.7	42.1	36.2	17.1	12.1	27.0	9.7	8.7	4.6	5.6	5.3	4.5
Total Asset Turnover 34	1.7	•	8.5	3.4	2.3	2.3	2.5	1.8	1.5	1.2	1.7	0.8
Inventory Turnover 35	30.7	•	87.4	59.1	129.8	8.5	29.6	39.4	26.3	23.1	3.6	36.6
Receivables Turnover 36	12.0	•	92.4	23.1	18.8	8.6	14.6	6.0	5.7	6.2	6.3	8.2
Total Liabilities to Net Worth 37	1.7	•	1.2	3.7	1.1	1.0	2.2	1.6	1.9	1.1	2.0	1.9
Current Assets to Working Capital 38	2.7	•	2.0	3.4	1.5	2.0	2.7	3.1	4.0	2.7	2.2	4.0
Current Liabilities to Working Capital 39	1.7	•	1.0	2.4	0.5	1.0	1.7	2.1	3.0	1.7	1.2	3.0
Working Capital to Net Sales 40	0.1	•	0.0	0.0	0.1	0.1	0.1	0.1	0.1	0.1	0.1	0.1
Inventory to Working Capital 41	0.1	•	0.0	0.0	0.0	0.1	0.2	0.1	0.1	0.1	0.1	0.1
Total Receipts to Cash Flow 42	3.0	1.8	3.1	3.0	3.1	3.1	3.4	3.7	3.7	3.0	2.2	3.1
Cost of Goods to Cash Flow 43	0.4	0.0	0.2	0.4	0.5	0.4	1.3	0.9	0.9	0.7	0.1	0.6
Cash Flow to Total Debt 44	0.9	•	5.0	1.4	1.4	1.5	1.1	0.8	0.6	0.8	1.2	0.4

Selected Financial Factors (in Percentages)

Debt Ratio 45	62.8	•	55.4	78.9	51.9	49.1	68.3	61.6	66.0	51.3	67.0	64.9
Return on Total Assets 46	17.5	•	81.9	33.9	21.0	26.2	28.1	14.5	11.6	9.8	11.8	11.0
Return on Equity Before Income Taxes 47	40.8	•	178.4	150.9	40.0	49.5	79.4	33.4	26.7	16.5	29.0	24.5
Return on Equity After Income Taxes 48	34.6	•	175.7	149.5	38.6	47.0	75.1	30.6	21.9	11.7	22.1	16.2
Profit Margin (Before Income Tax) 49	9.1	7.1	9.4	9.4	8.4	10.9	10.0	7.0	5.9	6.8	5.5	10.6
Profit Margin (After Income Tax) 50	7.7	6.9	9.2	9.3	8.1	10.3	9.4	6.4	4.9	4.8	4.2	7.0

Table I

Corporations with and without Net Income

HOSPITALS, NURSING, AND RESIDENTIAL CARE FACILITIES

MONEY AMOUNTS AND SIZE OF ASSETS IN THOUSANDS OF DOLLARS

Item Description for Accounting Period 7/10 Through 6/11	Total	Zero Assets	Under 500	500 to 1,000	1,000 to 5,000	5,000 to 10,000	10,000 to 25,000	25,000 to 50,000	50,000 to 100,000	100,000 to 250,000	250,000 to 500,000	500,000 to 2,500,000	2,500,000 and over
Number of Enterprises 1	20255	1813	13293	2016	2471	247	213	97	30	32	11	18	13
Revenues ($ in Thousands)													
Net Sales 2	137560262	2649867	11900623	5041538	13811475	3583270	5631090	5069935	3729704	7989871	4199919	14810181	59142789
Interest 3	1307679	3397	303	1280	2841	989	1879	6596	822	11767	5921	51863	1220023
Rents 4	531112	4543	0	1118	190	727	9165	11159	100	29660	6976	107546	359928
Royalties 5	0	0	0	0	0	0	0	0	0	0	0	0	0
Other Portfolio Income 6	1360471	1061590	10	101	46598	7123	4862	2134	1233	17573	1377	156820	61051
Other Receipts 7	9858369	51112	43973	2897	556638	24706	97327	83117	46158	701725	72115	303741	7874857
Total Receipts 8	150617893	3770509	11944909	5046934	14417742	3616815	5744323	5172941	3778017	8750596	4286308	15430151	68658648
Average Total Receipts 9	7436	2080	899	2503	5835	14643	26969	53329	125934	273456	389664	857231	5281434
Operating Costs/Operating Income (%)													
Cost of Operations 10	5.0	11.0	8.6	2.1	6.1	15.7	12.6	9.8	7.6	5.9	7.5	1.5	2.6
Salaries and Wages 11	42.6	46.0	38.4	32.5	43.3	32.5	33.6	38.2	42.0	43.7	40.8	45.5	45.0
Taxes Paid 12	5.5	7.5	4.8	3.8	6.7	6.2	5.6	6.2	5.9	7.4	5.5	5.9	4.8
Interest Paid 13	4.8	10.0	0.9	0.6	0.9	1.2	1.3	1.6	1.3	1.4	2.8	3.1	8.7
Depreciation 14	3.1	1.8	0.9	0.6	1.2	1.3	1.8	2.0	2.3	2.4	3.2	3.5	4.6
Amortization and Depletion 15	0.6	0.4	0.0	0.2	0.1	0.2	0.2	0.3	0.5	0.4	0.5	1.1	0.8
Pensions and Other Deferred Comp. 16	0.5	0.8	0.2	0.1	0.1	0.3	0.4	0.3	0.3	0.4	0.1	0.1	0.8
Employee Benefits 17	4.8	7.6	1.3	2.5	3.2	5.0	4.5	4.1	4.0	3.9	4.3	4.7	6.2
Advertising 18	0.4	0.3	0.9	0.1	0.2	0.3	0.7	0.4	0.3	0.3	0.1	0.4	0.4
Other Expenses 19	37.6	34.0	34.2	48.3	36.4	32.9	37.5	34.5	35.3	41.1	34.6	35.0	39.0
Officers' Compensation 20	1.5	4.4	7.3	3.0	1.9	1.2	1.4	0.9	0.9	0.6	0.5	0.2	0.6
Operating Margin 21	•	•	2.4	6.1	•	3.3	0.5	1.7	•	•	0.1	•	•
Operating Margin Before Officers' Comp. 22	•	•	9.6	9.1	1.9	4.5	1.9	2.7	0.6	0.7	0.7	•	•

Selected Average Balance Sheet ($ in Thousands)

Net Receivables 23	729	0	15	142	477	1822	3060	6543	16074	30115	58675	100166	573816
Inventories 24	10	0	0	1	2	12	78	213	567	1181	1950	2646	2608
Net Property, Plant and Equipment 25	2554	0	70	166	671	3393	4708	13612	25754	63276	181312	455814	2507369
Total Assets 26	6940	0	129	731	2060	7388	14350	34528	64658	161979	374574	1016698	7270589
Notes and Loans Payable 27	4378	0	153	291	1117	3673	8228	17980	33982	57576	186890	475356	5031937
All Other Liabilities 28	1706	0	87	155	610	3122	6272	9554	24737	50942	126397	201849	1627049
Net Worth 29	856	0	-112	286	333	593	-149	6994	5939	53461	61287	339493	611603

Selected Financial Ratios (Times to 1)

Current Ratio 30	1.3	•	0.5	2.2	1.7	0.9	1.2	1.5	1.2	1.4	1.4	1.3	1.2
Quick Ratio 31	1.0	•	0.4	1.7	1.4	0.7	0.9	1.3	1.0	1.2	1.2	1.1	0.9
Net Sales to Working Capital 32	23.5	•	•	10.8	12.5	•	31.1	12.3	26.3	14.7	14.5	17.1	22.1
Coverage Ratio 33	1.7	2.9	3.9	10.8	6.1	4.5	2.9	3.4	1.8	2.4	1.8	2.0	1.3
Total Asset Turnover 34	1.0	•	6.9	3.4	2.7	2.0	1.8	1.5	1.9	1.5	1.0	0.8	0.6
Inventory Turnover 35	33.2	•	1337.5	45.0	188.0	186.5	42.8	24.1	16.6	12.4	14.6	4.8	44.6
Receivables Turnover 36	9.7	•	63.9	17.7	11.7	10.6	8.9	9.0	6.9	8.3	7.9	6.8	8.7
Total Liabilities to Net Worth 37	7.1	•	•	1.6	5.2	11.5	•	3.9	9.9	2.0	5.1	2.0	10.9
Current Assets to Working Capital 38	5.0	•	•	1.8	2.4	•	7.6	3.0	6.0	3.2	3.7	4.3	5.3
Current Liabilities to Working Capital 39	4.0	•	•	0.8	1.4	•	6.6	2.0	5.0	2.2	2.7	3.3	4.3
Working Capital to Net Sales 40	0.0	•	•	0.1	0.1	•	0.0	0.1	0.0	0.1	0.1	0.1	0.0
Inventory to Working Capital 41	0.0	•	•	0.0	0.0	•	0.1	0.1	0.1	0.1	0.0	0.0	0.0
Total Receipts to Cash Flow 42	3.0	11.9	4.2	2.0	3.1	3.3	2.8	3.1	3.4	2.8	3.7	3.3	2.7
Cost of Goods to Cash Flow 43	0.1	1.3	0.4	0.0	0.2	0.5	0.4	0.3	0.3	0.2	0.3	0.1	0.1
Cash Flow to Total Debt 44	0.4	•	0.9	2.8	1.0	0.6	0.6	0.6	0.6	0.8	0.3	0.4	0.3

Selected Financial Factors (in Percentages)

Debt Ratio 45	87.7	•	186.3	61.0	83.8	92.0	101.0	79.7	90.8	67.0	83.6	66.6	91.6
Return on Total Assets 46	7.9	•	25.4	23.5	14.2	10.8	7.1	8.1	4.4	5.3	5.0	5.0	7.0
Return on Equity Before Income Taxes 47	25.7	•	•	54.6	73.2	104.8	•	28.1	21.3	9.5	13.7	7.4	18.8
Return on Equity After Income Taxes 48	20.4	•	•	52.9	72.4	97.4	•	25.2	17.2	7.1	7.9	5.1	13.3
Profit Margin (Before Income Tax) 49	3.2	18.5	2.7	6.2	4.4	4.3	2.5	3.8	1.0	2.0	2.2	3.0	2.5
Profit Margin (After Income Tax) 50	2.6	10.9	2.7	6.0	4.3	4.0	2.2	3.4	0.8	1.5	1.3	2.1	1.8

Table II
Corporations with Net Income

HOSPITALS, NURSING, AND RESIDENTIAL CARE FACILITIES

MONEY AMOUNTS AND SIZE OF ASSETS IN THOUSANDS OF DOLLARS

Item Description for Accounting Period 7/10 Through 6/11	Total	Zero Assets	Under 500	500 to 1,000	1,000 to 5,000	5,000 to 10,000	10,000 to 25,000	25,000 to 50,000	50,000 to 100,000	100,000 to 250,000	250,000 to 500,000	500,000 to 2,500,000	2,500,000 and over
Number of Enterprises **1**	12088	396	7758	1676	1771	180	155	79	17	25	6	•	•
Revenues ($ in Thousands)													
Net Sales **2**	121452212	1200667	9177319	4476410	10560209	2936644	4755728	4230744	2578970	6828545	3020734	•	•
Interest **3**	1275580	513	113	936	2380	937	1782	6506	314	6215	4629	•	•
Rents **4**	489669	3852	0	1118	1	5	7431	11139	0	7339	2018	•	•
Royalties **5**	0	0	0	0	0	0	0	0	0	0	0	•	•
Other Portfolio Income **6**	1337672	1052583	10	101	45065	6655	3639	2106	1157	7571	1367	•	•
Other Receipts **7**	9527232	39298	2724	2071	551426	24173	62473	81321	29261	580072	59365	•	•
Total Receipts **8**	134082365	2296913	9180166	4480636	11159081	2968414	4831053	4331816	2609702	7429742	3088113	•	•
Average Total Receipts **9**	11092	5800	1183	2673	6301	16491	31168	54833	153512	297190	514686	•	•
Operating Costs/Operating Income (%)													
Cost of Operations **10**	4.7	1.5	10.6	1.2	6.4	18.3	12.5	11.2	9.6	6.3	7.3	•	•
Salaries and Wages **11**	43.1	56.5	40.8	31.0	45.6	30.8	33.2	36.1	42.0	42.1	41.5	•	•
Taxes Paid **12**	5.4	7.5	4.3	3.3	7.1	6.4	5.8	6.3	5.7	7.7	6.2	•	•
Interest Paid **13**	5.0	18.8	0.8	0.5	0.7	0.5	1.0	1.5	0.9	1.2	2.0	•	•
Depreciation **14**	3.1	1.6	0.5	0.5	1.0	1.0	1.4	1.8	2.1	2.1	2.7	•	•
Amortization and Depletion **15**	0.6	0.2	0.0	0.2	0.1	0.1	0.2	0.3	0.3	0.3	0.2	•	•
Pensions and Other Deferred Comp. **16**	0.5	1.7	0.1	0.1	0.2	0.3	0.5	0.3	0.3	0.4	0.1	•	•
Employee Benefits **17**	4.9	12.0	1.1	2.6	3.6	5.0	4.2	3.7	3.7	3.8	4.1	•	•
Advertising **18**	0.4	0.3	0.9	0.1	0.2	0.3	0.7	0.4	0.2	0.3	0.1	•	•
Other Expenses **19**	36.9	33.3	29.3	49.8	31.4	30.5	35.8	34.6	32.2	39.9	33.1	•	•
Officers' Compensation **20**	1.2	8.4	5.4	2.9	1.7	1.4	1.2	1.0	0.8	0.7	0.6	•	•
Operating Margin **21**	•	•	6.1	7.8	1.9	5.3	3.5	2.8	2.1	•	2.1	•	•
Operating Margin Before Officers' Comp. **22**	•	•	11.5	10.7	3.6	6.7	4.7	3.8	2.9	•	2.6	•	•

Selected Average Balance Sheet ($ in Thousands)

Net Receivables 23	1096	0	14	143	491	1994	3451	6997	17829	32817	53663
Inventories 24	11	0	0	1	2	14	34	238	420	1316	1950
Net Property, Plant and Equipment 25	3466	0	66	124	677	2849	4661	13638	20569	61889	186365
Total Assets 26	10274	0	138	727	2241	7066	14656	34515	62303	158380	341680
Notes and Loans Payable 27	6472	0	207	206	972	2793	8206	17454	22253	56348	142967
All Other Liabilities 28	2500	0	82	152	538	3251	5633	9871	23480	49710	84996
Net Worth 29	1302	0	-151	369	731	1022	818	7190	16570	52322	113717

Selected Financial Ratios (Times to 1)

Current Ratio 30	1.3	•	2.4	1.9	0.9	1.2	1.5	1.3	1.5	1.2	
Quick Ratio 31	1.0	•	1.8	1.6	0.8	0.9	1.3	1.1	1.2	1.0	
Net Sales to Working Capital 32	22.1	•	10.6	11.4	•	26.9	11.1	20.8	13.4	40.9	
Coverage Ratio 33	1.9	3.7	16.7	11.8	13.6	6.2	4.4	4.7	4.3	3.1	
Total Asset Turnover 34	1.0	•	3.7	2.7	2.3	2.1	1.6	2.4	1.7	1.5	
Inventory Turnover 35	43.3	•	31.9	181.6	214.5	113.7	25.2	34.7	13.0	18.9	
Receivables Turnover 36	10.4	•	26.8	11.5	11.5	10.7	9.7	•	9.7	9.8	
Total Liabilities to Net Worth 37	6.9	•	1.0	2.1	5.9	16.9	3.8	2.8	2.0	2.0	
Current Assets to Working Capital 38	4.7	•	1.7	2.2	•	6.4	2.9	4.2	2.9	7.1	
Current Liabilities to Working Capital 39	3.7	•	0.7	1.2	•	5.4	1.9	3.2	1.9	6.1	
Working Capital to Net Sales 40	0.0	•	0.1	0.1	•	0.0	0.1	0.0	0.1	0.0	
Inventory to Working Capital 41	0.0	•	0.0	0.0	•	0.0	0.1	0.1	0.1	0.1	
Total Receipts to Cash Flow 42	2.9	4.1	1.9	3.1	3.4	2.8	2.9	3.5	2.8	3.6	
Cost of Goods to Cash Flow 43	0.1	0.4	0.0	0.2	0.6	0.3	0.3	0.3	0.2	0.3	
Cash Flow to Total Debt 44	0.4	1.0	3.9	1.3	0.8	0.8	0.7	0.9	0.9	0.6	

Selected Financial Factors (in Percentages)

Debt Ratio 45	87.3	•	210.0	49.2	67.4	85.5	94.4	79.2	73.4	67.0	66.7
Return on Total Assets 46	9.3	•	59.5	30.8	22.0	16.0	12.7	10.4	10.1	8.9	9.3
Return on Equity Before Income Taxes 47	34.9	•	•	57.0	61.8	102.5	191.1	38.6	29.8	20.7	19.0
Return on Equity After Income Taxes 48	29.1	•	•	55.5	61.3	96.6	179.6	35.1	27.2	17.6	13.3
Profit Margin (Before Income Tax) 49	4.5	49.7	6.1	7.9	7.6	6.4	5.1	5.2	3.3	4.0	4.3
Profit Margin (After Income Tax) 50	3.8	33.1	6.1	7.7	7.5	6.0	4.8	4.7	3.0	3.4	3.0

Table I

Corporations with and without Net Income

OTHER ARTS, ENTERTAINMENT, AND RECREATION

MONEY AMOUNTS AND SIZE OF ASSETS IN THOUSANDS OF DOLLARS

Item Description for Accounting Period 7/10 Through 6/11	Total	Zero Assets	Under 500	500 to 1,000	1,000 to 5,000	5,000 to 10,000	10,000 to 25,000	25,000 to 50,000	50,000 to 100,000	100,000 to 250,000	250,000 to 500,000	500,000 to 2,500,000	2,500,000 and over
Number of Enterprises 1	74236	16570	54189	1834	1190	253	84	38	25	26	17	11	0
Revenues ($ in Thousands)													
Net Sales 2	43104786	1770275	15500672	2367725	4642404	1788531	1349298	436077	1521705	2760208	3390867	7577024	0
Interest 3	158579	231	1094	497	4850	261	917	4624	3574	6626	15555	120350	0
Rents 4	80035	4716	1153	925	1771	211	0	90	5326	7935	16491	41416	0
Royalties 5	109736	204	164	0	0	0	0	2087	434	27901	10387	68558	0
Other Portfolio Income 6	206317	19671	27482	21955	22071	4907	3365	665	153	4604	80909	20537	0
Other Receipts 7	2216454	28795	246391	4203	144354	24041	16581	105920	251065	574611	605547	214948	0
Total Receipts 8	45875907	1823892	15776956	2395305	4815450	1817951	1370161	549463	1782257	3381885	4119756	8042833	0
Average Total Receipts 9	618	110	291	1306	4047	7186	16311	14460	71290	130072	242339	731167	•
Operating Costs/Operating Income (%)													
Cost of Operations 10	20.7	37.6	11.2	26.5	14.1	30.4	24.6	36.0	29.9	20.8	26.6	30.2	•
Salaries and Wages 11	17.1	7.0	11.9	11.0	19.1	11.8	21.4	28.1	32.4	41.0	31.8	12.3	•
Taxes Paid 12	4.1	2.0	2.1	2.9	3.5	2.6	2.7	3.7	4.0	3.1	7.9	8.6	•
Interest Paid 13	1.8	1.1	0.5	0.9	0.3	1.7	1.0	3.2	1.2	2.8	2.5	5.6	•
Depreciation 14	3.1	2.3	1.8	2.4	1.9	3.4	3.1	5.4	2.6	5.9	3.4	5.6	•
Amortization and Depletion 15	1.4	1.9	0.3	0.3	0.4	0.1	0.1	0.8	1.1	1.7	5.5	3.1	•
Pensions and Other Deferred Comp. 16	1.3	0.6	2.0	0.1	1.4	0.2	0.5	0.1	1.1	2.0	1.7	0.6	•
Employee Benefits 17	1.2	0.6	0.8	0.5	0.6	0.9	1.8	2.7	2.3	3.0	2.8	1.1	•
Advertising 18	2.4	2.8	0.8	8.6	1.9	2.0	1.0	2.7	2.5	5.4	0.8	3.6	•
Other Expenses 19	38.6	48.0	45.6	35.6	32.3	35.5	28.0	54.7	29.9	43.5	25.7	34.3	•
Officers' Compensation 20	9.9	9.5	18.9	5.2	12.1	6.3	4.6	2.3	3.5	1.8	2.6	1.7	•
Operating Margin 21	•	•	4.2	6.1	12.3	5.2	11.0	•	•	•	•	•	•
Operating Margin Before Officers' Comp. 22	8.3	•	23.1	11.3	24.5	11.4	15.7	•	•	•	•	•	•

Selected Average Balance Sheet ($ in Thousands)

	•	•	•	•	•	•	•	•	•	•	•	•
Net Receivables 23	35	0	2	24	97	526	1907	5248	7275	12729	26808	82806
Inventories 24	9	0	2	13	249	51	53	1158	1304	1378	2545	2661
Net Property, Plant and Equipment 25	138	0	11	261	364	959	4102	5604	11886	58209	83696	424799
Total Assets 26	534	0	54	659	2034	7184	16593	32904	71416	168786	371135	1468324
Notes and Loans Payable 27	237	0	56	365	689	3175	6761	14534	25637	58092	105426	651786
All Other Liabilities 28	175	0	11	144	521	2051	3047	21804	45967	63234	129986	440345
Net Worth 29	123	0	-14	150	824	1957	6785	-3434	-188	47460	135724	376193

Selected Financial Ratios (Times to 1)

	•	•	•	•	•	•	•	•	•	•	•	•
Current Ratio 30	1.3	•	2.3	1.7	1.9	1.5	2.2	1.3	1.0	1.3	1.2	1.0
Quick Ratio 31	0.8	•	1.8	1.4	0.9	1.4	1.5	0.7	0.7	0.7	0.8	0.4
Net Sales to Working Capital 32	13.6	•	14.0	12.0	6.5	6.4	3.9	3.3	•	9.7	10.4	•
Coverage Ratio 33	3.7	•	13.7	9.0	52.6	5.0	12.9	•	6.3	•	4.9	1.0
Total Asset Turnover 34	1.1	•	5.3	2.0	1.9	1.0	1.0	0.3	0.9	0.6	0.5	0.5
Inventory Turnover 35	14.1	•	15.8	26.9	2.2	42.4	74.8	3.6	13.9	16.0	20.8	78.2
Receivables Turnover 36	17.4	•	180.4	53.7	35.1	16.0	8.1	2.0	10.0	9.0	7.0	9.8
Total Liabilities to Net Worth 37	3.3	•	•	3.4	1.5	2.7	1.4	•	•	2.6	1.7	2.9
Current Assets to Working Capital 38	4.5	•	1.8	2.4	2.1	3.0	1.8	3.9	•	4.0	5.3	•
Current Liabilities to Working Capital 39	3.5	•	0.8	1.4	1.1	2.0	0.8	2.9	•	3.0	4.3	•
Working Capital to Net Sales 40	0.1	•	0.1	0.1	0.2	0.2	0.3	0.3	•	0.1	0.1	•
Inventory to Working Capital 41	0.2	•	0.1	0.0	0.4	0.1	0.0	0.6	•	0.1	0.2	•
Total Receipts to Cash Flow 42	2.7	3.8	2.2	2.8	2.4	2.7	2.7	2.9	3.3	3.4	3.2	3.4
Cost of Goods to Cash Flow 43	0.6	1.4	0.2	0.7	0.3	0.8	0.7	1.0	1.0	0.7	0.8	1.0
Cash Flow to Total Debt 44	0.5	•	1.9	0.9	1.4	0.5	0.6	0.1	0.3	0.3	0.3	0.2

Selected Financial Factors (in Percentages)

	•	•	•	•	•	•	•	•	•	•	•	•
Debt Ratio 45	77.0	•	125.8	77.3	59.5	72.8	59.1	110.4	100.3	71.9	63.4	74.4
Return on Total Assets 46	7.3	•	34.5	15.9	31.4	8.3	13.0	•	6.7	6.7	6.8	2.7
Return on Equity Before Income Taxes 47	23.1	•	•	62.3	76.0	24.5	29.3	45.8	•	•	14.7	0.3
Return on Equity After Income Taxes 48	21.4	•	•	60.8	74.0	24.4	28.9	46.3	•	•	12.2	•
Profit Margin (Before Income Tax) 49	4.9	•	6.0	7.2	16.1	6.8	12.4	•	6.6	6.6	10.0	0.1
Profit Margin (After Income Tax) 50	4.5	•	6.0	7.0	15.6	6.8	12.2	•	6.1	•	8.3	•

Table II

Corporations with Net Income

OTHER ARTS, ENTERTAINMENT, AND RECREATION

MONEY AMOUNTS AND SIZE OF ASSETS IN THOUSANDS OF DOLLARS

Item Description for Accounting Period 7/10 Through 6/11		Total	Zero Assets	Under 500	500 to 1,000	1,000 to 5,000	5,000 to 10,000	10,000 to 25,000	25,000 to 50,000	50,000 to 100,000	100,000 to 250,000	250,000 to 500,000	500,000 to 2,500,000	2,500,000 and over
Number of Enterprises	1	40057	7455	30717	1042	641	104	45	14	13	10	12	5	0
Revenues ($ in Thousands)														
Net Sales	2	25512339	477855	11154440	1669312	3340790	1191185	1102742	206407	820486	1186183	2481055	1881884	0
Interest	3	52867	11	756	489	4271	231	520	3763	3316	4010	12121	23381	0
Rents	4	52135	0	1150	925	1652	211	0	90	4771	209	16491	26636	0
Royalties	5	84318	0	0	0	0	0	0	2087	51	20568	249	61363	0
Other Portfolio Income	6	113749	9305	23	4783	14750	1254	3271	622	17	426	75235	4064	0
Other Receipts	7	1607481	17742	210393	9504	143393	56523	30010	35948	96544	277313	599854	130256	0
Total Receipts	8	27422889	504913	11366762	1685013	3504856	1249404	1136543	248917	925185	1488709	3185005	2127584	0
Average Total Receipts	9	685	68	370	1617	5468	12014	25257	17780	71168	148871	265417	425517	•
Operating Costs/Operating Income (%)														
Cost of Operations	10	16.4	7.8	13.8	15.7	13.2	36.7	23.8	15.7	34.2	8.5	24.0	10.2	•
Salaries and Wages	11	14.9	5.2	7.5	11.7	17.7	6.6	19.6	10.0	17.6	50.6	32.4	15.9	•
Taxes Paid	12	4.1	1.2	1.9	2.8	3.4	1.4	2.1	2.0	5.0	3.3	10.0	16.0	•
Interest Paid	13	1.2	2.2	0.3	0.6	0.2	0.0	0.6	2.7	1.0	2.9	1.8	7.7	•
Depreciation	14	2.2	1.8	0.8	0.8	1.2	0.6	2.9	1.0	3.0	3.5	2.1	13.0	•
Amortization and Depletion	15	1.1	0.5	0.2	0.3	0.3	0.0	0.1	1.0	0.4	2.9	4.5	4.9	•
Pensions and Other Deferred Comp.	16	1.6	0.0	2.1	0.1	2.0	0.2	0.6	0.1	0.5	3.2	2.0	0.7	•
Employee Benefits	17	1.1	0.2	0.7	0.7	0.5	0.4	1.6	0.8	0.7	3.1	3.4	0.8	•
Advertising	18	1.7	1.1	0.9	5.5	2.2	2.6	0.3	0.4	2.2	2.5	0.9	2.9	•
Other Expenses	19	35.3	56.0	43.1	42.4	23.2	18.1	23.3	68.1	25.1	31.7	27.7	29.6	•
Officers' Compensation	20	10.9	12.5	15.8	6.7	16.0	8.0	5.1	2.0	4.4	2.7	3.0	1.5	•
Operating Margin	21	9.4	11.6	12.8	12.7	20.2	25.2	19.9	•	6.0	•	•	•	•
Operating Margin Before Officers' Comp.	22	20.4	24.1	28.6	19.4	36.1	33.2	25.0	•	10.4	•	•	•	•

Selected Average Balance Sheet ($ in Thousands)

Net Receivables 23	26	0	2	43	97	210	1603	1555	5595	17886	30685	32786	•
Inventories 24	5	0	2	22	88	32	39	236	1431	991	2169	3707	•
Net Property, Plant and Equipment 25	135	0	9	171	252	346	4179	1178	15867	49557	57280	633270	•
Total Assets 26	468	0	59	685	2013	7639	16019	31760	67296	179994	387743	1126638	•
Notes and Loans Payable 27	123	0	27	180	250	1051	4751	5082	10406	64642	81735	315742	•
All Other Liabilities 28	146	0	12	163	581	279	2764	6418	47906	82246	127663	346855	•
Net Worth 29	199	0	20	341	1182	6309	8504	20259	8984	33105	178345	464041	•

Selected Financial Ratios (Times to 1)

Current Ratio 30	1.8	•	3.0	1.8	3.4	7.9	2.3	0.8	2.0	1.2	1.6	0.8	•
Quick Ratio 31	1.4	•	2.5	1.6	2.1	7.7	1.6	0.6	1.5	0.8	1.0	0.6	•
Net Sales to Working Capital 32	8.4	•	13.1	11.7	5.0	2.3	5.4	•	4.1	15.0	4.5	•	•
Coverage Ratio 33	15.2	9.0	23.4	49.8	159.5	728.0	37.6	7.1	19.3	4.7	10.5	2.3	•
Total Asset Turnover 34	1.4	•	6.2	2.3	2.6	1.5	1.5	0.5	0.9	0.7	0.5	0.3	•
Inventory Turnover 35	19.4	•	28.2	11.6	7.8	132.3	150.4	9.9	15.1	10.1	22.9	10.4	•
Receivables Turnover 36	21.0	•	290.5	38.4	34.3	68.1	12.9	10.5	14.6	6.3	7.4	5.7	•
Total Liabilities to Net Worth 37	1.4	•	1.9	1.0	0.7	0.2	0.9	0.6	6.5	4.4	1.2	1.4	•
Current Assets to Working Capital 38	2.2	•	1.5	2.3	1.4	1.1	1.8	•	2.0	7.1	2.7	•	•
Current Liabilities to Working Capital 39	1.2	•	0.5	1.3	0.4	0.1	0.8	•	1.0	6.1	1.7	•	•
Working Capital to Net Sales 40	0.1	•	0.1	0.1	0.2	0.4	0.2	•	0.2	0.1	0.2	•	•
Inventory to Working Capital 41	0.1	•	0.1	0.0	0.1	0.0	0.0	•	0.1	0.1	0.1	•	•
Total Receipts to Cash Flow 42	2.1	1.7	1.9	2.1	2.3	2.3	2.3	1.3	2.6	2.6	2.5	2.8	•
Cost of Goods to Cash Flow 43	0.3	0.1	0.3	0.3	0.3	0.8	0.5	0.2	0.9	0.2	0.6	0.3	•
Cash Flow to Total Debt 44	1.1	•	4.9	2.2	2.8	3.7	1.4	1.0	0.4	0.3	0.4	0.2	•

Selected Financial Factors (in Percentages)

Debt Ratio 45	57.5	•	65.9	50.1	41.3	17.4	46.9	36.2	86.7	81.6	54.0	58.8	•
Return on Total Assets 46	24.6	•	92.7	33.3	65.3	45.1	35.7	9.0	18.5	8.9	9.9	5.9	•
Return on Equity Before Income Taxes 47	54.2	•	266.3	63.9	110.4	54.5	65.4	12.1	131.7	38.0	19.4	7.9	•
Return on Equity After Income Taxes 48	52.2	•	265.8	62.7	107.8	54.5	64.8	11.9	124.6	34.2	16.7	5.9	•
Profit Margin (Before Income Tax) 49	16.9	17.3	14.8	13.6	25.0	30.0	22.7	16.7	18.7	10.6	16.7	9.8	•
Profit Margin (After Income Tax) 50	16.3	16.6	14.7	13.4	24.5	30.0	22.5	16.4	17.7	9.5	14.4	7.3	•

Table I

Corporations with and without Net Income

AMUSEMENT, GAMBLING, AND RECREATION INDUSTRIES

MONEY AMOUNTS AND SIZE OF ASSETS IN THOUSANDS OF DOLLARS

Item Description for Accounting Period 7/10 Through 6/11	Total	Zero Assets	Under 500	500 to 1,000	1,000 to 5,000	5,000 to 10,000	10,000 to 25,000	25,000 to 50,000	50,000 to 100,000	100,000 to 250,000	250,000 to 500,000	500,000 to 2,500,000	2,500,000 and over
Number of Enterprises **1**	47252	8433	30479	4020	3338	421	303	144	56	30	13	12	4
Revenues ($ in Thousands)													
Net Sales **2**	47526526	501341	10329021	2847829	7012123	2516598	2444112	2559046	2052534	3181834	3054163	6045159	4982766
Interest **3**	401119	165	2933	4903	4069	5020	3766	4946	19079	14397	8899	18719	314222
Rents **4**	159660	0	271	8164	3629	16564	3949	7823	14795	8174	18764	47665	29863
Royalties **5**	141394	0	0	55	0	1550	0	0	46	21170	54711	647	63214
Other Portfolio Income **6**	394442	17117	30525	16372	22596	25930	12953	41306	44483	31231	3862	96609	51457
Other Receipts **7**	3146907	40475	208637	463858	315937	184901	289546	117890	127427	113347	413236	806340	65315
Total Receipts **8**	51770048	559098	10571387	3341181	7358354	2750563	2754326	2731011	2258364	3370153	3553635	7015139	5506837
Average Total Receipts **9**	1096	66	347	831	2204	6533	9090	18965	40328	112338	273357	584595	1376709
Operating Costs/Operating Income (%)													
Cost of Operations **10**	21.5	11.1	31.7	17.5	23.8	28.7	22.0	19.0	11.6	33.6	15.6	5.6	17.2
Salaries and Wages **11**	21.8	9.5	12.9	24.2	20.8	27.0	30.3	29.2	27.3	19.2	25.3	29.2	19.4
Taxes Paid **12**	8.0	3.8	3.7	6.0	6.5	6.0	6.2	5.2	10.0	4.9	8.3	14.5	16.9
Interest Paid **13**	5.0	2.6	0.8	1.5	2.3	2.3	4.7	3.3	3.5	4.0	10.2	10.6	13.2
Depreciation **14**	8.4	7.9	3.1	7.6	6.4	7.8	10.4	8.5	8.5	7.5	9.7	11.1	18.5
Amortization and Depletion **15**	1.0	1.5	0.2	0.4	0.3	0.4	1.1	0.9	1.3	1.5	2.2	1.8	2.2
Pensions and Other Deferred Comp. **16**	0.2	0.3	0.0	0.3	0.4	0.4	0.1	0.5	0.6	0.2	0.4	0.1	0.1
Employee Benefits **17**	1.5	1.2	0.7	1.4	1.0	1.8	2.3	1.6	2.0	2.5	1.7	1.9	1.6
Advertising **18**	2.5	2.8	1.6	2.0	1.6	2.5	2.8	2.2	2.3	2.6	3.7	3.1	4.5
Other Expenses **19**	36.4	66.2	38.8	50.8	35.0	29.8	32.5	32.4	42.6	34.2	43.1	37.5	22.6
Officers' Compensation **20**	3.1	8.2	6.7	5.2	3.2	3.0	2.5	2.0	1.2	0.7	1.0	0.7	0.8
Operating Margin **21**	•	•	•	•	•	•	•	•	•	•	•	•	•
Operating Margin Before Officers' Comp. **22**	•	•	6.3	•	1.8	•	•	•	•	•	•	•	•

Selected Average Balance Sheet ($ in Thousands)

Net Receivables 23	53416	35992	11970	7658	2629	1749	900	418	113	21	1	50
Inventories 24	18698	8048	2815	2057	2178	825	320	126	70	10	4	22
Net Property, Plant and Equipment 25	1276963	699096	183964	83678	38268	20169	10348	5104	1087	382	54	752
Total Assets 26	3294348	1143316	376538	149220	70480	34491	15521	7090	2083	666	96	1384
Notes and Loans Payable 27	1500152	678861	240769	83957	23644	10555	7345	3638	1296	403	84	739
All Other Liabilities 28	348122	359896	156340	63134	17451	10497	3406	1403	352	126	17	338
Net Worth 29	1446074	104558	-20571	2120	29384	13438	4770	2049	436	137	-6	308

Selected Financial Ratios (Times to 1)

Current Ratio 30	0.8	0.6	0.4	0.8	1.6	1.1	1.4	0.9	1.5	1.0	1.1	0.9
Quick Ratio 31	0.6	0.4	0.3	0.6	1.1	0.8	0.9	0.7	1.2	0.8	0.8	0.7
Net Sales to Working Capital 32	•	•	•	•	6.1	42.3	8.6	•	9.6	97.8	110.6	•
Coverage Ratio 33	0.5	1.0	0.5	•	0.7	1.5	0.5	0.8	2.5	1.3	3.4	0.9
Total Asset Turnover 34	0.4	0.4	0.6	0.7	0.5	0.5	0.5	0.8	1.0	1.1	3.5	0.7
Inventory Turnover 35	11.5	3.5	13.0	17.3	2.0	4.1	5.5	13.6	7.1	12.1	28.1	9.7
Receivables Turnover 36	20.1	14.9	18.2	15.9	10.6	11.5	9.1	11.9	20.4	21.5	198.2	19.4
Total Liabilities to Net Worth 37	1.3	9.9	•	69.4	1.4	1.6	2.3	2.5	3.8	3.9	•	3.5
Current Assets to Working Capital 38	•	•	•	•	2.7	16.8	3.4	•	2.8	21.4	9.3	•
Current Liabilities to Working Capital 39	•	•	•	•	1.7	15.8	2.4	1.8	1.8	20.4	8.3	•
Working Capital to Net Sales 40	•	•	•	•	0.2	0.0	0.1	0.1	0.1	0.0	0.0	•
Inventory to Working Capital 41	•	•	•	•	0.3	1.8	0.4	•	0.4	1.0	1.3	•
Total Receipts to Cash Flow 42	9.5	4.3	4.3	5.4	4.2	3.9	4.8	5.0	3.8	2.7	4.0	4.3
Cost of Goods to Cash Flow 43	1.6	0.2	0.7	1.8	0.5	0.7	1.0	1.4	0.9	0.5	1.3	0.9
Cash Flow to Total Debt 44	0.1	0.1	0.1	0.1	0.2	0.2	0.2	0.2	0.3	0.5	0.8	0.2

Selected Financial Factors (in Percentages)

Debt Ratio 45	56.1	90.9	105.5	98.6	58.3	61.0	69.3	71.1	79.1	79.4	106.3	77.8
Return on Total Assets 46	2.6	4.7	3.4	•	1.4	2.6	1.2	1.7	6.0	2.1	10.0	3.3
Return on Equity Before Income Taxes 47	•	0.6	•	54.1	•	2.4	•	•	17.4	2.4	•	•
Return on Equity After Income Taxes 48	•	•	61.4	51.4	•	1.3	•	•	16.5	1.9	•	•
Profit Margin (Before Income Tax) 49	•	0.1	•	•	•	1.8	•	•	3.6	0.5	2.0	•
Profit Margin (After Income Tax) 50	•	•	•	•	•	1.0	•	•	3.4	0.4	1.9	•

Table II

Corporations with Net Income

AMUSEMENT, GAMBLING, AND RECREATION INDUSTRIES

MONEY AMOUNTS AND SIZE OF ASSETS IN THOUSANDS OF DOLLARS

Item Description for Accounting Period 7/10 Through 6/11		Total	Zero Assets	Under 500	500 to 1,000	1,000 to 5,000	5,000 to 10,000	10,000 to 25,000	25,000 to 50,000	50,000 to 100,000	100,000 to 250,000	250,000 to 500,000	500,000 to 2,500,000	2,500,000 and over
Number of Enterprises	1	22781	3465	15769	1725	1526	100	104	50	20	11	5	6	0
Revenues ($ in Thousands)														
Net Sales	2	22487682	263878	5672779	1870164	4251328	855180	1179527	1196110	938940	1130044	492041	4637691	0
Interest	3	110863	0	1915	4097	2521	886	814	1158	9023	5306	128	85015	0
Rents	4	67181	0	271	2405	2946	3296	821	4871	4107	4413	172	43879	0
Royalties	5	23135	0	0	0	0	1550	0	0	0	20028	1556	0	0
Other Portfolio Income	6	276728	9530	28420	14605	20886	24376	9933	35862	26419	26440	351	79906	0
Other Receipts	7	1922820	58227	56454	116975	308261	24676	131870	30232	67155	41102	356523	731345	0
Total Receipts	8	24488409	331635	5759839	2008246	4585942	909964	1322965	1268233	1045644	1227333	850771	5577836	0
Average Total Receipts	9	1093	96	365	1164	3005	9100	12721	25365	52282	111576	170154	929639	•
Operating Costs/Operating Income (%)														
Cost of Operations	10	15.6	7.6	14.9	20.9	20.0	42.2	24.2	15.0	6.1	15.7	20.2	5.3	•
Salaries and Wages	11	20.9	2.6	13.8	21.8	20.3	17.0	22.8	31.6	29.3	21.4	28.7	25.5	•
Taxes Paid	12	9.8	1.9	4.1	5.3	7.4	3.4	6.5	4.5	11.9	6.8	6.0	25.0	•
Interest Paid	13	3.0	2.1	0.8	0.9	1.2	1.9	4.7	1.2	2.3	2.9	14.8	7.5	•
Depreciation	14	6.1	7.5	3.0	3.8	2.8	4.8	8.9	8.0	9.2	6.6	15.7	11.0	•
Amortization and Depletion	15	0.7	0.1	0.1	0.1	0.1	0.5	0.1	0.6	1.0	1.5	1.4	1.9	•
Pensions and Other Deferred Comp.	16	0.3	•	0.0	0.3	0.6	0.4	0.1	0.0	0.5	0.3	1.3	0.2	•
Employee Benefits	17	1.4	1.7	0.9	1.3	0.6	1.4	2.3	1.7	2.0	2.9	3.8	1.7	•
Advertising	18	2.3	0.8	1.6	1.0	1.8	1.9	2.9	2.3	2.5	3.2	5.8	3.2	•
Other Expenses	19	34.5	55.3	44.2	35.0	34.5	16.4	25.7	26.6	30.6	33.1	50.7	28.2	•
Officers' Compensation	20	4.2	7.9	8.5	5.8	3.8	3.1	3.0	1.3	1.4	1.4	1.5	0.9	•
Operating Margin	21	1.4	12.4	8.0	3.5	6.7	6.8	•	7.3	3.2	4.1	•	•	•
Operating Margin Before Officers' Comp.	22	5.6	20.3	16.5	9.4	10.5	10.0	1.9	8.6	4.7	5.5	•	•	•

Selected Average Balance Sheet ($ in Thousands)

Net Receivables 23	45	0	1	17	134	500	1073	2559	2220	9181	5287	52724
Inventories 24	18	0	3	16	108	40	305	587	1084	2427	2947	9015
Net Property, Plant and Equipment 25	599	0	50	359	939	3679	9532	17813	45393	73832	141823	1021837
Total Assets 26	1145	0	99	653	2136	6097	15852	36351	74830	145798	334204	1882102
Notes and Loans Payable 27	513	0	36	362	768	3091	6925	9449	18876	52734	171422	1000692
All Other Liabilities 28	210	0	11	148	307	850	3051	7190	6808	43698	48027	376792
Net Worth 29	422	0	51	144	1061	2156	5876	19712	49147	49366	114756	504618

Selected Financial Ratios (Times to 1)

Current Ratio 30	1.4	•	2.5	1.1	1.9	2.0	1.4	1.2	2.3	1.2	1.4	0.9
Quick Ratio 31	1.0	•	1.9	0.9	1.5	1.8	1.0	0.9	1.9	0.9	1.0	0.5
Net Sales to Working Capital 32	14.7	•	18.2	37.9	6.5	9.5	8.6	17.5	4.1	13.8	6.1	•
Coverage Ratio 33	5.0	18.8	13.7	13.6	13.1	7.8	3.4	11.9	7.2	5.6	2.5	2.3
Total Asset Turnover 34	0.9	•	3.6	1.7	1.3	1.4	0.7	0.7	0.6	0.7	0.3	0.4
Inventory Turnover 35	8.4	•	19.2	14.4	5.2	90.1	9.0	6.1	2.6	6.6	6.8	4.5
Receivables Turnover 36	23.0	•	187.6	50.0	23.2	17.7	12.3	11.4	15.6	15.0	17.1	14.8
Total Liabilities to Net Worth 37	1.7	•	0.9	3.5	1.0	1.8	1.7	0.8	0.5	2.0	1.9	2.7
Current Assets to Working Capital 38	3.6	•	1.7	7.7	2.1	2.0	3.3	6.7	1.8	5.3	3.3	•
Current Liabilities to Working Capital 39	2.6	•	0.7	6.7	1.1	1.0	2.3	5.7	0.8	4.3	2.3	•
Working Capital to Net Sales 40	0.1	•	0.1	0.0	0.2	0.1	0.1	0.1	0.2	0.1	0.2	•
Inventory to Working Capital 41	0.3	•	0.2	0.5	0.3	0.0	0.4	0.5	0.1	0.5	0.2	•
Total Receipts to Cash Flow 42	2.8	1.3	2.6	2.7	2.5	4.3	3.5	3.0	2.7	2.7	1.6	3.2
Cost of Goods to Cash Flow 43	0.4	0.1	0.4	0.6	0.5	1.8	0.8	0.5	0.2	0.4	0.3	0.2
Cash Flow to Total Debt 44	0.5	•	2.9	0.8	1.0	0.5	0.3	0.5	0.7	0.3	0.3	0.2

Selected Financial Factors (in Percentages)

Debt Ratio 45	63.1	•	48.2	78.0	50.3	64.6	62.9	45.8	34.3	66.1	65.7	73.2
Return on Total Assets 46	13.1	•	37.4	19.6	20.6	21.2	11.3	9.6	10.6	11.3	11.1	7.2
Return on Equity Before Income Taxes 47	28.4	•	67.0	82.5	38.3	52.3	21.5	16.2	13.9	27.3	19.5	15.3
Return on Equity After Income Taxes 48	26.3	•	66.2	81.4	37.5	49.0	20.5	14.1	12.9	26.2	16.1	11.6
Profit Margin (Before Income Tax) 49	12.1	38.1	9.5	10.9	14.6	13.2	11.1	13.4	14.6	13.1	22.8	10.0
Profit Margin (After Income Tax) 50	11.2	38.1	9.4	10.8	14.3	12.3	10.6	11.6	13.5	12.6	18.8	7.6

Table I

Corporations with and without Net Income

ACCOMMODATION

MONEY AMOUNTS AND SIZE OF ASSETS IN THOUSANDS OF DOLLARS

Item Description for Accounting Period 7/10 Through 6/11	Total	Zero Assets	Under 500	500 to 1,000	1,000 to 5,000	5,000 to 10,000	10,000 to 25,000	25,000 to 50,000	50,000 to 100,000	100,000 to 250,000	250,000 to 500,000	500,000 to 2,500,000	2,500,000 and over
Number of Enterprises **1**	32286	4259	14967	3983	7266	1056	457	131	68	41	23	22	13
Revenues ($ in Thousands)													
Net Sales **2**	79608499	2845742	4466805	1886617	7687325	2931896	3828406	2829724	3426841	7102500	3443498	5217136	33932009
Interest **3**	1706621	11091	2449	1221	9853	1234	9420	8466	16341	20313	18633	238157	1369444
Rents **4**	1303424	43499	69	1011	3369	3831	12238	12013	20950	13369	17478	122174	1053425
Royalties **5**	2386795	10944	0	0	0	0	1232	0	0	2773	219594	30341	2121911
Other Portfolio Income **6**	2090845	317	3196	3630	45113	466	18297	10824	13642	5575	38062	14305	1937421
Other Receipts **7**	8776117	-28828	105329	40037	113894	47415	150318	24432	60107	151452	160322	193638	7757995
Total Receipts **8**	95872301	2882765	4577848	1932516	7859554	2984842	4019911	2885459	3537881	7295982	3907587	5815751	48172205
Average Total Receipts **9**	2969	677	306	485	1082	2827	8796	22026	52028	177951	169895	264352	3705554
Operating Costs/Operating Income (%)													
Cost of Operations **10**	15.5	10.1	8.3	7.6	14.6	24.6	37.9	15.0	27.7	20.9	15.2	11.7	12.4
Salaries and Wages **11**	28.2	12.2	18.5	15.4	18.0	16.9	14.6	20.2	9.4	15.1	20.7	25.3	42.8
Taxes Paid **12**	7.9	6.0	7.2	8.2	6.6	6.4	5.2	6.6	4.0	4.1	4.1	13.3	9.8
Interest Paid **13**	10.9	5.5	1.3	6.4	8.7	9.4	5.7	4.3	3.0	1.6	3.2	12.7	17.9
Depreciation **14**	7.6	8.2	3.0	6.9	8.2	13.6	7.1	6.3	5.0	3.7	8.2	12.7	8.0
Amortization and Depletion **15**	1.1	2.2	0.2	0.2	0.7	0.5	0.8	0.6	0.2	0.4	0.9	1.6	1.6
Pensions and Other Deferred Comp. **16**	0.5	0.3	0.0	0.2	0.0	0.2	0.1	0.2	0.2	0.1	0.7	0.3	0.9
Employee Benefits **17**	3.0	1.4	0.2	0.7	1.1	1.3	2.5	1.5	1.2	1.5	2.0	2.6	5.0
Advertising **18**	3.1	1.5	2.4	2.1	1.8	1.2	1.9	2.6	2.4	4.2	3.1	3.4	3.7
Other Expenses **19**	48.0	70.4	64.7	54.1	38.7	30.0	88.7	49.7	53.3	54.2	49.4	31.5	42.9
Officers' Compensation **20**	1.2	1.9	2.7	2.8	1.6	1.3	0.9	0.8	0.9	0.4	1.1	0.9	1.0
Operating Margin **21**	•	•	•	•	•	•	•	•	•	•	•	•	•
Operating Margin Before Officers' Comp. **22**	•	•	•	•	1.6	•	•	•	•	•	•	•	•

Selected Average Balance Sheet ($ in Thousands)

Net Receivables 23	264	0	4	15	56	116	796	1313	3439	6971	24628	68507	365150
Inventories 24	114	0	2	7	16	26	99	349	791	1732	2418	25932	203631
Net Property, Plant and Equipment 25	3379	0	93	589	1692	5068	10426	21492	43400	78746	185954	454280	4591240
Total Assets 26	7758		152	750	2130	6341	14887	34022	71764	158609	355404	903211	13258002
Notes and Loans Payable 27	4314		127	604	1954	5585	10402	20841	36435	44566	143863	418624	6966536
All Other Liabilities 28	2013		24	78	171	325	1877	5973	11377	73477	61142	118419	4098378
Net Worth 29	1431		0	67	5	431	2607	7208	23952	40566	150400	366168	2193087

Selected Financial Ratios (Times to 1)

Current Ratio 30	1.0	•	1.3	1.0	1.5	1.3	1.4	0.7	1.3	1.5	0.9
Quick Ratio 31	0.7	•	1.0	0.7	1.1	0.8	1.0	0.5	1.0	1.0	0.6
Net Sales to Working Capital 32	64.3	•	18.8	22.0	10.7	14.5	11.1	•	9.9	4.0	•
Coverage Ratio 33	0.6	•	0.7	1.1	•	0.6	0.7	•	2.4	0.6	1.1
Total Asset Turnover 34	0.3	2.0	0.6	0.5	0.6	0.6	0.7	1.1	0.4	0.3	0.2
Inventory Turnover 35	3.3	10.7	5.3	9.9	32.1	9.3	17.7	20.9	9.5	1.1	1.6
Receivables Turnover 36	8.7	106.0	38.6	16.1	11.3	13.9	12.1	26.0	5.8	3.3	6.6
Total Liabilities to Net Worth 37	4.4	636.8	10.2	431.9	4.7	3.7	2.0	2.9	1.4	1.5	5.0
Current Assets to Working Capital 38	25.0	•	4.0	4.5	3.1	4.2	3.4	•	4.2	2.9	•
Current Liabilities to Working Capital 39	24.0	•	3.0	3.5	2.1	3.2	2.4	•	3.2	1.9	•
Working Capital to Net Sales 40	0.0	0.1	0.1	0.0	0.1	0.1	0.1	•	0.3	0.3	•
Inventory to Working Capital 41	2.8	•	0.5	0.3	0.1	0.2	0.1	•	0.1	0.3	•
Total Receipts to Cash Flow 42	3.6	3.0	3.1	3.3	6.7	4.6	4.2	4.2	2.4	5.3	3.3
Cost of Goods to Cash Flow 43	0.6	0.3	0.2	0.2	2.5	0.7	1.2	0.9	0.4	0.6	0.4
Cash Flow to Total Debt 44	0.1	0.6	0.2	0.1	0.1	0.2	0.2	0.4	0.3	0.1	0.1

Selected Financial Factors (in Percentages)

Debt Ratio 45	81.5	99.8	91.0	99.8	82.5	78.8	66.6	74.4	57.7	59.5	83.5
Return on Total Assets 46	2.1	•	2.8	4.8	•	•	•	•	3.3	2.2	3.7
Return on Equity Before Income Taxes 47	•	•	•	225.2	•	•	•	•	4.6	•	1.2
Return on Equity After Income Taxes 48	•	•	•	195.9	•	•	•	•	2.7	•	•
Profit Margin (Before Income Tax) 49	•	•	•	1.0	•	•	•	•	4.6	•	1.0
Profit Margin (After Income Tax) 50	•	•	•	0.9	•	•	•	•	2.7	•	•

Table II
Corporations with Net Income

ACCOMMODATION

MONEY AMOUNTS AND SIZE OF ASSETS IN THOUSANDS OF DOLLARS

Item Description for Accounting Period 7/10 Through 6/11		Total	Zero Assets	Under 500	500 to 1,000	1,000 to 5,000	5,000 to 10,000	10,000 to 25,000	25,000 to 50,000	50,000 to 100,000	100,000 to 250,000	250,000 to 500,000	500,000 to 2,500,000	2,500,000 and over
Number of Enterprises	1	11259	516	4881	1870	3227	485	168	49	23	•	10	10	•
Revenues ($ in Thousands)														
Net Sales	2	32854620	1480079	2587471	1144713	4022516	1921408	2404652	746722	713585	•	2304796	2675683	•
Interest	3	756445	1004	502	36	8665	641	3672	3351	9874	•	2841	198303	•
Rents	4	315088	43499	69	0	447	0	5666	5463	7104	•	13570	47005	•
Royalties	5	1712991	6139	0	0	0	0	0	0	0	•	219594	55	•
Other Portfolio Income	6	1960314	147	171	0	43230	0	10718	9787	5052	•	22764	12289	•
Other Receipts	7	6686515	28903	24206	24483	50549	42959	26057	19351	35090	•	106642	70389	•
Total Receipts	8	44285973	1559771	2612419	1169232	4125407	1965008	2450765	784674	770705	•	2670207	3003724	•
Average Total Receipts	9	3933	3023	535	625	1278	4052	14588	16014	33509	•	267021	300372	•
Operating Costs/Operating Income (%)														
Cost of Operations	10	19.0	10.4	2.9	7.1	16.2	24.7	44.0	13.5	16.1	•	12.7	10.3	•
Salaries and Wages	11	31.8	13.7	19.0	11.7	15.0	16.6	14.4	23.2	21.2	•	17.3	21.1	•
Taxes Paid	12	7.8	8.0	5.7	7.5	6.5	6.1	4.2	8.5	6.7	•	3.4	18.0	•
Interest Paid	13	9.0	5.0	0.6	6.1	6.8	6.7	3.3	6.2	6.2	•	2.3	14.2	•
Depreciation	14	7.1	8.2	1.6	5.4	7.0	7.1	3.9	8.0	8.8	•	8.1	10.3	•
Amortization and Depletion	15	1.3	2.5	0.1	0.1	0.8	0.3	0.3	0.3	0.4	•	0.9	1.6	•
Pensions and Other Deferred Comp.	16	0.6	0.5	•	•	0.0	0.3	0.0	0.4	0.6	•	0.9	0.3	•
Employee Benefits	17	2.4	1.3	0.1	0.4	1.2	1.1	3.1	2.1	3.0	•	1.8	1.9	•
Advertising	18	3.0	2.6	2.7	2.4	1.3	0.8	0.9	2.9	3.3	•	4.1	3.1	•
Other Expenses	19	41.2	48.3	61.0	50.5	31.7	27.0	20.5	29.6	31.3	•	48.9	25.6	•
Officers' Compensation	20	1.4	0.3	0.9	1.9	2.8	1.6	1.3	1.1	1.4	•	1.5	0.7	•
Operating Margin	21	•	•	5.3	6.8	10.7	7.7	4.1	4.3	1.1	•	•	•	•
Operating Margin Before Officers' Comp.	22	•	•	6.2	8.8	13.6	9.3	5.4	5.4	2.5	•	•	•	•

Selected Average Balance Sheet ($ in Thousands)

Net Receivables 23	424	0	8	15	92	210	1666	1725	3267	21835	123123
Inventories 24	175	0	3	3	24	38	92	265	568	3722	26082
Net Property, Plant and Equipment 25	3531	0	69	619	1555	4795	9917	21239	42358	166697	420250
Total Assets 26	9432	0	156	773	2104	6489	14842	31780	69478	368110	809700
Notes and Loans Payable 27	5293	0	120	553	1474	5329	9930	23619	31422	128383	433201
All Other Liabilities 28	2017	0	26	70	148	286	1479	2570	9548	88437	93388
Net Worth 29	2122	0	10	150	483	874	3433	5591	28508	151291	283112

Selected Financial Ratios (Times to 1)

Current Ratio 30	1.8	•	2.1	1.6	2.0	2.2	1.9	1.0	1.9	1.7	2.0
Quick Ratio 31	1.3	•	1.7	1.4	1.7	1.5	1.5	0.8	1.3	1.0	1.3
Net Sales to Working Capital 32	4.8	•	19.0	20.4	7.6	9.9	8.5	•	4.3	7.1	2.3
Coverage Ratio 33	2.7	2.0	11.4	2.5	3.0	2.5	2.9	2.5	2.5	7.1	1.4
Total Asset Turnover 34	0.3	•	3.4	0.8	0.6	0.6	1.0	0.5	0.4	0.6	0.3
Inventory Turnover 35	3.2	•	4.5	16.8	8.4	25.8	68.2	7.8	8.8	7.9	1.1
Receivables Turnover 36	9.2	•	106.7	49.9	13.3	18.4	10.5	8.5	6.3	8.5	3.5
Total Liabilities to Net Worth 37	3.4	•	14.7	4.1	3.4	6.4	3.3	4.7	1.4	1.4	1.9
Current Assets to Working Capital 38	2.2	•	1.9	2.6	2.0	1.8	2.1	•	2.2	2.4	2.0
Current Liabilities to Working Capital 39	1.2	•	0.9	1.6	1.0	0.8	1.1	•	1.2	1.4	1.0
Working Capital to Net Sales 40	0.2	•	0.1	0.0	0.1	0.1	0.1	•	0.2	0.1	0.4
Inventory to Working Capital 41	0.3	•	0.1	0.1	0.1	0.1	0.1	•	0.0	0.1	0.3
Total Receipts to Cash Flow 42	2.4	2.2	2.6	2.4	2.5	3.2	4.4	3.1	2.9	2.0	4.0
Cost of Goods to Cash Flow 43	0.5	0.2	0.1	0.2	0.4	0.8	2.0	0.4	0.5	0.2	0.4
Cash Flow to Total Debt 44	0.2	•	1.4	0.4	0.3	0.2	0.3	0.2	0.3	0.5	0.1

Selected Financial Factors (in Percentages)

Debt Ratio 45	77.5	•	93.6	80.6	77.0	86.5	76.9	82.4	59.0	58.9	65.0
Return on Total Assets 46	7.6	•	23.3	11.9	11.9	10.1	9.0	7.5	6.8	10.2	6.4
Return on Equity Before Income Taxes 47	21.3	•	334.0	36.5	34.3	45.2	25.1	25.5	9.9	21.3	5.0
Return on Equity After Income Taxes 48	16.0	•	333.7	35.8	33.6	43.1	22.3	22.4	8.8	16.9	4.2
Profit Margin (Before Income Tax) 49	15.5	4.8	6.3	9.0	13.3	10.0	6.0	9.4	9.1	14.0	5.2
Profit Margin (After Income Tax) 50	11.6	4.0	6.3	8.8	13.0	9.5	5.4	8.2	8.1	11.1	4.4

Table I

Corporations with and without Net Income

FOOD SERVICES AND DRINKING PLACES

MONEY AMOUNTS AND SIZE OF ASSETS IN THOUSANDS OF DOLLARS

Item Description for Accounting Period 7/10 Through 6/11	Total	Zero Assets	Under 500	500 to 1,000	1,000 to 5,000	5,000 to 10,000	10,000 to 25,000	25,000 to 50,000	50,000 to 100,000	100,000 to 250,000	250,000 to 500,000	500,000 to 2,500,000	2,500,000 and over
Number of Enterprises 1	264853	40922	198848	12842	10461	1070	406	116	67	48	28	32	13
Revenues ($ in Thousands)													
Net Sales 2	343209513	7352278	109355903	23853267	41443587	13551376	11167826	6207828	7816527	12497675	12940363	30955822	66067061
Interest 3	319470	3662	7672	7603	8459	6450	8048	5105	3543	7799	28866	94531	137732
Rents 4	647130	55202	8126	1040	10022	5793	3265	4393	8271	32982	68511	288419	161106
Royalties 5	4085028	153223	1179	23	535	4781	45498	39586	88524	161162	716856	695553	2178108
Other Portfolio Income 6	1795171	163612	72838	78692	9482	24138	11888	19532	2830	18965	34067	676121	683005
Other Receipts 7	9273782	214609	586927	118244	452828	202413	329201	113870	77843	220721	148150	1365864	5443114
Total Receipts 8	359330094	7942586	110032645	24058869	41924913	13794951	11565726	6390314	7997538	12939304	13936813	34076310	74670126
Average Total Receipts 9	1357	194	553	1873	4008	12892	28487	55089	119366	269569	497743	1064885	5743856
Operating Costs/Operating Income (%)													
Cost of Operations 10	41.3	43.0	41.8	37.9	41.0	38.9	43.6	40.1	43.2	36.8	46.9	36.6	43.8
Salaries and Wages 11	19.3	20.2	17.8	20.5	18.0	19.2	19.5	19.5	20.0	20.8	20.6	25.2	18.7
Taxes Paid 12	4.3	5.3	4.3	4.4	3.9	3.6	4.1	4.1	3.7	3.9	3.9	4.0	4.7
Interest Paid 13	1.7	1.4	0.6	0.8	1.1	1.3	1.4	1.9	1.9	1.9	3.1	2.4	3.5
Depreciation 14	3.0	3.2	1.9	2.6	2.5	3.1	3.3	3.8	3.7	4.1	3.8	5.5	3.8
Amortization and Depletion 15	0.6	1.0	0.3	0.4	0.5	0.6	0.7	0.6	0.5	0.8	0.9	0.8	0.9
Pensions and Other Deferred Comp. 16	0.2	0.1	0.1	0.1	0.0	0.1	0.3	0.1	0.1	0.1	0.3	0.3	0.4
Employee Benefits 17	1.2	0.5	0.6	0.7	0.8	1.0	1.0	1.7	1.3	1.3	1.9	1.6	2.6
Advertising 18	2.3	1.7	1.8	2.2	3.0	3.6	3.3	3.5	2.4	2.4	2.2	2.8	2.0
Other Expenses 19	24.3	37.0	25.2	24.2	23.5	26.3	22.0	24.2	22.3	30.9	21.0	23.4	22.4
Officers' Compensation 20	2.5	3.4	4.8	3.1	2.6	1.0	1.4	1.1	1.0	0.8	0.7	0.9	0.5
Operating Margin 21	•	•	1.0	3.1	3.2	1.2	•	•	•	•	•	•	•
Operating Margin Before Officers' Comp. 22	1.8	•	5.8	6.2	5.8	2.2	0.8	0.5	0.9	•	•	•	•

Selected Average Balance Sheet ($ in Thousands)

Net Receivables 23	45	0	3	23	146	177	911	1844	3888	7492	21962	40445	487688
Inventories 24	20	0	7	27	43	190	438	785	2072	3137	9849	19107	114803
Net Property, Plant and Equipment 25	294	0	64	321	870	3237	6820	16028	36190	76115	118643	447026	1557788
Total Assets 26	888	0	126	675	1807	7074	14827	33577	72143	158965	352503	923850	8704260
Notes and Loans Payable 27	373	0	94	351	1056	3600	7438	17881	30297	69713	181961	290280	2759323
All Other Liabilities 28	301	0	26	137	343	1588	3262	7031	23484	49166	121772	299249	3719153
Net Worth 29	214	0	6	187	409	1885	4127	8664	18362	40086	48769	334320	2225785

Selected Financial Ratios (Times to 1)

Current Ratio 30	1.0	•	1.2	1.4	1.4	1.0	1.1	1.2	0.7	0.7	1.0	1.0	0.9
Quick Ratio 31	0.7	•	0.7	1.0	1.0	0.7	0.8	0.8	0.4	0.5	0.7	0.6	0.7
Net Sales to Working Capital 32	178.4	•	109.2	30.4	22.2	490.0	91.2	43.8	•	•	•	•	•
Coverage Ratio 33	3.6	•	3.7	6.1	4.8	3.3	3.1	2.2	2.2	0.8	1.8	4.0	4.1
Total Asset Turnover 34	1.5	•	4.3	2.8	2.2	1.8	1.9	1.6	1.6	1.6	1.3	1.0	0.6
Inventory Turnover 35	26.4	•	32.1	25.7	37.7	26.0	27.4	27.3	24.3	30.6	22.0	18.5	19.4
Receivables Turnover 36	30.4	•	209.5	65.6	34.5	79.0	32.8	27.1	26.6	41.8	25.3	27.3	10.6
Total Liabilities to Net Worth 37	3.1	•	20.0	2.6	3.4	2.8	2.6	2.9	2.9	3.0	6.2	1.8	2.9
Current Assets to Working Capital 38	22.8	•	7.1	3.3	3.3	60.8	12.9	6.6	•	•	•	•	•
Current Liabilities to Working Capital 39	21.8	•	6.1	2.3	2.3	59.8	11.9	5.6	•	•	•	•	•
Working Capital to Net Sales 40	0.0	•	0.0	0.0	0.0	0.0	0.0	0.0	•	•	•	•	•
Inventory to Working Capital 41	2.8	•	1.5	0.4	0.2	7.5	1.5	0.6	•	•	•	•	•
Total Receipts to Cash Flow 42	5.3	9.0	6.1	5.2	5.1	5.2	5.9	5.4	6.1	4.6	6.8	4.9	4.4
Cost of Goods to Cash Flow 43	2.2	3.9	2.5	2.0	2.1	2.0	2.6	2.2	2.6	1.7	3.2	1.8	1.9
Cash Flow to Total Debt 44	0.4	•	0.7	0.7	0.6	0.5	0.4	0.4	0.4	0.5	0.2	0.3	0.2

Selected Financial Factors (in Percentages)

Debt Ratio 45	75.9	•	95.2	72.3	77.4	73.3	72.2	74.2	74.5	74.8	86.2	63.8	74.4
Return on Total Assets 46	8.6	•	9.7	13.0	12.0	7.8	8.2	6.8	6.6	2.6	7.3	10.0	8.4
Return on Equity Before Income Taxes 47	25.7	•	147.7	39.3	41.8	20.3	20.0	14.3	14.0	23.7	•	20.7	24.8
Return on Equity After Income Taxes 48	19.3	•	143.8	38.5	41.0	19.8	18.8	12.5	11.8	13.7	13.7	14.0	16.0
Profit Margin (Before Income Tax) 49	4.3	•	1.6	3.9	4.3	3.0	3.0	2.3	2.2	•	2.5	7.2	10.9
Profit Margin (After Income Tax) 50	3.2	•	1.6	3.9	4.2	2.9	2.8	2.0	1.9	•	1.4	4.8	7.0

FOOD SERVICES AND DRINKING PLACES

Table II
Corporations with Net Income

MONEY AMOUNTS AND SIZE OF ASSETS IN THOUSANDS OF DOLLARS

Item Description for Accounting Period 7/10 Through 6/11	Total	Zero Assets	Under 500	500 to 1,000	1,000 to 5,000	5,000 to 10,000	10,000 to 25,000	25,000 to 50,000	50,000 to 100,000	100,000 to 250,000	250,000 to 500,000	500,000 to 2,500,000	2,500,000 and over
Number of Enterprises **1**	133524	12541	102663	9216	7762	827	312	78	48	•	17	23	•
Revenues ($ in Thousands)													
Net Sales **2**	266672775	2567233	73529259	19883832	35530574	11452575	8767318	3866972	5523331	•	8691416	25573981	•
Interest **3**	226060	3362	4087	5575	5850	4647	2413	4053	3311	•	3302	51848	•
Rents **4**	448314	34523	5569	585	9978	3321	343	2640	5776	•	11742	230596	•
Royalties **5**	3427701	109354	0	23	0	0	17509	9292	70941	•	583656	430157	•
Other Portfolio Income **6**	1707531	133060	54368	77234	5251	19554	11599	18333	2110	•	27923	659635	•
Other Receipts **7**	8364417	162428	368634	103524	289024	178081	237558	72349	64591	•	119003	1248042	•
Total Receipts **8**	280846798	3009960	73961917	20070773	35840677	11658178	9036740	3973639	5670060	•	9437042	27894259	•
Average Total Receipts **9**	2103	240	720	2178	4617	14097	28964	50944	118126	•	555120	1212794	•
Operating Costs/Operating Income (%)													
Cost of Operations **10**	41.3	39.4	41.1	37.1	41.1	39.2	42.9	41.1	46.4	•	50.1	38.3	•
Salaries and Wages **11**	18.8	19.5	17.3	20.8	17.3	17.9	19.6	16.4	17.7	•	18.2	24.5	•
Taxes Paid **12**	4.1	5.4	4.1	4.3	3.8	3.4	4.1	3.9	3.6	•	3.4	4.0	•
Interest Paid **13**	1.5	1.3	0.5	0.7	1.0	1.1	1.1	1.6	1.4	•	2.0	1.7	•
Depreciation **14**	2.8	2.3	1.2	2.2	2.1	2.9	3.1	3.5	3.5	•	4.0	5.9	•
Amortization and Depletion **15**	0.5	0.4	0.2	0.3	0.5	0.6	0.5	0.7	0.4	•	0.8	0.3	•
Pensions and Other Deferred Comp. **16**	0.2	0.1	0.0	0.1	0.0	0.1	0.1	0.1	0.1	•	0.3	0.3	•
Employee Benefits **17**	1.3	0.5	0.6	0.7	0.8	1.0	1.0	1.1	1.2	•	1.5	1.5	•
Advertising **18**	2.3	1.7	1.9	2.3	3.0	3.6	3.3	4.4	2.4	•	2.1	2.5	•
Other Expenses **19**	22.8	31.2	23.2	23.3	22.3	25.5	20.6	21.9	20.3	•	19.8	21.3	•
Officers' Compensation **20**	2.2	3.8	4.5	2.8	2.8	1.0	1.5	1.1	1.1	•	0.7	0.8	•
Operating Margin **21**	2.0	•	5.4	5.4	5.4	3.6	2.4	4.2	2.0	•	•	•	•
Operating Margin Before Officers' Comp. **22**	4.2	•	9.8	8.2	8.2	4.5	3.8	5.3	3.1	•	•	•	•

Selected Average Balance Sheet ($ in Thousands)

Net Receivables 23	72	0	3	26	157	194	878	1121	3295	•	26972	47102
Inventories 24	30	0	8	27	45	170	386	618	1976	•	11648	22357
Net Property, Plant and Equipment 25	434	0	60	298	838	3166	6773	16472	35016	•	129918	546143
Total Assets 26	1414	0	140	660	1839	7086	14666	33616	69249	•	354288	964466
Notes and Loans Payable 27	504	0	67	293	966	3667	6279	17403	26359	•	159025	274900
All Other Liabilities 28	497	0	30	114	343	1050	2862	4553	19050	•	117977	323331
Net Worth 29	412	0	43	254	530	2369	5525	11659	23840	•	77286	366236

Selected Financial Ratios (Times to 1)

Current Ratio 30	1.2	•	1.4	1.7	1.6	1.1	1.2	1.1	0.9	•	1.1	1.0
Quick Ratio 31	0.8	•	0.9	1.1	1.1	0.7	0.9	0.8	0.5	•	0.8	0.7
Net Sales to Working Capital 32	57.2	•	49.8	24.0	17.7	132.8	42.3	69.1	•	•	52.4	•
Coverage Ratio 33	5.9	10.1	12.8	9.7	7.2	5.7	5.9	5.3	4.3	•	3.9	6.9
Total Asset Turnover 34	1.4	•	5.1	3.3	2.5	2.0	1.9	1.5	1.7	•	1.4	1.1
Inventory Turnover 35	27.2	•	36.6	29.2	42.1	31.8	31.2	32.9	27.0	•	22.0	18.8
Receivables Turnover 36	29.9	•	222.1	66.0	38.0	84.7	34.3	39.4	28.0	•	24.1	27.6
Total Liabilities to Net Worth 37	2.4	•	2.3	1.6	2.5	2.0	1.7	1.9	1.9	•	3.6	1.6
Current Assets to Working Capital 38	7.6	•	3.4	2.5	2.6	16.3	5.8	9.0	•	•	9.8	•
Current Liabilities to Working Capital 39	6.6	•	2.4	1.5	1.6	15.3	4.8	8.0	•	•	8.8	•
Working Capital to Net Sales 40	0.0	•	0.0	0.0	0.0	0.0	0.0	0.0	0.0	•	0.0	•
Inventory to Working Capital 41	0.9	•	0.6	0.3	0.2	2.0	0.6	0.8	•	•	1.1	•
Total Receipts to Cash Flow 42	4.7	3.5	5.1	4.7	4.8	4.7	5.4	4.5	5.6	•	5.5	4.8
Cost of Goods to Cash Flow 43	2.0	1.4	2.1	1.8	2.0	1.9	2.3	1.9	2.6	•	2.8	1.8
Cash Flow to Total Debt 44	0.4	•	1.5	1.1	0.7	0.6	0.6	0.5	0.4	•	0.3	0.4

Selected Financial Factors (in Percentages)

Debt Ratio 45	70.8	•	69.5	61.6	71.2	66.6	62.3	65.3	65.6	•	78.2	62.0
Return on Total Assets 46	13.0	•	33.0	23.1	18.3	12.7	12.5	12.7	10.0	•	11.1	13.1
Return on Equity Before Income Taxes 47	37.1	•	99.9	54.0	54.5	31.4	27.5	29.8	22.3	•	37.6	29.5
Return on Equity After Income Taxes 48	30.4	•	98.8	53.2	53.6	30.9	26.4	27.8	19.9	•	27.2	21.0
Profit Margin (Before Income Tax) 49	7.7	11.7	6.0	6.4	6.3	5.4	5.4	7.0	4.6	•	5.7	9.8
Profit Margin (After Income Tax) 50	6.3	10.9	5.9	6.3	6.2	5.3	5.2	6.5	4.1	•	4.1	7.0

Table I

Corporations with and without Net Income

AUTOMOTIVE REPAIR AND MAINTENANCE

MONEY AMOUNTS AND SIZE OF ASSETS IN THOUSANDS OF DOLLARS

Item Description for Accounting Period 7/10 Through 6/11	Total	Zero Assets	Under 500	500 to 1,000	1,000 to 5,000	5,000 to 10,000	10,000 to 25,000	25,000 to 50,000	50,000 to 100,000	100,000 to 250,000	250,000 to 500,000	500,000 to 2,500,000	2,500,000 and over
Number of Enterprises **1**	110215	17817	82376	6536	3240	152	60	13	9	7	5	0	0
Revenues ($ in Thousands)													
Net Sales **2**	65944964	2148397	38847882	9087569	8356772	1391891	1397655	611336	1228935	769887	2104639	0	0
Interest **3**	14815	0	3423	5426	1621	587	713	1416	288	757	583	0	0
Rents **4**	23010	0	6536	929	2250	0	434	253	0	99	12508	0	0
Royalties **5**	101383	0	0	0	0	0	0	0	1951	44759	54672	0	0
Other Portfolio Income **6**	77333	1830	25517	17919	5782	511	4442	3371	13931	3796	232	0	0
Other Receipts **7**	301599	5640	142577	19082	44104	39016	9730	6852	-11750	8242	38113	0	0
Total Receipts **8**	66463104	2155867	39025935	9130925	8410529	1432005	1412974	623228	1233355	827540	2210747	0	0
Average Total Receipts **9**	603	121	474	1397	2596	9421	23550	47941	137039	118220	442149	•	•
Operating Costs/Operating Income (%)													
Cost of Operations **10**	49.1	45.0	46.8	53.8	51.1	55.4	59.2	30.6	60.5	44.9	56.0	•	•
Salaries and Wages **11**	13.0	11.8	13.3	9.2	15.3	9.7	12.8	29.0	14.1	20.8	9.8	•	•
Taxes Paid **12**	3.5	4.3	3.5	3.2	4.2	2.9	2.9	4.7	2.3	3.5	1.7	•	•
Interest Paid **13**	1.2	1.0	0.8	2.0	1.6	2.1	0.5	2.8	0.7	6.1	2.9	•	•
Depreciation **14**	1.9	2.1	1.5	2.6	2.5	2.2	2.4	6.2	2.3	2.6	2.3	•	•
Amortization and Depletion **15**	0.5	0.2	0.3	0.5	0.8	0.4	0.2	1.2	0.7	3.9	2.6	•	•
Pensions and Other Deferred Comp. **16**	0.3	0.0	0.2	0.9	0.3	0.1	0.2	0.2	0.3	0.2	0.5	•	•
Employee Benefits **17**	1.2	0.4	1.2	1.1	1.1	1.5	1.1	1.8	1.6	2.7	1.8	•	•
Advertising **18**	1.5	0.8	1.4	1.7	1.6	1.9	1.1	1.2	0.6	1.5	4.2	•	•
Other Expenses **19**	20.2	34.6	21.7	17.2	15.7	16.3	14.2	23.6	14.0	18.4	19.7	•	•
Officers' Compensation **20**	5.9	6.3	7.5	4.0	4.2	3.7	1.7	1.6	0.9	0.9	0.6	•	•
Operating Margin **21**	1.8	•	2.0	3.6	1.8	3.7	3.8	•	2.0	•	•	•	•
Operating Margin Before Officers' Comp. **22**	7.6	•	9.5	7.7	6.0	7.5	5.5	•	2.8	•	•	•	•

Selected Average Balance Sheet ($ in Thousands)

Net Receivables 23	16	0	8	46	98	680	1156	2940	11775	15899	8449
Inventories 24	19	0	12	59	120	635	948	2090	2003	3180	38454
Net Property, Plant and Equipment 25	88	0	36	329	847	2139	6378	13147	20688	27702	111533
Total Assets 26	217	0	95	675	1641	6727	14974	31348	75030	159985	442932
Notes and Loans Payable 27	141	0	78	470	990	2662	3786	17996	19733	77650	250901
All Other Liabilities 28	52	0	28	100	236	1360	1831	6553	28943	44697	196024
Net Worth 29	24	0	-11	104	414	2705	9356	6798	26353	37628	-3993

Selected Financial Ratios (Times to 1)

Current Ratio 30	1.4	•	1.3	1.8	2.3	1.6	1.1	1.0	0.9	0.9	0.8
Quick Ratio 31	0.9	•	0.9	1.1	1.5	1.1	0.6	0.6	0.6	0.6	0.1
Net Sales to Working Capital 32	28.6	•	45.3	15.5	9.6	9.8	40.7	•	•	•	•
Coverage Ratio 33	3.0	•	4.1	3.1	2.5	4.1	11.8	0.6	4.4	1.3	2.0
Total Asset Turnover 34	2.8	•	4.9	2.1	1.6	1.4	1.6	1.5	1.8	0.7	1.0
Inventory Turnover 35	15.1	•	19.1	12.6	11.0	8.0	14.6	6.9	41.2	15.5	6.1
Receivables Turnover 36	33.8	•	55.0	25.2	20.6	10.6	17.9	16.6	12.6	8.7	47.9
Total Liabilities to Net Worth 37	7.9	•	•	5.5	3.0	1.5	0.6	3.6	1.8	3.3	•
Current Assets to Working Capital 38	3.5	•	4.0	2.3	1.8	2.6	8.1	•	•	•	•
Current Liabilities to Working Capital 39	2.5	•	3.0	1.3	0.8	1.6	7.1	•	•	•	•
Working Capital to Net Sales 40	0.0	•	0.0	0.1	0.1	0.1	0.0	•	•	•	•
Inventory to Working Capital 41	1.0	•	1.1	0.7	0.5	0.7	1.7	•	•	•	•
Total Receipts to Cash Flow 42	6.5	5.9	6.1	6.5	8.1	5.6	7.1	9.1	9.3	9.6	6.2
Cost of Goods to Cash Flow 43	3.2	2.7	2.9	3.5	4.1	3.1	4.2	2.8	5.6	4.3	3.5
Cash Flow to Total Debt 44	0.5	•	0.7	0.4	0.3	0.4	0.6	0.2	0.3	0.1	0.2

Selected Financial Factors (in Percentages)

Debt Ratio 45	88.8	•	111.3	84.5	74.7	59.8	37.5	78.3	64.9	76.5	100.9
Return on Total Assets 46	10.5	•	16.4	12.5	6.3	11.9	8.3	2.7	5.6	5.7	5.5
Return on Equity Before Income Taxes 47	62.6	•	•	54.6	15.0	22.4	12.2	•	12.4	6.2	•
Return on Equity After Income Taxes 48	60.2	•	•	54.3	14.7	21.1	12.1	•	10.0	5.6	•
Profit Margin (Before Income Tax) 49	2.5	•	2.5	4.1	2.4	6.6	4.9	•	2.4	2.1	2.9
Profit Margin (After Income Tax) 50	2.4	•	2.5	4.1	2.4	6.2	4.9	•	1.9	1.9	1.9

Table II

Corporations with Net Income

AUTOMOTIVE REPAIR AND MAINTENANCE

MONEY AMOUNTS AND SIZE OF ASSETS IN THOUSANDS OF DOLLARS

Item Description for Accounting Period 7/10 Through 6/11	Total	Zero Assets	Under 500	500 to 1,000	1,000 to 5,000	5,000 to 10,000	10,000 to 25,000	25,000 to 50,000	50,000 to 100,000	100,000 to 250,000	250,000 to 500,000	500,000 to 2,500,000	2,500,000 and over
Number of Enterprises **1**	63202	7060	49738	4182	2025	134	43	5	•	•	•	0	0
Revenues ($ in Thousands)													
Net Sales **2**	45557183	723050	26773029	6169998	5627948	1129041	1325918	214417	•	•	•	0	0
Interest **3**	11362	0	2597	5348	979	347	712	3	•	•	•	0	0
Rents **4**	16762	0	3121	929	101	0	6	0	•	•	•	0	0
Royalties **5**	101340	0	0	0	0	0	0	0	•	•	•	0	0
Other Portfolio Income **6**	54747	434	18777	9529	1739	454	4426	2984	•	•	•	0	0
Other Receipts **7**	264415	4051	122566	9381	36484	38050	5204	-24	•	•	•	0	0
Total Receipts **8**	46005809	727535	26920090	6195185	5667251	1167892	1336266	217380	•	•	•	0	0
Average Total Receipts **9**	728	103	541	1481	2799	8716	31076	43476	•	•	•	•	•
Operating Costs/Operating Income (%)													
Cost of Operations **10**	48.6	33.1	46.5	55.0	45.8	51.7	59.2	21.5	•	•	•	•	•
Salaries and Wages **11**	12.4	8.5	12.4	8.9	16.1	11.1	12.8	41.3	•	•	•	•	•
Taxes Paid **12**	3.3	2.4	3.2	3.4	4.6	2.6	2.9	4.0	•	•	•	•	•
Interest Paid **13**	1.0	2.9	0.6	1.6	1.2	2.5	0.3	3.6	•	•	•	•	•
Depreciation **14**	1.4	1.7	1.0	1.7	1.8	1.7	2.1	8.6	•	•	•	•	•
Amortization and Depletion **15**	0.3	0.1	0.1	0.4	0.3	0.5	0.2	1.3	•	•	•	•	•
Pensions and Other Deferred Comp. **16**	0.3	•	0.1	1.3	0.4	0.1	0.2	0.0	•	•	•	•	•
Employee Benefits **17**	1.2	0.1	1.2	1.1	1.1	1.0	1.1	2.2	•	•	•	•	•
Advertising **18**	1.4	1.3	1.3	0.8	2.0	2.0	1.0	0.2	•	•	•	•	•
Other Expenses **19**	18.4	38.1	19.9	13.9	15.9	17.4	13.6	15.6	•	•	•	•	•
Officers' Compensation **20**	6.0	3.9	7.7	3.7	5.4	4.4	1.7	2.1	•	•	•	•	•
Operating Margin **21**	5.6	8.0	6.0	8.2	5.4	5.0	4.9	•	•	•	•	•	•
Operating Margin Before Officers' Comp. **22**	11.5	11.8	13.6	11.9	10.8	9.4	6.6	1.7	•	•	•	•	•

Selected Average Balance Sheet ($ in Thousands)

Net Receivables 23	21	0	9	55	132	489	1482	4525
Inventories 24	21	0	11	54	121	561	1190	2608
Net Property, Plant and Equipment 25	88	0	31	297	697	2221	5934	14610
Total Assets 26	242	0	97	679	1512	6884	14193	34658
Notes and Loans Payable 27	108	0	48	361	629	2694	2310	16696
All Other Liabilities 28	50	0	25	98	170	1256	4828	3736
Net Worth 29	84	0	24	220	713	2934	7055	14226

Selected Financial Ratios (Times to 1)

Current Ratio 30	1.7	•	1.7	2.1	2.8	2.0	1.1	1.3
Quick Ratio 31	1.1	•	1.2	1.3	1.9	1.3	0.8	0.8
Net Sales to Working Capital 32	18.4	•	25.3	12.4	7.3	7.4	91.7	19.4
Coverage Ratio 33	7.4	4.0	11.7	6.5	6.1	4.4	18.6	1.3
Total Asset Turnover 34	3.0	•	5.5	2.2	1.8	1.2	2.2	1.2
Inventory Turnover 35	16.6	•	22.8	14.9	10.5	7.8	15.3	3.5
Receivables Turnover 36	31.6	•	54.4	24.2	17.0	11.2	18.1	•
Total Liabilities to Net Worth 37	1.9	•	3.0	2.1	1.1	1.3	1.0	1.4
Current Assets to Working Capital 38	2.4	•	2.3	1.9	1.5	2.0	13.7	4.7
Current Liabilities to Working Capital 39	1.4	•	1.3	0.9	0.5	1.0	12.7	3.7
Working Capital to Net Sales 40	0.1	•	0.0	0.1	0.1	0.1	0.0	0.1
Inventory to Working Capital 41	0.6	•	0.5	0.5	0.4	0.5	3.5	1.2
Total Receipts to Cash Flow 42	5.4	3.1	5.2	5.5	6.1	5.0	7.1	9.5
Cost of Goods to Cash Flow 43	2.6	1.0	2.4	3.0	2.8	2.6	4.2	2.0
Cash Flow to Total Debt 44	0.8	•	1.4	0.6	0.6	0.4	0.6	0.2

Selected Financial Factors (in Percentages)

Debt Ratio 45	65.2	•	74.8	67.5	52.8	57.4	50.3	59.0
Return on Total Assets 46	22.6	•	39.4	22.2	13.3	13.4	13.1	5.7
Return on Equity Before Income Taxes 47	56.1	•	143.3	57.9	23.5	24.2	24.8	3.0
Return on Equity After Income Taxes 48	55.0	•	141.6	57.6	23.2	22.8	24.7	2.9
Profit Margin (Before Income Tax) 49	6.5	8.6	6.5	8.6	6.0	8.4	5.7	1.0
Profit Margin (After Income Tax) 50	6.4	8.6	6.4	8.6	6.0	7.9	5.6	0.9

OTHER REPAIR AND MAINTENANCE

Table I

Corporations with and without Net Income

MONEY AMOUNTS AND SIZE OF ASSETS IN THOUSANDS OF DOLLARS

Item Description for Accounting Period 7/10 Through 6/11	Total	Zero Assets	Under 500	500 to 1,000	1,000 to 5,000	5,000 to 10,000	10,000 to 25,000	25,000 to 50,000	50,000 to 100,000	100,000 to 250,000	250,000 to 500,000	500,000 to 2,500,000	2,500,000 and over
Number of Enterprises **1**	60040	11098	45206	1878	1548	113	129	40	16	•	0	0	4
Revenues ($ in Thousands)													
Net Sales **2**	40613506	719074	14007527	3809067	6906622	1496753	3212094	2351169	1483861	•	0	0	4778666
Interest **3**	106164	607	1506	3366	5540	1288	1756	553	914	•	0	0	89478
Rents **4**	10131	0	1380	1306	2328	1891	2608	475	0	•	0	0	31
Royalties **5**	150876	0	0	0	0	0	0	0	58	•	0	0	150708
Other Portfolio Income **6**	86811	5517	35963	11964	11817	1135	3767	1281	1841	•	0	0	1275
Other Receipts **7**	525382	22145	144088	14764	3618	2931	12045	7308	3632	•	0	0	290179
Total Receipts **8**	41492870	747343	14190464	3840467	6929925	1503998	3232270	2360786	1490306	•	0	0	5310337
Average Total Receipts **9**	691	67	314	2045	4477	13310	25056	59020	93144	•	•	•	1327584
Operating Costs/Operating Income (%)													
Cost of Operations **10**	55.8	40.7	43.3	54.8	52.3	67.0	64.6	67.6	62.7	•	•	•	83.4
Salaries and Wages **11**	11.6	6.9	13.8	11.4	15.8	7.4	8.9	10.6	9.2	•	•	•	4.0
Taxes Paid **12**	2.6	2.5	2.7	3.4	3.0	3.2	2.0	2.4	1.9	•	•	•	1.1
Interest Paid **13**	1.6	2.9	0.6	0.4	0.8	1.4	0.5	0.7	2.1	•	•	•	7.8
Depreciation **14**	1.8	2.1	1.9	1.8	1.0	3.9	3.0	1.6	3.6	•	•	•	0.5
Amortization and Depletion **15**	0.4	0.7	0.1	0.1	0.3	0.0	0.1	0.2	1.4	•	•	•	1.0
Pensions and Other Deferred Comp. **16**	0.4	•	0.4	0.4	0.2	1.0	0.5	0.7	0.2	•	•	•	0.2
Employee Benefits **17**	1.8	1.3	1.7	2.2	1.3	2.0	1.7	2.2	4.7	•	•	•	0.9
Advertising **18**	0.8	1.9	0.9	0.7	0.5	0.3	0.3	0.4	0.2	•	•	•	2.2
Other Expenses **19**	16.2	37.6	21.5	17.1	13.5	11.0	11.4	9.4	13.5	•	•	•	9.3
Officers' Compensation **20**	5.2	9.0	8.6	7.4	4.4	3.7	2.6	1.7	1.1	•	•	•	0.5
Operating Margin **21**	1.9	•	4.5	0.3	7.0	•	4.4	2.6	•	•	•	•	•
Operating Margin Before Officers' Comp. **22**	7.0	3.4	13.1	7.7	11.4	2.8	7.0	4.3	0.6	•	•	•	•

Selected Average Balance Sheet ($ in Thousands)

Net Receivables 23	84	0	12	177	452	1794	3175	9579	16298	•	460449
Inventories 24	40	0	10	127	297	1821	3535	6456	8667	•	26805
Net Property, Plant and Equipment 25	45	0	17	120	236	1152	3451	4948	10558	•	30142
Total Assets 26	389	0	66	722	1625	6481	14760	31059	66477	•	2406755
Notes and Loans Payable 27	166	0	36	167	663	3495	3196	5745	27448	•	1255487
All Other Liabilities 28	114	0	22	136	404	1993	4168	11720	18017	•	757997
Net Worth 29	109	0	8	420	558	994	7396	13594	21012	•	393270

Selected Financial Ratios (Times to 1)

Current Ratio 30	1.7	•	1.8	2.8	2.2	1.2	2.1	2.1	1.4	•	1.2
Quick Ratio 31	1.2	•	1.3	1.4	1.5	0.7	1.3	1.3	0.8	•	1.0
Net Sales to Working Capital 32	9.5	•	18.4	6.2	8.6	16.6	4.8	5.5	10.0	•	12.3
Coverage Ratio 33	3.5	0.4	10.5	4.0	10.7	0.7	10.7	5.2	1.0	•	1.0
Total Asset Turnover 34	1.7	•	4.7	2.8	2.7	2.0	1.7	1.9	1.4	•	0.5
Inventory Turnover 35	9.5	•	13.1	8.8	7.9	4.9	4.6	6.2	6.7	•	37.2
Receivables Turnover 36	9.2	•	29.9	11.9	10.7	6.3	8.3	7.4	6.1	•	3.3
Total Liabilities to Net Worth 37	2.6	•	6.9	0.7	1.9	5.5	1.0	1.3	2.2	•	5.1
Current Assets to Working Capital 38	2.5	•	2.2	1.6	1.9	5.3	1.9	1.9	3.6	•	6.6
Current Liabilities to Working Capital 39	1.5	•	1.2	0.6	0.9	4.3	0.9	0.9	2.6	•	5.6
Working Capital to Net Sales 40	0.1	•	0.1	0.2	0.1	0.1	0.2	0.2	0.1	•	0.1
Inventory to Working Capital 41	0.5	•	0.6	0.4	0.5	2.2	0.7	0.6	1.1	•	0.3
Total Receipts to Cash Flow 42	6.1	3.6	4.6	7.3	5.6	12.4	7.1	9.7	13.4	•	11.4
Cost of Goods to Cash Flow 43	3.4	1.5	2.0	4.0	2.9	8.3	4.6	6.6	8.4	•	9.5
Cash Flow to Total Debt 44	0.4	•	1.2	0.9	0.8	0.2	0.5	0.3	0.2	•	0.1

Selected Financial Factors (in Percentages)

Debt Ratio 45	72.0	•	87.4	41.9	65.7	84.7	49.9	56.2	68.4	•	83.7
Return on Total Assets 46	9.9	•	30.1	4.3	22.3	2.1	9.4	7.1	2.8	•	4.0
Return on Equity Before Income Taxes 47	25.1	•	215.7	5.6	59.0	•	17.1	13.2	•	•	0.8
Return on Equity After Income Taxes 48	23.4	•	213.3	4.0	58.2	•	14.6	10.1	•	•	•
Profit Margin (Before Income Tax) 49	4.0	•	5.8	1.2	7.4	•	5.1	3.0	•	•	0.3
Profit Margin (After Income Tax) 50	3.8	•	5.8	0.8	7.3	•	4.3	2.3	•	•	•

Table II

Corporations with Net Income

OTHER REPAIR AND MAINTENANCE

MONEY AMOUNTS AND SIZE OF ASSETS IN THOUSANDS OF DOLLARS

Item Description for Accounting Period 7/10 Through 6/11		Total	Zero Assets	Under 500	500 to 1,000	1,000 to 5,000	5,000 to 10,000	10,000 to 25,000	25,000 to 50,000	50,000 to 100,000	100,000 to 250,000	250,000 to 500,000	500,000 to 2,500,000	2,500,000 and over
Number of Enterprises	1	37386	4220	31233	628	1066	85	111	27	8	4	4	0	0
Revenues ($ in Thousands)														
Net Sales	2	30874762	494406	11479171	1313879	5532623	1049797	3078824	1783712	727692	671778	4742879	0	0
Interest	3	16887	580	518	1405	4826	1234	1266	480	575	1029	4974	0	0
Rents	4	8638	0	1380	1300	2328	1891	1290	449	0	0	0	0	0
Royalties	5	272	0	0	0	0	0	0	0	27	110	135	0	0
Other Portfolio Income	6	67330	5	33391	6129	9741	1118	3470	1142	566	19	11752	0	0
Other Receipts	7	159407	574	33890	325	14407	2549	10260	6407	2849	1306	86837	0	0
Total Receipts	8	31127296	495565	11548350	1323038	5563925	1056589	3095110	1792190	731709	674242	4846577	0	0
Average Total Receipts	9	833	117	370	2107	5219	12430	27884	66377	91464	168560	1211644	•	•
Operating Costs/Operating Income (%)														
Cost of Operations	10	54.6	39.0	42.1	52.3	48.9	65.9	64.0	65.1	64.4	38.5	81.9	•	•
Salaries and Wages	11	11.1	3.1	12.1	9.9	16.7	8.3	8.8	12.7	6.0	22.3	4.1	•	•
Taxes Paid	12	2.3	2.3	2.5	2.8	2.7	2.1	2.0	2.2	2.9	3.8	1.2	•	•
Interest Paid	13	0.6	0.1	0.5	0.3	0.6	1.4	0.5	0.4	2.6	1.4	0.5	•	•
Depreciation	14	1.7	1.7	1.9	3.8	0.7	3.7	2.8	1.2	3.4	1.2	0.7	•	•
Amortization and Depletion	15	0.3	0.2	0.1	0.1	0.3	•	0.1	0.1	0.7	1.7	0.9	•	•
Pensions and Other Deferred Comp.	16	0.4	•	0.4	0.3	0.2	1.4	0.5	0.8	0.2	0.2	0.2	•	•
Employee Benefits	17	1.6	1.6	1.7	0.7	1.1	1.9	1.7	1.1	4.9	4.3	1.0	•	•
Advertising	18	0.8	0.7	0.8	1.3	0.6	0.3	0.2	0.4	0.1	0.2	1.7	•	•
Other Expenses	19	15.1	32.2	20.4	16.7	13.8	9.8	11.0	9.6	7.8	21.7	7.4	•	•
Officers' Compensation	20	5.2	6.9	8.8	6.8	4.6	4.3	2.6	1.7	1.5	0.7	0.8	•	•
Operating Margin	21	6.4	12.2	8.7	5.0	9.8	0.8	5.7	4.6	5.4	4.0	•	•	•
Operating Margin Before Officers' Comp.	22	11.6	19.1	17.6	11.8	14.5	5.1	8.3	6.3	6.9	4.7	0.3	•	•

Selected Average Balance Sheet ($ in Thousands)

Net Receivables 23	103	0	11	151	550	1603	3441	10354	19235	36575	424846
Inventories 24	45	0	9	160	372	2067	3054	7999	8944	4692	30630
Net Property, Plant and Equipment 25	46	0	20	139	257	1177	2972	4296	9862	6725	25224
Total Assets 26	315	0	66	758	1684	6232	14995	30964	66286	188803	779483
Notes and Loans Payable 27	101	0	26	119	550	3606	2508	4716	25640	64859	287974
All Other Liabilities 28	98	0	18	152	409	1128	4637	9346	16778	43148	356516
Net Worth 29	115	0	23	487	725	1498	7850	16902	23867	80796	134993

Selected Financial Ratios (Times to 1)

Current Ratio 30	1.9	•	1.6	5.8	2.4	1.6	2.0	2.6	1.4	1.5	1.6
Quick Ratio 31	1.3	•	1.2	3.0	1.7	0.8	1.3	1.6	0.9	1.1	1.4
Net Sales to Working Capital 32	8.9	•	25.4	5.3	8.0	7.2	5.1	4.7	9.0	8.4	5.9
Coverage Ratio 33	13.1	103.7	19.7	20.1	19.2	2.0	13.5	13.6	3.3	4.1	4.3
Total Asset Turnover 34	2.6	•	5.6	2.8	3.1	2.0	1.8	2.1	1.4	0.9	1.5
Inventory Turnover 35	10.0	•	18.2	6.8	6.8	3.9	5.8	5.4	6.6	13.8	31.7
Receivables Turnover 36	9.2	•	37.1	9.0	9.8	5.8	9.4	7.7	•	•	•
Total Liabilities to Net Worth 37	1.7	•	1.9	0.6	1.3	3.2	0.9	0.8	1.8	1.3	4.8
Current Assets to Working Capital 38	2.1	•	2.6	1.2	1.7	2.6	2.0	1.6	3.6	2.9	2.6
Current Liabilities to Working Capital 39	1.1	•	1.6	0.2	0.7	1.6	1.0	0.6	2.6	1.9	1.6
Working Capital to Net Sales 40	0.1	•	0.0	0.2	0.1	0.1	0.2	0.2	0.1	0.1	0.2
Inventory to Working Capital 41	0.5	•	0.5	0.4	0.4	1.2	0.7	0.5	0.9	0.2	0.2
Total Receipts to Cash Flow 42	5.3	2.5	4.1	5.4	4.7	11.8	6.7	8.0	9.9	4.2	12.5
Cost of Goods to Cash Flow 43	2.9	1.0	1.7	2.8	2.3	7.8	4.3	5.2	6.4	1.6	10.2
Cash Flow to Total Debt 44	0.8	•	2.1	1.4	1.2	0.2	0.6	0.6	0.2	0.4	0.1

Selected Financial Factors (in Percentages)

Debt Ratio 45	63.5	•	65.6	35.7	56.9	76.0	47.7	45.4	64.0	57.2	82.7
Return on Total Assets 46	20.6	•	54.7	16.4	33.8	5.6	12.5	11.7	11.7	5.1	3.5
Return on Equity Before Income Taxes 47	52.1	•	151.0	24.3	74.3	11.6	22.1	19.9	22.6	9.0	15.6
Return on Equity After Income Taxes 48	49.5	•	149.7	20.1	73.3	9.2	19.4	16.3	19.2	6.9	11.3
Profit Margin (Before Income Tax) 49	7.2	12.4	9.3	5.7	10.4	1.4	6.3	5.1	5.9	4.3	1.8
Profit Margin (After Income Tax) 50	6.9	12.3	9.3	4.7	10.2	1.1	5.5	4.2	5.0	3.3	1.3

Table I

Corporations with and without Net Income

PERSONAL AND LAUNDRY SERVICES

MONEY AMOUNTS AND SIZE OF ASSETS IN THOUSANDS OF DOLLARS

Item Description for Accounting Period 7/10 Through 6/11	Total	Zero Assets	Under 500	500 to 1,000	1,000 to 5,000	5,000 to 10,000	10,000 to 25,000	25,000 to 50,000	50,000 to 100,000	100,000 to 250,000	250,000 to 500,000	500,000 to 2,500,000	2,500,000 and over
Number of Enterprises **1**	162399	38324	112353	6713	4514	275	130	43	21	•	•	13	•
Revenues ($ in Thousands)													
Net Sales **2**	76382760	2915807	27339768	8649982	13082040	4369130	1711561	1668232	1865547	•	•	12232109	•
Interest **3**	107847	4882	4585	1789	10578	1682	3373	4092	714	•	•	69382	•
Rents **4**	56357	47	3737	5986	822	1095	6934	920	331	•	•	29869	•
Royalties **5**	122966	0	0	0	1	589	1535	0	44	•	•	120797	•
Other Portfolio Income **6**	320853	51288	55690	22557	41113	8008	28310	3537	564	•	•	67843	•
Other Receipts **7**	1684098	16648	592224	506492	94044	62146	66370	28142	17795	•	•	232339	•
Total Receipts **8**	78674881	2988672	27996004	9186806	13228598	4442650	1818083	1704923	1884995	•	•	12841339	•
Average Total Receipts **9**	484	78	249	1369	2931	16155	13985	39649	89762	•	•	987795	•
Operating Costs/Operating Income (%)													
Cost of Operations **10**	30.1	14.8	25.8	34.7	24.0	69.7	32.9	36.3	33.9	•	•	30.6	•
Salaries and Wages **11**	20.5	15.4	20.9	18.8	25.2	8.5	20.3	15.0	22.6	•	•	21.1	•
Taxes Paid **12**	3.9	3.3	3.6	3.8	5.2	2.0	3.6	1.8	3.4	•	•	4.7	•
Interest Paid **13**	1.7	0.9	0.9	1.1	1.8	0.5	2.2	2.2	1.6	•	•	4.0	•
Depreciation **14**	3.1	2.6	2.3	2.4	2.3	2.6	4.9	4.8	3.0	•	•	5.5	•
Amortization and Depletion **15**	1.2	0.2	0.5	0.7	0.5	0.2	0.7	0.5	1.0	•	•	3.5	•
Pensions and Other Deferred Comp. **16**	0.4	0.1	0.2	0.5	0.5	0.4	0.5	0.6	0.2	•	•	0.8	•
Employee Benefits **17**	1.4	0.6	0.7	1.1	1.8	1.0	2.6	3.0	2.1	•	•	2.0	•
Advertising **18**	1.7	2.2	1.4	1.8	1.9	0.5	3.2	0.7	2.8	•	•	2.1	•
Other Expenses **19**	29.6	50.0	32.9	26.6	33.0	10.5	27.8	28.1	26.4	•	•	24.8	•
Officers' Compensation **20**	5.6	8.5	9.2	8.5	4.1	1.4	2.9	1.8	1.8	•	•	0.7	•
Operating Margin **21**	0.8	1.5	1.5	•	•	2.8	•	5.1	1.1	•	•	0.1	•
Operating Margin Before Officers' Comp. **22**	6.4	10.0	10.7	8.5	3.9	4.2	1.5	6.9	2.9	•	•	0.8	•

Selected Average Balance Sheet ($ in Thousands)

	1	2	3	4	5	6	7	8	9	10	11
Net Receivables 23	25	0	3	53	248	1200	1844	4117	9369	•	82058
Inventories 24	14	0	3	31	47	286	677	1701	3360	•	81978
Net Property, Plant and Equipment 25	106	0	27	272	790	2404	4180	8764	24342	•	447548
Total Assets 26	336	0	72	699	1847	6925	14984	34889	70450	•	1828502
Notes and Loans Payable 27	138	0	54	310	1060	1140	5168	12645	21906	•	516302
All Other Liabilities 28	116	0	14	114	481	2570	4015	17608	22174	•	842532
Net Worth 29	82	0	3	275	305	3214	5801	4636	26370	•	469668

Selected Financial Ratios (Times to 1)

	1	2	3	4	5	6	7	8	9	10	11
Current Ratio 30	1.5	•	1.2	1.9	1.8	1.6	1.7	1.4	1.0	•	1.4
Quick Ratio 31	1.0	•	0.9	1.4	1.3	1.4	1.3	0.6	0.8	•	0.7
Net Sales to Working Capital 32	16.2	•	77.2	10.8	9.1	13.8	6.1	9.7	•	•	10.6
Coverage Ratio 33	3.3	5.3	5.4	6.8	1.5	9.7	3.2	4.3	2.3	•	2.2
Total Asset Turnover 34	1.4	•	3.4	1.8	1.6	2.3	0.9	1.1	1.3	•	0.5
Inventory Turnover 35	10.3	•	21.8	14.3	14.7	38.8	6.4	8.3	9.0	•	3.5
Receivables Turnover 36	18.7	•	89.6	25.6	12.4	12.6	5.7	8.1	8.9	•	12.7
Total Liabilities to Net Worth 37	3.1	•	19.6	1.5	5.0	1.2	1.6	6.5	1.7	•	2.9
Current Assets to Working Capital 38	3.0	•	6.6	2.1	2.2	2.6	2.5	3.9	•	•	3.3
Current Liabilities to Working Capital 39	2.0	•	5.6	1.1	1.2	1.6	1.5	2.9	•	•	2.3
Working Capital to Net Sales 40	0.1	•	0.0	0.1	0.1	0.1	0.2	0.1	•	•	0.1
Inventory to Working Capital 41	0.5	•	1.1	0.3	0.2	0.2	0.2	0.5	•	•	1.0
Total Receipts to Cash Flow 42	4.5	2.9	4.3	4.0	4.3	8.1	4.4	4.8	4.9	•	4.9
Cost of Goods to Cash Flow 43	1.3	0.4	1.1	1.4	1.0	5.6	1.5	1.7	1.6	•	1.5
Cash Flow to Total Debt 44	0.4	•	0.8	0.8	0.4	0.5	0.3	0.3	0.4	•	0.1

Selected Financial Factors (in Percentages)

	1	2	3	4	5	6	7	8	9	10	11
Debt Ratio 45	75.5	•	95.2	60.7	83.5	53.6	61.3	86.7	62.6	•	74.3
Return on Total Assets 46	7.7	•	16.4	13.3	4.1	11.4	6.1	10.6	4.8	•	4.6
Return on Equity Before Income Taxes 47	21.8	•	274.6	28.8	8.0	22.1	10.7	61.0	7.3	•	9.7
Return on Equity After Income Taxes 48	19.4	•	270.8	28.0	7.1	20.9	9.1	57.5	5.1	•	6.1
Profit Margin (Before Income Tax) 49	3.8	4.0	3.9	6.1	0.8	4.5	4.7	7.3	2.2	•	4.8
Profit Margin (After Income Tax) 50	3.4	3.9	3.9	6.0	0.7	4.2	4.0	6.9	1.5	•	3.0

Table II
Corporations with Net Income

PERSONAL AND LAUNDRY SERVICES

MONEY AMOUNTS AND SIZE OF ASSETS IN THOUSANDS OF DOLLARS

Item Description for Accounting Period 7/10 Through 6/11	Total	Zero Assets	Under 500	500 to 1,000	1,000 to 5,000	5,000 to 10,000	10,000 to 25,000	25,000 to 50,000	50,000 to 100,000	100,000 to 250,000	250,000 to 500,000	500,000 to 2,500,000	2,500,000 and over
Number of Enterprises **1**	88722	17591	63494	4923	2357	231	72	26	13	•	0	•	•
Revenues ($ in Thousands)													
Net Sales **2**	57332434	1898594	20104491	7870880	8800888	4073096	1070711	1178166	1042939	•	0	•	•
Interest **3**	61980	4882	3114	1293	5636	1061	1968	2036	262	•	0	•	•
Rents **4**	16638	47	774	5958	573	652	6908	912	59	•	0	•	•
Royalties **5**	122201	0	0	0	1	589	1455	0	2	•	0	•	•
Other Portfolio Income **6**	266344	49055	41981	19012	39391	6495	26119	1583	529	•	0	•	•
Other Receipts **7**	939715	5743	539603	47108	70669	52421	44971	18271	7198	•	0	•	•
Total Receipts **8**	58739312	1958321	20689963	7944251	8917158	4134314	1152132	1200968	1050989	•	0	•	•
Average Total Receipts **9**	662	111	326	1614	3783	17897	16002	46191	80845	•	•	•	•
Operating Costs/Operating Income (%)													
Cost of Operations **10**	32.0	12.5	29.0	36.1	16.0	71.5	32.6	41.8	34.4	•	•	•	•
Salaries and Wages **11**	19.2	12.4	20.1	13.6	27.3	8.0	21.2	14.3	22.8	•	•	•	•
Taxes Paid **12**	3.8	2.8	3.4	3.7	5.5	1.8	3.4	2.0	3.5	•	•	•	•
Interest Paid **13**	1.2	1.2	0.9	0.9	1.4	0.3	0.6	1.4	1.6	•	•	•	•
Depreciation **14**	2.6	1.7	1.8	2.1	1.8	2.0	3.3	3.6	2.7	•	•	•	•
Amortization and Depletion **15**	1.1	0.1	0.3	0.6	0.4	0.2	0.3	0.6	1.5	•	•	•	•
Pensions and Other Deferred Comp. **16**	0.4	0.1	0.2	0.5	0.3	0.3	0.5	0.7	0.4	•	•	•	•
Employee Benefits **17**	1.4	0.7	0.7	0.9	1.6	0.8	2.9	2.8	2.0	•	•	•	•
Advertising **18**	1.6	1.7	1.4	1.8	1.9	0.4	2.6	0.8	1.3	•	•	•	•
Other Expenses **19**	25.9	45.9	27.6	25.1	35.9	9.8	27.5	21.0	21.2	•	•	•	•
Officers' Compensation **20**	5.2	8.4	8.1	8.0	3.9	1.2	2.0	1.6	2.0	•	•	•	•
Operating Margin **21**	5.5	12.5	6.4	6.7	3.9	3.7	3.1	9.4	6.7	•	•	•	•
Operating Margin Before Officers' Comp. **22**	10.7	20.9	14.6	14.7	7.8	4.9	5.1	11.0	8.6	•	•	•	•

Selected Average Balance Sheet ($ in Thousands)

Net Receivables 23	32	0	3	55	238	1299	2861	4413	11328
Inventories 24	20	0	3	39	48	296	779	1760	3712
Net Property, Plant and Equipment 25	105	0	25	289	803	1953	3684	7809	18247
Total Assets 26	359	0	76	721	1945	6747	15133	33518	69089
Notes and Loans Payable 27	130	0	43	313	945	942	2416	9715	17386
All Other Liabilities 28	96	0	16	94	453	2389	4383	13408	17457
Net Worth 29	134	0	17	314	547	3416	8334	10395	34245

Selected Financial Ratios (Times to 1)

Current Ratio 30	1.8	•	1.3	2.6	2.2	1.7	2.7	1.6	1.4
Quick Ratio 31	1.2	•	1.0	2.0	1.5	1.5	2.1	0.9	1.1
Net Sales to Working Capital 32	12.6	•	46.6	8.9	8.5	12.8	3.6	8.3	14.1
Coverage Ratio 33	7.5	14.2	11.9	9.6	4.6	19.5	18.5	9.1	5.6
Total Asset Turnover 34	1.8	•	4.1	2.2	1.9	2.6	1.0	1.4	1.2
Inventory Turnover 35	10.5	•	28.2	14.9	12.4	42.6	6.2	10.8	7.4
Receivables Turnover 36	20.7	•	96.8	33.0	16.1	13.1	4.4	8.3	7.0
Total Liabilities to Net Worth 37	1.7	•	3.5	1.3	2.6	1.0	0.8	2.2	1.0
Current Assets to Working Capital 38	2.3	•	3.9	1.6	1.9	2.3	1.6	2.5	3.8
Current Liabilities to Working Capital 39	1.3	•	2.9	0.6	0.9	1.3	0.6	1.5	2.8
Working Capital to Net Sales 40	0.1	•	0.0	0.1	0.1	0.1	0.3	0.1	0.1
Inventory to Working Capital 41	0.4	•	0.6	0.2	0.1	0.1	0.1	0.3	0.2
Total Receipts to Cash Flow 42	4.1	2.2	3.9	3.9	3.5	8.0	3.6	4.3	4.4
Cost of Goods to Cash Flow 43	1.3	0.3	1.1	1.4	0.6	5.7	1.2	1.8	1.5
Cash Flow to Total Debt 44	0.7	•	1.3	1.0	0.8	0.7	0.6	0.5	0.5

Selected Financial Factors (in Percentages)

Debt Ratio 45	62.8	•	77.8	56.4	71.9	49.4	44.9	69.0	50.4
Return on Total Assets 46	16.7	•	42.3	18.8	12.4	14.4	11.1	17.2	10.5
Return on Equity Before Income Taxes 47	38.9	•	174.5	38.7	34.6	27.0	19.1	49.4	17.4
Return on Equity After Income Taxes 48	36.2	•	173.1	37.8	33.6	25.7	17.1	46.8	14.6
Profit Margin (Before Income Tax) 49	8.0	15.7	9.4	7.6	5.1	5.2	10.7	11.3	7.4
Profit Margin (After Income Tax) 50	7.5	15.5	9.3	7.4	4.9	5.0	9.6	10.7	6.3

Table I
Corporations with and without Net Income

RELIGIOUS, GRANTMAKING, CIVIC AND PROFESSIONAL ORGANIZATIONS

MONEY AMOUNTS AND SIZE OF ASSETS IN THOUSANDS OF DOLLARS

Item Description for Accounting Period 7/10 Through 6/11	Total	Zero Assets	Under 500	500 to 1,000	1,000 to 5,000	5,000 to 10,000	10,000 to 25,000	25,000 to 50,000	50,000 to 100,000	100,000 to 250,000	250,000 to 500,000	500,000 to 2,500,000	2,500,000 and over
Number of Enterprises **1**	44994	5206	33260	3795	2422	196	84	17	10	•	•	0	•
Revenues ($ in Thousands)													
Net Sales **2**	9599437	201360	3105480	2037922	2471525	564219	638661	191309	250527	•	•	0	•
Interest **3**	109563	767	24866	21165	43802	7236	5278	2626	2226	•	•	0	•
Rents **4**	35789	1591	8303	5414	14316	1876	150	115	297	•	•	0	•
Royalties **5**	1936	0	0	1935	0	0	0	0	0	•	•	0	•
Other Portfolio Income **6**	100430	594	26426	40325	26060	3982	506	910	1160	•	•	0	•
Other Receipts **7**	3726097	9200	1183353	365882	689248	129135	145744	74585	53153	•	•	0	•
Total Receipts **8**	13573252	213512	4348428	2472643	3244951	706448	790339	269545	307363	•	•	0	•
Average Total Receipts **9**	302	41	131	652	1340	3604	9409	15856	30736	•	•		•
Operating Costs/Operating Income (%)													
Cost of Operations **10**	17.1	1.0	10.0	27.5	11.7	14.7	27.6	22.8	34.4	•	•		•
Salaries and Wages **11**	13.1	14.2	7.3	7.7	17.4	23.9	16.9	37.3	28.5	•	•		•
Taxes Paid **12**	2.8	2.2	2.5	1.4	3.3	3.8	3.5	7.8	2.9	•	•		•
Interest Paid **13**	1.0	0.2	1.1	0.5	0.9	1.8	1.5	6.3	1.1	•	•		•
Depreciation **14**	2.3	3.4	1.0	0.9	2.7	4.7	4.5	7.4	5.6	•	•		•
Amortization and Depletion **15**	0.2	0.4	0.1	0.0	0.1	0.1	0.1	3.4	0.4	•	•		•
Pensions and Other Deferred Comp. **16**	0.2	•	0.1	0.0	0.1	1.1	0.2	0.2	1.3	•	•		•
Employee Benefits **17**	1.6	•	0.4	0.8	2.1	2.7	3.9	4.1	2.5	•	•		•
Advertising **18**	1.7	0.9	4.5	0.0	0.4	1.7	0.3	0.5	0.7	•	•		•
Other Expenses **19**	95.9	89.6	105.9	74.7	91.4	60.0	59.8	45.9	37.9	•	•		•
Officers' Compensation **20**	3.4	•	5.0	4.4	0.6	6.8	1.8	1.2	2.3	•	•		•
Operating Margin **21**	•	•	•	•	•	•	•	•	•	•	•		•
Operating Margin Before Officers' Comp. **22**	•	•	•	•	•	•	•	•	•	•	•		•

Selected Average Balance Sheet ($ in Thousands)

Net Receivables 23	23	0	5	25	92	176	1719	5181	12730
Inventories 24	1	0	0	1	10	23	70	183	162
Net Property, Plant and Equipment 25	76	0	9	58	432	2597	8762	11963	24036
Total Assets 26	481	0	96	691	1944	6187	16641	35729	65408
Notes and Loans Payable 27	39	0	16	61	175	1325	1861	5762	7308
All Other Liabilities 28	218	0	18	120	300	1141	5119	10446	21751
Net Worth 29	224	0	63	510	1470	3720	9662	19521	36350

Selected Financial Ratios (Times to 1)

Current Ratio 30	1.9	•	4.4	6.8	5.1	1.7	1.6	1.4	1.4
Quick Ratio 31	1.2	•	4.1	6.3	4.8	1.4	1.2	1.3	1.3
Net Sales to Working Capital 32	1.4	•	1.5	1.1	1.0	2.5	3.4	2.8	4.7
Coverage Ratio 33	2.6	•	2.7	4.6	1.7	2.9	3.4	1.6	5.7
Total Asset Turnover 34	0.4	•	1.0	0.8	0.5	0.5	0.5	0.3	0.4
Inventory Turnover 35	36.1	•	98.8	217.0	12.1	18.4	30.0	14.0	53.1
Receivables Turnover 36	9.4	•	17.5	18.3	12.1	12.0	5.0	1.9	1.4
Total Liabilities to Net Worth 37	1.1	•	0.5	0.4	0.3	0.7	0.7	0.8	0.8
Current Assets to Working Capital 38	2.1	•	1.3	1.2	1.2	2.5	2.6	3.5	3.8
Current Liabilities to Working Capital 39	1.1	•	0.3	0.2	0.2	1.5	1.6	2.5	2.8
Working Capital to Net Sales 40	0.7	•	0.7	0.9	1.0	0.4	0.3	0.4	0.2
Inventory to Working Capital 41	0.0	•	0.0	0.0	0.0	0.0	0.0	0.0	0.0
Total Receipts to Cash Flow 42	1.2	1.5	1.2	1.6	1.3	1.8	1.9	2.5	3.0
Cost of Goods to Cash Flow 43	0.2	0.0	0.1	0.4	0.2	0.3	0.5	0.6	1.0
Cash Flow to Total Debt 44	0.7	•	2.3	1.9	1.7	0.6	0.6	0.3	0.3

Selected Financial Factors (in Percentages)

Debt Ratio 45	53.4	•	34.9	26.2	24.4	39.9	41.9	45.4	44.4
Return on Total Assets 46	1.2	•	2.9	1.8	0.8	2.4	2.3	3.2	2.3
Return on Equity Before Income Taxes 47	1.6	•	2.8	1.9	0.4	2.6	2.8	2.3	3.4
Return on Equity After Income Taxes 48	1.1	•	2.4	1.5	0.0	1.9	2.1	0.8	2.8
Profit Margin (Before Income Tax) 49	1.7	•	1.9	1.8	0.6	3.4	3.6	3.9	5.0
Profit Margin (After Income Tax) 50	1.2	•	1.6	1.4	0.0	2.5	2.7	1.5	4.1

Table II
Corporations with Net Income

RELIGIOUS, GRANTMAKING, CIVIC AND PROFESSIONAL ORGANIZATIONS

MONEY AMOUNTS AND SIZE OF ASSETS IN THOUSANDS OF DOLLARS

Item Description for Accounting Period 7/10 Through 6/11	Total	Zero Assets	Under 500	500 to 1,000	1,000 to 5,000	5,000 to 10,000	10,000 to 25,000	25,000 to 50,000	50,000 to 100,000	100,000 to 250,000	250,000 to 500,000	500,000 to 2,500,000	2,500,000 and over
Number of Enterprises **1**	24041	2033	17546	2708	1590	91	54	7	•	•	•	0	•
Revenues ($ in Thousands)													
Net Sales **2**	6094728	119192	1946549	1425867	1315096	312428	519333	68310	•	•	•	0	•
Interest **3**	83026	81	18220	18203	35233	5320	2726	323	•	•	•	0	•
Rents **4**	27081	1591	4398	5414	9579	1843	150	115	•	•	•	0	•
Royalties **5**	1935	0	0	1935	0	0	0	0	•	•	•	0	•
Other Portfolio Income **6**	93127	0	25721	40296	24709	430	465	161	•	•	•	0	•
Other Receipts **7**	2264390	7034	324757	265614	330496	88292	105061	37850	•	•	•	0	•
Total Receipts **8**	8564287	127898	2319645	1757329	1715113	408313	627735	106759	•	•	•	0	•
Average Total Receipts **9**	356	63	132	649	1079	4487	11625	15251	•	•	•		•
Operating Costs/Operating Income (%)													
Cost of Operations **10**	21.1	1.7	12.3	32.4	12.1	22.5	27.4	52.5	•	•	•		•
Salaries and Wages **11**	11.6	13.5	7.4	5.6	14.0	25.6	15.0	32.0	•	•	•		•
Taxes Paid **12**	2.5	1.5	3.2	1.3	2.3	3.5	2.6	6.5	•	•	•		•
Interest Paid **13**	0.5	•	0.1	0.3	1.1	0.9	0.7	0.3	•	•	•		•
Depreciation **14**	1.6	0.5	0.6	0.4	1.8	2.3	3.3	9.0	•	•	•		•
Amortization and Depletion **15**	0.1	•	0.0	0.0	0.0	•	0.0	0.0	•	•	•		•
Pensions and Other Deferred Comp. **16**	0.2	•	0.1	0.0	0.1	1.7	0.2	0.3	•	•	•		•
Employee Benefits **17**	1.4	•	0.1	0.5	1.9	2.5	4.1	2.2	•	•	•		•
Advertising **18**	1.1	1.1	2.4	0.0	0.5	3.0	0.4	0.7	•	•	•		•
Other Expenses **19**	88.8	74.5	77.8	70.8	90.7	52.8	57.9	29.7	•	•	•		•
Officers' Compensation **20**	4.8	7.8	7.8	6.4	0.5	6.6	2.2	1.7	•	•	•		•
Operating Margin **21**	•	7.1	•	•	•	•	•	•	•	•	•		•
Operating Margin Before Officers' Comp. **22**	•	7.1	•	•	•	•	•	•	•	•	•		•

Selected Average Balance Sheet ($ in Thousands)

Net Receivables 23	30	0	5	13	75	168	2567	10165
Inventories 24	1	0	0	12	32	100	146	
Net Property, Plant and Equipment 25	65	0	12	32	269	1428	6747	13321
Total Assets 26	673	0	113	681	1865	6077	17274	33887
Notes and Loans Payable 27	26	0	3	44	144	606	1370	1161
All Other Liabilities 28	359	0	19	75	244	1122	6398	10570
Net Worth 29	288	0	91	562	1478	4349	9506	22156

Selected Financial Ratios (Times to 1)

Current Ratio 30	1.8	•	6.7	7.8	6.6	3.6	1.7	1.7
Quick Ratio 31	1.0	•	6.3	7.4	6.3	3.5	1.3	1.7
Net Sales to Working Capital 32	1.2	•	1.3	1.0	0.7	1.2	2.9	1.4
Coverage Ratio 33	13.4	•	79.1	13.4	5.6	11.7	10.4	79.0
Total Asset Turnover 34	0.4	•	1.0	0.8	0.4	0.6	0.6	0.3
Inventory Turnover 35	37.0	•	154.7	347.0	8.2	24.2	26.3	35.1
Receivables Turnover 36	8.5	•	24.0	30.4	11.1	12.2	4.2	•
Total Liabilities to Net Worth 37	1.3	•	0.2	0.2	0.3	0.4	0.8	0.5
Current Assets to Working Capital 38	2.2	•	1.2	1.1	1.2	1.4	2.4	2.4
Current Liabilities to Working Capital 39	1.2	•	0.2	0.1	0.2	0.4	1.4	1.4
Working Capital to Net Sales 40	0.8	•	0.8	1.0	1.5	0.8	0.3	0.7
Inventory to Working Capital 41	0.0	•	0.0	0.0	0.0	0.0	0.0	0.0
Total Receipts to Cash Flow 42	1.2	1.5	1.6	1.7	1.2	1.8	1.7	2.4
Cost of Goods to Cash Flow 43	0.3	0.0	0.2	0.5	0.1	0.4	0.5	1.3
Cash Flow to Total Debt 44	0.5	•	3.2	2.7	1.8	1.1	0.7	0.3

Selected Financial Factors (in Percentages)

Debt Ratio 45	57.2	•	19.7	17.5	20.8	28.4	45.0	34.6
Return on Total Assets 46	2.5	•	7.3	2.8	2.9	5.8	4.3	6.2
Return on Equity Before Income Taxes 47	5.4	•	9.0	3.2	3.0	7.4	7.0	9.4
Return on Equity After Income Taxes 48	4.7	•	8.5	2.8	2.4	6.1	6.0	6.3
Profit Margin (Before Income Tax) 49	6.2	14.4	7.4	3.4	5.3	9.3	7.0	21.2
Profit Margin (After Income Tax) 50	5.4	13.5	7.0	2.9	4.2	7.7	5.9	14.3

INDEX

INDEX

Credit card issuing and other consumer credit, 281, 282
Credit Intermediation, 275, 276
Cut and sew apparel contractors and mftrs., 65, 66
Cutlery, hardware, spring and wire, machine shops, nut, bolt, 113, 114

D

Dairy products, 43, 44
Data processing, hosting, and related services, 271, 272
Database, directory, and other publishers, 259, 260
Depository credit intermediation, 277–280
Drugs and druggists' sundries, 185, 186

E

Educational services, 361, 362
Electric power generation, transmission, and distribution, 17, 18
Electrical contractors, 31, 32
Electrical equipment, appliance, and component manufacturing, 147–152
Electrical equipment, 149, 150
Electrical goods, 175, 176
Electrical lighting equipment and household appliance, 147, 148
Electronics and appliance stores, 209, 210
Employment services, 353, 354
Engine, turbine, and power transmission equipment, 133, 134

F

Fabricated metal product manufacturing, 111–122
Farm product raw material, 191, 192
Finance and insurance, 275–316
Food and beverage stores, 219, 220
Food, beverage, and liquor stores, 219–236
Food manufacturing, 37–50
Food services and drinking places, 381, 382
Forestry and logging, 3, 4
Forging and stamping, 111, 112
Foundries, 109, 110
Fruit and vegetable preserving and specialty food, 41, 42

Furniture and home furnishing stores, 207, 208
Furniture and related product manufacturing, 161, 162
Furniture, sports, toys, jewelry, other durable goods, 181, 182

G

Gasoline stations, 225, 226
General merchandise stores, 231, 232
Glass and glass product manufacturing, 101, 102
Grocery and related product, 189, 190

H

Hardware, plumbing, heating equipment, and supplies, 177, 178
Hardware stores, 213, 214
Health and personal care stores, 223, 224
Health care and social assistance, 363–374
Heavy and civil engineering construction, 27, 28
Home centers; paint and wallpaper stores, 211, 212
Hospitals, nursing and residential care facilities, 373, 374

I

Industrial machinery 125, 126
Information, 253–276
Insurance agencies and brokerages, 305, 306
Insurance carriers and related activities, 297–310
Intl. trade, secondary financing, other nondepository credit, 285, 286
Investment banking and securities dealing, 289, 290
Iron, steel mills, and steel product, 105, 106

L

Land subdivision, 29, 30
Lawn and garden equipment and supplies stores, 217, 218
Leather and allied product manufacturing, 69, 70
Legal services, 331, 332
Lessors of buildings, 315, 316